Handbook of Comparative Interventions for Adult Disorders

Handbook of Comparative Interventions for Adult Disorders

Second Edition

Edited by

Michel Hersen

and

Alan S. Bellack

John Wiley & Sons, Inc.

New York • Chichester • Weinheim • Brisbane • Singapore • Toronto

This book is printed on acid-free paper. ∞

Copyright © 1999 by John Wiley & Sons, Inc. All rights reserved.
Published simultaneously in Canada.

This publication is designed to provide accurate and authoritative information in regard to the subject matter covered. It is sold with the understanding that the publisher is not engaged in rendering professional services. If legal, accounting, medical, psychological or any other expert assistance is required, the services of a competent professional person should be sought.

Library of Congress Cataloging-in-Publication Data:

Handbook of comparative interventions for adult disorders / edited by
    Michel Hersen and Alan S. Bellack. — 2nd ed.
        p.   cm.
    Rev. ed. of: Handbook of comparative treatments for adult
disorders. c1990.
    Includes bibliographical references and indexes.
    ISBN 0-471-16342-2 (cloth : alk. paper)
    1. Psychotherapy—Handbooks, manuals, etc.   2. Behavior therapy—
Handbooks, manuals, etc.   3. Mental illness—Chemotherapy—
Handbooks, manuals, etc.   4. Psychodynamic psychotherapy—
Handbooks, manuals, etc.   I. Hersen, Michel.   II. Bellack, Alan S.
III. Handbook of comparative treatments for adult disorders.
    [DNLM: 1. Mental Disorders—therapy. 2. Psychotherapy.
3. Behavior Therapy. 4. Drug Therapy.   WM 420 H2311 1999]
RC480.5.H275 1999
616.89'14—dc21
DNLM/DLC
for Library of Congress   98-43529

Printed in the United States of America.

10 9 8 7 6 5 4 3 2 1

Contributors

Larry W. Bates
Auburn University
Auburn, Alabama

Jules R. Bemporad, M.D.
Mamaroneck, New York

Susan Berel
Pacific University
Forest Grove, Oregon

Cindy Brody
American University
Washington, DC

Stephen F. Butler, Ph.D.
Innovative Training Systems
Amherst, New Hampshire

Ricardo Castañeda, M.D.
Clinical Associate Professor
Department of Psychiatry
New York Medical Center
New York

Emil F. Coccaro, M.D.
Professor and Director, Clinical
    Neuroscience Research Unit
Department of Psychiatry
Medical College of Pennsylvania &
    Hahnemann University
Philadelphia, Pennsylvania

Katherine A. Comtois
Department of Psychiatry &
    Behavioral Sciences
University of Washington
Seattle, Washington

Kenneth L. Critchfield

John M. Davis, Ph.D.
Illinois State Psychiatric Institute
University of Illinois
Chicago, Illinois

Morris N. Eagle, Ph.D.
Derner Institute
Adelphi University
Garden City, New York

Michael Feinberg, M.D.
Department of Psychiatry
Hahnemann University
Philadelphia, Pennsylvania

Edna B. Foa, Ph.D.
Director, The Center for the
    Treatment and Study of Anxiety
Department of Psychiatry
Medical College of Pennsylvania &
    Hahnemann University
Philadelphia, Pennsylvania

David W. Foy, Ph.D.
Graduate School of Education and
    Psychology
Pepperdine University
Culver City, California

Martin E. Franklin, Ph.D.
Assistant Professor
Department of Psychiatry
Allegheny University of Health
    Science
Philadelphia, Pennsylvania

Arthur Freeman, Ph.D.
Philadelphia College of Osteopathic
  Medicine
Philadelphia, Pennsylvania

David M. Fresco

Marc Galanter, M.D.
Professor and Director, Division of
  Alcoholism and Drug Abuse
Department of Psychiatry
New York University School of
  Medicine
New York

Shirley M. Glynn, Ph.D.
West Los Angeles Veteran Affairs
Medical Center, Brentwood Division
Los Angeles, California

Alan M. Gross, Ph.D.
Department of Psychology
University of Mississippi
University, Mississippi

David A.F. Haaga, Ph.D.
Department of Psychology
American University
Washington, DC

Richard G. Heimberg, Ph.D.
Director, Social Phobia Program
Temple University
Philadelphia, Pennsylvania

Mardi J. Horowitz, M.D.
Professor of Psychiatry
Langley Porter Psychiatric Institute
San Francisco, California

Christine Howard
School of Professional Psychology
Pacific University
Forest Grove, Oregon

Lisa H. Jaycox
Allegheny University of Health
  Science
Philadelphia, Pennsylvania

Jon D. Kassel, Ph.D.
Department of Psychology
University of Illinois at Chicago
Chicago, Illinois

Richard Kavoussi, M.D.
Allegheny University of Health
  Science
Philadelphia, Pennsylvania

Jelena Kunovac, M.D.
Department of Psychiatry
University of California, San Diego
La Jolla, California

Eric R. Levensky
Department of Psychology
University of Washington
Seattle, Washington

Marsha M. Linehan, Ph.D.
Department of Psychology
University of Washington
Seattle, Washington

Brian Martis, M.D.

F. Dudley McGlynn, Ph.D.
Department of Psychology
Auburn University
Auburn, Alabama

Jonathan M. Meyer, Ph.D.
Department of Psychiatry &
  Behavioral Sciences
LAC/USC Medical Center
Los Angeles, California

Howard B. Moss, M.D.
Professor of Psychiatry
University of Pittsburgh Medical
  Center
Pittsburgh, Pennsylvania

Matthew T. O'Neill, B.S.

Carol Oster, Ph.D.
Professor and Associate Dean
Adler School of Professional
    Psychology
Chicago, Illinois

William S. Pollack, Ph.D.
McLean Hospital
Belmont, Massachusetts

Linda K. Porzelius, Ph.D.
School of Professional Psychology
Pacific University
Forest Grove, Oregon

Richard L. Pyle, M.D.
Associate Professor
Department of Psychiatry
University of Minnesota Medical
    School
Minneapolis, Minnesota

Dana Rabois
American University
Washington, DC

Heidi S. Resnick, Ph.D.
Crime Victims Research and
    Treatment Center
Medical University of South Carolina

Edward K. Silberman, M.D.
Department of Psychiatry
Jefferson Medical College
Philadelphia, Pennsylvania

George M. Simpson, M.D.
Professor of Research Psychiatry
Director of Clinical Research
LAC/USC Medical Center
Los Angeles, California

Murray B. Stein, M.D.
Department of Psychiatry
University of California, San Diego
La Jolla, California

Hans H. Strupp, Ph.D.
Department of Psychology
Vanderbilt University
Nashville, Tennessee

Holly A. Swartz, M.D.
Department of Psychiatry
Payne Whitney Psychiatric Clinic
New York Hospital
Cornell Medical Center
New York

Cynthia L. Turk

Marina Unrod, B.A.
University of Florida
Gainsville, Florida

Russell G. Vasile

Eric F. Wagner, Ph.D.
Florida International University
Miami, Florida

G. Stennis Watson
University of Mississippi
University, Mississippi

Terri L. Weaver, Ph.D.
Center for Trauma Recovery and
    Department of Psychology
St. Louis, Missouri

David L. Wolitzky, Ph.D.
Research Center for Mental Health
New York University
New York

Preface

THE TREATMENT of psychiatric disorders has undergone a dramatic change since the late 1960s. Prior to that, the field was saddled with an archaic and overgeneralized diagnostic system. More often than not, diagnoses were assigned on an ad hoc basis after an informal clinical interview. The resultant labels were apt to be unreliable, and they provided little clear information about etiology, course, or treatment needs. However, consequences of this process were not as bad as one might imagine because treatment options were severely limited. Traditional psychoanalytic techniques predominated. Behavior therapy and biological psychiatry were nascent disciplines, and ego and cognitive psychology were still in formative stages of development. The critical diagnostic distinction was either psychotic or nonpsychotic. The latter were apt to receive a standard form of long-term analytic therapy or low-potency benzodiazepines, whereas psychotic patients were likely to receive low-potency neuroleptics.

The therapeutic environment has changed dramatically in the last four decades. Behavior therapy has progressed through a series of developmental stages, from being an academic oddity to being a universal part of the treatment environment, crossing theoretical boundaries. Behavioral techniques have become the treatment of choice for a number of disorders.

Biological psychiatry has seen a similar development. Newer, more effective anti-anxiety, antidepressant, and antipsychotic pharmacological agents with dramatically fewer side effects are constantly being developed and tested. Concurrently, the various imaging strategies have enhanced our understanding of brain structure, functioning, and chemistry. Indeed, we now have a clearer view as to how neurotransmitters affect behavior. In the decade since the first publication of this handbook, developments in biological psychiatry have been staggering. Several of these are documented in the chapters that follow. Developments in psychotherapy strategies have not been as dramatic, but they are no less significant. Greater emphasis is on the environment, current functioning, observable cognitive phenomena, and use of active strategies. In general, dynamic strategies are much more flexible and are more specifically targeted to the specific life situation of the patient. These therapeutic developments have been associated with increased understanding of the etiology of many disorders, as well as with a substantially improved diagnostic system. It is now much more likely that treatment will be tailored to the needs (and diagnosis) of the individual patient. In psychotherapy, the influence of behavioral techniques, emphasizing documentation and accountability, has been seen in the numerous treatment manuals that have evolved. Such manuals have enabled researchers to derive more cogent conclusions from clinical trials, because of greater comparability and replicability of treatment from one therapist to another dealing with clients with identical diagnoses.

Perhaps the one down side to the evolution of treatment has been an explosion in the volume of literature on psychopathology and treatment issues. Scores of new journals publish highly specialized material, and hundreds of relevant books appear each year. It is almost impossible to be thoroughly up to date in the literature for a particular orientation or disorder, let alone to maintain catholic reading habits. As a consequence, important new developments are frequently missed, and perspectives on alternative approaches are all too quickly outdated. It would probably be safe to say that most professionals maintain stereotyped views of alternative models, based substantially on the literature extant during the individual's postgraduate training.

The *Handbook of Comparative Interventions for Adult Disorders* was again, as in the first edition, designed with this extremely large literature in mind. The intent was to present an overview of the best current thinking and techniques, from two or more different viewpoints, on each of the major adult disorders. It is our hope that this presentation will permit easy comparison for the student or professional. The contributors to this book, who are experts in the field, have been invited to describe how they think about their patients, how they conceptualize the respective disorders, how they design and implement treatment, and what they do when their favored approach does not work. To introduce each perspective, the first part of this book contains overviews of each of the major orientations. The remaining parts focus on individual disorders, with editorial commentary at the end of each section. To amplify the characterization of the treatment process, each of the chapters contains a description of the treatment of a typical case. The contributing authors were requested not to write prototypical literature reviews supporting one technique over another. Instead, the authors have attempted to communicate an understanding about how and why they approach cases in a particular way. There are obvious differences among the approaches across diagnostic categories, but more importantly there are some remarkable similarities.

We wish to acknowledge the many individuals who have contributed to the production of this handbook. First we thank our eminent contributors who agreed to share their expertise with us. Second, we thank our friends at John Wiley, and especially our editor, Jennifer Simon. Third, we appreciate the invaluable technical assistance provided by Carole Londerée, Sonia McQuarters, Eleanor Gil, and Erika Qualls.

MICHEL HERSEN
ALAN S. BELLACK

Forest Grove, Oregon
Baltimore, Maryland

Contents

PART ONE

MAJOR STRATEGIES

CHAPTER 1

Dynamic Psychotherapy

STEPHEN F. BUTLER, KENNETH L. CRITCHFIELD, and HANS H. STRUPP

PSYCHOTHERAPY IS often described as a "treatment," and because medical terminology (patient, therapist, diagnosis, etiology, etc.) has traditionally been used, the analogy of a physician ministering to a relatively passive patient readily springs to mind. The roles assumed by patient and therapist in psychotherapy have only superficial resemblance to this medical model. Psychotherapy is more accurately defined as a *collaborative* endeavor, or a partnership, in which the patient is expected to play an active part almost from the beginning. This active role is essential if patients are to become more autonomous, more self-directing, and more responsible for their feelings, beliefs, and actions. To feel better about themselves, their relationships with others, and their behavior, patients must learn to make changes within themselves and in their environments that permit them to feel and act differently. The process of therapy is designed not to change patients but to help patients change themselves.

In this sense, psychotherapy is a learning process, and the role of the therapist is analogous to that of a teacher or mentor. Psychotherapy is based on the assumption that feelings, cognitions, attitudes, and behaviors are the product of a person's life experience; that is, they have been learned. If something has been learned, modification of the previous learning can occur. Where learning is impossible (for example, in conditions attributable to genetic or biochemical factors), psychotherapy has little to offer directly, but even here psychotherapy can assist with coping. Similarly, if the disturbance is solely due to factors in the person's social milieu (poverty, oppression, imprisonment), or if patients do not desire change on their own (e.g., they are referred by a court or school system), psychotherapists encounter great difficulties. Thus, psychotherapy works best (1) if patients desire change of their own accord and are motivated to work toward it, (2) if the environment in which they live tolerates the possibility of change, and (3) if the inner obstacles to learning (defenses and rigidities of character) are not insurmountable.

No single definition of psychotherapy has found universal acceptance. Depending on the therapist's theoretical orientation and other factors, psychotherapy is seen by some as a psychosocial treatment, by others as a special form of education, and by still others as a means of promoting personality growth and self-actualization, to cite but a few divergent views. Most therapists agree, however, that psychotherapy involves both a human relationship and a set of techniques for bringing about personality and behavior change.

Historically, psychotherapy has roots in ancient medicine, religion, faith healing, and hypnotism. In the nineteenth century psychotherapy emerged as a prominent treatment for so-called nervous and mental diseases, and its practice became a medical art, restricted to psychiatrists. Around the middle of the twentieth century, other professions gained entry into the field, largely as a result of the growing demand for psychotherapy services. This broadened base of clinical and theoretical influence has led to modifications of the earlier disease-oriented treatment model. Today, the term *psychotherapy* is the generic term for psychological interventions that are designed to ameliorate emotional or behavioral problems of various kinds. Contemporary psychotherapy is characterized by a diversity of theoretical orientations (e.g., psychodynamic, client-centered, rational-emotive, behavioral, cognitive-behavioral, Gestalt) and treatment modalities (individual, group, family, marital).

In broadest terms, psychotherapy is concerned with personality and behavior *change*. The patient who seeks help for a psychological problem desires change (the patient wants to feel or act differently) and the psychotherapist agrees to assist the patient in achieving this goal. The major issues in psychotherapy relate to (1) *what* is to be changed, and (2) *how* change can be brought about. The first requires definition of the problem for which the patient is seeking help (depression, marital difficulties, shyness, nail biting, sexual dysfunctions, existential anxiety, etc.); the second pertains to the processes and techniques used to foster change (support, ventilation of feelings, interpretations, systematic desensitization, assertiveness training, etc.).

At this time, a considerable lack of consensus remains about how to define problems in therapy and how to foster change. Given the extraordinary complexity of the psychotherapy process, it is unlikely that any single currently existing perspective will emerge as clearly superior to the rest. Indeed, any ultimate theory of psychotherapy will certainly encompass the clinical wisdom embodied in all important perspectives. Although a mainly psychodynamic view is presented in this chapter, the attempt has been to eschew theoretical rhetoric in favor of discussing the fundamental elements of the therapeutic encounter, that is, the contributions of the patient, the therapist, and their relationship to the therapeutic encounter. In addition, conceptual and methodological concerns in the study of psychotherapy are examined; concerns that must be addressed if the field is to make appreciable scientific advances.

THE PATIENT: GENERAL CONSIDERATIONS

Perhaps the single most important characteristic of individuals who decide to consult a psychotherapist is that they are troubled. At times, they may be unaware of the cause of their suffering and unhappiness; more often, they have identified a set of circumstances they view as accounting for their disturbance. Typically, either they are dissatisfied with their lives and complain of troublesome feelings (anxiety, depression, etc.) or they see difficulties with some aspect of their behavior (phobia, impulsiveness, etc.). Often, they have tried various means of combating their difficulties, without notable success. Not uncommonly, patients have previously consulted medical specialists who refer them to a psychotherapist because the physician senses either the involvement of emotional factors or the futility of other treatment approaches.

However the patient comes to therapy, the therapist is confronted with a unique set of problems and, most important, a unique individual. Not only do prospective patients differ in the kinds of problems for which they seek help, but also they show great variations in (1) the degree of subjective distress they experience, (2) the urgency with which they desire relief, and (3) the eagerness with which they accept help once it is offered. A great deal of research has focused on the issue of what kinds of patients benefit most from psychotherapy (Garfield, 1994). For the most part, this research has not led to any clear-cut or simple results. People from all races, socioeconomic statuses, genders, and ages can benefit from therapy. These results underscore the importance of understanding the unique perspective of an individual patient in therapy, as opposed to their more general characteristics.

Further, prospective patients differ in their expectations of what a helping professional might do to bring about relief. Virtually everyone has retained from childhood the hope of magical solutions to problems—a wish that tends to become intensified when a person experiences anxiety and distress. A magical solution involves the patient's wish to be relieved of distress simply by submitting to a powerful figure (in this case the therapist). For the uninitiated, such wishes contribute to unrealistically high expectations of what psychotherapy can do. Alternatively, people whose experience with authority figures in the past has been profoundly disappointing may enter therapy with unrealistically low expectations. Such expectations occur not only among uneducated or unsophisticated patients, but also among those with broad educational and cultural backgrounds. At any rate, these expectations may have considerable bearing on a given patient's approach to psychotherapy and the evolving relationship with the therapist. A patient's unique understanding of therapy, as well as his or her transferential reactions toward therapy (that is, expectations based in parent-child and other important past relationships that are transferred to the therapy relationship) can be useful information that the therapist may use to determine the course of therapy.

As stated, patients typically want to feel better, to act differently, to stop some pattern of behavior, or to shed inhibitions that prevent them from engaging in behavior considered to be desirable. In most instances, patients tend to complain of a lack of will power and of feeling helpless. At the same time, they tend to blame their difficulties on other persons in their lives, referring to themselves (explicitly or implicitly) as victims. Whatever the nature of the complaint, the patient generally measures the outcome of therapy by improvements in feelings and behavior.

From the therapist's standpoint, the change desired by the patient is sometimes not possible, or at least not in the manner the patient desires. In many cases, although patients ostensibly desire change of a certain kind, they are unwittingly committed to maintenance of the status quo and actively oppose any change. For example, patients may express a wish to become more assertive, but it becomes apparent on exploration that they are actually searching for a human relationship that allows them to be passive and dependent.

The task of therapy involves helping the patient identify and overcome the self-imposed obstacles to change. Such obstacles are present from the beginning of a therapy, so that the patient's problem is often not what it initially appears to be. Clues about the deeper nature of a patient's problems may be evident in patterns of affect, cognition, or behavior that the patient experiences. A patient's wishes, fears, and expectations of others may also provide important information for a therapist. Still more clues may be found in the patient's relationships ranging from early experiences with caregivers, to current relationships, and even to the ongoing therapeutic relationship. Redefinitions of the problem and the goals of therapy may be indicated. As therapy proceeds, the patient and therapist (1) must work toward a mutual understanding of the problems and goals and (2) must neutralize the obstacles in order to develop a collaborative and constructive alliance. This is delicate and important work, and the achievement of this alliance alone often heralds increases in the patient's self-esteem and self-worth. Indeed, one of the most consistent findings in psychotherapy research is that the formation and maintenance of a good therapeutic relationship, from early in therapy, predicts better patient outcome (Henry, Strupp, Schacht, & Gaston, 1994; Orlinsky, Grawe, & Parks, 1994).

THE THERAPIST: GENERAL CONSIDERATIONS

The therapist attempts to be helpful to the patient or client. However, as a result of disagreements over both the purpose of psychotherapy and the way in which therapeutic change is to be brought about, there is little consensus concerning the precise role and function of the therapist even among primarily psychodynamic therapists. Some therapists view their primary task as providing patients with insight into their emotional conflicts; others seek to bring about a reorganization of the patient's cognitions and beliefs; still others work more directly toward behavioral change in the hope that successful experiences in one area will help patients gain greater self-confidence, which in turn may enable them to tackle other problems in living.

Most professionals agree that the therapist must acquire special skills, but for the aforementioned reasons, there is less agreement on the nature of these skills or on how to perfect them. Consequently, training programs for psychotherapists differ markedly in content, breadth, and duration (Strupp, Butler, & Rosser, 1988). It has even been asserted that naturally helpful persons (indigenous helpers, nonprofessionals, and paraprofessionals) may be as helpful as professionally trained therapists, thus calling into question the necessity for training in special skills or techniques.

Whatever the therapist's background or level of training, the therapist must necessarily form some notions or hypotheses about the patient's problem or difficulty, and decide what needs to be done to bring about an improvement in the patient's condition. Thus, therapists must become diagnosticians as they engage patients in activities they consider therapeutic. Both of these activities usually entail verbal (and nonverbal) communications, occurring in the context of a *relationship* that develops between patient and therapist.

In this therapeutic relationship, the patient expresses fears, hopes, and expectations, and views the therapist as a person who can provide relief from suffering. Some of the patient's expectations are realistic, but others, as already noted, are distorted, tinged with the hope of magic solutions.

Almost by definition, patients view themselves as persons in need of outside help. This places them, à priori, into a dependent position vis-à-vis the therapist. Thus, patients unwittingly tend to relate to the therapist as helpless children relate to a powerful parent (transference), thereby turning the therapeutic relationship into a quasi-parent-child relationship. Psychodynamic therapists, who essentially define the therapist as a specialist in detecting and resolving transferences, find this particularly interesting. Although there is no single agreed-upon definition of "transference," many psychodynamic therapists include in the definition any maladaptive interpersonal behavior patterns, usually learned in early important relationships, that create difficulties in the patient's current relationships and that also occur in the therapeutic relationship (Anchin & Kiesler, 1982; Butler & Binder, 1987; Gill, 1982; Henry et al., 1994; Strupp & Binder, 1984). Although some may object to the term *transference* as being too exclusively psychoanalytic a term, there is increasing recognition of the importance of the therapeutic relationship and the prior relational learning that may affect it by nonpsychodynamic theorists (e.g., behavior therapists: Wilson & Evans, 1977; cognitive therapists: Mahoney & Gabriel, 1987; Safran & Segal, 1990).

In the course of therapy, the therapist necessarily engages in a relationship with the patient and brings his or her personal influence to bear upon that relationship in order to bring about change. Of course, both the patient's and therapist's personalities determine the character and quality of their interaction, but it is the therapist who mainly defines the framework of the relationship and determines to a large extent how the relationship shall be used to achieve particular therapeutic ends. There is still a lively debate about the degree to which the therapist determines the outcome of therapy primarily by personal qualities or the degree to which the outcome is a function of the techniques employed by the therapist. It is likely that both sets of variables are interdependent and contribute significantly to the resulting therapeutic process and outcome (Butler & Strupp, 1986). Thus, whatever the role of technique, it is clear that the *personal qualities* of the therapist and their interaction with the patient's characteristics, expectations, and transference must be important factors in the equation (Beutler, Crago, & Arizmendi, 1986; Beutler, Machado, & Neufeldt, 1994; Parloff, Waskow, & Wolfe, 1978).

Finally, it is important to examine how the professional therapist differs from other helpful persons. Above all, the therapist creates a professional rather than a personal relationship with the patient. Although the patient may be lonely and in need of a friend, the therapist does not view the therapeutic task as fulfilling this need. Instead, the goal is to facilitate patients' interpersonal relationships with *others* and to help them cope more adaptively and effectively on their own. Consequently, the therapist seeks to avoid personal involvement with the patient, a stance frequently contrary to the patient's wishes.

This relative detachment allows the therapist to be more objective about the patient's difficulties. More important, the professional nature of this relationship (determined by time restrictions and the presence of a fee) enables the patient to communicate more freely by minimizing the potential for social consequences, such as shame, fear, anger, and retaliation from others. Thus, the therapeutic context makes possible the overt expression of hidden thoughts, fantasies, wishes, and so forth. As patients learn to trust the therapist and the safety of the therapeutic situation, the experience of acceptance and understanding contributes to greater self-acceptance and diminishes the patient's sense of isolation or aloneness. Armed with enhanced confidence, patients can often begin to tackle other troublesome problems in life.

Ideally, the professional therapist's interpersonal stance is one of collaboration, acceptance, respect, understanding, helpfulness, and warmth. This stance must be combined with deliberate efforts not to criticize, to pass judgment, to react emotionally to provocations, or to play an unwitting role in the harmful reenactment of transference scenarios. This deliberate effort is necessary because some patients expect to be criticized or harmed by people in positions of power or authority (perhaps mirroring experiences in other relationships), and they are particularly sensitive to the subtle implications of the words and actions of the therapist. If the therapist reenacts the role of a significant person in the past, such as critical, self-absorbed mother, then the therapist is at a disadvantage to help bring about change. In such instances, the therapist serves to reinforce relational problems. Indeed, unskillful use of a primary strategy for change in psychodynamic therapy, namely, the transference interpretation, may take on a pejorative quality. Research suggests that when this occurs, the therapist is cast in a hostile, dominant role that is harmful to the patient (Henry et al., 1994). When the therapist can maintain a collaborative and helpful stance in relation to the patient, particularly when the patient expects hostility and condemnation, this experience itself may contribute to positive changes in the patient. How to create such a relationship and to turn it to maximal therapeutic advantage is the challenge facing the psychodynamic therapist.

PSYCHOTHERAPY AND RESEARCH

Psychotherapy has always been a very practical undertaking, growing out of the clinician's desire to help a suffering human being in the most effective, economical, efficient, and humane way. The clinician's first question has always been Does a treatment help? Recognizing the importance of understanding why a treatment works, therapists have devised theories of psychotherapy. Of course, a treatment or a set of therapeutic procedures may work when the theory is wrong; or the theory may be reasonable, but the techniques inefficient or ineffective. The point to be made is that individual practitioners have no sure way of answering these questions because they must necessarily rely on the clinical method, that is, naturalistic observation of a few cases—their own. Furthermore, the history of science amply demonstrates that humanity's capacity for self-deception is so great that misconceptions (e.g., the geocentric view of the universe) may persist for centuries.

As modern psychotherapy gained momentum and its practitioners grew in number, questions were raised about the quality of the outcome, the nature of the problems to which psychotherapy might be applied, the relative effectiveness of different techniques, the adequacy of the underlying theoretical formulations, the training and qualification of therapists, the possibility of harmful effects, and many other issues. From its slow beginnings in the 1940s, research in psychotherapy has grown impressively in size and quality. It is a product of contemporary behavioral science, and as such, it exemplifies the application of modern scientific methodology to the solution of important clinical and theoretical problems. We now take a closer look at some of these problems.

THE PROBLEM OF THERAPY OUTCOME

The single most important problem, overshadowing all others and placing them in perspective, is the issue of psychotherapeutic effectiveness. The question has usually been, Is psychotherapy effective? Research efforts to address this question have been voluminous and sustained. In the years since Eysenck (1952) charged that psychotherapy produces no greater changes in emotionally disturbed individuals than naturally occurring life experiences, researchers and clinicians alike have felt compelled to answer the challenge.

Analyzing and synthesizing the data from 25 years of research on the efficacy of psychotherapy, Luborsky, Singer, and Luborsky (1975) concluded that most forms of psychotherapy produce changes in a substantial proportion of patients. These changes are often, but not always, greater than those achieved by control patients who did not receive therapy. Most contemporary reviews (e.g., Lambert & Bergin, 1994; Lambert, Shapiro, & Bergin, 1986) have reached similar conclusions. In a now-classic analysis, which summarizes our current understanding of the question, Is psychotherapy effective? M. Smith, Glass, and Miller (1980) demonstrated that across all types of therapy, patients, therapists, and outcome criteria, the average patient shows more improvement than 75 percent of untreated individuals. The preponderance of the evidence, it has become clear, does not support Eysenck's pessimistic conclusion. Overall, nearly every type of psychotherapy that has been subjected to analysis, including a number of purely psychodynamic therapies, has been shown to be more effective than no therapy at all. However, no single type of therapy or set of techniques has proven uniquely superior (Lambert & Bergin, 1994).

One difficulty encountered in investigations of differential efficacy of competing types of therapy is how to define *outcome*. When considering psychotherapy outcome, researchers and therapists alike have difficulty adequately conceptualizing and defining the notion of outcome. This lack of clarity is problematic for both psychotherapy researchers and for those charged with policy decisions regarding psychotherapy (Strupp, 1986). For example, insurance companies and government agencies increasingly are demanding accountability for treatments they are asked to reimburse.

The problem of defining psychotherapy outcome touches on many facets of human life, and conceptions of mental health and illness cannot be considered apart from the problems of philosophy, ethics, religion, and public policy. Inescapably, we deal with human existence and the person's place in the world, and ultimately, any adequate conception of outcome must confront questions of *value* (Strupp & Hadley, 1977). Someone must make a judgment about whether a person's concern with duty is a virtue or a symptom of compulsiveness; whether in one case we accept a patient's judgment that he or she feels better, whereas in another we set it aside, calling it "flight into health," "reaction formation," "delusional," and so forth. These decisions can only be made by reference to the values society assigns to feelings, attitudes, and actions. These values are inherent in conceptions of mental health and illness as well as in clinical judgments based on one of these models.

Freud (1916) already saw the outcome issue as a practical one, and this may well be the best way to treat it. When all is said and done, there may be common sense agreement on what constitutes a mentally healthy, nonneurotic person. Knight (1941) postulated three major rubrics for considering therapeutic change, which still seem eminently reasonable: (1) disappearance of presenting symptoms; (2) real improvement in mental functioning; and (3) improved adjustment to reality.

Most therapists and researchers, although they may disagree on criteria and operations for assessing these changes, would concur that therapeutic success should be demonstrable in the person's (1) feeling state (well-being), (2) social functioning (performance), and (3) personality organization (structure). The first is clearly the individual's subjective perspective; the second is that of society, including prevailing standards of conduct and "normalcy"; the third is the perspective of mental health professionals, whose technical concepts (e.g., ego strength, impulse control) partake of information and standards derived from the preceding sources but are ostensibly scientific, objective, and value free.

As Strupp and Hadley (1977) have shown, few therapists or researchers have taken seriously implications of this complex view of outcome. Therapists continue to assess treatment outcomes on the basis of global clinical impressions, whereas researchers persist in the assumption that quantitative indexes can be interpreted as if they were thermometer readings. In reality, values influence and suffuse every judgment of outcome.

Such outcome issues call into doubt the utility of the traditional, global question, Is psychotherapy effective? It has become increasingly apparent that psychotherapy is not a unitary process, nor is it applied to a unitary problem (Kiesler, 1966). Furthermore, therapists cannot be regarded as interchangeable units that deliver a standard treatment in uniform quantity or quality (see

Beutler et al., 1994; Parloff et al., 1978). Patients, too, cannot be considered a uniform variable. Instead, they respond differentially to various forms of therapeutic influence, depending on the complex interplay of personality, education, intelligence, nature of emotional difficulties, motivation, and other variables (Garfield, 1994). Finally, technique variables are thoroughly intertwined with the person of the therapist and cannot be considered in isolation (Butler & Strupp, 1986; Orlinsky, Grawe, & Parks, 1994; Orlinsky & Howard, 1986).

Accordingly, the problem of therapeutic outcomes must be reformulated as a standard scientific question: What specific therapeutic activities of specific therapists produce specific changes in specific patients under specific conditions? This question implies the scientific imperative of improving descriptions and understanding of therapists' in-session actions, other therapist variables, patient variables, and the ways in which these interact. In essence, psychotherapy researchers need to be asking still deeper questions about the nature of psychotherapy such as, How does psychotherapy work? for whom? and under what conditions. Progress along these lines, coupled with greater conceptual precision regarding outcome itself, will be essential if we are to address successfully questions regarding the relationship between therapist actions and patient outcomes. A number of researchers have recently turned to these issues utilizing new methodologies that focus on the process of therapy, the interaction of patient characteristics and approaches to treatment, and factors thought to be common to all therapies (Beutler, 1991; Bryk & Raudenbush, 1991; Rogosa, 1991; Shoham-Salomon & Hannah, 1991; Shoham & Rohrbaugh, 1995; B. Smith & Sechrest, 1991).

PATIENT VARIABLES AND THE PROBLEMS OF DIAGNOSIS

Although it may not always be recognized, therapy outcomes depend to a significant extent on patient characteristics. When a therapist encounters a new patient, the first task is to define the nature of the problem in need of treatment or amelioration. As previously mentioned, therapists must be diagnosticians who attempt to identify a problem in order to take appropriate therapeutic steps. This requires not only an understanding of the diagnostic categories into which many patients fit, but also an appreciation of the vast array of *individual differences* among patients, which may affect therapy. Deceptively simple, this problem is exceedingly fateful in its implications for therapy and research.

To illustrate, many therapists and researchers have come to realize that a phobia, a depression, or an anxiety state in one patient is not identical to a seemingly comparable problem in another. Accordingly, it may be hazardous to categorize or type patients on the basis of the presenting difficulty alone. Traditional diagnostic categories (e.g., *Diagnostic and Statistical Manual*, 4th ed., American Psychiatric Association [APA], 1994) *(DSM-IV)*, although helpful, are limited in their utility for psychotherapeutic practice and research. Other systems of classification (e.g., in terms of maladaptive interpersonal patterns, defensive styles, or ego functions), although sometimes useful, have shortcomings of their own.

The plain fact, long recognized by clinicians, is that patients differ on a host of dimensions, from intelligence, education, socioeconomic status, and age to such variables as psychological-mindedness, motivation for psychotherapy, organization of defenses, and rigidity of character. The latter grouping of patient qualities is part of a relatively stable constellation of person characteristics usually thought of as "personality." In a very real sense, the psychotherapist confronts not so much a diagnosed illness, but complex, organized patient qualities or personality characteristics that help or hinder the therapeutic process.

Human personality is *organized*, and personality organization often forms an integral part of the therapeutic problem. For example, phobic patients tend to be generally shy, dependent, and anxious in many situations (Andrews, 1966). Genetic, social, temperamental, and environmental factors of various kinds all influence the patient's current disturbance. From the psychodynamic perspective, the patient's life history, particularly interpersonal relationships in early childhood, may be crucially important for understanding and treating the current problem. This reflects the recognition that the current problem must be understood in the *context* of this person's life (Butler & Strupp, 1986) and of the unique constellation of variables that constitute this person's personality. The interest of clinicians in the Personality Disorders (Axis II of the *DSM-IV*) corresponds to an increasing awareness of this issue (cf. Frances, 1986).

The study of patient characteristics in relation to therapeutic change has for the most part focused on one basic issue: How do patient variables influence the course of psychotherapy? One ultimate goal is to answer the question, Which patient characteristics and problems are most amenable to which techniques conducted by which type of therapist in what kind of setting? Thus, rather than identifying patient characteristics associated with success across a broad band of different types of therapies, it is more important either to devise reasonably specific therapies that will benefit particular kinds of patients or to identify processes common to all therapies that may interact with patient characteristics (Gaston & Gagnon, 1996; Goldfried & Wolfe, 1996; Henry, 1996; Lambert & Lambert, 1997).

THE PROBLEM OF TECHNIQUE

Techniques are, of course, the core and raison d'être of modern psychotherapy and, as previously noted, are usually anchored in a theory of psychopathology or maladaptive learning. Psychoanalysis has stressed the interpretation of resistances and transference phenomena as the principal curative factors, contrasting these operations with the suggestions of early hypnotists. Behavior therapy, to cite another example, has developed its own armamentarium of techniques, such as systematic desensitization, modeling, aversive and operant conditioning, cognitive restructuring, and training in self-regulation and self-control. In general, the proponents of all systems of psychotherapy credit their successes to more or less *specific* operations, which are usually claimed to be uniquely effective. A corollary of this proposition is that a therapist is a professional who must receive systematic training in the application of the recommended techniques.

Only in the past decade or so have psychotherapy researchers turned to an examination of psychodynamic techniques and their relation to outcome. One technique in particular that has received attention is that of transference interpretation. In a recent review of the literature, Henry and colleagues (1994) concluded that although transference interpretations may indeed be beneficial, they also present unique risks to therapy, which may take a good deal of therapist skill and tact to handle. In particular, they noted that, consistent with the views of mainstream psychoanalytic thinkers, more interpretations are not necessarily better, and in some cases, too many or ill-considered interpretations may even damage the therapeutic alliance. Henry and colleagues also noted that therapists do not always deliver accurate transference interpretations, and some interpretations may be less accurate than had been previously assumed. One consequence of poorly timed or inaccurate interpretations is that the patient's level of defensiveness may rise, resulting in less openness to the therapy process and damage to the relationship overall.

As we have already mentioned, psychotherapy researchers have found little evidence that one approach to therapy or set of techniques is clearly superior to another, even under reasonably controlled conditions (Lambert et al., 1994; Luborsky et al., 1975; Sloane et al., 1975). The commonly accepted finding that approximately two-thirds of neurotic patients who enter outpatient psychotherapy of whatever description show noticeable improvement (Garfield, 1994; Lambert et al., 1994) likewise reinforces a skeptical attitude concerning the unique effectiveness of particular techniques. Finally, it often turns out that initial claims for a new technique cannot be sustained when the accumulating evidence is critically examined. For example, initial claims regarding the efficacy of systematic desensitization in the treatment of phobias appear not to have held up to long-term scrutiny (Marks, 1978).

An alternative hypothesis that has been advanced to account for the "no differences" finding asserts that psychotherapeutic change is predominantly a function of factors common to all therapeutic approaches (e.g., Frank, 1981). These factors are brought to bear on the human *relationship* between the patient and the healer. One version of this hypothesis holds that individuals, defined by themselves or others as patients, suffer from demoralization and a sense of hopelessness. Consequently, any benign human influence is likely to boost their morale, which in turn is registered as improvement. Primary ingredients of these factors, common to most forms of psychotherapy, include understanding, respect, interest, encouragement, acceptance, forgiveness, in short, the kinds of human qualities that since time immemorial have been considered effective in buoying the human spirit.

Frank identifies another important common factor in all psychotherapies, that is, their tendency to operate in terms of a conceptual scheme and associated procedures that are thought to be beneficial. Although the *contents* of the schemes and the procedures differ among therapies, they have common morale-building functions. They combat the patient's demoralization by providing an explanation, acceptable to both patient and therapist, for the patient's hitherto inexplicable feelings and behavior. This process serves to remove the mystery from the patient's suffering and eventually to supplant it with hope.

Frank's formulation implies that training in and enthusiasm for a special theory and method may increase the effectiveness of therapists, in contrast to nonprofessional helpers who may lack belief in a coherent system or rationale. This hypothesis also underscores the continuity between faith healers, shamans, and modern psychotherapists. The latter may operate on the basis of sophisticated scientific theories (by contemporary standards), but the function of these theories may intrinsically be no different from the most primitive rationale undergirding a faith healer's efforts. In both, techniques of whatever description are inseparable from the therapist's belief system, which in successful therapy is accepted and integrated by the patient. Of course, some patients more than others may be receptive to, and thus likely to benefit from, the therapist's manipulations.

Rogers (1956), from a different perspective, regarded a set of "facilitative conditions" (i.e., accurate empathy, genuineness, and unconditional positive regard) as necessary and sufficient conditions for beneficial therapeutic change. Thus, both Rogers and Frank deemphasize the effectiveness of therapeutic techniques per se and elevate relationship factors to a position of preeminence. From this perspective, management of the interpersonal relationship between patient and therapist may be considered a special technique in and of itself. It has been asserted that the relationship between patient and therapist not only facilitates the techniques specific to a given therapy, and that it provides a sense of hope and a rationale, but that it is also healing in another direct sense. By engaging in a relationship with a therapist, a patient is able to internalize and incorporate (introject) the relationship with the therapist so as to replace earlier maladaptive introjections (Henry & Strupp, 1994). It is in this sense that psychotherapy has been referred to as a "reconstructive" process (Benjamin, 1993). Early attempts to empirically establish the mechanism(s) by which the relationship may be linked to patient change have yielded positive results (Harrist, Quintana, Strupp, & Henry, 1994; Henry, Schacht, & Strupp, 1990; Quintana & Meara, 1990).

It is clear that the problem of technique has important ramifications for research and practice. For example, if further evidence can be adduced that techniques contribute less to good therapy outcomes than has been claimed, greater effort might be expended in selecting and training therapists who are able to provide the aforementioned common factors, and who are more sensitive and responsive to the relational processes that are a part of nearly every kind of therapy. We also need far more information about the kinds of therapeutic services that may be performed safely by individuals with relatively little formal training (paraprofessionals), as well as the limits set by their lack of comprehensive training. Furthermore, there may be patients for whom the establishment of any sort of positively toned relationship may be extremely difficult (e.g., personality-disordered patients), and whose treatment should be relegated to professionals specially trained in techniques designed to help create and maintain a therapeutic relationship with such patients. Nevertheless, there may be definite limitations to what techniques, per se, can accomplish (Frank, 1974). Limits may be set by patient characteristics and therapist qualities, which may include the therapist's level of training.

THE PERSON OF THE THERAPIST

As previously suggested, psychotherapy prominently involves the interaction of two or more *people,* and the therapeutic influence is by no means restricted to the formal techniques a therapist may use. The patient, like the therapist, reacts to the other as a total person; hence, both researchers and clinicians must become centrally concerned with the therapist as a human being. What has been said about enormous individual differences among patients applies, of course, with equal force to therapists. Indeed, it is difficult to fathom how, in early psychoanalysis, as well as in the later research studies, therapists could ever have been treated as interchangeable units, presumably equal in skill and personal influence (Kiesler, 1966). Therapists, like patients, obviously differ in as many dimensions as one cares to mention: age, gender, cultural background, ethnic factors, level of professional experience, psychological sophistication, maturity, empathy, tact, social values, to name but a few. Any or all of these may have a significant bearing on the therapist's theoretical orientation, the therapist's techniques, and the manner in which the therapist interacts with and influences a given patient.

When considering the unique effects of each therapist as an individual, many therapist qualities elude definition. This elusiveness has posed serious obstacles to research in this area, although it is possible to specify human qualities a good therapist should possess (Holt & Luborsky, 1958), as well as those that may be harmful to patients (Bergin, 1966; Strupp, Hadley, & Gomes-Schwartz, 1977). Research and practical interest in identifying and describing qualities of therapists that may be detrimental to patients is reminiscent of the ancient medical principle, Above all, do no harm. Clearly it is as important to know what a therapist should *not* do as it is to specify what the therapist *should do.*

Among the therapist variables that have been subjected to quantitative research are the therapist's personal adjustment and well-being; the facilitative conditions already mentioned (warmth, empathy, genuineness, etc.); the therapist's cognitive style; the therapist's level of professional experience; the therapist's professional status (professionals versus nonprofessionals or paraprofessionals); gender; age; socioeconomic status; ethnicity; and the therapist's social and cultural values. Effects of personality conflicts, needs, and attitudes of the therapist toward the patient have also been investigated in a variety of studies (Beutler et al., 1994; Orlinsky & Howard, 1986; Parloff et al., 1978). Of all the therapist variables that have been studied, one of the few relatively robust findings has been that the therapist's level of emotional well-being, impacts patient outcome. Beutler and colleagues summarize by stating:

> While one can currently conclude only that therapist mental health may be an important but not necessary condition for improvement in high-functioning clients, the possibility that emotional problems on the part of the therapist may negatively affect even relatively well-functioning clients should be given considerably more attention. (p. 238)

Furthermore, patient personality characteristics demonstrably influence the therapist's effectiveness, which suggests that patients should be selected more carefully to match the therapist's capabilities, or perhaps therapists should be more specifically trained to deal with different personalities. Although therapists appear to be differentially effective with particular patients (Strupp, 1980a, 1980b, 1980c, 1980d), it has proven difficult to isolate salient dimensions of the therapist's personality and to measure the impact of those dimensions. Indeed, it is becoming increasingly clear that variables of *individual* therapists, except perhaps for glaring defects in the therapist's personality, are not likely to provide the answers sought by researchers and clinicians. Instead, a combination of therapist attributes appears to form an integrated *gestalt*, to which the patient responds positively, negatively, or neutrally, other things being equal.

Clinical wisdom suggests that the effective therapist must be able to instill trust, confidence, hope, and conviction in the patient's personal strength and resilience. To have a therapeutic impact on the patient, the therapist's personality must have distinctive stimulus value or salience; therapists can never be impersonal technicians, nor can they apply therapeutic techniques in a vacuum. At times, therapists must be capable of encouraging patients to explore a particular feeling, belief, attitude, and so on; at other times, they must wait patiently for the patient to find his or her own solutions. They must be able to distinguish between the patient's neurotic and nonneurotic needs, and they must avoid getting entangled in the patient's neurotic maneuvers. Above all, they must make a careful assessment of how much help is needed, what kind of help is needed, and what obstacles prevent the patient from reaching a constructive solution.

THE THERAPEUTIC ALLIANCE

Psychoanalytic theorists (e.g., Greenson, 1967; Langs, 1973; Menninger & Holtzman, 1973) have identified the relationship between patient and therapist as a major therapeutic force. As Freud developed the technique of psychoanalytic therapy, he recognized that the patient must become an active partner who collaborates with the therapist in his or her own cure. Traditionally, psychoanalysts have postulated an "observing ego" (cf. Strupp & Binder, 1984, p. 39), which represents the reasonable and rational part of the patient's personality and is capable of forming an alliance with the therapist's efforts to analyze the irrational (transferential) aspects of the patient's personality. This alliance is the foundation for the necessary collaboration between therapist and patient that permits the analysis to proceed.

To the extent that factors within the patient or the therapist interfere with the establishment of a productive therapeutic alliance, therapeutic progress will be retarded or even vitiated. Premature termination or intractable dependency on the therapist are instances of such failures. It is also well known that patients who have relatively intact and strong egos have a better chance of succeeding in analytic therapy (Horwitz, 1974; Kernberg, 1976), and perhaps in other forms of therapy as well.

Research into the nature of the alliance, as well as its relation to outcome, has greatly increased over the past fifteen to twenty years in response to the work of Bordin (1974, 1979), who reframed the traditionally psychodynamic concept of the alliance as a factor common to all types of therapy. Although there is no precise consensual definition of the alliance, theorists have addressed such questions as, How does the alliance develop? How is it best conceptualized? What is its structure? What are the relative contributions of patient and therapist? and How does the alliance impact outcome? (Henry et al., 1994). Although these questions still remain largely unanswered, researchers agree that the alliance consists of aspects of the relationship between patient and therapist, such as their ability to collaborate on goals and tasks, their emotional bond, and their interpersonal behavior (Bordin, 1979; Henry & Strupp, 1994; Orlinsky & Howard, 1986). Despite differing definitions and measures of the alliance, researchers have observed a consistent moderate relationship between measures of the therapeutic alliance and measures of outcome (Horvath & Symonds, 1991). The link between alliance and outcome indicates that a better therapeutic alliance early in therapy predicts a better therapeutic outcome. This alliance–outcome relationship has been observed in a wide variety of therapeutic settings, patient populations, measures of outcome, and types of therapy (Henry et al., 1994).

Horvath and Symonds (1991), in a meta-analysis of alliance research, found that the predictive validity of the alliance differs depending on the perspective of the rater. Alliance ratings made by patients and independent observers are more highly predictive of outcome than ratings made by therapists. In discussing this finding, Henry and colleagues (1994), have raised the possibility that therapists may have a blind spot (p. 487) when it comes to judging the quality or strength of the alliance and that therapists may benefit from more training in the understanding, recognition, and enhancement of relational processes common to all types of therapy. If therapists are more aware of the ongoing relational process, they may be able to responsively adjust their own contributions to the therapeutic alliance according to the needs of patients.

Although it superficially resembles any good human relationship (of the kind discussed elsewhere in this chapter), the therapeutic alliance provides a unique starting point for the patient's growing *identification* with the therapist, a point stressed by the proponents of object relations theory (Fairbairn, 1952; Guntrip, 1971; Kernberg, 1976; Winnicott, 1965), who spearheaded advances in psychoanalytic theory. According to these authors, internalization of the therapist as a good object is crucial for significant psychotherapeutic change. Because internalization of bad objects has made the patient "ill," therapy succeeds to the extent that the therapist can be internalized as a good object. However, because patients tend to remain loyal to the early objects of childhood, defending them against modification, therapy inevitably becomes a struggle. From this perspective, patients' amenability to therapy (i.e., their ability to form a therapeutic alliance) is importantly influenced by their early relations with others. Consistent with these ideas, early work focused on a patient's contribution to the alliance points to the importance of a patient's pretherapy interpersonal functioning (e.g., Gaston, 1991; Kiesler & Watkins, 1989; Kokotovic & Tracey, 1990; Marmar, Weiss, & Gaston, 1989; Moras & Strupp, 1982; Wallner, Muran, Segal, & Schumann, 1992), quality of object-relations (e.g., Piper et al., 1991; Piper & McCallum, 1997), and the nature of their relationships with early caregivers (e.g., Christenson, 1991; Mallinckrodt, 1991).

CODA: THE FUTURE OF PSYCHODYNAMIC PSYCHOTHERAPY?

In the previous edition of this volume, which was written at the end of the 1980s, we concluded with speculation on the great potential that might arise from intensive integration of psychotherapy research and practice. We envisioned a close collaboration of clinicians and researchers geared specifically toward greater understanding of which therapist actions are most effective with which patients in a way that could be readily integrated into the clinical situation. The tone of these conclusions was optimistic and forward looking, building on principles of dynamic psychotherapy, but inclusive of other perspectives as well. The ultimate goal of this systematic process of exploration was to understand what the clinician could do when facing the complex patient presentations that occur daily in the clinician's office.

However, just as the first edition of this volume was published, a profound change began to take place in the practice of psychotherapy. Economic and political changes in the early 1990s resulted in the proliferation of managed care entities, which began a process of defining both mental illness and psychotherapy, based on economic and political realities rather than scientific and clinical ones. The initial salvo of these powerful institutions was to adopt completely a medical model of "mental illness" based on symptom presentation, and to limit the role of psychotherapy to the amelioration of the acute version of these symptoms. That is, if someone presents with a phobia, for instance, the clinician is expected to focus on the presenting complaint—the phobia. The clinician is discouraged by case reviewers and extreme time limitations from working with the patient on how these phobic symptoms mesh with other, maladaptive aspects of his or her personality. Removal of the symptom from the patient's personality, as should be apparent from this chapter, is antithetical to a psychodynamic approach.

Consider an example from one of our caseloads. A young mother presented with a phobia of driving on interstate highways. Although one might approach a simple phobia with systematic desensitization, for instance, this woman was incapable of "imagining" with the therapist, of attempting progressive relaxation, or of even closing her eyes in the therapist's office. Exploration revealed that the main effect of the phobia on her was her difficulty visiting her invalid father a few hours drive away in an adjoining state. Further exploration revealed that she was extremely focused on maintaining interpersonal control in virtually any situation. This caused difficulty with her husband, neighbors, children, and her father (who shared the controlling tendencies), and was evident in her refusal to consider a psychopharmacological evaluation. Thus, clearly the phobic symptoms were nested within a personality that demanded interpersonal control, even when it meant being out of control of which highways she could travel. This formulation does not insist that only a psychodynamic therapy could help this woman. Rather, the point is that divorcing the symptom presentation from the personality, as the managed care organizations would have the clinician do, is not consistent with clinical reality.

A recent *APA Monitor* front page article addressed the use of psychotherapy research by the managed care industry as justification for limiting benefits to very brief (and inexpensive) treatments (Sleek, 1997). This article pointed out how some benefit limits have been justified by insurance companies on the basis of selecting controlled research that showed symptom improvement to be achieved in very brief periods of time (such as six sessions). This ignores the fact that such research typically restricts patients to having only one problem, and specifically excludes those who present with active suicidal threat, have comorbid substance abuse problems, or present with other serious complicating factors that are commonly seen in clinical settings. The managed care companies also have ignored research concluding that improvements in psychotherapy tend to accrue with longer treatments (e.g., Kopta, Howard, Lowry, & Beutler, 1994). Finally, the difficulties of measuring outcomes in psychotherapy continue to plague researchers and clinicians alike. Indeed, one problem in psychotherapy research is that patients tend to feel better about the *decision to enter psychotherapy*, so that it is common for patients to report feeling more in control, less frightened, and more optimistic. Such "improvement" often registers on standard symptom measures as improvement, even before the person meets with the therapist. Difficulties such as these conspire against simple, straightforward research designs and methods to demonstrate the effectiveness of psychotherapy.

What does the future hold for dynamic psychotherapy and psychotherapy in general? There are attempts by dynamic authors to tailor dynamic theory and therapy to demands of the medical model by highlighting that several models of brief dynamic therapy are directed toward particular symptom presentations (e.g., Crits-Christoph & Barber, 1991; Levenson, Butler, & Beitman, 1997). Such approaches to the problem rest on the assumption that for dynamic psychotherapy to remain a viable force in the future, researchers and theorists will have to achieve greater precision about what the therapist is doing, with whom, and why.

Another approach to the dilemma facing psychotherapy is reflected in efforts to move psychotherapy research away from tightly controlled clinical trials (efficacy research) in rarefied, usually academic settings and toward examination of the treatment's effectiveness in traditional clinical settings. This approach is being advanced by the National Institute on Mental Health (NIMH) and APA (Sleek, 1997). There is an emphasis on improving the research so that the case for extended treatments can be made when such treatments are indicated. Perhaps in this way, it will be possible to re-include personality as central to the treatment of our patients.

As discussed earlier, psychotherapy research emerged in response to charges from Eysenck (1952) that psychotherapy was no better at achieving changes in emotionally disturbed individuals than naturally occurring life experiences. Thirty years later, psychotherapy and psychotherapy research face another, ill-considered challenge. Once again, the field will need to respond with creativity and diligence to those who would criticize it. One hopes that the resulting advances in knowledge will take the theory and practice of psychotherapy well into the next century.

REFERENCES

American Psychiatric Association. (1994). *Diagnostic and statistical manual of mental disorders* (4th ed.). Washington, DC: Author.

Anchin, J.C., & Kiesler, D.J. (1982). *Handbook of interpersonal psychotherapy.* New York: Pergamon Press.

Andrews, J. (1966). Psychotherapy of phobias. *Psychological Bulletin, 66, 455–480.*

Benjamin, L.S. (1993). *Interpersonal diagnosis and treatment of personality disorders.* New York: Guilford Press.

Bergin, A.E. (1966). Some implications of psychotherapy research for therapeutic practice. *Journal of Abnormal Psychology, 71, 235–246.*

Beutler, L.S. (1991). Have all won and must all have prizes? Revisiting Luborsky et al.'s verdict. *Journal of Consulting and Clinical Psychology, 59*(2), 226–232.

Beutler, L.S., Crago, M., & Arizmendi, T.G. (1986). Therapist variables in psychotherapy process and outcome. In S.L. Garfield & A.E. Bergin (Eds.), *Handbook of psychotherapy and behavior changes* (3rd ed., pp. 256–310). New York: Wiley.

Beutler, L.S., Machado, P.P.P., & Neufeldt, S.A. (1994). Therapist variables. In A.E. Bergin & S.L. Garfield (Eds.), *Handbook of psychotherapy and behavior change* (4th ed., pp. 229–270). New York: Wiley.

Bordin, E.S. (1974). *Research strategies in psychotherapy.* New York: Wiley.

Bordin, E.S. (1979). The generalizability of the psychoanalytic concept of the working alliance. *Psychotherapy: Theory, Research and Practice, 16, 252–260.*

Bryk, A.S., & Raudenbush, S.W. (1991). *Hierarchical linear models: Applications and data analysis methods.* Newbury Park, CA: Sage.

Butler, S.F., & Binder, J.L. (1987). Cyclical psychodynamics and the triangle of insight: An integration. *Psychiatry, 50, 218–231.*

Butler, S.F., & Strupp, H.H. (1986). "Specific" and "nonspecific" factors in psychotherapy: A problematic paradigm for psychotherapy research. *Psychotherapy, 23, 30–40.*

Christenson, J. (1991). *Understanding the patient–therapist interaction and therapeutic change in light of pre-therapy interpersonal relations.* Unpublished doctoral dissertation, Vanderbilt University, Nashville, TN.

Crits-Christoph, P., & Barber, J.P. (Eds.). (1991). *Handbook of short-term dynamic psychotherapy.* New York: Basic Books.

Eysenck, H.J. (1952). The effects of psychotherapy: An evaluation. *Journal of Consulting Psychology, 16,* 319–324.

Fairbairn, R. (1952). *Object relations theory of the personality.* New York: Basic Books.

Frances, A.J. (1986). Introduction to personality disorders. In A.M. Cooper, A.J. Frances, & M.H. Sacks (Eds.), *Psychiatry: The personality disorders and neuroses* (Vol. 1, pp. 171–189). New York: Basic Books.

Frank, J.D. (1974). Therapeutic components of psychotherapy: A 25-year progress report of research. *Journal of Consulting and Clinical Psychology, 47,* 310–316.

Frank, J.D. (1981). Therapeutic components shared by all psychotherapies. In J.H. Harvey & M.M. Parks (Eds.), *The master lecture series: Psychotherapy research and behavior change* (Vol. 1). Washington, DC: American Psychological Association.

Freud, S. (1960). Analytic therapy. In J. Strachey (Ed. and Trans.), *Standard edition of the complete psychological works of Sigmund Freud* (Vol. 16, pp. 448–463). London: Hogarth. (Original work published 1916)

Frieswyk, S.H., Allen, J.G., Colson, D.B., Coyne, L., Gabbard, G.O., Horwitz, L., & Newsom, G. (1986). Therapeutic alliance: Its place as a process and outcome variable in dynamic psychotherapy research. *Journal of Consulting and Clinical Psychology, 54,* 32–38.

Garfield, S.L. (1994). Research on client variables in psychotherapy. In A.E. Bergin & S.L. Garfield (Eds.), *Handbook of psychotherapy and behavior change* (4th ed., pp. 190–229). New York: Wiley.

Gaston, L. (1991). Reliability and criterion-related validity of the California psychotherapy alliance scales. *Psychological Assessment, 3,* 68–74.

Gaston, L., & Gagnon, R. (1996). The role of process research in manual development. *Clinical Psychology: Science and Practice, 3*(2), 13–24.

Gill, M.M. (1982). *Analysis of transference: Theory and technique.* New York: International Universities Press.

Goldfried, M.R., & Wolfe, B.E. (1996). Psychotherapy practice and research. *American Psychologist, 51*(10), 1007–1016.

Greenson, R. (1967). *The technique and practice of psychoanalysis.* New York: International Universities Press.

Guntrip, H. (1971). *Psychoanalytic theory, therapy, and the self.* New York: Basic Books.

Harrist, R.S., Quintana, S.M., Strupp, H.H., & Henry, W.P. (1994). Internalization of interpersonal process in time-limited dynamic psychotherapy. *Psychotherapy, 31*(1), 49–57.

Hartley, D.E., & Strupp, H.H. (1983). The therapeutic alliance: Its relationship to outcome in brief psychotherapy. In J. Masling (Ed.), *Empirical studies of psychoanalytic theories* (Vol. 1, pp. 1–37). Hillsdale, NJ: Analytic Press.

Henry, W.P. (1996). Structural analysis of social behavior as a common metric for programmatic psychopathology and psychotherapy research. *Journal of Consulting and Clinical Psychology, 64*(6), 1263–1275.

Henry, W.P., Schacht, T.E., & Strupp, H.H. (1990). Patient and therapist introject, interpersonal process, and differential psychotherapy outcome. *Journal of Consulting and Clinical Psychology, 58*(6), 768–774.

Henry, W.P., & Strupp, H.H. (1994). The therapeutic alliance as interperonal process. In A.O. Horvath & L.S. Greenberg (Eds.), *The working alliance: Theory, research, and practice* (pp. 51–84). New York: Wiley.

Henry, W.P., Strupp, H.H., Schacht, T.E., & Gaston, L. (1994). Psychodynamic approaches. In A.E. Bergin & S.L. Garfield (Eds.), *Handbook of psychotherapy and behavior change* (4th ed., pp. 467–508). New York: Wiley.

Holt, R.R., & Luborsky, L. (1958). *Personality patterns of psychiatrists: A study in selection techniques* (Vol. 1). New York: Basic Books.

Horowitz, M.J., Marmar, C., Weiss, D.S., DeWitt, K.N., & Rosenbaum, R. (1984). Brief psychotherapy of bereavement reactions: The relationship of process to outcome. *Archives of General Psychiatry, 41*, 438–488.

Horvath, A.O., & Symonds, D.B. (1991). Relationship between working alliance and outcome in psychotherapy: A meta-analysis. *Journal of Counseling Psychology, 38*, 139–149.

Horwitz, L. (1974). *Clinical practice in psychotherapy.* New York: Jason Aronson.

Kernberg, O.F. (1976). Some methodological and strategic issues in psychotherapy research: Research implications of the Menninger Foundation's Psychotherapy Research Project. In R.L. Spitzer & D.F. Klein (Eds.), *Evaluation of psychological therapies*. Baltimore: Johns Hopkins University Press.

Kiesler, D.J. (1966). Some myths of psychotherapy research and the search for a paradigm. *Psychological Bulletin, 65*, 110–136.

Kiesler, D.J., & Watkins, L.M. (1989). Interpersonal complementarity and the therapeutic alliance: A study of relationship in psychotherapy. *Psychotherapy, 26*, 183–194.

Knight, R.P. (1941). Evaluation of the results of psychoanalytic therapy. *American Journal of Psychiatry, 98*, 434–446.

Kokotovic, A.M., & Tracey, T.J. (1990). Working alliance in early phase of counseling. *Journal of Counseling Psychology, 37*, 16–21.

Kopta, S.M., Howard, K.I., Lowry, J.L., & Beutler, L.E. (1994). Patterns of symptomatic recovery in psychotherapy. *Journal of Consulting and Clinical Psychology, 62*, 1009–1016.

Lambert, M.J., & Bergin, A.E. (1994). The effectiveness of psychotherapy. In A.E. Bergin & S.L. Garfield (Eds.), *Handbook of psychotherapy and behavior change* (4th ed., pp. 143–190). New York: Wiley.

Lambert, M.J., & Lambert, J.M. (1997, June). *Do meta-analytic reviews confirm the Dodo bird verdict?* Paper presented at the annual convention of the Society for Psychotherapy Research, Geilo, Norway.

Lambert, M.J., Shapiro, D.A., & Bergin, A.E. (1986). The effectiveness of psychotherapy. In S.L. Garfield & A.E. Bergin (Eds.), *Handbook of psychotherapy and behavior changes* (3rd ed., pp. 157–211). New York: Wiley.

Langs, R. (1973). *The technique of psychoanalytic psychotherapy.* New York: Jason Aronson.

Levenson, H., Butler, S.F., & Beitman, B.D. (1997). *Concise guide to brief dynamic therapy.* Washington, DC: American Psychiatric Press.

Luborsky, L., Mintz, J., Auerbach, A., Christoph, P., Bachrach, H., Todd, T., Johnson, M., Cohen, M., & O'Brien, C.P. (1980). Predicting the outcome of psychotherapy: Findings of the Penn Psychotherapy Project. *Archives of General Psychiatry, 37*, 471–481.

Luborsky, L., Singer, B., & Luborsky, L. (1975). Comparative studies of psychotherapies: Is it true that "Everybody has won and all must have prizes?" *Archives of General Psychiatry, 32*, 995–1008.

Mahoney, M.J., & Gabriel, T.J. (1987). Psychotherapy and the cognitive sciences: An evolving alliance. *Journal of Cognitive Psychology, 1*(1), 39–59.

Mallinckrodt, B. (1991). Clients' representations of childhood emotional bonds with parents, social support, and formation of the working alliance. *Journal of Counseling Psychology, 38*, 401–409.

Marks, I.M. (1978). Behavioral psychotherapy of adult neurosis. In S.L. Garfield & A.E. Bergin (Eds.), *Handbook of psychotherapy and behavior change: An empirical analysis* (2nd ed., pp. 493–547). New York: Wiley.

Marmar, C.R., Weiss, D.S., & Gaston, L. (1989). Towards the validation of the California therapeutic alliance rating system. *Psychological Assessment, 1,* 46–52.

Menninger, K.A., & Holtzman, P.S. (1973). *Theory of psychoanalytic techniques* (2nd ed.). New York: Basic Books.

Moras, K., & Strupp, H.H. (1982). Pretherapy interpersonal relations, patients' alliance, and outcome in brief therapy. *Archives of General Psychiatry, 39,* 405–409.

Morgan, R., Luborsky, L., Crits-Christoph, P., Curtis, H., & Solomon, J. (1982). Predicting the outcomes of psychotherapy by the Penn helping alliance rating method. *Archives of General Psychiatry, 39,* 397–402.

Orlinsky, D.E., Grawe, K., & Parks, B.K. (1994). Process and outcome in psychotherapy—Noch Einmal. In A.E. Bergin & S.L. Garfield (Eds.), *Handbook of psychotherapy and behavior change* (4th ed., pp. 270–378). New York: Wiley.

Orlinsky, D.E., & Howard, K.I. (1986). Process and outcome in psychotherapy. In S.L. Garfield & A.E. Bergin (Eds.), *Handbook of psychotherapy and behavior change* (3rd ed., pp. 311–384). New York: Wiley.

Parloff, M.B., Waskow, I.E., & Wolfe, B.E. (1978). Research on therapist variables in relation to process and outcome. In S.L. Garfield & A.E. Bergin (Eds.), *Handbook of psychotherapy and behavior change* (2nd ed., pp. 233–282). New York: Wiley.

Piper, W.E., Azim, F.A., Joyce, S.A., McCallum, M., Nixon, G., & Segal, P.S. (1991). Quality of object relations vs. interpersonal functioning as predictors of alliance and outcome. *Journal of Nervous and Mental Disease, 179,* 432–438.

Piper, W.E., & McCallum, M. (1997, June). *Interaction of personality characteristics and forms of time-limited psychodynamic psychotherapy.* Paper presented at the annual meeting of the Society for Psychotherapy Research, Geilo, Norway.

Quintana, S.M., & Meara, N.M. (1990). Internalization of therapeutic relationships in short-term psychotherapy. *Journal of Counseling Psychology, 37*(2), 123–130.

Rogers, C.R. (1956). The necessary and sufficient conditions of therapeutic personality change. *Journal of Consulting Psychology, 21,* 95–103.

Rogosa, D. (1991). A longitudinal approach to ATI research: Models for individual growth and models for individual differences in response to intervention. In R.E. Snow & D.E. Wiley (Eds.), *Improving inquiry in social science: A volume in honor of Lee J. Cronbach* (pp. 221–248). Hillsdale, NJ: Erlbaum.

Safran, J., & Segal, Z. (1990). *Interpersonal process in cognitive therapy.* New York: Basic Books.

Shoham, V., & Rohrbaugh, M. (1995). Aptitude X treatment interaction (ATI) research: Sharpening the focus, widening the lens. In M. Aveline & D. Shapiro (Eds.), *Research foundations for psychotherapy research.* Sussex, England: Wiley.

Shoham-Salomon, V., & Hannah, M.T. (1991). Client-treatment interactions in the study of differential change processes. *Journal of Clinical and Consulting Psychology, 59*(2), 217–225.

Sleek, S. (1997, December). The "cherrypicking" of treatment research. *APA Monitor, 29,* 1, 21.

Sloane, R.B., Staples, F.R., Cristol, A.H., Yorkston, N.J., & Whipple, K. (1975). *Short-term analytically oriented psychotherapy vs. behavior therapy.* Cambridge, MA: Harvard University Press.

Smith, B., & Sechrest, L. (1991). Treatment of aptitude X treatment interactions. *Journal of Consulting and Clinical Psychology, 59*(2), 233–244.

Smith, M.L., Glass, G.V., & Miller, T.I. (1980). *The benefits of psychotherapy.* Baltimore: Johns Hopkins University Press.

Strupp, H.H. (1980a). Success and failure in time limited psychotherapy: A systematic comparison of two cases (Comparison 1). *Archives of General Psychiatry, 37,* 595–603.

Strupp, H.H. (1980b). Success and failure in time limited psychotherapy: A systematic comparison of two cases (Comparison 2). *Archives of General Psychiatry, 37,* 708–716.

Strupp, H.H. (1980c). Success and failure in time limited psychotherapy: With special reference to the performance of a lay counselor (Comparison 3). *Archives of General Psychiatry, 37,* 831–841.

Strupp, H.H. (1980d). Success and failure in time limited psychotherapy: Further evidence (Comparison 4). *Archives of General Psychiatry, 37,* 947–954.

Strupp, H.H. (1986). Psychotherapy: Research, practice and public policy (How to avoid dead ends). *American Psychologist, 41,* 120–130.

Strupp, H.H., & Binder, J.L. (1984). *Psychotherapy in a new key: A guide to time-limited dynamic psychotherapy.* New York: Basic Books.

Strupp, H.H., Butler, S.F., & Rosser, C.L. (1988). Training in psychodynamic therapy. *Journal of Consulting and Clinical Psychology, 56,* 689–695.

Strupp, H.H., & Hadley, S.W. (1977). A tripartite model of mental health and therapeutic outcomes: With special reference to negative effects in psychotherapy. *American Psychologist, 32,* 187–196.

Strupp, H.H., Hadley, S.W., & Gomes-Schwartz, B. *(1977). Psychotherapy for better or worse: The problem of negative effects.* New York: Jason Aronson.

Wallner, L., Muran, J.C., Segal, Z.V., & Schumann, C. (1992, June). *Patient pretreatment interpersonal problems and therapeutic alliance in short-term cognitive therapy.* Paper presented at the annual meeting of the Society for Psychotherapy Research, Berkeley, CA.

Wilson, G.T., & Evans, I.M. (1977). The therapist-client relationship in behavior therapy. In A.S. Gurman & A.M. Razin (Eds.), *Effective psychotherapy: A handbook of research.* New York: Pergamon Press.

Winnicott, D. (1965). *The family and individual development.* New York: Basic Books.

CHAPTER 2

Behavior Therapy

G. STENNIS WATSON and ALAN M. GROSS

BEHAVIOR THERAPY emerged in the years following World War II as psychologists applied principles of learning to therapeutic situations. Initially, behavior therapy referred to the use of classical and operant techniques in clinical settings; for example, Skinner's work with psychiatric patients or Wolpe's work with neurotic patients. In the 1970s and 1980s behavioral techniques were popularized when *behavior modification* became a household term. In the past decade the field of behavior therapy has continued to expand, and it now encompasses both original forms of behavior therapy and such evolving trends as cognitive behavioral therapy, group behavior therapy, and use of treatment manuals.

The term *behavior therapy* was first employed in the 1953 status report of Lindsley, Skinner, and Solomon to describe an operant conditioning paradigm used to treat patients with psychoses. A few years later, Lazarus described Wolpe's (1958) reciprocal inhibition techniques as behavior therapy (O'Donohue & Krasner, 1995). However, the roots of behavior therapy reside in much earlier formulations of learning principles and behavioral psychology. Two schools of learning, classical conditioning and operant conditioning, provided the theoretical and methodological foundations for early behavior therapy.

CLASSICAL CONDITIONING

The phenomenon of classical conditioning was described in the writings of Ivan Pavlov and in the doctoral dissertation of Edwin B. Twitmyer (Domjan, 1993). In the basic classical conditioning paradigm, an event (the unconditioned stimulus, US) that evokes a native response (the unconditioned response, UR) is paired with a second event (the conditioned stimulus, CS), and over repeated pairings the CS comes to evoke the same response (conditioned response, CR) as the US. When stimuli similar to the CS evoke the CR, *generalization* has taken place. When stimuli that differ from the CS fail to evoke the CR, *discrimination* has taken place. When the CS ceases to evoke the CR, *extinction* has occurred.

The Little Albert study of Watson and Raynor (1920, cited in Gerow, 1989) illustrates the implication of classical conditioning for behavior therapy. Watson and Raynor used a loud noise to condition an eleven-month-old child to cry in the presence of a white rat, a response that he repeated in the presence of a variety of objects that resembled the rat. If, as Watson and Raynor suggested, the child's behavior was indicative of a state of fear, then it may be inferred that fear is a learned response. If fear is a learned response to a conditioned stimulus, a behavior therapist should be able to use learning principles to extinguish the fear response and, perhaps, to pair the feared object with some unconditioned stimulus that evokes a satisfying response.

INSTRUMENTAL CONDITIONING

Concurrent with the work of Pavlov, the foundations were being laid for instrumental or operant conditioning. E.L. Thorndike formulated the law of effect, which states that "if a response in the presence of a stimulus is followed by a satisfying event, the association between the stimulus and the response is strengthened. If the response is followed by an annoying event, the association is weakened" (Domjan, 1993, p. 125). In the mid- and late twentieth century B.F. Skinner elucidated many of the principles of instrumental conditioning and carried learning principles into applied settings (Ferster & Skinner, 1957; Skinner, 1953).

In essence there is a family of instrumental conditioning procedures. In the positive reward procedure some behavior is followed by a satisfying (appetitive) stimulus, or reward, such that a person (or a nonhuman animal) behaves in a way that enhances the probability of the reward. In the positive punishment procedure some behavior is followed by an unpleasant (aversive) stimulus, or punishment, such that a person behaves in a way that decreases the probability of the punishment. In the negative reward procedure some behavior is followed by the removal of an aversive stimulus, such that a person behaves in a way that increases the probability of the removal of an aversive stimulus. In the negative punishment procedure some behavior is followed by the removal of an appetitive stimulus, such that a person behaves in a way that decreases the probability of removal of the appetitive stimulus. Avoidance occurs when a person learns to make a response that blocks the presentation of a punisher before it can be delivered.

The effects of instrumental conditioning are evident in many settings. For example, when a parent takes a child to a grocery store, they often pass by a candy display at the checkout line. The child may request a candy bar and the parent refuses. The child cries loudly; the parent gives in to the child; the child gets the candy and ceases crying; the parent is relieved. From one point of view the story illustrates positive reward: The child is rewarded with a candy bar for crying loudly, and most likely will cry again the next time candy is withheld. From another point of view the story illustrates negative reward: The child's crying annoys the parent, and the source of annoyance is removed. From a third point of view the parent may have learned an avoidance behavior: Giving the child a candy bar before the child begins to cry prevents an embarrassing or frustrating state in the parent's life. Thus, behavior, both adaptive and maladaptive, is maintained by the contingencies associated with behavior. For the parent to change the child's crying behavior, the parent will need to cease to reward the child for crying.

Social Learning

Historically, a third school, social learning theory, has exerted a strong influence on the evolution of behavior therapy. Both classical and instrumental conditioning explored learning in the context of a direct relationship between the person (or animal) being conditioned and the event supplying the stimuli or contingencies. The work of Albert Bandura suggested that learning may also occur by observation (Bandura, 1977b). For example, when children observed adults striking a rubber doll, the children imitated the adults and struck the doll (Bandura, Ross, & Ross, 1963). From social learning theory the concept of modeling has become accepted in the literature of behavior therapists and the popular press.

THE PRINCIPLES OF CONTEMPORARY BEHAVIOR THERAPY

Contemporary behavior therapy eludes simple description (Wixted, Bellack, & Hersen, 1990). It does not employ a single set of methods or a monolithic theory. The best way to understand behavior therapy is to explore the traditions from which it arose, and to grasp the vocabulary that those scientific traditions exported to applied settings. From those scientific traditions and from traditional and current practice of behavior therapy, a family of common principles can be extracted.

Empiricism

The therapy room is an applied laboratory where the clinician uses an experimental method to promote behavior change. Assessment of the problematic behavior is made through observation and carefully designed measures. Hypotheses are developed concerning the conditions that maintain maladaptive behaviors or aversive states. Variables are operationalized as objective and publicly verifiable phenomena to facilitate measurement. Interventions are formulated based on sound theory and experimentally validated methods. Assessment continues throughout the intervention. At the end of the treatment period, the clinician evaluates behavior change and the mechanisms for change. Hence, strengths of behavior therapy include the ability to examine whether a given treatment was effective for a given client and the ability to explore the capacity of that treatment to generalize to other clients or other problem behaviors.

LEARNING HISTORY AND CONTEXT

Behavior therapy assumes that a person's behavioral repertoire is learned through interaction with the environment and that present contingencies maintain behavior. Consequently, behavioral change is dependent on altering a person's environment or the way a person responds to his or her environment. Neither biology nor internal motives are primary concerns. Rather, antecedents, consequences, stimuli, and responses are the vehicles through which change is accomplished. For example, if a person with an insect phobia was treated in behavior therapy, the therapist would not explore the symbolic meaning of the phobia. The therapist would seek to disconnect the object feared (an insect) from the fear response, perhaps by exposing the person to insects repeatedly until the person ceased to respond fearfully to them.

IDIOGRAPHIC APPROACH

From the beginning, behaviorism has been a science of the individual. Lessons were derived from Pavlov's dogs, Watson's Little Albert, and Skinner's pigeons, not as groups of subjects, but as individuals. Sidman's (1960) classic text on laboratory methods in psychology emphasizes that each participant is an experiment in himself or herself and that successive participants are replications of the experiment undertaken with a single participant. This method has been retained in the clinical application of behaviorism. In both the laboratory and the clinic, group data have often been discredited because they do not reflect the performance of any specific individual, and may, in fact, obfuscate the true performance of a single individual (Barlow & Hersen, 1984). Consequently, the maladaptive behavior that a person seeks to change is best approached on an individual basis, and the single-case design has been adopted as the preferred method for behavior change. (See Barlow & Hersen, 1984, pp. 26–27, for M.B. Shapiro's contribution to this method in behavior therapy.)

FUNCTIONAL APPROACH

Behavior therapy takes a functional approach to diagnosis and treatment. Traditionally, there has been little concern with nosological labels, which define problems in medical rather than behavioral terms. The task of diagnosis is to describe a person's problematic behaviors in terms consistent with learning theory: antecedents and consequences, stimulus objects and learned responses, behavioral excesses or deficits, or events in the environment that alter a person's motivation to respond to stimuli. Such terminology is consistent both with the way in which maladaptive behavior is conceptualized in behavior therapy and with the interventions that will be made.

However, reluctance to use nosological labels has softened among some behavior therapists. In certain cases, such as posttraumatic stress disorder (PTSD) or specific phobias, nosological labels may be helpful in organizing clusters of symptoms that respond well to given treatments. This has permitted the development and validation of standardized treatments for several symptom constellations. (See Barlow, 1993.)

GOAL ORIENTATION

Behavior therapy is an action-oriented approach. Target behaviors are identified and goals for change are established. To the extent that target behaviors have been modified, the therapy is said to be successful. Furthermore, this approach often enlists the client as an active participant in therapy: identifying goals, completing assignments that propel the client toward the goals, and self-monitoring change as it occurs. In behavior therapy the therapist takes the role of educator, program director, or consultant. This contrasts with therapies that seek to help the client understand why he or she acts or perceives life experiences in a certain way, which confine the therapeutic process to the clinic, and confine the therapist to the role of explorer of the client's cognitive or intrapsychic processes.

Goal orientation facilitates a time-limited approach in behavior therapy. When goals are clear and measures of change are objective, then the end of therapy can be determined with some clarity. When objectives have been reached, then new goals must be established or therapy terminated.

ASSESSMENT

The behavior therapist asks, What the client's current behavior is? What the antecedents and consequences of this behavior are? What can be done to change the behavior? and How can change be evaluated? (Wilson, 1989). These questions demand a continuous assessment of the client's behavior and environment, from the initial consultation until the concluding session. Direct observation of behavior is a central feature of behavior therapy. Even the therapy room itself is a place where the therapist can observe a sample of client behaviors under well-specified conditions, and then draw inferences about the client's interpersonal behavior in other contexts. Behavior therapy is especially interested in behavior as it occurs in the contexts of interest, and a behavior therapist may observe the client in a naturalistic setting. Self-monitoring and descriptions of client behavior by other persons in the environment (e.g., a teacher, friend, or family member) may elucidate client behaviors. Because behavior is expected to change in relation to environmental changes, assessment throughout therapy is needed to answer the question, If the environment is modified in a specified fashion, how does the client's behavior shift? At the conclusion of therapy, assessment helps to describe behavioral changes that have occurred in response to interventions. Comparing data across clients allows behavior therapists to develop hypotheses about the generalizability of an intervention.

ASSESSMENT

Traditionally, the goals of behavioral assessment have been to identify target behaviors, determine controlling variables, facilitate the selection of treatment strategies, and evaluate the treatment outcome (Nelson & Hayes, 1981). These goals differ from those of measurement systems that seek to assess the individual against the context of a normal population or to assess psychological processes deep within the individual. Behavioral and nonbehavioral approaches to assessment share instruments and techniques (e.g., clinical interview, role playing, self-report measures, and standardized tests). However, the data of interest vary according to assumptions driving the therapy. In a clinical interview a behavior therapist is not interested in defense mechanisms or normative problem-solving abilities. The behavior therapist is attempting to assess the nature of the client's behavior and how the environment controls the behavior of the client. Likewise, a behavior therapist may give repeated administrations of the Beck Depression Inventory in order to establish changes in the client over time, but typically not to ask whether the client is more or less depressed than most people. In this sense, all measures in behavioral assessment are viewed as direct or indirect behavioral samples.

Pragmatic concerns (e.g., the demands of managed care or the practice of behavior therapy within a medical community, Peterson & Sobell, 1994) and the rise of treatment manuals (see Barlow, 1993) have added a fifth objective, clinical diagnosis. Diagnostic labels are inconsistent with the assumptions of behavior therapy, but their use may be a reality forced upon many behaviorally oriented clinicians. Therefore, structured interviews and checklists aimed at assigning diagnostic labels have become a part of the assessment used by behavior therapists.

As with all good measures, behavioral assessment measures should possess appropriate psychometric properties (Cone, 1981). The most basic of these is reliability, or consistency of measurement over time, between raters, within a test session, or within a given instrument. For example, if two observers are counting the number of times that a child initiates conversation with a peer, and their counts vary, then the researcher needs to explore whether one or both raters were casual in their counting, whether the variable of interest (initiating conversation) was operationalized adequately, or whether there was an instrument failure. In any case, unreliability will decrease the probability that meaningful patterns will appear in visual representations of the child's behavior. A second basic concept is validity, which describes a faithful relationship between a measure and the construct of interest. In behavioral assessment the issue of validity is seen in the use of self-report measures to determine the behavior of the client. To the extent that the client reports accurately, the measure may possess validity as an indicator of behavior. However, the client often cannot or chooses not to report accurately, so that the self-report measure may be a valid indicator of the client's desired, but not actual, behavior.

INTERVIEW TECHNIQUES

A clinical interview is an important beginning point in a complete functional assessment (Morganstern & Tevlin, 1981). The purposes are to establish rapport with the client, to gather enough data to specify the problems that the client is experiencing, and to observe a sample of the client's behavior. The interview may suggest treatment approaches that should be taken or raise additional issues that must be answered from different types of measures. At the conclusion, the interviewer should have a detailed understanding of the client's presenting problems in order to facilitate subsequent assessment and treatment.

Unstructured clinical interviews have the flexibility to explore a variety of issues and can provide the therapist with the opportunity to build rapport with a client. This flexibility may be especially critical with certain persons or with certain constellations of symptoms. For example, persons who show signs of posttraumatic stress disorder following rape must be approached with sensitivity, and yet, the therapist needs substantial details concerning the rape to construct an effective intervention (Resick & Schnicke, 1993; Resnick, Kilpatrick, & Lipovsky, 1991). An unstructured interview may permit the therapist to collect all the necessary data while maintaining a therapeutic relationship with the client. However, an unstructured interview is no more reliable or valid than the clinician that administers it. The clinician must be sufficiently skilled to elicit behaviors and information important to conceptualizing the client's case.

Structured clinical interviews have become common among many behavior therapists, and a number of instruments have been developed to assess symptoms and behavior generally or as they relate to specific problems. One of the most widely used of the general interview schedules has been the Structured Clinical Interview (SCID) (Spitzer, Williams, & Gibbon, 1987) for the *Diagnostic and Statistical Manual of Mental Disorders* (3rd ed. rev.) *(DSM-III-R)* (American Psychiatric Association [APA], 1987), and it appears likely that the revision of the SCID for the *DSM-IV* (American Psychiatric Association [APA], 1994) will continue to have a strong influence among clinicians (Calhoun & Resick, 1993). An alternative to the SCID is the Diagnostic Interview Schedule (DIS) (Robbins, Helzer, Croughan, & Ratcliff, 1981). A questionnaire specifically designed to facilitate behavioral assessment is the Behavioral Analysis History Questionnaire (BAHQ) (Cautela & Upper, 1976, in Cormier & Cormier, 1991, pp. 617–624). The advantage to a comprehensive structured interview is that it forces the clinician to assess the client across many domains, and, therefore, it has the potential to detect symptoms that might have been missed otherwise. The disadvantages of comprehensive structured interviews are the collection of data irrelevant to presenting problems (lack of economy) and the potential to impede the development of a therapeutic relationship.

As an alternative to a comprehensive interview, limited interview schedules have been created for a number of symptom areas. For example, clinicians treating persons with symptoms of anxiety can use the Anxiety Disorders Interview Schedule (ADIS) (DiNardo, Brown, & Barlow, 1994; also, Brown, O'Leary, & Barlow, 1993) or the Clinician Administered PTSD Scale (CAPS) (Blake et al., 1990; see J. Beck & Zebb, 1994). A widely used clinical interview for eating disorders is the Eating Disorder Examination (EDE) (Fairburn & Wilson, 1993; see Wilson & Pike, 1993). The edited volume by Barlow (1993) identifies limited interview schedules and self-report instruments for several disorders. The advantage of limited interview schedules is a focus on behaviors and symptoms of interest. However, they require that the clinician be relatively certain that the behaviors and symptoms assessed are the only ones of interest.

Client self-ratings form a useful adjunct to the clinical interview. Self-ratings may be relatively unstructured. For example, subjective units of distress (SUDS) ratings are a simple way to get at the client's current emotional state. Clients are instructed to provide a numerical indicator of distress on a 0–100 scale, with greater numbers indicating greater distress (Hope & Heimberg, 1993). Subjective units of distress can provide economical and reliable data on the client's subjective reactions to stimuli. On the other hand, clients self-rating scales can be highly structured, such as the Beck Depression Inventory (BDI) (A. Beck, 1978; A. Beck, Rush, Shaw, & Emery, 1979), which requires the client to answer 21 items on a 0–3 scale, and from which a total "depression score" is computed.

Both structured and unstructured client self-ratings come with a caveat. The behaviors sampled by self-ratings are not objective behaviors of the client; they are the client's awareness, interpretation, and presentation of behavior. Therefore, self-ratings are measures of the client's reporting tendencies, not actual behavior. Self-ratings are valid measures of objective behavior only in so far as the client is willing and able to report objective behavior. Furthermore, in behavior therapy self-ratings have idiographic value as indicators of individual change over a specified interval of time, rather than normative value (i.e., comparison of a client with a population average). For example, a behavior therapist can use a BDI to determine a client's admission of changes in eating, sleeping, concentration, or suicidality, but that therapist would be unlikely to use BDI scores to compare this client with some other client.

OBSERVATION OF BEHAVIOR

From the early days of behaviorism, observation of overt behavior has been the principal assessment technique (see Kazdin, 1981). Direct observation varies along two dimensions. First, behavior may be observed in a naturalistic setting (e.g., observing children playing on a playground) or in a contrived setting (e.g., placing a child alone with toys in a clinic room). Second, assessment may be obtrusive or unobtrusive: The observer may be hidden (e.g., behind an observing window), visible but minimally obtrusive (e.g., an observer sitting quietly near a child who is playing), or extremely obtrusive (e.g., an observer who is engaging a child in a conversation in order to note how the child responds to an unfamiliar adult). Numerous strategies have been developed for coding and recording directly observed behavior. For example, the observer may record how long a child talks to another child (duration), how many times the child initiates conversation in a given time interval (frequency), or the number of children with whom the child initiates conversation (frequency). Whether in a natural setting or contrived, and whether using measures of frequency or duration, the observer's task is to quantify units of publicly verifiable behavior.

Naturalistic observation is an assessment of behaviors as they occur in the client's usual life context. Therefore, it has a high degree of ecological validity.

For example, if an unnoticed observer sees a parent and a child in a grocery store arguing about whether the child may have candy, the observer can be reasonably certain that under similar circumstances the interaction will be repeated. The observer may be able to detect particular antecedents, consequences, and contextual variables that are associated with the interaction, and develop predictions about the conditions necessary for repetition of the interaction. Furthermore, these observational data have not been contaminated by self-report of a highly-emotional event.

There are a number of instances when naturalistic observation may be impractical, unethical, or impossible. For example, "it is seldom possible to perform behavioral observations of substance abusers while they are intoxicated, and if it were possible, the observations would need to occur over extended periods and in a variety of settings" (Sobell, Toneatto, & Sobell, 1994, p. 534). Direct observation of child sexual abuse by a client (without observer intervention into the abusive event) would be profoundly unethical. Furthermore, direct observation may require traveling to a distant or inconvenient location, and it may require a substantial amount of time from the observer. In these cases other approaches to assessment must be employed.

Observation of behavior in contrived situations offers an alternative to naturalistic observation. In some instances these observations are minimally intrusive. For example, if a client has reported excessive irritability and angry outbursts, the therapist may design an experiment to reveal the effects of client frustration: The client may be asked to complete some tedious or extraneous paperwork while waiting for therapy to begin; the client's behavior may be monitored by a confederate posing as a member of the office staff.

The Behavioral Avoidance Test (also known as the Behavioral Approach Test), or BAT, is frequently used in the assessment of clients with obsessive compulsive or phobic problems (J. Beck & Zebb, 1994; Steketee, 1994; Wixted et al., 1990). Typically, a list of feared objects is generated and then organized in a hierarchy of feared objects. The client is then asked to approach each, beginning with the least feared and ending with the most feared. The therapist may take subjective ratings (SUDS) or quantify specific behaviors as the client moves from one object to the next. In a similar assessment for clients who fear crowds, the therapist may ask the client to leave the office and walk as far away as he or she can. The point at which the client stops and returns to the office becomes a behavioral index of the client's fear. The BAT has several advantages: It can provide objective behaviors as measures, measure objects actually feared (ecological validity), and be repeated to evaluate therapeutic change over time.

Role play is used with a variety of symptom presentations. The best use of role play occurs after the therapist has collected enough data to define client problem behaviors and design scenarios that establish specific contexts of interest to the therapist. Then, the therapist can test hypotheses about the client's reactions to persons, events, and environments. For example, if a client reports a distressing relationship with a coworker, it may be impractical for the therapist to observe the client and coworker directly, and the therapist may elect to use role playing to understand how the client responds to the co-worker. It is important for the therapist to reconstruct the work environment and present the coworker accurately, if germane responses are to be elicited from the client. When role playing works effectively, the therapist can observe client behaviors and obtain client ratings of emotional states. (See Cormier & Cormier, 1991.)

When performing direct behavioral observations, the therapist must not lose sight of the concept of situational specificity, or, in behavioral terms, the influence of the environment on behavior. Role playing is a contrived event, and may be of little use if it does not sufficiently approximate the environment of interest. However, even seemingly nonobtrusive naturalistic observation should be scrutinized for ways in which the effect of observation modifies the client's normal response patterns. For example, presence of an unfamiliar adult on a school playground may alter how children interact with one another. In the most obvious case the children actively attend to the adult and not to one another. In a more insidious case, the children may attend to one another, but their behavior is behavior in the presence of an adult rather than typical recess play behavior.

Indirect methods of behavioral observation, in which the client or a person who knows the client reports the client's behavior, may be used to supplement the direct observational methods. Self-monitoring is a common technique of indirect observation of behavior. Target behaviors (or feelings) are selected, and the client records the frequency, latency, duration, or intensity of behaviors (Cormier & Cormier, 1991). Self-monitoring may be specific to particular client situations. For example, if a client presents at a university clinic requesting help with academic improvement, the therapist may ask the client to keep a record of when and how long he or she read, how many pages, at what times of the day, whether the client studied alone or with others, whether the client took study breaks, what specific distractors were in the study area, and subjective ratings of attention, concentration, and satisfaction with that study period. Likewise, self-monitoring may employ standardized forms, such as those described by Brown et al. (1993) for generalized anxiety disorder or by Riggs and Foa (1993) for obsessive compulsive disorder.

There are some cautions and limitations for using self-monitoring. First, because the client is aware that ratings are being taken, reactivity should be a concern: The client's behavior may change as a function of recording. Second, the client may overreport (e.g., a "cry for help") or underreport (e.g., social desirability) behaviors. Third, extensive rating programs require time and commitment from the client, and so the client must be enlisted as an active participant for self-ratings to be effective. Fourth, some clients simply are not able to collect self-ratings. In order to maximize the accuracy of self-ratings, target behaviors must be defined clearly, objectively, and completely; the client must be trained properly to make self-ratings; and a commitment must be obtained from the client to engage in the task. (See Cormier & Cormier, 1991.)

Collateral reports of client behaviors are common in the assessment of children or adults with mental retardation and developmental disorders, where teacher and parent ratings may form the basis for referral or diagnosis. Because most behavior occurs in a social context, collateral reports may be more helpful in behavioral assessment than current use suggests. For example, a spouse may supply details of behavior that the client failed to report, or the spouse may be able to add detail to the description of the environment in which the behavior occurs. Assets of collateral reports are that these data are available, frequently at low cost, and provide parallel measures against which client reports can be verified (Sobell et al., 1994). However, the therapist must remember to respect client confidentiality and to submit collateral data to the same scrutiny for reliability and validity as any other report measures.

PHYSIOLOGICAL MEASURES

Use of physiological and biochemical means of assessment have been popularized in some treatment areas but not in others. For example, urine, breath, hair, saliva, and blood tests are reliable and accurate in the detection of recent drug or alcohol use, and elevated blood levels of carbon monoxide and cotinine are indicators of tobacco use. Therefore, biochemical assays may be important in behavioral assessments of alcohol, drug, or tobacco treatment (Sobell et al., 1994). However, in general physiological measures have not demonstrated substantial clinical utility, even when they possess experimental validity (Beck & Zebb, 1994; Steketee, 1994).

ARCHIVAL DATA

Generally, existing records have not played a prominent role in behavioral assessment. This may be a natural consequence of behavior therapy's ahistorical focus. However, they should not be dismissed summarily. For example, employment, medical, academic, and legal records can provide evidence of how disrupted a client's life is.

THERAPY

Wixted et al. (1990) suggested three features that differentiated behavior therapy from other approaches to psychotherapy. First, behavior therapy is concerned with current thoughts, feelings, and behaviors. An assumption of behavior therapy is that knowledge of past traumatic events or of unconscious conflicts does not facilitate the process of therapy. Rather a client needs to learn either to respond differently when confronted with disturbing stimuli or to modify the environment so that those stimuli no longer control the client's responses. Second, most behavior therapies require the client's active participation. Typically, the behavior therapist helps the client identify objectifiable problems and to set goals for remediating the problems. Homework assignments are used to engage the client in therapeutic activities between sessions and to aid the process of generalization from the therapy room to the client's life context. Third, empirical validation is a hallmark of the behavior therapies. Behavior therapy grew out of a laboratory science and it continues to set experimental scrutiny as the gold standard for determining that a particular therapeutic technique is effective (see Emmelkamp, 1994).

CLASSICAL CONDITIONING MODELS

Classical conditioning models, the most well known of which is Wolpe's (1958) systematic desensitization, have a long history within the context of behavior therapy. As early as 1924, Mary Cover Jones, a student of J.B. Watson, treated children's phobias with a conditioning model in which she trained children to eat in the presence of a feared object (Wolpe, 1995). The basic assumption of these models is that the client has learned to pair some neutral stimulus with a negative emotion, and, therefore, these are relearning procedures. Treatment is effective when a stimulus that elicited negative emotions has been neutralized. These models are frequently used in the treatment of a variety of anxiety disorders, where their effectiveness has been demonstrated (Emmelkamp, 1994).

Systematic desensitization, a counterconditioning model in which a client's fear response is replaced by a pleasant response, has been used successfully with phobias and social anxiety (Wolpe, 1995). First, the client is provided with a rationale for this particular treatment. Second, the client is taught to relax. Third, the client and therapist compose a hierarchy of feared objects. Next, the therapist describes the least-feared object to the client; the client holds that image in mind for a short interval, at the end of which the therapist instructs the client to release the image and to relax. When anxiety associated with one item in the hierarchy has been reduced, then the therapist proceeds to the next item (see Cormier & Cormier, 1991). Wolpe (1958, 1995) explained the effect of this technique by the term *reciprocal inhibition,* or the inhibition of a weak response (e.g., fear) by a stronger and incompatible response (e.g., deep relaxation, see McGlynn, Moore, Rose, & Lazarte, 1995). However, extinction (Lomont, 1965) and self-control (Goldfried, 1971) have been proposed as alternative explanations for the effectiveness of systematic desensitization.

In exposure procedures clients are placed in the presence of high intensity, anxiety-provoking stimuli for long periods of time. Exposure may be to the actual object of fear (in vivo, or direct exposure) or by imagination (indirect exposure). Unlike systematic desensitization, no attempt is made to teach the client a competing satisfying emotional response. The client is simply subjected to an experience of anxiety, and the anxiety-response subsides (see Craske & Barlow, 1993, pp. 19–22, for a discussion of massed versus spaced exposure, graduated versus intense exposure, and controlled escape versus stimulus endurance). Flooding and systematic desensitization are equally effective in treating specific phobias, and exposure is a treatment of choice with obsessive compulsive disorder (Emmelkamp, 1994). Foa and colleagues have proposed a model of prolonged exposure for rape-related PTSD (Foa, Rothbaum, Riggs, & Murdock, 1991).

Relaxation techniques have been effective with panic disorder and generalized anxiety disorder (Emmelkamp, 1994). Methods include progressive muscle relaxation (PMR; Brown et al., 1993), imagery, and breathing exercises.

First, clients are taught to self-induce a state of relaxation, and then they are taught to evoke the state of relaxation when they are confronted by anxious feelings or intrusive thoughts.

OPERANT CONDITIONING MODELS

Operant models are based on the premise that people act on their environment in ways that maximize the likelihood of satisfying responses from the environment and minimize the likelihood of unsatisfying responses. The most basic versions of operant therapy reward individuals for adaptive behaviors and punish individuals for maladaptive behaviors. For example, if children complete their school assignments without having to be reminded, parents may reward the children with a trip to the movies or an arcade game. If the children do not complete their daily assignments, then the parents may punish the children by not allowing television viewing that evening. These methods have been used successfully in settings where the environment can be controlled and where specified response sets are desired. (See Watson & Gross, 1997, for a discussion of operant models used with persons with mental retardation and autism.)

Schedules of reinforcement directly affect the outcome of operant conditioning. Normally, a person will respond to a continuous reinforcement schedule at a moderate, steady rate, and will stop responding soon after reinforcement ceases. Variable interval schedules may produce less consistent, high-rate responding, but they are far more resistant to extinction than continuous schedules of reinforcement (Domjan, 1993). Recent work with schedules of reinforcement has focused on less traditional schedules, such as differential-reinforcement-of-other behaviors (DRO) (Mazaleski, Iwata, Vollmer, Zarcone, & Smith, 1993), multicomponent treatment models (Carr & Carlson, 1993; Iwata, Duncan, Zarcone, Lerman, & Shore, 1994), and applications of the matching law (Neef, Mace, Shea, & Shade, 1992; Noll, 1995).

The token economy (Ayllon & Azrin, 1968; Kazdin, 1977) employs both immediate and long-term reinforcement to modify behavior. In this procedure target behaviors are specified, and persons are rewarded with tokens for engaging in target behaviors. When a sufficient number of tokens have been received, then they may trade the tokens for a desired reward. For example, each time a child picks up his or her toys, the parent may reward that child with a gold star on a highly visible board; when the child has accrued a specified number of stars, the child gets to choose where the family will go for supper. Token economies have been used successfully across a variety of clinical settings, as well as in experimental models of behavior.

Self-control, self-reward, or *self-reinforcement* refer to behavioral models in which clients regulate their own behavior. According to Bandura (1971) several conditions are necessary for self-reinforcement: The individual (1) determines the performance criteria for the contingency, (2) controls access to the contingency, and (3) administers the contingency (Cormier & Cormier, 1991). Contingencies in this paradigm may be positive or negative rewards or punishments, just as in traditional operant models. For example, a student who has studied diligently for an examination may decide to reward himself or herself with a movie, or a student that has failed to study for an examination may decided that he or she cannot spend the evening with friends but must study instead. Self-control has been used in classroom-management, weight-loss programs, exercise programs, and treatment of depression (Cormier & Cormier).

Some behavior therapists may raise a difficult theoretical objection to the concept of self-control, in which the individual controls the contingencies. To the extent that the individual chooses to administer his or her own rewards and punishments, that individual is not under the control of the environment. A traditional behavior therapist may then ask what contingencies control the individual's choice to administer consequences for behavior, because an individual's behavior must by definition be under the control of the environment.

SELF-EFFICACY THEORY

According to self-efficacy theory, human functioning is not a mechanistic reaction to the environment but reflects the interaction of environment, behavior, and personal factors (including the person's affect, cognition, and biology). Therefore, self-efficacy theory stands in sharp distinction with conditioning models, in which behavior is a direct consequence of environmental forces. Self-efficacy theory posits that people possess cognitive capacities that facilitate their knowledge about events in the environment. Knowledge about environmental events allows the person to have a degree of self-motivation and self-direction. A basic tenet of self-efficacy theory is that a person's perceptions of his or her self-efficacy make causal contributions to that person's behavior (Bandura, 1977a; Cervone & Scott, 1995). The implication of this theory is that as clients gain a sense of confidence in their abilities to change, then change is more likely to occur. Therefore, a therapist who works from the stance of self-efficacy theory will be interested in the client's cognitions, especially as they relate to a sense of self-empowerment, in addition to the client's environment, behavior, and affect. Self-efficacy theory has been applied to simple phobias, agoraphobia, smoking cessation, and cardiac rehabilitation.

MODELS OF THERAPY IN A SOCIAL CONTEXT

Therapy within a social context is a natural extension of behavior therapy. It provides a naturalistic setting in which to assess client behavior, and it permits the client to practice behavior change in vivo. One of the concerns of therapy of all types is how to generalize gains made in the therapy room to the client's world. In many instances therapy in a social context allows clients to learn behavior changes in their world so that the initial generalization has already been made.

Social-skills training uses education and behavioral training to remediate deficits and excesses in social behavior. In a psychoeducational model, clients may be taught overtly how to interact in appropriate ways and given the opportunity to practice good interpersonal skills. In an operant model clients may not receive overt instruction, but they are rewarded for appropriate interpersonal behavior. Social-skills training has been applied to aggressive behavior (Middleton & Cartledge, 1995), autism (Kamps et al., 1992), residents with mental retardation and psychotic disorders (Stewart, Van Houten, & Van Houten, 1992), and depression (Donohue, Acierno, Hersen, & Van Hasselt, 1995). The interested reader is referred to recent special issues of the *Journal of Applied Behavior Analysis* (Summer 1992) and *Behavior Modification* (July 1993) for a series of articles on this topic.

Recently, behavioral group therapy has come into its own right. This format has been used to teach social competence (Rose & LeCroy, 1985), and to treat depression (Lewinsohn, Breckenridge, Antonuccio, & Teri, 1985), addictive disorders (Barrios, Turner, & Ross, 1985), sexual disorders (McGovern & Jensen, 1985), anxiety disorders (Emmelkamp & Kuipers, 1985), and chronic pain (Kulich & Gottlieb, 1985).

COGNITIVE-BEHAVIORAL MODELS

Cognitive-behavioral therapy (CBT) models retain the idiographic, action oriented focus of traditional behavior therapies, and they add an emphasis on altering maladaptive thought patterns as well as maladaptive behaviors and feelings. The behavioral component is much like that of traditional behavior therapy.

The cognitive component of cognitive-behavioral therapy, which owes a substantial debt to the work of Albert Ellis and Aaron Beck, is based on a cognitive learning model. In essence, as persons have experiences with the world, they form patterns of thinking (schemas) that reflect their experiences and shape their thoughts, feelings, and behavior. For example, a child with hypercritical parents may have learned the following report card schema: At the evaluation period the child receives Bs across all school subjects; the child takes the report card home to the parents; the parents criticize the child for "a poor performance" and take away 30 minutes of television viewing each night; the child responds with feelings of anger and frustration; each grading period becomes an anxiety provoking event because the child "knows" the sequence of events that follows Bs. The child may generalize parental criticisms to other evaluative situations, so that the child begins to believe that failure is inevitable and success is impossible.

In cognitive-behavioral therapy models, schemas direct a person's behavior by offering a framework of what to expect from the world and then by guiding behavior more or less automatically in accordance with the schemas. When schemas are not accurate representations of the world, they can cause a person to behave in maladaptive ways. Cognitive-behavioral therapists intervene by helping the client develop accurate schemas that guide the person into adaptive behavior. Using the example of the child who assimilated a tendency toward extreme self-criticism, the therapist may challenge aspects of the child's thinking, such as a self-label ("failure") or all-or-nothing thinking ("I can never do anything right"), to assist the child in developing schemas that lead to adaptive behavior.

CBT has been applied to a diversity of disorders including depression (Thase, Bowler, & Harden, 1991; Thase, Simons, Cahalane, & McGeary, 1991), body image and obesity (Rosen, Orosan, & Reiter, 1995), benzodiazepine discontinuation (Morin, Colecchi, Ling, & Sood, 1995), bulimia (Kettlewell, Mizes, & Wasylyshyn, 1992), pathological gambling (Ladouceur, Boisvert, & Dumont, 1994), and obsessions (Ladouceur, Freeston, Gagnon, Thibodeau, & Dumont, 1995).

Cognitive processing therapy for rape victims (CPT) (Resick & Schnicke, 1993) illustrates the application of CBT to rape-related PTSD. The two primary components of CBT are intense exposure to the rape and cognitive restructuring. First, clients are asked to develop full accounts of the rape (exposure). Next, they are taught to identify maladaptive ways in which they think about the rape (cognitive restructuring). Finally, they are asked to consider a set of issues (safety, trust, power and control, esteem, and intimacy) that relate to having been raped. The intention of this particular program is to guide rape victims back into the event and to allow them to reinterpret the event in ways that ameliorate PTSD symptoms.

MODELS INTEGRATING PHYSIOLOGY AND BEHAVIOR

The changing roles of behavior therapists are illustrated in the evolving relationship between physiological sciences and behaviorism. The Brelands' work with instinctive drift (i.e., the tendency of organisms to perform innate rather than learned behaviors) (Breland & Breland, 1961), demonstrated that animals behave within some naturally occurring parameters. Although psychology is not a physiological science, it does seek to explain how the products of anatomy and physiology (e.g., instinctive drift, behavioral potentials, hunger, or developmental milestones) affect behavior (Reese, 1996). Thus, behavioral psychologists may be quite at home treating a hyperactive child who is also taking methylphenidate, or working with patients with diabetes to live a symptom-free life style.

Treatments that combine the use of psychopharmacology and behavior therapy are relatively common. In residential programs schizophrenic patients may receive both neuroleptics and behavior modification to help reduce psychotic behavior. In counseling centers clients may receive a combination of antidepressant medications and cognitive therapy to treat major depression. In the treatment of children with attention deficit/hyperactivity disorder a combination of methylphenidate and behavior interventions is employed frequently as a means of controlling behavior (Ajibola & Clement, 1995; Johnson, Handen, Lubetsky, & Sacco, 1994; Rapport et al., 1996; see *Behavior Modification*, April 1992).

Behavioral medicine is the application of behavioral techniques to medical problems. For example, in many medical centers psychological interventions are used to assist with cardiac and physical rehabilitation. Some specific applications of behavioral medicine include encopresis (Reimers, 1996), nocturnal enuresis (Houts, 1991), obesity (Brownell & Wadden, 1991), smoking cessation (Klesges, Benowitz, & Meyers, 1991), and depression (Sheldon, Hollon, Purdon, & Loosen, 1991).

EMERGING ISSUES

Manualized Treatments

Behavior therapy is founded on an empirical approach to intervention. Single case approaches bring the scientific acumen of the lab to the consulting room, and a design such as an ABA design offers both basic and clinical researchers evidence that an intervention is effective (Barlow & Hersen, 1984). A natural outgrowth of behaviorism's evidential quest is experimental validation of a specified intervention for a specific constellation of symptoms. Two elements are essential for the success of experimentally validated treatments: One is a specified treatment approach, and the other is a consensus (if uneasy) concerning constellations of symptoms that may be treated as a diagnostic construct. The need for treatment manuals has produced well-defined treatment strategies for a number of disorders (see Barlow, 1993, 1996). Consensus concerning diagnostic constructs remains a point of contention for many behavior therapists.

It appears likely that use of manualized treatments will grow in popularity. Therefore, it is suggested that behavioral therapists need to develop an adequate nosology, construct standardized treatments that are effective with nosological categories, and validate the treatments for specific client populations and specific nosological categories. This means being able to state which groups of persons and symptoms are likely to respond to which treatments (convergent validity) and which are likely not to respond (discriminant validity).

Managed Care

In the 1990s, the medical and behavior health communities have undergone substantial changes in organization and in the delivery of treatment, and the trend toward these changes driven by a market place economy appears to continue. Although the ultimate outcome of these changes is difficult to predict, it does appear likely that managed care will alter delivery of behavioral health services in substantial ways. For example, therapists may have to provide evidence of the efficacy of a given treatment if it is to be reimbursed under managed care, or managed care organizations may dictate to therapists which treatments are acceptable. The practice of behavior therapy would benefit from systematic studies of the demands that managed care is presently making and those that are likely to be made in the future. With these data, members of the behavior therapy community would be better prepared to integrate their science with market-driven exigencies or to offer resistance to managed care demands that are not in the best interest of clients (see Mash & Hunsley, 1993).

COMPUTERS

Computers have become common in homes, offices, schools, and health facilities. Therefore, a natural question is, What role can computers play in behavior therapy? At the very least, their entertainment functions can serve as important reinforcers for children in modern North American culture, and computers can facilitate communication among professionals. Some authors have suggested that computers may actually be used in therapy. For example, the use of computers has been explored in treating obesity (Taylor, Agras, Losch, Plante, & Burnett, 1991) and self-injurious behavior (Hastings, Remington, & Hall, 1995). If computers are to be assimilated into therapy practice, then behavioral scientists need to explore issues of effectiveness and utility. As with other treatment modalities, researchers need to determine whether computer-based therapies provide positive treatment outcomes, and whether these positive outcomes can be made available economically.

CONTINUING ISSUES

Problems associated with generalizability, durability, and social validity continue to trouble the field of behavior therapy (Wixted et al., 1990). Generalizability and durability are core issues in both the experimental and applied sciences of behaviorism, and many issues of such important behavioral publications as the *Journal of Applied Behavior Analysis* devote space to discussions of generalization, discrimination, and maintenance of behavior. A particular way in which generalizability relates to behavior therapy is the question of treatment efficacy across groups. It appears that the move to develop experimentally validated treatments will extend the discussion of generalizability. Validation requires specification of populations for which a given treatment is efficacious and populations for which it is not efficacious. Moreover, behavior therapists need to be aware of the limits of available treatment and need to develop new interventions suitable for populations in which existing treatments fail.

Likewise, the durability of learning relates to behavior therapy in a particular way. Persons come to therapists with the expectation that their problems well be corrected. When this expectation is met, then a second expectation emerges, that problems will remain corrected. Behavioral scientists have long recognized that behavior is subject to extinction, new learning, behavioral momentum, competing stimuli, and innate parameters. Therefore, a therapist should not be surprised when successful treatment outcomes are nullified over time or with changing environments. A challenge for behavior therapists is to assimilate relevant lessons from experimental analysis of behavior and seek ways to apply these lessons to durability in therapy.

Finally, concern for the social validity of therapeutic change is driven by the ethics of behavior therapy, the needs of clients, and a consumer economy that is emerging in behavioral health care. This is not a matter of clinical versus statistical significance in the narrow sense. Rather, it involves providing services that consumers need to live adaptive lives, and providing these services as economically as possible. To this end, every client should be seen as an opportunity to define client needs, to develop or refine a treatment program, and to evaluate the effectiveness of therapy. However, this is the same scientific approach to intervention that has marked the best of behavior therapy.

REFERENCES

Ajibola, O., & Clement, P.W. (1995). Differential effects of methylphenidate and self-reinforcement on attention-deficit hyperactivity disorder. *Behavior Modification, 19,* 211–233.

American Psychiatric Association. (1987). *Diagnostic and statistical manual of mental disorders* (3rd ed. rev.). Washington, DC: Author.

American Psychiatric Association. (1994). *Diagnostic and statistical manual of mental disorders* (4th ed.). Washington, DC: Author.

Ayllon, T., & Azrin, N.H. (1968). *The token economy: A motivational system for therapy and rehabilitation.* New York: Appleton-Century-Crofts.

Bandura, A. (1971). Vicarious and self-reinforcement processes. In R. Glasser (Ed.), *The nature of reinforcement.* New York: Academic Press.

Bandura, A. (1977a). Self-efficacy: Toward a unifying theory of behavioral change. *Psychological Review, 84,* 191–215.

Bandura, A. (1977b). *Social learning theory.* Englewood Cliffs, NJ: Prentice-Hall.

Bandura, A., Ross, D., & Ross, S.A. (1963). Imitation of film-mediated aggressive models. *Journal of Abnormal and Social Psychology, 66,* 3–11.

Barlow, D.H. (Ed.). (1993). *Clinical handbook of psychological disorders: A step-by-step treatment manual* (2nd ed.). New York: Guilford Press.

Barlow, D.H. (1996). Health care policy, psychotherapy research, and the future of psychotherapy. *American Psychologist, 51,* 1050–1058.

Barlow, D.H., & Hersen, M. (1984). *Single case experimental designs: Strategies for studying behavior change* (2nd ed.). Boston: Allyn & Bacon.

Barrios, B.A., Turner, R.W., & Ross, S.M. (1985). Behavioral group treatment for addictive-appetitive disorders: Alcoholism, smoking, obesity, and drug abuse. In D. Upper & S.M. Ross (Eds.), *Handbook of behavioral group therapy* (pp. 331–420). New York: Plenum Press.

Beck, A.T. (1978). *Depression inventory.* Philadelphia: Center for Cognitive Therapy.

Beck, A.T., Rush, A.J., Shaw, B.F., & Emery, G. (1979). *Cognitive therapy of depression.* New York: Guilford Press.

Beck, J.G., & Zebb, B.J. (1994). Behavioral assessment and treatment of panic disorder: Current status, future directions. *Behavior Therapy, 25,* 581–611.

Blake, D.D., Weathers, F.W., Nagy, L.M., Kaloupek, D.G., Klauminzer, G., Charney, D., & Keane, T., (1990). A clinician rating scale for assessing current and lifetime PTSD: The CAPS-1. *Behavior Therapist, 13,* 137–188.

Breland, K., & Breland, M. (1961). The misbehavior of organisms. *The American Psychologist, 16,* 681–684.

Brown, T.A., O'Leary, T.A., & Barlow, D.H. (1993). Generalized anxiety disorder. In D.H. Barlow (Ed.), *Clinical handbook of psychological disorders: A step-by-step treatment manual* (2nd ed., pp. 137–188). New York: Guilford Press.

Brownell, K.D., & Wadden, T.A. (1991). The heterogeneity of obesity: Fitting treatments to individuals. *Behavior Therapy, 22,* 153–177.

Calhoun, K.S., & Resick, P.A. (1993). Post-traumatic stress disorder. In D.H. Barlow (Ed.), *Clinical handbook of psychological disorders: A step-by-step treatment manual* (2nd ed., pp. 48–98). New York: Guilford Press.

Carr, E.G., & Carlson, J.I. (1993). Reduction of severe behavior problems in the community using a multicomponent treatment approach. *Journal of Applied Behavior Analysis, 26*, 157–172.

Cervone, D., & Scott, W.D. (1995). Self-efficacy theory of behavioral change: Foundations, conceptual issues, and therapeutic implications. In W. O'Donohue & L. Krasner (Eds.), *Theories of behavior therapy: Exploring behavior change* (pp. 349–383). Washington, DC: American Psychological Association.

Cone, J.D. (1981). Psychometric considerations. In M. Hersen & A.S. Bellack (Eds.), *Behavioral assessment: A practical handbook* (2nd ed., pp. 38–68). New York: Pergamon Press.

Cormier, W.H., & Cormier, L.S. (1991). *Interviewing strategies for helpers: Fundamental skills and cognitive behavioral interventions.* Pacific Grove, CA: Brooks/Cole.

Craske, M.G., & Barlow, D.H. (1993). Panic disorder and agoraphobia. In D.H. Barlow (Ed.), *Clinical handbook of psychological disorders: A step-by-step treatment manual* (2nd ed., pp. 1–47). New York: Guilford Press.

DiNardo, P.A., Brown, T.A., & Barlow, D.H. (1994). *Anxiety disorders interview schedule of DSM-IV (ADIS-IV).* Albany, NY: Graywind.

Domjan, M. (1993). *The principles of learning and behavior* (3rd ed.). Pacific Grove, CA: Brooks/Cole.

Donohue, B., Acierno, R., Hersen, M., & Van Hasselt, V.B. (1995). Social skills training for depressed, visually impaired older adults: A treatment manual. *Behavior Modification, 19*, 379–424.

Emmelkamp, P.M.G. (1994). Behavior therapy with adults. In A.E. Bergin & S.L. Garfield (Eds.), *Handbook of psychotherapy and behavior change* (4th ed., pp. 379–427). New York: Wiley.

Emmelkamp, P.M.G., & Kuipers, A.C.M. (1985). Behavioral group therapy for anxiety disorders. In D. Upper & S.M. Ross (Eds.), *Handbook of behavioral group therapy* (pp. 443–471). New York: Plenum Press.

Fairburn, C.G., & Wilson, G.T. (Eds.). (1993). *Binge eating: Nature, assessment, and treatment.* New York: Guilford Press.

Ferster, C.B., & Skinner, B.F. (1957). *Schedules of reinforcement.* New York: Appleton-Century-Crofts.

Foa, E.B., Rothbaum, B.O., Riggs, D.S., & Murdock, T.B. (1991). Treatment of Post-traumatic Stress Disorder in rape victims: A comparison between cognitive-behavioral procedures and counseling. *Journal of Consulting and Clinical Psychology, 59*, 715–723.

Gerow, J.R. (1989). *Psychology: An introduction* (2nd ed.). Glenview, IL: Scott, Foresman.

Goldfried, M.R. (1971). Systematic desensitization as training in self-control. *Journal of Consulting and Clinical Psychology, 37*, 228–234.

Hastings, R.P., Remington, B., & Hall, M. (1995). Adults' responses to self-injurious behavior: An experimental analysis using a computer-simulation paradigm. *Behavior Modification, 19*, 425–450.

Hope, D.A., & Heimberg, R.G. (1993). Social phobia and social anxiety. In D.H. Barlow (Ed.), *Clinical handbook of psychological disorders: A step-by-step treatment manual* (2nd ed., pp. 99–136). New York: Guilford Press.

Houts, A.C. (1991). Nocturnal enuresis as a biobehavioral problem. *Behavior Therapy, 22*, 133–151.

Iwata, B.A., Duncan, B.A., Zarcone, J.R., Lerman, D.C., & Shore, B.A. (1994). A sequential, test-control methodology for conducting functional analyses of self-injurious behavior. *Behavior Modification, 18,* 289–306.

Johnson, C.R., Handen, B.L., Lubetsky, M.J., & Sacco, K.A. (1994). Efficacy of methylphenidate and behavioral intervention on classroom behavior in children with ADHD and mental retardation. *Behavior Modification, 18,* 470–487.

Kamps, D.M., Leonard, B.R., Vernon, S., Dugan, E.P., Delquadri, J.C., Gershon, B., Wade, L., & Folk, L. (1992). Teaching social skills to students with autism to increase peer interactions in an integrated first-grade classroom. *Journal of Applied Behavior Analysis, 25,* 281–288.

Kazdin, A.E. (1977). *The token economy: A review and evaluation.* New York: Plenum Press.

Kazdin, A.E. (1981). Behavioral observation. In M. Hersen & A.S. Bellack, (Eds.), *Behavioral assessment: A practical handbook* (2nd ed., pp. 101–124). New York: Pergamon Press.

Kettlewell, P.W., Mizes, J.S., & Wasylyshyn, N.A. (1992). A cognitive behavioral group treatment of bulimia. *Behavior Therapy, 23,* 657–670.

Klesges, R.C., Benowitz, N.L., & Meyers, A.W. (1991). Behavioral and biobehavioral aspects of smoking and smoking cessation: The problem of postcessation weight gain. *Behavior Therapy, 22,* 179–199.

Kulich, R.J., & Gottlieb, B.S. (1985). The management of chronic pain: A cognitive-functioning approach. In D. Upper & S.M. Ross (Eds.), *Handbook of behavioral group therapy* (pp. 489–507). New York: Plenum Press.

Ladouceur, R., Boisvert, J.-M., & Dumont, J. (1994). Cognitive-behavioral treatment for adolescent pathological gamblers. *Behavior Modification, 18,* 230–242.

Ladouceur, R., Freeston, M.H., Gagnon, F., Thibodeau, N., & Dumont, J. (1995). Cognitive-behavioral treatment of obsessions. *Behavior Modification, 19,* 247–257.

Lewinsohn, P.M., Breckenridge, J.S., Antonuccio, D.O., & Teri, L. (1985). A behavioral group therapy approach to the treatment of depression. In D. Upper & S.M. Ross (Eds.), *Handbook of behavioral group therapy* (pp. 303–329). New York: Plenum Press.

Lindsley, O.R., Skinner, B.F., & Solomon, H.C. (1953). *Studies in behavior therapy* (Status Report I). Waltham, MA: Metropolitan State Hospital.

Lomont, J.F. (1965). Reciprocal inhibition or extinction? *Behaviour Research and Therapy, 3,* 209–219.

Mash, E.J., & Hunsley, J. (1993). Behavior therapy and managed mental health care: Integrating effectiveness and economics in mental health practice. *Behavior Therapy, 24,* 67–90.

Mazaleski, J.L., Iwata, B.A., Vollmer, T.R., Zarcone, J.R., & Smith, R.G. (1993). Analysis of the reinforcement and extinction components in DRO contingencies with self-injury. *Journal of Applied Behavior Analysis, 26,* 143–156.

McGlynn, F.D., Moore, P.M., Rose, M.P., & Lazarte, A. (1995). Effects of relaxation training on fear and arousal during *in vivo* exposure to a caged snake among *DSM-III-R* simple (snake) phobics. *Journal of Behavior Therapy and Experimental Psychiatry, 26,* 1–8.

McGovern, K.B., & Jensen, S.H. (1985). Behavioral group treatment methods for sexual disorders and dysfunctions. In D. Upper & S.M. Ross (Eds.), *Handbook of behavioral group therapy* (pp. 421–442). New York: Plenum Press.

Middleton, M.B., & Cartledge, G. (1995) The effects of socials skills instruction and parental involvement on the aggressive behaviors of African American males. *Behavior Modification, 19,* 192–210.

Morganstern, K.P., & Tevlin, H.E. (1981). Behavioral interviewing. In M. Hersen & A.S. Bellack (Eds.), *Behavioral assessment: A practical handbook* (2nd ed., pp. 71–100). New York: Pergamon Press.

Morin, C.M., Colecchi, C.A., Ling, W.D., & Sood, R.K. (1995). Cognitive behavior therapy to facilitate benzodiazepine discontinuation among hypnotic-dependent patients with insomnia. *Behavior Therapy, 26,* 733–745.

Neef, N.A., Mace, F.C., Shea, M.C., & Shade, D. (1992). Effects of reinforcer rate and reinforcer quality on time allocation: Extension of matching theory to educational settings. *Journal of Applied Behavior Analysis, 25,* 691–699.

Nelson, R.O., & Hayes, S.C. (1981). Nature of behavioral assessment. In M. Hersen & A.S Bellack (Eds.), *Behavioral assessment: A practical handbook* (2nd ed., pp. 3–37). New York: Pergamon Press.

Noll, J.P. (1995). The matching law as a theory of choice in behavior therapy. In W. O'Donohue & L. Krasner (Eds.), *Theories of behavior therapy: Exploring behavior change* (pp. 129–144). Washington, DC: American Psychological Association.

O'Donohue, W., & Krasner, L. (1995). Theories in behavior therapy: Philosophical and historical contexts. In W. O'Donohue & L. Krasner (Eds.), *Theories of behavior therapy: Exploring behavior change* (pp. 1–22). Washington, DC: American Psychological Association.

Peterson, L., & Sobell, L.C. (1994). Introduction to the State-of-the-Art Review series: Research contributions to clinical assessment. *Behavior Therapy, 25,* 523–531.

Rapport, M.D., Loo, S., Isaacs, P., Goya, S., Denney, C., & Scanlan, S. (1996). Methylphenidate and attentional training: Comparative effects on behavior and neurocognitive performance in twin girls with attention-deficit/hyperactivity disorder. *Behavior Modification, 20,* 428–450.

Reese, H.W. (1996). How is physiology relevant to behavior analysis? *Behavior Analyst, 19,* 61–70.

Reimers, T.M. (1996). A biobehavioral approach toward managing encopresis. *Behavior Modification, 20,* 469–479.

Resick, P.A., & Schnicke, M.K. (1993). *Cognitive processing therapy for rape victims: A treatment manual.* Newbury Park, CA: Sage.

Resnick, H.S., Kilpatrick, D.G., & Lipovsky, J.A. (1991). Assessment of rape-related posttraumatic stress disorder: Stressor and symptom dimensions. *Psychological Assessment, 3,* 561–572.

Riggs, D.S., & Foa, E.B. (1993). Obsessive compulsive disorder. In D.H. Barlow (Ed.), *Clinical handbook of psychological disorders: A step-by-step treatment manual* (2nd ed., pp. 189–239). New York: Guilford Press.

Robbins, L.N., Helzer, J.D., Croughan, J., & Ratcliff, K.S. (1981). The national institute of mental health diagnostic interview schedule: It's history, characteristics, and validity. *Archives of General Psychiatry, 38,* 381–389.

Rose, S.D., & LeCroy, C.W. (1985). Improving children's social competence: A multimodal behavioral group approach. In D. Upper & S.M. Ross (Eds.), *Handbook of behavioral group therapy* (pp. 173–202). New York: Plenum Press.

Rosen, J.C., Orosan, P., & Reiter, J. (1995). Cognitive behavior therapy for negative body image in obese women. *Behavior Therapy, 26,* 25–42.

Sheldon, R.C., Hollon, S.D., Purdon, S.E., & Loosen, P.T. (1991). Biological and psychological aspects of depression. *Behavior Therapy, 22,* 201–228.

Sidman, M. (1960). *Tactics of scientific research: Evaluating experimental data in psychology.* New York: Basic Books.

Skinner, B.F. (1953). *Science and human behavior.* New York: Macmillan.

Sobell, L.C., Toneatto, T., & Sobell, M.B. (1994). Behavioral assessment and treatment planning for alcohol, tobacco, and other drug problems: Current status with emphasis on clinical applications. *Behavior Therapy, 25,* 533–580.

Spitzer, R.L., Williams., J.B., & Gibbon, M. (1987). *Structured clinical interview for the DSM-III-R non-patient version.* New York: New York State Psychiatric Institute.

Steketee, G. (1994). Behavioral assessment and treatment planning with obsessive compulsive disorder: A review emphasizing clinical application. *Behavior Therapy, 25,* 613–633.

Stewart, G., Van Houten, R., & Van Houten, J. (1992). Increasing generalized social interactions in psychotic and mentally retarded residents through peer-mediated therapy. *Journal of Applied Behavior Analysis, 25,* 335–339.

Taylor, C.B., Agras, W.S., Losch, M., Plante, T.G., & Burnett, K. (1991). Improving the effectiveness of computer-assisted weight loss. *Behavior Therapy, 22,* 229–236.

Thase, M.E., Bowler, K., & Harden, T. (1991). Cognitive therapy of endogenous depression: Part 2. Preliminary findings in 16 unmedicated inpatients. *Behavior Therapy, 22,* 469–477.

Thase, M.E., Simons, A.D., Cahalane, J.F., & McGeary, J. (1991). Cognitive therapy of endogenous depression: Part 1. An outpatient clinical replication series. *Behavior Therapy, 22,* 457–467.

Watson, G.S., & Gross, A.M. (1997). Treatment of mental retardation and developmental disorders. In M. Hersen & R.T. Ammerman (Eds.), *Handbook of prevention and treatment with children and adolescents: Interventions in a real world context* (pp. 495–520). New York: Wiley.

Wilson, G.T. (1989). Behavior therapy. In R.J. Corsini & D. Wedding (Eds.), *Current psychotherapies* (4th ed., pp. 241–282). Itasca, IL: Peacock.

Wilson, G.T., & Pike, K.M. (1993). Eating disorders. In D.H. Barlow (Ed.), *Clinical handbook of psychological disorders: A step-by-step treatment manual* (2nd ed., pp. 278–317). New York: Guilford Press.

Wixted, J.T., Bellack, A.S., & Hersen, M. (1990). Current directions: Behavior therapy. In A.S. Bellack & M. Hersen (Eds.), *Handbook of comparative treatments for adult disorders* (pp. 17–33). New York: Wiley.

Wolpe, J. (1958). *Psychotherapy by reciprocal inhibition.* Stanford, CA: Stanford University Press.

Wolpe, J. (1995). Reciprocal inhibition: Major agent of behavior change. In W. O'Donohue & L. Krasner (Eds.), *Theories of behavior therapy: Exploring behavior change* (pp. 23–57). Washington, DC: American Psychological Association.

CHAPTER 3

Cognitive Behavior Therapy

DAVID A.F. HAAGA, DANA RABOIS, and CINDY BRODY

COGNITIVE BEHAVIOR therapy (CBT) is a set of therapy systems sharing the assumptions that: (1) Dysfunctional thinking contributes to the maintenance, perhaps even the initial onset, of psychopathology, and (2) changes in cognition mediate clinical improvement (Haaga & Davison, 1991). Like behavior therapy in general, CBT focuses on alleviation of current problems and symptoms, skill building to enable patients to become their own therapists after a relatively brief course of treatment, by applying theory and research from basic psychology and by empirically testing the efficacy of treatment methods. CBT diverges from other approaches to behavior therapy by emphasizing change in cognitive contents, processes, and structures as a causal factor in psychotherapy.

In its attention to people's capacities for constructing a wide range of idiosyncratic, sometimes self-defeating meanings of any given experience, CBT resembles humanistic and psychodynamic therapies. It differs from these approaches, though, in that the CBT therapist is typically far more directive and explicitly educative, aiming to help patients learn cognitive conceptualizations of their symptoms and how such symptoms might be managed or reduced.

Well over a dozen variants of CBT have been identified (Mahoney, 1988). Two key distinctions to be considered among them are the degree of emphasis on restructuring vs. replacement of maladaptive thoughts (e.g., Arnkoff, 1986) and the extent to which evidence that the treatment works is available.

By *restructuring* we refer to efforts to identify, challenge, and thereby reshape the patient's current cognitions. Cognitive therapy (A. Beck, 1964), discussed further in the following section, and rational emotive behavior therapy (REBT; Ellis, 1962, 1993) exemplify restructuring approaches. In REBT, therapists teach patients how to identify the irrational beliefs that underlie their problem behaviors and excessively negative emotional reactions to events. The core quality of irrationality is demandingness, grandiose thinking that someone or some situation must be a particular way. Demandingness is contrasted with preferential thinking, in which one may have strong wishes but recognizes that there is no law of the universe dictating that conditions and people be arranged in accordance with these wishes. Irrational beliefs, once identified, are vigorously disputed on grounds of logic (e.g., Just because you want love and approval, how does it follow that everyone must love and admire you or else you cannot stand it?), empiricism (Where is the evidence in your past experience that you literally cannot stand to be rejected?), and utility (What are you getting out of running your life on the basis that you cannot stand rejection, and what would be the consequences of relaxing this demand and reframing it as a preference?).

Replacement strategies, on the other hand, essentially bypass the evaluation or disputation of current cognitive styles in favor of instilling new, putatively healthy ones. For example, problem-solving therapists (e.g., D'Zurilla, 1986) teach patients how to use a generally applicable, five-step approach to problems, including extensive emphasis on cognitive aspects of problem solving (e.g., appraisal of problems as normal, high self-efficacy for applying the model, decision-making guidelines). There is, however, little focus on evaluating and thoroughly testing or challenging the patient's current beliefs about optimal strategies for addressing personal problems. Similarly, stress-inoculation training (e.g., Meichenbaum, 1986) teaches patients specific self-statements to employ when anticipating and then confronting stressors, again with little attempt to unearth and challenge preexisting cognitive patterns.

CBT systems differ, not only in prioritization of cognitive restructuring vs. replacement, but also in the extent of empirical support amassed in outcome studies. Judgments about empirical support are of course controversial. REBT, for instance, has fared well in quantitative reviews (Engels, Garnefski, & Diekstra, 1993) of the effects of psychotherapy, but less well in qualitative reviews of the methodological adequacy of clinical trials of this approach (Kendall et al., 1995).

Although there is no perfect solution to the problem of how to identify CBT systems with adequate empirical support, for the purposes of this chapter we will utilize the list of empirically validated treatments identified by the Task Force on Promotion and Dissemination of Psychological Procedures of Division 12 of the American Psychological Association (Chambless et al., 1996). This report singles out cognitive therapy (CT) of depression and adaptations of CT applied to panic disorder, generalized anxiety disorder (GAD), social phobia, irritable bowel syndrome, chronic pain, and bulimia as the CBT systems meeting the criteria for designation as "well-established treatments." Accordingly, we focus in the "Conceptualization" section to follow on CT, and throughout the chapter we mainly review studies of CT as applied to the disorders just listed.

CONCEPTUALIZATION

Cognitive therapy was originally based on Beck's cognitive model of depression. In brief, the model describes depressed persons' automatic (intrusive, difficult to control) thoughts as highly negative, reflecting themes of loss, and forming a "cognitive triad" of negative thinking about the self, the personal environment, and the future (A. Beck, 1987). These automatic thoughts are believed to be maintained by biased cognitive processes such as overgeneralization (e.g., concluding from a setback in one area that one will fare poorly in all areas of functioning) and selective abstraction (forming conclusions on the basis of an isolated negative aspect of the event while ignoring other, positive features).

According to the theory, these readily identified negative thoughts and cognitive biases reflect activation by personally relevant stressors of latent dysfunctional beliefs. For example, a person with rigid, dysfunctional beliefs about achievement (e.g., If I am not the best, then I am a failure) might react to a setback in this domain (e.g., being passed over for promotion) by experiencing negative automatic thoughts about the self as a loser and the future as hopeless, with corresponding intense sadness, loss of interest in working toward goals, and other symptoms of depression.

Cognitive therapists target the dysfunctional beliefs hypothesized to contribute to the onset of depression after first teaching the patient skills for questioning and reevaluating the negative automatic thoughts themselves. The intended style of the therapy is collaborative, as therapist and patient together work to examine and evaluate the validity of automatic thoughts associated with depression. In the early stages of treatment, much of this work is carried out via behavioral methods designed to elevate mood directly and to provide an opportunity to test negative thoughts (e.g., If you think you cannot accomplish anything, test that conceptualization by attempting the following simple tasks, working your way gradually up a graded series of such tasks). Such behavioral experiments are typically debriefed collaboratively to determine whether, for instance, the patients' depressive thinking has led them to discount the significance of any accomplishments that may have been made. A component analysis of CT for depression indicated that this behavioral activation aspect of treatment may be quite powerful in its own right, perhaps sufficient in itself if carried out thoroughly to constitute the entire therapy (Jacobson et al., 1996).

In standard CT practice, however, behavioral activation strategies give way as treatment proceeds, and patients are helped to learn cognitive skills for evaluating automatic thoughts as well (i.e., to question the evidence for those thoughts; to consider whether any equally viable alternative conceptualizations of what has happened are possible; to decatastrophize their implications if true; and to look for whether anything can be done constructively about the sometimes truly dreadful situations the patient confronts).

With other disorders, the use of behavioral strategies and automatic-thought-questioning strategies in CT is similar, but the content of targeted cognitions differs (e.g., exaggerated expectations of imminent biological catastrophe in panic disorder, of rejection and humiliation in social phobia). Detailed descriptions of cognitive-therapy procedures specific to a range of disorders are available (e.g., A. Beck, Emery, & Greenberg, 1985; A. Beck, Rush, Shaw, & Emery, 1979; see also Chapters 6 and 12 of this volume). In the remainder of this chapter we review patient and therapist variables qualifying the effects of CT, and we draw conclusions about its utility in managed-care contexts accordingly.

PATIENT VARIABLES

Although CBT has been found efficacious in the treatment of several disorders, not every patient responds favorably. A number of studies have examined patient characteristics as potential predictors of response to CBT, frequently in the context of CT for depression.

DEMOGRAPHICS

Gender, age, socioeconomic status, and education have generally failed to correlate with treatment outcome in studies of CT for depression (Jarrett, Eaves, Grannemann, & Rush, 1991; Sotsky et al., 1991). Married patients fared better than did divorced, widowed, or separated patients in CT for depression (Jarrett et al., 1991; Sotsky et al., 1991). This effect was not replicated in a study of CBT for panic disorder with agoraphobia (Clair, Oei, & Evans, 1992).

INTELLIGENCE

It is sometimes thought that high intelligence should be associated with favorable response to CBT on the grounds that CBT "requires the understanding of logical arguments and evaluation of beliefs" (Whisman, 1993, p. 256). Yet, Haaga, DeRubeis, Stewart, and Beck (1991) found that neither fluid nor crystallized intelligence was significantly predictive of outcome of CT for patients diagnosed with major depression, dysthymia, or generalized anxiety disorder.

Intelligence may be too general a construct to capture the aptitude useful for profiting from the verbal, educative tactics emphasized in CT. A recent experiment found right-ear accuracy for syllables (but not complex tones) in dichotic listening tasks to be a strong predictor of favorable response to CT for depression (Bruder et al., 1997). Right-ear accuracy for syllables reflects left-hemisphere advantage for verbal processing. The mechanism of this effect, or indeed its replicability, remains unknown, but the authors conjectured that "patients with greater left-hemisphere superiority for verbal processing may have been better able to use the language-dominant hemisphere in learning to reinterpret negative life events" (Bruder et al., 1997, p. 143).

DYSFUNCTIONAL COGNITION

Given that CBT theoretically works by virtue of challenging dysfunctional thinking, it might seem that patients with high levels of dysfunctional thinking would benefit most from this approach. With respect to CT for depression, however, it appears that the opposite is true. Patients with *low* levels of dysfunctional attitudes seem to respond best to CT (Jarrett et al., 1991; Sotsky et al., 1991). Patients with severely dysfunctional beliefs may be insufficiently flexible in their thinking to make effective use of cognitive interventions (Simons,

Gordon, Monroe, & Thase, 1995). Whisman (1993) noted, though, that high cognitive dysfunction is associated with severity of depression, poor social support, and a high number of prior depressive episodes, all of which may contribute to poor prognosis in any treatment (Norman, Miller, & Dow, 1988). For example, pharmacotherapy has been less effective for patients with high scores on a measure of dysfunctional attitudes as well (Sotsky et al., 1991).

The relation between low cognitive dysfunction and favorable response to CT for depression may in any event be qualified by variation in the recent occurrence of negative life events. In one study, patients with high levels of dysfunctional attitudes who also had experienced a negative life event were likely to respond well to cognitive therapy (Simons et al., 1995). A recent, major negative life event combined with biased thinking about it may give the cognitive therapist something specific to work with, rather than an overall generalized dysfunctional attitude that may be pervasive and difficult to change (Simons et al., 1995).

SYMPTOM SEVERITY

Findings are mixed with respect to the impact of symptom severity on CT response and may vary by disorder. Agoraphobic patients with panic who reported a more severe symptom presentation responded better to CBT than those with less impairment in one clinical trial (Clair et al., 1992). However, GAD patients with higher levels of anxiety responded better to behavioral therapy than CBT (Butler, 1993). In CBT for bulimia, severity was negatively related to response in that patients with lower desired body weight, higher frequency of laxative use, and a history of self-harm were less likely to "engage" successfully in therapy (Coker, Vize, Wade, & Cooper, 1993).

BIOLOGICAL PRESENTATION

Endogenous depression was expected to be less responsive to cognitive-behavior therapy based on the presumption that it is biologically based and more likely to respond to pharmacotherapy (Whisman, 1993). Some studies corroborate this prediction (e.g., McKnight, Nelson-Gray, & Barnhill, 1992; Persons, Burns, & Perloff, 1988), whereas others do not (Blackburn, Bishop, Glen, Whalley, & Christie, 1981; Jarrett, Rush, Khatami, & Roffwarg, 1990; Simons & Thase, 1992). Results may vary with the indicator used to assess endogeneity. Abnormal dexamethasone-suppression-test response has predicted poor outcome (McKnight et al., 1992), and this finding appears to be independent of depression severity itself (Thase, Simons, & Reynolds, 1996).

PERSONALITY DISORDER COMORBIDITY

In general, a comorbid personality-disorder diagnosis is considered to be predictive of poor response to short-term treatment of Axis I disorders (Reich & Vasile, 1993). Cognitive therapists have generally concluded from clinical experience that personality disorders complicate and lengthen treatment (e.g., J.S. Beck, 1996). However, whether or under what circumstances CBT's effectiveness is hindered by the presence of comorbid personality disorders is somewhat unclear. Research on panic disorder patients found that responders and nonresponders to CBT did not differ on clinical diagnosis of personality disorders (Rathus, Sanderson, Miller, & Wetzler, 1995). Likewise, whereas a diagnosis of borderline personality disorder in particular predicted poor outcome in CT for depressed patients (Burns & Nolen-Hoeksema, 1992), the presence of personality disorders in the NIMH Treatment of Depression Collaborative Research Program study did not predict poor response to CT (Shea et al., 1990).

THERAPIST VARIABLES

In an analysis of four outcome studies, Luborsky et al. (1986) found that therapist effects on outcome were greater than the effects attributable to the type of therapy received. The influence of the individual therapist may be even greater in naturalistic settings than in formal outcome studies using therapy manuals to guide practice. A meta-analysis of therapist effects on outcome found that use of therapy manuals tended to minimize differences between therapists in attained outcomes (Crits-Christoph et al., 1991).

What differences among therapists have such a profound influence on how much patients benefit from psychotherapy? This question has received much attention in psychotherapy research. Therapist factors that have been studied in relation to outcome in CBT are reviewed in this section.

PROFESSIONAL TRAINING AND EXPERIENCE

Berman and Norton (1985) found that professional and paraprofessional therapists were equally effective in treating a variety of patient groups. Five different treatments were represented in the therapist sample, one of which was cognitive-behavior therapy. Their results suggested that professional and paraprofessional therapists might achieve different levels of effectiveness depending on the length of the treatment. Professionals performed somewhat better in the studies using treatments lasting fewer than 13 weeks, whereas paraprofessionals were more effective in studies of treatments continuing more than 12 weeks. The differences, although present, were quite small, with a maximum-effect size of 0.19. Results of this study suggest that therapists' professional status might not be a crucial factor influencing outcome. Perhaps factors such as specific competence in the treatment being offered are more important than what kind of degree a therapist obtains.

Burlingame and colleagues (Burlingame, Fuhriman, Paul, & Ogles, 1989) investigated the relationship of therapist experience in general and therapist training in time-limited therapy to therapy outcome. Therapists identified with a variety of orientations, including cognitive behavioral. In this study, patients of therapists with more clinical experience had better outcomes than those of the less experienced therapists. Also, therapists who received more training in time-limited therapy had clients who had better outcomes, regardless of the therapists' overall level of experience.

A meta-analysis of therapist effects in psychotherapy outcome studies found the experience level of therapists to be highly related to the size of the therapist effects in each study (Crits-Christoph et al., 1991). The use of highly experienced therapists greatly reduced the amount of therapy outcome variance that was due to the therapists. Therapist experience, therefore, was found to minimize the differences in outcome that were due to therapist factors.

Finally, Burns and Nolen-Hoeksema (1992) studied therapist experience with specific reference to CBT for depression and anxiety disorders. Patients of therapists who had one year or less of experience did not improve as much as those of therapists with two or more years of prior clinical work. Perhaps therapists with more experience are more likely to be perceived by patients as having more credibility or more expertise (Ilardi & Craighead, 1994). They could be more skilled at providing patients with hope and the expectation that cognitive-behavior therapy will be effective for them.

TECHNICAL FIDELITY

In their study of what determines change in cognitive therapy for depression, DeRubeis and Feeley (1990) found that when therapists implemented the focused, practical techniques of cognitive therapy early in treatment, such as setting and following an agenda, their patients had greater reductions in depression.

THERAPIST EMPATHY AND CREDIBILITY

The relationship between the therapist and client during cognitive therapy has been seen as an important, but not crucial factor in the change process. In particular, a positive working alliance has been viewed as necessary, but not sufficient, for cognitive therapy to be effective (A. Beck et al., 1979). In reviewing eight studies of cognitive-behavior therapy for depression, though, Ilardi and Craighead (1994) discovered that much of the improvement in depressive symptoms occurred within the first three weeks of therapy, before specifically cognitive techniques, such as teaching skills for questioning one's negative automatic thoughts, are a major focus of CT sessions (A. Beck et al., 1979). This suggests that early symptom reduction may depend a great deal on "nonspecific" factors such as the therapist's credibility in presenting a CT rationale and ability to empathize with patients and form a positive alliance.

Several studies have examined the role of therapist empathy in promoting positive outcome in CBT. In 1985, Persons and Burns examined mood change during one session of cognitive therapy received by depressed and anxious patients. Both negative mood and degree of belief in automatic thoughts significantly decreased during the session. Patients' perceptions of therapist empathy related to mood improvement during the session. However, as Persons and Burns pointed out (1985) their results leave open the possibility that changes in patients' automatic thoughts lead to mood improvement, which causes them to rate the relationship with the therapist positively. Also, the ratings of therapist empathy were only taken once, and the rated session was not during the early phase of therapy, where the role of empathy in improvement might be the most evident (Ilardi & Craighead, 1994).

Burns and Nolen-Hoeksema (1992) found that the empathy expressed by therapists during cognitive-behavioral therapy for depression had a moderate-to-large causal effect on patients' recovery. They used structural equation modeling to examine the role of empathy in causing the alleviation of depression. Results showed that the patients who rated their therapists as the most warm and empathic evidenced significantly greater improvement than those who gave their therapists the lowest ratings on these constructs (Burns & Nolen-Hoeksema). In addition, these results showing a causal effect of empathy on improvement controlled for the possible reciprocal causality of improvement on perceived therapist empathy. However, it should be noted that patients in this study rated their therapists after treatment was completed. In their retrospective reflections about their therapists, patients who improved the most may have had positively biased opinions stemming from the benefits they obtained from therapy (Ilardi & Craighead, 1994). If patients had been rating their therapists' empathy throughout the course of therapy, a clearer interpretation of the results could possibly be offered.

Marmar and colleagues (Marmar, Gaston, Gallagher, & Thompson, 1989) contrasted the relationship of patient and therapist perceptions of therapeutic alliance with outcome in depression in the elderly. In the cognitive-therapy condition, the only aspect of the alliance that related to positive outcome was that of patient commitment. In general, patient perceptions of the alliance were more predictive of reduction in depression symptoms than therapist scores on alliance measures (Marmar et al., 1989). This result suggests that the patient's contribution to the working relationship could be even more important than the therapist's in predicting outcome in cognitive-behavior therapy (Ilardi & Craighead, 1994; Krupnick et al., 1996).

PRESCRIPTIVE TREATMENT AND MANAGED CARE

The relative brevity of CBT, combined with empirical support for its efficacy in the treatment of several common disorders, makes it a highly viable approach in the context of managed care. Even relative to other structured, effective treatments, CBT may be rapid in showing benefits. In one study, CBT for depression effected significant change, maintained at one-year follow-up, within the first 8 sessions, whereas change with interpersonal-dynamic therapy was more evident after session 12 (Shapiro et al., 1995). An 8-session version of interpersonal-dynamic therapy was not as effective at one-year follow-up, suggesting that CBT is a cost-efficient short-term-therapy technique.

Also helpful for prescriptive purposes would be information on the types of patients for which CBT is the treatment of choice and the types of patients for which it is inferior to alternative methods. In evaluating existing data to make such decisions, it is necessary to bear in mind the important distinction between prognostic findings, which tell us what patients do best in CBT, and prescriptive findings, which tell us what treatment (CBT vs. alternatives) is best for a given patient. These need not be the same (Hollon & Najavits, 1988). For example, as noted earlier, some studies indicate that low cognitive dysfunction predicts favorable response to CBT for depression (Sotsky et al., 1991). It would be misleading, however, to conclude on the basis of this prognostic finding that CBT should be recommended to patients with low dysfunction. It is possible that low cognitive dysfunction is prognostic of good treatment responses in general, and such patients might do even better in an alternate treatment. Conversely, a variable could fail to predict response to CT yet prove useful for prescribing it. For example, if patients of high or low general intelligence all do moderately well in CT (Haaga et al., 1991), whereas the highly intelligent respond very well and the less intelligent very poorly to an alternative treatment, then it would be sensible to administer CT only to the less intelligent patients.

Most outcome research on CBT has examined such prognostic indicators (Whisman, 1993), but several prescriptive findings have been reported, as reviewed in this section.

Symptom Severity

The NIMH Treatment of Depression Collaborative Research Program found that high depression severity was associated with poorer outcome in CBT relative to antidepressant medication, whereas group differences were not evident among the less severely depressed (Elkin et al., 1995). However, several studies of similar design have failed to replicate this result (for a review, see Hollon, DeRubeis, & Evans, 1996). Thus, severity of depression cannot at this time be considered a robust prescriptive indicator.

Learned Resourcefulness and "Cognitive" Rationale

Learned resourcefulness (Rosenbaum, 1980) refers to people's abilities to use constructive problem-solving strategies, to delay gratification, and to perceive oneself as efficacious in regulating internal events. People scoring high on this dimension responded better to CT relative to pharmacotherapy for depression, suggesting that it might be a useful prescriptive variable (Simons, Lustman, Wetzel, & Murphy, 1985). However, later studies failed to replicate these results (e.g., Wetzel, Murphy, Carney, Whitworth, & Knesevich, 1992). A possible explanation for this inconsistent pattern is that learned resourcefulness may be associated with preferential response to CT only among the initially more severely depressed patients (Burns, Rude, Simons, Bates, & Thase, 1994).

Just as general intelligence may be giving way to a more specific marker of left-hemisphere dominance for verbal processing as a favorable prognosticator for response to CT (see earlier discussion), so, too, learned resourcefulness may be overinclusive as a marker of a favorable prescriptive indicator. A couple of studies suggest that more specific aspects of patients' worldviews may be pertinent. In one study of CT for depression, about one-half of patients responded very rapidly (within 2 weeks), seemingly on the basis of finding the CT rationale for depression to be a good fit for their circumstances (Fennell & Teasdale, 1987). These patients did not differ from less responsive ones in pretreatment severity, but they did score higher on "depression about depression" (Teasdale, 1985), that is, severely negative reactions to the experience of being depressed itself. Furthermore, depressed patients endorsing abstract, general ("existential") reasons for being depressed fared especially well in CT and less well in a component treatment involving only behavioral activation strategies (Addis & Jacobson, 1996).

Considerably more research is needed before these findings could be employed prescriptively with great confidence. However, a picture seems to be emerging of a subset of depressed patients, who are demoralized about the meaningfulness of their lives and discouraged about the implications of their having been depressed, who respond very favorably to a CT rationale about flexible thinking and alternative construals of the situations they confront. On a less positive note, for the sake of balance, we close with a consideration of two possible negative indicators for prescription of CT: severe marital discord and high levels of dispostional resistance.

MARITAL DISTRESS

Severe marital discord may contraindicate individual CT for depression. Behavioral marital therapy might address the depression just as well, and it might address the relationship problems better, than does individual CT (O'Leary & Beach, 1990).

DISPOSITIONAL RESISTANCE

Due to CBT's more directive style, it was suggested that the resistance of a patient would interfere with therapy, thus leading to poor outcome (Beutler, Mohr, Grawe, Engle, & MacDonald, 1991). Studies examining the relationship between a patient's resistance, or a "propensity to resist the influence of authorities" (p. 20), found that resistance level interacted with treatment condition for group cognitive therapy (Beutler, Machado, Engle, & Mohr, 1993). Cognitive therapy was more effective than other self-directed treatments for patients with low resistance potential, whereas patients with high resistance responded more favorably to self-directed treatments (Beutler et al., 1993).

SUMMARY

Cognitive behavior therapy is a set of active, directive, skill-training therapies sharing the assumption that dysfunctional thinking contributes to the maintenance of psychopathology and that cognitive change mediates clinical improvement. Beck's cognitive therapy (CT) and adaptations of it have received considerable empirical support as an effective treatment for depression, panic,

GAD, social phobia, irritable bowel syndrome, chronic pain, and bulimia. CT utilizes both behavioral and cognitive techniques in the context of a collaborative patient-therapist relationship. CT is well-suited for the managed care context because it is relatively brief and, therefore, efficient. The search for patient or therapist characteristics useful in determining when to prescribe CT as opposed to alternative psychological interventions has proven difficult. However, there are some indications that CT works best for those patients whose relative strengths (e.g., left-hemisphere advantage for verbal processing, learned resourcefulness, strong belief in cognitive rationale for depression and its treatment, willingness to comply with the directives of credible authorities) match the requirements of the therapy, and for therapists with experience and training in brief therapy and an ability to convey empathy clearly to patients.

REFERENCES

Addis, M.E., & Jacobson, N.S. (1996). Reasons for depression and the process and outcome of cognitive-behavioral psychotherapies. *Journal of Consulting and Clinical Psychology, 64,* 1417–1424.

Arnkoff, D.B. (1986). A comparison of the coping and restructuring components of cognitive restructuring. *Cognitive Therapy and Research, 10,* 147–158.

Beck, A.T. (1964). Thinking and depression: II. Theory and therapy. *Archives of General Psychiatry, 10,* 561–571.

Beck, A.T. (1987). Cognitive models of depression. *Journal of Cognitive Psychotherapy: An International Quarterly, 1,* 5–37.

Beck, A.T., Emery, G., & Greenberg, R.L. (1985). *Anxiety disorders and phobias: A cognitive perspective.* New York: Basic Books.

Beck, A.T., Rush, A.J., Shaw, B.F., & Emery, G. (1979). *Cognitive therapy of depression.* New York: Guilford Press.

Beck, J.S. (1996). Cognitive therapy of personality disorders. In P.M. Salkovskis (Ed.), *Frontiers of cognitive therapy* (pp. 165–181). New York: Guilford Press.

Berman, J.S., & Norton, N.C. (1985). Does professional training make a therapist more effective? *Psychological Bulletin, 98,* 401–407.

Beutler, L.E., Machado, P.P., Engle, D., & Mohr, D. (1993). Differential patient x treatment maintenance among cognitive, experiential, and self-directed psychotherapies. *Journal of Psychotherapy Integration, 3,* 15–31.

Beutler, L.E., Mohr, D.C., Grawe, K., Engle, D., MacDonald, R. (1991). Looking for differential treatment effects: Cross-cultural predictors of differential psychotherapy efficacy. *Journal of Psychotherapy Integration, 1,* 121–141.

Blackburn, I.M., Bishop, S., Glen, A.I.M., Whalley, L.J., & Christie, J.E. (1981). The efficacy of cognitive therapy in depression: A treatment trial using cognitive therapy and pharmacotherapy, each alone and in combination. *British Journal of Psychiatry, 139,* 181–189.

Bruder, G.E., Stewart, J.W., Mercier, M.A., Agosti, V., Leite, P., Donovan, S., & Quitkin, F.M. (1997). Outcome of cognitive-behavioral therapy for depression: Relation to hemispheric dominance for verbal processing. *Journal of Abnormal Psychology, 106,* 138–144.

Burlingame, G.M., Fuhriman, A., Paul, S., & Ogles, B.M. (1989). Implementing a time-limited therapy program: Differential effects of training and experience. *Psychotherapy, 26,* 303–313.

Burns, D.D., & Nolen-Hoeksema, S. (1992). Therapeutic empathy and recovery from depression in cognitive-behavioral therapy: A structural equation model. *Journal of Consulting and Clinical Psychology, 60,* 441–449.

Burns, D.D., Rude, S., Simons, A.D., Bates, M.A., & Thase, M.E. (1994). Does learned resourcefulness predict the response to cognitive behavioral therapy for depression? *Cognitive Therapy and Research, 18,* 277–290.

Butler, G. (1993). Predicting outcome after treatment for generalized anxiety disorder. *Behavior Research and Therapy, 31,* 211–213.

Chambless, D.L., Sanderson, W.C., Shoham, V., Johnson, S.B., Pope, K.S., Crits-Christoph, P., Baker, M., Johnson, B., Woody, S.R., Sue, S., Beutler, L., Williams, D.A., & McCurry, S. (1996). An update on empirically validated therapies. *Clinical Psychologist, 49,* 5–18.

Clair, A.L., Oei, T.P.S., & Evans, L. (1992). Personality and treatment response in agoraphobia with panic attacks. *Comprehensive Psychiatry, 33,* 310–318.

Coker, S., Vize, C., Wade, T., Cooper, P.J. (1993). Patients with bulimia nervosa who fail to engage in cognitive behavior therapy. *International Journal of Eating Disorders, 13,* 35–40.

Crits-Christoph, P., Baranackie, K., Kurcias, J.S., Beck, A.T., Carroll, K., Perry, K., Luborsky, L., McLellan, A.T., Woody, G.E., Thompson, L., Gallagher, D., & Zitrin, C. (1991). Meta-analysis of therapist effects in psychotherapy outcome studies. *Psychotherapy Research, 1,* 81–91.

DeRubeis, R.J., & Feeley, M. (1990). Determinants of change in cognitive therapy for depression. *Cognitive Therapy and Research, 14,* 469–482.

D'Zurilla, T.J. (1986). *Problem-solving therapy: A social competence approach to clinical intervention.* New York: Springer.

Elkin, I., Shea, M.T., Watkins, J.T., Gibbons, R.D., Sotsky, S.M., Pilkonis, P.A., & Hedeker, D. (1995). Initial severity and differential treatment outcome in the National Institute of Mental Health Treatment of Depression Collaborative Research Program. *Journal of Consulting and Clinical Psychology, 63,* 841–847.

Ellis, A. (1962). *Reason and emotion in psychotherapy.* New York: Lyle Stuart.

Ellis, A. (1993). Changing rational-emotive therapy (RET) to rational emotive behavior therapy (REBT). *Behavior Therapist, 16,* 257–258.

Engels, G.I., Garnefski, N., & Diekstra, R.F.W. (1993). Efficacy of rational-emotive therapy: A quantitative analysis. *Journal of Consulting and Clinical Psychology, 61,* 1083–1090.

Fennell, M.J.V., & Teasdale, J.D. (1987). Cognitive therapy for depression: Individual differences and the process of change. *Cognitive Therapy and Research, 11,* 253–271.

Haaga, D.A.F., & Davison, G.C. (1991). Cognitive change methods. In F.H. Kanfer & A.P. Goldstein (Eds.), *Helping people change: A textbook of methods* (4th ed., pp. 248–304). Elmsford, NY: Pergamon Press.

Haaga, D.A.F., DeRubeis, R.J., Stewart, B.L., & Beck, A.T. (1991). Relationship of intelligence with cognitive therapy outcome. *Behaviour Research and Therapy, 29,* 277–281.

Hollon, S.D., DeRubeis, R.J., & Evans, M.D. (1996). Cognitive therapy in the treatment and prevention of depression. In P.M. Salkovskis (Ed.), *Frontiers of cognitive therapy* (pp. 293–317). New York: Guilford Press.

Hollon, S.D., & Najavits, L. (1988). Review of empirical studies of cognitive therapy. In A.J. Frances & R.E. Hales (Eds.), *American Psychiatric Press review of psychiatry* (Vol. 7, pp. 643–666). Washington, DC: American Psychiatric Press.

Ilardi, S.S., & Craighead, W.E. (1994). The role of nonspecific factors in cognitive-behavior therapy for depression. *Clinical Psychology: Research and Practice, 1,* 138–156.

Jacobson, N.S., Dobson, K.S., Truax, P.A., Addis, M.E., Koerner, K., Gollan, J.K., Gortner, E., & Prince, S.E. (1996). A component analysis of cognitive-behavioral treatment for depression. *Journal of Consulting and Clinical Psychology, 64,* 295–304.

Jarrett, R.B., Eaves, G.G., Grannemann, B.D., & Rush, A.J. (1991). Clinical, cognitive, and demographic predictors of response to cognitive therapy for depression: A preliminary report. *Psychiatry Research, 37,* 245–260.

Jarrett, R.B., Rush, A.J., Khatami, M., & Roffwarg, H.P. (1990). Does the pretreatment polysomnogram predict response to cognitive therapy in depressed outpatients? A preliminary report. *Psychiatry Research, 33,* 285–299.

Kendall, P.C., Haaga, D.A.F., Ellis, A., Bernard, M., DiGiuseppe, R., & Kassinove, H. (1995). Rational-emotive therapy in the 1990s and beyond: Current status, recent revisions, and research questions. *Clinical Psychology Review, 15,* 169–185.

Krupnick, J.L., Sotsky, S.M., Simmens, S., Moyer, J., Elkin, I., Watkins, J., & Pilkonis, P.A. (1996). The role of the therapeutic alliance in psychotherapy and pharmacotherapy outcome: Findings in the National Institute of Mental Health Treatment of Depression Collaborative Research Program. *Journal of Consulting and Clinical Psychology, 64,* 532–539.

Luborsky, L., Crits-Christoph, P., McLellan, A.T., Woody, G., Piper, W., Liberman, B., Imber, S., & Pilkonis, P. (1986). Do therapists vary much in their success? Findings from four outcome studies. *American Journal of Orthopsychiatry, 56,* 501–512.

Mahoney, M.J. (1988). The cognitive sciences and psychotherapy: Patterns in a developing relationship. In K.S. Dobson (Ed.), *Handbook of cognitive-behavioral therapies* (pp. 357–386). New York: Guilford Press.

Marmar, C.R., Gaston, L., Gallagher, D., & Thompson, L.W. (1989). Alliance and outcome in late-life depression. *Journal of Nervous and Mental Disease, 177,* 464–472.

McKnight, D.L., Nelson-Gray, R.O., & Barnhill, J. (1992). Dexamethasone suppression test and response to cognitive therapy and antidepressant medication. *Behavior Therapy, 23,* 99–111.

Meichenbaum, D. (1986). Cognitive-behavior modification. In F.H. Kanfer & A.P. Goldstein (Eds.), *Helping people change: A textbook of methods* (3rd ed., pp. 346–380). Elmsford, NY: Pergamon Press.

Norman, W.H., Miller, I.W., & Dow, M.G. (1988). Characteristics of depressed patients with elevated levels of dysfunctional cognitions. *Cognitive Therapy and Research, 12,* 39–52.

O'Leary, K.D., & Beach, S.R.H. (1990). Marital therapy: A viable treatment for depression and marital discord. *American Journal of Psychiatry, 147,* 183–186.

Persons, J.B., & Burns, D.D. (1985). Mechanisms of action of cognitive therapy: The relative contributions of technical and interpersonal interventions. *Cognitive Therapy and Research, 10,* 539–551.

Persons, J.B., Burns, D.D., & Perloff, J.M. (1988). Predictors of drop-out and outcome in cognitive therapy for depression in a private practice setting. *Cognitive Therapy and Research, 12,* 557–575.

Rathus, J.H., Sanderson, W.C., Miller, A.L., & Wetzler, S. (1995). Impact of personality functioning on cognitive behavioral treatment of panic disorder: A preliminary report. *Journal of Personality Disorders, 9,* 160–168.

Reich, J.H., & Vasile, R.G. (1993). Effect of personality disorders on the treatment outcome of Axis I conditions: An update. *Journal of Nervous and Mental Disease, 181,* 475–484.

Rosenbaum, M. (1980). A schedule for assessing self-control behaviors: Preliminary findings. *Behavior Therapy, 11,* 109–121.

Shapiro, D.A., Rees, A., Barkham, M., Hardy, G., Reynolds, S., & Startup, M. (1995). Effects of treatment duration and severity of depression on the maintenance of gains after cognitive-behavioral and psychodynamic-interpersonal psychotherapy. *Journal of Consulting and Clinical Psychology, 63,* 378–387.

Shea, M.T., Pilkonis, P.A., Beckham, E., Collins, J.F., Elkin, I., Sotsky, S.M., & Docherty, J.P. (1990). Personality disorders and treatment outcome in the NIMH Treatment of Depression Collaborative Research Program. *American Journal of Psychiatry, 147,* 711–718.

Simons, A.D., Gordon, J.S., Monroe, S.M., & Thase, M.E. (1995). Toward an integration of psychologic, social, and biologic factors in depression: Effects on outcome and course of cognitive therapy. *Journal of Consulting and Clinical Psychology, 63,* 369–377.

Simons, A.D., Lustman, P.J., Wetzel, R.D., & Murphy, G.E. (1985). Predicting response to cognitive therapy of depression: The role of learned resourcefulness. *Cognitive Therapy and Research, 9,* 79–89.

Simons, A.D., & Thase, M.E. (1992). Biological markers, treatment outcome, and 1 year follow-up in endogenous major depression: EEG sleep studies and response to cognitive therapy. *Journal of Consulting and Clinical Psychology, 60,* 392–401.

Sotsky, S.M., Glass, D.R., Shea, M.T., Pilkonis, P.A., Collins, J.F., Elkin, I., Watkins, J.T., Imber, S.D., Leber, W.R., Moyer, J., & Oliveri, M.E. (1991). Patient predictors of response to psychotherapy and pharmacotherapy: Findings of the NIMH Treatment of Depression Collaborative Research Program. *American Journal of Psychiatry, 148,* 997–1008.

Teasdale, J.D. (1985). Psychological treatments for depression: How do they work? *Behaviour Research and Therapy, 23,* 157–165.

Thase, M.E., Simons, A.D., & Reynolds, C.F. (1996). Abnormal electroencephalographic sleep profiles in major depression: Association with response to cognitive-behavioral therapy. *Archives of General Psychiatry, 53,* 99–108.

Wetzel, R.D., Murphy, G.E., Carney, R.M., Whitworth, P., & Knesevich, M.A. (1992). Prescribing therapy for depression: The role of learned resourcefulness, a failure to replicate. *Psychological Reports, 70,* 803–807.

Whisman, M.A. (1993). Mediators and moderators of change in cognitive therapy of depression. *Psychological Bulletin, 114,* 248–265.

CHAPTER 4

Pharmacotherapy

JONATHAN M. MEYER and GEORGE M. SIMPSON

ALTHOUGH THE psychoactive properties of medicinal plants have been known for millennia, only in the last 50 years have mechanisms been delineated for various drugs, and specific criteria arrived at for their usage. Nevertheless, psychopharmacology is still in its relative infancy, and it continues to evolve along with complex developments in the fields of neural science, pharmacology, psychotherapy, and mental health epidemiology.

The modern history of psychopharmacology commenced with the synthesis of barbiturates in the early twentieth century. These were the first compounds to be effective anxiolytics without the central nervous system (CNS) complications associated with bromide use. The majority of the modern classes of psychoactive drugs were discovered by midcentury, but their specific applications for psychosis (phenothiazines), bipolar disorder (lithium salts), depression (monoamine oxidase inhibitors [MAOIs], tricyclic antidepressants [TCAs]) generally appeared as serendipitous side effects of the original intended usage. The initial optimism with these compounds was subsequently tempered by the realization that these drugs also possessed their own unique deleterious effects. Tardive dyskinesia became associated with long-term antipsychotic administration, renal and thyroid dysfunction with lithium usage, hypertensive crises with monoamine oxidase inhibitors, cardiac arrhythmias and lethal overdose with tricyclic antidepressants.

The goal of modern pharmacology involves the attempt to separate a drug's therapeutic effects from adverse side effects. This task has been assisted by molecular techniques permitting clarification of specific receptor subtypes on neurons, advances in imaging techniques that permit visualization of brain regions where drug activity occurs, and subsequent correlation of this information with symptoms and current models of psychopathology. Although the science of pharmacotherapy has benefited from these technological developments, the information derived from epidemiologic studies and clinical trials may be the greater contributor to the goal of clarifying indications for both psychotherapeutic and biological treatments in specific disorders.

Naturalistic data from epidemiologic inquiries and clinical studies has assumed increasing importance as both researchers and clinicians strive to define syndromes and disorders that carry prognostic significance for treatment. The diagnostic criteria in the fourth edition of the *Diagnostic and Statistical Manual of Mental Disorders* (*DSM-IV;* American Psychiatric Association [APA], 1994) for the major mood, anxiety and psychotic disorders are intended to group individuals whose illness carries a unique natural history and response to treatment, both psychological and pharmacological. Thus, individuals who meet the criteria for a major depressive episode with melancholic features, as a group, are likely to have a similar response to tricyclic antidepressants regardless of precipitants or social stressors. For the psychotic disorders (e.g., schizophrenia, severe mood disorders), pharmacotherapy is essential; however, for many anxiety and depressive disorders, the decision to employ medications must take into account numerous factors including illness severity, effectiveness of nonbiologic treatment, past response to psychotherapy and medications, patient preference and motivation for various forms of treatment. The importance of patient and clinician variables in arriving at an effective treatment plan will be discussed in a separate section later in this chapter.

This chapter is not intended as a guide to pharmacological treatment, but rather as an overview of some basic concepts of pharmacotherapy. The initial section will be devoted to those defining principles of drug actions and therapeutics: pharmacokinetics, pharmacodynamics, the importance of accurate diagnosis, and a rational approach to the use of medications. Current medications in use for treatment of the common classes of anxiety, psychotic, and mood disorders will be surveyed in the second section, with an emphasis on the multiple usages of medications, as well as important side effects. The last section is devoted to those variables in clinical practice inherent in the clinician and patient relationship, which may have an impact on treatment, with a brief focus on the impact of practice in the managed care setting.

RATIONAL THERAPEUTICS

As alluded to in the introduction, arriving at a diagnosis for the presenting complaint is the single most important determinant in the potential outcome of any therapy. Although there is considerable pressure in this era of managed care to evaluate a patient and prescribe a course of treatment in the first session, there is rarely clinical necessity to commit an individual to a particular treatment so early in the therapeutic relationship. Utilizing additional time for evaluation can permit the clinician to differentiate among psychiatric disorders that share common symptomatology, and to properly investigate possible medical causes of symptoms that may have been overlooked. Thus, an 18-year-old woman who appears to have developed a depressive disorder as part of adjustment to living away from home at college may actually have subclinical hypothyroidism. A man with a first manic episode at age 42 may be demonstrating the sequelae of undiagnosed human immunodeficiency virus (HIV) infection. The middle-aged woman who complains of morning anxiety might be suffering from mild alcohol withdrawal. The numerous medical and substance related disorders that present with psychiatric manifestations should be taken into account as part of the clinical formulation, and likely candidates excluded as part of the routine pretreatment evaluation (Marsh, 1997). An appreciation of the patient's medical history is always useful even when not directly related to the presenting problems for several reasons:

1. Physical illness may be an ongoing source of stress.
2. Medications taken for physical illnesses may themselves have side effects that can affect mood and cognition.
3. Physical illness and medication may alter the metabolism and effectiveness of psychotropic agents.

Gelenberg and Schoonover (1991) have outlined some useful principles to guide the use of pharmacologic agents for psychiatric disorders:

1. Use nonbiological treatments when they are as effective as pharmacotherapy.
2. Do not deny a patient appropriate medication.
3. Choose the drug with the best risk/benefit ratio.
4. Understand the pharmacokinetics of psychotropic agents.
5. Learn the differences between preparations.
6. Prescribe the simplest regimen to increase compliance.
7. Avoid polypharmacy whenever possible.
8. Provide the most cost effective treatment.
9. Exercise special care with the medically ill patient.
10. Establish an ongoing therapeutic relationship.
11. Complete each drug trial.

These basic precepts are profound in their simplicity, as they embody the essential goal of any treatment: ensure the best choice, do more good than harm, make it easy to follow and affordable, and give the medication sufficient time to work. Item number two stands alone as a caveat against the tendency to attribute disorders occurring in the context of multiple stressors to a "reactive" cause, and thereby minimize the need for treatment. Almost every mental health professional at times has said to themselves, "I would be depressed too if I had . . ."; however, if the symptom severity and duration warrant a diagnosis of major depressive disorder, for example, the patient should not be deprived of treatment, including medication if necessary.

BASIC CONCEPTS IN PHARMACOTHERAPY

PHARMACOKINETICS

An appreciation of pharmacotherapy necessarily begins with the basics of pharmacokinetics, which concerns itself with what happens to a substance when it enters the body. Pharmacokinetics refers specifically to the absorption, distribution, metabolism or transformation of a drug, and to its excretion. All of these properties carry implications for achieving the desired effect, minimizing side effects, and arriving at a dosing schedule that optimizes these properties while fostering patient compliance.

Absorption

Absorption determines the rate at which a compound enters the body from its site of administration and becomes distributed within the body. Presently, there are many modes clinically available for drug delivery. Oral, sublingual, inhalational, nasal, rectal, parenteral (intramuscular (IM) injection, or via intravenous (IV) administration), and transdermal routes are all commonly employed. Each carries advantages and disadvantages depending on the clinical need (see Table 4.1), and the choice must be determined by the clinician for each scenario.

The oral form is generally the most common method of drug administration due to the favorable factors noted above. The compliance issue must always be considered, especially if the patient has a history of treatment failure. In some instances, such as schizophrenia, it may loom as the primary problem. Once a drug is ingested by mouth, its passage from inside the intestine across the mucosal lining to the bloodstream is governed by passive processes dependent on gastrointestinal (GI) motility and blood flow, the acidic (pH) environment of the stomach, presence of food, and inherent properties of the drug itself. Because biological membranes are composed of a fatty lipid bilayer, drugs that are fat soluble (e.g., lipophilic) are absorbed readily, which may lead to a more rapid onset of action. In general, one will not note the effects of any orally

Table 4.1
Comparison of Routes for Drug Administration

Route	Absorption	Positives	Negatives
Transdermal	Slow	Compliance Stable drug levels	Limited to small dosages Limited availability for most drugs
Oral	Variable	Convenient Usually safe Cheaper	Dependent on patient compliance Erratic absorption for certain drugs Nausea First pass effect
Intramuscular	Prompt	Reliable	Pain Not available for certain drugs Only small amounts can be administered
Intravenous	Absorption not an issue	Ideal for emergency situations Exact dose titration Large volumes may be administered	Risk of infection Rapid onset must be closely monitored

ingested drug in less than 30- to 45-minutes; with poorly absorbed drugs, the effect may not be apparent for several hours, if at all. Many compounds are poorly or erratically absorbed from the GI tract due to destruction by stomach acid or chemical properties of the drug, which make it poorly soluble in lipids (hydrophilic). Another process contributing to lower than desired serum drug levels after oral administration is the "first-pass" effect of hepatic metabolism. Anything absorbed across intestinal membranes enters the veins draining the intestines and proceeds to the liver, whose function is to extensively metabolize nutrients and drugs. As much as 90 percent of an orally administered dose may be inactivated by this first-pass effect, thereby limiting the amount available to enter the general circulation (Benet, Kroetz, & Sheiner, 1996). The bioavailability of an oral preparation refers to the sum total of these issues related to absorption, and it is expressed as a percentage of the orally administered dose. For those compounds that can be absorbed via the mucous membrane linings of the mouth, nose, rectum, or lungs there is no first-pass effect, because they enter directly into the systemic circulation.

Intravenous (IV), intramuscular (IM), and transdermal routes offer a similar advantage in avoiding first-pass hepatic metabolism. Medications given by IV also bypass the absorptive phase, allowing one to achieve rapid serum levels. IM medications are absorbed very rapidly, although there are some long-acting depot preparations designed to be slowly absorbed from the muscle tissue over a period of weeks. Nicotine might properly be considered the first psychotropic agent available in a transdermal patch. Although the transdermal route also bypasses the first-pass liver metabolism, it requires many hours to achieve modest serum levels of the compound because of the thickness of the skin layer. Its advantages lie in the ability to maintain relatively constant blood levels in a delivery system that maximizes compliance.

Distribution

Once the drug has been absorbed into the bloodstream, it is then distributed throughout the body by the general circulation. This important fact is the bane of all who prescribe medications. The drug intended to treat depression will also go to the heart, liver, kidneys and GI tract where its pharmacological action results in unwanted side effects. Depending on a drug's lipid solubility and the relative blood circulation of a particular organ, there will be differential concentrations of the drug both within and outside of cells in various body regions. There is a physiologic and microanatomic blood-brain barrier that resists the entrance into the brain by most compounds; the distribution of drugs into the central nervous system (CNS) is therefore governed mostly by lipid solubility. Also, many drugs will temporarily bind to serum proteins in the blood, thereby reducing the amount of free drug available to exert its effects. This may have significant clinical relevance when an individual on medication commences a second drug that is more tightly bound to plasma proteins, thereby displacing much of the former. Although there has been no change in the dose of the first drug, the patient may have deleterious effects resulting from the increase in unbound or free drug in the bloodstream.

Biotransformation and Excretion

With the exception of medications that are excreted via the GI tract and not absorbed, such as the antiulcer drug sucralfate, or simple salts like lithium chloride, which are excreted solely by the kidney, all compounds undergo some degree of transformation in the liver. Although orally administered drugs are subject to first-pass metabolism in the liver prior to entering the general circulation, all medications in the blood will eventually pass through the liver circulation and be subjected to the effects of various liver enzymes. The product of this enzymatic action may be active or inactive metabolites, which are subsequently excreted by the kidney. Interindividual differences in enzyme activity, especially between various ethnic groups, is a subject of intense scrutiny at this time as it may help to explain variations in both efficacy and side effects (Lin, Anderson, & Poland, 1995). Enzymatic activity also declines with age, making the elderly more susceptible to toxicity from prolonged higher levels of the parent drug and its active metabolites (Catterson, Preskorn, & Martin, 1997).

The time required for the blood concentration of a drug to be reduced 50 percent is referred to as the half-life. Knowledge of a drug's half-life, and that of its primary metabolites, is important in deciding upon an appropriate dosing interval to achieve maximum clinical effect while minimizing side effects. Especially relevant to the development of side effects is the possibility that compounds with very long half-lives may accumulate in the system, resulting in potential toxicity over a period of days or weeks. When administered on a regular schedule appropriate to the half-life, a balance will generally ensue between absorption and excretion after approximately five half-lives, resulting in a steady state of equilibrium. Monitoring of steady-state levels is important for some drugs that require a well-defined serum level to be clinically effective, and to avoid toxicity. An excellent example is lithium, for which a level of 0.9 meq/l is therapeutic, 0.3 meq/l subtherapeutic, and 1.8 meq/l potentially toxic (Schou, 1997). The clinical half-life of any medication may be affected by many factors such as age, ethnicity, coexisting medical illness, and the use of other medications or substances that may impede each other's metabolism. The various chemicals in cigarette smoke stimulate the liver to metabolize drugs more extensively, shortening the half-life of many medications. Carbamazepine is an antiseizure drug employed for bipolar disorder that also shares this property of inducing hepatic activity.

In general, metabolites and variable amounts of free drug are excreted via the kidney. With age, the glomerular filtration rate will decrease necessitating dosage adjustments in some instances, especially if there is evidence of significant renal dysfunction.

PHARMACODYNAMICS

"Pharmacodynamics can be defined as the study of the biochemical and physiological effects of drugs and their mechanisms of actions" (Ross, 1996, p. 29). Once absorbed, a certain fraction of the drug will be distributed to the intended organ, where its effects are exerted at the cellular level. Although the majority of agents employed by psychiatrists are designed to be active within the CNS, there are medications utilized that may not have primary CNS effects. The beta-adrenergic blockers are employed specifically to slow the heart rate and ameliorate the peripheral effects of anxiety, and are especially helpful for performance anxiety.

The Synapse

The cell is the basic building block of all living tissues, and possesses receptors upon which endogenous and exogenous chemicals act to influence cellular function. Within the CNS, and at other sites involving neurons, the binding of chemical neurotransmitters is transduced into electrical activity propagated down the length of the cell to its terminus, where it releases a transmitter to affect its neighbor. Figure 4.1 demonstrates the basic structure of the synapse where two neurons interface. The presynaptic neuron synthesizes and packages the neurotransmitter into vesicles that fuse with the cell membrane when the cell is stimulated, causing the transmitter to be released into the synaptic cleft. Some of this chemical may diffuse away, but a great amount will bind to receptors on the postsynaptic cell. For certain neurotransmitters (serotonin, norepinephrine, dopamine), unbound transmitter will be taken up into the presynaptic cell via a reuptake pump. Drugs have been identified that will effect every step in this process of transmitter synthesis: vesicle storage, release, receptor binding, and transmitter reuptake. However, given the immense complexity of connections within the CNS via billions of neurons and receptor subtypes, the clinical effect may not directly correlate with the putative cellular action. The selective serotonin reuptake inhibitors (SSRI) for example, are not only antidepressants, but also effective for obsessive compulsive disorder (OCD) and panic disorder. Conversely, panic disorder is a clinical entity which responds to drugs of four different classes: high potency benzodiazepines, SSRIs, monoamine oxidase inhibitors (MAOI), and the tricyclic antidepressant (TCA) imipramine.

Receptors

Receptors are membrane-bound proteins designed to respond preferentially to a specific chemical. The nature of this response is dictated by the receptor configuration. When stimulated, the benzodiazepine receptor opens a central channel, permitting the entrance of a chloride ion that hyperpolarizes the cell, making it more resistant to stimulation. Other classes of receptors are connected to second messenger systems within the cell, which amplify the effect of receptor binding in ways that impact cellular functions. Stimulation of the D_1 subtype of dopamine receptors results in increased intracellular levels of the second messenger cyclic-AMP (cAMP), whereas binding of dopamine to cells with the D_2 subtype decreases cAMP levels. Both PET scanning and molecular-biology techniques have combined in identifying the receptor subtypes implicated in psychiatric disorders, as well as those responsible for unwanted side effects. It is now appreciated that blockade of greater than 80

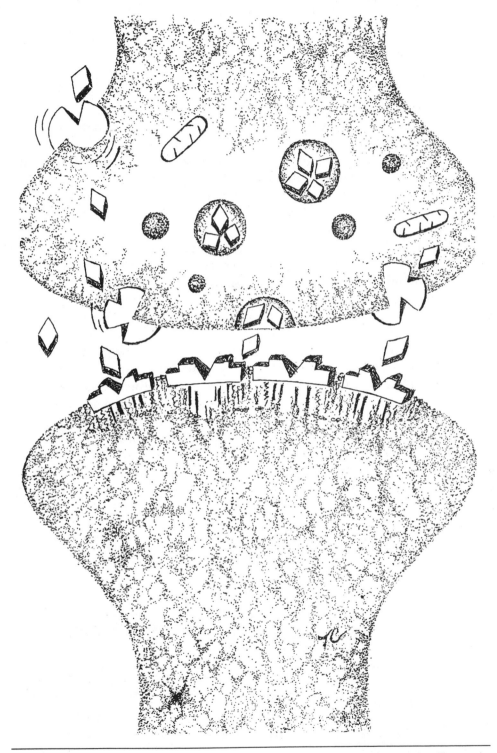

Figure 4.1 Synapse. Presynaptic Neuron (above) with Vesicles Containing Transmitter which Binds to Postsynaptic Receptors upon Release. Reuptake Pumps are Located on the Presynaptic Neuron.

percent of the D_2 neurons within the brain results in extrapyramidal side effects, whereas 50 percent to 70 percent receptor occupancy achieves the desired antipsychotic effect (Brucke, 1992).

Dose-Response and Time

Arriving at the appropriate dose to generate a clinical response without unduly burdening the patient with side effects is the holy grail of psychopharmacology. For some drugs, there are well-defined serum levels in which a drug is active. Lithium is an excellent example of a drug with a narrow therapeutic window. Although increasing the dosage of most drugs will typically result in greater clinical effect, there is usually an upper limit beyond which side effects predominate; moreover, the effectiveness may fail to increase or may even decrease outside the therapeutic window. These dose-response relationships generally fall into one of three distinct patterns (Figure 4.2). Although imipramine is a TCA with a linear dose response, another TCA, nortriptyline, possesses an inverted curvilinear response curve. Antipsychotics tend to manifest a sigmoidal dose-response relationship.

Adequate completion of a pharmacological trial to assess efficacy depends on the nature of the disorder as well as the agents employed. Benzodiazepines are effective within hours of oral administration for relieving generalized anxiety, but require one to four weeks to achieve maximum control of panic disorder. A significant clinical response to antidepressant therapy is noted after three weeks of treatment at the earliest, and six weeks is often considered the minimum to adequately assess antidepressant efficacy. Those taking clozapine for schizophrenia may continue to demonstrate improvement in certain outcome measures even after six months of continuous therapy (Baldessarini & Frankenberg, 1991). In the following section, pharmacologic treatments available for the major categories of psychiatric disorders will be surveyed to clarify the pitfalls and possibilities of drug treatment.

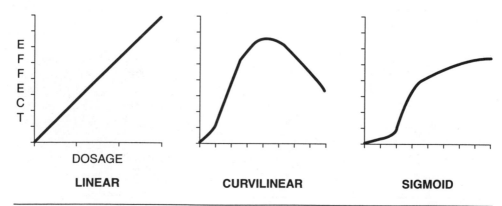

Figure 4.2 Typical Dose-Response Curves. Both the Curvilinear and Sigmoid Curves Illustrate the Presence of a Therapeutic Window Beyond which Increasing Dosage Generates Minimal Improvement.

TREATMENT OF MAJOR DISORDERS

PSYCHOSIS

Over forty years later, we continue to grapple as a society with the impact that the discovery of antipsychotic medication has had on the medical, legal, and social approaches to those with mental illness. Worldwide, 1 percent of the population suffers from schizophrenia (Marder, 1996). Prior to the realization of chlorpromazine's antipsychotic effects in the mid-1950s, electroconvulsive therapy (ECT) offered only modest benefit for treatment, necessitating the warehousing of large populations of chronically psychotic patients. Although the use of antipsychotic medications represents one of the most effective symptomatic treatments available to psychiatry, the presence of significant numbers with schizophrenia among this country's homeless attests to the ongoing social dimensions of this disorder, and to the failure of policy makers to appreciate the limitations of delivering medication to psychotic patients in the community. Issues surrounding schizophrenia illustrate the concept that medications should be considered one aspect of a treatment plan, which includes the psychosocial aspects of illness. Even with medication compliance, the addition of psychosocial programs significantly impacts the rate of relapse (Falloon, Boyd, & McGill, 1982; Goldstein, Rodnick, & Evans, 1978; Hogarty, Anderson, & Reiss, 1991; Hogarty, Schooler, & Ulrich, 1979; Kopelowicz, Liberman, Mintz, & Zarate, 1997).

Psychosis implies a state in which reality testing is significantly impaired by either delusions, hallucinations, or gross disorganization of thought processes. Psychosis may be an acute process, as part of a severe depressive or manic episode, the sequelae of heavy recent substance use, a complication of medical illness, or a more chronic disorder as with schizophrenia, delusional disorder, or serious CNS insults, such as trauma or degenerative diseases (e.g., brain tumor, Alzheimer's disease, HIV-associated dementia), which may have psychotic symptoms as epiphenomena. Because of the wide range of underlying etiologies that may present with psychotic symptoms, determining the cause is vitally important to ensure adequate treatment of both the psychotic symptoms, and any organic precipitants. The first presentation of psychosis in any individual merits an appropriate medical evaluation tailored to the age, risk factors, and clinical course.

Once the association between chlorpromazine's dopamine blocking activity and its antipsychotic properties were understood, the dopamine model of psychotic disorders led to the development of dozens of antipsychotic agents sharing the ability to block postsynaptic dopamine receptors. Although clinical efficacy was linked specifically to the blockade of the D_2 subtype of dopamine receptors within the cerebral cortex, the concomitant blockade of D_2 receptors in the basal ganglia resulted in extrapyramidal side effects (EPS) (Waddington, 1995). EPS evident with short-term usage of typical dopamine-blocking antipsychotic drugs includes acute dystonia (muscle spasms or contractions in neck muscles or tongue), akathisia (restlessness), and Parkinson's syndrome (stiffness, shuffling gait, and tremor). Although these are all reversible, the long-term administration of dopamine blocking agents was noted in certain patients to progress to tardive dyskinesia (TD). TD is characterized by involuntary movements of the lips, tongue, and digits, and in severe cases extremities or trunk. Discontinuation of dopamine blocking medication often allows the syndrome to wane until clinically imperceptible, but for some patients the symptoms are permanent, and they can be physically or socially disabling. Moreover, the removal of antipsychotic therapy in a patient with schizophrenia results in clinical relapse of psychotic symptomatology (Herz et al., 1997).

Synthesized in 1958 in Bern, Switzerland, clozapine is a dibenzodiazepine compound structurally derived from tricyclic models. It lacks the classic antipsychotic effects on repetitive behavior in animals given amphetamines, properties that are dependent on a high level of D_2 blockade. Because of concerns about potentially fatal drops in the numbers of white blood cells, clozapine was not released in the United States until 1990 (Alvir, Lieberman, & Safferman, 1993). These concerns, along with a rigid monitoring system imposed by the manufacturer on physicians and pharmacies, limited the utilization of clozapine, despite data demonstrating superior efficacy in schizophrenia without EPS. This unique property of controlling psychosis without inducing EPS demonstrated to psychopharmacologists that the clinical effect of an antipsychotic could be separated from its liability to cause EPS (Carlsson, 1995). The other distinguishing characteristic of clozapine lay in its ability to ameliorate the negative symptoms of schizophrenia: apathy, avolition, alogia. Whereas all typical antipsychotics were equally effective in controlling the positive symptoms of schizophrenia (hallucinations, delusions, disorganized thoughts or behavior), there was little impact on the disabling cluster of negative symptoms. Moreover, only two-thirds of patients responded in a significant manner to typical antipsychotics, whereas 30 percent to 61 percent of treatment-refractory schizophrenics responded to clozapine, quickly establishing it as the gold standard, despite the necessity of weekly white blood cell monitoring (Marder, 1996).

Clozapine thus has become the model for a new class of so-called atypical antipsychotics (see Table 4.2), which share the pharmacologic property of blocking a subtype of postsynaptic serotonin receptors (5-HT_2), with weaker D_2 binding than among typical antipsychotics (Farde, Nordstrom, Nyberg, Halldin, & Sedvall, 1994). As of this writing, two agents (risperidone, olanzapine) have been released, and many more are on the horizon (Lieberman, 1996; Weiden, Aquila, & Standard, 1996).

Table 4.2
Atypical Antipsychotics

Drug	Dosage (mg/day)
Clozapine	300–900
Risperidone	4–12
Olanzapine	10–20
Quetiapine	200–750
Ziprasidone	10–80

Although the binding of antipsychotics to receptors in the brain can be demonstrated within hours after oral ingestion, the clinical effects of both typical and atypical drugs require days to weeks to develop in patients with schizophrenia; moreover, complete remission with a return to a prior level of function is exceedingly uncommon in this disease. This chronicity and multifaceted nature of symptoms clearly distinguishes schizophrenia and schizoaffective disorder from other psychoses. The sole exception is a pure delusional disorder that is easily differentiated from schizophrenia by the absence of affective blunting, hallucinations, bizarre or disorganized thoughts or behavior (Manschreck, 1996). The acute psychoses that accompany severe mood episodes, delirium, or substance use respond more rapidly to treatment with complete remission of the psychotic component of the illness (Coryell, 1996; McElroy, Keck, & Strakowski, 1996).

The typical antipsychotics (see Table 4.3) are generally divided into two groups depending on relative potency. Although equally effective, low-potency drugs such as chlorpromazine cause more weight gain due to blockade of histamine H_1 receptors, and more sedation due to blockade of acetylcholine receptors. This anticholinergic property is somewhat protective against acute EPS, but at the expense of memory impairment, dry mouth, constipation, blurred vision, increased heart rate, and urinary retention in males. High-potency antipsychotics like haloperidol generally lack anticholinergic and antihistaminic side effects, but in turn they have an increased incidence of EPS. Anticholinergic drugs such as benztropine (Cogentin) and trihexyphenidyl (Artane) are prescribed at times solely for the prophylaxis or treatment of EPS in patients receiving high-potency agents (Kimura, Meyer, & Simpson, 1996; Meyer, & Simpson, in press). The continued development of novel atypical antipsychotics may obviate concerns about prophylactic use of anticholinergic drugs or of EPS in general.

One aspect of schizophrenia that has not been changed significantly with the advent of atypical antipsychotic medications is the problem with compliance. In addition to avoiding unpleasant side effects, the chronically psychotic patient often lacks insight into the fact that a mental illness exists, leading to noncompliance with medication that is deemed unnecessary. Ensuring compliance with

Table 4.3
Typical Antipsychotics

Generic Name	Equivalent Dose (mg)
Chlorpromazine	100
Thioridazine	50
Loxapine	15
Molindone	10
Perphenazine	10
Thiothixene	5
Trifluoperazine	5
Fluphenazine	2
Haloperidol	1–2

an oral regimen is a daunting task; however, there are long-acting depot preparations of haloperidol and fluphenazine, which enable patients with schizophrenia to be maintained with an IM injection every four or every two weeks, respectively, albeit with the potential for EPS associated with these high-potency typical antipsychotics (Kane, Woerner, & Sarantakos, 1986). The possibility of a depot preparation for an atypical agent offers much promise and hope for the millions of patients and families struggling with this illness.

Mood Disorders

Appropriate pharmacotherapy of mood presents a complex problem because of the heterogeneity that exists even within populations who meet criteria for similar disorders. Again, it is important that individuals presenting for treatment, especially when pharmacological agents may be employed, have underlying medical etiologies investigated. Although mania is less commonly seen as the direct physiologic result of physical illness or medications, there is a seemingly endless list of possibilities to consider for the depressive disorders. The clinical presentation and recent history, including medications, physical symptoms, and substance use, will help to narrow the focus of investigation and to guide treatment.

Bipolar Disorder

The two major classes of mood disorders are characterized primarily by the presence or absence of manic (or hypomanic) symptoms. Those illnesses that present with prolonged elevated mood are limited to bipolar disorder and cyclothymia. There are two forms of bipolar disorder: Type I is characterized by manic episodes lasting a minimum of seven days (or less if hospitalization is required), often with a subsequent major depressive episode, although this is not necessary to establish the diagnosis; Type II individuals have hypomanic symptoms lasting a minimum of four days, again with alternating major depressive episodes. During periods of hypomania, the patient may have a decreased need for sleep, rapid speech, increased goal-directed behavior (e.g., work, sex, spending money), and impulsivity, but the impairment is, by definition, not severe enough to mandate hospitalization. Should hospitalization be necessary or should psychotic symptoms such as grandiose or paranoid delusions develop, one is dealing with a manic episode. Cyclothymia is characterized by short, less severe episodes of hypomania and depression.

The three mood stabilizers in common usage are lithium, and two anti-seizure drugs carbamazepine (Tegretol) and divalproex sodium (Depakote). The effect on a manic episode may require one to two weeks, often necessitating the adjunctive use of antipsychotics or of the benzodiazepine clonazepam (Klonopin), which has some weak antimanic properties. Lithium levels must be carefully monitored due to potential toxicity, and patients on chronic therapy must also have routine laboratory assessment of thyroid and kidney function. Side effects of lithium therapy include increased urinary volume, tremor, hair loss, acne, and weight gain. The latter is often cited as a major reason for individuals to discontinue long-term treatment. For years, lithium has been considered the optimum medication for treatment of bipolar disorders; however, there are certain groups that do not respond as well to lithium as to Depakote or combination therapy (Swann et al., 1997). A subset of patients refractory to all forms of combination therapy with mood stabilizers have responded to clozapine (Calabrese et al., 1996). Although ECT is extremely effective at aborting a manic episode, obtaining consent from a manic individual presents a major hurdle.

Depressive Disorders

The depressive disorders represent a much more heterogeneous group of illnesses in which specific therapies can be assessed only in the light of accurate diagnosis. When specific diagnostic symptoms are sought during the evaluation, reliable diagnosis is often, but not always, possible (Holzer, Nguyen, & Hirschfeld, 1996; McCullough et al., 1996). Moreover, milder depressive episodes have many treatment options available for the clinician, with the mode of therapy often determined by the practitioner's expertise. There are a clear subset of patients who develop recurrent depressive episodes, and they respond favorably to maintenance antidepressant treatment (Kupfer et al., 1992). For such individuals, long-term drug therapy is more cost-effective than maintenance interpersonal therapy (IPT) alone; however, with the first presentation of a major depressive disorder it is difficult to predict those who may progress to recurrent episodes (Kamlet et al., 1995). Among patients with recurrent depression, the presence of abnormal sleep EEG profiles was a predictor of poor response to interpersonal therapy (Thase et al., 1997). For patients with chronic depressive disorders, the combination of psychotherapy and pharmacotherapy is superior to either treatment alone (Friedman & Kocsis, 1996). Antidepressant therapy has also proven to be of benefit in dysthymia, and dysphoric symptoms associated with menstrual cycles (Freeman, Rickels, & Sondheimer, 1996; Kocsis et al., 1997).

The development of SSRIs in the 1980s has revolutionized the treatment of depression only in the sense that drugs became available that possessed a more favorable side-effect profile than the TCAs or MAOIs, thereby extending the spectrum of use to individuals with milder symptoms. However, for certain individuals with atypical depression or with major depression with melancholic or psychotic features, the SSRIs may not be as effective as MAOIs in the former or as TCAs for the latter groups (Karasu et al., 1996). Nevertheless, the SSRIs have permitted thousands of patients to receive treatment for depression for whom TCAs and MAOIs were contraindicated or intolerable. The time course to improvement for all classes of antidepressants is three to six weeks.

The five SSRIs currently licensed in the United States (see Table 4.4) have comparable efficacy for depression, and are differentiated primarily by half-life and by pharmacokinetic interactions with other medications. Common side effects include sour stomach or loose stools, sexual side effects (especially delayed orgasm), and transient complaints of headache, anxiety, or difficulty sleeping. They generally lack the anticholinergic and antihistaminic side

Table 4.4
Selective Serotonin Reuptake Inhibitors
Available in the United States

Trade Name	Generic Name	Dosage for Major Depression (mg)
Prozac	Fluoxetine	20–40
Zoloft	Sertraline	50–150
Paxil	Paroxetine	20–40
Luvox	Fluvoxamine	50–200
Celexa	Citalopram	10–60

effects of the TCAs, and, unlike TCAs, they are not lethal in overdose. For these reasons, the SSRIs are considered first line agents for the treatment of most forms of depression. Seasonal affective disorder, which responds to solar spectrum light therapy, is one notable exception. Nefazodone is another effective antidepressant recently available that modulates serotonergic activity via reuptake inhibition and blockade of a subtype of postsynaptic serotonin receptors.

The tricyclic antidepressants exert their therapeutic effect via blockade of serotonin and norepinephrine reuptake. These compounds are very effective, and have well-defined serum levels for clinical response, which are not available for the SSRIs. Imipramine and amitriptyline are tertiary amines that are more sedating than their primary metabolites, desipramine and nortriptyline. Imipramine is also effective for panic disorder, and its halogenated derivative, clomipramine (Anafranil), is quite effective for OCD. Monoamine oxidase inhibitors irreversibly bind to the enzyme responsible for the degradation of several neurotransmitters. Because the majority of monoamine oxidase is present in the liver, blockade of this enzyme by MAOIs mandates that patients on these medications must adhere to a strict diet to avoid ingesting tyramine which, when not metabolized, can result in dangerous elevations of blood pressure. Tyramine is present in aged cheeses and meats, red wines, and foreign or strong beers. For similar reasons, patients must also use caution with any medication that is chemically related to the stimulating neurotransmitters. MAOIs are used infrequently, but are uniquely effective in atypical depression characterized by increased sleep, carbohydrate craving, and interpersonal sensitivity. They also have uses in panic disorder and social phobia, as will be discussed later.

There are several antidepressants used that do not fall clearly into any of the above classes of agents. Bupropion (Wellbutrin) and venlafaxine (Effexor) are two such compounds (Leonard, 1996; Stoudemire, 1996). Remeron (mirtazapine) is a recently released antidepressant whose novel mechanism of action involves antagonism of presynaptic alpha$_2$-adrenergic receptors (de Boer, Nefkens, van Helvoirt, & van Delft, 1996; Haddjeri, Blier, & de Montigny, 1995, 1996). At times, depression refractory to one class of agents may respond to another, to a combination of drugs, or to augmentation strategies employing lithium, psychostimulants or thyroid hormone. Only in seriously ill medical populations, for whom a three-week latency to symptom relief is not clinically acceptable, are the psychostimulants dextroamphetamine and methylphenidate employed for major depression because of their rapid onset of action. ECT still remains the gold standard among all somatic therapies with response rates of up to 94 percent in patients with past depressive episodes, compared with 50 percent to 70 percent for medications (Dubovsky, 1995).

ANXIETY DISORDERS

Diagnostically and therapeutically, the anxiety disorders may present a challenge due to the presence of comorbid anxiety disorders in the same individual (Goldenberg et al., 1996). As with depression, there are several different classes of agents from which to choose for many anxiety disorders. Although recent comparative trials have helped clarify the indications for certain medications, clinician preference and experience often dictates the choice of pharmacotherapy, especially when the patient presents with a mixed anxiety disorder.

The benzodiazepines (see Table 4.5) represent a class of medications that are immediately effective for almost all forms of anxiety, but they carry clinical concerns because of sedation, potential for abuse, and physiologic dependence. Nevertheless, they are widely prescribed to control anxiety of various types, as hypnotics for sleep induction, and to mitigate the effects of severe alcohol withdrawal. The latter property derives from the fact that alcohol, barbiturates, and benzodiazepines are all agonists at gamma-aminobutyric acid (GABA) receptors, and, thus, exhibit cross-tolerance. Unlike barbiturates, benzodiazepines are rarely fatal in overdosage, although respiratory depression can occur, especially when combined with alcohol. Although short-acting benzodiazepines such as Halcion and Restoril are used primarily as hypnotics, Xanax is an effective antipanic agent, although its half-life mandates dosing three times a day. Benzodiazepines should only be used for short-term treatment of sleep disorders due to anxiety, and they are contraindicated if any suspicion exists of sleep apnea.

Buspirone is a serotonergic drug that has been shown to be effective for generalized anxiety disorder, and it lacks the side effects or abuse potential of the benzodiazepines. The onset of action occurs over two to three weeks, making it

Table 4.5
Equivalent Benzodiazepine Potencies

Trade Name	Generic Name	Equivalent Dosage (mg)
Klonopin	Clonazepam	.25
Xanax	Alprazolam	.50
Halcion	Triazolam	.50
Ativan	Lorazepam	1
Valium	Diazepam	5
Restoril	Temazepam	15
Serax	Oxazepam	15
Librium	Chlordiazepoxide	25

unpopular with some patients who are accustomed to the immediate effect of the benzodiazepines (Schweizer, 1995).

Serotonergic drugs also have important uses in both panic disorder and OCD. In controlled studies, SSRIs have proved superior to imipramine, and the high-potency benzodiazepines Xanax and Klonopin (Bakish et al., 1996; Boyer, 1995; Rosenberg, 1993). The MAOIs are perhaps the most effective pharmacologic agents available for panic, but are generally third-line drugs due to the dietary restrictions (Pollack & Smoller, 1995). When pharmacotherapy is indicated for OCD, a serotonergic drug is required, as the benzodiazepines are not effective for this disorder. Typically patients will require one and a half to three times the antidepressant dose of an SSRI or clomipramine for effective symptom relief, with 8 to 12 weeks required for clinical response (Higgins, 1996; Hollander et al., 1996; Trivedi, 1996). Although classified under the somatoform disorders, body dysmorphic disorder (BDD) involves the preoccupation with an imagined defect in appearance and responds to similar therapeutic regimens as OCD (Phillips, 1996a, 1996b). Posttraumatic stress disorder (PTSD) may also respond to SSRIs, even in the absence of significant mood symptoms (Marmar et al., 1996).

Social phobia will respond to judicious use of benzodiazepines or beta-adrenergic blocking drugs (e.g., propranolol, atenolol), in conjunction with behavioral, cognitive behavioral, or group therapy (Mancini & Ameringen, 1996). Interestingly, the MAOIs are also quite effective, but again have limited usage as primary agents.

EATING DISORDERS

Although pharmacotherapy is not the primary treatment modality in these disorders, medications have proven beneficial in many instances (Jimerson, Wolfe, Brotman, & Metzger, 1996; Mirin et al., 1996; Yager et al., 1996). Anorexia nervosa responds less well to pharmacological adjuncts; however, in bulimia, the SSRIs and other antidepressants have demonstrated effectiveness in several studies by reducing the frequency of binge eating and self-induced vomiting episodes (Keel & Mitchell, 1997; Walsh et al., 1997).

SUBSTANCE USE DISORDERS

For the substance use disorders, medications have always been utilized during the detoxification process for those drugs with significant physiologic withdrawal symptoms, especially alcohol, benzodiazepines, and opiates. For relapse prevention in alcoholism, recent studies have demonstrated that the opiate antagonist naltrexone decreases craving and increases time of sobriety (Berg, Pettinati, & Volpicelli, 1996; Obrien, Volpicelli, & Volpicelli, 1996; Omalley, Jaffe, Rode, & Rounsaville, 1996).

Nicotine dependence is a problem with a tremendous impact on the health care budget, but which is often minimized during mental health evaluation (American Psychiatric Association, 1996). Nicotine-containing transdermal patches or gum are only modestly effective when used as the sole method for smoking cessation, and are associated with almost 90 percent incidence of relapse if not combined with behavioral treatments (Richmond, Kehoe, & de Almeida Neto, 1997; N. Schneider et al., 1995; Smith & Winters, 1995). Irritability and craving are part of the one- to two-week withdrawal process, but more significant mood symptoms may arise. In one study the discontinuation of smoking was associated with a 2 percent incidence of depression in those with no prior history of depression, but increased to 17 percent in those with one prior depressive episode, and to 30 percent in those with recurrent depression (Covey, Glassman, & Stetner, 1997).

DEMENTIA

Although the underlying pathology of disorders such as Alzheimer's disease is progressive and not reversible with treatment, pharmacotherapy has routinely been employed to treat the mood and psychotic complications of the dementias (Alexopoulos, 1996; Tariot, 1996). In recent years, two drugs have become available that modify the course of memory impairment in dementia of the Alzheimer type that results from the loss of neurons producing the neurotransmitter acetylcholine. Tacrine and Aricept inhibit the activity of acetylcholinesterase, an enzyme present within cholinergic synapses, thereby increasing the amount of acetylcholine available from the remaining neurons. These drugs not only delay progression of cognitive impairment for many months, but do delay the time to nursing home placement from 7 to 13 months in those who continue on medication compared to comparable patients off medication (L. Schneider, 1996).

PERSONALITY DISORDERS

Individuals with personality disorders are at greater risk for Axis I disorders, especially depression and substance use. Medications are employed for the typical indications as with other patients with Axis I conditions, but the response is often less robust and associated with greater patient complaints of side effects (Scott, Harrington, House, & Ferrier, 1996; Thase, 1996). Pharmacotherapy may also be used adjunctively to relieve the dysphoria and impulsivity associated with borderline personality disorder (Gunderson & Phillips, 1995). Care must be exercised in these patients due to the chronic suicidality that may accompany the symptom cluster in this disorder. A recent case report has also documented naltrexone as reducing self-injurious behavior in a patient with borderline personality disorder (McGee, 1997).

OTHER CLINICAL VARIABLES

CLINICIAN AND PATIENT ATTRIBUTES

The overriding purpose for performing research on medication in a double-blind fashion rests on the considerable influence that the clinician's attitude toward the treatment may have on the patient and the outcome. A strong desire on the part of the clinician or patient for a certain clinical outcome results in a skewed perception of the true benefit (Hemila, 1996). These effects are nonetheless real and are responsible for the reports of both clinical improvement and side effects among patients receiving placebo in double-blind trials (Kocsis et al., 1997; N. Schneider et al., 1995).

As in all medical mental health settings, patients bring to the clinical encounter preconceived notions about their problem and treatment derived from personality characteristics, social experience, cultural norms, and the influences of the psychiatric illness itself upon cognition. The practitioner prescribing pharmacotherapy must appreciate and utilize techniques garnered from behavioral, psychodynamic, and cognitive behavioral therapies to establish a treatment alliance with the patient that maximizes compliance and the potential clinical benefit of medication. In large urban settings, one must necessarily be attuned to the variety of sociocultural beliefs about psychological and psychiatric illness, and the specific significance attached to the use of medication within that context of beliefs for a particular patient. Overlying these issues is the impact of heritable biological variations among racial and geographic groups on drug kinetics. Lastly, the individual's level of insight and motivation to pursue a trial of pharmacotherapy can present a major treatment obstacle among the more severe Axis I and Axis II disorders.

MANAGED CARE AND THE FUTURE

Managed care exerts an overwhelming influence on the provision of mental health care through such mechanisms as "carving out" mental health treatment from other medical care, restricting duration and frequency of visits, and formulary restrictions. The thrust of managed care models has focused on the utilization of primary care physicians for most treatment in a theoretical attempt to limit costs associated with specialized physician care (Stoudemire, 1996, 1997). A review of approximately 13,000 patients in one health maintenance organization (HMO) with diagnoses of otitis media (inner ear infection), arthritis, hypertension, asthma, or ulcer disease demonstrated two important findings: (1) A significant portion of patients with a specific diagnosis of major depression were receiving no antidepressant medication; (2) Cost-containment strategies markedly limited psychiatric referral, frequency of visits, and the use of SSRIs (Horn, 1997). HMO policy makers often overlook the fact that attendant with the social and economic costs to the patient of undertreated psychiatric disorders is increased utilization of medical services (Hirschfeld et al., 1997). Moreover, in two large scale studies within HMO systems, comparing the total cost of SSRIs to TCAs including physician time, expenses for medical monitoring, and expenses for the treatment of side effects, SSRIs demonstrated comparable cost to TCA use, with superior outcome measures for the SSRIs based on quality-adjusted lifetime years (Revicki et al., 1997; Sclar et al., 1995).

These studies and other outcomes research will hopefully provide strong weapons in the armamentarium of the clinician in justifying ongoing psychotherapy and pharmacotherapy (Gabbard, Lazar, Hornberger, & Spiegel, 1997). The goal of pharmacotherapy in psychiatric disorders is not simply symptom relief, but restoration of the individual to the highest potential level of functioning in all spheres: psychological, social, and biological. Until managed care organizations can see beyond the quarterly balance sheet, overall cost-assessment data can be employed by appealing to those aspects of biological functioning that appear to have the most direct economic impact on medical service utilization.

Despite whatever institutional hurdles are present to providing care, this is an exciting period in the history of psychopharmacology. The decade of the brain has resulted in profound advances in our knowledge of brain functions in health and sickness, permitting the subsequent development of medications with greater efficacy and fewer adverse effects than had previously been thought possible. Much as the unleashing of atomic energy in the New Mexico desert in 1945 heralded a new era whose possibilities were dimly foreseen by physicists working 10 years prior, the potential development of unforeseen agents to alter mood, behavior, and cognition will exert its effects beyond our imagined realms of biology and medicine.

REFERENCES

Alexopoulos, G.S. (1996). The treatment of depressed demented patients. *Journal of Clinical Psychiatry, 57*(Suppl. 14), 14–20.

Alvir, J.M., Lieberman, J.A., & Safferman, A.Z. (1993). Clozapine-induced agranulocytosis: Incidence and risk factors in the United States. *New England Journal of Medicine, 329,* 162–167.

American Psychiatric Association. (1994). *Diagnostic and statistical manual of mental disorders* (4 ed.). Washington, DC: American Psychiatric Association.

American Psychiatric Association. (1996). Practice guideline for the treatment of patients with nicotine dependence. *American Journal of Psychiatry, 153*(Suppl. 10), 1–31.

Bakish, D., Hooper, C.L., Filteau, M.J., Charbonneau, Y., Fraser, G., West, D.L., Thibaudeau, C., & Raine, D. (1996). A double-blind placebo-controlled trial comparing fluvoxamine and imipramine in the treatment of panic disorder with or without agoraphobia. *Psychopharmacology Bulletin, 32*(1), 135–141.

Baldessarini, R., & Frankenberg, F. (1991). Clozapine: A novel antipsychotic agent. *New England Journal of Medicine, 324,* 746–754.

Benet, L.Z., Kroetz, D.L., & Sheiner, L.B. (1996). Pharmacokinetics. In L.S. Goodman, A. Gilman, J.G. Hardman, & A.G. Gilman (Eds.), *The pharmacological basis of therapeutics* (9th ed.). New York: McGraw-Hill.

Berg, B.J., Pettinati, H.M., & Volpicelli, J.R. (1996). A risk-benefit assessment of naltrexone in the treatment of alcohol dependence. *Drug Safety, 15*(4), 274–282.

Boyer, W. (1995). Serotonin uptake inhibitors are superior to imipramine and alprazolam in alleviating panic attacks: A meta-analysis. *International Clinical Psychopharmacology, 10*(1), 45–49.

Brucke, T. (1992). Striatal dopamine D2-receptor blockade by typical and atypical neuroleptics. *Lancet, 339,* 497.

Calabrese, J.R., Kimmel, S.E., Woyshville, M.J., Rapport, D.J., Faust, C.J., Thompson, P.A., & Meltzer, H.Y. (1996). Clozapine for treatment-refractory mania. *American Journal of Psychiatry, 153*(6), 759–764.

Carlsson, A. (1995). The dopamine theory revisited. In S.R. Hirsch & D.R. Weinberger (Eds.), *Schizophrenia* (pp. 379–400). Cambridge, MA: Blackwell Science.

Catterson, M., Preskorn, S., & Martin, R. (1997). Pharmacodynamic and Pharmacokinetic Considerations in Geriatric Psychopharmacology. *Psychiatric Clinics of North America, 20*(1), 205–218.

Coryell, W. (1996). Psychotic depression. *Journal of Clinical Psychiatry, 57*(Suppl. 3), 27–31.

Covey, L.S., Glassman, A., & Stetner, F. (1997). Major depression following smoking cessation. *American Journal of Psychiatry, 154*(2), 263–265.

de Boer, T.H., Nefkens, F., van Helvoirt, A., & van Delft, A.M. (1996). Differences in modulation of noradrenergic and serotonergic transmission by the alpha-2 adrenoceptor antagonists, mirtazapine, mianserin and idazoxan. *Journal of Pharmacology and Experimental Therapeutics, 277*(2), 852–860.

Dubovsky, S.L. (1995). Electroconvulsive therapy. In H.I. Kaplan & B.J. Sadock (Eds.), *Comprehensive textbook of psychiatry* (6th ed., pp. 2129–2140). Baltimore: Williams & Wilkins.

Falloon, I., Boyd, J., & McGill, C. (1982). Family management in the prevention of exacerbations of schizophrenia. *New England Journal of Medicine, 306*, 1437–1440.

Farde, L., Nordstrom, A.L., Nyberg, S., Halldin, C., & Sedvall, G. (1994). D1-, D2-, and 5-HT2-receptor occupancy in clozapine-treated patients. *Journal of Clinical Psychiatry, 55*(Suppl. B), 67–69.

Freeman, E.W., Rickels, K., & Sondheimer, S.J. (1996). Fluvoxamine for premenstrual dysphoric disorder: A pilot study. *Journal of Clinical Psychiatry, 57*(Suppl. 8), 56–60.

Friedman, R., & Kocsis, J. (1996). Pharmacotherapy for chronic depression. *Psychiatric Clinics of North America, 19*(1), 121–132.

Gabbard, G.O., Lazar, S.G., Hornberger, J., & Spiegel, D. (1997). The economic impact of psychotherapy: A review. *American Journal of Psychiatry, 154*(2), 147–155.

Gelenberg, A.J., & Schoonover, S.C. (1991). Introduction: The practice of pharmacotherapy. In A.J. Gelenberg, E.L. Bassuk, & S.C. Schoonover (Eds.), *The practitioner's guide to psychoactive drugs*. New York: Plenum Press.

Goldenberg, I., White, K., Yonkers, K., Reich, J., Warshaw, M., Goisman, R., & Keller, M. (1996). The infrequency of "pure culture" diagnoses among the anxiety disorders. *Journal of Clinical Psychiatry, 57*(11), 528–533.

Goldstein, M., Rodnick, E., & Evans, J. (1978). Drugs and family therapy in the aftercare of acute schizophrenics. *Archives of General Psychiatry, 35*, 1169–1177.

Gunderson, J.G., & Phillips, K.A. (1995). Personality disorders. In H.I. Kaplan & B.J. Sadock (Eds.), *Comprehensive textbook of psychiatry* (6th ed., pp. 1425–1462). Baltimore: Williams & Wilkins.

Haddjeri, N., Blier, P., & de Montigny, C. (1995). Noradrenergic modulation of central serotonergic neurotransmission: acute and long-term actions of mirtazapine. *International Clinical Psychopharmacology, 10*(Suppl. 4), 11–17.

Haddjeri, N., Blier, P., & de Montigny, C. (1996). Effect of the alpha-2 adrenoceptor antagonist mirtazapine on the 5-hydroxytryptamine system in the rat brain. *Journal of Pharmacology and Experimental Therapeutics, 277*(2), 861–871.

Hemila, H. (1996). Vitamin C, the placebo effect, and the common cold: A case study of how preconceptions influence the analysis of results. *Journal of Clinical Epidemiology, 49*(10), 1079–1084.

Herz, M.I., Liberman, R., Lieberman, J., Marder, S., McGlashan, T., Wyatt, R., & Wang, P. (1997). Practice guideline for the treatment of patients with schizophrenia. *American Journal of Psychiatry, 154*(4), Supplement.

Higgins, E.S. (1996). Obsessive-compulsive spectrum disorders in primary care: The possibilities and the pitfalls. *Journal of Clinical Psychiatry, 57*(Suppl. 8), 7–10.

Hirschfeld, R.M., Keller, M.B., Panico, S., Arons, B.S., Barlow, D., Davidoff, F., Endicott, J., Froom, J., Goldstein, M., Gorman, J.M., Guthrie, D., Marek, R.G., Maurer, T.A., Meyer, R., Phillips, K., Ross, J., Schwenk, T.L., Sharfstein, S.S., Thase, M.E., & Wyatt, R.J. (1997). The national depressive and manic-depressive association consensus statement on the undertreatment of depression. *Journal of the American Medical Association, 277*(4), 333–340.

Hogarty, G., Anderson, C., & Reiss, D. (1991). Family psychoeducation, social skills training, and maintenance chemotherapy in the after-care treatment of schizophrenia II: Two-year effects of a controlled study on relapse and adjustment. *Archives of General Psychiatry, 48,* 340–347.

Hogarty, G., Schooler, N., & Ulrich, R. (1979). Fluphenazine and social therapy in the aftercare of schizophrenic patients: Relapse analysis of a two-year controlled study of fluphenazine decanoate and fluphenazine hydrochloride. *Archives of General Psychiatry, 36,* 1283–1294.

Hollander, E., Kwon, J.H., Stein, D.J., Broatch, J., Rowland, C.T., & Himelein, C.A. (1996). Obsessive-compulsive and spectrum disorders: Overview and quality of life issues. *Journal of Clinical Psychiatry, 57*(Suppl. 8), 3–6.

Holzer, C., Nguyen, H., & Hirschfeld, R. (1996). Reliability of diagnosis in mood disorders. *Psychiatric Clinics of North America, 19*(1), 73–84.

Horn, S.D. (1997). Overcoming obstacles to effective treatment: Use of clinical practice improvement methodology. *Journal of Clinical Psychiatry, 58*(Suppl. 1), 15–19.

Jimerson, D., Wolfe, B., Brotman, A., & Metzger, E. (1996). Medications in the treatment of eating disorders. *Psychiatric Clinics of North America, 19*(4), 739–754.

Kamlet, M.S., Paul, N., Greenhouse, J., Kupfer, D., Frank, E., & Wade, M. (1995). Cost utility analysis of maintenance treatment for recurrent depression. *Controlled Clinical Trials, 16*(1), 17–40.

Kane, J.M., Woerner, M., & Sarantakos, S. (1986). Depot neuroleptics: A comparative review of standard, intermediate, and low-dose regimens. *Journal of Clinical Psychiatry, 47*(Suppl.), 30–33.

Karasu, T.B., Docherty, J.P., Gelenberg, A., Kupfer, D.J., Merriam, A., & Shadoan, R. (1996). *Practice guideline for major depressive disorder in adults: American Psychiatric Association Practice Guidelines.* Washington, DC: American Psychiatric Association.

Keel, P., & Mitchell, J. (1997). Outcome in bulimia nervosa. *American Journal of Psychiatry, 14*(3), 313–321.

Kimura, M., Meyer, J.M., & Simpson, G.M. (1996). Anticholinergic prophylaxis revisited. *Psychiatric Annals, 26*(9), 602–603.

Kocsis, J.H., Zisook, S., Davidson, J., Shelton, R., Yonkers, K., Hellerstein, D., Rosenbaum, J., & Halbreich, U. (1997). Double-blind comparison of sertraline, imipramine, and placebo in the treatment of dysthymia: Psychosocial outcomes. *American Journal of Psychiatry, 154*(3), 390–395.

Kopelowicz, A., Liberman, R., Mintz, J., & Zarate, R. (1997). Comparison of efficacy of social skills training for deficit and nondeficit negative symptoms in schizophrenia. *American Journal of Psychiatry, 154*(3), 424–425.

Kupfer, D.J., Frank, E., Perel, J.M., Cornes, C., Mallinger, A.G., Thase, M.E., McEachran, A.B., & Grochocinski, V.J. (1992). Five-year outcome for maintenance therapies in recurrent depression. *Archives of General Psychiatry, 49*(10), 769–773.

Leonard, B.E. (1996). New approaches to the treatment of depression. *Journal of Clinical Psychiatry, 57*(Suppl. 4), 26–33.

Lieberman, J.A. (1996). Atypical antipsychotic drugs as a first-line treatment of schizophrenia: A rationale and hypothesis. *Journal of Clinical Psychiatry, 57*(Suppl. 11), 68–71.

Lin, K.-M., Anderson, D., & Poland, R. (1995). Ethnicity and psychopharmacology. *Psychiatric Clinics of North America, 18*(3), 635–647.

Mancini, C., & Ameringen, M.V. (1996). Paroxetine in social phobia. *Journal of Clinical Psychiatry, 57*(11), 519–522.

Manschreck, T. (1996). Delusional disorder: The recognition and management of paranoia. *Journal of Clinical Psychiatry, 57*(Suppl. 3), 32–38.

Marder, S.R. (1996). Management of schizophrenia. *Journal of Clinical Psychiatry, 57*(Suppl. 3), 9–13.

Marmar, C.R., Schoenfeld, F., Weiss, D.S., Metzler, T., Zatzick, D., Wu, R., Smiga, S., Tecott, L., & Neylan, T. (1996). Open trial of fluvoxamine treatment for combat-related posttraumatic stress disorder. *Journal of Clinical Psychiatry, 57*(Suppl. 8), 66–70.

Marsh, C. (1997). Psychiatric presentations of medical illnesses. *Psychiatric Clinics of North America, 20*(1), 181–204.

McCullough, J., Kornstein, S., McCullough, J., Belyea-Caldwell, S., Kaye, A., Roberts, W.C., Plybon, J., & Kruus, L. (1996). Differential diagnosis of chronic depressive disorders. *Psychiatric Clinics of North America, 19*(1), 55–72.

McElroy, S., Keck, P., & Strakowski, S. (1996). Mania, psychosis, and antipsychotics. *Journal of Clinical Psychiatry, 57*(Suppl. 3), 14–26.

McGee, M.D. (1997). Cessation of self-mutilation in a patient with borderline personality disorder treated with naltrexone [letter]. *Journal of Clinical Psychiatry, 58*(1), 32–33.

Meyer, J.M., & Simpson, G.M. (in press). Anticholinergics and amantadine. In H.I. Kaplan & B.J. Sadock (Eds.), *Comprehensive textbook of psychiatry* (7th ed.). Baltimore: Williams & Wilkins.

Mirin, S., Batki, S., Bukstein, O., Isbell, P., Kleber, H., Schottenfeld, R., Weiss, R., & Yandow, V. (1996). Practice guideline for the treatment of patients with substance use disorders: alcohol, cocaine, opioids. In A.P. Association (Ed.), *American psychiatric association practice guidelines* (pp. 209–320). Washington, DC: American Psychiatric Association.

Obrien, C.P., Volpicelli, L.A., & Volpicelli, J.R. (1996). Naltrexone in the treatment of alcoholism: a clinical review. *Alcohol, 13*(1), 35–39.

Omalley, S.S., Jaffe, A.J., Rode, S., & Rounsaville, B.J. (1996). Experience of a "slip" among alcoholics treated with naltrexone or placebo. *American Journal of Psychiatry, 153*(2), 281–283.

Phillips, K.A. (1996a). Body dysmorphic disorder: Diagnosis and treatment of imagined ugliness. *Journal of Clinical Psychiatry, 57*(Suppl. 8), 61–65.

Phillips, K.A. (1996b). Pharmacologic treatment of body dysmorphic disorder. *Psychopharmacology Bulletin, 32*(4), 597–605.

Pollack, M.H., & Smoller, J.W. (1995). The longitudinal course and outcome of panic disorder. *Psychiatric Clinics of North America, 18*(4), 785–801.

Revicki, D.A., Brown, R.E., Keller, M.B., Gonzales, J., Culpepper, L., & Hales, R.E. (1997). Cost-effectiveness of newer antidepressants compared with tricyclic antidepressants in managed care settings. *Journal of Clinical Psychiatry, 58*(2), 47–58.

Richmond, R.L., Kehoe, L., & de Almeida Neto, A.C. (1997). Effectiveness of a 24-hour transdermal nicotine patch in conjunction with a cognitive behavioural programme: One year outcome. *Addiction, 92*(1), 27–31.

Rosenberg, R. (1993). Drug treatment of panic disorder. *Pharmacology and Toxicology*, 72(6), 344–353.

Ross, E.M. (1996). Pharmacodynamics. In L.S. Goodman, A. Gilman, J.G. Hardman, & A.G. Gilman (Eds.), *The pharmacological basis of therapeutics* (9th ed.). New York: McGraw-Hill.

Schneider, L. (1996). New therapeutic approaches to Alzheimer's disease. *Journal of Clinical Psychiatry*, 57(Suppl. 14), 30–36.

Schneider, N.G., Olmstead, R., Mody, F.V., Doan, K., Franzon, M., Jarvik, M.E., & Steinberg, C. (1995). Efficacy of a nicotine nasal spray in smoking cessation: A placebo-controlled, double-blind trial. *Addiction*, 90(12), 1671–1682.

Schou, M. (1997). Forty years of lithium treatment. *Archives of General Psychiatry*, 54(1), 9–13.

Schweizer, E. (1995). Generalized anxiety disorder. Longitudinal course and pharmacologic treatment. *Psychiatric Clinics of North America*, 18(4), 843–857.

Sclar, D.A., Robison, L.M., Skaer, T.L., Galin, R.S., Legg, R.F., Nemec, N.L., Hughes, T.E., Buesching, D.P., & Morgan, M. (1995). Antidepressant pharmacotherapy: Economic evaluation of fluoxetine, paroxetine and sertraline in a health maintenance organization. *Journal of Internal Medicine Research*, 23(6), 395–412.

Scott, J., Harrington, J., House, R., & Ferrier, I.N. (1996). A preliminary study of the relationship among personality, cognitive vulnerability, symptom profile, and outcome in major depressive disorder. *Journal of Nervous and Mental Disorders*, 184(8), 503–505.

Smith, T.M., & Winters, F.D. (1995). Smoking cessation: A clinical study of the transdermal nicotine patch. *Journal of the American Osteopathic Association*, 95(11), 655–656, 661–662.

Stoudemire, A. (1996a). New antidepressant drugs and the treatment of depression in the medically ill patient. *Psychiatric Clinics North America*, 19(3), 495–514.

Stoudemire, A. (1996b). Psychiatry in medical practice. Implications for the education of primary care physicians in the era of managed care: Part 1. *Psychosomatics*, 37(6), 502–508.

Stoudemire, A. (1997). Psychiatry in medical practice. Implications for the education of primary care physicians in the era of managed care: Part 2. *Psychosomatics*, 38(1), 1–9.

Swann, A., Bowden, C., Morris, D., Calabrese, J., Petty, F., Small, J., Dilsaver, S., & Davis, J.M. (1997). Depression during mania: Treatment response to lithium or divalproex. *Archives of General Psychiatry*, 54(1), 37–42.

Tariot, P.N. (1996). Treatment strategies for agitation and psychosis in dementia. *Journal of Clinical Psychiatry*, 57(Suppl. 14), 21–29.

Thase, M., Buysse, D., Frank, E., Cherry, C., Cornes, C., Mallinger, A., & Kupfer, D. (1997). Which depressed patients will respond to interpersonal psychotherapy? The role of abnormal EEG sleep profiles. *American Journal of Psychiatry*, 154(4), 502–509.

Thase, M.E. (1996). The role of Axis II comorbidity in the management of patients with treatment-resistant depression. *Psychiatric Clinics of North America*, 19(2), 287–309.

Trivedi, M.H. (1996). Functional neuroanatomy of obsessive-compulsive disorder. *Journal of Clinical Psychiatry*, 57(Suppl. 8), 26–36.

Waddington, J.L. (1995). The clinical psychopharmacology of antipsychotic drugs in schizophrenia. In S.R. Hirsch & D.R. Weinberger (Eds.), *Schizophrenia* (pp. 341–357). Cambridge, MA: Blackwell Science.

Walsh, B.T., Wilson, G.T., Loeb, K., Devlin, M., Pike, K., Roose, S., Fleiss, J., & Water-naux, C. (1997). Medication and psychotherapy in the treatment of bulimia nervosa. *American Journal of Psychiatry, 154*(4), 523–531.

Weiden, P., Aquila, R., & Standard, J. (1996). Atypical antipsychotic drugs and long-term outcome in schizophrenia. *Journal of Clinical Psychiatry, 57*(Suppl. 11), 53–60.

Yager, J., Andersen, A., Devlin, M., Mitchell, J., Powers, P., & Yates, A. (1996). *Practice guideline for eating disorders: American Psychiatric Association Practice Guidelines.* Washington, DC: American Psychiatric Association.

PART TWO

DEPRESSION

AFFECTIVE DISORDERS are among the most prevalent psychiatric dysfunctions and have been widely acknowledged as a major public-health problem. Consequently, there has been a tremendous volume of research on their etiology and treatment since the late 1970s, stimulated in no small part by the financial support of both the NIMH (National Institute of Mental Health) and pharmaceutical companies. In contrast to a number of other disorders examined in this volume, this research has led us to the development of a number of new and effective treatments. There is evidence to support the use of several psychosocial interventions, as well as a number of pharmacological strategies. In recognition of the diversity and significance of these various approaches, we have opted to include four chapters in this section: Interpersonal Psychotherapy (IPT), Cognitive-Behavior Therapy (CBT), Psychodynamic Therapy, and Pharmacotherapy. Each of these approaches has proven to be effective with at least some subsets of depressed patients in more than one well-controlled clinical trial.

The chapters in this section present exceptionally clear portraits of the clinical applications of the various interventions. Although it is evident that there are significant differences among the approaches, it is also apparent that there is considerable agreement on a number of strategic issues. The authors of all four chapters are in agreement about the value of medication with the more impaired patients. Mania, melancholia, and psychosis are uniformly viewed as indicators for pharmacotherapy and/or electroconvulsive therapy-ECT. Conversely, chronic mild depression (e.g., dysthymic disorder) is viewed as possibly more responsive to psychotherapy (including CBT and IPT) than to pharmacotherapy. There is also agreement that atypical patients, including those with character disorders, present unique problems for any approach.

Despite obvious conceptual differences, there is considerable strategic and tactical overlap among the psychosocial approaches. Bemporad and Vasile (Chapter 4), Freeman and Oster (Chapter 5), and Swartz (Chapter 6) all emphasize the role of interpersonal factors in precipitating and/or main-taining depression. Although IPT is primarily and explicitly focused on enhancing social behavior, both CBT and psychodynamic therapy also pay considerable attention to the patient's social environment and interpersonal difficulties. Although the precise techniques vary, all three approaches en-courage the patient to practice new behaviors in social interactions at home and in the community.

All three approaches also place considerable emphasis on the role of mala-daptive cognitions in the etiology and/or maintenance of the illness. Of course, this is the major focus of CBT. However, IPT devotes considerable attention to cognitive phenomena in the context of social perception, including modifi-cation of inaccurate cognitive appraisals of others. Similarly, Bemporad and Vasile indicate that recent psychodynamic thinking emphasizes the role of faulty beliefs and assumptions about significant others (notably parents) in the etiology of depression, and that a major task of therapy is to point out and cor-rect these cognitive errors. We have previously argued that the literature sup-ports the conclusion that a number of different psychosocial interventions for depression (especially including IPT, and CBT) are equally effective. Perhaps this result occurs because of the overlap in the various approaches.

Despite the existence of a number of effective strategies, one cannot be overly sanguine about our ability to treat depression. The chapters in this section raise a number of significant concerns. Feinberg points out that depression is a recur-rent disorder; more than 50 percent of unipolar patients and 80 percent of bipolars are likely to have at least one relapse. Yet, comparatively little is known about long-term maintenance strategies. Side effects and medical risks of the major medications make continued treatment a circumspect option for many patients. Psychotherapy would appear to be an attractive alternative to long-term pharmacotherapy. But, the long-term effects of psychotherapy, alone or in some combination with pharmacotherapy, are uncertain. Important data on long-term maintenance is coming from the work of Ellen Frank and her col-leagues at the University of Pittsburgh. Their data increasingly demonstrate the need for long-term maintenance, especially for patients who have manifested a history of recurrent episodes. It is hoped that ongoing clinical trials of mainte-nance strategies will shed some light on this issue over the next few years.

Bemporad and Vasile raise the important issue that many cases of depres-sion are secondary to physical illnesses, including a number of endocrinologi-cal and hormonal disorders. Such cases often are misdiagnosed by both mental health professionals and primary care physicians. This is an interesting and important issue, given the emphasis in managed care to shift treatment to pri-mary care physicians. As pointed out in other sections of this volume, depres-sion is also frequently associated with other psychiatric disorders including obsessive-compulsive disorder, panic and agoraphobia, social phobia, and bor-derline personality. In some cases, the treatments are parallel, and differential diagnosis may not be absolutely critical (e.g., SSRIs for depression and panic disorder, CBT for depression and social phobia). However, fortuitous treatment based on inaccurate diagnosis is the exception rather than the rule. Even when the same medication may be appropriate for two different disorders, the required dosages, titration schedules, and so forth may be different. Categories such as atypical, treatment-resistant double depression, and so on reflect the uncertain status of our understanding. Similarly, dual diagnosis or retrospective diagnosis based on treatment response is not satisfactory. The only way to resolve these problems and to deliver the most effective treatment is to improve the diagnostic system and associated assessment instruments.

CHAPTER 5

Dynamic Psychotherapy

JULES R. BEMPORAD and RUSSELL G. VASILE

PSYCHOANALYTIC FORMULATIONS OF DEPRESSION

The earliest attempts to encompass depression from a psychodynamic point of view appear to have been direct applications of the then-prevailing psychoanalytic theory. In this manner, Abraham (1911/1960a) considered depression at first to be a blockage of libido and later (1916/1960b) to be a regression to pre-Oedipal modes of gratification and object relations.

It was not until publication of *Mourning and Melancholia* in 1917 that Freud (1960) turned his attention to depressive states and formulated an original interpretation that was specific to these disorders. This work explained depression as resulting from anger directed inward toward a lost love object, which, by incorporation, had become part of the ego.

A decade later, Rado (1927/1956) modified this basic formulation according to the general changes that had been introduced by the structural theory. In Rado's revision, the superego becomes the punishing agent, and the pre-Oedipal introjection is conceived of as a dual process, with the good aspects of the parents becoming part of the superego, while the bad aspects become a part of the ego. These works are representative of the classical period of psychoanalytic thought, during which basic mental structures were proposed and then used to account for various clinical phenomena. During this formative and creative period of psychoanalytic thought, great emphasis was given to intrapsychic structures, processes, and conflicts, with theory becoming more complex and farther removed from the presenting clinical data.

DEPRESSION AS A BASIC AFFECT

A radically new way of conceptualizing depression arose in the 1950s and 1960s, which not only showed the influence of ego psychology but also reflected a disenchantment with both complicated and unprovable metapsychological theories; it also stemmed from the wish to propose simpler models that were conceptually closer to observable clinical manifestations. This newer view was initiated by Bibring (1953), who postulated that depression be considered a basic state of the ego, which cannot be reduced further, and which arises automatically when the individual is in a situation that forces the person to give up strongly held narcissistic aspirations. Because different frustrations or deprivations may cause different people to feel powerless in trying to attain needed narcissistic goals, depression could not be the universal manifestation of an oral fixation or of retroflected anger following object loss. Rather, the feeling of depression is seen as the emotional expression of the ego's helplessness in maintaining a desired sense of self. Bibring's innovative interpretations shifted the focus of study from the internal, intersystemic conflicts that were thought to produce depression intrapsychically to those situations that precipitated a sense of ego helplessness. Taking the experience of depression as a given, he also speculated on the type of person who would have difficulty overcoming or defending against lowered self-esteem following narcissistic frustration.

A decade after Bibring's postulation, Sandler and Joffee (1965) furthered this line of reasoning by suggesting that depression be considered a negative emotion, much like anxiety. Depression was said to arise whenever the individual experienced loss of a former state of well-being. In the case of depression following loss of a loved one, these authors postulated that it was not loss of the object per se that provoked dysphoria, but rather the loss of the state of well-being that the object supplied. A consequence of considering depression to be a basic affect is that this emotional state is closely related to the body's normal physiological processes. Therefore, depression could be caused or alleviated, at times, by altering specific chemical reactions. Depression, as is discussed in the following text, may result either from psychological events that, in turn, alter basic neurochemical processes or, in some instances, from a direct intervention in those processes themselves.

Another significant contribution was Sandler and Joffee's delineation of two stages in the depressive sequence. The first type of depression immediately follows loss of a state of well-being. This stage of depression was called a "psychobiological reaction" and was believed to be a ubiquitous, if not a normal, response. Most individuals would be able to overcome such initial dysphoria by finding new ways to obtain a state of well-being, and so their depressions are self-limited and, perhaps, even beneficial. However, some individuals cannot mobilize themselves to alter this condition of deprivation, and they go on to experience the second form of depression, which is the "clinical episode." The predisposition to clinical depression, therefore, resides in the particular individual's inability to find sources of well-being after a loss or frustration.

This two-stage sequence also proposes that depression be viewed as a process that culminates over time as the individual faces a future bereft of needed gratification. In this sense, clinical depression is more than a reactive dysphoria, which passes with time as the individual readjusts the internal narcissistic equilibrium. Clinical depression entails an alteration in one's sense of self and has definite clinical and psychodynamic features that go beyond the transient unhappiness secondary to the usual vicissitudes of life. Clinical depression may be seen as a way of organizing experience and as the reemergence of childhood modes of thinking and relating toward oneself and others that are no longer appropriate to adult life.

In chronic depressions, it is postulated that external events reverberate with dimly conscious and threatening views of the self and others, confirming a negativistic world view, which now appears unalterable. These dreaded assumptions, believed to be based on childhood experiences, usually consist of the acceptance that one will never be loved, or that one does not deserve to be loved by one's needed others, or that one can never be a worthwhile human being, or that one will always suffer at the mercy of a world beyond one's control. When reality appears to prove, either in actuality or in distorted fantasy, the veracity of these assumptions, the individual automatically experiences a depressive affect appropriate to the content of these assumptions.

Bowlby (1980) has enumerated these underlying beliefs and the childhood experiences from which they are thought to derive. These experiences are not single events but long-term patterns of familial interaction that may occur singly or in combination. One pattern of interaction is the child's "bitter experience of never having attained a stable or secure relationship with the parents despite having made repeated efforts to do so, including having done his [or her] utmost to fulfill their demands and perhaps also unrealistic expectations they may have had of him [or her]" (p. 247). Another relates to the child having been "told repeatedly how unlovable, and /or how inadequate, and /or how incompetent he [or she] is" (p. 247). Last is the possibility that the child was "more likely than others to have experienced actual loss of a parent . . . with consequences to [herself or] himself that, however disagreeable they might have been, [she or] he was impotent to change" (p. 248).

Arieti and Bemporad (1978) have enumerated basic belief systems in depressives that are not dissimilar from those described by Bowlby. These authors have found a common theme in the lifestyle of the depressive to be a "bargain relationship," in which the individual forms an unspoken pattern with the parent, agreeing to remain in a position of childish dependency in return for security and protection. Implicit in this bargain is the notion that the individual will achieve in order to bring honor or praise to the family but will not pursue independent avenues of gaining self-worth. Further assumptions are that no one but the parent could possibly love or care for the individual and that without the parent figure, the individual would be helpless in a hostile and overwhelming world. In this manner, the future depressive's abilities are perverted so that they bring no measure of worth in or of themselves, but they are used only in the frantic need to maintain a relationship with an allegedly needed other. These persons grow up believing they are somehow unable to face the challenges of life alone, that they are doomed to failure or isolation without the magical protection of the powerful parent figure, and that they are unworthy of genuine love or caring from others.

Most individuals prone to depression evolve intrapsychic defenses or particular modes of existence to protect themselves from realization of these painful self-estimations. Some manipulate others to give them constant demonstrations of affection or care in order to reassure themselves that they are loved; others become overconscientious workers, to ensure the approval of surrogate parental figures while pursuing wealth or power to compensate for a sense of inner inferiority and weakness. Still others must live according to unrealistic, scrupulous moral standards to confirm their worth. When these defensive maneuvers are removed by an external occurrence, such as the loss of a source of love, or of financial security, or the emergence of unremitting erotic longings, these individuals are forced to come to grips with their most dreaded beliefs about themselves, together with an overwhelming sense of despair. Depression is, thus, precipitated by an external event which, in the minds of predisposed individuals, reactivates an atavistic sense of lovelessness, powerlessness, and hopelessness of ever gaining a sense of adequacy and security.

Psychodynamic psychotherapy also aims at stripping away defensive operations that obscure underlying beliefs. However, in therapy, this goal is achieved in a gradual and supportive manner, and in the context of a trusted relationship. While the underlying beliefs emerge as negative self-evaluations, or while they are acted out in the patient-therapist transference, their validity can be examined, and their inapplicability to adult behavior can be recognized. Furthermore, limitations that these beliefs imposed on the individual can be understood and can serve as motivation for change.

DIAGNOSTIC ISSUES AND PROBLEMS

Suitability for psychodynamic psychotherapy rests on the capacity of the individual to mobilize sufficient observing ego processes: (1) to maintain a therapeutic alliance, (2) to constructively use the transference neurosis to develop insight, and (3) to build on this insight to develop a corrective emotional experience. For psychodynamic psychotherapy to proceed, there must be a capacity to explore current relationships, including the real patient-therapist relationship in psychotherapy, the transference relationship, and past relationships, all of which exist in a dynamic equilibrium.

Any factors that might interfere with the cognitive and emotional capacities to engage in this process could potentially undermine any role for psychodynamic psychotherapy. Hence, careful attention to diagnostic issues and problems is vital in the initial assessment of the patient who seeks psychodynamic psychotherapy.

The tasks of assessing the depressed patient's suitability for psychotherapy involve recognition of the differential diagnosis of mood disorders and their implications for treatment interventions. The primary versus secondary distinction refers to those depressions that occur independently of other conditions versus those depressions with an onset that is clearly associated with another medial or psychiatric condition.

Although most depressions are primary, it is critical for the psychotherapist to recognize the multiple etiologies of secondary depressive disorders, because their treatment is dependent on appropriate diagnosis. A variety of medications may be associated with psychiatric symptoms as an unwarranted side effect. Substance abuse may become manifest with depressive symptoms; for example, amphetamine or cocaine withdrawal may produce profound endogenous depressive symptoms. Alcoholism has been demonstrated to be strongly associated with affective illness and may exacerbate underlying disorders of mood. Failure to assess these conditions, which may be subtle or covert in initial presentation, will undermine any psychotherapeutic initiatives.

Medical illnesses, including hypothyroidism and other endocrine disorders, anemia, cerebrovascular diseases, tumors, and other neurologic conditions, may be present along with symptoms of depression. For example, the differential diagnosis of dementia versus pseudodementia due to depression in the elderly may be particularly vexing and required neuropsychological testing for clarification (McAllister, 1983).

Within the primary depressive disorders, the unipolar versus bipolar, or manic-depressive distinction, is paramount. Assessing severity and duration of depressive symptoms and the presence or absence of psychotic manifestations is vital to appropriate selection of a psychodynamic treatment program. Psychotic manifestations in depression may include delusions or hallucinations—including nihilistic content, such as the belief that one's intestines are cancerous—or they may take the form of command hallucinations, such as a voice telling a patient to jump from a window. Psychotic depression usually requires prompt somatic therapy treatment, either electroconvulsive therapy (ECT) or a combination neuroleptic-antidepressant medication, because response to psychotherapy alone would be expected to be poor (American Psychiatric Association, 1978). It is, therefore, vital to ascertain the presence or absence of psychotic features. In the *DSM-IV*, melancholia is a subset of the primary depressions. Melancholia is defined by marked neurovegetative depressive features; this subcategory of depressed patients almost invariably requires somatic treatment for sufficient improvement prior to productively utilizing psychotherapy. Attention must be drawn to the presence or absence of suicidal ideation or intent. Particularly important are historical factors, including the past history of attempts and their degree of lethality (R. Brown, Sweeney, Kocsis, & Frances, 1984).

Studies exploring combined pharmacotherapy and psychotherapy of major depression have suggested that the patient's overall rate of improvement is likely to be facilitated by combined therapy, as opposed to either treatment modality alone. Neurovegetative symptoms of depression tend to improve most rapidly with somatic therapy, whereas measures of social adjustment tend to show greater amelioration with psychotherapy (Conte, Plutchik, Wild, & Karasu, 1986; DiMascio, Weissman, & Prusoff, 1979; Klerman & Schecter, 1982). In a combined psychotherapy and psychopharmacology treatment situation, the therapist should explore with the patient feelings about being placed on medication and should examine expectations concerning the potential benefits and limitations of the medications, administered in the context of overall psychotherapeutic treatment (Docherty, Marder, & van Kammen, 1977; Gutheil, 1982).

Of equal importance is the assessment of patients with borderline or narcissistic characters. The diagnosis of borderline personality disorder, as documented in the *DSM-IV*, includes identity confusion, inappropriate affect, rapid idealization or devaluation of significant others, emotional instability, and impulsive self-destructiveness, as well as feelings of emptiness and depression. The therapist must be able to assess and to diagnose borderline personality disorder and to develop a psychotherapy that is best suited to that disorder. The specific vulnerability of borderline patients in psychotherapy includes their capacity to develop a rapid, unmanageable transference to the therapist, which often involves marked oscillations between intensive overidealization and powerful devaluation and rage. This phenomenon is further exacerbated by an unstructured psychotherapy that searches for unconscious factors in the patient's distress, and this may lead to an unmanageable transference process (Adler, 1986).

For borderline or narcissistic patients, in general, a more highly structured psychotherapy is indicated. Although there is debate in the literature as to what precise approach is psychodynamically best suited for these patients, there is little question that their vulnerability to affective disruption requires a modification of the psychodynamic technique, which would be appropriate for the healthier depressed patient. For example, dream interpretation, which might be well-suited for a neurotic depressed patient, would be inappropriate in the treatment of the borderline patient who is actively depressed and in a state of regression.

The narcissistic personality disorder patient, particularly in the context of the transference, does not experience the same vulnerability to psychotic disruption that is associated with the borderline patient. Several authors have viewed these patients as existing on a continuum with the borderline personality disorder, with a critical difference being the narcissistic patients' firmer grasp of a sense of self and their capacity to tolerate a certain psychological aloneness and self-other differentiation. Nonetheless, psychotherapy of these patients is also fraught with potential complexities. Many of these patients cannot tolerate interpretations, and they require a kind of admiring, uncritical stance for long periods of time before feeling a capacity to self-critically explore their own contribution to becoming depressed.

The literature is replete with strategems for coping with the narcissistic disordered patient, with emphasis placed on the importance of empathy and nurturing on the one hand, but, on the other hand, certain authors feel that confrontation of the patient's inevitable hostile devaluing transference is required to achieve therapeutic results. These patients present feelings of emptiness, isolation, and conflicts around intimate relationships. They will also exhibit in fantasy a preoccupation with their own omnipotence, brilliance, and special qualities, and they expect a strong degree of admiration and uncritical approval on the part of the therapist.

A pattern of counterdependent devaluing hostility will become evident early in the psychotherapy of these patients. Their preoccupation with grandiose achievements conceals a profound sense of emptiness, unlovability, and defectiveness. As with the neurotically depressed patient, ultimately, amelioration of their despair will involve important grief work around disappointed wishes, hopes, and aspirations, be they for love, approval, or for accomplishment of deeply valued goals. But unlike the more typically neurotically depressed patient, a narcissistic patient's psychotherapy will be threatened with disruption early and often if the therapist is unaware of the extraordinary sensitivity to interpretations and self-observation that the narcissistic patient may experience as intensely hostile and unemphathic.

Although the borderline personality disorders and narcissistic personality disorders represent a significant psychodynamic challenge in the psychotherapy of depression, a challenge of a different nature arises in those patients who exhibit disorders more characteristic of an obsessive nature. These patients tend to cathect thinking, as opposed to feeling, which may become a significant impediment if one attempts to conduct psychodynamic psychotherapy. The patient may be temperamentally poorly suited for a psychodynamic relationship that involves exploration of feelings in the patient's current relationships in the world, as well as in the real and transferential relationship to the therapist. These patients may become impatient with subtle emotional concepts and shades of feelings and tend to find security in a more highly structured cognitive psychotherapy. The patient may prefer to feel a certainty of progress, if progress can be quantified or described in some manifest, behavioral fashion. Elsewhere in this volume, approaches in cognitive and behavioral therapy are carefully explored. It suffices to say that in the evaluation of the patient for psychodynamic psychotherapy, the therapist must keep in mind the temperamental capacity of the patient to tolerate and emotionally invest in psychodynamic psychotherapy.

The issue of social rehabilitation and milieu and group therapies requires careful attention, particularly in the socially isolated and the elderly. The role of hospitalization in affording respite from overwhelming psychosocial stressors also requires consideration, although, in general, suicidal ideation or behavior is the key indication for hospitalization (Ross, 1987).

Treatment options for the psychotherapy of the depressed patient involve assessments of the patient's underlying character traits, defenses, and overall ego functioning. Alternatives to insight-oriented psychodynamic psychotherapy prominently include interpersonal psychotherapy, a highly structured, educative here-and-now treatment approach, as well as cognitive and behavioral methodologies. Supportive short-term psychotherapy would appear best suited for adjustment disorders, depressed mood, bereavement disorders, and demoralization. Supportive psychotherapy: (1) focuses on behavior in the here and now, (2) is time limited, and (3) does not rely on the activation of transference or an exploration of unconscious determinants of illness.

The various forms and causes of depressive disorders underscore the importance of selecting appropriate treatment for each patient. Intensive psychodynamic psychotherapy, as described in the next section, is best suited for those patients who present chronic characterological depression in which psychopathology is a basic part of the individual's life-style, encompassing personal relationships, values, and modes of self-assessment.

TREATMENT STRATEGIES OF INTENSIVE
PSCYHODYNAMIC PSYCHOTHERAPY

The aim of psychodynamic psychotherapy is to increase individual's conscious knowledge of crucial aspects of their psychological makeup and functioning of which they were previously unaware or only dimly aware. It is assumed that although kept out of awareness, these aspects of the personality have a major effect on the experience and behavior of the individual. Once these unconscious aspects have been identified, integrated into the rest of the personality, and evaluated in terms of their validity, individuals can live their lives in a freer, more satisfying and constructive manner. Therefore, there are two major tasks in the therapeutic process: The first is to make the here-and-now experience between patient and therapist reveal those unconscious processes that still influence and direct the individual's current life, and the second is to help the patient understand how the present is different, in terms of autonomy and control, from those times in the distant past when the unconscious aspects were learned and subsequently repressed.

Although most therapists would agree that atavistic parts of the self are inappropriately carried into the present, there is disagreement as to the actual conceptual nature of these archaic aspects. Originally, it was believed that memories laden with painful emotions were repressed but continued to exert their pathogenic effect. Later, forbidden instinctual desires or fantasies were thought to make up the content of the repressed aspects of the psyche. Both of these views are still held today, although, in recent decades, a growing body of literature has added a third component to the contents of the repressed. This more recent contribution suggests that archaic beliefs and assumptions of childhood often underlie the seemingly irrational behavior and emotional reactions of most individuals (Arieti & Bemporad, 1978; Beck, 1967; Bowlby, 1980). This more cognitive school asserts that individuals continue to live out their existence according to outmoded and maladaptive systems of belief that were formed in childhood and that continue to exist outside of awareness.

Because all individuals are assumed to harbor atavistic beliefs formulated in childhood, the nature, extent, and dread of these beliefs may determine the predisposition to psychopathology. Most, if not all, individuals will experience a period of dysphoria following a significant loss or disappointment. However, most will, in time reinstate avenues of obtaining meaning and worth from their activities. Similarly, sadness and loss of interest may follow deprivation or frustration, but individuals will continue to have relatively realistic appraisals of themselves or of others. However, if individuals have not altered a distorted childhood view of the self and, in fact, have defended against acknowledging these self-evaluations because of the psychic pain inherent in such awareness, then the abrupt discovery of this self-view would cause greater and longer-lasting dysphoria. Finally, many individuals create an interpersonal network based on these childhood beliefs, such as relationships based on excessive dependency or inhibition over pleasurable pursuits, which greatly hampers their ability to find ways of overcoming dysphoria.

STAGES OF THERAPY

For purposes of exposition, the therapeutic process can be separated into three stages, each with its own specific goals. However, this division is artificial at best, because throughout therapy, new material may be uncovered, new transference distortions may appear, and new defensive resistances may emerge. Furthermore, everyday life does not stand still during the extensive period of therapy, so that events outside the office often influence the course of treatment. With these provisos in mind, the usual progress of therapy with a depressed individual can be presented as consisting of three sequential stages.

STAGE 1: SETTING THE COURSE OF THERAPY

The initial stage concerns the proper setting of the course of therapy, the handling of immediate transference reactions, and the relating of the precipitating event to the individual's particular personality style and unconscious beliefs. One of the most difficult steps in the therapy of depressives is the first one. These patients begin therapy in the midst of an episode; they feel overcome with painful dysphoria, they feel hopeless and helpless, and they desire only relief from the misery. It may be difficult for them to talk of anything other than their suffering, and asking them to reflect on their experience may only bring about more pain or may seem a pointless exercise that will not ease their distress. At the same time, they may ask for reassurances that they will recover or that the therapist will take care of them, often proclaiming that the therapist is their last hope or that the therapist's extensive knowledge or skill enable the therapist to cure their disorder. This initial state of demandingness, actual misery, dependency, and often ingratiating behavior presents numerous difficulties for the therapist who desires to proceed with the uncovering process and to reveal those intrapsychic factors responsible for the illness.

Jacobson (1971, 1975) has described how depressed patients may overvalue the therapist and experience an initial improvement in their symptoms because they believe they have found a source of care and nurturance. There is the danger that the patient may become overly involved with obtaining gratification from the therapist and may try to obtain this gratification by devotion and excessive loyalty to the therapeutic process. When the expected care is not forthcoming, however, the patient may become incensed, may feel cheated, or may experience an exacerbation of symptoms.

During initial sessions, the therapist must walk a fine line, being wary of becoming the center of patients' lives or their only hope of salvation while extending a warm and encouraging stance that will facilitate trust and the mutual exploration of intrapsychic material. A further difficulty is breaking the repetitive litany of complaints and/or self-preoccupation with the symptoms of the disorder. New topics may be introduced by the therapist for exploration, and in those cases where the dysphoric mood or negative signs so overwhelm patients' ability to participate in therapy, antidepressant medication is certainly indicated. These pharmacological agents are in no way contraindicated, and aside from the natural rule of easing any individual's pain, they help in making patients more accessible to the therapeutic process. Finally, patients should be encouraged to be completely honest about their judgments and feelings about loved ones, colleagues, and the therapist. This openness is crucial because the depressive has frequently been raised in an atmosphere of secrecy and manipulativeness, where voiced criticism or hostility was certain to result in psychological abandonment or guilt-provoking responses.

Once therapy has begun on a more or less neutral course, the focus should turn to the inward search for those inner beliefs that were brought to light by the precipitating event and for those defensive operations that served to keep those very beliefs at a safe distance. This connection is not consistently obvious at the outset, and it may become clarified only after a considerable period of therapy; however, associations stemming from the context in which the depression occurred will lead the way to revealing the individual's mode of obtaining self-esteem and defending against feelings of unworthiness, guilt, and shame.

Case Illustration

One depressed woman, for example, stated that she became symptomatic when she could no longer keep up with her work and felt herself to be a failure. This explanation was partially true but did not go far enough in describing her actual situation. Later it was revealed that she began to feel anxious and dysphoric when her boss, upon whom she depended for a sense of worth and who had transferentially become her psychological father, hired another female assistant. This threatened the patient's imagined special status with the boss, and she anticipated that he would favor the new employee, who was erroneously perceived as more able, attractive, and likable than the patient. Much of this reaction was a recapitulation of the events surrounding the birth of a younger sibling when the patient was 5 years old. Just as in childhood, she attempted to win back the father's preferential regard by working harder and harder, in order to obtain praise and reassurance.

However, in contrast to her father, the boss did not sufficiently recognize her increased effort, causing her to apply herself even harder so that her work did become too much for her. Therefore, she did become depressed as a result of being overwhelmed by her work; however, the initiative to do more and more was of her own choosing, and the basic reason for it was to become reinstated as the boss/father's favorite. Her failure to achieve this goal was identified as the real cause of her decompensation. Finally, she was not aware of her need for a father surrogate's approval in order to feel worthy and whole. Yet, lacking that approval, she sensed herself unlovable, inadequate, and at times wicked and vile, without really knowing why.

The first stage of therapy comprises: (1) resolving the initial dependency and transference distortions, (2) understanding that the clinical episode results from aberrant premorbid personality functioning, and (3) beginning to connect the precipitating event with deep-seated belief systems.

STAGE 2: MODIFYING BELIEF SYSTEMS

The second stage consists of the gradual identification of atavistic belief systems, their evaluation in terms of current possibilities, and their eventual modification. This is not an easy task, because although these basic beliefs result in repetitive experiences of dysphoria, they also serve to structure the psychic life of the depressive individuals and allow them a sense of security and emotional safety, albeit transient and precarious. The basic struggle revolves around depressives relinquishing their excessive need for external sources of worth, which are adult transformations of their childhood interpersonal situations, and their daring to develop new, more appropriate, and less precarious modes of feeling worthwhile. This process produces a great deal of anxiety in individuals who believe that giving up old values will leave them totally without structure or support and that they will be abandoned, criticized, or somehow damaged if they dare to assert their need for autonomous satisfaction.

> For example, an executive was awarded an all-expenses paid vacation as the result of her outstanding work performance. As the time of her departure approached, she was haunted by incessant worries: (a) that in her absence her job would be given to someone else, (b) that her apartment would be burglarized, and (c) that her parents would become sick and die. The irrationality of these fears is evidenced by the fact that her work forced her to travel at least once a month, which she was able to do without trepidation. It was only when she was to travel for her own pleasure rather than to comply with the needs of others that she developed her multiple fears.

As with the executive's, these irrational emotional reactions are traced back to childhood, when they were indeed appropriate to the family system of beliefs. Gradually, the individual senses more clearly how these beliefs and how this structuring of experience were developed in order to avoid rejection, criticism, or guilt, and to ensure acceptance by needed adults. Concurrent with this process of reality testing, transference distortions manifest themselves as the patient unwittingly creates a new parental surrogate—complete with all the biases, restrictions, and manipulations—in the therapist. Usually, these distortions can be observed in the unwarranted behavior of the patient toward the therapist, although quite often, a dream is reported in which the therapist is confused with the original parent. When the therapist refuses to act out the expected parental role and instead identifies and examines the reactions the patient anticipates from the therapist, the therapist can make clear, in a vivid, living manner, the nature of the original relationship as it continues to affect the present. Of greatest importance is the realization of the concept of self that had been formed during crucial years of personality development. The patient comprehends, with some inescapable discomfort, that beneath the personal facade of a mature, responsible, and often successful adult, there remains a hated, helpless and needy child who had never felt truly loved or appreciated, who lived in fear of criticism or abandonment, and who never dared to act on true, deeply felt desires or ambitions.

As patients realize the atavistic nature of these attitudes, they begin the slow process of change, venturing to try new modes of relating to significant others, of obtaining worth, and of estimating themselves. These timorous forays are rewarded in the therapy by pointing out the sense of freedom and satisfaction that accompany these trial attempts and by pointing out that the terrible consequences that were anticipated have not transpired. More and more attempts are made and discussed in the therapeutic situation. Concurrently, the therapist begins to be seen as a concerned helper, with human limitations, rather than an omniscient and punitive parental image. Personal material, which had previously been avoided because of the fear of the reaction it might elicit, is now openly reported without the expectation of criticism and with the comfortable understanding that one need not be perfect in the eyes of others or oneself.

The middle stage of therapy generally comprises: (1) the identification of persistent childhood beliefs, (2) the influence of those beliefs on current behavior and sense of self, (3) defensive maneuvers created to compensate for negative self-regard, and (4) a decided effort to alter these old assumptions.

STAGE 3: CONSOLIDATING AND INTEGRATING THE NEW BELIEFS

The final stage concerns the consolidation of a new sense of self, together with managing reactions of others to this alteration. It is hoped that patients will exhibit a new integrity in their intimate relationships, free from the fear of being rejected or of needing reassurance. Humor, anger, and spontaneous enjoyment become a larger part of the individual's experience. A more relaxed view toward oneself, and a less critical evaluation of others, comes about as the childhood "shoulds" are modified. These changes not infrequently provoke dismay, and even anger, in significant others who had become accustomed to patients' prior ingratiating and overconscientious mode of being. Such reactions are seen in employers, parents, and colleagues, but most often in spouses of older depressives. Although these individuals do not want patients to reexperience episodes of clinical depression, they are loathe to adjust to a new type of relationship. At this time, patients require an impartial confidant who will understand these obstacles objectively, and will share in patients' resolve to maintain those changes that were so arduously created.

INTERPERSONAL PSYCHOTHERAPY

This form of psychotherapy shares some basic concepts and techniques with more traditional psychodynamic treatment, although it differs markedly in important aspects. The basis for interpersonal psychotherapy (IPT) is the belief that depression is best understood in an interpersonal context, particularly in regard to existing social supports and the individual's social effectiveness. Meyer, Sullivan, and others have stressed the importance of the interpersonal and social milieu in the prevention of or vulnerability to mental illness. In 1978, G. Brown and Harris demonstrated the protective effect of strong social supports in the susceptibility to depression in a large sample of British working-class women. Therefore, IPT aims to clarify the psychosocial context in which the depression had its onset and to alter the individual's social functioning to facilitate recovery and prevent further episodes.

These theoretical and practical tenets are much in agreement with psycho-dynamic therapy. The major difference resides in IPT's limiting its therapeutic endeavor to the conscious "here and now" and avoiding investigation of un-conscious beliefs, transference manifestations, overall self-evaluations, and handling of anger or guilt. Practitioners of IPT describe three components in depression: (1) the symptomatic clinical presentation, (2) the individual's so-cial adjustment and interpersonal relationships, and (3) enduring personality traits resulting from childhood experience. IPT attempts to intervene only in the first two components, whereas traditional therapy, while not ignoring these, concentrates its efforts on the third component.

Despite such self-acknowledged limitation, IPT has been shown to be quite effective in clinical trials, although its benefits become apparent only after 6 to 8 months of therapy. Further advantages are that the technique can be de-scribed objectively in a treatment manual, that it is less time-intensive than traditional therapy, and that, as a result of its communicability, it can be tested empirically. Evaluations at one year after termination of IPT have been favor-able; however, longer term studies of its effectiveness remain to be performed.

Case Illustration

Mr. A. was a relatively typical individual with depression, a middle-aged executive who was seen after a brief psychiatric hospitalization, where he had been admitted in a state of agitation and despair. During his inpatient stay, he had been started on a tricyclic antidepressant and a benzodiazepine, with beneficial results. These medications had relieved his vegetative symptoms and some of his anxiety, but he still felt hopeless, finding each day a torment, and he was plagued with the idea that he was a failure and a disgrace to his family.

The acute episode had begun a few weeks after Mr. A. had decided on a major career change. For the previous 10 years, he had worked for a large advertising agency in a major city; He had begun as a salesman, and, because of his great talent for selling the firm's product to clients, he had worked his way up to the director-ship of the sales division. Mr. A. had a knack for pleasing clients, he was full of en-tertaining stories and self-effacing humor, and he had a disarming manner that ingratiated himself and his firm to prospective customers. He displayed the same sort of upbeat and friendly attitude within the firm, where he was uniformly liked, and he seemed to have an encouraging word for all of the employees.

However, Mr. A. demonstrated an insatiable need for praise and reassurance from his superiors, and he would, at times, badger them with pointless questions or small-talk banter in order to wrest from them an opinion that he was properly performing his job. His need to hear that he was doing well seemed independent of the sales figures from which the firm's principals actually derived evaluations. An-other difficulty at work was that, although superficially friendly and caring, he had never developed a close relationship with any of his colleagues, preferring to spend his free time with or in search of, a superior.

His domestic situation revealed more serious problems. Mr. A. was often away on sales trips, during which he appeared to be unaware that he had a wife and children. Upon his return home, he would expect to be greeted with a great show of welcome and would become morose and withdrawn if any gift he brought back was not praised lavishly. At home, he subtly competed with his children for his wife's nurturance and attention, being easily offended if he felt she were neglecting him.

A further problem area related to a lifelong propensity toward excessive worry and self-criticism and a lack of gratifying leisure activities. Mr. A. would replay situations in his mind, constantly seeking out instances in which he would have offended an important person or had not been sufficiently pleasant or friendly. He suffered greatly whenever he failed to conclude a sale, blaming himself and feeling depressed. At those times, he reacted to such setbacks as if he were a total failure as a person. He believed that success of a business transaction depended solely on his being a likable or lovable person, and he dismissed the importance of the quality of the product or other relevant factors. Most of his waking thoughts were filled with the impression he made on clients or superiors, and he derived little pleasure or meaning from anything else.

Although Mr. A. described a chronic state of dysphoria, exacerbated by his belief that he failed to please his bosses, he had never suffered a major depressive episode until shortly after he made the decision to leave his job and go into business for himself. At that time, he experienced increasing anxiety and terrifying premonitions of failure. He sensed himself to be unable to work and to be doomed to failure. He was convinced that he was basically an inadequate and unlikable person whose prior success had been a sham, that if people really knew him, they would dislike him. These dreaded thoughts were accompanied by sleeplessness, anorexia, and a total lack of motivation. He refused to get out of bed and demanded infantile gratification from his wife. It was at this point that he was hospitalized.

During his inpatient treatment, he was started on medication and supportive therapy. He was discharged after a few weeks, with marked symptomatic improvement, but he was still plagued by self-doubts, feelings of futility, and a terrible sense of failure. He had not been able to follow through on his business venture and felt a mixture of relief and shame over his missed opportunity, Instead, he found employment at another advertising firm, where he was again placed in charge of sales.

Therapy began approximately one month after he was discharged from the hospital. He was on maintenance medication, had started back to work, and he was attempting to resume his former life. He presented a mixture of glib, ingratiating statements together with a deep sense of self-hatred and despair. It was as if he had to keep up a pattern of small talk to avoid falling into a bottomless well of melancholia. Mr. A. was bewildered by his depressive episode and could not understand why such a terrible event had occurred in his life. He was frightened that he would become acutely depressed again, asking for reassurance that he was over the worst part of his disorder. On these occasions, it was suggested that he begin to look at what might have precipitated his clinical episode if he wished to avoid further decompensation. Mr. A. reacted to these suggestions with a sense of injury, feeling disappointed with the therapist's lack of positive assurance. However, he covered up these feelings with his usual facade of effusive good humor and small talk, which he believed would please the therapist. Mr. A. was confronted with those maneuvers as they occurred and encouraged to express his true feelings, however, disagreeable.

In this manner, Mr. A. started to explore his relationships to imagined authority figures, his suppression of negative affects, and his particular vulnerabilities that so often resulted in dysphoric episodes. As he related his past, he recalled with sadness and bitterness that his father was full of criticism and that he could never wrench a word of praise from him. His childhood environment had been dominated by his father, who was an exacting patriarch, tyrannical in his rule over the family. The father made everyone else feel inadequate and frightened, seeming to undermine any sense of accomplishment. Good behavior, excellent grades, and community achievements were taken as a matter of course as a proper means of carrying on some lofty family tradition. Failure to meet these high standards met with humiliation and guilt-inducing lectures. Mr. A.'s father also presented the extrafamilial world as a hostile and threatening jungle from which he protected his family through his superior talents and ability. Without him, the family could not cope and would be exploited by the alleged brutality of nonfamilial society.

Mr. A.'s mother concurred in these biased appraisals. She was remembered as an anxious, submissive woman who was terrified of upsetting her domineering husband. She also believed strongly in loyalty to the immediate family, using negative comparisons about neighbors as a means of inducing guilt if any of the children formed close relationships outside the extended family.

Mr. A. grew up believing that his sense of worth depended on getting praise or approval from his father, a feat that was never achieved. He always felt himself somehow unworthy and deficient for not living up to his father's standards, which he believed were fair and objective. He also believed that he would be doomed to failure in any pursuit without the support of a powerful father figure. Sensing himself unequal to meet the challenges of the adult world. He had developed an ability to disarm the father and ward off his criticism by assuming a pleasant, self-effacing, persona and committing to memory a host of entertaining stories that would divert his father's stern negativism. Although these were a successful defense against criticism, this facade never allowed him to experience or express his true feelings or true aspirations.

As Mr. A. reflected on his past, he became aware that he had always required the support and esteem of some father figure. Without this nurturing figure, he felt lost and helpless. Such insight helped explain his decompensation; because forming his own company necessitated his giving up his dependent relationship with the boss, who had transferentially assumed the father role. This business venture also would have forced him to move away from his childhood family, whom he believed still magically protected him.

Mr. A. also became aware of how his superficial mode of interaction had been created as a means of placating the father, and that it now had become generalized to almost all relationships, so that these were empty and ungratifying. This insight was achieved partially by interpretations of his behavior toward the therapist, who became yet another individual to win over and from whom to obtain assurance.

A few months after therapy had begun, Mr. A. reported a long series of dreams, all of which focused on his father. In some, the father was reprimanding him for some shortcoming or was punishing him for some misdeed, whereas in others, the father abandoned the patient, causing great anxiety and sadness. These dreams helped to demonstrate and clarify Mr. A.'s excessive dependence on his father, and, by relating the dreams to events in his working life, showed his dependence on surrogate paternal figures.

Eventually, Mr. A. became aware of his overriding need to win approval from his father and from his father's substitutes: (1) to feel worthy and whole, (2) to remain psychologically loyal to the family in order to continue being loved by his mother, and (3) to hide his true feelings so that others would find him likable. He also was able to conceptualize his enduring childhood sense of himself as helpless and unworthy if he was left alone or if he dared to gratify his own desires.

Once these childhood beliefs and the defensive maneuvers that had been constructed to fend off a dreaded view of the self were brought to consciousness, the slow process of change was initiated. This involved an extensive reevaluation of his relationships and of himself. As he ventured to try some more genuine assertion of himself, he would experience old fears, which in turn revived memories of how his autonomy had been eroded in childhood. For example, Mr. A. remembered his parents threatening to send him away from home if he disobeyed them; later, as a teenager, his budding interest in girls was ridiculed and shamed. He also recalled his mother threatening to abandon him if he did not demonstrate unswerving fidelity to her commands, as well as her using him as a go-between with her husband. These revelations helped him to understand the genesis of his current beliefs, defenses, and interpersonal maneuvers. He continued to make appropriate steps, by being more tolerant of setbacks and failure in himself and in others. He no longer felt he had to entertain or play up to others in order to be liked; he relied on his own judgment and enjoyed his achievements directly rather than for the praise they brought. He related to others more honestly, both in therapy and in other relationships.

These changes brought about varying responses from those individuals with whom Mr. A. had close contact. His wife was delighted with lessened dependency on her, but at work, some of his colleagues were not as pleased with Mr. A.'s new honesty and straightforward manner. These reactions were discussed in therapy, which was now used as a source of support in the process of change. During this same period, Mr. A. began to pursue activities for their own sake rather than for how those activities would impress others. He took up golf more seriously and enjoyed his gradually increasing proficiency. He had played previously, but he had used the game to conclude business deals or to feel part of an idealized group.

These alterations gradually solidified, and the frequency of therapy was decreased to once every 2 weeks, until it was stopped by mutual agreement.

SUMMARY

In treating a depressed patient through the modality of pscyhodynamic psychotherapy, the clinician is choosing a specific treatment method predicated on assessments of the patient's underlying character structure, pattern of psychological conflict, and ego strengths. A capacity to grasp the impact of unconscious conflict and tolerate powerful affects as they emerge in the transference are important factors in selecting patients for this treatment modality. The clinician must be aware of possible biological factors contributing to depressive symptoms that may occur in conjunction with psychodynamic psychotherapy.

Psychodynamic psychotherapy contrasts with other psychotherapies that are used to treat depressive disorders. The case illustration highlights principles of case selection for psychodynamic psychotherapy and illuminates key therapeutic tactics as the treatment unfolds.

REFERENCES

Abraham, K. (1960a). Notes on the psychoanalytic treatment of manic depressive insanity and allied conditions. In *Selected papers on psychoanalysis*. New York: Basic Books. (Original work published 1911)

Abraham, K. (1960b). The first pregenital stage of libido. In *Selected papers on psychoanalysis*. New York: Basic Books. (Original work published 1916)

Adler, G. (1986). Psychotherapy of the narcissistic personality disorder. *American Journal of Psychiatry, 143,* 4.

American Psychiatric Association. (1978). *Task force on electroconvulsive therapy of the American Psychiatric Association: Electroconvulsive therapy* (Task Force Report No. 14). Washington, DC: Author.

Arieti, S., & Bemporad, J. (1978). *Severe and mild depression.* New York: Basic Books.

Beck, A. (1967). *Depression.* New York: Hoeber.

Bibring, E. (1953). The mechanism of depression. In P. Greenacre (Ed.), *Affective disorders.* New York: International Press.

Bowlby, J. (1980). *Loss.* New York: Basic Books.

Brown, G.W., & Harris, T. (1978). *Social origins of depression.* London: Tavistock.

Brown, R.P., Sweeney, E., Kocsis, J., & Frances, A. (1984). Involutional melancholia revisited. *American Journal of Psychiatry, 141,* 1.

Conte, H.R., Plutchik, R., Wild, K.V., & Karasu, T.B. (1986). Combined psychotherapy and pharmacotherapy for depression. *Archives of General Psychiatry, 43,* 471–479.

DiMascio, A., Weissman, M.M., & Prusoff, B.A. (1979). Differential symptom reduction by drugs and psychotherapy in acute depression. *Archives of General Psychiatry, 36,* 1450–1456.

Docherty, J.P., Marder, S.R., & van Kammen, D.P. (1977). Psychotherapy and pharmacotherapy: Conceptual issues. *American Journal of Psychiatry, 134,* 529–533.

Drugs that cause psychiatric symptoms. (1984). *The Medical Letter, 26.*

Freud, S. (1960). Mourning and melancholia. In *Collected papers* (Vol. 4). New York: Basic Books. (Original work published in 1917)

Gutheil, T.G. (1982). The psychology of psychopharmacology. *Bulletin of the Menninger Clinic, 46,* 321–330.

Jacobson, E. (1971). *Depression.* New York: International Universities Press.

Jacobson, E. (1975). The psychoanalytic treatment of depressed patients. In E.J. Anthony & T. Benedek (Eds.), *Depression and human existence.* Boston: Little, Brown.

Klerman, G., & Schecter, G. (1982). Drugs and psychotherapy. In E.S. Paykel (Ed.), *Handbook of affective disorders.* New York: Guilford Press.

Klerman, G., Weissman, M.M., Rounsaville, B.J., & Chevron, B.S. (1984). *Interpersonal psychotherapy of depression.* New York: Basic Books

McAllister, T.W. (1983). Overview: Pseudodementia. *American Journal of Psychiatry, 140,* 5.

Rado, S. (1956). The problem of melancholia. In *Collected papers* (Vol. 1). New York: Grune & Stratton. (Original work published in 1927)

Ross, J.L. (1987). Principles of psychoanalytic hospital treatment. *Bulletin of the Menninger Clinic, 49,* 409–416.

Sandler, J., & Joffee, W.G. (1965). Notes on childhood depression. *International Journal of Psychoanalysis, 46,* 80–96.

CHAPTER 6

Cognitive Behavior Therapy

ARTHUR FREEMAN and CAROL OSTER

FROM BIBLICAL reports of King Saul's black moods to Hippocrates' humoral view of melancholia, to Shakespeare's melancholic Dane, to Freud, through to contemporary psychological and neurobiological understandings of the syndrome, depression has been a part of the human condition through all of recorded history. Depression has been called the common cold of emotional disorders. For some this cold may be the equivalent of a periodic case of the sniffles, annoying, but time limited. For others, depression is episodic, occurring frequently, with the symptoms having a noticeable and possibly significant impact on functioning and personal comfort. For yet others, depression is a long-term visitor, unwelcome, but so constant that it has become how that individual learns to define themselves, that is, I am a depressive.

The depressive response may be reactive to an external stressor (e.g., loss) or it may be more characteristic of the patient's pattern of responding to the world, as in the self-defining experience of dysthymia. At its extreme form, it can contribute to a virtual total withdrawal from interpersonal behavior, and it can lead to thoughts or actions leading to self-damage or suicide. The frequency, amplitude, or depth of the depression may vary from patient to patient. The particular combination or permutation of depressive symptoms may similarly vary.

The basic syndrome of depression, however, is so common that it can be identified cross-culturally. For example, the Beck Depression Inventory (BDI, 1996b) has been translated, validated, and is currently in active use in over 20 countries around the world, without revision of the content. One might be concerned that an assessment tool developed in the United States and standardized on a North American group might not be sensitive or appropriate to the depression seen in such diverse cultures as China, Sweden, Israel, and Italy. However, the BDI, evaluating the basic components of depression, has become part of the standard evaluation battery for depression internationally. Although depression appears to be a universal response with many manifestations, it is nonetheless a response that can be limited in severity and decreased in frequency. Its affect on life can be muted, decreased, or even eliminated. The typical symptoms of depression are well defined and agreed to by practitioners representing diverse theoretical treatment models.

COGNITIVE THERAPY

Cognitive Therapy (CT) is a short term, active, structured, directive, collaborative, psychoeducational, and dynamic model of psychotherapy that utilizes a broad range of cognitive and behavioral techniques to affect changes in mood, thought, and action. Cognitive therapy, as developed, researched, and practiced by Aaron T. Beck (1967, 1976; Beck, Rush, Shaw, & Emery, 1979) and his colleagues, is one of several cognitive-behavioral models of therapy. Included in this group are the works of Ellis (1962, 1973, 1985), Lazarus (1976, 1981), and Meichenbaum (1977), and a number of offshoots of each of these major theoreticians. The major therapeutic focus in the cognitive-behavioral models is to help patients examine the manner in which they construe and understand the world (cognitions) and to experiment with new ways of responding (behavior). By learning to understand the idiosyncratic way in which they perceive self, world, and experience, and the prospects for the future, patients can be helped to alter negative affect and to behave more adaptively. CT was among the earliest models, and it was developed specifically in response to the need to treat depression (Beck, 1967, 1977; Beck et al., 1979). Given this early focus on depression, the efficacy of CT has been most studied in its application to this disorder (Beck, 1991; Blackburn, Bishop, Glen, Walley, & Christie, 1981; Dobson, 1989; Haaga, Dyck, & Ernst, 1991; Hollon et al., 1992; Hollon & Najavits, 1988; Hollon, Shelton, & Davis, 1993; Murphy et al., 1977; Robinson, Berman, & Neimeyer, 1990; Wetzel & Reich, 1989). Given the two decades since the publication of the now classic, *Cognitive Therapy of Depression* (Beck et al., 1979), the plethora of studies, and information in the popular press, there still linger many misconceptions of what CT is and what it is not, what it does and what it does not do. For example, the following misconceptions articulated by Freeman (1983) and Freeman, Simon, Pretzer, and Fleming (1990) persists:

1. Cognitive therapy is "the power of positive thinking."
2. Negative thoughts cause psychopathology.
3. Cognitive therapy is simple.
4. Cognitive therapy is talking people out of their problems.
5. Cognitive therapy ignores emotion and behavior.
6. Cognitive therapy ignores the past.
7. Cognitive therapy is superficial.
8. The therapeutic relationship is unimportant.
9. Cognitive therapy is finished in 15 sessions or less.
10. Cognitive therapy and medication are antithetical.

11. Cognitive therapy is just a collection of techniques without a unifying theory.
12. The goal of cognitive therapy is to eliminate emotion.
13. Cognitive therapy is only appropriate for bright, verbal intellectually oriented patients.
14. Cognitive therapy is not useful for seriously disturbed patients who need inpatient treatment.

Regardless of the manifestation of the depressive symptoms and course of depression, the CT approach to the conceptualization and treatment of depression starts with the observation and identification of both the common and idiosyncratic cognitive structures, processes, vulnerabilities, and the emotional, cognitive, and behavioral products. This chapter will describe the assessment of depression, the general cognitive conceptualization of depression, and the treatment strategies that have evolved from this conceptualization.

The internal processes in depression do not exist to the exclusion of contextual or external events, and the external manifestations do not exist without some internal monitoring, whether at or below the level of awareness. A patient could be depression resistant regardless of the severity of loss-related events in the patient's life (e.g., Henny Youngman's oft repeated one-liner, "Take my wife . . . please."). Conversely, an individual may be depression prone to events and circumstances that to the observer appear neutral or even positive (e.g., "What? I won the lottery? Oh my, that puts me into the highest tax bracket.").

Rather, the cognitive perspective is a diathesis-stress model: That is, life events, thoughts, behaviors and moods are inextricably tied to each other in a reciprocal manner. Cognitions, behaviors, and moods all serve future and past functions in a complex process of information processing, behavioral regulation, and motivation (Freeman & Oster, 1997). Further, the cognitive perspective implicates early life events and learning in the creation of patterns of information processing called *schema*. These schema may predispose patients to specific emotional, cognitive, and behavioral vulnerabilities, and they may maintain emotional difficulties once behavioral, cognitive and mood patterns are initiated.

Cognition is likely to be related to mediation (vulnerability) and moderation (expression and maintenance) of depression (Ingram, Miranda, & Segal, 1998). Two levels of cognition are viewed as influencing these processes. These two levels can be easily described as deep cognitions and surface cognitions, respectively (Dobson & Shaw, 1987; Kwon & Oei, 1994; Rude & Rehm, 1991; Stiles & Gotestam, 1989).

Deep cognitions are predisposing vulnerability factors that mediate the development of depression. Deep cognitions have been given a number of labels, including schema, attitudes, basic assumptions, and core beliefs. Kwon and Oei (1994) describe this level of cognition as consisting of stable, cross-situational, and basic components of cognitive organization. Consistent with the model proposed by Beck et al. (1990), we will use the term schema as the inclusive term. Among the most powerful techniques in CT involves using the various cognitive techniques to challenge dysfunctional thinking. The CT model posits an interaction between the individual's thoughts and emotions. For example, Patient A awakes in the morning and thinks, "Another lousy day. Nothing to do. It wouldn't make a difference, since I'm such a hopeless case." Patient A may begin to feel more and more depressed as a consequence of such dysfunctional thinking. Patient B awakes and is overcome by feelings of depression. He may lay in bed and think, "Another lousy day. I've just gotten up and I'm already depressed. There is nothing I can do to ease my depression. I'm a hopeless case." Whether the therapist focuses on the preceding cognition or the subsequent attribution, the focus is a cognitive focus.

COGNITIVE MODEL OF DEPRESSION

Beck (1967) in the earliest formulation of his cognitive theory of depression, posited three structures that are consistent across culture and theoretical model. These are the cognitive triad, cognitive distortions, and schema. The triad represents an accumulation of thought content. The distortions describe the way in which thoughts are structured. Finally, the schema can be characterized as representing the patient's belief system.

THE COGNITIVE TRIAD

The cognitive triad for depression (Beck, 1967; Beck et al., 1979) describes the patient's negative views of self, of world or experience, and of the future. Virtually all patient problems can be subsumed under one, or a combination, of these areas. The accumulated content in each of these three areas is evident in the patient's overt and covert cognitions, including verbal and visual representations. Affect and behavior will typically correspond with the negative content of these views. For example, if individuals view themselves as physically unattractive, they may feel sad, disappointed in their looks, and may then avoid situations where physical attractiveness might be seen as a prerequisite for success (e.g., dating).

The therapist can start to focus and structure the therapy from the onset of treatment by paying special attention to the depressive triad. Personal issues relating to self, world, and future differ for each patient so that each constituent of the triad does not necessarily contribute equally to the depression. By assessing the degree of contribution of each of the three factors, the therapist can begin to develop a conceptualization of the patient's problem(s). This conceptualization can be shared with the patient and used to help the patient have a better understanding of the focus of the therapy, which will be basic to the development of collaborative treatment strategies.

The negative view of self is labeled as low self-esteem or poor self-image. This is expressed in verbalizations reflecting beliefs such as, "I am stupid," or, "There is something flawed in my make-up." The negative view of the world involves the individual believing that their problems come more from the ubiquitous "thems" of the world, or the problems that they experience come from the more vague "its." They might verbalize and believe that, "They are unfair to me," "They should not have done that," or "It is too hard," "It shouldn't be that way." If, for example, the patient's concerns are predominantly self and world, they might make statements reflecting low self-esteem and negative views of world and experience, but when questioned about hopelessness and suicidal potential, this patient might say, "Kill myself? Oh No! I'll just continue to live my poor, miserable life because I deserve to."

If, however, the patient's concerns focus on self and future, the verbalizations would include those reflecting low self-esteem and suicidal thoughts (e.g., "What good am I? I deserve to die. The world seems to get along pretty well, it's me that is at variance with the rest of the world.").

Finally, if patients' concerns involve a negative view of the world and the future, they may include a diatribe against the ills and evils of the world, and a multitude of reasons about why the best course of action in dealing with the awful world is death. Suicidal impulses are often based on a desire for retribution or as a means of getting even with others. When asked about self-esteem or personal contributions to their difficulty, this patient type will often go on in great detail about how they have tried and not succeeded, but they are victimized because of the world's problems. They see themselves as innocent victims. This perceptual/response style is common among Axis II patients (Beck & Freeman, 1990; Freeman & Leaf, 1989; Freeman et al., 1990). By including the patient in the assessment and understanding of each of the triadic factors, the therapeutic collaboration can begin early and can be directed at specific areas of concern rather than on vague, global, and amorphous treatment issues. For example, negative views of the self and world were found in one study to be more common in depressed patients' thinking than were negative views of the future (Blackburn, Eunson, & Bishop, 1986). Negative views of the future are characteristic of the thinking of suicidal patients (Freeman & Reinecke, 1994; Salkovskis, Atha, & Storer, 1990). Negative views of the world are reported more often by patients who experience increased anger with depression (Blackburn et al., 1986).

COGNITIVE DISTORTIONS

Distortions are basically idiosyncratic views that may or may not be consensually validated. An individual can distort in a variety of ways. These distortions can be positive or negative. The patient who distorts in a positive direction may be the "fool that rushes in where angels fear to tread." The positive distorter may view life in an unrealistically positive way. He or she may take chances that most people would avoid, for example, starting a new business, investing in a risky stock. If successful, the positive distorter is vindicated. The positive distorter can, however, take chances that may put themselves in situations of great danger, for example, experiencing massive chest pains and not consulting a physician ("I'm too young/healthy for a heart attack"). Excessive positive distortion is typically termed *denial* because of the potential neglect of realistic negative factors. At the extreme, the patient in a manic episode exhibits great neglect of consequences and sees the world with a positive bias that can create chaos for the patient and for those associated with them.

The distortions can be viewed as *minor delusions.* This would be in contrast to the delusional beliefs typical of psychotic individuals. For example, the depressed patient may state (and believe) that they are unloved and unlovable. If we were to gather all the individuals in the patient's life and interview them about how loved or unlovable the patient is, and 98.3 percent of the individuals interviewed state that the identified patient is greatly and easily loved, the depressed patient may either focus on the 1.7 percent who validated their negative belief, or dismiss the 98 percent as unreliable reporters. For some severely depressed patients, these dysfunctional beliefs assume an almost fixed delusional quality that appears to be immutable.

Distortions become the initial focus of CT. The therapist works with the patient to make the distortions manifest by tracking "automatic thoughts," or the spontaneous thoughts associated with certain moods or situations. These spontaneously generated thoughts are then evaluated for content, degree of patient belief, style, and the impact on the patient's life. The distortions become the thematic directional signs that point to the underlying schema. The main purpose of labeling the style or content of the distortion is to provide a conceptual tool to help patients understand their thoughts, and to begin to alter those thoughts that are dysfunctional. Reinforcing patients for questioning the possibility of an idea being a distortion and testing alternatives is far more important than the rightness of the label. The distortions that follow are in no way a comprehensive list of all of the possible distortions the therapist might encounter. The distortions occur in many combinations and permutations. Any distortion can be depressive. They are presented here in isolation for the sake of discussion. Typical distortions include:

1. *Dichotomous thinking*—"I'm either a success or a failure." "The world is either black or white."
2. *Arbitrary inference/mind reading*—"They probably think that I'm incompetent." "I just know that they disapprove."
3. *Emotional reasoning*—"Because I feel inadequate I am inadequate." "I believe that I must be funny to be liked, so it is fact."
4. *Personalization*—"That comment wasn't just random, it must have been directed toward me." "Problems always emerge when I'm in a hurry."
5. *Overgeneralization*—"Everything I do turns out wrong." "It doesn't matter what my choices are, they always fall flat."
6. *Catastrophic thinking*—"If I go to the party, there will be terrible consequences." "I better not try because I might fail, and that would be awful."
7. *Should statements*—"I should visit my family every time they want me to." "They should be nicer to me."
8. *Externalization of self-worth*—"My worth is dependent upon what others think of me." "They think, therefore I am."

9. *Comparing*—"I am not as competent as my coworkers or supervisors." "Compared to others, there is clearly something flawed about me."
10. *Disqualifying the positive*—"This success experience was only a fluke." "The compliment was unwarranted."
11. *Perfectionism*—"I must do everything perfectly or I will be criticized and be a failure." "Doing a merely adequate job is akin to being a failure."
12. *Selective abstraction*—"The rest of the information doesn't matter. This is the salient point." "I must focus on the negative details while I ignore and filter out all the positive aspects of a situation."
13. *Magnification*—"That mistake that I made will cause the end of the world as we know it." "All others have far greater value than I do."
14. *Minimization*—"I have little or nothing to offer." "The flaws of others are not relevant, only my errors."

There are also a number of fallacies, for example:

1. *Control*—"If I'm not in complete control all of the time, I will be totally out of control."
2. *Change*—"If my situation were different, all of my problems would be over."
3. *Worrying*—"If I worry about something enough, it will be resolved."
4. *Ignoring and denying*—"If I ignore it, maybe it will go away." "If I don't pay attention, I will not be held responsible."
5. *Fairness*—"Life should be fair." "People should all be fair."
6. *Being right*—"I must prove that I am right because being wrong is unthinkable." "To be wrong is to be a bad patient."
7. *Attachment and dependence*—"I can't live without a man/woman." "If I was in a relationship, all of my problems would be solved."
8. *Heaven's reward*—"If I do everything perfectly here, I will be rewarded later." "I have to muddle through this life, and then maybe things will be better later." (Freeman & Zaken-Greenburg, 1989)

Although all of the above distortions are stated in the first person, they can also apply to expectations of others, including family, social, religious, or gender groups (McGoldrick, Pearce, & Giordano, 1982). The novice cognitive therapist might be inclined to charge ahead challenging each of the patient's distorted thoughts. Our goal is to not just displace the distortions, but to help the patient develop the skills to question and later challenge their negative distortions. A more complex and sophisticated goal is to help the patient to understand the schema that generate the distortions.

SCHEMA

An essential focus of CT is on understanding and making manifest the patient's underlying schema. These schemas or basic rules of life begin to be established as a force in cognition and behavior from the earliest points in life, and are well fixed by the middle childhood years. They are the accumulation of the individual's learning and experience within the family group, the religious group, ethnic, gender, or regional subgroups, and the broader society. The particular extent or effect that a schema has on an individual's life depends on: (1) how strongly that schema is held, (2) how essential the individual sees that schema to their safety, well-being, or existence, (3) their previous learning vis-à-vis the importance and essential nature of a particular schema, (4) how early a particular schema was internalized, and (5) how powerfully and by whom was the schema reinforced (for an extended discussion of the schema see Beck et al., 1990).

In seeking to alter a particular schema that has endured for a long period of time, it would be necessary to help the individual to deal with the belief from as many different perspectives as possible. A pure cognitive strategy would leave the behavioral and affective elements untouched. The pure affective strategy is similarly limited, and, of course, the strict behavioral approach is limited by its disregard for cognitive-affective elements. In many cases, we find that an individual's particular schema are consensually validated by significant others, communities, or cultures.

Whether a depressed individual develops a schema that is held with moderate strength and is amenable to change, or a depressed individual operates with a schema that is powerful and is apparently immutable, we may posit several possibilities: (1) In addition to the schema, the individual maintains a powerful associated belief that they cannot change; (2) the belief system is powerfully reinforced by parents or significant others; (3) although the belief system may not be especially reinforced, any attempt to believe the contrary may not be reinforced or even punished, that is, a child may be told, "You're no good" (a second possibility would be that the child is not specifically told that they lack worth but any attempt to assert worth would be ignored); (4) the parents or significant others may offer instruction contrary to developing a positive image, for example, "It's not nice to brag" or "It's not nice to toot your own horn because people will think less of you." These components develop in response to early life experiences, through both social and operant learning. Schema may operate actively, determining a majority of the patient's daily behavior, or may be latent, triggered by specific events. They may be compelling and hard to resist, or noncompelling and easily countered or resisted (Beck et al., 1990; Freeman, 1998; Freeman & Leaf, 1989). The schema may appear to be contradictory, for example, a compelling schema may be, "I can only eat food that is prepared in accordance with religious dietary laws." If, however, one is starving, this schema may be compromised by the equally compelling belief, "I must survive." As illustrated in Figure 6.1, schema exist on a shift potential continuum from those that are *paralyzed* (i.e., cannot change under any circumstance) to those that are *chaotic* (i.e., are in a constant state of shift and change).

Schema are ideas that guide the process by which a patient organizes, interprets, understands, and structures receptive and expressive information about the individual's internal and external world. They guide the patient's selection

Schematic Paralysis	Schematic Rigidity	Schematic Stability	Schematic Flexibility	Schematic Instability
Ossified	*Dogmatic*	*Steady*	*Creative*	*Chaotic*

Figure 6.1 Schematic Shift Potential.

of information to attend to or to seek, they guide pattern-search procedures, and they provide "default values" when information is missing (Dent & Teasdale, 1988; Hollon & Garber, 1990). Schema develop through the process of adaptation described by Piaget (Rosen, 1985, 1989). The individual's first attempt to deal with internal or external stimuli is to ask, "What are you and where do you fit within my past experience/knowledge?" If enough similarities are found between the existing knowledge structures and the stimuli, the new event is *assimilated* into existing knowledge. However, if sufficient dissimilarities exist, knowledge structures and rules are altered to accommodate the contrasts that are detected and *accommodation* occurs. If the alterations are quite small, the individual may need to make only those minimal changes necessary for coping. If, on the other hand, the dissimilarities are broad, entirely new categories may be created using pieces of information and hierarchies already encoded.

Schema, automatic thoughts, and the distortions evident in them, combine to contribute both distally and proximally to the patient's experience of depression. Schema, as distal structures and processes, result in a depressogenic style of global, internal, and stable negative attribution (Abramson, Seligman, & Teasdale, 1978). This style mediates the development of depression by creating a cognitive vulnerability that acts in concert with negative life events in a stress-diathesis model. In addition, schema contribute, with life events, to the development of negative cognitive content at the level of automatic thoughts.

Automatic thoughts in depressed patients are proximal events that cohere around negative attributions and expectations of self, world or experience, and future. At this level, cognitions operate in conjunction with negative life events, mood (distress), and behavior to maintain and moderate the expression of an existing depression.

COGNITIVE THERAPY OF DEPRESSION

The approach taken in CT of depression is typically short term. Clinical trials have generally included time periods of 12 to 20 weeks as a reasonable trial of cognitive therapy (Blackburn et al., 1981; Rush, Beck, Kovacs, & Hollon, 1977; Thase, Bowler, & Harden, 1991). In practice, the time period is adjusted to the particular circumstances of the patient, including the co-occurrence of Axis I disorders (e.g., anxiety), Axis II disorders, other psychological disorders, and the life events experienced or anticipated in the course of therapy. Although most improvement is noted in the first weeks of therapy (for example, Berlin,

Mann, & Grossman, 1991; Kavanagh & Wilson, 1989), relapse prevention may require sessions beyond 16 or 20 (Shea et al., 1992; Thase et al., 1991).

Cognitive therapists are active and directive. The work is often of a psycho-educational nature. The patient will typically be helped to learn skills, behaviors, or methods of altering cognitions and behaviors. The therapist takes a proactive stance to setting agendas, determining the direction of the therapy, and actively structuring the therapy. However, there are limits to the directiveness of the therapist. CT is a collaborative model. Because a major goal is for patients to acquire the ability to address cognitions and behaviors on their own, the course of therapy must begin with, and see an increase in, the ability of patients to set the direction, focus, and pace of the therapy. The collaborative approach increases the patients' sense of efficacy, and counters negative attributions about self, world, and future.

Nonspecific factors impact on the success of cognitive therapy, as they do on all other therapies (Frank, 1985). These include the development of a good working relationship, the empathy expressed by the therapist, the patient's experience of universality, and the patient's experience of hope within the therapy.

Schema are not eradicated, but modified. Automatic thoughts are not necessarily stopped, but managed and countered. The therapist helps the patient to develop a range of cognitive and behavioral coping strategies for present and future exigencies of life, with the effect of altering mood. The patient's ability to control negative cognitions and the patient's perception of self-efficacy about this control at termination predict a sustained response to cognitive therapy (Kavanaugh & Wilson, 1989).

The primary targets of CT for depression are the negative automatic thoughts that maintain the depression and the schema (assumptions and beliefs) that predispose the patient to depression in the first place (Kwon & Oei, 1994). CT carefully examines the individual's relatively unstable, temporary, and situation-specific thoughts termed *automatic thoughts*, which are more basic and available than the schema (Beck, 1979; Beck et al., 1979; Kwon & Oei, 1994). They arise quickly and automatically, and appear to be habitual or reflexive. They do not seem to be subject to conscious control by the patient, and they are uncritically accepted by the patient, to whom they seem perfectly plausible. Most often the patient is unaware of the fleeting thought, although they may be keenly aware of the emotion that precedes, accompanies, or follows it (Freeman et al., 1990). Automatic thoughts are accessible through introspection and self-report, and they represent the conclusions drawn by the patient on the basis of the information processing rules that they presently follow. That is, they are the products of the processes and structures that comprise the schema (Beck, 1966, 1976, 1977; Freeman, 1986; Freeman & Leaf, 1989; Freeman et al., 1990).

ASSESSMENTS

A number of measures of automatic thoughts or surface cognitions exist, although not all of these instruments were designed with that construct in mind.

These include the Automatic Thoughts Questionnaire (ATQ) (Hollon & Kendall, 1980), the Beck Depression Inventory (BDI) (Beck, 1996b), the Beck Hopelessness Scale (BHS) (Beck, 1996c), the Beck Anxiety Inventory (BAI) (Beck, 1996a), and others.

Automatic thoughts are most often assessed by directly asking the patient about their thoughts. When the therapist or patient notes a change in affect, a simple probe, "What are you thinking right now?" interrupts the automatic processing and encourages the patient to think about their thinking (metacognition) (Beck et al., 1979; Hollon & Garber, 1990; Meichenbaum, 1994). The automatic thought that is most easily elicited is often only a partial thought or "cognitive stem." For example, a depressed patient might state, "That task is far too difficult for me to ever complete it . . ." Although that may have a depressing property, the last part of the thought, ". . . and I will be destroyed" or, ". . . and there is nothing that I can do about it," is far more likely to lead to depression. If the patient ended the stem by thinking, ". . . so I better seek some help" or, ". . . it would make sense to get some additional training," there would be less likelihood that the complete thought would be depressogenic.

The major focus of the therapy is to help patients to become aware of and to evaluate ways in which they construct the meaning of their experiences, and to experiment with new ways of responding, both cognitively and behaviorally. Although cognition is a major focus of therapy, cognitive therapists also utilize a broad range of behavioral approaches, to meet both cognitive and behavioral ends (Freeman et al., 1990; Stravynski & Greenberg, 1992).

Altering dysfunctional cognitions, at both the deep and surface levels, appears to follow a typical pattern, whether patient led or therapist led. A task analysis conducted by Berlin et al. (1991) identified three sequential requirements:

1. Coming to view cognitive-emotional appraisals as hypothetical or subjective, and, therefore, worthy of testing, investigation, or examination.
2. Generating alternative appraisals, and using these as a basis for action and further thought or as a basis for pattern search or schema identification.
3. Generating more adaptive, useful, or accurate core assumptions, and using them as a basis for cognition and action.

ASSESSMENT AND SOCIALIZATION TO THE COGNITIVE THERAPY MODEL

Both the course of therapy as a whole and a single session of CT follow a basic guideline. The first tasks in cognitive therapy are assessment of the patient's life and circumstances, conceptualization of the problem according to the cognitive model, socializing the patient to the cognitive model, and identifying goals and appropriate interventions consonant with the patient's needs and consistent with the CT model. These tasks overlap and are intertwined with each other. Assessment is often, and should be, therapeutic. Socializing a patient to the therapy model is an intervention that in itself may produce significant change.

DIAGNOSTIC PROFILING SYSTEM
(© FREEMAN, 1998) REVISED EDITION

Date of Assessment:_____

Session#:_____Evaluator:_____

Patient Name:_____ Patient#: _____Location:_____

Birthdate: _____Age: _____Race: _____ Gender: _____ Birthorder: _____Marital/Children:_____

Employment: _____Education: _____Disability: _____Medication:_____

Physician: _____Referral Question:_____

Instructions: Record the diagnosis including the code number. Briefly identify the criteria for the selected diagnosis. Working with the patient either directly or as part of the data gathering of the clinical interview, SCALE the SEVERITY of EACH CRITERION for the patient at the PRESENT TIME. Indicate the level of severity on the grid.

DIAGNOSIS (DSM/ICD) with Code:
Axis I: _____

Axis II: _____

Axis III: _____

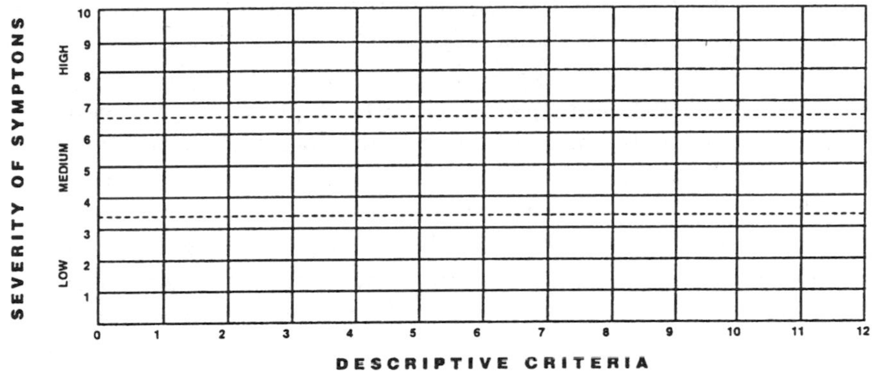

CRITERIA:

1 _____   7 _____

2 _____   8 _____

3 _____   9 _____

4 _____   10 _____

5 _____   11 _____

6 _____   12 _____

Do you believe that the above noted criteria are a reasonably accurate sample of the patient's behavior? **YES or NO**

If **NO**, please indicate why:_____

Are there any reasons to believe that this individual is an imminent danger to himself/herself or others? **YES or NO**

If **YES**, please indicate the danger._____

Figure 6.2   Diagnostic Profiling System.

A basic tool for both evaluating the depression and targeting areas for treatment (Figure 6.2) is the Diagnostic Profile System (DPS) (Freeman, 1998). It should be noted that the DPS assessment is not intended to help the therapist label the patient or their style, but to determine points of intervention with the potential for change and methods of initiating the desired change.

Preparation and socialization for CT may be through the therapist's didactic explanations, through reading brochures or books (Burns, 1980; Freeman &

DeWolfe, 1989, 1991), through video (Schotte, Maes, Beuten, Vandenbossche, & Cosyns, 1993), or by a limited explanation of the therapy, with the therapist demonstrating the basic therapy model by intertwining it within the context of the therapy. The severity of the patient's depression, as measured by the BDI (Beck, 1996b), impacts negatively on the perceived helpfulness of preparatory procedures, as would be predicted by the model. Patients report that the most helpful aspects of preparation are explanations of the symptoms, causes, and therapy of depression, and examples of the thoughts, actions, and feelings common to depression (Schotte et al., 1993). Many patients respond positively to completing the BDI by commenting that they feel reassured that there is a single measure that so delineates their depression that they are encouraged that others share the problem and they might be able to be helped.

Taking a thorough history is useful when specific attention is paid to: (1) the patient's triadic view of self, world, and future; (2) the attributional and expectancy style of the evident distortions; and (3) to the developmental history of the patient's schema. The therapist may evaluate life events that are perceived by the patient to have triggered the current episode of depression. In addition, the therapist's evaluation of the individual's social supports will relate to relapse and recurrence prevention.

From the assessment, the therapist develops a conceptualization of the patient's depression. The process of developing a conceptualization follows the steps in observation, hypothesis formation, and hypothesis testing that we ask the patient to follow in the therapy itself. The assessment itself becomes an explicit model for the patient to follow:

1. What is the problem? How does it affect the patient? The patient and therapist develop an exhaustive problem list. It is assumed that the schema that create the vulnerability for depression will manifest themselves in a number of cognitions, behaviors, and emotions. Examining the range of problems will often point to the underlying schema.

2. How do patients explain their problems to themselves? What is their causal model? What are their attributions and expectancies regarding their depression? These relate to the cognitive structures and processes that are assumed to create vulnerability to depression (schema), and that have an effect on the automatic thoughts.

3. How does the interaction of the patient's cognition, behavior, and life events result in depression? The therapist and patient explore the sources of stress and support in the environment, and the patient's response to or use of them. Are there other explanations other than the one the patient holds that might account for these connections?

4. What evidence is there for the patient's model and for any other models or hypotheses? How are the patient's cognitions, behaviors, and environment maintaining the depression?

5. How did the patient come to think and behave the way they do? The therapist and patient construct hypotheses about how the patient's cognitive biases and distortions developed by examining the patient's childhood

experiences related to schema. This is a search for antecedents, original stimulus-response connections, and social-learning episodes.

6. How would this hypothesis explain current and past events? What predictions could be made about the ways that the patient's schema and automatic thoughts will be evident in and will affect the patient's feelings and behavior within and outside of the therapy? What would be the evidence?

7. If the hypothesis is correct, what does that suggest, in terms of intervention? If the hypotheses are accurate they will explain past behavior, make sense of present behavior, and will predict future behavior.

The therapist and the patient may have different theories or models of the patient's depression. The goal is not to argue and to try to convince the patient of the correctness of the therapist's model, but to help the patient to be aware of their model as a theory or hypothesis about self, world, and future. Theories and models can be assessed for goodness of fit with new information and with experience. It is therapeutic for the patient to see that models can be revised when the fit is not good enough or is no longer useful. That is, the primary goal of the first stage of therapy is to help them to distance themselves from their model in order to evaluate it.

STRUCTURE OF A TYPICAL SESSION

A typical session of cognitive therapy begins with agenda setting. Depressed patients often have difficulty organizing themselves in order to problem solve. In fact, the lack of organization is emblematic of the depressive syndrome. By collaboratively setting an agenda, the therapist models a problem-solving approach and offers a structure that makes the therapy easier for the patient. A typical session agenda might include:

1. Greeting the patient and reconnecting after the time off.
2. Review of any weekly assessments the patient fills out prior to the session, such as the BDI, the BAI, and other scales. This allows specific issues to be put on the day's agenda. (The assessment forms are typically available in the waiting room prior to the session.)
3. A brief overview of the weeks interactions and problems. The patient can be asked to recount specifics of the week's events, including the reaction to the last session.
4. A review of homework, what worked, what was learned, what problems were encountered, and the emotions, behaviors, and cognitions that attended the homework.
5. Setting an agenda that would include a specific problem focus for the session. Priorities are determined collaboratively, according to both patient preference and consonance with the model. This might involve identifying and questioning automatic thoughts related to an event of the week, skill building, hypothesis testing, and so forth. This points out the need

for further information for, or next steps in problem solving, and thus directs attention to the next homework that needs to be done.

6. A wrap-up and review of the session, and feedback to the therapist. Time is always left before the close of the session for the patient to review and outline what he or she has gotten from the session. Goals and accomplishments of the session are identified, and homework for the next session is reviewed and tied to goals. The patient is asked for responses to the session. This gives the session closure and solidifies gains made.

THERAPEUTIC INTERVENTIONS

We would differentiate between the terms *strategy* and *intervention*. Strategy is used to describe an overall goal of the therapy. For example, a goal with a depressed patient might be increased concentration. We use the term *intervention* to delineate specific techniques that are used to reach the goal. For example, writing down desired goals helps to limit concentration difficulties.

Several cognitive and behavioral techniques can be used by the therapist to help to question both the distortions and the schema that underlie those distortions. These techniques are taught to the patients to help them respond in more functional ways. A rule of thumb in treating severely depressed patients would be that the greater the severity of the depression, the greater the proportion of behavioral to cognitive interventions the therapist will use. This is illustrated in Figure 6.3.

The precise mix of cognitive and behavioral techniques will depend on the patient's skill, the therapist's skill, the level of depression, and the treatment goals. For the severely depressed patient, the initial goals of treatment would be focused on the patient doing basic self-help tasks, such as coping with the activities of daily living (ADLs). In working on ADLs, graded task assignments

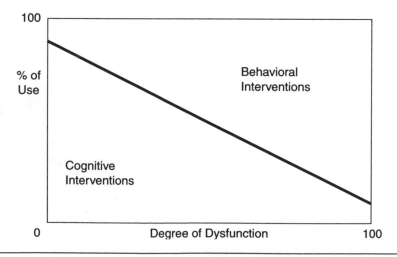

Figure 6.3 Relationship of Cognitive and Behavioral Interventions.

can be used with great success. Starting with the easiest tasks at the bottom of a hierarchy of difficulty and moving through successively more difficult tasks can help the patient achieve a greater sense of personal efficacy. This personal efficacy can then be used as evidence for the cognitive work in therapy.

COGNITIVE TECHNIQUES

1. *Determining idiosyncratic meaning.* The therapist cannot assume that a term or statement used by a patient is completely understood by the therapist until the patient is asked for meaning and clarification. This also models for the patient the need for active listening skills to both self and others, improved communication, and a means for checking out assumptions. For example, "What do you mean by that?"

2. *Questioning the evidence.* We all use certain evidence to maintain our ideas and beliefs. It is essential to teach the individual to identify and then to question the evidence that they are using to maintain and strengthen an idea or belief. Questioning the evidence also requires examining the source of data. The patient who is depressed often gives equal weight to all sources. For example, a spouse, on his way to the toilet appears to frown when the patient (his wife) passes. This may be used by the patient as "evidence" that she is unloved and thus may as well kill herself. Many patients have the ability to ignore major pieces of data (selective abstraction) and focus on the few pieces of data that support their depressive and dysfunctional view. By having the patient question the evidence with family members or significant others, a fuller accounting can be had. If the patient's view is accurate and supported by the evidence, the therapist can help to structure alternative ways of either perceiving the data or changing behaviors, so that the evidence is either modified or no longer exists. For example, "Let's make a list of the information that you are using to keep this issue such a strong part of your life?"

3. *Reattribution.* A common statement made by patients is, "It's all my fault." This is commonly heard in situations of relationship difficulty, separation, or divorce. Although one cannot dismiss this out of hand, it is unlikely that a single patient is totally responsible for everything that goes wrong in a relationship. The depressed patient often takes responsibility for events and situations that are only minimally attributable to them. The therapist can help the patient distribute responsibility amongst all relevant parties. If the therapist takes a position of total support (i.e., "It wasn't your fault." "She isn't worth it," " You're better off without her," or "There are other fish in the ocean."), the therapist ends up sounding like friends and family that the patient has already dismissed as being a cheering squad, and not understanding the patient's position. The therapist can, by taking a middle ground, help the patient to reattribute responsibility and not take all the blame, nor unrealistically shift all blame to others (e.g., "Can we identify which issues are yours and which are his?").

4. *Examining options and alternatives.* Many individuals see themselves as having lost all options, and they become hopeless. Typically, suicidal patients

see their options and alternatives as so limited that, among their few choices, death might be the easiest or simplest choice. This cognitive strategy involves working with the patient to generate additional options (e.g., "What else can you do?").

5. *Decatastrophizing.* This is also called the what-if technique. This involves helping the patient to evaluate if they are overestimating the catastrophic nature of a situation. Questions that might be asked of the patient include, "What is the worst thing that can happen," or "And if it does occur, what would be so terrible?" This technique has the therapist working against a Chicken-Little style of thinking. If patients see an experience (or life itself) as a series of catastrophes and problems, the therapist can work toward reality testing. Patients can be helped to see that the consequence of their life actions are not all or nothing, and, thereby, they are less catastrophic. It is important that this technique be used with great gentleness and care so that the patient does not feel ridiculed or made fun of by the therapist.

6. *Examining fantasized consequences.* In this technique the patients are asked to fantasize a situation and to describe their images and attendant concerns. Often patients describe their concerns and in the direct verbalization, they can see the irrationality of their ideas. If the fantasized consequences are realistic, the therapist can work with the patient to realistically assess the danger and develop coping strategies. This technique allows patients to bring imaged events, situations, or interactions that have happened previously into the consulting room. The images can become grist for the therapeutic mill. The fantasy, being colored by the same dysfunctional thinking that alters many of the patient perceptions, may be overly negative.

7. *Advantages and disadvantages.* Examining the advantages and disadvantages of maintaining a particular belief or behavior can help patients gain balance and perspective. This technique can be used to examine the advantages and disadvantages of acting a certain way (e.g., dressing a certain way), thinking a certain way (e.g., thinking of what others will think of you), feeling a particular way (e.g., sad). For example, "Let's look at the pros and cons of your continuing in this relationship."

8. *Turning adversity to advantage.* Sometimes a seeming disaster can be used to advantage. Losing one's job can be a disaster but may, in some cases, be the entry point to a new job or even a new career. Having a deadline imposed may be seen as oppressive and unfair, but it may be used as a motivator. There is, once again, a balancing that puts the patient's experience into a perspective. The patient may accuse the therapist of being an unrealistic Pollyanna. The therapist can point out that the positive view is no less real than the patient's unrealistically negative view.

9. *Guided association/discovery.* Through simple questions such as, "Then what?" "What would that mean?" "What would happen then?" the therapist can help the individual explore the significance they see in events. This collaborative, therapist-guided technique stands in opposition to the technique of free association, which is basic to the psychoanalytic process and involves the use of what we call chained or guided association. For example, the therapist

provides the conjunctions to the patients verbalizations. The use of statements like, "And then what?" "What evidence do we have that that is true?" allow the therapist to guide the patients along various therapeutic paths, depending on the conceptualization and therapeutic goals.

10. *Use of exaggeration or paradox.* By taking an idea to its extreme, the therapist can often help to move the family to a more central position vis-à-vis a particular belief. Care must be taken to not insult, ridicule, or embarrass the patient, given their hypersensitivity to criticism and ridicule. The therapist who chooses to use the paradoxical or exaggeration techniques must have: (1) a strong working relationship with the patient, (2) exquisite timing, (3) the good sense to know when to back away from the technique, and (4) an excellent sense of humor. Some patients may experience the therapist who uses paradoxical strategies as making light of their problems.

Exaggeration techniques are useful because there seems to be room at the extreme for only one patient. When the therapist takes a more extreme stance, i.e., focusing on the absolutes "never," "always," "no one," "everyone," the patient will often be forced to move from their extreme view to a position closer to center.

11. *Scaling.* For those patients who see things as all or nothing, the technique of scaling or seeing things as existing on a continuum can be very helpful. The scaling of a feeling can help patients utilize the strategy of gaining distance and perspective. For example, "On a scale of 0 to 10, how depressed were you last night?"

12. *Externalization of voices.* By having the therapist take the part of the internal voice, the patient can get practice in adaptive responding. The patient will verbalize the internal thoughts and the therapist can first model being adaptive to the patient's verbalizations. After modeling a more adaptive voice, the therapist can, via a graded manner, become an increasingly more difficult dysfunctional voice for the patients to respond to. The patient hears the dysfunctional voices in their head. When they externalize the voices, both patient and therapist are in better positions to deal with the voices/messages in a variety of ways. The therapist can hear the tone, content, and general context of the suicidal thoughts and generate strategies for intervention.

13. *Self-instruction.* We all give ourselves orders, directions, instructions, or information necessary to solve problems. According to Meichenbaum's model (1977), the child moves from overt verbalization of self-instructions to subvocalization to nonverbalization. This same process can be developed in the adult. The patient can start with direct verbalization which, with practice, will become part of the behavioral repertoire. In some cases, patients can be taught counter-instructions. In this technique, the therapist is not introducing anything new. Rather, the patients are being helped to utilize and strengthen a technique that we all use at various times.

14. *Thought stopping.* Dysfunctional thoughts often have a snowball effect for the individual. What may start as a small and insignificant problem can, if left to roll along, gather weight, speed, and momentum. Thought stopping is best used when the thought process is just beginning, not in the middle of the

process. The patient can picture a stop sign, "hear" a bell, picture a wall. A therapist hitting the desk sharply or ringing a small bell can serve to help the patient to stop the thoughts. The memory of that intervention has both a distractive and aversive quality.

15. *Distraction.* It is almost impossible to maintain two thoughts, at the same strength, simultaneously. Distraction or refocusing of attention may be achieved by focusing on some aspect of the environment, engaging in mental exercise or imagery, or initiating physical activity. It is helpful if the distraction activity can also serve to challenge the patient's catastrophizing. Although this is a short-term technique, it is very useful to allow patients the time to establish some degree of control over their thinking. This time can then be used to utilize other cognitive techniques. By having patients focus on complex counting, addition or subtraction, they are rather easily distracted from other thoughts. (One should take care that the patient is not math or number phobic, in which case the counting may work to increase anxiety.) For example, having the patient count to 200 by 13s is very effective, whereas counting by 2, 5, 10, or 11 is not as effective because these number sequences are overlearned.

16. *Direct disputation.* Although we do not advocate arguing with a patient, there are times when direct disputation is necessary. A major guideline for necessity is the imminence of a dangerous behavior, such as a suicide attempt. In this situation, the therapist must directly and quickly work to challenge the hopelessness. Although it might appear to be the treatment technique of choice, the therapist risks becoming embroiled in a power struggle or argument with the patient. Disputation coming from outside the patient may, in fact, engender passive resistance and a passive-aggressive response that might include suicide. Disputation, argument, or debate are potentially dangerous tools and must be used carefully, judiciously, and with skill.

BEHAVIORAL TECHNIQUES

The first goal is to utilize direct behavioral strategies and techniques, to help to gather data and test dysfunctional thoughts and behaviors. The second is to develop the patient's repertoire of responses. A major issue for many depressed patients is their limited response repertoire. The behavioral work can be used in the session, and it can be practiced as homework. This might include acting differently, practicing active listening, being verbally or physically affectionate, asserting oneself, or doing things in a new way.

1. *Activity scheduling.* The activity schedule is one of the most useful forms in the CT therapist's armamentarium. For patients who are feeling overwhelmed, the activity schedule can be used to first assess present time use, and then to plan more effective time use.

2. *Mastery and pleasure ratings.* The activity schedule can also be used to assess and plan activities that offer patients both a sense of personal efficacy (mastery, 1–10), and pleasure (1–10). The greater the mastery and pleasure, the lower the rate of depression.

3. *Social-skills training.* If reality testing is good, and patients actually lack specific skills, it is incumbent upon the therapist to either help them gain the

skills or to make a referral for skills training. The skill acquisition may involve anything from teaching patients how to properly shake hands to practicing conversational skills.

4. *Assertiveness training.* As with the social skills training, assertiveness training may be an essential part of the therapy. Patients who are socially anxious can be helped to develop responsible assertive skills (Jakubowski & Lange, 1978).

5. *Bibliotherapy.* Several excellent books can be assigned as readings for homework. These books can be used to socialize or educate patients to the basic CT model, emphasize specific points made in the session, or to introduce new ideas for discussion at future sessions.

6. *Graded task assignments (GTA).* GTAs involve a shaping procedure of small sequential steps that lead to the desired goal. By setting out a task and then arranging the necessary steps in a hierarchy, patients can be helped to make reasonable progress with a minimum of stress. As patients attempt each step, the therapist can be available for support and guidance.

7. *Behavioral rehearsal/role-playing.* The therapy session is the ideal place to practice many behaviors. The therapist can serve as teacher and guide, offering direct feedback on performance. The therapist can monitor the patient's performance, offer suggestions for improvement, and model new behaviors. In addition, anticipated and actual road blocks can be identified and worked on in the session. There can be extensive rehearsal before the patient attempts the behavior in vivo.

8. *Relaxation training.* The patient for whom anxiety is a concomitant of the depression can profit from relaxation training. The relaxation training can be progressive muscle relaxation or imagined relaxation. Both can be taught in the office and then practiced by the patient for homework. Ready-made relaxation tapes can be purchased or the therapist may easily tailor a tape for a patient. The therapist-made tape can include the patient's name and can focus on particular symptoms. The tape can be modified, as needed.

HOMEWORK

CT can be distinguished by its approach to transfer and generalization through the use of intersession homework. Systematic extension of the work of therapy to nontherapy hours results in faster, more comprehensive improvement (Burns & Auerbach, 1992; Meichenbaum, 1987; Neimeyer & Feixas, 1990). Skills, new cognitions, and new behaviors must be applied in vivo. Learning and changes relative to one situation must be actively generalized to similar situations. In this way, new learning becomes natural and automatic aspects of the patient's behavioral and cognitive repertoire.

Homework can be cognitive or behavioral. Most often, it is both. Homework early in therapy focuses on helping the patient to interrupt automatic routines, and to observe the connections between thought, behavior, and mood. Thus, early homework tasks may include observing automatic thoughts through the use of the DTR, activity scheduling, collecting evidence for and against the patient's attributions and expectancies, and mastery and pleasure ratings. In the middle of therapy, homework includes trying out new behaviors through graded task assignments; acting differently in order to gather information about alternative hypotheses; noticing, catching, interrupting and responding to negative thoughts and behaviors; and enacting a plan designed to lead to a specific goal.

Homework may be an unfortunate term to use in describing the things a patient does between sessions to extend the therapy into their life. It carries connotations that, for some, may sound authoritarian, suggesting that homework is assigned. In CT, homework should arise naturally, out of the content of the session, and it should relate both to the therapist's (and the patient's) conceptualization of the patient's depression and to the clinical model. That is, the task should be something known to be likely to facilitate desired changes.

Patients' adherence to recommendations that they act between sessions to further their therapy is affected by the way the homework is conceived, the follow-up that occurs, and the complexity of the tasks themselves. A number of suggestions to increase adherence have been given by Meichenbaum and Turk (1987).

1. *Homework should be collaboratively developed.* The therapist can lead the discussion in such a way that patients themselves develop ideas for the work that is needed. The therapist lays the groundwork by asking questions, reflecting on what is already known of the skills the patient has and what is missing, and then going public with a rationale or theories.

2. *Tasks should be simple.* For tasks that are beyond the patient's skill level, the smaller the task, and the greater the likelihood of success, the better. For a more skilled patient, more challenging tasks are better. Regardless, the task must be able to be performed with reasonable time and effort.

3. *Provide the patient with a choice.* If more than one method exists to monitor behaviors or thoughts, using the one the patient prefers increases the likelihood of follow-through. Choice, or the perception of choice, enhances a patient's sense of control and self-efficacy.

4. *Specify what will be done, when, and how.* Moderately specific plans result in better adherence than overly specific ones, because they offer the patient opportunity for creativity and allow a margin of error for nonadherence to an overly specific and rigid plan, particularly with longer-term goals. Moderately specific plans give the patient choices and engage them in decision making.

5. *Engage significant others in the task.* In reinforcing the patient for completing or engaging in the task, and in determining the task whenever possible.

6. *Directly, and in a stepwise fashion, teach monitoring skills.* Including recording, interpreting, and using the results.

7. *Specify contingencies that follow adherence or nonadherence.* Specify the results the patient can expect from the task or the purpose of the task.

8. *Go public with the rationale for the task.* Better yet, have the patient identify the rationale as part of collaboratively designing the task.

9. *Offer mild counter-arguments about completion of the task.* For example, anticipate difficulties, drawbacks, obstacles the patient is likely to face in attempting the task. Help the patient to plan cognitive and behavioral responses to obstacles, and to identify partial success or partial completion as useful.

10. *Provide the patient with feedback on adherence and on the accuracy of their performance of the task.* Defocus from the product, and focus on the attempt; effort and new information are more important than specific results.

11. *Record positive behaviors rather than negative ones.* Assign "do" tasks rather than "don't do" tasks. Particularly when the task involves interrupting an old routine, plan a substitute behavior or cognition. In the absence of a better plan, the patient will fall back on old behaviors and cognitions.

12. *Help the patient to internally attribute success and improvements that result from adherence.* Depressed patients tend to self-attribute blame, and they tend to see good events or results as being due to uncontrollable, external forces. Internal attribution of success enhances self-efficacy. Shelton and Levy (1981) suggested a homework assignment should specify what patients are to do, how often or how many times they should do it, how they are to record their efforts, what they are to bring to the next appointment (e.g., the record), and the consequences or contingencies attendant on either adherence or nonadherence.

THE COURSE OF THERAPY

A number of factors affect the treatment plan early in therapy. The severity of the depression, as assessed by the BDI, self-report, report of significant others or other measures, or patient request/demand, may indicate the need for medication. A number of studies suggest that more severely depressed patients respond better and more rapidly to cognitive therapy when combined with pharmacotherapy than to cognitive therapy alone (Bowers, 1990; Shea et al., 1992). In general, the more severely depressed the patient is, the greater the need for pharmacological assessment, and the more behavioral and concrete the initial interventions need to be.

In general, the initial interventions are aimed at helping the patient to interrupt automatic information processing, which contains the dysfunctional, habitual, and uncritically accepted negative thoughts and behaviors, and to increase deliberate information processing. The therapist teaches the patient to notice, catch, and interrupt automatic thoughts (Beck et al., 1979; Freeman et al., 1990). This is most often done through simple questioning and through some form of the Daily Record of Dysfunctional Thoughts, better known as the Daily Thought Record (DTR) (Figure 6.4). The use of the DTR is taught step by step, practiced in sessions, and can then be used as homework. The DTR helps to obtain examples of the patient's automatic thoughts in vivo to use for assessment, to encourage the patient's independent evaluation of their thinking, to increase the patient's self-efficacy and hope, to facilitate generalization and transfer of learning, and to decrease attendant anxiety through distraction.

The DTR is not implemented completely in the first session(s) in which it is introduced, but as the patient is able to understand and use the format, the DTR may be tailored to individual situations and personal characteristics. We routinely "discover" the format of the DTR collaboratively with the patient by using guided discovery, asking the patient what would be worth knowing and what information might be useful next. For example, we ask the patient to describe a situation. The therapist might simply write the situation on a notepad.

Date	Situation Briefly describe the situation	Emotion(s) Rate 0–100%	Automatic Thoughts Try to quote thoughts then rate your belief in each thought 0–100%	Rational Response Rate degree of belief 0–100%	Outcome Re-rate emotions

Figure 6.4 Daily Record of Automatic Thoughts.

The patient is then asked about the emotions that were attendant to the situations. They are then asked their level of emotion: "How depressed were you on a scale from 0 to 10?" This helps the patient to learn the important new skill of scaling and to recognize that the present situation will often fall somewhere on a continuum rather than at an extreme. Setting idiosyncratic anchor points can be easily done; for example: "Think of the time that you were more depressed than you have ever been before. Label that as 0. Now think of the time in your life when you were the least depressed. Let's label that as 10."

The patient is then asked about the automatic thoughts that were related to the situation and feelings. The thoughts are also rated in terms of the patient's level of belief in the thought(s). The final column invites the patient to restructure the thought. We can alter the column headings for specific problems or for children or adolescents. The basic goals and format (situation, thoughts, behaviors) are constant, however. The goal is not to have the patient become expert at filling out forms, but to have them develop a model for problem solving. The process can begin with the thought, the emotion, or the situation. If the patient presents an emotion (e.g., "I'm very sad"), the therapist needs to inquire about the situations that might engender the emotion and the attendant thoughts. If the patient presents with a thought (e.g., "I'm a loser"), the therapist needs to ascertain the feelings and the situation. Finally, the patient may present a situation (e.g., "My husband left me"). The therapist needs to determine the thoughts and the emotions. Statements such as, "I feel like a loser" need to be reframed as thoughts, and the emotions that are a concomitant of the thought elicited. The following examples demonstrate the use of the DTR.

Often, patients phrase their thoughts as questions (e.g., "Why does this always happen to me?" "Why can't I maintain a relationship?" or "Why doesn't my life turn out better?"). A heuristic view is that questions are generally functional. It is important to ask questions, and then to answer them (e.g., "Does this always happen to me?" "Why do I have difficulty in maintaining relationships?" or "What has caused my life to be less than I had hoped for?"). The dysfunctional thoughts are more generally declarative rather than interrogatory (e.g., "This always happens to me," "I can't maintain a relationship," and "My life is less than I had hoped for"). In the course of guided discovery, the patient may experience some strong emotion. This can signify that the patient has arrived at a perception of a core belief, usually relevant to their perception of self. This is an optimum moment for intervention: the affectively coded, state-dependent learning and the state are both activated. Alternative explanations, attributions, expectancies that are discovered or provided at this moment have maximum impact. Examining alternatives or generating options of thought, affect, and behavior involves considering the existence of other possible views or explanations of the situations to which the patient attends, and then exploring those views or explanations. Both Socratic questioning ("I wonder what other explanations you have considered?") and stochastic questioning ("Could another explanation be that . . .") are used in helping the patient to develop a list of alternatives. Listing alternatives breaks down the all-or-nothing thinking characteristic of depressed patients, initiates reattribution, and interrupts premature termination of data-search routines.

Demanding immediate or hasty abandonment of the patient's causal model or demanding immediate allegiance to an alternative explanation are likely to result in failure. The patient needs to explore and consider the social, emotional, personal, and behavioral consequences of altering their causal model (Berlin, Mann, & Grossman, 1991). Further, one cannot give up a dysfunctional hypothesis or schema until an equal or better working model is proposed and accepted.

Several cognitive techniques can be used to question a single set of conclusions. For example:

Situation: My girlfriend told me that she didn't want to see me anymore.

Emotion(s): Sad (98%), Angry (50%), Scared (70%)

Dysfunctional thought: "I cannot maintain a relationship"

Sample adaptive responses:

What do you mean by "a relationship"? (idiosyncratic meaning)

What evidence are you using that you cannot maintain a relationship? (evidence)

Has it always been you who has caused relationships to end? (Reattribution)

Have you never maintained a relationship for *any* length of time? (exaggeration)

On a scale from 1 to 10, where would you place the quality of the relationship? (scaling)

The utilization of the techniques are limited only by the creativity of the therapist.

Other early interventions are similarly aimed at assessment and hypothesis formation, encouraging movement, distraction, and interrupting automatic processing. For example, more severely depressed patients are asked to complete an activity schedule. The patient keeps track of their activities over the course of a week, several days, or, for the severely depressed patient, one day. Their perception that, "I just can't seem to get anything done," is an example of low self-efficacy, negative expectations, minimizing the positive and maximizing the negative. Activity scheduling counters these by allowing the patient and therapist to examine what the patient has in fact done over the course of several days. Further, the activity schedule identifies the frequency of reinforcing or rewarding activities.

The activity schedule is also used to schedule tasks, to increase self-efficacy and counter hopelessness, to break down large tasks into small steps, and to counter all-or-nothing behavior and thought patterns. Pleasant activities can be scheduled to increase reinforcement. Depressed individuals have difficulty identifying alternatives. Their recall is mood-congruent (Bradley & Mathews, 1988; Pace & Dixon, 1993). They often have difficulty identifying pleasant activities they have engaged in. It becomes important for the therapist to assess the patient's potential for pleasure and range of activities, and to cue the patient's recall or creation of pleasant alternatives that can be used as self-reinforcers.

The activity schedule can later include pleasure and mastery ratings. Although this is often listed as a behavioral technique, the purpose of such ratings from the cognitive therapy perspective is to affect expectancies. Patients are asked to make predictions about their abilities to cope with and enjoy anticipated activities or events. This assesses patients' negative expectancies. Depressed patients typically overestimate the difficulty of the task and underestimate both their ability to cope and the potential for pleasure.

After the scheduled event takes place, the patient is asked to rerate their mastery of and pleasure in the task or event. The difference between expectancy and experience demonstrates the effect of cognition on behavior and mood. The activity being rated is often one that the patient would have withdrawn from or avoided, due to negative predictions. Because, most often, the patient's mastery and pleasure is greater than anticipated, the patient is encouraged that feelings are not reality, and the decision to act in a certain way is removed one step from affectively based automatic processing.

Changes in affect within the session are cues to probe for "hot cognitions" by asking, "What are you thinking right now?" The patterns in content, stimulus, and behavioral or emotional consequence are identified.

Another intervention that is useful early in therapy is helping the patient to label the content, frequency, and pattern of their cognitive distortions. The purpose of labeling distortions is not to diagnose the patient or their thinking, but to point out patterns or bias in the patient's information seeking and interpretation, to interrupt automatic processing, and to give the patient a tool for thinking about their thinking so that information processing becomes deliberate.

The first phase of therapy brings to light the patient's explanatory model (schema, core beliefs, attributional style), the biases in their information search-and-sort habits, and the ways in which cognition, behavior, life events and mood are related for the patient. Although a complicated stage, it is usually accomplished in relatively short order. Making the patient's heuristic process apparent is itself a therapeutic experience, and results in symptom relief and change. In fact, the biggest drop in self-reported symptoms of depression is routinely identified as occurring in the first four weeks of cognitive therapy (Berlin et al., 1991).

In the middle phase of CT the focus is to generate, test, and practice alternative behaviors, attributions, expectancies, and hypotheses. That is, the goal is to modify maladaptive automatic thoughts and behavior patterns, and their underlying schema. This requires that patients become consciously aware, on an ongoing basis, of their information-processing and meaning-making activities (Hollon & Garber, 1988, 1990). Creating this level of awareness is akin to asking patients to alter the way they walk, to create a new way of carrying themselves physically. It is, at best, awkward and usually uncomfortable. Self-reported symptoms of depression in the middle phase may fluctuate (Berlin et al., 1991).

We often use metaphor to explain and predict this experience for patients. When individuals first learn to drive, they engage in frequent and overt self-instruction. As driving is overlearned, overt self-talk fades and becomes intermittent. Ultimately, driving is an automatic process that requires little thought or conscious decision-making. However, if the car acts up, if there is an accident, or if the weather turns foul, self-examination and self-talk reappears. Altering automatic thoughts and schema requires overt self-instruction and metacognition. Predicting this experience and the discomfort that accompanies it is a paradoxical technique aimed at normalizing the experience for the patient, and at alleviating secondary distress. In this middle phase of therapy the therapist helps the patient to generate, test, and practice alternative behaviors, attributions, expectancies, and hypotheses. Maladaptive automatic thoughts and behavior patterns, and their underlying schema, can be modified. Ideally, patients are consciously aware, on an ongoing basis, of their information-processing and meaning-making activities. New patterns of thought and behavior have been practiced in vivo, in a variety of situations, and are becoming automatic.

Ending Phase of Therapy

The last phase of therapy is devoted to further generalization and transfer of learning, self-attribution for gains made, and relapse prevention. Because the goal of CT is not cure, but more effective coping, the therapy is seen as time-limited. When formal assessments such as the BDI, the patient's reported symptoms, observations of significant others, and the therapist's observation confirm decreased depression, greater activity, higher levels of adaptive functioning, and increased skills, the therapy can move toward termination.

Termination and Relapse Prevention

Termination in CT begins in the first session. Because the goal of CT is not cure, but more effective coping, the cognitive therapist does not plan for therapy ad infinitum. The therapist's goal is to assist patients in acquiring the skills to deal with the internal and external stressors. When the depression inventory, patient report, therapist observation, and the feedback from significant others confirm more adaptive function, decreased depression, or greater activity the therapy can move toward termination. The termination is accomplished gradually to allow time for ongoing modifications and corrections. Sessions can be tapered off from once weekly to biweekly. From that point, sessions can be set on a monthly basis, with follow-up sessions at 3 and 6 months, until therapy is ended. Patients can still call and set an appointment in the event of an emergency. Sometimes, patients will call simply to get some information, a reinforcement of a particular behavior, or to report a success. With the cognitive therapist in the role of a consultant/collaborator, this continued contact is appropriate and important.

Relapse

It appears that even those patients who relapse within the current episode of depression continue for some time following termination to attempt to apply the skills and methods learned in the therapy. Thus, even those that eventually relapse take longer to do so than for other therapies or for pharmacotherapy. Correlates of relapse include a history of prior depressive episodes, greater severity of symptoms at intake, slower response to therapy, unmarried status, and higher BDI and DAS scores at termination (Beach, 1990, 1992; Clark et al., 1992; Evans et al., 1985; Rush & Eaves, 1986; Simians, Murphy, & Leaven, 1986; Theresa et al., 1991; Theresa & Simians, 1992).

Relapse prevention strategies address a number of key factors. Goals of therapy and initial symptoms are reviewed. Progress is measured both against initial symptoms and against goals. It is important for the patient to identify how far they have come, and to develop a scale against which to measure current concerns and moods.

The patient is asked to account for changes made: What changed? How did that come about? What did the patient do to affect this change? The purpose is to self-attribute the successes experienced. Further, the patient is asked to identify new learning, attitudes, and skills, and to contrast these with old ones. We often have patients list the things that they will take away from the therapy, and we ask them to plan where to keep this list for easy referral and reminder. The patient is asked to anticipate stressors. The therapist ensures that the list developed includes events similar to those that brought the patient into therapy, events similar to those assumed to be the origin of the underlying depressogenic schema and anticipated life events, such as developmental transitions the patient or their family will encounter. The patient is asked to imagine as vividly as possible that these events are occurring or have occurred, and to identify the skills, reattributions, and new patterns of behavior or cognition that can be called to bear on the stressor. This behavioral and imagined rehearsal is conducted in as specific detail as possible, with an emphasis on coping thoughts and behaviors, self-attribution of efforts and success, and referral to the use of new resources. Both resourcefulness and utilization of therapy as a resource are promoted.

Finally, the meaning of the therapy to the patient and to their life, and the meaning of the relationship with the therapist, is addressed. The goal is to integrate the experience of therapy into the personal narrative of the patient so that it is seen as part of, rather than apart from, their life.

SUMMARY

Beck's cognitive therapy was developed specifically in response to depression. The role of cognitions in depression is often misinterpreted to be one of simple linear causality: Negative cognitions cause depression. If this were true, the implications for treatment would be further simple linear reasoning: Positive thinking cures depression. Another misunderstanding of the CT model is that the cognitive perspective implicates internal processes in depression to the exclusion of contextual events. The implication would be that a patient could be depression-resistant regardless of events in the patient's life. The cognitive perspective is a diathesis-stress model where life events, thoughts, behaviors, and moods are inextricably tied to each other in a reciprocal manner. Cognitions, behaviors, and moods all serve feed-forward and feed-back functions in a complex process of information processing, behavioral regulation, and motivation. Further, the cognitive perspective implicates early life events and learning in the creation of patterns of information processing.

Cognitive therapists are active, directive, and psychoeducational in nature. The collaborative approach increases the patient's sense of efficacy, and it counters negative attributions about self, world, and future. The primary targets of cognitive therapy for depression are both the negative automatic thoughts that maintain the depression and the schema (assumptions and beliefs) that predispose the patient to depression in the first place. Although cognition is a major focus of therapy, cognitive therapists also utilize a broad range of behavioral approaches, to meet affective, cognitive, and behavioral ends.

CT has matured significantly over the last two decades. From a peripheral model seen largely as mechanistic and technique focused, it has become a central and mainstream model of treatment. From its first focus on depression, it has become a general model of psychotherapy that has been demonstrated to be effective across the broad range of emotional disorders. The cross-cultural interest in cognitive therapy is an expression of the nature of the model as process oriented as opposed to models that are content oriented and may not fit diverse cultures. Finally, CT has become an expression of the therapy *zeitgeist* and serves as a meeting place for therapists from a range of theoretical positions.

REFERENCES

Beck, A.T. (1967). *Depression: Causes and treatment.* Philadelphia: University of Pennsylvania Press.

Beck, A.T. (1976). *Cognitive therapy and the emotional disorders.* New York: International Universities Press.

Beck, A.T. (1996a). *Beck anxiety inventory.* San Antonio: The Psychological Corporation.

Beck, A.T. (1996b). *Beck depression inventory.* San Antonio: The Psychological Corporation.

Beck, A.T. (1996c). *Beck hopelessness scale.* San Antonio: The Psychological Corporation.

Beck, A.T., Freeman, A., & Associates. (1990). *Cognitive therapy of personality disorders.* New York: Guilford Press.

Beck, A.T., Rush, A.J., Shaw, B.F., & Emery, G. (1979). *Cognitive therapy of depression.* New York: Guilford Press.

Berlin, S.B., Mann, K.B., & Grossman, S.F. (1991). Task analysis of cognitive therapy for depression. Annual conference of the society for psychotherapy research. *Social Work Research and Abstracts, 27*(2), 3–11.

Blackburn, I., Bishop, S., Glen, A.I.M., Walley, L.J., & Christie, J.E. (1981). The efficacy of cognitive therapy in depression: A treatment using cognitive therapy and pharmacotherapy, each alone and in combination. *British Journal of Psychiatry, 139,* 181–189.

Blackburn, I.M., Eunson, K.M., & Bishop, S. (1986). A two year naturalistic follow-up of depressed patients treated with cognitive therapy, pharmacotherapy and a combination of both. *Journal of Affective Disorders, 10,* 67–75.

Bowers, W. (1989). Cognitive therapy with inpatients. In A. Freeman, K.M. Simon, L. Beutler, & H. Arkowitz (Eds.), *Comprehensive handbook of cognitive therapy.* New York: Plenum Press.

Bradley, B.P., & Mathews, A. (1988). Memory bias in recovered clinical depressives: Information processing and the emotional disorders [Special issue]. *Cognition and Emotion, 2*(3), 235–245.

Craighead, W.E., Craighead, L.W., & Ilardi, S.S. (1998). Psychosocial treatments for depressive disorder. In P.E. Nathan & J.M. Gorman (Eds.), *A guide to treatments that work.* New York: Oxford University Press.

Dent, J., & Teasdale, J.D. (1988). Negative cognition and the persistence of depression. *Journal of Abnormal Psychology, 97*(1), 29–34.

DeRubeis, R.J., Evans, M.D., Hollon, S.D., Gaarvey, M.J., Grove, W.M., & Tuason, V.B. (1990). Cognitive change and symptom change in cognitive therapy and pharmacotherapy for depression. *Journal of Consulting and Clinical Psychology, 58,* 862–869.

Dobson, K. (1989). A meta-analysis of the efficacy of cognitive therapy for depression. *Journal of Consulting and Clinical Psychology, 57,* 414–419.

Dobson, K.S., & Shaw, B.F. (1987). Specificity and stability of self-referent encoding in clinical depression. *Journal of Abnormal Psychology, 98,* 34–40.

Ellis, A. (1962). *Reason and emotion in psychotherapy.* New York: Lyle Stuart.

Ellis, A. (1973). *Humanistic psychotherapy: The rational-emotive approach.* New York: Julian Press.

Ellis, A. (1977). The basic clinical theory of rational-emotive therapy. In A. Ellis & R. Grieger (Eds.), *Comprehensive handbook of rational-emotive therapy.* New York: Springer.

Ellis, A., & Harper, R. (1961). *New guide to rational living.* New York: Crown.

Evans, M.D., Hollon, S.D., DeRubeis, R.J., Piasech, J.M., Grove, W.M., Garvey, M.J., & Tuason, V.B. (1992). Differential relapse following cognitive therapy and pharmacotherapy for depression. *Archives of General Psychiatry, 49,* 802–808.

Frank, J. (1985). Therapeutic components shared by all psychotherapies. In M. Mahoney & A. Freeman (Eds.), *Cognition and psychotherapy* (pp. 49–80). New York: Plenum Press.

Freeman, A. (1988). *The diagnostic profile system.* Unpublished manuscript.

Freeman, A., & DeWolf, R. (1989). *Woulda, coulda, shoulda.* New York: Morrow.

Freeman, A., & DeWolf, R. (1991). *The 10 dumbest mistakes smart people make.* New York: HarperCollins.

Freeman, A., & Leaf, R. (1989). Cognitive therapy of personality disorders. In A. Freeman, K.M. Simon, L. Beutler, & H. Arkowitz (Eds.), *Comprehensive handbook of cognitive therapy.* New York: Plenum.

Freeman, A., & Reinecke, M. (1994). *Cognitive therapy of suicidal behavior.* New York: Springer.

Freeman, A., Simon, K.M., Pretzer, J., & Fleming, B. (1990). *Clinical applications of cognitive therapy.* New York: Plenum Press.

Freeman, A., & Zaken-Greenburg, F. (1989). Cognitive family therapy. In C. Figley (Ed.), *Psychological stress.* New York: Brunner/Mazel.

Haaga, D.A.F., Dyck, M.J., & Ernst, D. (1991). Empirical status of cognitive theory of depression. *Psychological Bulletin, 110,* 215–236.

Hollon, S.D., & Garber, J. (1990). Cognitive therapy of depression: A social cognitive perspective. *Personality and Social Psychology Bulletin, 16,* 58–73.

Hollon, S.D., & Kendall, P.C. (1980). Cognitive self-statements in depression: Development of an automatic thoughts questionnaire. *Cognitive Therapy and Research, 3,* 383–396.

Hollon, S.D., & Najavits, L. (1988). Review of empirical studies of cognitive therapy. In A.J. Frances & R.E. Hales (Eds.), *American Psychiatric Press review of psychiatry* (Vol. 7, pp. 643–666). Washington, DC: American Psychiatric Press.

Hollon, S.D., Shelton, R.C., & Davis, D.D. (1993). Cognitive therapy for depression: Conceptual issues and clinical efficacy. *Journal of Consulting and Clinical Psychology, 61,* 270–275.

Jakubowski, P., & Lange, A.J. (1978). *The assertive option.* Champaign, IL: Research Press.

Kavanagh, D.J., & Wilson, P.H. (1989). Prediction of outcome with group cognitive therapy for depression. *Behaviour Research and Therapy, 27*(4), 333–343.

Kwon, S.-M., & Oei, T.P.S. (1994). The roles of two levels of cognitions in the development, maintenance, and treatment of depression. *Clinical Psychology Review, 14*(5), 331–358.

Lazarus, A. (Ed.). (1976). *Multimodal behavior therapy.* New York: Springer.

Lazarus, A. (1981). *The practice of multimodal therapy.* New York: McGraw-Hill.

McGoldrick, M., Pearce, J.K., & Giordano, J. (Eds.). (1982). *Ethnicity and family therapy.* New York: Guilford Press.

McMullin, R. (1987). *Handbook of cognitive therapy techniques.* New York: Norton.

Meichenbaum, D. (1977). *Cognitive behavior modification.* New York: Plenum Press.

Meichenbaum, D. (1994). *A clinical handbook/practical therapist manual for assessing and treating adults with post traumatic stress disorder (PTSD).* Waterloo, ON, Canada: Institute Press.

Miranda, J., & Persons, J.B. (1991). *Implications of the mood-state hypothesis for studies of the process of cognitive therapy.* Paper presented at the annual meeting of the American Psychological Association, San Francisco.

Miranda, J., Persons, J.B., & Byers, C.N. (1990). Endorsement of dysfunctional beliefs depends on current mood state. *Journal of Abnormal Psychology, 99,* 237–241.

Murphy, G.E., Simons, A.D., Wetzel, R.D., & Lustman, P.J. (1984). Cognitive therapy versus tricyclic antidepressants in major depression. *Archives of General Psychiatry, 41*, 33–41.

Neimeyer, R.A., & Feixas, G. (1990). The role of homework and skill acquisition in the outcome of group cognitive therapy for depression. *Behavior Therapy, 21*(3), 281–292.

Pace, T.M., & Dixon, D.N. (1993). Changes in depressive self-schemata and depressive symptoms following cognitive therapy. *Journal of Counseling Psychology, 40*(3), 288–294.

Riskind, J.H., Rholes, W.S., & Eggers, J. (1982). The Velton mood induction procedure: Effects on mood and memory. *Journal of Consulting and Clinical Psychology, 50*, 3–13.

Robinson, L.A., Berman, J.S., & Neimeyer, R.A. (1990). Psychotherapy for the treatment of depression: A comprehensive review of controlled outcome research. *Psychological Bulletin, 108*, 30–49.

Rosen, H. (1985). *Piagetian concepts of clinical relevance.* New York: Columbia University Press.

Rosen, H. (1989). Piagetian theory and cognitive therapy. In A. Freeman, K.M. Simon, L. Beutler, & H. Arkowitz (Eds.), *Comprehensive handbook of cognitive therapy.* New York: Plenum Press.

Rude, S.S., & Rehm, L.P. (1991). Response to treatment for depression: The role of initial status on targeted cognitive and behavioral skills. *Clinical Psychology Review, 11*(5), 493–514.

Rush, A.J., Beck. A.T., Kovacs, M., & Hollon, S. (1977). Comparative efficacy of cognitive therapy and imipramine in the treatment of depressed outpatients. *Cognitive Therapy and Research, 1*, 17–37.

Salkovskis, P.M., Atha, C., & Storer, D. (1990). Cognitive behavioural problem solving in the treatment of patients who repeatedly attempt suicide: A controlled trial. *British Journal of Psychiatry, 157*, 871–876.

Schotte, C., Maes, M., Beuten, T., Vandenbossche, G., & Cosyns, R. (1993). A videotape as introduction for cognitive behavioral therapy with depressed inpatients. *Psychological Reports, 72*(2), 440–442.

Shea, M.T., Elkin, I., Imber, S.D., & Sotsky, S.M., et al. (1992). Course of depressive symptoms over follow-up: Findings from the National Institute of Mental Health treatment of depression collaborative research program. *Archives of General Psychiatry, 49*(10), 782–787.

Stiles, T.C., & Gotestam, K.G. (1989). The role of automatic thoughts in the development of dysphoric mood: An analogue experiment. *Cognitive Therapy and Research, 13*(2), 161–170.

Stravynski, A., & Greenberg, D. (1992). The psychological management of depression. *Acta Psychiatrica Scandinavica, 85*(6), 407–414.

Thase, M.E., Bowler, K., & Harden, T. (1991). Cognitive behavior therapy of endogenous depression: II. Preliminary findings in 16 unmedicated patients. *Behavior Therapy, 22*, 469–477.

Wetzel, R.D. (1976). Hopelessness, depression, and suicidal intent. *Archives of General Psychiatry, 33*, 1069–1073.

Wetzel, R.D., & Reich, T. (1989). The cognitive triad and suicidal intent in depressed men inpatients. *Psychological Reports, 65*, 1027–1032.

CHAPTER 7

Interpersonal Psychotherapy

HOLLY A. SWARTZ

CONCEPTUALIZATION

Interpersonal Psychotherapy (IPT) is a time-limited, focused psychotherapy developed by Klerman and Weissman for the treatment of depression (Klerman, Weissman, Rounsaville, & Chevron, 1984). Unlike many other psychotherapies, IPT was designed to treat a specific disorder (depression) and has been systematically evaluated in research trials. A practical, user-friendly approach to treating depression, IPT has withstood the rigors of outcome studies and is now entering the armamentarium of discerning clinicians.

THEORETICAL ROOTS

In the 1970s Klerman and Weissman described a psychotherapy that derived from extant theoretical models and psychosocial data. Bowlby's theories of attachment (Bowlby, 1977), Sullivan's interpersonal focus (Sullivan, 1953), and Meyer's emphasis on social relations (Meyer, 1957) provided important theoretical roots for this new treatment. Data from Brown and Harris (1978) provided evidence that confiding interpersonal relationships were protective against depression, and Parker (1978) contributed an appreciation for the role of multiple intimate interpersonal relationships in the prevention of complicated bereavement. The epidemiologic research of Weissman, Klerman, Paykel, Prusoff, and Hanson (1974) and Henderson, Byrne, Duncan-Jones, Scott, and Adcock (1980), respectively, demonstrating higher rates of marital discord among depressed women and more impaired social relationships among a population at risk for developing neuroses, provided substantiating data for an "interpersonal stressor" model of depression. Conversely, data from Coyne (1976) and others underscored the importance of the erosive

Support provided by the Reader's Digest Fund and New York Community Trust. The author wishes to thank John C. Markowitz, M.D. for reviewing a draft of this chapter.

139

effects of depression in an interpersonal context, as impairments in mood, communication, and activity rupture the social bond.

IPT thus developed from both a theoretical belief in and factual demonstration of the reciprocal interactions between mood and life events. Although its empirical validity is important from a scientific standpoint, its intuitive plausibility contributes to IPT's clinical success. Both clinicians and patients easily accept the idea that current relationships and life events affect/influence mood. In fact, many depressed patients present with an identified interpersonal precipitant that they believe contributed to the onset of their mood disorder.

A Treatment for Depression

Many psychotherapies do not target specific disorders and have not been tested in randomized clinical trials (Swartz & Markowitz, 1997). Detractors of psychotherapy have questioned their theoretical value, and insurance companies have ceased to reimburse for many of these treatments. By contrast, Klerman and Weissman recognized the importance of demonstrating efficacy for any treatment, be it pharmacological or psychological. They developed IPT as a focused psychotherapy for depression that could be tested in head-to-head comparisons with antidepressant medication (DiMascio et al., 1979). Given a homogeneous sample (e.g., depressed patients) and a homogeneous treatment (IPT), researchers identified and measured specific outcome variables (e.g., depressive symptoms). The efficacy of IPT was established rapidly whereas open-ended, nonhomogeneous psychodynamic treatments, despite a century of experience, remain essentially untested.

A disorder-specific psychotherapy such as IPT offers clear advantages to the patient: an illness is diagnosed and treated. Long standing neurotic issues may remain unaddressed, but symptom remission invariably provides tremendous relief. In the wake of its success with depression, IPT has been modified and retested for use with other disorders and depressive subtypes (Weissman & Markowitz, 1994). In its original incarnation, however, IPT is structured for the acute treatment of moderate to severe, outpatient, nondelusional major depressive disorder.

A Time-Limited Treatment

In the 1970s time-limited treatments became more common, as social factors (e.g., deinstitutionalization of psychiatric patients, fiscal concerns) placed more demands on limited outpatient resources (Swartz & Markowitz, 1997). IPT was thus developed at a time when the exigencies of health care favored the development of briefer, "testable" therapies. IPT's circumscribed duration (12 to 16 weeks) meets the clinical needs of an acutely depressed patient population and the methodological demands of research design (as already mentioned, it can be evaluated in head-to-head trials with medications).

Time limitation is an important motivational ingredient in IPT. Because the therapist defines treatment duration at the outset, patient and therapist are aware of the proverbial ticking clock, spurring the therapist to greater activity and the patient to rapid change. In their experience with depressed, HIV-positive patients, Markowitz, Klerman, and Perry (1992) noted that the additive effects of a life-shortening illness and a time-limited therapy sped their patients to major life changes and the enactment of treasured, previously deferred, wishes. Because motivation ebbs in depression, brevity is an important, antiregressive attribute of IPT that facilitates a more rapid return to health. IPT has been described as a therapy of change and the time limit is a crucial element in this process (Swartz & Markowitz, 1998).

IPT shares with other time-limited therapies several important, but nonspecific, characteristics. Like all time-limited therapies, IPT is designed to have a coherent beginning, middle, and end. This distinguishes time-limited treatments from arbitrarily brief open-ended therapies that are inadvertently truncated by attrition or other external forces. All time-limited therapies require a treatment focus. In IPT this translates into selective attention to depressive symptoms and a carefully chosen interpersonal-problem area. The patient's specific interpersonal-problem area forms the backbone of an IPT treatment (see "Treatment Strategies"). IPT does not address chronic issues such as character pathology, distant familial conflict, or other psychiatric disorders. Both the patient and the therapist must agree to this treatment focus and must actively disregard extraneous issues. It is reassuring to both therapists and patients that once the depression is treated, many patients are better equipped to manage stressors, even if they are not explicitly addressed in the treatment. Also, so-called character pathology may seem to resolve as the depression abates, reinforcing the axiom that trait diagnoses are impossible to make in the setting of an active Axis I disorder (Hirschfield et al., 1983).

The IPT therapist, like most time-limited therapy practitioners, takes an active role in the treatment. Unlike the neutral psychoanalyst who avoids overt structuring of sessions to permit the evolution of an uncontaminated transference, the IPT therapist works intensively to maintain the treatment focus and intervenes when necessary with practical suggestions, role play, and psychoeducation. The therapist maintains a warm, encouraging stance that counters the depressed patient's pessimism with an equal and opposite optimistic realism. In psychodynamic terms, the IPT therapist cultivates a positive transference. He or she handles negative transference as treatment-interfering behaviors: For instance, tardiness or lack of participation would be defined as sequelae of depression. The therapist might intervene by saying, "It's hard to feel enthusiastic about therapy when your depression makes it hard to enjoy anything." In addition, the therapist might address it on a practical level, saying, "We only have five sessions left; if you arrive late, we might not have enough time to get to the bottom of your problem with your wife."

HERE-AND-NOW TREATMENT

Psychodynamic theory, the predominant psychotherapy paradigm during the past century, concentrates on early life events such as childhood conflicts and parental relationships. Given the ubiquity of psychoanalytic doctrine, there may be a tacit assumption that psychotherapy should be about the past. On the contrary, IPT is a here-and-now treatment focusing on current symptoms, recent relationships, and recent life events. Although the IPT therapist may elicit a history of past relationships to identify a pattern of behavior perpetuating current interpersonal problems, the sessions themselves focus on the past week's activities. If the patient strays into the past, the therapist gently returns the focus to the present.

Here and now does *not* refer to the relationship between the patient and therapist (i.e., transference). Instead, patients are encouraged to talk about recent conversations, interactions, and dilemmas with real people in their lives. The therapist actively engages patients in an examination of their reactions to these current relationships/events and helps patients to enact change when appropriate.

MEDICAL MODEL

IPT conceptualizes the patient's "problem" as an illness. Using standardized instruments such as *DSM-IV* criteria (American Psychiatric Association, 1994) and the Hamilton Rating Scale for Depression (Ham-D) (Hamilton, 1960), the IPT therapist diagnoses a depression. Patients learn that their lack of energy, poor sleep, feelings of helplessness, etc. are symptoms of a mood disorder. This approach, in addition to reflecting a thorough psychiatric evaluation and accurate diagnosis, relieves patients of any guilt associated with this syndrome. Rather than reinforcing the depressed patients' tendency to blame themselves, IPT stresses the biologic (rather than a moral) etiology of depression.

The medical model is incorporated throughout the IPT treatment. During the initial phase of treatment (sessions 1 to 3), the therapist gives the patient the "sick role" (Parsons, 1951). This maneuver encourages the patient to actively participate in treatment (the patient's job), identifies the symptoms as a manifestation of the disorder (rather than a weakness), and relieves the patient of unmanageable social obligations. Early sessions incorporate significant psychoeducation, helping the patient to become an "expert" on depression. IPT equates depression with medical illnesses, such as pneumonia or broken bones. The therapist makes direct statements about genetics, neurotransmitters, treatability, and so on. Although not necessary to IPT's success, antidepressant medications are easily combined with IPT, because both approaches appreciate the physiologic, medical aspects of depression.

During the course of treatment, therapists generally administer serial Ham-Ds, helping the patient to see (presumably) diminishing scores as treatment progresses. In addition to helping patients recognize the symptoms of depression, the repeated administration of a standardized symptom inventory legitimizes the disorder for the patient. The end of treatment includes further psychoeducation about the risk of recurrence or relapse and strategies for managing potential recurrences or relapses (including seeking an evaluation for further treatment).

A RESEARCH TOOL

It is important to remember that IPT was developed as a research tool. Its very structure reflects those roots. For instance, the duration of treatment was determined by the requirements of a medication trial: 12 to 16 weeks permits a direct comparison with a typical medication cell. One of the first systematic IPT studies compared IPT, amitriptyline, IPT-plus-amitriptyline, and non-scheduled psychotherapy for the treatment of acute depression (DiMascio et al., 1979). In addition to establishing its efficacy as an acute treatment, researchers have investigated the role of IPT (generally administered at less frequent intervals) as continuation and maintenance therapy (Frank et al., 1990; Reynolds et al., 1992).

The manual (Klerman et al., 1984) was developed to allow different therapists to reliably deliver the same standardized treatment in research trials, and the incorporation of serial Ham-D's reflects the importance of serial measures in the evaluation of outcome. IPT's practitioners primarily have been therapists connected with academic centers who participate in psychotherapy research trials. Clinicians have only recently had the opportunity to learn the technique from the research community. Given its demonstrated efficacy, ease of use, and, increasing popularity in nonresearch settings, IPT is enjoying expanding clinical appeal.

IPT AND OTHER PSYCHOTHERAPEUTIC APPROACHES

In IPT, Klerman and Weissman attempted to synthesize and systematize the techniques that many therapists were already using to treat depressed patients. Rather than inventing an entirely new technique, Klerman and Weissman borrowed from other psychotherapies to create a coherent approach to depression:

> In developing IPT, our goal was not to create a new psychotherapy but to make explicit and operational a systematic approach to depression based on theory and empirical evidence. The fact that much of IPT is part of what many, perhaps most, psychotherapists do in brief treatment is a reflection of the extent to which the interpersonal approach has permeated the mental health field and psychotherapeutic practice in the United States (Klerman et al., 1984, p. 17).

The IPT trainee might detect elements of supportive therapy, psychodynamic psychotherapy, and cognitive therapy in IPT. Like cognitive therapy (CT), IPT is structured and symptom focused; unlike CT, IPT requires the affective involvement of the patient with a focus on feelings rather than thoughts. Like psychodynamic therapy, IPT is an affectively charged therapy, with an appreciation for the centrality of human relationships; unlike psychodynamic therapy, IPT is a pragmatic treatment that relies on practical strategies to affect change in interpersonal problems rather than complex theories about drives, unconscious conflicts, and defenses (Markowitz, Svartberg, & Swartz, 1998). Like supportive therapy, IPT uses strategies like communication analysis and social skills retraining to help the patient improve coping and social skills; unlike supportive therapy, IPT offers an explanation for the patient's problems and a focused strategy to resolve them.

In IPT training sessions, therapists trained in other modalities invariably comment that parts of IPT resemble other approaches. The model is admittedly eclectic. IPT's user-friendly quality in part stems from therapists' easy acclimation to IPT. Although the overall philosophy is new to the clinician, IPT draws upon extant skills. It is fresh but familiar; innovative but intelligible. Therapists schooled in other psychotherapies easily learn and implement IPT strategies. In summary, IPT is novel in its whole rather than its parts.

DIAGNOSTIC ISSUES AND PROBLEMS

As described above, IPT uses a medical model to understand depression. IPT is a treatment for Major Depressive Disorder that relies heavily on *DSM-IV* criteria both for diagnosis and treatment. During the initial phase of IPT, the clinician conducts a thorough psychiatric interview, clearly establishing the diagnosis of a depressive episode. Symptoms are reviewed in great detail, and the patient's illness is labeled. Rather than posing a problem, *DSM-IV* is the IPT's therapist's ally. Symptoms are signposts of the disorder for the patient, and the therapist uses them to link mood to life events. As symptoms wane, the patient and therapist point to these markers as evidence of improvement. Resolution of symptoms is an important outcome measure in trials evaluating the efficacy of IPT.

Unlike most psychotherapies, IPT treats specific psychiatric disorders. Flying in the face of psychodynamic tradition, IPT organizes its case formulation around the diagnosis of a disorder, which is stated explicitly to the patient (Markowitz & Swartz, 1997). The IPT therapist literally says, "You have an illness called depression." Thus, subsyndromal or "neurotic problems" are inappropriate for a pure IPT approach. On the other hand, it is probably reasonable (although it has not been formally evaluated) to incorporate IPT techniques into an eclectic treatment for a patient with, among other complaints, depressive symptoms.

After researchers demonstrated its efficacy for the treatment of depression, IPT was adapted for use with a variety of disorders (Klerman & Weissman, 1993), but in each incarnation, IPT remained a diagnosis-driven treatment. For instance, when treating chronic depression, IPT therapists formally diagnose Dysthymic Disorder, helping patients to see their problems as symptoms of a disorder rather than a character flaw (Markowitz, 1997). When treating depressed, HIV-positive patients, the therapist diagnoses two disorders, major depression and HIV (Swartz & Markowitz, 1998). When treating bulimia, the therapist diagnoses an eating disorder (Fairburn, Jones, Peveler, Hope, & O'Connor, 1993). Diagnosis remains an organizing feature of IPT.

TREATMENT STRATEGIES

IPT is divided into three parts: initial sessions, intermediate sessions, and termination. Each phase of treatment has separate goals and strategies, unified by an overarching focus on the relationship between mood and life events. In the section that follows, I will describe treatment strategies associated with each phase, illustrated by case vignettes. All clinical data have been altered to protect patients' identities and confidentiality. Interested readers are referred to Klerman et al.'s manual (1984) for a fuller description of these techniques.

Initial Sessions

The first few (one to three) sessions of IPT are devoted to a thorough *psychiatric evaluation*, a review of important relationships (the *interpersonal inventory*), and a determination of the *interpersonal problem area*. The patient is diagnosed with a depression and offered an *interpersonal formulation* that links the depression to the problem area. The initial phase of treatment ends when the patient accepts the formulation and agrees to the treatment focus (i.e., the depression and interpersonal problem area) and the practical aspects of treatment (e.g., fees, exact treatment duration, frequency of sessions, etc.).

The IPT therapist conducts the kind of thorough initial interview typical of a comprehensive medical model psychiatric evaluation. The therapist carefully elucidates information about the nature, duration, and progression of psychiatric symptoms. The clinician obtains the patient's prior psychiatric history, family psychiatric history, and medical history. Administering a Ham-D during the initial interview helps determine the severity of depressive symptoms and establishes a baseline for future comparisons. Using these data, the therapist diagnoses a depression, rules out confounding comorbidities (e.g., substance abuse, psychosis), and makes treatment recommendations (e.g., hospitalization, medication, IPT). In the process of diagnosing a depression, the therapist explicitly reviews symptoms and gives the patient the *sick role* (Parsons, 1951).

The skilled therapist seamlessly weaves an interpersonal inventory into the psychiatric assessment. A more detailed search for a precipitant, the interpersonal inventory consists of a review of all important past and present relationships as they relate to the current depressive episode. The therapist asks about the patient's life circumstances and requests a description of the important people in his or her life. In addition to outlining the cast of characters in the patient's life, the therapist probes the quality of those relationships, asking the patient to describe satisfying and unsatisfying aspects of relationships, unmet expectations with others, and aspects of relationships that the patient would like to change. The therapist listens closely for omissions, such as the harried paralegal who does not mention his boss, or the "happily" married housewife who labels her marriage to an absent, high-powered executive as "fine," but does not volunteer details. The interpersonal rationale offered by the therapist represents a practical but nonetiologic model for understanding and resolving the patient's depression.

The therapist listens for perturbations in relationships that may correspond temporally to the onset or maintenance of the depressive symptoms. The therapist uses this information to establish a problem area that will subsequently form the backbone of treatment. In IPT, there are four problem areas:

1. *Grief:* Grief or complicated bereavement requires the death of an important person in the patient's life. Symptoms must exceed those characteristic of the normal mourning process. Grief is *not* used to describe
psychodynamic losses (e.g., the loss of a job, loss of function from aging),
which, in IPT, would be called role transitions.
2. *Interpersonal disputes:* An interpersonal dispute refers to any relationship
in which there are nonreciprocal expectations. Examples include a man
who wants to have a third child but whose wife does not, a secretary who
is reduced to tears daily by a demanding boss, and a devoted art history
student whose parents insist she apply to medical school.
3. *Role transition:* A role transition is any major life event. This category
subsumes many potential stressors including new employment, unemployment, matriculation, graduation, retirement, marriage, divorce, giving birth, moving, etc.
4. *Interpersonal deficits:* This final option is a "default" category, and it
probably implies a worse prognosis. These patients suffer from a long-
standing history of impoverished social relationships and are unable to
identify an acute interpersonal stressor. When possible, one of the first
three problem areas is preferentially selected as a treatment focus.

The therapist, in consultation with the patient, selects a problem area that is
affectively meaningful to the patient and appears related to the depression.
Ideally, the patient and therapist agree to focus on one, or at most two, problem area(s).

At the end of the initial phase of treatment, the therapist offers the patient
an interpersonal formulation that links the problem area to the depression.
The formulation should be personalized, including details and metaphors
elicited during the evaluation. The therapist describes a model for understanding the patient's experience, without making frank statements about causality.
Finally, the formulation lays out a focused plan for treatment and instills hope.
An example of an interpersonal formulation follows:

> You've been very depressed for the past several months. The problems that you're
> describing—poor sleep, poor appetite, inability to concentrate, loss of pleasure, loss
> of sex drive, feelings of hopelessness—are typical symptoms of depression. I don't
> think these physical symptoms are a product of your HIV illness per se because, as
> your medical doctor has told both of us, you're physically very healthy. Instead, I
> understand them as part of a depression.
>
> When your lover Tom died from AIDS two years ago, you had many of these feel-
> ings, but they seemed to get much better over time. Although you still miss Tom and
> feel sad about his death, you were feeling well until your HIV test came back six
> months ago. Because you and Tom practiced safe sex, it sounds like you never imag-
> ined you would seroconvert. I think that you are having difficulty handling the
> change from being someone who is HIV-negative to someone who is HIV-positive.
> This isn't easy information for anyone to handle, but it seems to be particularly trou-
> blesome for you. As you pointed out, memories of Tom's difficult death probably
> make this harder for you now. We call this change a role transition, and I think that

your difficulties around testing positive have contributed significantly to the development of your depression.

Over the next twelve weeks, I propose that we focus on how you cope with this role transition, with being HIV-positive. We'll discuss your feelings about this big, unexpected change in your life and, explore options for different—or not so different—goals and wishes as an HIV-positive man. We'll talk about many of the things you brought up in our discussions so far—that is, how it affects your sex life, career choices, your elderly parents, memories of Tom's illness, etc. I expect that as we get a better handle on this role transition, your depression will improve as well.

Because the patient's symptoms seemed temporally related to the news of seroconversion, rather than to the death of Tom, the case was formulated as a role transition instead of complicated bereavement. However, the patient must agree to the formulation. In the unlikely event that the therapist and patient disagree, the therapist would listen carefully to the patients concerns and adjust the formulation. For instance, if the patient just discussed had felt strongly that his problem stemmed from Tom's death and not from testing positive, it would probably have made sense to reformulate the case as complicated bereavement. Because the formulation is practical rather than etiological, there is no need to quibble over the "correct" explanation for the depression (in fact, most episodes are multifactorial). The IPT therapist's job is to identify a problem area that makes sense and is salient to the patient.

INTERMEDIATE SESSIONS

During the middle phase of treatment, the therapist focuses on both the patient's mood and problem area. Each session begins with the deceptively simple question, "How have you been since we last met?" This inquiry, while maintaining a focus on the here and now, will be answered with either a mood response, such as, "I've been feeling depressed," or an event response, such as, "My husband and I have been fighting less." Following the patient's lead, the therapist gathers more information about either mood or the event. The therapist then inquires about the unspoken issues (i.e., mood, if only events are described, and events, if only mood is described). The therapist then links the mood to an event or visa versa. An example follows:

Mr. A. responded to the opening inquiry of a session with a mood response. "I'm a wreck," he said. He elaborated that he had been feeling especially sad and unmotivated since Sunday and had barely slept in two days. When asked, "What happened over the weekend?," Mr. A. reported that he had spent Saturday watching TV. On further probing, he admitted that he considered the "wasted day" evidence of his "uselessness." Because Mr. A.'s problem area was a role transition, involving the shift from high-powered lawyer to retiree, the therapist helped the patient understand that his mood shift on Sunday was directly linked to Saturday's TV marathon, including its attendant social isolation. The therapist said, "Because you used to go to the office on Saturdays, you were at a particular loss about how to manage your time this past Saturday. This had a direct impact on your mood. Although you feel 'useless,' I think this feeling of worthlessness is a symptom of your depression that will improve as we solve the difficulties associated with your role transition. Maybe we should think together about what you would *like* to do with your Saturdays."

The process of reviewing depressive symptoms and relating them to life events is central to each IPT session across problem areas. In addition, each problem area is characterized by a specific set of goals and treatment strategies outlined in the manual. A synopsis of the approach and a case example for each problem area follows.

In complicated bereavement or grief, the IPT therapist facilitates the mourning process, helps the patient reestablish interest in life, and encourages the development of substitutes for what has been lost:

Ms. B.'s depressive symptoms began soon after her first routine mammogram (which was normal) and two years after her mother's death from breast cancer. She was diagnosed with a major depressive episode and complicated bereavement. During the first part of treatment, Ms. B.'s therapist helped to reinstitute the mourning process by asking Ms. B. to describe the details of her relationship with her mother, especially around the time leading up to her death. Ms. B. reported that she was in graduate school in another city during the first few years of her mother's illness. Although she knew the severity of her mother's condition, she blocked it out by throwing herself into her dissertation. She found that she had less and less contact with her mother during this period because "the fantasy that everything was *status quo* came crashing down around me any time I went home for a visit." Ms. B.'s mother's condition deteriorated just as Ms. B. was finalizing plans to travel abroad for two months to complete her dissertation research. She postponed her trip and returned to the family home to care for her terminally ill mother. "Instead of studying important documents, I cleaned bedpans for two months."

With the help of her therapist, Ms. B. was able to acknowledge both sadness and the anger about her mother's death. She expressed regrets about not spending time with her mother while she was in relatively good health and admitted that the demands of caring for a dying parent at home made it difficult for her to enjoy "quality time" with her mother at the end. She also verbalized for the first time her anger about having had to postpone work on her dissertation. In order to facilitate the mourning process, her therapist encouraged Ms. B. to visit her mother's grave, review photo albums of a family trip prior to her mother's diagnosis, and to discuss with her siblings their memories of their mother. Ms. B. was also encouraged to discuss with her own physician her fears about vulnerability to breast cancer and recommendations for follow up.

Although Ms. B. had finished her dissertation in the two years following her mother's death, she remained socially isolated. The therapist encouraged Ms. B. to participate in a few organized social activities to decrease her isolation. As Ms. B.'s depression lifted, she became more involved with a hiking club and agreed to participate in a summer trip to Colorado.

In an interpersonal-role dispute, the goals of treatment include identifying the dispute, choosing a course of action, modifying expectations, and improving communication. In particular, the therapist focuses on the impact of *nonreciprocal expectations* in the relationship and examines parallels in other relationships to help the patient understand how the dispute is perpetuated. The approach to a role dispute has been described as "unilateral couples therapy," (Markowitz, 1997) although it is permissible in IPT to include a "significant other" for a few sessions in order to facilitate treatment:

Ms. C., a 28-year-old single woman, came to treatment after losing her fifth waitressing job in a one-year period. She met criteria for a major depressive episode. Initially attributing her deteriorating mood to unemployment, Ms. C. subsequently revealed a covert dispute with her mother that antedated the onset of job difficulties. Two years prior to evaluation, Ms. C. had moved from an expensive apartment into her mother's house in order to save enough money to fulfill her dream of moving to Paris to paint and sculpt. Her mother had agreed to accept $200 per month for rent, and Ms. C. expected to put the bulk of her paycheck into her "Paris savings account." She also reserved a small amount of cash each month to purchase art supplies.

Without directly discouraging her, Ms. C.'s mother showed little support for her daughter's art work. For instance she expressed irritation about "the mess" generated by Ms. C.'s projects, and she criticized her daughter's attempts to learn French in preparation for Paris as "high and mighty." As the months went by, her mother asked Ms. C. to contribute large sums of money to unpaid household bills in addition to the agreed upon rent. As Ms. C. pointed out, her mother "didn't twist [her] arm, but knew what buttons to push." Resentfully, Ms. C. put all of her income toward the family debt. She was unable to save money for Paris or purchase art supplies for painting at home. As she became discouraged about the possibilities of ever moving to Paris or making a living as an artist, she developed "an attitude" at work that led to successive terminations.

Ms. C. identified a pattern of "getting pushed around" in relationships. For instance, a prior romantic relationship ended because of multiple infidelities on her partner's side, which Ms. C. permitted to continue for many months. In another instance, Ms. C. cared for a semi-invalid roommate (an acquaintance, but not a close friend) for many months, despite mounting resentment. The therapist identified for Ms. C. a pattern of communication problems—specifically, difficulty with self-assertion—that contributed to the current role dispute and depression.

The focus of treatment was to improve communication with her mother. Because the dispute was at an impasse, the therapist pushed Ms. C. to bring the dispute into the open. With help from the therapist (which included encouragement, communication analysis, and role play), Ms. C. told her mother directly about her angry feelings and explored their nonreciprocal expectations about money. She explained the importance of her finances to her Paris plans and underscored her intent to persevere with her artwork. To Ms. C.'s amazement, her mother offered little resistance to the discussion. Ms. C. learned that her mother was skeptical about Ms. C.'s intentions to save for Paris, assuming that it was "a pipe dream." Her mother responded well to her direct comments, saying, "I only want you to be happy" and offered to repay her daughter.

Once the channels of communication opened, the mother and daughter quickly resolved the financial piece, agreeing to a slightly higher rent and a timely repayment schedule. They also agreed to set aside part of an unused basement room as studio space to contain the mess that disturbed Ms. C.'s mother. As the patient continued to communicate more directly with her mother, she regained sight of her dream and felt willing to make the interim compromises necessary to achieve her goal. Her depression lifted and she found new employment. She took a job in a better paying, upscale restaurant, which involved more difficult work but promised more rapid accumulation of savings. She also reported that her mother displayed one of her paintings in the living room, taking an interest in her artwork for the first time.

The goals of solving a problematic role transition include helping the patient to mourn and accept the loss of the old role, to develop a more balanced representation (the good and the bad) of both the old role (which is often idealized) and the new role (which is generally devalued), and to master the skills required by the new role:

Mr. D., a 32-year-old single man, was the owner of a small computer company that had enjoyed remarkable success over the past two years. He had grown the business from a one-man operation to a bustling organization with fifteen employees. Mr. D. was puzzled that, despite his apparent successes, he had become increasingly depressed over the prior six months.

In therapy, the patient discussed his mixed feelings about his work. He enjoyed the excitement and time pressures of a growing business, but he felt increasingly isolated from friends and family. He found himself working seven days a week either at the office or on his home computer. He also felt increasingly frustrated by the administrative demands on his time, which prevented him from participating in the pleasurable process of designing web pages (his company's product).

His therapist encouraged Mr. D. to talk about the early days of his business, which he remembered as a happy, exciting time when he created "magic on a shoe string budget" and reveled in "having a job that felt more like play than work." On further probing, Mr. D. admitted that he had had many financial worries at that time. He had experienced pressure from his parents to succeed (he had opened the business instead of taking a law-related job after law school), and he often doubted his capabilities. He acknowledged that although there were many aspects of the struggling-entrepreneur role that he enjoyed, he also disliked its inherent uncertainty and the financial risk.

As the patient reviewed his experiences in the old role, his therapist encouraged him to verbalize his concerns about the new role and talk about changes he might like to make. Mr. D. was initially self-critical, saying, "I have it all and I'm still miserable." With the therapist's help, the patient identified some aspects of his current role that could be improved. Mr. D. verbalized a wish to expand his social life and limit the time demands of his business. With encouragement, Mr. D. left the city for an entire weekend to spend time in the country with college buddies. Noting a definite improvement in mood following the break from work, Mr. D. scheduled more non-work-related activities into his routine, including a weekly basketball game with law school friends and a semiregular lunch with a former colleague. As the depression improved, Mr. D. hired a part-time administrator to manage some of the "boring stuff," leaving him free to participate in the design end of the business. His Hamilton scores returned to the normal range.

Patients with interpersonal deficits relate a long history of isolation and poor interpersonal skills. This is a "default category," selected only when none of the other problem areas pertain. Typically, the patient denies any acute stressors. The goal of treatment, therefore, is to decrease social isolation, using past relationships and the relationship with the therapist as models for new relationships:

> Ms. E., a 42-year-old speech therapist, lived alone in a small apartment. She was a conscientious employee, but she rarely left her apartment for nonwork functions. She had severed ties with her family many years ago, but she maintained contact with a single homebound friend, with whom she spoke weekly by telephone.
>
> Ms. E. was married briefly in her late twenties. The man had pressed her to marry him, and she acquiesced because "my therapist said I should." The marriage ended one year later. The IPT therapist seized upon this relationship as a possible model for new relationships. The therapist asked Ms. E. many questions about her exhusband including, "What was good about the relationship?" "What did you two enjoy together?" and "What were the biggest problems?" Attributing the end of the relationship to sexual incompatibility ("I hated it and he wanted sex every night"), Ms. E. admitted that they enjoyed attending scientific lectures together. In fact, they had met at an amateur astronomers' night at the local planetarium. The therapist suggested that Ms. E. attend some lectures now in order to decrease her isolation. Ms. E. admitted a wish to attend an ornithology seminar, but she feared going alone. With great therapist encouragement, Ms. E. asked a coworker to accompany her. Much to the patient's relief, her coworker agreed.
>
> Whenever possible, the therapist helped Ms. E. to increase her social contacts. For instance, when she went to lectures, the therapist encouraged Ms. E. to stay for any attendant social events. Benefiting from role-play practice sessions, Ms. E. successfully asked another lecture participant to join her for coffee after a seminar.
>
> In the middle of treatment, the therapist was 15 minutes late for a session. Ms. E. made the indirect comment, "I wish I could take long lunch breaks like you." The therapist used this interaction as an opportunity to help Ms. E. express herself more directly in relationships. The therapist pointed out that Ms. E. sounded angry and, in fact, had a right to be angry. The therapist suggested some alternative approaches to the indirect comment, such as direct expression of anger and disappointment, and requests to make amends (e.g., rescheduling the missed 15 minutes). The therapist also suggested that these approaches could be used with her new lecture-circuit acquaintances.
>
> Although Ms. E. did not form close relationships with any of her new contacts, she enjoyed the seminars and felt pleased to "be part of the living world again." Her mood improved greatly.

TERMINATION

In the final two to four sessions, the therapist reiterates the date and time of the final session and actively elicits responses to the end of treatment (if the patient does not spontaneously offer them). Termination provides an opportunity to review treatment gains, which are usually significant, and to identify unaddressed problems.

IPT termination is like a graduation. The therapist helps the patient express sad feelings about the end of treatment, but underscores patient progress in treating the depressive episode and in improving work, love relationships, etc. Although concerns about the patient's ability to manage without the therapist's help are inevitable, the therapist counters with examples of the patient's hard work outside the office. The therapist commends the patient's real-world victories and reminds the patient that IPT has helped develop skills needed to improve relationships without the therapist's help. Termination promotes patient independence while grieving the loss of the treatment relationship.

In the event of partial or nonresponse, the therapist suggests alternative treatments and makes appropriate referrals for follow-up. The therapist and patient also review the symptoms of depression and identify warning signs that might lead the patient to a reevaluation in the future.

ALTERNATIVE TREATMENT OPTIONS

IPT, cognitive behavioral therapy (CBT), a wide range of pharmacotherapies, and electroconvulsive therapy (ECT) are clearly supported by extant data as efficacious treatments of depression. Although widely used in clinical practice, psychodynamic psychotherapies have not been systematically tested in outcome trials. Although clinicians can select from this relatively broad menu of treatment options, few data exist to guide them through the difficult decision maze of differential therapeutics (Frances, Clarkin, & Perry, 1984).

Data from a post hoc comparison of IPT, CBT, imipramine, and placebo for the treatment of depression suggest that patients with severe social dysfunction (i.e., severe interpersonal deficits) may not benefit from IPT, whereas patients with poor cognitive functioning may not respond to CBT. Severely depressed patients responded better to imipramine and IPT, whereas less severely depressed patients improved with any kind of treatment (Sotsky et al., 1991). This analysis suggests that less severely depressed patients will get better with nonspecific approaches, whereas more severely depressed patients should receive IPT or antidepressants. The most severely depressed patients require hospitalization, pharmacotherapy, and possibly ECT.

The additive value of combination therapy (e.g., IPT plus a serotonin reuptake inhibitor), although intuitively reasonable, has yet to be clearly demonstrated in clinical trials. On the other hand, no data suggest that combination treatment is detrimental to the patient: Combined treatment has never done worse, and sometimes does better than monotherapy (Manning, Markowitz, & Frances, 1992). In practice, clinicians routinely prescribe medication and psychotherapy together for depressed patients.

If a patient fails IPT or shows only a partial response, despite good participation in treatment, referral to a different modality is indicated. The next step is largely a matter of personal preference, but a depression unabated after four months of psychotherapy probably deserves a trial of antidepressant medication. A reassessment of the initial diagnosis is also indicated.

PRESCRIPTIVE TREATMENT
AND MANAGED CARE

In a managed-care environment, IPT shines because (1) it is manualized, (2) it is time-limited, and (3) its efficacy is well documented in research trials.

As previously discussed, IPT is a 12- to 16-week psychotherapy described in detail in the manual by Klerman et al. (1984). The specificity of this treatment offers consumer appeal to insurers, healthcare providers, and patients; it is focused, reproducible, and of circumscribed duration. Patients and managed care companies can be certain that IPT delivers the same product across trained therapists, with expected relief arriving within three to four months. Most importantly, they know that IPT works, as demonstrated in several large randomized clinical trials.

The NIMH Treatment of Depression Collaborative Research Program (TDCRP) is a landmark study in the history of psychotherapy outcome trials (Elkin et al., 1989). In the TDCRP, 250 outpatients at multiple sites, meeting *DSM-III* criteria for depression were randomly assigned to one of four treatment cells: IPT, CBT, imipramine plus clinical management (CM), or placebo plus CM. Patients in all four groups showed improvement, with nonstatistically significant differences among them: patients treated with imipramine did nonsignificantly better that those receiving IPT who in turn did much better than patients receiving CBT. CBT was, in turn, somewhat better than CM. As discussed previously, the more severely depressed patients in this study responded significantly better to imipramine or to IPT than to placebo (Sotsky et al., 1991).

In a study with a similar design to the TDCRP, Markowitz et al. (1998) treated 101 depressed, HIV-positive outpatients with either IPT, CBT, supportive therapy (SP), or imipramine-plus-SP. They found that patients improved in all four conditions, but that patients treated with IPT or imipramine had better outcomes than patients receiving CBT or SP alone.

Frank and colleagues, at the University of Pittsburgh, examined the role of maintenance therapies in the treatment of recurrent depression (Frank et al., 1990). One hundred twenty-five patients with multiply recurrent major depression were randomly assigned to one of five treatment cells: a maintenance, monthly form of IPT (IPT-M) alone, IPT-M plus imipramine, IPT-M plus placebo, medication clinic (MC) plus placebo, or MC plus imipramine. IPT-M was administered monthly, whereas imipramine was dosed to high therapeutic levels (mean dose > 200 mg/day). Both imipramine and IPT-M yielded significantly longer survival times (i.e., relapse prevention) than did placebo. Outcomes that included imipramine (alone or with IPT) were superior to those that did not. IPT-M, alone or with placebo, yielded results intermediate to imipramine and placebo. IPT-M conferred no additional benefit to treatment with imipramine.

SUMMARY

Interpersonal Psychotherapy is a time-limited treatment for depression developed in the 1970s by Klerman and Weissman. Originally conceived as a research intervention to establish psychotherapy's efficacy relative to standard treatment (e.g., medication), IPT is enjoying growing clinical popularity in its third decade of life. With demonstrated efficacy in several large, randomized clinical trials, IPT is one of few psychotherapies to enjoy both empirical support and end-user applause. A treatment that codifies (but also adds to) what most psychotherapists do in brief treatment, IPT is practical, systematic, optimistic, and efficacious. In addition to bringing relief to many depressed patients, IPT provides a solution to therapists trying to balance the time demands of managed care with their own demands for clinical excellence.

REFERENCES

American Psychiatric Association. (1994). *Diagnostic and statistical manual of mental disorders* (4th ed.). Washington, DC: Author.

Bowlby, J. (1977). The making and breaking of affectional bonds: II. Some principles of psychotherapy. *British Journal of Psychiatry, 10*, 421–431.

Brown, G.W., & Harris, T. (1978). *Social origins of depression: A study of psychiatric disorders in women.* New York: Free Press.

Coyne, J.C. (1976). Depression and the response of others. *Journal of Abnormal Psychology, 85*, 186–193.

DiMascio, A., Weissman, M.M., Prusoff, B.A., Neu, C., Zwilling, M., & Klerman, G.L. (1979). Differential symptom reduction by drugs and psychotherapy in acute depression. *Archives of General Psychiatry, 36*, 1450–1456.

Elkin, I., Shea, M.T., Watkins, J.T., Imber, S.D., Sotsky, S.M., Collins, J.F., Glass, D.R., Pilkonis, P.A., Leber, W.R., Docherty, J.P., Fiester, S.J., & Parloff, M.B. (1989). National Institute of Mental Health treatment of depression collaborative research program: General effectiveness of treatments. *Archives of General Psychiatry, 46*, 971–982.

Fairburn, C.G., Jones, R., Peveler, R.C., Hope, R.A., & O'Connor, M. (1993). Psychotherapy and bulimia nervosa: Longer term effects of interpersonal psychotherapy, behavior therapy, and cognitive behavior therapy. *Archives of General Psychiatry, 50*, 419–428.

Frances, A., Clarkin, J.F., & Perry, S. (1984). *Differential therapeutics in psychiatry: The art and science of treatment selection.* New York: Brunner/Mazel.

Frank, E., Kupfer, D.J., Perel, J.M., Cornes, C., Jarrett, D.B., Mallinger, A.G., Thase, M.E., McEachran, A.B., & Grochocinski, V.J. (1990). Three-year outcomes for maintenance therapies in recurrent depression. *Archives of General Psychiatry, 47*, 1093–1099.

Hamilton, M. (1960). A rating scale for depression. *Journal of Neurology, Neurosurgery, and Psychiatry, 25*, 56–62.

Henderson, S., Byrne, G., Duncan-Jones, P., Scott, R., & Adcock, S. (1980). Social relationships, adversity and neurosis: A study of associations in general population sample. *British Journal of Psychiatry, 136*, 574–583.

Hirschfeld, R.M.A., Klerman, G.L., Clayton, P.J., Keller, M.B., McDonald-Scott, P., & Larkin, B.H. (1983). Assessing personality: Effects of the depressive state on trait measurement. *American Journal of Psychiatry, 140*, 695–699.

Klerman, G.L., & Weissman, M.M. (Eds.). (1993). *New applications of interpersonal therapy.* Washington, DC: American Psychiatric Press.

Klerman, G.L., Weissman, M.M., Rounsaville, B.J., & Chevron, E.S. (1984). *Interpersonal psychotherapy of depression.* New York: Basic Books.

Manning, D.W., Markowitz, J.C., & Frances, A.J. (1992). A review of combined psychotherapy and pharmacotherapy in the treatment of depression. *Journal of Psychotherapy Practice and Research, 1,* 103–116.

Markowitz, J.C. (1997). *Interpersonal psychotherapy for dysthymic disorder.* Washington, DC: American Psychiatric Press.

Markowitz, J.C., Klerman, G.L., & Perry, S.W. (1992). Interpersonal psychotherapy of depressed HIV-seropositive patients. *Hospital and Community Psychiatry, 43,* 885–890.

Markowitz, J.C., Kocsis, J.H., Fishman, B., Spielman, L.A., Jacobsberg, L.B., Frances, A.J., Klerman, G.L., & Perry, S.W. (1998). Treatment of depressive symptoms in HIV-positive patients. *Archives of General Psychiatry, 55,* 452–457.

Markowitz, J.C., Svartberg, M., & Swartz, H.A. (1998). Is IPT time-limited psychodynamic psychotherapy? *Journal of Psychotherapy Practice and Research, 7,* 185–195.

Markowitz, J.C., & Swartz, H.A. (1997). Case formulation in interpersonal psychotherapy of depression. In T.D. Eells (Ed.), *Handbook of psychotherapy case formulation* (pp. 192–222). New York: Guilford Press.

Meyer, A. (1957). *Psychobiology: A science of man.* Springfield, IL: Charles C. Thomas.

Parker, G. (1978). *The bonds of depression.* Sydney: Angus and Robertson.

Parsons, T. (1951). Illness and the role of the physician: A sociological perspective. *American Journal of Orthopsychiatry, 21,* 452–460.

Reynolds, C.F., Frank, E., Perel, J.M., Imber, S.D., Cornes, C., Morycz, R.K., Mazumdar, S., Miller, M.D., Pollock, B.G., Rifai, A.H., Stack, J.A., George, C.J., Houck, P.R., & Kupfer, D.J. (1992). Combined pharmacotherapy and psychotherapy in the acute and continuation treatment of elderly patients with recurrent major depression: A preliminary report. *American Journal of Psychiatry, 149,* 1687–1692.

Sotsky, S.M., Glass, D.R., Shea, M.T., Pilkonis, P.A., Collins, J.F., Elkin, I., Watkins, J.T., Imber, S.D., Leber, W.R., Moyer, J., & Olivieri, M.E. (1991). Patient predictors of response to psychotherapy and pharmacotherapy: Findings in the NIMH treatment of depression collaborative research program. *American Journal of Psychiatry, 148,* 997–1008.

Sullivan, H.S. (1953). *The interpersonal theory of psychiatry.* New York: Norton.

Swartz, H.A., & Markowitz, J.C. (1997). Time-limited psychotherapy. In A. Tasman, J. Kay, & J.A. Lieberman (Eds.), *Psychiatry* (Vol. 2, pp. 1405–1417). Philadelphia: W.B. Saunders.

Swartz, H.A., & Markowitz, J.C. (1998). Interpersonal psychotherapy for the treatment of depression in HIV-positive men and women. In J.C. Markowitz (Ed.), *Interpersonal psychotherapy* (pp. 129–155). Washington, DC: American Psychiatric Press.

Weissman, M.M., Klerman, G.L., Paykel, E.S., Prusoff, B.A., & Hanson, B. (1974). Treatment effects on the social adjustment of depressed patients. *Archives of General Psychiatry, 30,* 771–778.

Weissman, M.M., & Markowitz, J.C. (1994). Interpersonal psychotherapy: Current status. *Archives of General Psychiatry, 51,* 599–606.

CHAPTER 8

Pharmacotherapy

MICHAEL FEINBERG

DISORDERS OF mood (affective disorders) are very common, especially among the elderly and the chronically medically ill. These conditions range from normal grief reactions, adjustment disorders, and dysthymia to severe, incapacitating reactions that may result in death. The lifetime risk of suicide in major affective disorders is 10 percent to 15 percent, but this statistic does not begin to represent the cost to society of this group of notoriously underdiagnosed and undertreated illnesses. Perhaps one-fourth to one-third of episodes are diagnosed, and a minority of these are adequately treated (Greenberg, Stiglin, Finkelstein, & Berndt, 1993; Isacsson, Boethius, & Bergman, 1992; Katon, Von Korff, Lin, Bush, & Ormel, 1992; Kind & Sorensen, 1993).

Major depression is a common, disabling disorder. Estimates of lifetime prevalence are as high as 25 percent for females and 12 percent for males. Other studies estimate a range from 6 percent to 17 percent (Kessler et al., 1994; Regier et al., 1988). It is more common in women, among first-degree relatives of depressed patients (1.5–3 times greater), and among persons suffering from chronic general medical illness and substance abuse. Depression is seen throughout the life cycle, and throughout the world (The Cross National Collaboration Group, 1992; Klerman & Weissman, 1989). The average age of onset is the late twenties, but the illness may begin at any age. The symptoms of major depression typically develop over days to weeks, and an untreated episode typically lasts 4 to 12 months. It is estimated that over 50 percent of people who have such an episode will eventually have another episode and that during the interepisode period 20 percent to 30 percent of patients may have persistent residual symptoms and social or occupational impairment (American Psychiatric Association, 1993).

Accurate diagnosis of the patient with mood disturbance can be challenging and even confusing, but more accurate diagnosis and careful selection of appropriate treatment increases the probability of a good response. The *Diagnostic and Statistical Manual (DSM-IV)* offers guidelines for standardized diagnosis

156

of mood disorders. Major Depressive Episode (MDE) is classified on several, conceptually independent axes. These include:

1. Severity
   a. Mild
   b. Moderate
   c. Severe
      i. Without psychotic features
      ii. With psychotic features
         (1) Mood-congruent
         (2) Mood-incongruent

2. Course
   a. Episode number
      i. Single episode
      ii. Recurrent
   b. In partial remission
   c. In full remission
   d. Chronic course
   e. Time of onset
      i. Seasonal pattern
      ii. Postpartum

3. Other features
   a. Melancholic
   b. Catatonic
   c. Atypical

Not all human grief, misery, and disappointment are indications for medical treatment, and even severe affective disorders have a high rate of spontaneous remission given sufficient time (often a matter of months). The antidepressant and antimanic agents are thus generally reserved for the more severe and otherwise incapacitating disorders of mood, and the most satisfactory results tend to occur in patients who have moderately severe illnesses with endogenous or melancholic characteristics (see American Psychiatric Association, 1994; Baldessarini, 1989; Peselow, Sanfilipo, Difiglia, & Fieve, 1992).

There are data suggesting that several of these diagnostic subtypes predict response to treatment: severity, presence of psychosis, and melancholic features. The last of these overlaps with the presence of specific biological abnormalities that are not included in *DSM*.

HISTORY OF ANTIDEPRESSANTS

Monoamine oxidase inhibitors (MAOIs) were the first antidepressants discovered. In 1952, iproniazid, an antitubercular drug and MAO inhibitor, was noted to elevate the mood of depressed tuberculosis patients. MAOIs have been successfully used as antidepressants, but fell out of favor because of side effects and the need for dietary restrictions.

The next class of antidepressants, the tricyclics, are structurally similar to the phenothiazine group of antipsychotic drugs. While searching for a better antipsychotic drug, Kuhn (1958), cited in (Baldessarini, 1996) found fortuitously that imipramine had a remarkable antidepressant effect. Commonly referred to as tricyclics or TCAs, this group includes both tricyclic and tetracyclic antidepressants.

MAO inhibitors and tricyclic antidepressants, the first successful antidepressants, were discovered by chance. Such chance discoveries proved to be of seminal importance. First, they provided the first scientifically proven drug treatment for major depression. Second, they demonstrated that major depression was amenable to medical intervention just like other medical conditions such as hypertension and diabetes.

The next class of antidepressants to be introduced was the serotonin selective reuptake inhibitors (SSRIs). Fluoxetine (Prozac), introduced in 1988, was the first SSRI used in the United States. Currently, five SSRIs are available in the United States: fluoxetine (Prozac), paroxetine (Paxil), sertraline (Zoloft), citalopram (Celexa), and fluvoxamine (Luvox—FDA approved for treatment of OCD only).

Other additions to the antidepressant armamentarium that do not specifically belong to any of the above classes of medications are usually referred to as atypical antidepressants. They include bupropion (Wellbutrin), trazodone (Desyrel), venlafaxine (Effexor), nefazodone (Serzone), and mirtazapine (Remeron).

MECHANISM OF ANTIDEPRESSANT ACTIVITY

The search for a biochemical cause for affective disorders has been long, hard, and mostly unsuccessful. The Greeks postulated that melancholia was caused by an excess of black bile, but researchers failed to identify this substance in the intervening 2,000 years. In the last 30 years, many studies have suggested that such disorders arise as a consequence of malfunction of one or more neuronal pathways of the limbic region of the brain. The monoamine theory of depression originally postulated that the symptoms of the illness arise as a consequence of decreased availability of serotonin and/or norepinephrine at the presynaptic nerve terminal. Thirty years of research and millions of dollars have produced no evidence to support this theory unequivocally, and have led to significant changes in it.

The two monoamines usually thought to be involved in the pathogenesis of affective disorders are serotonin (also known as 5-hydroxytryptamine or 5-HT) and norepinephrine (NE). These amines are released from the presynaptic nerve terminal and stimulate the postsynaptic neuron. Their action is usually terminated by reuptake, in which the transmitters are taken up into the presynaptic terminal and either recycled into storage vesicles or degraded by MAO. A minority of the transmitter is metabolized to inactive compounds without reuptake. The proposed mechanism(s) of action of antidepressant drugs usually involve their pharmacological actions on these and other neurotransmitter systems.

Tricyclic antidepressants inhibit the reuptake of norepinephrine and serotonin by presynaptic neurons in the central nervous system (CNS). Selective serotonin reuptake inhibitors (SSRIs) inhibit the uptake of serotonin into presynaptic nerve terminals, thereby increasing the availability of serotonin at the nerve endings. This blockade of reuptake might lead, in turn, to increased stimulation of the postsynaptic neuron. MAOIs have a different mechanism of action: they inhibit monoamine oxidase, which catalyzes the degradation of serotonin, epinephrine, norepinephrine, and other monoamines in the presynaptic nerve. This might mean greater amounts of neurotransmitter available for release into the synapse, and increased stimulation.

Antidepressants achieve their effects, both therapeutic and toxic, either by inhibition of presynaptic uptake of norepinephrine, serotonin, or perhaps dopamine at nerve endings or by blockade of postsynaptic receptors (Richelson, 1988). They also bind nonspecifically to a wide variety of receptors. The SSRIs are considered to be highly selective inhibitors of serotonin uptake with limited affinity for receptors associated with other neurotransmitters. Venlafaxine inhibits both norepinephrine and 5-HT uptake. Nefazodone has a pharmacologic profile distinct from the SSRIs and other antidepressant drugs in that it is a potent 5-HT receptor antagonist as well as a serotonin reuptake inhibitor. Bupropion does not seem to have any significant action at the synapse, but may act centrally on noradrenergic transmission by the Locus Coeruleus.

Most antidepressants are thought to act by increasing concentrations of norepinephrine and/or serotonin in the synaptic cleft. This increase occurs almost immediately, but the medication's therapeutic effect is not appreciable for two to three weeks. Reuptake inhibition and the increase in neurotransmitter concentrations are thought to act as a trigger for a complex sequence of adaptive changes involving various neurotransmitters and receptors. The changes in central serotonergic and/or noradrenergic function induced by most of the antidepressants would appear to be necessary, though not sufficient, for therapeutic activity.

Many antidepressants with a high degree of selectivity for serotonergic systems have been developed in recent years. There is no clinical evidence to suggest that these drugs are more effective or have a faster onset of action than the older, nonspecific tricyclic antidepressants. Their major advantage would appear to be a reduction in their anticholinergic effects and relative lack of cardiovascular toxicity in overdose or in patients with preexisting disease of the myocardial conduction system.

Over the last decade, drug discovery and development in psychiatry has gone from being a process based almost exclusively on serendipity to one of rational drug development based on selecting a target of interest (i.e., molecular targeting). This type of rational drug development is now possible because of the improved understanding of central and peripheral mechanisms of action relevant to both desired and undesired effects.

OVERVIEW OF SOMATIC TREATMENT OF DEPRESSION

After the diagnosis of major depression has been established, the clinician must select a treatment modality and decide how to administer it, taking into account the benefit-to-risk ratio. Successful treatment of patients with major depression is promoted by a thorough assessment of the patient's symptoms; past general medical and psychiatric history; psychological makeup and conflicts; life stressors; family, psychosocial, and cultural environment; and preference for specific treatments and approaches. The expansion in the number of treatment options requires the physician to carefully consider the advantages and disadvantages of various options when developing a treatment plan.

Clinicians initiating treatment of a major depressive episode have at their disposal a variety of psychotherapeutic approaches, a number of medications, electroconvulsive therapy, and light therapy. These various interventions may be used alone or in combination.

Antidepressant medication has been shown to treat all forms of MDE effectively. Barring contraindications to these agents, antidepressant medications are first-line treatments for MDE in the following conditions:

1. The depression is severe. (Patients with mild depression may be treated with psychotherapy alone or with a combination of medication and psychotherapy. Even mild depression, if unresponsive to psychotherapy, should be considered for antidepressant medication therapy.)
2. There are psychotic features (in which case the addition of an antipsychotic to the antidepressant is required for maximum efficacy).
3. There are melancholic features (the presence of melancholic features increases the likelihood of response to somatic intervention) or atypical symptom features (in which case the MAOIs have been found to be especially effective).
4. Prophylactic maintenance treatment is indicated. Frank et al. (1990) found that maintenance medication clearly prevents recurrences, whereas monthly maintenance psychotherapy delays recurrences but does not prevent them.
5. The patient has shown prior positive response to medication or the patient prefers medication.
6. Treatment by a competent psychotherapist trained in a depression-specific psychotherapy is not available.

New guidelines and a discussion of these issues can be found in Schulberg, Katon, Simon, and Rush (1998). Approximately 65 percent to 70 percent of depressed patients respond to antidepressant therapy, and ECT is effective in another 10 percent to 15 percent of patients (Andrews & Nemeroff, 1994). Treatment consists of an acute phase, during which remission is induced, a continuation phase, during which remission is preserved, and a maintenance phase, during which the susceptible patient is protected against the recurrence of subsequent depressive episodes.

PHARMACOLOGIC TREATMENT OF DEPRESSION

The treatment of psychiatric disorder in general and of depression in particular has improved considerably in the last decade, due in large part to the development of effective and well-tolerated antidepressants, such as SSRIs. The antidepressant drugs do not markedly influence the brain of a mentally healthy human but, rather, correct an abnormal condition. The TCAs, MAOIs, and SSRIs are antidepressants for depressed individuals but have relatively little or no effect as general euphoriants or stimulants in most mentally healthy persons. Several classes of antidepressants are available today. These drug classes and individual agents within classes are distinguished not so much by efficacy as by their side-effect profiles, and their efficacy in various subtypes of depression.

Until recently, the standard first-line treatment for depression had been tricyclic antidepressant drugs. Although very effective, these drugs have significant liabilities, such as toxicity in overdose, cardiotoxicity, and troublesome and often debilitating side effects that adversely affect patient compliance. Newer antidepressants, especially the SSRIs, have replaced TCAs as the first choice drugs because of their generally preferable side-effect profiles and safety in overdose. Some patients respond only to a drug from a different class or cannot tolerate the side effects of both TCAs and SSRIs.

General Guidelines

All pharmacologic treatments for depression begin acting with the first dose, but specific antidepressant effects may take weeks to become evident, even when the patient is on the steady-state dose. Side effects begin immediately, as do some nonspecific therapeutic effects. These include decreased anxiety (for most antidepressants), decreased disturbance of sleep (especially for imipramine and amitriptyline), and increased appetite (for tricyclic antidepressants and phenelzine). Once the patient has responded, he or she should remain on the effective dose of antidepressant for 4 to 6 months; patients will relapse if the drug is stopped too soon. It is probably not a coincidence that untreated episodes typically last from 4 to 12 months. Melancholia is a chronic, recurrent illness, and the modal cycle length is one year. If treatment is stopped at the wrong time, patients may suffer a recurrence. This may be prevented by maintenance treatment, which might include antidepressants, mood stabilizing drugs, and psychotherapy.

TRICYCLIC ANTIDEPRESSANTS AND RELATED COMPOUNDS

Available in the United States for over 30 years, the tricyclic antidepressants (TCAs) are relatively inexpensive and have been repeatedly demonstrated to be effective in treating major depression (Ball & Kiloh, 1959; Elkin et al., 1989; Rogers & Clay, 1975; Stewart et al., 1983). The mechanism of therapeutic action of the TCAs is thought to involve inhibition of norepinephrine and/or serotonin reuptake in the central nervous system (CNS). As with other antidepressants, full doses of TCAs must be administered for several weeks before concluding that the patient will not respond.

Initiation of Treatment

Patients to be started on TCAs should have an initial medical work up to prevent serious adverse reactions. An EKG probably should be obtained for all patients, but especially women over 40 and men over 30. The initial dose must be small and should be raised gradually, reaching the expected steady-state dose in one to two weeks. The clinician can raise the dosage for inpatients more quickly than for outpatients because of their closer clinical supervision.

Probably the most important factor in choosing a particular TCA is the individual side-effect profile. The tertiary amine TCAs, amitriptyline and imipramine, tend to have more severe side effects than their secondary amine metabolites, nortriptyline and desipramine (Baldessarini, 1996; Szabadi, Gaszner, & Bradshaw, 1980). The major side effects of the TCAs are attributed to inhibition of one or more neurotransmitter receptors, including the histaminergic, cholinergic, serotonergic, and dopaminergic receptors. Therapy with a tertiary TCA such as imipramine or amitriptyline, should be initiated with a low daily dose of 50 mg administered at bedtime. The daily dose is then increased in 50-mg increments in 2 to 4 day intervals to 200 to 300 mg/day. Some patients may require higher doses for maximal therapeutic response or lower doses because of adverse effects. This is of importance because patients vary widely in their propensity to metabolize TCAs.

Nortriptyline is the TCA of choice for many clinicians because of its well-established therapeutic plasma level window (50–150 ng/mL) and relatively more favorable side-effect profile compared with imipramine and amitriptyline.

It should be explained to patients that although sleep and appetite may improve in 1 or 2 weeks, TCAs usually take 3 to 4 weeks to have antidepressant effects, and a complete trial should last 6 weeks at the steady state dose.

The anticholinergic side effects of the TCAs are the most common reasons for discontinuing treatment. They include dry mouth, constipation, urinary retention, blurred vision, sinus tachycardia, and memory dysfunction. Blockade of histamine receptors in the CNS by TCAs is associated with sedation, drowsiness, and weight gain (Richelson, 1990). Cardiotoxicity associated with TCAs may be life-threatening in patients with preexisting cardiac disease. This is particularly pertinent to TCA overdose in which conduction delays, arrhythmias, and other untoward cardiac effects are often fatal (Glassman, Roose, & Bigger, 1993; Jefferson, 1975). Cardiac effects, such as orthostatic hypotension, dizziness, and cardiac conduction delays (e.g., first-degree AV block; bundle branch block) and arrhythmias (including sudden death after myocardial infarction) may occur with TCA therapy.

There is considerable evidence that plasma levels of TCAs are related to the probability of therapeutic response. Plasma level criteria are best established for imipramine (total plasma TCA level over 200 ng/mL) and nortriptyline (plasma level between 50 and 150 ng/mL). There is no documented association between plasma level and clinical response for other classes of antidepressants. This becomes especially significant in treating patients who appear to be unresponsive to antidepressant drug treatment, because the plasma level becomes a criterion for the adequacy of treatment.

The average acute lethal dose of TCA is about 10 times the steady-state daily dose. Prescriptions for patients at risk (i.e., those with a history of suicide attempts or suicidal ideation) should be limited to a 1-week supply.

In summary, TCAs are efficacious antidepressants and are relatively inexpensive, but they are no longer first-line treatment for depression because of their untoward side effects and low therapeutic index.

MONOAMINE OXIDASE INHIBITORS

The two MAOIs available for the treatment of depression in the United States are phenelzine and tranylcypromine. Commercial production of isocarboxazid has been discontinued.

Patients starting treatment should have a medical examination, as with those starting TCAs. MAOI therapy should be started with low doses that are generally increased (Klein, Gittelman, Quitkin, & Rifkin, 1980). The usual steady-state dose for phenelzine is 1 mg/kg/day; for tranylcypromine, 0.67 mg/kg/day. These drugs tend to be stimulating and should be given in divided doses early in the day, with the last dose at or before 3 P.M. Such multiple daily dose regimen may be associated with noncompliance. Like all antidepressants, the MAOIs must be administered for 3 to 4 weeks before any significant improvement in depression occurs, although decreased anxiety occurs quite early.

Side effects associated with MAOIs include dizziness, orthostatic hypertension, weight gain, and delayed orgasm (McDaniel, 1986). They suppress rapid eye movement (REM) sleep completely, though the occasional patient complains of nightmares.

In 1962, a case report described the death from a hypertensive crisis of a patient who was treated with tranylcypromine. The drug was withdrawn from the market until the cause of this sudden death was clarified. As noted earlier, patients taking MAOIs have unusually large stores of norepinephrine in presynaptic nerve terminals. This could be displaced by substances with a similar chemical structure if these were taken up into the nerve terminal. In this case, the compound was tyramine, which is present in many fermented foods, especially some cheeses and wines, and in meat or fish which is not very fresh. MAO is present in the small intestine, where it ordinarily metabolizes tyramine present in food, but MAOIs inhibit this enzyme and tyramine is absorbed (Baldessarini, 1996). Foods to be avoided during MAOI therapy include aged cheese, pickled or smoked fish, and fermented sausages. We now realize that the dietary restrictions that must be followed by patients taking MAOIs are not as difficult or as extensive as was previously thought.

The MAOIs are involved with several clinically significant drug interactions. Over-the-counter cold medications containing sympathomimetics may cause hypertensive crisis just as tyramine can. Concurrent administration of

MAOIs and other antidepressants is difficult or dangerous and, with SSRIs, potentially lethal, not to be undertaken lightly. Meperidine (Demerol) has also caused a dangerous interaction.

In summary, the MAOIs are not first-line antidepressants because of the requisite dietary restrictions and unfavorable side-effect profile. Nonetheless, the MAOIs do have a place in the treatment of depression (Pare, 1985), particularly in anxious patients and in those with atypical depression that is characterized by hypersomnia and/or hyperphagia, refractory depression, panic attacks, social phobia (Liebowitz et al., 1988), and bulimia.

SELECTIVE SEROTONIN REUPTAKE INHIBITORS

The SSRIs are currently considered first-line therapy for depression because they are easy to prescribe and have a superior side-effect/safety profile (Drugs for psychiatric disorders, 1997). The drugs in this class are not equally selective in affecting serotonin reuptake: paroxetine is the most selective. All cause decreased dopaminergic transmission, possibly by decreasing release of dopamine from presynaptic terminals. The SSRI antidepressants marketed in the United States include fluoxetine, paroxetine, sertraline, and fluvoxamine, the last approved only for treatment of OCD in the United States. The usual starting doses for the first two may also be the steady-state daily doses, and there is no need to search for an effective dose. SSRIs are often administered as a single daily dose with food. Fluoxetine and paroxetine are usually prescribed at an initial dose of 20 mg/day. The usual daily dose of fluoxetine may be as high as 80 mg/day, though some researchers have found no increased benefit over 40 mg/day. The daily dose of paroxetine may be as high as 50 mg, though doses above 30 mg/day might not provide extra benefit in treating depression. Sertraline is prescribed at a range of 50 to 200 mg/day; however, most patients require 100 mg/day or more to achieve full clinical response. Once daily dosing of the SSRIs can improve patient compliance.

The major side effects of the SSRIs are nausea, headache, dry mouth, insomnia, nervousness/agitation, sweating, dizziness, tremor, and sexual dysfunction. These side effects rarely result in discontinuation of the medication because most are transient. For example, treatment-emergent nausea and headache frequently resolve within 10 to 14 days of beginning SSRI therapy. The side-effect profiles of the SSRIs currently available in the United States are more alike than different. However, sertraline is frequently associated with loose stools and diarrhea. Fluoxetine is often associated with anxiety, nervousness, insomnia, and anorexia. Paroxetine may cause dry mouth and may be associated with mild somnolence. Unlike the TCAs, the SSRIs do not significantly alter the electrocardiogram. Interference with dopaminergic transmission may partially explain the nervousness or agitation associated with these drugs. It may also explain the not infrequent complaints of sedation, affective flattening, and leaden slowing made by patients who have been taking these drugs for long periods.

Sexual dysfunction, which may be the most problematic and under-reported side effect associated with the SSRIs, is manifest as ejaculatory delay and impotence in men and anorgasmia in women (Zajecka, Fawcett, Schaff, Jeffriess, & Guy, 1991). These drugs are effective treatment for premature ejaculation in some cases.

Drug-drug interactions with SSRIs are common. As discussed above, the combination of SSRIs and MAOIs can lead to the serotonin syndrome (Sternbach, 1991). SSRIs inhibit certain subtypes of the hepatic cytochrome P_{450} enzyme system, which metabolizes most drugs (Richelson, 1998). As a result, drugs metabolized by this enzyme system may exhibit marked increases in plasma concentration when co-administered with SSRIs. This may, in turn, cause serious side effects, including lethal cardiac arrhythmias. There are significant differences among these drugs in the presence or absence of active metabolites and in half lives, which influence the choice of drug. Norfluoxetine, an active metabolite of fluoxetine, has a very long half-life of about a week. At the other extreme, the half-life of paroxetine is about 18 hours, and there are no active metabolites. Any drug with a long half-life will tend to accumulate in older patients, while drugs with short half-lives tend to produce withdrawal symptoms.

As with other antidepressants, there is a 3- to 5-week lag before the full therapeutic effects of the SSRIs are apparent. Therefore, response should be monitored every 1 to 2 weeks during initiation of therapy. After 6 weeks of therapy, the response should be assessed and the dose increased for patients with partial response. Patients showing no improvement after 6 weeks of full-dose therapy should be considered for alternative therapy.

It is of paramount importance that, in contrast to the TCAs and MAOIs, the SSRIs are markedly safer when taken in overdose. Overdoses of TCAs are often fatal; therefore, in a population of patients prone to suicide attempts, use of TCAs may represent a treatment risk that is far greater than that associated with the SSRIs.

OTHER ANTIDEPRESSANTS

Bupropion

Bupropion (Wellbutrin) was first synthesized in 1966 and approved by the Food and Drug Administration (FDA) for use in depression in 1985. It is chemically unrelated to other antidepressants. The neurochemical mechanism of action of bupropion remains obscure, although it does exert relatively weak effects at noradrenergic, dopaminergic, and serotonergic systems. Bupropion was withdrawn shortly after it came to market because some patients taking the drug had seizures. Subsequent studies showed that the seizure risk was unacceptably high in anorexic patients and those with an underlying high risk of seizures; the incidence of drug-induced seizures did not differ from that for traditional antidepressants in other depressed patients and in daily doses below 450 mg. The drug was reintroduced into the United States in 1989. (See Feinberg (1990) for a review.)

In adult outpatients, bupropion is initially prescribed at 75 mg twice daily, and the dose is gradually increased to approximately 300 mg/day, with some patients requiring up to 450 mg/day. The most serious side effect of bupropion is the propensity to induce seizures in patients with no prior seizure history. The seizure rate is 0.4 percent to 4 percent, depending on the dose; seizures may be avoided by administering the total daily dose in divided doses. Other reported side effects of Bupropion include dry mouth, constipation, headache, insomnia, agitation, and nausea. Because bupropion may cause agitation (32%) and insomnia (19%), the last dose of the day should be administered well before bedtime. Other significant advantages of bupropion are a low risk of cardiotoxicity, infrequent effect on sexual function and relative safety in overdose (Salzman, 1993). Bupropion can be combined with SSRIs in the management of treatment-refractory depression.

Trazodone

Trazodone is not structurally related to the TCAs, SSRIs, or the MAOIs. It was the first antidepressant available in the United States that was not lethal in overdose, unless the patient also consumed considerable quantities of alcohol. Trazodone is quite sedating and is used alone or in combination to relieve insomnia. Therapy is generally begun with doses of 50 to 100 mg at bedtime, and the daily dose is gradually increased to 200 to 600 mg. Major side effects include sedation, orthostatic hypertension, dizziness, headache, and nausea. Unlike any of the other antidepressants, trazodone can produce priapism, which in some cases has required surgical intervention (Drugs that cause sexual dysfunction, 1992), and which may lead to irreversible impotence.

Nefazodone

Nefazodone has been shown to treat people with moderate to severe depression effectively. It effects both noradrenergic and serotonergic transmission. Nefazodone is usually started at 50 to 75 mg twice a day and gradually titrated upward to 300 to 600 mg/day. Doses of 450 to 600 mg/day may be necessary for full clinical response.

The incidence of sexual dysfunction, in both men and women, is significantly less than with SSRIs, though impotence is occasionally a problem. No change in weight has been observed throughout the course of treatment, and no symptoms suggesting decreased dopaminergic transmission have been reported. The overall favorable side-effect profile of nefazodone is evident in the low rate of treatment discontinuation due to adverse experiences during clinical trials. Nefazodone may have an anti-anxiety effect and improve sleep decreasing night and early morning awakenings. Some patients complain of excessive sedation.

Venlafaxine

Venlafaxine is a phenylethylamine, chemically unrelated to other antidepressants now on the market, and inhibits both norepinephrine and serotonin reuptake with little effect on other neurotransmitter systems (Andrews & Nemeroff, 1994). It must be administered in two or three divided doses per day, a regimen that may reduce compliance. Patients respond to a relatively wide range of daily doses of venlafaxine and treatment is usually started at 50 to 75 mg/day and titrated upward to as high as 375 mg/day. Nausea occurs when therapy is initiated and may be severe; nausea may be minimized by beginning treatment with lower doses of 25 mg and gradually titrating up to therapeutic doses. Anorexia (11%) and insomnia (18%) also occur during venlafaxine use. Blood pressure should be monitored during venlafaxine therapy because higher doses can be associated with sustained increases in blood pressure. Increased heart rate and serum cholesterol levels also occur. Venlafaxine may be effective in treatment of depression refractory to other drugs, especially at doses of 300 to 375 mg/day.

Mirtazapine

Mirtazapine (Remeron) came to market in the United States in 1996. It has an unusual profile of action on central neurotransmission: mirtazapine enhances noradrenergic transmission by blocking presynaptic a_2 receptors. Smith and his colleagues (Smith, Hollingsworth, Garcia-Sevilla, & Zis, 1983) had postulated that increased function of these receptors might be central to the pathophysiology of depression. The norepinephrine released may then cause release of serotonin by stimulating serotonergic neurons. The drug also blocks postsynaptic 5-HT_2 and 5-HT_3 receptors, but not 5-HT_1 receptors. The net result is stimulation of 5-HT_1 receptors (Wheatley, van Moffaert, Timmerman, & Kremer, 1998). It is usually started at 15 mg/day at bedtime, and the dose can be increased to 45 mg/day. Adverse effects include somnolence, dry mouth, and weight gain.

Citalopram

Citalopram (Celexa) is the latest (1998) addition to the antidepressants available in the United States, though it has been available in Europe since 1989. The major difference between citalopram and other SSRIs lies in its having less of an inhibitory effect on cytochrome P450 enzymes than the other SSRIs or nefazodone. This inhibition may be a major cause of adverse drug interactions. There is some evidence that citalopram may be fatal in overdose (Citalopram for depression, 1998).

ELECTROCONVULSIVE THERAPY

Electroconvulsive therapy (ECT) is arguably the safest and most effective antidepressant treatment for patients with severe depression (Avery & Winokur, 1984; Prudic & Sackheim, 1990). Patients may have a full therapeutic response in less than three weeks. ECT was more commonly used before the introduction of antidepressants and since has been minimally used in the United States. This is in part a result of an undeserved reputation among the public that the treatment is dangerous and induces brain damage. The use of succinylcholine to produce paralysis prevented broken bones and brain damage caused by hypoxia. Alterations in the delivery of the electrical stimulus, including unilateral treatment of the nondominant hemisphere, have further decreased the transient memory loss associated with ECT. Klein and his colleagues (1980) present a skeptic's view of ECT.

ECT may be preferred to other treatments in several situations. These include: severe depression that requires rapid response (e.g., high risk of suicide, cachexia); contraindications to the use of medication (e.g., pregnancy, severe medical illness); psychotic depression; failure to respond to medication; catatonia; and previous positive response to ECT. In typical drug trials, about 67 percent of depressed patients respond to an antidepressant, while over 90 percent respond to ECT. ECT has been found to be effective for 50 percent to 70 percent of patients who have failed to respond to antidepressant medications. Maintenance therapy with antidepressant medication is usually necessary with patients who have received ECT given the 30 percent to 60 percent probability of relapse if treatment is stopped too soon. Whether initially stabilized with medication or with ECT, patients who exhibit repeated episodes of moderate or severe depression despite maintenance with a combination of an antidepressant and lithium or patients who are medically ineligible for such treatment can be treated with monthly maintenance ECT.

The chief side effects of ECT are cognitive. Treatment is associated with a transient post-ictal confusional state and with a longer period of anterograde and retrograde memory interference. ECT has the highest rate of response of any form of antidepressant treatment and should be considered in virtually all cases of moderate or severe major depression not responsive to pharmacologic intervention (Prudic & Sackheim, 1990).

Treating Refractory Depression

There are a number of antidepressants currently available to treat depression. Nierenberg and White (1990) wrote an excellent review with suggestions for successive treatments. If a patient fails an adequate trial with one antidepressant, then a representative of another class of antidepressant with a different mechanism of action or side-effect profile should be prescribed next. The standard is 6 weeks' treatment with imipramine or nortriptyline at an adequate plasma drug level. When a patient has had only partial response to antidepressants, several strategies may be employed, including the addition of lithium at full therapeutic plasma levels (Austin, Souza, & Goodwin, 1991). Thyroid hormone (tri-iodothyronine, 25–50 mg/day) is a second-line augmentation strategy. The TCAs, venlafaxine, or MAOIs are rational agents for treating severe, refractory depression. SSRIs may be effective in combination with TCAs in refractory patients, provided plasma TCA concentrations are monitored. The addition of psychostimulants, such as amphetamine or methylphenidate, may be effective in some cases. Electroconvulsive therapy (ECT) is effective for antidepressant non-responsive depression with melancholic or psychotic features (Klein, Gittelman, Quitkin, & Rifkin, 1980). Some refractory patients, especially those without melancholic or psychotic features, may be more appropriately and effectively treated with psychotherapy instead of, or in addition to, drugs.

Few drugs are universally effective, and all have side effects. The value of any new compound is ultimately determined by the extent to which it provides improved efficacy and tolerability over existing drugs. It is already evident that some serotonin selective drugs provide a measurable advance over traditional treatments.

Despite the comparative advantages of current antidepressants, clinical limitations remain. There is still a delay in onset of therapeutic effects, usually 1 to 3 weeks. Absent careful diagnosis and expert treatment, there is an efficacy ceiling of approximately 65 percent for any single antidepressant drug. Side effects continue to discourage compliance or detract from quality of life when patients do comply.

SEASONAL AFFECTIVE DISORDER

Some individuals suffer annual episodes of depression beginning in the fall or spring, usually at the same time each year. About 85 percent of these patients have annual recurrences of major depressive disorder, not seasonal affective disorder. The remainder may suffer from Seasonal Affective Disorder (Thase, 1986). Their depressive episodes frequently include atypical features such as hypersomnia and overeating, and these patients are less likely to have the specific abnormalities of sleep and endocrine function associated with MDD (Rosenthal et al., 1984). The entire range of treatments for depression may be used to treat seasonal affective disorder, either in combination with or as an alternative to light therapy. However, patients with atypical symptoms may be more likely to respond to phototherapy than those with endogenous or melancholic symptoms (Stinson & Thompson, 1990).

In some patients with seasonal affective disorder, depressive manifestations respond to supplementation of environmental light by means of exposure to bright white artificial light in the morning and/or evening hours, usually for 2 to 5 hours a day (Rosenthal et al., 1985). Time of day of exposure has not been clearly shown to be important (Jacobsen, Wehr, Skwerer, Sack, & Rosenthal, 1987; James, Wehr, Sack, Parry, & Rosenthal, 1985; Rosenthal et al., 1985). Possible side effects include headache, eyestrain, irritability, and insomnia. Concerns have been raised about possible adverse ocular effects of phototherapy. As a sole form of treatment, light therapy may be recommended as a time-limited trial (Rosenthal et al., 1985; Stinson & Thompson, 1990), primarily in outpatients with clear seasonal patterns and atypical features.

BIPOLAR DISORDER

Kraepelin (1921) united all affective disorders under the rubric "manic-depressive insanity," partly as a reaction to increasingly complicated diagnostic systems. Leonhard (1968) separated this into unipolar (depression only) and bipolar (cyclic episodes of both mania and depression) disorders, and Dunner and his colleagues further divided bipolar disorder into types I and II, where bipolar II patients had been hypomanic but never manic. About 1.3 percent of the U.S. population has bipolar disease (0.8% bipolar I and 0.5% bipolar II), and its prevalence seems to be rising. There is no apparent gender difference in prevalence.

Lithium (Li) was first used to treat manic episodes in the late 1940s, but it was not approved for clinical use in the United States until 1970. Despite lithium's marked antimanic activity, response to it is inadequate for almost half of those with bipolar illness. Over the next decade, the antimanic and antidepressant effects of the anticonvulsants valproate (VPA) and carbamazepine (CBZ) were found to be therapeutically useful in people with bipolar disorders. Clinical trials subsequently demonstrated that the efficacy of these agents in acute mania is comparable to that of lithium.

The safe and effective treatment of bipolar depression presents a particularly difficult clinical challenge. There is a risk that treating bipolar depressed patients with an antidepressant will induce mania or lead to "rapid cycling" (more than four affective episodes per year), although the degree of risk remains unclear (Lewis & Winokur, 1982; Wehr & Goodwin, 1987; Wehr, Sack, Rosenthal, & Cowdry, 1988). The management of manic, mixed, and depressive mood states in bipolar disorder relies on lithium or other mood-stabilizing agents as the primary treatment. An antidepressant can be added cautiously and temporarily to treat depression, but the additional benefit of sustained combinations has not been proven.

LITHIUM

In 1949, John F.J. Cade reported the successful therapeutic effects of lithium in a patient with manic episodes. In the 1950s and the 1960s Mogens Schou conducted the critical experiments which eventually resulted in the approval of lithium for the treatment of mania by the U.S. Food and Drug Administration (FDA) in 1970. The introduction of lithium into psychiatry in 1949 changed utterly the course and prognosis of manic-depressive illness. It is not a sedative, depressant, or euphoriant, and this characteristic differentiates lithium from other psychotropic agents. The precise mechanism of action of lithium as a mood-stabilizing agent remains unknown, although many cellular actions of lithium have been described.

There is more evidence that lithium prevents recurrence of mania or depression in both bipolar and unipolar patients than there is for any other treatment (Davis, 1976). Yet 20 percent to 30 percent of manic-depressives have partial or no response to ongoing treatment with lithium (Gerbino, Oleshansky, & Gershon, 1978). Many of these patients are rapid cyclers, who have four or more affective episodes per year.

For most adult patients, the clinician should start lithium carbonate at 900 to 1200 mg/day. The starting dosage in patients who are elderly or who have renal impairment should be 300 mg once or twice daily. The usual eventual dosage is between 900 and 1,800 mg a day. Immediate-release lithium, given in a single bedtime dose, has been shown to have less short term effect on renal function than other dosage regimens (Hetmar et al., 1986; Plenge et al., 1982; Schou et al., 1982). This regimen may also decrease the chance of long-term renal damage. Lithium is not prescribed by dose, but by blood level, because of its low therapeutic index. Lithium cannot be used safely in patients who cannot be tested regularly. Concentrations between 0.7 and 1.25 mEq per liter are considered to be effective and safe, and levels between 0.9 and 1.1 mEq per liter are favored for treatment of acutely manic or hypomanic patients. Somewhat lower values (0.8 to 1.0 mEq per liter) are considered adequate for long-term use for prevention of recurrent illness (Gelenberg et al., 1989). Lithium levels above 2 mEq per liter are toxic. These concentrations refer to serum or plasma samples obtained between 11 and 13 hours after the preceding dose. The need for regularly monitoring serum lithium levels and maintaining them within a narrow therapeutic range, problems of compliance, and the danger of accidental or suicidal overdose may further complicate long-term treatment.

The most common adverse effects of lithium treatment are gastric distress, weight gain, tremor, fatigue, and mild cognitive impairment. Gastrointestinal symptoms can include nausea, decreased appetite, vomiting, and diarrhea and can often be reduced by dividing the dosage, administering the lithium with food or giving it in a single bedtime dose. Weight gain results from increased appetite and from a poorly understood effect of lithium on carbohydrate metabolism. Lithium affects thyroid function both acutely and chronically, and this can also lead to weight gain.

Treatment of acute mania and the prevention of recurrences of manic-depressive illness in otherwise-healthy adults or adolescents are the only currently FDA approved uses in the United States. In addition, on the basis of compelling evidence of efficacy, lithium also is used as an adjunct when response to an antidepressant alone is unsatisfactory (Austin, Souza, & Goodwin, 1991; Baldessarini & Tohen, 1988; Joffe, Singer, Levitt, & MacDonald, 1993).

MAINTENANCE AND PROPHYLACTIC ANTIDEPRESSANT TREATMENT

Most depressive disorders have a lifetime course. For the majority of patients, the risk for future episodes increases and the length of the well interval between episodes decreases with each new episode. Patients whose first episode occurs later in life have a higher probability of recurrence than those whose first episode comes earlier. As the number of episodes becomes larger and the patient older, episodes tend to be more severe, less responsive to conventional antidepressants, and thus more destructive. Current studies suggest that maintenance treatment may prevent recurrence and thus improve quality of life. Episodes of major depression tend to remit spontaneously over 6 to 12 months, more quickly in bipolar patients. There is a high risk of relapse following premature discontinuation of successful antidepressant treatment. To minimize this risk, it is best to continue antidepressant medication for 4 to 6 months* following apparent full clinical recovery. Frank et al. (1991) suggested

---

*This risk is estimated at 50 percent within 6 months and 65 percent to 70 percent at one year of follow-up, rising to 85 percent by 3 years (Baldessarini & Tohen, 1988). The available data indicate that patients treated for a first episode of uncomplicated depression who exhibit satisfactory response to an antidepressant agent should continue to receive a full therapeutic dose of that agent for at least 16 to 20 weeks after achieving full remission (Prien & Kupfer, 1986).

that depressive illness occurring less than four months after treatment is stopped should be regarded as part of the original illness (relapse) rather than an occurrence of a new episode (recurrence). It is, therefore, necessary that patients have been symptom free for a period of at least 4 months before response to prophylaxis can be validly assessed.

Many depressed patients with recurrent episodes have lesser levels of symptoms and disability between major episodes, and so require consideration of long-term maintenance medication to reduce the risk of recurrence [see Greden (1993); Thase (1992)]. Such treatment has been tested for as long as 5 years, using relatively high doses of imipramine, with evidence that early dose reduction led to a higher risk of relapse (Frank et al., 1993; Kupfer et al., 1992; Thase, 1992). Frank and her colleagues (1990, 1993) conclude that, for patients who have suffered several recurrences, full-dose maintenance treatment is most effective prophylactic strategy. Maintenance dosages need to be comparable to established treatment dosages until it is proven that lower doses are efficacious; such data now are lacking. When medication is selected for long-term treatment, strong consideration should be given to the agent's side-effect profile, since compliance is essential for success.

Greden (1993) suggests that long-term or lifetime maintenance appears indicated for patients who have had multiple prior episodes and those who are older at the time of onset. The following patients are likely to benefit from lifetime treatment:

1. Those who are 50 years or older at time of onset.
2. Those who are 40 years of age or older at time of onset and who have experienced two or more episodes of major depression.
3. Those who have had three or more episodes, regardless of their age of onset or current age.

Multiple prior episodes might be defined as two or more episodes within 4 years, as suggested by Schou (1989), who discusses the criteria for lithium maintenance in a book written for a wide audience, including patients and their families. He adds that patients with fewer, more severe episodes should also be considered for maintenance treatment. This would include patients who made a serious suicide attempt or who were otherwise in danger and those who were psychotic.

The ideal outcome for patients with mood disorders is maintenance of euthymia rather than multiple resolutions of acute episodes. For most patients with this lifetime disorder, that objective appears achievable. If medication is ultimately tapered and discontinued, patients should be carefully monitored during and immediately after discontinuation to ensure that remission is stable. Patients who have had multiple prior episodes of depression should be considered for maintenance medication treatment. Specific forms of psychotherapy, psychoanalysis, or psychotherapeutic management may be used to reduce the effect of stresses and conflicts that might cause recurrence of depression or undermine medication compliance (American Psychiatric

Association, 1993). Available data suggest that antidepressants generally have acceptable risk in long-term use. While more systematic studies of safety need to be collected over the long term, few long-term adverse consequences have been reported. In comparison, repeated episodes of severe depression have major and profound risks of disability, divorce, financial ruin, morbidity, and death.

Frank, Kupfer, and their colleagues (Frank et al., 1990; Kupfer et al., 1992) have shown that specific psychotherapy is an important part of a maintenance program. They used interpersonal therapy and imipramine to show that psychotherapy had a protective effect, but did not add to the effect of imipramine alone.

If it is absolutely necessary to discontinue medication, this should be done gradually, cautiously, with close monitoring, with ongoing use of nonpharmacologic treatment if possible, and with a strategic plan for prompt intervention when anticipated relapse occurs.

SUMMARY

Depression is a normal mood, a symptom of a wide variety of mental and physical disorders, and a specific syndrome. Patients with depressive illness fall into a number of poorly differentiated diagnostic categories, and the correct diagnosis of patients with depressed mood can be difficult and confusing. Depressed patients can respond well to a variety of specific psycho- and pharmacotherapies, and to combinations of these modalities. Selecting safe and effective treatment(s) for each patient can also be complicated and difficult and includes a component of trial and error. We discuss with the patient the diagnosis and treatment of depression, including short- and long-term strategies, with an emphasis on pharmacological treatment.

REFERENCES

American Psychiatric Association. (1993). Practice guidelines for major depressive disorder in adults. *American Journal of Psychiatry, 150,* S1–S26.

American Psychiatric Association. (1994). *Diagnostic and statistical manual of mental disorders* (4th ed.). Washington, DC: Author.

Andrews, J.M., & Nemeroff, C.B. (1994). Contemporary management of depression. *American Journal of Medicine, 97,* S6A24–S6A32.

Austin, M.P., Souza, F.G., & Goodwin, G.M. (1991). Lithium augmentation in antidepressant-resistant patients: a quantitative analysis. *British Journal of Psychiatry, 159,* 510–514.

Avery, D., & Winokur, G. (1984). The efficacy of electroconculsive therapy and antidepressants in depression. *Biological Psychiatry, 12,* 507–523.

Baldessarini, R.J. (1989). Current clinical status of antidepressants: Clinical pharmacology and therapy. *Journal of Clinical Psychiatry, 50,* 117–126.

Baldessarini, R.J. (1996). Drugs and the treatment of psychiatric disorders, depression, and mania. In J.G. Hardman, L.E. Limbird, P.B. Molinoff, R.W. Ruddon, & A.G.

Gilman (Eds.), *The pharmacological basis of therapeutics* (9th ed., pp. 431–460). New York: McGraw-Hill.

Baldessarini, R.J., & Tohen, M. (1988). Is there a long-term protective effect of mood-altering agents in unipolar depressive disorder? In D.E. Casey & A.V. Christensen (Eds.), *Psychopharmacology: Current trends* (pp. 130–139). Berlin: Springer-Verlag.

Ball, J.R.B., & Kiloh, L.G. (1959). A controlled trial of imipramine in the treatment of depressive states. *British Medical Journal, 2,* 1052–1055.

Citalopram for depression. (1998). *The Medical Letter on Drugs and Therapeutics, 40,* 113–114.

The Cross National Collaboration Group. (1992). The changing rate of major depression. *Journal of the American Medical Association, 268,* 3098–3105.

Davis, J.M. (1976). Overview: Maintenance therapy in psychiatry: II. Affective disorders. *American Journal of Psychiatry, 133,* 1–13.

Drugs for psychiatric disorders. (1997). *The Medical Letter on Drugs and Therapeutics, 39,* 33–40.

Drugs that cause sexual dysfunction: An update. (1992). *The Medical Letter on Drugs and Therapeutics, 34,* 73–78.

Elkin, I., Shea, T., Watkins, J.T., Imber, S.D., Sotsky, S.M., Collins, J.F., Glass, D.R., Pilkonis, P.A., Leber, W.R., Docherty, J.P., Fiester, S.J., & Parloff, M.B. (1989). National Institute of Mental Health treatment of depression collaborative research program: General effectiveness of treatments. *Archives of General Psychiatry, 46,* 971–982.

Feinberg, M. (1990). Bupropion: New therapy for depression. *American Family Physician, 41,* 1787–1790.

Frank, E., Kupfer, D.J., Jarrett, R.B., Keller, M.B., Lavori, P.W., Rush, A.J., & Weissman, M.M. (1991). Conceptualization and rationale for consensus definitions of terms in major depressive disorder: Remission, recovery, relapse, and recurrence. *Archives of General Psychiatry, 48,* 851–855.

Frank, E., Kupfer, D.J., Perel, J.M., Cornes, C., Jarrett, D.B., Mallinger, A.G., Thase, M.E., McEachran, A.B., & Grochocinski, V.J. (1990). Three-year outcomes for maintenance therapies in recurrent depression. *Archives of General Psychiatry, 47,* 1093–1099.

Frank, E., Kupfer, D.J., Perel, J.M., Cornes, C., Mallinger, A.G., Thase, M.E., McEachran, A.B., & Grochocinski, V.J. (1993). Comparison of full-dose versus half-dose pharmacotherapy in the maintenance of recurrent depression. *Journal of Affective Disorders, 27,* 139–145.

Gelenberg, A.J., Kane, J.M., Keller, M.B., Lavori, P., Rosenbaum, J.F., Cole, K., & Lavelle, J. (1989). Comparison of standard and low serum levels of lithium for maintenance treatment of bipolar disorder. *New England Journal of Medicine, 321,* 1489–1493.

Gerbino, L., Oleshansky, M., & Gershon, S. (1978). Clinical use and mode of action of lithium. In M.A. Lipton, A. DiMascio, & A.F. Killam (Eds.), *Psychopharmacology: A generation of progress.* New York: Raven Press.

Glassman, A.H., Roose, S.P., & Bigger, J.T., Jr. (1993). The safety of tricyclic antidepressants in cardiac patients. Risk-benefit reconsidered. *Journal of the American Medical Association, 269,* 2673–2675.

Greden, J.F. (1993). Antidepressant maintenance medications: When to discontinue and how to stop. *Journal of Clinical Psychiatry, 54,* S39–S45.

Greenberg, P.E., Stiglin, L.E., Finkelstein, S.N., & Berndt, E.R. (1993). The economic burden of depression in 1990. *Journal of Clinical Psychiatry, 54,* 405–418.

Hetmar, O., Bolwig, T.G., Brun, C., Ladefoged, J., Larsen, S., & Rafaelsen, O.J. (1986). Lithium: Long term effects on the kidney: I. Renal function in retrospect. *Acta Psychiatrica Scandinavica, 73,* 574–581.

Isacsson, G., Boethius, G., & Bergman, U. (1992). Low level of antidepressant prescription for people who later commit suicide: Fifteen years of experience from a population-based drug database in Sweden. *Acta Psychiatrica Scandinavica, 85,* 444–448.

Jacobsen, F.M., Wehr, T.A., Skwerer, R.A., Sack, D.A., & Rosenthal, N.E. (1987). Morning versus midday phototherapy of seasonal affective disorder. *American Journal of Psychiatry, 144,* 1301–1305.

James, S.P., Wehr, T.A., Sack, D.A., Parry, B.L., & Rosenthal, N.E. (1985). Treatment of seasonal affective disorder with light in the evening. *British Journal of Psychiatry, 147,* 424–428.

Jefferson, J.W. (1975). A review of the cardiovascular effects and toxicity of tricyclic antidepressants. *Psychosomatic Medicine, 37,* 160–179.

Joffe, R.T., Singer, W., Levitt, A.J., & MacDonald, C.A. (1993). A placebo-controlled comparison of lithium and triiodothyronine augmentation of tricyclic antidepressant in unipolar refractory depression. *Archives of General Psychiatry, 50,* 387–393.

Katon, W., Von Korff, M., Lin, E., Bush, T., & Ormel, J. (1992). Adequacy and duration of antidepressant treatment in primary care. *Medical Care, 30,* 67–76.

Kessler, R.C., McGonagle, K.A., Zhao, S., Nelson, C.B., Hughes, M., Eshleman, S., Wittchen, H.-U., & Kendler, K.S. (1994). Lifetime and 12-month prevalence of *DSM-III-R* psychiatric disorders in the United States: Results from the national comorbidity survey. *Archives of General Psychiatry, 51,* 8–19.

Kind, P., & Sorensen, J. (1993). The costs of depression. *International Journal of Clinical Psychopharmacology, 7,* 191–195.

Klein, D.F., Gittelman, R., Quitkin, F., & Rifkin, A. (1980). *Diagnosis and drug treatment of psychiatric disorders: Adults and children* (2nd ed.). Baltimore: Williams & Wilkins.

Klerman, G.L., & Weissman, M.M. (1989). Increasing rates of depression. *Journal of the American Medical Association, 261,* 2229–2235.

Kraepelin, E. (1921). *Manic-depressive insanity and paranoia.* Edinburgh: Livingstone.

Kupfer, D.J., Frank, E., Perel, J.M., Cornes, C., Mallinger, A., Thase, M.E., McEachran, A.B., & Grochocinski, V.J. (1992). Five-year outcome for maintenance in recurrent depression. *Archives of General Psychiatry, 49,* 769–773.

Leonhard, K. (1968). *Aufteilung der endogenen Psychosen* (4th ed.). Berlin: Aufl Akademie Verlag.

Lewis, J.L., & Winokur, G. (1982). The induction of mania. *Archives of General Psychiatry, 39,* 303–306.

Liebowitz, M.R., Gorman, J.M., Fyer, A.J., et al. (1988). Pharmacotherapy of social phobia: An interim report of a placebo-controlled comparison of phenelzine and atenolol. *Journal of Clinical Psychiatry, 49,* 252–257.

McDaniel, K.D. (1986). Clinical pharmacology of monoamine oxidase inhibitors. *Clinical Neuropharmacology, 9,* 207–234.

Nierenberg, A.A., & White, K. (1990). What next? A review of pharmacologic strategies for treatment resistant depression. *Psychopharmacology Bulletin, 26,* 429–660.

Pare, C.M.B. (1985). The present status of monoamine oxidase inhibitors. *British Journal of Psychiatry, 146,* 576–584.

Peselow, E.D., Sanfilipo, M.P., Difiglia, C., & Fieve, R.R. (1992). Melancholic/endogenous depression and response to somatic treatment and placebo. *American Journal of Psychiatry, 149,* 1324–1334.

Plenge, P., Mellerup, E.T., Bolwig, T.G., Brun, C., Hetmar, O., Ladefoged, J., Larsen, S., & Rafaelsen, O.J. (1982). Lithium treatment: Does the kidney prefer one daily dose instead of two? *Acta Psychiatrica Scandinavica, 66,* 121–128.

Prien, R.F., & Kupfer, D.J. (1986). Continuation drug therapy for major depressive episodes: How long should it be maintained? *American Journal of Psychiatry, 143,* 18–23.

Prudic, J., & Sackheim, H.A. (1990). Refractory depression and electroconvulsive therapy. In S. Roose & A.H. Glassman (Eds.), *Treatment strategies for refractory depression* (pp. 111–128). Washington, DC: American Psychiatric Press.

Regier, D.A., Boyd, J.H., Burke, J.D., Jr., Rae, D.S., Myers, J.K., Kramer, M., et al. (1988). One-month prevalence of mental disorders in the United States: Based on five epidemiological catchment area sites. *Archives of General Psychiatry, 45,* 977–986.

Richelson, E. (1988). Synaptic pharmacology of antidepressants: An update. *McLean Hospital Journal, 13,* 67–88.

Richelson, E. (1990). Antidepressants and brain neurochemistry. *Mayo Clinic Proceedings, 65,* 1227–1236.

Richelson, E. (1998). Pharmacokinetic interactions of antidepressants. *Journal of Clinical Psychiatry, 59*(Suppl. 10), 22–26.

Rogers, S.C., & Clay, P.M. (1975). A statistical review of controlled trials of imipramine and placebo in the treatment of depressive illness. *British Journal of Psychiatry, 127,* 599–603.

Rosenthal, N.E., Sack, D.A., Carpenter, C.J., Parry, B.L., Mendelson, W.B., & Wehr, T.A. (1985). Antidepressant effects of light in seasonal affective disorder. *American Journal of Psychiatry, 142,* 163–170.

Rosenthal, N.E., Sack, D.A., Gillin, J.C., Lewy, A.J., Goodwin, F.K., Davenport, Y., Mueller, P.S., Newsome, D.A., & Wehr, T.A. (1984). Seasonal affective disorder: A description of the syndrome and preliminary findings with light therapy. *Archives of General Psychiatry, 41,* 72–80.

Salzman, C. (1993). Pharmacologic treatment of depression in the elderly. *Journal of Clinical Psychiatry, 54,* S23–S28.

Schou, M. (1989). *Lithium treatment of manic-depressive illness* (4th ed.). Basel: Karger.

Schou, M., Amdisen, A., Thomsen, K., Vestergaard, P., Hetmar, O., Mellerup, E.T., Plenge, P., & Rafaelsen, O.J. (1982). Lithium treatment regimen and renal water handling: The significance of dosage pattern and tablet type examined through comparison of results from two clinics with different treatment regimens. *Psychopharmacology (Berlin), 77,* 387–390.

Schulberg, H.C., Katon, W., Simon, G.E., & Rush, A.J. (1998). Treating major depression in primary care practice. An update of the agency for health care policy and research practice guidelines. *Archives of General Psychiatry, 55,* 1121–1127.

Smith, C.B., Hollingsworth, P.J., Garcia-Sevilla, J.A., & Zis, A.P. (1983). Platelet alpha-2 adrenoceptors are decreased in number after antidepressant therapy. *Progress in Neuropsychopharmacology and Biological Psychiatry, 7,* 241–247.

Sternbach, H. (1991). The serotonin syndrome. *American Journal of Psychiatry, 148,* 705–713.

Stewart, J.W., Quitkin, F.M., Liebowitz, M.R., McGrath, P.J., Harrison, W.M., & Klein, D.F. (1983). Efficacy of desipramine in depressed outpatients. *Archives of General Psychiatry, 40,* 202–207.

Stinson, D., & Thompson, C. (1990). Clinical experience with phototherapy. *Journal of Affective Disorders, 18,* 129–135.

Szabadi, E., Gaszner, P., & Bradshaw, C.M. (1980). The peripheral anticholinergic activity of tricyclic antidepressants: Comparison of amitriptyline and desipramine in human volunteers. *British Journal of Psychiatry, 137,* 433–439.

Thase, M.E. (1986). Defining and treating seasonal affective disorder. *Psychiatric Annals, 16,* 733–737.

Thase, M.E. (1992). Long-term treatments of recurrent depressive disorders. *Journal of Clinical Psychiatry, 53,* 32–44.

Wehr, T.A., & Goodwin, F.K. (1987). Can antidepressants cause mania and worsen the course of affective illness? *American Journal of Psychiatry, 144,* 1403–1411.

Wehr, T.A., Sack, D.A., Rosenthal, N.E., & Cowdry, R.W. (1988). Rapid cycling affective disorder: Contributing factors and treatment responses in 51 patients. *American Journal of Psychiatry, 145,* 179–184.

Wheatley, D.P., van Moffaert, M., Timmerman, T., & Kremer, C.M.E. (1998). Mirtazapine: Efficacy and tolerability in comparison with fluoxetine in patients with moderate to severe major depressive disorder. *Journal of Clinical Psychiatry, 59,* 306–312.

Zajecka, I., Fawcett, J., Schaff, M., Jeffriess, H., & Guy, C. (1991). The role of serotonin in sexual dysfunction: Fluoxetine-associated orgasm dysfunction. *Journal of Clinical Psychiatry, 52,* 66–68.

PART THREE

PANIC AND AGORAPHOBIA

ALL THREE chapters in this section reflect the substantial changes that recently have occurred in the conceptualization of panic and agoraphobia. Previously, panic was viewed as little more than an intense form of the same excessive anxiety characteristic of all anxiety disorders. It was given little attention in either etiological models or treatment programs. In contrast, current views hold that panic is a significant phenomenon in its own right. It is still not clear if it is physiologically distinct from other forms of anxiety, but its severity and distinct quality apparently make it phenomenologically different. Agoraphobia has been viewed narrowly as a fear of open spaces, not unlike other specific phobias. Here too, recent findings document that it has a much more pervasive impact and that concurrent Axis II diagnoses compound the difficulties in treating this resistive disorder.

Wolitsky and Eagle present the psychoanalytic interpretation of anxiety in general. Most of the comments about the efficacy of psychoanalytic treatment are at the theoretical level, given the "absence of even informal follow-up reports" (see Chapter 9) from this group of therapists. However, those authors, albeit the lack of hard data, suggest that initial treatment be symptom focused, followed by some combination of pharmacological, supportive, insight-oriented, cognitive, and in vivo strategies. They argue that, by resolving core conflicts, further symptomatic behavior is less likely to be evinced.

McGlynn and Bates present the cognitive behavioral approach to panic and agoraphobia, noting that the two syndromes are assessed and treated separately. Current behavioral treatments for panic include breathing retraining, interoceptive exposure, muscular relaxation, and cognitive restructuring. The major approach for agoraphobia involves some sort of in vivo exposure (therapist assisted or self-directed). The research has documented efficacy of a number of these treatment methods, but multi-element protocols seem to predominate. Silberman reviews the extensive pharmacological literature, which documents effectiveness of several classes of medication, including atypical benzodiazepines, tricyclic antidepressants, other cyclic and serotonerigic antidepressants, and MAOIs. Treatment dropouts and relapses after termination of medication remain notable problems. However, these problems are no worse than they are in the treatment of many other disorders, and overall success rates appear to be notable in some instances. The importance of collaborative treatment planning is underscored. The physician is cautioned to discuss the range of medications available and the potential side effects with patients.

Several procedural and conceptual commonalities are apparent in the three chapters. First and foremost, all three approaches recognize the importance of exposure to the feared situation. Exposure represents the key aspect of behavioral interventions, but its precise role in pharmacotherapy and psychoanalytic therapy is less clear. Patients receiving the latter two approaches are urged to expose themselves once panic and anticipatory anxiety begin to subside. However, exposure is sometimes viewed simply as a facilitative strategy that speeds overall recovery rather than as an activity that is essential if recovery is to occur. Unfortunately, the existing literature does not resolve this issue. Further research is necessary in order to determine precisely how and when exposure should be conducted, both with and without associated medication. Similarly, additional work is needed to analyze the relative effects of medication and exposure on panic (when used separately) and on avoidance (when used in combination).

Finally, all three chapters recognize the significant advance provided by *DSM-IV* in categorization of patients, and all three indicate that the current system does not provide enough information about treatment choices. A variety of pharmacological agents has proven to be effective in treatment, despite dramatically different chemical structures and sites of action. Similarly, diverse behavioral strategies have yielded significant results. Such diversity suggests some higher-order etiology that can be redressed in a variety of ways, or a very heterogeneous category that includes a number of different disorders with similar phenomenology. This is the most perplexing and pressing issue in the search for improved outcome and for a reduction in the number of nonresponders.

CHAPTER 9

Psychoanalytic Approaches

DAVID L. WOLITZKY and MORRIS N. EAGLE

CONCEPTUALIZATION OF THE DISORDERS

Our aim in this chapter is to provide an account of the psychoanalytically oriented treatment of three *DSM-IV* anxiety disorders—panic disorder with agoraphobia (300.21), panic disorder without agoraphobia (300.01), and agoraphobia without history of panic disorder (300.22). We proceed by presenting the psychoanalytic conceptualization of anxiety and its implications for diagnosis and treatment of these disorders (American Psychiatric Association [APA], 1994). We also include some case illustrations and comment briefly on alternative treatment approaches.

According to traditional or classical psychoanalytic theory (Meissner, 1985), anxiety is a central aspect of virtually every psychiatric disorder. It can be (1) acute, quite intense, and unbound, as in panic disorder; (2) chronic, more moderate, and also unbound, as in generalized anxiety disorder; or, (3) manifestly absent a good deal of the time, as in circumscribed phobic disorders, in which it is bound to specific objects or situations that often can be avoided.

The acute, intense form of anxiety is what Freud called *traumatic anxiety*. It is a state of feeling overwhelmed with uncontrollable fear, terror, and a conviction of impending catastrophe or doom. The patient feels that his or her actual survival is at stake, and such great apprehension typically is accompanied by a variety of physical manifestations (e.g., dizziness, dyspnea, chest pain tachycardia), which further intensify fears of loss of control, insanity, and or dying.

In its milder forms, anxiety is seen by Freud as a signal of the potential onset of traumatic anxiety. This signal is the occasion for the automatic instigation of defenses aimed at reducing the anxiety.

Anxiety, in its signal or traumatic form, unlike fear, is not a response to a realistic, external danger, from which one could escape. The nature of the danger in anxiety is an internal one—in particular, an unconscious, instinctual wish that is assumed to be dangerous, especially if it reaches consciousness and is expressed through action.

There are typical danger situations associated with different phases of psychosexual development. In order, these are (1) loss of the love object, (2) loss of the object's love, (3) castration anxiety in males, and (4) superego anxiety or guilt. Although each of these dangers predominates at different developmental phases, they each build on one another and typically have overlapping unconscious meanings.

These so-called danger situations share the common point that they can all lead to the traumatic situation of the excessive, overwhelming excitation of nongratified instinctual drives. The traumatic danger represented by the loss of the love object, for example, is due to the threat that libidinal and aggressive wishes would not be able to be discharged, with the result that accumulated excitation would overwhelm and damage the nervous system and render the ego helpless.

Signal anxiety is a developmental achievement. Its presence presupposes the capacity for anticipation based on memories of traumatic situations and of experiences of gradations of anxiety. It is also based on the judgment that certain instinctual wishes are dangerous because they have led to or will meet with actual and/or fantasized disapproval and punishment. These judgments become internalized, creating intrapsychic conflict (most notably between the id and the superego). Ego deficits and ego regressions impair the effective operation of anxiety signals and make the patient more vulnerable to traumatic anxiety. These conditions make it more likely that ego defenses (of which repression is the prototype) will fail to contain the anxiety, and that symptoms (e.g., phobias) will develop as a second line of defense. Symptoms are understood as expressing, often symbolically, both the forbidden wish and the attempt to defend against its awareness and expression, and they vary according to whether they show more manifest evidence of the wish or of the defense against the wish. It is recognized that there are individual differences (perhaps, in part, genetically based) in susceptibility to anxiety, capacity to tolerate it, and ways of defending against it. In traditional Freudian theory, all symptoms and defensive behavior are based on anxiety. Within the category of defensive behavior, we include not only the classic, mental mechanisms of repression, denial, projection, isolation of affect, and so on, but also symptomatic behavioral patterns and attitudes (e.g., inability to make a commitment to a relationship, avoidance of certain situations or ideas).

It is not only defensive behavior that is instigated by anxiety. Development of character or personality style, ego interests, values, and so on are all regarded, in part, as expressing ways of coping with anxiety and as compromise means of achieving instinctual gratification within the context of a tolerable level of anxiety. In this formulation, anxiety is accorded a central, regulating role in all behavior. The distinction between so-called symptom neurosis and character neurosis is seen as one of degree. Fluctuations in the level of symptomatic behaviors and in the intensity and pervasiveness in the expression of personality styles or traits are thought to reflect shifts in the dynamic equilibrium between strivings to gratify conflictual wishes and defensive efforts to prohibit their gratification. As Brenner (1982) puts it, "The mind functions in such a way as to afford to drive derivatives the fullest degree of satisfaction compatible with a tolerable degree of anxiety and/or depressive affect" (p. 119). At the same time, it is recognized in psychoanalytic theory that personality growth, successful adaptation, creativity, and good reality-testing require tolerance of anxiety. There is also a place in the theory for behavior and functioning that is relatively conflict-free and in which anxiety plays a minimal role.

Psychological symptoms reflect the sense of danger (i.e., anticipation of the feared consequences) associated with the gratification of conflicted libidinal and/or aggressive wishes. The person (ego) judges that such gratification would bring catastrophic consequences. When agoraphobia is a prominent part of the symptom picture (as part of a panic disorder or as agoraphobia without a history of panic disorder), anxiety associated with the drive gratification is displaced and projected onto leaving home, so that being housebound enables the patient to avoid the full-blown panic attacks. In either its free-floating or bound form, anxiety symptoms indicate the failure of repression and other defenses to keep the unconscious wishes sufficiently far from awareness and action and are a second line of defense against an awareness of the underlying conflicts.

Although we have summarized only Freud's last theory of anxiety, it needs to be stressed that it is no longer accurate to speak of the psychoanalytic theory of anxiety or phobias. There have been several influential psychodynamic theories of anxiety since Freud's formulations. In the interest of brevity, we do not present these theories here, but we refer the interested reader to a review (Eagle & Wolitzky, 1988). Two common features of these later theories are (1) the centrality of anxiety in explanations of personality development and psychopathology, and (2) the rejection of Freud's emphasis on conflict-laden instinctual wishes as the trigger for anxiety. Theorists since Freud, particularly object-relations theorists and self-psychologists following Kohut (1971, 1977, 1984), are inclined to view symptoms of anxiety less in terms of repressed, instinctual conflicts and more in terms of conflicts regarding (1) developmental challenges such as separation and individuation (Mahler, Pine, & Bergman, 1975), (2) both actual and internalized object relationships with others (Guntrip, 1968), and (3) one's sense of self-cohesion (Kohut, 1971, 1977, 1984). For example, Kohut (1971, 1977, 1984), whose views are embraced by many clinicians as a workable alternative to traditional Freudian theory, gives primary importance to the self as the supraordinate factor in personality functioning. In his view, the primary source of intense anxiety is the fear of fragmentation or loss of cohesion of one's self, not the feared consequences of drive gratification. The effect on drive gratification is viewed as the result of self-pathology, not its cause.

The classic Freudian interpretation of agoraphobia as expressing unconscious sexual fantasies has largely, but not entirely (e.g., Brenner, 1982), given way in later conceptualizations to an emphasis on separation anxiety and/or anxiety concerning self-cohesion as a key element in this and other anxiety disorders, as well as in most other forms of psychopathology. The point is that many psychoanalytic clinicians probably currently practice from a multimodal perspective (Silverman, 1986), in which drive theory, ego psychology, object-relations theories, and self-psychology are all regarded as useful, potential guidelines for understanding the patient (Pine, 1985). Even though some of the basic theoretical assumptions of these models are incompatible, it is argued that use of multiple models has greater clinical utility than adherence to a single model. In actual practice, which of these clinical perspectives or combinations of perspectives is given greater emphasis in the clinical understanding and interpretation of agoraphobic and panic-disorder symptoms seems to depend, in part, on the therapist's preferred theoretical orientation and on the nature of the patient's productions.

A few orienting comments are in order for readers unfamiliar with the evolution and current status of psychoanalytic theorizing. The history of psychoanalytic theory can be characterized by shifts in emphasis from Freud's earliest drive theories to his conception of ego psychology (with its focus on defense and adaptation) to the development of British object-relations theories (e.g., Fairbairn) to the appearance of Kohut's self-psychology with its focus on self-cohesion as the central feature of personality functioning. These interrelated theoretical changes involve (1) a decreasing emphasis on the instinctual drives as the wellsprings of human motivation, (2) a shift from a primarily intrapsychic etiology of pathology to a stress on environmental trauma and maternal failure, (3) a focus on pre-Oedipal rather than Oedipal sources of psychopathology, and (4) a concern with developmental arrests rather than intrapsychic conflict as the basis for psychopathology. Thus, for many contemporary psychoanalysts who have been influenced by object-relations theories and by self-psychology conflicts between attachment and autonomy and issues of self-cohesion are considered more central in psychopathology, including panic and agoraphobia, than are sexual conflicts. More traditional Freudians feel that the pendulum has swung too far in this direction and that what began as a corrective to an overemphasis on the sexual drives has resulted in ignoring them rather than in an integrated theory that makes appropriate room for all relevant aspects of human motivation. Traditional Freudians would argue that sexual conflicts are intimately intertwined with conflicts concerning dependency, and that the latter can often defensively mask the centrality of the former.

Relative emphases on drive, ego-psychological, object-relational, and self-psychological theories will shape the explanations of all forms of psychopathology, including panic and agoraphobia. Kessler (1996), for example, argues that contemporary views of panic and agoraphobia are reminiscent of Freud's prepsychoanalytic theory of "actual neuroses." For instance, anxiety neurosis, as noted earlier, was considered to be purely somatic in origin, that is, caused by undischarged sexual drives. This view prevailed before Freud fully articulated his concepts of the dynamic unconscious, infantile sexuality, and unconscious fantasy. Thus, explanations of anxiety attacks from the perspective of the actual neuroses (rather than the psychoneuroses) did not include any psychological content. Kessler views it as an interesting irony that current nondynamic theories of panic (e.g., biological and cognitive-behavioral) are akin to Freud's pre-1900 theories. He also claims that current psychoanalytic theories based on the concept of deficit are similarly in danger of seeing panic symptoms as devoid of psychological meaning (e.g., as a direct consequence of an "enfeebled self"). He cites Compton's (1992a) observation that some analysts do not believe that there is conscious or unconscious mental content in panic attacks and Cooper's (1985) assessment of biological theories of panic as "largely contentless biological dysregulation" (p. 1398), leading Cooper to the conclusion that to focus on a psychodynamic understanding of panic symptoms is a "cruel misunderstanding" (p. 1398) in that one would be holding the patient "responsible" for symptoms that had no psychological basis. The idea of contentless anxiety (i.e., without psychodynamic significance) can be traced back to Freud's concept of actual neurosis (Freud, 1962/1898).

Kessler (1996) also claims that Bowlby's (1989) theories ". . . emphasizing the notion of external insult producing disease, are really biologic theories in psychological disguise" (p. 512). He likens them to Klein's purely biological theory, in which the mental content of a panic attack is irrelevant (Klein & Rabkin, 1981). This seems to us an overstatement in support of the argument that to explain panic as the direct result of separation anxiety (Bowlby, 1989) or and "enfeebled self" (Kohut, 1977) have in common the idea of a ". . . passive, unmotivated experiencing of an unaltered childhood state" (p. 513), a kind of fixed defect. The problem with Kessler's (1996) view is that to feature childhood separation anxiety as part of the explanation of panic disorder is not an inherently nondynamic explanation if it is linked with the subsequent attachment-autonomy intrapsychic conflicts of late adolescence and early adulthood. It seems to us that the real thrust of Kessler's (1996) critique is that biological, object-relational, and self-psychological views of panic and agoraphobia are in danger of crowding out more traditional psychoanalytic inferences concerning sexual conflicts. His point is well-taken, if the case examples that he presents are at all representative of cases of panic disorder.

For example, Kessler (1996) summarizes a case that is chock full of sexual material that is presumably implicated in the patient's panic attacks. This female patient's first panic attack occurred while she was in the first trimester of her first pregnancy as she crossed the street to buy a chocolate bar. Here is the chain of clinical inference and clinical evidence presented to support the inference that buying the chocolate bar had unconscious sexual meanings associated with the panic attack:

1. In response to her father having left his marriage when the patient was 5 years old, she developed fantasies of oral impregnation via oral incorporation of the penis as a way of dealing with the loss of the father as well as a means of expressing her "vengeful anger" (p. 519).
2. On the first Christmas without him, she allegedly tried to swallow a Christmas tree bulb (apparently linked in Kessler's mind with the idea of oral incorporation, although Kessler stops short of claiming that the Christmas tree bulb symbolically represents the paternal phallus).
3. She had frequent daydreams of her father's death and had the fantasy that she would take on the care of his son from his second marriage.

4. She had long-standing symptoms of choking and gagging.
5. Symptoms of nausea, dizziness, and stomachaches arose prior to the analyst's vacations, and she placed crackers on her night table, something she had done for morning sickness during her pregnancies (here Kessler implies but does not explicitly claim that her anticipation of his loss during vacation recapitulated the loss of the father and likewise led to an intensification of unconscious fantasies of oral incorporation).
6. Apparently she periodically received chocolates from her father, and these gifts aroused feelings of nausea and worries that the chocolates might be poisonous; the patient had a chronic fear of botulism and feared that she had toxoplasmosis during pregnancy (Kessler infers that these symptoms ". . . expressed a pregnancy wish, but also punishment for incestuous and castrating wishes" [p. 519]).
7. Some time after receiving the chocolates from her father the patient began to smell chocolates while in the analyst's office and had begun to buy bars of chocolate after every analytic session, preferring those that contained peanuts but ". . . she slipped of course and said 'penis'" (p. 519).
8. She had, in an earlier session, ". . . almost hallucinated a 'brown penis' like her father's and she remarked that a chocolate bar looked like a 'brown penis'" (p. 520).

It was at that point that she recalled her initial panic attack when she crossed the street to purchase a bar of chocolate during her first pregnancy.

Kessler (1996) presents additional clinical details to buttress his claim that this patient's panic attacks were closely linked to her sexual conflicts. These include:

1. The patient recalled two episodes of sexual molestation in childhood (fellatio and fingering of her vagina).
2. She worried about her children being sexually molested and said that she would rather they be ". . . killed than sexually abused" (p. 520).
3. She had a spontaneous panic attack when she looked in the dictionary for the word *scrotum*, while sitting in her son's bed.
4. Her first dream in analysis included the idea of performing in a porno film.
5. She developed dyspareunia after becoming more sexually active with her husband, feeling that he ". . . was stabbing her with his penis" (p. 520).
6. After a brief sexual affair with a college student she feared that his parents would try to kill her or have her arrested for child molestation.
7. She had fantasies of that following pleasurable intercourse she would be bound and raped.
8. She had fantasies that if she were to become lost while driving and have to ask directions at a gas station she would be assaulted sexually.
9. She feared that if she were driving with her husband he would feel that she wanted to emasculate him.

10. She reported dreams of women who could fly, walk on stilts, climb mountains, drive trucks, and had men's names.
11. She had a panic attack while driving to her first session, engaged in the fantasy of being seduced by the analyst.

Although the case report does not explicitly attempt to tie all these observations to her panic attacks, the implication is that they form an essential part of the context of her sexual conflicts. In addition to her panic symptoms, the patient was seen to have a personality disorder with masochistic and hysterical features and other neurotic symptoms (e.g., obsessive-compulsive symptoms such as, that she might jump out of the window or stab her children), hypochondriasis, and conversion symptoms.

We have reviewed this case report at length in order to highlight a few points. First, returning to a point made earlier, rarely do panic patients come to psychodynamically oriented clinicians presenting a single syndrome that troubles them.

Second, we want to share with the reader the kind of data from which analysts make psychodynamic formulations. The data consist almost entirely of selectively reported case material, based on process notes rather than on verbatim recording. The clinician naturally reports material that supports his or her theoretical orientation and would be expected to have an understandable tendency not to see or seriously consider hypotheses that favor an alternate theoretical viewpoint. Of course, even in systematically conducted psychotherapy-outcome research there is a correlation between which type of treatment is superior and the theoretical allegiance of the investigator (Luborsky, 1984). To what extent the material is skewed by prior interpretations is unclear, a fact that weakens the probative value of the "evidence" (cf. Grunbaum, 1984). The ratio of inference to data is often quite high (although it is actually somewhat less so in Kessler's [1996] case report).

Third, having indicated some of the liabilities and pitfalls of relying on case material, the reader can perhaps appreciate the richness of the clinical material that emerges in dynamic therapy and understand why analysts would be disinclined to regard panic attacks as lacking in psychological meaning. Thus, when a biologically oriented psychiatrist hears a panic patient indicate that she fears she might rip off her clothes and run naked down the street (Klein, 1981), and the psychiatrist views it as the patient's attempt to think of something upsetting enough to explain the attack (Klein, 1981) or considers the attribution of psychological meanings to it by the therapist as simply an example of the therapist's creative imagination, we can see how easily clinicians with these different theoretical persuasions can part company.

Fourth, a problem within the field of psychoanalysis is that, even with the same clinical observations, clinicians of differing psychoanalytic orientations will tend to favor inferences in line with their theoretical perspective. Because the data typically are polysemous, that is not hard to do. Thus, someone could challenge Kessler's emphasis on sexual conflicts. It is true that the patient reported many details that manifestly referred to sexual matters. For example, she had her first panic attack while going to buy a chocolate bar, and there is evidence of the link between chocolate and her father. Even if it is true (and Kessler does not tell us whether he made this interpretation to the patient) that, in the patient's mind, the idea of eating chocolate is unconsciously equated with a wish to orally incorporate the father's phallus and to have a child with him, we do not know why the arousal of this wish would necessarily lead to a panic attack. Why was the anxiety signal in relation to these presumed wishes not effective in instituting defensive measures that would have averted panic? Why would these wishes necessarily give rise to anxiety in the first place? Can we assume that the patient found such wishes reprehensible because of their incestuous and aggressive meanings? If so, did she unconsciously fear punishment and retaliation from her superego and her father? Was she concerned that her father would abandon her again? Does she harbor feelings that her father abandoned her in the first place because of her aggressive and sexual feelings toward him? If so, is not her anxiety at bottom a fear of loss of the object and/or the object's love? In this latter formulation, her sexual preoccupations are merely manifest content and metaphors for earlier developmental issues of separation and loss. Thus, what one takes as metaphor versus the core, underlying meanings expressed by the metaphor is at least partly a function of one's theoretical predilections.

Fifth, perhaps the most valuable point we can take from Kessler's case report is that panic attacks have multiple meanings derived from patient's conflicts at all psychosexual levels (oral, anal, and genital). Surely, the traditional Freudian is likely to seek and find in the analytic material some basis for inferring that her preoccupation with chocolate was overdetermined, that, in addition to the fact of her father sending her chocolate, chocolate also had some anal referent (e.g., an unconscious equation between brown penis and stool). Thus, contrary to the biological view and to some psychoanalytic views (e.g., Kohut's 1977 notion of contentless anxiety), the patient's associations should not be regarded as ". . . a sort of readout of mental (dys)functioning . . . [but] as emerging from the usual matrix of multiple, psychic determinants." (Kessler, 1996, p. 513). This, in our view, is the most useful point of view for understanding clinical phenomena.

Regardless of the issue of interpretive emphasis (and its unknown correlation with treatment outcome), all clinicians agree on the importance of a highly detailed inquiry into the specifics of a set of symptoms. For example, it is not sufficient to know that the patient has a barbershop phobia. One wants to know the circumstances surrounding its onset, the relative degree of fear of each element that ordinarily evokes fear in such a situation—the sense of being confined, the public nature of the situation, the possibility of mutilation, and so on. Such knowledge will enable the psychoanalytic clinician to help the patient understand the idiosyncratic meanings of the phobia. Having stressed the importance of discovering the meanings of the patient's symptoms from the patient's material and not from the imposition of a favorite theory, it should be noted that a large part of the clinical and nonclinical evidence, at least in the case of agoraphobia, points to the central role of difficulties and conflicts in the area of separation-individuation and autonomy. Here is a case, we believe, in which the post-Freudian formulation of agoraphobia (e.g., Fairbairn, 1952, p. 43), in terms of conflicts between "the regressive lure of identification" (by which he means infantile dependence) and the "progressive urge toward separation," is more in accord with both the clinical and the research evidence than the early Freudian account that focuses on prostitution fantasies (see Eagle, 1979). This is not to say that Freud was necessarily incorrect in inferring that unconscious sexual fantasies played a key role in the onset of agoraphobia in the patients that he encountered in the late 1800s. Agoraphobic and panic symptoms can have roots in one or more of the psychosexual stages of development, depending on the individual patient's personal history and the cultural milieu in which psychological development takes place. However, it may well be that the sexual fantasies were linked to issues of independence and autonomy. In the current cultural context, repression of sexual fantasies appears almost always to be secondary to conflicts over attachment and autonomy in the production and maintenance of panic and agoraphobia.

Based on data from clinical interviews, psychoanalytic clinicians believe that panic patients find it hard to acknowledge and manage negative feelings (particularly anger) because these feelings threaten ties to significant attachment figures (e.g., Busch, Cooper, Klerman, Shapiro, & Shear, 1991; Shear, Cooper, Klerman, Busch, & Shapiro, 1993). Consistent with this formulation, Busch, Shear, Cooper, Shapiro, and Leon (1995) found that panic disorder patients, compared with dysthymic patients, scored significantly higher on the defenses of reaction formation and undoing.

We should note that on the descriptive level, the psychodynamic conceptualization of agoraphobia is entirely compatible with some accounts that have emerged from a behavioral tradition. As an example of the latter, consider Mathews, Gelder, and Johnston's (1981) integrated model of agoraphobia. According to their model, the factors that would predispose one to agoraphobia include early family factors (e.g., overprotection, fostering of overdependency) and high trait anxiety (which, it should be noted, might well have a genetic component—for example, see Lader & Wing, 1966). At some particular time, increased nonspecific stress then leads to an acute anxiety attack while outdoors. Given the added factors of an individual's dependent and avoidant style, as well as a tendency to attribute the causes of anxiety to external situations, a probable outcome is the development of agoraphobic symptoms. Once the agoraphobic symptoms develop, the maintaining factors include secondary gain and the anticipatory fear of another anxiety or panic attack (see also Beck & Emery, 1985).

Note that the foregoing model is entirely consistent with and, indeed, implicitly includes such psychodynamic factors as fostering of overdependency and defensive style (e.g., avoidance and externalization). Indeed, the description by Mathews et al. (1981), of the relationship between the initial outbreak of intense anxiety and the subsequent development of agoraphobia, is remarkably similar to Fenichel's (1945) account in which "panic anxiety" in a particular situation is experienced and in which the phobia is maintained by a "secondary traumatic neurosis," the hallmark of which is fear of anxiety itself (see also Schur, 1971, who observes that this fear of anxiety is a key factor in perpetuating a phobia). Fenichel goes on to note that people who develop phobias are especially prone to anxiety and to a state of heightened inner tension (which is obviously parallel to Mathews et al.'s high trait anxiety). Fenichel's description is quite dramatic. He describes the state of the phobic—the prone person—as "a powder keg in which the danger signal of the ego acts like a match" (Fenichel, 1945, p. 195).

One of the more important issues of interest in a psychodynamic perspective, and one that is relatively ignored in behavioral theory accounts of agoraphobia (including Mathews et al.'s 1981 account), is the role of intrapsychic conflict. According to the psychodynamic point of view, although there might be some fortuitous elements in generating the patient's initial outbreak of intense anxiety, key causal factors will have to do with intrapsychic conflict. Thus, an individual may have his or her major anxiety attack in the street and then come to avoid that situation. However, from a psychodynamic perspective, the street is not itself a fortuitous element in the whole story, but itself represents core conflictual issues, namely, those having to do with separation and symbiotic versus autonomous functioning.

Indeed, the multiple and sometimes shifting nature of the phobic situation (e.g., sitting in restaurants or theaters, being in cars or trains, being alone) suggests the essential irrelevance of the actual physical situation. Anything that can be symbolically equated with separation, being cut off from home, or the need for autonomous functioning, can serve as the phobic stimulus. In short, although Fenichel describes the onset of the initial anxiety attack as analogous to "a match in a powder keg" (given the individual's chronic state of heightened tension), the stimulus that serves as the match in the case of agoraphobia must itself have anxiety-producing properties associated with particular psychological meanings.

Thus, it is not simply a matter of chance that the initial anxiety attack occurs in the street, but rather that the street, insofar as it represents such meanings as separation, aloneness, and so on, triggers core conflicts and thereby is an anxiety-eliciting stimulus. It is interesting to note that in some cases of agoraphobia, the initial anxiety occurs not simply when the patient is in the street, but when the patient is *crossing* a street, a bridge, a plaza, and so on. It is as if the act of crossing comes to symbolize, with great force, the transition and conflict between the symbiotic safety of home and the dangers associated with separation from home.

In emphasizing separation anxiety, we do not mean to imply that this factor is central in all phobias and in the anxiety and panic that can be associated with the phobic object or situation. Issues of separation appear particularly prominent in cases of agoraphobia. Other phobias and panic attacks often are related to conflicts concerning sexual and/or aggressive impulses.

There are other determinants of panic and agoraphobic symptoms posited by nonanalytic theories that, in our view, are entirely compatible with a psychoanalytic account. For example, cognitive models of panic disorder stress the patient's readiness to overinterpret bodily sensations as threatening a full-blown panic attack. For instance, a patient might feel convinced that heart palpitations are signaling an imminent heart attack. Clark and Beck (1988) refers to these threatening perceptions as "catastrophic misinterpretations." Anger, exercise, or jitteryness from caffeine can contribute to the onset of a panic attack. The fact that patients report threatening thoughts during panic attacks after they focus on their bodily sensations has been taken as strong evidence in favor of a cognitive model of panic (Clark, 1988). Further support of the cognitive model is seen in Clark's finding that laboratory-induced panic in panic-disorder patients and in healthy subjects leads to similar physiological sensations, but that only the patients misinterpret the sensations. The fact that cognitive restructuring can alleviate the panic symptoms also is evidence in support of the cognitive model (Clark & Beck, 1988).

Barlow's (1988) integrated model posits a biologically based vulnerability to false alarms, which, through classical conditioning, become "learned alarms," leading panic-disorder patients to fear that a panic attack is imminent and to adopt avoidance patterns to forestall the anticipated attack. Hyperventilation theories and Klein's (1992, 1993) contention that panic-disorder patients have a dysfunctional suffocation threshold in relation to carbon dioxide levels suggests that physiological factors need to be included in a comprehensive theory of panic disorder.

From a psychoanalytic perspective, it would be argued that cognitive and physiological factors are perhaps necessary but probably rarely sufficient to produce a panic disorder. That is, these factors would likely increase the probability of such a disorder in the context of significant intrapsychic problems. Thus, the psychoanalytic formulation for panic disorder, particularly serious panic disorder accompanied by agoraphobia would be as follows: Vulnerability to panic increases in individuals with:

1. A biological vulnerability to anxiety,
2. A recent history of psychological stress involving real or imagined loss and/or threats to self-esteem,
3. Decreased effectiveness of defenses,
4. Increased intensity of intrapsychic conflict (particularly regarding dependence-independence and hostility), and
5. Decreased confidence in one's ability to cope effectively with intrapsychic issues.

Given this context, an experience that further alters the dynamic balance of the aforementioned factors in a negative direction, i.e., increases the strain on the tenuous defensive patterns, will trigger an anxiety attack. Subsequent to the first major panic attack, hypochondriacal misattributions of bodily sensations and/or carbon dioxide hypersensitivity (and any other biologically based predispositions to anxiety) will make the individual more susceptible to recurrent attacks, especially in the absence of a favorable shift in the dynamic equilibrium posited above. (It would be consistent with a psychoanalytic perspective to allow for the possibility that individual differences in the cognitive distortions of bodily sensations and in carbon dioxide sensitivity contribute to the probability of the initial attack, although these elements would likely play an even stronger role in the onset of subsequent attacks.) Anticipatory anxiety of further panic attacks and the associated fear of total loss of control and a state of utter helplessness will lead to the avoidance of situations that one senses will trigger the attack and to the amplification of minor anxiety signals. Thus, an integrated psychoanalytic model incorporates all the determinants emphasized in rival accounts (see Busch, Cooper, & Klerman, 1991 for an account like the one already outlined), but claims that clinically significant panic, that is, panic that clearly impairs adaptive functioning on an ongoing basis (Katerndahl & Realini, 1997), would not occur in the absence of continued intrapsychic conflict, usually concerning issues of separation and loss, and other interpersonal difficulties.

In our clinical experience, when panic and agoraphobic symptoms are a prominent part of the clinical picture, we invariably find significant current and prior psychopathology. At least in these more complex cases, it appears unlikely that cognitive misattributions of bodily sensations would be sufficient to trigger a panic attack, although, as noted above, proneness to such distortions might make panic attacks more likely. That is, panic patients typically have a premorbid history that includes free-floating anxiety, separation anxiety, low self-esteem, fear of their own anger and of alienating others, shyness, and behavioral inhibition (Biederman, Rosenbaum, Chaloff, & Kagan, 1995).

In the case of panic disorder with agoraphobia, the latter behavior is an attempt to reduce the probability of further panic attacks. In cases of agoraphobia without a history of panic disorder, we assume that the person has suffered from subthreshold panic and has developed the agoraphobia as an extreme safety measure to avoid the possibility of a full-blown panic attack. Although the *DSM-IV* lists agoraphobia without a history of panic disorder as a possible diagnosis, this diagnosis is rarely used (McNally, 1994).

In general, we would say that it is reasonable to suppose that biological factors contribute to individual differences in proneness to and tolerance of free-floating anxiety, as well as in the capacity of the person to "bind" anxiety in the form of symptoms. In other words, adaptive psychological functioning involves the effective operation of signal anxiety. According to the psychoanalytic theory of anxiety, the threat of a full-blown traumatic anxiety is apprehended by the ego and is followed automatically by the activation of defenses designed to forestall further anxiety. It is true that the theory does not clearly specify the nature of the signal and the process by which defense is instituted. Nonetheless, we can posit that the ability of the ego to recognize signal (minimal) levels of anxiety is impaired, partly for biological reasons, and that this impairment is due to some combination of an already high level of free-floating anxiety, a sudden increase in arousal that quickly overwhelms the ego, and a tendency to amplify, via cognitive distortion of bodily sensations, the rising tide of anxiety. In this formulation, when the defenses are ineffective, due, in part, to the increased pressure of the underlying wishes, symptoms appear (e.g., a phobia). Full-blown panic, in this view, would result when neither the defensive maneuvers nor the symptom were sufficient to bind the anxiety. This state of what Freud called traumatic anxiety is one in which there is the overpowering fear of total annihilation or dissolution of the ego as expressed in patients' fears of loss of control, of going crazy, and of dying.

The psychoanalytic account, when it takes appropriate account of nondynamic factors (e.g., biological vulnerability to panic) appears to offer a better understanding of panic and agoraphobia than rival accounts that focus on one primary element (e.g., carbon dioxide hypersensitivity). Our contention that biological or cognitive explanations of panic are incomplete is clearly evident in a study which showed that laboratory-induced panic via a 5.5 percent CO_2-inhalation procedure was a function of the presence or absence of a "safe" companion (Carter, Hollon, Carson, & Shelton, 1995). In further support of an integrated psychodynamic theory of panic is the repeated finding that there is a high degree of comorbidity in that patients with panic disorder will very often simultaneously qualify for another Axis I and/or Axis II diagnosis. For example, many studies have pointed to the strong association between panic, agoraphobia and depression (Breise, Charney, & Heninger, 1986; Lesser, 1990). Even clinicians with a primarily cognitive/behavioral orientation will acknowledge the contribution of psychodynamic factors to the formation of phobic symptoms and to the reactions of patients to cognitive/behavioral interventions.

Two further considerations seem to argue in favor of a psychoanalytic model for panic and agoraphobia. First, although some writers have emphasized the idea of so-called spontaneous panic attacks, clinical inquiry will often reveal both the presence of recent stresses that compromise the effectiveness of ego defenses as well as subtle, symbolic meanings in the apparently innocuous external situations in which the first panic attack occurs. For example, a male patient of ours had been having numerous sexual affairs with a variety of women. He often brought them to his mother's country house, where he would have sex in his mother's bed. For over two years these experiences were not associated with any psychological symptoms. However, on the occasion that he brought to this house a woman who clearly reminded him of his mother (something an external observer would not know) he had a massive panic attack in bed. It became evident in the course of the patient's associations that this woman unconsciously represented a forbidden, incestuous object. As long as the previous women did not remind him of his mother, he could unconsciously gratify his incestuous longings without anxiety. However, in the instance of his panic attack, we assume that his ordinary defenses were ineffective in the face of the intensified unconscious wish. One might, of course, argue that it is always easy retrospectively to find a psychoanalytic explanation for just about any behavior. We grant that it would be stronger evidence of a psychoanalytic model if we could predict which people would have panic attacks under which conditions. Although we cannot rule out the possibility that some so-called spontaneous panic attacks are without psychodynamic precipitants, we believe that most of them probably entail the increased activation of unconscious conflicts. The research literature supports the idea that recent life-event stressors are greater in the period just before the onset of panic (e.g., Lteif & Mavissakalian, 1995). The clinical example already described would not be captured in a life-events kind of inquiry.

The second factor that appears to support a psychodynamic conceptualization of panic and agoraphobia is the fact that the onset of these disorders typically occurs in late adolescence and early adulthood. Unless there are biological theories of which we are unaware that suggest a greater physiologically based vulnerability at this age, we would regard the onset at this age to be consistent with the age-appropriate developmental challenge of resolving the conflict between dependency and autonomy, the dynamic issue typically encountered in patients with these disorders.

DIAGNOSTIC ISSUES AND PROBLEMS

According to the *DSM-IV* (APA, 1994), there are three categories in which the diagnosis of agoraphobia or panic disorder can be made:

1. Agoraphobia without history of panic disorder (300.22)
2. Panic disorder with agoraphobia (300.21)
3. Panic disorder without agoraphobia (300.01)

The third diagnosis is made if the patient does not meet the criteria for the first two disorders.

Psychodynamically oriented clinicians treat many patients who do not strictly meet the *DSM-IV* criteria for these or other disorders. In fact, the prototypical patient is apt to approximate simultaneously several of the *DSM-IV* Axis I and Axis II categories but not fit formally into any of them. Given the complexity of etiological factors, the usual presence of multiple symptoms and character problems, the tendency to embark on the same general approach to treatment at least for problems within the neurotic range, and the uncertain relationship between diagnosis and response to treatment, the *DSM-III-R* classification is generally of limited utility to psychodynamically oriented clinicians. Behaviorally oriented clinicians also have misgivings about the *DSM-IV* classifications of agoraphobia and panic disorder (Bowen & Kohut, 1979; Emmelkamp, 1988; Goldstein & Chambless, 1978; Hallam, 1978; Marks, 1970).

In the interest of brevity, we do not include a more detailed discussion of diagnostic difficulties or problems with the *DSM* scheme. Suffice it to say that psychodynamically oriented clinicians will want to assess the structure and functioning of the patient's overall personality in order to understand the psychological significance of the symptoms. This appraisal of the patient's level of adaptation (including reality testing, adequacy of defenses, affect tolerance, etc.) will serve as a guide to treatment prognosis and planning (e.g., the relative balance of supportive versus uncovering treatment techniques).

McNally (1994) offers a useful discussion of the origins and evolution of the concept of panic disorder. He notes that it was not until the 1980 *DSM-III* classification that panic disorder was considered a discrete syndrome, and that it was not until the 1994 *DSM-IV* that an essential element in the diagnosis of panic disorder includes persistent anticipatory anxiety regarding the possibility of recurrent but unexpected panic attacks. In the 1987 *DSM-III-R*, panic disorder with agoraphobia was recognized, because most cases of agoraphobia followed the onset of panic.

According to McNally (1994), Freud failed to distinguish between anxiety and spontaneous panic, a distinction that McNally feels is required because imipramine ameliorates panic but not anxiety (Klein, 1964). Other writers (e.g., Barlow, 1988) note findings that contradict Klein's original finding that imipramine selectively ameliorates panic but not chronic anxiety. Furthermore, onset of panic is sudden, as compared with anxiety. It evokes a sense of imminent danger, rather than worry, and is more likely to be accompanied by fears of dying or going crazy. In our view, what Freud called "traumatic anxiety" is what we today call a panic attack. It is true that he emphasized the quantitative difference more than any qualitative distinction, although he did point to the sense of utter helplessness that comes with the ego feeling overwhelmed. In fact, he regarded this extreme state of the dissolution of the ego as the bedrock anxiety that underlies all forms of anxiety and fear, and in that sense seems to have implied a qualitative distinction between anxiety and panic.

As is well known, Freud's initial view of anxiety was primarily a somatic one, in that he thought that undischarged sexual energy was converted into anxiety. Therefore, he initially classified anxiety neurosis as an "actual" neurosis (along with neurasthenia and hypochondriasis) to be distinguished from the psychoneuroses (primarily hysteria, obsessive-compulsive neurosis, and phobia), which he felt had a psychological origin (i.e., the repression of libidinal wishes caused anxiety). In both categories of neurosis, the anxiety was caused by the lack of full and direct discharge of sexual energy. Freud later revised this theory (without fully abandoning the idea of some link between sexual tension and anxiety) to one in which anxiety is the motive for defense. McNally (1994) seems not to realize this momentous change in Freud's thinking, because he still attributes to Freud a view of the sexual, somatic etiology of panic. He does note the "striking similarities" (p. 4) between Freud's description of anxiety neurosis and the current description of panic disorder and credits Freud with describing the recollection of prior anxiety attacks and the anticipatory fear of another one as important in understanding agoraphobia.

The *DSM-III* still retained Freud's descriptive account of anxiety neurosis but divided it into panic disorder and generalized anxiety disorder, and it divided phobic neurosis into simple phobia, social phobia, and agoraphobia. The *DSM-IV* contains the classification mentioned at the beginning of this chapter. It should be noted that, although Freud made diagnostic classifications and analysts continue to do so today, they do not view syndromes as distinct from one another but as multiple, simultaneous expressions of the same core dynamic issues. Psychoanalytic clinicians do not think in terms of comorbidity in the way the framers of the *DSM* did.

TREATMENT STRATEGIES

In many respects, psychotherapy for panic disorder and for agoraphobia shares the same general principles of treatment that are relevant to the other syndromes among the so-called anxiety disorders, as well as to most of the other functional, nonpsychotic disorders in *DSM-IV*. Before we can offer a meaningful discussion of treatment strategies, we need to present at least briefly the main principles of the overall theory of psychoanalytic psychotherapy.

PRINCIPLES OF PSYCHOANALYTIC PSYCHOTHERAPY

The main features of the traditional psychoanalytic theory of psychotherapy can be summarized as follows:

1. The patient is suffering from pathological compromise formations (e.g., symptoms) based on repressed conflicts.
2. These conflicts become expressed in the context of the therapeutic relationship, particularly in the form of transference and resistance.
3. This process is facilitated when the treatment situation is unstructured and fosters the free associations that will allow the unconscious, unresolved conflicts to be expressed via dreams, memories, reactions to the therapist, and so on.
4. The analyst listens with free-floating attention and a neutral (i.e., nonbiased), nonjudgmental attitude, which facilitates the therapeutic alliance, that is, the patient's desire to cooperate despite conflicting attitudes about wanting to recover.
5. These conditions promote the development of an analyzable transference. For many clinicians the core of psychoanalytic treatment is the analysis of the transference. It is also considered vital for therapists to be aware of and employ their own countertransference reactions in understanding patients and in intervening appropriately.
6. The analyst's interpretations of the patient's unconscious conflicts and forms of resistance as manifest in the transference will yield insights into the nature and influence of the neurotic anxieties associated with these conflicts.
7. Through the repetitive, increasingly conscious, experiencing of long-standing conflicts, in the context of affectively vivid here-and-now transference reactions and their multiple meanings, patients gradually work through their difficulties by shifting to more realistic, less anxious, more adaptive emotional and behavioral patterns inside and outside the treatment situation. Repeated insight into disavowed, split-off, disowned, anxiety-laden wishes, conflicts, and fantasies (in Freud's terminology, the id or drive derivatives) allows them to become more integrated into the ego, particularly when the insights are accompanied by behavioral changes that can show patients that their fears will not overcome them.
8. In addition to insight, there are other important ingredients of the therapeutic relationship that are considered to facilitate change. Clinicians

who favor an object-relations or a self-psychology approach tend, relatively speaking, to deemphasize insight in favor of the following factors:

(1) The actual experience of a new, benign, relationship with a nonjudgmental parental figure helps reduce the harshness of the patient's superego.

(2) The patient has an opportunity to form a new identification; the patient can form an identification with the analyst's approach (i.e., with the analytic attitude) and can introject and later identify with the analyst as a person.

(3) The analyst and the analyst-patient relationship can provide a safe, supportive base that can foster the patient's progressive urges toward greater autonomy and individuation (as against regressive longings to merge and cling to infantile dependence).

(4) In Kohut's view (1984), analysts serve a critical function by allowing patients to use the analysts as mirroring and idealized self-objects to aid in the patients' efforts to regulate their own tension states.

(5) The therapist's empathy, as experienced by the patient, is held to be a vital element in therapeutic change. This component is stressed particularly by Kohut (1984) and his followers, who regard feeling understood (and its positive implications for the experience of affirmed selfhood) as the ultimately curative factor, the factor that gives insight its impact.

Although we can make conceptual distinctions among these several relationship factors and between these factors and insight, in actual practice, it is virtually impossible to accord these elements differential weightings in attempting to account for therapeutic change. To take one obvious example, the experience of an emotionally vivid insight conveyed through a well-timed interpretation usually will also simultaneously arouse a feeling of being profoundly understood. Thus, psychoanalytic insight is an experience that occurs in the context of a relationship.

PRACTICE OF PSYCHOANALYTIC TREATMENT OF PANIC DISORDER AND OF AGORAPHOBIA

Assessment

Based on the foregoing general principles of psychoanalytic psychotherapy, the therapist will begin with an assessment of the presenting symptoms and complaints, in the context of an evaluation of the patient's overall current functioning. This initial appraisal will include inquiries concerning the history, severity, duration, intensity, and precipitants of the patient's panic attacks and/or agoraphobic behavior. It will also focus on other problems the patient may be experiencing. As discussed earlier, panic disorder and/or agoraphobia rarely if ever occur as circumscribed, isolated symptoms in an otherwise nonneurotic, well-functioning individual.

In judging the prospective patient's suitability for dynamic psychotherapy we take account of the following factors: (1) positive motivation to change, (2) presence of an optimal degree of suffering, (3) access to affective experience and tolerance of anxiety, (4) adequate ego strength, psychological mindedness, and reality testing, (5) a reasonably decent history of satisfying object relations, and (6) a capacity to form a working alliance with the therapist. The final variable has been shown, in fact, to predict treatment outcome (Luborsky, 1984). Of course, this list of clinical criteria could make one question whether people who meet these criteria are in need of psychotherapy. In practice, the extent to which these criteria are met is a relative matter. There is now a cumulative body of research that indicates that the factors just listed are associated with better treatment outcomes (Luborsky, Crits-Christoph, Mintz, & Auerbach, 1988; see especially pp. 315–353 for a summary of these findings).

This initial assessment will enable the therapist to judge whether patient's quality of life is so impaired as to require a rapid reduction in symptoms. For instance, if the patient's job is in jeopardy or if the threat of panic attacks seriously impairs the patient's functioning in going on job interviews, then an immediate focus on the symptoms is called for. The therapist might recommend a psychiatric consultation for medication, instruct the patient about how to breathe, suggest relaxation exercises, and so on. The therapist will be alert to the possible meanings to the patient of these kinds of direct interventions and later in the treatment will explore these meanings with the patient.

The initial assessment also will include an evaluation of the possibility of other clinically significant factors, principally depression (and suicidal risk) and personality disorder. The latest, world-wide, epidemiological data (Weissman et al., 1997) indicate that for patients with panic disorder, the likelihood of agoraphobia ranges from 22.5 percent to 58.2 percent. Agoraphobia is found without panic disorder in only 1.4 percent to 6.5 percent of patients. Put another way, the odds ratio for the comorbidity of panic disorder and agoraphobia ranges from 7.5 percent to 21.4 percent. It was also found that 22.5 percent to 68.2 percent of depressed patients also show evidence of panic disorder. These findings, from several different countries, highlight the consistency of comorbidity. In this connection, it should be noted that although the *DSM* emphasizes separate, discrete nosological entities, analytically oriented clinicians typically do not assess patients within this framework. That is, they view psychopathology not as a set of discrete syndromes, but as interrelated aspects of the personality struggling to adapt in the face of inner and outer stresses that excessively strain the person's defenses.

Approach to Treatment

The clinician's assessment of the degree of overall disturbance and the nature of the patient's current life situation will serve not only as an influence on the degree of early, direct intervention (e.g., pharmacotherapy) but also as a guide to the relative emphasis on a supportive versus an expressive approach. In general, "the greater the psychiatric severity, the more supportive and less expressive the therapy needs to be" (Luborsky, 1984, p. 56). That is, the more disturbed the patient and the more intractable or painful the symptom (whether agoraphobia, panic, or any other problem), the more likely the therapist will be to employ explicitly noninterpretive modes of intervention and/or to offer interpretations that border on advice or suggestion.

Given the state of the field of clinical practice, conceptualization and diagnosis of a disorder quite often do not clearly point to a particular treatment strategy. That is, the principles of treatment outlined above serve as a general framework for the treatment of a wide variety of Axis I and Axis II disorders, once psychosis and organicity have been ruled out and the diagnosis of borderline personality disorder (from a psychoanalytic perspective) has been considered. Relatively speaking, in the case of agoraphobia and panic disorders, conceptualization and diagnosis *do* suggest something about treatment strategies and approaches. For example, agoraphobic patients tend to be primarily women whose relationships to their often overprotective and controlling mothers reveal a pattern that has been variously referred to as "anxious attachment" (Bowlby, 1973), "painful ambivalence" (Buglass, Clarke, Henderson, Kreitman, & Presley, 1977), and "hostile dependency" (Quadrio, 1984). Their core problem can be seen as one involving extreme difficulties along the developmental dimension of separation-individuation and autonomy. The agoraphobic symptom itself can be understood as rather graphically portraying this core issue: The desire to break away and achieve autonomy is enacted by actual or fantasied forays into the outside world, but due to experiencing too much anxiety and very strong dependency wishes, the patient does not successfully carry out this desire. As noted earlier, this entire pattern quite often gets repeated or even intensified in the marital relationship. What are the implications of this understanding of agoraphobia for treatment?

In our experience, it is useful to view the agoraphobic symptom as a rather dramatic and troubling expression of the unresolved developmental issue of growing up, separating, and leaving home (both physically and psychologically). We often communicate this point of view to the patient, based on early, suggestive, and often striking evidence that emerges during the initial consultations, and we suggest to the patient that psychotherapy can represent an opportunity to deal more fully with this set of unresolved issues (see the case illustration, later in this chapter). Generally, patients experience some relief at hearing this initial formulation, because, although they may present the outbreak of the agoraphobic symptom as sudden, ego-alien, and bewildering, at some level, they often know that they have had difficulties with separation, individuation, and autonomy (of course, they do not refer to their difficulties in these terms) and that they have experienced milder symptoms linked to agoraphobia (e.g., varying degrees of school avoidance or discomfort, varying degrees of other expressions of separation anxiety) a good part of their lives. The initial relief comes from hearing a simple description of what, at some deep level, they knew all along to be the case. At the same time, a cautionary note is in order, because we do not want to impose a premature closure on the clinical data. Therefore, one has to gauge whether there is more to be gained or lost in offering early interpretations of the meanings of the symptoms. In general, the therapeutic approach in analytically oriented treatment is to facilitate as much as possible the patient's own discovery of the meanings of their behavior and experience.

Course of Treatment

On the basis of both our own experience and what we can glean from the literature, a number of common elements and a general pattern of treatment course in psychotherapy with agoraphobic patients can be discerned. Different patients show varying degrees of clear awareness of the possible psychological significance of their agoraphobic symptoms. Some patients can verbalize quite readily the links between their agoraphobic symptoms and earlier difficulties with leaving home or even between the symptom and an earlier enmeshed relationship, generally with the mother. Some of these highly verbal patients also acknowledge that, similar to their relationship with mother (or father), they feel trapped in their relationship with their husband (or wife). In general, the early phase of treatment is taken up with, to borrow Quadrio's (1984, p. 845) words, "deepening awareness of earlier levels of ambivalent dependency, of poor separation, and of passive-aggressive mechanisms." Much of this phase of treatment can be summed up by saying that patients become aware that they have been living according to the "pathogenic belief" (Weiss & Sampson, 1986) that if "I leave my parent" (or spouse) and lead a separate, independent life "I will not survive." This is not, after all, such a great insight insofar as it is quite close to the actual experience of the agoraphobic symptom. Ideally, during this phase of treatment, patients also become aware of the degree to which their current marital relationships (if, of course, they are married) duplicates their early hostile-dependent relationships with their parents. A similar pattern should emerge in the patient's relationship with the therapist, and later in this initial phase of treatment, appropriate transference interpretations will be made.

In the last several years, psychodynamically-oriented clinicians have recognized the desirability of publishing treatment manuals as research and training guidelines for general psychotherapy (e.g., Luborsky, 1984) as well as for specific forms of treatment with particular patient populations (e.g., Kernberg, 1975). Milrod, Busch, Cooper, and Shapiro (1997) published what appears to be the first manual specifically focused on psychodynamic psychotherapy for panic-disorder patients. This manual is far from a specific how-to-do-it set of technical recommendations. Rather it is a statement of general principles and guidelines of psychodynamic psychotherapy, with particular reference to panic patients.

It needs to be acknowledged that guidelines for the psychodynamic psychotherapy of panic are based entirely on clinical experience and not any body of systematic, controlled studies using comparison groups receiving rival treatments. It is probably for this reason that McNally (1994), in his otherwise thorough and highly informative book on panic disorder, does not cover psychodynamic treatments. He refers to the writings of analytic clinicians as "speculations" and notes that ". . . few empirical studies have been stimulated by the psychodynamic perspective . . ." (p. 105). Although his position is accurately stated, it is hard to ignore the wealth of clinical experience that has given rise to the psychoanalytic understanding of panic and agoraphobia. Thus, we continue to describe the treatment of these syndromes, mindful of the fact that the necessary efficacy and effectiveness studies remain to be done.

With this important caveat in mind, we wish to present guidelines as stated by Milrod et al. (1997, pp. 19–20). We quote them at length because, as far as we are aware, this is the first time that a psychoanalytically oriented, organized treatment plan for panic and agoraphobia has been articulated.

> Phase I: Treatment of acute panic. To lessen panic symptoms, we believe that it is necessary to uncover the unconscious meaning of these symptoms. The following strategy is used:
>
> A. Initial evaluation and early treatment
>   1. Exploration of circumstances and feelings surrounding panic onset
>   2. Exploration of personal meanings of panic symptoms
>   3. Exploration of feelings and content of panic episodes
> B. Psychodynamic conflicts in panic disorder
>   1. Separation and independence
>   2. Anger recognition, management, and coping with expression
>   3. Sexual excitement and its perceived dangers
> C. Expected responses to phase I of treatment
>   1. Panic symptom relief
>   2. Reduction in agoraphobic symptoms
>
> Phase II: Treatment of panic vulnerability. To lessen vulnerability to panic, we hypothesize that core dynamisms must be understood and altered . . . often through their emergence in the transference. The following strategy is used:
>
> A. Addressing conflicts in the transference
> B. Working through
> C. Expected responses to phase II of treatment
>   1. Improvement in relationships
>   2. Less conflicted experience of separation, anger, sexuality
>   3. Reduction in vulnerability to panic recurrence
>
> Phase III: Termination. To address . . . severe difficulties with separation and independence, . . . this time-limited psychotherapy will permit the patient to re-experience these conflicts directly with the therapist so that underlying fantasies can begin to be articulated, understood, and rendered less frightening. Patient reaction to termination must be addressed for a minimum of the final third of treatment:
>
> A. Re-experiencing of separation and anger themes in the transference as termination approaches
> B. Expected responses to phase II of treatment
>   1. Possible temporary recrudescence of symptoms as these feelings are experienced in therapy
>   2. New ability to manage separation and independence.

According to Milrod et al. (1997), phase I can be expected to take three months; if phase II and phase III are included, the treatment usually lasts 9 to

12 months. In cases of panic disorder in the context of severe personality disorder, more than 12 months is required to ameliorate the symptoms and to reduce the probability of a relapse. At another point in their text, the authors state that phase I usually is successful in producing symptom relief in ". . . approximately 12 to 20 weeks . . . ," which is a bit longer than what was stated earlier. They also recommend a frequency of at least two sessions per week. In other words, they are claiming that symptom relief can typically be achieved in 24 to 40 sessions. If the patient also is agoraphobic, then phase I will usually last a bit longer. Milrod (1995, p. 18) claims, "This outcome is comparable with results reported with cognitive-behavioral and psychopharmacological treatments."

These assertions appear to be based on a series of 32 cases treated by Milrod and her colleagues and on a survey of 35 successfully treated cases in the literature, where duration of psychodynamic psychotherapy was available for 17 patients. No information is provided regarding unsuccessful, short-term outcomes, either in their series of cases or in the ones they found in the literature, yet we assume that there had to be some refractory cases that are not being noted or discussed. In short, we have to acknowledge that we are without firm outcome data from these series of case studies, nor do we have any systematic clinical trials comparing different forms and durations of treatment. Therefore, as Compton (1992b, p. 418), himself an analyst, recognizes, "The burden of showing that psychoanalysis does as well as, or something more than, exposure therapy rests upon psychoanalysts."

Furthermore, it is not clear from the Milrod et al. (1997) manual what the criteria are for combining psychodynamic psychotherapy with cognitive-behavioral therapy techniques (e.g., exposure and/or pharmacotherapy). The implication is that these forms of treatment are used in cases judged to be particularly difficult. In any case, Milrod et al. clearly advocate the use of these forms of treatment and feel that they can facilitate psychodynamic understanding and, thus, are useful adjuncts to psychodynamic treatment.

Milrod (1995) makes a case for the potential benefit of long-term therapy. The available follow-up data on treatment of panic and agoraphobia suggest a picture of chronic difficulties and not uncommon relapse and recurrence in panic patients treated with pharmacotherapy and/or cognitive-behavioral therapy. For example, as many as 50 percent of panic patients seem to require medication indefinitely, and panic patients show a high degree of comorbidity with depression. When both syndromes are present they each tend to be more severe than either one alone. These particular patients have been ill longer, and they respond less well to pharmacotherapy than do those that present with either depression or panic disorder (Lydiard, 1991). Thus, relapse is fairly likely following short-term treatment. Even though there is not yet hard evidence that long-term, psychodynamic psychotherapy prevents relapse or recurrence, there is the plausible expectation that it provides an opportunity for increased ego resilience and decreased psychological vulnerability. In short, even if cognitive-behavioral therapy and pharmacotherapy bring more rapid symptom relief than psychodynamic psychotherapy, analysts believe that the latter treatment is beneficial for the patient's quality of life over the long term.

Indeed, this proposition is just that—a promise and not a finding—and it needs to be put to systematic, empirical test.

Additional Interventions

Exposure. Two interventions are often necessary, particularly with agoraphobic patients, which clearly depart from a strict psychoanalytic stance in the treatment. One is to encourage patients to take steps to expose themselves to the phobic situation. Many patients who come for treatment have already made this attempt on their own in varying degrees. Insofar as they remain agoraphobic, these efforts need to be encouraged. As Mathews et al. (1981) suggest, however, a critical therapeutic factor in the treatment of agoraphobia is increased exposure (without a companion) to the phobic situation while experiencing less than the traumatic anxiety anticipated. This appears to be a necessary step whatever one's therapeutic approach—behavioral or psychodynamic. *Whatever* makes increased exposure without traumatic anxiety possible, and thereby reduces avoidance behavior, will lead to symptomatic improvement.

The value of encouraging exposure to the phobic situation, something recognized by clinicians of all persuasions, would seem to have no place in the theory of psychoanalytic psychotherapy. However, as Freud notes, for those patients who completely avoid the phobic situation, exposure is important only insofar as it activates the anxiety and conflicts that underlie it so that these origins can be explored. The idea that exposure could contribute significantly to the amelioration of symptoms by means of extinction alone is not part of the psychodynamic view, even though it actually may turn out to be the case that it is so.

Although some orthodox psychoanalytic clinicians (e.g., Abend, 1989) argue that one should make every effort to rely exclusively on interpretation to achieve symptomatic improvement, most contemporary analytically oriented therapists will at least indirectly encourage the patient to face the phobic situation. For example, an interpretation that *implies* that the patient has an irrational fear of a situation or object can be experienced by the patient as conveying the tacit suggestion that it is safe and necessary to confront what is feared. However, in seeking to maintain analytic purity, Abend (1989, p. 399) claims that "It is no longer even considered appropriate analytic technique to urge patients to enter the avoided phobic situations, although that was at one time accepted practice, even among psychoanalysts of the most traditional stripe. The change in technique reflects strongly the accumulated and more accurate understanding arrived at in the recent period of psychoanalytic theory, which holds that the patients' defenses, manifested in treatment as resistance to progress, cannot merely be swept aside or overpowered." Abend goes on to imply that, although it might take longer to achieve amelioration of the symptom using the approach that he advocates, the patient will be more immune to a relapse. This is a statement of the alleged superiority of a cure based on insight and conflict resolution as opposed to a so-called transference cure that relies on the analyst's authority and suggestions. Of course, this claim has to be put to empirical test. Even if Abend's approach results in more stable improvement, he ignores the issue of the consequences of the patient's prolonged suffering. Furthermore, direct encouragement to face the phobic situation, although it does not sweep aside the patient's defenses, does bypass them temporarily and, as Freud suggested long ago, the activation of anxiety otherwise avoided can potentially facilitate the therapeutic process.

Spousal Involvement in Treatment. Another intervention often indicated, particularly for agoraphobics when the patient shows little or no improvement, is to invite the patient's spouse to participate in varying degrees, in the treatment. (Of course, this is done only with the patient's agreement.) The spouse may participate in only a few sessions or, when it is deemed advisable, in an ongoing conjoint therapy. There are clinicians who believe that conjoint therapy is generally advisable for agoraphobic patients. This is the case as the agoraphobic symptom serves to maintain a marital system in which the agoraphobic spouse reenacts in the marriage the early relationship of hostile dependency and early difficulties with separation and autonomy and in which the patient's spouse subtly encourages the agoraphobic spouse's dependency and helplessness because of personal inadequacies, extreme jealousy, (Hafner, 1979) denial of dependency, and fear of being abandoned (Quadrio, 1984). Indeed, there is evidence in one study that some patients' spouses were adversely affected when their agoraphobic mates showed symptomatic improvement (Hafner, 1976, 1984, 1986).

Pharmacotherapy. In cases of severely impaired functioning, patients' suffering and preoccupation with their symptoms usually will not allow them to engage readily in an exploratory psychotherapy. Medication is necessary to take the edge off the symptoms, enough that patients can tolerate the residual anxiety and have the freedom to engage in psychotherapy.

Themes of Treatment

To return to the context of individual therapy, we have already noted that during the earlier phase of treatment, many patients become aware of the pathogenic belief that "If I leave home and lead an independent life as a separate person, I will not survive." Only in a later phase of treatment does the patient begin to become aware of the more deeply buried pathogenic belief to the effect that "if I leave home and lead an independent life as a separate person, my parent will not survive." In other words, the patient becomes more aware of the degree to which survivor guilt and separation guilt have dominated and continue to dominate much of the agoraphobic's life (Modell, 1984). Obviously, there are individual differences about these themes. However, we have been impressed with the degree to which *some* variation of the theme is commonly seen in agoraphobia (see the case illustration).

There is a danger of taking patients' manifest presentations to represent the core intrapsychic issues. For example, if one takes at face value, rather than as metaphors, patients' descriptions of their panic or agoraphobia as expressing a fragmenting sense of self (in the case of panic) or of fear and guilt about separation and autonomy (agoraphobia), one might miss the possibility that these concerns could, although significant in their own right, simultaneously be masking other conflicts (e.g., of an Oedipal nature). (See Kessler, 1996, for case material that bears on this issue.) Of course, all these factors could be relevant and might not be masking a primary factor or element.

Candidates for Psychoanalytic Treatment

It is our strong impression that the foregoing psychodynamic approach is most suitable for that subcategory of agoraphobic and panic patients who are somewhat psychologically minded, who have a reasonably rich and differentiated inner life to which they have access, who have demonstrated a reasonable level of developmental achievements and psychological differentiation, and who are conflicted about their agoraphobic symptom. It is also our view that there is a subcategory of agoraphobic patients, particularly those who also experience panic and related symptoms apart from the usual agoraphobic situations, who do not fit the preceding description. These patients tend to be relatively undifferentiated, to show a somewhat primitive personality organization, to have a lifestyle in which the agoraphobic symptom does not seem to represent a major impediment to carrying out vital life goals (partly because of more limited life goals), and who (while distressed) do not seem especially conflicted about their agoraphobic symptoms. This latter category of patients is more likely to experience panic attacks or threats of panic attacks in an apparently random manner and somewhat independent of venturing outside the home. The seemingly random nature of the panic experiences is another factor that makes psychodynamic treatment more difficult. As far as treatment for this group of patients is concerned, it seems to us that behavior therapy (including group behavior therapy), primarily in vivo exposure, often combined with pharmacological treatment, are interventions likely to be far more appropriate than psychodynamic therapy of any kind.

Apparent Claustrophobic Symptoms

One important dynamic issue has not been discussed much. The fact is that many agoraphobic patients also experience other symptoms, some of which appear to fall under the rubric of claustrophobic symptoms, the apparent opposite of agoraphobia. For example, it is not uncommon for agoraphobic patients to report that when going to movies or plays, they must sit right on the aisle. If they sit in the middle of the row, they feel trapped (see the case illustration). There are at least two ways in which one can interpret these claustrophobic symptoms, these feelings of being trapped. One way is to say that the usual "combination of agoraphobic with claustrophobic symptoms . . . nicely expresses the conflict [between wanting to break out and not being able to]—when she is in, she wants to get out; when she is out, she wants to get back in. Dependency and separation are the fundamental conflicts" (Quadrio, 1984, p. 82). This interpretation is consistent with Fairbairn's (1952, p. 43) claim that agoraphobia is primarily an expression of conflict between the desires for infantile dependence and for separation and autonomous growth, "the regressive lure of identification and the progressive urge for separation."

According to the preceding view, the claustrophobic symptoms represent the patients' desire to get out once they are in—that is, the urge toward separation. An alternative to this view is that the seemingly claustrophobic symptoms represent an extension of the agoraphobic symptoms, insofar as the apparently claustrophobic situations all have in common the fact that they are experienced as potential barriers to rush back home should the urgent need or impulse to do so arise. This view is consistent with many agoraphobic patients' subjective experience. Thus, the reported reason that the patient (M.C., discussed in the case illustration section) had to have an aisle seat is that she would be free to rush back home to safety should she panic and feel the need to reach a safe base. Sitting in the center of a row was symbolically experienced as being cut off or blocked from safety. In other words, it is not that the patient wants out in the sense of being free to separate, but rather that the patient is out (i.e., in the theater, train, elevator, or any other place away from home) and now wants a sure way of getting *back in* to the safety of home (or any temporary safety).

The preceding issue is not simply a theoretical one, nor one of esoteric interest only. It is a question of the appropriate and correct interpretation to the patient, one that is in tune with the patient's experience and inner world. What Kohut (1984) refers to as "empathic resonance" is undoubtedly important for all patients, including agoraphobic patients. If the agoraphobic patient's experience of being trapped consists essentially in feeling cut off from the safety of home, it would not be especially therapeutic to interpret this experience as representing an urge toward separation. Often, at a deeper level, the fear of being trapped reflects the patient's anxiety surrounding the wish to fuse with another person.

We are not suggesting that in the so-called claustrophobic experience, agoraphobic patients do not experience intense conflicts between symbiotic dependence and separation. It is clear that they do. Indeed, the very act of venturing out and going, say, to a movie, but having to sit in a position that permits the feeling that they can get back home as soon as possible, is already a compromise expressing that conflict. Agoraphobic patients' characteristic relationships of hostile dependence or anxious attachment with a parent and later with a spouse are probably the strongest and most important expressions of the conflict between symbiotic dependence and separation and autonomy. They often feel burdened and engulfed by the symbiotic dependence (and its elements of guilt and what Winnicott (1958) referred to as "impingement"), and they want out of this kind of relationship. However, the experience of separation anxiety and survivor guilt are strong forces propelling the patient back *into* the dependent relationship. The result of this in-out conflict (see Guntrip, 1968) is the characteristic relationship of hostile dependence, and it leads to episodes of separation attempts and fantasies, followed by regressive returns. Particularly in long-term psychodynamic treatment, the therapist should be sensitive to expressions of this pattern in the transference.

From the perspective of Bowlby's (1973) attachment theory, agoraphobia can be understood as an attachment pathology. More specifically, it can be viewed as a dysregulation of, or imbalance between, the exploratory and attachment systems. From this standpoint, one would predict that of those people who experience panic attacks, only those with significant attachment pathology (i.e., lacking an internalized safe base) will become agoraphobic.

Conclusions

Based on our own experiences and what we have learned from colleagues' experiences, we have become impressed with the special importance of early multimodal treatment (including pharmacological treatment) for people who have experienced their first or second panic attack. Whatever the reasons for the onset of panic attacks, the fact is that the experience of panic often quickly becomes associated with avoidant and other maladaptive feelings and behaviors, which, once developed and crystallized, become locked in and recalcitrant. Early treatment in these cases is important to prevent the reinforcement and crystallization of the avoidant (such as manifestations of agoraphobia) and other maladaptive behavior.

Our comments on treatment are based almost exclusively on case reports, our own clinical experiences, and the received wisdom of the psychodynamic approach. Although one should not ignore these sources and this sort of evidence, clearly they do not represent good substitutes for systematic, well-controlled, and clinically relevant therapeutic outcome and process studies. As for the availability of these kinds of studies, although some form of psychotherapy (which presumably contains some psychodynamic features) is often included in comparisons of the therapeutic effectiveness of different treatment modalities, we do not know of any study that systematically evaluates the relative effectiveness of long-term psychodynamic treatment of agoraphobia and panic disorders. This is obviously a serious gap in our knowledge.

Finally, and somewhat related to the foregoing, we want to emphasize the overriding importance of being informed about treatment approaches other than one's own and knowing when to make an appropriate referral to one of those other treatment approaches. There is an all-too-human tendency to assume implicitly the suitability of a treatment approach for just about any kind of patient if the approach is the one in which the clinician has been trained and is the one the clinician believes to be most efficacious. The overwhelmingly strong likelihood is that this is not the case. One good way of counteracting an excessively parochial or partisan attitude is by being both reasonably knowledgeable about alternative treatment approaches and reasonably aware of the literature dealing with the issue of which approach is most suitable for which set of problems.

In any case, there are few definitive answers to key questions in the area of treatment process and effectiveness. In presenting the psychodynamic approach to treatment of agoraphobia and panic disorder, we have not wanted to suggest that this approach is superior (or inferior) to all others. Rather, we have aimed to give the reader a clear conception of some of the basic assumptions and other ingredients of this approach. Armed with other background knowledge, readers can then make independent judgments regarding the appropriateness and usefulness of psychodynamic treatment for particular cases of agoraphobia and panic disorders.

THE RELATIVE BALANCE OF SUPPORTIVE AND EXPRESSIVE (INTERPRETIVE) THERAPEUTIC TECHNIQUES

We indicated earlier that encouraging patients to expose themselves to the phobic situation often is a necessary step in the treatment of agoraphobia. It has become a basic feature of psychoanalysis and psychoanalytically oriented psychotherapy to keep suggestion to the minimum possible, on the grounds that substituting therapists' authority for parents' authority would limit patients' growth and freedom to develop along lines most suited to their nature and goals. Thus, the radical feature of psychoanalytic treatment, and the aspect that differentiates it from other forms of therapy (such as those noted in the final sections of this chapter), is the seemingly paradoxical effort by the therapist to use the influence of parental authority to offer interpretations that often, at least implicitly, refer to the patient's excessive reliance on real and imagined internalized parental standards and prohibitions.

There are many cases in which the patient's level of disturbance, immediate symptoms, or current life circumstances do not permit a completely nondirective psychoanalytic approach. Freud (1919/1974, p. 168) was aware that the widespread application of analytic technique would "compel us to alloy the pure gold of analysis freely with the copper of direct suggestion." He also noted in the same paper that certain symptoms require a direct approach; the treatment of phobias (as opposed to hysteria) has "already made it necessary to go beyond our former limits." Freud (1919/1974, p. 165) stated that: "One can hardly master a phobia if one waits till the patient lets the analysis influence him to give it up. He will never in that case bring into the analysis the material indispensable for a convincing resolution of the phobia." Freud (1919/1974) thus viewed forced exposure as a necessary *first* step, to be followed by an exploration of the underlying conflicts. The question of the conditions under which it is necessary or desirable to attempt *directly* to alter a symptom is part of the larger issue of the place of deliberately supportive, noninterpretive interventions in psychoanalytically oriented psychotherapy. Ordinarily, the change hoped for by the psychoanalytic clinician is not that the patient engage in a specific behavior at the behest of the therapist. Rather, the therapist hopes to facilitate the patient's freedom to choose more readily among incompatible wishes as these wishes become less fraught with anxiety and peril. (See, in this connection, Schafer's excellent 1970 paper on the psychoanalytic visions of reality and its elaboration by Messer and Winokur in their 1980 discussion of the possibilities of integrating psychodynamic and behavioral approaches to treatment.)

In actual practice, the more disturbed the patient and the more intractable, painful, disabling, and life-threatening the symptom (whether agoraphobia or any other symptom), the more the therapist will be inclined to employ explicit and direct modes of intervention and to recommend or insist on adjunctive treatments (e.g., pharmacotherapy). For example, if the patient's agoraphobia has progressed to the point where he or she is unwilling to leave home alone, we take this as evidence that the ego has been unable to limit anxiety to an internal signal that could activate a less crippling defense. The patient's adaptive capacities are seriously compromised, and strong secondary gains from the symptom have to be suspected. As suggested earlier, these patients often choose jealous, insecure, sexually inadequate husbands who collude with them in maintaining the symptoms. It is more likely, compared with simple phobias, that one will find both a history of significant difficulty negotiating the separation-individuation phase of development (Mahler et al., 1975) and evidence of borderline and narcissistic features. To the extent that these qualities are present, the therapist will depart more from a predominantly expressive approach (however, see Kernberg, 1975) and may include pharmacotherapy, marital therapy, or a multimodal approach in the treatment of agoraphobia.

Our discussion has focused on the psychotherapy of agoraphobia. The considerations and treatment strategies advanced herein apply as well to the psychotherapy of patients with panic disorder. The precipitants of the panic attacks, the particular symptoms that are prominent features of the attacks, and the patient's associations to these factors are explored in an effort to help the patient understand and resolve the underlying conflicts. The conflicts are likely to be more varied than in the case of agoraphobia. The extent to which the therapist relies on explicitly ego-supportive measures and on medication is a function of the frequency and severity of the attacks, the degree to which the patient experiences distress and impaired functioning between attacks, and the therapist's assessment of the patient's ego strength, characterological difficulties, and capacity to benefit from insight-oriented psychotherapy. This approach, of course, does not reflect a view that patients who are not likely to benefit from insight-oriented therapy are somehow inferior.

Case Illustrations

M.C. was a 28-year-old woman who had been married two-and-one-half years. Two months before coming for treatment, she had given birth to a baby boy. The pregnancy had been a difficult one and had included toxemia. The patient's husband had taken a new job in a smaller city about 50 miles from the city in which the patient grew up and in which she and her husband and her parents now lived. The husband had rented a house in the smaller city and expected that after the baby was born, they would all move to their new home. This anticipated move to the new city appeared to precipitate the outbreak of agoraphobic symptoms. Because they had given up their apartment (in anticipation of the move to the new house) and because the patient felt quite anxious being alone, she, her husband, and their new baby moved into the patient's parents' house (which, among other things, involved a 50-mile commute each way for her husband).

When the patient appeared for treatment (she was brought to treatment and driven back home by her husband), she could not leave the house without intense anxiety (she could barely manage going across the street for some minor grocery shopping). She also reported that she experienced a chronic, if manageable, level of anxiety even while at home. The patient also reported that she was quite anxious about her new baby, worried that he might succumb to crib death, and concerned about whether she could take good enough care of him. M.C.'s extreme reluctance to move to the new city presented a dilemma in which symptomatic improvement meant moving to what she experienced as a loathsome place, whereas remaining agoraphobic protected her from this fate.

Hence, whatever else was going on, it was clear that the secondary gain derived from the agoraphobic symptom would serve to maintain that symptom and would constitute a powerful and difficult obstacle to improvement. It seemed that before therapy could proceed very far, this no-win issue had to be confronted. The therapist then saw the patient and her husband together for two sessions in which he spelled out the aforementioned situation. The husband responded that he was getting tired of the long commute and would try to get a job in the city in which they were now living. Fortunately, after a number of joint sessions, the plan to move to the new city was relinquished by both the patient and her husband. Hence, the patient's agoraphobic symptom could be dealt with relatively free of at least one blatant and strong secondary-gain issue.

It should be noted that were the agoraphobic symptom linked solely to the move to the new city (which in its specificity, might make one think of malingering or volitional manipulation), it would presumably disappear or at least become less pervasive and intense, once the plan to move to the new city was relinquished. In fact, this was not the case. Although M.C. felt relieved and grateful about not having to move, her agoraphobic symptom continued at the same level.

At this point, let us briefly introduce some historical and familial material. Although never manifestly agoraphobic, the patient did experience mild phobic symptoms in the past. She reported, for example, that eating in a restaurant, other than a self-service fast-food restaurant, was always a somewhat tense and anxious experience, particularly during the interval between the time the waiter or waitress took her order and the time the food arrived. Having given her order, the patient felt that she had to remain in the restaurant, at least until the food arrived, and she, therefore, felt trapped. M.C. had other experiences similar to her restaurant phobia. For example, whenever possible, she sat on the aisle during a movie or theater performance, because sitting in the middle of the row also made her feel trapped.

One additional item of information played a very important role in the course of the treatment. M.C.'s mother suffered from a kidney disease requiring dialysis, and the patient reported that ever since she was about eight or nine years of age, it was her job to change the filters for her mother's kidney dialysis machine. This task had become habitual and was taken for granted, and, she reported, she never thought much about it.

Therapy proceeded on a semi-weekly basis and mild-to-moderate improvements occurred. For example, after about two months of treatment, M.C. became capable of driving to the sessions unaccompanied by her husband. On weekends, she, her husband, and their baby took short auto trips. If these trips went beyond a particular length of time and distance, M.C. would panic, and they would turn back. However, they would make another foray the next weekend.

From the beginning of treatment, the therapist shared with M.C. his understanding of her agoraphobic symptom as expressing a developmental issue, specifically as one involving separation from parents (particularly, mother) and living one's own independent life—in short, as a difficulty in growing up to become an independent adult. She began to see her earlier preagoraphobic symptoms (i.e., anxiety in restaurants, having to occupy an aisle seat in the theater) as more subtle expressions of the same developmental issue. As we discussed, it was as if the pervasive feeling, "if I leave home, I will not survive," had finally come to a head in the agoraphobic symptom.

The next phase of treatment was characterized by M.C. being able to make increasingly longer and further trips (including solitary shopping and family auto trips to the country on weekends). She related that when she became anxious during these trips, she would conjure up comments and interpretations the therapist had made in the therapy sessions and would repeat them to herself. This would serve to reduce her anxiety. In other words, during this time, much like children use their favorite teddy bears or blankets to assuage anxiety, M.C. employed images, memories, and comments of the therapist as soothing transitional objects (Winnicott, 1958). Consistent with this idea, during this time, M.C. also reported dreams in which the therapist would appear and in which he was making a reassuring comment or interpretation.

Still later in the treatment, one was struck by the fact that M.C.'s dreams now included the therapist's words, but she was now saying them to herself. The therapist was no longer directly in the dreams. Then something occurred that truly constituted a turning point (Stone, 1982) one of the very few dramatic ones that a therapist is likely to experience. It may be recalled that M.C. prepared the filters for her mother's kidney dialysis machine for many years. This hardly came up at all as a topic for discussion in the treatment. All the more surprising, then, that at the beginning of one session, M.C. announced that she had decided that she would no longer be responsible for this task and had so informed her mother, who appeared to accept this decision with equanimity. We should also note that the therapist made no comment or interpretation in response to M.C.'s announcement because he wanted to see what the patient herself would feel, think, and say after making this decision.

Then came a dramatic turn of events. At the next session, M.C. reported that her mother had gone to visit a relative, who lived a few hundred miles away, and had to return suddenly, because she had not brought enough filters with her and, thereby, had literally endangered her life. While relating this incident, M.C. suddenly and emotionally exclaimed: "No wonder I had to move back home. This way I can oversee both my mother and M." (her new baby). During the next and last phase of treatment, M.C. became more and more aware of the degree to which she had internalized her mother's implicit message, "If you leave me and live your own life, I [i.e., mother] will not survive." It was relatively easy to become aware of the feeling that "If I leave home I will not survive," because that feeling was very close to the actual experience of the agoraphobic symptom itself. But what was a revelation was the awareness that she had been living according to what Weiss and Sampson (1986) call the "pathogenic belief" that "if I leave mother, she will not survive."

We referred to the preceding dialysis incident as a turning point, not only because it led to a powerful insight, but also because, from that point on, M.C. made steady and rapid progress, eventually became virtually symptom free and, with her husband and baby, moved into their own apartment. One perhaps sobering note: Although from a reality point of view, the apartment was attractive and reasonably priced, the fact is that it was found by M.C.'s parents and just happened to be across the street from the parents' home. M.C. was certainly aware of the complex significance of this fact and tried to see certain realistic advantages to her parents' propinquity, such as the ready availability of babysitters. Thus, in becoming symptom free, M.C. accepted the compromise of both moving into her own apartment and remaining physically close to her parents; this suggests, perhaps, the limited success of the treatment. However, at the last follow-up, five years after the termination of treatment, M.C. continued to be symptom free. She seemed reasonably content in her marriage and happy with her child. Because her little boy was now in school, she had taken a part-time job, which, she reported, was giving her a good deal of satisfaction.

In concluding this section, we note that in our clinical experience (which for the most part has been with private rather than with clinic patients) we have encountered many cases in which there are a number of mild variants of agoraphobic symptoms. These cases do not qualify for a formal diagnosis but perhaps can be characterized as a subclinical agoraphobia. The patient does not restrict travel, or need a companion in order to leave home, or experience intense anxiety on venturing out alone. However, there often is a clearly perceptible, mild discomfort (a low level signal anxiety, if you will) associated with leaving home. This is the sort of feeling that can be largely unattended to and masked by a subtle feeling of safety and security on returning to the familiar environment of one's home. Of course, the boundary between the psychological state just described and the normal feeling of comfort associated with being at home often is not clear cut. Likewise, the boundary line between avoidance of leaving home and preference for being at home (i.e., between an ego inhibition and a personality style) can be fuzzy.

Although it fails to meet the strict criteria for agoraphobia without history of panic disorder, the aforementioned, subtle avoidance behaviors are of strong interest to the psychoanalytic therapist in terms of their implications for such issues as self-esteem, sense of self, defenses against envy, separation anxiety, sexual and aggressive conflicts, degree of ego inhibition, identification with one's parents, perpetuation of maladaptive patterns, and the like.

Often, the patterns alluded to are not readily discernible on the basis of the limited information gathered during diagnostic interviews but emerge clearly during the course of psychotherapy. As a clinical illustration, we can cite the case of a divorced professional woman approaching her fortieth birthday who was being seen twice a week in psychoanalytic psychotherapy. This woman lives in a large, metropolitan area and works about two miles from home. She has no difficulty in going to and from work or in attending work-related meetings elsewhere in the city. However, she reports an uneasiness in being far from home and away from her dog when she ventures out for social occasions (e.g., to meet a friend) or during her leisure time (e.g., to go shopping or to visit a museum). Only in these circumstances does she make reference to her "shtetl mentality" as a cultural reference to her immigrant parents who lived in a European Jewish ghetto. In one session, she mentioned that she had spent a little time with a woman friend and felt that she "had to get home." She was relieved that the woman did not suggest having dinner together, complained that she was tired of listening to this woman talk about her plans, and felt strongly that she wanted to be by herself. After leaving her friend she forced herself to walk for a while before getting on the subway to go home, feeling like a "tiny girl in a big city," and finally felt relaxed once she returned home. Her thoughts then turned to not wanting to get close to anyone for fear that it would be "too draining," that she could not set limits, and that, therefore, it was "easier to avoid contact with people." Subsequent associations included a recent phone conversation in which she "had to get off the phone," for fear that she would either say something hostile or appear incompetent. This eventually led to childhood memories of feeling emotionally sapped and depleted by having to care for her chronically ill mother and her older, seriously ill sibling, and feeling criticized by her father for not wholeheartedly carrying out this burdensome responsibility assigned to her by him, and then to ongoing issues and conflicts around deprivation, depletion, death wishes, envy, rivalry, and guilt.

There are two points to be highlighted in this case example. First, this patient's level of discomfort in being away from home varied, not with the distance from home, but with the *meanings* of the social situations in which she found herself. For instance, she could readily go on European vacations alone and without any anxiety. Although one often reads that the further from home the patient is the more anxious she is, with this patient, and with many others, our experience has been that it is not the distance from home that is critical in triggering agoraphobic symptoms, but the kinds of intrapsychic conflicts activated in particular situations. Second, for the psychoanalytic clinician it is these conflicts rather than the symptoms per se that are the main focus of therapeutic work.

ALTERNATIVE TREATMENT OPTIONS

There are several alternative approaches to the treatment of agoraphobia and panic. We describe briefly a number of them.

Nonbehavioral Psychotherapy

Quite apart from the specific context of agoraphobia and panic disorders, there are a number of different schools, techniques, and approaches of nonbehavioral psychotherapy. These include, for example, client-centered therapy, Jungian therapy, Gestalt therapy, and so on. Although there is little doubt that patients with agoraphobia and panic have been treated with all these different approaches, we know of no studies comparing their relative efficacy.

Conjoint and Family Therapy

There is a good deal of evidence that complex marital and family interactions and pathology are centrally implicated in the development and maintenance of agoraphobia (e.g., Kleiner & Marshall, 1985). Indeed, Quadrio (1984) states that agoraphobia is "a defense mechanism protecting the marital system or the marital dyad" (p. 81). Hence, the argument goes, effective treatment requires conjoint therapy (Barlow, O'Brien, & Last, 1984, report that including husbands facilitates treatment and improvement in work, social, and family functioning). Some family therapists go further and argue that effective treatment of agoraphobia requires, not simple conjoint, but family therapy. However, it should be kept in mind that some impassioned family therapists believe that family therapy is indicated for virtually all kinds of pathology. Unfortunately, there are mainly anecdotal reports and little systematic evidence to guide the clinician here.

As noted earlier, our own view is that even in individual psychodynamic psychotherapy, it is sometimes advisable to see the patient's spouse for a few sessions or to recommend conjoint therapy. However, we also believe that very often, individual psychotherapy alone is quite appropriate. Given the relatively wide consensus that agoraphobia centrally involves issues of separation, individuation, and infantile dependence versus autonomy, it is often advisable to work only with the individual patient in these areas. It is our belief that growth and improvement is not entirely a matter of effecting changes in the marital or family system. To imply to patients that it is, seems to us to reinforce, in subtle ways, the very overenmeshment with family and overdependency that often characterizes agoraphobic patients. Consistent with our clinical view, Hafner's (1988) review of research on marital therapy for agoraphobia suggests that its usefulness is not yet clear.

BEHAVIORAL AND COGNITIVE THERAPY

These techniques of various kinds represent an obvious alternative treatment strategy. Of the various behavioral approaches available (e.g., systematic desensitization, imaginal flooding, and in vivo exposure), there is some evidence that in vivo exposure is the most effective for treatment of agoraphobia. Comparisons of methods of in vivo exposure (group exposure, self-directed exposure, therapist-directed exposure, spouse-assisted exposure) suggest some effectiveness for each approach.

Michelson, Mavissakalian, and Marchione (1985) compared graduated exposure, paradoxical intention, and progressive muscle relaxation in patients with agoraphobia and panic attacks. They found reductions in the frequency of panic attacks of 55 percent, 50 percent, and 60 percent, respectively. A three-month follow-up maintained these gains. Marshall and Segal (1986) conclude that graduated exposure with the spouse present, done in cohesive groups, combined with spouse-assisted home practice is best. However, follow-up data generally are not encouraging. For example, in one four-year follow-up, less than 20 percent of patients were symptom-free (McPherson, Brougham, & McLaren, 1980). Also, Barlow (1981) reports a median dropout rate of 22 percent, and Barlow et al. (1984) note a failure rate of about 30 percent among those patients who undertook in vivo exposure treatment.

Given the failure rate, dropout rate, and relapse rate of in vivo exposure, cognitive therapy strategies and pharmacotherapy have been used separately and in conjunction with in vivo exposure. The combination of in vivo exposure and imipramine (e.g., Telch, Agras, Taylor, Roth, & Gallen, 1985) appears promising, whereas the addition of cognitive therapy appears to be equivocal (Emmelkamp, Kuipers, & Eggeraat, 1978; Emmelkamp & Mersch, 1982; Taylor & Arnow, 1988; Williams & Rappoport, 1983).

In a review of cognitive therapy, Clark and Beck (1988) state that "its contribution to the treatment of phobias is not well defined in current research" (p. 381), but they claim that the cognitive-therapy procedures used were inadequate.

GROUP TREATMENTS

The various kinds of group treatment, including group psychotherapy and group exposure, have been employed in the treatment of agoraphobia and panic and obviously represent an economical alternative to individual treatment.

PHARMACOLOGICAL TREATMENTS

Particularly in the last number of years, pharmacological treatment for agoraphobia, panic, and generalized anxiety has become more common. Such treatment can be and has been combined with any of the aforementioned treatment approaches. There is also evidence that different drugs tend to be selectively effective for different diagnostic categories. Thus, imipramine and phenelzine have been reported to be especially effective for cases of panic disorder, including those associated with agoraphobia or lactate-induced panic (e.g., Sheehan, Ballenger, & Jacobson, 1980), whereas antianxiety benzodiazepines are held to be more effective for generalized anxiety (Ballenger, 1986). A review (Taylor & Arnow, 1988) of nine studies using imipramine from 8 to 26 weeks at dosages from 122 mg up to 300 mg shows consistent evidence of reductions in the frequency and intensity of panic attacks, as well as diminished depression. However, the dropout rate in these studies ranged from 17 percent to 30 percent, and the relapse rate within the first two years following treatment can be as high as 30 percent (Kelly, Guirguis, Frommer, Mitchell-Heggs, & Sargant, 1970; Zitrin, Wein, Woerner, & Ross, 1983). According to Taylor and Arnow fewer than 50 percent of panic disorder patients showed a stable benefit from drug treatment if one combines relapse rate, dropouts, and patient intolerance. Therefore, they recommend an integrated approach that includes medication, education, relaxation techniques, changes in exercise and diet, paradoxical interventions, and cognitive-therapy techniques (e.g., modification of self-statements).

Hyperventilation and carbon dioxide breathing also have been used to treat panic disorder (see Taylor & Arnow, 1988, for an account of this work, as well as for a useful discussion of the indications and contraindications for pharmacological treatments).

MULTIMODAL APPROACH

This approach is often recommended for treatment of agoraphobia and panic, but the term itself is somewhat ambiguous. It can refer to different permutations and combinations of available treatment approaches. For example, the term *multimodal* can refer to (1) the combination of pharmacotherapy with individual behavioral therapy or individual psychotherapy, (2) pharmacotherapy with group therapies of various kinds, or (3) pharmacotherapy with conjoint or family therapy. *Multimodal* can also refer to different kinds of interventions entirely within the context of psychotherapy—for example, the combination of individual psychodynamic psychotherapy with conjoint therapy and even with some form of exposure therapy.

Whatever the particular combination of different techniques and interventions, the central point made by those who advocate a multimodal approach to the treatment of agoraphobia and panic is the need for flexibility in treating these frequently recalcitrant disorders. Remaining a purist and sticking to one approach, whether it is psychodynamic or behavioral or family oriented, may make the therapist feel comfortable, however, it may not always be in the best interests of the patient. A syndrome such as agoraphobia is often pervasive and implicates many different aspects and levels of the patient's life: biochemical, intrapsychic, behavioral, marital, family, and social. Often, many of these different aspects must be addressed in order for treatment to be effective (e.g., Taylor & Arnow, 1988).

One practical problem involved in trying to implement a multimodal approach is the difficulty inherent in trying to coordinate different interventions and approaches. In some more limited and modest multimodal treatment, the therapist alone can carry out the different interventions. However, when a wide range of interventions are involved, each requiring different skills, training, and experience, it may be unrealistic (on occasion, even grandiose) for the therapist to believe that he or she is expert in all of them. On such occasions, issues of referral and coordination arise, which, if not handled appropriately, may confuse the patient and disrupt treatment.

PSYCHODYNAMIC BEHAVIOR THERAPY

Finally, we want to describe an alternative treatment strategy (Feather & Rhoads, 1972; Rhoads & Feather, 1974), which has been used mainly and only very rarely in the treatment of circumscribed phobias. We believe that this approach perhaps has been undeservedly neglected and that it may have potential for the treatment of agoraphobia and panic. Very briefly, the basic idea underlying psychodynamic behavior therapy is that the patient is desensitized, not to be overt phobic stimulus, but to the unconscious symbolic meaning of the stimulus, which is determined through prior careful clinical interviewing. In one paper, Feather and Rhoads describe the treatment of public speaking phobias, in which they attempt to desensitize patients, not to the phobic situation itself, but to the preconscious and unconscious *fantasies and meanings* associated with public speaking. For example, some patients have fantasies of urinating in their clothes or hurling obscenities at the audience, and it is these situations and fantasies, rather than public speaking itself, to which patients are desensitized.

It seems to us that this approach might be meaningfully extended in a number of ways. One also can employ behavioral techniques other than desensitization, such as imaginal flooding. Also, one can vary the level of unconscious meanings to which the behavioral techniques of desensitization and flooding are applied. For example, if on the basis of clinical data for a particular patient, one has reason to believe that anxiety over public speaking is, at an unconscious level, related to Oedipal wishes and fears (e.g., fantasy of hurling obscenities at the audience is, in turn, linked to wishes to destroy father and fear of retaliation), one could apply the behavioral techniques to these Oedipal wishes and fears.

COMPARISONS OF DIFFERENT TREATMENT APPROACHES

The primary focus on this chapter has been the psychoanalytically oriented treatment of agoraphobia and panic disorder. We have briefly described alternative treatment approaches but have not commented on their relative efficacy or on the several different theoretical emphases within a psychodynamic framework.

Apart from an interest in brevity and our understanding that the main focus should be a clinical one, there is, to our knowledge, no body of research that indicates a clear superiority for a particular method of treatment among the three main therapeutic approaches—that is, psychodynamic, cognitive-behavioral, pharmacological—or for combinations of these approaches. In fact, there has been virtually no high-quality research that bears on the question of relative efficacy. The large-scale meta-analytic studies of treatment outcome for a variety of disorders (Prioleau, Murdock, & Brody, 1983; Shapiro & Shapiro, 1982; Smith, Glass, & Miller, 1980) offer little confidence that we will soon have an answer to the question of treatment of choice for panic disorder and agoraphobia. Among the shortcomings of the treatment-outcome research assessed in these meta-analytic reviews are (1) small number of sessions, (2) use of inexperienced therapists, (3) absence of treatment manuals against which conformity with the technique and the competence of the therapist are assessed, (4) tendency to exclude complex cases and to use nonpatients, (5) failure to use multiple indexes of outcome and multiple perspectives (i.e., therapist, patient, and independent judges), and (6) the finding that effect size (i.e., mean of the treatment group minus mean of the control as comparison group, divided by the standard deviation of the control or comparison group) is a function of the theoretical allegiance of the investigators. Smith et al. (1980), for example, report a 0.29 mean difference in mean effect size in a comparison of the studies done by researchers who presumably were neutral (effect size = 0.66) with the studies conducted by those who had a prior belief in the superiority of the technique being assessed (effect size = 0.95).

Shear (1995, 1996) has written a number of excellent papers on panic and agoraphobia. She presents evidence (Shear, Pilkonis, Cloitre, & Leon, 1994) that a nonprescriptive therapy for panic disorder (later called "emotion-focused treatment" by Shear and Weiner, 1997) did as well as cognitive-behavior treatment in ameliorating symptoms at posttreatment and at six-month follow-up. Both treatments began with three sessions of a psychoeducational approach so that it was not possible to measure the specific impact of the two treatments and whether in fact they added anything more than what might be beneficial in the psychoeducational sessions (Shear & Baslow, 1998).

In another paper (Shear, 1996), drawing on Bowlby's work and on neurobiological studies, Shear presents a cogent case for the role of attachment disturbances in panic disorder and agoraphobia. Interestingly, Klein (1964) first conceived of panic disorder as linked to separation anxiety but arrived at an essentially nonpsychological explanation of the phenomenon. Shear also points out (Shear & Weiner, 1997) that panic-disorder patients tend to avoid negative emotions and tend to deny any link between the onset of symptoms and an emotionally significant experience. For this reason, the clinician might come to the erroneous conclusion that a panic attack was a spontaneous event lacking important psychological precipitants.

With respect to the issue of type of patient studied, Hafner (1988) notes that simple, compared with complex, agoraphobia (Goldstein & Chambless, 1978; Hafner, 1977, 1982) is overrepresented in clinical research, often for good methodological reasons. The so-called complex cases are those in which other, significant psychopathology and marital conflict are part of the initial clinical picture. Bowen and Kohut (1979), for example, found that more than 90 percent of their agoraphobic patients also had a primary affective disorder. A treatment outcome study on the relative effectiveness of different types of therapy that excluded such subjects would yield results with limited generalizability. For example, in their study of agoraphobia, Zitrin et al. (1983) excluded patients with more than moderate levels of depression. Although this may have been necessary and desirable from the standpoint of research methodology, it obviously poses problems of generalizability. Thus, the finding by Klein, Zitrin, Woerner, and Ross (1983) of no difference among agoraphobic patients in degree of symptomatic improvement when comparing behavior therapy and supportive therapy, even if replicated repeatedly, cannot automatically be generalized to the more complex and apparently more typical cases of agoraphobia seen in clinical practice by psychoanalytically oriented therapists. We refer here to the difference between efficacy and effectiveness.

As Hafner (1988) reminds us, apparently only about half the agoraphobic patients referred for treatment, in the context of a research project, ever complete treatment, and a high percentage of those relapse. The other half either drops out (Mavissakalian & Michelson, 1982) or fails to meet the inclusion criteria of the research protocol (Jannoun, Munby, Catalan, & Gelder, 1980). It is probably patients from these two subgroups that come to the attention of psychodynamically oriented therapists. Therefore, it is not surprising that a reader of an earlier draft of this chapter, commenting on the differences between our treatment approach and that of a colleague who is a biologically oriented research psychiatrist, said that he and we "could be seeing different species!"

Suppose it could be shown decisively that, compared with psychodynamic therapy, pharmacotherapy and/or behavior therapy offered a greater and more rapid amelioration of the symptoms of agoraphobia and panic disorder. These methods would then become the treatment of choice for a symptom-focused approach to these disorders. They clearly have the advantage of economy. Thus, Marks (1987) believes that behavioral therapy is the treatment of choice for most phobic disorders and also reports that psychiatrists and nurses (it is not clear why he limits his comments to these professions) can learn the treatment methods of behavior therapy in a very brief period of time and that the application of this approach frequently requires the clinician to devote no more time than is typical in pharmacological or other routine psychiatric treatments.

However, unless it also could be shown that these methods had a positive feedback on the other *DSM-IV* Axis I and Axis II diagnoses often associated with agoraphobia and panic disorder, we still would need to know which treatment approach or combination and sequence of approaches would be most beneficial, both short term and in the long run, for patients with multiple diagnoses. Only when the necessary body of research has been done to answer this complex question will we be able to move beyond clinical experience in deciding the legitimate place of psychoanalytically oriented (supportive and insight) psychotherapy in the treatment of panic disorder and of agoraphobia.

SUMMARY

For a variety of historical, ideological, and philosophical reasons that we do not articulate here, most psychodynamically oriented, compared with biologically oriented or cognitive-behaviorally oriented therapists, come from a tradition in which formal research on the efficacy of treatment and the necessity for accountability are not highly valued. Even today, for example, most psychodynamically oriented therapists view tape recording of sessions as an infringement that compromises the effectiveness of treatment. Clinical experience acquired through supervision and clinical lore are the main guidelines for treatment. Not surprisingly, the meta-analyses of therapy outcome (cf. Parloff, 1984) include so few comparisons that reflect the work of experienced psychodynamically oriented therapists that it is not yet possible to be guided by the research literature, even if one were so inclined.

In light of these unfortunate limitations, as well as the absence of even informal follow-up reports from psychodynamically oriented clinicians, and given the somewhat positive but less than superlative results of medication and of behavioral, cognitive, and other approaches, what practical recommendations can we make for a psychoanalytically informed approach to the treatment of panic disorder and agoraphobia? First, initial treatment should be symptom focused to the extent that the symptoms are disabling. When impairment is significant, some combination of pharmacological, supportive, cognitive, and in vivo exposure measures should be employed. These methods should be used in the context of a therapeutic atmosphere that promotes a good working alliance and a sense of safety, trust, and respect. These qualities will enhance the patient's experience of being in a helping relationship and should facilitate hope. This phase of providing symptomatic relief is regarded as *preliminary* to a psychotherapy that would combine supportive and insight-oriented features in a proportion that reflects the patient's motivation and capacity for self-understanding and tolerance for troublesome thoughts and feelings. To the degree that the patient can resolve the underlying core conflicts, by making and internalizing needed behavioral and characterological changes (see Luborsky et al., 1988), further symptomatic behavior and psychic pain should be less likely to occur, given average expectable environmental conditions, or, as Freud (1937/1957, p. 321) put it, "it still of course remains an open question how much of this immunity is due to a benevolent fate which spares him [or her] too searching a test."

REFERENCES

Abend, S. (1989). Psychoanalytic psychotherapy. In C. Linderman (Ed.), *Handbook of phobia therapy* (pp. 393–403). Northvale, NJ, and London: Jason Aronson.

American Psychiatric Association. (1994). *Diagnostic and statistical manual of mental disorders* (4th ed., rev.). Washington, DC: Author.

Ballenger, J.C. (1986). Pharmacotherapy of the panic disorders. *Journal of Clinical Psychiatry, 47*(Suppl.), 27–32.

Barlow, D.H. (1981). On the relation of clinical research to clinical practice: Current issues, new directions. *Journal of Consulting and Clinical Psychology, 49,* 147–155.

Barlow, D.H. (1988). *Anxiety and its disorders.* New York: Guilford Press.

Barlow, D.H., O'Brien, G.T., & Last, C.G. (1984). Couples treatment of agoraphobia. *Behavior Therapy, 15,* 41–58.

Beck, A.T., & Emery, G. (1985). *Anxiety disorders and phobias.* New York: Basic Books.

Biederman, J., Rosenbaum, J.F., Chaloff, J., & Kagan, J. (1995). Behavioral inhibition as a risk factor for anxiety disorders. In J.S. March (Ed.), *Anxiety disorders in children and adolescents* (pp. 61–81). New York: Guilford Press.

Bowen, R.C., & Kohut, J. (1979). The relationship between agoraphobia and primary affective disorders. *Canadian Journal of Psychiatry, 24,* 317–322.

Bowlby, J. (1973). *Attachment and loss: Vol. 2. Separation.* New York: Basic Books.

Bowlby, J. (1989). The role of attachment in personality development and psychopathology. In S.I. Greenspan & G.H. Pollock (Eds.), *The course of life: Infancy* (Vol 1, pp. 229–270). Madison, CT: International Universities Press.

Breise, A., Charney, D.S., & Heninger, G.R. (1986). Major depression in patients with agoraphobia and panic disorders. *Archives of General Psychiatry, 43,* 1029–1036.

Brenner, C. (1982). *The mind in conflict.* New York: International Universities Press.

Buglass, D., Clarke, J., Henderson, A.S., Kreitman, N., & Presley, A.S. (1977). A study of agoraphobic housewives. *Psychological Medicine, 7,* 73–86.

Busch, F.N., Cooper, A.M., & Klerman, G.L. (1991). Neurophysiological, cognitive-behavioral, and psychoanalytic approaches to panic disorder: Toward an integration. *Psychoanalytic Inquiry, 11,* 316–322.

Busch, F.N., Milrod, B.L., Cooper, A.M., & Shapiro, T. (1995). Psychodynamic approaches to panic disorder. *Journal of Psychotherapy Practice and Research, 5*(1), 73–83.

Busch, F.N., Shear, M.K., & Cooper, A.M. (1995). An empirical study of defense mechanisms in panic disorder. *Journal of Nervous Mental Disease, 183,* 299–303.

Carter, M., Hollon, S.D., Carson, R., & Shelton, R.C. (1995). Effects of a safe person on induced stress following a biological challenge in panic disorders with agoraphobia. *Journal of Abnormal Psychology, 104*(1), 156–163.

Clark, D.M. (1988). A cognitive model of panic attacks. In S. Rachman & J.D. Maser (Eds.), *Panic: Psychological perspectives* (pp. 71–89). Hillsdale, NJ: Erlbaum.

Clark, D.M., & Beck, A.T. (1988). Cognitive approaches. In C.G. Last & M. Hersen (Eds.), *Handbook of anxiety disorders* (pp. 362–385). New York: Pergamon Press.

Compton, A. (1992a). The psychoanalytic view of phobias: I. Freud's theories of phobias and anxiety. *Psychoanalytic Quarterly, 61*(2), 206–229.

Compton, A. (1992b). The psychoanalytic view of phobias: III. Agoraphobia and other phobias of adults. *Psychoanalytic Quarterly, 61*(3), 400–425.

Cooper, A. (1985). Will neurobiology influence psychoanalysis? *American Journal of Psychiatry, 142*(12), 1395–1402.

Eagle, M. (1979). Psychoanalytic formulations of phobias. In L. Saretsky, G.D. Goldman, & D.S. Milman (Eds.), *Integrating ego psychology and object relations theory* (pp. 97–118). Dubuque, IA: Kendall/Hunt.

Eagle, M., & Wolitzky, D.L. (1988). Psychodynamics. In C.G. Last & M. Hersen (Eds.), *Handbook of anxiety disorders* (pp. 251–277). New York: Pergamon Press.

Emmelkamp, P.M.G. (1988). Phobia disorders. In C.G. Last & M. Hersen (Eds.), *Handbook of anxiety disorders* (pp. 66–86). Elmsford, NY: Pergamon Press.

Emmelkamp, P.M.G., Kuipers, A.C., & Eggeraat, J.B. (1978). Cognitive modification versus prolonged exposure in vivo: A comparison with agoraphobics as subjects. *Behaviour Research and Therapy, 16*, 33–41.

Emmelkamp, P.M.G., & Mersch, P. (1982). Cognition and exposure in vivo in the treatment of agoraphobia: Short term and delayed effects. *Cognitive Therapy and Research, 6*, 77–78.

Fairbairn, W.R.D. (1952). *Psychoanalytic studies of the personality.* London: Tavistock; Routledge & Kegan Paul.

Faravelli, C. (1985). Life events preceding the onset of panic disorder. *Journal of Affective Disorder, 9*, 103–105.

Feather, B.W., & Rhoads, J.M. (1972). Psychodynamic behavior therapy. *Archives of General Psychiatry, 26*, 496–511.

Fenichel, O. (1945). *The psychoanalytic theory of neurosis.* New York: Norton.

Freud, S. (1957). Analysis terminable and interminable. In *Collected papers.* London: Hogarth. (Original work published 1937)

Freud, S. (1962). The sexual etiology of the neuroses. In J. Strachey (Ed. and Trans.), *Standard edition* (Vol. 3, pp. 261–285). London: Hogarth. (Original work published 1898)

Freud, S. (1974). *Lines of advance in psycho-analytic therapy.* In J. Strachey (Ed. and Trans.), *Standard edition.* London: Hogarth. (Original work published 1919)

Goldstein, A.J., & Chambless, D.L. (1978). A reanalysis of agoraphobia. *Behavior Therapy, 9*, 47–59.

Grunbaum, A. (1984). *The foundations of psychoanalysis.* Berkeley: University of California Press.

Guntrip, H. (1968). *Schizoid phenomena, object relations and the self.* New York: International Universities Press.

Hafner, R.J. (1976). Fresh symptom emergence after intensive behaviour therapy. *British Journal of Psychiatry, 129*, 378–383.

Hafner, R.J. (1977). The husbands of agoraphobic women and their influence on treatment outcome. *British Journal of Psychiatry, 131*, 289–294.

Hafner, R.J. (1979). Agoraphobic women married to abnormally jealous men. *British Journal of Medical Psychology, 52*, 99–104.

Hafner, R.J. (1982). The marital context of the agoraphobic syndrome. In D.L. Chambless & A.J. Goldstein (Eds.), *Agoraphobia: Multiple perspectives on theory and treatment.* New York: Wiley.

Hafner, R.J. (1984). The marital repercussions of behavior therapy for agoraphobia. *Psychotherapy, 21*(4), 53–54.

Hafner, R.J. (1986). *Marriage and mental illness.* New York: Guilford Press.

Hafner, R.J. (1988). Marital and family therapy. In C.G. Last & M. Hersen (Eds.), *Handbook of anxiety disorders.* New York: Pergamon Press.

Hallam, R.S. (1978). Agoraphobia: A critical review of the concept. *British Journal of Psychiatry, 133*, 314–319.

Jannoun, L., Munby, M., Catalan, J., & Gelder, M. (1980). A home-based treatment program for agoraphobia: Replication and controlled evaluation. *Behavior Therapy, 11*, 294–305.

Kagan, J., Reznik, J.S., & Snidman, N. (1990). Origins of panic disorder. In J. Ballenger (Ed.), *Neurobiology of panic disorder* (pp. 71–87). New York: Wiley.

Katerndahl, D.A., & Realini, J.P. (1997). Comorbid psychiatric disorders in subjects with panic attacks. *Journal of Nervous and Mental Disease, 185*(11), 669–674.

Kelly, D., Guirguis, W., Frommer, E., Mitchell-Heggs, N., & Sargant, W. (1970). Treatment of phobic states with antidepressants: A retrospective study of 245 patients. *Journal of Psychiatry, 116,* 387–389.

Kernberg, O. (1975). *Borderline conditions and pathological narcissism.* New York: Aronson.

Kessler, R.J. (1996). Panic disorder and the retreat from meaning. *Journal of Clinical Psychoanalysis, 5*(4), 505–528.

Klein, D.F. (1964). Delineation of two drug-responsive anxiety syndromes. *Psychopharmacologia, 5,* 397–408.

Klein, D.F. (1981). Anxiety reconceptualized. In D.F. Klein & J.G. Rubkin (Eds.), *Anxiety: New research and changing concepts.* New York: Raven Press.

Klein, D.F. (1992). Panic disorders: Old wine in new bottles? [Comment]. *Integrative Psychiatry, 8*(2), 85–86.

Klein, D.F. (1993). False suffocation alarms, spontaneous panics, and related conditions: An integrative hypothesis. *Archives of General Psychiatry, 50,* 306–317.

Klein, D.F., & Gorman, J.M. (1987). A model of panic and agoraphobic development. *Acta Psychiatrica Scandinavia, 76,* 87–95.

Klein, D.F., & Rubkin, J.G. (Eds.). (1981). *Anxiety: New research and changing concepts.* New York: Raven Press.

Klein, D.F., Zitrin, C.M., Woerner, M.G., & Ross, D.C. (1983). Treatment of phobias: II. Behavior therapy and supportive psychotherapy. Are there any specific ingredients? *Archives of General Psychiatry, 40,* 139–145.

Kleiner, L., & Marshall, W.L. (1985). Relationship difficulties and agoraphobia. *Clinical Psychology Review, 5,* 581–595.

Kohut, H. (1971). *The analysis of the self.* New York: International Universities Press.

Kohut, H. (1977). *The restoration of the self.* New York: International Universities Press.

Kohut, H. (1984). *How does analysis cure?* Chicago: University of Chicago Press.

Lader, M.H., & Wing, L. (1966). *Physiological measures, sedative drugs and morbid anxiety* (Maudsley Monograph No. 14). London: Oxford University Press.

Lesser, I.M. (1990). Panic disorders and depression: Co-occurrence and treatment. In J.C. Ballenger (Ed.), *Clinical aspects of panic disorders* (pp. 181–191). New York: Wiley-Liss.

Lteif, G.N., & Mavissakalian, M.R. (1995). Life events and panic disorders/agoraphobia. *Comprehensive Psychiatry, 36*(2), 118–122.

Luborsky, L. (1984). *Principles of psychoanalytic psychotherapy: A manual for supportive-expressive treatment.* New York: Basic Books.

Luborsky, L., Crits-Christoph, P., Mintz, J., & Auerbach, A. (1988). *Who will benefit from psychotherapy?* New York: Basic Books.

Lydiard, B.R. (1991). Coexisting depression and anxiety and special diagnosis and treatment issues. *Journal of Psychiatry, 52*(Suppl.), 48–54.

Mahler, M., Pine, F., & Bergman, A. (1975). *The psychological birth of the human infant: Symbiosis and individuation.* New York: Basic Books.

Marks, I.M. (1970). The classification of phobic disorders. *British Journal of Psychiatry, 116,* 377–386.

Marks, I.M. (1987). *Fears, phobias and rituals.* New York: Oxford University Press.

Marshall, W.L., & Segal, Z. (1986). Phobia and anxiety. In M. Hersen (Ed.), *Pharmacological and behavioral treatment: An integrative approach* (pp. 260–288). New York: Wiley.

Mathews, A.M., Gelder, M.G., & Johnston, D.W. (1981). *Agoraphobia: Nature and treatment.* London: Tavistock.

Mavissakalian, M., & Michelson, L. (1982). Agoraphobia: Behavioral and pharmacological treatments, preliminary outcome, and process findings. *Psychopharmacology Bulletin, 18,* 91–103.

McNally, R.J. (1994). *Panic disorders: A critical analysis.* New York: Guilford Press.

McPherson, F.M., Brougham, L., & McLaren, S. (1980). Maintenance of improvement in agoraphobic patients treated by behavioral methods—a four year follow-up. *Behaviour Research and Therapy, 18,* 150–152.

Meissner, W.W. (1985). Theories of personality and psychopathology: Classical psychoanalysis. In H.I. Kaplan & B.J. Sadock (Eds.), *Comprehensive textbook of psychiatry.* Baltimore: Williams & Wilkins.

Messer, S.B., & Winokur, M. (1980). Some limits to the integration of psychoanalytic and behavior therapy. *American Psychologist, 35,* 818–827.

Michelson, L., Mavissakalian, M., & Marchione, K. (1985). Cognitive and behavioral treatments of agoraphobia: Clinical, behavioral, and psychophysiological outcomes. *Journal of Consulting and Clinical Psychology, 53,* 913–925.

Milrod, B.L. (1995). The continuing usefulness of psychoanalysis in the treatment for panic disorder. *Journal of American Psychoanalytic Association, 43,* 151–162.

Milrod, B.L., Busch, F.N., Cooper, A.M., & Shapiro, T. (1997). *Manual of panic-focused psychodynamic psychotherapy.* Washington, DC: American Psychiatric Association Press.

Milrod, B.L., & Shear, M.K. (1991a). Dynamic treatment of panic disorder: A review. *Journal of Nervous Mental Disorders, 179,* 741–743.

Milrod, B.L., & Shear, M.K. (1991b). Psychodynamic treatment of panic: Three case histories. *Hospital Community Psychiatry, 42,* 311–312.

Modell, A. (1984). *Psychoanalysis in a new context.* New York: International Universities Press.

Parloff, M. (1984). Psychotherapy research and its incredible credibility crisis. *Clinical Psychology Review, 4,* 95–109.

Pine, F. (1985). *Developmental theory and clinical process.* New Haven, CT: Yale University Press.

Prioleau, L., Murdock, M., & Brody, N. (1983). An analysis of psychotherapy versus placebo studies. *Behavioral and Brain Sciences, 6,* 275–310.

Quadrio, C. (1984). The families of agoraphobic women. *Australian and New Zealand Journal of Psychiatry, 18,* 164–170.

Rhoads, J.M., & Feather, B.W. (1974). Application of psychodynamics to behavior therapy. *American Journal of Psychiatry, 131,* 17–20.

Sanderson, W.C., & McGinn, L.K. (1997). Psychological treatment of anxiety disorder patients with comorbidity. In S. Wetzler, W.C. Sanderson, et al. (Eds.), *Treatment strategies for patients with psychiatric comorbidity* (pp. 75–104). New York: Wiley.

Schafer, R. (1970). The psychoanalytic vision of reality. *International Journal of Psychoanalysis, 51,* 270–297.

Schur, M. (1971). Metapsychological aspects of phobias in adults. In M. Kanzer (Ed.), *The unconscious today: Essays in honor of Max Schur.* New York: International Universities Press.

Schwartz, V. (1994). The panic disorder psychodynamic model. *American Journal of Psychiatry, 151*(5), 786–787.

Shapiro, D.A., & Shapiro, D. (1982). Meta-analysis of comparative therapy outcome studies: A replication and refinement. *Psychological Bulletin, 92,* 581–604.

Shear, M.K. (1995). Psychotherapy for panic disorder. *Psychiatric Quarterly, 66*(4), 321–328.

Shear, M.K. (1996). Factors on the etiology and pathogenesis of panic disorder: Revisiting the attachment-separation paradigm. *American Journal of Psychiatry, 153*(Suppl.), 125–136.

Shear, M.K., & Barlow, D.H. (1998). Cognitive behavioral treatment compared with nonprescriptive treatment of panic disorder [Reply]. *Archives of General Psychiatry, 55*(7), 665–666.

Shear, M.K., Cloitre, M., & Heckelman, L. (1995). Emotion-focused treatment for panic disorders: A brief dynamically informed therapy. In J.P. Barber & P. Crits-Christopher, et al. (Eds.), *Dynamic therapies for psychiatric disorders (Axis 1)* (pp. 267–293). New York: Basic Books.

Shear, M.K., Cooper, A.M., Klerman, G.L., & Busch, F.N. (1993). A psychodynamic model of panic disorder. *American Journal of Psychiatry, 150*(6), 859–866.

Shear, M.K., Pilkonis, P.A., Cloitre, M., & Leon, A.C. (1994). Cognitive behavioral treatment compared with nonprescriptive treatment of panic disorder. *Archives of General Psychiatry, 51*(5), 395–401.

Shear, M.K., & Weiner, K, (1997). Psychotherapy for panic disorder. *Journal of Clinical Psychiatry, 153*(Suppl. 2), 38–45.

Sheehan, D.V., Ballenger, J., & Jacobson, G. (1980). Treatment of endogenous anxiety with phobic, hysterical and hypochondriacal symptoms. *Archives of General Psychiatry, 37*, 51–59.

Silverman, D. (1986). A multi-model approach: Looking at clinical data from three theoretical perspectives. *Psychoanalytic Psychology, 3*, 121–132.

Smith, M.C., Glass, G.V., & Miller, J.I. (1980). *The benefits of psychotherapy.* Baltimore: Johns Hopkins University Press.

Stone, M. (1982). Turning points in psychotherapy. In S. Slipp (Ed.), *Curative factors in dynamic psychotherapy* (pp. 259–279). New York: McGraw-Hill.

Strupp, H.H., & Binder, J. (1984). *Psychotherapy in a new key: A guide to time limited dynamic psychotherapy.* New York: Basic Books.

Taylor, C.B., & Arnow, B. (1988). *The nature and treatment of anxiety disorders.* New York: Free Press.

Telch, M., Agras, W.S., Taylor, C.B., Roth, W.T., & Gallen, C. (1985). Combined pharmacological and behavioral treatment for agoraphobia. *Behaviour Research and Therapy, 23*, 325–335.

Weiss, J., & Sampson, H. (1986). *The psychoanalytic process.* New York: Guilford Press.

Weissman, M.M., Bland, R.C., Canino, G.J., & Faravelli, C. (1997). The cross-national epidemiology of panic disorder. *Archives of General Psychiatry, 54*(4), 305–309.

Weissman, M.M., Canino, G.J., Greenwald, S., & Peter, R. (1995). Current rates and symptom profiles of panic disorder in six cross-national studies. *Clinical Neuropharmacology, 18*(2), S1–S6.

Williams, S.L., & Rappoport, A. (1983). Cognitive treatment in the natural environment for agoraphobics. *Behavior Therapy, 14*, 299–313.

Winnicott, D.W. (1958). *Collected papers: Through pediatrics to psychoanalysis.* New York: Basic Books.

Zitrin, C.M., Wein, W.F., Woerner, M.G., & Ross, D.C. (1983). Treatment of phobias: I. Comparison of imipramine hydrochloride and placebo. *Archives of General Psychiatry, 40*, 125–137.

CHAPTER 10

Cognitive Behavior Therapy

F. DUDLEY MCGLYNN and LARRY W. BATES

A VAST literature is devoted to panic disorder and panic disorder with agoraphobia, including over 2,000 articles from the last 10 years. The concepts of panic disorder and agoraphobia are undergoing rapid change, as are presumptive explanations and approaches to assessment and intervention. Here we present contemporary, behavioral approaches to conceptualizing, assessing, and treating panic and agoraphobia. By *behavioral* approaches we mean those associated historically with the behavior-therapy movement and the cognitive-behavior therapy (CBT) arm of that movement.

CONCEPTUALIZATION

Panic refers to a sudden experience of extreme biological and cognitive fearfulness that reaches a zenith in about 10 minutes, then gradually subsides. *Agoraphobia* refers to behavioral avoidance of situations in which panic is deemed likely. Panic occurs with and without agoraphobia; agoraphobia usually occurs in association with panic (discussed later).

BIOLOGICAL CONCEPTUALIZATION OF PANIC DISORDER

Biological theorists (e.g., Klein & Klein, 1989a) have proffered the Neo-Kraepelinian argument that panic disorder is an identifiable entity that reflects unique neurochemical disease. Grist for the biologists' theoretical mill has come from at least four empirical sources: a seemingly unique response of panic attacks to the antidepressant imipramine (Klein, 1964); a seemingly unique responsivity among panic patients to various biological challenge tests (see Woods & Charney, 1988); an apparent pattern of panic-disorder heritability (Torgersen, 1983); and the apparent absence of peripheral stimulus control over panic phenomena (Klein, 1981). However, continued examination of the aforementioned empirical claims (e.g., Margraf, Ehlers, & Roth, 1986; M. Roth,

225

1984; Telch, 1988) has yielded doubt about the extent to which they support any straightforward biological explanation of panic disorder (see especially McNally, 1990). For example, the response of panic to imipramine turned out to be not unique (Kahn et al., 1986), and the unique responsivity of panic patients to biological challenge is not physiological (Margraf et al., 1986). Furthermore, there is little agreement about the biological subsystems that provide foundations for panic disorder (e.g., Charney et al., 1990; Nutt & Lawson, 1992; Roy-Byrne, Mellman, & Uhde, 1988).

Hyperventilation (ventilation that exceeds metabolic requirements) has received the most attention as a likely precursor to panic physiology. Some theories treat hyperventilation as a necessary or sufficient condition for panic (e.g., Ley, 1985; Lum, 1981). These theories are related to research literatures that: compare the symptoms of hyperventilation to those of panic, study the panic-like consequences of deliberate hyperventilation, study the respiratory consequences of anxiety, and evaluate the effects on panic of so-called respiratory treatments. The research shows overlap between panic and hyperventilation but not sufficient overlap to support a simple hyperventilatory theory of panic origins (for a review see Margraf, 1993). One response to problems for the simple hyperventilation theory has been to incorporate hyperventilation and related phenomena into more complex theories along with psychological factors (discussed later).

PSYCHOLOGICAL CONCEPTUALIZATION OF PANIC DISORDER

Psychological theorists have likewise proffered several explanations of the origins of panic disorder. Common to standard formulations is the notion that panic disorder amounts to fear that is related to unexpected bodily events, for example, events associated with hyperventilation (Hibbert, 1984; Ley, 1985; Lum, 1981). In one formulation of the relation between bodily events and panic (Goldstein & Chambless, 1978; Wolpe & Rowan, 1988), the bodily events function as interoceptively conditioned stimuli for panic, i.e. panic is an interoceptively conditioned response (Razran, 1961) to the bodily event cues that precede it. In another formulation of the relation, panic arises from cognitive catastrophizing that is prompted by the bodily events (Clark, 1986) among persons who believe that the events signal imminent danger (Clark, 1988; Reiss & McNally, 1985). Grist for the psychological theorist's mill comes from several arenas of research in which panic patients are studied. Representative arenas are research on interoceptive acuity (e.g., Ehlers, 1989, cited in Ehlers, 1993), and research on attentional biases (e.g., Mathews & MacLeod, 1985) and memory biases (e.g., McNally, Foa, & Donnell, 1989) for information related to threat.

Interoceptive Acuity

Owing to the prominence of bodily signals in panic phenomena, some research has focused on the obvious possibility that bodily events among panic patients differ from bodily events among others. Following the lead of Pennebaker (1982), the target of research has been differential bodily change; either in the form of spontaneous fluctuation (e.g., W. Roth et al., 1986), or in the form of response to stressful events (e.g., W. Roth et al., 1992). By and large the research has failed to describe important differences between panic patients and others (see Ehlers, 1993).

Other research has focused on the perception of bodily events (usually cardiac events) among panic patients and others. Ehlers and Breuer (1992), for example, found superior accuracy of heartbeat counts uniquely among panic patients when panic patients were compared to occasional panickers, specific phobics, and normal comparison subjects. However, they found superior accuracy of heartbeat counts among both panic patients and generalized-anxiety-disorder patients, when those two groups were compared with depressed patients. Furthermore, there have been other comparisons in which panic patients' perception of heartbeats has not differed from perception among normal controls (e.g., Ehlers, Margraf, & Roth, 1988). The hypothesis that enhanced cardiac awareness plays a role in the events of panic has received nontrivial support; but the finding of superior cardiac awareness among panic patients is not robust.

Attentional Bias

Virtually all theoretical approaches to anxiety begin with the notion that anxiety is a response to danger. It follows that selective attention to danger signals would characterize anxious persons. Burgess, Jones, Robertson, Radcliffe, and Emerson (1981) provided the first demonstration of attentional bias for threat cues among agoraphobics. Agoraphobic and normal subjects listened to two prose passages simultaneously; they orally reiterated one of them, and listened for out-of-context threats and neutral words in both. The agoraphobics detected more threats than neutral out-of-context words imbedded in the passage that was not orally reiterated; the control subjects did not.

Several investigators have used the Stroop color-naming paradigm to compare reactivity to threat cues among panic disorder patients versus others. In the Stroop preparation, subjects are instructed to name the colors of printed words quickly; variations in latencies to naming imply that the meanings of the words have influenced the processing of color information. Ehlers, Margraf, Davies, and Roth (1988) compared color-naming latencies for threatening versus neutral words among panic-disorder patients versus normal subjects. Among patients, the color-naming latencies for threat words (related to bodily danger, physical separation, embarrassment) were longer than for neutral words. Among normal subjects the opposite result occurred. Thus, threatening word meanings somehow influenced processing of color-related information among the patients. Similar phenomena have been reported independently (e.g., McNally, Riemann, & Kim, 1990). The implications of panic patients' unique performances in Stroop preparations remain to be worked out in detail. However, the picture is emerging that panic patients do sometimes exhibit attentional biases for disorder-specific threat information (see Ehlers, 1993; McNally, 1990).

Memory Bias

Interest in panic patients' attentional bias vis-à-vis threat-related information has been paralleled by interest in any memory bias for such information that might exist. Both explicit (purposeful, conscious) and implicit (incidental, automatic) memory processes have been investigated. McNally et al. (1989) reported a representative experiment. Panic patients and normal subjects were asked to rate the extent to which each of a list of anxiety-related and other adjectives described them accurately. Later they responded to a surprise recall test for the words they had rated. Panic patients recalled more anxiety-related words than other words; normal subjects recalled more other words than anxiety-related words. A similar phenomenon was reported by Cloitre and Liebowitz (1991) using a free-recall paradigm. In general, demonstrations of memory bias for threat-related information among panic-disorder patients are noteworthy, but work remains both experimentally and conceptually.

Psychobiological Theories of Panic

As with the biological approach (already discussed), a straightforward and trustworthy psychological account about the origins of panic has not yet been accomplished. The interoceptive-conditioning model is entirely post hoc, and it distinguishes inadequately between conditioned and unconditioned stimuli and responses (cf. Acierno, Hersen, & van Hasselt, 1993; McNally, 1994). The cognitive account is weakened by the observation (e.g., Wolpe & Rowan, 1988) that cognitive catastrophizing *follows* panic, and by the observation (Rachman, Lopatka, & Levitt, 1988) that panic occurs in the absence of cognitive catastrophizing.

Multi-element theories for thinking about the ontogeny of panic have been articulated by Barlow (1988), Clark (1988), Ehlers and Margraf (1989), and Rapee (1987), among others. There are differences between the various formulations, but their commonality is more important. Barlow's model is representative. In his model the foundations of panic disorder are stressful interpersonal and/or somatic events in the lives of persons who are predisposed biologically, and sometimes psychologically, to develop panic disorder. The cumulative effect of life stress and predisposition is an initial panic attack: an event that sets the stage for associatively learned fear of the interoceptive and exteroceptive signals that are present during the episode.

Panic, Anxiety, and Fear

The history of the modern concept of panic begins in 1959 when Klein observed that imipramine alleviated panic attacks but not chronic anxiety. The implication of Klein's observation was that panic and anxiety differed neurobiologically. One consequence has been three decades of controversy over how we should proceed conceptually given both similarities and differences among the phenomena termed *anxiety, spontaneous panic,* and *phobic fear* (e.g., Barlow, 1988; Craske, 1991; Klein, 1993; Marks, 1987).

One controversial question is how we should conceptualize the relation between panic and anxiety. Barlow (1988) is among those who have argued that panic and anxiety can be conceptualized as different affective phenomena. Panic is an extreme manifestation of the more basic affect of fear; as such, panic is solely concerned with preparing the organism to escape from imminent danger. Anxiety is a multidimensional affect related to vigilance/scanning and to appraisal/coping vis-à-vis threat, including but not limited to imminent danger. Marks (1987) is among those who have argued that panic and anxiety are fundamentally the same; panic and anxiety occupy different positions on the same continuum of physiological arousal/negative affectivity.

Another controversial question is how we should conceptualize the relation between panic and phobic fear. In this case Barlow (1988) has argued against making a distinction. As was already noted, panic is construed as intense fear that mobilizes escape from imminent danger. Similarly, Craske (1991) reviewed considerable evidence that panic and fear are the same aside from their stimulus control; fear is cued by environmental events that signal danger; panic is cued by bodily events that signal danger. On the other hand, data that support the propriety of making a distinction between panic and fear have been provided by Rapee, Sanderson, McCauley, and DiNardo (1992) among others. Interviews with phobic panic-disorder patients about their experiences during phobic encounters versus panic attacks suggested that panic is differentially associated with fear of dying, with fear of going crazy or losing control, and with parathesias.

McNally (1994) reviewed the salient arguments and data that bear on the issue of how to conceptualize panic, anxiety, and fear. He concluded that a distinction between panic and anxiety can be defended, that the difference between panic and phobic fear is less straightforward, that better data are needed, and that better data are more likely to be acquired if panic and fear are presumed to differ. We would add simply that a strong potential for confusion due to reification of constructs is inherent in these kinds of discussions.

PANIC AND AGORAPHOBIA

In *DSM-III* (American Psychiatric Association, 1980) there was no connection between panic disorder and agoraphobia; panic disorder was a subtype of anxiety neurosis, agoraphobia was a subtype of a separate disorder called phobic neurosis. Cursory review of articles about agoraphobia that appeared in the mainstream behavior-therapy literature of the 1970s confirms that a separation existed between panic and agoraphobia in that verbal community at one time. During the 1980s, however, the frequent coincidence of panic and agoraphobia was established. In turn, the *DSM-III-R* (APA, 1987) contained panic disorder, panic disorder with agoraphobia, and agoraphobia without history of panic disorder. It was also during the 1980s that behavior therapists linked panic and agoraphobia (e.g., Barlow, 1988).

Notwithstanding the realizations just described, problems have been encountered during attempts to link agoraphobia with panic, both theoretical problems and empirical ones. One impediment to developing an understanding of the linkage between agoraphobia and panic has been premature attempts to couch the issues in terms of dual-process theory. The dual-process fear-mediation theory of avoidance (Mowrer, 1939, 1960) has been with us for over half a century and has never worked really well, not even when used to guide controlled experiments with animal subjects (D'Amato, 1970; Herrnstein, 1969). Nonetheless, behaviorally oriented clinicians have been quick to extend the theory to the case of panic-related agoraphobia. Not only has such theoretical allegiance been misdirected, but also it has served to forestall serious and potentially more fruitful theoretical ventures. Seemingly, the intuitive comfort of the dual-process fear-mediation theory of avoidance has outweighed its demonstrable failures in garnering our theoretical allegiance.

Aside from the problematic theoretical legacy, there is lack of clarity in the empirical literature linking panic and agoraphobia. Some individuals have panic disorder and do not develop agoraphobia. Other people develop agoraphobia soon after their first panic attack. Still others develop agoraphobia gradually after extended periods following the onset of panic disorder. Various attempts have failed to identify factors that discriminate convincingly between panic sufferers who do and who do not become agoraphobic. Among the factors that do *not* separate agoraphobic and nonagoraphobic panic sufferers are: severity of panic attacks, age at panic onset, and duration of panic disorder. Among the factors that sometimes separate agoraphobic from nonagoraphobic panic sufferers are cognitive behaviors such as catastrophizing about the likelihood and consequences of panicking (see McNally, 1994). (There are empirical issues also concerning people who seemingly develop agoraphobia without history of panic. At issue is whether agoraphobia develops in the absence of panic as the diagnostic terminology denotes or evolves out of comorbid anxiety conditions or subclinical panic that is present but undiagnosed.)

Panic and agoraphobia both refer to complex event domains that differ between persons and differ within persons across times and settings. However, our theoretical attempts to link panic and agoraphobia lend a monolithic character to events within both domains (i.e., little allowance is made for nuances of behavioral topography or somatic response patterning). Such oversimplification compounds problems associated with an untoward theoretical legacy and a vague empirical picture. Fortunately, the task of describing linkages between agoraphobic events and panic events need not be completed for clinicians to proceed. As will be shown, clinicians deal with panic and agoraphobia as separate domains of problems.

Comorbidity

Most of the comorbidity data are available for panic disorder and agoraphobia as defined in terms of *DSM-III-R* (APA, 1987). Comorbidity rates for *DSM-III-R* Axis I diagnoses among patients diagnosed with panic disorder have ranged from 65 percent to 88 percent (see J. Beck & Zebb, 1994). The most common concurrent Axis I diagnoses are Specific Phobia and Social Phobia, Dysthymia and Major Depression, and Alcohol Abuse/Dependence. Comorbidity figures for Axis I diagnoses among patients who have panic disorder with agoraphobia have ranged from 51 percent to 91 percent of patients (J. Beck & Zebb, 1994). For the most part, comorbidity figures reiterate those among patients who have panic disorder. However, some comorbid conditions seem to be associated more with agoraphobia than with panic disorder, for example, major depression (Starcevic, Uhlenhuth, Kellner, & Pathak, 1992).

Mixed panic and agoraphobia cohorts have been used typically in studies of comorbidity involving Axis II diagnoses (J. Beck & Zebb, 1994). Rates of personality-disorder diagnoses among these patients have ranged from 25 percent to 60 percent. Cluster C is overrepresented among comorbid diagnoses.

Some research in the arena of comorbidity has examined changes in rates of comorbid diagnoses as agoraphobia becomes increasingly restrictive. Among the Axis I comorbid conditions that become more prevalent with severe agoraphobia are Alcohol Use/Dependence, Major Depression, and Hypochondriasis (Himle & Hill, 1991; Starcevic, Kellner, Uhlenhuth, & Pathak, 1992). Personality disorders also become more prevalent along with severe agoraphobia.

DIAGNOSTIC ISSUES AND PROBLEMS *(DSM-IV)*

Panic in *DSM-IV*

According to *DSM-IV* (APA, 1994) panic is a discrete period of intense fear or discomfort, in which four or more of thirteen listed symptoms develop abruptly and reach a peak within 10 minutes. The listed symptoms are various bodily phenomena plus dissociative experiences and fears of losing control and of dying. Following Klein and Klein (1989b), *DSM-IV* goes on to distinguish between three types of panic based on apparent stimulus control. *Unexpected* panic attacks have no known controlling stimulus; they occur spontaneously or "out of the blue." *Situationally predisposed* panic attacks occur under probabilistic stimulus control from situational cues; some situations render an attack more likely than do others. *Situationally bound* panic attacks occur under strong stimulus control; panic occurs almost invariably and immediately upon exposure to the controlling cues.

The major criteria for diagnosing panic disorder have been changed across the last three versions of the *DSM*. In *DSM-III* (APA, 1980), the diagnosis of panic disorder required criterional panic attacks. In *DSM-III-R* (APA, 1987) the diagnosis of panic disorder could be based on either criterional panic attacks or fearful preoccupation with panic. In *DSM-IV* the diagnosis of panic disorder requires *both* criterional panic attacks and fearful preoccupation with panic. Because phenomena akin to repeated panic attacks occur not infrequently in other anxiety disorders, fearful preoccupation with panic attacks is the major distinguishing feature of panic disorder.

Behavioral Assessment of Panic

A useful distinction can be made between behavioral assessment and behaviorally oriented clinical assessment. Behavioral assessment refers to assessment activities that are congruent philosophically with one or more varieties of psychological behaviorism. (In brief, behavioral assessment mirrors either the premise that behavior is a determined product of specific environmental regulation, or the premise that behavior is a dynamic product of moment-to-moment interactions between environmental and organismic determinants.) Behaviorally oriented clinical assessment, on the other hand, refers to the evolved assessment practices of clinicians who identify themselves as behavior therapists. The narrative that follows is about behaviorally oriented clinical assessment.

Self-Report Assessment of Panic: Structured Interviewing

The interview structure most commonly used in evaluating anxiety disorders was developed by Barlow and his colleagues. The Anxiety Disorders Interview Schedule (ADIS) (DiNardo, O'Brien, Barlow, Waddell, & Blanchard, 1983) incorporated items developed by the authors with material from the Schedule for Affective Disorders and Schizophrenia (Endicott & Spitzer, 1979), the Hamilton Anxiety Rating Scale (Hamilton, 1959), and the Hamilton Rating Scale for Depression (Hamilton, 1960). It was intended for use with the *DSM-III* (APA, 1980) anxiety-disorder criteria, but was expanded to incorporate information about the histories of anxiety problems, information about situational and cognitive factors that influence anxiety, and about depressive, psychotic, addictive, and organic symptoms. The ADIS-IV (Brown, DiNardo, & Barlow, 1994) is the current version of the ADIS geared to the anxiety-disorder classifications of *DSM-IV* (APA, 1994).

Throughout several iterations of the ADIS there has been careful work on fundamentals, such as interrater reliabilities of *DSM* diagnoses (Barlow, 1987; DiNardo, Moras, Barlow, Rapee, & Brown, 1993). There has also been evident concern with the continuity or flow of actual interviewing. The ADIS-IV begins with demographic information, followed by basic questions about the presenting complaint, and by queries about recent life stresses. The remainder of the interview deals with anxiety disorders, mood and somatoform disorders, mixed anxiety and depression, substance use, obvious psychotic/conversion symptoms, and relevant medical conditions. There is an ADIS-IV-L (lifetime version) that prompts relatively detailed answers about previous episodes. The ADIS-IV is used for assessing anxiety disorders in clinics worldwide. It is recommended here as the preferred means of choosing parameters for behavioral assessment in the individual case.

Self-Report Assessment of Panic: Questionnaires

Questionnaires are used mostly for research purposes because, by and large, they are insufficiently idiographic for routine use in clinical assessment. When questionnaires are used clinically, they serve as components of multifaceted assessment protocols that are organized around convergent validation strategies.

Bouchard, Pelletier, Gauthier, Côté, and Laberge (1997) provided a review of 14 questionnaires used in assessing panic and agoraphobia. These questionnaires were classified as involving global or specific information, and they were discussed in terms of psychometric desiderata. Specific questionnaires about panic include the Agoraphobic Cognitions Questionnaire (Chambless, Caputo, Bright, & Gallager, 1984), the Agoraphobic Cognitions Scale (Hoffart,

Friis, & Martinsen, 1992), the Anxiety Sensitivity Index (Reiss, Peterson, Gursky, & McNally, 1986), the Body Sensations Questionnaire (Chambless et al., 1984), the Catastrophic Cognitions Questionnaire-Modified (Khawaja, Oei, & Baglioni, 1994), the Panic Appraisal Inventory (Telch, 1987), the Panic Attack Questionnaire and Panic Attack Symptoms Questionnaire (Clum, Broyles, Borden, & Watkins, 1990), the Panic Belief Questionnaire (Greenberg, 1988), and the Self-Efficacy to Control Panic Attacks Questionnaire (Gauthier, Bouchard, Côté, Laberge, & French, 1993). These instruments can be subdivided into those that assess panic-related symptoms, and those that assess panic-related thinking. Questionnaires about panic-related symptoms can be useful in identifying panic phenomena to target during treatment. Those that assess panic-related thinking might be of value in identifying the type or quality of panic-related cognition that is germane to the individual case (e.g., fear of fear, fear of negative consequences, fear of bodily sensations). In general, however, much work remains in the effort to provide adequately norm-referenced and standardized questionnaires for routine use with panic patients.

The most influential questionnaire that deals with panic-related thinking is the Anxiety Sensitivity Index or ASI (above). Anxiety sensitivity refers to the habitual tendency of a person to display catastrophic thinking in the presence of particular bodily sensations. The ASI is a 16-item questionnaire about fearful preoccupation with potentially adverse consequences of anxiety. Data have shown that ASI scores have adequate test-retest stability, that ASI scores account for unique variability in anxiety ratings, that ASI scores discriminate between anxiety-disordered and normal respondents, and that ASI scores can be used to discriminate panic patients from patients who have other anxiety disorders (S. Taylor, 1995).

The most recent questionnaire to appear is the Bodily Sensations Interpretation Questionnaire (Clark et al., 1997). It has 27 items that provide an index of the degree to which respondents interpret various somatic and other events as signals of impending catastrophe. Initial research suggests that scores on the questionnaire discriminate reliably between patients with panic and those with other anxiety disorders.

Self-Report Assessment of Panic: Self-Monitoring

Self-monitoring was not prominent in the anxiety-assessment literature until it was made relevant by the modern concept of panic as a discrete and identifiable (i.e., recordable) response array. In self-monitoring, the patient keeps ongoing records of some aspect(s) of the behavior of interest (e.g., frequency, intensity, duration). Record forms are provided and the patient is instructed to turn in the forms regularly. C. Taylor, Fried, and Kenardy (1990) provided patients with a hand-held computer that prompted and stored ratings related to panic at each hour.

In the self-monitoring of panic, provision is made for recording the frequencies and durations of episodes as well as specific symptoms and contexts (see Craske & Waikar, 1994). Structured forms prompt the patient to record whether he or she was alone during the attack or with a spouse, friend, or stranger; to record whether the attack occurred in a stressful situation; and to record whether the attack was expected. Various bodily sensations and themes of catastrophic thinking are listed, also; the patient is instructed to rate each bodily event and cognitive theme along a dimension of severity.

Self-monitoring is susceptible to many of the same sources of inaccuracy that influence other assessment activities. Self-monitoring also presents problems associated with reactivity, that is, behavior changes produced by the activities of behavior recording (see Nelson, 1977). Nonetheless informative uses of self-monitoring have appeared in the literature on panic disorder. For example, Basoglu, Marks, and Sengun (1992) used self-monitoring to track panic and anxiety phenomena among 39 patients diagnosed as having panic disorder with agoraphobia. Self-monitoring showed that panic occurs at the end of long anxious periods.

Psychophysiological Assessment of Panic

Data about panic attacks can be obtained by deliberately producing panic in the clinic. Sodium lactate, caffeine, and yohimbine have been used to produce panic pharmacologically (Shear & Fyer, 1988), but carbon dioxide inhalation has received the most attention (Sanderson & Wetzler, 1990). Group data have shown that panic patients report more panic phenomena during carbon dioxide inhalation than do normal comparison subjects. However, rates of panic induction for panic patients versus others are not sufficiently different to recommend carbon dioxide challenge testing as a diagnostic method.

By contrast with biological challenge testing, ambulatory monitoring of heart rate (e.g., C. Taylor, Telch, & Haavik, 1983) is well suited for panic assessment. In their application of hand-held computers to the tasks of self-monitoring, C. Taylor et al. (1990) had 12 panic-disorder patients wear a cardiac monitor. The device recorded heart rate continuously and supplied 10-second records of the ECG signal when the software recognized the signal as atypical. Ambulatory devices for recording bioelectric signals doubtlessly will become increasingly prominent in panic assessment, because they solve the problem of external or ecological validity that characterized much laboratory and clinic assessment. However, ambulatory assessment of heart rate is not without problems vis-à-vis panic; some panic attacks occur without identifiable heart-rate signatures, and some seemingly pathognomonic heart-rate phenomena occur in the absence of panic (see C. Taylor et al., 1986).

BEHAVIORAL ASSESSMENT OF AGORAPHOBIA

Self-Report Assessment of Agoraphobia: Questionnaires

The Mobility Inventory (Chambless, Caputo, Jasin, Gracely, & Williams, 1985) prompts reports about 26 common agoraphobic situations when alone and when accompanied. Craske, Rachman, and Tallman (1986) have shown that it reliably discriminates between agoraphobic patients and patients with other anxiety disorders.

Relative severity of agoraphobia can be assessed with the 23-item Fear Questionnaire (Marks & Mathews, 1979). This instrument provides four main ratings and three subscales, including the agoraphobia subscale. Normative data from the general population were reported by Mizes and Crawford (1986).

Self-reports about cognition associated with agoraphobia can be acquired with the Agoraphobia Cognitions Questionnaire (Chambless et al., 1984). This 14-item questionnaire is a companion to the Body Sensations Questionnaire (already mentioned) and is utilized for understanding cognition vis-à-vis several behavioral, social, and physiological situations that provoke anxiety. The Agoraphobia Cognitions Scale (Hoffart et al., 1992) can be used to assess cognition related specifically to bodily incapacitation, embarrassment, and loss of control.

Self-Report Assessment of Agoraphobia: Self-Efficacy

Treatment for agoraphobia often entails multiple self-directed exposure trials of considerable difficulty. Self-efficacy vis-à-vis the various exposure tasks is sometimes measured to allow prediction about the strength and persistence of self-exposure efforts (Bandura 1977, 1986). Williams (1990) has provided a standardized format called the Self-Efficacy Scales for Agoraphobia on which patients rate their perceived efficacy vis-à-vis several locomotor performances. These scales are beginning to appear in comparative behavior therapy outcome research (e.g., Hoffart, 1995).

Self-Report Assessment of Agoraphobia: Safety Signals

Safety signals are people, places, or things that promote a sense of well-being. They can influence a patient's ability to complete exposure tasks as well as the severity of distress experienced. Therefore, knowledge about safety signals is valuable in developing exposure tasks (Rachman, 1984). Typically an understanding of safety-signal phenomena is developed from the initial interview. Barlow (1988) catalogued the frequency of several safety signals among 125 agoraphobic patients.

Assessment of Motoric Behavior

Naturalistic behavioral avoidance tests (BATs) are used typically to assess motor behavior among agoraphobics. In the simplest case (e.g., Emmelkamp, 1982), the patient is instructed to walk as far as possible along a specified route and to return immediately when no further progress is anticipated. The route can be specified as one that leaves a place of safety (e.g., home, neighborhood) or as one that approaches a place of danger (e.g., a crowded supermarket). Sometimes patients are instructed to leave a corroborative marker at the point of maximum progress. In a more elaborate approach an individualized hierarchy of adaptively germane and increasingly fearsome locomotor performances is specified; the patient is instructed to undertake each in turn (e.g., Mathews, Gelder, & Johnston, 1981). In a still more elaborate application, locomotor behavior among agoraphobics is assessed under standardized conditions so that data can be compared across patients (Agras, Leitenberg, & Barlow, 1968). At the SUNY-Albany Center for Stress and Anxiety Disorders, a standard 1.2-mile course, punctuated with stopping stations, has been established. Patients proceed until they are too distressed to continue; their success is monitored at the stopping stations.

Naturalistic behavioral testing overcomes the external-validity problems that compromise many varieties of clinical assessment. However, high-quality assessment still requires representative sampling across problematic situations.

TREATMENT OF PANIC

The psychological treatment of panic disorder is described in several readily available sources (Bouman & Emmelkamp, 1996; Craske & Barlow, 1993; Craske & Waikar, 1994). The narratives below summarize the major therapeutic strategies, and characterize the current literature about clinical efficacy.

BREATHING RETRAINING

Rationale

Hyperventilation exists when the rate of carbon dioxide production is lower than the rate of carbon dioxide expiration, resulting in respiratory alkalosis, defined as pH > 7.45 (Ley, 1985). Studies indicate that voluntary hyperventilation promotes paniclike symptoms in some patients (Clark, Salkovskis, & Chalkley, 1985), that hyperventilation is contiguously associated with naturally occurring panic (Hibbett, 1986, cited in Clark, 1986), and that patients with panic disorder have abnormally low CO_2 levels at rest (Gorman et al., 1986; Lum, 1976; Rapee, 1986; Salkovskis, Jones, & Clark, 1986). The physiological consequences of respiratory alkalosis include heart palpitations, shortness of breath, and dizziness. People may misattribute the symptoms to a variety of causes (e.g., heart attack) and move toward panic as described earlier. During hyperventilation, thoracic breathing is coupled with tense abdominal muscles to produce shallow, rapid breaths and hyperventilation. Breathing retraining promotes abdominal breathing in a slow, rhythmic pattern.

General Procedures

Typically, the therapist models correct breathing after placing one hand on the stomach and one hand on the chest. During inhalations, the hand on the stomach should rise while the hand on the chest remains relatively motionless. Rhythmic breathing can be facilitated by inhaling through the nose and exhaling through the mouth at a pace of about 8 to 12 respirations per minute. It is helpful early on to use an audiotaped script to pace inhalations and exhalations. Patients are instructed to practice abdominal breathing two to three times per day. Therapy should include discussions of progress in breathing practice and of effects of breathing on panic. Detailed information about breathing retraining is readily available (see Bouman & Emmelkamp, 1996; Clark et al., 1985; Craske & Barlow, 1993). The following case is a representative sample of the use of breathing retraining in our clinic. We will use parts of this case throughout this chapter along with other examples:

> Burt was an elderly man with a three-year history of panic disorder with agoraphobia. After initial assessment, he was educated about panic and agoraphobia and was taught to relax and to breathe abdominally prior to initiating interoceptive exposure. He had been firm in his belief that his problem was related to some unknown physical ailment, not to panic. One day he entered the clinic and announced that he was having a panic attack and must leave. The therapist convinced Burt to remain. His heart rate was 128 bpm, he stated that he was having trouble catching his breath, and he was sweating. He was encouraged to begin abdominal breathing while the therapist guided his respiration count and provided feedback about his breathing. After 10 minutes, his heart rate had fallen to 74 beats per minute, although he stated that he was still quite fearful. He continued slow rhythmic breathing while the therapist explained the bodily changes that had taken place. After about 10 more minutes, Burt proclaimed that his attack was over and he felt fine. His heart rate at this point was 68 beats per minute. This session was pivotal in helping Burt realize that his symptoms were related to panic. Afterward he was more fully engaged in the therapy.

Therapy Outcome Literature

Garssen, de Ruiter, and van Dyck (1992) reviewed the small literature on breathing retraining and panic, then posited that breathing retraining may only be a "rational placebo." Ley (1993) reviewed the same literature and concluded that breathing retraining is an effective treatment. Overall, the research results for breathing retraining are ambiguous. Part of the difficulty characterizing breathing retraining outcomes is that typically research methods, including some experimental breathing regimens, have been weak. Another aspect of the difficulty is that typically breathing retraining has been studied as a component of complex intervention.

INTEROCEPTIVE EXPOSURE

Rationale

Exposure to fear signals has been a centerpiece of behavioral fear therapy for three decades. As noted earlier, modern theories of panic incorporate bodily events as fear signals; either as interoceptive conditioned stimuli for panic, or as precursors to catastrophic thinking that eventuates in panic. Contemporary uses of interoceptive exposure reflect a new variation of an established practice: that is, assessment of frightening bodily cues followed by repetitive exposure to those cues in a controlled and safe setting.

General Description of Procedure

First, a hierarchy of feared somatic sensations is constructed. The therapist models each of several exercises, encourages the patient to repeat them, and asks the patient to rate the fear experienced. The exercises are then arranged in a hierarchical fashion with the most feared exercise at the top.

Detailed guidelines for conducting interoceptive exposure are readily available (Craske & Barlow, 1993; Rapee & Barlow, 1989). The major techniques are described only briefly here. Exposure to respiratory symptoms is accomplished most often by voluntary hyperventilation. Patients are asked simply to breathe deeply and rapidly through their nose and mouth (40 inhalations per min) for about one to three minutes (Ley, 1985). Exposure to cardiac symptoms is accomplished by aerobic exercises, such as brisk walking, running in place, climbing stairs, and so forth. Exposure to symptoms such as dizziness, lightheadedness, and loss of balance is accomplished by exercises that involve rapidly changing the head position in respect of one's vertical or horizontal plane. For example, the therapist may have patients repeatedly place the head between the legs then quickly reorient themselves to a sitting position. Musculoskeletal tension can be produced easily by using muscle tensing instructions or by tensing exercises, such as holding a push-up or sit-up.

In general exercises such as those just mentioned are used to promote repeated exposure to increasingly fearsome bodily events. Thirty-second exposure durations are sought; successive exercise routines may take two minutes or longer.

> We have already introduced Burt. At one stage of therapy Burt performed several interoceptive exposure exercises. For respiratory symptoms, we first suggested hyperventilation, but Burt refused because of sinus congestion. He was able to hold his breath for 90 seconds. To stimulate cerebrovascular symptoms, Burt was asked to swivel in a chair for 30 seconds, then 60 seconds. He stated that this exercise caused nausea and dizziness. He rated his anxiety after the exercise as about 25 on a 100-point scale and as being very different from his panic symptoms. He was asked to maintain a push-up for about 90 seconds, but this produced no tension akin to his panic symptoms. For cardiac symptoms we asked Burt to run in place, but he stated that he preferred brisk walking to running because it was "better on the back." We then asked Burt to walk briskly from his car to the therapy room at his next visit. Burt walked into his next therapy session and stated that he was having nervous symptoms like a panic attack; specifically, his heart was pounding, he was walking unsteadily, and he was having trouble breathing. He gave a fear rating of 60 for that brisk walk and felt its effects were quite similar to a mild panic attack. We continued to use this exercise to produce cardiac symptoms and encouraged the use of breathing retraining, deep muscle relaxation, and cognitive restructuring to cope with the symptoms until brisk walking no longer produced paniclike symptoms.
>
> Unfortunately, no exercise other than the walking produced symptoms that mimicked panic to any appreciable degree. This case, however, does give one an appreciation for some of the subtleties of interoceptive exposure. Each patient is unique and no exercise will produce paniclike symptoms in everyone. For Burt, brisk walking provided for interoceptive exposure to some paniclike symptoms and allowed for rehearsal of coping strategies.

Treatment Outcome

Barlow and colleagues developed a panic-control treatment that utilizes a variety of exercises to provoke somatic sensations (Barlow, Craske, Cerny, & Klosko, 1989). The full panic-control treatment includes education about panic physiology, interoceptive exposure, some cognitive restructuring, and situational exposure (discussed later), as needed. In testing the efficacy of panic-control treatment, Barlow et al. assigned over 60 patients with panic disorder randomly to one of four conditions: wait list, applied progressive muscle relaxation, exposure and cognitive restructuring, and muscle relaxation combined with exposure and cognitive restructuring. A total of 56 patients completed the project; a relatively large percentage of subjects dropped out of the relaxation treatment (33%). Among patients who completed a protocol, all three treatments reduced panic frequency. Exposure plus cognitive restructuring and exposure plus cognitive restructuring plus relaxation were most effective. Respectively, 85 percent and 87 percent of patients reported zero panic attacks at posttreatment, as compared to 36 percent of patients on the wait list and 60 percent of those who received relaxation alone. However, as Barlow et al. pointed out only 50 percent of those who received the most effective regimens reached high end-state functioning as defined in the project. Craske, Brown, and Barlow (1991) reported a 24-month follow-up of these patients. The data suggested that interoceptive exposure can be an effective treatment for reducing panic frequency.

RELAXATION TRAINING

Relaxation techniques have long been among the tools utilized by behavior therapists in dealing with anxiety-related problems. Jacobson (1938) pioneered the use of relaxation training and developed exercises referred to as progressive relaxation training. Wolpe (1958) popularized a shortened version of the technique. Bernstein and Borkovec (1973) provided a widely used manual that afforded standardization of relaxation procedures. Notwithstanding this long history, research on relaxation training as a treatment for panic is in short supply (Barlow et al., 1989; Barlow, O'Brien, & Last, 1984; C. Taylor, Kenigsberg, & Robinson, 1982).

Rationale

In its earliest uses (Jacobson, 1938), relaxation training was used to reduce a person's arousal level while at rest. Wolpe (1958) used relaxation to attenuate emotional responsiveness to anxiety-cue stimuli. Research by others (e.g., Paul & Trimble, 1970) provided support for that usage. Öst (1987) is the most recent in a series of practitioners who use relaxation as a coping strategy during stressful encounters. By employing relaxation techniques during phobic or panic situations, patients presumably are better able to tolerate exposure.

General Description of Procedure

Applied relaxation (Öst, 1987) consists of six phases of training. In the first phase (progressive relaxation), patients receive two sessions of progressive relaxation (Wolpe & Lazarus, 1966) and are instructed to practice at home. In the second phase (relaxation-only), detailed progressive relaxation instructions are replaced with a general instruction to relax, using the tension-relaxation cycles progressively. In the third phase (cue-controlled relaxation), the self-instruction to relax is paired with the relaxed state (see also Russell & Sippich, 1973). The therapist says, "Inhale," before each inhalation and, "Relax," before exhalation. The patient is then instructed to think these words while breathing. Typically, time to relax is reduced to about two to three minutes after this session. In the remaining phases, training is focused on relaxing on cue and doing so in the face of stress.

Treatment Outcome

Öst (1988) reported a between-groups experiment in which 14 patients with panic disorder and four patients with generalized-anxiety disorder received either progressive muscle relaxation (Bernstein & Borkovec, 1973) or applied relaxation training (Öst, 1987) over 14 sessions. Assessments of panic frequency, duration, and intensity were performed two weeks before treatment, after treatment, and 6 to 29 months later. Of seven panic-disorder patients who received progressive muscle relaxation, five were panic-free after treatment; four of seven remained panic-free at follow-up. Applied relaxation rendered 100 percent of panic-disordered patients free of panic at both posttreatment and follow-up.

Öst and Westling (1995) compared CBT (A. Beck, Emery, & Greenberg, 1985) to applied relaxation training (Öst, 1987). Patients with panic disorder were assessed prior to treatment, given 12 sessions of therapy, and reassessed at posttreatment and one year later. There were no significant differences between patients assigned to the two therapy groups; both CBT and applied relaxation training eliminated panic in over 80 percent of those who completed treatment.

Michelson, Mavissakalian, and Marchione (1988) compared the effects of relaxation training, graduated exposure, and paradoxical intention (Ascher, 1981) among patients who had panic disorder with agoraphobia. All three interventions were somewhat effective; about half of the patients from each treatment condition showed high end-state functioning at both posttreatment and follow-up. The primary difference between groups was that patients who had received either relaxation or exposure were less reactive psychophysiologically than were those who had received paradoxical intention. Of some concern was that just over half the treated patients reached high end-state functioning and that no significant end-state differences were found.

COGNITIVE RESTRUCTURING

Rationale

Cognitive theoretical explanations of panic (e.g., Clark, 1986, 1988) were discussed earlier. The basic idea is that bodily events give rise to untoward thinking, and untoward thinking spirals into panic. Cognitive therapies are designed to alter the content of thought.

General Description of Procedure

Descriptions of cognitive-therapy procedures and of those designed specifically for panic disorder are found in several publications (e.g., A. Beck, 1988;

Clark & Beck, 1988; Craske & Barlow, 1993; Rapee & Barlow, 1989). Cognitive restructuring is a mainstream cognitive-therapy approach; it typically includes identifying and challenging untoward cognitions.

Treatment begins with a detailed interview about symptomatology and about thought content that precedes and accompanies panic symptoms. Treatment proceeds by teaching patients to recognize and challenge misconceptions regarding the symptoms, their meaning, and their consequences.

The untoward thinking of panic sufferers can be classified into two major themes, namely, overpredicting the likelihood of adversity and catastrophizing about the consequences of adversity. Hence, focus on estimating and catastrophizing is of primary importance during cognitive restructuring. Challenging misappraisals consists basically of having patients rationally reconsider likely events and consequences. For example, graduate students might fear failing the doctoral qualifying exam and might believe that failure will end their career, when, in fact, failure is unlikely and would only mean that they must repeat the exam. The following is a representative sample from a session at our clinic:

THERAPIST: Tell me about the attack that happened while you were driving yesterday. Can you remember what preceded the attack?

PATIENT: All I know is that I was driving and then my chest got tight. I began to have trouble catching my breath. My heart started pounding and I was afraid that I was having a heart attack.

THERAPIST: I thought you had an ECG last week and the doctor stated that you were not suffering from a heart condition.

PATIENT: That's true, but what if he was wrong?

THERAPIST: I know that having a heart attack is a fear of yours. But what did you do yesterday, given that you thought you were having a heart attack? Did you call the ambulance on your cell phone?

PATIENT: No. I just got off of the road and got out of the car until it passed.

THERAPIST: So although you believed you were having a heart attack, you did nothing in the way of helping yourself, if this was the case?

PATIENT: I guess not. Well, the doctor told me last week that it wasn't a heart attack. But this one may have been.

THERAPIST: In retrospect, was the attack you had yesterday a heart attack?

PATIENT: No, I guess not.

THERAPIST: This has happened several times in the past. How many times has it resulted in a heart attack?

PATIENT: None.

THERAPIST: So what is the probability that if you experience these same symptoms again that it is a heart attack?

PATIENT: I guess it's pretty low, since the doctor has given me the green light and I've never had a heart attack.

THERAPIST: So does it help you to believe that these symptoms are heart attacks?

PATIENT: No, it hasn't changed a thing. I keep having the attacks anyway.

THERAPIST: Well, let's review the symptoms for panic and those for a heart attack and how to use some coping skills for when you have the attacks—other than just getting out of the car.

Treatment Outcome

Cognitive therapy is an integral part of many multimodal therapy plans that typically include relaxation training and some exposure-based components. However, it has been investigated without other components to allow clinicians to judge its efficacy as a stand-alone treatment. Salkovskis, Clark, and Hackmann (1991) used a multiple-baseline design across patients to investigate the effectiveness of cognitive therapy in the treatment of seven patients who had panic disorder with moderate to severe agoraphobia. The patients were assigned randomly to baselines of differing lengths, followed by two sessions of cognitive therapy. Five of these patients received focal cognitive therapy, which included a focus on changing catastrophic misinterpretations of bodily sensations. The remaining two patients received nonfocal cognitive therapy, which concentrated on concerns other than misinterpretations of somatic sensations, followed by two sessions of focal treatment. Marked reductions in panic-attack frequency were found in four of five patients during the focal condition; no such reductions were found among patients during the nonfocal condition. In all, six of seven patients showed marked reductions in panic frequency after brief focal cognitive therapy; two achieved complete cessation of panic.

The largest body of research has compared the effects of cognitive therapies to the effects of various relaxation-training regimens. In some of these experiments cognitive therapy has been relatively more beneficial than relaxation training (Arntz & van den Hout, 1996; J. Beck, Stanley, Baldwin, Deagle, & Averill, 1994; Clark et al., 1994). In others of the experiments the results for cognitive therapy and relaxation training have been equivalent (Öst & Westling, 1995). A box-score tally of the comparative outcomes gives an edge to cognitive therapy. One is struck, however, that the research outcomes mirror reliably the a priori allegiances of the investigators. Hence, cognitive therapy may have earned its apparent superiority by virtue of having garnered more adherents, rather than vice versa.

In one noteworthy experiment, Clark et al. (1994) compared cognitive therapy, applied relaxation, and imipramine in the treatment of panic disorder. Seventy-two patients were assigned randomly to one of the three treatment conditions or to a wait list. Two psychological therapies entailed 12 weekly sessions of either cognitive therapy or a modified version of applied relaxation. Patients receiving imipramine were maintained on medication until a six-month assessment, then they were gradually withdrawn. Results at three months indicated that both the percentage of panic-free patients and the percentage of those who achieved high end-state functioning were higher among cognitive-therapy patients than among patients in either the applied relaxation or imipramine conditions. At six months there was no difference between cognitive therapy and imipramine treatment; both were superior to applied relaxation. At 15 months the results of cognitive therapy were again superior to both imipramine and applied relaxation on most measures. Those who received imipramine had by then been completely withdrawn from the medication.

TREATMENT OF AGORAPHOBIA

SITUATIONAL EXPOSURE

Rationale

Exposure therapy grew out of the persuasive argument (Marks, 1975) that exposure to fearsome circumstances is the common element of most successful anxiety therapies. Exposure therapy proceeds by promoting in vivo exposure to feared circumstances for as long as possible or until sometime after fear has subsided. Fear diminution based on exposure is styled as reflecting habituation, extinction, self-efficacy enhancement, cognitive alteration, and so on. However, these theoretical interpretations of fear reduction are legacies of the original anxiety therapies on which exposure is based, not data-based interpretations of exposure effects. Furthermore, the theoretical accounts afford little in the way of guiding the details of exposure procedure.

There are comparative outcome experiments that provide guidance concerning procedural choices, e.g. self-directed versus therapist-guided exposure, massed versus spaced exposure, partner-assisted versus nonassisted exposure, and gradual versus intense exposure (Bouman & Emmelkamp, 1996). However, the data are without clear-cut implications for clinical practice save for the principle that exposure should be prolonged and harmless. The choice of particular variants to use with any patient is governed more by the clinical considerations than scientific ones.

General Description of Procedure

There is no uniform set of procedures known as exposure therapy. By and large, there is an effort to promote prolonged and up-close exposure in ways that reflect clinical concerns such as time, cost, risk of drop-out, etc. However, some facets of exposure treatment for agoraphobia are becoming more or less routine. One typical facet is construction of a hierarchy of feared encounters. This is done following one of the well-known methods associated with systematic desensitization (Wolpe, 1973). Once the fear/avoidance hierarchy is developed, it serves to guide in vivo rehearsals that are graduated in fearsomeness and in exposure time, that is, rehearsals one to two hours each day for three to seven days per week. Friends, spouses, or therapists are sometimes utilized to facilitate exposure, and then they are eventually faded out. Utilization of self-directed exposure warrants that the specifics of the assignment be previewed at length. Details of each exposure assignment (e.g., when, where, with whom, duration, how, etc.) are very specific, for example: "Ride in the rear section of the bus while your partner remains in the front section, from the Collum St. terminal to 71st Street, and return to the Collum St. terminal."

In some approaches (e.g., Bouman & Emmelkamp, 1996) patients are instructed to use self-monitoring and are encouraged to utilize a diary for recording each exposure exercise as well as other anxiety-provoking situations that present themselves. Patients record the exposure task, their anxiety level, the time and interval of exposure, and whether the exposure was partner-assisted or alone. Most formats include instructions for cognitive strategies and breathing that are coupled with exposure practice. In general, therapists or self-help books review the exposure tasks, the coping strategies utilized, and the cognitions experienced. Negative thought content during exposure is identified and corrected. The following is a portion of a representative case example from our clinic involving discussion about buying groceries:

THERAPIST: How did your shopping go this week?

PATIENT: Well, I did like you said and bought something every day this week at the supermarket. But I cheated a little.

THERAPIST: Well, by going everyday maybe we accomplished something. Now what do you mean by cheating a little?

PATIENT: The first two times I only bought candy at the display rack and checked out at the express lane. But I actually bought a few things the other times. You know, regular stuff like real food.

THERAPIST: Tell me about the first time you bought candy. What kind of sensations were you experiencing; how did it feel?

PATIENT: Well, I was only in there for just a little while and I kept wondering if I could do it during the daylight hours with it being so crowded. My heart was beating fast for awhile but I don't guess it was so bad. I just didn't want to panic again, so I didn't do it correctly out of fear of panicking.

THERAPIST: But you did not panic?

PATIENT: No. I was scared but didn't really panic.

THERAPIST: Did you try the coping strategies you've learned?

PATIENT: Not until later. On the third trip I bought some food to make burgers. That time I almost panicked because the lines were pretty long, a lot longer than early in the morning. But I backed down an aisle and began slowing my breathing down. This took the edge off the anxiety and I was able to get in one of the shorter lines and purchase my food.

THERAPIST: Great. So you used the breathing technique and it reduced your anxiety.

PATIENT: Yeah. I felt a big relief when I got to the car, but I did it. It had been a long time since I had been shopping like that.

Treatment Outcome

Guided exposure has been the primary component of behavioral treatment for agoraphobia for some time (Barlow, 1988; Emmelkamp, 1982; Emmelkamp & Wessels, 1975; Mathews et al., 1981). Therefore, a sizable literature about the effects of technique variation is available. For example, prolonged exposure is more efficacious than is brief exposure (Stern & Marks, 1973). Group exposure and individual exposure appear to be about equally effective (Emmelkamp & Emmelkamp-Benner, 1975; Hafner & Marks, 1976). The results for spouse-assisted versus nonassisted exposure are mixed (e.g., Barlow et al., 1984; Cobb, Mathews, Childs-Clarke, & Blowers, 1984; Emmelkamp, 1990). Michelson and Marchione (1991) reviewed the treatment of agoraphobia and concluded that graduated, prolonged, therapist-assisted in vivo exposure is most effective. Using meta-analysis they found that self-directed practice is about 25 percent effective, whereas therapist-assisted practice results in 50 percent to 65 percent improvement. It is not clear that severity of agoraphobia dictates therapist involvement. It is clear that more responsibility for treatment can be given to the patient than was thought at one time.

TREATMENT OUTCOME OF COMBINED
COGNITIVE-BEHAVIORAL INTERVENTIONS

As is probably clear from the narrative to this point, the therapy-outcome literature concerned with panic and/or agoraphobia is based on research that evaluates competing treatments. A sizable body of research takes the next step and
combines various treatments into multielement treatment procedures.

Michelson et al. (1990) used such a treatment package for panic that included applied relaxation, breathing retraining, interoceptive exposure, and in
vivo coping homework assignments. Ten outpatients who had panic disorder
received 13 group sessions. All achieved high end-state functioning and none
had spontaneous panic after treatment.

Telch et al. (1993) evaluated another multimodal group therapy using 67 patients who had panic disorder with and without agoraphobia. Patients were assigned to either 8 weeks of cognitive-behavioral group therapy or to a wait list.
Group therapy consisted of education, cognitive therapy, breathing retraining,
and interoceptive exposure. Among patients who received treatment, 85 percent were panic-free at posttreatment, as compared to 30 percent of patients on
the wait list. A full 83 percent of the treated patients remained panic-free at a
six-month follow-up; 63 percent met the criteria for full recovery relative to
only 9 percent of the wait-list patients.

Craske, Maidenberg, and Bystritsky (1995) evaluated a shortened version of
the cognitive-behavioral treatment used by Barlow et al. (1989) to treat panic
disorder. Thirty subjects were assigned randomly to either the brief CBT or to
nondirective therapy for four weekly sessions. Brief CBT involved education,
cognitive restructuring, breathing retraining, and interoceptive exposure.
Nondirective therapy entailed education, nondirective listening, and discussion of panic, stress, etc. Among patients who received CBT, 53 percent became
panic-free; 23 percent of the others did so. That difference was not significant,
but only patients who received CBT showed significant reductions in worry
about panic and ratings of phobic distress.

CONDENSING BEHAVIOR THERAPY

Positive results from cognitive-behavioral interventions for panic and agoraphobia have prompted efforts to streamline therapy. Typically this involves
using shortened protocols or reducing therapist contact with the patient. Two
examples of such efforts are summarized here.

Côté, Gauthier, Laberge, Cormier, and Plamondon (1994) assigned 21 panic
patients to either a standard or a reduced-therapist-contact regimen of manualized CBT. Those in the standard contact group met with a therapist for each
of 17 weeks, while those in the reduced-contact group had eight meetings with
the therapist and seven brief telephone contacts. The protocol included standard elements, such as education, breathing, relaxation training, cognitive restructuring, interoceptive exposure, and in vivo exposure. Patients in both
groups improved significantly in virtually all areas. About 73 percent of patients assigned to the two regimens were panic-free at posttreatment and six

months later. This experiment suggests that therapist contact can be reduced in treating panic when a manualized format of multimodal CBT is provided.

Clum and his associates (Clum, 1990; Gould & Clum, 1995; Gould, Clum, & Shapiro, 1993) have also studied minimal-therapist-contact panic treatment. Although an initial experiment by Gould et al. (1993) found no differences in panic-attack frequency or agoraphobic avoidance between wait-list control and self-help treatment protocols, a follow-up study by Gould and Clum (1995) was more promising. Twenty-five women with panic disorder with or without agoraphobia were assigned to either a wait-list condition or a self-help condition with minimal therapist contact. The self-help condition included access to a self-help book (Clum, 1990), watching a videotape of a role-play therapy session, and receiving an audiotape for relaxation training. Subjects were contacted by telephone at midtreatment and posttreatment and questioned about the contents of the book. They mailed their progress records weekly. Between-groups analyses revealed no differences in frequency of panic at posttreatment, but two months later those in the self-help group had significantly fewer panic attacks than before, while those on the wait list had slightly more. Furthermore, at follow-up 69 percent of the self-help subjects were panic-free as compared to 25 percent of the wait-list subjects. These results suggest that when self-help programs are structured appropriately, they can lead to unambiguous improvement in panic disorder. It remains to be seen if self-help methods can be rendered comparable to therapist-directed treatment.

ALTERNATIVE TREATMENT OPTIONS

The major alternative approaches to helping patients who have panic disorder/agoraphobia are discussed in the other chapters here. Our narrative has sought to portray mainstream cognitive behavioral work. Still other methods of treatment have been employed occasionally. Most of these variations simply allow the patient to have more or less control of matters or add/delete some aspect of treatment. One unique strategy, described by Margraf (1990), is known as vagal innervation. Vagal innervation entails lowering heart rate by stimulating vagal receptors; for example, by massaging the caroted artery. Sartory and Olajide (1988) found that what they refer to as vagal innervation techniques are effective among patients who are fearful of suddenly increased heart rate. However, this treatment has not garnered noteworthy scientific interest.

PRESCRIPTIVE TREATMENT
AND MANAGED CARE

For most of the history of psychiatry and clinical psychology, the activities of clinicians have been guided by grand models of psychopathology; assessments were standardized and interventions were more or less uniform across presenting complaints. With the advent of behavior therapy in the 1960s some practitioners in clinical psychology, and a few in psychiatry, began to change. Guided by a growing empirical literature, clinicians began to adapt treatment methods to disorder categories; matching treatments to clients became a popular, though seldom realized, rallying point. One contemporary manifestation of the evolution of behavior therapy is termed prescriptive practice: "the prescription of a highly specified, thoroughly evaluated treatment regimen in order to ameliorate a highly specified, thoroughly assessed complaint" (Acierno, Hersen, & Ammerman, 1994, p. 3).

Progress in the assessment and treatment of panic disorder and agoraphobia has positioned that arena to be an early testing ground for prescriptive psychological work. The materials needed for standardizing psychological practices are available in several sources (Bouman & Emmelkamp, 1996; Craske & Barlow, 1993; Craske & Waikar, 1994) and consensus is developing about the current state of the art in dealing with these disorders from a cognitive-behavioral perspective.

At the same time much research remains in developing bona fide prescriptive assessments and treatments. This will always be true in research-anchored practice, because the progress of science is marked inevitably by the appearance of improved questions. As just one example, benefit might result from work on Ley's (1992) tripartite classification of panic. According to Ley, panic attacks can be divided into three kinds, based on differences across the symptom categories of fear, dyspnea, palpitations, catastrophic thinking, and additional *DSM* symptoms. The three categories of panic, in turn, set the stage for three recommended modes of treatment. Continuing work on matching the treatment to the client could use Ley's formulation as heuristic for planning both assessment and intervention. The effort would be emblematic of the kind needed to use panic and agoraphobia as a proving ground for prescriptive practice.

The theme of guarded optimism holds also for the interface of professional psychology with the environment of managed care. The challenge of accountability is met these days by data. The challenge of cost containment is addressed by such initiatives as self-directed treatment. Again, much work remains. Whether clinical psychology in some recognizable form can flourish in a managed-care environment and in competition with pharmacotherapy remains to be seen. Clearly, however, the assessment and treatment of panic disorder and agoraphobia is among the arenas where definitive battles will be fought.

SUMMARY

Panic is sudden, extreme fearfulness that entails both bodily and cognitive phenomena. Agoraphobia refers to avoidance of settings where panic is deemed likely. Panic occurs without agoraphobia, but agoraphobia rarely occurs without a history of something akin to panic. Biological theorists have not achieved accord in describing the biological systems responsible for panic. Psychological theorists highlight the importance of associative and/or cognitive-mediational mechanisms that produce irrational fear of benign bodily sensations. Notwithstanding areas of contention, psychobiological models of panic exist that share important features; predisposition plus life stress produces panic that tends to recur and sometimes motivates agoraphobia. The connection of agoraphobia to panic, however, is poorly understood.

Clinicians deal with panic and agoraphobia more or less separately. Panic is assessed by structured interviewing, questionnaires, self-monitoring and, sometimes, via ambulatory psychophysiological monitoring. Agoraphobia is assessed with structured interviewing, questionnaires, and naturalistic behavioral testing; assessment is sometimes supplemented with tests of self-efficacy for treatment, and with interviewing designed to pinpoint safety signals that can be used during treatment.

The rationales, procedures, and known outcomes of the major treatments for panic are described. Breathing retraining is credible and promising, but the relevant research is weak. Interoceptive exposure is the centerpiece of panic treatment; a package termed panic control treatment demonstrably reduces panic frequency and often produces improved end-state function. A muscular relaxation training regimen termed *applied relaxation* is promising as well. Correcting catastrophic thinking is also a mainstay of panic treatment. The effects of cognitive restructuring are at least as significant as are those of applied relaxation.

The major treatment for agoraphobia is guided in vivo exposure in which confrontations with feared settings are intimate and prolonged. Usually variants of the aforementioned treatments for panic are brought to bear also to facilitate coping during exposure. Therapist-assisted exposure is the most efficacious, but evidence shows the promise of self-directed exposure involving minimal therapist contact.

Much of the treatment-outcome literature has evaluated multi-element protocols that combine the aforementioned procedures. The work has produced impressive results when viewed against the backdrop of psychological intervention over this century. Some work has been directed toward economizing by condensing therapy.

Alternative approaches to treating panic and agoraphobia are discussed in the companion chapters. Panic disorder and agoraphobia will continue to provide a proving ground for standardizing and "prescribing" psychological treatment in the era of managed care. Notwithstanding impressive progress, much work remains to understand panic and agoraphobia and to develop more beneficial and cost-effective psychological intervention.

REFERENCES

Acierno, R.E., Hersen, M., & Ammerman, R.T. (1994). Overview of the issues in prescriptive treatments. In M. Hersen & R.T. Ammerman (Eds.), *Handbook of prescriptive treatments for adults.* New York: Plenum Press.

Acierno, R.E., Hersen, M., & van Hasselt, V.B. (1993). Interventions for panic disorder: A critical review of the literature. *Clinical Psychology Review, 13,* 561–578.

Agras, W.S., Chapin, H.N., & Oliveau, D.C. (1972). The natural history of phobia. *Archives of General Psychiatry, 26,* 315–317.

Agras, W.S., Leitenberg, H., & Barlow, D.H. (1968). Social reinforcement in the modification of agoraphobia. *Archives of General Psychiatry, 19,* 423–427.

American Psychiatric Association. (1980). *Diagnostic and statistical manual of mental disorders* (3rd ed.). Washington, DC: Author.

American Psychiatric Association. (1987). *Diagnostic and statistical manual of mental disorders* (3rd ed., rev.). Washington, DC: Author.

American Psychiatric Association. (1994). *Diagnostic and statistical manual of mental disorders* (4th ed.). Washington, DC: Author.

Arntz, A., & van den Hout, M. (1996). Psychological treatments of panic disorder without agoraphobia: Cognitive therapy versus applied relaxation. *Behaviour Research and Therapy, 34,* 113–121.

Ascher, L.M. (1981). Employing paradoxical intention in the treatment of agoraphobia. *Behaviour Research and Therapy, 19,* 533–542.

Bandura, A. (1977). Self-efficacy: Toward a unifying theory of behavioral change. *Cognitive Therapy and Research, 1,* 287–310.

Bandura, A. (1986). Tests of the generality of self-efficacy theory. *Cognitive Therapy & Research, 4,* 39–66.

Barlow, D.H. (1987). The classification of anxiety disorders. In G.L. Tischler (Ed.), *Diagnosis and classification in psychiatry: A critical appraisal of DSM-III.* Cambridge, England: Cambridge University Press.

Barlow, D.H. (1988). *Anxiety and its disorders: The nature and treatment of anxiety and panic.* New York: Guilford Press.

Barlow, D.H., Craske, M.G., Cerny, J.A., & Klosko, J.S. (1989). Behavioral treatment of panic disorder. *Behavior Therapy, 20,* 261–282.

Barlow, D.H., O'Brien, G.T., & Last, C.G. (1984). Couples treatment of agoraphobia. *Behavior Therapy, 20,* 261–282.

Basoglu, M., Marks, I.M., & Sengun, S. (1992). A prospective study of panic and anxiety in agoraphobia with panic disorder. *British Journal of Psychiatry, 160,* 57–64.

Beck, A.T. (1988). Cognitive approaches to panic disorder: Theory and therapy. In S. Rachman & J.D. Maser (Eds.), *Panic: Psychological perspectives.* Hillsdale, NJ: Erlbaum.

Beck, A.T., Emery, G., & Greenberg, R.L. (1985). *Anxiety disorders and phobias: A cognitive perspective.* New York: Basic Books.

Beck, J.G., Stanley, M.A., Baldwin, L.E., Deagle, III, E.A., & Averill, P.M. (1994). Comparison of cognitive therapy and relaxation training for panic disorder. *Journal of Consulting and Clinical Psychology, 62,* 818–826.

Beck, J.G., & Zebb, B.J. (1994). Behavioral assessment and treatment of panic disorder: Current status, future directions. *Behavior Therapy, 25,* 581–611.

Bernstein, D.A., & Borkovec, T.D. (1973). *Progressive relaxation training: A manual for the helping professions.* Champagne, IL: Research Press.

Bouchard, S., Pelletier, M.H., Gauthier, J.G., Côté, G., & Laberge, B. (1997). The assessment of panic using self-report: A comprehensive survey of validated instruments. *Journal of Anxiety Disorders, 11,* 89–111.

Bouman, T.K., & Emmelkamp, M.G. (1996). Panic disorder and agoraphobia. In V.B. Van Hasselt & M. Hersen (Eds.), *Sourcebook of psychological treatment manuals for adult disorders.* New York: Plenum Press.

Brown, T.A., DiNardo, P.A., & Barlow, D.H. (1994). *Anxiety disorders interview schedule for DSM-IV (ADIS-IV).* Albany, NY: Graywind.

Burgess, I.S., Jones, L.M., Robertson, S.A., Radcliffe, W.N., & Emerson, E. (1981). The degree of control exerted by phobic and non-phobic verbal stimuli over the recognition behaviour of phobic and non-phobic subjects. *Behaviour Research and Therapy, 19,* 233–243.

Chambless, D.L., Caputo, G.C., Bright, P., & Gallagher, R. (1984). Assessment of fear in agoraphobics: The body sensations questionnaire and the agoraphobic cognitions questionnaire. *Journal of Consulting and Clinical Psychology, 52,* 1090–1097.

Chambless, D.L., Caputo, G.C., Jasin, S.E., Gracely, E.J., & Williams, C. (1985). The mobility inventory for agoraphobia. *Behaviour Research and Therapy, 23,* 35–44.

Charney, D.S., Woods, S.W., Price, L.H., Goodman, W.K., Glazer, W.M., & Heninger, G.R. (1990). Noradrenergic dysregulation in panic disorder. In J.C. Ballenger (Ed.), *Neurobiology of panic disorder* (pp. 91–105). New York: Wiley-Liss.

Clark, D.M. (1986). A cognitive approach to panic. *Behaviour Research and Therapy, 24,* 461–470.

Clark, D.M. (1988). A cognitive model of panic attacks. In S. Rachman & J.D. Maser (Eds.), *Panic: Psychological perspectives* (pp. 71–89). Hillsdale, NJ: Erlbaum.

Clark, D.M., & Beck, A.T. (1988). Cognitive approaches. In C.G. Last & M. Hersen (Eds.), *Handbook of anxiety disorders* (pp. 362–385). Elmsford, NY: Pergamon Press.

Clark, D.M., Salkovskis, P., & Chalkley, A. (1985). Respiratory control as a treatment for panic attacks. *Journal of Behavior Therapy and Experimental Psychiatry, 16,* 23–30.

Clark, D.M., Salkovskis, P.M., Hackmann, A., Middleton, H., Anastasiades, P., & Gelder, M. (1994). A comparison of cognitive therapy, applied relaxation and imipramine in the treatment of panic disorder. *British Journal of Psychiatry, 164,* 759–769.

Clark, D.M., Salkovskis, P.M., Öst, L.-G., Breitholtz, E., Koehler, K.A., Westling, B.E., Jeavens, A., & Gelder, M. (1997). Misinterpretation of body sensations in panic disorder. *Journal of Consulting and Clinical Psychology, 65,* 203–213.

Cloitre, M., & Liebowitz, M.R. (1991). Memory bias in panic disorder: An investigation of the cognitive avoidance hypothesis. *Cognitive Therapy and Research, 15,* 371–386.

Clum, G.A. (1990). *Coping with panic.* Pacific Grove, CA: Brooks/Cole.

Clum, G.A., Broyles, S., Borden, J., & Watkins, P.L. (1990). Validity and reliability of the panic attack symptoms and cognitions questionnaires. *Journal of Psychopathology and Behavioral Assessment, 12*(1), 233–245.

Cobb, J.P., Mathews, A.M., Childs-Clark, A., & Blowers, C.M. (1984). The spouse as cotherapist in the treatment of agoraphobia. *British Journal of Psychiatry, 144,* 282–287.

Côté, G., Gauthier, J.G., Laberge, B., Cormier, H.J., & Plamondon, J. (1994). Reduced therapist contact in the cognitive behavioral treatment of panic disorder. *Behavior Therapy, 25,* 123–145.

Craske, M.G. (1991). Phobic fear and panic attacks: The same emotional states triggered by different cues? *Clinical Psychology Review, 11,* 599–620.

Craske, M.G., & Barlow, D.H. (1993). Panic disorder and agoraphobia. In D.H. Barlow (Ed.), *Clinical handbook of psychological disorders* (2nd ed.). New York: Guilford Press.

Craske, M.G., Brown, T.A., & Barlow, D.H. (1991). Behavioral treatment of panic disorder: A two-year follow-up. *Behavior Therapy, 22,* 289–304.

Craske, M.G., Maidenberg, E., & Bystritsky, A. (1995). Brief cognitive-behavioral versus nondirective therapy for panic disorder. *Journal of Behavior Therapy and Experimental Psychiatry, 26,* 113–120.

Craske, M.G., Rachman, S.J., & Tallman, K. (1986). Mobility, cognitions, and panic. *Journal of Psychopathology and Behavioral Assessment, 8,* 199–210.

Craske, M.G., & Waikar, S.V. (1994). Panic disorder. In M. Hersen & R.T. Ammerman (Eds.), *Handbook of prescriptive treatments for adults.* New York: Plenum Press.

D'Amato, M.R. (1970). *Experimental psychology: Methodology, psychophysics, and learning.* New York: McGraw-Hill.

DiNardo, P.A., Moras, K., Barlow, D.H., Rapee, R.M., & Brown, T.A. (1993). Reliablility of the *DSM-III-R* anxiety disorder categories using the anxiety disorders interview schedule–revised (ADIS-R). *Archives of General Psychiatry, 50,* 251–256.

DiNardo, P.A., O'Brien, G.T., Barlow, D.H., Waddell, M.T., & Blanchard, E.B. (1983). Reliability of *DSM-III* anxiety disorder categories using a new structured interview. *Archives of General Psychiatry, 40,* 1070–1074.

Ehlers, A. (1993). Interoception and panic disorder. *Advances in Behavior Research and Therapy, 15,* 3–21.

Ehlers, A., & Breuer, P. (1992). Increased cardiac awareness in panic disorder. *Journal of Abnormal Psychology, 101,* 371–382.

Ehlers, A., & Margraf, J. (1989). The psychophysiological model of panic attacks. In P.M.G. Emmelkamp, W.T.A.M. Everaerd, F.W. Kraaimaat, & M.J.M. van Son (Eds.), *Fresh perspectives on anxiety disorders* (pp. 1–30). Amsterdam, The Netherlands: Swets & Zeitlinger.

Ehlers, A., Margraf, J., Davies, S., & Roth, W.T. (1988). Selective processing of threat cues in subjects with panic attacks. *Cognition and Emotion, 2,* 201–219.

Ehlers, A., Margraf, J., & Roth, W.T. (1988). Selective information processing, interoception and panic attacks. In I. Hand & H.U. Wittchen (Eds.), *Panic and phobias 2* (pp. 129–148). Berlin: Springer.

Emmelkamp, P.M.G. (1982). *Phobic and obsessive-compulsive disorders: Theory, research, and practice.* New York: Plenum Press.

Emmelkamp, P.M.G. (1990). Anxiety and fear. In A.S. Bellack, M. Hersen, & A.E. Kazdin (Eds.), *International handbook of behavior modification and therapy* (pp. 238–305). New York: Plenum Press.

Emmelkamp, P.M.G., & Emmelkamp-Benner, A. (1975). Effects of historically portrayed modeling and group treatment of self-observation: A comparison with agoraphobics. *Behaviour Research and Therapy, 13,* 135–139.

Emmelkamp, P.M.G., & Wessels, H. (1975). Flooding in imagination versus flooding *in vivo:* A comparison with agoraphobics. *Behaviour Therapy and Research, 13,* 7–16.

Endicott, J., & Spitzer, R.L. (1979). Use of the research diagnostic criteria and the schedule for affective disorders and schizophrenia to study affective disorders. *American Journal of Psychiatry, 136,* 52–56.

Garssen, B., de Ruiter, C., & van Dyck, R. (1992). Breathing retraining: A rational placebo? *Clinical Psychology Review, 12,* 141–153.

Gauthier, J., Bouchard, S., Côté, G., Laberge, B., & French, D. (1993). Development of two scales measuring self-efficacy to control panic attacks. *Canadian Psychology, 30*(2a), 305.

Goldstein, A.J., & Chambless, D.L. (1978). A reanalysis of agoraphobia. *Behavior Therapy, 9,* 47–59.

Gorman, J.M., Cohen, B.S., Liebowitz, M.R., Fyer, A.J., Ross, D., Davies, S.O., & Klein, D.F. (1986). Blood gas changes and hypophosphatemia in lactate induced panic. *Archives of General Psychiatry, 43,* 1067–1071.

Gould, R.A., & Clum, G.A. (1995). Self-help plus minimal therapist contact in the treatment of panic disorder: A replication and extension. *Behavior Therapy, 26,* 533–546.

Gould, R.A., Clum, G.A., & Shapiro, D. (1993). The use of bibliotherapy in the treatment of panic: A preliminary investigation. *Behavior Therapy, 24,* 241–252.

Greenberg, R.L. (1988). Panic disorder and agoraphobia. In J.M.G. Williams & A.T. Beck (Eds.), *Cognitive therapy in clinical practice: An illustrative casebook* (pp. 25–49). London: Routledge & Kegan Paul.

Hafner, R.J., & Marks, I.M. (1976). Exposure *in vivo* in agoraphobics: Contributions of diazepam, group exposure, and anxiety evocation. *Psychological Medicine, 6,* 71–88.

Hamilton, M. (1959). The assessment of anxiety states by rating. *British Journal of Medical Psychology, 32,* 50–55.

Hamilton, M. (1960). A rating scale for depression. *Journal of Neurology, Neurosurgery and Psychiatry, 23,* 56–62.

Herrnstein, R.J. (1969). Method and theory in the study of avoidance. *Psychological Review, 76,* 49–69.

Hibbert, G.A. (1984). Ideational components of anxiety: Their origin and content. *British Journal of Psychiatry, 144,* 618–624.

Himle, J.A., & Hill, E.M. (1991). Alcohol abuse and the anxiety disorders: Evidence from the epidemiologic catchment area survey. *Journal of Anxiety Disorders, 5,* 237–245.

Hoffart, A. (1995). A comparison of cognitive and guided mastery of agoraphobia. *Behaviour Research and Therapy, 22,* 59–70.

Hoffart, A., Friis, S., & Martinsen, E.W. (1992). Assessment of fear among agoraphobic patients: The agoraphobic cognitions scale. *Journal of Psychopathology and Behavioral Assessment, 14,* 175–187.

Jacobson, E. (1938). *Progressive relaxation.* Chicago: University of Chicago Press.

Kahn, R.J., McNair, D.M., Lipman, R.S., Covi, L., Rickels, K., Downing, R., Fisher, S., & Frankenthaler, L.M. (1986). Imipramine and chlordiazepoxide in depressive and anxiety disorders: II. Efficacy in anxious outpatients. *Archives of General Psychiatry, 43,* 79–85.

Khawaja, N.G., Oei, T.P.S., & Baglioni, A.J. (1994). Modification of the catastrophic cognition questionnaire (CCQ-M) for normals and patients: Exploratory and LISREL analyses. *Journal of Psychopathology and Behavioral Assessment, 16,* 325–342.

Klein, D.F. (1964). Delineation of two drug-responsive anxiety syndromes. *Psychopharmacologia, 5,* 397–408.

Klein, D.F. (1981). Anxiety reconceptualized. In D.F. Klein & J.G. Rabkin (Eds.), *Anxiety: New research and changing concepts* (pp. 235–263). New York: Raven Press.

Klein, D.F. (1993). False suffocation alarms, spontaneous panics, and related conditions: An integrative hypothesis. *Archives of General Psychiatry, 50,* 306–317.

Klein, D.F., & Klein, H.M. (1989a). The definition and psychopharmacology of spontaneous panic and phobia. In P. Thyer (Ed.), *Psychopharmacology of anxiety* (pp. 135–162). New York: Oxford University Press.

Klein, D.F., & Klein, H.M. (1989b). The nosology, genetics, and theory of spontaneous panic and phobia. In P. Thyer (Ed.), *Psychopharmacology of anxiety* (pp. 163–195). New York: Oxford University Press.

Ley, R. (1985). Blood, breath, and fears: A hyperventilation theory of panic attacks and agoraphobia. *Clinical Psychology Review, 5,* 271–285.

Ley, R. (1992). The many faces of Pan: Psychological and physiological differences among three types of panic attacks. *Behaviour Research and Therapy, 30,* 347–357.

Ley, R. (1993). Breathing retraining in the treatment of hyperventilatory complaints and panic disorder: A reply to Garssen, de Ruiter, and van Dyck. *Clinical Psychology Review, 13,* 393–408.

Lum, L.C. (1976). The syndrome of habitual chronic hyperventilation. In O.W. Hill (Ed.), *Modern trends in psychosomatic medicine* (Vol. 3). London: Buttersworth.

Lum, L.C. (1981). Hyperventilation and anxiety state. *Journal of the Royal Society of Medicine, 74,* 1–4.

Margraf, J. (1990). Panic and agoraphobia: Behavior therapy. In A.S. Bellack & M. Hersen (Eds.), *Handbook of comparative treatments for adult disorder* (1st ed., pp. 144–175). New York: Wiley.

Margraf, J. (1993). Hyperventilation and panic disorders: A psychophysiological connection. *Advances in Behavior Research and Therapy, 15,* 49–74.

Margraf, J., Ehlers, A., & Roth, W.T. (1986). Sodium-lactate infusions and panic attacks: A review and critique. *Psychosomatic Medicine, 48,* 23–51.

Marks, I.M. (1975). Behavioral treatments of phobic and obsessive-compulsive disorders: A critical appraisal. In M. Hersen, R.M. Eisler, & P.M. Miller (Eds.), *Progress in behavior modification* (Vol. 1, pp. 66–143). New York: McGraw-Hill.

Marks, I.M. (1987). *Fears, phobias, and rituals.* New York: Oxford University Press.

Marks, I.M., & Mathews, A.M. (1979). Brief standard self-rating for phobic patients. *Behaviour Research and Therapy, 17,* 263–267.

Mathews, A.M., Gelder, M.G., & Johnston, D.W. (1981). *Agoraphobia: Nature and treatment.* New York: Guilford Press.

Mathews, A.M., & MacLeod, C. (1985). Selective processing of threat cues in anxiety states. *Behaviour Research and Therapy, 23,* 563–569.

McNally, R.J. (1990). Psychological approaches to panic disorder: A review. *Psychological Bulletin, 108,* 403–419.

McNally, R.J. (1994). *Panic disorder: A critical analysis.* New York: Guilford Press.

McNally, R.J., Foa, E.B., & Donnell, C.D. (1989). Memory bias for anxiety information in patients with panic disorder. *Cognition and Emotion, 3,* 27–44.

McNally, R.J., Riemann, B.C., & Kim, E. (1990). Selective processing of threat cues in panic disorder. *Behaviour Research and Therapy, 28,* 407–412.

Michelson, L., & Marchione, K. (1991). Behavioral, cognitive, and pharmacological treatments of panic disorder with agoraphobia: Critique and synthesis. *Journal of Consulting and Clinical Psychology, 59,* 100–114.

Michelson, L., Marchione, K., Greenwald, M., Glanz, L., Testa, S., & Marchione, N. (1990). Panic disorder: Cognitive-behavioral treatment. *Behaviour Research and Therapy, 28,* 141–151.

Michelson, L., Mavissakalian, M., & Marchione, K. (1988). Cognitive, behavioral, and psychophysiological treatments of agoraphobia: A comparative outcome investigation. *Behavior Therapy, 19,* 97–120.

Mizes, J.S., & Crawford, J. (1986). Normative values on the Marks and Mathews fear questionnaire: A comparison as a function of age and sex. *Journal of Psychopathology and Behavioral Assessment, 8,* 253–262.

Mowrer, O.H. (1939). A stimulus-response analysis of anxiety and its role as a reinforcing agent. *Psychological Review, 46,* 553–565.

Mowrer, O.H. (1960). *Learning theory and behavior.* New York: Wiley.

Nelson, R.O. (1977). Methodological issues in assessment via self-monitoring. In J.D. Cone & R.P. Hawkins (Eds.), *Behavioral assessment: New directions in clinical psychology* (pp. 217–240). New York: Brunner/Mazel.

Nutt, D., & Lawson, C. (1992). Panic attacks: A neurochemical overview of models and mechanisms. *British Journal of Psychiatry, 160,* 165–178.

Öst, L.G. (1987). Applied relaxation: Description of a coping technique and review of controlled studies. *Behaviour Research and Therapy, 25,* 397–409.

Öst, L.G. (1988). Applied relaxation vs. progressive relaxation in the treatment of panic disorder. *Behaviour Research and Therapy, 26,* 13–22.

Öst, L.G., & Westling, B.E. (1995). Applied relaxation vs. cognitive behavior therapy in the treatment of panic disorder. *Behaviour Research and Therapy, 33,* 145–158.

Paul, G.L., & Trimble, R.W. (1970). Recorded vs. "live" relaxation training and hypnotic suggestion: Comparative effectiveness for reducing physiological arousal and inhibiting stress response. *Behavior Therapy, 1,* 285–302.

Pennebaker, J.W. (1982). *The psychology of physical symptoms.* New York: Springer.

Rachman, S. (1984). Agoraphobia: A safety-signal perspective. *Behaviour Research and Therapy, 22,* 59–70.

Rachman, S., Lopatka, C., Levitt, K. (1988). Experimental analyses of panic: II. Panic patients. *Behaviour Research and Therapy, 26,* 33–40.

Rapee, R. (1986). Differential response to hyperventilation in panic disorder and generalized anxiety disorder. *Journal of Abnormal Psychology, 95,* 24–28.

Rapee, R. (1987). The psychological treatment of panic attacks: Theoretical conceptualization and review of evidence. *Clinical Psychology Review, 7,* 427–438.

Rapee, R.M., & Barlow, D.H. (1989). Psychological treatment of unexpected panic attacks: Cognitive/behavioural components. In R. Baker (Ed.), *Panic disorder: Theory, research, and therapy.* New York: Wiley.

Rapee, R.M., Sanderson, W.C., McCauley, P.A., & DiNardo, P.A. (1992). Differences in reported symptom profile between panic disorder and other *DSM-III-R* anxiety disorders. *Behaviour Research and Therapy, 30,* 45–52.

Razran, G. (1961). The observable unconscious and the inferable conscious in current Soviet psychophysiology: Interoceptive conditioning, semantic conditioning, and the orienting reflex. *Psychological Review, 68,* 81–147.

Reiss, S., & McNally, R.J. (1985). Expectancy model of fear. In S. Reiss & R.R. Bootzin (Eds.), *Theoretical issues in behavior therapy* (pp. 107–121). San Diego, CA: Academic Press.

Reiss, S., Peterson, R.A., Gursky, D.M., & McNally, R.J. (1986). Anxiety, sensitivity, anxiety frequency and the prediction of fearfulness. *Behaviour Research and Therapy, 26,* 1–8.

Roth, M. (1984). Agoraphobia, panic-disorder and generalized anxiety disorder: Some implications of recent advances. *Psychiatric Development, 2,* 31–52.

Roth, W.T., Margraf, J., Ehlers, A., Taylor, C.B., Maddock, R.J., Davies, S., & Agras, W.S. (1992). Stress test reactivity in panic disorder. *Archives of General Psychiatry, 49,* 301–310.

Roth, W.T., Telch, M.J., Taylor, C.B., Sachitano, J.A., Gallen, C.C., Kopell, M.L., McClenahan, K.L., Agras, W.S., & Pfefferbaum, A. (1986). Autonomic characteristics of agoraphobia with panic attacks. *Biological Psychiatry, 21,* 1133–1154.

Roy-Byrne, P., Mellman, T.A., & Uhde, T.W. (1988). Biologic findings in panic disorder: Neuroendocrine and sleep-related abnormalities. *Journal of Anxiety Disorders, 2,* 17–29.

Russell, R.K., & Sippich, J.F. (1973). Cue-controlled relaxation in the treatment of test anxiety. *Journal of Behavior Therapy and Experimental Psychiatry, 4,* 47–49.

Salkovskis, P., Clark, D., & Hackmann, A. (1991). Treatment of panic attacks using cognitive therapy without exposure or breathing retraining. *Behaviour Research and Therapy, 29,* 161–166.

Salkovskis, P.M., Jones, D.R.O., & Clark, D.M. (1986). Respiratory control in the treatment of panic attacks: Replication and extension with concurrent measurement of behavior and pCO_2. *British Journal of Psychiatry, 148,* 526–532.

Sanderson, W.C., & Wetzler, S. (1990). Five percent carbon dioxide challenge: Valid analogue and marker of panic disorder? *Biological Psychiatry, 27,* 689–701.

Sartory, G., & Olajide, D. (1988). Vagal innervation techniques in the treatment of panic disorder. *Behaviour Research and Therapy, 26,* 431–434.

Shear, M.K., & Fyer, M.R. (1988). Biological and psychopathological findings in panic disorder. In A.J. Frances & R.E. Hales (Eds.), *American psychiatric press review* (Vol. 7, pp. 29–53). Washington, DC: American Psychiatric Press.

Starcevic, V., Kellner, R., Uhlenhuth, E.H., & Pathak, D. (1992). Panic disorder and hypochondriacal fears and beliefs. *Journal of Affective Disorders, 24,* 73–85.

Starcevic, V., Uhlenhuth, E.H., Kellner, R., & Pathak, D. (1992). Patterns of comorbidity in panic disorder and agoraphobia. *Psychiatry Research, 42,* 171–183.

Stern, R.S., & Marks, I.M. (1973). A comparison of brief and prolonged flooding in agoraphobics. *Archives of General Psychiatry, 28,* 210–216.

Taylor, C.B., Fried, L., & Kenardy, J. (1990). The use of real-time computer diary for data acquisition and processing. *Behaviour Research and Therapy, 28,* 93–97.

Taylor, C.B., Kenigsberg, M.L., & Robinson, J.M. (1982). A controlled comparison of relaxation and diazepam in panic disorder. *Journal of Clinical Psychiatry, 43,* 423–425.

Taylor, C.B., Sheikh, J., Agras, S., Roth, W.T., Margraf, J., Ehlers, A., Maddock, R.J., & Gossard, D. (1986). Ambulatory heart rate changes in patients with panic attacks. *American Journal of Psychiatry, 143,* 478–482.

Taylor, C.B., Telch, M.J., & Haavik, D. (1983). Ambulatory heart rate changes during panic attacks. *Journal of Psychosomatic Research, 17,* 1–6.

Taylor, S. (1995). Anxiety sensitivity: Theoretical perspectives and recent findings. *Behaviour Research and Therapy, 33,* 243–258.

Telch, M.J. (1987). *The panic appraisal inventory* (Unpublished scale). Austin: University of Texas.

Telch, M.J. (1988). Combined pharmacologic and psychological treatments for panic sufferers. In S. Rachman & J.D. Maser (Eds.), *Panic: Psychological perspectives.* Hillsdale, NJ: Erlbaum.

Telch, M.J., Lucas, J.A., Schmidt, N.B., Hanna, H.H., Jaimez, T.L., & Lucas, R.A. (1993). Group cognitive-behavioral treatment of panic disorder. *Behaviour Research and Therapy, 31,* 279–287.

Torgersen, S. (1983). Genetic factors in anxiety disorders. *Archives of General Psychiatry, 40,* 1085–1089.

Williams, S.L. (1990). Guided mastery treatment of agoraphobia: Beyond stimulus exposure. *Progress in Behavior Modification, 26,* 89–121.

Wolpe, J. (1958). *Psychotherapy by reciprocal inhibition.* Stanford, CA: Stanford University Press.

Wolpe, J. (1973). *The practice of behavior therapy* (2nd ed.). New York: Pergamon Press.

Wolpe, J., & Lazarus, A.A. (1966). *Behaviour therapy techniques.* New York: Pergamon Press.

Wolpe, J., & Rowan, V.C. (1988). Panic disorder: A product of classical conditioning. *Behaviour Research and Therapy, 26,* 441–450.

Woods, S.W., & Charney, D.S. (1988). Applications of the pharmacologic challenge strategy in panic disorders research. *Journal of Anxiety Disorders, 2,* 31–49.

CHAPTER 11

Pharmacotherapy

EDWARD K. SILBERMAN

DIAGNOSTIC CONSIDERATIONS

Central to the medical-biological conception of panic disorder and agoraphobia is identification of the panic attack as a unique syndrome different from other forms of anxiety. The current psychiatric conception of panic disorder and agoraphobia is based on the work of Klein and his coworkers, who described a group of patients "with sudden onset of subjectively inexplicable panic attacks, accompanied by hot and cold flashes, rapid breathing, palpitations, weakness, unsteadiness, and a feeling of impending death . . . they were often lively, popular, and friendly when not anxious" (Klein & Fink, 1962). Such patients, in contrast to those with more diffuse and less intense generalized anxiety or anticipatory anxiety, were unresponsive to phenothiazine tranquilizers, but experienced symptom relief from imipramine or monoamine oxidase inhibitors (MAOIs). This description is very similar to the distinction between panic and anticipatory anxiety made by Freud, (Freud, 1962, 1963), although Freud did not pursue the possible meaning of this difference.

Klein suggested that the distinct response of panic attacks to antidepressants might reflect their etiology as a "disorder of an innate (i.e., biological) separation anxiety mechanism" (Klein, 1964). Similarly, the biological view of panic attacks implies that they are endogenous (Sheehan, Ballenger, & Jacobsen, 1980), that is, stemming from a disturbance of physiology, rather than being a learned response to external stimuli. Clinically, this has usually been translated to mean that spontaneity is the defining feature of true panic attacks, as opposed to phobic or anticipatory anxiety that would be linked to external triggers (Sheehan et al., 1980; Zitrin, Klein, Woerner, & Ross, 1983). However, although many panic-disorder patients do report having attacks with no apparent external stimulus, the requirement of spontaneity is not logically necessary for a biological conception of the disorder (and is not used at all, for example, in attempting to delineate endogenous or biological forms of depression). The concept of spontaneity has also been hard to validate. Patients whose initial panic attack is situationally triggered appear quite similar to those with spontaneous attacks (Garvey, Noyes, & Cook, 1987). In addition, externally triggered panic attacks are experienced very similarly by patients to those which are internally triggered (Barlow et al., 1985). Physiological concomitants have been found to be similar whether panic attacks are spontaneous, triggered by phobic stimuli, or stimulated physiologically (Liebowitz et al., 1985; Nutt, Glue, Lawson, & Wilson, 1990; Taylor et al., 1986; S. Woods, Charney, McPherson, Gradman, & Heninger, 1987). Furthermore, it is hard to be certain when panics are truly spontaneous and when they arise in response to stimuli that are not noticed by the patient. Subtle alterations in bodily sensations, to which panic-prone patients might overreact, have been proposed as one possible type of covert stimulus for panic attacks (Barlow, 1986).

In the currently prevalent view, agoraphobia is not a separate disorder, but a secondary avoidant reaction to the fear of having a panic attack when in a public place where escape is not possible or help is not available. This formulation depends on the empirically testable proposition that panic attacks inevitably precede the onset of phobic avoidance in agoraphobic patients. Although most clinical experience and some systematic research support this hypothesis, others, such as Marks (Marks et al., 1983), contend that agoraphobia itself is primary in substantial numbers of patients. Furthermore, *DSM-IV* provides a category of agoraphobia without panic attacks. Thus, the extent to which agoraphobia exists independently of panic attacks remains unsettled in the current literature.

A conservative view of the biological abnormality of panic disorder, therefore, would be a physiologically lowered threshold for intense anxiety reactions to either internal or external stimuli. Such, intense paroxysmal anxiety, with accompanying autonomic, cardiac, respiratory, and gastrointestinal symptoms, comprises a syndrome with possible distinct biological features, which is highly likely to respond to pharmacological treatments regardless of whether there are accompanying phobic or avoidant features.

BIOLOGICAL CONCEPTUALIZATION OF PANIC DISORDER

The current psychiatric conception of panic disorder as a primary neurophysiological disturbance is based on inference from a number of lines of evidence. First, there is the phenomenologic distinction between panic-type anxiety and generalized anxiety. Second, family studies have supported a genetic contribution to panic disorder (Crowe, Noyes, Pauls, & Slymen, 1983; Crowe, Noyles, Wilson, Elston, & Wood, 1987) as well as links to depressive disorders (Breier, Charney, & Heninger, 1986; Leckman, Merikanges, Pauls, Prusoff, & Weissman, 1983). Thus, depression and panic disorder may be part of a spectrum of biochemically mediated disorders that respond to antidepressant treatment. Third, a variety of biochemical challenges induce panic attacks in patients with panic disorder, but not in those with only generalized anxiety or normal controls. Biological theories have attempted to associate panic attacks with dysregulation of neurochemical systems, to localize panic disorder anatomically, and to associate panic attacks with altered respiratory physiology.

NEUROTRANSMITTER ALTERATIONS

A great deal of the speculation and research about neurochemical mediators of panic has been based on the role of the locus coeruleus (LC) in mediating anxiety. The LC is a pontine nucleus containing 70 percent of the brain's adrenergic neurons. These neurons, which have widespread projections to the cerebral cortex, limbic structures, brain stem, cerebellum, and spinal cord, are hypothesized to be part of the neuronal system mediating arousal/alertness and the accompanying affect of anxiety (Redmond, 1979). Redmond (1977) has shown that electrical or chemical stimulation of the LC in monkeys produces behaviors similar to those produced in response to danger under natural conditions. A connection to humans is made by the observation that drugs that suppress firing of the LC (including morphine, ethanol, benzodiazepines, tricyclic antidepressants, and clonidine) tend to have antianxiety effects. Conversely, yohimbine and piperoxan, which have been shown to increase LC firing, also tend to produce anxiety or panic in human subjects (Uhde, Boulenger, Vittone, & Post, 1984).

Despite the plausibility of an adrenergic-LC theory of panic disorders, clinical studies of adrenergic function in panic disorder have produced complex, variable, and apparently contradictory results. Although some researchers have found elevations of epinephrine, norepinephrine, and their metabolites in patients at baseline or during panic attacks (Ballenger et al., 1984; Ko et al., 1983) the association between adrenergic variables and symptoms in naturally occurring panics has been inconsistent. Both naturally occurring and lactate-induced panics are striking for their lack of associated adrenergic or hormonal changes (Gaffney, Fenton, Lane, & Lake, 1988; S. Woods et al., 1987). Autonomic measures such as increased heart rate, reflecting increased beta-adrenergic activity, have been found to distinguish panic attacks from non-panic intense anxiety (Taylor et al., 1986). However, not all panic attacks are accompanied by elevated heart rate.

Yohimbine, an α_2 adrenergic receptor antagonist stimulates firing of the LC and produces panic-type anxiety in panic-disorder patients more frequently than in normal controls (Uhde et al., 1984). Clonidine is an α_2 receptor agonist. Some (Charney, Heninger, & Breier, 1984; Nutt, 1989) but not all (Uhde et al., 1989) investigators have found that panic-disorder patients have greater than normal decreases in blood pressure and plasma 3-methoxy H-hydroxy pharylglycol (MHPG) levels (a metabolite of norepinephrine) following clonidine administration, suggesting presynaptic α_2 = adrenergic hypersensitivity. At the same time, growth hormone response to clonidine has been found blunted in panic-disorder patients (Charney & Heninger, 1986; Nutt, 1989), indicating possible subsensitivity of postsynaptic α_2 receptors. Thus, there is evidence for exaggerated sensitivity to both α_2 agonists and antagonists in panic disorder.

Evidence from clinical pharmacological studies has been similarly equivocal. Drugs such as clonidine and propranolol, which have very direct adrenergic effects, have been less impressive therapeutically than tricyclic antidepressants and MAOIs (Gorman et al., 1983; Uhde et al., 1989). Similarly, although tricyclics are considerably more potent than alprazolam in reducing MHPG production, they are about equal in their therapeutic effect (Charney et al., 1988). Results of trials with nonadrenergic antidepressants bupropion and trazodone have been mixed (Mavissakalian, Perel, Bowler, & Dealy, 1987; Sheehan, Davidson, Manshrek, & Fleet, 1983). Levels of desmethylimipramine, a purely adrenergic metabolite of imipramine, do not predict degree of relief from panic symptoms (Mavissakalian, Perel, & Michelson, 1984). *Volatility* may best describe the dysfunction of the nonadrenergic system in panic disorder. Variability of MHPG has been found significantly greater in patients than controls, and diminished in parallel with symptomatic improvement following fluoxetine treatment (Coplan et al., 1977).

Because it is now well established that endogenous receptors mediate the anxiolytic effect of benzodiazepines, investigators have speculated that dysfunction of such receptors may play a role in panic attacks. Benzodiazepine receptors in panic patients have been found subsensitive compared to those of controls (Roy-Byrne, Cowley, Greenblatt, Shader, & Honner, 1990). Furthermore, flumazenil, a benzodiazepine receptor inverse agonist has been found to increase anxiety in panic patients, but not in controls (Nutt et al., 1990). This finding may be evidence that benzodiazepine receptors in panic disorder have a set point altered in the direction of inverse-agonist effects. Such a change in set point might explain why high-, but not low-potency benzodiazepines effectively block panic attacks.

Finally, the efficacy of serotonergic antidepressants in treating panic attacks, as well as known serotonergic influences on the LC, suggest that alterations in the serotonin system may be involved in producing panic anxiety. M-chloro-phenyl-piperazine (MCPP), a serotonin agonist, produces anxiety in panic patients at lower doses than it does in normal controls (Charney et al., 1987); serotonin uptake blockers, like adrenergic antidepressants, tend to exacerbate anxiety initially, and alleviate it gradually over several weeks. This may reflect initial stimulation of hypersensitive serotonin receptors, followed by down-regulation (Kahn et al., 1988). Paradoxically, however, precursors of serotonin have been found to decrease rather than increase anxiety when administered acutely (Westenberg & Den Boer, 1989).

. ANATOMIC LOCALIZATION

Gorman, Liebowitz, Fyer, and Stein (1989) have proposed a model that integrates the anatomy of anxiety-mediating systems with neurochemical data. In their integration, panic attacks are a brainstem phenomenon based in the LC and medulary chemoreceptors and mediated by norepinephrine and serotonin. Anticipatory anxiety is produced and regulated in the limbic lobe, and it increases progressively with repeated stimulation (kindling) from brain-stem structures during panic attacks. The γ–ammino hoxylic acid (GABA) system is proposed as the chemical mediator of anticipatory anxiety, and it is modulated by benzodiazepine anxiolytic medication. Finally, phobic avoidance is viewed as originating in the frontal lobe as part of its function of evaluating the meaning of anxiety and formulating a plan for responding to it.

Partial confirmation of this model has bee provided by positron emission tomography (PET) studies, which have demonstrated increased right versus left parahippocampal blood flow and bilateral temporal pole blood flow in patients during panic attacks (Reiman et al., 1986, 1989). The latter change was also found in healthy controls during periods of anticipatory anxiety, suggesting that the temporal lobes may be part of a final common pathway for anxiety responses.

Altered Respiratory Physiology

Klein (1993) has attempted to integrate the diverse results of challenge studies with other biochemical and clinical findings in his "false suffocation alarm" hypothesis. This hypothesis extends long-standing speculation on dysfunction of respiratory control as a possible etiology for panic attacks. Carr and Sheehan (1984) have pointed out that "air hunger" and hyperventilation are prominent features of panic. They have suggested that the operative mechanism is increased central nervous system (CNS) sensitivity to elevations in hydrogen ion concentrations (i.e., increased acidity) in medullary chemoreceptor zones. Thus, lactate-induced drops in pH in these zones might stimulate the respiratory drive, with concomitant subjective symptoms of panic. A similar mechanism would apply when acidosis is induced by breathing air with high carbon dioxide content, which has been shown to produce panic attacks as reliably as lactate in patients, but not in controls (S. Woods, Charney, Goodman, & Heninger, 1988).

Carr and Sheehan (1984) also propose that paniclike symptoms induced by hyperventilation of room air, which causes not acidosis but alkalosis, might result from reflex cerebral ischemia and acidosis occurring in response to the elevations in peripheral pH. An alternate view of the ventilatory-control hypothesis is that CNS response to carbon dioxide concentration, rather than to hydrogen-iron concentration (pH), is altered in panic-disorder patients (Gorman et al., 1988). If the internal set point for carbon dioxide concentration were too low, the respiratory drive would be too easily triggered, with accompanying subjective symptoms of air hunger and anxiety. Lactate is metabolized first to bicarbonate and then to carbon dioxide, which would trigger the respiratory drive and panic attacks.

The carbon dioxide sensitivity theory is not consistent with a number of research findings, however. First, the exaggerated ventilatory responses in panic patients predicted by the theory have not been found consistently (Gorman et al., 1988; S. Woods, Charney, et al., 1988). Second, the theory would not explain why lactate infusions are more strongly panicogenic than bicarbonate infusions (Gorman, Dattisto, et al., 1989). Third, D-lactate, which is not metabolized to carbon dioxide, also induces panic attacks (Gorman et al., 1990).

Klein's resolution of these paradoxes proposes: (1) that a suffocation false alarm, rather than hypersensitivity to either pH or carbon dioxide, is responsible for panic attacks, and (2) that paniclike anxiety can be split into two distinct subtypes—one with prominent air hunger/shortness of breath, related to false sense of suffocation, and a second without such air hunger, which may be an intense form of generalized anxiety. Thus, lactate which, like carbon dioxide, increases in suffocation and causes cerebral vasolidation may be a direct signal to the suffocation alarm mechanism. Furthermore, lactate, bicarbonate, and isoproterenol show a different physiologic profile from yohimbine, caffeine, CPP, and flumezenil, although all provoke panic attacks. Klein cites evidence that challenges with the former substances are not associated with activated cortisol or noradrenergic metabolism and have their panicogenic effects blocked better by tricycles antidepressants than benzodiazepines. Challenges with the latter group result in dexamethasone escape, elevated cortisol levels, and elevated MHPG and have their effects blocked by benzodiazepines, but not by tricycles.

Klein further postulates that primary suffocation-alarm panics might give rise to secondary fear-based panics, akin to intense anticipatory anxiety, which would have relatively few respiratory symptoms. He predicts that symptoms marked by prominent respiratory distress and hyperventilation would respond preferably to antidepressants, and those without those symptoms would respond preferably to benzodiazepines.

Klein's theory is attractive as the best integration to date of phenomenology and experimental data, but it remains to be confirmed. In support of the hypothesis, people with high fear of suffocation have been found to have increased prevalence of panic disorder (Taylor & Rachman, 1994), whereas children with decreased sensitivity to suffocation (central hypoventilatory syndrome) have lower than expected rates of panic-related symptoms (Pine et al., 1994). In contrast, subjective and physiologic indicators of carbon dioxide sensitivity have not been found to predict which patients would panic in response to carbon dioxide challenge (Schmidt, Telch, & Jaimez, 1996). Similarly, Klein's predictions about treatment response have not consistently been confirmed. Patients with prominent suffocation symptoms during panic attacks have been found to respond just as well to cognitive therapy as those without such symptoms (Taylor et al., 1996). Also, the approximately equivalent efficacy of antidepressants and benodiazepines in unselected populations of panic patients (discussed later) and lack of bimodal response patterns within these groups do not support sharply distinct subgroups of medication responders. Studies suggesting that benzodiazepines treat spontaneous panic attacks more effectively than situational ones (Greenblatt, Harmatz, & Shader, 1993) would similarly contradict Klein's predictions. It may be that once the disorder is established in an individual, anxiety triggers may originate at brainstem, limbic, or cortical levels, and feed back or forward to other levels of the CNS. This would blur distinctions between theoretically different types of panic-related symptoms.

A weakness in all extant biological theories of panic disorder is that they do not explain the well-known fluctuations over time of the disease (Noyes et al.,

1990). A complete theory would have to account for the strong social and cognitive influences on panic symptoms as well (Sanderson, Rapee, & Barlow, 1989). Conversely, psychological theories that postulate hypersensitivity to somatic sensations do not deal with the biology of altered learning and the failure to habituate, which such a theory implies.

MEDICATIONS FOR PANIC/AGORAPHOBIA

In the medical model of panic/agoraphobia, drug therapy is the central aspect of the treatment plan. Along with medication prescription, it is also important to provide the patient with education about the illness, support, and a certain amount of instruction to face feared situations once the medication has had a chance to work. These nonpharmacological aspects of treatment are often not systematically studied by psychopharmacologists, so that the minimum necessary directive-behavioral elements and the extent of their interaction with drug therapy remain open to question.

The vast majority of the literature on drug treatment of panic disorder and agoraphobia deals with tricyclic, selective serotonergic, or MAOI-type antidepressants, and with benzodiazepines. Within these categories, most research has been focused on imipramine, phenelzine, and alprazolam, although there is no reason to think that these medication are unique in their therapeutic efficacy.

IMIPRAMINE

Imipramine is the drug most systematically studied for treatment of panic disorder and agoraphobia, demonstrating efficacy compared to placebo in about 70 percent of double-blind studies. Imipramine's efficacy in treating panic attacks appears to be independent of its antidepressant effect, because studies have found either no relationship or negative correlations between degree of depression and antianxiety effects (Mavissakalian, 1987a; Nurnberg & Coccaro, 1982; Zitrin et al., 1983). There is, however, more question about which symptoms are primary targets of imipramine in panic patients.

Klein usd a mathematical path analysis to evaluate the causal chain in improvement of drug-treated agoraphobic patients (Klein, Ross, & Cohen, 1987). His results suggest that drug therapy decreases avoidance by first reducing panics. This conclusion supports the common clinical observation that alleviation of panic attacks precedes reduction in agoraphobia. Not all studies have supported the specific antipanic effect of imipramine, however. Telch et al. (1985) found no specific antipanic effect at all, whereas Mavissakalian and coworkers reported a dose response for phobic and anticipatory anxiety but not for panic (Mavissakalian & Perel, 1985). Some have found a direct antiphobic response to imipramine that correlates with the drug's antidepressant, but not antipanic effects (McNair & Kahn, 1981). Mavissakalian (1996) has reported that fear, unreality, and respiratory symptoms respond most quickly to imipramine therapy, whereas palpitations, tingling, and sweating respond more slowly.

Although early studies demonstrated the benefit of adding imipramine to behavioral therapies, the efficacy of imipramine alone is now well established (Garakani, Zitrin, & Klein, 1984; Mavissakalian & Perel, 1989, 1995; Rizley, Kahn, McNair, & Frakenthaler, 1986; Sheehan et al., 1980). Klein and coworkers found no added benefit of combining imipramine with formal exposure therapy versus supportive therapy, in which patients are urged to face feared situations (Klein, Zitrin, Woerner, & Ross, 1983). However, Telch, Agras, Taylor, Roth, and Gallen (1985) found that imipramine alone was not helpful when patients were told to continue avoidant behavior during the first eight weeks of treatment. Mavissakalian (1993) reviewed studies of combined imipramine and exposure therapy and concluded that each modality conferred extra benefit when added to the other. The weight of the evidence, therefore, suggests an interaction between medication and supportive/directive aspects of treatment, whether delivered formally or informally.

The dose response and the time course of action of imipramine are somewhat less well understood for treatment of panic disorder than for depression, but they seem to be generally similar. The average dose reported in controlled studies is about 160 mg daily, which is comparable to the usual minimum antidepressant dose. Mavissakalian and Perel (1985) have reported that more patients respond at doses above than at doses below 150 mg daily, and Munjack et al. (1985) found a 20 percent response in those taking less than 50 mg, but a 67 percent in those taking more than 50 mg. However, Ballenger et al. (1984) reported better response in the 100 mg to 150 mg range than in the 200 mg to 250 mg range. One possible reason for these differences is that side effects might be more pronounced at the higher doses, and they may begin to interfere with overall efficacy as doses are raised above optimal levels. Furthermore, some patients seem to get good therapeutic responses at doses as low as 10 mg or 15 mg daily with proportionately low blood levels (Jobson, Linnoila, Gillan, & Sullivan, 1978). At present, there is no way of predicting who might respond at very low levels.

The relationship of response to blood levels support the idea of a therapeutic window. Mavissakalian et al. (1984) found a positive correlation between imipramine (IMI), but not desipramine (DMI), blood levels, and response. The mean combined IMI + DMI levels in their study was 241 ng/ml. Ballenger et al. (1984) reported a trend toward better outcomes in those maintained in the 100 ng/ml to 150 ng/ml than in the 200 ng/ml to 250 ng/ml range, whereas Mavissakalian and Perel (1995) found a peak effectiveness for phobic symptoms in the 110 ng/ml to 140 ng/ml range. Unlike the results for phobic symptoms, there was no decrement in efficacy above 140 ng, although there was no added benefit either.

It is difficult to make a general statement about overall response rates with imipramine, because rates depend on which symptoms are targeted and what degree of improvement is required to define a responder. The range of response rates in published reports is 0 percent to 80 percent, with a mean of about 78 percent substantially improved on medication. Most, though not all, of these rates have been measured in terms of antipanic effects. By comparison, the range of reported placebo responses is 33 percent to 72 percent, with a mean of 51 percent. Thus, a great many potentially medication-responsive patients may do equally well on placebo (Mavissakalian, 1987b).

Time of onset of antipanic action is similar to antidepressant action, that is, generally from two to four weeks. However, some authors have reported continued improvement as far as five or six months into treatment, so that maximum benefit may require a fairly lengthy trial (Zitrin et al., 1983). A major factor affecting time of onset is the difficulty in getting patients up to a therapeutic dose because of poorly tolerated side effects. In addition to the usual anticholinergic and hypotensive effects, panic patients appear to be especially prone to amphetamine-like effects of imipramine, including feelings of increased anxiety, energy, tension, restlessness, or shakiness, with or without concomitant palpitations, diaphoresis, tremulousness, and sleep disturbance. Difficulty tolerating such symptoms is undoubtedly a major factor in the rather high medication dropout rate (Noyes, Garvey, Cook, & Samuelson, 1989b), which in 12 studies averaged 27 percent, with a range of 18 percent to 43 percent. One must view this number in the perspective of the placebo dropout rate, which averages 20 percent or more in those studies reporting it (Evans et al., 1985; Marks et al., 1983; Mavissakalian & Perel, 1985; Telch et al., 1985; Zitrin, Klein, & Woerner, 1980; Zitrin et al., 1983). Thus, it is the extreme somatic sensitivity of panic patients as much as the properties of the medication itself that makes pharmacological treatment difficult.

There is general agreement that substantial numbers of patients will relapse when taken off medication, but there are few systematic data about it in the literature. Zitrin et al. (1983) report a 27 percent relapse rate six months after the start of treatment; at two years, there was a relapse of 35 percent among patients treated with imipramine plus supportive therapy, and of 20 percent in those treated with the drug plus exposure therapy. The authors do not make clear what proportion of patients were off medication at the time of relapse. More recent studies suggest that half or more of patients stably maintained on tricyclic antidepressants for two to three years will experience clinically significant return of anxiety within the first several months after medication withdrawal (Nagy, Krystal, & Charney, 1993; Noyes, Garvey, & Cook, 1989). In these studies, about two-thirds of patients were substantially improved on long-term maintenance therapy, although relatively few were entirely free of symptoms.

Patients have a tendency to take less medication over time, with some studies suggesting that 50 percent of the acute dose of imipramine is sufficient for long-term maintenance (Mavissakalian & Perel, 1992a; Nagy et al., 1993). Patients blindly tapered after six months of full-dose therapy have been compared for long-term outcome to patients on half-dose therapy after an additional 12 months (Mavissakalian & Perel, 1992b). Six months after taper, 83 percent of the former group, but only 25 percent of the extended-treatment group had relapsed. Thus, as with depression, there may be a minimum critical treatment period after which liability to relapse declines substantially.

At present, the literature offers few predictors of imipramine response in patients with anxiety syndromes. Long duration of illness, increased severity or frequency of attacks, prominent depressive symptoms, relative lack of panic attacks compared to other types of anxiety, and predominance of simple phobia have all been associated with poorer outcome (Mavissakalian & Michelson, 1986; Rickels, Schweizer, Weiss, & Zavodnick, 1993; Sheehan et al., 1980; Zitrin et al., 1980). Personality pathology has been associated with poorer global outcome, but not with antipanic effects of medication (Reich, 1988).

OTHER CYCLIC AND SEROTONERGIC ANTIDEPRESSANTS

The question of whether serotonergic potency is a necessary attribute for efficacy in panic disorder is unsettled in the current literature. Finding that antipanic and antiphobic effects are more directly related to imipramine levels than desmethyl-imipramine levels, Mavissakalian and Perel (1996) conclude that the serotonergic parent compound is the active component of treatment. In support of this idea, many uncontrolled and fewer controlled studies of serotonergic antidepressants have demonstrated their efficacy (Den Boer & Westenberg, 1995; van Vliet, 1996), whereas studies of nonserotonergic antidepressants, such as maprotiline and bupropion (Den Boer & Westenberg, 1988; Sheehan et al., 1983) have found them ineffective in panic disorder. However, controlled studies of lofepramine and desipramine, both noradrenergic drugs, have found them to be effective (Fahy, O'Rourke, Brophy, & Schazmamm, 1992; Lidyard, Morton, Emmanuel, & Zouberg, 1993). Thus, although highly adrenergic antidepressants might not be the first choice for panic disorder, they should not be ruled out as therapeutic possibilities.

As with imipramine, tolerability may be a major limiting factor in clinical use of selective serotonergic antidepressants. In some studies, over 25 percent of patients were unable to tolerate the usual 20-mg dose of fluoxetine because of initial increase in anxiety, making it necessary to begin with doses as low as 5 mg daily and increase slowly over several weeks in order to reach therapeutic doses (Louie, Lewis, & Lannon, 1993; Schneier et al., 1990). Treatment emergent depression in the face of successful alleviation of panic attacks has been reported when patients received fluvoxamine, but not tricyclic antidepressants or clonazepam (Fux, Taub, & Zohar, 1993). All such patients had a prior history of depression and may represent a problematic group for treatment with serotonergic antidepressants.

MONOAMINE OXIDASE INHIBITORS

The antipanic effect of MAOIs has been less thoroughly studied than that of imipramine and other cyclic antidepressants. The literature contains six controlled studies (five dealing with phenelzine) (Lipsedge et al., 1973; Mountjoy, Roth, Garside, & Leitch, 1977; Sheehan et al., 1980; Solyom et al., 1973; Solyom, Solyom, LaPierre, Pecknold, & Morton, 1981; Tyrer, Candy, & Kelly, 1973), and a number of uncontrolled clinical trials of MAOIs in panic/agoraphobic patients. Interpretation of these reports is difficult, because many of them deal with a mixture of anxiety disorders, use relatively small numbers of patients, and administer medication in modest doses. Furthermore, few of them use specific measures of antipanic response. Despite these shortcomings, all published reports find some type of anxiolytic effect of MAOIs, with an average response rate of about 80 percent.

As with imipramine, target symptoms of phenelzine cover a broad range and are not limited to reduction of panic attacks. In the best MAOI study to date, Sheehan et al. (1980) reported reduction in somatic, depressive, and obsessive symptoms, reduction in phobic anxiety, and improvement in work and social functioning, in addition to reduction in frequency and severity of panic attacks. The authors observed that improvement in phobic avoidance tends to lag behind panic reduction by about three months. The Sheehan study also provides the only controlled comparison of phenelzine and imipramine, showing a nonsignificant trend toward superiority of the former drug on most measures.

Doses of phenelzine have been reported in the range of 30 mg to 90 mg daily, but most studies have not used more than 45 mg. The possibility that this might represent underdosage is supported by Tyrer et al. (1973), who found that raising the dose as high as 90 mg converted many of the initial nonresponders. It seems possible, therefore, that the extant literature somewhat underestimates the efficacy of MAOIs in panic/agoraphobic patients. There are no published data on the relationship of platelet MAOI activity to therapeutic effect.

Time of improvement ranges from three to eight weeks of treatment, with a mean of about four weeks. Only about 20 percent of patients across studies failed to complete treatment, suggesting that MAOIs may be somewhat better tolerated by panic-agoraphobic patients than cyclic antidepressants. Commonly reported side effects include dizziness, postural hypotension, dry mouth, blurred vision, edema, decreased libido or potency, weight gain, sweating, nausea, and headache. As with other types of antidepressants, the initial period of treatment is the most difficult in terms of side effects, which generally diminish after one to two weeks.

Studies that have compared behavioral treatments to phenelzine have tended to find few qualitative or quantitative differences in response (Lipsedge et al., 1973; Solyom et al., 1973). Combined drug and behavioral treatment is superior to either treatment alone in some, but not all, studies (Solyom et al., 1981); some degree of supportive psychotherapy accompanies medication prescription in most published reports, but such therapy generally has not been controlled or carefully described. Although there is some suggestion that MAOIs may work more quickly than behavioral treatment, estimates of relapse rates off medication range from 66 percent to 100 percent in those studies reporting it, which is considerably greater than that following behavioral treatment.

At present there is little guidance for predicting either which patients will respond to MAOIs or which drug within the class may be most effective. In addition to phenelzine, iproniazid has been found effective in a controlled trial (Lipsedge et al., 1973), and tranylcypromine and isocarboxazid have also been reported effective (Kelly, Guirguis, Frommer, Mitchell-Heggs, & Sargant, 1970). Greater levels of depression, personality pathology, and longer duration of illness have been associated with poorer outcome in some, but not all studies.

In summary, the present evidence suggests that MAOIs are as good as other types of antidepressants in their effect on panic/agoraphobia. As in treatment of depression, such medications are seldom drugs of first choice because of the necessity for a low-tyramine diet and the possibility of dangerous drug interactions.

ALPRAZOLAM AND OTHER BENZODIAZEPINES

Although Klein suggested in early reports that benzodiazepine-type anxiolytics were ineffective for panic attacks, interest in possible antipanic properties of these medications has revived considerably since the late 1970s. The major focus of attention has been on the triazolobenzodiazepine alprazolam, although other high-potency benzodiazepines or low-potency drugs at high enough doses are effective as well.

Controlled studies of alprazolam in panic disorder have shown the effectiveness of the drug with a mean response rate of about 75 percent compared to a placebo response ranging from 31 percent to 63 percent (Ballenger et al., 1988; Charney et al., 1988; Dunner, Ishiki, Avery, Wilson, & Hyde, 1986; Lesser et al., 1992; Rizley et al., 1986; Sheehan et al., 1984; Swinson, Pecknold, & Kuch, 1986). Although the numbers of patients treated in most studies is small, a large-scale study of alprazolam, using over 500 patients, reported very similar findings (Ballenger et al., 1988). Alprazolam has been found to reduce both spontaneous and situational panic attacks, as well as anticipatory anxiety.

Dose and blood-level-response studies of alprazolam (Alexander & Alexander, 1986; Greenblatt et al., 1993; Lesser et al., 1992) have produced the following findings: (1) the relationship of dose to plasma level averages about 1 mg/day for each 10 ng/ml in blood level; (2) the relationship of dose to blood level is highly variable among individuals; (3) generalized anxiety tends to respond at the lowest dose/blood levels, panic attacks at higher levels, and phobic anxiety at higher levels yet; (4) clinically significant relief from panic and anticipatory anxiety usually occurs at lower levels than clinically significant side effects; (5) the threshold blood level for major improvement in panic attacks has been reported variously as 20 ng/ml to 40 ng/ml.

Clinically, these findings imply that many patients may require 4 mg to 6 mg daily doses to control their panic attacks and that such doses are generally well tolerated. At the same time, metabolism of alprazolam varies widely among patients, and much higher or lower doses may be appropriate in a given case. The relative resistance of phobic anxiety to treatment is consistent with the general observation that phobic avoidance is not immediately responsive to medication, and may require a period of relearning of responses conditioned by panic attacks.

Alprazolam appears to be both faster in onset and better tolerated than antidepressants. Virtually all reports have described a clinically significant response in 1 week or less, although continued improvement has been found after six or seven weeks of treatment. In sharp contrast to antidepressants, the placebo drop-out rate in alprazolam studies (about 28 percent) exceeds the drop-out rate of patients on active drug (about 12 percent). By far the most common side effect is sedation, which is reported in more than two-thirds of patients taking the drug. Other common side effects include slurred speech, fatigue, and changes in cognitive ability, most often confusion and amnesia. Serious side effects such as delirium, combativeness, and hepatotoxicity appear to occur in no more than 1 percent of patients (Noyes et al., 1988). Manic reactions also occasionally occur in panic patients with no known bipolar history, just as such reactions occur in some depressed patients (Pecknold & Fleury, 1986).

Although patients commonly require an increase in their therapeutic dose during the first several months of treatment (Liebowitz et al., 1986) they do not tend to need continually escalating doses. In fact, after several years of treatment, patients generally use somewhat less medication than originally prescribed (J. Woods, Katz, & Winger, 1988; J. Woods & Winger, 1995). Similarly, despite widespread concern on the part of clinicians and regulatory agencies, studies to date have failed to find evidence that people who are not otherwise substance abusers abuse or misuse benzodiazepines. However, physiologic dependence on benzodiazepines and concomitant withdrawal syndromes are well-established realities, and it is important both for the clinician and the patient to understand them and how they differ from addiction.

If abruptly withdrawn from benzodiazepines 60 percent to 100 percent of patients who have taken them for a year or more will have a clinically apparent withdrawal reaction (Rickels, Schweizer, Case, & Greenblatt, 1990). Peak severity of withdrawal occurs at about two days with short half-life drugs, and four to seven days with long half-life drugs. Even when tapered more gradually, at rates of 20 percent to 30 percent of the maintenance dose weekly, 75 percent to 100 percent of patients taking alprazolam become significantly symptomatic during the withdrawal period (Fyer, Liebowitz, & Gorman, 1987; Noyes, Garvey, Cook, & Suelzer, 1991). Patients tapered from long half-life benzodiazepines at this rate also suffer withdrawal symptoms and in one study, 32 percent were unable to remain medication-free for five weeks (Schweizer, Rickels, Case, & Greenblatt, 1990).

Benzodiazepine discontinuation reactions have been divided into phenomena of relapse—a return of the original symptoms; rebound—recurrence of such symptoms with greater severity than before treatment; and withdrawal—the appearance of new symptoms that had not been part of the pretreatment syndrome. One study using this classification found that of patients tapered from alprazolam at a rate of 1 mg every three to seven days, 35 percent experienced rebound and 35 percent withdrawal (Pecknold, Swinson, Kuch, & Lewis, 1988). The most common withdrawal symptoms were cramps or spasms, gastrointestinal discomfort, paresthesias, and altered sensory perception. Benzodiazepine discontinuation may more rarely provoke grand mal seizures.

Because of Klein's early report of lack of efficacy of benzodiazepine anxiolytics for panic disorder, it was initially thought that alprazolem might be unique as an antipanic agent within this class of drugs. However, studies of diazepam, clonazepam, and lorazepam have found them about equally effective and well tolerated (Dunner et al., 1986; Fontaine, 1985; Noyes et al., 1984, 1996). Clonazepam has increasingly come to replace alprazolam as a benzodiazepine of first choice for panic disorder, because it has approximately twice the potency per weight and a longer half-life, allowing many patients to do well on twice-daily dosing (Herman, Rosenbaum, & Brotman, 1987). For the same reasons, discontinuation of clonazepam may be easier than alprazolam for some patients. Possibly because of its rapid onset of action, high potency, and short half-life, many clinicians find alprazolam especially difficult for patients to discontinue.

Patients taking high potency benzodiazepines for panic disorder and agoraphobia have been followed for periods from 8 months to four years (Nagy, Krystal, Woods, & Charney, 1989; Pollack et al., 1993; Schweizer, Rickels, Weiss, & Zavodnick, 1993). These studies have all found that patients maintain their improvements without need for escalation of dose. However, attenuated panic attacks, anticipatory anxiety, or phobias remain in about 40 percent of patients. Furthermore, attempting to taper medication results in relapse in one-third to two-thirds of patients, and 50 percent to 80 percent are still taking medication at the end of the study period (Rickels et al., 1993; Abelson & Curtis, 1993).

Patients with more severe anxiety symptoms, those with agoraphobia, and those with comorbid personality disorders have generally been found to be more symptomatic after both acute and long-term treatment with benzodiazepines, and less likely to be able to stay off medication (Nagy et al., 1989; Noyes et al., 1990; Rickels et al., 1993). Patients with hypothalamic-pituitary-adrenal axis overactivity, as measured by elevated 24-hour serum cortisol levels or an abnormal dexamethasone suppression test also have been found to respond poorly to benzodiazepine treatment (Coryell, Noyes, & Reich, 1991; Abelson & Curtis, 1996).

Other predictors of outcome have been less consistently demonstrated. Longer duration of illness predicts poorer outcome in most, but not all studies (Abelson & Curtis, 1993; Basoglu et al., 1994; Noyes et al., 1990; Pollack et al., 1993). Presence of depressive symptoms or past history of depression predict poorer outcome in some studies (Basoglu et al., 1994; Noyes et al., 1990; Pollack et al., 1993), but not in others (Keller et al., 1993). Furthermore, some investigations have found benzodiazepines to be effective in treating depression comorbid with panic disorder (Keller et al., 1993), while others have not (Nagy et al., 1989). These inconsistencies may, in part, reflect the heterogeneity of depressive symptoms in panic-disorder patients.

Spiegel and Bruce (1997) have recently reviewed the literature on combining benzodiazepines with cognitive-behavioral therapy. They conclude that more studies are needed, but evidence to date does not support a general added benefit of combined versus montherapy. However, there may be advantages to combining treatments in individual cases, such as adding benzodiazepines for patients with severe anxiety in the early stages of cognitive-behavioral therapy, or adding cognitive-behavioral therapy for patients whose agoraphobia is resistant to benzodiazepine treatment. When treatments are combined, laboratory and clinical data support tapering medication before or concurrently with psychotherapy.

OTHER MEDICATIONS

A variety of other medications have been reported to be effective for panic disorder, but none has a clearly established place in the therapeutic armamentarium. Although the adrenergic theory of panic attacks would predict an important place for adrenergic antagonists, results to date have been unimpressive. Some reports suggest that propranolol, in doses ranging from 30 mg to 160 mg daily, may alleviate panic attacks (Heiser & DeFrancisco, 1976; Munjack et al., 1985), but others have failed to confirm this (Gorman et al., 1983; Noyes et al., 1984). Trials with clonidine have produced similarly ambiguous results (Hoehn-Saric, Merchant, Keyser, & Smith, 1982; Liebowitz, Fyer, McGrath, & Klein, 1981).

More recently, there has been interest in the possible efficacy of anticonvulsant drugs (other than clonazepam) for panic disorder. Although there are little data as yet, evidence to date supports efficacy of valproate, but not carbamazepine in alleviating panic anxiety (Keck, McElroy, Turgul, Bennett, & Smith, 1993; Lum, Fontaine, Elie, & Ontiversos, 1990; Uhde, Stein, & Past, 1988). The relationship of antipanic efficacy to EEG status is not clearly delineated in these reports.

TREATMENT STRATEGIES

Successful treatment of panic-agoraphobia requires skillful management of the psychological context in which medications are given as well as judicious prescription of the medications themselves. Treatment that includes careful attention to: (1) patient education, (2) treatment planning, and (3) choice of medication will maximize the effectiveness of pharmacotherapy.

PATIENT EDUCATION

Once a solid diagnosis of panic disorder with or without agoraphobia is made, it is very important to give the patient an accurate, simple model of the disease. Many patients with this condition are chronically demoralized, suspecting that some personal failing is responsible for their symptoms. Others fear that something is seriously wrong with them physically. Patients often report spending much time in psychotherapy attempting to deal with possible underlying emotional issues, but getting no symptomatic relief. Family members may view the symptoms as attention-getting or dependent maneuvers that the patient can willfully control.

Explaining that biological, possibly genetic factors are thought to be necessary for developing the disease, and that it bears no specific relationship to any personality type or life situation can help lift patients' self-esteem and alleviate blame and stigma within their families. The physician's description of the most commonly experienced panic symptoms and the circumstances under which they occur usually helps patients to feel understood and that their condition is not bizarre, unique, or life-threatening. For patients (probably a majority) in whom spontaneous panic attacks precede the onset of phobic avoidance, the fear-of-becoming-afraid model of agoraphobia can have considerable explanatory power and pave the way for acceptance of medications. The most important and useful points in presenting the medical view of panic/agoraphobia are that panic attacks, whether or not associated with current stressors or feared situations, have a life of their own, do not necessarily remit with environmental changes, and may need to be treated pharmacologically.

It is also important to keep in mind that personality traits and interpersonal stresses may affect the course of the illness. Studies have shown that although personality factors do not influence the antipanic response to medications, they do influence outcome in terms of overall level of functioning (Reich, 1988). It is, therefore, important to assess the degree to which family conflict or maladaptive patterns of behavior play a part in the patient's current life. Where these are prominent, their effects on the patient's ability to cope with the illness should be stressed, and adjunctive psychotherapy may be recommended.

TREATMENT PLANNING

Collaborative treatment planning, important in any form of psychiatric treatment, is essential to success with panic/agoraphobic patients. Such patients feel a great need to be in control, and often they are both highly apprehensive about medications and hypersensitive to their effects. Patients should be told that the primary action of the medication is to block panic attacks, but that it will probably also help diminish general anxiety and improve overall sense of well-being. Patients with avoidant behaviors should be encouraged to begin to try to face feared situations once they notice attenuation of their panic attacks. They must be helped to understand the need to test their susceptibility to panicking by exposing themselves to various situations and thus, gaining confidence over time.

The physician should also discuss the range of medication options, the side effects of each type of medication, and the major points for and against each. The patient's reaction to such a discussion is an important guide to choice of a starting regimen. The patient's history of toleration and effectiveness of prior treatments should also influence medication choice. Whichever medication is chosen, patients should receive a full description of likely side effects; the danger of frightening patients away from treatment is not as great as that of losing them when unanticipated side effects are noticed. When prescribing benzodiazepines, one should educate patients about the difference between physiologic dependency and addiction. Unfortunately, many physicians as well as lay people confuse these two conditions, and may tell patients that such medications will turn them into addicts. They may need to be reassured that withdrawal effects can be well tolerated if discontinuation is planned and managed collaboratively. It is also important for the physician to be available by telephone between appointments so that the patient can check in about troublesome physical symptoms and receive reassurance or revised medication instructions. The knowledge that someone is available to help exerts a powerful moderating effect on the symptoms, so that an appropriate degree of availability is in itself an active ingredient of the treatment.

CHOICE OF MEDICATION

There is no universally best type of medication for treatment of panic/agoraphobia. Benzodiazepines are easily tolerated and fast acting, but they must be taken several times daily and may have unpleasant or even dangerous withdrawal effects. Cyclic antidepressants are generally free of these liabilities, but often they are poorly tolerated. MAOIs may be the most potent antipanic agents currently available, but they necessitate a special diet and carry the risk of potentially dangerous medication interactions. Furthermore, there are presently no known patient variables that predict differential drug response. Thus, the patient's preferences about medication may be the best determinant of where to start.

If the patient has no past history of medication treatment and no strong predilections, it is reasonable to begin with low doses of a benzodiazepine, because these drugs are well tolerated and may ameliorate the early side effects of an antidepressant if it becomes necessary to add one. Furthermore, such a starting regimen capitalizes on the tendency of panic patients to be placebo responders. Clonazepam, started in doses of 0.5 mg to 1.0 mg twice daily, is a frequent drug of first choice. Benefits and side effects can be gauged within a week of treatment, after which the dose can be adjusted as needed.

It is especially important when using benzodiazepines to educate the patient to the use of standing, rather than PRN, dosing. As-needed use of such medication tends to increase self-vigilance and anticipatory anxiety, and sets off internal struggles about when to use the medication. By the time the patient takes the PRN dose, it may be too late to abort the attack, which may then prompt additional doses, followed by a miniwithdrawal and rebound anxiety. Instead, the physician must assure the patient that standing doses will be adjusted until the panics are well controlled.

Patients who fail to respond satisfactorily to benzodiazepines should be considered for an antidepressant trial. Cyclic antidepressants and SSRIs should be chosen based on how well their side-effect profiles fit the patient's needs. Most published studies have used a starting dose of 25 mg of imipramine, with increases of 25 mg every 2 to 3 days, but either higher or lower doses might be used depending upon the patient's apprehensiveness about medication and past history of medication trials. SSRIs should also be started at lower doses than the doses used for depression. Some patients are so sensitive to side effects, particularly the early feelings of shakiness and tension, that they may require months to arrive at a therapeutic dose. In such cases, reassurance, support, and gentle persistence are essential to a successful outcome. Dividing the dose may help to alleviate side effects. Concomitant treatment with benzodiazepines may be very helpful in moderating the stimulant effects of antidepressants as well as patients' secondary anxiety responses to them. Many patients will ultimately do well on one medication alone, so that an attempt should be made to taper benzodiazepines slowly once an effective dose of antidepressant has been reached. There is little data to guide the clinician when results with the first antidepressant are unsatisfactory. As with treatment of depression, an antidepressant of another type may be better. Some reports suggest that partial response with an antidepressant of one type may be augmented by adding a second one of another type (Tiffon et al., 1994).

MAOIs are available as third-line medications. Most published clinical experience has been with phenelzine. A starting dose of 15 mg may be increased to 45 mg daily in divided doses over the course of a week. The dose must be pushed up to 90 mg daily in some patients to achieve maximum therapeutic benefit.

From the point of view of time and cost to the patients, it may be most efficient to begin with medication, education, and support, but not formal psychotherapy. This becomes an especially important consideration if the patient's insurance pays for medication maintenance but does not support more expensive treatments. Indications for psychotherapy include failure to tolerate medication, a patient's wish to be medication free, resistance of symptoms (such as phobic avoidance) to medication/support alone, and the discovery that psychological or interpersonal factors play a prominent role in maintaining the anxiety.

Although there are no clear guidelines for maintenance therapy, it appears that patients are about evenly divided between those who will eventually do well off medication and those who will not. On the one hand, there is generally little reason to press patients to withdraw from medication; most drugs that are effective for panic disorder are safe for long-term use, and patients may need considerable time for rehabilitation after many years of uncontrolled panic attacks. On the other hand, periodic attempts to taper medication constitutes good general practice.

When tapering medication, it is important to explain that the disorder is chronic in some people, and the patient should not consider it a personal failure if the taper is unsuccessful. Benzodiazepines should be tapered on a flexible schedule in collaboration with the patient, who must be well educated about withdrawal, rebound, and relapse phenomena. Patients should not proceed to the next level of taper until they are comfortable at the present level. Depending on dose, an initial taper rate of 15 percent to 25 percent/week is usually appropriate, but often the last 25 percent of taper must be slowed considerably. Patients whose working relationship with the prescriber allows them a sense of control will have a much smoother discontinuation process than those who feel pressured or abandoned.

Case Illustrations

Case 1: The patient is a 26-year-old married woman with one child. She has a long psychiatric history, going back to her teenage years, which were notable for school truancy and polysubstance abuse. Her family history includes a mother with several mental breakdowns and a father who chronically uses antianxiety medication. The patient dates the onset of her anxiety disorder to her early teen years, when she began to have spontaneous panic attacks, characterized by intense fear, palpitations, and air hunger. She began avoiding public transportation and other public situations from which she could not exit easily (such as school) soon after the onset of panics. The drugs she abused were various but mostly were restricted to alcohol, marijuana, and prescription medications such as barbiturates and diazepam. Although she did not finish high school, she successfully completed a general education diploma course when she was 19 years old, walking three miles each way to attend classes. She had a series of clinging relationships with one boyfriend after another, and married when she was 20. At the time she presented for treatment, she had recently discovered that her husband was having an affair.

The patient had participated in behavioral therapy several times, for several months at a time. The therapy did not help her panic attacks, but it moderated her avoidant behavior to some extent. However, she always dropped out because of the difficulty of getting to her appointments. She had been tried briefly on imipramine, which did help the panic attacks, but she stopped taking it because it made her feel "like a zombie" and made her very dizzy whenever she stood up. Therefore, she feared that the medication was making her sicker. At the time of presentation she had stopped using most drugs, but she sedated herself with alcohol and diazepam, which she got from physicians, friends, and relatives. The diazepam was used erratically, according to when she felt she needed it, in doses up to 70 mg daily.

The patient was brought for treatment by her husband, who complained of dependency and "hysterical" behavior. After going over her history, the physician reviewed the diagnosis and nature of the disorder with the patient and her husband. It was explained that the patient was probably not a primary substance abuser, but had been attempting to self-medicate with whatever was available. The initial goals of treatment were: (1) to get control of the panic attacks, which were occurring at the rate of several daily, and (2) to reduce and regularize the patient's use of diazepam. An antidepressant was chosen as the drug of first choice, because the patient was still having panic attacks on large doses of benzodiazepine, had continuing difficulty using such medications appropriately, and had a history of good antipanic response to imipramine. Nortriptyline was chosen because it is similar to imipramine but has a more favorable side-effect profile.

Because the patient was extremely apprehensive about starting another antidepressant, she was begun on only 10 mg daily and told to call in after 3 days to report the effect or earlier if she had any questions or concerns. She was also asked to restrict her diazepam intake to 10 mg three times daily, to be taken regularly every day. The patient called after the second dose of medication, saying that she was more anxious than before taking it. Following discussion, she was able to distinguish between the physical sense of tremulousness related to the medication and her usual symptoms of anxiety. She agreed to take the same dose until her next appointment the following week. By that time, she was tolerating the medication well enough to raise the dose to 10 mg twice daily. At this dose, she felt "freaked out" and very jumpy, but she was able to tolerate 20 mg alternating with 10 mg every other day.

By the end of the third month of treatment, the patient was taking 50 mg of nortriptyline and noticing some moderation of her panic attacks. She described feeling as if a panic attack were about to come but never developed hyperventilation or the full severity. She was less successful in regulating her diazepam intake, often taking extra doses during stressful situations, such as fights with her husband.

During her appointments the patient was helped to distinguish between panic anxiety, anticipatory anxiety, and somatic sensations associated with medication. She was counseled about the danger of rebound anxiety following high doses of benzodiazepines. She was encouraged to begin to venture into feared situations as her panic attacks moderated, but for some time she continued to demand that her husband accompany her when she went outside her home. Several sessions were spent with the patient and her husband, reviewing the course of her illness and considering the ways in which it had interfered with her functioning in the marriage. With the advice of the physician, the couple agreed to a course of marital counseling to address issues of control and dependency in the relationship.

Over the next few months, the patient was able to become less avoidant and to begin to perform routine errands outside the house. Her dose of nortriptyline was gradually increased to 100 mg daily, first in divided doses, and then taken all at bedtime. At this dose, she was entirely free of panic attacks and able to stay on a steady dose of diazepam, 30 mg daily. As her concerns about panic attacks diminished and her relationship with her husband improved, she agreed to withdraw from diazapam over a one-month period. She was maintained on nortriptyline alone, with monthly psychiatric appointments, and no recurrence of panic attacks or return to inappropriate self-medication. She continued to insist on monthly psychiatric visits and continued to be somewhat dependent in her marriage, although less clinging and demanding.

Case 2: The patient is a 45-year-old married man with three children. He had grown up in a household with an irritable father who drank to excess and was physically abusive. After a troubled adolescence, he graduated from college, married, and began a successful career in business. However, he was typically gloomy in outlook, had little social life, and had a chronic tendency to overeat and be overweight.

At age 34 he began to have episodes of palpitations, tingling of the arms and legs, churning stomach, chest pain, and fear that he was about to have a heart attack. The attacks occurred as frequently as several weekly, and the patient became constantly tense and apprehensive in anticipation of the next attack. The attacks seemed to bear no relation to ongoing events, but occurred most often when he was driving his car.

After several visits to hospital emergency rooms and thorough evaluation by his doctor revealed no medical cause of his symptoms, the patient concluded that they were "emotional." He did not curtail his usual activities, but talked himself through attacks when they occurred. He also entered weekly insight-oriented psychotherapy, where he examined his emotionally distant style and its probable antecedents. After one year of therapy he noted closer relationships with family members, but no effect on his symptoms.

The patient reluctantly consulted a psychiatrist about medication at the urging of his wife. He expressed fear of being "hooked" or controlled by medications, and thought he should be able to handle his symptoms without them. The psychiatrist confirmed the diagnosis of panic disorder, explained the probable biologic basis of the symptoms, and suggested several books on anxiety disorders for general readership. He also suggested the possibility that the patient had been living with untreated, low-grade depression for many years (Dysthymic Disorder). After a week of considering it, doctor and patient decided on a trial of antidepressants, which might improve his mood-related symptoms as well as his anxiety.

He was begun on sertraline, which was chosen over tricyclic antidepressants because it is not associated with weight gain. However, he was unable to tolerate minimum 25-mg dose of this medication, complaining of jumpiness, headaches, and upset stomach. Medication was changed to fluoxetine concentrate, starting with 1 mg mixed with juice, and increasing by 1 mg every 2 days. Side effects were similar to those on sertraline, but much milder, and tolerable. At 10 mg daily, the dose was held constant for one month to monitor effects and allow blood levels to come to equilibrium. By the end of this period, the patient noted markedly diminished intensity of symptoms, which still occurred once or twice weekly, but never progressed into a full-blown attack. He no longer complained of side effects. However, there was no change in his outlook, social energy, or tendency to overeat.

Medication was raised to 20 mg gradually over the next two weeks and then switched to the more convenient capsule form. Two months later, the patient and his wife noted that he was more energetic, less gloomy, and more interested in socializing. Although he remained overweight, he noticed that he had less of a craving for sweets than previously, which had contributed to his overeating. The frequency of panic symptoms had diminished to several times monthly, and they remained limited in intensity. Doctor and patient planned to continue the medication indefinitely, with office visits at three to four-month intervals or as needed.

REFERENCES

Abelson, J., & Curtis, G. (1993). Discontinuation after successful treatment of panic disorders: A naturalistic follow-up study. *Journal of Anxiety Disorders, 7*, 107–117.

Abelson, J., & Curtis, G. (1996). Hypothalamic-pituitary-adrenal axis activity in panic disorder: Prediction of long-term outcome by pre-treatment cortical levels. *American Journal of Psychiatry.*

Alexander, P.E., & Alexander, D.D. (1986). Alprazolam treatment for panic disorder. *Journal of Clinical Psychiatry, 47*, 301–304.

Ballenger, J.C., Burrows, G.D., DuPont, R.L., Lesser, I.M., Noyes, R., Pecknold, J.D., Rifkin, A., & Swinson, R.P. (1988). Alprazolam in panic disorder and agoraphobia: Results from a multicenter trial. I. Efficacy in short-term treatment. *Archives of General Psychiatry, 45*, 413–422.

Ballenger, J.C., Peterson, G.A., Laraia, M., Hucek, A., Lake, C.R., Jimerson, D., Cox, D.J., Trockman, C., Ship, J., & Wilkinson, C. (1984). A study of plasma catecholamines in agoraphobia and the relationship of serum tricyclic levels to treatment response. In J.C. Ballenger (Ed.), *Biology of agoraphobia.* Washington, DC: American Psychiatric Press.

Barlow, D.H. (1986). A psychological model of panic. In B.F. Shaw, F. Cushman, Z.V. Segal, & T.M. Vallis (Eds.), *Anxiety disorders: Theory, diagnosis, and treatment.* New York: Plenum Press.

Barlow, D.H., Vermilyea, J.A., Blanchard, E.B., Vermiliyea, B.B., DiNardo, P.A., & Cery, J.A. (1985). The phenomenon of panic. *Journal of Abnormal Psychology, 94*, 320–328.

Basoglu, M., Marks, I., Swinson, R., Noshirvani, H., O'Sullivan, G., & Kuch, K. (1994). Pre-treatment predictors of treatment outcome in panic disorder and agoraphobia treated with alprazolam and exposure. *Journal of Affective Disorders, 30*, 123–132.

Breier, A., Charney, D.S., & Heninger, E.R. (1986). Agoraphobia with panic attacks: Development, diagnostic stability, and course of illness. *Archives of General Psychiatry, 43*, 1929–1936.

Carr, D.B., & Sheehan, D.V. (1984). Panic anxiety: A new biological model. *Journal of Clinical Psychiatry, 45,* 323–330.

Charney, D.S., & Heninger, G.R. (1986). Abnormal regulation of noradrenergic function in panic disorder. *American Journal of Psychiatry, 143,* 1042–1054.

Charney, D.S., Heninger, G.R., & Breier, A. (1984). Noradrenergic function in panic anxiety. Effects of yohimbine in healthy subjects and patients with agoraphobia and panic disorder. *Archives of General Psychiatry, 41,* 751–763.

Charney, D.S., Woods, S.W., Goodman, W.K., & Heninger, E.R. (1987). Serotonin function in anxiety: II. Effects of the serotonin agonist MCPP in panic disorder patients and healthy subjects. *Psychopharmacology, 92,* 14–24.

Charney, D.S., Woods, S.W., Goodman, W.K., Rifkin, G., Kinch, M., Aiden, B., Quadrino, L.M., & Heninger, G.R. (1988). Drug treatment of panic disorder: The comparative efficacy of imipramine, alprazolam, and triazolam. *Journal of Clinical Psychiatry, 47,* 580–586.

Coplan, J., Papp, L., Pire, D., Martinez, J., Cooper, T., Rosenblum, L., Klein, D., & Gorman, J. (1977). Clinical improvement with fluoxetine therapy and noradrenergic function in patients with panic disorder. *Archives of General Psychiatry, 54,* 643–648.

Coryell, W., Noyes, R., & Reich, J. (1991). The prognostic significance of HPA axis disturbance in panic disorder: a three-year follow-up. *Biological Psychiatry, 29,* 96–102.

Crowe, R.R., Noyes, R., Pauls, D.L., & Slymen, D. (1983). A family study of panic disorder. *Archives of General Psychiatry, 40,* 1075–1079.

Crowe, R.R., Noyes, R., Wilson, A.F., Elston, R.C., & Wood, L.J. (1987). A linkage study of panic disorder. *Archives of General Psychiatry, 44,* 933–937.

Den Boer, J., & Westenberg, H. (1995). Serotonergic compounds in panic disorder, obsessive-compulsive disorder, and anxious depression: A concise review. *Human Psychopharmacology, 10,* 5173–5183.

Dunner, D.L., Ishiki, D., Avery, D.H., Wilson, L.G., & Hyde, T.S. (1986). Effect of alprazolam and diazepam on anxiety and panic attacks in panic disorder: A controlled study. *Journal of Clinical Psychiatry, 47,* 458–480.

Evans, L., Schneider, P., Ross-Lee, L., Wiltshire, G., Eadie, M., Kenardy, J., & Hoey, H. (1985). Plasma serotonin levels in agoraphobia [letter]. *American Journal of Psychiatry, 142,* 267.

Fahy, T., O'Rourke, D., Brophy, J., & Schazmamm, W. (1992). The Galway study of panic disorder: A placebo controlled trial. *Journal of Affective Disorders, 25,* 63–75.

Fontaine, R. (1985). Clonazepam for panic disorders and agitation. *Psychosomatics, 20*(Suppl. 12), 13–18.

Freud, S. (1962). Obsessions and phobias: Their psychological mechanism and their etiology. In J. Strachey (Ed. & Trans.), *The standard edition of the complete psychological works of Sigmund Freud* (Vol. 3). London: Hogarth Press.

Freud, S. (1963). Introductory lectures on psychoanalysis: Lecture 25. Anxiety. In J. Strachey (Ed. & Trans.), *The standard edition of the complete psychological works of Sigmund Freud* (Vol. 16). London: Hogarth Press.

Fux, M., Taub, M., & Zohar, J. (1993). Emergence of depressive symptoms during treatment for panic disorder with specific 5-hydroxytryptophan reuptake inhibitors. *Acta Psychiatrica Scandinavica, 88,* 235–237.

Fyer, A., Liebowitz, M., & Gorman, J. (1987). Discontinuation of alprazolm treatment in panic patients. *American Journal of Psychiatry, 144,* 303–308.

Gaffney, F.A., Fenton, B.J., Lane, L.D., & Lake, C.R. (1988). Hemodynamic, ventilatory, and biochemical responses of panic patients and normal controls with sodium lactate infusion and spontaneous panic attacks. *Archives of General Psychiatry, 45,* 53–60.

Garakani, H., Zitrin, C.M., & Klein, D.F. (1984). Treatment of panic disorder with imipramine alone. *American Journal of Psychiatry, 141,* 446–448.

Garvey, M.J., Noyes, R., & Cook, B. (1987). Does situational panic disorder represent a specific panic disorder subtype? *Comprehensive Psychiatry, 28,* 324–333.

Gorman, J., Goetz, R., Dillon, D., Liebowitz, M.R., Fyer, A.J., Davies, S., & Klein, D.F. (1990). Sodium D-lactate infusion of panic disorder patients. *Neuropsychopharmacology, 3,* 181–189.

Gorman, J.M., Dattisto, D., Goetz, R.R., Dillon, D., Liebowitz, M.R., Fyer, A., Kahn, J., Sandberg, D., & Klein, D.F. (1989). A comparison of sodium bicarbonate and sodium lactate infusion in the induction of panic attacks. *Archives of General Psychiatry, 46,* 145–150.

Gorman, J.M., Fyer, M.R., Goetz, R., Askanazi, J., Liebowitz, M.R., Fyer, A.J., Kinney, J., & Klein, D.F. (1988). Ventilatory physiology of patients with panic disorder. *Archives of General Psychiatry, 40,* 1079–1082.

Gorman, J.M., Levy, G.F., Liebowitz, M.R., McGrath, P., Appleby, I.L., Dillon, D.J., Davies, S.O., & Klein, D.F. (1983). Effect of acute B-adrenergic blockade on lactate-induced panic. *Archives of General Psychiatry, 40,* 1079–1082.

Gorman, J.M., Liebowitz, M.R., Fyer, A.J., & Stein, J. (1889). A neuroanatomical hypothesis for panic disorder. *American Journal of Psychiatry, 1216,* 148–161.

Greenblatt, D.J., Harmatz, J.S., & Shader, R.I. (1993). Plasma alprazolam concentrations. Relation to efficacy and side effects in the treatment of panic disorder. *Archives of General Psychiatry, 50,* 715–722.

Heiser, J.F., & DeFrancisco, D. (1976). The treatment of pathological panic states with propranolol. *American Journal of Psychiatry, 133,* 1384–1393.

Herman, J.B., Rosenbaum, J.F., & Brotman, A.W. (1987). The alprozalam to clonazepam switch for the treatment of panic disorder. *Journal of Clinical Psychopharmacology, 7,* 175–178.

Hoehn-Saric, R., Merchant, A.F., Keyser, M.L., & Smith, V.K. (1982). Effects of clonidine on anxiety disorders. *Archives of General Psychiatry, 38,* 1278–1282.

Jobson, K., Linnoila, M., Gillan, J., & Sullivan, J.L. (1978). A successful treatment of severe anxiety attacks with tricyclic antidepressants: A potential mechanism of action. *American Journal of Psychiatry, 135,* 863–864.

Kahn, R., Asnis, G., Wetzler, S., & van Praag, H.M. (1988). Neuroendocrine evidence for serotonin receptor hypersensitivity in panic disorder. *Psychopharmacology, 96,* 360–364.

Keck, P., McElroy, S., Turgul, K., Bennett, J., & Smith, J. (1993). Antiepileptic drugs for treatment of panic disorder. *Neuropsychobiology, 27,* 150–153.

Keller, M., Lavori, P., Goldenberg, I., Baker, L., Pollack, M., Sachs, G., Rosenbaum, J., Deltito, J., Leon, A., Shear, K., & Herman, G. (1993). Influence of depression on the treatment of panic disorder with imipramine, alprazolam, and placebo. *Journal of Affective Disorders, 28,* 27–38.

Kelly, D., Guirguis, W., Frommer, E., Mitchell-Heggs, N., & Sargant, W. (1970). Treatment of phobic states with antidepressants: A retrospective study of 246 patients. *British Journal of Psychiatry, 116,* 387–398.

Klein, D.F. (1964). Delineation of two drug-responsive anxiety syndromes. *Psychopharmacologia, 5,* 347–408.

Klein, D.F. (1993). False suffocation alarms, spontaneous panics, and related conditions. An integrative hypothesis. *Archives of General Psychiatry, 50,* 306–317.

Klein, D.F., & Fink, M. (1962). Behavioral reaction patterns with phenothiazines. *Archives of General Psychiatry, 7,* 444–454.

Klein, D.F., Ross, D.C., & Cohen, P. (1987). Panic and avoidance in agoraphobia. Application of path analysis and treatment studies. *Archives of General Psychiatry, 44,* 377–385.

Klein, D.F., Zitrin, C.M., Woerner, M.G., & Ross, D.C. (1983). Treatment of phobias: II. Behavior therapy and supportive psychotherapy: Are there any specific ingredients? *Archives of General Psychiatry, 40,* 139–145.

Ko, G.N., Elsworth, J.D., Roth, R.H., Rifkin, B.G., Leigh, H., & Redmond, D.E. (1983). Panic induced elevation of plasma MHPG levels in phobic-anxious patients. *Archives of General Psychiatry, 40,* 425–430.

Leckman, J.F., Merikanges, K.R., Pauls, D.L., Prusoff, B.A., & Weissman, M.M. (1983). Anxiety disorders associated with episodes of depression: Family study data contradict *DSM-III* convention. *American Journal of Psychiatry, 140,* 880–882.

Lesser, I., Lidyard, R.B., Antal E., Rubin, R., Ballenger, J., & DuPont, R. (1992). Alprazolam plasma concentrations and treatment response in panic disorder and agoraphobia. *American Journal of Psychiatry, 149,* 1556–1562.

Lidyard, R.B., Morton, W., Emmanuel, N., & Zouberg, J. (1993). Preliminary report: Placebo-controlled, double-blind study of the clinical and metabolic effects of desipramine in panic disorder. *Psychopharmacology Bulletin, 29,* 185–188.

Liebowitz, M.R., Fyer, A.J., Gorman, J.M., Campeas, R., Levin, A., Davies, S., Goetz, D., & Klein, D.F. (1986). Alprazolam in the treatment of panic disorders. *Journal of Clinical Psychopharmacology, 6,* 13–20.

Liebowitz, M.R., Fyer, A.J., McGrath, P., & Klein, D.F. (1981). Clonidine treatment of panic disorder. *Psychopharmacology Bulletin, 17,* 122–123.

Liebowitz, M.R., Gorman, J.M., Fyer, A.J., Levitt, M., Dillon, D., Levy, G., Appleby, I.L., Anderson, S., Palij, M., Davies, S., & Klein, D.F. (1985). Lactate provocation of panic attacks: II. Biochemical and physiological findings. *Archives of General Psychiatry, 42,* 709–714.

Lipsedge, M.S., Hajioff, J., Huggins, P., Napier, L., Peerce, J., Pike, D.J., & Rich, M. (1973). The management of severe agoraphobia: A comparison of iproiazid and systematic desensitization. *Psychopharmacologia, 32,* 67–80.

Louie, A., Lewis, T., & Lannon, R. (1993). Use of low-dose fluoxetine in major depression and panic disorder. *Journal of Clinical Psychiatry, 54,* 435–438.

Marks, I.M., Gray, S., Cohen, D., Hill, R., Mawson, D., Ramm, E., & Stern, R. (1983). Imipramine and brief therapist-aided exposure in agoraphobics having self-exposure homework. *Archives of General Psychiatry, 40,* 153–162.

Mavissakalian, M. (1987a). Initial depression and response to imipramine in agoraphobia. *Journal of Nervous and Mental Disease, 175,* 358–361.

Mavissakalian, M. (1987b). The placebo effect in agoraphobia. *Journal of Nervous and Mental Disease, 175,* 95–99.

Mavissakalian, M. (1993). Combined behavioral therapy and pharmacotherapy of agoraphobia. *Journal of Psychiatric Research, 27(* Suppl. 1), 179–191.

Mavissakalian, M. (1996). Phenomenology of panic attacks: responsiveness of individual symptoms to imipramine. *Journal of Psychopharmacology, 16,* 233–237.

Mavissakalian, M., & Michelson, L. (1986). Agoraphobia: Relative and combined effectiveness of therapist-assisted in vivo-exposure and imipramine. *Journal of Clinical Psychiatry, 47,* 117–122.

Mavissakalian, M., & Perel, J. (1985). Imipramine in the treatment of agoraphobia: Dose-response relationship. *American Journal of Psychiatry, 142,* 1032–1036.

Mavissakalian, M., & Perel, J. (1989). Imipramine dose-response relationship in panic disorder with agoraphobia. Preliminary findings. *Archives of General Psychiatry.*

Mavissakalian, M., & Perel, J. (1992a). Clinical experiments in maintenance and discontinuation of imipramine therapy in panic disorder with agoraphobia. *Archives of General Psychiatry, 49,* 318–323.

Mavissakalian, M., & Perel, J. (1992b). Protective effects of imipramine maintenance treatment in patients with panic disorder and agoraphobia. *American Journal of Psychiatry, 149,* 1053–1057.

Mavissakalian, M., & Perel, J. (1995). Imipramine treatment of panic disorder with agoraphobia: Dose ranging and plasma level-response relationships. *American Journal of Psychiatry, 152,* 673–682.

Mavissakalian, M., & Perel, J. (1996). The relationship of plasma, imipramine and N-desmethylimipramine to response to panic disorder. *Psychopharmacology Bulletin, 32,* 143–147.

Mavissakalian, M., Perel, J., Bowler, K., & Dealy, R. (1987). Trazodone in the treatment of panic disorder and agoraphobia with panic attacks. *American Journal of Psychiatry, 144,* 785–787.

Mavissakalian, M., Perel, J., & Michelson, J. (1984). The relationship of plasma imipramine and N-desmethyl imipramine to improvement in agoraphobia. *Journal of Clinical Psychopharmacology, 4,* 36–40.

McNair, D.M., & Kahn, R.J. (1981). Imipramine compared with a benzodiazepine for agoraphobia. In D.M. Klein & J. Rabkin (Eds.), *Anxiety: New research and changing concepts.* New York: Raven Press.

Mountjoy, C.Q., Roth, M., Garside, R.F., & Leitch, I.M. (1977). A clinical trial of phenelzine in anxiety depressive and phobic neuroses. *British Journal of Psychiatry, 131,* 486–492.

Munjack, D.J., Rebal, R., Shaner, R., Staples, F., Braun, R., & Leonard, M. (1985). Imipramine versus propranolol in the treatment of panic attacks: A pilot study. *Comprehensive Psychiatry, 26,* 80–89.

Nagy, L., Krystal, J., & Charney, D. (1993). Long-term medication and panic disorder after short-term behavioral group treatment: 2–4 year naturalistic follow-up study. *Journal of Clinical Psychopharmacology, 13,* 16–24.

Nagy, L., Krystal, J., Woods, S., & Charney, D. (1989). Clinical and medication outcome after short-term alprazolam and behavioral group treatment in panic disorder. *Archives of General Psychiatry, 46,* 993–999.

Noyes, R., Anderson, D.J., Clancy, J., Crowe, R.R., Slymen, D.J., Ghoneim, M.M., & Hinrichs, J.V. (1984). Diazepam and propranolol in panic disorder and agoraphobia. *Archives of General Psychiatry, 41,* 287–292.

Noyes, R., Burrows, G., Reich, J., Judd, F., Garvey, M., Norman, T., Cook, B., & Marriott, P. (1996). Diazepam vs. Alprazolam for the treatment of panic disorder. *Journal of Clinical Psychiatry, 57,* 349–355.

Noyes, R.E., DuPont, R.L., Pecknold, J.C., Rifkin, A., Rubin, R.T., Swinson, R.P., Ballenger, J.C., & Burrows, G.D. (1988). Alprazolam in panic disorder and agoraphobia: Results from a multicenter trial: II. Patient acceptance, side effects, and safety. *Archives of General Psychiatry, 45,* 423–428.

Noyes, R., Garvey, M., & Cook, B.L. (1989). Follow-up of patients with panic attacks treated with tricyclic antidepressants. *Journal Affective Disorders, 16,* 244–257.

Noyes, R., Garvey, M., Cook, B.L., & Samuelson, L. (1989). Problems with trycyclic antidepressant use in patients with panic disorder or agoraphobia. *Journal Clinical Psychiatry, 50*, 163–169.

Noyes, R., Garvey, M., Cook, B.L., & Suelzer, M. (1991). Controlled discontinuation of benzodiazepine treatment for patients with panic disorder. *American Journal of Psychiatry, 148*, 517–523.

Noyes, R., Reich, J., Christianson, J., Swelzer, M., Pfohl, B., & Coryell, W. (1990). Outcome of Panic Disorder: Relationship to diagnostic subtypes and comorbidity. *Archives of General Psychiatry, 47*, 809–818.

Nurnberg, H.G., & Coccaro, E.F. (1982). Response of panic disorder and resistance of depression to imipramine. *American Journal of Psychiatry, 139*, 1060–1062.

Nutt, D.J. (1989). Altered central alpha 2-adrenoreceptor sensitivity in panic disorder. *Archives of General Psychiatry, 46*, 165–169.

Nutt, D.J., Glue, P., Lawson, C., & Wilson, S. (1990). Flumezenil provation of panic attacks. Evidence for altered benzodiazepine receptor sensitivity in panic disorder. *Archives of General Psychiatry, 47*, 917–925.

Pecknold, J.C., & Fleury, D. (1986). Alprazolam-induced manic episode in two patients with panic disorder. *American Journal of Psychiatry, 143*, 652–653.

Pecknold, J.C., Swinson, R.P., Kuch, K., & Lewis, C.P. (1988). Alprazolam in panic disorder and agoraphobia: Results from a multicenter trial: III. Discontinuation effects. *Archives of General Psychiatry, 45*, 429–436.

Pine, D., Weese-Mayer, D., Silvestri, J., Davies, M., Whitaker, A., & Klein, D. (1994). Anxiety and congenital central hypoventilation syndrome. *American Journal of Psychiatry, 151*, 864–870.

Pollack, M.H., Otto, M., Tesar, G.E., Cohen, L., Melter-Brody, S., & Rosenbaum, J. (1993). Long-term outcome after acute treatment with alphazolam or clonazepam for panic disorder. *Journal Clinical Psychopharmacology, 13*, 257–263.

Redmond, D.E. (1977). Alterations in the function of the locus coeruleus: A possible model for studies of anxiety. In I. Hannin & E. Usdin (Eds.), *Animal models in psychiatry and neurology*. New York: Pergamon Press.

Redmond, D.E. (1979). New and old evidence for the involvement of a brain norepinephrine system in anxiety. In W.E. Fann, A.D. Kokorny, & I. Karacan (Eds.), *Phenomenology and treatment of anxiety*. New York: Spectrum.

Redmond, D.E., & Huang, Y.M. (1979). Current concepts: II. New evidence for a locus coeruleus-norepinephrine connection with anxiety. *Life Science, 25*, 2149–2162.

Reich, J.H. (1988). *DMS-III* personality disorders and the outcome of treated panic disorder. *American Journal of Psychiatry, 145*, 1149–1152.

Reiman, E., Raichle, M., Robins, E., Butler, F.K., Herscovitch, P., Fox, P., & Perlmutter, J. (1986). The application of position emission tomography to the study of panic disorder. *American Journal of Psychiatry, 143*, 469–477.

Reiman, E., Raichle, M., Robins, E., Mintun, M., Fusselman, M., Fox, P., Price, J., & Hackman, K. (1989). Neuroanatomical correlates of a lactate-induced anxiety attack. *Archives of General Psychiatry, 46*, 493–500.

Rickels, K., Schweizer, E.E., Case, G., & Greenblatt, D. (1990). Long-term therapeutic use of benzodiazepines: I. Effects of abrupt discontinuation. *Archives of General Psychiatry, 47*, 899–907.

Rickels, K., Schweizer, E.E., Weiss, S., & Zavodnick, S. (1993). Maintenance drug treatment for panic disorder: II. Short and long-term outcome after drug taper. *Archives of General Psychiatry, 50*, 61–68.

Rizley, R., Kahn, R.J., McNair, D.M., & Frankenthaler, L.M. (1986). A comparison of alprozalam and imipramine in the treatment of agoraphobia and panic disorder. *Psychopharmacology Bulletin, 22,* 167–172.

Roy-Byrne, P., Cowley, D., Greenblatt, D., Shader, R., & Honner, D. (1990). Reduced benzodiazepine sensitivity in panic disorder. *Archives of General Psychiatry, 47,* 534–535.

Sanderson, W.C., Rapee, R.Y., & Barlow, D.H. (1989). The influence of an illusion of control on panic attacks induced via the inhalation 5.5 percent carbon dioxide-enriched air. *Archives of General Psychiatry, 46,* 157–162.

Schmidt, N., Telch, M., & Jaimez, T. (1996). Biological challenge manipulation of PCO_2: A test of Klein's (1993) suffocation alarm theory of panic. *Journal of Abnormal Psychology, 105,* 446–454.

Schneier, F., Liebowitz, M., Davies, S., Fairbanks, S., Mollender, E., Campeas, R., & Klein, D. (1990). Fluoxetine in panic disorder. *Journal of Clinical Psychopharmacology, 10,* 119–121.

Schweizer, E., Rickels, K., Case, G., & Greenblatt, D. (1990). Long-term therapeutic use of benzodiazepines: II. Effects of gradual taper. *Archives of General Psychiatry, 47,* 408–915.

Schweizer, E., Rickels, K., Weiss, S., & Zavodnick, S. (1993). Maintenance drug treatment of panic disorder: I. Results of a prospective, placebo-controlled comparison of alprazolam and imipramine. *Archives of General Psychiatry, 50,* 51–60.

Sheehan, D.V., Ballenger, J., & Jacobsen, G. (1980). Treatment of endogenous anxiety with phobic, hysterical and hypochondriacal symptoms. *Archives of General Psychiatry, 37,* 51–59.

Sheehan, D.V., Coleman, J.H., Greenblatt, D.J., Jones, K.J., Levine, P.H., Orsulak, P.J., Peterson, M., Schildkraut, J.J., Uzogare, E., & Watkins, D. (1984). Some biochemical correlates of panic attacks with agoraphobia and their response to a new treatment. *Journal of Clinical Psychopharmacology, 4,* 66–75.

Sheehan, D.V., Davidson, J., Manshrek, T., & Fleet, J. (1983). Lack of efficacy of a new antidepressant (buproprin) in the treatment of panic disorder with phobias. *Journal of Clinical Psychopharmacology, 3,* 28–31.

Solyom, C., Solyom, L., LaPierre, Y., Pecknold, J., & Morton, L. (1981). Phenelzine and exposure in the treatment of phobias. *Biological Psychiatry, 16,* 239–247.

Solyom, L., Heseltine, G.F.D., McClure, D.J., Solyom, C., Ledwidge, B., & Steinberg, G. (1973). Behavior therapy versus drug therapy in the treatment of neurosis. *Canadian Psychiatric Association Journal, 18,* 25–32.

Spiegel, D.A., & Bruce, T.J. (1997). Benzodiazepines and exposure-based cognitive behavioral therapies for panic disorder: Conclusions from combined treatment trials. *American Journal of Psychiatry, 154,* 773–781.

Swinson, R.P., Pecknold, J.C., & Kuch, K. (1986). Psychopharmacological treatment of panic disorder and related states: A placebo controlled study of alprazolam. *Progress in Neuro-psychopharmacology and Biological Psychiatry, 11,* 105–113.

Taylor, C.B., & Rachman, S. (1994). Klein's suffocation theory of panic. *Archives of General Psychiatry, 51,* 505–506.

Taylor, C.B., Sheikh, J., Agras, W.S., Roth, W.T., Margraf, J., Ehlers, A., Maddock, R.J., & Gossard, D. (1986). Ambulatory heart rate changes in patients with panic attacks. *American Journal of Psychiatry, 143,* 478–482.

Taylor, C.B., Woody, S., Koch, W., & McLean, P. (1996). Suffocation false alarms and efficacy of cognitive behavioral therapy for panic disorder. *Behavior Therapy, 27,* 115–126.

Telch, M.J., Agras, W.S., Taylor, C.B., Roth, W.T., & Gallen, C.C. (1985). Combined pharmacological and behavioral treatment for agoraphobia. *Behavior Therapy and Research, 23,* 325–335.

Tiffon, L., Coplan, J.D., Pepp, L.A., & Gorman, J.M. (1994). Augmentation strategies with tricyclic or fluoxetine treatment in seven partially responsive panic disorder patients. *Journal of Clinical Psychiatry, 55,* 66–69.

Tyrer, P., Candy, J., & Kelly, D. (1973). A study of the clinical effects of phenelzine and placebo in the treatment of phobic anxiety. *Psychopharmacologia, 32,* 237–254.

Uhde, T.W., Boulenger, J.P., Vittone, B.J., & Post, R.M. (1984). Historical and modern concepts of anxiety: A focus on adrenergic function. In J. Ballenger (Ed.), *Biology of agoraphobia.* Washington, DC: American Psychiatric Press.

Uhde, T.W., Stein, M., & Post, R. (1988). Lack of efficacy of carbamazepine in the treatment of panic disorder. *American Journal of Psychiatry, 145,* 1104–1109.

Uhde, T.W., Stein, M., Vittone, B.J., Siever, L., Boulenge, J.P., Klein, E., & Mellman, T. (1989). Behavioral and psysiologic effects of short-term and long-term administration of clonidine in panic disorder. *Archives of General Psychiatry, 46,* 170–177.

Van Vliet, I., Den Boer, J., Westenberg, H., & Slaap, B. (1996). A double-blind comparative study of lofepramine and fluvoxamine in outpatients with panic disorder. *Journal of Psychopharmacology, 16,* 299–306.

Westenberg, H., & Den Boer, J. (1989). Serotonin function in panic disorder: effect of L-5-hydroxytryptophan in patients and controls. *Psychopharmacology, 98,* 283–285.

Woods, J.H., Katz, J., & Winger, G. (1988). Use and abuse of benzodiazepines. Issues relevant to prescribing. *Journal of the American Medical Association, 260,* 3476–3480.

Woods, J.H., & Winger, G. (1995). Current benzodiazepine issues. *Psychopharmacology, 118,* 107–115.

Woods, S.W., Charney, D.S., Goodman, W.K., & Heninger, G.R. (1988). Carbon dioxide-induced anxiety: Behavioral, physiologic, and biochemical effects of carbon dioxide in patients with panic disorder and healthy subjects. *Archives of General Psychiatry, 45,* 43–52.

Woods, S.W., Charney, D.S., McPherson, C.A., Gradman, A.H., & Heninger, G.R. (1987). Situational panic attacks: Behavioral, physiologic, and biochemical characterization. *Archives of General Psychiatry, 44,* 365–375.

Zitrin, C.M., Klein, D.F., & Woerner, M.G. (1980). Treatment of agoraphobia with group exposure in-vivo and imipramine. *Archives of General Psychiatry, 37,* 63–73.

Zitrin, C.M., Klein, D.F., Woerner, M.G., & Ross, D.C. (1983). Treatment of phobias: I. Comparison of imipramine hydrochloride and placebo. *Archives of General Psychiatry, 40,* 125–138.

PART FOUR

SOCIAL PHOBIA

THIS SECTION contains excellent and thought-provoking chapters on cognitive behavioral, skills training, and pharmacological treatments for social phobia. It is one of only two sections of this book that does not contain a chapter on verbal psychotherapy. After consultation with a number of colleagues who are expert on verbal psychotherapies, we concluded that there was not a sufficiently well-defined psychotherapeutic approach for social phobia to justify a separate chapter. That is not to say that psychotherapists do not treat patients who present interpersonal fears and a sense of social inadequacy. To the contrary, we believe that it reflects the historical place of social phobia in the literature. As indicated by all three chapters in this section, social phobia has not received much attention until the past few years. It was variously assumed to be clinically unimportant, infrequent, or a manifestation of other, more significant pathology. Consequently, it was not subject to careful scientific scrutiny, and it was treated with procedures developed for other dysfunctions (e.g., benzodiazepines, systematic desensitization).

It has now become apparent that social phobia is a very common disorder that can cause substantial distress and disruption of daily functioning. It appears to have notable etiological and phenomenological differences from other anxiety disorders, which result in varied treatment needs. For example, monoamine oxiadase inhibitors (MAOIs) seem to be more effective than either antidepressants (which have proven effective in treating panic disorder) or beta blockers (which are useful in reducing performance anxiety). Similarly, exposure and cognitive therapy alone do not appear to be as effective as a combination of the two. Unfortunately, all three chapters emphasized the tentativeness of these conclusions. For example, both the Turk et al., chapter on cognitive behavior therapy and the Franklin et al., chapter on social skills underscore that overall outcomes for these behavioral approaches have been positive, but there are little data to document whether exposure, skills training, or cognitive change are sufficient and necessary for change to occur, or which combinations are the most effective. There simply have not been enough methodologically sound studies to allow for great confidence in treatment recommendations.

One factor that seems to have plagued the clinical trials has been inconsistency in diagnosis. Different studies have employed different populations of patients with some degree of social anxiety. This is especially true of the literature that antedates *DSM-III-R*. In many cases, it would seem to be impossible to compare trials conducted at different time periods between social phobia and the more common performance anxieties (e.g., fear associated with musical performance). Two other nosological distinctions are less clear-cut. First, there seem to be notable differences between the specific social phobias, such as fear of public speaking or of urination in public restrooms, and the generalized type, which is characterized by multiple social fears and avoidance. These two subgroups appear to have different responses to both pharmacological and behavioral interventions. It may be that the generalized type is etiologically different from the specific type; alternatively, it may simply be a more severe variation. In contrast, the case for pharmacotherapy seems to be clearer. As with other anxiety disorders and depression, specific seratonim reuptake inhibitors (SSRIs) appear to be established as a first-line treatment, with monoamine oxiadase inhibitors (MAOIs) and tricyclic antidepressants available for nonresponders.

Similar confusion pertains to the distinction between social phobia and avoidant personality disorder (APD). It seems illogical to have distinct nosological categories that exhibit the same phenomenology and respond to more or less the same treatments, especially in the absence of clear data on differences in etiology or course. It would seem to be critical to resolve these two diagnostic dilemmas if we are to conduct replicable treatment trials and develop effective interventions. Moreover, the entire issue of treatment for APD requires further study. Axis II disorders have characteristically been viewed as treatment resistant. It may be that effective treatments for this disorder will alter this conception; conversely, existence of an effective treatment may (tacitly or otherwise) remove the disorder from Axis II.

None of the three chapters discussed combined behavioral-pharmacological interventions at length. There are some data to suggest that pharmacotherapy has better short-term outcomes than behavioral treatments but that the latter produce better maintenance. However, these preliminary findings need to be replicated. Several trials are underway, and the forthcoming results should be telling. Overall, the current literature offers considerable promise for the development of effective treatments, but much more work is required.

CHAPTER 12

Cognitive Behavior Therapy

CYNTHIA L. TURK, DAVID M. FRESCO, and RICHARD G. HEIMBERG

CONCEPTUALIZATION
OF THE DISORDER

According to the fourth edition of the *Diagnostic and Statistical Manual of Mental Disorders (DSM-IV)* (American Psychiatric Association, 1994, p. 411), the essential feature of social phobia is "a marked and persistent fear of social or performance situations in which embarrassment may occur." Individuals with social phobia fear that their behavior will be judged by others to be inadequate (e.g., not knowing the right thing to say in a conversation) or that their anxiety symptoms (e.g., trembling hands, shaking voice) will be noticed by others, resulting in negative interpersonal evaluation. The situations feared may concern performance (e.g., public speaking, writing in public) or social interaction (e.g., having a conversation, interacting with a member of the opposite sex). The diagnosis of social phobia captures a heterogeneous group of patients in terms of number and types of situations feared and extent of impairment. Although an individual with social phobia may experience marked distress regarding one specific situation, such as eating in public, and otherwise exhibit satisfactory functioning, it is more common for individuals with social phobia to report fear and avoidance of multiple social situations (Holt, Heimberg, Hope, & Liebowitz, 1992; Turner, Beidel, Dancu, & Keys, 1986).

Social phobia was once thought to be a relatively rare disorder (APA, 1980). Recent epidemiological data, however, suggest that it is among the most prevalent of mental health problems. Based on the responses of over 13,000 people in four communities who participated in the Epidemiological Catchment Area (ECA) study, the lifetime prevalence rate of social phobia was reported to be 2.4 percent (Schneier, Johnson, Hornig, Liebowitz, & Weissman, 1992). However, respondents in the ECA study were asked about impairment resulting from only three situations relevant to social phobia. The more recent National

Comorbidity Survey (NCS), based on a stratified, multistage probability sample of over 8,000 noninstitutionalized individuals throughout the United States, inquired about fear and impairment in six social situations: public speaking, using public restrooms, eating or drinking in public, talking to other people, writing while being observed, and participating in a meeting, class, or going to a party (Walker & Stein, 1995). The NCS, which utilized *DSM-III-R* (APA, 1987) criteria, revealed a lifetime prevalence rate of 13.3 percent for social phobia, making it the third most common psychiatric disorder, exceeded only by major depressive disorder and alcohol dependence (Kessler et al., 1994).

Another study, which used the same interview as the NCS, reported a lifetime prevalence rate of 16 percent among 470 adults randomly sampled from Basle, Switzerland (Wacker, Müllejans, Klein, & Battegay, 1992). A fourth study, which assessed social anxiety in 526 adults randomly sampled from telephone directories in Winnipeg, Manitoba, revealed a point prevalence rate of 7.1 percent, similar to the 12-month rate of 7.9 percent reported in the NCS (Stein, Walker, & Forde, 1994). These respondents were surveyed about their level of anxiety in seven social situations. The authors concluded that prevalence rates for social phobia are largely determined by the diagnostic threshold set to determine distress or impairment and by the range of social situations assessed. Furthermore, studies focusing on severe cases or on a narrow range of social situations may underestimate the frequency of social phobia in the general population (Stein et al., 1994).

Social phobia is more common among women than among men in the general population (Kessler et al., 1994; Schneier et al., 1992). In clinical samples, however, the genders are more equally represented (Chapman, Mannuzza, & Fyer, 1995). Social phobia is typically reported to begin between early and late adolescence (see Hazen & Stein, 1995, Table 1.4, for a summary of studies of age at onset for social phobia). However, studies that report only average age of onset may obscure important information. A close examination of the ECA data reveals a bimodal distribution for age of onset, with peaks at younger than age 5 and at 11 to 15 years old (Juster, Brown, & Heimberg, 1996; Schneier et al., 1992).

Although social phobia is quite prevalent in the general population, it seems likely that many individuals avoid treatment because they fear scrutiny in the treatment setting, they view their anxiety as a fixed personality trait, or they believe their problems to be unsolvable (Heimberg & Barlow, 1988). As a result, many individuals with social phobia may not seek treatment until they suffer from additional problems, such as another anxiety disorder, depression, or substance abuse. In fact, in the ECA study, individuals with social phobia that was not complicated by any disorder other than dysthymia or simple phobia were no more likely to seek treatment than individuals without a psychiatric disorder (Schneier et al., 1992). Nevertheless, social phobia was associated with significant functional impairment. Persons with uncomplicated social phobia utilized medical services more frequently and were more likely be dependent on welfare or disability than individuals with no psychiatric disorder (Davidson, Hughes, George, & Blazer, 1993; Schneier et al., 1992). They are also less likely to be married (Schneier et al., 1992), they experience decreased educational and occupational achievement (Davidson et al., 1993; Liebowitz, Gorman, Fyer, & Klein, 1985; Schneier et al., 1994; Turner et al., 1986), they report impaired social functioning and social support (Davidson et al., 1993; Liebowitz et al., 1985; Schneier et al., 1994; Turner et al., 1986), and they judge their quality of life to be very low (Safren, Heimberg, Brown, & Holle, 1997).

We now briefly summarize a cognitive behavioral model of social phobia that integrates much of the previous work in social anxiety and social phobia (e.g., Beck & Emery, 1985; Buss, 1980; Clark & Wells, 1995; Heimberg & Barlow, 1988; Heimberg, Juster, Hope, & Mattia, 1995; Juster et al., 1996; Leary & Atherton, 1986). Individuals with social phobia possess the belief that some or all social situations are dangerous because of their potential for negative evaluation. Negative evaluation is perceived as leading to painful consequences, such as rejection, embarrassment, loss of social standing, and/or damaged self-esteem. For individuals with social phobia, the presence of other people (an audience) sets the cycle of anxiety in motion. For some, the feared audience may be colleagues watching them give a formal presentation. For others, it may be strangers who may incidentally observe them in public places. Individuals with social phobia construct a mental representation of how their behavior and appearance are perceived by the audience. This mental representation may be distorted in a number of ways, with flaws that are perceived as potential sources of negative evaluation being particularly salient. For example, individuals with social phobia judge their own performance as poor, regardless of its actual quality (Heimberg, Hope, Dodge, & Becker, 1990), and they overestimate the extent to which their anxiety is visible to others (Bruch, Gorsky, Collins, & Berger, 1989; McEwan & Devins, 1983). The mental representation of self as perceived by the audience shifts as a function of interpretations of internal feedback (e.g., feeling warm means "I'm blushing") and external feedback (e.g., the other person's expression means "I look foolish"). Moreover, individuals with social phobia preferentially allocate attentional resources to threatening social/evaluative information (Hope, Rapee, Heimberg, & Dombeck, 1990; Mattia, Heimberg, & Hope, 1993; McNeil et al., 1995), increasing the probability that they will detect negative or ambiguous cues from the social environment. In addition to monitoring how they are perceived by the audience, persons with social phobia also project the performance standard expected of them by the audience. The more they believe their performance and appearance fall short of their estimate of the audience's expectations, the more likely negative evaluation and its accompanying catastrophic consequences are predicted to be. The prediction of negative evaluation evokes behavioral, cognitive, and physical symptoms of anxiety. These symptoms then serve as information about how individuals are being perceived by the audience, which feeds back into the cycle of anxiety and competes with their abilities to attend to and function in the ongoing social situation, and so on, in a circular process. A fuller explication of this model is provided by Rapee and Heimberg (1997).

Although this formulation focuses on the maintenance of social anxiety, Rapee and Heimberg (1997) also address factors that may be important in the development of the core fear of negative evaluation seen in social phobia. They suggest that a genetic predisposition (see Fyer, Mannuzza, Chapman, Liebowitz, & Klein, 1993; Kendler, Neale, Kessler, Heath, & Eaves, 1992; Mannuzza et al., 1995) to interpret situations as threatening may be shaped by early life experiences into a specific sensitivity to negative social evaluation. Family factors potentially influential in this shaping process may include parental modeling of evaluation fears, restricted exposure to social interaction as a normative part of the family environment, use of shame as a disciplinary technique, and exposure to a distant but overprotective parenting style (Arrindell et al., 1989; Bruch & Heimberg, 1994; Bruch, Heimberg, Berger, & Collins, 1989). Early life difficulties with peers or dating partners may also exacerbate social fears (Bruch et al., 1989). These issues have been recently reviewed by Rapee (1997).

DIAGNOSTIC ISSUES AND PROBLEMS

As previously noted, the diagnosis of social phobia captures a heterogeneous group of patients in terms of the nature of their social fears and their overall functionality. In this section, we review the research examining various subgroups of individuals within the larger diagnostic category of social phobia. Furthermore, we present issues relating to differential diagnosis as well as comorbidity and its implications.

SOCIAL PHOBIA SUBTYPES AND AVOIDANT PERSONALITY DISORDER

DSM-III originally described social phobia as a specific fear of being embarrassed, humiliated, and scrutinized by others in one to two performance-oriented social situations. However, research and clinical experience suggested that individuals who experience fear in a limited number of situations actually represent a small subset of individuals with social phobia who present for treatment. More commonly, these individuals endorse multiple fears (Liebowitz, et al., 1985; Turner et al., 1986). In response to these findings, the *DSM-III-R* differentiated two main subgroups of individuals with social phobia. The *generalized* type (GSP) was to be specified when most social situations are feared. Although some researchers have advocated other subtyping schemes (see Heimberg, Holt, Schneier, Spitzer, & Liebowitz, 1993), the *DSM-IV* retained this dichotomous subtyping system. Persons whose fears do not extend to most social situations were grouped together into the *nongeneralized* subtype (non-GSP) of social phobia, "a heterogeneous group that includes persons who fear a single performance situation as well as those who fear several, but not most, social situations" (APA, 1994, p. 413). Non-GSP was not further divided, because the *DSM-IV* work group on social phobia judged that there was insufficient empirical justification to do so (Schneier et al., 1996).

Individuals with GSP and non-GSP have been reliably differentiated on a number of demographic and clinical features. On demographic variables, Heimberg, Hope, et al. (1990) found that individuals with GSP were younger, less educated, and more likely to be unemployed than individuals with non-GSP.

Similarly, individuals with GSP are more often single and have an earlier age of onset than individuals with non-GSP (Mannuzza et al., 1995). On a variety of self-report indices, individuals with GSP subtype endorse higher levels of depression, social anxiety, avoidance, and fear of negative evaluation (Brown, Heimberg, & Juster, 1995; Turner, Beidel, & Townsley, 1992).

The subtypes of social phobia have also been differentiated on clinician-rated distress and impairment. Clinicians in Turner et al. (1992) rated individuals with GSP higher on the Hamilton (1959) Anxiety Scale and the Clinical Global Impressions Scale (Guy, 1976). Similarly, Herbert, Hope, and Bellack (1992) reported that individuals with GSP had significantly lower Global Assessment of Functioning scores than individuals with the non-GSP subtype. Individuals with GSP also received more concurrent Axis I and Axis II diagnoses as assessed with a structured diagnostic interview.

Heimberg, Hope, et al. (1990) compared patients with GSP to patients with non-GSP (with a specific fear of public speaking) during a behavior test that was individualized to reflect a salient fear of each patient. Individuals with GSP and non-GSP did not differ on their self-ratings of anxiety or quality of performance. However, independent assessors rated individuals with GSP as more anxious during the task and more functionally impaired than individuals with non-GSP. The two groups also demonstrated very different patterns of heart-rate reactivity to the behavior test. Individuals with non-GSP exhibited a sharp increase in heart rate (+20 bpm) during the first minute of the task that gradually fell, but never returned, to baseline. Individuals with GSP experienced a small increase in heart rate (+5 bpm) that was sustained throughout the task. The pattern of findings led Heimberg, Hope, et al. (1990) to conclude that GSP may be characterized by objectively worse performance, whereas individuals with non-GSP may be characterized by a negative cognitive bias and more extreme physiological reactivity.

Heimberg, Hope, et al. (1990) individualized the behavior test for each participant. Hence, it did not represent a standardized behavioral challenge, and differences in the test situations may have accounted for a portion of the differences between persons with GSP and non-GSP. Levin et al. (1993) overcame this difficulty by administering a standard public speaking test to all participants. Similar to Heimberg, Hope, et al., coders rated persons with GSP as more anxious during the behavior test. Greater heart-rate reactivity was again demonstrated in non-GSP, albeit with a different pattern. Individuals with non-GSP exhibited acute increases in heart rate, during a baseline phase, that gradually declined over the course of the behavior test. In contrast to Heimberg, Hope, et al., individuals with GSP reported more anxiety during the task than individuals with non-GSP. Finally, Levin et al. assessed participants on a series of biochemical indices (e.g., cortisol, epinephrine, and norepinephrine) but failed to demonstrate differences between groups. In summary, except for the cardiac reactivity findings presented above, most subtyping studies support the notion that social phobia subtypes differ by degree rather than in kind.

In much the way that non-GSP and GSP have been examined, so have differences between social phobia and avoidant personality disorder (APD). Like social phobia, APD first appeared as a diagnostic category in *DSM-III*. Social phobia was more narrowly defined than in later editions of the *DSM*, and severe interpersonal anxiety was classified as APD rather than social phobia. In *DSM-III-R*, the rules were changed so that diagnoses of social phobia and APD could be given to the same person, and the diagnostic criteria for both disorders became more similar. The core disturbance of APD was changed to an extreme fear of negative evaluation rather than discomfort in interpersonal relationships. The diagnosis of APD could now be earned by meeting four of seven criteria rather than five of five (Heimberg, 1996). In the *DSM-IV*, the core feature remains a "pervasive pattern of social inhibition, feelings of inadequacy, and hypersensitivity to negative evaluation . . ." (p. 664). These changes to the diagnostic criteria for APD, as well as the evolution of the social phobia criteria already described, have led researchers to question whether the two diagnostic entities represent distinct disorders or whether they represent the same disorder differing only in degree. Indeed, research supports the position that social phobia and APD belong on a continuum that has been artificially separated at the boundary between Axis I and Axis II (Heimberg, 1996). Individuals with APD almost always have a diagnosis of social phobia, whereas many individuals with social phobia do not also have APD (Widiger, 1992). Individuals with GSP (median = 58%) are more likely than individuals with non-GSP (median = 18%) to also meet criteria for avoidant personality disorder (Heimberg, 1996). Most investigators have concluded, as did Holt, Heimberg, and Hope (1992), that the co-occurrence of GSP and APD describes those persons with the most severe social phobias and the poorest global functioning. For example, individuals with both GSP and APD report greater depression and have a larger number of additional diagnoses (Feske, Perry, Chambless, Renneberg, & Goldstein, 1996; Johnson & Lydiard, 1995).

DIFFERENTIAL DIAGNOSIS

One difficulty in arriving at a reliable diagnosis of social phobia is the similarity of symptoms within the anxiety and mood disorders. The anxiety disorders share overlapping features (e.g., fear and avoidance), whereas social phobia and depression may both be characterized by social withdrawal. However, a number of factors have been shown to reliably differentiate social phobia from other disorders. These factors include differences in the nature and number of feared situations, differences in specific symptoms of anxiety, and differences on demographic variables, such as age of onset and gender.

Panic Disorder (and/or Agoraphobia)

Like social phobia, individuals suffering from panic disorder with agoraphobia may avoid both social and performance situations. However, they avoid situations for fear of having a spontaneous panic attack and being unable to obtain help in that situation, not specifically for fear of negative evaluation (Ball, Otto, Pollack, & Uccello, 1995; Heckelman & Schneier, 1995; Mannuzza, Fyer, Liebowitz, & Klein, 1990). Hazen and Stein (1995) describe the ways in which social phobia and panic disorder may differ. Individuals with either disorder may suffer from panic attacks. In social phobia, these attacks are situationally bound and occur when entering or anticipating a feared social situation. By contrast, in panic disorder, there is a history of at least one unexpected attack, and subsequent attacks do not occur exclusively in social situations. Second, individuals with social phobia and panic disorder differ in the content of their thoughts. In social phobia, the content of automatic thoughts revolves around fear of embarrassment and negative evaluation whereas, in panic disorder, the thoughts center on fear of catastrophic consequences such as a heart attack, death, or loss of control. Third, a review of epidemiological studies suggests that social phobia has an earlier age of onset than panic disorder (early to middle adolescence versus mid-20s; Hazen & Stein, 1995).

In one study examining the specific fears of 140 patients with a primary anxiety disorder (agoraphobia, social phobia, or simple phobia), individuals with social phobia reported significantly higher levels of distress on five items (being teased; entering a room with other people seated; being with a person of the opposite sex; strangers; and being watched while working) from the Wolpe (1983) Fear Survey (Stravynski, Basoglu, Marks, & Sengun, 1995). Individuals with agoraphobia scored higher on 14 items whose content dealt with being alone, travel, physiological sensations, and the prospect of surgery. Regardless of the specific nature of the fears, individuals with social phobia endorsed fewer items than agoraphobics (Stravynski et al., 1995). Finally, anxiety symptoms can also reliably differentiate social phobia from panic disorder (with or without agoraphobia). Individuals with social phobia are more likely to endorse certain symptoms, particularly those that can be observed by others, such as blushing, muscle twitching (Amies, Gelder, & Shaw, 1983), dry mouth (Reich, Noyes, & Yates, 1988), trembling, and sweating (Gorman & Gorman, 1987), whereas individuals with panic disorder tend to experience dizziness, palpitations, chest pain, breathing problems, ringing in the ears, blurred vision, numbness, feeling faint, and a fear of dying (Amies et al., 1983; Hazen & Stein, 1995; Reich et al., 1988).

Generalized Anxiety Disorder (GAD)

Despite having clearly articulated diagnostic criteria, GAD and social phobia share clinical features that complicate differential diagnosis. For example, individuals with GAD report higher levels of social anxiety than individuals with any anxiety disorder other than social phobia (Rapee, Sanderson, & Barlow, 1988). Similar to persons with GAD, individuals with social phobia devote excessive time to worrying and ruminating about social situations. In contrast to persons with social phobia, however, individuals with GAD spend excessive time in uncontrollable worry that is not exclusive to social situations. Rather, a hallmark feature of worry in GAD is heightened focus on possible catastrophic consequences across several domains of one's life. An examination of the anxiety symptoms reported by individuals with social phobia versus GAD has also been successful in differentiating these disorders. Individuals with social phobia report more frequent occurrence of sweating, flushes, and breathing problems, whereas individuals with GAD report more frequent occurrences of headaches and fear of dying (Cameron, Thyer, Nesse, & Curtis, 1986; Reich et al., 1988). Further, individuals with GAD suffer from insomnia more than individuals with social phobia (Versiani, Mundim, Nardi, & Liebowitz, 1988). Still, differences on these anxiety symptoms may not be sufficient to reliably differentiate social phobia from GAD in a clinical setting (Heckelman & Schneier, 1995). Additional research is needed to more sensitively differentiate social phobia and GAD.

Depression

The social withdrawal common to mood disorders can resemble the behavioral avoidance that occurs frequently in anxiety disorders. A clinician must probe to determine if social avoidance/withdrawal occurs because of low energy or anhedonia (i.e., depression) or because of fear of negative evaluation (i.e., social phobia). One telling difference is that individuals with social phobia feel that they would be more comfortable in social situations if they could overcome their fear of negative evaluation, whereas depressed individuals maintain that they lack the energy or desire to engage others in social contact (Heckelman & Schneier, 1995).

DIAGNOSTIC COMORBIDITY AND TREATMENT COMPLICATIONS

Social phobia commonly co-occurs with other disorders, and it typically predates the onset of the comorbid disorder (Davidson et al., 1993; Schneier et al., 1992). Among individuals with social phobia examined in the ECA study, the comorbid disorders with the highest lifetime prevalence rates were simple phobia (59%), agoraphobia (45%), alcohol abuse (19%), major depression (17%), drug abuse (13%), and dysthymia (13%) (Schneier et al., 1992).

A number of studies have suggested that social phobia complicates the onset, course, and treatment of other disorders. The comorbidity of social phobia and alcohol abuse has received attention because individuals with social phobia may begin to abuse alcohol in an attempt to self-medicate anxiety symptoms (see Kushner, Sher, & Beitman, 1990, for a review of the relationship between alcohol problems and anxiety disorders). Elevated rates of social phobia have been found among alcoholics (Chambless, Cherney, Caputo, & Rheinstein, 1987; Mullaney & Trippett, 1979; Smail, Stockwell, Canter, & Hodgson, 1984), and research suggests that a significant percentage of individuals with social phobia abuse alcohol (Amies et al., 1983; Schneier, Martin, Liebowitz, Gorman, & Fyer, 1989; Thyer et al., 1986). Among individuals with comorbid social phobia and substance abuse, social phobia may interfere with treatment in traditional chemical dependence programs, given that interventions in these programs are typically administered in group formats. Furthermore, avoidance of aftercare appointments or Alcoholics Anonymous or Narcotics Anonymous meetings due to social anxiety may increase the probability of relapse following treatment. However, these issues await empirical research.

Two studies offer initial evidence that social phobia (or social anxiety) has significant consequences for survivors of trauma. Orsillo, Heimberg, Juster, and Garrett (1996) reported that 32 percent of combat veterans with posttraumatic stress disorder (PTSD) had a comorbid diagnosis of social phobia. They were also more likely than combat veterans without PTSD to meet criteria for social phobia. Further, heightened social anxiety was predicted by an inhospitable homecoming from Vietnam. Social phobia may also be a serious complication to the treatment of combat-related PTSD, because this treatment often involves self-disclosure of negative aspects of one's self in a group setting. Similar findings have been reported among women who have survived sexual assault and rape (Brown, 1996). Women with elevated levels of social anxiety prior to rape endorsed higher levels of depression and PTSD symptoms, reported telling fewer people about the rape, and were more likely to judge the reactions of the people they did tell as negative (Brown, 1996). Thus, social anxiety may interfere with a rape survivor's willingness or ability to disclose the details of a rape to confidants or service providers.

Finally, results from a large cross-cultural study that pooled data from four international sites (USA, Edmonton, Puerto Rico, Korea) suggest that the presence of social phobia increases the likelihood of a suicide attempt in individuals with any psychiatric disorder (Weissman et al., 1996). Log odds ratios ranged from 1.9 (USA) to 4.1 (Korea).

TREATMENT STRATEGIES

The literature on cognitive-behavioral approaches to the treatment of social phobia has grown rapidly since 1980. Although social phobia is now known to be a chronic and debilitating disorder, there is growing evidence that it can be treated effectively in a limited time frame and that treatment gains may be maintained. Many recent studies focus on the efficacy of treatments that include exposure to phobic stimuli combined with cognitive restructuring techniques. In this section, we will provide a rationale for the use of exposure and cognitive restructuring in the treatment of social phobia and describe cognitive-behavior group therapy (CBGT), our treatment protocol, which integrates these techniques. We will review the literature supporting the efficacy of CBGT and report on other studies examining the effectiveness of exposure and cognitive restructuring techniques in the treatment of social phobia. Because of space limitations, readers are referred to Heimberg and Juster (1995) for a more detailed and thorough critical analysis of many of the studies presented here.

Long recognized as the most effective treatment of specific phobias, agoraphobia, and obsessive-compulsive disorder (Barlow & Wolfe, 1981), exposure techniques have been increasingly used in the treatment of social phobia. As with other anxiety disorders, exposure exercises are typically conducted according to a hierarchy, proceeding from least to most anxiety-provoking social situation. According to a habituation model, repeated, prolonged exposure to phobic stimuli can be expected to result in anxiety reduction. However, it has been hypothesized that exposure alone may not be sufficient in the treatment of social phobia, because the core feature of the disorder is essentially a cognitive construct (fear of negative evaluation) and because many individuals with social phobia report the persistence of anxiety, despite regularly confronting feared social situations (Butler, 1985). This hypothesis is controversial but consistent with the previously presented cognitive-behavioral model of social phobia, in which negative cognitions play a primary role in the maintenance of social fears.

THE CBGT PROTOCOL

CBGT incorporates both exposure and cognitive techniques (see Heimberg et al., 1995, or Hope & Heimberg, 1993, for more detailed discussions of CBGT procedures). CBGT has three principal components: within-session exposure exercises, cognitive restructuring before and after the within-session exposure exercises, and homework assignments for in vivo exposures, which explicitly incorporate cognitive restructuring skills learned in group. It has been most commonly conducted in a format of 12 weekly sessions of two to two and one-half hours each. The groups are comprised of four to seven patients, with six considered to be an optimal number to allow adequate individual attention and a reasonable group size if dropouts or absences occur. Group composition is balanced in terms of age, gender, and subtype of social phobia. Ideally, a man and a woman serve as cotherapists in order to provide maximum flexibility in constructing within-session exposure exercises.

The first two sessions of CBGT are largely didactic in nature, giving patients time to habituate to the group setting before formal exposure exercises are introduced. During these sessions, patients are given a cognitive-behavioral explanation of social phobia, provided with a rationale for the three components of treatment, and introduced to cognitive restructuring concepts through a series of structured exercises. Patients begin to expose themselves to speaking within the group setting by briefly talking about themselves, stating their primary social fears, declaring their treatment goals, and contributing to discussions during cognitive restructuring exercises.

The remaining sessions are primarily devoted to within-group exposure exercises integrated with cognitive restructuring work. Prior to each session, the therapists generate several possible exposures for each patient, based on the individual's treatment goals and hierarchy of feared social situations. The situation selected is typically one that has been rated as 50 or greater by the patient on a 0 to 100 anxiety scale. Three patients are selected to be the focus of exposure exercises each week. For patients not participating in an exposure exercise, homework is reviewed. For the remainder of the session, they contribute to cognitive restructuring discussions, provide feedback and support, and, in later groups, serve as role players. They also benefit from observing other group members model cognitive coping skills and continued performance despite anxiety.

A specific exposure exercise begins with one of the therapists proposing a situation for attention (e.g., a conversation with a coworker at the coffee machine). The patient is given an opportunity to provide additional information to make the situation more personally relevant and realistic. The patient is then asked to identify automatic thoughts that come to mind as the patient thinks about the situation, and these thoughts are recorded on a newsprint easel. With the assistance of the other patients, the target patient labels the cognitive distortions in the thoughts, poses a series of questions to dispute each one, and develops an overall rational response. Therapists and group members then assist the patient in developing nonperfectionistic, behavioral goals (e.g., "I will ask the other person five questions and state one personal opinion," as opposed to "I will have a conversation with this person without anxiety").

The typical duration of an exposure exercise is 10 minutes, although therapists may use clinical judgment to either extend or shorten a role play. During the first few exposure exercises, one of the therapists serves as the role-play partner. The other therapist prompts the patient to give anxiety ratings and to repeat the rational response aloud each minute. This therapist also monitors the patient's progress toward the behavioral goals (e.g., by counting the number of questions the patient asks). During later sessions, other patients and additional clinic staff are incorporated into exposure exercises. Upon its conclusion, the therapists debrief the patient about the exposure. The patient is asked whether the agreed-upon goals were achieved. Feedback regarding goal attainment is provided by the therapist who monitored the role play (e.g., the patient asked eight questions and offered three personal opinions). In this postprocessing, the therapists are careful not to allow the patient to disqualify attainment of behavioral goals or to substitute perfectionistic, anxiety-focused goals. Therapists also turn to other group members for further validation of their feedback and use the postprocessing as an opportunity to draw parallels between patients. The pattern of minute-by-minute anxiety ratings is reviewed and discussed (pattern of declining anxiety over time, anxiety increased when there was a pause in the conversation, anxiety declined when the patient used cognitive coping skills, etc.). The patient is asked to asses the effectiveness of the rational response and whether any new automatic thoughts surfaced during the role play. Lastly, the patient is asked what was learned from the exposure.

Therapists work with patients at the end of each session to develop homework assignments for the next week. Patients are encouraged to expose themselves to real-life social situations similar to the ones role played in group. Engaging in the assigned exposure activity is only part of the homework. Using written instructions, patients complete a preexposure cognitive restructuring routine similar to the one conducted in group. Written instructions are also used to assist patients in conducting a rational self-analysis after the in vivo exposure has ended.

Case Illustration

Several reports of the treatment of individual patients who participated in CBGT have previously been published (see Heimberg & Juster, 1994; Heimberg et al., 1995; Hope & Heimberg, 1990, 1993, 1994). In the interest of space, we refer readers to these sources for complete discussion of the clinical application of CBGT. Herein, we provide a summary of the treatment of one such case (Heimberg et al., 1995).

Bob was a 50-year-old, married man with an eleventh-grade education. He was financially successful, owning and operating a successful mechanical contracting firm. As owner, Bob was responsible for the conduct of numerous meetings, and it was this aspect of his life that precipitated his request for treatment. He experienced extreme anxiety in these almost-daily meetings and put them off whenever possible. Bob reported a history of public speaking fears present since grade school, but he had no history of previous treatment. It appeared that any situation in which Bob was (or anticipated being) the center of attention induced significant anxiety. In the first two sessions of CBGT, in which structured exercises are employed to help patients identify their negative cognitions and how these thoughts affect their anxiety, Bob identified the thoughts that he would be anxious, that his audience would detect this anxiety, and that they would view him negatively as a result. He feared that his anxiety would be evident in blushing, that his voice would crack, and that he would not be able to think clearly. As a result, the meeting would not go well, and he would be overwhelmed by the realization that he had performed incompetently in front of his employees. He was afraid that he would be viewed as an impostor, someone who did not belong because of his limited education.

Over the course of the remaining sessions, Bob was the target of several in-group exposure exercises, and these were followed by homework assignments related to the conduct of meetings at work. He also participated in the exposure exercises of other patients and learned much about this process by helping others before he was very able to apply the concepts to himself. His exposure exercises progressed from (1) carrying on a conversation with two other people, in which he was the center of attention as he spoke to them about a topic with which he felt comfortable (fishing), (2) making an extemporaneous presentation to the therapy group about his business, (3) reading a story aloud from a popular magazine, (4) conducting a meeting within the group that was similar to one of the meetings at work after preparing to do so during the week between sessions, and (5) conducting another meeting of this type without prior preparation.

In cognitive restructuring activities prior to the first exposure, Bob was provided with a list of questions with which to dispute the negative cognitions just described and the additional thought, "Anxiety equals failure," which was identified at that time. On the basis of this disputation effort, he developed rational alternative thoughts: "It's OK to be anxious" and "It's OK to be average." As we have stated elsewhere (Hope & Heimberg, 1990), although these responses may have the flavor of a cliché, they are the product of great struggle on the part of the patient to cast off old beliefs and are often regarded by the patient as new and radical ideas. Bob was also asked to establish specific behavioral goals for the exercise, which would not depend on the absence of anxiety or of normal human speech dysfluencies. He suggested that he would be able to answer six questions asked of him by the other role players and ask three questions of his own. In fact, he answered 18 questions and asked six. His anxiety ratings began at 75 (on a 0 to 100 scale) and reached a low of 30 after seven minutes. Bob learned that he could converse with others despite initially high anxiety and that his attempts at cognitive coping seemed to break the viscious circle of his negative thoughts, thereby helping him to keep anxiety at more manageable levels.

In preparation for his second exposure, Bob identified the thought that he would forget to tell the audience something important and that this would have serious consequences, both for their evaluation of him and for their safety on the job. Cognitive restructuring activities were focused on normalizing his expectation of perfect performance and decatastrophizing the impact of imperfect performances. Behavioral goals were again negotiated, and easily surpassed during the role play. Anxiety diminished to manageable levels after an early spike.

Because Bob exhibited some difficulty in organizing his thoughts for presentation, his next two exposures provided more structure, first by giving him something specific to read, second by giving him time to prepare his materials before the group session. In preparation for the reading, he noted that he would lose his place and pause, and that pauses would be taken as inappropriate. Cognitive restructuring activities were focused on these ideas. Countering ideas were raised about the possibility that someone who pauses might be perceived as thoughtful and that pauses are commonly observed in the speeches of political figures. The reading and the structured presentation exercises were completed successfully, but Bob's anxiety appeared to decrease more slowly than it had in previous exercises. Postprocessing of the structured presentation exercise revealed a hidden goal of not being nervous and the subsequent disqualification of some of his recent success. Feedback from group members was solicited about the degree of anxiety that they could perceive and what effect it had on their evaluations of Bob, and these appeared to be quite helpful. In his next exposure exercise, he conducted a similar meeting without preparation and was able to do so with substantially lower anxiety levels.

Bob also completed a number of homework assignments during the course of the 12-week program. In the first few weeks, these assignments involved the monitoring of thoughts, identification of cognitive distortions in the thoughts, and disputation and formulation of rational responses. Thereafter, homework assignments involved the application of cognitive coping skills to the conduct of meetings in the workplace, which Bob was able to do more and more regularly and with decreasing anxiety. Thereafter, Bob's group also received six monthly sessions of booster cognitive behavior treatment, and this focus was continued.

Bob's progress through treatment was assessed with structured interview, self-report, and behavioral measures, the details of which are described in Heimberg et al. (1995). At the end of the booster sessions, an independent assessor determined that Bob no longer met criteria for social phobia, his self-reported anxiety was substantially reduced, and a behavioral test in which he gave maximal ratings before treatment was completed with little distress. In real life, Bob also did well. He conducted meetings at regular intervals without overwhelming anxiety. He never came to look forward to these meetings, but they were no longer a source of distress, and anxiety was no longer viewed as a weakness.

REVIEW OF THE CBGT LITERATURE

Heimberg, Becker, Goldfinger, and Vermilyea (1985) reported on the efficacy of an early version of CBGT, differing from the current version primarily in that it included imaginal exposure in addition to the techniques described above. Using a multiple baseline design, Heimberg et al. (1985) demonstrated that six of seven patients with *DSM-III* social phobia achieved significant posttreatment improvement on self-report, behavioral, and physiological measures of anxiety and maintained these gains over three- and six-month follow-up periods. In the next study, CBGT was compared to educational-supportive group therapy (ES) in the treatment of 49 patients with *DSM-III* social phobia (Heimberg, Dodge, et al., 1990). ES, a therapy consisting of lectures, discussions, and support, was developed to serve as a control for therapist attention, credibility of the treatment rationale, and positive outcome expectations. In fact, patient ratings of treatment credibility and outcome expectations were similar for CBGT and ES. Following treatment, 75 percent of CBGT patients were classified as having made significant improvement by clinical assessors, compared to 40 percent of ES patients. CBGT patients also reported less anxiety before and during an individualized behavior test than ES patients. Both groups showed similar improvement over baseline on self-report measures. Six-month follow-up assessments revealed an attenuation of posttreatment improvement on self-report measures for ES patients; however, CBGT patients maintained their gains on self-report measures and remained more improved than ES patients on assessor and behavior test anxiety ratings. The superiority of CBGT over ES has been replicated in a sample of patients with *DSM-III-R* social phobia (Lucas & Telch, 1993). In this study, CBGT, ES, and an individual version of the CBGT protocol (ICBT) were compared. Patients treated with CBGT and ICBT made similar treatment gains, both superior to ES.

Nineteen patients who received treatment in the Heimberg, Dodge, et al. (1990) study participated in a long-term follow-up (Heimberg, Salzman, Holt, & Blendell, 1993). The interval between treatment and follow-up ranged from 4.5 to 6.25 years. Although follow-up participants were originally less impaired than nonparticipants, no pretreatment differences were found between CBGT and ES patients in the follow-up sample. At long-term follow-up, 89 percent of CBGT patients were classified as no longer exhibiting significant impairment according to independent assessor ratings, compared to 44 percent of ES patients. Furthermore, compared to ES patients, CBGT patients reported less social anxiety and were rated by independent judges as less anxious and more socially skilled during an individualized behavior test.

Hope, Heimberg, and Bruch (1995) conducted a comparative study of CBGT to Exposure Alone (EA) and a waiting-list control. EA was conducted in that same format as CBGT but with material relevant to a habituation model of exposure replacing cognitive restructuring activities. CBGT and EA produced equivalent treatment credibility and group cohesion ratings. At posttreatment, CBGT and EA were superior to the waiting-list control on independent assessor ratings, self-report measures, and ratings of performance quality during a behavioral test. Contrary to expectations, both CBGT and EA patients made improvements on cognitive measures, with CBGT patients showing no clear advantage. Furthermore, although not statistically significant, only 36 percent of CGBT patients were judged by an independent assessor to have achieved subclinical levels of social anxiety at posttreatment, compared to 70 percent of EA patients. Therefore, CBGT was less effective in this study than in those reviewed above. Attrition was five times greater for CBGT than EA, although this was not a significant difference. Hope et al. (1995a) speculated that the reduced efficacy of CBGT might have been the result of a disruption of group process due to CBGT attrition, which, in most cases, was unrelated to therapy.

Three studies compare the efficacy of CBGT to that of pharmacological interventions. Gelernter et al. (1991) compared CBGT to alprazolam, phenelzine, and pill placebo in the treatment of 65 patients with *DSM-III* social phobia. All groups exhibited significant improvement at posttreatment on self-report measures of anxiety and cognitive self-statements. This study, however, is limited by its exclusive reliance on self-report for comparisons of the four treatments, the emphasis in the medication conditions on self-directed exposure (which may have been the active element of the treatments), and the fact that CBGT was conducted in groups of 10, allowing less time for individual attention than the typical group size of six.

CBGT was compared to clonazepam in a recently completed study of 45 patients with *DSM-III-R* social phobia (Otto et al., 1997). Similar improvements were observed in each group on self-report measures and clinician ratings at weeks 4 and 8. At posttreatment (week 12), both groups were significantly improved over baseline, but clonazepam showed a slight advantage over CBGT on three self-report measures. Unfortunately, the interpretation of this difference is complicated by attrition of relatively more impaired clonazepam patients between the 8-week and 12-week assessments. Using more conservative criteria than in other CBGT studies, independent assessor ratings classified 20 percent of clonazepam and 25 percent of CBGT patients who began treatment as being in remission at posttreatment.

The largest study of the comparative efficacy of CBGT and pharmacotherapy for social phobia was conducted by Heimberg and Liebowitz (Heimberg et al., 1998; Liebowitz et al., 1997). One hundred thirty-three patients from two study sites were randomly assigned to CBGT, phenelzine, pill placebo, or ES (the attention-control condition devised by Heimberg, Dodge, et al., 1990), and 107 patients completed 12 weeks of treatment. At posttest, independent assessors classified 21/28 CBGT patients (75%) and 20/26 phenelzine patients (77%) as having made clinically significant response (58%, 65%, respectively, if dropouts are counted as treatment failures). These rates surpassed those achieved by either control condition and did not differ from each other. However, phenelzine patients achieved their response more quickly, as demonstrated by their superior showing at an assessment conducted after six weeks of treatment, and they were also significantly more improved than CBGT patients on some measures after 12 weeks. Thereafter, only patients who showed a positive response to CBGT or phenelzine were continued through six additional months of maintenance treatment and a 6-month follow-up. At the end of these additional phases, 50 percent of previously-responding phenelzine patients had relapsed, compared to only 17 percent of patients who had received CBGT. The difference in relapse between treatments was especially pronounced for patients with generalized social phobia. The overall pattern of results suggests that phenelzine might have slightly greater immediate efficacy, but that CBGT may confer greater protection against relapse. The combination of these two treatments has not yet been evaluated although a study by our research group is currently addressing this question.

FACTORS INFLUENCING CBGT OUTCOME

Several studies have examined the influence of social phobia subtype and APD on response to CBGT. Individuals with generalized social phobia appear to begin and end treatment more impaired than individuals with nongeneralized social phobia; however, both subtypes exhibit similar degrees of improvement over the course of treatment (Brown et al., 1995; Hope, Herbert, & White, 1995). These results suggest that patients with generalized social phobia may require additional therapy time in order to overcome their anxiety. Furthermore, individuals with and without a comorbid diagnosis of APD have been shown to make similar treatment gains (Brown et al., 1995; Hope, Herbert, et al., 1995). Thus, APD does not appear to identify a subtype of social anxiety which is especially resistant to treatment, as typically implied by a diagnosis of a personality disorder. In fact, Brown et al. (1995) found that 47 percent of patients with a comorbid diagnosis of APD before treatment no longer qualified for that diagnosis after treatment.

Other factors that may affect CBGT outcomes have been examined. Homework is typically viewed as an integral component of cognitive-behavior therapy. In CBGT, homework primarily involves practice of cognitive coping skills and exposure to real-life social situations. Homework compliance has been associated with positive outcomes at posttreatment (Leung & Heimberg, 1996) and six-month follow-up (Edelman & Chambless, 1995). Likelihood of homework compliance has not been found to be associated with level of pretreatment social anxiety (Edelman & Chambless, 1995; Leung & Heimberg, 1996) or with pretreatment perceptions of control over outcomes (Leung & Heimberg, 1996).

Expectancies that patients with social phobia have about their ability to benefit from CBGT have also been examined (Safren, Heimberg, & Juster, 1997). Positive expectancies predicted better treatment response, even after accounting for pretreatment severity. Lower expectancies were associated with longer duration of social phobia and poorer pretreatment functioning according to clinician ratings and self-reports of anxiety and depression. Safren, Heimberg, and Juster (1997) suggest that the modification of negative expectancies should be a priority early in treatment because of their association with poorer outcomes.

Woody, Chambless, and Glass (1997) examined changes in self-focused attention over the course of CBGT and corresponding changes in symptoms of social anxiety. CBGT was modified to incorporate two strategies intended to decrease self-focused attention: training in diaphragmatic breathing and instruction in increasing attention to external stimuli. Patients were significantly improved following treatment according to six composite measures of outcome. Self-focused attention significantly decreased over time. Reductions in self-focused attention were not accompanied by increases in attention to external stimuli but were associated with reductions in social interaction anxiety and negative self-assessment. For the subset of patients who primarily suffered from public speaking fears, reductions in self-focused attention were strongly related to decreases in speech anxiety.

OVERVIEW OF OTHER COGNITIVE-BEHAVIOR TREATMENTS

A number of cognitive-behavioral approaches have proven efficacious in the treatment of social phobia. Rational-emotive therapy (RET; Ellis, 1962) and variations of RET have been shown to be effective in several studies (e.g., Emmelkamp, Mersch, Vissia, & van der Helm, 1985; Kanter & Goldfried, 1979; Mersch, Emmelkamp, Bögels, & van der Sleen, 1989; Scholing & Emmelkamp, 1993a, 1993b). In RET, patients are taught to view social situations as activating events that trigger beliefs that have emotional and behavioral consequences. Therapy then focuses on helping patients to identify and dispute irrational beliefs activated by feared social situations. Self-instructional training (SIT), based on Meichenbaum's (1985) stress inoculation training, has also demonstrated positive treatment results (e.g., Emmelkamp et al., 1985; Jerremalm, Jansson, & Öst, 1986). In SIT, patients are taught to observe and record negative thoughts and feelings experienced during social situations. Therapist and patient then work together to develop a set of realistic, coping thoughts appropriate for when the patient is anticipating the difficult social situation, when the patient is in the situation, and when the patient is thinking about the situation after it has concluded. Patients practice using these more adaptive thought patterns in imaginal rehearsal, during role-plays, and/or in similar real-life situations.

Social phobia patients treated with exposure alone have shown improvements following therapy (Fava, Grandi, & Canestrari, 1989). Exposure alone has been demonstrated to be superior to progressive relaxation training (Al-Kubaisy et al., 1992; Alström, Nordlund, Persson, Hårding, & Ljungqvist, 1984), pill placebo (Turner, Beidel, & Jacob, 1994), a waiting list control (Newman, Hofmann, Trabert, Roth, & Taylor, 1994), and a control therapy consisting of education, self-exposure instructions, and unspecified anxiolytic medication (Alström et al., 1984). Turner, Beidel, Cooley, Woody, and Messer (1994) reported on a pilot study evaluating social-effectiveness therapy (SET), which includes a large exposure component. SET is a multicomponent treatment package that combines group and individual formats and that includes in vivo and/or imaginal flooding, programmed practice, education, and social skills training. Seventeen generalized social phobics began SET but only 13 were included in the final analyses, because four, each with an Axis II diagnosis, dropped out. Significant decreases were noted from pretreatment to posttreatment for self-reported social anxiety, clinician ratings, and behavior test anxiety ratings. At posttreatment, 84 percent of patients completing treatment were classified as functioning at a level similar to nonpatients. Eight of the 13 patients completing this study participated in a two-year follow-up (Turner, Beidel, & Cooley-Quille, 1995). Self-report and clinician ratings indicated maintenance of treatment gains or additional improvement during the follow-up interval, although three of the eight patients had received additional treatment in the interim.

Because cognitive approaches are typically combined with exposure techniques, it is unclear whether the cognitive techniques enhance treatment effectiveness beyond what might be obtained by exposure alone (Heimberg & Juster, 1995). In a meta-analysis examining this issue, Feske and Chambless (1995) compared 12 social phobia treatment trials testing exposure plus cognitive restructuring to nine trials testing exposure alone. Exposure plus cognitive restructuring and exposure alone did not differ in dropout rates and yielded similar effect sizes on both posttreatment and follow-up measures of social anxiety, cognitive symptoms, and depression/anxiety. In another meta-analysis, Gould, Buckminster, Pollack, Otto, and Yap (1997) evaluated 24 trials that examined cognitive-behavior and pharmacological therapies, which included a control condition. Cognitive-behavioral therapy and pharmacological treatment produced similar effect sizes for reductions in social anxiety, and both effect sizes were significantly different from zero. Within the category of cognitive-behavior therapy, cognitive restructuring with exposure and exposure alone yielded similar attrition rates and effect sizes. Lastly, another recent meta-analysis examined 42 treatment trials in order to compare six conditions: waiting list control, placebo, exposure, cognitive restructuring without exposure, cognitive restructuring with exposure, and social skills training (Taylor, 1996). Drop-out rate did not differ across the 6 conditions. The four active therapies and placebo produced greater effect sizes than the waiting-list control; however, only cognitive restructuring with exposure had a significantly larger effect size than placebo.

Whether cognitive coping skills enhance the effects of exposure may be influenced by whether the cognitive techniques are presented as a separate module in treatment or integrated with exposure procedures. In their recent review, Heimberg and Juster (1995) predicted that integrated cognitive-behavior treatments would ultimately be shown to be more effective than exposure alone. They noted that evidence favored integrated cognitive-behavior therapy over exposure alone in three studies (Butler, Cullington, Munby, Amies, & Gelder, 1984; Mattick & Peters, 1988; Mattick, Peters, & Clarke, 1989) but results were mixed in other studies (e.g., Hope, Heimberg, et al., 1995). In two recent studies, Scholing and Emmelkamp (1993a, 1993b) examined cognitive techniques administered in isolation or integrated with exposure. Patients with DSM-III-R social phobia, who reported fear of showing anxiety symptoms, such as blushing, sweating, or trembling, were randomly assigned to exposure followed by cognitive therapy, cognitive therapy followed by exposure, or integrated cognitive-behavior treatment (Scholing & Emmelkamp, 1993a). Treatments were administered in four-week blocks separated by a four-week no-treatment block. After completion of treatment, patients in all conditions showed improvement on self-reports of avoidance, negative cognitions, and somatic symptoms; no differences were found between treatment methods. In the next study, patients given a DSM-III-R diagnosis of generalized social phobia were randomly assigned to exposure alone, cognitive therapy followed by exposure, or integrated cognitive-behavior therapy (Scholing & Emmelkamp, 1993b). As in Scholing and Emmelkamp (1993a), treatment was administered in four-week blocks and the same dependent measures were examined. Surprisingly, following the first block of treatment, the decrease in self-reported somatic symptoms was greater for exposure therapy and cognitive therapy than for integrated treatment. This difference, however, was not present after the second block of treatment or at three-month follow-up. At three-month follow-up, patients receiving integrated treatment (15%) were less likely to need further treatment than patients treated with exposure only (37%) or cognitive therapy followed by exposure (30%). Integrated cognitive-behavioral treatments may require more time for the patient to learn and implement the skills, but treatment gains may be better maintained than is the case for cognitive therapy or exposure alone.

Whether cognitive techniques are an essential component of the treatment of social phobia remains an unresolved and controversial topic (Heimberg & Juster, 1995). However, it appears likely that cognitive change is central to good clinical outcomes. Change in fear of negative evaluation from pretreatment to posttreatment has been shown to predict end-state functioning (Mattick & Peters, 1988; Mattick, Peters, & Clarke, 1989). Some studies have found treatments that incorporate a cognitive restructuring component to produce superior outcomes, especially on cognitive indices of improvement (Butler et al., 1984; Emmelkamp et al., 1985; Jerremalm et al., 1986; Kanter & Goldfried, 1979). However, cognitive interventions may not be necessary to engender cognitive change. Exposure alone may provide sufficient disconfirmatory information to alter dysfunctional beliefs (Hope, Heimberg, et al., 1995; Mattick & Peters, 1988; Newman et al., 1994).

Before conclusions are drawn regarding the necessity of cognitive interventions and the role of cognitive change in successful treatment outcome, several issues should be considered. The first issue concerns the measures used to demonstrate cognitive change. Questionnaire measures commonly used as indices of cognitive change correlate highly with social phobia symptom measures. When change is noted on these measures, the observed gains may be a product of change in the portion of variance shared with symptom measures. In other words, change on commonly used questionnaire measures of cognition may reflect changes in cognition, anxiety, or both (Heimberg, 1994). One approach to this problem is to utilize tasks that assess information processing but rely less on self-report. Changes in patients' biases in attending to and encoding threatening social information would be predicted following successful treatment (see Mattia et al., 1993). Second, as pointed out by Newman et al. (1994), many purely behavioral interventions may implement exposure-only procedures in a manner that facilitates cognitive change. Specifically, exposure-only treatments that include therapist and/or group member feedback regarding patient skill, visibility of anxiety symptoms, ability to cope with anxiety, etc., share many features with cognitive approaches, although these aspects of therapy may not be labeled as cognitive interventions by noncognitive therapists. Third, although studies that find equivalent outcomes for exposure versus exposure plus cognitive restructuring typically interpret this pattern to mean that cognitive restructuring does not add to the efficacy of exposure, alternative interpretations are available. It is also reasonable to suggest that cognitive restructuring activities reduce the amount of exposure necessary for effective treatment.

ALTERNATIVE TREATMENTS

In addition to exposure-only or cognitive-behavior treatments of social phobia, social-skills training (SST), applied relaxation (AR), and pharmacological interventions have also been evaluated. Because separate chapters in this volume are devoted to both SST and pharmacological treatments of social phobia, we restrict our consideration of other therapies to a brief discussion of AR.

Relaxation-based approaches to the treatment of social phobia arose from the idea that the physiological symptoms of anxiety prevented individuals from performing optimally in social situations and that being relaxed would allow them to overcome the effects of anxiety. However, relaxation techniques in and of themselves do not effectively help an individual overcome social phobia (Al-Kubaisy et al., 1992; Alström et al., 1984). Rather, relaxation strategies are most effective when individuals are trained to apply them in feared social situations (Jerremalm et al., 1986; Öst, Jerremalm, & Johansson, 1981). For Öst (1988), AR consists of teaching the patient to attend to early signs of anxiety and to apply relaxation skills as a means of coping rather than becoming incapacitated by the anxiety. The first part of AR is devoted to teaching the individual to monitor his/her own physiological signs of anxiety. Individuals are then taught progressive muscle relaxation (a technique that involves alternating between tensing and relaxing a number of muscle groups throughout the body). Once progressive relaxation is mastered, the individual is instructed to relax in response to a cue, such as the word *relax*, without first tensing his/her muscles. The individual is next instructed to employ relaxation during non-anxiety-provoking physical activities. Only then is the individual encouraged to apply these relaxation skills in situations that elicit anxiety. In this last phase, individuals with social phobia use relaxation during in-session role plays and in between-session situations that typify the social situations they fear. Details of AR studies are reported in the following paragraphs. They suggest that AR is superior to waitlist controls and may match the efficacy of other active therapies for some patients (e.g., SIT; Jerremalm et al., 1986; SST; Öst et al., 1981).

PRESCRIPTIVE TREATMENT AND MANAGED CARE

Clearly, our understanding of the effectiveness of exposure and cognitive techniques in the treatment of social phobia has greatly increased since social phobia was labeled the "neglected anxiety disorder" 15 years ago (Liebowitz et al., 1985). A few studies have attempted to improve upon the gains achieved with cognitive-behavioral therapy by matching treatment to patient characteristics. We provide a review of those studies and suggest directions for future research. Lastly, we summarize the research that has examined the issue of cost-effectiveness in the treatment of social phobia.

Matching Treatments to Patient Characteristics

Investigators who study social phobia have attempted to match patients' characteristics to therapy modalities in order to maximize their treatment gains.

However, results from these studies have generally been modest and not extremely supportive of the effort (Butler & Wells, 1995; Heimberg & Juster, 1995). Öst et al. (1981) systematically evaluated whether subsets of individuals with social phobia would demonstrate a differential response to either SST or AR. On some measures, patients who performed relatively more poorly on a behavioral test made greater therapy gains in SST than in AR, whereas patients who exhibited relatively greater cardiac reactivity to the behavior test fared better in AR than in SST.

One study compared patients with relatively greater heart-rate reactivity during a behavioral test to patients who reported a relatively higher frequency of negative thoughts during the test. Jerremalm et al. (1986) randomly assigned these individuals to AR, self-instructional training (SIT), or a wait-list control. Cognitive reactors reduced their number of negative thoughts regardless of which active treatment they received. Further, cognitive reactors treated with SIT demonstrated greater improvement than those treated with AR on several measures. Finally, physiological reactors responded equally well to AR and SIT. Mersch et al. (1989) studied behavioral reactors who were assessed in a manner similar to Öst et al. (1981) and cognitive reactors who were assessed to be less rational and cognitively skilled. Participants were treated with either SST or RET. Behavioral and cognitive reactors responded equally well after treatment as well as 14 months later (Mersch, Emmelkamp, & Lips, 1991).

Despite the inconclusive results in studies of the treatment-matching hypothesis, Butler and Wells (1995) highlight the importance of continuing to identify patient characteristics that are salient for specific therapy modalities, especially because individuals with social phobia are a heterogeneous group. One as yet untested approach is to match on the basis of the personality characteristics (rather than response profiles) of individuals with social phobia. The literature on cognitive therapy of depression suggests that personality variables may predict response to treatment. Briefly, Beck (1983) describes two dispositional characters who are vulnerable to depression when specific life events occur. The sociotropic character has extreme interpersonal concerns and may become depressed in the face of stressful interpersonal events. The autonomous character has extreme achievement concerns and may become depressed following an achievement failure. A similar theory, proposed by Blatt (Blatt, Quinlan, Chevron, McDonald, & Zuroff, 1982), focusing on dependency and self-criticism, has also enjoyed strong support. Recent data suggest that these personality characteristics may demonstrate differential response to treatment. Blatt (1992) reported that dependent clients responded better to supportive-expressive therapy, whereas self-critical clients responded more favorably to traditional psychoanalysis. Peselow, Robins, Sanfilipo, and Block (1992) found that highly autonomous clients demonstrated a superior response to antidepressant drug therapy compared to highly sociotropic clients. Finally, Zettle, Haflich, and Reynolds (1992) provide initial evidence that sociotropic clients fare best in group cognitive psychotherapy, whereas autonomous clients fare best in individual cognitive therapy.

Although all the work just reviewed pertains to depression, two recent studies have extended Beck's (1983) theory by demonstrating that sociotropy and autonomy are relevant and meaningful to social phobia (Brown, Juster, Heim-berg, & Winning, 1998; Fresco, Heimberg, Winning, & Brown, 1997). Treatment-matching studies that assign individuals with social phobia to treatments on the basis of sociotropy and autonomy have not yet been conducted. However, given the promising work in the treatment of depression, this effort warrants future consideration.

Treatment of Patients with Comorbid Conditions or Complicating Symptoms

One area that has yet to be considered in the treatment of social phobia is the development of treatments that address the presence of a concurrent disorder or complicating symptom. Many patients with social phobia have comorbid di-agnoses, and these individuals may present a more dysfunctional clinical pro-file than patients with uncomplicated social phobia (Andersch & Hanson, 1993; Bellodi, Battaglia, Diaferia, & Draisci, 1993). For example, clinical experi-ence suggests that comorbid panic disorder may interfere with social phobic patients' willingness to expose themselves to certain feared social situations, and many patients with social phobia may have panic attacks without meeting criteria for panic disorder (Jack, Heimberg, & Mennin, 1997). Thus, an area de-serving of further attention is the integration of techniques into the treatment of social phobia that address the concerns of additional symptoms or disorders. In the case of social phobia and panic disorder (or panic attacks), treatments for social phobia which incorporate panic control strategies (e.g., Woody et al., 1997) may have substantial merit.

Cost Effectiveness

Lucas and Telch (1993) examined the relative efficacy of group and individual cognitive-behavior treatments for social phobia. Both approaches were more ef-fective than a wait-list condition and quite similar in the magnitude of therapeu-tic effect. However, the group treatment cost less than one-third as much as the individual treatment. Another recent study suggests that the cost of the group treatment may be further reduced without diminishing its efficacy (Gruber, Moran, Roth, & Taylor, 1997). In that study, the standard 12-week CBGT protocol was compared to a brief (8-week) version, which incorporated computer-assisted homework assignments (CaCBGT). CBGT and CaCBGT were shown to produce superior outcomes on all measures relative to a waiting-list condition at posttreatment and were similar in effectiveness at six-month follow-up.

Gould et al. (1997) included cost calculations in their meta-analysis of cognitive-behavior and pharmacological treatments for social phobia. Although a complete description of their analyses is beyond the scope of this chapter, group cognitive-behavior interventions were found to cost less than half the amount of individual cognitive-behavioral or pharmacological treatment, if cal-culations are constrained to the first year of treatment. However, because many patients remain on medication for 2 years or more, the total cost of an episode of pharmacological treatment was found to range between 2.75 and 7.23 times the cost of cognitive-behavior group treatment (depending on the cost of the specific medication).

SUMMARY

Social phobia is a diagnostic category that captures a heterogeneous group of patients in terms of number and type of social situations feared. It is associated with significant suffering and interference in academic, occupational, and social functioning. Treatments including an exposure component have been shown to reduce social anxiety. Although many researchers and theorists hypothesize that cognitive factors are important in the maintenance of social phobia and that cognitive coping skills should be integrated into the treatment of social phobia, the question of whether treatment gains achieved with exposure are enhanced or better maintained with the addition of cognitive coping skills awaits additional research. However, evidence is accumulating that supports the efficacy of both group and individually administered cognitive-behavior treatments for social phobia.

REFERENCES

Al-Kubaisy, T., Marks, I.M., Logsdail, S., Marks, M.P., Lovell, K., Sungur, M., & Araya, R. (1992). Role of exposure homework in phobia reduction: A controlled study. *Behavior Therapy, 23*, 599–621.

Alström, J.E., Nordlund, C.L., Persson, G., Hårding, M., & Ljungqvist, C. (1984). Effects of four treatment methods on social phobic patients not suitable for insight-oriented psychotherapy. *Acta Psychiatrica Scandinavica, 70*, 97–110.

American Psychiatric Association. (1980). *Diagnostic and statistical manual of mental disorders* (3rd ed.). Washington, DC: Author.

American Psychiatric Association. (1987). *Diagnostic and statistical manual of mental disorders* (3rd ed., Rev.). Washington, DC: Author.

American Psychiatric Association. (1994). *Diagnostic and statistical manual of mental disorders* (4th ed.). Washington, DC: Author.

Amies, P.L., Gelder, M.G., & Shaw, P.M. (1983). Social phobia: A comparative clinical study. *British Journal of Psychiatry, 142*, 174–179.

Andersch, S.E., & Hanson, L.C. (1993). Comorbidity of panic disorder and social phobia. *European Journal of Psychiatry, 7*, 59–64.

Arrindell, W.A., Kwee, M.G.T., Methorst, G.J., van der Ende, J., Pol, E., & Moritz, B.J.M. (1989). Perceived parental rearing styles of agoraphobic and socially phobic inpatients. *British Journal of Psychiatry, 155*, 526–535.

Ball, S.G., Otto, M.W., Pollack, M.H., & Uccello, R. (1995). Differentiating social phobia and panic disorder: A test of core beliefs. *Cognitive Therapy and Research, 19*, 473–481.

Barlow, D.H., & Wolfe, B.E. (1981). Behavioral approaches to anxiety disorders: A report on the NIMH-SUNY, Albany, research conference. *Journal of Consulting and Clinical Psychology, 49*, 448–454.

Beck, A.T. (1983). Cognitive therapy of depression: New perspectives. In P.J. Clayton & J.E. Barrett (Eds.), *Treatment of depression: Old controversies and new approaches* (pp. 265–290). New York: Raven Press.

Beck, A.T., & Emery, G. (1985). *Anxiety disorders and phobias: A cognitive perspective.* New York: Basic Books.

Bellodi, L., Battaglia, M., Diaferia, G., & Draisci, A. (1993). Lifetime prevalence of depression and family history of patients with panic disorder and social phobia. *European Psychiatry, 8*, 147–152.

Blatt, S.J. (1992). The differential effect of psychotherapy and psychoanalysis with anaclitic and introjective patients: The Menninger psychotherapy research project revisited. *Journal of the American Psychoanalytic Association, 40,* 691–724.

Blatt, S.J., Quinlan, D.M., Chevron, E.S., McDonald, C., & Zuroff, D. (1982). Dependency and self-criticism: Psychological dimensions of depression. *Journal of Consulting and Clinical Psychology, 50,* 113–124.

Brown, E.J. (1996). *Self-disclosure, social anxiety, and symptomatology in rape victims-survivors: The effects of cognitive and emotional processing.* Unpublished dissertation, State University of New York at Albany, Center for Stress and Anxiety Disorders, Albany.

Brown, E.J., Heimberg, R.G., & Juster, H.R. (1995). Social phobia subtype and avoidant personality disorder: Effect on severity of social phobia, impairment, and outcome of cognitive behavioral treatment. *Behavior Therapy, 26,* 467–486.

Brown, E.J., Juster, H.R., Heimberg, R.G., & Winning, C.D. (1998). Stressful life events and personality styles: Relation to impairment and treatment outcome in patients with social phobia. *Journal of Anxiety Disorders, 12,* 233–251.

Bruch, M.A., Gorsky, J.M., Collins, T.M., & Berger, P. (1989). Shyness and sociability reexamined: A multicomponent analysis. *Journal of Personality and Social Psychology, 57,* 904–915.

Bruch, M.A., & Heimberg, R.G. (1994). Differences in perceptions of parental and personal characteristics between generalized and nongeneralized social phobics. *Journal of Anxiety Disorders, 8,* 155–168.

Bruch, M.A., Heimberg, R.G., Berger, P., & Collins, T.M. (1989). Social phobia and perceptions of early parental and personality characteristics. *Anxiety Research, 2,* 57–65.

Buss, A.H. (1980). *Self-consciousness and social anxiety.* San Francisco: Freeman.

Butler, G. (1985). Exposure as a treatment for social phobia: Some instructive difficulties. *Behaviour Research and Therapy, 23,* 651–657.

Butler, G., Cullington, A., Munby, M., Amies, P., & Gelder, M. (1984). Exposure and anxiety management in the treatment of social phobia. *Journal of Consulting and Clinical Psychology, 52,* 642–650.

Butler, G., & Wells, A. (1995). Cognitive-behavioral treatments: Clinical applications. In R.G. Heimberg, M.R. Liebowitz, D.A. Hope, & F.R. Schneier (Eds.), *Social phobia: Diagnosis, assessment, and treatment* (pp. 310–333). New York: Guilford Press.

Cameron, O.G., Thyer, B.A., Nesse, R.M., & Curtis, G.C. (1986). Symptom profiles of patients with *DSM-III* anxiety disorders. *American Journal of Psychiatry, 143,* 1132–1137.

Chambless, D.L., Cherney, J., Caputo, G.C., & Rheinstein, B.J.G. (1987). Anxiety disorders and alcoholism: A study with inpatient alcoholics. *Journal of Anxiety Disorders, 1,* 29–40.

Chapman, T.F., Mannuzza, S., & Fyer, A.J. (1995). Epidemiology and family studies of social phobia. In R.G. Heimberg, M.R. Liebowitz, D.A. Hope, & F.R. Schneier (Eds.), *Social phobia: Diagnosis, assessment, and treatment* (pp. 21–40). New York: Guilford Press.

Clark, D.M., & Wells, A. (1995). A cognitive model of social phobia. In R.G. Heimberg, M.R. Liebowitz, D.A. Hope, & F.R. Schneier (Eds.), *Social phobia: Diagnosis, assessment, and treatment* (pp. 69–93). New York: Guilford Press.

Davidson, J.R.T., Hughes, D.L., George, L.K., & Blazer, D.G. (1993). The epidemiology of social phobia: Findings from the Duke epidemiological catchment area study. *Psychological Medicine, 23,* 709–718.

Edelman, R.E., & Chambless, D.L. (1995). Adherence during sessions and homework in cognitive-behavioral group treatment of social phobia. *Behaviour Research and Therapy, 33*, 573–577.

Ellis, A. (1962). *Reason and emotion in psychotherapy.* New York: Lyle Stuart.

Emmelkamp, P.M.G., Mersch, P.P.A., Vissia, E., & van der Helm, M. (1985). Social phobia: A comparative evaluation of cognitive and behavioral interventions. *Behaviour Research and Therapy, 23*, 365–369.

Fava, G.A., Grandi, S., & Canestrari, R. (1989). Treatment of social phobia by homework exposure. *Psychotherapy and Psychosomatics, 52*, 209–213.

Feske, U., & Chambless, D.L. (1995). Cognitive behavioral versus exposure only treatment for social phobia: A meta-analysis. *Behavior Therapy, 26*, 695–720.

Feske, U., Perry, K.J., Chambless, D.L., Renneberg, B., & Goldstein, A. (1996). Avoidant personality disorder as a predictor for treatment outcome among generalized social phobics. *Journal of Personality Disorders, 10*, 174–184.

Fresco, D.M., Heimberg, R.G., Brown, E.J., & Winning, C.D. (1997). *Comorbidity and dysphoria in social phobia: The role of sociotropy and autonomy.* Submitted for publication.

Fyer, A.J., Mannuzza, S., Chapman, T.F., Liebowitz, M.R., & Klein, D.F. (1993). A direct family interview study of social phobia. *Archives of General Psychiatry, 50*, 286–293.

Gelernter, C.S., Uhde, T.W., Cimbolic, P., Arnkoff, D.B., Vittone, B.J., Tancer, M.E., & Bartko, J.J. (1991). Cognitive-behavioral and pharmacological treatments for social phobia: A controlled study. *Archives of General Psychiatry, 48*, 938–945.

Gorman, J.M., & Gorman, L.K. (1987). Drug treatment of social phobia. *Journal of Affective Disorders, 13*, 183–192.

Gould, R.A., Buckminster, S., Pollack, M.H., Otto, M.W., & Yap, L. (1997). Cognitive-behavioral and pharmacological treatment for social phobia: A meta-analysis. *Clinical Psychology: Science and Practice, 4*, 291–306.

Gruber, K., Moran, P.J., Roth, W.T., & Taylor, C.B. (1997). *Computer-assisted cognitive-behavioral group therapy for social phobia: A treatment comparison.* Submitted for publication.

Guy, W. (Ed.). (1976). *ECDEU assessment manual for psychopharmacology* (DHEW Publication No. ADM, pp. 218–222). Washington, DC: Government Printing Office.

Hamilton, M. (1959). The assessment of anxiety states by rating. *British Journal of Medical Psychology, 32*, 50–55.

Hazen, A.L., & Stein, M.B. (1995). Clinical phenomenology and comorbidity. In M.B. Stein (Ed.), *Social phobia: Clinical and research perspectives* (pp. 3–41). Washington, DC: American Psychiatric Press.

Heckelman, L.R., & Schneier, F.R. (1995). Diagnostic issues. In R.G. Heimberg, M.R. Liebowitz, D.A. Hope, & F.R. Schneier (Eds.), *Social phobia: Diagnosis, assessment, and treatment* (pp. 3–20). New York: Guilford Press.

Heimberg, R.G. (1994). Cognitive assessment strategies and the measurement of outcome of treatment for social phobia. *Behaviour Research and Therapy, 32*, 269–280.

Heimberg, R.G. (1996). Social phobia, avoidant personality disorder and the multiaxial conceptualization of interpersonal anxiety. In P.M. Salkovskis (Ed.), *Trends in cognitive and behavioural therapies* (Vol. 1, pp. 43–61). Chichester, England: Wiley.

Heimberg, R.G., & Barlow, D.H. (1988). Psychosocial treatments for social phobia. *Psychosomatics, 29*, 27–37.

Heimberg, R.G., Becker, R.E., Goldfinger, K., & Vermilyea, J.A. (1985). Treatment of social phobia by exposure, cognitive restructuring, and homework assignments. *Journal of Nervous and Mental Disease, 173*, 236–245.

Heimberg, R.G., Dodge, C.S., Hope, D.A., Kennedy, C.R., Zollo, L., & Becker, R.E. (1990). Cognitive-behavioral group treatment of social phobia: Comparison to a credible placebo control. *Cognitive Therapy and Research, 14*, 1–23.

Heimberg, R.G., Holt, C.S., Schneier, F.R., Spitzer, R.L., & Liebowitz, M.R. (1993). The issue of subtypes in the diagnosis of social phobia. *Journal of Anxiety Disorders, 7*, 249–269.

Heimberg, R.G., Hope, D.A., Dodge, C.S., & Becker, R.E. (1990). *DSM-III-R* subtypes of social phobia: Comparison of generalized social phobics and public speaking phobics. *Journal of Nervous and Mental Disease, 178*, 172–179.

Heimberg, R.G., & Juster, H.R. (1994). Treatment of social phobia in cognitive behavioral groups. *Journal of Clinical Psychiatry, 55*(6, Suppl.), 38–46.

Heimberg, R.G., & Juster, H.R. (1995). Cognitive-behavioral treatments: Literature review. In R.G. Heimberg, M.R. Liebowitz, D.A. Hope, & F.R. Schneier (Eds.), *Social phobia: Diagnosis, assessment, and treatment* (pp. 261–309). New York: Guilford Press.

Heimberg, R.G., Juster, H.R., Hope, D.A., & Mattia, J.I. (1995). Cognitive-behavioral group treatment: Description, case presentation, and empirical support. In M.B. Stein (Ed.), *Social phobia: Clinical and research perspectives* (pp. 293–321). Washington, DC: American Psychiatric Press.

Heimberg, R.G., Liebowitz, M.R., Hope, D.A., Schneier, F.R., Holt, C.S., Welkowitz, L.A., Juster, H.R., Campeas, R., Bruch, M.A., Cloitre, M., Fallon, B., & Klein, D.F. (1998). Cognitive-behavioral group therapy versus phenelzine in social phobia: I. 12-week outcome. *Archives of General Psychiatry, 55*, 1133–1141.

Heimberg, R.G., Salzman, D.G., Holt, C.S., & Blendell, K.A. (1993). Cognitive-behavioral group treatment for social phobia: Effectiveness at five-year followup. *Cognitive Therapy and Research, 17*, 325–339.

Herbert, J.D., Hope, D.A., & Bellack, A.S. (1992). Validity of the distinction between generalized social phobia and avoidant personality disorder. *Journal of Abnormal Psychology, 101*, 332–339.

Holt, C.S., Heimberg, R.G., & Hope, D.A. (1992). Avoidant personality disorder and the generalized subtype of social phobia. *Journal of Abnormal Psychology, 101*, 318–325.

Holt, C.S., Heimberg, R.G., Hope, D.A., & Liebowitz, M.R. (1992). Situational domains of social phobia. *Journal of Anxiety Disorders, 6*, 63–77.

Hope, D.A., & Heimberg, R.G. (1990). Dating anxiety. In H. Leitenberg (Ed.), *Handbook of social and evaluative anxiety* (pp. 217–246). New York: Plenum Press.

Hope, D.A., & Heimberg, R.G. (1993). Social phobia and social anxiety. In D.H. Barlow (Ed.), *Clinical handbook of psychological disorders: A step-by-step treatment manual* (pp. 99–136). New York: Guilford Press.

Hope, D.A., & Heimberg, R.G. (1994). Social phobia. In C. Last & M. Hersen (Eds.), *Adult behavior therapy casebook* (pp. 125–138). New York: Plenum Press.

Hope, D.A., Heimberg, R.G., & Bruch, M.A. (1995). Dismantling cognitive-behavioral group therapy for social phobia. *Behaviour Research and Therapy, 33*, 637–650.

Hope, D.A., Herbert, J.D., & White, C. (1995). Diagnostic subtype, avoidant personality disorder, and efficacy of cognitive behavioral group therapy for social phobia. *Cognitive Therapy and Research, 19*, 285–303.

Hope, D.A., Rapee, R.M., Heimberg, R.G., & Dombeck, M. (1990). Representation of the self in social phobia: Vulnerability to social threat. *Cognitive Therapy and Research, 14*, 177–189.

Jack, M., Heimberg, R.G., & Mennin, D. (1997). *Social situational panic: Relationship to social phobia with and without panic disorder.* Manuscript in preparation.

Jerremalm, A., Jansson, L., & Öst, L.G. (1986). Cognitive and physiological reactivity and the effects of different behavioral methods in the treatment of social phobia. *Behaviour Research and Therapy, 24,* 171–180.

Johnson, M.R., & Lydiard, R.B. (1995). Personality disorders in social phobia. *Psychiatric Annals, 25,* 554–563.

Juster, H.R., Brown, E.J., & Heimberg, R.G. (1996). Sozialphobie [Social phobia]. In J. Margraf (Ed.), *Lehrbuch der verhaltenstherapie* [Textbook of behavior therapy] (pp. 43–59). Berlin: Springer-Verlag.

Kanter, N.J., & Goldfried, M.R. (1979). Relative effectiveness of rational restructuring and self-control desensitization in the reduction of interpersonal anxiety. *Behavior Therapy, 10,* 472–490.

Kendler, K.S., Neale, M.C., Kessler, R.C., Heath, A.C., & Eaves, L.J. (1992). The genetic epidemiology of phobias in women: The interrelationship of agoraphobia, social phobia, situational phobia, and simple phobia. *Archives of General Psychiatry, 49,* 273–281.

Kessler, R.C., McGonagle, K.A., Zhao, S., Nelson, C.B., Hughes, M., Eshleman, S., Wittchen, H.U., & Kendler, K.S. (1994). Lifetime and 12-month prevalence of *DSM-III-R* psychiatric disorders in the United States. Results from the National Comorbidity Survey. *Archives of General Psychiatry, 51,* 8–19.

Kushner, M.G., Sher, K.J., & Beitman, B.D. (1990). The relation between alcohol problems and the anxiety disorders. *American Journal of Psychiatry, 147,* 685–695.

Leary, M.R., & Atherton, S.C. (1986). Self-efficacy, social anxiety, and inhibition in interpersonal encounters. *Journal of Social Clinical Psychology, 4,* 256–267.

Leung, A.W., & Heimberg, R.G. (1996). Homework compliance, perceptions of control, and outcome of cognitive-behavioral treatment of social phobia. *Behaviour Research and Therapy, 34,* 423–432.

Levin, A.P., Saoud, J.B., Strauman, T., Gorman, J.M., Fyer, A.J., Crawford, R., & Liebowitz, M.R. (1993). Responses of "generalized" and "discrete" social phobics during public speaking. *Journal of Anxiety Disorders, 7,* 207–221.

Liebowitz, M.R., Gorman, J.M., Fyer, A.J., & Klein, D.F. (1985). Social phobia: Review of a neglected anxiety disorder. *Archives of General Psychiatry, 42,* 729–736.

Liebowitz, M.R., Heimberg, R.G., Schneier, F.R., Hope, D.A., Davies, S., Holt, C.S., Goetz, D., Juster, H.R., Lin, S.-H., Bruch, M.A., Marshall, R.D., & Klein, D.F. (1997). *Cognitive-behavioral group therapy versus phenelzine in social phobia: II. Long-term outcome.* Submitted for publication.

Lucas, R.A., & Telch, M.J. (1993, November). *Group versus individual treatment of social phobia.* Paper presented at the annual meeting of the Association for Advancement of Behavior Therapy, Atlanta.

Mannuzza, S., Fyer, A.J., Liebowitz, M.R., & Klein, D.F. (1990). Delineating the boundaries of social phobia: Its relationship to panic disorder and agoraphobia. *Journal of Anxiety Disorders, 4,* 41–59.

Mannuzza, S., Schneier, F.R., Chapman, T.F., Liebowitz, M.R., Klein, D.F., & Fyer, A.J. (1995). Generalized social phobia. Reliability and validity. *Archives of General Psychiatry, 52,* 230–237.

Mattia, J.I., Heimberg, R.G., & Hope, D.A. (1993). The revised Stroop color-naming task in social phobics. *Behavior Research and Therapy, 31,* 305–313.

Mattick, R.P., & Peters, L. (1988). Treatment of severe social phobia: Effects of guided exposure with and without cognitive restructuring. *Journal of Consulting and Clinical Psychology, 56,* 251–260.

Mattick, R.P., Peters, L., & Clarke, J.C. (1989). Exposure and cognitive restructuring for social phobia: A controlled study. *Behavior Therapy, 20,* 3–23.

McEwan, K.L., & Devins, G.M. (1983). Is increased arousal in social anxiety noticed by others? *Journal of Abnormal Psychology, 92,* 417–421.

McNeil, D.W., Ries, B.J., Taylor, L.J., Boone, M.L., Carter, L.E., Turk, C.L., & Lewin, M.R. (1995). Comparison of social phobia subtypes using Stroop tests. *Journal of Anxiety Disorders, 9,* 47–57.

Meichenbaum, D. (1985). *Stress inoculation training.* New York: Pergamon Press.

Mersch, P.P., Emmelkamp, P.M., Bögels, S.M., & van der Sleen, J. (1989). Social phobia: Individual response patterns and the effects of behavioral and cognitive interventions. *Behaviour Research and Therapy, 27,* 421–434.

Mersch, P.P., Emmelkamp, P.M., & Lips, C. (1991). Social phobia: Individual response patterns and the long-term effects of behavioral and cognitive interventions. A follow-up study. *Behaviour Research and Therapy, 29,* 357–362.

Mullaney, J.A., & Trippett, C.J. (1979). Alcohol dependence and phobias: Clinical description and relevance. *British Journal of Psychiatry, 135,* 565–573.

Newman, M.G., Hofmann, S.G., Trabert, W., Roth, W.T., & Taylor, C.B. (1994). Does behavioral treatment of social phobia lead to cognitive changes? *Behavior Therapy, 25,* 503–517.

Orsillo, S.M., Heimberg, R.G., Juster, H.R., & Garret, J. (1996). Social phobia and PTSD in Vietnam Veterans. *Journal of Traumatic Stress, 9,* 235–252.

Öst, L.G. (1988). Applied relaxation: Description of an effective coping technique. *Scandinavian Journal of Behaviour Therapy, 17,* 83–96.

Öst, L.G., Jerremalm, A., & Johansson, J. (1981). Individual response patterns and the effects of different behavioral methods in the treatment of social phobia. *Behaviour Research and Therapy, 19,* 1–16.

Otto, M.W., Pollack, M.H., Gould, R.A., Worthington, J.J., Heimberg, R.G., McArdle, E.T., & Rosenbaum, J.F. (1997). *A comparison of the efficacy of clonazepam and cognitive-behavioral group therapy for the treatment of social phobia.* Submitted for publication.

Peselow, E.D., Robins, C.J., Sanfilipo, M.P., & Block, P. (1992). Sociotropy and autonomy: Relationship to antidepressant drug treatment response and endogenous-nonendogenous dichotomy. *Journal of Abnormal Psychology, 101,* 479–486.

Rapee, R.M. (1997). Potential role of childrearing practices in the development of anxiety and depression. *Clinical Psychology Review, 17,* 47–67.

Rapee, R.M., & Heimberg, R.G. (1997). A cognitive-behavioral model of anxiety in social phobia. *Behaviour Research and Therapy.*

Rapee, R.M., Sanderson, W.C., & Barlow, D.H. (1988). Social phobia features across the DSM-III-R anxiety disorders. *Journal of Psychopathology and Behavioral Assessment, 10,* 287–299.

Reich, J.H., Noyes, R., & Yates, W. (1988). Anxiety symptoms distinguishing social phobia from panic and generalized anxiety disorders. *Journal of Nervous and Mental Disease, 176,* 510–513.

Safren, S.A., Heimberg, R.G., Brown, E.J., & Holle, C. (1997). Quality of life in social phobia. *Depression and Anxiety, 4,* 126–133.

Safren, S.A., Heimberg, R.G., & Juster, H.R. (1997). Client expectancies and their relationship to pretreatment symptomatology and outcome of cognitive-behavioral group treatment for social phobia. *Journal of Consulting and Clinical Psychology.*

Sanderson, W.C., DiNardo, P.A., Rapee, R.M., & Barlow, D.H. (1990). Syndrome comorbidity in patients diagnosed with a DSM-III-R anxiety disorder. *Journal of Abnormal Psychology, 99,* 308–312.

Schneier, F.R., Heckelman, L.R., Garfinkel, R., Campeas, R., Fallon, B.A., Gitow, A., Street, L., Del Bene, D., & Liebowitz, M.R. (1994). Functional impairment in social phobia. *Journal of Clinical Psychiatry, 55,* 322–331.

Schneier, F.R., Johnson, J., Hornig, C.D., Liebowitz, M.R., & Weissman, M.M. (1992). Social phobia: Comorbidity and morbidity in an epidemiologic sample. *Archives of General Psychiatry, 49,* 282–288.

Schneier, F.R., Liebowitz, M.R., Beidel, D.C., Fyer, A.J., George, M.S., Heimberg, R.G., Holt, C.S., Klein, A.P., Lydiard, R.B., Mannuzza, S., Martin, L.Y., Nardi, E.G., Roscow, D.B., Spitzer, R.L., Turner, S.M., Uhde, T.W., Vasconcelos, I.L., & Versiani, M. (1996). Social phobia. In T.A. Widiger, A.H. Frances, H.A. Pincus, M.J. First, R. Ross, & W. Davis (Eds.), *DSM-IV source book* (Vol. 2, pp. 507–548). Washington, DC: American Psychiatric Press.

Schneier, F.R., Martin, L.Y., Liebowitz, M.R., Gorman, J.M., & Fyer, A.J. (1989). Alcohol abuse in social phobia. *Journal of Anxiety Disorders, 3,* 15–23.

Scholing, A., & Emmelkamp, P.M.G. (1993a). Cognitive and behavioural treatments of fear of blushing, sweating or trembling. *Behaviour Research and Therapy, 31,* 155–170.

Scholing, A., & Emmelkamp, P.M.G. (1993b). Exposure with and without cognitive therapy for generalized social phobia: Effects of individual and group treatment. *Behaviour Research and Therapy, 31,* 667–681.

Smail, P., Stockwell, T., Canter, S., & Hodgson, R. (1984). Alcohol dependence and phobic anxiety states: I. A prevalence study. *British Journal of Psychiatry, 144,* 53–57.

Stein, M.B., Walker, J.R., & Forde, D.R. (1994). Setting diagnostic thresholds for social phobia: Considerations from a community survey of social anxiety. *American Journal of Psychiatry, 151,* 408–412.

Stravynski, A., Basoglu, M., Marks, M., & Sengun, S. (1995). The distinctiveness of phobias: A discriminant analysis of fears. *Journal of Anxiety Disorders, 9,* 89–101.

Taylor, S. (1996). Meta-analysis of cognitive-behavioral treatments for social phobia. *Journal of Behavior Therapy & Experimental Psychiatry, 27,* 1–9.

Thyer, B.A., Parrish, R.T., Himle, J., Cameron, O.G., Curtis, G.C., & Nesse, R.M. (1986). Alcohol abuse among clinically anxious patients. *Behaviour Research and Therapy, 24,* 357–359.

Turner, S.M., Beidel, D.C., Cooley, M.R., Woody, S.R., & Messer, S.C. (1994). A multicomponent behavioral treatment for social phobia: Social Effectiveness Therapy. *Behaviour Research and Therapy, 32,* 381–390.

Turner, S.M., Beidel, D.C., & Cooley-Quille, M.R. (1995). Two-year follow-up of social phobics treated with social effectiveness therapy. *Behaviour Research and Therapy, 33,* 553–555.

Turner, S.M., Beidel, D.C., Dancu, C.V., & Keys, D.J. (1986). Psychopathology of social phobia and comparison to avoidant personality disorder. *Journal of Abnormal Psychology, 95,* 389–394.

Turner, S.M., Beidel, D.C., & Jacob, R.G. (1994). Social phobia: A comparison of behavior therapy and atenolol. *Journal of Consulting and Clinical Psychology, 62,* 350–358.

Turner, S.M., Beidel, D.C., & Townsley, R.M. (1992). Social phobia: A comparison of specific and generalized subtypes and avoidant personality disorder. *Journal of Abnormal Psychology, 101,* 326–331.

Versiani, M., Mundim, F.D., Nardi, A.E., & Liebowitz, M.R. (1988). Tranylcypromine in social phobia. *Journal of Clinical Psychopharmacology, 8,* 279–283.

Wacker, H.R., Müllejans, R., Klein, K.H., & Battegay, R. (1992). Identification of cases of anxiety disorders and affective disorders in the community according to *ICD-10* and *DSM-III-R* by using the composite international diagnostic interview (CIDI). *International Journal of Methods in Psychiatric Research, 2,* 91–100.

Walker, J.R., & Stein, M.B. (1995). The epidemiology of social phobia. In M.B. Stein (Ed.), *Social phobia: Clinical and research perspectives* (pp. 43–75). Washington, DC: American Psychiatric Press.

Weissman, M.L., Bland, R.C., Canino, G.J., Greenwald, S., Lee, C.-K., Newman, S.C., Rubio-Stipec, M., & Wickramaratne, P.J. (1996). The cross-national epidemiology of social phobia: A preliminary report. *International Clinical Psychopharmacology, 11*(Suppl. 3), 9–14.

Widiger, T.A. (1992). Generalized social phobia versus avoidant personality disorder: A commentary on three studies. *Journal of Abnormal Psychology, 101,* 340–343.

Wolpe, J. (1983). *The practice of behavior therapy.* New York: Pergamon Press.

Woody, S.R., Chambless, D.L., & Glass, C.R. (1997). Self-focused attention in the treatment of social phobia. *Behaviour Research and Therapy, 35,* 117–129.

Zettle, R.D., Haflich, J.L., & Reynolds, R.A. (1992). Responsivity of cognitive therapy as a function of treatment format and client personality dimensions. *Journal of Clinical Psychology, 48,* 787–797.

CHAPTER 13

Social Skills Training

MARTIN E. FRANKLIN, LISA H. JAYCOX, and EDNA B. FOA

CONCEPTUALIZATION

DSM-IV (American Psychiatric Association, 1994) defines social phobia as a marked or persistent fear of embarrassment or humiliation in one or more social or performance situations in which the person is exposed to unfamiliar people or to possible scrutiny by others. Exposure to feared situations almost invariably provokes anxiety that may even take the form of a panic attack, feared situations are avoided or else endured with extreme distress, and the fear cannot be better accounted for by substance use or a general medical condition. Because some fleeting social anxiety is very common in children and adolescents, individuals under age 18 must have symptoms that endure for at least six months for a diagnosis to be given.

Prevalence estimates of social phobia have varied widely, depending on the diagnostic system used. Epidemiological data using the *DSM-III* definition of social phobia suggested a six-month prevalence of 2.7 percent and a lifetime prevalence of 3.8 percent (Davidson, Hughes, George, & Blazer, 1993). Because the *DSM-III-R* and *DSM-IV* criteria are somewhat less restrictive than the *DSM-III* criteria, studies using the former two definitions have yielded higher prevalence estimates. For example, Kessler et al. (1994) have estimated lifetime prevalence for social phobia to be 13.3 percent, and Stein, Walker, and Forde (1994), a point prevalence of 7 percent. In addition to being relatively common, social phobia typically begins in childhood or early adolescence, has a chronic course, rarely remits spontaneously, and is associated with increased risk for suicide attempts (Amies, Gelder, & Shaw, 1983). Social phobia, therefore, poses a serious public health problem.

This chapter was supported in part by NIMH grant #49430 awarded to the third author. We would like to thank Bartholomew Brigidi for his assistance in preparing this chapter.

DSM-IV also specifies that if fears include most social situations, subtype of generalized social phobia (GSP) should also be given. Research suggests that most social phobics fear and avoid multiple situations (Turner, Beidel, Dancu, & Keys, 1986). Thus, the majority probably fall within the generalized subtype (GSP), although the criteria used to define *multiple* social situations is subject to interpretation. GSP is a chronic and debilitating disorder that often severely disrupts social and occupational functioning (Heimberg, Dodge, Hope, Kennedy, & Zollo, 1990). The disorder is associated with extreme distress, with failure to establish and maintain both casual and intimate relationships, and with underemployment (Scholing & Emmelkamp, 1990). GSP patients have been found to show greater life interference and clinical severity than those with non-GSP (Herbert, Hope, & Bellack, 1992; Holt, Heimberg, & Hope, 1992; Turner, Beidel, & Townsley, 1992). It also appears, from recent studies that have examined response to cognitive behavioral interventions, that GSPs are less likely to be classified as improved at posttreatment than are non-GSPs (Brown, Heimberg, & Juster, 1995; Hope, Herbert, & White, 1995; Turner, Beidel, Cooley, Messer, & Woody, 1994). Thus, the issue of social-phobia subtype is clinically important.

Two major views about social phobia have stimulated the research on psychopathology and treatment of this disorder. One view emphasizes the role of deficient social skills (e.g., Marzillier, Lambert, & Kellett, 1976), and the other highlights the role of cognitive distortions (e.g., Clark & Wells, 1995). Empirical data lend support to both views. For example, Stopa and Clark (1993) found that observers rated the performance of social phobics in a role-played conversation with a confederate as poorer than that of nonphobics *and* that social phobics rated their own performance as poorer than did the observer. However, the issue of whether performance deficits are characteristic of social phobia remains unresolved, because there have also been some negative findings with respect to differences in observer ratings between social phobics and controls on certain performance tasks (e.g., Pilkonis, 1977; Rapee & Lim, 1992). One possible explanation for the equivocal findings on between-group performance differences is that these assessment studies typically included a mixture of GSPs and non-GSPs, which may have masked real differences between patients and normals that would have been apparent if only GSPs were included.

A related hypothesis that has gained wide interest of late is that GSPs have more social-skills problems than non-GSPs. Results from studies examining this hypothesis have been mixed. One study failed to find differences between GSPs and non-GSPs on social skills (Turner et al., 1992); a second study found GSPs' performance poorer than discrete social phobia patients (Heimberg, Becker, Dodge, & Hope, 1990); and a third study found no differences between the subtypes in speech performance but poorer social skills for GSPs during role-played interactions (Herbert et al., 1992). A recent study indicated that compared to social phobics with specific public speaking fears, GSPs with avoidant personality disorder (APD) showed poorer social skills during both a speech task and a conversation role play; the ratings of GSPs without avoidant personality fell between the other two groups (Tran & Chambless, 1995). Taken together, these observations indicate that GSPs may have poorer social skills than do non-GSPs on some tasks but not others. These findings are consistent with clinical observations, suggesting significant variation in social skills in social phobia patients, even among GSPs.

In the last decade, the conceptualization of social phobia has emphasized cognitive factors in the development and maintenance of the disorder (Beck & Emery, 1985; Clark & Wells, 1995; Foa & Kozak, 1985; Rapee & Heimberg, 1997). This emphasis led to development of treatments that have focused on cognitive interventions and exposure exercises aimed at changing the mistaken thinking implicated in social phobia. Indeed, several studies of treatment response to cognitive-behavioral interventions have indicated that change in social-phobia-relevant cognitions following treatment are important mediators of improvement (e.g., Foa, Franklin, Perry, & Herbert, 1996; Lucock & Salkovskis, 1988; Mattick, Peters, & Clarke, 1989).

The wide acceptance of cognitive theories of social phobia has led naturally to an emphasis on cognitive restructuring techniques and exposure in recent treatment research. Additionally, because many treatment studies have included both GSPs and non-GSPs, the need for and potential helpfulness of SST may have been obscured. As already mentioned, GSPs, especially those with APD, may suffer from significant performance problems as well as cognitive distortions. Thus, the addition of social-skills training (SST) procedures, designed to remediate these performance problems directly, may enhance the effectiveness of cognitive-behavioral interventions for GSP. Moreover, the available treatments for social phobia have typically shown moderate efficacy for GSP, as will be discussed later. Thus, there remains a need to develop cognitive-behavioral treatment packages specifically for use with GSPs. The addition of SST to existing treatments emphasizing cognitive restructuring and exposure may be what is needed in light of the psychopathology of GSP.

One further comment on the theoretical underpinnings of SST and use of SST in conjunction with other cognitive-behavioral techniques is warranted. Although SST procedures are typically conceptualized as targeting specific performance deficits and are designed to increase positive reinforcement from the environment, they may also serve an important function in helping to address cognitive distortions. For example, a common cognition encountered in social-phobia treatment is the distortion, "I won't know what to say." Cognitive techniques are typically utilized to address this concern, but there is an added potential benefit from social-skills training. By teaching the patient what to say and how to say it and by practicing these techniques repeatedly in session, credible evidence to disconfirm the dysfunctional thought has been generated. Later, when the patient encounters this same cognition again while participating in social encounters outside treatment, the individual can counter the thought, "I won't know what to say," with a rational response developed from cognitive restructuring methods and strengthened by repeated practice and constructive feedback received in SST.

DIAGNOSTIC ISSUES AND PROBLEMS

In considering the special issues and problems associated with diagnosing social phobia, the first problem confronting the clinical evaluator at intake is whether a patient is experiencing sufficient functional impairment or distress to warrant a diagnosis. Because many people either describe themselves as shy or report experiencing at least some social anxiety in certain situations, it is important in diagnosing social phobia to ask patients in detail about whether this anxiety has resulted in significant hardships via lost educational, employment, and/or social opportunities, or has prevented them from going about their day-to-day activities. If there is little evidence of functional impairment upon detailed inquiry, the diagnosis may still be given if social fears are viewed by the patient as a major source of distress. That being said, the problem of whether an individual's social fears are sufficiently severe to warrant a diagnosis is a larger stumbling block for epidemiologists than for clinicians involved in the treatment of social phobia, because most patients seeking treatment for social fears present with substantial functional impairment and distress about how social anxiety is affecting their lives. For the diagnostician screening patients for treatment programs, the problems of associated psychopathology and differentiating among comorbid symptoms present a much greater challenge.

We will now review the most common associated Axis I disorders in descending order of their reported co-occurrence with social phobia in the epidemiologic catchment area (ECA) study on social phobia (Schneier, Chin, Hollander, & Liebowitz, 1992). Notably, Schneier et al. found that 69 percent of those individuals diagnosed with social phobia had at least one other lifetime Axis I psychiatric disorder. Treating the social-phobia patient with a comorbid condition raises certain problems that we will review later. In addition, distinguishing between social phobia and other disorders can also pose difficulties, and we will discuss some of the more problematic differential diagnoses.

Simple phobia was the most common comorbid disorder reported in the ECA study, occurring in 59 percent of diagnosed social phobics. Clinically, the additional diagnosis of simple phobia seldom poses any serious impediments to treating the socially phobic patient, except on those rare occasions when confronting the patient's specific fear (e.g., elevators, heights) is necessary in order to get to or stay in the treatment situation. In addition, specific fears of needles can occasionally hinder compliance with necessary study procedures in clinical outcome studies that include blood drawings. Patients avoiding routine blood work required as part of study participation may need treatment of these fears in order to help them remain in the study.

Agoraphobia was diagnosed in 45 percent of the socially phobic ECA participants, making it the second most frequent comorbid condition. Moreover, the differential diagnosis between social phobia and panic attacks and related avoidance can be especially difficult, because a subset of socially phobic patients report experiencing panic symptoms before, during, and/or after confronting threatening social situations. Many socially phobic patients also report fear that others in social situations will notice that they are nervous; this is especially true for patients who exhibit overt behavioral indicators of anxiety such as blushing, trembling, or stuttering. In order to make an accurate diagnosis, the diagnostician must determine whether the primary source of the fear is physical sensations themselves or public embarrassment upon exhibiting signs of anxiety. Additional information that would help determine whether the patient is suffering from panic disorder instead of social phobia includes the presence of nocturnal panic attacks, high frequency of uncued panic attacks, and greater comfort in the presence of others (Heckelman & Schneier, 1995).

Alcohol abuse was the next most frequent comorbid condition, occurring in 19 percent of diagnosed social phobics. Clinically, careful assessment of the quantity, frequency, specific situations in which the person is drinking, and difficulties directly associated with drinking (e.g., frequently driving drunk, blackouts) is especially important, even when it can be clearly established that social phobia preceded the alcohol abuse. In cases where the symptoms are severe enough to warrant a diagnosis of alcohol dependence, this problem should be addressed regardless of the severity of social phobia. However, one must make treatment recommendations for the alcohol problem in light of the comorbid social phobia. For instance, an alcohol treatment program with a strong or exclusive emphasis on group processes may not be maximally effective for those social-phobia patients whose symptoms would greatly hinder active involvement in treatment. Within cognitive-behavior therapy (CBT), we also try to address drinking behavior that might in and of itself be considered subclinical, but poses a potential threat to social phobia treatment efficacy. We tell patients that use of alcohol to relieve social anxiety, even if not sufficiently severe to be considered alcohol abuse, is functionally similar to other types of avoidance behaviors (e.g., sitting in the last row in class, pretending to read when someone sits next to you on the train) that serve to maintain social anxiety. Therefore, patients are strongly encouraged to try their best to limit all avoidant behaviors, including self-medication with alcohol, in order to receive the maximum treatment benefit possible. Other comorbid substance abuse, which was diagnosed in 13 percent of the ECA social-phobia sample, is treated in accordance with the strategy delineated for alcohol-related problems.

In the ECA study, major depression (17%) and dysthymia (13%) also co-occurred with higher frequency in those diagnosed with social phobia than in those without social phobia. In our ongoing controlled treatment outcome study of generalized social phobia (Foa & Davidson, 1998), approximately 20 percent of patients screened at intake to date received a diagnosis of current major depression (unpublished data). When a patient presents to the clinic with features of both social phobia and depression, it is important to establish whether social avoidance is secondary to depressive symptoms such as loss of interest and energy, or whether fear of embarrassment and humiliation is the primary motivator of continued avoidance. Specificity of negative thinking may also provide relevant diagnostic information. Some studies have suggested that distorted thinking in social phobia is confined to socially relevant concerns (e.g., Foa et al., 1996), whereas depressed patients appear to be generally negative about themselves and the world at large. However, content specificity is not an absolute rule of thumb, as other data indicate that untreated social phobics who did not meet diagnostic criteria for comorbid major depression were equally likely to assign a negative interpretation to an ambiguous event description whether or not its content was socially relevant (Franklin, Fitzgibbons, Freshman, Coles, & Foa, 1997). When patients presenting for social-phobia treatment meet criteria for both diagnoses, the clinician must also evaluate whether the depressive symptoms will interfere substantially with the patient's ability to complete treatment exercises. In such cases, it may be preferable to treat depressive symptoms before asking the patient to confront their social fears.

Obsessive-compulsive disorder (OCD) was also a common comorbid diagnosis, occurring in 11 percent of the ECA sample. When both disorders are present, it is important clinically to determine the primary diagnosis and to make adjustments in treatment if the secondary diagnosis is negatively affecting treatment of the primary diagnosis. For instance, a patient with primary social phobia and comorbid OCD was experiencing difficulty with cognitive restructuring tasks in social-phobia group treatment, because of compulsive checking of homework sheets, repeated reassurance seeking about whether she understood the assignment perfectly well, and so on. In that case, the therapists recommended that the patient engage in exposure exercises to target OCD symptoms, such as intentionally making spelling errors and stray marks on written assignments, and refraining from asking questions more than once (ritual prevention), both during and between sessions. This intervention led to a reduction in obsessive fear over time, as well as an increase in attention to social-phobia-related treatment tasks. Another problem that arises occasionally is distinguishing the mental reviewing of OCD from the rumination following social interactions that is frequently reported by individuals with social phobia. One patient seen in our clinic reported extreme anxiety during and after most of his face-to-face social encounters, and reported that he spent so much time thinking about these interactions afterwards that he was unable to function effectively at work. Upon detailed inquiry, he explained that his primary fear was that he might inadvertently spit on the person he was talking with, and that he was intentionally reviewing the conversation afterwards to check whether or not he did. Moreover, after reviewing these interactions many times, the patient would typically become satisfied that he did not in fact spit on the other conversant, and his anxiety would diminish substantially. Thus, despite presence of social fears and considerable mental reviewing of conversations, we diagnosed OCD instead of social phobia and treated the patient accordingly. In contrast to our OCD patient, social phobics will more typically report that their rumination about social interactions is involuntary, making them feel worse rather than better. Focus on unusual content during mental reviewing of social interactions (e.g., whether the patient swore at the other conversant and now doesn't remember doing so) is also suggestive of OCD rather than social phobia.

In addition to comorbid Axis I disorders, there is a great deal of overlap between GSP and APD. In *DSM-III-R* (APA, 1987), the addition of the GSP subtype created considerable overlap in symptoms with APD, and both diagnoses could be given to the same individual. Tran and Chambless (1995) recently found that 55 percent of clients who met criteria for GSP also met criteria for APD; other researchers have found similarly high rates of overlap between GSP and APD, with less overlap between APD and the discrete subtype. There does not appear to be any clear evidence that GSP with or without APD are qualitatively distinct. Thus, the distinction between GSP with and without APD may be largely one of severity, with the additional diagnosis of APD suggesting greater severity. Clinically, we have found that many of our most severe GSP patients with APD have more well-established habits of avoiding social situations in which success is not assured, and, therefore, have needed additional support and encouragement to attend group sessions and complete exposure homework exercises in which such guarantees cannot be provided.

TREATMENT STRATEGIES

SST is a structured therapy that is designed to teach specific skills that will enable a client to perform effectively in a variety of situations. Performing effectively means that the client will receive maximum positive reinforcement from the environment (Bellack, Hersen, & Himmelhoch, 1996). This focus will help clients with GSP to learn that social interactions are beneficial rather than harmful, despite the anxiety they initially feel. Thus, the goal of SST is to help the client to elicit positive reinforcement from others.

Social skills include a mixture of verbal and nonverbal responses, and thus are quite complex. Of course, assessment of social skills and training itself will depend a great deal on clinical judgment. The clinician should always be striving to help the client achieve positive responses from others in their own environment, and thus must be sensitive to differences in style and in the client's cultural and environmental milieu. Several components of social skills have been identified, and knowledge of these components can help the clinician identify problem areas and target specific components for training. These include speech content, paralinguistic elements (voice volume, pace, pitch, and tone), nonverbal behaviors (proxemics, kinesics, eye contact, facial expression), and the timing of responses or interactive balance (see Foa, Herbert, Franklin, & Bellack, 1995, for a detailed review).

SST generally proceeds as follows: assessment of client's baseline skills, rationale for modification, education about the skill to be taught, demonstration of the skill, first role play, feedback and positive reinforcement, second role play, feedback and positive reinforcement, and more optional role plays. At least two role plays are required so that the client can have the opportunity to respond to feedback, and additional role plays should be implemented until the client reaches an acceptable performance criterion.

EFFICACY STUDIES OF SST

Several empirical studies have examined the efficacy of SST with individuals with social phobia. Even prior to the advent of social phobia in *DSM-III*, a controlled study compared systematic desensitization (SD) and SST to a wait-list control group among socially inadequate psychiatric inpatients (Marzillier et al., 1976). These patients reported social or interpersonal difficulties as their chief complaint, anxiety or nervousness in a wide range of social situations, and they complained of or showed clear social skills deficits. SST consisted of repeated role plays with the therapist, who modeled appropriate ways of coping with social situations and gave feedback between role plays. Both treatments were offered in a 15-week, individual format. Results showed that patients treated with SD and SST evinced improvements in their social lives (number and range of social contacts) as compared to those in the wait-list group. However, neither of the active treatments differed from the wait-list group on measures of social anxiety, social skills, or clinical adjustment at the end of the treatment period. Despite the apparent importance of using a control group demonstrated by this study, few of the later studies reviewed below included a control group.

A second study also tested SD and SST among two types of patients with social failure: those deemed unskilled or primary, and those deemed socially phobic or secondary (Trower, Yardley, Bryant, & Shaw, 1978). Patients were classified as belonging to one group or the other, based on the primary presenting problem: anxiety and avoidance in the social phobia group, and awkwardness, unease, and poor relationships in the unskilled group. SST in this study consisted of coaching the patient on component events and skills, modeling by role partner, behavioral rehearsal, and modification of the performance in light of feedback. Both treatments consisted of 10 individual sessions. The authors expected that the unskilled patients would respond more to SST, whereas the socially phobic patients would benefit more from SD. Results indicated that the unskilled patients responded to SST, as evidenced by a reduction in difficulties in social situations, increased social activities, and improved social skills. The socially phobic group responded equally well to both therapies. The authors proposed that these results indicate a dual role for SST: one of behavior acquisition as well as one of anxiety reduction. They suggested that the anxiety reduction could occur via counter-conditioning (Wolpe & Lazarus, 1966), with assertive responses inhibiting anxiety responses, or via reality testing (Bandura, Jeffery, & Gajdos, 1975).

One study compared SD, flooding, and SST among 30 social phobics (Shaw, 1979). The treatments consisted of 10 individual sessions, and followed the same format as described in the Trower et al. (1978) study. Patients in all three treatments showed significant improvement at posttest, with no significant differences found between the treatments. Because the study did not include a control condition, it is possible that nonspecific factors such as therapist contact accounted for the observed changes at posttreatment. In light of the absence of clear between-group differences, Shaw suggests that factors such as acceptability of the therapy to patients and cost of procedures should guide treatment selection.

SST with nonprofessional therapists was tested on 16 individuals with social phobia as defined in *DSM-III* (Falloon, Lloyd, & Harpin, 1981). Patients in this study also received propranolol or placebo throughout treatment. Although there was no psychosocial control group, patients waited four weeks before active treatment began. SST in this program was conducted over four weeks with a nonprofessional therapist and another patient. Two target problems were identified, and each was worked on for two weeks. The first two-week period began with a six-hour training session with the nonprofessional therapist and patient, in which the patient worked on the problem in the clinic and then in real-life settings. Instructions, modeling, and feedback were given throughout this training session. After this long session, the patient practiced the problem area with a different patient-partner outside of the clinic at least twice, and again the following week with a third partner. This procedure was repeated during the next two-week period with the second target problem. There were no changes on any assessments during the four-week waiting period. During the treatment period, all patients showed significant reduction on all outcome measures, and there were no differences between those patients who received propranolol and those who received placebo. Gains were maintained at six-month follow-up.

SST was also tested alone and with cognitive modification on patients with *DSM-III* social phobia (Stravynski, Marks, & Yule, 1982). The design of this study included a three- to nine-week baseline period, during which repeated assessments were made. Treatment was conducted in a group or individual format, for 12 one-and-one-half-hour sessions. No improvement occurred during the baseline period, and patients who received either treatment improved equally after treatment on measures of social anxiety, isolation, relationships with coworkers, depression, and irrational social beliefs. Thus, it appeared that cognitive modification did not enhance the treatment effect of SST.

In an examination of individual response patterns in treatment, social phobics were divided into two groups on the basis of a social interactions test and heart-rate monitoring: behavioral and physiological reactors (Ost, Jerremalm, & Johansson, 1981). Half of each group was then randomly assigned to SST, a behaviorally focused treatment, or applied relaxation (AR), a physiologically based treatment. SST consisted of a combination of parts of personal-effectiveness training (Liberman, King, DeRisi, & McCann, 1975) and SST (Trower et al., 1978). Early sessions focused on analysis of problem areas and training the patient with the format of the skills training. Training itself consisted of a dry run, feedback and modeling when appropriate, and then repeated role plays, until the patient felt comfortable with the situation and the therapist deemed further training unnecessary. All patients were treated in a 10-session, individual format. Results indicated that both treatments produced significant reductions on most measures. For behavioral reactors, SST yielded better results than AR on six of ten measures; however, all of these were self-report measures. For physiological reactors, AR yielded superior results on three of ten outcome measures.

Another study followed a similar format to Ost et al. (1981) in order to examine different response patterns between behavioral and cognitive reactors (Mersch, Emmelkamp, Bogels, & van der Sleen, 1989). Patients were classified as one of these two types on the basis of a behavioral test and a cognitive measure, and were then randomly assigned to SST or rational emotive therapy (RET). Both treatments were conducted in a group format for eight weekly sessions. SST consisted of discussing and practicing social situations, and training via modeling by the therapist or other patients and behavioral rehearsal. Half the time in therapy was spent on structured exercises, such as basic communication skills, and the other half was spent in addressing patients' particular problems. Results indicated that in both treatments patients felt more skilled and less anxious at posttreatment and six-week follow-up, but there was no indication that the RET was superior for cognitive reactors or that the SST was superior for behavioral reactors.

SST was compared to in vivo exposure conducted individually or in a group format among two groups of patients with social inhibition: those with primary social phobia or primary social-skills deficits (Wlazlo, Schroeder-Hartwig, Hand, Kaiser, & Munchau, 1990). SST in this study was based on personal-effectiveness training (Liberman et al., 1975), and was carried out in a group format of 25 twice-weekly sessions, for a total of 37.5 hours over three months. The group exposure (GE) and individual exposure (IE) treatments were shorter in duration: GE lasted 34 hours over one month, and the IE lasted 12 hours over one month. Individuals were not randomly assigned to treatments, but rather assigned on the basis of when they applied for treatment. In addition, treatment modalities overlapped somewhat with each other, with some exposure instructions given within SST, and some skills training done within exposure. Results indicated that all three conditions showed significant gains at posttreatment on measures of social anxiety and skills deficits, as well as on other measures of neurotic complaints and attributional style. There were few differences between the social phobia and social-skills deficits groups in outcome. Because of the methodological problems described above, results of this study are difficult to interpret.

An open trial of a multicomponent treatment offered promising results for those individuals diagnosed with GSP (Turner, Beidel, Cooley, et al., 1994). This treatment, social effectiveness training (SET), consisted of education about social anxiety and SST in a group format, and exposure (flooding and programmed practice) in an individual format. The SST component included instruction modeling, behavioral rehearsal, feedback, and reinforcement. Particular focus was made on social environment awareness (e.g., choosing appropriate topics, listening), interpersonal-skill enhancement (e.g., establishing and maintaining friendships), and presentation-skill enhancement (e.g., making short speeches). Significant changes were noted on measures of social anxiety, physiological and subjective measures of anxiety during a behavioral task, social skills, and global severity. These changes were maintained in a subsample of patients assessed two years following treatment (Turner, Beidel, & Cooley-Quille, 1995).

In summary, many of the studies on SST completed to date have suffered from methodological problems, making them difficult to interpret. In particular, very few studies included a control group: Only one study used a wait-list control group (Marzillier et al., 1976), and two others included a baseline assessment period (Falloon et al., 1981; Stravynski et al., 1982). Furthermore, the Marzillier et al. study found no difference between the active treatment and the wait-list group on several measures. Further, comparison studies that have been performed are likely to lack statistical power to detect differences because of low numbers of subjects (Donohue, Van Hasselt, & Hersen, 1994). Another problem that has plagued these studies involves the diagnostic criteria. Most studies did not differentiate between GSPs and non-GSPs. This distinction is apparently important, because GSPs appear to be less responsive to CBT (Brown et al., 1995; Turner, Beidel, & Jacob, 1994). Thus, the magnitude of treatment effects in the studies described above is difficult to determine, because they are tested on an undetermined mixture of GSPs and non-GSPs. One exception is the Turner, Beidel, Cooley, et al. (1994) and Turner et al. (1995) studies, in which all clients were GSPs. Some researchers did attempt to classify social phobics into groups (e.g. cognitive vs. behavioral reactors), but these subtyping systems generally failed to differentiate individuals in terms of their responses to different treatments. These subtyping systems may not have divided social phobics in an optimal manner, because most if not all social phobics report dysfunctional thinking, whereas only some appear to suffer from substantial social-skills problems. Future research will be necessary to determine the efficacy of multicomponent CBT packages including SST for GSP in comparison to control treatments. Although there is evidence that individuals with GSPs are more severe, more impaired, and have greater decrements on measures of behavior (e.g., Heimberg et al., 1990), whether GSPs would be especially responsive to such multicomponent interventions still awaits further evaluation.

The next section describes a group consisting of six individuals with GSP, and it highlights the social-skills training of two group members. Names and identifying information have been changed to preserve confidentiality. The group format in this case was a 14-week CBT, led by a team of two therapists (MEF and LHJ), and following the format of the *Comprehensive Cognitive Behavior Therapy Manual for Generalized Social Phobia* (Foa et al., 1995).

Case Illustration

Following an initial telephone screening for eligibility and interest in the social phobia treatment program available at our center, patients participated in a structured diagnostic interview (SCID-IV; First, Spitzer, Gibbon, & Williams, 1995) that included evaluation of generalized social phobia symptoms, other anxiety disorders, mood disorders, alcohol and other substance abuse/dependence, psychotic symptoms, as well as APD and borderline personality disorder. Patients who met entry criteria and wished to participate in our treatment-outcome study completed self-report measures of social anxiety (e.g., Social Phobia and Anxiety Inventory, Turner, Beidel, Dancu, & Stanley, 1989) and other psychopathology (e.g., Beck Depression Inventory; Beck, Ward, Mendelson, Mock, & Erbaugh, 1961). Patients also participated in videotaped role-play assessments of conversational and speech skills. Patients were then randomly assigned to treatments. Patients assigned to group treatment met individually with one of the therapists to identify problem areas to target in treatment (e.g., unassertiveness, poor eye contact, stiff posture) and to construct a fear hierarchy for use during the group. Therapists had access to all data collected during the assessment procedures, and used this information to help develop the treatment plan.

The first treatment group consisted of introductions of group members, instruction about the group format, and education about the cognitive-behavior theory underlying treatment. The second session introduced cognitive therapy, including identification of negative automatic thoughts, discussion of cognitive distortions, and challenging negative thoughts via Socratic questioning to derive a rational response. In this session, the rationale for SST was also described, and therapists briefly demonstrated effective use of several social skills (e.g., eye contact, use of context in conversation) that would be emphasized in subsequent treatment exercises. The third and fourth sessions consisted of repeated SST on four elemental areas: initiating conversations, maintaining conversations, ending conversations, and negotiation. In these two sessions, each client participated in two rounds of three to four role plays of each skill, thus participating in at least 24 brief (30 to 60 seconds) role plays in front of the group. After each role play, clients were given specific feedback from the group leaders and other group members. Sessions 5 to 13 consisted of two or three longer role plays with individual clients, with additional participation of other group members in providing feedback, playing less central roles in other patients' role-play exercises, and so on. Prior to each role play conducted, beginning in session 5, each client would pick a situation from their fear hierarchy, identify negative thoughts, and with the help of the group, generate a rational response. With the patient's input, the therapists identified two or three specific social skills to target during the role play, and demonstrated appropriate use of these skills when needed. Then the client participated in three role plays, using their rational response and receiving feedback on social skills after each practice. The first two role plays typically lasted two to three minutes, and the third lasted three to five minutes. Session 14, the final group meeting, ended with a party and feedback given to each group member about gains they had made as well as areas for continued work.

In the group we describe below, six clients (two women, four men) began treatment. One male patient dropped out of the group after session 3, leaving five patients for the duration of the therapy. We will focus on two men in the group, one with some apparent deficits in social skills, and the second with above average skills.

George was a 27-year-old, single Caucasian male who was working in an accounting firm and taking classes at night. He had few friends and little social activity other than with his parents, with whom he lived. George reported high levels of anxiety both at work and with acquaintances, and was highly avoidant of initiating social interactions with others. George was visibly anxious in early group sessions, with a frozen facial expression, moist brow, and rapid speech. He reported going blank several times in early sessions and thus could not always report his cognitions or help to generate a scenario for role play. In session 3, the first social skills targeted for George involved slowing his speech and attempting to smile when initiating and maintaining conversations. Because smiling was very difficult, given his rigid facial muscles, we instead emphasized verbal social reinforcement (e.g., making a positive statement about the interaction). George was very concerned that he would go blank during conversations, so another skill that was highlighted for him was reflective listening. The therapist encouraged George to listen carefully to the other person, reflecting some of the information back to them, and asking relevant questions, to help him focus on the interaction instead of on his anxiety. He reported that this skill was very helpful in "getting me out of my head," and was able to be more effective in the role plays. Other skills that were addressed throughout treatment were George's stiff posture, lack of body movement during interactions, and lack of inflection in his speech. His sense of humor was encouraged and reinforced whenever possible, as it showed his personality, allowed him to smile naturally, and to receive positive reinforcement from others in the environment.

In addition, George also received instruction about the verbal content of his interactions with others. Because George had little experience with initiating social interactions or especially with dating, some skills training was also necessary for these areas. George had avoided asking others on dates because of the enormous amount of pressure he felt to find a girlfriend, which he believed would be accomplished by meeting attractive strangers and asking them out on a date almost immediately. Some basic education about dating was introduced by the therapists and reinforced by the group. For instance, the women in the group told him that they prefer to see a man as a friend first, where there is no explicit pressure to begin dating, and then to move into a romantic relationship more slowly. This feedback helped George to focus primarily on meeting individuals whom he liked, rather than on finding a girlfriend. In addition, the cognitive portion of the program focused on these same themes, so that his rational responses were statements like, "My goal is to enjoy the interaction, and then see how things go," to replace the automatic thought, "If I blow this I won't date anyone for a long time." Thus, the cognitive and social skills portions of the program reinforced the same idea for George, thereby reducing his anxiety and allowing him to be more effective in establishing new relationships. Between sessions, George worked on these same issues by getting involved in activities outside of work, such as bicycling in local races, going to happy hour with coworkers, and going to the gym regularly. He was able to successfully initiate conversations with other people in these situations, and he found that such activities provided a natural context for the conversations (e.g., bicycling).

Another group member, Joseph, was a 34-year-old, single Caucasian male who was working as a car salesman, and had social skills appropriate for his job. He reported unbearable levels of anxiety both at work and in personal relationships, yet he appeared poised and calm. He was involved in a long-term relationship and attended many social gatherings, but always with distress. At first glance, it seemed that Joseph would need little remediation of social-skills deficits. However, in the first few role plays in session 3, some important skills issues were identified. First, Joseph had a tendency to speak rapidly and not to listen very well, and, therefore, his responses did not always match the situation. For instance, after inquiring how his coworker was doing in a role-played interaction in session 3, she responded that she'd been having a hard time lately. His response, light and jocular, was seen as ineffective, given the context of the conversation. The therapists implemented reflective listening for Joseph, in an attempt to slow his speech and to build an empathic response through reflection or asking questions. He found this very helpful, and immediately began to use the technique at work and in personal relationships. A second issue for Joseph became apparent when he reported difficulty moving from impersonal relationships to more intimate ones. He reported not wanting to "let people in" to get to know him, lest they see his vulnerabilities and hurt him. This issue was addressed via cognitive therapy as well as SST. In SST, Joseph practiced revealing a "weakness," such as telling others at a social gathering that he was slightly uncomfortable because he didn't know anyone at a party. He reported immediate relief of his anxiety at the end of the first role-played interaction in which he practiced this skill, because he no longer had to make special efforts to hide his anxiety. In later treatment sessions, this skill of selective self-disclosure was also practiced repeatedly in simulated business settings, where he became more comfortable in meetings when he raised a difficulty he was having instead of trying to hide it. Here again, working on the specific verbal content of the interactions proved to be as useful as working on his thinking about the interactions. Cognitive therapy exercises converged nicely with the SST foci by directly challenging the idea that, if others know a slight flaw or weakness, they will reject him.

SPECIAL PROBLEMS IN SST

As was illustrated in the foregoing examples, clients can have very different levels of social-skills abilities and still benefit from skills training. It can be problematic, however, when a client has a particularly odd or peculiar social style. In a group setting, this difference can be harder to handle, because of comparisons made between group members and because of the task of giving constructive criticism in front of other group members. For instance, Alex was a 52-year-old, single Caucasian male who lived with his brother and was unemployed. His eye contact was invariably unbroken with the other conversant and his facial expression was stiff, with sporadic and intense smiles that were not linked to environmental cues. The other group members appeared to be highly aware of his deficits, but his contributions to the group and his sense of humor helped other group members respond positively to him despite these differences. The challenge to the therapists in this case was to balance feedback so that it would be truthful, so as to maintain credibility with other group members, but not overwhelm Alex with criticism. This meant setting aside the smaller issues and beginning with the inappropriate smiling and overly intense eye contact. Unfortunately, Alex was keenly aware of the difference between himself and other group members, and he dropped out of the group after five sessions because he thought his social anxiety was too severe. In cases such as this one, individual therapy may prove to be more suitable, because patients can get constructive feedback more slowly in a less threatening environment.

A special problem occurs when the skills problems directly affect other group members. A 42-year-old male client who was extremely anxious around women also felt very pressured to begin a relationship with a women. In terms of social skills, the client was similar to many socially anxious individuals because he found it difficult to make eye contact. However, in the presence of women, he would fix his gaze on their breasts, including women in the group. Such problematic behavior was addressed by the female therapist during role plays, where he was directed to practice eye contact and shifting gaze by periodically looking over the other conversant's shoulder instead. In addition, it was necessary to address this problematic behavior individually with the client when a woman in the group complained that it made her uncomfortable. These interventions ultimately proved effective; the patient reported having been unaware of this behavior and the discomfort it was causing, and he began to practice making more appropriate eye contact throughout the group.

ALTERNATIVE TREATMENT OPTIONS

There are several alternatives to SST for social phobia. First, there are other variations of treatment that incorporate cognitive-behavior techniques, such as exposure therapy alone, cognitive therapy alone, or treatments that combine all three elements (exposure, cognitive therapy, and SST). In addition, several pharmacotherapies have been found to be superior to placebo. Other forms of therapy, such as psychoanalysis, have no known efficacy (Bellack & Hersen, 1990).

COGNITIVE-BEHAVIOR THERAPIES WITHOUT SST

Cognitive therapy is an established treatment for social phobia that reflects the increasing influence of cognitive theories of pathological anxiety. It is directed at correcting the cognitive distortions that hypothetically underlie social phobia symptoms. Several studies have demonstrated the efficacy of variants of such treatment (e.g., DiGiuseppe, McGowan, Simon, & Gardner, 1990; Mattick & Peters, 1988; Mattick et al., 1989; Mersch et al., 1989; Scholing & Emmelkamp, 1993).

The efficacy of a cognitively oriented treatment for social phobia, referred to as cognitive-behavior group therapy (CBGT), was examined by Heimberg, Becker, Goldfinger, and Vermilyea (1985) and Heimberg et al. (1990). The treatment is conducted in small groups over a 12-week period and integrates cognitive restructuring and exposure homework. Heimberg et al. (1990) reported that after 12 weeks of such treatment, 75 percent of the CBGT group were responders, contrasted to 40 percent of the psychotherapy control group. These gains were maintained after a six-month follow-up. Notably, at five-year follow-up, CBGT remained superior to the psychotherapy comparison treatment (Heimberg, Salzman, Holt, & Blendell, 1993), although approximately half the sample was unavailable for evaluation at this test point. Studying CBGT, Hope et al. (1995) obtained results similar to those of Heimberg et al. (1990), with a trend suggesting that GSPs were less likely than non-GSPs to be classified as improved at posttreatment.

Exposure therapies, which involve prolonged confrontation with feared situations either in imagination, in vivo, or in role plays, have also shown promising efficacy for social phobia (e.g., Al-Kubaisy et al., 1992; Butler, Cullington, Munby, Amies, & Gelder, 1984; Emmelkamp, Mersch, Vissia, & van der Helm, 1985; Mattick & Peters, 1988; Mattick et al., 1989; Turner, Beidel, & Jacob, 1994). Three studies have revealed that the addition of cognitive restructuring, SST, or anxiety-management procedures to exposure improved outcome (Butler et al., 1984; Mattick & Peters, 1988; Mattick et al., 1989); two studies, one of which involved three case reports, failed to find evidence for such additive effects (Biran, Augusto, & Wilson, 1981; Hope et al., 1995). In the aggregate, these studies suggest that exposure is at least somewhat effective for social phobia, and certain additional procedures may enhance its efficacy.

PHARMACOTHERAPY

Three controlled trials of phenelzine have demonstrated its effectiveness for social phobia (Gelernter et al., 1991; Liebowitz et al., 1992; Versiani et al., 1992). However, the side-effect profile and associated restrictions on diet and concomitant medications diminish the desirability of phenelzine for some patients. Although two other monoamine oxidase inhibitors (MAOI), moclobemide and brofaromine, have also been found to be effective with social phobia (Van Vliet, den Boer, & Westenberg, 1991; Versiani et al., 1992), these compounds are currently unavailable in the United States. Moreover, recent trials with moclobemide have not clearly demonstrated its efficacy, possibly because of inadequate dosing (Potts & Davidson, 1995).

Two benzodiazepines, clonazepam and alprazolam, have been found superior to placebo for social phobia (Davidson et al., 1993; Gelernter et al., 1991). In the Davidson et al. study, the placebo responder rate was 20 percent and clonazepam, 78 percent. Notably, in a follow-up to the clonazepam trial, patients who had received clonazepam had typically continued to take their medication and were doing better than who had taken placebo (Sutherland, Colkert, Davidson, & Tupler, 1996). These positive results notwithstanding, patients' vulnerability to physiological dependence and the difficulties of discontinuation are disadvantages of the benzodiazepines. In controlled trials of atenolol and buspirone, neither compared well to placebo, and both have been found inferior to behavior therapy (Clark & Agras, 1991; Liebowitz et al., 1992; Turner, Beidel, & Jacob, 1994).

Positive effects have been found for three selective serotonin reuptake inhibitor (SSRI) drugs relative to placebo. Van Vliet, den Boer, and Westerberg (1994) noted good results for fluvoxamine (46% vs. 7% responders), Katzelnick et al. (1995) observed greater benefit for sertraline in a cross-over design (50% vs. 9% responders), and Stein et al. (1996), studying GSPs only, noted greater relapse when paroxetine was discontinued than when it was continued for three months on an open-label basis. Although the SSRIs appear to offer potential for symptom relief in social phobia without serious side effects and are typically better tolerated than are the older generation MAOIs, more placebo-controlled, double-blind studies are needed to demonstrate their efficacy (Potts & Davidson, 1995).

COMPARISONS OF PHARMACOTHERAPY AND PSYCHOTHERAPY IN SOCIAL PHOBIA

The published studies that have included drug and behavioral therapies for social phobia leave the issue of relative and combined efficacy substantially unresolved. Gelernter et al. (1991) found no difference between cognitive-behavior techniques and pharmacotherapy; Falloon et al. (1981) found no additive effect for propanolol plus SST compared to SST plus placebo. However, both of these studies suffered from some methodological problems, making the results difficult to interpret.

On the other hand, two studies have shown some advantage of cognitive-behavior treatment over medication. Clark and Agras (1991) examined the effects of cognitive-behavior treatment plus buspirone, cognitive-behavior treatment plus placebo, buspirone alone, and placebo alone in a sample of socially phobic musicians. Results indicated that buspirone alone did not differ from placebo alone, but cognitive-behavior treatment with or without buspirone resulted in significant improvements over placebo. Turner, Beidel, and Jacob (1994) compared individual behavior therapy (exposure), atenolol, and pill placebo. Results indicated that behavior therapy was consistently superior to placebo, whereas atenolol was not. At posttreatment, 56 percent of behavior therapy patients were classified as greatly improved, compared to 13 percent of the atenolol group and 6 percent of the placebo group. Because even the most effective monotherapy (behavior therapy) yielded only partial improvement, the authors concluded that treatments incorporating multiple interventions, such as SST, exposure, and perhaps medication, are desirable for social phobia. A third study compared phenelzine, pill placebo, CBGT, and educational support (Heimberg et al., 1994, reported in Heimberg & Juster, 1995). Results indicated that phenelzine and CBGT were superior to both pill placebo and educational support at posttreatment, with phenelzine superior to CBGT on some posttreatment measures. However, there appeared to be a higher rate of relapse in the phenelzine group compared to CBGT during the no-treatment follow-up phase of the study.

Two important problems are common to most of the existing studies that compared drug and psychosocial treatments. First, patients were not identified according to subtype of social phobia, so it is unclear whether the results are generalizable to the typically more severe and impaired GSPs. Second, except for the Falloon et al. (1981) and the Clark and Agras (1991) studies, combination treatments involving pharmacotherapy plus psychosocial therapy were not evaluated. The importance of evaluating the effect of combined pharmacological and psychosocial treatments has been highlighted by several investigators (e.g., Agras, 1990). Drawing on data from studies on other anxiety disorders, it seems likely that combining medication and psychotherapy may be especially helpful in preventing relapse upon drug discontinuation. Studies implementing such designs need to be conducted in social-phobia treatment-outcome research.

INDIVIDUAL VERSUS GROUP TREATMENT

It is not clear whether the delivery of CBT techniques including SST is best in a group or in an individual format, because studies comparing the two modalities have found them to be equivalent on most outcome measures (e.g., Scholing & Emmelkamp, 1993; Wlazlo et al., 1990). Disadvantages of group treatment are that the prospect of group sessions can be quite daunting to individuals with severe GSP, and, therefore, may result in more treatment refusals. Each patient receives less direct individual-therapy time, although each does get the opportunity for vicarious treatment and exposure to the social atmosphere of the group. In addition, logistical constraints with a group format include waiting periods for some patients until a group is formed, difficulties with scheduling a time for the group that works for all group members, and an inability to reschedule missed sessions readily. On the other hand, advantages of a group format include greater cost efficiency, the capacity for receiving believable feedback on social skills and other issues from other group members suffering from similar problems, and the naturalistic exposure to a group setting inherent in group treatment.

PRESCRIPTIVE TREATMENT AND MANAGED CARE

As managed care has become a major part of the mental health care system, it is important to evaluate treatments in relation to these systems. In general, the managed-care environment is conducive to short-term treatments, such as the cognitive-behavior programs involving SST described in this chapter, first, because the efficacy of such treatments has been documented. Despite some methodological problems in the particular studies, the majority of patients who completed the cognitive-behavior programs for social phobia reported feeling less anxious and more skilled at the end of treatment. Second, such treatments target the specific symptoms of social phobia and are time limited. Third, consistent with the stated managed-care mission of providing effective treatment while holding down costs, careful evaluation of treatment outcome and discontinuation of ineffective interventions are standard practices in CBT.

Despite the ways in which CBT involving SST and managed care appear to be compatible, there are impediments that remain to be addressed. For example, the group comprehensive cognitive-behavior therapy (CCBT) program described earlier requires that patients attend weekly group therapy sessions for 14 weeks. Despite the fact that group and individual formats appear to be about equally effective in treating social phobia (e.g., Wlazlo et al., 1990), many insurance policies arbitrarily do not cover the cost of group treatments. Such omission seems particularly short sighted, because the cost per patient is usually lower in a group format, and in some settings with a large client flow, groups can be implemented with minimal waiting time for patients. In order to ensure that managed-care companies give this and other treatment-relevant issues full consideration as they make policy decisions, it is imperative that relationships between CBT providers and managed-care companies be established, fostered, and maintained. This seems to be the most efficient way to ensure that effective treatments, such as CBT involving SST for social phobia, will be made more available in sufficient numbers of sessions for a wider range of mental health consumers. Thus, although contending with these bureaucracies poses difficulties, the potential payoff is of sufficient importance to warrant our best efforts to do so.

SUMMARY

The nature and treatment of social phobia has received considerable attention in the last decade, and at present there are a number of empirically validated cognitive-behavior and pharmacotherapy alternatives available. In this chapter we reviewed one type of treatment in detail, cognitive-behavior treatment involving SST. Although there is some empirical evidence for the efficacy of SST in social phobia, many of the studies of this treatment have been compromised by methodological problems (e.g., lack of control groups, small sample sizes). Thus, whether SST should be considered a stand-alone treatment for social phobia awaits further empirical support. Its use in combination with other treatment procedures, such as cognitive restructuring and exposure, has raised considerable interest recently, especially in light of studies indicating that GSPs evidence performance decrements on behavior tasks. Although the cause of these performance problems has been a matter of debate (e.g., Heimberg & Juster, 1995), the fact that GSPs evidence skills problems and appear to be less responsive to CBGT (Brown et al., 1995) and exposure alone (Turner, Beidel, & Jacob, 1994) suggests that SST may serve a useful adjunctive-treatment role because it specifically targets skills and performance problems. However, this hypothesis awaits further investigation. Toward that end, a controlled study of CCBT for GSP, a multicomponent group-treatment program involving exposure, cognitive restructuring, and SST, is currently in progress (Foa & Davidson, 1998). Results of this investigation will provide information about the relative efficacy of CCBT, fluoxetine, CCBT plus fluoxetine, CCBT plus pill placebo, and pill placebo alone in the treatment of GSP.

Although much is known about social phobia and its treatment, there is a great deal yet to be learned. Even among those patients classified as treatment responders, it seems that reduction of social phobia symptoms rather than remission is typical. Additionally, some patients respond minimally to the available treatments. Further study of treatment response by social phobia subtype, symptom severity, presence of comorbid disorders, etc., is needed to help guide the development of maximally effective treatments for even the most disabled patients. Another important issue at hand is the establishment of working relationships with managed-care systems, because these organizations have increasing influence over access to treatment. If collaborations with managed-care organizations are not fostered, policy makers within these systems are likely to remain uninformed about the types of treatments that are most effective for social phobia and the number of sessions needed to provide these interventions adequately. In the end, if insurers do not cover the cost of these treatments, even the social-phobia treatments found most effective in research studies will be of limited value because they will not be available to the community at large.

REFERENCES

Agras, W.S. (1990). Treatment of social phobias. *Journal of Clinical Psychiatry, 51,* 52–55.

Al-Kubaisy, T., Marks, I.M., Logsdail, S., Marks, M.P., Lovell, K., Sungur, M., & Araya, R. (1992). Role of exposure homework in phobia reduction: A controlled study. *Behavior Therapy, 23,* 599–621.

Alstrom, J.E., Nordlund, C.L., & Persson, G. (1984). Effects of four treatment methods on social phobic patients not suitable for insight-oriented psychotherapy. *Acta Psychiatrica Scandinavica, 70,* 97–110.

American Psychiatric Association. (1987). *Diagnostic and statistical manual of mental disorders* (3rd ed. Rev.). Washington, DC: Author.

American Psychiatric Association. (1994). *Diagnostic and statistical manual of mental disorders* (4th ed.). Washington, DC: Author.

Amies, P.L., Gelder, M.G., & Shaw, P.M. (1983). Social phobia: A comparative clinical study. *British Journal of Psychiatry, 142,* 174–179.

Bandura, A., Jeffery, R.W., & Gajdos, E. (1975). Generalizing change through participant modeling with self-directed mastery. *Behaviour Research and Therapy, 13,* 141–152.

Beck, A.T., & Emery, G. (1985). *Anxiety disorders and phobias: A cognitive perspective.* New York: Basic Books.

Beck, A.T., Ward, C., Mendelson, M., Mock, J.E., & Erbaugh, J.K. (1961). An inventory for measuring depression. *Archives of General of Psychiatry, 4,* 561–571.

Bellack, A.S., & Hersen, M. (1990). Editorial commentary on social phobia. In A.S. Bellack & M. Hersen (Eds.), *Handbook of comparative treatments for adult disorders* (pp. 240–241). New York: Wiley.

Bellack, A.S., Hersen, M., & Himmelhoch, J. (1996). Social skills training for depression: A treat manual. In V.B. van Hasselt & M. Hersen (Eds.), *Sourcebook of psychological treatment manuals for adult disorders* (pp. 179–200). New York: Plenum Press.

Biran, M., Augusto, F., & Wilson, G.T. (1981). In vivo exposure vs. cognitive restructuring in the treatment of scriptophobia. *Behavior Research Therapy, 19,* 525–532.

Brown, E.J., Heimberg, R.G., & Juster, H.R. (1995). Social phobia subtype and avoidance personality disorder: Effect on severity of social phobia, impairment, and outcome of cognitive-behavioral treatment. *Behavior Therapy, 26,* 467–486.

Butler, G., Cullington, A., Munby, M., Amies, P., & Gelder, M. (1984). Exposure and anxiety management in the treatment of social phobia. *Journal of Consulting and Clinical Psychology, 52.*

Clark, D.B., & Agras, W.S. (1991). The assessment and treatment of performance anxiety in musicians. *American Journal of Psychiatry, 148,* 598–605.

Clark, D.B., & Wells, A. (1995). A cognitive model of social phobia. In R.G. Heimberg, M.R. Liebowitz, D.A. Hope, & F.R. Schneier (Eds.), *Social phobia: Diagnosis, assessment, and treatment* (pp. 69–93). New York: Guilford Press.

Davidson, J.R.T., Hughes, D.L., George, L.K., & Blazer, D.G. (1993). The epidemiology of social phobia: Findings from the epidemiological catchment area study. *Psychological Medicine, 23,* 709–718.

DiGiuseppe, R., McGowan, L., Simon, K.S., & Gardner, F. (1990). A comparative outcome study of four cognitive therapies in the treatment of social anxiety. *Journal of Rational-Emotive and Cognitive-Behavior Therapy, 8,* 129–146.

Donohue, B.C., Van Hasselt, V.B., & Hersen, M. (1994). Behavioral assessment and treatment of social phobia. *Behavior Modification, 18,* 262–288.

Emmelkamp, P.M.G., Mersch, P.P., Vissia, E., & van der Helm, M. (1985). Social phobia: A comparative evaluation of cognitive and behavioral interventions. *Behavior Research and Therapy, 23,* 365–369.

Falloon, I.R.H., Lloyd, G.G., & Harpin, R.E. (1981). Real-life rehearsal with nonprofessional therapists. *Journal of Nervous and Mental Disorder, 169,* 180–184.

First, M.B., Spitzer, R.L., Gibbon, M., & Williams, J.B. (1995). *Structured clinical interview for DSM-IV axis I disorders—patient edition* (SCID-I/P,version 2.0). New York: Guilford Press.

Foa, E.B., & Davidson, J.R.T. (1998). *Fluoxetine and cognitive-behavior therapy for social phobia.* Unpublished data.

Foa, E.B., Franklin, M.E., Perry, K.J., & Herbert, J.D. (1996). Cognitive biases in generalized social phobia. *Journal of Abnormal Psychology, 105*(3), 433–439.

Foa, E.B., Herbert, J.D., Franklin, M.E., & Bellack, A.S. (1995). *Comprehensive cognitive behavior therapy for generalized social phobia.* Unpublished manuscript.

Foa, E.B., & Kozak, M.J. (1985). Treatment of anxiety disorders: Implications for psychopathology. In A.H. Tuma & J.D. Maser (Eds.), *Anxiety and the anxiety disorders* (pp. 421–452). Hillsdale, NJ: Erlbaum.

Franklin, M.E., Fitzgibbons, L.A., Freshman, M., Coles, M., & Foa, E.B. (1997, November). *Does treatment for social phobia ameliorate negative interpretation bias?* Poster presented at the 31st annual meeting of the Association for Advancement of Behavior Therapy, Miami, FL.

Gelernter, C.S., Uhde, T.W., Cimbolic, P., Arnkoff, D., Vittone, B.J., Tancer, M., Tancer M.E., & Bartko, J.J. (1991). Cognitive-behavior and pharmacological treatments of social phobia: A controlled study. *Archives of General Psychiatry, 48,* 938–945.

Heckelman, L.R., & Schneier, F.R. (1995). Diagnostic issues. In R.G. Heimberg, M.R. Liebowitz, D.A. Hope, & F.R. Schneier (Eds.), *Social phobia: Diagnosis, assessment and treatment* (pp. 3–20). New York: Guilford Press.

Heimberg, R.G., Becker, R.E., Dodge, C.S., & Hope, D.A. (1990). *DSM-III-R* sub-types of social phobia: Comparison of generalized social phobia and public speaking phobics. *Journal of Nervous and Mental Disease, 178,* 172–179.

Heimberg, R.G., Becker, R.E., Goldfinger, K., & Vermilyea, J.A. (1985). Treatment of social phobia by exposure, cognitive restructuring, and homework assignments. *Journal of Nervous and Mental Disease, 173,* 236–245.

Heimberg, R.G., Dodge, C.S., Hope, D.A., Kennedy, C.R., & Zollo, L.J. (1990). Cognitive behavioral group treatment for social phobia: Comparison with a credible placebo control. *Cognitive Therapy and Research, 14,* 1–23.

Heimberg, R.G., & Juster, H.R. (1995). Treatment of social phobia in cognitive-behavioral groups. *Journal of Clinical Psychiatry, 56,* 38–46.

Heimberg, R.G., Salzman, D.G., Holt, C.S., & Blendell, K. (1993). Cognitive-behavioral group treatment for social phobia: Effectiveness at five-year followup. *Cognitive Therapy and Research, 17,* 325–339.

Herbert, J.D., Hope, D.A., & Bellack, A.S. (1992). Validity of the distinction between generalized social phobia and avoidant personality disorder. *Journal of Abnormal Psychology, 101,* 332–339.

Holt, C.S., Heimberg, R.G., & Hope, D.A. (1992). Avoidant personality disorder and the generalized subtype of social phobia. *Journal of Abnormal Psychology, 101,* 318–325.

Hope, D.A., Herbert, J.D., & White, C. (1995). Diagnostic sub-type, avoidant personality disorder, and efficacy of cognitive-behavioral group therapy for social phobia. *Cognitive Therapy and Research, 19,* 399–417.

Katzelnick, D.J., Kobak, K.A., Greist, J.H., Jefferson, J.W., Mantle, J.M., & Serlin, R.C. (1995). Sertraline in social phobia: A double-blind, placebo-controlled crossover study. *American Journal of Psychiatry, 152,* 1368–1371.

Kessler, R.C., McGonagle, K.A., Zhao, S., Nelson, C.B., Hughes, M., Eschleman, S., Wittchen H.-U., & Kendler, K.S. (1994). Lifetime and 12-month prevalence of *DSM-III-R* psychiatric disorders in the United States—Results from the national comorbidity survey. *Archives of General Psychiatry, 51,* 8–19.

Liberman, R.P., King, L.W., DeRisi, W.J., & McCann, M. (1975). *Personal effectiveness.* Champaign, IL: Research Press.

Liebowitz, M.R., Schneier, R.R., Campeas, R., Hollander, E., Horrerer, J., Fyer, A., Gorman, J.M., Papp, L., Davies, S.O., Gully, R., & Kleing D.F. (1992). Phenelzine vs. atenolol in social phobia: A placebo-controlled comparison. *Archives of General Psychiatry, 49,* 290–300.

Lucock, M.P., & Salkovskis, P.M. (1988). Cognitive factors in social anxiety and its treatment. *Behaviour Research & Therapy, 26,* 297–302.

Marzillier, J.S., Lambert, C., & Kellett, J. (1976). A controlled evaluation of systematic desensitization and social skills training for socially inadequate psychiatric patients. *Behavior Research and Therapy, 14,* 225–238.

Mattick, R.P., & Peters, L. (1988). Treatment of severe social phobia: Effects of guided exposure with and without cognitive restructuring. *Journal of Consulting and Clinical Psychology, 56,* 251–260.

Mattick, R.P., Peters, L., & Clarke, J.C. (1989). Exposure and cognitive restructuring for social phobia: A controlled study. *Behavior Therapy, 20,* 3–23.

Mersch, P.P.A., Emmelkamp, P.M.G., Bogels, S.M., & van der Sleen, J. (1989). Social phobia: Individual response patterns and the effects of behavioral and cognitive interventions. *Behavior Research Therapy, 27,* 421–434.

Ost, L.G., Jerremalm, A., & Johansson, J. (1981). Individual response patterns and the effects of different behavioral methods in the treatment of social phobia. *Behavior Research Therapy, 19,* 1–16.

Pilkonis, P.A. (1977). The behavioral consequences of shyness. *Journal of Personality, 45,* 596–611.

Potts, N.L.S., & Davidson, J.R.T. (1995). Pharmacological treatments: Literature review. In R.G. Heimberg, M.R., Liebowitz, D.A. Hope, & F.R. Schneier (Eds.), *Social phobia: Diagnosis, assessment, and treatment* (pp. 344–365). New York: Guilford Press.

Rapee, R.M., & Heimberg, R.G. (1997). A cognitive-behavioral model of anxiety in social phobia. *Behavior Research Therapy, 35,* 741–756.

Rapee, R.M., & Lim, L. (1992). Discrepancy between self and observer ratings of performance in social phobia. *Journal of Abnormal Psychology, 101,* 728–731.

Schneier, F.R., Chin, S.J., Hollander, E., & Liebowitz, M.R. (1992). Fluoxetine in social phobia. *Journal of Clinical Pharmacology, 12,* 62–63.

Scholing, A., & Emmelkamp, P.M.G. (1990). Social phobia: Nature and treatment. In H. Leitenberg (Ed.), *Handbook of social and evaluation anxiety.* New York: Plenum Press.

Scholing, A., & Emmelkamp, P.M.G. (1993). Exposure with and without cognitive therapy for generalized social phobia: Effects of individual and group treatment. *Behaviour Research and Therapy, 31,* 667–681.

Shaw, P. (1979). A comparison of three behavior therapies in the treatment of social phobia. *British Journal of Psychiatry, 134,* 620–623.

Stein, M.B., Chartier, M.J., Hazen, A.L., Kroft, C.D.L., Chale, R.A., Cote, D., & Walker, J.R. (1996). Paroxetine in the treatment of generalized social phobia: Open-label treatment and double-blind placebo-controlled discontinuation. *Journal of Clinical Psychopharmacology, 16,* 218–222.

Stein, M.B., Walker, J.R., & Forde, D.R. (1994). Setting diagnostic thresholds for social phobia: Considerations from a comorbidity survey of social anxiety. *American Journal of Psychiatry, 151,* 408–412.

Stopa, L., & Clark, D.M. (1993). Cognitive processes in social phobia. *Behaviour Research and Therapy, 31,* 255–267.

Stravynski, A., & Greenberg, D. (1989). Behavioural psychotherapy for social phobia and dysfunction. *International Review of Psychiatry, 1,* 207–218.

Stravynski, A., Marks, I., & Yule, R. (1982). Social skills problems in neurotic outpatients. *Archives of General Psychiatry, 39,* 1378–1385.

Sutherland, S.M., Colkert, J.T., Davidson, J.R.T., & Tupler, L.A. (1996). A 2-year follow-up of social phobia: Status after a brief medication trial. *Journal of Nervous and Mental Disease, 184,* 731–738.

Tran, G.Q., & Chambless, D.L. (1995). Psychopathology of social phobia: Effects of subtype and of avoidant personality disorder. *Journal of Anxiety Disorders, 9,* 489–501.

Trower, P., Yardley, K., Bryant, B.M., & Shaw, P. (1978). Treatment of social failure: A comparison of anxiety-reduction and skills-acquisition procedures on two social problems. *Behavior Modification, 2*(1), 41–60.

Turner, S.M., Beidel, D.C., Cooley, M.R., Messer, S.C., & Woody, S.R. (1994). A multicomponent behavioral treatment for social phobia: Social effectiveness therapy. *Behaviour Research and Therapy, 32,* 381–390.

Turner, S.M., Beidel, D.C., & Cooley-Quille, M.R. (1995). Two-year follow-up of social phobics treated with social effectiveness therapy. *Behavior Research Therapy, 33,* 553–555.

Turner, S.M., Beidel, D.C., Dancu, C.V., & Keys, D.J. (1986). Psychopathology of social phobia and comparison to avoidant personality disorder. *Journal of Abnormal Psychology, 95,* 389–394.

Turner, S.M., Beidel, D.C., Dancu, C.V., & Stanley, M.A. (1989). An empirically derived inventory to measure social fears and anxiety: The social phobia and anxiety scale. *Psychological Assessment, 1,* 35–40.

Turner, S.M., Beidel, D.C., & Jacob, R.G. (1994). Social phobia: A comparison of behavior therapy and atenolol. *Journal of Consulting and Clinical Psychology, 62,* 350–358.

Turner, S.M., Beidel, D.C., & Townsley, R.M. (1992). Social phobia: A comparison of specific and generalized sub-types and avoidant personality disorder. *Journal of Abnormal Psychology, 101,* 326–331.

Van Vliet, I.M., den Boer, J.A., & Westenberg, G.M. (1991). Psychopharmacological treatment of social phobia: Clinical and biochemical effects of brofaromine, a selective MAO-A inhibitor. *European Psychopharmacology, 8,* 21–29.

Van Vliet, I.M., den Boer, J.A., & Westenberg, H.G.M. (1994). Psychopharmacological treatment of social phobia: A double-blind placebo-controlled study with fluvoxamine. *Psychopharmacology, 115,* 128–134.

Versiani, M., Nardi, A.E., Mundim, F.D., Alves, A.B., Liebowitz, M.R., & Amrein, R. (1992). Pharmacotherapy of social phobia: A controlled study with moclobemide and phenelzine. *British Journal of Psychiatry, 161,* 353–360.

Wlazlo, Z., Schroeder-Hartwig, K., Hand, I., Kaiser, G., & Münchau, N. (1990). Exposure in vivo vs. social skills training for social phobia: Long-term outcome and differential effects. *Behavior Research and Therapy, 28,* 181–193.

Wolpe, J., & Lazarus, A.A. (1966). *Behavior therapy techniques.* New York: Pergamon Press.

CHAPTER 14

Pharmacotherapy

JELENA KUNOVAC and MURRAY B. STEIN

CLINICAL AND epidemiological evidence have shown that social phobia is far more prevalent than once thought, affecting as many as 1 in 10 individuals (Magee, Eaton, Wittchen, McGonagle, & Kessler, 1996).

Patients with social phobia can be treated effectively with either medication, cognitive-behavior therapy (CBT) or the combination of both. Efficacy has been reported in a number of open and double-blind, placebo-controlled studies for several different classes of medication, including beta-blockers, monoamine oxidase inhibitors (MAOIs), high potency benzodiazepines, and selective serotonin reuptake inhibitors (SSRIs).

BETA-BLOCKERS

Beta-blockers were evaluated in numerous studies for their efficacy in reducing performance anxiety (e.g., Tyrer & Lader, 1974). The first study (Granville-Grossman & Turner, 1966) reported in the literature suggested that only the autonomically mediated symptoms, such as heart palpitations, tremor, and sweating were significantly improved by propranolol, whereas symptoms of anxiety, tension, and irritability were not improved. During the 1970s and early 1980s, 13 studies that evaluated efficacy of beta-blockers in the treatment of various types of performance anxiety were reported in the literature (see Sutherland & Davidson, 1995). In 10 of the 13 studies, significant benefit from beta-blockers in performance results, relief of anxiety, or both was reported (Sutherland & Davidson, 1995).

SINGLE-DOSE STUDIES

Single-doses of beta-blockers have been found effective in reducing performance anxiety in several double-blind, placebo-controlled studies. The drug is usually given in a single dose between 30 minutes and several hours before the performance, depending on the pharmacokinetic characteristics of the particular drug. Alprenolol (50 to 100 mg), oxprenolol (40 mg), atenolol (100 mg), and propranolol were all more effective than placebo in reducing anxiety and heart rate (Brantigan, Brantigan, & Joseph, 1982; James, Griffith, Pearson, & Newby, 1977; Liden & Gottfries, 1974; Neftel et al., 1982).

MULTIPLE-DOSE STUDIES

In a small open study of 10 patients diagnosed with social phobia using *DSM-III* criteria, Gorman, Liebowitz, Fyer, Campeas, and Klein (1985) administered 50 to 100 mg of atenolol for at least six weeks. Improvement was observed in both generalized and specific social phobic symptoms.

Liebowitz et al. (1992) conducted an eight-week double-blind, placebo-controlled study of MAOI phenelzine and beta-blocker atenolol in patients meeting *DSM-III* criteria for social phobia. Seventy-four patients who completed eight weeks of treatment with either phenelzine, atenolol, or placebo entered eight-week maintenance phase. Sixty-four percent of patients on phenelzine were considered responders, compared to 30 percent on atenolol and 23 percent on placebo. Authors failed to observe differences in response between placebo and atenolol. When patients were analyzed separately, accordingly to discrete and generalized social phobia (GSP) subtype, there was a higher response rate to phenelzine in the generalized group. The study included an eight-week maintenance phase with minimal further changes within each treatment group.

The latest study reported in the literature (Turner, Beidel, & Jacob, 1994) also showed no benefit of atenolol over placebo in the treatment of social phobia. Seventy-two patients with social phobia were randomly assigned to behavioral or drug treatment with atenolol (up to 100 mg) or placebo for three months. No difference was observed between atenolol and placebo, whereas behavioral treatment was superior to placebo.

Thus, although beta-blockers appear to be of some use in specific social anxiety-provoking situations, such as public speaking and performance anxiety, there is scant evidence demonstrating their efficacy in patients actually diagnosed with social phobia.

BENZODIAZEPINES

Although many investigators have viewed benzodiazepines (BDZs) as the most effective group of drugs for the majority of anxiety disorders, there are only a few reports in the literature of the use of these agents in social phobia. The high potency BDZs, alprazolam and clonazepam, are the most extensively studied benzodiazepines in the treatment of social phobia.

Several open-label studies supported the efficacy of clonazepam in social phobia (Munjack, Baltazar, Bohn, Cabe, & Appleton, 1990; Ontiveros & Fontaine, 1990; Reiter, Pollack, Rosenbaum, & Cohen, 1990). In a long-term treatment study, Davidson, Ford, Smith, and Potts (1991) treated 26 social-phobia patients for a mean of 11.3 months (range 1 to 29) with the treatment doses ranging from 0.5 to 5 mg/day, and mean daily dose of 2.1 mg. All the patients requiring doses of greater than 1.5 mg/day during the initial treatment phase were able to lower their doses over time while maintaining their clinical gains. Five patients successfully withdrew from medication. The reported response rate was 85 percent, with half of these rated as very much improved and half as much improved. The studies showed that side effects associated with clonazepam treatment are frequent and could be troublesome. The most commonly reported were loss of libido and cognitive disturbance.

Davidson and colleagues (Davidson, Potts, Richichi, & Krishnan, 1993) conducted what is to date the only double-blind, placebo-controlled trial of clonazepam. The results indicated superior efficacy of clonazepam on most measures, including performance and generalized social anxiety, interpersonal sensitivity, fears of negative evaluation, and disability measures (Davidson et al., 1993). Seventy-eight percent of patients on clonazepam and 20 percent of patients on placebo were rated as at least much improved on clinical global improvement scale. Treatment was continued for up to 10 weeks. Treatment doses ranged from 0.5 mg/day to 3.0 mg/day, with a mean dose of 2.4 mg/day. A statistically significant difference between clonazepam and placebo was observed as early as week 1 on a global improvement measure, and from week 2 onward on almost all other outcome measures. Maximum improvement was achieved by week 8 on scales measuring fear, avoidance, anxious cognitions, and disability. The most common side effects of clonazepam included sedation and anorgasmia.

In an 8-week study, Reich and Yates (1988) administered a mean daily dose of 2.9 mg of alprazolam (dosage range 1 to 10 mg/daily) to 14 social-phobia patients. Significant improvement on all symptom measures was observed within the first two weeks of treatment, with a reduction in disability evident by weeks 3 and 4. Ten patients were rated as very much improved and four as much improved at the end of the treatment. The medication was tapered off over one week after the end of the study. A rapid reemergence of symptoms was observed one week after completion of the drug taper.

The efficacy of alprazolam was further supported in another open-label trial by Lydiard, Laraia, Howell, and Ballenger (1988), who reported that four patients with social phobia experienced moderate-to-marked improvement with alprazolam treatment (3 to 8 mg/day). One patient showed an additional benefit after addition of phenelzine.

The only published double-blind, placebo-controlled study, compared phenelzine, alprazolam and cognitive-behavior group therapy (CBGT) in a 12-week study of 65 subjects (Gelernter et al., 1991). In this study, conducted at the National Institute of Mental Health, a very rigid criterion was used to measure treatment response, identifying responders as those whose rating on the social-phobia subscale of the Fear Questionnaire fell into the normal range for the general population. Using this criterion, 69 percent of the phenelzine group were responders, 38 percent of the alprazolam group, 24 percent of the

CBGT group and 20 percent of placebo group qualified as responders. Alprazolam treatment was, however, associated with a higher relapse rate than phenelzine at two months follow-up after the discontinuation of treatment.

Thus, there is reasonable support for the use of benzodiazepines to treat social phobia. Their use should be balanced against the risks of abuse, misuse, and dependence with this class of drugs. Clinicians should avoid using the benzodiazepines in patients with a history of drug or alcohol abuse—the latter of which is particularly common in social phobics—but in other cases the benzodiazepines represent a reasonable alternative to antidepressant medications. In terms of choosing among the benzodiazepines, there are no empirical data to inform this decision. Practically speaking, the longer half-life of clonazepam (and the resultant ability to administer it once or twice daily) offers a practical advantage over alprazolam, which needs to be taken three to four times daily.

ANTIDEPRESSANTS

Antidepressants have been used to treat patients with social phobia almost since social phobia became an official diagnosis. MAOIs, SSRIs, and other antidepressants have all been studied with varying results in patients with social phobia. The MAOIs have been the treatment of choice for years, but their considerable side effects limit their use. The SSRIs are well established in treating social phobia and many clinicians nowadays choose an SSRI as their first-line agent.

MAOIs

Almost from their introduction, MAOIs have been used successfully to treat various anxiety syndromes. The nonspecific, irreversible MAOIs are the medications with the best proven efficacy in social phobia.

In most studies, a reduction in social anxiety is seen after treatment with phenelzine or tranylcypromine (Gelernter et al., 1991; Liebowitz et al., 1988, 1992; Versiani et al., 1992; Versiani, Mundim, Nardi, & Liebowitz, 1988). In three published double-blind, placebo-controlled trials, phenelzine was found effective for about two-thirds of patients (Gelernter et al., 1991; Liebowitz et al., 1992; Versiani et al., 1992). The results of these studies are reported elsewhere in this chapter.

There are no double-blind, placebo-controlled studies evaluating the efficacy of tranylcypromine in social phobia. An open study of a one-year treatment with tranylcypromine in dosages between 40 and 60 mg/day found marked improvement in 62 percent of patients and moderate improvement in 17 percent (Versiani et al., 1988). The response was maintained over a period of one year. Side effects were common and alcohol abuse was associated with a poor outcome. Although no empirical data exist, our clinical experience suggests that some patients who are nonresponders to phenelzine may respond to tranylcypromine, and vice versa. Consequently, treatment failure to the first MAOI does not necessarily represent treatment resistance to this class of drugs in general, and switching to an alternate MAOI, after a 14-day wash-out period, may be worthwhile.

The utility of irreversible, nonspecific MAOIs is limited by the high risk of hypertensive crisis if dietary precautions are not strictly followed. Also, the propensity for serious drug interactions with MAOIs limit their appeal. MAOIs also cause a relatively high rate of adverse effects, including postural hypotension, daytime drowsiness, insomnia, weight gain, and sexual dysfunction.

REVERSIBLE INHIBITORS OF MONOAMINE OXIDASE TYPE A

Safer and better tolerated reversible inhibitors of monoamine oxidase A (RIMAs), moclobemide and brofaromine, also have been found effective in some but not all studies of the treatment of social phobia. Versiani et al. (1992) conducted a double-blind, placebo-controlled study comparing phenelzine (25 patients), moclobemide (26 patients), and placebo (23 patients). The patients entered an eight-week acute treatment phase followed by an eight-week maintenance phase and then an eight-week placebo discontinuation phase. Phenelzine was increased up to 90 mg/day; moclobemide was started from 100 mg/day and increased to a maximum of 600 mg/day. Among patients who completed 16 weeks of treatment, 90 percent of the phenelzine group, 82 percent of the moclobemide group, and 43 percent of the placebo group were classified as responders. Both drugs were significantly superior to placebo by week 8, with phenelzine being superior to moclobemide on only the Liebowitz Social Anxiety Scale subscale for avoidance. The two drug groups differed most in rates of side effects, particularly during the eight-week maintenance phase, with 95 percent of patients taking phenelzine experiencing side effects compared to only 12 percent of patients in moclobemide group.

The international multicenter clinical trial group on moclobemide has recently completed a large study which included 578 patients (Katschnig et al., 1997). The study was a double-blind, fixed-dose parallel group and was designed to compare the efficacy of 300 mg and 600 mg of moclobemide to placebo. After a one-week placebo run-in period, patients were randomly assigned to placebo, 300 mg or 600 mg moclobemide group for 12 weeks. The results showed that 600 mg of moclobemide was effective and statistically superior to placebo at weeks 8 and 12. Although 300 mg dose showed better efficacy than placebo on all measures, only about half of them were statistically significantly different from placebo. Moclobemide was well tolerated; the most common side effect reported was insomnia.

Despite the apparent utility of moclobemide in the aforementioned study, two subsequent studies have failed to demonstrate the superiority of moclobemide to placebo in the treatment of social phobia (Noyes, Moroz, Davidson, & Liebowitz, 1997; Schneier et al., 1998). At the present time, moclobemide is not being marketed in the United States, but it is available in Canada and throughout much of the rest of Europe, Scandinavia, Australia, and South America. These most recent double-blind studies notwithstanding (Noyes et al., 1997; Schneier et al., 1998), moclobemide continues to be used to treat social phobia in these countries, with some apparent success. Still, it is probably fair to conclude that moclobemide is not among the most robust of the pharmacologic treatments available for social phobia.

A double-blind, placebo-controlled study using brofaromine (which is not currently commercially available) in the treatment of social phobia was published by Van Vliet, den Boer, and Westenberg (1992). Thirty patients diagnosed with *DSM-III-R* criteria for social phobia participated in a 12-week study. Patients who were considered improved continued for another 12 weeks. The dose of brofaromine was increased from 50 to 150 mg daily over three weeks. In the brofaromine group, 12 of 15 patients were considered responders, compared to 2 of 15 in the placebo group. Superiority of brofaromine to placebo was observed in reducing scores on the Liebowitz Social Anxiety Scale and the Hamilton Anxiety Scale. The most common reported side effects in the brofaromine group included insomnia, nausea, loss of appetite, and weight loss.

The results of a multicenter, placebo-controlled, double-blind study were recently reported in the literature (Lott et al., 1997). In a 10-week treatment of either placebo or brofaromine 102 patients were randomized. Brofaromine was given in a maximal dose of 150 mg/day, depending on treatment response. At the end of the study, brofaromine was statistically significantly superior to placebo in reducing scores from baseline on the Liebowitz Social Anxiety Scale. The side effects associated with brofaromine were insomnia, dizziness, dry mouth. anorexia, tinnitus, and tremor.

SEROTONIN SELECTIVE REUPTAKE INHIBITORS

A review of open-label trials and controlled trials supports the efficacy of SSRIs in the treatment of social phobia. Most of the published studies are, however open label and samples are very small. Double-blind studies with several of the SSRIs are either in progress or have already been completed, but details have not yet been published.

In a 12-week, open clinical trial, paroxetine was administered to 18 patients with a primary diagnosis of GSP (Mancini & van Ameringen, 1996). The starting dose was 10 mg of paroxetine daily. The dose was increased according to clinical response and side effects. At the end of the study, 83 percent of patients were considered responders (moderate or marked improvement). Stein et al. (1996) conducted an 11-week forced escalation open-label study of paroxetine in the treatment of GSP, followed by a double-blind, placebo-controlled discontinuation. Among 30 patients who completed 11 weeks of open-label treatment, 23 were considered responders on the basis of a clinician rating of either very much improved or much improved on the Clinical Global Impression Scale. Sixteen responders were randomized to an additional 12 weeks of either paroxetine or placebo on a double-blind basis. Five of eight subjects switched to placebo relapsed during the follow-up period, compared to only one of eight subjects who continued taking paroxetine. The findings suggest that relapse rates are high if medication is discontinued early.

In a double-blind, placebo-controlled study, Van Vliet, den Boer, and Westenberg (1994) investigated the efficacy of fluvoxamine in 30 social phobics *(DSM-III-R)*. Patients were treated with 150 mg of fluvoxamine or placebo for

12 weeks. Improvement was defined as a 50 percent or greater reduction in the anxiety subscale of the Liebowitz Social Anxiety Scale. Of patients on fluvoxamine, 46 percent were rated as substantially improved, comparing to seven percent (one patient) in placebo group. Treatment with fluvoxamine resulted in a decrease in social anxiety, as well as social avoidance. Although the level of phobic avoidance decreased, the difference at endpoint between fluvoxamine and placebo failed to reach statistical difference.

There are a total of four open-label and one double-blind, placebo-controlled trials of sertraline in patients with social phobia reported in the literature. An open-label study (van Ameringen, Mancini, & Streiner, 1994) first suggested the efficacy of sertraline in social phobia. In a double-blind crossover study, 12 patients were randomized to 10 weeks of sertraline (50–200 mg/day, flexible dosing) and 10 weeks of placebo (Katzelnick et al., 1995). The maximum mean daily dose of sertraline was 133.5 mg. A statistically significant improvement in scores on the Liebowitz Social Anxiety Scale was observed in the sertraline group, but not in the placebo group (50% of the patients, compared to 9%).

Fluoxetine, the most widely prescribed SSRI for the treatment of depression, was evaluated for the treatment of social phobia. To our knowledge, there are no controlled studies reported in the literature. Four open-label, small-sample-size studies indicated that 20 to 80 mg of fluoxetine daily was of value for treating social phobia (Black, Uhde, & Tancer, 1992; Schneier, Chin, Hollander, & Liebowitz, 1992; Sternbach, 1992; van Ameringen, Mancini, & Streiner, 1993).

In another open-label study, three patients were treated with 20 mg of citalopram—an SSRI which, at the time of this writing, is awaiting release in the United States for the treatment of depression—for 12 to 24 months (Lepola, Koponen, & Leinonen, 1994). In this small study, citalopram was believed to be efficacious. More recently, Bouwer and Stein (1998) published results of a series of 22 generalized social phobic patients who were treated with open-label citalopram. In that study, patients were started on 20 mg per day of citalopram and, if tolerated, this was increased to 40 mg per day by week 2; total duration of treatment was 12 weeks. All patients completed the study, and the medication was generally very well tolerated. Overall, 19 patients (86%) were considered responders to treatment on the basis of Clinical Global Impression of Change scores. These preliminary findings suggest that citalopram is likely to prove to be a well-tolerated, efficacious agent in the management of generalized social phobia.

Buspirone Augmentation of SSRIs

Although SSRIs are emerging as a first-line treatment for social phobia, there are some disadvantages associated with their use. First, improvement typically takes several weeks to become apparent, and second, adverse effects such as nausea, insomnia, and especially sexual dysfunction are frequently reported by patients. Furthermore, it is likely that only 50 percent to 60 percent of patients will respond to SSRIs, leaving a substantial proportion of social phobics as nonresponders. In this regard, there have been some recent efforts to augment SSRI response with other pharmacotherapeutic agents.

Van Ameringen, Mancini, and Streiner (1996) evaluated the efficacy of buspirone augmentation of SSRIs in social phobia. Ten patients, who obtained only a partial response to an adequate trial of SSRI, received buspirone in addition to the SSRI for eight weeks in an open trial. The mean dose of buspirone at the end point was 45 mg/day. The dose range was 30 to 60 mg/day. Seven patients (70%) were considered responders (moderate or marked improvement) providing clinical evidence that buspirone augmentation may be a useful clinical strategy in social phobic patients who show partial response to SSRIs. Five of the 10 patients had treatment-related side effects, but none of these necessitated withdrawal from the open trial. Fatigue, nausea, jitteryness and "fogginess" were observed. The utility of buspirone as an augmenting agent under double-blind conditions has yet to be demonstrated.

VENLAFAXINE

Venlafaxine is an antidepressant with dual activity at both serotonin and norepinephrine transporters. Kelsey (1995) suggested that venlafexine might be efficacious in treating social phobia, particularly in patients who do not respond to SSRIs. Nine patients with social phobia participated in an open-label trial of venlafexine. Eight of them had previously been treated with an SSRI and either failed to respond to it or could not tolerate the medication. Among nine patients, eight had a marked improvement in social phobia symptoms on venlafexine. To the best of our knowledge, double-blind, placebo-controlled studies of venlafaxine for social phobia are not currently available.

NEFAZODONE

Nefazodone is an antidepressant with serotonin receptor type 2 (5-HT2) antagonist properties, which has very little sexual dysfunction associated with its use. Given the high rates of anorgasmia and delayed ejaculation associated with SSRI use—which, in the authors' experience, is a common reason for discontinuing treatment among social phobics taking SSRIs—the availability of a medication without these problems would be a significant advantage. Van Ameringen and colleagues (van Ameringen, Mancini, & Oakman, 1997) treated 23 patients with a primary *DSM-IV* diagnosis of GSP with 100mg or more of nefazodone in an open-label clinical trial. Of 23 patients, 21 completed the 12-week trial, and 16 (70%) were considered responders (defined as moderate or marked improvement). If the findings are replicated in placebo-controlled trials, nefazodone will become a welcome addition to the therapeutic armamentarium for generalized social phobia.

OTHER MEDICATIONS

Buspirone is an azapirone acting as a full receptor agonist at the somatodendritic serotonin type-1A (5-HT1A) autoreceptor and as a partial agonist at the postsynaptic 5-HT1A receptor. It is marketed for the treatment of generalized anxiety disorder.

The results of open-label studies suggested that buspirone might be effective in the treatment of social phobia (Munjack et al., 1991; Schneier et al., 1993). Reduction of social anxiety and social avoidance was reported in patients with social phobia (Munjack et al., 1991; Schneier et al., 1993). These findings were not confirmed in what is so far the only double-blind, placebo-controlled study (Van Vliet, den Boer, Westenberg, & Pian, 1997). Thirty patients with social phobia, diagnosed according to *DSM-IV* criteria, were treated with either buspirone (30 mg daily) or placebo for 12 weeks. Overall, buspirone was well tolerated, but no statistical difference between buspirone and placebo on any of the outcome measures was found. The results of this study remind us that double-blind studies often fail to confirm the usefulness of medications that appear promising in open-label studies.

Ondansetron is a 5-HT3 antagonist currently marketed in the United States as an antiemetic. Preliminary results of a randomized, double-blind, placebo-controlled multicenter trail showed that ondansetron was significantly more effective than placebo at the end of week 10 (DeVaugh-Geiss & Bell, 1994). The Duke Brief Social-Phobia Scale was used as the primary efficacy variable. Although ondansetron was significantly superior to placebo, the authors felt the "effect size" was small, and the medication is not being further developed for social phobia.

SELECTING A MEDICATION

A review of the published literature regarding the treatment of social phobia brings the conclusion that the most effective medication treatments for social phobia are MAOIs, SSRIs, and benzodiazepines. In selecting the medication, several factors should be considered, primarily efficacy, side effects of medication, and the diagnostic subtype of social phobia.

Some authorities propose that some forms of non-GSP, such as those limited to performance situations, should be treated with PRN (as needed) medication, primarily single doses of beta-blockers or benzodiazepines used 30 to 60 minutes prior to the situation (Marshall & Schneier, 1996). Because they are devoid of abuse potential, beta-blockers are often considered first-line treatment. An electrocardiogram is recommended prior to the initiation of the therapy. Atrioventricular block, asthma, and diabetes are among the major contraindications. Dose must be determined for each individual, based on consideration of side effects (e.g., postural hypotension, bradycardia, anergia) and efficacy. It is recommended that patients try out the medication in a "safe" setting on more than one occasion in order to find the optimal dose for them. This may require several visits to the physician before they are ready to use the medication in a performance situation.

If beta-blockers are ineffective—which, in the authors' experience, is more often the case than not—then short-acting benzodiazepines, such as lorazepam or alprazolam, may be tried on a PRN basis, also 30 to 60 minutes prior to the situation. In general, the benzodiazepines tend to be effective and well tolerated for the treatment of performance-related social anxiety. However, sedation may be a limiting factor in their use for a minority of patients. Also, benzodiazepines are rarely associated with anterograde memory loss or acute disinhibition, either of which seems to occur on an idiosyncratic basis. It is, therefore, wise to counsel patients to try out the medication at least once or twice prior to using it in an important performance situation.

When the patient is diagnosed with GSP, indicating that their social anxiety is pervasive and spans many social situations, then the use of as-needed medication is no longer practical. For such patients, continuous-treatment SSRIs should be the treatment of choice. Numerous studies have confirmed their efficacy in the treatment of social phobia. Adverse effects are very common, but they usually wear off after several weeks of therapy, and they rarely result in patients choosing to discontinue the medication. The most bothersome side effect, which does not abate with time, is sexual dysfunction. In some cases, this side effect can be managed with weekend "drug holidays," as long as SSRIs with relatively short half-lives (e.g., sertraline, fluvoxamine, or paroxetine) are used.

If SSRIs are not effective or not tolerated, a trial of MAOI is warranted. Unfortunately, reversible MAOIs are not available in the United States. Dietary precautions should be strictly followed. Finally, if neither SSRIs nor MAOIs have relieved symptoms of social phobia, BDZ should be tried, using either alprazolam or clonazepam.

SOCIAL PHOBIA AND MANAGED CARE

There is currently very little information available that might inform an approach to social phobia in the era of managed care. Three questions come to mind: Can primary care physicians recognize social phobia? If they can, should they be treating social phobia? If the answer is yes to the first two questions, when should primary care physicians refer the patient to a psychiatrist? Unlike depression and panic disorder, where primary care physicians can recognize and identify these conditions, general practitioners are not aware of the relatively high prevalence and associated disability of social phobia (Weiller, Bisserbe, Boyer, Lepine, & Lecrubier, 1996). We need to provide primary care physicians with the data on the typical characteristics of a patient with social phobia, as well as with the data regarding comorbidity between social phobia and depression and substance abuse. Primary care physicians need guidelines for making diagnosis. Because it is very unlikely that the patient will go to a primary care physician complaining about social-phobia symptoms, such protocols would recommend asking questions about social-phobia symptoms if several major psychiatric conditions, such as major depression or alcohol abuse, are present. Also, all care givers should keep in mind that there is an ongoing trend in managed care to use the least extensively trained provider. Patients with psychiatric disorders other than psychoses are typically referred to social workers or counselors. If these mental healthcare workers are educated to recognize social phobias, then, perhaps, referral to an experienced psychologist (for appropriate behavioral interventions) or psychiatrist can be initiated.

We know for certain that social phobia is associated with poorer self-rated health (Weiller et al., 1996) and with reduced quality of life (Safren, Heimberg, Brown, & Holle, 1997). There are currently no data available about the direct or indirect costs of social phobias to the healthcare system or to society in general (e.g., time away from work; reduced work productivity). When these data become available, they will enable health policy makers to generate an appropriate response to this underrecognized and neglected public-health problem. Whether managed-care companies will respond to these plans remains to be seen.

Case Illustration

Jonas is a 40-year-old male computer programmer who presented to a psychiatrist complaining of depression. He described feeling down, disinterested, and anergic for the prior year. When questioned further, he admitted to feeling unhappy for most of his life, and that this unhappiness was associated with chronic feelings of low self-worth and dissatisfaction with his life. In the prior year, however, there was a definite worsening of his mood, to the point that he had become frequently tearful, and thought about life not being worth living (though he had no thoughts about doing anything to end his life). He reported an increase in his appetite in the past six to nine months, associated with carbohydrate and sugar craving, leading to a 15-pound weight gain. He described feeling frequently anxious and restless, and he slept only four to five hours per night, even though he felt chronically tired and napped during the daytime whenever he could. His concentration was poor, and he felt that his performance at work was not as good as it should have been, though his output was not materially affected and none of his superiors had voiced any complaints.

When asked to describe his feeling of anxiety, Jonas stated that he was "anxious all the time," though this had been the case for only the past year or so. Prior to that, he stated that he was usually "laid back," except when in the company of other people. He stated that he had "always" been shy, and that this had been a problem for him throughout his life. He spontaneously reported that this shyness had shaped much of his life. Specifically, he stated that he had never been able to date, and that he had seen this as a "major flaw" in his character. Beginning in high school, when confronted with his inability to talk to girls, he adopted the habit of calling himself a coward. He also saw his choice of career as cowardly: "I went into computers because I knew I could sit in my little corner, do my work, and not have to talk to people." Now at age 40, he found himself bored with his career, but too frightened by the prospect of interviewing for other jobs or going back to school to even consider those options. He also found himself isolated and alone, feeling like an outsider among his small circle of long-time friends, and wondering whether he was going to spend the rest of his life as a hermit.

When directly queried about this, Jonas reported fear and avoidance of a vast array of situations. These included talking to more than one person at a time (either in formal or informal situations), eating in public, using public restrooms, talking to people in authority (he dreaded conversations with his boss), talking to women in any context but especially in unstructured social contexts (e.g., lunchroom at work; parties), and numerous other situations.

Jonas had seen numerous counselors over the years for various periods of time, the longest being an 18-month course of once-a-week therapy with a clinical psychologist approximately 10 years prior. At that time, the focus of therapy was to help him deal with the death of his father, which had precipitated an episode of profound depression that lasted several years. Although he had talked to this (and other) therapists about his severe shyness, this had apparently never become a direct focus of treatment. He had also seen a psychiatrist approximately four years prior, again for depressive symptoms, and took imipramine briefly but discontinued it because of side effects (weight gain and headaches).

At this initial assessment, Jonas was felt to suffer from Dysthymia of longstanding duration, Major Depressive Disorder of 9 to 12 months duration, and Social Phobia (Generalized Type). An Axis II diagnosis of Avoidant Personality Disorder was also considered, though additional information needed to be collected at future visits to confirm this diagnosis. The therapist felt that, given the severity of his anergia and trouble concentrating, his depressive symptoms might best be addressed pharmacotherapeutically, at least initially. The therapist also judged that pharmacotherapy had a good chance of alleviating his social anxiety.

Jonas was started on paroxetine, an SSRI, at a dose of 20 mg every morning. He was seen again in two weeks, at which time he reported some daytime sleepiness and nausea when he first started taking the medication, but that these were diminishing as time went on. He was seen two weeks later, at which time he reported improvement in his sleep, some reduction in his anxiety and restlessness, and some brightening of his mood. He reported no side effects at the time. When asked about his level of self-consciousness when in the presence of others, he reported that this was no different than usual. Taking this into consideration, his paroxetine dose was increased to 30 mg every morning.

He was seen again two weeks later, at which time he reported that his mood, energy, and concentration were significantly improved. Furthermore, he described several situations involving interaction with peers at work "where I wasn't nearly as anxious as I thought I'd be. It was really something!" He was encouraged to even more actively seek out opportunities for social interaction, to test out whether the medication was working. His dosage was not changed.

He returned four weeks later stating that his depression was no longer a problem, and that he had noted substantial improvement in his social anxiety symptoms. He described the change in his social-phobia symptoms as nothing short of "miraculous." He lamented the fact that "it took so long for me to get on this medication," and a good deal of the session was spent talking about "all the opportunities I've missed." Toward the end of the session, Jonas remarked that he was considering asking a female colleague out for a drink, but that he was concerned about how long it was taking for him to reach orgasm and ejaculation. He had apparently been aware of this since shortly after starting the medication, and it had worsened slightly upon the increase from 20 to 30 mg. It was only now, though, when he was considering the possibility of a romantic encounter, that he expressed concern about this side effect.

On further questioning, Jonas reported that when masturbating, he had noticed that it took him several minutes longer to ejaculate and, moreover, that his sensation of orgasm felt dulled when it did finally arrive. In discussion with his psychiatrist, Jonas made it clear that he had no desire to discontinue the medication, because he felt that he was benefitting tremendously from its use. It was considered that a sexual encounter was probably not imminent and, when it did happen, his sexual functioning was likely to be objectively fine, and that probably only he would be aware of any difference from his nonmedicated state in this regard. Jonas was relieved by this discussion. His psychiatrist also told him that if the delayed ejaculation proved to be a problem in the future, several options were available. These might include temporary reductions in dosage (e.g., to 10 mg/day for the weekend), adding in medication(s) that would potentially reduce the delayed ejaculation, or switching to another medication. It was also discussed with the patient that CBT might be indicated as an alternative solution to his social anxiety, and that this could be started sometime in the future.

PSYCHOSOCIAL ALTERNATIVES TO PHARMACOTHERAPY FOR SOCIAL PHOBIA

We consider cognitive-behavior therapy to be a proven alternative to pharmacotherapy. When we discuss treatment options with a new patient suffering from social phobia, we describe the availability of two kinds of treatment: pharmacotherapy and specific psychotherapy (i.e., CBT). We point out that both genres of therapy are generally effective, and that choosing which one to start with is usually just a matter of patient preference. In reality, though, we often find that patients' insurance and the availability of therapists skilled in CBT for social phobia represent additional factors that strongly influence the initial approach to treatment. Almost every insurance plan provides access to treatment with an SSRI (although not necessarily for the stated diagnosis of social phobia), but far fewer give the patient (or, for that matter, the treating primary care physician) the right to insist that a therapist be seen, much less what kind of therapist or for how long.

We are thus often faced with the practical reality that adequate pharmacotherapy is likely to be readily available, whereas adequate CBT for social phobia is not. For this reason, it is more likely than not that our initial approach to treating a patient with social phobia will involve pharmacotherapy, rather than CBT. There is also at least one scenario in which our preference would clearly be to start with pharmacotherapy, namely, when a patient is seriously depressed. Although we recognize that this remains controversial, our impression is that anergic, disheartened, concentration-impaired patients are not good candidates for psychotherapy.

It should be mentioned that when we talk about using pharmacotherapy for social phobia, we do not do so in a cognitive-behavioral void. In fact, it is our practice to provide self-help and other reading materials to educate patients about social phobia. We make liberal use of cognitive and behavioral interventions as part of our treatment with medications. This inevitably includes helping the patient to challenge their unrealistic thoughts about the dangers of social situations, and to reexamine their assessment of risk and the potential for a negative outcome. It also includes a hefty dose of encouragement to "push" the patient into anxiety-provoking situations, partly to test out the efficacy of the medication, but partly also to convince patients that they can do these things. So, although we are a long way from suggesting that formal CBT should—or could—be provided in this setting, we genuinely believe that the liberal use of these fairly simple (i.e., simple enough that even psychopharmacologists can learn them!) cognitive-behavior interventions are an integral part of good pharmacotherapy for social phobia.

When would we consider referring a patient to a psychotherapist for formal CBT? Any time a patient expresses an interest in what we typically describe as an "active, educationally based approach to learning how to deal with your social anxiety," and access to a skilled therapist is not an issue, we would strongly consider referring such a patient for a course of CBT. In such a case, we would remain in close contact with the patient and the therapist, and we would offer to initiate pharmacotherapy at some point in the future if the CBT alone was not proving effective. Conversely, we would strongly consider referring a patient for CBT if pharmacologic therapy was proving ineffective or only modestly effective.

In fact, this *sequential* approach to treatment is our favored model for treating social phobia. In the absence of empirical data, we have had to rely on our clinical experience in this regard, and it tells us that many patients do well with either mode of treatment (i.e., pharmacotherapy or specific psychotherapy) alone. To us, this indicates that it is not likely to be cost effective to treat patients simultaneously with pharmacotherapy and CBT for their social phobia. Rather, our preference is to start with one of these treatment modalities, to get as much out of them as possible, and then to sequentially *add on* the other treatment modality if response is inadequate.

The other indication to refer for CBT is a pharmacologically treated patient is doing well, has made good progress in terms of their social phobia, and the time has come (e.g., 12 to 15 months later) to consider discontinuing medication. Once again, the literature has little to offer us with respect to guidelines for long-term pharmacotherapy, but clinical experience has taught us that many patients do relapse when medication is discontinued. Our impression is that the patients who have the most social exposure while on medication, and those who have had the opportunity to improve their self-confidence to the greatest extent (almost always through "positive" experiences when they have taken behavioral risks, e.g., asked someone out for a date and were amazed when the person didn't laugh at them!), are the least likely to relapse when medication is discontinued. This leads us to believe—although once again we must remind the reader that empirical evidence is lacking—that relapse rates might be systematically reduced were patients to participate in a course of CBT prior to medication discontinuation. Consequently, we often refer patients for CBT after they have consolidated gains on pharmacotherapy, in the hope that this will lead to more long-lasting change if and when medication is eventually discontinued.

REFERENCES

Black, B., Uhde, T.W., & Tancer, M.E. (1992). Fluoxetine for the treatment of social phobia [letter]. *Journal of Clinical Psychopharmacology, 12,* 293–295.

Bouwer, C., & Stein, D.J. (1998). Use of the selective serotonin reuptake inhibitor citalopram in the treatment of generalized social phobia. *Journal of Affective Disorders, 49,* 79–82.

Brantigan, C.O., Brantigan, T.A., & Joseph, N. (1982). Effect of beta-blockade and beta-stimulation on stage fright. *American Journal of Medicine, 72,* 88–94.

Davidson, J.R.T., Ford, S.M., Smith, R.D., & Potts, N.L. (1991). Long-term treatment of social phobia with clonzaepam. *Journal of Clinical Psychiatry, 52*(Suppl. 11), 16–20.

Davidson, J.R.T., Potts, N., Richichi, E., & Krishnan, K.R. (1993). Treatment of social phobia with clonazepam and placebo. *Journal of Clinical Psychopharmacology, 13,* 423–428.

DeVaugh-Geiss, J., & Bell, J. (1994, December). *Multicenter trial of a 5-HT$_3$ antagonist, ondansetron, in social phobia.* Poster presented at the 33rd annual meeting of the American College of Neuropsychopharmacology, San Juan, Puerto Rico.

Gelernter, C.S., Uhde, T.W., Cimbolic, P., Arnkoff, D.B., Vittone, B.J., Tancer, M.E., & Bartko, J.J. (1991). Cognitive-behavioral and pharmacological treatment of social phobia. *Archives of General Psychiatry, 48,* 938–945.

Gorman, J.M., Liebowitz, M.R., Fyer, A.J., Campeas, R., & Klein, D.F. (1985). Treatment of social phobia with atenolol. *Journal of Clinical Psychopharmacology, 5,* 298–301.

Granville-Grossman, K.L., & Turner, P. (1966). The effect of propranolol on anxiety. *Lancet, 1,* 788–790.

James, I.M., Griffith, H.W., Pearson, R.M., & Newby, P. (1977). Effect of oxprenolol on stage fright in musicians. *Lancet, 2,* 952–954.

Katschnig, H., Stein, M., Buller, R. (on behalf of the International Multicenter Clinical Trial Group on Moclobemide in Social Phobia). (1997). Moclobemide in social phobia: A double-bind, placebo-controlled clinical study. *European Archives of Psychiatry and Clinical Neuroscience, 247,* 71–80.

Katzelnick, D.J., Kobak, K.A., Greist, J.H., Jefferson, J.W., Mantle, J.M., & Serlin, R.C. (1995). Sertraline in social phobia: A double-bind, placebo-controlled crossover study. *American Journal of Psychiatry, 152,* 1368–1371.

Kelsey, J.E. (1995). Venlafaxine in social phobia. *Psychopharmacology Bulletin, 31,* 767–771.

Lepola, U., Koponen, H., & Leinonen, E. (1994). Citalopram in the treatment of social phobia: A report of three cases. *Pharmacopsychiatry, 27,* 186–188.

Liden, S., & Gottfries, C. (1974). Beta-blocking agents in the treatment of catecholamine-induced symptoms in musicians [letter]. *Lancet, 2,* 529.

Liebowitz, M.R., Gorman, J.M., Fyer, A.J., Campeas, R., Levin, A.P., Sandberg, D., Hollander, E., Papp, L., & Goetz, D. (1988). Pharmacotherapy of social phobia: An interim report of a placebo-controlled comparison of phenelzine and atenolol. *Journal of Clinical Psychiatry, 49,* 252–257.

Liebowitz, M.R., Schneier, F., Campeas, R., Hollander, E., Hatterer, J., Fyer, A., Gorman, J., Papp, L., Davies, S., Gully, R., & Klein, D.F. (1992). Phenelzine vs. atenolol in social phobia: A placebo-controlled comparison. *Archives of General Psychiatry, 49,* 290–300.

Lott, M., Greist, J.H., Jefferson, J.W., Kobak, K.A., Katzelnick, D.J., Katz, R.J., & Schaettle, S.C. (1997). Brofaromine for social phobia: A multicenter placebo-controlled, double-blind study. *Journal of Clinical Psychopharmacology, 17,* 255–260.

Lydiard, R.B., Laraia, M.T., Howell, E.F., & Ballenger, J.C. (1988). Alprazolam in the treatment of social phobia. *Journal of Clinical Psychiatry, 49,* 17–19.

Magee, W.J., Eaton, W.W., Wittchen, H.-U., McGonagle, K.A., & Kessler, R.C. (1996). Agoraphobia, simple phobia, and social phobia in the national comorbidity survey. *Archives of General Psychiatry, 53,* 159–168.

Mancini, C., & van Ameringen, M. (1996). Paroxetine in social phobia. *Journal of Clinical Psychiatry, 57,* 519–522.

Marshall, R.D., & Schneier, F.R. (1996). An algorithm for the pharmacotherapy of social phobia. *Psychiatric Annals, 26,* 210–216.

Munjack, D.J., Baltazar, P.L., Bohn, P.B., Cabe, D.D., & Appleton, A.A. (1990). Clonazepam in the treatment of social phobia: a pilot study. *Journal of Clinical Psychiatry, 51*(Suppl. 5), 35–40.

Munjack, D.J., Burns, J., Baltazar, P.L., Brown, R., Leonard, M., Nagy, R., Koek, R., Crocker, B., & Schafer, S. (1991). A pilot study of buspirone in the treatment of social phobia. *Journal of Anxiety Disorders, 5*, 87–98.

Neftel, K.A., Adler, R.H., Kappell, L., Rossi, M., Kaser, H.E., Bruggesser, H.H., & Vorkauf, H. (1982). Stage fright in musicians: A model illustrating the effect of beta-blockers. *Psychosomatic Medicine, 44*, 462–469.

Noyes, R., Moroz, G., Davidson, J.R.T., & Liebowitz, M.R. (1997). Moclobemide in social phobia: A controlled dose-response trial. *Journal of Clinical Psychopharmacology, 17*, 247–254.

Ontiveros, A., & Fontaine, R. (1990). Social phobia and clonazepam. *Canadian Journal of Psychiatry, 35*, 439–441.

Reich, J., & Yates, W. (1988). Family history of psychiatric disorders in social phobia. *Comprehensive Psychiatry, 29*, 72–75.

Reiter, S.R., Pollack, M.H., Rosenbaum, J.F., & Cohen, L.S. (1990). Clonazepam for the treatment of social phobia. *Journal of Clinical Psychiatry, 51*, 470–472.

Safren, S.A., Heimberg, R.G., Brown, E.J., & Holle, C. (1997). Quality of life in social phobia. *Depression and Anxiety, 4*, 126–133.

Schneier, F.R., Chin, S.J., Hollander, E., & Liebowitz, M.R. (1992). Fluoxetine in social phobia [letter]. *Journal of Clinical Psychopharmacology, 12*, 62–64.

Schneier, F.R., Goetz, D., Campeas, R., Fallon, B., Marshall, R., & Liebowitz, M.R. (1998). Placebo-controlled trial of moclobemide in social phobia. *British Journal of Psychiatry, 172*, 70–77.

Schneier, F.R., Saoud, J.B., Campeas, R., Fallon, B.A., Hollander, E., Coplan, J., & Liebowitz, M.R. (1993). Buspirone in social phobia. *Journal of Clinical Psychopharmacology, 13*, 251–256.

Stein, M.B., Chartier, M.J., Hazen, A.L., Kroft, C.D.L., Chale, R.A., Cote, D., & Walker, J.R. (1996). Paroxetine in the treatment of generalized social phobia: Open-label treatment and double-blind placebo-controlled discontinuation. *Journal of Clinical Psychopharmacology, 16*, 218–222.

Sternbach, H. (1992). Fluoxetine treatment of social phobia [letter]. *Journal of Clinical Psychopharmacology, 12*, 62–64.

Sutherland, S.M., & Davidson, J.R.T. (1995). Beta-blockers and benzodiazepines. In M.B. Stein (Ed.), *Social phobia: Clinical and research perspectives* (pp. 323–346). Washington, DC: American Psychiatric Press.

Turner, S.M., Beidel, D.C., & Jacob, R.G. (1994). Social phobia: A comparison of behavior therapy and atenolol. *Journal of Consulting & Clinical Psychology, 62*, 350–358.

Tyrer, P.J., & Lader, M.H. (1974). Response to propranolol and diazepam in somatic and psychic anxiety. *British Medical Journal, 2*, 14–16.

van Ameringen, M., Mancini, C., & Oakman, J. (1997). *Nefazodone in social phobia*. Proceedings of the 1997 annual meeting of the Canadian Psychiatric Association, Calgary, Alberta, Canada.

van Ameringen, M., Mancini, C., & Streiner, D.L. (1993). Fluoxetine efficacy in social phobia. *Journal of Clinical Psychiatry, 54*, 27–32.

van Ameringen, M., Mancini, C., & Streiner, D.L. (1994). Sertraline in social phobia. *Journal of Affective Disorders, 31*, 141–145.

van Ameringen, M., Mancini, C., & Wilson, C. (1996). Buspirone augmentation of selective serotonin reuptake inhibitors in social phobia. *Journal of Affective Disorders, 39*, 115–121.

van Vliet, I.M., den Boer, J.A., & Westenberg, H.G.M. (1992). Psychopharmacologic treatment of social phobia: Clinical and biochemical effects of brofaromine, a selective MAO-A inhibitor. *European Neuropsychopharmacology, 2*, 21–29.

van Vliet, I.M., den Boer, J.A., & Westenberg, H.G.M. (1994). Psychopharmacological treatment of social phobia: A double blind placebo controlled study with fluvoxamine. *Psychopharmacology, 115,* 128–134.

van Vliet, I.M., den Boer, J.A., Westenberg, H.G.M., & Pian, K.L.H. (1997). Clinical effects of buspirone in social phobia: A double-blind placebo-controlled study. *Journal of Clinical Psychiatry, 58,* 164–168.

Versiani, M., Mundim, F.D., Nardi, A.E., & Liebowitz, M.R. (1988). Tranylcypromine in social phobia. *Journal of Clinical Psychopharmacology, 8,* 279–283.

Versiani, M., Nardi, A.E., Mundim, F.D., Alves, A.B., Liebowitz, M.R., & Amrein, R. (1992). Pharmacotherapy of social phobia: A controlled study with moclobemide and phenelzine. *British Journal of Psychiatry, 161,* 353–360.

Weiller, E., Bisserbe, J.-C., Boyer, P., Lepine, J.P., & Lecrubier, Y. (1996). Social phobia in general health care: An unrecognized under treated disabling disorder. *British Journal of Psychiatry, 168,* 169–174.

PART FIVE

OBSESSIVE-COMPULSIVE DISORDER

OBSESSIVE-COMPULSIVE DISORDER (OCD) presents one of the most perplexing pictures of any dysfunction discussed in this volume. It is associated with a considerable range of severity. At the mild end, it encompasses idiosyncratic rituals that appear as little more than curious eccentricities, such as rechecking doors and windows. At its extreme, the disorder can be incapacitating, requiring 8 to 10 hours to perform simple chores, such as washing hands. Many OCDs are misdiagnosed as psychotic because their obsessions appear to be delusional. OCD is often associated with depression, and it has occasionally been viewed as an affective disorder; but treatment outcome data do not support this assumption.

OCD also has a superficial relationship to a number of other disorders that have a ruminative or compulsive quality, including social phobia associated with fear of urinating or eating in public; kleptomania and compulsive gambling; eating disorders, including compulsive dieting, bulimia, and anorexia; extreme, monosymptomatic hypochondriacal fears (e.g., fear of getting cancer or AIDS); and tics, such as Tourette's syndrome and trichotillomania. It is unclear whether some (or all) of these dysfunctions represent subcategories of the core OCD disturbance or whether they simply represent phenomenologically similar conditions. This same question pertains to OCD patients with and without concomitant depression, as well as patients with delusion-like symptoms (overvalued ideators). A related uncertainty is the prevalence of the disorder. It had been thought to be relatively rare: less than 1 percent of the population. More recent studies make it one of the most widespread anxiety disorders, with a prevalence between 1 percent and 3 percent.

There are two primary etiological models for the disorder: biological and behavioral. The former hypothesizes a dysfunction in the serotonin system, which results in decreased availability of serotonin. The problem could be in decreased production, inefficient receptors, or excessive reuptake. The primary evidence for this hypothesis is the differential effectiveness of tricyclic antidepressants that inhibit reuptake, notably clomipramine. The behavioral model posits that obsessions are conditioned anxiety stimuli and that compulsions are maintained by their capacity to reduce anxiety. Cognitive versions of the behavioral model also consider the role of illogical assumptions and attributions, such as the belief that anything that is not controllable is dangerous and, therefore, must be corrected. Foa and Franklin emphasize that the most useful definitions of obsessions and compulsions focus on their ability to increase and decrease anxiety, respectively, in contrast to the traditional distinction between cognitive or overt behavioral events. The primary support for this position comes from laboratory work demonstrating predicted increases in anxiety when patients are exposed to their phobic object (e.g., dirt), followed by sharp decreases on performance of the compulsive ritual (e.g., washing, reciting certain sequences of numbers). The behavioral hypothesis also receives indirect support from the effectiveness of behavioral treatment programs.

These two hypotheses have led to the development of the two predominant treatments for OCD: clomipramine and behavior therapy. O'Neill, Davis, and Martis provide a comprehensive review of the available pharmacotherapy options for OCD, of which clomipramine remains the treatment of choice. However, the picture has changed since the first edition of this book because of the availability of SSRIs, which are a good second choice, especially in patients who cannot tolerate the side effects of clomimpramine. However, the results seem to be more modest than those achieved with pharmacological treatment of other disorders (e.g., panic, depression). OCD may simply be a difficult disorder to treat, with lower placebo response rates, less symptom reduction, and higher rate of relapse. This may be especially the case if the primary symptoms are obsessions rather than compulsions, and if there is substantial depression.

Foa and Franklin have a more sanguine view of the treatment prospects for OCD. They report success rates of up to 75 percent with an intensive treatment program consisting of exposure and response prevention. Results suggest that behavioral treatment is more effective and more durable than pharmacotherapy, but questions remain about cost and acceptability to patients. Clearly, many patients will prefer medication to the time-consuming and effortful demands of exposure and response prevention. Ongoing trials of combined treatments should indicate whether combinations offer any advantage in time, compliance, or outcome.

This brief discussion underscores the need for further research on this disorder. OCD is, apparently, much more prevalent than had previously been thought: It is not a rare condition. Current treatments are much more effective than might have been imagined 10 years ago, when OCD was viewed as almost completely refractory. Nevertheless, we need to learn much more about the appropriate classification of subcategories, about the interaction of treatments, about the maintenance of treatment gains (especially when the initial treatment gains only produced a partial response), and about the treatment of patients who cannot tolerate the side effects of pharmacotherapy or the discomfort associated with behavior therapy.

CHAPTER 15

Cognitive Behavior Therapy

EDNA B. FOA and MARTIN E. FRANKLIN

CONCEPTUALIZATION OF THE DISORDER

DEFINITION

According to the *DSM-IV* (American Psychiatric Association, 1994), obsessive compulsive disorder (OCD) is characterized by recurrent obsessions and/or compulsions that interfere substantially with daily functioning. Obsessions are "persistent ideas, thoughts, impulses, or images that are experienced as intrusive and inappropriate and cause marked anxiety or distress" (p. 418). Common obsessions are repeated thoughts about contamination, causing harm to others, and doubting whether one locked the front door. Compulsions are "repetitive behaviors . . . or mental acts . . . the goal of which is to prevent or reduce anxiety or distress" (p. 418). Common compulsions include handwashing, checking, and counting.

Compared to the previous definition of OCD in *DSM-III-R* (APA, 1987), the *DSM-IV* definition includes several noteworthy changes. In *DSM-IV*, obsessions and compulsions are defined as functionally related: Obsessions are defined as thoughts, images, or impulses that *cause* marked anxiety or distress, and compulsions are defined as overt (behavioral) or covert (mental) actions that are performed in an attempt to *reduce* the distress brought on by obsessions or according to rigid rules. This modification is supported by findings from the recently completed *DSM-IV* field study on OCD, in which over 90 percent of participants reported that their compulsions aim to either prevent harm associated with their obsessions or to reduce obsessional distress (Foa et al., 1995).

Data from the *DSM-IV* field study also indicated that the vast majority (over 90 percent) of obsessive compulsives manifest both obsessions and behavioral

This chapter was supported in part by grant #MH45404 awarded to the first author.

rituals. When mental rituals are included, only 2 percent of the sample reported pure obsessions (Foa et al., 1995). Behavioral rituals (e.g., handwashing) are equivalent to mental rituals (e.g., silently repeating special prayers) in their functional relationship to obsessions; both serve to reduce obsessional distress, prevent feared harm, or restore safety. Thus, the traditional view that obsessions are mental events and compulsions are behavioral events requires revision; although all obsessions are indeed mental events, compulsions are either mental or behavioral. Identification of mental rituals is an especially important aspect of treatment planning, as obsessions and compulsions are addressed via different techniques.

Another definitional shift in *DSM-IV* was the deemphasis of the requirement for insight in diagnosing OCD. It has been argued that a continuum of insight or strength of belief better represents the clinical picture of OCD than the previously prevailing view that *all* obsessive compulsives recognize the senselessness of their obsessions and compulsions (Kozak & Foa, 1994). The growing consensus about a continuum of insight (Foa et al., 1995; Insel & Akiskal, 1986; Lelliott, Noshirvani, Basoglu, Marks, & Monteiro, 1988) led to the inclusion of a subtype of OCD with *poor* insight to include individuals who indeed have obsessions and compulsions but do not recognize their senselessness.

CLASSIFICATION

Modern classification schemes for OCD have focused on ritualistic activity (i.e., compulsions) rather than on the obsessive content. Although many patients have more than one form of ritual, the predominant one determines how the individual's OCD symptoms will be classified. Thus, patients are described as washers, checkers, orderers, and so on.

Ritualistic washing is the most common compulsion and is typically performed to decrease discomfort associated with contamination obsessions. For example, individuals who fear contact with AIDS germs clean themselves and their environment excessively in order to prevent either contracting AIDS themselves or spreading it to others. Some washers do not fear that a specific disaster will befall them if they refrain from compulsive washing. Rather, the state of being contaminated itself generates tremendous discomfort. To decrease this distress, they feel compelled to engage in washing rituals.

Another common compulsion is repetitive checking, which is performed in order to prevent an anticipated catastrophe. Individuals who fear that a burglar will enter their home, take their valuables, and possibly harm their family will repeatedly check doors and windows to decrease the likelihood of this actually happening. Likewise, individuals who dread that while driving they will run over a pedestrian and fail to notice it will repeatedly retrace their driving route in search of possible victims. Repeaters are similar to checkers in that they too are typically driven by the wish to prevent disasters; however, they differ from checkers in that their rituals are unrelated logically to their feared consequences. For example, it is logical (if excessive) to check the front door lock many times if one fears a burglary, but illogical to walk up and down the stairs repeatedly to prevent a loved one's death in a motor vehicle accident.

Other compulsions include ordering, counting, and hoarding. Hoarding is atypical because many hoarders engage in little compulsive activity, but are perhaps better characterized as avoidant. Instead of going to great lengths to collect materials to save, many hoarders simply avoid discarding items they encounter in everyday life (e.g., newspapers, string) for fear of not having them available in the future. Over long periods of time, consistent avoidance of discarding can result in overwhelming accumulations, even in the absence of active gathering rituals. Hoarded material can also vary from items of some monetary value (e.g., complete sets of Sports Illustrated magazines) to those that are worthless (e.g., chicken bones, empty milk containers); diagnosis is more complicated when the hoarded material can be viewed as collectibles.

COGNITIVE AND BEHAVIORAL THEORIES

Several theories have been advanced to account for the etiology and maintenance of OCD. An early account was proposed by Dollard and Miller (Dollard & Miller, 1950) and is based on Mowrer's (Mowrer, 1939, 1960) two-stage theory of fear acquisition and maintenance of avoidance behavior. According to this theory, a neutral event that has been paired with an innate aversive event takes on the aversive properties of that event and consequently elicits distress and an accompanied fearful response. Distress can be conditioned to mental events (e.g., thoughts) as well as to physical events (e.g., floors, bathrooms). In a second stage, after fear of the neutral event had been established, escape or avoidance behavior (i.e., compulsions) evolves to reduce fear. Avoidance is maintained by the negative reinforcement associated with its ability to attenuate fear. Although Mowrer's theory does not adequately account for fear acquisition (Rachman & Wilson, 1980), it is consistent with observations about the maintenance of compulsive rituals: obsessions increase anxiety/distress and compulsions reduce it (e.g., Roper & Rachman, 1976; Roper, Rachman, & Hodgson, 1973).

Some cognitive theorists have suggested that OCD arises from exaggeration of negative consequences (e.g., Carr, 1974). However, clinical observations suggest that exaggerated evaluation of danger is typical of *all* anxiety disorders. These theories do not address the characteristics that distinguish OCD from other disorders.

A more thorough cognitive analysis of OCD was offered by Salkovskis (1985), proposing that five assumptions are specifically characteristic of OCD: (1) thinking of an action is akin to actually doing it; (2) failure to try to prevent harm to self or others is morally comparable to causing the harm; (3) responsibility for harm is not diminished by mitigating factors; (4) failure to perform rituals in response to harm-related thoughts is akin to an actual intention to harm; and (5) one should exercise control over one's thoughts.

Salkovskis' thoughtful paper sparked interest in examining the role of responsibility in the psychopathology of OCD (Ladouceur et al., 1995; Rachman, Throdarson, Shafran, & Woody, 1995; Rheaume, Freeston, Dugas, Letarte, & Ladouceur, 1995). Most of these investigations were conducted on nonclinical samples using individuals with high scores on self-report measures of OCD. One study by Lopatka and Rachman (1995) utilized patients who met *DSM-III-R* criteria (APA, 1987) for OCD. In this study, the authors examined the hypothesis that a manipulation that increases responsibility would increase the urge to check, the amount of discomfort experienced, and the estimated probabilities of bad outcome, whereas deflating levels of responsibility would decrease scores on these variables. Although subjects in the high-responsibility condition did perceive a higher degree of responsibility compared to subjects in the low-responsibility condition, they did not differ in urges to perform checking rituals, in discomfort, or in their estimates regarding the probability of anticipated harm. However, individuals in the low-responsibility condition experienced a decrease in urge to check, in discomfort, and in estimated probability of anticipated harm. Thus, the hypothesis regarding the role of responsibility in OCD checking was only partially supported.

To further examine the role of responsibility in OCD, Foa, Amir, Bogert, and Molnar (1997) developed the Obsessive Compulsive Responsibility Scale (OCRS) that includes high risk, low risk, and obsessive-compulsive relevant scenarios. For each scenario, OCD and nonpatient participants were asked to estimate the degree of urge to rectify the situation, distress upon leaving the situation unrectified, and personal responsibility for harm to others if the unrectified situation were to result in harm. Results indicated that in low and obsessive-compulsive relevant situations, individuals with OCD reported greater urge, distress, and responsibility than did nonpatients. However, no group differences were detected on the high-risk situations: both groups indicated by far the highest values for this type of situation. These results seem to indicate that nonpatients better differentiate situations that merit attention and corrective action from situations in which the risk is too low to merit concern. Although individuals with OCD can also make such discriminations, they tend to display inflated responsibility for low-risk situations.

Clinical observations have led some investigators to hypothesize that memory deficits for actions underlie compulsive checking (e.g., Sher, Frost, & Otto, 1983). However, the results of experimental investigations of this hypothesis are equivocal. Some support for an action-memory deficit was found in nonclinical checkers (e.g., Rubenstein, Peynirgioglu, Chambless, & Pigott, 1993; Sher et al., 1983). In contrast, a study using a clinical sample found that, compared to nonpatients, checkers *better* recalled their fear-relevant actions (e.g., plugging in an iron, unsheathing a knife), but not fear-irrelevant actions (e.g., putting paper clips in a box; Constans, Foa, Franklin, & Mathews, 1995).

Foa and Kozak (1985) hypothesized that obsessive compulsives often assume that, in the absence of clear evidence for safety, a situation must be dangerous; conversely, they fail to conclude that in the absence of clear evidence for danger a situation must be safe. For example, in order to feel safe, an OCD sufferer may want to have a guarantee that the doorknob is clean before touching it, whereas a person without OCD would assume that the doorknob is safe and would not hesitate touching it unless there were clear danger cues. Because such guarantees are not possible in everyday life, rituals that are performed to reduce the likelihood of harm can never really provide the level of desired safety and must be repeated.

DIAGNOSTIC ISSUES AND PROBLEMS

The high comorbidity of OCD with other disorders, as well as the similarity between the criteria for OCD and other *DSM-IV* disorders, can pose diagnostic difficulties.

OBSESSIONS VERSUS RUMINATIONS

It is sometimes difficult to differentiate depressive ruminations from obsessions. The distinction rests primarily on thought content and on the patient's reported resistance to such thoughts. Unlike obsessions, ruminations are generally pessimistic ideas about the self or the world, and content frequently shifts in rumination. Additionally, depressive ruminators tend not to suppress their ruminations the way that individuals with OCD attempt to suppress obsessions. In cases where depression and OCD co-occur, both phenomena may be present but only obsessions should be targeted with exposure exercises.

TOURETTE'S SYNDROME AND TIC DISORDERS

In order to differentiate the stereotyped motor behaviors that characterize Tourette's Syndrome and tic disorders from compulsions, the functional relationship between these behaviors and any obsessive thoughts must be examined. Motor tics are generally experienced as involuntary and are not aimed at neutralizing distress brought about by obsessions. There is no conventional way of differentiating them from pure compulsions, but OCD with pure compulsions is extremely rare (Foa et al., 1995). There appears to be a high rate of comorbidity between OCD and tic disorders (e.g., Pauls et al., 1986); thus, both disorders may be present simultaneously in a given patient. As is the case with ruminations and obsessions, differentiating among tics and compulsions in patients with both disorders is especially important, as both are treated via different methods.

DELUSIONAL DISORDER AND SCHIZOPHRENIA

Individuals with OCD may present with obsessions of delusional intensity (see Kozak & Foa, 1994, for review). Approximately 5 percent of OCD patients report complete conviction that their obsessions and compulsions are realistic, with an additional 20 percent reporting strong but not fixed conviction. Therefore, it is important to consider the diagnosis of OCD "with poor insight" even if these beliefs are very strongly held. The differentiation of delusional disorder from OCD can depend on the presence of compulsions in OCD (Eisen, Beer, Pato, Venditto, & Rasmussen, 1997). In OCD, obsessions of delusional intensity are usually accompanied by compulsions.

It is important to recognize that the content of obsessions in OCD may be quite bizarre, as in the delusions of schizophrenia, but bizarreness does not in itself preclude a diagnosis of OCD. For example, one OCD patient seen at our center was fearful that small bits of her "essence" would be forever lost if she passed too close to public trash cans. In schizophrenia, other symptoms of formal thought disorder must also be present, such as loose associations, hallucinations, flat or grossly inappropriate affect, and thought insertion or projection. A dual diagnosis is appropriate when an individual meets criteria for both OCD and schizophrenia.

OTHER ANXIETY DISORDERS

OCD can co-occur with other anxiety disorders, and diagnostic criteria are sometimes similar among anxiety disorders, but the symptoms associated with each diagnosis can usually be distinguished. For example, the excessive worries characteristic of generalized anxiety disorder (GAD) may appear similar to OCD but, unlike obsessions, worries are excessive concerns about real life circumstances and are experienced by the individual as appropriate (ego syntonic). In contrast, obsessive thinking is more likely to be unrealistic or magical, and obsessions are usually experienced by the individual as inappropriate (ego dystonic). There are, however, exceptions to this general rule: individuals with either GAD or OCD may both worry about everyday matters such as their children getting sick. However, if worried about their children catching cold, parents with GAD may focus their concern on the long-term consequences (e.g., falling behind in school, development of a life-long pattern of debilitation), whereas OCD parents might focus more on the contamination aspect of illness (e.g, their child being infested with cold germs). The problem of distinguishing obsessions from worries in a given patient is most relevant when the patient exhibits no compulsions, but, as just mentioned, pure obsessionals comprise only about 2 percent of OCDs (Foa et al., 1995).

In the absence of rituals, the avoidance associated with specific phobias can also appear similar to OCD. For example, excessive fear of germs and specific phobia can both result in persistent avoidance of cats. However, unlike an individual with OCD, a cat phobic can successfully avoid cats for the most part or reduce distress quickly by escaping cats when avoidance is impractical. In contrast, the individual with OCD who is obsessed with cat germs continues to feel contaminated even after the cat is gone, and sometimes the known presence of a cat in the vicinity several hours earlier can also produce obsessional distress, even if there is no possibility that the cat will return. This distress often prompts subsequent avoidance behaviors (e.g., taking off clothing that might have been near the contaminating cat), not typically observed in specific phobias.

HYPOCHONDRIASIS AND BODY DYSMORPHIC DISORDER (BDD)

The health concerns that characterize hypochondriasis and the preoccupation with imagined physical defects of body dysmorphic disorder are both formally similar to the obsessions of OCD. The best way to differentiate these disorders from OCD is to examine for content specificity of the fear-provoking thoughts. Most individuals with hypochondriasis or BDD are singly obsessed, whereas most individuals with OCD have multiple obsessions.

TREATMENT STRATEGIES

Until the middle of the 1960s, OCD was considered nonresponsive to available psychodynamic and pharmacologic treatments. Around that time, several behavioral techniques derived from learning theory also began being used to treat OCD. Although investigations of these interventions were generally limited by methodologic problems (small sample sizes, no control groups), results appeared to indicate that treatments using some form of exposure to feared situations or thoughts were somewhat effective, as were treatments that used reinforcement procedures to inhibit ritualizing (for a review see Foa, Steketee, & Ozarow, 1985). These early studies served to generate new hypotheses about treatment efficacy in OCD, and helped lead to the development of combined exposure and ritual prevention procedures that have since proven highly effective.

Meyer's (Meyer, 1966) initial report on a behavioral procedure that included prolonged exposure to obsessional cues and strict prevention of rituals led to a dramatic shift in OCD treatment. This exposure-and-response-prevention (EX/RP) procedure was found to be extremely successful at posttreatment in 10 of 15 cases and partially effective in the remainder; at long-term follow-up only two patients had relapsed (Meyer & Levy, 1973; Meyer, Levy, & Schnurer, 1974). Although these findings were certainly encouraging, it was only later that EX/RP was compared to other interventions and the parameters of effective EX/RP treatment were explored.

Numerous controlled and uncontrolled studies of the combined EX/RP procedure have been conducted since Meyer and colleagues reported their initial findings, and the results have indicated that the majority of EX/RP treatment completers meet responder criteria at posttreatment and maintain their gains over long periods of time. In a review (Foa & Kozak, 1996) of 12 outcome studies ($N = 330$) that reported on treatment responders, 83 percent of treatment completers responded to EX/RP at posttreatment. In 16 studies reporting long-term follow-up data ($N = 376$; Mean follow-up = 29 months), 76 percent were responders. These findings appear to be quite robust, as they were compiled across a number of different treatment sites, procedural variations, etc.

With respect to the parameters of effective EX/RP treatment, it appears that prolonged continuous exposure is better than short interrupted exposure (Rabavilas, Boulougouris, & Stefanis, 1976), with 90 minute exposures serving as a useful, although not infallible, rule of thumb. Gradual exposure to the most distressing items does not appear more effective than immediate exposure to these items (Hodgson, Rachman, & Marks, 1972), although patients typically prefer the former.

Beginning with Meyer's (1966) work, most studies on the efficacy of exposure therapy for OCD also included some form of ritual prevention (e.g., Foa & Goldstein, 1978; Rachman, Hodgson, & Marks, 1971). To separate the effects of these procedures, Foa, Steketee, Grayson, Turner, and Latimer (1984) randomly assigned washers to receive treatment by exposure only (EX), ritual prevention only (RP), or their combination (EX/RP). Treatments were conducted intensively (15 daily two-hour sessions conducted over three weeks) and followed by a therapist visit to the patient's home to ensure generalization of gains. Results indicated that although all groups improved, EX/RP was superior to EX and RP on almost every symptom measure at posttreatment and follow-up. Notably, patients who received EX reported lower posttreatment anxiety when confronting feared contaminants than patients who had received RP, whereas the RP group reported greater decreases in urge to ritualize than did the EX group. The implication of these findings is that EX and RP affect different OCD symptoms, and that treatments including *both* components are more effective.

Optimal frequency of exposure sessions has not been established. Although excellent results have generally been found with intensive EX/RP programs involving 15 daily treatment sessions conducted over three weeks (e.g., Foa, Kozak, Steketee, & McCarthy, 1992), some programs involving weekly sessions have also produced quite favorable outcomes (e.g., de Araujo, Ito, Marks, & Deale, 1995). No study has directly compared weekly and intensive EX/RP programs. In our center, we typically see patients with at least moderately severe OCD, and some who also have comorbid conditions. In light of the typical severity and complexity of our cases, we generally conduct intensive EX/RP treatment. For less severe patients who are highly motivated to complete exposure and ritual prevention assignments between sessions, weekly or twice weekly sessions may also be successful. The presence of clinically significant comorbid depression or other complicating factors also may lead us to recommend intensive- over nonintensive-therapy regimens.

The importance of therapist guidance of exposure exercises in EX/RP treatment has yet to be clarified. Although studies with OCD have not found enhancement of immediate (Emmelkamp & van Kraanen, 1977) or long-term effects (Marks et al., 1988) in groups receiving therapist-assisted exposure compared to self-exposure, therapist presence did enhance outcome of specific phobia treatment compared to self-exposure (Ost, 1989). Moreover, methodological issues (e.g., small sample size), in those studies conducted using OCD samples, complicate interpretation of the negative findings for therapist presence. Clinical experience with OCD patients in our center suggests that therapist presence is important in conducting exposure exercises, and, therefore, we continue to provide therapist-assisted exposures in treatment sessions augmented by patient-controlled exposure homeworks between sessions.

The inclusion of imaginal exposure to an in vivo EX/RP program appeared to enhance long-term outcome in two studies (Foa, Steketee, Turner, & Fischer, 1980; Steketee, Foa, & Grayson, 1982), but it did not affect long-term outcome in another study (de Araujo et al., 1995). Methodological differences between the procedures used in these studies precludes strong conclusions about the source of the disparate findings. Clinically, we find imaginal exposure helpful for those patients whose obsessional fears focus on disastrous consequences not readily addressed with in vivo exposure (e.g., burning in hell). For patients who do not report any feared disasters that would result from refraining from rituals, imaginal exposure may not be needed.

The efficacy of formal cognitive therapy in treating OCD is also unclear. One study found that the addition of a cognitive therapy (self-instructional training) to an EX/RP regimen hindered outcome compared to EX/RP without cognitive therapy (Emmelkamp, van der Helm, van Zanten, & Plochg, 1980). Two studies have since found no differences between Rational Emotive Therapy (RET) and EX/RP treatments (Emmelkamp & Beens, 1991; Emmelkamp, Visser, & Hoekstra, 1988). Notably, in comparison to the EX/RP treatments found to yield the most improvement (e.g., Foa et al., 1992), the EX/RP treatments used in these studies involved fewer and shorter sessions, and did not include therapist-assisted exposure. Evaluation of posttreatment symptom reduction for EX/RP as conducted in these studies indicates that these mitigating factors may have attenuated outcome somewhat for EX/RP. Thus, the comparison between these treatments and the cognitive therapies are difficult to interpret.

The issue of whether or not formal cognitive therapy improves the efficacy of EX/RP is of theoretical interest but of limited practical utility, because of the customary use of informal cognitive techniques in EX/RP treatment. During exposure sessions, therapists in our center routinely do informal cognitive therapy by discussing risk assessment, overestimation of probability, emotional reasoning, and other cognitive concepts with the patient. The focus of our treatment remains on the EX/RP procedures, however, so that such discussions take place during exposure exercises rather than at their expense. Indeed, removal of informal cognitive procedures from EX/RP and of behavioral assignments from cognitive therapy greatly attenuated outcomes for both of the purer therapies (van Oppen et al., 1995). Thus, we take the position that EX/RP is actually a cognitive-behavior treatment in which exposure and ritual prevention should be emphasized but informal cognitive procedures should also be utilized.

Case Illustration

Russell, a 35-year-old man, was afflicted since late adolescence by obsessive thoughts of harming others by driving "carelessly." Despite never having been involved in even a minor traffic accident, Russell remembered worrying about striking pedestrians or other vehicles with his car ever since receiving his learner's permit. He was especially distressed after hitting a bump or hearing an unexpected noise while driving. When this happened, Russell would check in his rearview mirror repeatedly until convinced that he did not cause an accident. If checking in the mirror did not reduce his anxiety sufficiently, he would feel compelled to retrace his driving route to check for injured pedestrians lying along the roadside.

Russell was less anxious when accompanied by passengers because he thought that they would inform him if an accident occurred. Nevertheless, he would compulsively question his passengers about the possibility that he inadvertently harmed a pedestrian. This particular ritual was especially frustrating for Russell's wife, and she insisted that she should drive instead of Russell to avoid these interrogations. For a short time this arrangement worked satisfactorily. However, soon Russell began to obsess about accidents even when he was just a passenger: he still felt responsible to check for injured pedestrians and to warn his wife repeatedly about potential hazards.

In addition to the fears of harming others while driving, Russell also feared harming people via his imagined carelessness in other situations, such as while doing home repairs. For example, if he hammered a nail into a piece of wood, Russell felt compelled to check repeatedly to ensure that the sharp end of the nail did not penetrate through the wood and thus pose a potential hazard to his three children. Russell checked such things long after it was evident to others and even to himself that the repair posed no risk, as if "I couldn't trust my own senses because the stakes were so high." Russell also feared harming his family by making a financial mistake (e.g., inadvertently writing checks for a much larger amount than needed), and he would reread his checks many times until satisfied that the amounts were correct. Eventually Russell stopped writing checks and using his credit cards whenever possible to avoid potential financial disasters resulting from his carelessness.

Russell's anxiety about harming others caused him extreme distress and his compulsive checking and retracing of driving routes resulted in chronic lateness for work and other appointments. The persistent reassurance seeking became a serious source of marital stress. Although Russell recognized it was unlikely that he would actually harm people in the ways that he feared, this insight did not attenuate the frequency or intensity of his intrusive thoughts.

At the urging of a trusted friend who had been treated successfully for OCD and with the support of his wife, Russell sought help in our center and was treated with cognitive-behavior treatment by EX/RP. The first three treatment sessions (six hours) were spent planning exposures to feared situations, such as driving, making home repairs, and paying bills. Exposure exercises were arranged hierarchically, with those evoking moderate distress (e.g., driving on highways where pedestrians would not be present) introduced earlier and more difficult situations, later (e.g., driving on crowded city streets). Beginning with the first day of exposure to feared situations (treatment session 4), Russell was instructed to refrain from all checking behavior, reassurance seeking, and passive avoidance of situations that might cause distress.

During the first treatment session, Russell drove on a local highway with the therapist in the passenger seat. Russell was instructed to refrain from all compulsive checking throughout the drive, and was informed that requests for reassurance would be rejected by the therapist and by others because reassurances are compulsions and needed to be prevented in order for treatment to be effective. During the first part of the first exposure session Russell was extremely anxious, but as expected his anxiety began to decrease gradually. Upon return to the clinic after an hour of driving, Russell engaged in imaginal exposure, in which he provided a detailed account of one of his worst fears. An example of imaginal exposure is as follows: Russell's decreased vigilance resulted in his actually killing a pedestrian while driving; he was arrested for murder and was informed that the victim was a child; he was convicted, incarcerated, and his family was left in financial ruin. A detailed, five-minute script of this disastrous scenario was audiotaped, and Russell listened to it several times during the session and then listened to it for at least an hour at home that same night.

In each subsequent session, Russell continued to confront his fears of harming others while driving and while working around the house by using imaginal and in vivo exposure exercises. During these sessions, Russell and the therapist pointed to the fact that refraining from retracing his routes and other checking behavior did not result in harm to others. Discussion during sessions also addressed Russell's tendency to accept unsubstantiated evidence that he had caused an accident. Thus discussion was aimed at teaching Russell to differentiate between unrealistic (e.g., a noise of unknown origin) and realistic (e.g., a human head on the windshield) worries.

By treatment session six, Russell, accompanied by the therapist, drove on crowded city streets and near schools, with the exposure culminating with a drive through Philadelphia's Italian Market, a section with narrow streets and heavy pedestrian traffic. For homework following this session, Russell began the fairly complex task of constructing a swing set in his backyard, a task he had been avoiding for fear of doing it incorrectly and inadvertently killing one of his children. Russell's urges to perform compulsions, which were initially quite high and difficult to resist, decreased gradually over the course of treatment. By the second week, he was able to refrain completely from acting upon his compulsive urges, and the frequency and intensity of his obsessions diminished considerably. At the end of the third week of treatment, Russell was able to resume normal functioning and even began to enjoy going for drives with his family. When obsessions did arise, Russell designed and completed exposure exercises in order to confront these fears directly without engaging in the rituals and avoidance behaviors that only served to reinforce these obsessive fears.

Following intensive treatment, Russell had weekly, one-hour therapy visits for six weeks, after which therapy contacts consisted of occasional brief telephone calls. At six-month follow-up, Russell maintained his treatment gains. Whenever he experienced obsessive fears he handled them by confronting the feared situation (e.g., driving on crowded streets) without performing rituals. This change in his attitude towards his symptoms was necessary to maintain his treatment gain. In the three years since treatment ended, Russell has continued to maintain his improvement. To ensure that he does not fall back into old habits, Russell has left response prevention reminders to himself in places where he used to ritualize heavily (e.g., toolkit, checkbook). He returned to virtually normal functioning at work, and he undertook a major indoor repair job in his home with few difficulties.

ALTERNATIVE TREATMENT

Pharmacotherapy by SRIs is an established treatment for OCD. The tricyclic antidepressant clomipramine (Anafranil) was the first medication approved by the FDA for OCD, and its usefulness has been documented in a number of double-blind controlled trials (DeVeaugh-Geiss, Landau, & Katz, 1989; Marks, Stern, Mawson, Cobb, & McDonald, 1980; Thoren, Asberg, Chronholm, Jornestedt, & Traskman, 1980; Zohar & Insel, 1987). More recently, fluoxetine (Prozac) has also been found effective for OCD (Fontaine & Chouinard, 1985; Jenike, Buttolph, Baer, Ricciardi, & Holland, 1989; Montgomery et al., 1993). Another SRI recently approved by the FDA for OCD, fluvoxamine (Luvox), has also been found effective (Perse, Greist, Jefferson, Rosenfeld, & Dar, 1987; Price, Goodman, Charney, Rasmussen, & Heninger, 1987). Other SRIs such as paroxetine (Paxil) and sertraline (Zoloft) have also been found effective (e.g., Greist, Chouinard, et al., 1995; Zohar, Judge, & Paroxetine Study group, 1996).

Although response rates of up to 60 percent have been observed across the many SRI studies, the average symptom reductions are typically quite modest, ranging from five to eight points on the severity section of the Yale-Brown Obsessive Compulsive Scale (Y-BOCS) (Goodman et al., 1989). In contrast, mean Y-BOCS reductions of 14 and 15 points respectively were observed in two patient groups receiving intensive EX/RP as part of a study on relapse prevention procedures (Hiss, Foa, & Kozak, 1994). Conclusions about the relative efficacy of the different SRIs are difficult because of a paucity of head-to-head comparisons. However, Greist, Jefferson, Kobak, Katzelnick, and Serlin (1995) conducted a meta-analysis of the available large-scale, double-blind controlled studies that suggests that clomipramine is superior to fluoxetine, fluvoxamine, and sertraline, and that the latter do not differ from one another in efficacy. However, the side-effect profile of clomipramine is generally less favorable than those associated with the selective SRIs.

Long-term improvement appears to depend heavily on continuation of the pharmacotherapy, as relapse occurs after discontinuation (Thoren et al., 1980). Ninety percent of a group who had improved with clomipramine were found to relapse within a few weeks after a blind drug withdrawal (Pato, Zohar-Kadouch, Zohar, & Murphy, 1988). A comparably high relapse rate was reported with fluvoxamine (Mallya, White, Waternaux, & Quay, 1992). Although somewhat lower relapse rates have been found following fluoxetine discontinuation (Fontaine & Chouinard, 1989), the problem is also substantial for this medication as well.

The availability of EX/RP and pharmacotherapy, two treatments that are partially effective individually, has prompted studies of their combined efficacy. Substantial improvement with EX/RP accompanied by a small additive effects of clomipramine, was found in 40 obsessive compulsives immediately post treatment by Marks and colleagues (1980). Unfortunately, assessment of the individual effect of clomipramine could not be made because the drug-only period was too short (4 weeks) to allow optimal assessment. Marks et al. (1988) later found that adjunctive clomipramine had a small transitory (8 week) additive effect to EX/RP; again, EX/RP was more potent than clomipramine. Although the study's design precluded evaluation of the long-term effects of EX/RP, a six-year follow-up study revealed no long-term effect for clomipramine. Interestingly, better compliance during exposure treatment was predictive of long-term outcome (O'Sullivan, Noshirvani, Marks, Monteiro, & Lelliot, 1991).

Fluvoxamine and EX/RP have been found to produce comparable reductions in OCD symptoms immediately after treatment and at six-months follow-up, and combined treatment produced slightly more improvement in depression than did EX/RP alone (Cottraux et al., 1990). The posttreatment superiority of the combined treatment for depression, however, was not evident at follow-up.

At Allegheny University of the Health Sciences (AUHS), an uncontrolled study examined the long-term effects (mean 1.5 years posttreatment) of intensive EX/RP and fluvoxamine or clomipramine in 62 patients with OCD (Hembree, Cohen, Riggs, Kozak, & Foa, 1992). Patients were treated with serotonergic drugs, intensive EX/RP, or EX/RP plus one of the two medications. Patients who were taking medication at follow-up ($N = 25$) did equally well regardless of whether they had received medication alone or EX/RP in addition to medication. However, patients who were medication free at follow up ($N = 37$) showed a different pattern: those who had received EX/RP alone or EX/RP plus medication were less symptomatic than those who had only received medication. Thus, patients who received EX/RP maintained their gains more than patients treated with serotonergic medication that was subsequently discontinued.

A multicenter controlled study in progress at the Medical College of Pennsylvania—Hahnemann University and Columbia University is examining the relative and combined efficacy of intensive EX/RP, clomipramine, and combined treatment (Kozak, Liebowitz, & Foa, in press). Preliminary findings with treatment-completer data indicate that the active treatments appear superior to pill placebo, EX/RP appears superior to clomipramine, and the combined treatment does not appear superior to EX/RP alone; similar but less robust patterns have also been found with intent to treat data. However, the design adopted for this study may not be optimal for promoting an additive medication effect, because EX/RP treatment was largely completed before medication effects could be achieved.

In summary, there is considerable evidence for the efficacy of EX/RP and SRIs, but information about the relative efficacy is scarce. Until more definitive studies are completed, the evidence suggests that EX/RP is associated with greater treatment response and maintenance of gains than is pharmacotherapy with SRIs. Thus, it appears that EX/RP may be the treatment of choice for OCD patients willing or able to complete it. However, if EX/RP expertise is not available, if the patient refuses it, or is extremely depressed, SRIs should be prescribed. Although combined treatment is frequently advocated as the treatment of choice for OCD (e.g., Greist, 1992), there is no clear evidence from controlled studies for the long-term advantages of this procedure compared to EX/RP alone.

PRESCRIPTIVE TREATMENT AND MANAGED CARE

At first glance, the managed-care environment appears conducive to manualized short-term treatment, such as the intensive cognitive behavioral program described in this chapter for OCD. First, the efficacy of the treatment is already extremely well documented. The majority of patients who complete the program benefit substantially as measured, not only by symptom reduction of OCD but also by increased general functioning. Second, treatments are time limited and designed to target specific symptoms rather than more general life issues. Third, there is emphasis on routine evaluation of treatment outcome, as well as adjustment of procedures or termination of treatment if it is found ineffective for a given patient.

Although the aforementioned discussion suggests compatibility of EX/RP with managed care policies, there are inconsistencies as well. For example, the

EX/RP program described above requires that patients are seen by their therapists every day and sessions are typically at least 90-minutes long. This requirement is not compatible with general practice of mental health providers, and thus with general guidelines of managed care organizations, which typically calls for weekly 45-minute sessions. Although there is no head to head comparison of weekly versus daily treatment with OCD, results with panic-disordered patients suggest the superiority of intensive treatment (Foa, Jameson, Turner, & Payne, 1980). Moreover, clinical observations suggest that although motivated patients with mild to moderate OCD can benefit from weekly sessions, those with severe OCD usually do not. For them, the significant short-term investment in money and effort may result in long-term savings, both in terms of therapy time and other measures of cost effectiveness, such as regained productivity.

How does the incorporation of cognitive behavior therapy (CBT) into managed-care systems compare to incorporating medication treatment? Initially, the provision of pharmacotherapy seems exceedingly easier, because professionals who can deliver pharmacotherapy are more readily available than cognitive behavioral treatment experts. It is important to note, however, that the training of a psychiatrist is quite expensive, perhaps more so than training of proficiency in CBT. And yet, because of the well-documented relapse upon withdrawal from medication, this treatment is probably much more costly in the long run than intensive CBT. As part of their mission to reduce costs yet continue to provide effective treatments, managed care organizations will be well served to encourage and promote training in well documented CBT programs such as EX/RP for OCD.

SUMMARY

At present the treatment outcome literature suggests that there are two treatments of established efficacy for OCD: CBT involving EX/RP and pharmacotherapy with SRIs. Across multiple studies, EX/RP treatment generally has been associated with greater response rates, greater percentages of symptom reduction, and greater maintenance of gains than pharmacotherapy. However, until well-controlled direct comparisons of these individual treatments and combination treatment are completed, it remains difficult to draw definitive conclusions about their relative and combined efficacy. Previous studies designed to examine these questions have been complicated by methodological problems.

Although already established as effective, EX/RP and pharmacotherapy are not universally accepted or successful for all patients. Future research should continue to examine ways in which the monotherapies can be combined to increase patient retention and treatment response. Many OCD patients prefer pharmacotherapy to EX/RP because they fear the latter will prove too distressing for them; perhaps premedication with an SRI will yield sufficient symptom reduction and thereby make subsequent EX/RP treatment more acceptable for these patients. Additionally, it may be that patients discontinuing pharmacotherapy for financial, medical, or other reasons who are treated with EX/RP during and following drug withdrawal are less vulnerable to relapse. These research questions have yet to be examined.

As clinical researchers continue to examine the efficacy of EX/RP in comparison to other treatments and to explore the effects of procedural variations (e.g., frequency of sessions) on immediate and long-term outcome, attention must also be paid to the effects of managed care on treatment delivery. If treatments are developed for OCD that cannot be incorporated into the managed-care environment in which many clinicians practice, their practical value and impact is diminished. Working relationships between managed-care companies and clinical research centers need to be established to help prevent the arbitrary exclusion of well-established CBT protocols from the lists of reimbursible treatments. Educating managed-care policy makers about the long-term efficacy and cost effectiveness of treatments such as EX/RP may result in greater acceptability of such treatments, as well as increased flexibility for providing these treatments, even when some treatment parameters (e.g., longer sessions) are inconsistent with existing policies and requirements.

REFERENCES

American Psychiatric Association. (1987). *Diagnostic and statistical manual of mental disorders* (3rd ed., Rev.). Washington, DC: Author.

American Psychiatric Association. (1994). *Diagnostic and statistical manual of mental disorders* (4th ed.). Washington, DC: Author.

Brown, T.A., DiNardo, P.A., & Barlow, D.H. (1995). *Anxiety disorders interview schedule for DSM-IV (ADIS-IV)*. New York: University at Albany, State University of New York.

Carr, A.T. (1974). Compulsive neurosis: A review of the literature. *Psychological Bulletin, 81,* 311–318.

Constans, J.I., Foa, E.B., Franklin, M.E., & Mathews, A. (1995). Memory for actions in obsessive compulsives with checking rituals. *Behaviour Research and Therapy, 33,* 665–671.

Cooper, J. (1970). The Leyton obsessional inventory. *Psychological Medicine, 1,* 48–64.

Cottraux, J., Mollard, E., Bouvard, M., Marks, I., Sluys, M., Nury, A.M., Douge, R., & Ciadella, P. (1990). A controlled study of fluvoxamine and exposure in obsessive-compulsive disorder. *International Clinical Psychopharmacology, 5,* 17–30.

de Araujo, L.A., Ito, L.M., Marks, I.M., & Deale, A. (1995). Does imagined exposure to the consequences of not ritualising enhance live exposure for OCD? A controlled study: I. Main outcome. *British Journal of Psychiatry, 167,* 65–70.

DeVeaugh-Geiss, J., Landau, P., & Katz, R. (1989). Treatment of OCD with clomipramine. *Psychiatric Annals, 19,* 97–101.

Dollard, J., & Miller, N.E. (1950). *Personality and psychotherapy: An analysis in terms of learning, thinking and culture.* New York: McGraw-Hill.

Eisen, J.L., Beer, R., Pato, M.T., Venditto, & Rasmussen, S.A. (1997). *American Journal of Psychiatry, 154,* 271–273.

Emmelkamp, P.M.G., & Beens, H. (1991). Cognitive therapy with obsessive-compulsive disorder: A comparative evaluation. *Behaviour Research and Therapy, 29,* 293–300.

Emmelkamp, P.M.G., van der Helm, M., van Zanten, B.L., & Plochg, I. (1980). Treatment of obsessive compulsive patients: The contribution of self-instructional training to the effectiveness of exposure. *Behaviour Research and Therapy, 18,* 61–66.

Emmelkamp, P.M.G., & van Kraanen, J. (1977). Therapist-controlled exposure in vivo: A comparison with obsessive-compulsive patients. *Behaviour Research and Therapy, 15,* 491–495.

Emmelkamp, P.M.G., Visser, S., & Hoekstra, R.J. (1988). Cognitive therapy vs. exposure in vivo in the treatment of obsessive compulsives. *Cognitive Therapy and Research, 12,* 103–114.

First, M.B., Spitzer, R.L., Gibbon, M., & Williams, J.B.W. (1995). *Structured clinical interview for the DSM-IV Axis I disorders (SCID).* Washington, DC: American Psychiatric Press.

Foa, E.B., Amir, N., Bogert, K., & Molnar, C. (1997). *Inflated perception of responsibility for harm in obsessive-compulsive disorder.* Manuscript in preparation.

Foa, E.B., & Goldstein, A. (1978). Continuous exposure and complete response prevention in the treatment of obsessive-compulsive neurosis. *Behavior Therapy, 9,* 821–829.

Foa, E.B., Jameson, J.S., Turner, R.M., & Payne, L.L. (1980). Massed vs. spaced exposure sessions in the treatment of agoraphobia. *Behaviour Research and Therapy, 18,* 333–338.

Foa, E.B., & Kozak, M.J. (1985). Treatment of anxiety disorders: Implications for psychopathology. In A.H. Tuma & J.D. Maser (Eds.), *Anxiety and the anxiety disorders* (pp. 421–452). Hillsdale, NJ: Erlbaum.

Foa, E.B., & Kozak, M.J. (1996). Obsessive compulsive disorder: Long-term outcome of psychological treatment. In M. Mavissakalian & R. Prien (Eds.), *Long-term treatments of anxiety disorders.* Washington, DC: American Psychiatric Press.

Foa, E.B., Kozak, M.J., Goodman, W.K., Hollander, E., Jenike, M., & Rasmussen, S. (1995). DSM-IV field trial: Obsessive-compulsive disorder. *American Journal of Psychiatry, 152,* 654.

Foa, E.B., Kozak, M.J., Salkovskis, P.M., Coles, M.E., & Amir, N. (1997). *The validation of a new obsessive compulsive disorder scale: The obsessive compulsive inventory (OCI).* Manuscript in preparation.

Foa, E.B., Kozak, M.J., Steketee, G.S., & McCarthy, P.R. (1992). Treatment of depressive and obsessive-compulsive symptoms in OCD by imipramine and behavior therapy. *British Journal of Clinical Psychology, 31,* 279–292.

Foa, E.B., Steketee, G.S., Grayson, J.B., Turner, R.M., & Latimer P. (1984). Deliberate exposure and blocking of obsessive-compulsive rituals: Immediate and long-term effects. *Behavior Therapy, 15,* 450–472.

Foa, E.B., Steketee, G.S., & Ozarow, B.J. (1985). Behavior therapy with obsessive-compulsives: From theory to treatment. In M. Mavissakalian (Ed.), *Obsessive-compulsive disorders: Psychological and pharmacological treatments* (pp 49–120). New York: Plenum Press.

Foa, E.B., Steketee, G.S., Turner, R.M., & Fischer, S.C. (1980). Effects of imaginal exposure to feared disasters in obsessive-compulsive checkers. *Behaviour Research and Therapy, 18,* 449–455.

Fontaine, R., & Chouinard, G. (1985). An open clinical trial of fluoxetine in the treatment of obsessive-compulsive disorder. *Journal of Clinical Psychopharmacology, 6,* 98–101.

Fontaine, R., & Chouinard, G. (1989). Fluoxetine in the long-term maintenance treatment of OCD. *Psychiatric Annals, 19,* 88–91.

Freund, B., Steketee, G.S., & Foa, E.B. (1987). Compulsive activity checklist (CAC): Psychometric analysis with obsessive compulsive disorder. *Behavioral Assessment, 9,* 67–79.

Goodman, W.K., Price, L.H., Rasmussen, S.A., Masure, C., Fleishman, C., Hill, C., Heninger, G., & Charney, D.S. (1989). The Yale-Brown obsessive compulsive scale

(Y-BOCS) I: Development, use and reliability. *Archives of General Psychiatry, 46,* 1006–1011.

Greist, J.H. (1992). An integrated approach to treatment of obsessive compulsive disorder. *Journal of Clinical Psychiatry, 53,* 38–41.

Greist, J.H., Chouinard, G., DuBuff, E., Halaris, A., Kim, S.W., Koran, L., Liebowitz, M.L., Lydiard, R.B., Rasmussen, S., White, K., & Sikes, C. (1995). Double-blind parallel comparison of three dosages of sertraline and placebo in outpatients with obsessive-compulsive disorder. *Archives of General Psychiatry, 52,* 289–295.

Greist, J.H., Jefferson, J., Kobak, K.A., Katzelnick, D.J., & Serlin, R.C. (1995). Efficacy and tolerability of serotonin transport inhibitors in obsessive compulsive disorder: A meta-analysis. *Archives of General Psychiatry, 52,* 53–60.

Hembree, E.A., Cohen, A., Riggs, D.S., Kozak, M.J., & Foa, E.B. (1992). *The long-term efficacy of behavior therapy and serotonergic medications in the treatment of obsessive-compulsive ritualizers.* Unpublished manuscript.

Hiss, H., Foa, E.B., & Kozak, M.J. (1994). Relapse prevention program for treatment of obsessive-compulsive disorder. *Journal of Consulting and Clinical Psychology, 62,* 801–808.

Hodgson, R.J., & Rachman, S. (1977). Obsessional-compulsive complaints. *Behaviour Research and Therapy, 15,* 389–395.

Hodgson, R.J., Rachman, S., & Marks, I.M. (1972). The treatment of chronic obsessive-compulsive neurosis: Follow-up and further findings. *Behaviour Research and Therapy, 10,* 181–189.

Insel, T.R., & Akiskal, H.S. (1986). Obsessive-compulsive disorder with psychotic features: A phenomenologic analysis. *American Journal of Psychiatry, 143,* 1527–1533.

Jenike, M.A., Buttolph, L., Baer, L., Ricciardi, J., & Holland, A. (1989). Open trial of fluoxetine in obsessive compulsive disorder. *American Journal of Psychiatry, 146,* 909–911.

Kozak, M.J., & Foa, E.B. (1994). Obsessions, overvalued ideas, and delusions in obsessive-compulsive disorder. *Behaviour Research and Therapy, 32,* 343–353.

Kozak, M.J., Liebowitz, M.L., & Foa, E.B. (in press). Cognitive behavior therapy and pharmacotherapy for OCD: The NIMH-sponsored collaborative study. In W. Goodman, M. Rudorfer, & J. Maser (Eds.), *Obsessive compulsive disorder: Contemporary issues in treatment.* Mahwah, NJ: Erlbaum

Ladouceur, R., Rheaume, J., Freeston, M.H., Aublet, F., Jean, K., Lachance, S., Langlois, F., & de Polomandy-Morin, K. (1995). Experimental manipulations of responsibility: An analogue test for models of obsessive-compulsive disorder. *Behaviour Research & Therapy, 33,* 937–946.

Lelliott, P.T., Noshirvani, H.F., Basoglu, M., Marks, I.M., & Monteiro, W.O. (1988). Obsessive-compulsive beliefs and treatment outcome. *Psychological Medicine, 18,* 697–702.

Lopatka, C., & Rachman, S. (1995). Perceived responsibility and compulsive checking: An experimental analysis. *Behaviour Research & Therapy, 33,* 673–684.

Mallya, G.K., White, K., Waternaux, C., & Quay, S. (1992). Short- and long-term treatment of obsessive-compulsive disorder with fluvoxamine. *Annals of Clinical Psychiatry, 4,* 77–80.

Marks, I.M., Lelliot, P., Basoglu, M., Noshirvani, H., Monteiro, W., Cohen, D., & Kasvikis, Y. (1988). Clomipramine, self-exposure, and therapist-assisted exposure for obsessive compulsive rituals. *British Journal of Psychiatry, 152,* 522–534.

Marks, I.M., Stern, R.S., Mawson, D., Cobb, J., & McDonald, R. (1980). Clomipramine and exposure for obsessive compulsive rituals: I. *British Journal of Psychiatry, 136,* 1–25.

Meyer, V. (1966). Modification of expectations in cases with obsessional rituals. *Behaviour Research and Therapy, 4,* 273–280.

Meyer, V., & Levy, R. (1973). Modification of behavior in obsessive-compulsive disorders. In H.E. Adams & P. Unikel (Eds.), *Issues and trends in behavior therapy* (pp. 77–136). Springfield, IL: Charles C. Thomas.

Meyer, V., Levy, R., & Schnurer, A. (1974). The behavioural treatment of obsessive-compulsive disorders. In H.R. Beech (Ed.), *Obsessional states* (pp. 233–258). London: Methuen.

Montgomery, S.A., McIntyre, A., Osterheider, M., Sarteschi, P., Zitterl, W., Zohar, J., Birkett, M., Wood, A.J., & The Lilly European OCD Study Group. (1993). A double-blind, placebo-controlled study of fluoxetine in patients with *DSM-III-R* obsessive-compulsive disorder. *European Neuorpsychopharmacology, 3,* 143–152.

Mowrer, O.A. (1939). A stimulus-response analysis of anxiety and its role as a reinforcing agent. *Psychological Review, 46,* 553–565.

Mowrer, O.A. (1960). *Learning theory and behavior.* New York: Wiley.

Öst, L.-G. (1989). One-session treatment for specific phobias. *Behaviour Research and Therapy, 27,* 1–7.

O'Sullivan, G., Noshirvani, H., Marks, I., Monteiro, W., & Lelliot, P. (1991). Six-year follow-up after exposure and clomipramine therapy for obsessive compulsive disorder. *Journal of Clinical Psychiatry, 52,* 150–155.

Pato, M.T., Zohar-Kadouch, R., Zohar, J., & Murphy, D.L. (1988). Return of symptoms after discontinuation of clomipramine in patients with obsessive-compulsive disorder. *American Journal of Psychiatry, 145,* 1521–1525.

Pauls, D.L., Towbin, K.E., Leckman, J.F., Gwendolyn, E.P., Zahner, G.E., & Cohen, D.J. (1986). Gilles de la Tourette's syndrome and obsessive-compulsive disorder: Evidence supporting a genetic relationship. *Archives of General Psychiatry, 43,* 1180–1182.

Perse, T.L., Greist, J.H., Jefferson, J.W., Rosenfeld, R., & Dar, T. (1987). Fluvoxamine treatment of obsessive compulsive disorder. *American Journal of Psychiatry, 144,* 1543–1548.

Price, L.H., Goodman, W.K., Charney, D.S., Rasmussen, S.A., & Heninger, G.R. (1987). Treatment of severe obsessive-compulsive disorder with fluvoxamine. *American Journal of Psychiatry, 144,* 1059–1061.

Rabavilas, A.D., Boulougouris, J.C., & Stefanis, C. (1976). Duration of flooding sessions in the treatment of obsessive-compulsive patients. *Behaviour Research and Therapy, 14,* 349–355.

Rachman, S., Hodgson, R.J., & Marks, I.M. (1971). The treatment of chronic obsessive compulsive neurosis. *Behaviour Research and Therapy, 9,* 237–247.

Rachman, S., Throdarson, D.S., Shafran, R., & Woody, S.R. (1995). Perceived responsibility: Structure and significance. *Behaviour Research and Therapy, 33,* 779–784.

Rachman, S.J., & Wilson, G.T. (1980). *The effects of psychological therapy.* Oxford, England: Pergamon Press.

Rheaume, J., Freeston, M.H., Dugas, M.J., Letarte, H., & Ladouceur, R. (1995). Perfectionism, responsibility and obsessive-compulsive symptoms. *Behaviour Research & Therapy, 33,* 785–794.

Roper, G., & Rachman, S. (1976). Obsessional-compulsive checking: Experimental replication and development. *Behaviour Research and Therapy, 14,* 25–32.

Roper, G., Rachman, S., & Hodgson, R. (1973). An experiment of obsessional checking. *Behaviour Research and Therapy, 11,* 271–277.

Rubenstein, C.S., Peynirgioglu, Z.F., Chambless, D.L., & Pigott, T.A. (1993). Memory in sub-clinical obsessive-compulsive checkers. *Behaviour Research & Therapy, 31,* 759–765.

Salkovskis, P.M. (1985). Obsessional compulsive problems: A cognitive behavioral analysis. *Behaviour Research and Therapy, 23,* 571–583.

Sanavio, E. (1988). Obsessions and compulsions: The Padua inventory. *Behaviour Research and Therapy, 26,* 169–177.

Sher, K.J., Frost, R.O., & Otto, R. (1983). Cognitive deficits in compulsive checkers: An exploratory study. *Behaviour Research and Therapy, 21,* 357–364.

Steketee, G.S., Foa, E.B., & Grayson, J.B. (1982). Recent advances in the treatment of obsessive-compulsives. *Archives of General Psychiatry, 39,* 1365–1371.

Taylor, S. (1995). Assessment of obsessions and compulsions: Reliability, validity, and sensitivity to treatment effects. *Clinical Psychology Review, 15,* 261–296.

Thoren, P., Asberg, M., Chronholm, B., Jornestedt, L., & Traskman, L. (1980). Clomipramine treatment of obsessive-compulsive disorder. *Archives of General Psychiatry, 46,* 335–341.

van Oppen, P., de Haan, E., van Balkom, A.J.L.M., Spinhoven, P., Hoogduin, K., & van Dyck, R. (1995). Cognitive therapy and exposure in vivo in the treatment of obsessive compulsive disorder. *Behaviour Research and Therapy, 33,* 379–390.

Zohar, J., & Insel T.R. (1987). Drug treatment of obsessive-compulsive disorder: Drug treatment of anxiety disorders [Special issue]. *Journal of Affective Disorders, 13,* 193–202.

Zohar, J., Judge, R., & Paroxetine Study Group. (1996). Paroxetine versus clomipramine in the treatment of obsessive-compulsive disorder. *British Journal of Psychiatry, 169,* 468–474.

CHAPTER 16

Pharmacotherapy

MATTHEW T. O'NEILL, JOHN M. DAVIS, and BRIAN MARTIS

VIRTUALLY ALL of what we know about Obsessive Compulsive Disorder (OCD) has unfolded over just the past three decades. The therapeutic effectiveness of the Serotonin Reuptake Inhibitors (SRIs) and Exposure with Response Prevention (ERP), as well as evidence of a genetic relationship between Tourette's Syndrome (TS) and OCD and the discovery of an infection-triggered subtype of OCD (Swedo et al., 1998) have altered the perception of OCD as a "purely psychogenic" illness. We continue to learn more about this unique disorder from phenomenological studies, the development of reliable and valid measures of outcome like the Yale-Brown Obsessive Compulsive Scale (YBOCS; Goodman, Price, Rasmussen, Mazure, Delgado, et al., 1989; Goodman, Price, Rasmussen, Mazure, Fleischmann, et al., 1989); evidence from genetic, epidemiological, neurochemical, neuroimaging studies and studies of animal models.

DIAGNOSIS AND CLINICAL FEATURES

Obsessive Compulsive Disorder is characterized by obsessions (repetitive ideas, thoughts, impulses, or images) and compulsions (repetitive mental acts or motor behaviors) usually performed in response to the obsessions. These intrusive thoughts and actions are experienced as irrational or ego-dystonic, which the patient usually tries to resist, often causing marked distress and consuming considerable amounts of time thus significantly impairing personal, social, and occupational functioning (American Psychiatric Association, 1994).

We gratefully acknowledge the Stanley Foundation for support of this work. The authors also gratefully thank Dr. Edwin Cook Jr., Dr. Jean Marc Mienville, Mike Bennett, Margo McClelland, and Betty Hartley and Dr. Jefferson of the OCD Resource Center, for help with various aspects of the writing of this chapter.

Surprisingly, even though these core symptoms of OCD are quite characteristic, the average time from onset to diagnosis is roughly 5 to 10 years. This is often due to:

- The secretive nature of the sufferers (shame, fear of being viewed as "crazy");
- Patients feeling embarrassed when talking about their behavior;
- Common first presentation to non-psychiatric health professionals;
- Presence of masking comorbid conditions (like depression or substance abuse); and
- Inexperience of the evaluating clinician (not familiar with varying clinical manifestations) (Rasmussen & Eisen, 1990).

Presently the *DSM-IV* classifies OCD as an anxiety disorder which may not be accurate. Though anxiety is a very prominent and distressing symptom there are characteristic differences between OCD and other anxiety disorders. The early age of onset (Rasmussen & Tsuang, 1986), and the response of obsessions to serotonergic agents (Greist, Jefferson, Kobak, Katzelnick, & Serlin, 1995; Jenike, 1993), but not to tricyclics or anxiolytics, characterizes OCD as a disorder distinct from anxiety disorders. Additionally, the high rate of comorbidity of OCD and TS, as well as the high-incidence of OCD among families of TS patients (Pauls, Leckman, Towbin, Zahner, & Cohen, 1986) suggests OCD is a genetically influenced disease. Furthermore, the existence of similar obsessions observed among patients, irrespective of age, socioeconomic factors, or cultural backgrounds characterizes OCD as a distinct, biologically based disorder. Indeed, cleaning and counting compulsions have been reported among ages varying from young children to middle-aged adults, and across numerous cultures from the far east to inner cities in the United States (Okasha, Saad, Khalil, el Dawla, & Yehia, 1994; Saz, Copeland, de la Camara, Lobo, & Dewey, 1995; Weissman et al., 1994).

EPIDEMIOLOGY, COURSE, AND GENETICS

Once thought of as very rare, recent studies have shown that the prevalence of this disorder is far greater than the 0.05 percent initially reported by Rudin (Rudin, 1953). Recently, the incidence of OCD was estimated at 0.55 per 1000 person-years, based on the data from the Epidemiological Catchment Area (ECA) Study (Nestadt, Bienvenu, Cai, Samuels, & Eaton, 1998). Most contemporary studies report a prevalence as high as 1 percent to 2 percent (Karno, Golding, Sorenson, & Burnam, 1988). However, some authors have raised questions about the validity of diagnoses by lay interviewers (M. Stein, Forde, Anderson, & Walker, 1997), and the temporal stability of OCD diagnoses in the ECA studies (Nelson & Rice, 1997). Even so, the minimal prevalence of 1 percent represents a significant number of affected individuals (approximately 2.5 million in the United States) with significant individual and familial suffering, as well as a sizable economic burden (Hollander et al., 1998). (See Table 16.1.)

Table 16.1
Epidemiological Studies

Authors	Study	Prevalence	Additional
Robins et al. (1984)	Lifetime prevalence of psychiatric disorders in three US sites	Lifetime prevalence of 2.5%	
Flament et al. (1988)	Adolescents	Age-corrected point prevalence of 1–2%	
Bland et al. (1988)	Age of onset of psychiatric disorders	3.0%	
Karno et al. (1988)	Epidemiology of OCD in 5 U.S. communities	2.5%; 1.9–3.3% (1.2–2.4 with DSM III exclusions) across 5 U.S. communities	
Weissman et al. (1994)	Cross national epidemiology of OCD	2% in the U.S., Canada and Puerto Rico (Worldwide approximately 2% except Taiwan); higher risk of Major Depression and Anxiety disorders, cultural factors may affect symptom presentation	4 continents, 7 surveys using the DIS
M. Stein, Forde, et al. (1997)	OCD in the community	1 month weighted previously dropped from 3.1 to 0.6% when reappraise by clinicians	Raises questions of overdiagnosis by lay interviewers

OCD is a chronic disorder which requires treatment throughout life. The severity of symptoms have been noted to fluctuate over time. The average age of onset has been reported as approximately 20 to 25 years (Bland, Stebelsky, Orn, & Newman, 1988; Karno et al., 1988). Nonetheless, approximately 65 percent of patients with OCD experience onset of the illness before the age of 25 (Rasmussen & Tsuang, 1986), and less than 5 percent of patients experience onset after 45. Adult onset OCD is slightly female predominant (Weissman et al., 1994), whereas a higher frequency of affected males is observed among the childhood and adolescent population (Rasmussen & Eisen, 1990). The most common comorbidities observed in OCD are Affective Disorders (31%) and Substance Abuse (24%) (Karno et al., 1988).

Hereditary factors are involved in the expression of OCD, and there seems to be an overlap with TS that is known to be a genetically transmitted disease. Twin studies (Rasmussen & Tsuang, 1986), and studies reporting a high prevalence of OCD among relatives of probands with OCD or TS (Pauls, Towbin, Leckman, Zahner, & Cohen, 1986) substantiate this. Unfortunately, the heritability pattern and the specific genetic substrates involved in the expression of OCD or TS are not understood conclusively. Associations between OCD and a 5-HT2A receptor polymorphism (Enoch et al., 1998), the catechol-o-methyl transferase gene (Karayiorgou et al., 1997), and the serotonin transporter gene (McDougle, Epperson, Price, & Gelernter, 1998) have been demonstrated recently in studies which await replication. Future genetic studies will hopefully clarify the heritability pattern and contribute to an understanding of the disorder.

OVERVIEW OF TREATMENT

Initially OCD was thought to be resistant to treatment due to the failure of psychoanalytically based therapies. However, it is now well established that behavioral and pharmacological treatments can independently, and in concert, reduce OCD symptomatology. The treatment strategy that may reduce obsessive-compulsive symptoms and maximally improve the quality of patients lives combines Exposure with Response Prevention (ERP) with pharmacological therapy (Jenike, 1993). Furthermore, for treatment strategies to be effective and comprehensive, attention to and intervention in the personal, familial, social, and occupational areas of the patient are essential due to the pervasiveness and chronicity of the disorder. The following sections are generally restricted to the drug treatment of OCD.

CLOMIPRAMINE (CMI)

> We believe that even if clomipramine is not a definite treatment for obsessive neurosis in every case, it opens a hopeful research pathway to the pharmacological treatment of these patients. After about 5 weeks, the patient becomes stronger in confronting his obsessions and little by little they start interfering less with his normal behavior (Lopez-Ibor, 1968).

> What struck us, besides the fast action of clomipramine, is the high percentage of excellent results. Indeed, when one browses the literature on obsessions, one rarely sees favorable percentages over 20 percent to 30 percent. Our own experience has revealed excellent results in Obsessive Compulsive Disorder, but never as frequent as with clomipramine (van Renynghe de Voxvrie, 1968).

Though CMI is considered a tricyclic structurally, it is functionally categorized as a SRI due to its highly potent 5HT-reuptake inhibiting properties. CMI is not considered a Selective Serotonin Reuptake Inhibitor (SSRI) because its active metabolite nor-clomipramine is a norepinephrine reuptake inhibitor. CMI was first observed to have antiobsessive potential in 1967 when it was administered intravenously to subjects with comorbid depression (Fernandez & Lopez-Ibor, 1967; van Renynghe de Voxvrie, 1968). By 1980, there was adequate evidence to prove this initial observation beyond a reasonable doubt. However it was not until the late 1980s that CMI was studied in the United States and approved by the Food and Drug Administration specifically for the treatment of OCD. In the decades prior to this there were no pharmacotherapies available in the United States with a proven, clinically relevant efficacy. The ignorance of foreign studies and failure of the National Institute of Mental Health and the manufacturer Ciba Geigy to perform studies in the United States from 1967 through the mid-1980s is extremely unfortunate.

OCD and Depression

As noted earlier, these initial studies involving patients with OCD recorded a substantial prevalence of comorbid depression. Indeed, affective disorders are the most prevalent complications of OCD (Black, Goldstein, Noyes, & Blum, 1995; Karno et al., 1988), and initially it was unclear whether improvements in OCD were secondary to improvements in depression. In order to study whether CMI had specific antiobsessive effects, depressed and nondepressed individuals were studied. Furthermore, a series of studies were conducted comparing the efficacy of CMI to other tricyclic agents commonly used in the treatment of depression.

Table 16.2
Controlled Studies of Clomipramine in OCD

Report	n	OCD, Diagnostic Info.	Description	Weeks	Result
Karabanow (1977)	20		100mg/d CMI (n=10) vs. placebo (n=10), double blind	6	CMI > placebo; all responded to CMI, 0 of 10 to placebo
Marks et al. (1980)	40		225mg/d CMI (n=20) vs. placebo (n=20), double blind	32	CMI effect diminished after week 10–18.
Montgomery (1980)	14	Without depression	75mg/d CMI vs. placebo, blind crossover	4 of ea.	Significant effect with CMI in weeks 1, 3, and 4; 64.5% response rate, 5% placebo response rate
Flament et al. (1985)	19	Half refractory	200mg/d max CMI vs. placebo, blind crossover	5 of ea.	CMI > placebo
Mavissakalian et al. (1985)	12		CMI (n=7) or placebo (n=5), double blind	12	Significant improvement of OCD with CMI vs. placebo; equal improvement of depression with CMI or placebo
Jenike et al. (1989)	27		Up to 300mg/d CMI (n=13) vs. placebo (n=14), double blind	10	CMI > placebo, significantly; small placebo effect
Greist et al. (1990)	32	No depression	250 or 300mg/d CMI (n=16) vs. placebo (n=16), double blind	10	11 of 15 improved with CMI, 2 of 16 on placebo
Mavissakalian et al. (1990)	25	No depression	200mg/d CMI (n=13) vs. placebo (n=12), double blind	10	CMI > placebo, significantly
CMI collaborative group (1991)	520	No depression	Two studies: CMI up to 300mg/d (n=118, 134) vs. placebo (n=120, 129), double blind	10	YBOCS reduced 38% and 44% vs. 3% and 5% for placebo
DeVeaugh-Geiss et al (1992)	60	Children and adolescents	CMI (n=31) vs. placebo (n=29), double blind	8	CMI reduced OCD by 37% by YBOCS (8% with placebo) CMI significantly effective during 1 year open label
Ackerman et al (1994)			Analysis of responders to CMI from the CMI Collaborative Group study (below)		Few patients with HAM-D scores >16, but depression correlated with least response; low or high scores for depression correlated with a high response rate

Studies of CMI in which depressed individuals were either included or excluded (see Table 16.2) demonstrated that:

- The degree of initial depression does not predict the response of obsessive compulsive symptomatology to CMI.
- The improvement in depression observed with CMI therapy does not correlate with the degree of improvement in OCD.
- The time-course of improvement observed with OCD is longer than that observed in depression.

Furthermore, the studies in which CMI was compared to other tricyclics proved (see Table 16.3) that available tricyclic antidepressants other than CMI do not effectively treat OCD symptoms. The potent inhibition of serotonin reuptake, not catecholamine reuptake, led to improvement in OCD, implicating serotonin as an important neurotransmitter in the pathophysiology of OCD.

Before the advent of SSRIs, CMI was the most widely employed antiobsessive agent. It still remains a first-line drug treatment option. The dose of CMI for OCD is usually up to 250 mg/day. 12 weeks are an adequate length for a trial. CMI is associated with a number of side effects which may compromise compliance.

Table 16.3
CMI vs. TCA

Report	n	OCD, Info.	Description	Weeks	Result
Rapoport et al. (1980)	9		CMI vs. desipramine vs. placebo, blind crossover	3–5 of ea.	No significant effect with either CMI or desipramine incomparison to placebo
Thoren et al. (1980)	24		CMI vs. nortriptyline vs. placebo (3 groups), double blind	5	CMI: 42% reduction; nortryptyline: 21% reduction; placebo: 7% reduction of OCD scale score
Ananth et al. (1981)	20		CMI (n=10) vs. amitriptyline (n=10), double blind	4	7 of 10 with CMI, 3 of 10 with amitriptyline; no effect between groups, trend favoring CMI over amitriptyline zimelidine significantly more effective than imipramine
Prasad (1984a)	6		Imipramine (n=3) vs. zimelidine (n=3; an SRI), double blind	4	Zimelidine significantly more effective than imipramine
Volavka et al. (1985)	16		CMI (n=11) vs. imipramine (n=12), double blind	12	CMI > imipramine
Leonard et al. (1989)	48	Child and adolescents	CMI vs. desipramine, blind crossover	5 of ea.	CMI >> desipramine, desipramine phase associated with relapse
Leonard et al. (1991)	20	Child and adolescents	Double-blind desipramine substitution to maintenance CMI (3 mo. CMI—2 mo. desipramine or CMI—3 mo. CMI)	NA	CMI effective, 1 of 9 responded to desipramine
Kindler et al. (1993)	10		CMI vs. desipramine, crossover	6 of ea.	CMI >> desipramine

Intravenous CMI Loading

Administration of intravenous CMI is an apparently successful strategy by which a significant antiobsessive response has been obtained with fewer side effects. Indeed, the initial reports of CMI's antiobsessive potential had employed iv administration (Fernandez & Lopez-Ibor, 1967; van Renynghe de Voxvrie, 1968). More recent reports continue to substantiate the effectiveness of this approach by demonstrating a rapid response to iv CMI (4.5 days in one study) when compared to oral CMI (4 weeks) (Capstick, 1971; Koran, Sallee, & Pallanti, 1997; Warneke, 1992). This combination of a rapid response and a decreased frequency of side effects may be particularly beneficial for patients acutely incapacitated by OCD, or resistant to standard treatments. One large controlled study, however, observed an acute exacerbation of OCD symptomatology upon iv administration (Mundo, Bellodi, & Smeraldi, 1995). In the same study, subsequent oral CMI was successful after 10 weeks.

Venlafaxine

Like CMI, venlafaxine blocks both 5-HT and NE reuptake. Venlafaxine is speculated to be efficacious in the treatment of OCD, although large studies confirming this have yet to be performed. In several small studies and case reports, however, venlafaxine has been shown to be modestly effective. One study evaluated a dose of 225 mg/day, which they noted, may have been too low of a dose for a significant effect to arise (Yaryura-Tobias & Neziroglu, 1996). Other studies of venlafaxine have employed doses of up to 375 mg/day (Rauch, O'Sullivan, & Jenike, 1996). These studies observed results during weeks 5 to 12.

SELECTIVE SEROTONIN REUPTAKE INHIBITORS (SSRIs)

Controlled trials have shown beyond doubt that the SSRIs (fluoxetine, fluvoxamine, paroxetine, and sertraline) are useful in the treatment of OCD. These SSRIs are roughly as effective as CMI (see Table 16.4), are safer, easier to use, and better tolerated making them a first choice among clinicians. Compared to their usage in depression, somewhat higher dosages may be needed with a response time approximately twice as long (8–12 weeks). Patients must also be educated about the SSRI withdrawal syndrome which is associated with short half-life SSRIs when discontinuing or changing medications. If combining an SSRI (e.g., fluoxetine) with CMI, it should be remembered that SSRIs can cause a 2- to 3-fold increase in plasma levels of CMI. In this case dosages should be adjusted and plasma levels should be monitored. Table 16.5 summarizes the controlled studies of SSRIs. See Table 16.6 for a list of SSRIs and dosages used in OCD.

- *Fluoxetine.* Two large double-blind, placebo-controlled studies have proven the antiobsessive potential of fluoxetine. In one study, quantities of 20, 40, and 60 mg/day were found to diminish symptoms in a dose-response manner, while in another only the 60 mg/day dose was significantly superior to placebo. Trials in these studies lasted 8 to 13 weeks. 12 weeks is sufficient for a trial.

Table 16.4
CMI vs. SSRIs

Report	n	Diagnosis	Description	Weeks	Result
Pigott et al. (1990)	32	OCD	CMI vs. fluoxetine, crossover	10	Both effective
Saiz et al. (1992)	55	OCD	Fluoxetine 40mg/d vs. CMI 150mg/d, blind	8	Effective, equally
Lopez-Ibor et al. (1996)	55	OCD	40mg/d fluoxetine (n=30) vs. 150mg/d CMI (n=25), blind	8	Both effective
Tamimi et al. (1991)	23	OCD	CMI 300mg/d max vs. fluvoxamine 300mg/d, open	12	Effective, equally
Smeraldi et al. (1992)	10	OCD	Fluvoxamine 200mg/d vs. CMI 200mg/d, blind	12	Effective, equally
Freeman et al. (1994)	64	OCD	Fluvoxamine 100–250mg/d (n=34) vs. CMI 100–250mg/d (n=30)	10	Effective, equally
Koran et al. (1996)	73	OCD	Fluvoxamine 300mg/d max vs. CMI 250mg/d max	10	Effective, equally
Mundo et al. (1996)	128	OCD	Fluvoxamine vs. CMI 300mg/d for each drug	10	Effective, equally
Milanfranchi et al. (1997)	26	OCD, no comorbidity	Fluvoxamine vs. CMI, double blind	7	Effective, equally

- *Fluvoxamine.* A number of small studies and two large double-blind studies have proven the antiobsessive efficacy of fluvoxamine. In the larger controlled trials, flexible doses ranging from 100–300 mg/day effectively reduced obsessive compulsive symptoms compared to placebo. One trial reported a significant response as early as 4 weeks and the other at 6 weeks.
- *Sertraline.* The antiobsessive effects of sertraline have been demonstrated by three large controlled studies. One 8-week study administered flexible doses of sertraline (50–200 mg/day) and demonstrated significant therapeutic response compared to placebo. Another group reported a significant response as early as 3 weeks and then again from weeks 6 to 12. A third, larger study reported significant improvement with 50, 100, and 200 mg/day doses after 12 weeks.
- *Paroxetine.* Two large, controlled studies have substantiated the antiobsessive effectiveness of paroxetine. In one study paroxetine was found to be equally effective as CMI in reducing obsessive compulsive symptomatology. Additionally, a dose-effect response was observed when paroxetine was administered in doses of 20, 40, and 60 mg/day. These trials lasted 12 weeks.
- *Citalopram.* Recently released in the United States, citalopram is one of the most specific and potent SSRIs presently available. Only three small, uncontrolled studies of citalopram have been undertaken showing favorable results. One study found it equally efficacious as paroxetine and fluvoxamine (Mundo, Bianchi, & Bellodi, 1997). Presently, citalopram is FDA approved only for the treatment of depression.

Table 16.5
Controlled Studies of SSRIs in OCD

Report	n	OCD, Diagnostic Info.	Description	Weeks	Result (vs. Placebo)
Fluvoxamine					
Perse et al. (1987)	16		Fluvoxamine (*n*=16) vs. placebo (*n*=3)	20	13 of 16 responded
Goodman (1989)	42	Half with MDD	Fluvoxamine 300mg/d max vs. placebo (*n*=21)	6–8	9 of 21 on fluvoxamine, 0 of 21 on placebo
Cottraux et al. (1990)	60		Fluvoxamine 300mg/d, with ERP vs. placebo	48	Fluvoxamine > placebo, significantly
Jenike et al. (1990)	38		Fluvoxamine 300mg/d (*n*=18) vs. placebo	10	Fluvoxamine > placebo, non-significant
Mallya et al. (1992)	28		Fluvoxamine 300mg/d (*n*=14) vs. placebo	10	6 of 14 on fluvoxamine, 1 of 14 on placebo
Westenberg et al. (1993)	20	MDD allowed	Fluvoxamine 100mg tid vs. placebo	8	Fluvoxamine superior to placebo
Greist (1995)	160		Fluvoxamine 100–300mg/d (*n*=64) vs. placebo (*n*=76)	10	30 of 79 to fluvoxamine, 12 of 70 to placebo; fluvoxamine > placebo, significantly
Goodman et al. (1996)	160		Fluvoxamine 100–300mg/d (*n*=78) vs. placebo (*n*=78)	10	Fluvoxamine > placebo, significantly
Fluoxetine					
Riddle et al. (1992)	14	Children and adolescents	Fluoxetine 20mg/d (*n*=7) vs. placebo (*n*=7), blind crossover	8	44% decrease in C-YBOCS with fluoxetine vs. 27% decrease with placebo
Montgomery et al. (1993)	217		Fluoxetine 20 (*n*=53), 40 (*n*=52), and 60mg/d (*n*=55) vs. placebo (*n*=144)	8	Almost 50% response rate with 40 and 60mg; trend for 60>40>20mg
Tollefson et al. (1994)	355		Fluoxetine 20 (*n*=87), 40 (*n*=89), and 60mg/d (*n*=90) vs. placebo (*n*=89)	13	Fluoxetine > placebo, significantly; 60>40>20mg
Sertraline					
Chouinard et al. (1990)	87		Sertraline 200mg/d (*n*=43) vs. placebo (*n*=44)	8	Sertraline superior to placebo, 56% vs. 32%
Jenike et al. (1990)	19		Sertraline 200mg/d (*n*=10) vs. placebo (*n*=9)	10	Slight but non-significant trend for sertraline to be better than placebo
Greist et al. (1995)	325		Sertraline 50, 100, 200mg/d (*n*=241) vs. placebo (*n*=84)	12	93 of 240 on sertraline, 25 of 84 on placebo improved
Paroxetine					
Wheadon et al. (1993)	348		Paroxetine 20 (*n*=88), 40 (*n*=86), 60mg/d (*n*=85) vs. placebo	12	Paroxetine > placebo, trend for 60>40>20
J. Zohar & Judge (1996)	406		Paroxetine 60mg/d (*n*=201) vs. CMI (99) vs. placebo (99)	12	Paroxetine = CMI, both superior to placebo
Citalopram					
Thomsen (1997)	23	Children and adolescents	Citalopram 40mg/d, open	10	Significant reduction of scores
Koponen et al. (1997)	27		Citalopram 40 or 60mg/d, open	10	22 of 27, with 50% reduction in YBOCS
Mundo (1997)	30		Fluvoxamine 300mg/d max, paroxetine 60mg/d max, citalopram 60mg/d max	10	No differences between treatments

Table 16.6
Dosages of SRIs *

Agent	Dose (mg/day)	Duration	Washout Period (if Switching to an MAOI)
clomipramine	up to 250	12 weeks	2 weeks
fluoxetine	up to 80	12 weeks	at least 6 weeks
fluvoxamine	up to 250	12 weeks	2 weeks
sertraline	up to 200	12 weeks	2 weeks
paroxetine	up to 60	12 weeks	2 weeks
citalopram	up to 60	12 weeks	—

*Adapted from Rauch and Jenike, 1994.

OTHER AGENTS

- *MAOIs.* Comparisons of MAOIs and SSRIs (see Table 16.7) have shown patients' symptoms respond better to CMI than MAOIs. Clinically, certain patients have responded to MAOIs when other agents have failed. Accordingly, patients not responding to conventional SSRIs may be given a trial of a MAOI. Combining SSRIs and MAOIs may dangerously elevate

Table 16.7
Other Agents

Report	n	OCD, Diagnostic Info.	Description	Weeks	Results
MAOIs					
Insel et al. (1982)	12		100–300mg/d CMI vs. chlorgyline, crossover	6	CMI effective, relapse upon discontinuation
Vallejo et al. (1992)	26		CMI 225mg/d (*n*=14) vs. phenelzine 75mg/d (*n*=12)	12	Effective, equally
Jenike et al. (1997)	54		Phenelzine (60mg/d) vs. fluvoxetine (80mg/d) vs. placebo, blind	10	Fluvov > phenel, some patients responded to phenelzine
Trazodone					
Prasad (1984b)	8		Trazodone, no dose reported	6	6 of 8
Baxter (1985)	2	With MDD	Trazodone 400mg/d and 300mg/d	NA	Improvement in both cases
Lydiard (1986)	1		Trazodone up to 100mg/d	NA	Effective; remission upon discontinuation
Kim (1987)	1		Trazodone 150mg/d	NA	Effective, relapse upon discontinuation
Hermesh (1990)	9	Refract to CMI, Li	1 Trazodone 250mg b.i.d.	6	3 of 9, relapse upon discontinuation
Pigott, Heureax, et al. (1992)	21		Trazodone monotherapy (*n*=12) vs. placebo (*n*=6)	NA	No effect
Sunkureddi & Markovitz (1993)	1	Tricho, refractory	Trazodone	6	General improvement in tricho, and OCD

synaptic levels of 5-HT by inhibiting reuptake and degradation pathways and result in potentially fatal outcomes; such a combination should be avoided except in special circumstances. See Table 16.6 for recommended washout periods.

- *Trazodone.* Trazodone has been shown to have antidepressant properties and several small case studies suggest it may have potential in the treatment of OCD. Trazodone is not strictly speaking, an SSRI. The exact mechanism by which trazodone acts is complex, although blockage of 5-HT reuptake is thought to occur as is antagonism of 5-HT2 receptors. One small controlled study of trazodone in OCD did not report a significant positive effect. However, additional studies are needed to characterize trazodone's role in OCD. At present, it is not considered one of the front line agents but may be tried in augmentation (see Table 16.7).

AUGMENTATION

Roughly 50 percent of patients with OCD do not respond to standard first-line pharmacotherapeutic approaches. Even in responders to SSRIs, symptoms are reduced only to approximately 50 percent of their pretreatment levels. Though this often results in significant functional improvement, and many patients are left with residual symptoms. Accordingly, the augmentation of standard pharmacotherapies has been explored, unfortunately with little success in controlled trials. We will first discuss efforts to augment SSRIs with serotonergic agents and later discuss subtypes of OCD in which dopaminergic blockers may be useful.

SEROTONERGIC AGENTS

- *Buspirone* is a 5-HT1A partial agonist. Two open studies (Jenike, Baer, & Buttolph, 1991; Markovitz, Stagno, & Calabrese, 1990) and several case reports of successful augmentation with buspirone have been refuted by controlled studies (Grady et al., 1993; McDougle et al., 1993; Pigott, L'Heureux, Hill, et al., 1992). However, buspirone is an agent with a fairly benign side effect profile and trials on individual bases or in cases resistant to SSRIs may still be considered.

- *Lithium* is known to enhance serotonergic neurotransmission and is considered an effective augmenting agent in the treatment of Major Depression. In two controlled studies it failed to demonstrate efficacy as an augmenting agent for OCD (McDougle, Price, Goodman, Charney, & Heninger, 1991; Pigott et al., 1991). However, several cases suggest that certain patients may improve with lithium augmentation (Golden, Morris, & Sack, 1988; Rasmussen, 1984; Stern & Jenike, 1983).

In a few case reports (Rasmussen, 1984) and open studies (Yaryura-Tobias & Bhagavan, 1977), administration of the metabolic precursor l-tryptophan has resulted in modest therapeutic effects. The largest study of l-tryptophan in OCD investigated l-tryptophan as an open monotherapy, obtaining small but significant results at 4 weeks (Montgomery, Fineberg, Montgomery, & Bullock, 1992). It should be noted that previous reports of l-tryptophan administration resulting in Eosinophilia Myalgia syndrome, which led to a ban on its clinical use in the United States, were traced to contaminants from one manufacturer.

- *Clonazepam* has been studied both as an adjuvant and as monotherapy in patients with OCD. While the mechanism of clonazepam's action is not well understood, it is thought to increase serotonergic neurotransmission. One open study (Hewlett, Vinogradov, & Agras, 1990) and one controlled (Hewlett, Vinogradov, & Agras, 1992) demonstrated significant reduction of symptoms when clonazepam was administered as a monotherapy. There is also indication that patients not responding to SSRIs may respond to clonazepam. Clonazepam may be used as an adjuvant to SSRIs as well.

DOPAMINERGIC AGENTS

These agents will be discussed in the context of tic related disorders and psychotic spectrum disorders:

Tourette's Syndrome, Tic Disorder and OCD

Tourette's Syndrome (TS) is a chronic disorder in which the patient exhibits motor and phonic tics. The prevalence of TS has been estimated to be 0.05 percent to 1 percent. The average age of onset is 5 to 7 years with a 3 times greater number of male cases than female (Shapiro, Shapiro, Young, et al., 1988). TS is a lifetime disorder, although symptom severity has been observed to vary with time (Bruun et al., 1976; Erenberg, Cruse, & Rothner, 1987).

A preponderance of genetic and epidemiological research confirms an overlap between TS or, more generally, tic-disorder (TD), and OCD.

- Approximately 30 percent to 50 percent of TS patients have OCD (Pauls, Towbin, et al., 1986).
- In the NIMH cohort, 7 percent to 57 percent of children with OCD experienced tics and 15 percent qualified for a comorbid diagnosis of TS (Leonard et al., 1992; Swedo, Rapoport, Leonard, Lenane, & Cheslow, 1989).
- Among first-degree relatives of TS patients one group reported an 8 percent prevalence of TS, 15 percent chronic tics, and 16 percent OCD (Pauls, Raymond, Stevenson, & Leckman, 1991).
- Among first-degree relatives of subjects with OCD a high prevalence of TS (1.8%) and TD (14%) was observed by another group (Leonard et al., 1992).

Phenomenological studies and treatment studies suggest that patients with comorbid OCD and tic disorders may be a clinically unique subtype. For example, patients with tic-related OCD were found to report more aggressive, religious, and sexual obsessions as well as more checking, counting, ordering, touching, and hoarding compulsions than did patients with non-tic-related OCD (Leckman et al., 1994). Additionally, a number of reports have demonstrated that patients with tic related OCD appear to experience a more severe disorder than OCD or TS alone, with respect to symptomatology (Coffey et al., 1998; A. Zohar et al., 1997) and neuropsychological dysfunction (Alarcon, Libb, & Boll, 1994; de Groot, Yeates, Baker, & Bornstein, 1997; see Green & Pitman, 1990 for an extensive discussion). This subtype may require combination therapy with both SSRIs and antipsychotic agents. Haloperidol, pimozide, and more recently risperidone have been used in combination with SSRIs with some success in this subgroup of patients (see Table 16.8). Only rarely has the administration of SSRIs exacerbated the TS symptomology (Hauser & Zesiewicz, 1995).

OCD and Psychotic Disorders

Sometimes the differentiation of an obsession, an overvalued idea, and a delusion can be difficult. Some patients with OCD have been described in which the obsessions are of delusional proportions (Ballerini & Stangehellini, 1989; Insel & Akiskal, 1986). This is sometimes referred to as Obsessive Compulsive Psychosis (not a *DSM-IV* recognized category), or OCD with poor insight *(DSM-IV)*. Characteristically, the patient considers their obsessional thoughts or fears to be real, and compulsive actions are interpreted as necessary. The comorbidity of OCD in schizophrenia is reportedly 8 percent to 24 percent, which represents a significant overlap (Cassano, Pini, Saettoni, Rucci, & Dell'Osso, 1998; Eisen, Beer, Pato, Venditto, & Rasmussen, 1997; Karno et al., 1988). Such presentations deserve more diagnostic attention as several investigators have indicated that comorbid schizotypy was a poor prognostic indicator for drug response in OCD (Jenike, Baer, Minichiello, Schwartz, & Carey, 1986; Ravizza, Barzega, Bellino, Bogetto, & Maina, 1995). Concomitant administration of SSRIs and antipsychotics is a viable approach to treating this constellation of symptomatology, which has been effective in a number of cases (J. Zohar, Kaplan, & Benjamin, 1993).

Interestingly, in schizophrenic patients treated with clozapine, and more recently risperidone and olanzapine, there have been numerous reports of new-onset obsessive compulsive symptoms or clinical OCD (L. Allen & Tejera, 1994; al-Mulhim & Atwal, 1998; Eales & Layeni, 1994; Kopala & Honer, 1994; Morrison, Clark, Goldfarb, & McCoy, 1998; Patel & Tandon, 1993). In several cases, the OCD symptoms abated when these agents were discontinued, suggesting a direct pharmacological effect. Since these agents have unique 5-HT2 (as well as 5-HT6, possibly 5-HT7, and D4) blocking properties it suggests that the effects of 5-HT antagonism may be involved in the pathophysiology of OCD. This phenomenon has not usually been observed with administration of traditional neuroleptics to schizophrenics, and appears to respond to SSRIs.

Despite the above reports, antipsychotics may prove useful augmentative agents for cases not complicated by disorders such as TS or schizophrenia. One controlled trial, as well as a number of open trials, support the usage of neuroleptics for augmentation of SSRIs. Haloperidol and pimozide have been

Table 16.8
OCD with TS or Tics

Report	n	Diagnostic Information	Description	Weeks	Results
Yaryura-Tobias & Neziroglu (1975)	2	One with OCD, one with OCD and TS	Refractory to other TS treatments, CMI 150mg/d	NA	Amelioration of TS (both cases) and OCD
Riddle et al. (1988)	3	OCD with TS	Fluoxetine 20mg/d, open addition to TS medications	NA	Tics 1/3 better in one; 1/3 worse in another; no change in the third
Delgado et al. (1990)	1	OCD with TS	Fluvoxamine and pimozide	NA	Double blind discontinuation revealed that both were necessary for relief of tics and OCD
Ratzoni et al. (1990)	1	OCD with TS, adolescents	CMI monotherapy	NA	Effective relief of depression and TS; relapse upon discontinuation, effective upon reinstatement; 2 year effective maintenance
Riddle et al. (1990)	10	OCD with TS, children and adolescents	Fluoxetine 10 or 40mg/d, open addition to TS medications	20	5 or 10 responded (all had some degree of OCD) no change in TS
Como & Kurlan (1991)	26	OCD with TS	Fluoxetine 20 and 40mg/d, "TS medications allowed"	12–32	21 of 26 patients showed significant improvement of OCD, no effect on tics reported
Kurlan et al. (1993)	11	Ts with OCD, children	Fluoxetine 20–40mg/d, double blind	NA	No effect on OCD, indications of efficacy for TS; no indication of negative effects
McDougle et al. (1994)	8	OCD with TS, all refractory to fluvox alone	Adjuvant haloperidol 10mg/d max to fluvoxamine 300mg/d max, double blind	NA	8 of 8 experienced reduction of OC symptoms; no placebo response, no haloperidol effect on subjects without tics
Giakas (1995)	1	OCD with TS, refractory OCD	Fluoxetine with risperidone 6mg/d	NA	Significant improvement in OCD and TS with risperidone; fluoxetine and CMI alone inadequate
Eapen et al. (1996)	30	TS with OC behavior, half children	Fluoxetine addition to TS medications	12	At 6 and 12 weeks 23 of 30 experienced improvement in OCD; in one case fluoxetine exacerbated aggression
Saxena et al. (1996)	5	OCD with TS, SRI refractory OCD	SSRIs with adjuvant 2.75/d risperidone	NA	1 of 5 responded, 3 discontinued for akathisia
Stein, Bower, et al. (1997)	3	TS, with comorbid OCD refractory to SSRIs	SSRIs with adjuvant risperidone 3–4mg/d	NA	1 of 3 responded, 1 intollerant
Scahill et al. (1997)	5	OCD with TS, comorbid	Fluoxetine monotherapy 20mg/d, double blind	20	Fluoxetine effective for OCD, fluoxetine discontinuation led to exacerbation of OCD; no indication of negative effect on TS

administered successfully in 20 of 34 cases, with efficacy observed generally at 4 weeks (McDougle et al., 1990, 1994). Not surprisingly, a positive response was associated with, but was not limited to, the presence of tic disorders. Though serious side effects such as tardive dyskinesia remain a concern with these agents, the doses used are usually in the lower range.

In two open studies, and several case reports of refractory OCD, augmentation of SSRIs with risperidone resulted in symptom reduction in 25 of 41 cases (Ravizza, Barzega, Bellino, Bogetto, & Maina, 1996b; Saxena, Wang, Bystritsky, & Baxter, 1996; Stein, Bouwer, Hawkridge, & Emsley, 1997). Risperidone monotherapy for OCD has been shown to be useful in a small open study as well (Jacobsen, 1995). Again, it should be noted that like haloperidol, response of OCD patients to risperidone was sometimes, but not exclusively, associated with comorbidities such as tics and psychosis. More controlled studies are needed to substantiate risperidone's therapeutic role in OCD, and presently its use should be limited to cases not responding to SSRIs. Investigators have reported varied response times to adjuvant risperidone ranging from a few days to a few weeks. Four to 8 weeks are likely an adequate trial for augmentation.

MAINTENANCE TREATMENT AND DISCONTINUATION STUDIES

In most patients, OCD is a chronic, life-long illness requiring long-term therapy. Many patients who discontinue their medication relapse, even after years of treatment (Thoren, Asberg, Cronholm, Jornestedt, & Traskman, 1980). The high rate of relapse observed in placebo-controlled, double-blind discontinuation studies, is compelling evidence supporting long-term treatment (Pato, Hill, & Murphy, 1990; Pato, Zohar-Kadouch, Zohar, & Murphy, 1988). For this reason, most clinicians choose to treat patients indefinitely. Clinicians have, in most cases, employed maximal doses of SSRIs when treating OCD. Whether high doses need be sustained during long-term treatment is not clear. SSRIs often cause numerous side effects, the severity of which may compromise compliance, and it has been speculated that doses could be tapered after the initial response. Several studies have demonstrated successful dosage reductions of SSRIs; one study even reported no difference between full and half doses of several SSRIs (Mundo, Bareggi, Pirola, Bellodi, & Smeraldi, 1997; Pato et al., 199; Ravizza, Barzega, Bellino, Bogetto, & Maina, 1996a).

REFRACTORY OCD

Though the definition of refractory OCD is not widely agreed upon, most researchers consider failed responses to 3 trials of adequate length with SSRIs (including one trial with CMI), to augmentation and combination strategies, and to ERP as treatment resistant OCD. Causes of pseudo-resistance should carefully be ruled out before labelling a patient treatment resistant. Additionally, patients and families who have undergone failed treatments are often very discouraged and demand special attention. Treatment strategies for truly

Table 16.9
Stepwise Strategy for Resistant or Refractory Cases

Start	SRIs:	CMI
		fluvoxamine
		fluoxetine
		sertraline
		paroxetine
Consider	Combination of SRIs with CMI	
Consider	Augmentation agents:	
		clonazepam
		risperidone (especially in cases with tics or pschosis)
		neuroleptics (especially in cases with tics or pschosis)
		buspirone
		lithium
Consider	Alternative monotherapies:	
		venlafaxine
		clonazepam
		MAOIs (after an adequate washout):
		phenelzine
		tranylcypromine
Consider	Intravenous CMI (up to 350mg/infusion x 14 infusions)	
Consider	Neurosurgery consultation	

refractory patients should follow systematic algorithms proceeding from the best-studied agents to drugs less often employed, and, lastly, to experimental protocols. A stepwise strategy for the treatment of resistant or refractory cases adapted from Rauch and Jenike is presented in Table 16.9. These should be informed choices made by the patient and his or her family. (For a detailed discussion, see Rauch & Jenike, 1994.)

NEUROSURGERY

Neurosurgical treatment of OCD has not yet been tested in double-blind studies. Nonetheless cingulotomy, subcaudate tractotomy, limbic leukotomy, and anterior capsulotomy, or combinations thereof continue to remain an option for the truly refractive and severely debilitated patient (Mindus & Jenike, 1992; Mindus et al., 1994). The development of the gamma knife, which carefully places lesions in brain areas without the need for craniotomy greatly reduces the complications and discomfort previously associated with neurosurgery and may facilitate research. Jenike (1998) discusses the reluctant necessity of surgery for some cases in a recent article.

EXPERIMENTAL AGENTS AND SOMATIC TREATMENTS

The antiobsessive potential of numerous agents has been reported, usually as open studies or as case reports. Compounds as diverse as inositol, flutamide, aminoglutethimide, amphetamines, opioid agents, and hallucinogens have been noted to exhibit some antiobsessive properties, mostly in case reports. Of particular note, inositol (Fux, Levine, Aviv, & Belmaker, 1996) and flutamide (for OCD in males) (Peterson, Zhang, Anderson, & Leckman, 1998) have shown some antiobsessive properties in open studies. An extensive table of experimental agents employed in the treatment of OCD is presented by Hewlett (1997) in a recent book. Routine use of these agents cannot be recommended without substantiation from controlled trials.

REPETITIVE TRANSCRANIAL MAGNETIC STIMULATION

Recently there has been considerable excitement over the possible therapeutic effects of Repetitive Transcranial Magnetic Stimulation in many psychiatric disorders including depression (the most studied) and a few studies in patients with OCD (George, Wassermann, & Post, 1996; Greenberg et al., 1997). Further studies may demonstrate the possible efficacy and safety of this treatment modality. Currently it is experimental.

ELECTRO-CONVULSIVE THERAPY (ECT)

ECT is not recommended for treatment of the core symptoms of OCD based on scientific evidence. Comorbid conditions like MDD or OCD with acute suicidality may, however, compel its use. It has also been employed occasionally when all other treatments have failed and the patient's suffering is immense (Janicak, Davis, Preskorn, & Ayd, 1997).

OC SPECTRUM DISORDERS

There is also a growing body of literature suggesting that many psychiatric disorders are part of a spectrum of OCD-related disorders, the so-called Obsessive Compulsive Spectrum Disorders (Hollander & Wong, 1995b). Evidence in support of this hypothesis comes predominantly from phenomenological similarities and the response of some of these disorders to the SSRIs. Though this is a superficially attractive hypothesis, it has been criticized to be over-inclusive and the clinical meaningfulness of such a grouping is not absolutely clear. Studies of families and first-degree relatives must be performed to prove a true relationship. However, pathological gambling, pathological jealousy (D. Stein, Hollander, & Josephson, 1994), certain paraphilias, compulsive skin picking (Simeon et al., 1997), and compulsive buying (Black, Monahan, & Gabel, 1997) are several disorders manifesting phenomenological similarities that have prompted therapeutic trials with SSRIs. Future studies may establish relationships among these various spectrum disorders.

TRICHOTILLOMANIA

The *DSM-IV* defines trichotillomania (TTM) as an impulse control disorder in which there is recurrent pulling of one's hair resulting in noticeable hair loss, clinically significant distress or impairment in social, occupational, or other important areas of functioning (APA, 1994).

Christensen estimated the prevalence of *DSM-IV* TTM to be 0.6 percent (Christenson, Pyle, & Mitchell, 1991). Like OCD, TTM is often a childhood onset disorder. The mean age of onset was found to be 13 years in one study (Christenson, Mackenzie, & Mitchell, 1991) and 10.6 in another (D. Stein, Simeon, Cohen, & Hollander, 1995). As with OCD, patients are considerably reluctant to seek treatment, and the latency between onset and initiation of treatment may be as much as two decades (Christenson & Crow, 1996).

There appears to be a relationship between TTM and OCD. A number of TTM sufferers (13%) repeatedly have experienced comorbid OCD (Christenson & Crow, 1996). There has also been a higher frequency of OCD among first-degree relatives of hair-pullers (Lenane et al., 1992). Also similar to OCD, a large number of individuals experience comorbid depression (52%), anxiety, substance abuse, or social phobias. Additionally, both disorders reportedly have followed clinically after exposure to infectious agents (D. Stein, Wessels, et al., 1997; Swedo et al., 1998), and both have been found to have a high frequency of personality disorders (Christenson, Chernoff-Clementz, & Clementz, 1992; Joffe, Swinson, & Regan, 1988). Similar to OCD with tics, adjuvant pimozide was found to effectively augment SSRIs in 6 of 7 patients.

However, the nature of the association is not entirely clear. The absence of obsessional thinking in TTM, occasional lack of ego dystonicity, positive response to lithium, and the less than robust response to SSRIs argue against a close association. Only one of the two controlled studies of SSRIs in TTM found a significant effect compared to placebo (Table 16.10).

Body Dysmorphic Disorder

Persons with Body Dysmorphic Disorder (BDD) are often excessively preoccupied with aspects of their bodily appearance to the extent that their lives are impaired. Such persons may even subject themselves to numerous cosmetic surgeries to fix imagined imperfections, which may often lead to exacerbation of the condition (Andreasen & Bardach, 1977).

BDD is considered by some to be a variant of OCD due to a number of similarities (McKay, Neziroglu, & Yaryura-Tobias, 1997). Estimated prevalence rates for BDD are 0.1 percent to 1 percent, with comorbid OCD occurring in 7 percent to 37 percent of cases (Hollander & Wong, 1995a; Wilhelm, Otto, Zucker, & Pollack, 1997). BDD is equally common in men and women. As with OCD, there is an adolescent age of onset, frequent comorbid depression, and delusional or nondelusional subtypes. Additionally, patients often experience significant social and occupational impairment and approximately 30 percent of patients are housebound (Phillips, 1991; Phillips, McElroy, Keck, Pope, & Hudson, 1993; Simeon, Hollander, Stein, Cohen, & Aronowitz, 1995).

For diagnostic purposes, a modified version of the Yale-Brown Obsessive Compulsive Scale has been developed (Phillips et al., 1997). Clinicians should also be aware that BDD has often been misdiagnosed as OCD because of

Table 16.10
Trichotillomania

Report	n	Description	Weeks	Result
Swedo et al. (1989)	13	Desipramine vs. CMI, double blind crossover	10 of ea.	CMI effective, no desipramine effect
Christenson (1991)	10	Lithium carbonate	8–56	8 of 10 responded
Christenson (1991)	15	Fluoxetine 80mg/d vs. placebo, double blind crossover	6 of ea.	No effect
Stein (1992)	7	SRIs with adjuvant pimozide 1–2mg/d	NA	6 of 7 responded
Koran (1992)	13	Fluoxetine 80mg/d, open	8–12	9 of 13 responded
Jacobsen (1995)	5	1–6mg/d risperidone	4	Effective for tricho, improvement in OCD (3 of 3)
Streichenwein (1995)	16	fluoxetine 80mg/d vs. placebo, double blind crossover	12 of ea.	No effect
D. Stein, Bower, et al. (1997)	5	SSRIs with adjuvant risperidone 1–2 mg/d	4	3 of 5 responded; discontinuation with relapse
Stein (1997)	13	Citalopram 60mg/d max, open	12	5 of 13 responded
Stanley (1997)	13	Fluvoxamine 300mg/d max, open	12	No significant effect
Ninan (1998)	12	Venlafaxine 375mg/d max, open	12	8 of 12 responded, effective

concomitant OCD symptoms (Hollander & Phillips, 1993). While a number of pharmacological approaches have been undertaken, SSRIs have been the most widely effective, usually in doses equivalent to those used with OCD (Table 16.11).

SPECIAL POPULATIONS

CHILDREN AND ADOLESCENTS

OCD is predominantly a childhood and adolescent onset disorder and that psychiatric comorbidity commonly arises among children and adolescents with OCD. Comorbid depression, anxiety disorders, disruptive behavior disorders, and substance abuse (in adolescents) as well as tic-related disorders are common. Accordingly, early recognition and treatment is important and clinicians should inquire specifically about the presence of obsessions and compulsions. Acute separation anxiety, depression, aggressive behavior, and oppositional defiant behavior may be indicative of underlying OCD symptomatology.

Medication is often indicated. The patient and parents should be made aware of side effects and off-label use of some agents should be documented. School interventions are usually necessary and modified ERP may be particularly useful as well (see *How I Ran OCD Off My Land*, March & Mulle, 1998). Counseling families to avoid a punitive approach and conversely to

Table 16.11
Body Dysmorphic Disorder

Report	n	Description	Weeks	Result
Hollander (1989)	5	CMI	NA	5 of 5 responded
Hollander & Phillips (1993)	50	Retrospective study of SRIs and TCAs	NA	SRIs effective compared to baseline scores, 'slight improvement' with TCAs
Hollander (1994)	19	Imipramine vs. fluvoxamine	NA	Fluvoxamine effective, no effect with imipramine
Phillips (1994)	100	Retrospective comparison of SRIs, TCAs, MAOIs	NA	43 of 76 with SRIs, 4 of 41 with TCAs, 5 of 17 with MAOIs
Phillips (1995)	4	SRIs	NA	4 of 4 improved
Perugi (1996)	12	Fluvoxamine 300mg/d max, open	10	10 of 12 improved
Phillips (1996)	13	SRI with buspirone	8	6 of 13 improved
Phillips (1998)	30	Fluvoxamine, open	16	19 of 30 responded

avoid becoming over-involved is recommended (Rapoport, Leonard, Swedo, & Lenane, 1993).

Interestingly, viral or Group A Beta-Hemolytic Streptococcal infections have been associated with development of a number of neuropsychiatric symptoms in children, including OCD. This has been named Pediatric Auto-Immune Neuropsychiatric Disorders Associated with Streptococcal infection or PANDAS. While not conclusively proven, auto-antibodies resulting from the infection are thought to crossreact with elements of the basal ganglia causing neuropsychiatric symptoms. A trait marker for susceptibility to rheumatic fever labeled D8/17 is also expressed more often among childhood onset OCD or Tourette's (Murphy et al., 1997; Swedo et al., 1997). Penicillin prophylaxis, plasmapheresis, and SSRIs have been used in the management of some of these cases with some success (Swedo et al., 1998). The notion of reversible versus irreversible alterations in the basal ganglia possibly accounting for the more intractable cases of adult OCD is intriguing and merits study (A. Allen, 1997).

PREGNANCY AND PUERPERIUM

Exacerbation of OCD has been noted to occur premenstrually, during pregnancy, and during the postpartum period (Williams & Koran, 1997). In pregnancy, ERP is the treatment of choice, especially during the first trimester, unless the risk/benefit ratio compels use of medication. If pharmacological treatment is indicated, the increasing data on relatively safe use of certain SSRIs make them the agents of choice (Goldstein, 1995; Goldstein, Corbin, & Sundell, 1997). CMI is not recommended as it has been associated with seizures in the neonate (Schimmell, Katz, Shaag, Pastuszak, & Koren, 1991). As with most drug-treatments during pregnancy, such decisions to treat need to be a collaborative, well-informed, and well-documented process with follow-up on the child.

Developmentally Disabled

OCD can be a difficult diagnosis to make in this population due to similarities between ritualistic and stereotypic behaviors. However, disabling obsessive compulsive features have been noted in various developmental and chromosomal disorders (Dykens, Leckman, & Cassidy, 1996; Hellings & Warnock, 1994; Vitiello, Spreat, & Behar, 1989).

Several studies have found reduction of obsessive-compulsive symptoms with administration of CMI (McDougle et al., 1992). Furthermore, Gordon administered CMI and desipramine in crossover fashion and reported positive results only with CMI (Gordon, State, Nelson, Hamburger, & Rapoport, 1993). This implicates serotonin, and not norepinephrine, in the perseverative behaviors of autism. Generally SSRIs may be used in these cases (Cook, Rowlett, Jaselskis, & Leventhal, 1992; Cook, Terry, Heller, & Leventhal, 1990; Koshes, 1997; McDougle et al., 1992, 1996; Wiener & Lamberti, 1993). A controlled study of risperidone (as an adjuvant and monotherapy) has demonstrated significant effectiveness in the treatment of behavioral disturbances associated with mental retardation (Vanden Borre et al., 1993). Risperidone has been effective in the treatment of autism as well (McDougle, Holmes, et al., 1998).

Elderly and Neurologically Impaired

Rarely does the first onset of OCD occur after the age of 45. However, due to the chronicity of the disorder, OCD is observed in older populations—apparently with a similar 1 percent frequency as in younger populations (Saz et al., 1995). Recently, an increasing number of cases of OCD among older women was noted in an examination of the Epidemiological Catchment Area survey (Nestadt et al., 1998). In one study, the symptomatology among this group generally did not differ from younger manifestations, however, a higher frequency of "fear of having sinned" obsessions was noted (Kohn, Westlake, Rasmussen, Marsland, & Norman, 1997).

Often latter onsets are the result of underlying organic etiologies, the possibility of which should be investigated (Swoboda & Jenike, 1995). Addressing the underlying disorder, sensitivity to dosing, and drug interactions in this population are important. Clinicians are advised to begin with reduced doses of SSRIs (Jenike, 1991; Kunik, Pollock, Perel, & Altieri, 1994; Newhouse, 1996).

OCD AND MANAGED CARE

Clinicians often must design a treatment paradigm for a patient within the context of a managed care plan. In such cases, the clinician *must* be the patient's advocate and aim to provide the highest standard of care based on current knowledge of treatment. OCD being a chronic illness, emphasis should be given to the long-term management of the disorder and, importantly, to resource allocation. Often a specialist consultation initially, or more importantly in difficult cases, may save the patient suffering and resources (e.g., specialist psychopharmacological consultation).

Often the clinician may not have the expertise to provide behavioral therapy (ERP) or this may not be an integral part of the services covered by an insurance plan. In such cases, the clinician should not assume limitation but strongly recommend (explaining the effectiveness of such treatments) that the insurance company cover this (off of the plan) treatment. Patients and families should be educated and encouraged to be their own advocates directly as well as by involvement in advocacy groups. The Obsessive Compulsive Foundation has invaluable resources that should be explored when patients have difficulties accessing effective treatments. (See the Web site address at the end of the chapter.)

SUMMARY

Clearly, the approach to evaluating and treating patients with OCD and related disorders has changed significantly over the past several decades. The availability of effective drug and behavioral therapies for some patients is heartening though more research is necessary since most have some persistent symptoms. All patients with OCD require treatment with ERP and some may require a combination of pharmacotherapy and ERP for maximal and lasting response. While both treatments certainly can be started at the same time, it is unclear whether ERP or pharmacotherapy should be employed first. However, if ERP is begun first and the OCD does not quickly remit, drug treatment should soon follow. A patient not responding to ERP may become discouraged, drop out, and hence, never receive SSRIs. A treatment plan which addresses personal, familial, social, and occupational functioning, is necessary for successful treatment. Additional clinical, biological, genetic, and pharmacological studies are needed to meet the challenge of providing effective relief to people suffering from this disorder.

The following general guidelines should be kept in mind while working with patients and families dealing with OCD:

- Confirm the diagnosis (careful history of symptoms, onset, course, relationship to infections, prior treatment history).
- Carefully look for comorbid conditions (especially substance abuse) and include on treatment plan.
- Evaluate neuromedical status and possible contributing factors.
- Assess the effect of the disorder on development, self-esteem, social and occupational areas, and especially family dynamics and address these.
- Family members may have OCD or related disorders.
- Encourage patient and family empowerment through education and involvement in support groups and OCF.
- Be alert to the dynamics of medication management with patients with OCD. A collaborative, team approach is important and will improve patient compliance with the treatment strategy.
- Work closely with competent professionals with expertise in exposure and response prevention, family therapy, and marital therapy if referring out for therapy.

- Do not hesitate to consult experts in the field in a difficult clinical situation.
- Follow responses to treatment and side effects.

RESOURCES

The following are selected OCD related Web sites that may be useful for patients and their families as well as clinicians. We do not endorse the services or recommendations that these sites may provide, but offer them as a resource for information:

http://www.ocfoundation.org/indright.htm

http://pages.prodigy.com/alwillen/ocf.html

http://members.aol.com/afocd/afocd.htm

http://www.ocdresource.com

http://www.mentalhealth.com/dis/p20-an05.html

http://www.ocdhelp.org

http://www.health-center.com/english/brain/ocd

http://www.fairlite.com/ocd

http://www.ocdhelp.org/faq.html

REFERENCES

Ackerman, D.L., Greenland, S., Bystritsky, A., Morgenstern, H., & Katz, R.J. (1994). Predictors of treatment response in obsessive-compulsive disorder: multivariate analyses from a multicenter trial of clomipramine. *Journal of Clinical Psychopharmacology, 14*, 247–254.

Alarcon, R.D., Libb, J.W., & Boll, T.J. (1994). Neuropsychological testing in obsessive-compulsive disorder: a clinical review. *Journal of Neuropsychiatry and Clinical Neuroscience, 6*, 217–228.

Allen, A.J. (1997). Group A streptococcal infections and childhood neuropsychiatric disorders: relationships and therapeutic implications. *CNS Drugs, 8*, 267–275.

Allen, L., & Tejera, C. (1994). Treatment of clozapine-induced obsessive-compulsive symptoms with sertraline [letter]. *American Journal of Psychiatry, 151*, 1096–1097.

al-Mulhim, A., & Atwal, S. (1998). Provocation of obsessive-compulsive behaviour and tremor by olanzapine [letter] [In Process Citation]. *Canadian Journal of Psychiatry, 43*, 645.

American Psychiatric Association. (1994). *Diagnostic and statistical manual of mental disorders* (4th ed.). Washington, DC: Author.

Ananth, J., Burgoyne, K., Smith, M., & Swartz, R. (1995). Venlafaxine for treatment of obsessive-compulsive disorder [letter]. *American Journal of Psychiatry, 152*, 1832.

Ananth, J., Pecknold, J.C., van den Steen, N., & Engelsmann, F. (1981). Double-blind comparative study of clomipramine and amitriptyline in obsessive neurosis. *Progress in Neuropsychopharmacology, 5*, 257–262.

Andreasen, N.C., & Bardach, J. (1977). Dysmorphophobia: Symptom or disease? *American Journal of Psychiatry, 134*, 673–676.

Ballerini, A., & Stangehellini, G. (1989). Phenomenological questions about obsession and delusion. *Psychopathology, 22,* 315–319.

Baxter, L.R., Jr. (1985). Two cases of obsessive-compulsive disorder with depression responsive to trazodone. *Journal of Nervous and Mental Disorders, 173,* 432–433.

Black, D.W., Goldstein, R.B., Noyes, R.J., & Blum, N. (1995). Psychiatric disorders in relatives of probands with obsessive-compulsive disorder and co-morbid major depression or generalized anxiety. *Psychiatric Genetics, 5,* 37–41.

Black, D.W., Monahan, P., & Gabel, J. (1997). Fluvoxamine in the treatment of compulsive buying. *Journal of Clinical Psychiatry, 58,* 159–163.

Bland, R.C., Stebelsky, G., Orn, H., & Newman, S.C. (1988). Psychiatric disorders and unemployment in Edmonton. *Acta Psychiatrica Scandinavia, 338*(Suppl.), 72–80.

Bruun, R.D., Shapiro, A.K., Shapiro, E., Sweet, R., Wayne, H., & Solomon, G.E. (1976). A follow-up of 78 patients with Gilles de la Tourette's syndrome. *American Journal of Psychiatry, 133,* 944–947.

Capstick, N. (1971). Chlorimipramine in obsessional states (a pilot study). *Psychosomatics, 12,* 332–335.

Cassano, G.B., Pini, S., Saettoni, M., Rucci, R., & Dell'Osso, L. (1998). Occurrence and clinical correlates of psychiatric comorbidity in patients with psychotic disorders. *Journal of Clinical Psychiatry, 59,* 60–68.

Ceccherini-Nelli, A., & Guazzelli, M. (1994). Treatment of refractory OCD with the dopamine agonist bromocriptine [letter]. *Journal of Clinical Psychiatry, 55,* 415–416.

Chouinard, G., Goodman, W., Greist, J., Jenike, M., Rasmussen, S., White, K., Hackett, E., Gaffney, M., & Bick, P.A. (1990). Results of a double-blind placebo controlled trial of a new serotonin uptake inhibitor, sertraline, in the treatment of obsessive-compulsive disorder. *Psychopharmacology Bulletin, 26,* 279–284.

Christenson, G.A., Chernoff-Clementz, E., & Clementz, B.A. (1992). Personality and clinical characteristics in patients with trichotillomania. *Journal of Clinical Psychiatry, 53,* 407–413.

Christenson, G.A., & Crow, S.J. (1996). The characterization and treatment of trichotillomania. *Journal of Clinical Psychiatry, 57*(Suppl. 8), 42–49.

Christenson, G.A., Mackenzie, T.B., & Mitchell, J.E. (1991). Characteristics of 60 adult chronic hair pullers [see comments]. *American Journal of Psychiatry, 148,* 365–370.

Christenson, G.A., Mackenzie, T.B., Mitchell, J.E., & Callies, A.L. (1991). A placebo-controlled, double-blind crossover study of fluoxetine in trichotillomania. *American Journal of Psychiatry, 148,* 1566–1571.

Christenson, G.A., Popkin, M.K., Mackenzie, T.B., & Realmuto, G.M. (1991). Lithium treatment of chronic hair pulling. *Journal of Clinical Psychiatry, 52,* 116–120.

Christenson, G.A., Pyle, R.L., & Mitchell, J.E. (1991). Estimated lifetime prevalence of trichotillomania in college students [see comments]. *Journal of Clinical Psychiatry, 52,* 415–417.

Clomipramine Collaborative Study Group. (1991). Clomipramine in the treatment of patients with obsessive-compulsive disorder [see comments]. *Archives of General Psychiatry, 48,* 730–738.

Coffey, B.J., Miguel, E.C., Biederman, J., Baer, L., Rauch, S.L., O'Sullivan, R.L., Savage, C.R., Phillips, K., Borgman, A., Green-Leibovitz, M.I., Moore, E., Park, K.S., & Jenike, M.A. (1998). Tourette's disorder with and without obsessive-compulsive disorder in adults: Are they different? *Journal of Nervous and Mental Disorders, 186,* 201–206.

Como, P.G., & Kurlan, R. (1991). An open-label trial of fluoxetine for obsessive-compulsive disorder in Gilles de la Tourette's syndrome. *Neurology, 41,* 872–874.

Cook, E.H., Jr., Rowlett, R., Jaselskis, C., & Leventhal, B.L. (1992). Fluoxetine treatment of children and adults with autistic disorder and mental retardation. *Journal of the American Academy of Child and Adolescent Psychiatry, 31,* 739–745.

Cook, E.H., Jr., Terry, E.J., Heller, W., & Leventhal, B.L. (1990). Fluoxetine treatment of borderline mentally retarded adults with obsessive-compulsive disorder [letter]. *Journal of Clinical Psychopharmacology, 10,* 228–229.

Cottraux, J., Mollard, E., Bouvard, M., Marks, I., Sluys, M., Nury, A.M., Douge, R., & Cialdella, P. (1990). A controlled study of fluvoxamine and exposure in obsessive-compulsive disorder. *International Clinical Psychopharmacology, 5,* 17–30.

de Groot, C.M., Yeates, K.O., Baker, G.B., & Bornstein, R.A. (1997). Impaired neuropsychological functioning in Tourette's syndrome subjects with co-occurring obsessive-compulsive and attention deficit symptoms. *Journal of Neuropsychiatry and Clinical Neuroscience, 9,* 267–272.

Delgado, P.L., Goodman, W.K., Price, L.H., Heninger, G.R., & Charney, D.S. (1990). Fluvoxamine/pimozide treatment of concurrent Tourette's and obsessive-compulsive disorder. *British Journal of Psychiatry, 157,* 762–765.

DeVeaugh-Geiss, J., Moroz, G., Biederman, J., Cantwell, D., Fontaine, R., Greist, J.H., Reichler, R., Katz, R., & Landau, P. (1992). Clomipramine hydrochloride in childhood and adolescent obsessive-compulsive disorder—a multicenter trial. *Journal of the American Academy of Child and Adolescent Psychiatry, 31,* 45–49.

Disorder, E.C.P.F.O.-C. (1997). Treatment of obsessive-compulsive disorder. *Journal of Clinical Psychiatry, 58*(Suppl. 4), 2–72.

Dykens, E.M., Leckman, J.F., & Cassidy, S.B. (1996). Obsessions and compulsions in Prader-Willi syndrome. *Journal of Child Psychology and Psychiatry, 37,* 995–1002.

Eales, M.J., & Layeni, A.O. (1994). Exacerbation of obsessive-compulsive symptoms associated with clozapine [see comments]. *British Journal of Psychiatry, 164,* 687–688.

Eapen, V., Trimble, M.R., & Robertson, M.M. (1996). The use of fluoxetine in Gilles de la Tourette syndrome and obsessive compulsive behaviours: Preliminary clinical experience. *Progress in Neuropsychopharmacology and Biological Psychiatry, 20,* 737–743.

Eisen, J.L., Beer, D.A., Pato, M.T., Venditto, T.A., & Rasmussen, S.A. (1997). Obsessive-compulsive disorder in patients with schizophrenia or schizoaffective disorder [see comments]. *American Journal of Psychiatry, 154,* 271–273.

Enoch, M.A., Kaye, W.H., Rotondo, A., Greenberg, B.D., Murphy, D.L., & Goldman, D. (1998). 5-HT2A promoter polymorphism-1438G/A, anorexia nervosa, and obsessive-compulsive disorder [letter]. *Lancet, 351,* 1785–1786.

Erenberg, G., Cruse, R.P., & Rothner, A.D. (1987). The natural history of Tourette syndrome: A follow-up study. *Annuals of Neurology, 22,* 383–385.

Fernandez, E., & Lopez-Ibor, J. (1967). La monoclorimipramina en enfermos psiquiatricos resistentes a otros tratamientos. *Actas Luso Esp Neurol Psiquiatr Cienc, 26,* 119–147.

Flament, M.F., Rapoport, J.L., & Kilts, C. (1985). A controlled trial of clomipramine in childhood obsessive compulsive disorder. *Psychopharmacology Bulletin, 21,* 150–152.

Flament, M.F., Whitaker, A., Rapoport, J.L., Davies, M., Berg, C.Z., Kalikow, K., Sceery, W., & Shaffer, D. (1988). Obsessive compulsive disorder in adolescence: An epidemiological study. *Journal of the American Academy of Child and Adolescent Psychiatry, 27,* 764–771.

Freeman, C.P., Trimble, M.R., Deakin, J.F., Stokes, T.M., & Ashford, J.J. (1994). Fluvoxamine versus clomipramine in the treatment of obsessive compulsive disorder: a multicenter, randomized, double-blind, parallel group comparison. *Journal of Clinical Psychiatry, 55,* 301–305.

Fux, M., Levine, J., Aviv, A., & Belmaker, R.H. (1996). Inositol treatment of obsessive-compulsive disorder. *American Journal of Psychiatry, 153,* 1219–1221.

George, M.S., Wassermann, E.M., & Post, R.M. (1996). Transcranial magnetic stimulation: A neuropsychiatric tool for the 21st century. *Journal of Neuropsychiatry and Clinical Neuroscience, 8,* 373–382.

Giakas, W.J. (1995). Risperidone treatment for a Tourette's disorder patient with co-morbid obsessive-compulsive disorder [letter]. *American Journal of Psychiatry, 152,* 1097–1098.

Golden, R.N., Morris, J.E., & Sack, D.A. (1988). Combined lithium-tricyclic treatment of obsessive-compulsive disorder. *Biological Psychiatry, 23,* 181–185.

Goldstein, D.J. (1995). Effects of third trimester fluoxetine exposure on the newborn. *Journal of Clinical Psychopharmacology, 15,* 417–420.

Goldstein, D.J., Corbin, L.A., & Sundell, K.L. (1997). Effects of first-trimester fluoxetine exposure on the newborn. *Obstetrics and Gynecology, 89,* 713–718.

Goodman, W.K., Kozak, M.J., Liebowitz, M., & White, K.L. (1996). Treatment of obsessive-compulsive disorder with fluvoxamine: a multicentre, double-blind, placebo-controlled trial. *International Clinical Psychopharmacology, 11,* 21–29.

Goodman, W.K., Price, L.H., Rasmussen, S.A., Delgado, P., Heninger, G.R., & Charney, D.S. (1989). Efficacy of fluvoxamine in obsessive-compulsive disorder: A double-blind comparison with placebo. *Archives of General Psychiatry, 46,* 36–44.

Goodman, W.K., Price, L.H., Rasmussen, S.A., Mazure, C., Delgado, P., Heninger, G.R., & Charney, D.S. (1989). The Yale-Brown Obsessive Compulsive Scale. II. Validity. *Archives of General Psychiatry, 46,* 1012–1016.

Goodman, W.K., Price, L.H., Rasmussen, S.A., Mazure, C., Fleischmann, R.L., Hill, C.L., Heninger, G.R., & Charney, D.S. (1989). The Yale-Brown Obsessive Compulsive Scale. I. Development, use, and reliability. *Archives of General Psychiatry, 46,* 1006–1011.

Gordon, C.T., State, R.C., Nelson, J.E., Hamburger, S.D., & Rapoport, J.L. (1993). A double-blind comparison of clomipramine, desipramine, and placebo in the treatment of autistic disorder. *Archives of General Psychiatry, 50,* 441–447.

Grady, T.A., Pigott, T.A., L'Heureux, F., Hill, J.L., Bernstein, S.E., & Murphy, D.L. (1993). Double-blind study of adjuvant buspirone for fluoxetine-treated patients with obsessive-compulsive disorder. *American Journal of Psychiatry, 150,* 819–821.

Green, R.C., & Pitman, R.K. (1990). *Obsessive compulsive disorders: Theory and management.* St. Louis: Mosby-Year Book.

Greenberg, B.D., George, M.S., Martin, J.D., Benjamin, J., Schlaepfer, T.E., Altemus, M., Wassermann, E.M., Post, R.M., & Murphy, D.L. (1997). Effect of prefrontal repetitive transcranial magnetic stimulation in obsessive-compulsive disorder: A preliminary study. *American Journal of Psychiatry, 154,* 867–869.

Greist, J.H., Chouinard, G., DuBoff, E., Halaris, A., Kim, S.W., Koran, L., Liebowitz, M., Lydiard, R.B., Rasmussen, S., White, K., & Sikes, C. (1995). Double-blind parallel comparison of three dosages of sertraline and placebo in outpatients with obsessive-compulsive disorder. *Archives of General Psychiatry, 52,* 289–295.

Greist, J.H., Jefferson, J.W., Kobak, K.A., Katzelnick, D.J., & Serlin, R.C. (1995). Efficacy and tolerability of serotonin transport inhibitors in obsessive-compulsive disorder. A meta-analysis [see comments]. *Archives of General Psychiatry, 52,* 53–60.

Greist, J.H., Jefferson, J.W., Rosenfeld, R., Gutzmann, L.D., March, J.S., & Barklage, N.E. (1990). Clomipramine and obsessive compulsive disorder: A placebo-controlled double-blind study of 32 patients [see comments]. *Journal of Clinical Psychiatry, 51,* 292–297.

Greist, J.H., Jenike, M.A., Robinson, D., & Rasmussen, S.A. (1995). Efficacy of fluvoxamine in obsessive compulsive disorder: Results of a multicentre, double blind, placebo controlled trial. *European Journal of Clinical Research, 7,* 195–204.

Hauser, R.A., & Zesiewicz, T.A. (1995). Sertraline-induced exacerbation of tics in Tourette's syndrome. *Mov Disorders, 10,* 682–684.

Hellings, J.A., & Warnock, J.K. (1994). Self-injurious behavior and serotonin in Prader-Willi syndrome. *Psychopharmacology Bulletin, 30,* 245–250.

Hermesh, H., Aizenberg, D., & Munitz, H. (1990). Trazodone treatment in clomipramine-resistant obsessive-compulsive disorder. *Clinical Neuropharmacology, 13,* 322–328.

Hewlett, W.A. (1997). *Novel pharmacological treatments of OCD.* New York: Marcel Dekker.

Hewlett, W.A., Vinogradov, S., & Agras, W.S. (1990). Clonazepam treatment of obsessions and compulsions. *Journal of Clinical Psychiatry, 51,* 158–161.

Hewlett, W.A., Vinogradov, S., & Agras, W.S. (1992). Clomipramine, clonazepam, and clonidine treatment of obsessive-compulsive disorder. *Journal of Clinical Psychopharmacology, 12,* 420–430.

Hollander, E., Cohen, L., Simeon, D., Rosen, J., DeCaria, C., & Stein, D.J. (1994). Fluvoxamine treatment of body dysmorphic disorder. *Journal of Clinical Psychopharmacology, 14,* 75–77.

Hollander, E., Liebowitz, M.R., Winchel, R., Klumker, A., & Klein, D.F. (1989). Treatment of body-dysmorphic disorder with serotonin reuptake blockers. *American Journal of Psychiatry, 146,* 768–770.

Hollander, E., & Phillips, K.A. (1993). *Body image and experience disorders.* Washington, DC: American Psychiatric Press.

Hollander, E., Stein, D.J., Kwon, J.H., Rowland, C., Wong, C.M., Broatch, J., & Himelein, C. (1998). Psychosocial function and economic costs of obsessive-compulsive disorder. *CNS Spectrums, 3,* 48–58.

Hollander, E., & Wong, C.M. (1995a). Body dysmorphic disorder, pathological gambling, and sexual compulsions. *Journal of Clinical Psychiatry, 56*(Suppl. 4), 7–13.

Hollander, E., & Wong, C.M. (1995b). Obsessive-compulsive spectrum disorders. *Journal of Clinical Psychiatry, 56*(Suppl. 4), 3–6, 53–55.

Insel, T.R., & Akiskal, H.S. (1986). Obsessive-compulsive disorder with psychotic features: A phenomenologic analysis. *American Journal of Psychiatry, 143,* 1527–1533.

Insel, T.R., Alterman, I., & Murphy, D.L. (1982). Antiobsessional and antidepressant effects of clomipramine in the treatment of obsessive-compulsive disorder. *Psychopharmacology Bulletin, 18,* 115–117.

Jacobsen, F.M. (1995). Risperidone in the treatment of affective illness and obsessive-compulsive disorder. *Journal of Clinical Psychiatry, 56,* 423–429.

Janicak, P.G., Davis, J.M., Preskorn, S.H., & Ayd, Jr., F.J. (1997). *Principles and practice of psychopharmacotherapy.* Baltimore: Williams & Wilkins.

Jenike, M.A. (1991). Geriatric obsessive-compulsive disorder. *Journal of Geriatric Psychiatry and Neurology, 4,* 34–39.

Jenike, M.A. (1993). Obsessive-compulsive disorder: Efficacy of specific treatments as assessed by controlled trials. *Psychopharmacology Bulletin, 29,* 487–499.

Jenike, M.A. (1998). Neurosurgical treatment of obsessive compulsive disorder. *British Journal of Psychiatry, 173*(Suppl. 35), 79–90.

Jenike, M.A., Baer, L., & Buttolph, L. (1991). Buspirone augmentation of fluoxetine in patients with obsessive-compulsive disorder. *Journal of Clinical Psychiatry, 52,* 13–14.

Jenike, M.A., Baer, L., & Minichiello, W.E. (1990). *Obsessive compulsive disorders: Theory and management.* St. Louis: Mosby-Year Book.

Jenike, M.A., Baer, L., Minichiello, W.E., Rauch, S.L., & Buttolph, M.L. (1997). Placebo-controlled trial of fluoxetine and phenelzine for obsessive-compulsive disorder. *American Journal of Psychiatry, 154,* 1261–1264.

Jenike, M.A., Baer, L., Minichiello, W.E., Schwartz, C.E., & Carey, R.J., Jr. (1986). Coexistent obsessive-compulsive disorder and schizotypal personality disorder: A poor prognostic indicator [letter]. *Archives of General Psychiatry, 43,* 296.

Jenike, M.A., Baer, L., Summergrad, P., Minichiello, W.E., Holland, A., & Seymour, R. (1990). Sertraline in obsessive-compulsive disorder: A double-blind comparison with placebo. *American Journal of Psychiatry, 147,* 923–928.

Jenike, M.A., Baer, L., Summergrad, P., Weilburg, J.B., Holland, A., & Seymour, R. (1989). Obsessive-compulsive disorder: A double-blind, placebo-controlled trial of clomipramine in 27 patients. *American Journal of Psychiatry, 146,* 1328–1330.

Jenike, M.A., Hyman, S., Baer, L., Holland, A., Minichiello, W.E., Buttolph, L., Summergrad, P., Seymour, R., & Ricciardi, J. (1990). A controlled trial of fluvoxamine in obsessive-compulsive disorder: Implications for a serotonergic theory [see comments]. *American Journal of Psychiatry, 147,* 1209–1215.

Joffe, R.T., Swinson, R.P., & Regan, J.J. (1988). Personality features of obsessive-compulsive disorder. *American Journal of Psychiatry, 145,* 1127–1129.

Kaplan, H.I., & Sadock, B.J. (1991). *Synopsis of psychiatry: Behavioral sciences, clinical psychiatry* (6th ed.). Baltimore: Williams & Wilkins.

Karabanow, D. (1977). Double blind controlled study in phobias and obsessions. *Journal of International Medical Research, 5*(Suppl.), 42–48.

Karayiorgou, M., Altemus, M., Galke, B.L., Goldman, D., Murphy, D.L., Ott, J., & Gogos, J.A. (1997). Genotype determining low catechol-O-methyltransferase activity as a risk factor for obsessive-compulsive disorder. *Proceedings of the National Academy of Science, 94,* 4572–4575.

Karno, M., Golding, J.M., Sorenson, S.B., & Burnam, M.A. (1988). The epidemiology of obsessive-compulsive disorder in five US communities. *Archives of General Psychiatry, 45,* 1094–1099.

Kim, S.W. (1987). Trazodone in the treatment of obsessive-compulsive disorder: A case report [letter]. *Journal of Clinical Psychopharmacology, 7,* 278–279.

Kindler, S., Fux, M., Insel, T., & Zohar, J. (1993). *Comparison of clomipramine and desipramine in obsessive-compulsive disorder and panic disorder.* Paper presented at the first International Obsessive Compulsive Disorder Conference, Capri, Italy.

Kohn, R., Westlake, R.J., Rasmussen, S.A., Marsland, R.T., & Norman, W.H. (1997). Clinical features of obsessive-compulsive disorder in elderly patients. *American Journal of Geriatric Psychiatry, 5,* 211–215.

Kopala, L., & Honer, W.G. (1994). Risperidone, serotonergic mechanisms, and obsessive-compulsive symptoms in schizophrenia [letter]. *American Journal of Psychiatry, 151,* 1714–1715.

Koponen, H., Lepola, U., Leinonen, E., Jokinen, R., Penttinen, J., & Turtonen, J. (1997). Citalopram in the treatment of obsessive-compulsive disorder: An open pilot study. *Acta Psychiatrica Scandinavia, 96,* 343–346.

Koran, L.M., McElroy, S.L., Davidson, J.R.T., Rasmussen, S.A., Hollander, E., & Jenike, M.A. (1996). Fluvoxamine versus clomipramine for obsessive-compulsive disorder: A double blind comparison. *Journal of Clinical Psychopharmacology, 16,* 121–129.

Koran, L.M., Ringold, A., & Hewlett, W. (1992). Fluoxetine for trichotillomania: An open clinical trial. *Psychopharmacology Bulletin, 28,* 145–149.

Koran, L.M., Sallee, F.R., & Pallanti, S. (1997). Rapid benefit of intravenous pulse loading of clomipramine in obsessive-compulsive disorder. *American Journal of Psychiatry, 154,* 396–401.

Koshes, R.J. (1997). Use of fluoxetine for obsessive-compulsive behavior in adults with autism [letter]. *American Journal of Psychiatry, 154,* 578.

Kunik, M.E., Pollock, B.G., Perel, J.M., & Altieri, L. (1994). Clomipramine in the elderly: Tolerance and plasma levels. *Journal of Geriatric Psychiatry and Neurology, 7,* 139–143.

Kurlan, R., Como, P.G., Deeley, C., McDermott, M., & McDermott, M.P. (1993). A pilot controlled study of fluoxetine for obsessive-compulsive symptoms in children with Tourette's syndrome. *Clinical Neuropharmacology, 16,* 167–172.

Leckman, J.F., Grice, D.E., Barr, L.C., de Vries, A.L., Martin, C., Cohen, D.J., McDougle, C.J., Goodman, W.K., & Rasmussen, S.A. (1994). Tic-related vs. non-tic-related obsessive compulsive disorder. *Anxiety, 1,* 208–215.

Lenane, M.C., Swedo, S.E., Rapoport, J.L., Leonard, H., Sceery, W., & Guroff, J.J. (1992). Rates of obsessive compulsive disorder in first degree relatives of patients with trichotillomania: A research note. *Journal of Child Psychology and Psychiatry, 33,* 925–933.

Leonard, H.L., Lenane, M.C., Swedo, S.E., Rettew, D.C., Gershon, E.S., & Rapoport, J.L. (1992). Tics and Tourette's disorder: A 2- to 7-year follow-up of 54 obsessive-compulsive children. *American Journal of Psychiatry, 149,* 1244–1251.

Leonard, H.L., Lenane, M.C., Swedo, S.E., Rettew, D.C., & Rapoport, J.L. (1991). A double-blind comparison of clomipramine and desipramine treatment of severe onychophagia (nail biting). *Archives of General Psychiatry, 48,* 821–827.

Leonard, H.L., Swedo, S.E., Rapoport, J.L., Koby, E.V., Lenane, M.C., Cheslow, D.L., & Hamburger, S.D. (1989). Treatment of obsessive-compulsive disorder with clomipramine and desipramine in children and adolescents. A double-blind crossover comparison. *Archives of General Psychiatry, 46,* 1088–1092.

Lopez-Ibor, J.J., Jr. (1968). *Intravenous perfusions of monochlorimipramine: Technique and results.* Paper presented at the Proceedings of the VI International Congress of the Collegium Internationale Neruo-Psychopharmacologicum, Tarragona, Spain.

Lopez-Ibor, J.J., Jr., Saiz, J., Cottraux, J., Note, I., Vinas, R., Bourgeois, M., Hernandez, M., & Gomez-Perez, J.C. (1996). Double-blind comparison of fluoxetine versus clomipramine in the treatment of obsessive compulsive disorder. *European Neuropsychopharmacology, 6,* 111–118.

Lydiard, R.B. (1986). Obsessive-compulsive disorder successfully treated with trazodone. *Psychosomatics, 27,* 858–859.

Mallya, G.K., White, K., Waternaux, C., & Quay, S. (1992). Short and long term treatment of obssesive compulsive disorder with fluvoxamine. *Annals of Clinical Psychiatry, 4,* 77–80.

March, J., & Mulle, K. (1998). *OCD children and adolescents: A cognitive-behavioral treatment manual.* New York: Guilford Press.

Markovitz, P.J., Stagno, S.J., & Calabrese, J.R. (1990). Buspirone augmentation of fluoxetine in obsessive-compulsive disorder [see comments]. *American Journal of Psychiatry, 147,* 798–800.

Marks, I.M., Stern, R.S., Mawson, D., Cobb, J., & McDonald, R. (1980). Clomipramine and exposure for obsessive compulsive rituals. *British Journal of Psychiatry, 136,* 1–25.

Mavissakalian, M.R., Jones, B., Olson, S., & Perel, J.M. (1990). Clomipramine in obsessive-compulsive disorder: Clinical response and plasma levels. *Journal of Clinical Psychopharmacology, 10,* 261–268.

Mavissakalian, M.R., Turner, S.M., Michelson, L., & Jacob, R. (1985). Tricyclic antidepressants in obsessive-compulsive disorder: Antiobsessional or antidepressant agents? II. *American Journal of Psychiatry, 142,* 572–576.

Mawson, D., Marks, I.M., & Ramm, L. (1982). Clomipramine and exposure for chronic obsessive-compulsive rituals: III. Two year follow-up and further findings. *British Journal of Psychiatry, 140,* 11–18.

McDougle, C.J., Epperson, C.N., Price, L.H., & Gelernter, J. (1998). Evidence for linkage disequilibrium between serotonin transporter protein gene (SLC6A4) and obsessive compulsive disorder [In Process Citation]. *Molecular Psychiatry, 3,* 270–273.

McDougle, C.J., Goodman, W.K., Leckman, J.F., Holzer, J.C., Barr, L.C., McCance-Katz, E., Heninger, G.R., & Price, L.H. (1993). Limited therapeutic effect of addition of buspirone in fluvoxamine-refractory obsessive-compulsive disorder. *American Journal of Psychiatry, 150,* 647–649.

McDougle, C.J., Goodman, W.K., Leckman, J.F., Lee, N.C., Heninger, G.R., & Price, L.H. (1994). Haloperidol addition in fluvoxamine-refractory obsessive-compulsive disorder. *Archives of General Psychiatry, 51,* 302–308.

McDougle, C.J., Goodman, W.K., Price, L.H., Delgado, P.L., Krystal, J.H., Charney, D.S., & Heninger, G.R. (1990). Neuroleptic addition in fluvoxamine-refractory obsessive-compulsive disorder. *American Journal of Psychiatry, 147,* 652–654.

McDougle, C.J., Holmes, J.P., Carlson, D.C., Pelton, G.H., Cohen, D.J., & Price, L.H. (1998). A double-blind, placebo-controlled study of risperidone in adults with autistic disorder and other pervasive developmental disorders. *Archives of General Psychiatry, 55,* 633–641.

McDougle, C.J., Naylor, S.T., Cohen, D.J., Volkmar, F.R., Heninger, G.R., & Price, L.H. (1996). A double-blind, placebo-controlled study of fluvoxamine in adults with autistic disorder. *Archives of General Psychiatry, 53,* 1001–1008.

McDougle, C.J., Price, L.H., Goodman, W.K., Charney, D.S., & Heninger, G.R. (1991). A controlled trial of lithium augmentation in fluvoxamine-refractory obsessive-compulsive disorder: Lack of efficacy [see comments]. *Journal of Clinical Psychopharmacology, 11,* 175–184.

McDougle, C.J., Price, L.H., Volkmar, F.R., Goodman, W.K., Ward-O'Brien, D., Nielsen, J., Bregman, J., & Cohen, D.J. (1992). Clomipramine in autism: Preliminary evidence of efficacy [see comments]. *Journal of the American Academy of Child and Adolescent Psychiatry, 31,* 746–750.

McKay, D., Neziroglu, F., & Yaryura-Tobias, J.A. (1997). Comparison of clinical characteristics in obsessive-compulsive disorder and body dysmorphic disorder. *Journal of Anxiety Disorders, 11,* 447–454.

Milanfranchi, A., Ravagli, S., Lensi, P., Marazziti, D., & Cassano, G.B. (1997). A double-blind study of fluvoxamine and clomipramine in the treatment of obsessive-compulsive disorder. *International Clinical Psychopharmacology, 12,* 131–136.

Mindus, P., & Jenike, M.A. (1992). Neurosurgical treatment of malignant obsessive compulsive disorder. *Psychiatric Clinics of North America, 15,* 921–938.

Mindus, P., Rauch, S., Nyman, H., Baer, L., Edman, G., & Jenike, M. (1994). Capsulotomy and cingulotomy as treatments for malignant obsessive compulsive disorder: An update. In *Current insights in obsessive compulsive disorder.* New York: Wiley.

Montgomery, S.A. (1980). Clomipramine in obsessional neurosis: A placebo-controlled trial. *Pharmacological Medicine, 1,* 189–195.

Montgomery, S.A., Fineberg, N., Montgomery, D.B., & Bullock, T. (1992). *L-tryptophan in obsessive-compulsive disorder—a placebo controlled study.* Abstract P-127 #2 384–385 of the fifth Congress of the European College of Neuropsychopharmacology, Marbella, Spain.

Montgomery, S.A., McIntyre, A., Osterheider, M., Sarteschi, P., Zitterl, W., Zohar, J., Birkett, M., & Wood, A.J. (1993). A double-blind, placebo-controlled study of fluoxetine in patients with *DSM-III-R* obsessive-compulsive disorder. The Lilly European OCD study group. *European Neuropsychopharmacology, 3*, 143–152.

Montgomery, S.A., Montgomery, D.B., & Fineberg, N. (1990). Early response with clomipramine in obsessive compulsive disorder—a placebo controlled study. *Progress in Neuropsychopharmacology and Biological Psychiatry, 14*, 719–727.

Morrison, D., Clark, D., Goldfarb, E., & McCoy, L. (1998). Worsening of obsessive-compulsive symptoms following treatment with olanzapine [letter]. *American Journal of Psychiatry, 155*, 855.

Mundo, E., Bareggi, S.R., Pirola, R., Bellodi, L., & Smeraldi, E. (1997). Long-term pharmacotherapy of obsessive-compulsive disorder: a double-blind controlled study. *Journal of Clinical Psychopharmacology, 17*, 4–10.

Mundo, E., Bellodi, L., & Smeraldi, E. (1995). Effects of acute intravenous clomipramine on obsessive-compulsive symptoms and response to chronic treatment. *Biological Psychiatry, 38*, 525–531.

Mundo, E., Bianchi, L., & Bellodi, L. (1997). Efficacy of fluvoxamine, paroxetine, and citalopram in the treatment of obsessive-compulsive disorder: A single-blind study. *Journal of Clinical Psychopharmacology, 17*, 267–271.

Mundo, E., Smeraldi, E., & Bellodi, L. (1996). Fluvoxamine in the treatment of obsessive-compulsive disorder: A double blind comparison with clomipramine. *European Neuropsychopharmacology, 6*(Suppl. 4), 139–140.

Murphy, T.K., Goodman, W.K., Fudge, M.W., Williams, R.C., Jr., Ayoub, E.M., Dalal, M., Lewis, M.H., & Zabriskie, J.B. (1997). B lymphocyte antigen D8/17: A peripheral marker for childhood-onset obsessive-compulsive disorder and Tourette's syndrome? *American Journal of Psychiatry, 154*, 402–407.

Nelson, E., & Rice, J. (1997). Stability of diagnosis of obsessive-compulsive disorder in the epidemiologic catchment area study. *American Journal of Psychiatry, 154*, 826–831.

Nestadt, G., Bienvenu, O.J., Cai, G., Samuels, J., & Eaton, W.W. (1998). Incidence of obsessive-compulsive disorder in adults. *Journal of Nervous and Mental Disorders, 186*, 401–406.

Newhouse, P.A. (1996). Use of serotonin selective reuptake inhibitors in geriatric depression. *Journal of Clinical Psychiatry, 57*(Suppl. 5), 12–22.

Ninan, P.T., Knight, B., Kirk, L., Rothbaum, B.O., Kelsey, J., & Nemeroff, C.B. (1998). A controlled trial of venlafaxine in trichotillomania: Interim phase I results. *Psychopharmacology Bulletin, 34*, 221–224.

Okasha, A., Saad, A., Khalil, A.H., el Dawla, A.S., & Yehia, N. (1994). Phenomenology of obsessive-compulsive disorder: A transcultural study. *Comprehensive Psychiatry, 35*, 191–197.

Patel, B., & Tandon, R. (1993). Development of obsessive-compulsive symptoms during clozapine treatment [letter; comment]. *American Journal of Psychiatry, 150*, 836.

Pato, M.T., Hill, J.L., & Murphy, D.L. (1990). A clomipramine dosage reduction study in the course of long-term treatment of obsessive-compulsive disorder patients. *Psychopharmacology Bulletin, 26*, 211–214.

Pato, M.T., Zohar-Kadouch, R., Zohar, J., & Murphy, D.L. (1988). Return of symptoms after discontinuation of clomipramine in patients with obsessive-compulsive disorder. *American Journal of Psychiatry, 145*, 1521–1525.

Pauls, D.L., Leckman, J.F., Towbin, K.E., Zahner, G.E., & Cohen, D.J. (1986). A possible genetic relationship exists between Tourette's syndrome and obsessive-compulsive disorder. *Psychopharmacology Bulletin, 22*, 730–733.

Pauls, D.L., Raymond, C.L., Stevenson, J.M., & Leckman, J.F. (1991). A family study of Gilles de la Tourette syndrome. *American Journal of Human Genetics, 48*, 154–163.

Pauls, D.L., Towbin, K.E., Leckman, J.F., Zahner, G.E., & Cohen, D.J. (1986). Gilles de la Tourette's syndrome and obsessive-compulsive disorder. Evidence supporting a genetic relationship. *Archives of General Psychiatry, 43*, 1180–1182.

Perse, T.L., Greist, J.H., Jefferson, J.W., Rosenfeld, R., & Dar, R. (1987). Fluvoxamine treatment of obsessive-compulsive disorder. *American Journal of Psychiatry, 144*, 1543–1548.

Perugi, G., Giannotti, D., Di Vaio, S., Frare, F., Saettoni, M., & Cassano, G.B. (1996). Fluvoxamine in the treatment of body dysmorphic disorder (dysmorphophobia). *International Clinical Psychopharmacology, 11*, 246–254.

Peterson, B.S., Zhang, H., Anderson, G.M., & Leckman, J.F. (1998). A double-blind, placebo-controlled, crossover trial of an antiandrogen in the treatment of Tourette's syndrome [In Process Citation]. *Journal of Clinical Psychopharmacology, 18*, 324–331.

Phillips, K.A. (1991). Body dysmorphic disorder: The distress of imagined ugliness [see comments]. *American Journal of Psychiatry, 148*, 1138–1149.

Phillips, K.A. (1996). An open study of buspirone augmentation of serotonin-reuptake inhibitors in body dysmorphic disorder. *Psychopharmacology Bulletin, 32*, 175–180.

Phillips, K.A., Atala, K.D., & Albertini, R.S. (1995). Case study: Body dysmorphic disorder in adolescents. *Journal of the American Academy of Child and Adolescent Psychiatry, 34*, 1216–1220.

Phillips, K.A., Dwight, M.M., & McElroy, S.L. (1998). Efficacy and safety of fluvoxamine in body dysmorphic disorder. *Journal of Clinical Psychiatry, 59*, 165–171.

Phillips, K.A., Hollander, E., Rasmussen, S.A., Aronowitz, B.R., DeCaria, C., & Goodman, W.K. (1997). A severity rating scale for body dysmorphic disorder: Development, reliability, and validity of a modified version of the Yale-Brown obsessive compulsive scale. *Psychopharmacology Bulletin, 33*, 17–22.

Phillips, K.A., McElroy, S.L., Keck, P.E., Jr., Hudson, J.I., & Pope, H.G., Jr. (1994). A comparison of delusional and nondelusional body dysmorphic disorder in 100 cases. *Psychopharmacology Bulletin, 30*, 179–186.

Phillips, K.A., McElroy, S.L., Keck, P.E., Jr., Pope, H.G., Jr., & Hudson, J.I. (1993). Body dysmorphic disorder: 30 cases of imagined ugliness [see comments]. *American Journal of Psychiatry, 150*, 302–308.

Pigott, T.A., L'Heureux, F., Hill, J.L., Bihari, K., Bernstein, S.E., & Murphy, D.L. (1992). A double-blind study of adjuvant buspirone hydrochloride in clomipramine-treated patients with obsessive-compulsive disorder. *Journal of Clinical Psychopharmacology, 12*, 11–18.

Pigott, T.A., L'Heureux, F., Rubenstein, C.S., Bernstein, S.E., Hill, J.L., & Murphy, D.L. (1992). A double-blind, placebo controlled study of trazodone in patients with obsessive-compulsive disorder. *Journal of Clinical Psychopharmacology, 12*, 156–162.

Pigott, T.A., Pato, M.T., Bernstein, S.E., Grover, G.N., Hill, J.L., Tolliver, T.J., & Murphy, D.L. (1990). Controlled comparisons of clomipramine and fluoxetine in the treatment of obsessive-compulsive disorder. Behavioral and biological results [see comments]. *Archives of General Psychiatry, 47*, 926–932.

Pigott, T.A., Pato, M.T., L'Heureux, F., Hill, J.L., Grover, G.N., Bernstein, S.E., & Murphy, D.L. (1991). A controlled comparison of adjuvant lithium carbonate or thyroid hormone in clomipramine-treated patients with obsessive-compulsive disorder. *Journal of Clinical Psychopharmacology, 11*, 242–248.

Prasad, A.J. (1984a). A double blind study of imipramine versus zimelidine in treatment of obsessive compulsive neurosis. *Pharmacopsychiatry, 17*, 61–62.

Prasad, A.J. (1984b). Obsessive-compulsive disorder and trazodone [letter]. *American Journal of Psychiatry, 141*, 612–613.

Rapoport, J.L., Elkins, R., & Mikkelsen, E. (1980). Clinical controlled trial of chlorimipramine in adolescents with obsessive-compulsive disorder. *Psychopharmacology Bulletin, 16*, 61–63.

Rapoport, J.L., Leonard, H.L., Swedo, S.E., & Lenane, M.C. (1993). Obsessive compulsive disorder in children and adolescents: Issues in management. *Journal of Clinical Psychiatry, 54*(Suppl.), 27–30.

Rasmussen, S.A. (1984). Lithium and tryptophan augmentation in clomipramine-resistant obsessive-compulsive disorder. *American Journal of Psychiatry, 141*, 1283–1285.

Rasmussen, S.A., & Eisen, J.L. (1990). Epidemiology of obsessive compulsive disorder. *Journal of Clinical Psychiatry, 51*(Suppl.), 10–14.

Rasmussen, S.A., & Tsuang, M.T. (1986). Epidemiologic and clinical findings of significance to the design of neuropharmacologic studies of obsessive-compulsive disorder. *Psychopharmacology Bulletin, 22*, 723–729.

Ratzoni, G., Hermesh, H., Brandt, N., Lauffer, M., & Munitz, H. (1990). Clomipramine efficacy for tics, obsessions, and compulsions in Tourette's syndrome and obsessive-compulsive disorder: A case study. *Biological Psychiatry, 27*, 95–98.

Rauch, S.L., & Jenike, M.A. (1994). *In current insights in obsessive compulsive disorder.* New York: Wiley.

Rauch, S.L., O'Sullivan, R.L., & Jenike, M.A. (1996). Open treatment of obsessive-compulsive disorder with venlafaxine: A series of ten cases [letter]. *Journal of Clinical Psychopharmacology, 16*, 81–84.

Ravizza, L., Barzega, G., Bellino, S., Bogetto, F., & Maina, G. (1995). Predictors of drug treatment response in obsessive-compulsive disorder. *Journal of Clinical Psychiatry, 56*, 368–373.

Ravizza, L., Barzega, G., Bellino, S., Bogetto, F., & Maina, G. (1996a). Drug treatment of obsessive-compulsive disorder (OCD): Long-term trial with clomipramine and selective serotonin reuptake inhibitors (SSRIs). *Psychopharmacology Bulletin, 32*, 167–173.

Ravizza, L., Barzega, G., Bellino, S., Bogetto, F., & Maina, G. (1996b). Therapeutic effect and safety of adjunctive risperidone in refractory obsessive-compulsive disorder (OCD). *Psychopharmacology Bulletin, 32*, 677–682.

Riddle, M.A., Hardin, M.T., King, R., Scahill, L., & Woolston, J.L. (1990). Fluoxetine treatment of children and adolescents with Tourette's and obsessive compulsive disorders: Preliminary clinical experience. *Journal of the American Academy Child Adolescent Psychiatry, 29*, 45–48.

Riddle, M.A., Leckman, J.F., Hardin, M.T., Anderson, G.M., & Cohen, D.J. (1988). Fluoxetine treatment of obsessions and compulsions in patients with Tourette's syndrome [letter]. *American Journal of Psychiatry, 145*, 1173–1174.

Riddle, M.A., Scahill, L., King, R.A., Hardin, M.T., Anderson, G.M., Ort, S.I., Smith, J.C., Leckman, J.F., & Cohen, D.J. (1992). Double-blind, crossover trial of fluoxetine and placebo in children and adolescents with obsessive-compulsive disorder. *Journal of the American Academy Child Adolescent Psychiatry, 31*, 1062–1069.

Robins, L.N., Helzer, J.E., Weissman, M.M., Orvaschel, H., Gruenberg, E., Burke, J.D., Jr., & Regier, D.A. (1984). Lifetime prevalence of specific psychiatric disorders in three sites. *Archives of General Psychiatry, 41*, 949–958.

Rudin, E. (1953). Beitrag zur Grage der Zwangsdrankheit insbesondere ihrere hereditaren Beziehungen. *Archiv fur Psychiatrie und Nervenkrankenheiten, 191*, 14–54.

Saiz, J., Lopez-Ibor, J.J., Jr., Vinas, R., & Hernandez, M. (1992). The clomipramine challenge test in obsessive compulsive disorder. *International Clinical Psychopharmacology, 7*(Suppl. 1), 41–42.

Saxena, S., Wang, D., Bystritsky, A., & Baxter, L.R., Jr. (1996). Risperidone augmentation of SRI treatment for refractory obsessive-compulsive disorder. *Journal of Clinical Psychiatry, 57*, 303–306.

Saz, P., Copeland, J.R., de la Camara, C., Lobo, A., & Dewey, M.E. (1995). Cross-national comparison of prevalence of symptoms of neurotic disorders in older people in two community samples. *Acta Psychiatrica Scandinavia, 91*, 18–22.

Scahill, L., Riddle, M.A., King, R.A., Hardin, M.T., Rasmusson, A., Makuch, R.W., & Leckman, J.F. (1997). Fluoxetine has no marked effect on tic symptoms in patients with Tourette's syndrome: A double-blind placebo-controlled study. *Journal of Child Adolescent Psychopharmacology, 7*, 75–85.

Schimmell, M.S., Katz, E.Z., Shaag, Y., Pastuszak, A., & Koren, G. (1991). Toxic neonatal effects following maternal clomipramine therapy. *Journal of Toxins and Clinical Toxicology, 29*, 479–484.

Shapira, N.A., McConville, B.J., Pagnucco, M.L., Norman, A.B., & Keck, P.E., Jr. (1997). Novel use of tramadol hydrochloride in the treatment of Tourette's syndrome [letter]. *Journal of Clinical Psychiatry, 58*, 174–175.

Shapiro, A.K., Shapiro, E.S., Young, J.G., & Feinberg, T.E. (1988). *Gilles de la Tourette syndrome.* New York: Raven Press.

Simeon, D., Hollander, E., Stein, D.J., Cohen, L., & Aronowitz, B. (1995). Body dysmorphic disorder in the *DSM-IV* field trial for obsessive-compulsive disorder. *American Journal of Psychiatry, 152*, 1207–1209.

Simeon, D., Stein, D.J., Gross, S., Islam, N., Schmeidler, J., & Hollander, E. (1997). A double-blind trial of fluoxetine in pathologic skin picking. *Journal of Clinical Psychiatry, 58*, 341–347.

Smeraldi, E., Erzegovesi, S., Bianchi, I., Pasquali, S., Cocchi, S., & Ronchi, P. (1992). Fluvoxamine vs clomipramine treatment in obsessive compulsive disorder: A preliminary study. *New Trends in Experimental and Clinical Psychiatry, 8*, 63–65.

Stanley, M.A., Breckenridge, J.K., Swann, A.C., Freeman, E.B., & Reich, L. (1997). Fluvoxamine treatment of trichotillomania. *Journal of Clinical Psychopharmacology, 17*, 278–283.

Stein, D.J., Bouwer, C., Hawkridge, S., & Emsley, R.A. (1997). Risperidone augmentation of serotonin reuptake inhibitors in obsessive-compulsive and related disorders [see comments]. *Journal of Clinical Psychiatry, 58*, 119–122.

Stein, D.J., Bouwer, C., & Maud, C.M. (1997). Use of the selective serotonin reuptake inhibitor citalopram in treatment of trichotillomania. *European Archives of Psychiatry and Clinical Neuroscience, 7*, 234–236.

Stein, D.J., & Hollander, E. (1992). Low-dose pimozide augmentation of serotonin reuptake blockers in the treatment of trichotillomania. *Journal of Clinical Psychiatry, 53*, 123–126.

Stein, D.J., Hollander, E., & Josephson, S.C. (1994). Serotonin reuptake blockers for the treatment of obsessional jealousy. *Journal of Clinical Psychiatry, 55*, 30–33.

Stein, D.J., Simeon, D., Cohen, L.J., & Hollander, E. (1995). Trichotillomania and obsessive-compulsive disorder. *Journal of Clinical Psychiatry, 56*(Suppl. 4), 28–35.

Stein, D.J., Wessels, C., Carr, J., Hawkridge, S., Bouwer, C., & Kalis, N. (1997). Hair pulling in a patient with Sydenham's chorea [letter]. *American Journal of Psychiatry, 154*, 1320.

Stein, M.B., Forde, D.R., Anderson, G., & Walker, J.R. (1997). Obsessive-compulsive disorder in the community: An epidemiologic survey with clinical reappraisal. *American Journal of Psychiatry, 154,* 1120–1126.

Stern, T.A., & Jenike, M.A. (1983). Treatment of obsessive-compulsive disorder with lithium carbonate. *Psychosomatics, 24,* 671–673.

Streichenwein, S.M., & Thornby, J.I. (1995). A long-term, double-blind, placebo-controlled crossover trial of the efficacy of fluoxetine for trichotillomania. *American Journal of Psychiatry, 152,* 1192–1196.

Sunkureddi, K., & Markovitz, P. (1993). Trazodone treatment of obsessive-compulsive disorder and trichotillomania [letter]. *American Journal of Psychiatry, 150,* 523–524.

Swedo, S.E., Leonard, H.L., Garvey, M., Mittleman, B., Allen, A.J., Perlmutter, S., Lougee, L., Dow, S., Zamkoff, J., & Dubbert, B.K. (1998). Pediatric autoimmune neuropsychiatric disorders associated with streptococcal infections: Clinical description of the first 50 cases. *American Journal of Psychiatry, 155,* 264–271.

Swedo, S.E., Leonard, H.L., Mittleman, B., Allen, A.J., Rapoport, J.L., Dow, S.P., Kanter, M.E., Chapman, F., & Zabriskie, J. (1997). *American Journal of Psychiatry, 154,* 110–112.

Swedo, S.E., Leonard, H.L., Rapoport, J.L., Lenane, M.C., Goldberger, E.L., & Cheslow, D.L. (1989). A double-blind comparison of clomipramine and desipramine in the treatment of trichotillomania. *New England Journal of Medicine, 321,* 497–501.

Swedo, S.E., Rapoport, J.L., Leonard, H., Lenane, M., & Cheslow, D. (1989). Obsessive-compulsive disorder in children and adolescents. Clinical phenomenology of 70 consecutive cases. *Archives of General Psychiatry, 46,* 335–341.

Swoboda, K.J., & Jenike, M.A. (1995). Frontal abnormalities in a patient with obsessive-compulsive disorder: The role of structural lesions in obsessive-compulsive behavior. *Neurology, 45,* 2130–2134.

Tamimi, R., Mavissakalian, M., Jones, B., & Olson, S. (1991). Clomipramine versus fluvoxamine in obsessive compulsive disorder. *Annals of Clinical Psychiatry, 3,* 275.

Thomsen, P.H. (1997). Child and adolescent obsessive-compulsive disorder treated with citalopram: Findings from an open trial of 23 cases. *Journal of Child Adolescent Psychopharmacology, 7,* 157–166.

Thoren, P., Asberg, M., Cronholm, B., Jornestedt, L., & Traskman, L. (1980). Clomipramine treatment of obsessive-compulsive disorder: I. A controlled clinical trial. *Archives of General Psychiatry, 37,* 1281–1285.

Tollefson, G.D., Rampey, A.H., Jr., Potvin, J.H., Jenike, M.A., Rush, A.J., Kominguez, R.A., Koran, L.M., Shear, M.K., Goodman, W., & Genduso, L.A. (1994). A multicenter investigation of fixed-dose fluoxetine in the treatment of obsessive-compulsive disorder. *Archives of General Psychiatry, 51,* 559–567.

Vallejo, J., Olivares, J., Marcos, T., Bulbena, A., & Menchon, J.M. (1992). Clomipramine versus phenelzine in obsessive-compulsive disorder. A controlled clinical trial. *British Journal of Psychiatry, 161,* 665–670.

Vanden Borre, R., Vermote, R., Buttiens, M., Thiry, P., Dierick, G., Geutjens, J., Sieben, G., & Heylen, S. (1993). Risperidone as add-on therapy in behavioural disturbances in mental retardation: A double-blind placebo-controlled cross-over study. *Acta Psychiatrica Scandinavia, 87,* 167–171.

van Renynghe de Voxvrie, G. (1968). L'Anafranil dans l'obsession. *Acta Neurol. Belg., 68,* 787–792.

Vitiello, B., Spreat, S., & Behar, D. (1989). Obsessive-compulsive disorder in mentally retarded patients. *Journal of Nervous and Mental Disorders, 177,* 232–236.

Volavka, J., Neziroglu, F., & Yaryura-Tobias, J.A. (1985). Clomipramine and imipramine in obsessive-compulsive disorder. *Psychiatry Research, 14,* 85–93.

Warneke, L.B. (1992). Intravenous clomipramine for OCD [letter; comment]. *Canadian Journal of Psychiatry, 37,* 522–523.

Weissman, M.M., Bland, R.C., Canino, G.J., Greenwald, S., Hwu, H.G., Lee, C.K., Newman, S.C., Oakley-Browne, M.A., Rubio-Stipec, M., Wickramaratne, P.J., Wittchen, H.-U., & Yeh, E.-K. (1994). The cross national epidemiology of obsessive compulsive disorder. The Cross National Collaborative Group. *Journal of Clinical Psychiatry, 55*(Suppl.), 5–10.

Westenberg, H.G.M., De Leeuw, A.S., & Den Boer, J.A. (1993). *Serotonin reuptake blockers in obsessive compulsive disorder: A controlled trial with fluvoxamine.* Paper presented at the International Obsessive Compulsive Disorder Conference, Capri, Italy.

Wheadon, D.E., Bushnell, W.D., Steiner, M., & Meltzer, H.Y. (1993). *A dixed dose comparison of 20, 40, or 60mg paroxetine to placebo in the treatment of obsessive compulsive disorder.* Paper presented at the annual meeting of the American College of Neuropsychopharmacology, Honolulu, Hawaii.

Wiener, K., & Lamberti, J.S. (1993). Sertraline and mental retardation with obsessive-compulsive disorder [letter]. *American Journal of Psychiatry, 150,* 1270.

Wilhelm, S., Otto, M.W., Zucker, B.G., & Pollack, M.H. (1997). Prevalence of body dysmorphic disorder in patients with anxiety disorders. *Journal of Anxiety Disorders, 11,* 499–502.

Williams, K.E., & Koran, L.M. (1997). Obsessive-compulsive disorder in pregnancy, the puerperium, and the premenstruum. *Journal of Clinical Psychiatry, 58,* 330–336.

Yaryura-Tobias, J.A., & Bhagavan, H.N. (1977). L-tryptophan in obsessive-compulsive disorders. *American Journal of Psychiatry, 134,* 1298–1299.

Yaryura-Tobias, J.A., & Neziroglu, F. (1975). The action of chlorimipramine in obsessive-compulsive neurosis: A pilot study. *Current Therapeutical Research and Clinical Experience, 17,* 111–116.

Yaryura-Tobias, J.A., & Neziroglu, F.A. (1996). Venlafaxine in obsessive-compulsive disorder [letter; comment]. *Archives of General Psychiatry, 53,* 653–654.

Zajecka, J.M., Fawcett, J., & Guy, C. (1990). Coexisting major depression and obsessive-compulsive disorder treated with venlafaxine [letter]. *Journal of Clinical Psychopharmacology, 10,* 152–153.

Zohar, A.H., Pauls, D.L., Ratzoni, G., Apter, A., Dycian, A., Binder, M., King, R., Leckman, J.F., Kron, S., & Cohen, D.J. (1997). Obsessive-compulsive disorder with and without tics in an epidemiological sample of adolescents. *American Journal of Psychiatry, 154,* 274–276.

Zohar, J., & Judge, R. (1996). Paroxetine versus clomipramine in the treatment of obsessive-compulsive disorder. OCD Paroxetine Study Investigators. *British Journal of Psychiatry, 169,* 468–474.

Zohar, J., Kaplan, Z., & Benjamin, J. (1993). Clomipramine treatment of obsessive compulsive symptomatology in schizophrenic patients. *Journal of Clinical Psychiatry, 54,* 385–388.

PART SIX

POSTTRAUMATIC STRESS DISORDER

IN ACCORDANCE with *DSM-IV*, the cardinal feature of posttraumatic stress disorder (PTSD) is the development of characteristic symptoms following a psychologically distressing event that is outside the range of usual human experience. Excluded from making the diagnosis, then, would be marital conflict, business losses, chronic illness, and simple bereavement. However, severely traumatic, physically threatening, or life-threatening events, such as threat to one's children, seeing another individual maimed or killed in an accident or fire, rape, being a prisoner of war, combat experiences in war, or the horror of cataclysmic events (e.g., floods, hurricanes, tornadoes, earthquakes) definitely are considered to be contributors to the diagnosis. The reaction to such events (immediate or delayed) is marked by a reliving of the experience in the form of intrusive thoughts or dreams, avoidance of stimuli associated with the original trauma, persistent symptoms of increased arousal not present before the trauma, and diminished responsiveness or psychic numbness to the world.

Although posttraumatic stress disorder first appeared formally in the psychiatric nomenclature in *DSM-III*, its forebears had been referred to as "shell shock" and "traumatic war neurosis." However, it is with *DSM-III*, *DSM-III-R*, and *DSM-IV* that the range of disorders subsumed under this rubric has increased beyond those traumas only associated with war.

Despite some of the commonalities across the analytic and behavioral approaches to conceptualizations of PTSD, there obviously are some marked distinctions in focus and, of course, in treatment. The analytic view, presented as a feedback loop (Horowitz), posits that the traumatic event is stored in the conscious mind and undergoes repetition. Because repetition results in painful effects, the memory still poses a threat to the individual. Such pain elicits varying degrees of defense, ranging from conscious inhibition (suppression) to unconscious inhibition (repression). In addition, Horowitz poists that "meaning plays a role in personal appraisals of events and their consequences, and habits, traits, and styles of personality braid in with the trauma in causing effects."

The learning model (Weaver, Resnick, Glynn, & Foy) is based on Mowrer's two-factor theory, in which the original trauma results in a classically conditioned emotional response, with subsequent avoidance of all stimuli associated with the trauma, motivated by fear and maintained via fear reduction. Thus, in the case of rape as the traumatic event, the unconditioned stimulus yields an unconditioned response of extreme fear (including psychological, cognitive, and physiological aspects). Through classical conditioning, associated stimuli with the rape (e.g., place and time of day) become conditioned stimuli and are able to evoke either a full or a partial conditioned response of fear.

In both the analytic and the behavioral conceptions of PTSD, learning (albeit different in each case) is implicated as the underlying mechanism, with subsequent avoidance as the maintaining factor. Both approaches, however, underscore the importance of paying attention to the unique features of each case presentation.

With respect to treatment, Horowitz describes a time-limited dynamic therapy that can be carried out in 12 sessions. This treatment is both phase oriented and personality oriented, with phase orientation dealing with the patient's current degree of control over the tendency to repeat memories and reactions to traumatic events. The personality oriented phase focuses on the link between the event and the patient's self-concept and use of habitual defense strategies. By contrast, Weaver et al. describe a novel group-administered cognitive-behavioral treatment (Trauma Focused Group Therapy: TFGT) that incorporates prolonged exposure, cognitive restructuring, and relapse prevention training, set in a developmental perspective. Since publication of the first edition of this book, there have been additional randomized controlled trials documenting the value of using prolonged exposure, cognitive restructuring, and skills training. Manualized treatment protocols have allowed for a more precise implementation of strategies, thus resulting in improved research.

CHAPTER 17

Dynamic Psychotherapy

MARDI J. HOROWITZ

CONCEPTUALIZATION

Posttraumatic stress disorders are only one of many types of stress-response syndromes. Others include adjustment disorders and complicated grief disorders. All these diagnoses fit within the larger category of stress-response syndromes, and can be treated in ways to be discussed in this chapter.

Events that incite posttraumatic stress disorders are marked by their severity. Nonetheless, the preexisting personality of the patient always plays a role in how the event is experienced, interpreted, defended against, or mastered. In the main, stressful life experiences are injuries and losses or, at least, the threat of such traumas. The most serious of these threats involve fears of death, helpless terror, or brutality of other people. Yet there are also traumas arising from subjugation of the self to rules that seem alien to personal values or even human nature.

POPULATIONS

Experimental, field, and clinical studies of posttraumatic stress disorders indicate general response tendencies to serious life events. Although varying in resiliency, areas of personal vulnerability, and available support systems, populations exhibit extremes of conscious experience. These extremes are characterized

This chapter is a product of empirical research and theory formation funded by the National Institutes of Health (Heart, Lung, and Blood: NHLBI) and Mental Health (NIMH) from 1967–1984 and the Program on Conscious and Unconscious Mental Processes of the John D. and Catherine T. MacArthur Foundation (1984–1994). Important colleagues listed in part include, in alphabetical order, George Bonnonno, Tracy Eells, Nigel Field, Art Holea, Nancy Kaltreider, Janice Krupnick, Charles Marmar, Constance Milbank, Stephen Reidbord, Alan Skolnikoff, Charles Stinson, Daniel Weiss, Nancy Wilner, and Hans Znoj.

by both unusual episodes of intrusion and unusual episodes of avoidance or de-nial of the implications embedded in the stressful life experiences.

PHASES OF REACTION

Contrasting phases marked by intrusive experiences or denial-type experi-ences tend to alternate after a stressful event. Phases of intrusion and denial may overlap; individuals may enter or move through one phase more quickly than another depending on the nature of the event. Prototypically, however, an emotional outcry occurs first, followed by a period of relative denial, which in turn is followed by intrusive experiences. The person then may work gradually through the stressful life event and reach a relative completion of response.

NORMAL AND ABNORMAL

If any of these phases becomes excessively intense, or is blocked, pathological intensifications may develop. The discomfort of such pathological intensifica-tions is what leads the person to seek psychotherapy. Figure 17.1 shows this concept of phases of response to serious life events.

SIGNS AND SYMPTOMS

Table 17.1 shows a variety of intrusive signs and symptoms found in a post-traumatic stress disorder. A similar listing of signs and symptoms related to denial and numbing experiences is found in Table 17.2.

THEORY OF EXPLANATION

The psychodynamic theory of the development of such symptoms as listed in Figure 17.1 and Tables 17.1 and 17.2 was first formulated by Josef Breuer and Sigmund Freud in the context of hysteria (1895). Freud (1920) later devised a more advanced model in which the repetition compulsion was seen to super-cede the libidinal drive and pleasure principle in mental functioning. Contem-porary psychodynamics has revised Freud's theory into a general systems model with a feedback loop of defensive control of emotion (Horowitz, 1997). In this view of symptom formation, the information from the traumatic event is stored and tends to be repeated in the conscious mind. Such repetition would lead to painful levels of negative emotion, because the event was an injury or loss, and the memory is still threatening to the individual. To avoid being over-whelmed with emotional responses upon recollection, the person might im-pose various degrees of defense.

In my cognitive-dynamic integration of theories, I omitted Freud's theories about psychic energy because they are no longer an agreed-upon part of psy-chodynamic theory (Horowitz, 1998). However, modern psychodynamics still embrace the principle that memory of traumatic events is repeated and the mo-tive for such repetition is the need to master the information contained in such events. This contemporary model seeks to explain the persistence of recurrent

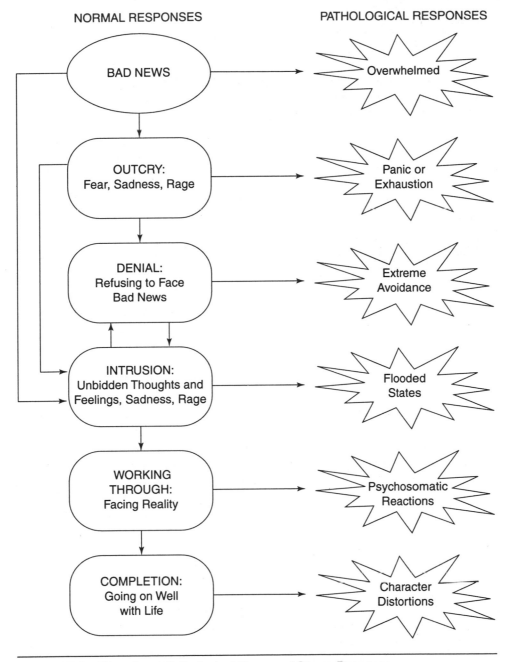

Figure 17.1 Normal and Pathological Phases of Stress Response.

recollection of the stressful event, and the maladaptive distortions of character that may result from a failure to integrate such memories, as in instances of excessive and prolonged inhibitions. Recovery is viewed as a combination of shock-mastery and reschematization of identity substrates.

A stressful life event is by definition out of accord with inner working models and existing mental schemas (Bowlby, 1969). It contains either too much or

Table 17.1

Symptoms and Signs Related to Intrusive Experience and Behavior

- Hypervigilance, including hypersensitivity to associated events
- Startle reactions
- Illusions or pseudohallucinations, including sensation of recurrence
- Intrusive-repetitive thoughts, images, emotions, and behaviors
- Overgeneralization of associations
- Inability to concentrate on other topics because of preoccupation with event-related themes
- Confusion or thought disruption when thinking about event-related themes
- Labile or explosive entry into intensely emotional and undermodulated states of mind
- Sleep and dream disturbances, including recurrent dreams
- Symptoms of exhaustion from chronic hyper arousal including tremor, nausea, diarrhea, and sweating
- Search for lost persons or situations, compulsive repetitions

From Horowitz, M.: Stress Response Syndromes, 1997b, p. 25.

too little of some familiar situation, or, as is much more often the case, it presents an entirely new threat to the equilibrium of the person and to their affiliations. The importance of these new perceptions means that they have high priority for retention in memory. That type of memory apparently tends to actively repeat in conscious experience unless a control maneuver is employed to specifically inhibit it.

An active memory storage exists, I hypothesize, which contains memories of traumatic events. It tends to repeat such memories as conscious representations until there is an accord between the information in the memory and working models of the event. This need to bring inner mental models up to date with a changing reality can be called a *completion tendency.* Moreover, the repeated representation does not contain only perceptions of external facts; a

Table 17.2

Symptoms and Signs Related to Denial or Numbing Experiences and Behavior

- Daze
- Selective inattention
- Inability to appreciate significance of stimuli
- Amnesia (complete or partial)
- Inability to visualize memories
- Disavowal of meanings of stimuli
- Constriction and inflexibility of thought
- Presence of fantasies to counteract reality
- A sense of numbness or unreality, including detachment and estrangement
- Overcontrolled states of mind, including behavioral avoidances
- Sleep disturbances (e.g., too little or too much)
- Tension-inhibition responses of the autonomic nervous system, with felt sensations such as bowel symptoms, fatigue, and headache
- Frantic overactivity to jam attention with stimuli
- Withdrawal from ordinary life activities

From Horowitz, M.: Stress Response Syndromes, 1997b, p. 26.

mixture of external and internal sets of information are reorganized according to schemas and then experienced. Thus, the active memory collates awareness of the traumatic event with information about earlier emotional responses and beliefs, and may include errors in terms of what really happened.

Because the information in active memory is so unusual and also so important, it will be difficult to process. Many repetitions of processing may be necessary. Such processing may proceed awake and asleep; dreams may be important memory and schema integrators in ways we do not yet fully understand.

A complete working-through process (shown as a phase of response in Figure 17.1) may require many repetitions and changes in inner schemas. As completion is approached, intrusion and denial will be experienced less. Until that time, however, intrusive experiences may occur as the pressure for repeated representation of the traumatic memories leads to interruption of other topics of thought.

Denial experiences occur as inner inhibitory control processes overpower the repetition tendency. Other effects of the control processes may include conscious experiences, such as feeling numb, or awareness of avoiding certain topics that might arouse the intense negative emotions associated with the traumatic events. Denial states are not necessarily to be evaluated or judged as pathological; they may be a period of adaptive self-restoration, if not prolonged excessively.

In other words, the controls that modulate the degree of reaction have the purpose of maintaining emotional equilibrium within tolerable limits. The outcomes may be adaptive or maladaptive. Adaptive outcomes might be called *coping*. Maladaptive outcomes might be called *pathological levels of defense*. Failure of self-regulation, also called a *failure of defense,* is a third type of outcome, and involves being so flooded with emotion that one cannot plan and take realistic action.

THEORY OF THERAPEUTIC ACTION

The concept of defense is very important to psychodynamic case formulation because psychotherapists often work either to increase or to decrease the control processes of the patient. In patients who have excessive inhibitions, the therapist might first seek to counteract these and help the patient access warded-off themes. Subsequently, the patient can begin to deal with emotions related to the traumatic experience and the emotional themes and person schemas activated through associative processes.

In patients who have maladaptive failures of control, the therapist may help to restructure activities, thought, and emotion to feel more in control. In patients using aberrant schemas and beliefs to organize their conscious views and preconscious or unconscious schemas about what happened, the therapist helps differentiate reality and fantasy, and helps to work through preexisting, focally relevant, neurotic or psychotic levels of conflict.

Very often the therapist is following a middle course, helping the patient to set aside extreme defenses, and to consciously and effectively modulate out-of-control trains of ideas, feelings, and behaviors, using more moderate control processes. The therapeutic relationship helps the patient tolerate some of the painful experience and working through of memories. As tolerance increases, control processes become progressively less necessary; the patient is able both to deliberately remember and to think of other things besides the traumatic event. Above all, the patient is able to reschematize a sense of self as articulating with a world that was changed by the traumatic events.

DIAGNOSTIC ISSUES AND PROBLEMS

Preexisting character structure consists, in part, of the schemas of self and other that the individual might use to interpret a traumatic experience, together with the individual's habitual control processes. It also consists of the person's capacity for integrating dissimilar self schemas into supraordinate forms. Other elements of this structure include the habitual styles of schema management used to regulate emotional experience and states of mind, the controls exercised on conscious representation, and an individual's inhibition or facilitation of various intentions to act.

Different character styles may be represented as prototypes. An individual will fit a given prototype only to a degree. Only those with a relatively rigid set of patterns will fit the prototype well, whereas others present a more mixed and less conforming picture.

Information-processing style may be seen while observing short-order patterns in the subject's flow of thought and emotion on a topic. The stressful life event is an apt topic for such observation, because habitual defensive styles are sometimes thrown into bold relief by intense emotional themes. However, the schemas of self and other are more commonly seen in medium- or long-order patterns. Those patterns may be observed directly in the patients' interpersonal behavior or inferred indirectly from their stories of how they have behaved with others over longer periods of time. The repetitive roles and actions for self and other in these stories may be especially useful for the therapist.

A grasp of how to formulate personality patterns is important in helping an individual work through the specific meaning of a traumatic event; one can then note the individual's own habitual style of responding to stressful events (Horowitz, 1997b). In working through the meaning of the stressful event, the person may also benefit by reducing character rigidity or armor (Reich, 1949; Shapiro, 1965).

Some patterns in a prototype of a histrionic personality style are shown in Table 17.3. The characteristic global attentiveness observed in this type often makes the experience of a traumatic event especially shocking. The tendency to short circuit a topic makes it important for the therapist to increase the time the patient spends on the topic by offering comments about it. Patients' attention-seeking behaviors may lead others to think that they are using their status as victims of trauma to get something they want. Professionals may be misled into thinking that the person is being manipulative rather than experiencing a serious PTSD. Therapists should be careful to avoid such errors.

Table 17.3
Patterns in the Histrionic Personality Style Prototype

Information-Processing Style

Short order patterns—observe in the flow of thought and emotion on a topic.

- Global deployment of attention.
- Unclear or incomplete representations of ideas and feelings, possibly with lack of details or clear labels in communication, nonverbal communications not translated into words or conscious meanings.
- Only partial or unidirectional associational lines.
- Short circuit to apparent completion of problematic thoughts.

Traits

Medium order patterns—observe in interviews.

- Attention-seeking behaviors, possibly including demands for attention, and/or the use of charm, vivacity, sex appeal, childishness.
- Fluid change in mood and emotion, possibly including breakthroughs of feeling.
- Inconsistency of apparent attitudes.

Interpersonal Relations

Long order patterns—observe in a patient's history.

- Repetitive, impulsive, stereotyped interpersonal relationships often characterized by victim–aggressor, child–parent, and rescue or rape themes.
- "Cardboard" fantasies and self-object attitudes.
- Drifting but possibly dramatic lives with an existential sense that reality is not really real.

From Horowitz, M.: Stress Response Syndromes, 1997b, p. 160.

The prototype of the compulsive personality style is shown in Table 17.4. The sharp focus on peripheral details may mislead professionals into thinking that such individuals do not have emotional intrusions when they are by themselves. Nevertheless, although the compulsive or obsessional typology may be associated with marked low affect in conversations, when alone such individuals with PTSD may have episodes of searingly intense emotion. These individuals exhibit a tendency to have power and control struggles with a psychotherapist, but it usually does not surface while the individual is in the intrusive phase of a stress-response syndrome. Instead, it may arise when the relationship with the therapist sustains the individual to feel safe enough that he or she then enters a denial phase of response. It is important at that point to recognize what is happening and to help the individual maintain a focus on working through the stressful event. Otherwise, the individual may insist that the event is no longer an important focus. The goal is dose-by-dose coping, staying within a zone of some suffering without feeling overwhelmed or out of control.

The narcissistic personality style, too, has ways of coloring the signs and symptoms observed in PTSD, as well as characteristic effects on the working-through process. It is especially important to recognize that such patients may lie about aspects of their role in the traumatic event to create a safe space in the therapy in which they can tell the truth about it without the revulsion of shame

Table 17.4
Patterns in the Compulsive Personality Style Prototype

Information-Processing Style

Short order patterns—observe in the flow of thought and emotion on a topic.
- Sharp focus of attention on details.
- Clear representation of ideas, meager representation of emotions.
- Shifting organization and implications of ideas rather than following an associational line to conclusion as directed by original intent or intrinsic meanings.
- Avoiding completion on decision of a given problem, instead switching back and forth between attitudes.

Traits

Medium order patterns—observe in interviews.
- Doubt, worry, overly detailed productivity and/or procrastination.
- Single-minded, unperturbable, intellectualizing.
- Tense, deliberate, unenthusiastic.
- Rigid, ritualistic.

Interpersonal Relations

Long order patterns—observe in a patient's history.
- Develops regimented, routine, and continuous interpersonal relationships low in "life," vividness, or pleasure. Often frustrating to be with.
- Prone to dominance-submission themes or power and control struggles.
- Duty filling, hardworking, seeks or makes strain and pressure, does what one should do rather than what one decides to do.
- Experiences self as remote from emotional connection with others, although feels committed to operating with others because of role or principles.

From Horowitz, M.: Stress Response Syndromes, 1997b, p. 172.

they might otherwise experience. The self-centered behavior should not mislead clinical evaluators into thinking these people have not been traumatized or that they are unworthy of professional care. The focus on reviewing the meaning to self of the traumatic event may be especially difficult to maintain if the patient's priority is recovering a sense of cohesion in identity. The same division into short-, medium-, and long-order patterns is used in Table 17.5 as was used in Tables 17.3 and 17.4.

It is possible to regard narcissistic controls as a distinct dimension of self-regulatory traits. That is, the person may primarily tend to use either a histrionic or compulsive style of controlling emotion in interpersonal situations, and may also slide meanings to protect self-esteem.

TREATMENT STRATEGIES

The treatment strategy will depend on the formulation of both the personality style and the nature of the individual's response to the event. Elapsed time after the event will also be a factor. In general, the longer an individual waits before seeking help, the longer the treatment may take. This seems paradoxical at first; however, the longer therapy is deferred, the deeper the individual may

Table 17.5
Patterns in the Narcissistic Personality Style Prototype

Information-Processing Style
Short order patterns—observe in the thought and emotions on a topic.
- Slides meanings of information that might damage self-concept. Also uses denial, disavowal, and negation for this purpose.
- Attention to sources of praise and criticism.
- Shifts subject-object focus of meanings, externalizes bad attributes, internalizes good attributes.
- Occasionally dissociates incompatible psychological attitudes into separate clusters.

Traits
Medium order patterns—observe in interviews.
- Self-centered.
- Overestimates or underestimates self and others.
- Self-enhancement in accomplishments real or fantasied, in garb or demeanor.
- Avoids self-deflating situations.
- Variable demeanors depending on state of self-esteem and context:
  - Charm, "wooing-winning" quality, controlling efforts, or charisma.
  - Superiority, contemptuousness, coldness, or withdrawal.
  - Shame, panic, helplessness, hypochondriasis, depersonalization, or self-destructiveness.
  - Envy, rage, paranoia, or demands.

Interpersonal Relations
Long order patterns—observe in patient's history.
- Often impoverished interpersonally or oriented to power over others or controlling use of others as accessories (self-objects).
- Absence of "I-thou" feelings.
- Social climbing or using others for positive reflection.
- Avoidance of self-criticism by goading others to unfair criticism.
- Discarding of persons no longer of use.
- Pseudo twinning relationship.

From Horowitz, M.: Stress Response Syndromes, 1997b, p. 187.

have become embedded in some type of pathological belief about the event. Such enduring schemas take more time to change.

Time-limited dynamic psychotherapy can lift a tendency to avoid an event, and sometimes a single session or two of crucial work starts an individual on a normal working-through process (Horowitz, 1999). Consider the mourning process as an example. Individuals can seldom go through a mourning process for a loved one who has died in less than a year. In instances of pathological grief, the individual may suffer far longer than that or experience overwhelming feelings during the year, and in some instances avoid mourning altogether. Psychotherapy does not seek to eliminate the painful sadness and other feelings that occur; neither must it continue until the person has completed a normal mourning process. Its purpose is to help the individual get on track of a normal mourning process, away from some type of pathological deflection or

Table 17.6

A Prototype for a Psychotherapy for Posttraumatic Stress Disorder

Approximate Sequence	Therapeutic Alliance	Patient Activity	Therapist Activity
1. State Stabilization	Initial hope because expert help is available. Then traumatic event related to life context of patient at the time it occurred, and current problems to what now can happen.	Patient tells story of traumatic event and current symptoms and problems; describes goals.	Takes psychiatric history, makes diagnoses and early formulations. Acts to stabilize states if indicated. Establishes preliminary focus as relation of traumatic event to "the self."
2. Safety	Patient tests therapy situation to see if precipitation into dreaded emotional states might occur. The therapeutic alliance is deepened if a sense of comparative safety occurs with these tests.	Patient adds associations expanding meaning to self of the trauma and its sequelae.	Realignment of focus to more specific issues. If denial or distortions are excessive, interprets both defenses and warded-off contents. Links warded-off emotions and ideas to traumatic event.
3. Work on Meanings and Identity	Resentments, sorrows, or worries that magical reparations will not occur may threaten the therapeutic alliance.	Works on what has been avoided because it seemed too overwhelming before therapy.	Linking of current reactions to preexisting beliefs about self, others, and how the world works and to possible future adaptive changes in identity.
4. Improving Coping and Resilience	Irrational expectations of treatment may be clarified and alternative views of the future suggested.	Makes plans for improving future coping.	Time of termination is discussed and work yet to do is clarified.
5. Reviewing and Revising	Meaning of termination as active rather than passive to counteract a view that a traumatic abandonment is about to happen.	Working through central conflicts and issues of termination as related to topics about the trauma. Giving up the therapist as restorer of what was lost, and bolstering plans for realistic and assertive future actions.	Clarification of conflicts and how these relate to past personality, traumatic events and the pending termination; clarification of unfinished issues for future contemplation.
6. Ending	Saying goodbye without resentment, sorrow, or worry.	Realization and clarification of work to be continued on own in times to come.	Acknowledgment of real gains and real future work. Additional recommendations. Set up for booster sessions as indicated.

From Horowitz, M.: Stress Response Syndromes, 1997b, p. 153.

overintensification. Then an individual can suffer the necessary pangs of grief without continuing therapy if they have the intuition, and it is warranted, that this is their way through it.

The choice between a brief or a time-unlimited dynamic psychotherapy depends on each individual case. A time-limited dynamic therapy will be described here as a prototype for what may happen during the course of a dynamic psychotherapy (Horowitz, 1997a). Table 17.6 gives such a sample outline, which utilized a time-limited 12-session dynamic therapy for stress disorders.

Dynamic therapy focusing on a traumatic event is both phase oriented and personality oriented. Phase orientation begins with an assessment of the patient's current degree of control over his or her tendency to repeat memories of, and reactions to, the traumatic events. The variety of goals for treatment is determined by each patient's prevailing state as summarized in Table 17.7. These states are due in part to the trauma and in part to preexisting character

Table 17.7
Priorities of Treatment by Phases of Patient's Response

Patient's Current State	Treatment Goal
Under continuing impact of external stress event.	—Terminate external event or remove patient from contiguity with it. —Provide a temporary relationship. —Help with decisions, plans, or working-through.
Swings to intolerable levels: —Ideational-emotional attacks. —Paralyzing denial and numbness.	—Reduce amplitude of oscillations to swings of tolerable intensity of ideation and emotion. —Continue emotional and ideational support.
Frozen in overcontrol state of denial and numbness with or without intrusive repetitions.	—Help patient "dose" reexperience of event and implications that help remember for a time, put out of mind for a time, remember for a time, and so on. —During periods of recollection, help patient organize and express experience. Increase sense of safety in therapeutic relationship so patient can resume processing the event.
Able to experience and tolerate episodes of ideation and waves of emotion.	—Help patient work through associations: the conceptual, emotional, object relations, and self-image implications of the stress event. —Help patient relate this stress event to earlier threats, relationship models, self-concept, and future plans.
Able to work through ideas and emotions on one's own.	—Work through loss of therapeutic relationship. —Terminate treatment.

structure and temperament. Formulation of these interactions and future possibilities leads to a plan for what techniques to use.

The nuances of psychotherapy technique may be based upon a conceptualization of the patient's personality style. In order to get into this issue, it is important to examine the problem of establishing a focus. An aspect of the focus in PTSD is the event itself. In addition, however, some type of link exists between the experience of the event and some aspect of the patient's self.

Early in treatment the facts about the event and the nature of the response may suffice as a focus, if only because one cannot know in a few interviews all there is to know that is relevant about a patient. Thus, the focus may be something like, "Our purpose, if you agree, will be to understand the impact of this event upon you." That sounds straightforward and simple; nonetheless, establishing the link between the patient's stressful life event and his or her self-concepts often comes as a surprise. Indeed, it is often what the patient has been trying to ward off. When a very simple focus, such as the link between the stress event and the self-concept of the subject, is employed initially, it can be realigned in midtherapy to deal with particular topics that are especially conflicted.

The type of habitual defenses associated with different personality styles will affect not only the way the focus is realigned, but also how the topic of the focus is processed over time. The goal of the treatment is to allow the person to have full access to associations to the traumatic event, to differentiate reality and fantasy about it, and to reach a variety of appropriate conclusions. Rendered graphically, the goal is to flow down the column shown at the left of Table 17.8. This series of control processes begins with helping the patient confront the topic of the trauma. Putting associations together in a sequence follows, and then progresses to revising inner and enduring schemas while practicing new modes of behavior made necessary by realities in the stressful event. The control processes in this column each have a variety of rows representing subdivisions into one of three categories: adaptive levels of regulation; maladaptive levels of regulation; and states of relative failure of regulation, efforts, or capacities. The therapist encourages the patient to use control processes at the adaptive level of regulation.

Each prototype style mentioned previously can be thought of as if it were a defect in following the normal working-through process. For each defect, a corresponding type of corrective is proposed that might be used in therapy. Tables 17.9, 17.10, and 17.11 illustrate prototypes for such cases, which require a longer exposition than space here allows. Full discussions are available elsewhere in the kind of detail necessary to make a psychodynamic view clear (Horowitz, 1997a, 1997b; Horowitz et al., 1996).

ALTERNATIVE TREATMENT OPTIONS

Within a case one might use a variety of treatment strategies. I see psychodynamic formulation as an overarching bridge. One always considers the effects of any technique (including prescribing medications) on the overall picture, as well as issues of transference and expectation. For example, if the patient

Table 17.8
Regulation of Sequences of Conscious Representations

Processes	Outcomes		
	Regulation		Dysregulation
Types of Control	Adaptive	Maladaptive	
Representing next thought			
Facilitation of associations	Contemplation of implications	Rumination and doubting	
Inhibition of associations	Dosing; selective inattention; careful choice of what is expressed; suppression	Denial; disavowal; repression; isolation; numbing; communicative reluctance; somatization; acting out	
Sequencing ideas			
Seeking information	Understanding: learning new skills	Intellectualization	Intrusion of ideas; emotional flooding; indecision; paralysis of action
Switching concepts	Emotional balancing	Undoing; reaction formation; displacement	
Sliding meanings and valuations	Humor, wisdom	Exaggeration; minimization; devaluation; reaction formation	
Arranging information into decision trees	Problem solving	Rationalization	
Revising working models	Learning; identifications; acceptance	Externalization; introjection	
Practicing new modes of thinking and acting	Replace previous automatic reactions with new ways of responding	Counterphobic behavioral patterns	

From Horowitz, M.: Introduction to Psychodynamics, 1988, p. 202.

Table 17.9
Some "Defects" of the Histrionic Personality Style Prototype
and How They Might be Counteracted in Psychotherapy

Function	Style as "Defect"	Therapeutic Counter
Perception	Global or selective inattention	Ask for details
Representation	Impressionistic rather than accurate	"Abreaction" and reconstruction
Translation of images and enactions into words	Limited	Encourage talk / Provide verbal labels
Associations	Limited by inhibitions	Encourage production
	Misinterpretations based on schematic stereotypes, deflected from reality to wishes and fears	Repetition / Clarification
Problem solving	Short circuit to rapid but often erroneous conclusions	Keep subject open / Interpretations
	Avoidance of topic when emotions are unbearable	Support

From Horowitz, M.: Stress Response Syndromes, 1997b, p. 165.

Table 17.10
Some "Defects" of the Compulsive Personality Style Prototype
and How They Might be Counteracted in Psychotherapy

Function	Style as "Defect"	Therapeutic Counter
Perception	Detailed and factual	Ask for overall impressions and statements about emotional experiences
Representation	Isolation of ideas from emotions	Link emotional meanings to ideational meanings
Translation of images into words	Misses emotional meaning in a rapid transition to partial word meanings	Focus attention on images and felt reactions to them
Associations	Shifts sets of meanings back and forth	Hold attention to the topic Interpretation of defense and warded-off meanings
Problem solving	Endless rumination without reaching decisions	Interpretation of reasons for warding off clear decisions

From Horowitz, M.: Stress Response Syndromes, 1997b, p. 180.

Table 17.11
Some "Defects" of the Narcissistic Personality Style Prototype
and How They Might be Counteracted in Psychotherapy

Function	Style as "Defect"	Therapeutic Counteraction
Perception	Focuses on praise and blame	Avoids being provoked into either praising or blaming but is realistically supportive
	Denies "wounding" information	Uses tactful timing and wording to counteract denials by selective confrontation
Representation	Dislocates bad traits from self to other	Repeatedly reviews in order to clarify who is who in terms of the sequence of acts and intentions in a recalled interpersonal transaction
Translation of images into words	Slides meanings	Consistently defines meanings; encourages decisions as to most relevant meanings and how much to weight them
Associations	Overbalances when finding routes to self-enhancement	Holds to other meanings: cautiously deflates grandiose beliefs
Problem solving	Distorts reality to maintain self-esteem	Points out distortion while (tactfully) encouraging and supporting reality fidelity
	Obtains illusory gratifications	Supports patient's self-esteem during period of surrender of illusory gratification (helped by the real interest of the therapist, by identification with the therapist, and by identification with the therapist as a noncorrupt person). Finds out about and gradually discourages unrealistic gratifications from therapy.
	Forgives self too easily	Helps develop appropriate sense of responsibility

From Horowitz, M.: Stress Response Syndromes, 1997b, p. 187.

has a phobic avoidance of a situation that would be adaptive to confront, but which is associated with traumatic anxiety, the therapist might encourage desensitization.

Similarly, biological treatments, including psychopharmacological agents, have to be considered. Use of antianxiety agents may be helpful to people who have overwhelming anxiety; however, some memory impairment and other side-effects may be a consequence of using certain agents. Excessive or prolonged use can lead not only to psychological addiction, but conceivably might slow down a working-through process. In my own experience, I have preferred to prescribe very small doses and single doses rather than using medication routinely every six hours or so.

Some people may have a major depressive disorder precipitated by traumatic life events, and the use of antidepressants is considered in such disorders. While the person is in a severely depressed mood it may be difficult or impossible for them to process all the extended meanings of a traumatic event. Medication may lift the severe vegetative signs, which in turn may be followed by marked progress in the psychological dimensions.

Family therapy may also be very important, not only for families who have been jointly exposed to serious life events, such as earthquakes or floods, but also to help integrate an individual who has had an unusual experience that differs substantially from other family members.

PRESCRIPTIVE TREATMENT AND MANAGED CARE

The treatment of some cases of PTSD will require a consideration of personality-based problems, and the stress by personality interaction. This consideration goes two ways: What is the contribution of prestress-event temperament and character to the patient's reactions to the current trauma, and what contribution may working through or failure to work through the current trauma make to future identity organization. Most managed care settings, at this writing, attempt to limit treatment length. This means that problems of these interventions desensitize emotional associations, increase coping efforts, and restore equilibrium by providing transient support with interpretation of any irrational belief, personality are often avoided, because assessing enduring traits takes interview time, and careful formulation takes clinician time. A route to excellent care may still be followed, but the patient may have to continue on a fee-for-service basis if insurance will not cover the important working through of stress by personality interactions. Moreover, the patient can have a short series of immediate sessions to facilitate emotional work and adaptation to life after the trauma, with a follow-up and then additional later sessions as needed to work through the personality and identity reschematization issues.

SUMMARY

Traumatic events cause a complex cascade of interacting effects. A trauma is seldom a discrete event, even though a catastrophe may be named, as in saying "my life changed after the tornado." The damage caused may be to finances, family ties, and personal meanings. The traumatized person may disrupt other supports as part of a reaction to the main stressor event. Phases of response may not be linear, as in gradually reduced symptoms, but episodic, as in periods of intrusive images and pangs of urgent feelings or impulses after a time of seeming quiescence due to avoidances and inhibitions. Moreover, meaning plays a role in personal appraisals of events and their consequences, and habits, traits, and styles of personality become entwined with the trauma in causing effects. For these reasons, PTSD cases require careful clinical evaluation, formulations, combinations of individually oriented interventions, and follow-up. With such a careful approach, excellent results may often be achieved.

REFERENCES

Bowlby, J. (1969). *Attachment and loss: Attachment* (Vol. 1). New York: Basic Books.

Breuer, J., & Freud, S. (1957–1974). Studies on hysteria. In J. Strachey (Ed. and Trans.), *The standard edition of the complete psychological works of Sigmund Freud* (Vol. 2). London: Hogarth Press. (Original work published 1895)

Freud, S. (1920). Beyond the pleasure principle. In J. Strachey (Ed. and Trans.), *The standard edition of the complete psychological works of Sigmund Freud* (Vol. 18). London: Hogarth Press.

Horowitz, M.J. (1987). *States of mind* (2nd ed.). New York: Plenum Press.

Horowitz, M.J. (1988). *Introduction to psychodynamics.* New York: Basic Books.

Horowitz, M.J. (1997a). *Formulation as a basis for planning psychotherapy.* Washington, DC: American Psychiatric Press.

Horowitz, M.J. (1997b). *Stress response syndromes* (3rd ed.). Northvale, NJ: Aronson.

Horowitz, M.J. (1998). *Cognitive psychodynamics: From conflict to character.* New York: Wiley.

Horowitz, M.J. (1999). *Manual for treatment of stress response syndromes.* San Francisco: University of California at San Francisco.

Horowitz, M.J., Marmar, C., Krupnick, J., Wilner, N., Kaltreider, N., & Wallerstein, R. (1998). *Personality styles and brief psychotherapy.* Northvale, NJ: Aronson.

CHAPTER 18

Behavior Therapy

TERRI L. WEAVER, HEIDI S. RESNICK,
SHIRLEY M. GLYNN, and DAVID W. FOY

THIS CHAPTER on behavior therapy for posttraumatic stress disorder (PTSD) is intended to provide a practical overview of cognitive behavioral methods that are currently in use or under intensive development for treating psychological problems experienced by survivors of extreme or traumatic events. The orientation of our work is optimistic because it reflects the considerable progress made in the past 10 years in the development and validation of behavioral treatments for a relatively new disorder that was first included in psychiatric nosology in 1980. Considerable progress has also been made in the empirical validation of PTSD diagnostic criteria to identify appropriate criterion A events and to establish the universality of symptomatic features across survivor populations and types of traumatic events.

In the sections that follow, we present an interactional cognitive-behavioral conceptual model in which principles of classical and operant conditioning, as well as principles of information processing theory, are incorporated to explain the development of PTSD symptoms and to guide assessment and treatment planning. We also provide an overview of multisite field trial research, which was conducted to help establish the current *DSM-IV* formulation of PTSD. Three primary types of behavioral treatment—exposure, cognitive restructuring, and skills training—are described and updated with respect to specific examples of their clinical applications. The use of prolonged exposure as a primary treatment approach for rape-related PTSD is detailed in a case illustration. Last, alternative behavioral treatment options are described.

Funding for Dr. Weaver's portion of this chapter was provided in part by the National Institutes of Mental Health Grant NIH-1-R01-MH51509-03, Patricia A. Resick, Ph.D., principal investigator. Points of view or opinions expressed within this manuscript are those of the authors and do not necessarily represent the official position or policies of the National Institutes of Mental Health.

CONCEPTUALIZATION OF THE DISORDER

Since the inception of the field of traumatic stress studies, researchers have been intrigued by the critical issue of why some individuals develop PTSD and others do not, even when they have been exposed to the same life-threatening event. The evolution of etiologic models of traumatic stress responses has transitioned from early, single-factor models, emphasizing either the predominant role of personal preexisting vulnerabilities (stress evaporation), or a purely environmental model highlighting traumatic stressor severity (residual stress), to current prevailing PTSD conceptualizations that incorporate interactions between three domains of explanatory variables—(1) preexisting personal variables, (2) traumatic stressor exposure characteristics, and (3) posttrauma environment, including loss of psychological and tangible resources (cf. Jones & Barlow, 1990).

Mowrer's two-factor theory (1960) provides a learning-based foundation for behavioral approaches to PTSD by explaining the origin and persistence of symptoms of PTSD through the operation of both classical and operant conditioning principles. In this formulation the initial trauma reaction becomes a classically conditioned emotional response, and subsequent avoidance responses are motivated by fear, and reinforced by fear reduction. Other learning principles that have been postulated as factors in the maintenance of anxiety and distress include stimulus generalization and higher order conditioning. By the process of stimulus generalization, new stimuli that are similar to the conditioned stimuli that elicit anxiety may also acquire this capacity. Higher-order conditioning is a process whereby previously neutral stimuli that are paired with trauma-related conditioned stimuli, such as cognitions about the event, may acquire an independent capacity to elicit fear. Through these processes, a great variety of stimuli in the environment may come to elicit anxiety and motivate further restriction of activity for trauma victims.

An advantage of this basic learning model is that it predicts that severity of distress will be directly related to the intensity of trauma exposure. This dose-response relationship between trauma exposure and related distress is consistent with findings from many etiologic studies in adults (e.g., Resnick, Kilpatrick, Dansky, Saunders, & Best, 1993), as well as children and adolescents (e.g., Foy, Madvig, Pynoos, & Camilleri, 1996). Treatment strategies based on the learning model include strategies that help the survivor to cope with the resulting anxiety and fear that they experience when encountering trauma-related cues, such as in stress-innoculation training (SIT) (Kilpatrick, Veronen, & Resick, 1982), or assist the survivor in enduring the anxiety and fear until it begins to dissipate, such as in prolonged exposure therapy (PE) (Foa, Hearst, Dancu, Hembree, & Jaycox, 1994).

This basic learning model is limited, however, because it cannot account for positive cases of PTSD following low exposure, nor does it account for noncases among those individuals who are highly exposed. In addition, although learning theories appear to be particularly well equipped to explain the development of trauma-related fear, anxiety, and sexual dysfunction, there are a number of trauma victims (e.g., individuals who were sexually abused in childhood), who do not present with primary complaints of fear. These individuals are often more disturbed by negative thoughts such as blame and guilt and non-fear-related emotions such as disgust. Therefore, other theorists (e.g., Chemtob, Roitblat, Hamada, Carlson, & Twentyman, 1988; Foa, Steketee, & Rothbaum, 1989; Kubany & Manke, 1995; Resick & Schnicke, 1993) have utilized information processing theory and emphasized the importance of a more thorough examination of the cognitive meaning of the trauma as a way of explaining these assault-related sequelae.

For example, Resick and Schnicke (1993) suggest that trauma survivors suffer from a variety of reactions in addition to fear and these reactions often prevent them from integrating the event because they are inconsistent with preexisting schema (cognitive structures representing knowledge about the self or about the world). Instead of integration, the event is either changed to fit prior beliefs (e.g., assimilation—a rape is reclassified as, "not a rape because I knew the rapist") or prior beliefs are altered to an extreme degree to encompass the event (e.g., overaccommodation: After being raped by someone known, "I can't trust anyone"). Negative cognitions such as these may then serve as triggers for other negative self-appraisals (e.g., "I deserve to have bad things happen to me") and maladaptive behaviors (e.g., engaging in high-risk behaviors), which may then contribute to anxiety, depression, shame, and lowered self-worth, all of which may coexist with PTSD (Kubany & Manke, 1995). Drawing upon information-processing theories, cognitive-restructuring treatment strategies are used to help the survivor to challenge these beliefs and to develop a view of the self and the world, which is more flexible and balanced, assisting in the integration of the traumatic event. Treatment strategies utilizing cognitive restructuring include cognitive-processing therapy (Resick & Schnicke, 1993), cognitive-processing therapy for sexual abuse (Chard, Weaver, & Resick, 1997), and cognitive therapy for trauma-related guilt (Kubany & Manke, 1995).

Given the complexity of the etiological factors implicated in the development of PTSD, our cognitive-behavioral conceptualization of PTSD (Foy, 1992) is an interactional model that is used to account for the interplay of trauma characteristics (agent), personal factors (host), and other factors (environment) in the development of acute or chronic PTSD. Such a model allows for individual differences on other important factors, such as prior trauma history, available social support, and cognitive attributions made about the cause and meaning of the trauma (Foa & Meadows, 1997) to be incorporated in case conceptualization and treatment. Before discussing the treatment strategies in detail, a review of the diagnostic category of PTSD will be reviewed.

DIAGNOSTIC ISSUES AND PROBLEMS (*DSM-IV*)

PTSD Update

Diagnostic criteria included in the fourth edition of the American Psychiatric Association's *Diagnostic and Statistical Manual of Mental Disorders (DSM-IV)*

(APA, 1994) differ somewhat from those in the previous *DSM-III-R* edition (APA, 1987). Kilpatrick et al. (1998) found gaps in existing PTSD literature to indicate that several aspects of the criteria specified in *DSM-III-R* had not been sufficiently evaluated empirically, particularly among populations not exposed to combat stressors. Specifically, in terms of criterion A, which defines stressor events that may lead to PTSD symptomatology, evidence from epidemiological studies (Breslau, Davis, Andreski, & Peterson, 1991; Kessler, Sonnega, Bromet, Hughes, & Nelson, 1995; Norris, 1992; Resnick, Kilpatrick, Dansky, Saunders, & Best, 1993) showed that such events were not rare, as implied in *DSM-III-R*. Moreover, there was a paucity of research evaluating the degree to which events currently excluded from criterion A (e.g., bereavement, illness) might be associated with symptoms of PTSD as defined by criteria B (reexperiencing), C (avoidance), and D (arousal). Finally, the prevalence and types of initial distress associated with exposure to criterion A events had not been studied. Further data on the validity of the clusters of B, C, and D symptoms, and the requirements for the longitudinal course of PTSD (e.g., that symptoms persist for at least one month) were needed for subsequent description in the *DSM-IV* (Davidson et al., 1996).

To address these issues, a multisite PTSD field trial study was conducted (Kilpatrick et al., in press). A major goal of the study was to empirically examine associations between a variety of stressor events and PTSD symptoms. In addition to considering events that were included in *DSM-III-R* criterion A, designated as "High Magnitude" events, Kilpatrick et al. also evaluated rates of PTSD symptoms associated with events that were excluded from criterion A, such as bereavement and chronic illness, designated as low-magnitude events. Factor structure of the B, C, and D symptom groupings was examined, and different duration options were evaluated for criterion E in terms of effects on overall prevalence. A total of 528 subjects, including 128 nontreatment seekers from two of the five study sites completed structured interview assessments of lifetime incidents of combat, accident, disaster, contact sexual assaults, physical assaults, and homicide of a close friend or family member; as well as past year reports of serious illness of self or a family member, death of a close friend or family member, marital discord, or job loss or financial difficulties. Of note, the field trial study was not a population-based study but rather, was a study designed to examine the phenomenology and etiology of PTSD within a (largely) treatment-seeking group.

Data indicated that the majority of subjects experienced a combination of high- and low-magnitude events (71%). Only 13 percent of the sample reported low-magnitude events, whereas 15 percent reported high-magnitude events alone, and 1 percent reported no events. A majority of subjects (64%) had experienced more than one high-magnitude event. Lifetime rate of PTSD (defined by *DSM-III-R* symptom criteria) was 45 percent among the full sample, 78 percent of whom were treatment seeking. Results related to high-magnitude events indicated that 75 percent occurred prior to age 18, with 50 percent occurring prior to age 11. Rates of PTSD were highest in association with physical or sexual assault, or combat experiences. Among the group of 66 respondents with low-magnitude events only, there were eight PTSD positive cases (12%), six of whom reported symptoms specific to deaths or serious illnesses in the past year. Two other individuals met PTSD criteria in response to being fired and being divorced, respectively. Both reported that the circumstances were sudden and unexpected. These data indicate that PTSD was rare in the absence of high-magnitude events, and occurred primarily in situations related to death or serious illness.

Results of the PTSD Field Trial, along with reviews of other studies addressing validity of symptom criteria (Davidson et al., 1996), were used to guide modifications in criteria included in *DSM-IV* (APA, 1994). Criterion A no longer specifies that the stressor event be outside the realm of usual human experience. The stressor criterion description does emphasize specific event characteristics as well as the individual's emotional response, and could include death, illness, or physical injury that may result from causes other than assault, accident, disaster, or combat.

Grouping criteria were reevaluated based on data from the Field Trial study and other factor analytic data (e.g., Keane, 1993). Based on this reevaluation, symptom item D6 "physiological reactivity on exposure to cues that symbolize or resemble an aspect of the traumatic event" is now included as B5 within the reexperiencing cluster of symptoms (p. 428). In addition to the factor analytic data, this symptom item conceptually reflects arousal in response to reminders rather than general arousal. Thus, to meet criterion B, one of five symptoms must have been persistently experienced since the event. Criterion C still requires the presence of three of seven symptoms (thus requiring at least one of the "numbing" type symptoms to meet the criterion), and criterion D now requires two or more of five symptoms of persistent arousal. There are also some phrasing changes in descriptions of symptoms including specification of internal or external cues as precipitants of distress.

DSM-IV specifies a duration of required symptoms (criterion E) for more than one month to receive a PTSD diagnosis as data on the symptom duration was supported by the field trial. The disorder is classified as acute if the duration is greater than one month, but less than three months, or chronic if the duration is three months or greater. In addition, delayed onset is specified in cases in which symptom onset is at least six months after the stressor event. A final important change in *DSM-IV* is the inclusion of criterion F, which specifies that "The disturbance causes clinically significant distress or impairment in social, occupational, or other important areas of functioning" (p. 429).

INTRODUCTION OF ACUTE STRESS DISORDER IN *DSM-IV* (308.3)

The *DSM-IV* includes a new diagnostic category to be assigned to individuals who display a pattern of anxiety, dissociative, and other symptoms following a criterion A stressor as defined earlier. The disturbance must last for at least two days and not more than four weeks and must have onset within four weeks of the criterion A event. The *DSM-IV* specifies that the individual has three or more dissociative symptoms (that may have begun during the trauma exposure). Symptoms include: (1) subjective sense of numbing, detachment, or absence of emotional responsiveness; (2) reduction in awareness of surroundings; (3) derealization; (4) depersonalization; and (5) dissociative amnesia. In addition, at least one reexperiencing symptom, one symptom of active avoidance of reminders; symptom(s) of increased arousal; and impairment in social, occupational, or other areas of functioning are required.

The utility of this diagnostic category remains to be evaluated. It is advantageous to be able to assign a diagnosis (that does not automatically imply chronicity) that will allow early interventions posttrauma. Previously there was no such category, and individuals may have been diagnosed with an adjustment disorder, despite the severity of the stressor event. Consistent assessment of criterion A2 may be useful to determine how well acute stress disorder captures the pattern of initial responses posttrauma. It is possible that the heavy emphasis on dissociative symptoms might actually exclude many individuals who would otherwise meet symptom criteria. In the Field Trial findings, numbing and dissociative symptoms were identified as components of both the acute and longer-term PTSD responses. However, acute panic and other positive symptoms of PTSD were more prominent.

COMORBIDITY: OTHER ANXIETY, MOOD, SUBSTANCE ABUSE DISORDERS

In a large scale epidemiological study of PTSD prevalence and comorbidity, Kessler and colleagues (1995) examined rates of specific anxiety, affective, substance use, and conduct disorder separately for men and women. Among men, PTSD was associated with significantly increased odds of all other anxiety disorders including generalized anxiety disorder (GAD), panic disorder, simple phobia, and agoraphobia. Rates of major depression, dysthymia, and mania were also significantly greater among men with PTSD, as was conduct disorder. Rates of both alcohol abuse/dependence and drug abuse/dependence were significantly greater in association with PTSD. Approximately 88 percent of the men with PTSD had at least one comorbid diagnosis, while 55 percent of the men without PTSD had at least one of the other *DSM* diagnoses.

Among women, rates of all other anxiety disorders were significantly greater in association with PTSD. For women, agoraphobia and panic disorder were associated with the greatest increased odds in association with presence of PTSD. Major depression and the other affective-disorder diagnoses occurred at increased rates among those with PTSD, as did alcohol and drug abuse and conduct disorders. Rate of any other diagnosis among women with PTSD was 79 percent versus 46 percent among those without PTSD.

Kessler et al. (1995) also attempted to estimate order of onset of PTSD or other comorbid disorders by comparing age of onset of comorbid disorders to upper and lower bound age estimates for onset of a given disorder among individuals who reported only one disorder (e.g., depression). Using this method they estimated PTSD most often occurred prior to affective disorders and substance-use disorders, and more often followed the onset of other anxiety disorders. Among women, it was estimated that PTSD more often preceded conduct disorder whereas the reverse was true for men. It should be noted that the accuracy of these estimates of onset of disorder were also dependent upon the extent to which traumatic stressors occurring in childhood were sensitively detected.

These comorbidity data were consistent with previous reports indicating the majority of those with PTSD have histories of other comorbid diagnoses (Breslau et al., 1991; Kulka et al., 1990) and emphasize the importance of the need for comprehensive assessment of diagnoses of major Axis I and Axis II diagnoses. The presence of high rates of comorbidity also suggest the importance of monitoring relevant symptom areas over the course of treatment. Further research is needed to determine whether comorbid conditions improve significantly with successful treatment of PTSD. There is some preliminary evidence that depression comorbid with PTSD remits during the treatment of PTSD for female rape victims and survivors of childhood sexual abuse (Chard, 1996; Resick, Nishith, & Astin, 1996). In some cases, particularly with substance abuse disorders, the use of multicomponent treatment strategies targeting PTSD and other comorbidity profiles is indicated.

COMPREHENSIVE ASSESSMENT OF PTSD IN STRESSOR AND SYMPTOM DOMAINS

Before beginning a course of behavior therapy, the foregoing discussion underscores the need for a comprehensive approach to the assessment of factors, which influence the course of treatment. In fact, pretreatment and ongoing assessment really forms the underpinnings of behavior therapy. Although time, assessment conditions, and resources may limit a comprehensive evaluation, ideally, behavioral assessment is multimodal, because measurements are made of two or more modes of behavior (e.g., assessment of thoughts, feelings, and behavior) and multimethod, because two or more methods are used to gather information (e.g., utilization of structured interviews, behavioral observation, and client self-report) (Spiegler & Guevremont, 1998). Relevant factors for assessment include: the stressor event exposure, PTSD and comorbid diagnostic conditions, and nonexposure variables such as social support.

STRESSOR ASSESSMENT

Assessment of the stressor characteristics includes assessing aspects of the experience that brought the client to treatment (referred to here as the index event) and assessing for prior trauma history, which may be amplifying the response to the index event. Emerging evidence has found that traumatized groups, such as battered women (Astin, Ogland-Hand, Coleman, & Foy, 1995; Weaver & Clum, 1996), rape survivors (Resnick, Kilpatrick, et al., 1993), sexual-abuse survivors (Russell, 1983; Wyatt, Guthrie, & Notgrass, 1992), and combat veterans (King, King, Foy, & Gudanowski, 1996), frequently have multiple trauma experiences.

It is critical that assessment of stressor event exposure, like efforts to assess symptoms, be conducted thoroughly, and in a reliable and valid fashion. Several structured interview and some self-report instruments have been developed to assess comprehensive stressor event history: the Potential Stressful Events Interview (PSEI) (Kilpatrick et al., 1998); the National Women's Study Event History—PTSD Module (Kilpatrick, Resnick, Saunders, & Best, 1989); the Traumatic Stress Schedule (TSS) (Norris, 1990); and the Trauma Assessment for Adults (TAA) (Resnick, 1996). Although it is beyond the scope of the present chapter to present a detailed overview of trauma assessment instruments and strategies, other recently published resources are available for this purpose (Norris & Riad, 1996; Resnick, Falsetti, Kilpatrick, & Freedy, 1996; Stamm, 1996).

Given the possibility that the victim may present with exposures to different traumatic events (e.g., a rape and a childhood history of physical abuse) or multiple exposures to a single type of traumatic event (e.g., multiple combat experiences), the behavior therapist may be uncertain of which event to focus on in therapy. Typically, clients are able to identify which experience was most traumatic for them and this experience should be treated first. It is also likely that this worst event will be evidenced in the content-related PTSD symptoms (e.g., flashbacks, intrusive memories, cue-related avoidance). Often, after the worst experience is treated, the recovery generalizes to the other trauma experiences. However, even when the generalization does not occur, treatment targeting secondary traumatic events tends to proceed more quickly after treating the worst trauma, as requisite skills/techniques have been mastered.

PTSD ASSESSMENT AND ASSESSMENT OF COMORBID DISORDERS

There are a number of clinical diagnostic interviews that can be used to assess for PTSD and possible comorbid conditions of depression, panic, or substance abuse. These semistructured interviews include the Structured Clinical Interview for *DSM-IV* (SCID) (First, Spitzer, Gibbon, & Williams, 1996) and the Diagnostic Interview Schedule (DIS) (Robins, Helzer, Cottler, & Goldring, 1988). These semistructured interviews yield a categorical diagnosis for these Axis I disorders. Axis II disorders can be assessed using the Structured Clinical Interview for *DSM-III-R* Personality Disorders (SCID-II) (Spitzer, Williams, Gibbon, & First, 1990).

Additional information regarding the severity of the PTSD can be determined using a semistructured interview, which was specifically designed for the assessment of PTSD: the Clinician Administered Assessment for PTSD (CAPS) (Blake et al., 1996). This semistructured interview yields a frequency and an intensity score for each of the PTSD criteria, permitting an examination of symptom severity. There are also several self-report instruments, which provide continuous ratings of PTSD severity including the PTSD Symptom Scale (PSS) (Foa, Riggs, Dancu, & Rothbaum, 1993) and the Modified PTSD Symptom Scale (MPSS-SR) (Resick, Falsetti, Resnick, & Kilpatrick, 1991). One efficient assessment approach would be to have clients complete the self-report instrument first, and proceed with the more intensive diagnostic interviews if they are endorsing a number of symptoms. Additional self-report instruments for the assessment of other comorbid conditions include the Beck Depression

Inventory (BDI) (Beck, Steer, Ball, & Ranieri, 1996) for depression and the Physical Reactions Scale (Falsetti & Resnick, 1992) for symptoms of panic. Self-report instruments are also useful for evaluating symptom change during the course of treatment (see case study for a model for assessment).

ASSESSMENT OF NONEXPOSURE FACTORS

Social support is increasingly recognized as important in the recovery from noncombat and combat trauma. In examining the stress reactions of civil disaster workers, McCammon, Durham, Allison, and Williamson (1988) found that those with the greatest perceived levels of social support reported significantly lower levels of PTSD symptoms. Similarly, Madakasira and O'Brien (1987) found that, among survivors of a hurricane, the only significant predictor of severe PTSD at five months was lower social support. Neither demographic nor hurricane exposure variables were significantly predictive. With regard to rape survivors, Kimerling and Calhoun (1994) reported that social support was related to decreased psychological distress in the year after an assault, and Harvey, Orbuch, Chwalisz, and Garwood (1991) found that confiding to a helpful (rather than critical) friend or relative was associated with positive adjustment after a sexual assault. In terms of recovery from combat-related PTSD, Solomon, Mikulincer, and Avitzur (1988) reported that the availability of social support led to an improvement in PTSD symptoms among combat veterans over a two-year period. Assessment of the client's level of social support can be conducted using the Social Adjustment Scale (SAS) (Weissman & Paykel, 1974).

An assessment of the client's strategies for coping with the PTSD and stressors in general, is also important to assess in the pretreatment interview. Patterns of PTSD-related coping can be gleaned from the client's responses to the avoidance questions on the CAPS or other PTSD diagnostic interviews. Some typical types of avoidance include overworking (e.g., clients working three part-time jobs and going to school), excessive house cleaning, and utilization of drugs or alcohol. These patterns of avoidance suggest that the client copes by limiting negative affective experiences, and this pattern will have to be addressed in treatment. In contrast, clients may have established more adaptive methods of coping, such as using exercise and seeking social support. Regardless, coping style will have to be considered in treatment planning (see section on case conceptualization and treatment planning).

TREATMENT STRATEGIES

Behaviorally based treatments for victims of trauma can be categorized according to exposure, cognitive restructuring, and coping-skills types. A fourth type is represented by a combination of the three basic forms, and this is most frequently used in actual clinical settings. All the treatments include a didactic component educating the survivor about the diagnosis of PTSD and any comorbid disorders (Falsetti, 1997). This educational opportunity includes a discussion of the symptoms, base rates, and etiological origins of PTSD. This discussion also focuses heavily on the role of avoidance in the maintenance of PTSD, along with predictions that clients may be tempted to avoid treatment, given the growing association that develops between the treatment setting, the therapist, and the memories of the trauma. Similarly, initial sessions in each of the treatments focus on orienting and educating the client to the treatment process and presenting data on treatment efficacy, highlighting the collaborative and educative process endemic to behavior therapy (Spiegler & Guevremont, 1998). One controlled clinical trial (Resick et al., 1996) has successfully utilized a clip from a television show and newspaper articles, describing the treatments, to educate incoming clients to the treatment process. Each of the treatments will be described in detail and the decision-making process regarding the choice of a treatment option will follow.

EXPOSURE TREATMENTS

There are now at least seven randomized controlled trials of exposure therapy that have reported encouraging results for significant reductions in PTSD or PTSD symptoms (see Table 18.1).

Procedurally, there is consistency across clinical reports of exposure therapy for PTSD, because 10 to 15 reexposure trials are used to achieve reduction of conditioned negative arousal (Foy, 1992). Treatment sessions range from 60 to 120 minutes in length and are usually scheduled on a weekly or twice-weekly basis. Relaxation procedures may be used before and after exposure trials. Some clinical reports describe a therapist-directed exposure procedure (e.g., Keane & Kaloupek, 1982), whereas more recent accounts, such as our case illustration in this chapter, feature a client self-directed exposure style.

Foa (Foa, Hearst, et al., 1994) developed a prolonged exposure (PE) therapy manual that combines flooding and systematic desensitization techniques. The goal is to expose clients to the conditioned fear stimuli utilizing imaginal and in vivo techniques, thus reducing the avoidant behaviors and decreasing the fear network (Foa & Kozak, 1986). In PE, clients attend between 9 and 12 ninety-minute sessions during which they recount the details of the assault repeatedly in the present tense describing their full sensory experience. Clients are asked to monitor their fear/anxiety level throughout this imaginal exposure using a subjective unit of distress (SUDS) rating. Outside of the session clients systematically conduct in vivo exposures to cues in the environment that they have been avoiding. The client is asked to stay in the safe, but fear producing, situation for at least 45 minutes or until the anxiety level is significantly reduced on the SUDS rating scale. Often the client will enlist a coach, someone who stays with them, initially, and subsequently, plays a smaller and smaller role.

COGNITIVE RESTRUCTURING STRATEGIES

Cognitive restructuring strategies deal with the meaning assigned to the traumatic experience(s) by the survivor and elaborations on the meanings of the

Table 18.1
Randomized Controlled Trials of Exposure Therapy for PTSD

Study	Setting	Subject Population	Intervention	Results	Measures
Keane, Fairbank, Caddell, & Zimering (1989)	Mixed	24 male veterans	Implosive therapy (IT; relaxation and exposure) vs. wait list [WL])	IT better than WL at posttreatment and at 6-month follow-up	PTSD re-experiencing, depression, anxiety
Brom, Kieber, & Defares (1989)	Out-pt.	112 survivors of various traumas	Traumatic de-sensitization (TD; relaxation and exposure) vs. hynotherapy vs. psychodynamic therapy vs. WL	All 3 groups equal and better than WL at posttreatment and 3-month follow-up	Intrusion and avoid-ance symptoms, gen-eral distress
Cooper & Clum (1989)	Out-pt.	22 male veterans	Flooding (F) and customary care (CC; individual and group treat-ment) vs. CC	F plus CC better than CC at post-treatment and at 3-month follow-up	Anxiety, sleep distur-bance, nightmares, avoidance
Boudewyns & Hyer (1990)	In-pt.	58 male veterans	Exposure vs. supportive counseling (SC)	Exposure better than SC at 6-month follow-up	Composite adjustment
Foa, Rothbaum, Riggs, & Murdock (1991)	Out-pt.	45 female sexual assault survivors	Exposure vs. stress inoculation training (SIT) vs. SC vs. WL	Exposure was equal to SIT, which was better than SC, which was equal to WL at posttreatment; Exposure better than all others at 3-month follow-up	PTSD B, C, D, symptom clusters
Foa, Freund, Hembree, Dancu, Franklin, Perry, Riggs, & Moinar (1994)	Out-pt.	76 female assault survivors	Exposure vs. SIT vs. exposure and SIT vs. WL	All 3 groups equal and better than WL at posttreatment and at 6-month follow-up	PTSD B, C, D, symptom clusters
Glynn et al. (1997)	Out-pt.	42 male veterans	Exposure vs. ex-posure plus be-havioral family therapy (BFT) vs. WL	Exposure was equal to exposure plus BFT better than WL	PTSD B & D symptom clusters

original event(s) that adversely affect the individual's current life assumptions about safety, trust, and power/control.

Variously termed cognitive restructuring (Carroll & Foy, 1992), cognitive processing (Resick & Schnicke, 1992), or emotional processing (Foa, Hearst, et al., 1994), these cognitive strategies involve systematic therapeutic examination of the individual's attributions of predictability, controllability, and culpability about the traumatic experience and their relationships to current life assumptions. Pretrauma, impact, and posttraumatic time frames are used to track critical changes made in life assumptions that may reflect overgeneralization of fear from the traumatic event(s). The therapist's role is to guide the client's self-exploration of meanings assigned to the traumatic experience(s) and assist in challenging misinterpretations and overgeneralizations that may contribute to trauma-related symtomatology.

One cognitive behavior treatment, currently under examination using a controlled randomized design for the treatment of rape survivors, is Cognitive Processing Therapy (CPT) (Resick & Schnicke, 1993). CPT is a 12-session treatment protocol, specifically designed to address cognitive distortions associated with the traumatic event. In addition, CPT does include some exposure, albeit written exposure. After the introductory sessions, the client writes out a complete description of the trauma experience in full detail. (If there are multiple experiences of trauma, the survivor writes about the most distressing experience.) After completing the writing, the client is instructed to read this account every day between sessions and to feel all feelings associated with the account. In the session, the client reads the account to the therapist and begins identifying problematic cognitions that have been created or reinforced by the assault. This process is repeated with the client rewriting the account at least one more time, and, when necessary, writing the account a third time or writing the account of another incident.

In the second phase of treatment, the therapist helps the client address "stuck points" or cognitive distortions utilizing homework sheets for Antecedents, Behaviors, and Consequences (ABC) (1) challenging questions, (2) faulty thinking patterns, and (3) challenging beliefs. After self-blame and other assimilation issues have been resolved, focus is placed on maladaptive thoughts in the areas of safety, trust, power/control, self-esteem, and intimacy. For example, some clients (after a rape) report having the thought that all men are dangerous. This may be a preexisting thought that was reinforced by the rape, or it may be a thought that was created and overgeneralized from the rape. By working with the homework sheets, the client and therapist challenge this thought in a number of different ways. For instance, the client may be asked if the thought was based on habitual thinking rather than fact, if the thought was created by over generalization of the assault experience, and/or if the thought was more of a certainty or a probability. The client is then asked to restate the thought in a more balanced format, such as, "Some men are dangerous, but all men are not dangerous." This challenging process and thought reformation is addressed in each of the five modules with an individualized emphasis for each client. Resick and Schnicke (1993) have utilized CPT in both group and individual therapy formats with equal long-term significant gains in rape survivors.

Resick and colleagues are currently comparing the relative effectiveness of CPT with PE, and a minimal contact support condition for the treatment of rape-related PTSD and depression. Preliminary findings of 47 participants completing treatment revealed that both CPT and PE resulted in significant decreases in diagnoses of PTSD and depression, compared with the wait-list condition (Resick et al., 1996). With the inclusion of more participants, differential efficacy for the two treatments on symptom domains can be examined.

Chard (Chard et al., 1997) has altered CPT to create Cognitive Processing Therapy for Sexual Abuse (CPT-SA) for the treatment of adult survivors of incest and childhood sexual abuse and is in the process of completing a controlled clinical trial on the treatment. Pilot data show that this treatment offered in either a group/individual or individual alone, format, resulted in at least a 50 percent decrease in symptoms of PTSD and depression for 95 percent of the clients (Chard, 1996).

Kubany and colleagues have developed cognitive therapy for trauma-related guilt (CT-TRG) (Kubany & Manke, 1995), which includes education about guilt, a debriefing/exposure phase in which clients retell their story to set the context for the event, and a cognitive restructuring phase, in which faulty conclusions related to specific guilt issues are addressed. Authors note that this treatment is not designed as a total treatment package for PTSD, but rather, is a specific treatment intervention, targeting a very important trauma-related symptom. At this time, a controlled clinical trial has not been completed on this treatment.

Skills Training

A third behavioral strategy for dealing with problems associated with victimization is a skills-training approach. Early clinical reports (e.g., Kilpatrick et al., 1982) incorporated relaxation training into treatment of trauma victims. Teaching relaxation skills to reduce unpleasant levels of autonomic arousal represents an additional coping strategy or skill that clients can then use under a variety of conditions. Another important area in which skills training is often indicated involves family or dyadic functioning. Communication skills training can be employed to treat predictable problems in intimate relationships following victimization. In particular, survivors' self-disclosure skills and spouses' active listening skills can be targeted to counteract the frequent tendency in victim dyads to avoid discussion of intense negative feelings associated with the traumatic experience (Carroll, Rueger, Foy, & Donahoe, 1985).

Training in other kinds of coping skills may also be indicated in individual cases. Anger management, problem solving, and assertion represent other kinds of specific skills for which structured behavioral training methods are available. More recently (Foy & Ruzek, in press), attention has been paid to other skill areas, such as coping with symptoms (e.g., Subjective Units of Discomfort Scale [SUDS] monitoring and thought stopping) and relapse prevention skills (e.g., enhancing social support and emergency planning for high risk situations and lapses).

A well-investigated form of anxiety-management training for PTSD survivors is stress-inoculation training (SIT) (Meichenbaum, 1974). SIT typically involves two phases: (1) education about anxiety responses and PTSD, and (2) instruction in skills for coping with anxiety, including such techniques as muscle relaxation, deep breathing, covert modeling, thought stopping, role playing, and guided self-dialogue (Calhoun & Atkeson, 1991). Participants typically select two or three of these techniques to master during the course of treatment, which can be conducted individually or in groups. Kilpatrick et al. (1982) originally utilized it with sexual assault survivors.

A number of studies have systematically evaluated the role of SIT in the treatment of trauma recovery, with generally positive results. Frank et al. (1988) reported that both systematic desensitization and anxiety management techniques similar to SIT were equally effective in reducing depression and anxiety among a group of rape survivors, regardless of whether they sought treatment soon after the assault, or some months later. Resick, Jordan, Girelli, Hutter, and Marhoefer-Dvorak (1988) found that three different brief group therapies (SIT, assertiveness training, or supportive counseling) all produced significant decreases in PTSD symptoms. Foa, Rothbaum, Riggs, and Murdock (1991) reported that two cognitive-behavioral procedures, SIT and PE, relieved PTSD symptoms more effectively than supportive counseling (SC) or no treatment. Although SIT was the most effective intervention at posttreatment, PE evidenced a trend toward being more effective at three-month follow-up. Therefore, the authors concluded that an optimal program might combine elements of both SIT and PE. However, when Foa and her colleagues (Foa, Freund, et al., 1994) tested this hypothesis in a subsequent study, it was not supported. These investigators randomized assault survivors with PTSD to receive either PE alone, SIT alone, a combination of the two treatments, or wait-list control. They found that although all three active treatments improved more than the control at posttreatment and six-month follow-up, there were no active treatment group differences. Because these investigators chose to equate therapist contact time in the three groups, the exposure and skills building interventions were abbreviated in the combined condition. Therefore, Foa and Meadows (1997) posited that shortening these treatments may have resulted in the failure to find superiority for the combined conditions.

Case Conceptualization and Treatment Planning

Given the aforementioned treatment strategies, the behavior therapist is faced with a decision-making process in order to determine which type of trauma-focused treatment to utilize. Falsetti (1997) has outlined a detailed decision tree, and some of those recommendations are summarized here. First, sessions with all clients should begin with an educational component, orienting the client to their diagnosis, whether the diagnosis is PTSD only, PTSD and depression, PTSD and panic, and so forth. Next, the client's level of coping skills and level of distress should be examined. If clients present as particularly fragile or are utilizing a number of maladaptive or destructive coping skills, then beginning with a coping skills treatment, such as SIT, is advised. If the client is substance dependent, then the therapist may want to incorporate an integrated substance abuse treatment plan before commencing with trauma-focused treatment. If the client presents with primary complaints of trauma-related anxiety and fear, then commencing with an exposure-based treatment may be considered, followed by a cognitive restructuring if the client has lingering cognitive distortions related to the trauma. If the client presents with primary complaints of self-blame, shame, or difficulties with intimacy or esteem, then beginning with one of the cognitive restructuring treatments may be considered, followed by prolonged exposure. These recommendations are intended to be very general guidelines to initiate thinking about the sequencing and matching of treatments to the individual client's constellation of presenting problems.

The following case illustrates an approach to treating rape-related PTSD in which principles of PE were utilized in a course of brief behavioral therapy for a client presenting to a randomized controlled clinical trial, comparing PE to CPT.

Case Illustration

Identifying Information
Ms. J. was a 25 year old, married, caucasian female who was living at home with her husband. She completed 2 years of college and was currently working in retail sales. During treatment, Ms. J. discovered that she was pregnant. She self-referred to therapy to address symptoms of PTSD from her rape by an ex-boyfriend nine years earlier.

Traumatic Event
At the age of 15, Ms. J. went out one Friday evening with some new girlfriends. She told her parents that she was going to spend the night with one of the friends but went to a party instead. All of the teenagers were drinking at the party. In order to ease her anxiety about being with friends whom she did not know well, Ms. J. also began drinking heavily. Soon Ms. J. saw that her ex-boyfriend, a football player, had arrived at the party and she quickly noted that he was very intoxicated and was acting very loud and unruly. Later in the evening, Ms. J. went upstairs to use the restroom. There was a long line at the hallway restroom and someone told her about another bathroom inside the master bedroom. After using the restroom, Ms. J. entered the master bedroom to find her ex-boyfriend in the room. She was initially happy to see him but he soon began making her uncomfortable as he attempted to kiss and to touch her. She repeatedly stated that she was not interested in having any physical contact with him. She then tried to flee the room and discovered that he had locked the door. She screamed loudly and fought him with all of her strength but he was able to use his body to hold her down and to violently pull off her clothes. She continued to fight but he pinned her down and raped her. At one point during the rape, the weight from his body on her chest made her feel as if she was suffocating and she thought that she was going to die. After the rape, two of her girl friends came up to the bedroom. In spite of the room being in shambles, they did not appear to recognize the seriousness of the situation. Ms. J. was then forced to listen to her friends talking about how couples fight now and then and to hear them say that she and her boyfriend would probably make up in a few days. Ms. J. then had to go back downstairs and sit with her ex-boyfriend (rapist) until she could get a ride home. This rape was Ms. J.'s first sexual experience.

Presenting Complaints
Prior to treatment Ms. J. was assessed by an independent evaluator for a screening evaluation. She met *DSM-III-R* criteria for chronic PTSD related to the sexual assault, based on the Clinician Administered PTSD Scale (CAPS; Blake et al., 1990). Specifically, she reported intrusive symptoms when exposed to reminders of the rape; these reminders included being around men who had the same physical stature as her ex-boyfriend, being at parties, and having friendships with other women; effortful and noneffortful avoidance symptoms; these symptoms included using cognitive distraction and overworking to avoid thoughts or feelings related to the rape, an inability to recall some details related to the rape, diminished interest in daily activities, and a general sense of detachment; and arousal symptoms,

which included recurrent difficulties with sleep, irritability, diminished concentration, and exaggerated startle. Assessment for additional Axis I disorders was conducted using the Structured Clinical Interview for *DSM-III-R* (SCID) (Spitzer, Williams, & Gibbon, 1987). Ms. J. did not meet criteria for any other Axis I diagnosis. At the time of the pretreatment evaluation Ms. J. was not using any medication.

Following the clinical diagnostic evaluation, Ms. J. was assessed using a series of assessment procedures including self-report and behavioral components. These measures included a PTSD intensity score derived from the self-report version of the PTSD Symptom Scale (PSS) (Foa et al., 1993); self-reported cognitive and vegetative symptoms of depression using the Beck Depression Inventory (BDI) (Beck, Ward, Mendelsohn, Mock, & Erbaugh, 1961); a self-report inventory of psychological symptoms and potentially fear-producing stimuli using the Rape Aftermath Symptom Test (RAST) (Kilpatrick, 1988); and a self-report measurement of common physical symptoms and sensations using the Pennebaker Inventory of Limbic Languidness (PILL) (Pennebaker, 1982). At pretreatment, Ms. J. reported symptoms of mild dysphoria (BDI = 13), circumscribed fears, including fears of being in a strange place, having people behind you, and shadows (all rated as situations that were very much feared), and physical symptoms, including weekly headaches, dizziness, and feeling faint. Ms. J. reported having a very supportive husband and family. Additional assessment ratings included utilization of a SUDS ratings in response to imaginal exposures to the rape and in response to in vivo exposures to rape-related stimuli.

Ms. J. was evaluated at pretreatment, therapy sessions 4 and 8, posttreatment, and at three months and nine months following completion of treatment. An independent evaluator, who was not familiar with the course or nature of the Ms. J.'s treatment, conducted diagnostic interviews at pretreatment, posttreatment, and at the three- and nine-month follow-up. The posttreatment and follow-up evaluations included the CAPS and SCID-III-R for diagnostic interviews, and self-report instruments (PSS, RAST, & PILL). Assessment data for the BDI was available at pretreatment and nine-month follow-up only, and the PSS and the SUDS ratings were the only assessment measures that were used during the course of treatment.

Treatment

Ms. J. was seen for nine therapy sessions, using the standardized PE protocol (Foa, Hearst, et al., 1994), which uses imaginal exposure and in vivo exposure techniques to help survivors process the emotional content of traumatic events. During the imaginal exposure, Ms. J. was instructed to imagine the rape as vividly as possible and describe the rape out loud. This process was repeated several times over a 45- to 60-minute time period with the goal of reducing the client's anxiety and distress levels. During in vivo exposure, Ms. J. confronted anxiety-provoking, but realistically safe, situations in her life that she had been avoiding since the rape. Focusing on situations that are realistically safe, she was instructed to stay in the situation until her anxiety decreased to manageable levels.

The first session was 60-minutes long and focused on educating Ms. J. about PTSD, particularly focusing on the role of avoidance and giving her the rationale for therapy. She was also instructed in breathing retraining in this initial session. In session 2, Ms. J. was taught about the common reactions to assault and participated in information gathering to generate a hierarchy (a list of activities that increase in difficulty) for in vivo exposures. In vivo exposures ranged from activities that were rated as moderate in difficulty, such as ordering a meal by herself in a strange place, driving a long distance by herself, inviting friends to go and do something, to activities that were rated as extremely difficult, such as looking at pictures of an old apartment (where she lived when her PTSD was at its worst), going to a bar with friends from work, and being around a muscular guy alone.

Prolonged imaginal exposure accompanied by continued between-session work on the in vivo exposures to feared situations and objects was introduced from sessions 3 to 9, all of which were 90 minutes in length. During the imaginal exposure, Ms. J. was instructed to imagine the assault scene as vividly as possible, "as if it were happening now," and to describe it out loud, using the present tense. Ms. J. was able to recount her story an average of two times during the imaginal exposure sessions, and the exposure portion lasted about 45 minutes. The verbal descriptions and the reliving of her trauma were recorded on audio tapes. Ms. J. listened to these tapes daily for homework. On average, Ms. J. spent 7.8 hours between sessions doing homework. Her preexposure, maximum in exposure and postexposure SUDS ratings are listed in Table 18.2 for imaginal exposures.

STATISTICALLY SIGNIFICANT CHANGE

A statistical method for analyzing single-case subject designs (Mueser, Yarnold, & Foy, 1991) was used to examine the efficacy of PE treatment. Using statistically significant change as the guide to evaluating change across sessions is superior to visual inspection, given that this approach is systematic and not subject to biases such as serial dependency of the data. This method also goes beyond subjective analysis of "significant," corrects for the "error" in the client's score, and evaluates the change in the client's score above and beyond chance variation.

Raw scores for each of the self-report measures are listed in Table 18.3. Table 18.4 presents descriptive statistics (means and standard deviations), reliabilities (rs), and critical-difference scores (CDS) for the within-session and outcome measures. Table 18.5 summarizes the results of the statistical tests comparing the pretreatment assessment of each variable with each of the five subsequent assessments for the PSS, each of the three subsequent assessments for the RAST and PILL, and with the single subsequent assessment for the BDI.

Table 18.2
Behavioral Recording of SUDS Ratings across Therapy Sessions

Session	SUDS Ratings (Maximum)		
	Preexposure	Exposure	Postexposure
1	N/A	N/A	N/A
2	N/A	N/A	N/A
3	75	100	25
4	50	100	30
5	45	65	15
6	35	50	25
7	35	50	25
8	25	45	20

Table 18.3

Raw Scores of Psychopathology Measures

Measure	Assessment Points					
	1 (Pre)	2 (S4)	3 (S8)	4 (Post)	5 (3 mo)	6 (9 mo)
PTSD Measures:						
PSS-Total[1]	19	19	2	0	1	5
(a) Reexperiencing	1	7	0	0	0	0
(b) Avoidance	10	4	0	0	0	1
(c) Arousal	8	8	2	0	1	4
RAST	27	N/A	N/A	9	5	7
General Psychopathology:						
PILL[2]	20	N/A	N/A	17	18	12
BDI	13	N/A	N/A	N/A	N/A	3

[1] PSS (PTSD Symptom Scale)

[2] Pill (Pennebaker Inventory of Limbic Languidness)

Table 18.4

Descriptive Statistics, Ipsative Z Scores, Test-Retest Reliabilities (Rel), and Critical Difference (CD) Scores for Outcome Measures

Measure	M	SD	Ipsative Z Scores						Rel	CD
			Z1	Z2	Z3	Z4	Z5	Z6		
PTSD Measures:										
PSS-Total	7.7	8.9	1.26	1.26	−.64	−.87	−.75	−.30	0.74	2.05
(a) Reexp.	1.3	2.8	−.46	2.04	−.46	−.46	−.46	−.46	0.66	2.34
(b) Avoid.	2.5	4.0	1.88	.38	−.63	−.63	−.63	−.38	0.56	2.67
(c) Arous.	3.8	3.5	1.20	1.20	−.51	−1.09	−.8	.06	0.71	2.16
RAST	12	10.1	1.48	N/A	N/A	−.30	−.69	−.50	0.85	1.27
General Psychopathology:										
PILL	16.8	3.4	.94	N/A	N/A	06	.35	−1.41	0.79	1.50
BDI	8	7.1	.70	N/A	N/A	N/A	N/A	−.58	0.65	1.37

Table 18.5

Statistically Significant Changes in Psychopathology from Pretreatment Assessment

Measure	S4	S8	Post	3 mo	9 mo
PTSD Measures:					
PSS-Total	0	0	+	0	0
(a) Reexp.	+	0	0	0	0
(b) Avoid	0	0	0	0	0
(c) Arous.	0	0	+	0	0
RAST	N/A	N/A	+	+	+
General Psychopathology:					
PILL	N/A	N/A	0	0	+
BDI	N/A	N/A	N/A	N/A	0

0: Not Significant; +: Significant at overall $p < .05$.

COURSE OF TREATMENT AND SIGNIFICANT CHANGE

The discussion will focus on aspects of clinical and statistical change. All of the discussion of the SUDS ratings refers to Table 18.2, discussion of clinical change refers to Table 18.3, and statistical analyses refer to Table 18.4.

Visual inspection of Ms. J.'s self-reported PTSD symptoms illustrate a dramatic decrease in the total PTSD score from session 4 (score = 19) to session 8 (score = 2) (see Table 18.3). These scores were reduced further at posttreatment (score = 0) with minor fluctuations at three and nine months. This change in Ms. J.'s PTSD score was statistically significant at posttreatment. Minor fluctuation in the total score rendered the change nonsignificant at the two follow-up assessment points, but the total scores were well within the nonclinical range.

Ms. J. reported a statistically significant increase in her reexperiencing scores at session 4. This increase in intrusive symptoms is commonly seen after the first imaginal exposure, which began in the previous session (session 3). Although Ms. J.'s avoidance decreased to nearly zero scores after session 4, this change was not statistically significant.

Ms. J. was able to experience and process increasingly more intense emotions, particularly fear-related emotions, over the course of her imaginal exposures. Her most intense exposure experience was in session 4 (the second exposure). During this exposure Ms. J. had a flashback in which she vividly saw her perpetrator's face. In spite of her fear and distress at having this flashback, Ms. J. was able to complete the imaginal exposure for that session and she reported a tremendous sense of relief at its conclusion. Subsequent exposures yielded lower maximum SUDS ratings (range = 50–65 compared with an initial maximum of 100) with the last session yielding a low-moderate maximum rating of 45 (see Table 18.2). Ms. J.'s arousal symptoms were significantly decreased at posttreatment with minor increases at three- and nine-month assessment points, rendering these scores insignificantly changed from baseline, but still clinically reduced. Ms. J. reported several spontaneous insights during the course of the imaginal exposures. She noted after several exposures that she now knows why she avoids developing friendships with women with blond hair (her friends at the party were blond) and now knows why she became estranged from a very close male friend after he started body building and became physically larger (her rapist was large and muscular).

Ms. J. made great strides in her in vivo exposures. Her self-report of phobic avoidance was significantly reduced at all assessment points and her SUDS ratings on all prescribed activities were dramatically reduced. In fact, her SUDS ratings for all prescribed activities were rated at posttreatment as either a 0 or a 10, with a single exception; she continued to rate being around a muscular male alone, as evoking a SUDS rating of 35. However, this rating was reduced from a 75 and was well within the low range of distress.

Finally, Ms. J.'s self-reported physical complaints were significantly reduced at the nine-month follow-up assessment, suggesting that the PTSD treatment may have been associated with some benefit for general (possibly stress-related) health complaints. Ms. J.'s BDI, or self-reported depression score was unchanged at the 9-month assessment point, although both the pretreatment and the 9-month assessment scores were well within the nonclinical range.

CLINICAL FUNCTIONING AT FOLLOW-UP

At the posttreatment, and three- and nine-month follow-up, Ms. J. was found to be PTSD negative based on the diagnostic evaluation using the CAPS. She also continued to be negative for any Axis I diagnosis using the SCID. Ms. J.'s functioning at nine months was particularly impressive given that she recently experienced a number of extremely stressful events. Between the three- and nine-month assessment, she experienced gestational diabetes and her child was born four weeks early. Within several weeks of her child's birth, her husband was critically injured during an airplane accident while crop dusting. Ms. J. was now in the position of helping her husband to recover from his injuries and simultaneously caring for a new infant. The young couple was forced to move back home to Ms. J.'s parents. They were also facing continued financial difficulties with calls from bill collectors, and Ms. J. was forced to seek work outside of the home. Ms. J. also reported that her husband was having difficulties with some PTSD-like symptoms following his accident. She stated that she instructed him to "face the memories" and that they repeatedly talked about his experiences. Informal follow-up several weeks later revealed that the couple was beginning to adjust to their new circumstances and that Ms. J. was beginning to interview for new jobs.

ALTERNATIVE TREATMENT OPTIONS

FAMILY TREATMENTS

There have been few systematic investigations of the role of the family in recovery from a traumatic experience, even though several authors have highlighted the importance of the family unit as both a buffer for the impact of the traumatic stressor and as social support for the trauma survivors recovery (Smith, 1983). Figley (1990) suggested that the family could be incorporated as a critical entity in recovery from a traumatic event by confronting the trauma as a family unit. Harris (1991) presented a compelling argument for the need to include the family unit in PTSD treatment. He suggested that an effective approach to treating PTSD should: (1) involve the family in assessing the problem confronting the individual and the family unit resulting from the trauma; (2) examine the possible solution to the problem by gauging the family's strengths and weaknesses; and (3) include problem solving around realistic obstacles so that solutions may be implemented. In addition, involvement of the family unit may well be an effective relapse-prevention strategy.

There have been many descriptions of family-based interventions to assist in recovering from PTSD. These include works by Figley (1990), Johnson, Feldman, and Lubin (1995), Matsakis (1994), and Rabin and Nardi (1991). These typically evolved from a clinical orientation of family systems, in which the entire family was assumed to have been traumatized if one member has been. Often, the interventions included psychoeducation about normal responses to trauma. Unfortunately, none has been evaluated in a randomized clinical trial.

Glynn et al. (1997) recently reported on a study investigating the results of augmenting exposure treatment for combat-related PTSD with behavioral family therapy (BFT) (Falloon, Boyd, & McGill, 1984). After a thorough assessment of all participants, BFT sessions were initiated with education on the etiology, course, treatment, and prevalence of PTSD. After education, skills training was provided on communication, anger management, and problem solving. Many behavioral strategies, including rehearsal, coaching, prompting, shaping, positive reinforcement, and homework, were utilized. Family members were taught problem-solving techniques to manage life stress more effectively. An integral aspect of BFT involved out-of-session assignments to promote generalization. Approximately one-third of session time was allocated to this issue. It was here that specific avoidance behaviors could be addressed over the six months of the treatment.

The design in the Glynn et al. study called for veterans and a family member to be randomly assigned to one of three conditions: (1) waiting list; (2) 18 sessions of twice weekly exposure therapy; or (3) 18 sessions of twice weekly exposure therapy followed by 16 sessions of behavioral family therapy. As hypothesized, participation in exposure therapy resulted in reductions of PTSD positive symptoms (e.g., re-experiencing and hyperarousal), but not PTSD negative symptoms (e.g., numbing and avoidance). These gains were maintained at six-month follow-up. However, participation in behavioral family therapy had no additional effects on either positive or negative PTSD symptoms. Small sample size and the chronicity of the PTSD in this sample 30 years after the war may have negatively influenced results. BFT with a more acute population, in which anxiety rates are higher, numbing less prevalent, and avoidance behaviors less entrenched, might be expected to produce stronger positive results.

Deblinger (Deblinger & Heflin, 1996) has designed a cognitive behavioral intervention for sexually abused children, which includes direct intervention with the children and with the nonoffending parent. In this treatment program, the child intervention includes coping-skills training, gradual exposure, and education regarding child sexual abuse, healthy sexuality, and personal safety/risk-reduction skills. The intervention for the nonoffending parent includes coping-skills training, gradual exposure, and behavior-management skills. There are also joint parent-child sessions. Deblinger and colleagues (Deblinger, Lippmann, & Steer, 1996) have conducted a controlled clinical trial for the treatment, in which 100 participating families were randomly assigned to one of four experimental conditions: (1) child intervention only, (2) mother intervention only, (3) mother/child intervention, and (4) community care comparison. This study revealed significant reductions in the children's PTSD symptoms for the children assigned to direct interventions (child only, and mother/child) compared with the other two nondirect interventions and significant reductions in the children's externalizing behaviors and parental effectiveness for the mothers assigned to the direct interventions (mother only, and mother/child) compared with the other two interventions. This controlled clinical trial demonstrated the importance of parental participation and direct intervention with the victimized children for treating the complex symptomatology associated with the sexual abuse of children.

Prescriptive Treatment and Managed Care

There is growing recognition of the need to address violent victimization in patients within medical and primary care settings (Koss, Koss, & Woodruff, 1991). Physicians, like those in the mental health field could benefit from training and materials to guide assessment of violence histories in their patients, to better prepare them to address the needs of patients whom they do identify (Sugg & Inui, 1992). Victimization history has been found to be prevalent in association with a variety of medical complaints including chronic pain, gastrointestinal problems, and lowered perceptions of health (Goodman, Koss, & Russo, 1993). Screening for victimization in the primary care setting could allow for appropriate referrals to mental health and other social services that may allow for more appropriate treatment of mental health sequelae of violence, rather than medical care for somatic complaints that may be nonorganic. Such strategies could reduce health care costs and allow opportunities for health care professionals to provide supportive responses to their patients as well. Simple screening procedures developed for the assessment of violence histories are critical components in training health care providers to perform routine risk identification for violence exposure among their patients.

In this managed care era of increased emphasis on cost efficiency and clinician accountability, the development of new cognitive-behavioral treatment for PTSD features manualized treatment delivered in a group format. One such treatment, Trauma Focus Group Therapy (TFGT) is under intensive development through a Veterans Affairs Cooperative Study (Friedman & Schnurr, 1995). As described by Foy, Ruzek, Glynn, Riney, and Gusman (in press), TFGT is administered to groups composed of four to six members lead by two facilitators, and it is specifically designed to overcome some of the implementation difficulties associated with individually administered exposure therapy (Foy et al., 1996). Over the course of 30 weekly sessions, TFGT emphasizes systematic prolonged exposure and cognitive restructuring applied to each individual's selected combat-related traumatic experience, and relapse prevention training to enhance members' coping skills and resources for maintaining control over specific PTSD and related symptoms. The cognitive-behavioral model of TFGT is set in a developmental perspective, taking into account important relationships and experiences occurring across the entire lifespan. It features an autobiographical emphasis that combines both an individual narrative approach as well as the group concept of bearing witness to members' public recounting of their significant life experiences. In addition, TFGT incorporates extensive trauma processing by encouraging group members to repeatedly experience their personal tragic events through assigned homework, as well as vicariously being exposed to the experiences of other group members. Relapse prevention planning is a final core component of TFGT. Emphasis on mobilizing coping resources to be used in predictable high-risk situations is intended to help maintain treatment gains between sessions and after TFGT is completed.

PHARMACOTHERAPY

The number of clinical trials examining pharmacotherapy as an adjunctive or primary treatment for PTSD have been growing (for comprehensive reviews see Davidson & van der Kolk, 1996; Yehuda, Marshall, & Giller, 1998). Currently, as detailed in Yehuda, Marshall, and Giller (1998), there are only seven controlled trials that have been conducted and only four of these trials met the highest standards of experimental rigor (i.e., randomized, prospective, blinded assessment, appropriate exclusion/inclusion criteria, state-of-the-art diagnostic methods, adequate sample size for statistical power and appropriate statistical analyses). The remaining studies consisted of open trials, case studies, and retrospective research. Additional limitations of pharmacological research include the fact that the populations studied were predominantly male, combat veterans, with very chronic refractory cases of PTSD. These characteristics obviously limit generalizability.

Keeping these limitations in mind, existing studies have found no single medication that effectively targets all the symptom clusters of PTSD. However, there is some indication that particular subsets of symptoms may respond to different medications. The range of psychotropic drugs that have been examined for their impact on PTSD and related symptomatology include monoamine oxidase inhibitors (MAOIs), tricyclic antidepressants (TCAs), selective serotonin reuptake inhibitors (SSRIs), lithium, anticonvulsants, beta-adrenergic blockers, and benzodiazepines (Davidson & van der Kolk, 1996). Of the medications that have been studied, SSRIs appear to hold relatively greater promise because they have been the first group of pharmacological agents that demonstrated the potential for targeting all three PTSD symptom clusters.

Given the limited effectiveness of pharmacotherapy, most agree that their use should be accompanied by psychotherapy. Specifically, pharmacotherapy can be helpful as an adjunctive treatment when symptom severity or comorbid symptoms (e.g., high levels of anxiety, numbing, depression, dissociation, impulsive aggression, or paranoia) interfere with the individual's ability to initiate, fully engage, or stay in trauma-focused treatment. If using pharmacotherapy as an adjunctive treatment, it is important to remember that most of the medications have side effects, which can lead to noncompliance. Therefore, adherence strategies may also have to be addressed within the trauma-focused treatment.

SUMMARY

In the past 10 years much progress has been made in the validation of PTSD as a diagnostic entity, as well as cognitive-behavioral treatment for PTSD. Diagnostic criteria for the disorder have been empirically validated, and much work on establishing PTSD epidemiology has been accomplished. Cognitive-behavioral conceptual models of PTSD are now multifactorial and interactional in nature, allowing for the effects of important mediating variables, such as prior traumatic experience and social support, to be considered. Randomized controlled trials have shown positive treatment outcome for standardized therapies utilizing prolonged exposure, cognitive restructuring, and skills training. In clinical applications, cognitive-behavioral treatments most often feature a combination of exposure, cognitive restructuring, and coping skills. Manualized treatment, with detailed session by session guides, is currently available for conducting individual cognitive-behavioral PTSD therapy, and intensive developmental work is underway for a similar manualized group format.

REFERENCES

American Psychiatric Association. (1987). *Diagnostic and statistical manual of mental disorders* (3rd ed. rev.). Washington, DC: Author.

American Psychiatric Association. (1994). *Diagnostic and statistical manual of mental disorders* (4th ed.). Washington, DC: Author.

Astin, M.C., Ogland-Hand, S.M., Coleman, E.M., & Foy, D.W. (1995). Posttraumatic stress disorder and childhood abuse in battered women: Comparisons with maritally distressed women. *Journal of Consulting and Clinical Psychology, 63,* 308–312.

Beck, A.T., Steer, R.A., Ball, R., & Ranieri, W.F. (1996). Comparison of Beck depression inventories-IA and -II in psychiatric outpatients. *Journal of Personality Assessment, 67,* 588–597.

Beck, A.T., Ward, C.H., Mendelsohn, M., Mock, J., & Erbaugh, J. (1961). An inventory for measuring depression. *Archives of General Psychiatry, 4,* 561–571.

Blake, D.D., Weathers, F.W., Nagy, L.M., Kaloupek, D.G., Charney, D.S., & Keane, T.M. (1996). *Clinician-administered PTSD scale for DSM-IV: Current and lifetime diagnostic version.* Boston: Behavioral Science Division, Boston VA Medical Center.

Blake, D.D., Weathers, F.W., Nagy, L.M., Kaloupek, D.G., Klauminzer, G., Charney, D.S., & Keane, T.M. (1990). A clinician rating scale for assessing current and lifetime PTSD: The CAPS-1. *Behavior Therapist, 18,* 187–188.

Boudewyns, P.A., & Hyer, L. (1990). Physiological response to combat memories and preliminary treatment outcome in Vietnam veteran PTSD patients with direct therapeutic exposure. *Behavior Therapy, 21,* 63–87.

Breslau, N., & Davis, G.C. (1992). Posttraumatic stress disorder in an urban population of young adults: Risk factors for chronicity. *American Journal of Psychiatry, 149,* 671–676.

Breslau, N., Davis, G.C., Andreski, P., & Peterson, E. (1991). Traumatic events and posttraumatic stress disorder in an urban population of young adults. *Archives of General Psychiatry, 48,* 216–222.

Brom, D., Kleber, R.J., & Defares, P.B. (1989). Brief psychotherapy for posttraumatic stress disorder. *Journal of Consulting and Clinical Psychology, 57,* 607–612.

Calhoun, K.S., & Atkeson, B.M. (1991). *Treatment of rape victims: Facilitating psychosocial adjustment.* New York: Pergamon Press.

Carroll, E.M., & Foy, D.W. (1992). Assessment and treatment of combat-related posttraumatic stress disorder in a medical center setting. In D.W. Foy (Ed.), *Treating PTSD: Cognitive-behavioral strategies* (pp. 39–68). New York: Guilford Press.

Carroll, E.M., Rueger, D.B., Foy, D.W., & Donahoe, C.P. (1985). Vietnam combat veterans with posttraumatic stress disorder: Analysis of marital and cohabiting adjustment. *Journal of Abnormal Psychology, 94,* 329–337.

Chard, K.M. (1996). Cognitive processing therapy for sexual abuse (CPT-SA). In P.A. Resick (Chair.), *Treating sexual assault/sexual abuse pathology: Recent findings.* Paper presented at the 30th annual meeting of the Association for the Advancement of Behavior Therapy, New York.

Chard, K.M., Weaver, T.L., & Resick, P.A. (1997). Adapting cognitive processing therapy for work with survivors of child sexual abuse. *Cognitive and Behavioral Practice, 4,* 31–52.

Chemtob, C., Roitblat, H.L., Hamada, R.S., Carlson, J.G., & Twentyman, C.T. (1988). A cognitive action theory of post-traumatic stress disorder. *Journal of Anxiety Disorders, 2,* 253–275.

Cooper, N.A., & Clum, G.A. (1989). Imaginal flooding as a supplementary treatment for PTSD in combat veterans: A controlled study. *Behavior Therapy, 20,* 381–391.

Davidson, J., Foa, E.B., Blank, A.S., Brett, E.A., Fairbank, J., Green, B.L., Herman, J.L., Keane, T.M., Kilpatrick, D.G., March, J.S., McNally, R.J., Pitman, R.K., Resnick, H.S., & Rothbaum, B.O. (1996). Posttraumatic stress disorder. In T.A. Widiger, A.J. Frances, H.A. Pincus, R. Ross, M.B. First, & W.W. Davis (Eds.), *DSM-IV sourcebook* (Vol. 2, pp. 577–605). Washington, DC: American Psychiatric Association.

Davidson, J., & van der Kolk, B.A. (1996). The psychopharmacological treatment of posttraumatic stress disorder. In B.A. van der Kolk, A.C. McFarlance, & L. Weisaeth (Eds.), *Traumatic stress: The effects of overwhelming experience on mind, body, and society* (pp. 510–524), New York: Guilford Press.

Deblinger, E., & Heflin, A.H. (1996). *Treating sexually abused children and their nonoffending parents: A cognitive behavioral approach.* Thousand Oaks, CA: Sage.

Deblinger, E., Lippmann, J., & Steer, R. (1996). Cognitive behavioral interventions for sexually abused children: Initial findings of a treatment outcome study. In P.A. Resick (Chair.), *Treating sexual assault/sexual abuse pathology: Recent findings.* Paper presented at the 30th annual meeting of the Association for the Advancement of Behavior Therapy, New York.

Emery, V.O., Emery, P.E., Shama, D.K., Quinana, N.A., & Jassani, A.K. (1991). Predisposing variables in PTSD patients. *Journal of Traumatic Stress, 4,* 325–343.

Engel, C.C., Engel, A.L., Campbell, S.J., McFall, M.E., Russo, J., & Katon, W. (1993). Posttraumatic stress disorder symptoms and precombat sexual and physical abuse in desert storm veterans. *Journal of Nervous and Mental Disease, 181,* 683–688.

Escobar, J.I., Randolph, E.T., Puente, G., Spiwak, F., Asamen, J.K., Hill, M., & Hough, R.L. (1983). Posttraumatic stress disorder in Hispanic Vietnam veterans: Clinical phenomenology and sociocultural characteristics. *Journal of Nervous and Mental Disease, 171,* 585–596.

Falloon, I.R.H., Boyd, J.L., & McGill, C.W. (1984). *Family care of schizophrenia.* New York: Guilford Press.

Falsetti, S.A. (1997). The decision-making process of choosing a treatment for patients with civilian trauma-related PTSD. *Cognitive and Behavioral Practice, 4,* 99–121.

Falsetti, S.A., & Resnick, H.S. (1992). *The physical reactions scale.* Charleston, SC: The National Crime Victims Research and Treatment Center, Medical University of South Carolina.

Figley, C.R. (1990). *Helping traumatized families.* New York: Brunner/Mazel.

First, M.B., Spitzer, R.L., Gibbon, M., & Williams, J.B.W. (1996). *Structured clinical interview for DSM-IV axis I disorders—non-patient edition.* New York: Biometrics Research Department, New York State Psychiatric Institute.

Foa, E.B., Freund, B.F., Hembree, E., Dancu, C.V., Franklin, M.E., Perry, K.J., Riggs, D.S., & Moinar, C. (1994, November). *Efficacy of short-term behavioral treatments of PTSD in sexual and non-sexual assault victims.* Paper presented at the 28th annual meeting of the Association for the Advancement of Behavior Therapy, San Diego, CA.

Foa, E.B., Hearst, D.E., Dancu, C.V., Hembree, E., & Jaycox, L.H. (1994). *Prolonged exposure (PE) manual.* Unpublished manuscript, Medical College of Pennsylvania, Eastern Pennsylvania Psychiatric Institute.

Foa, E.B., & Kozak, M.J. (1986). Emotional processing of fear: Exposure to corrective information. *Psychological Bulletin, 99,* 20–35.

Foa, E.B., & Meadows, E.A. (1997). Psychosocial treatments for posttraumatic stress disorder: A critical review. *Annual Review of Psychology, 48,* 449–480.

Foa, E.B., Riggs, D.S., Dancu, C.V., & Rothbaum, B.O. (1993). Reliability and validity of a brief instrument for assessing post-traumatic stress disorder. *Journal of Traumatic Stress, 6,* 459–473.

Foa, E.B., Rothbaum, B.O., Riggs, D., & Murdoc, T. (1991). Treatment of posttraumatic stress disorder in rape victims: A comparison between cognitive-behavioral procedures and counseling. *Journal of Consulting and Clinical Psychology, 59,* 715–723.

Foa, E.B., Steketee, G., & Rothbaum, B.O. (1989). Behavioral/cognitive conceptualizations of post-traumatic stress disorder. *Behavior Therapy, 20,* 155–176.

Foy, D.W. (1992). Introduction and description of the disorder. In D.W. Foy (Ed.), *Treating posttraumatic stress disorder: Cognitive behavioral strategies* (pp. 1–12). New York: Guilford Press.

Foy, D.W., Madvig, B.T., Pynoos, R.S., & Camilleri, A. (1996). Etiologic factors in the development of posttraumatic stress disorder in children and adolescents. *Journal of School Psychology, 34,* 133–145.

Foy, D.W., Ruzek, J.I., Glynn, S.M., Riney, S.A., & Gusman, F.D. (1997). Trauma focus group therapy for combat-related PTSD. *In Session: Psychotherapy in Practice, 3,* 59–73.

Foy, D.W., Wood, J.L., King, D.W., King, L.A., & Resnick, H.S. (1997). Los Angeles symptoms checklist: Psychometric evidence with an adolescent sample. *Assessment, 4,* 377–383.

Frank, E., Anderson, B., Stewart, B.D., Dancu, C., Hughes, C., & West, D. (1988). Efficacy of cognitive behavior therapy and systematic desensitization in the treatment of rape trauma. *Behavior Therapy, 19,* 403–420.

Friedman, M.J., & Schnurr, P.P. (1995). *Group treatment of PTSD.* Department of Veterans Affairs Cooperative Study #420, Veterans Affairs Research Service.

Glynn, S.M., Eth, S., Randolph, E.T., Foy, D.W., Urbaitis, M., Boxer, L., Paz, G.G., Leong, G.B., Firman, G., Salk, J.D., Katzman, J.W., & Crothers, J. (in press). A test of behavioral family therapy to augment exposure for combat-related PTSD. *Journal of Consulting and Clinical Psychology.*

Goodman, L.A., Koss, M.P., & Russo, N.F. (1993). Violence against women: Physical and mental health effects. Part I: Research findings. *Applied & Preventive Psychology, 2,* 79–89.

Harris, C.J. (1991). A family crisis-intervention model for the treatment of post-traumatic stress reaction. *Journal of Traumatic Stress, 4,* 195–207.

Harvey, J.H., Orbuch, T.L., Chwalisz, K.D., & Garwood, G. (1991). Coping with sexual assault: The roles of account-making and confiding. *Journal of Traumatic Stress, 4,* 515–531.

Johnson, D.R., Feldman, S.F., & Lubin, H. (1995). Critical interaction therapy: Couples therapy in combat-related posttraumatic stress disorder. *Family Process, 34,* 401–412.

Jones, J.C., & Barlow, D.H. (1990). The etiology of posttraumatic stress disorder. *Clinical Psychology Review, 10,* 299–328.

Keane, T.M. (1993). Symptomatology of Vietnam veterans with posttraumatic stress disorder. In J.R.T. Davidson & E.B. Foa (Eds.), *Posttraumatic stress disorder DSM-IV and beyond: Recent research and future development* (pp. 113–143). Washington, DC: American Psychiatric Press.

Keane, T.M., Fairbank, J.A., Caddell, J.M., & Zimering, R.T. (1989). Implosive (flooding) therapy reduces symptoms of PTSD in Vietnam combat veterans. *Behavior Therapy, 20,* 149–153.

Keane, T.M., & Kaloupek, D.G. (1982). Imaginal flooding in the treatment of a posttraumatic stress disorder. *Journal of Consulting and Clinical Psychology, 50,* 138–140.

Kessler, R.C., Sonnega, A., Bromet, E., Hughes, M., & Nelson, C.B. (1995). Posttraumatic stress disorder in the national comorbidity survey. *Archives of General Psychiatry, 52,* 1048–1060.

Kilpatrick, D.G., Resnick, H.S., Freedy, J.R., Pelcovitz, D., Resick, P., Roth, S., & van der Kolk, B. (1998). The posttraumatic stress disorder field trial: Evaluation of the PTSD construct: Criteria A through E. In T.A. Widiger, A.J. Frances, H.A. Pincus, R. Ross, M.B. First, & W.W. Davis (Eds.), *DSM-IV sourcebook* (Vol. 4, pp. 803–844). Washington, DC: American Psychiatric Association.

Kilpatrick, D.G., Resnick, H.S., Saunders, B.E., & Best, C.L. (1989). *The national women's study PTSD module.* Charleston: Crime Victims Research and Treatment Center, Department of Psychiatry, Medical University of South Carolina.

Kilpatrick, D.G., Veronen, L.J., & Resick, P.A. (1982). Psychological sequelae to rape: Assessment and treatment strategies. In D.M. Doleys & R.L. Meredith (Eds.), *Behavioral medicine: Assessment and treatment strategies* (pp. 473–497). New York: Plenum Press.

Kilpatrick, D.J. (1988). Rape aftermath symptom test. In M. Hersen & A.S. Bellack (Eds.), *Dictionary of behavioral assessment techniques* (pp. 366–367). Oxford, England: Pergamon Press.

Kimerling, R., & Calhoun, K.S. (1994). Somatic symptoms, social support, and treatment seeking among sexual assault victims. *Journal of Consulting and Clinical Psychology, 62,* 333–340.

King, D.W., King, L.A., Foy, D.W., & Gudanowski, D.M. (1996). Prewar factors in combat-related posttraumatic stress disorder: Structural equation modeling with a national sample of female and male Vietnam veterans. *Journal of Consulting and Clinical Psychology, 64,* 520–531.

Koss, M.P., Koss, P.G., & Woodruff, W.J. (1991). Deleterious effects of criminal victimization on women's health and medical utilization. *Archives of Internal Medicine, 151,* 342–347.

Kubany, E.S., & Manke, F.P. (1995). Cognitive therapy for trauma-related guilt: Conceptual bases and treatment outlines. *Cognitive and Behavioral Practice, 2,* 27–61.

Kulka, R.A., Schlenger, W.E., Fairbank, J.A., Hough, R.L., Jordan, B.K., Marmar, C.R., & Weiss, D.S. (1990). *Trauma and the Vietnam war generation.* New York: Brunner/Mazel.

Madakasira, S., & O'Brien, K.F. (1987). Acute posttraumatic stress disorder in victims of a natural disaster. *Journal of Nervous and Mental Disease, 175,* 286–290.

McCammon, S., Durham, T.W., Allison, E.J., & Williamson, J.E. (1988). Emergency workers' cognitive appraisal and coping with traumatic events. *Journal of Traumatic Stress, 1,* 353–371.

Meichenbaum, D. (1974). *Cognitive behavior modification.* Elmsford, NY: Plenum Press.

Mowrer, O.H. (1960). *Learning theory and behavior.* New York: Wiley.

Mueser, K.T., Yarnold, P.R., & Foy, D.W. (1991). Statistical analysis for single-case designs. *Behavior Modification, 15,* 134–155.

Norris, F.H. (1990). Screening for traumatic stress: A scale for use in the general population. *Journal of Applied Social Psychology, 20,* 1704–1718.

Norris, F.H. (1992). Epidemiology of trauma: Frequency and impact of different potentially traumatic events on different demographic groups. *Journal of Consulting and Clinical Psychology, 60,* 409–418.

Norris, F.H., & Riad, J.K. (1996). Standardized self-report measures of civilian trauma and PTSD. In J. Wilson & T. Keane (Eds.), *Assessing psychological trauma and PTSD: A practitioner's handbook.* New York: Guilford Press.

Pennebaker, J.W. (1982). *The psychology of physical symptoms* (pp. 169–171). New York: Springer-Verlag.

Rabin, C., & Nardi, C. (1991). Treating posttraumatic stress disorder couples: A psychoeducational program. *Community Mental Health Journal, 27,* 209–224.

Resick, P.A., Falsetti, S.A., Resnick, H.S., & Kilpatrick, D.G. (1991). *The modified PTSD symptoms scale-self report.* St. Louis: University of Missouri & Charleston, SC: Crime Victims Research and Treatment Center, Medical University of South Carolina.

Resick, P.A., Jordan, C.G., Girelli, S.A., Hutter, C.K., & Marhoefer-Dvorak, S. (1988). A comparative victim study of behavioral group therapy for sexual assault victims. *Behavior Therapy, 19,* 385–401.

Resick, P.A., Nishith, P., & Astin, M.C. (1996). Preliminary results of an outcome study comparing cognitive processing therapy and prolonged exposure. In P.A. Resick (Chair.), *Treating sexual assault/sexual abuse pathology: Recent findings.* Paper presented at the 30th annual meeting of the Association for the Advancement of Behavior Therapy, New York.

Resick, P.A., & Schnicke, M.K. (1992). Cognitive processing therapy for sexual assault victims. *Journal of Consulting and Clinical Psychology, 60,* 748–756.

Resick, P.A., & Schnicke, M.K. (1993). *Cognitive processing therapy for rape victims.* Newbury Park, CA: Sage.

Resnick, H.S. (1996). Psychometric review of trauma assessment for adults (TAA). In B.H. Stamm (Ed.), *Measurement of stress, trauma, and adaptation.* Lutherville, MD: Sidran Press.

Resnick, H.S., Best, C.L., Kilpatrick, D.G., Freedy, J.R., & Falsetti, S.A. (1993). *Trauma assessment for adults-self-report.* Charleston: The National Crime Victims Research and Treatment Center, Medical University of South Carolina.

Resnick, H.S., Falsetti, S.A., Kilpatrick, D.G., & Freedy, J.R. (1996). Assessment of rape and other civilian trauma-related PTSD: Emphasis on assessment of potentially traumatic events. In T.W. Miller (Ed.), *Theory and assessment of stressful life events.* Madison, CT: International Universities Press.

Resnick, H.S., Kilpatrick, D.G., Dansky, B.S., Saunders, B.E., & Best, C.L. (1993). Prevalence of civilian trauma and posttraumatic stress disorder in a representative national sample of women. *Journal of Consulting and Clinical Psychology, 61,* 984–991.

Robins, L., Helzer, J., Cottler, L., & Goldring, E. (1988). *NIMH diagnostic interview schedule version III revised (DIS-III-R).* St. Louis: Washington University Press.

Russell, D.E.H. (1983). The incidence and prevalence of intrafamilial and extrafamilial sexual abuse of female children. *Child Abuse and Neglect, 7,* 133–146.

Smith, S.M. (1983). Disaster: Family disruption in the wake of natural disaster. In C.R. Figley & H.I. McCubbin (Eds.), *Stress and the family: Volume II. Coping with catastrophe.* New York: Brunner/Mazel.

Solomon, Z., Mukulincer, M., & Avitzur, E. (1988). Coping, locus of control, social support, and combat-related post-traumatic stress disorder: A prospective study. *Journal of Personality and Social Psychology, 55,* 279–285.

Spiegler, M.D., & Guevremont, D.C. (1998). *Contemporary behavior therapy* (3rd ed.). Pacific Grove, CA: Brooks/Cole.

Spitzer, R.L., Williams, J.B.W., & Gibbon, M. (1987). *Structured clinical interview for DSM-III-R (SCID).* New York: Biometrics Research Department, New York State Psychiatric Institute.

Spitzer, R.L., Willaims, J.B.W., Gibbon, M., & First, M.B. (1990). *Structured clinical interview for DSM-III-R personality disorders* (SCID-II, Version 1.0). Washington, DC: American Psychiatric Press.

Stamm, B.H. (1996). *Measurement of stress, trauma, and adaptation.* Lutherville, MD: Sidran Press.

Sugg, K., & Inui, T. (1992). Primary care physicians' response to domestic violence. *Journal of the American Medical Association, 23,* 3157–3160.

Weaver, T.L., & Clum, G.A. (1996). Interpersonal violence: Expanding the search for long-term sequelae within a sample of battered women. *Journal of Traumatic Stress, 9*(4), 797–817.

Weissman, M.M., & Paykel, E.S. (1974). *The depressed woman: A study of social relationships.* Chicago: University of Chicago Press.

Wyatt, G.E., Guthrie, D., & Notgrass, C.M. (1992). Differential effects of women's child sexual abuse and subsequent sexual revictimization. *Journal of Consulting and Clinical Psychology, 60*(2), 167–173.

Yehuda, R., Marshall, R., & Giller, E.L. (1998). Psychopharmacological treatment of post-traumatic stress disorder. In P.E. Nathan & J.M. Gorman (Eds.), *A guide to treatments that work* (pp. 377–397). New York: Oxford University Press.

PART SEVEN

ANOREXIA AND BULIMIA

IN RECENT years, clinical research investigators have focused increased attention on the treatment of anorexia nervosa (AN) and bulimia nervosa (BN), two eating disorders exhibiting primarily in young women. In addition to the obvious nutritional and psychological aspects of anorexia and bulimia, each of the disorders has very serious dental and medical sequelae, ranging from deteriorated dentition, to hormonal imbalance, to death in anorexia nervosa. Indeed, in anorexia nervosa, the mortality rate at times has been reported to be as high as 20 percent.

Not only has there been keen scholarly interest in these two recalcitrant eating disorders, but there has been a parallel upsurge of articles in the public media as well, fueled by the death of a famous popular singer from the effects of anorexia and the confession of an equally famous actress who suffered from bulimia. As a consequence of such publicity, the demand for treatment has increased (exponentially), and many new treatment programs for individuals suffering from eating-disorders have appeared on the therapeutic scene. Unfortunately, however, many such programs promise more than they can deliver, given both our current knowledge of the etiology and assessment of anorexia and bulimia and the psychotherapeutic, behavioral, and pharmacological approaches to their remediation and prevention.

We should note that the authors of the two chapters in this section are modest in their descriptions of what is known about the eating disorders in general and about the efficacy of the extant treatment strategies. Indeed, the fierce and acrimonious competition of proponents of differing theoretical persuasions previously encountered in the eating disorders literature is remarkably absent. Doctrinaire positions are not held, and each investigator, representing different schools of thought, is open to the empirical contributions of the other. Perhaps this tack is taken in light of the enormous psychological and biological complexities of anorexia and bulimia.

In considering the descriptions of anorexia and bulimia, Pyle and Porzelius, Berel, and Howard appear to have similar conceptualizations, albeit their different theoretical perspectives. In looking at anorexia and bulimia, clear diagnostic delineations between the two disorders are presented, with anorexia often requiring protracted inpatient care, given the high mortality rate. On the other hand, bulimics almost always can be managed on an outpatient basis.

With increased study, both from a diagnostic and treatment perspective, it has become clear that anorexia and bulimia are not unitary disorders, but that there are subclasses within each diagnostic entity that respond differentially to treatment. Indeed, in the case of anorexia, two distinct subgroups have been identified: (1) restrictive anorexics who abstain from eating but do not binge, and (2) bulimic anorexics who maintain a very low weight by purging after binging.

In spite of the commonalities in treating anorexics and bulimics, there are some pronounced differences. Indeed, in the case of anorexia nervosa, the first order of business is to restore the patient's weight to as close to normal (according to population statistics) as possible. In a structured inpatient setting, nutritional strategies, behavioral methods, or in dire cases, forced tube feeding, all have proven to be effective. But weight restoration is only part of the battle. In anorexia nervosa, there are many concomitant issues, such as perceptions of personal control, family disruption, distorted body image, and affective symptoms. Moreover, relapse prevention is critical, given recedivism rates of 50 percent or more.

In light of the control issues in anorexia, it is not surprising that Pyle underscores the importance of the therapeutic relationship and the sensitivity of the therapist. A treatment showing promise is interpersonal therapy. Most interesting in this chapter is the author's endorsement of cognitive behavior therapy as the treatment of choice. He also underscores studies documenting the importance of increasing self-esteem and normalizing body image. According to Porzelius et al., cognitive behavioral approaches appear to have much value in the treatment of bulimia and much promise in the treatment of anorexia. Cognitive-behavioral treatment manuals, available for BN and AN, provide specific, point-by-point instructions, which should serve to promote use by clinicians, and to further research.

CHAPTER 19

Dynamic Psychotherapy

CONCEPTUALIZATION

Concerns with weight and food restriction are less pervasive among young females today than when they were considered normative (Rodin, Silberstein, & Striegel-Moore, 1983). Food restriction, often used to enhance thinness, has been shown to be associated with increased desire to binge-eat (that is, the consumption of very large amounts of food in a short period of time) (Wardle, 1980). It is understandable, then, that a significant number of college females report having engaged in binge-eating. A significant number also report purging behaviors, such as self-induced vomiting and laxative abuse to rid the body of unwanted food. Three out of ten female college students report a fear of becoming fat, suggesting that eating problems remain common among college-age women.

These disordered eating habits and attitudes, when severe, can be associated with development of the serious eating disorder syndromes anorexia nervosa (AN) and bulimia nervosa (BN) (*DSM-IV*; American Psychiatric Association, 1994). Such syndromes constitute a major problem among women between the ages of 18 and 25, and they are associated with adverse emotional, vocational, social, financial, and physical consequences.

ANOREXIA NERVOSA

Essential features of AN are "refusal to maintain body weight over a minimal normal weight for age and height; intense fear of gaining weight or becoming fat, even though underweight; a distorted body image; and amenorrhea (in females). (The term *anorexia* is a misnomer because loss of appetite is rate.) Disturbance in body image is manifested by the way in which a person's body weight, size, or shape is experienced. People with this disorder say that they feel fat or that parts of their body are fat, when they are obviously underweight or even emaciated. They are preoccupied with their body size and usually dissatisfied with some feature of their physical appearance. The weight loss is usually accomplished by a reduction in total food intake, often with extensive exercising. Frequently, there is also self-induced vomiting or use of laxatives or diuretics. The person usually comes to professional attention when weight loss (or failure to gain expected weight) is marked. By the time the person is profoundly underweight, there are other signs, such as hypothermia, bradycardia, hypotension, edema, lanugo (neonatal-downlike hair), and a variety of metabolic changes. In most cases amenorrhea follows weight loss, but it is not usual for amenorrhea to appear before noticeable weight loss has occurred (APA, 1987).

People with AN tend to limit themselves to a narrow selection of low-calorie foods. In addition, they may hoard, conceal, crumble, or throw away food. Most people with this disorder steadfastly deny or minimize severity of their illness and are uninterested in, or resistant to, therapy. Many of the adolescents have delayed psychosexual development, and adults may have a markedly decreased interest in sex. Compulsive behavior, such as hand washing, may also be present during the illness (APA, 1987). The prognosis for AN is guarded. In addition, the long-term outcome for AN treatment still leaves much to be desired, particularly with respect to social adjustment and chronic medical complications.

BULIMIA NERVOSA

The essential features of BN are "recurrent episodes of binge-eating (rapid consumption of a large amount of food in a discrete period of time); a feeling of lack of control over eating behavior during the eating binges; self-induced vomiting, use of laxatives or diuretics, strict dieting or fasting, or vigorous exercise in order to prevent weight gain; and persistent overconcern with body shape and weight" (APA, 1987).

The food consumed during a binge is often high calorie and easily ingested, with a texture that facilitates rapid eating. The food is usually eaten surreptitiously. A binge is usually terminated by abdominal discomfort or induced vomiting, which decreases the physical pain of abdominal distention, allowing either continued eating or termination of the binge. In some cases, vomiting itself may be desired, so that the person either will binge in order to vomit or will vomit after eating a small amount of food. Although eating binges may be pleasurable, disparaging self-criticism and a depressed mood often follow.

People with BN invariably exhibit great concern about their weight and make repeated attempts to control it by dieting, vomiting, or using cathartics or diuretics. They often feel that their lives are dominated by conflicts about eating (APA, 1987). The prognosis for successful recovery for most patients treated in outpatient programs for uncomplicated BN seems quite good. However, intermediate and long-range follow-up studies indicate that this illness runs a fluctuating course, with alternating periods of relapse and remission.

Many patients with eating disorders do not meet *DSM* diagnostic criteria. They may resemble patients with BN who no longer binge-eat (common in chronic cases) or patients with AN who do not meet weight criteria or who deny one or more of the diagnostic criteria in order to conceal their illness.

RISK FACTORS FOR BOTH DISORDERS

Available research has suggested some obvious and some probable risk factors. The risk factors that have been defined by existing epidemiological studies are gender, age, and socioeconomic status. These disorders are primarily confined to females with a median age of onset of about 18 years for BN and somewhat younger for AN. Higher socioeconomic status is considered to be a risk factor for AN but not for BN. Many authors have suggested that psychosocial pressure for thinness, and more recently for physical fitness and to exercise, contribute to the apparent increase in incidence of eating disorders (Garner, Garfinkel, Schwartz, & Thompson, 1980).

Several antecedents, sufficiently documented by existing studies, may be considered probable risk factors for eating disorders. Eating disorders may be more frequent among individuals with a higher familial prevalence of depression and/or chemical dependency (Hudson, Pope, Jonas, & Yurgelun-Todd, 1983; Pyle, Mitchell, & Eckert, 1981; Strober, Salkin, Burroughs, & Morrell, 1982). Increased stress, perceived stress, or personal loss have been antecedent to the development of eating disorders in retrospective studies, but they have not been studied systematically (Pyle et al., 1981; Strober, 1984). An association between onset of BN and strict dieting and presence of depression and alcohol abuse have all been reported, and they may be viewed as risk factors as well (Mitchell, Hatsukami, Eckert, & Pyle, 1985; Pyle et al., 1981). Sudden weight gain or loss have also been reported as antecedent to eating disorders (Fairburn, 1983).

Other characteristics associated with eating disorders have been suggested as either consequence or potential risk factors, including social isolation, impaired social adjustment, and low self-esteem (Hatsukami, Owen, Pyle, & Mitchell, 1982; Weiss & Ebert, 1983). Loss of control (impulsivity) has been described in bulimics and bulimic anorexics (Garner, Garfinkel, & O'Shaughnessy, 1985; Hatsukami et al., 1982). In addition, issues regarding body image, exercise, and maturity fears have all been implicated with AN as consequences or risk factors (Bruch, 1978; Garner & Garfinkel, 1980). Prospective studies may provide valuable data about status of these characteristics as either risk factors for or consequences of eating disorders.

DIAGNOSTIC ISSUES AND PROBLEMS (DSM-IV)

ENGAGING THE PATIENT IN THERAPY

Engaging the patient in therapy is often difficult. In summarizing this problem in AN, Hsu (1986) recommended that "the clinician establish a treatment alliance by openly acknowledging the significance of the anorexic patient's striving for thinness and control, while . . . stressing the negative and possibly dangerous effects of her [or his] endeavor, such as resultant depression, malnutrition, fatigue, insomnia, restlessness, social isolation, and constant preoccupation with food and exercising." He further points out that the clinician should explain the effects of starvation and outline the course and outcome of the illness while emphasizing the benefits of treatment with the assurance that the treatment will not destroy the patient's specialness or control. In addition, because cooperation of the family may determine whether the patient enters treatment, joint meetings with the patient and the family to discuss the illness and the treatment are considered to be essential. Literature for the patient and the family to read may also be of value (Garfinkel & Garner, 1982). Hsu (1986) also points out that little data exist on the percentage of patients who refuse treatment and their eventual outcome, noting that in Crisp's series, 30 percent of the patients declined the offer of treatment, and their outcome appeared to be poor (Hsu, Crisp, & Harding, 1979). Because AN patients and their families tend to deny the illness, particularly its severity, negative reactions are often noted from treatment staff, who view patients with AN as being willfully resistant to treatment, leaving them with a feeling of extreme exasperation (Brotman, Stern, & Herzog, 1984).

Patients with BN may leave therapists with the same feeling, for although they may be more motivated to seek treatment, they have difficulty tolerating therapeutic interventions that do not produce immediate relief of symptoms or that do not have sufficient structure and definition to reduce their feelings of being out of control (Pyle & Mitchell, 1985).

When Is Inpatient Care Indicated?

All clinicians offering psychotherapy for eating disorders, especially AN, need to consider the timing of inpatient admission. Use of inpatient admission as a contingency for failure to maintain weight in outpatient therapy for AN, has been made much more difficult in the United States, because admission criteria are set up on the basis of insurance company standards. For many years, it was considered that a patient who weighed less than 70 percent of average of "ideal" weight would require admission for weight restoration (Hsu, 1986). Hospitalization is definitely indicated for (1) weight loss of more than 30 percent over 3 months; (2) severe metabolic disturbance, such as pulse lower than 40 per minute or temperature lower than 36°C, systolic blood pressure less than 70 mm of mercury and serum potassium under 2.5 moles/liter despite oral potassium replacement; (3) severe depression or suicide risk; and (4) severe binge-eating and purging (with a risk of aspiration) (Herzog & Copeland, 1985).

Another relevant issue is that of involuntary hospitalization for the patient who absolutely refuses treatment despite obvious need. Because adult patients with AN seem capable of making judgments about treatment, requests for involuntary treatment may often be refused by the same courts who might not hesitate to commit patients for chemical-dependency treatment. Consequently, families will require support to develop new intervention contingencies, which may include withdrawal of emotional or physical support until the family member enters treatment.

The role of hospitalization for BN is unclear because the reported treatment studies involving treatment success have been outpatient studies. Inpatient admission may be indicated for those patients with more severe loss of control over their eating and more severe character pathology, including borderline, histrionic, or dependent personality features. Until these mitigating factors are more clearly studied and confirmed through controlled studies, lack of positive treatment results reported to date would suggest against inpatient care.

THE MANAGEMENT OF BULIMIC BEHAVIORS

Historically, there have been several controversies about management of bulimic behaviors: One was the intensive versus nonintensive approach. The former is designed to provide sufficient support for interruption of the daily habitual binge-purging process, and the latter allows patients to proceed more at their own pace, contracting for either cessation or reduction of the bulimic behaviors.

The time for confronting interpersonal, environmental, or psychological precipitants that maintain disordered eating has been open to discussion. Garner (1985b) feels that this should be done early, whereas others would wait until the habitual daily behavior is reduced so that environmental and psychological cues can be more easily determined before confronting the precipitants for binge-purge behavior (Fairburn, 1981; Pyle & Mitchell, 1985).

DEPRESSION

Significant depression has been associated with both AN and BN (Cantwell, Sturzenberger, Borroughs, Salkin, & Green, 1977; Hudson, Laffer, & Pope, 1982). Most researchers now believe such depression to be secondary to the syndromes. In fact, depression ratings are reduced for those patients with BN who have positive treatment outcome (Garner et al., 1988). Nevertheless, a subgroup of patients has (1) had episodes of major depression prior to the onset of their eating disorder, (2) symptoms of major depression with vegetative signs during the disorder, or (3) mood disturbances following normalization of eating behaviors. A trial on antidepressant medication may be indicated for these patients, even though the therapist does not elect to use antidepressant therapy as a primary treatment for the eating disorder.

WEIGHT ISSUES

Weight Restoration and Psychotherapy

Hsu (1986) pointed out the importance of psychotherapeutic intervention in weight restoration, including individual and family therapy, so that the patient does not feel that eating and weight gain are the only goals of treatment. He believes that (1) a carefully planned, structured inpatient program implemented consistently by a competent treatment team is effective in a vast majority of cases in restoring weight, (2) coercive treatments, overrestrictive measures, and pharmacotherapy are usually unnecessary; and (3) such measures, if used at all, should be used only in refractory cases or when definite clinical indications are present. Other clinicians have also emphasized the importance of introducing psychotherapy, noting that behavioral therapy alone is only good for providing short-term weight gain (Garfinkel & Garner, 1982) and that behavior modification techniques may be "potentially dangerous methods," as they may completely remove control from a patient who is struggling to maintain some control (Bruch, 1974).

Clinicians also disagree about the time of discharge for patients who are undergoing weight restoration as inpatients. Crisp (1980) has long advocated that weight restoration should match the population mean weight for height at the onset of illness, to allow both the patient and the family to reexperience the existential issues that precipitated the psycholgical regression. Others have aimed at restoration of the patient to either an age-appropriate weight (Casper, 1982) or a low-average weight (Garfinkel & Garner, 1982).

The advent of managed care has required that we rethink and modify our treatment approaches to weight restoration.

Weight Maintenance in BN

Programs at major centers no longer recommend diets of 1200 calories or less for patients involved in treatment of BN (even those who are overweight). Treatment protocols for BN usually advocate sufficient food intake to provide balanced daily nutrition to maintain weight and to prevent hunger. Disagreement occurs about the weight that should be maintained. Programs may (1) advocate no target weight but specify the caloric intake, (2) require a minimal weight of 90 percent of the ideal norm, (3) require caloric intake to maintain current weight, or (4) require an individualized weight based on family history and estimation of set-point weight (Garner, Rockert, Olmsted, Johnson, & Coscina, 1985).

RELAPSE PREVENTION

Both AN and BN have fluctuating courses in response to environmental stresses. Relapse occurs within a year in about 50 percent of patients treated in hospitals for AN (Hsu, 1980). Although these data covered studies from 1954 to 1978, the 50 percent relapse rate has not been appreciably reduced since then, indicating the need to develop techniques to strengthen therapist-patient bonds and to improve continuity of care during the transition between inpatient and outpatient care. More emphasis has been placed on relapse prevention for BN, and this concern is being partially addressed through exposure to high-risk foods and situations.

THE CHRONIC PATIENT

The short history of BN has limited collection of data about chronicity; however, many patients with AN have been followed for more than a decade. In general, a longer duration of illness consistently predicts poor outcome (Dally, 1969). Consequently, alternative treatment approaches may need to be considered for patients with multiple hospitalizations. Crisp (1980) has cautioned that coercive treatments may precipitate depression and suicide in chronic patients. Perhaps chronic patients should be admitted when weight is dangerously low, but they should not be required to attain a target weight (Hsu, 1986). Hsu and Lieberman (1982) described a paradoxical approach in which they suggested to the chronic patient that it might actually be better to maintain the best adjustment possible in the absence of weight restoration after so many years of illness.

THE THERAPIST

Treatment of both AN and BN require therapists who have extensive knowledge of the illness. The issue of whether therapists are more effective if they have experienced eating disorders has not been resolved. However, it appears that in lieu of actual experience, extensive knowledge of the eating disorder is equally well accepted by patients.

In the case of AN, the patient must develop a high degree of trust in a therapist's expertise, because it is exceedingly difficult for the patient to accept the need for weight restoration. Weight restoration is highly frightening for the anorectic patient, and this fear can only be abated by the patient's trust that the therapist is competent and will provide adequate care. With weight gain, anorexic patients perceive total loss of control over eating, and further weight restoration awakens fears of having a mature body and menses. The therapist must also be very empathic and able to bridge lack of affect and affective expression in patients with AN.

In the case of BN, patients are wary of coming into therapy with therapists who are not well informed about eating disorders. Knowledge about eating disorders is also essential for completing the educational process that must occur as a part of normalizing eating behavior. Also, the gender of the therapist may be an important issue that has not been sufficiently studied. Although female therapists are often used in the treatment of females with AN, they offer both advantages and disadvantages. Female therapists may have difficulty because of (1) the female anorectic patient's conflict with her mother, (2) her natural competition with women, and (3) the career-home conflicts of anorectic patients. Advantages for female therapists are (1) the identification that occurs with the female anorexic patient; (2) the openness that anorectics can thereby generate, as opposed to their reluctance to be open with males; and (3) the ability of the patient with AN to pick up assertiveness from her female therapist, which she would not be able to do with a male therapist (Frankenburg, 1984).

IATROGENESIS

In our treatment of eating disorders, we must ensure that the clinician does nothing to worsen the patients' condition. Garner (1985a) pointed out a number of iatrogenic factors that may worsen the clinical condition of eating-disorder patients, such as (1) failure to attend to food and weight issues in psychotherapy, (2) unrealistic target weights in treatment, (3) behavior modification without attention to psychological issues, (4) classical psychoanalysis, (5) use of tube feeding, (6) abstinence models, (7) well-intentioned prevention campaigns featuring prominent people who have eating disorders, and (8) self-help and support groups with actively bulimic members.

PROBLEM PATIENTS

Patients with comorbid conditions, including personality disorders, substance abuse (particularly alcohol), physical and sexual abuse, posttraumatic stress syndrome, and multiple personality are all associated with poor treatment outcome. All these problems may be present in the same individual. Patients meeting the diagnostic criteria for borderline personality may comprise 10 percent to 25 percent of the bulimic population. Abuse of alcohol and benzodiazapines are common and abuse of cocaine are frequent in this group. Physical and sexual abuse are also frequently reported, with frequency depending on the criteria used to define abuse. In addition, patients who report verbal abuse, particularly public humiliation have less favorable outcome (Rorty, Yager, & Rossotto, 1994). The comorbidity of eating disorders with diabetes is especially critical because of the continual variations in food intake present in many patients. Different treatment strategies may be indicated for each of these comorbid problems.

TREATMENT STRATEGIES

Consistent with the shorter chronology of documented diagnosis of BN, the treatment literature related to psychotherapy of AN is more extensive but includes fewer controlled psychotherapy studies than that for BN. Almost all researchers have emphasized the importance of psychotherapy for AN, although Russell (1970) advocates a basic nursing-support approach, with emphasis by the physician on honesty, empathy, and support. Bruch (1973, 1982, 1985) wrote extensively on the theory and practice of psychotherapy for AN, emphasizing fact finding and careful attention to the patient's feelings, sensations, and ideas. More recently, application of cognitive treatment approaches (Garner & Bemis, 1982) has provided a second viable treatment technique. Family therapy for AN has become very popular, but it is clearly more feasible for younger patients still living at their parents' home (Minuchin, Rosman, & Baker, 1978; Russell, Szmukler, Dare, & Eisler, 1987). Early reports of successful psychotherapy for BN stressed individual cognitive-behavior therapy (Fairburn, 1981) and group approaches (Boskind-Lodahl & White, 1978; Johnson, Connors, & Stuckey, 1983). Application of behavioral therapy, such as developing alternatives to binge-eating and using exposure and response prevention techniques (J. Rosen & Leitenberg, 1982) have been accepted as important components of psychotherapy for bulimia nervosa.

The multimodal approach developed for psychotherapy of eating disorders usually includes behavioral techniques for weight restoration and maintenance, for controlling bulimic behaviors, or for relapse prevention. Specific treatment techniques for eating disorders involving behavioral therapy are covered in Chapter 20. Treatment techniques specific to males with eating disorders have not been developed or studied.

Even though controlled treatment studies are lacking, there are many areas of common agreement for treatment of eating disorders in general and for AN in particular. Most researchers emphasize the multidimensional, heterogeneous nature of eating disorders. Consequently, comprehensive treatment may appropriately include family, individual, and group therapy, at times using behavioral, cognitive, and psychodynamic principals. All major programs emphasize normalizing food intake through structured eating, meal plans, or food diaries. In addition, phasing or sequencing of treatment approaches for both AN (Garner, Garfinkel, & Irving, 1986) and BN (Fairburn, 1985; Pyle & Mitchell, 1985) has received increasing attention.

A number of treatment concepts for AN have endured the test of time: (1) a focus on food and nutrition; (2) normalization of weight; (3) importance of the therapeutic relationship and engaging patient to improve self-concept; (4) importance of recognition of affect and the expression of affect; (5) clarification of family interactional patters and the improvement of family communication; (6) confrontation of developmental issues around separation and autonomy, sexual fears, and identity formation; (7) understanding of physical and psychological consequences of the illness, including the effects of starvation with its associated behavior, emotions, and thoughts; and (8) confrontation of the patients' internal conflict about their own illness (Garner & Garfinkel, 1985).

INDIVIDUAL PSYCHODYNAMIC PSYCHOTHERAPY

Psychodynamic psychotherapy continues to be the major psychotherapeutic modality for the treatment of patients with AN. Bruch (1973, 1978, 1982, 1985) defined the phenomenology of AN, in which self-starvation represents the struggle for autonomy, competence, control, and self-respect. She proposed a fact-finding psychotherapy aimed at correcting specific conceptual defects and distortions that evolved out of faulty developmental experiences. Therapy aims to help the patient discover a "genuine self" by encouraging and confirming authentic expressions of the patient's thoughts and feelings. Rather than exploring the symbolic significance of symptoms, experiences are reevaluated in order to understand how conceptual disturbances, largely derived from previous relationships, have interfered with the development of autonomy and self-confidence. Bruch (1985) cautioned that during psychotherapy, low weight must be corrected without disturbing the tenuous sense of autonomy that remains for the patient. At the same time, Bruch advocated clarifying family interactions to ally the entire family with the treatment effort.

Bruch believed that therapy should be initiated by identifying the symptom as one related to decreased self-worth and self-value, pointing out the effects of starvation, and indicating that the therapy is for the benefit of the patient, not the patient's parents. Patients were encouraged to reduce their posture of "helpless passivity, hateful submissiveness, and indiscriminate negativism." Ongoing therapy centered on repeated review about both the patient's need to be good and to please others, and the identification and reinforcement of a new personality based on internal needs rather than environmental expectations. The patient is also encouraged to identify developmental delays, and to confront (with the therapist) family mechanisms that encourage those delays. Patients also are helped to reduce their expectations for superperformance and to curb grandiose aspirations. Finally, the therapist works with patients to reduce their isolation from peers and family.

The second major force in the development of psychodynamic psychotherapy for AN has been Crisp (1980). Crisp emphasizes the phobic avoidance of weight and the fears of sexual maturity manifested by patients with AN. This developmental model assumes that AN represents an attempt to cope with the fears and conflicts associated with psychobiological maturity. The dieting and consequent starvation, then, become the mechanisms for the patient's regression to a prepubertal state. Such a model requires that weight restoration be continued to the point where developmental concerns arrested by the weight loss again surface. Individual therapy may then be directed toward developing more adult strategies for coping.

Goodsitt (1985) has borrowed from the self-theory of Kohut (1971) to develop a psychoanalytically oriented psychotherapy similar to that of Bruch. Casper's (1982) emphasis on self-esteem deficits addresses similar issues. Garner (1985b) has underscored the common themes present in individual therapy of AN. These include (1) the struggle for autonomy, independence, and individuality; (2) the inability of patient and family to handle adolescence and to break childhood bonds; and (3) the need for control, mastery, and competence in which the patient selects being thin as an area of mastery. Other elements of individual therapy include concerns about body image, emotional expressiveness, assertiveness, social skills, perfectionism, and depression. In addition, Garner notes contraindications to individual psychodynamic psychotherapy, including severe starvation and metabolic abnormalities, severe depression or decompensation, poor motivation for change or failure to develop a trusting relationship, severely limited intellectual capacity or complete lack of psychological awareness, family relationships that sabotage therapeutic goals, or a preadolescent onset of the disorder.

In summary, psychodynamic psychotherapy has been recommended as a primary treatment for AN but has not been adequately demonstrated as an effective treatment for BN. No controlled studies have evaluated the efficacy of individual psychodynamic psychotherapy for either condition.

INDIVIDUAL COGNITIVE AND COGNITIVE-BEHAVIORAL THERAPIES

The cognitive-behavioral approach to the treatment of both AN and BN is based on the premise that the central features of these disorders are irrational dysfunctional beliefs and values concerning body shape and weight. Individual cognitive-behavioral therapy was first recommended for bulimia nervosa (Fairburn, 1981) and shortly after for AN (Garner & Bemis, 1982). It has remained a primary treatment for bulimia nervosa.

Fairburn's open study (1981) used individual therapy that included self-monitoring, goal-setting, problem-solving, and cognitive-restructuring techniques for an average duration of seven months. The first stage consisted of eight appointments in four weeks, with an emphasis on establishing some degree of control over the habitual daily bulimic behavior, using behavioral techniques (which included self-monitoring, a prescribed pattern of regular eating, and stimulus-control measures similar to those used in behavioral treatment for obesity). Patients were also given education about body-weight regulation, dieting, and the adverse effects of vomiting and laxative abuse for weight control. The second stage, of approximately eight appointments in eight weeks, included training in (1) strategies designed to reduce the tendency to diet, (2) problem-solving techniques, and (3) cognitive-restructuring procedures to modify isolated environmental cues that trigger binge-purging behavior. In the final stage, lasting six weeks, with three appointments, emphasis was on assessment of progress and relapse prevention, Fairburn was one of the first to recommend introduction of forbidden foods into the diets of patients with BN as part of the later stages of treatment. Fairburn's posttreatment results found that 9 of 11 subjects reported fewer than one binge-purge episode per month; his follow-up results at one year revealed that five out of the six patients contacted were having binge-purge episodes no more frequently than once ever two to three months. These encouraging results influenced many clinicians to embrace these techniques.

Fairburn, Kirk, O'Connor, and Cooper (1986) later compared this approach for BN treatment with short-term psychotherapy, which was also associated with impressive treatment outcome. It was modeled after B. Rosen's (1979) brief psychotherapy, adapted on the basis of Bruch's (1973) writings on AN and Stunkard's (1980) psychotherapeutic approach to overweight people who binge-eat. This approach necessitates that eating problems be conceptualized as a maladaptive solution for other underlying difficulties. Freeman, Barry, Dunkeld-Turnbull, and Henderson (1988) compared weekly individual cognitive-behavior therapy, following Beck, Rush, Shaw, and Emery's model (1979), with individual behavioral therapy, supportive group therapy, and a waiting-list control. Individual cognitive-behavioral treatment techniques included identification and recording of automatic thoughts through self-monitoring and restructuring of those thoughts, dealing initially with maladaptive cognitions relating to eating and weight, and then progressing to general psychological issues including depression, self-esteem, and assertiveness. Only minimal attempts were used to alter the abnormal behavior. Of the 92 original subjects 65 completed treatment. All three treatment groups improved significantly in the frequency of bulimia behavior. Efficacy of individual cognitive-behavioral therapy was more evident during follow-up when binge-purging frequencies were further reduced and when this group was significantly superior to group therapy subjects, with regard to irritability, depression, and anxiety. There were no significant differences, however, between the two individual therapies. In this study, all three therapies were effective, with cognitive-behavioral and group therapies having higher dropout rates. Ordman and Kirschenbaum (1985) had less positive results with individual cognitive-behavior therapy and exposure and response prevention, when compared with a brief intervention waiting list control. Only 20 percent of the 10 subjects in the study were in remission after treatment and 30 percent were unchanged.

The main proponents of individual cognitive-behavior therapy for AN have been Garner and Bemis (1982, 1985). Their techniques were derived from the Beck et al. (1979) cognitive-behavioral treatment of depression. This approach involves a commitment to clear specification of treatment methods and an objective assessment of change in target behaviors. Modifications to conventional cognitive therapy are adopted in the treatment of AN. Specific areas that should be pursued are (1) idiosyncratic beliefs related to food and weight, (2) interaction of physical and psychological aspects of the disorder, (3) the patient's desire to retain certain focal symptoms, and (4) prominence of fundamental self-concept deficit related to self-esteem and trust of internal state.

These early studies suggested that individual cognitive-behavior therapy is an effective treatment for BN and that other individual therapies also may be effective treatments in the hands of able clinicians.

Although both individual and group cognitive-behavioral treatment approaches are widely supported by a majority of clinicians, a significant study by Fairburn's group comparing behavioral, cognitive behavioral, and interpersonal therapy, with short, intermediate, and long-term follow-up confirms not only the premise that many individual therapies may be effective, but also that the effectiveness of these therapies may be more evident at different points in time (Fairburn, Norman, Welch, O'Connor, Doll, & Peveler, 1995).

INTERPERSONAL PSYCHOTHERAPY

Interpersonal Psychotherapy (IPT) assumes that negative affect stems from dissatisfaction with relationships and social impairment. Fairburn and his group found that IPT yielded better long-term results for treatment of BN when used as a controlled group compared with cognitive behavioral therapy and behavior therapy (Fairburn et al., 1995). Of interest is the fact that IPT in these studies did not address disordered eating behavior. Improvement in behavior was assumed to be related to developing satisfying stable relationships and having a more fulfilling social life (Reiss & Johnson-Sabine, 1995). IPT, in dealing with interpersonal relationships, improves the socialization process, increases the number of contacts and strong affiliations with other individuals, and creates a carry over effect that reduces social isolation, increases self-esteem, and eventually improves patients capacity to be more tolerant of their body configuration. Because body dissatisfaction and its associated low self-esteem is a major factor in relapse, IPT has proven to be a valuable approach.

GROUP PSYCHOTHERAPY

Group psychotherapy potentially offers a cost-effective approach for large numbers of young men and women who are seeking treatment for BN. In fact, an initial cognitive-behavior group approach has been recommended as a cost-effective approach to treat less severe cases (Brotman, Alonso, & Herzog,

1985). On the other hand, group psychotherapy for AN, which is discussed later in this section, has limited advantages, except as an adjunctive treatment.

Bulimia Nervosa

Several attributes of group psychotherapy offer specific benefits for the treatment of BN. Group treatment may provide sufficient structure and support (1) to permit interruption of the chronic habitual nature of the behavior, (2) to promote reduction of the social isolation and loneliness that accompany BN, (3) to increase greatly the number of people offering insight and support about the behavior, and (4) to permit group members to increase their own self-esteem by assisting other group members (Pyle & Mitchell, 1985).

Seven different group formats have been used to test cognitive-behavior therapies as part of four controlled studies and one uncontrolled study. These studies have included (1) cognitive restructuring (as a control for other experimental groups) (Wilson, Rossiter, Kleifled, & Lindholm, 1986; Yates & Sambrailo, 1984); (2) cognitive-behavioral and behavioral principles (Kirkley, Schneider, Agras, & Beckman, 1985; Lee & Rush, 1986; Schneider & Agras, 1985); (3) cognitive restructuring and EAP (Wilson et al., 1986); and (4) cognitive-behavior therapy, behavioral techniques, and ERP (Yates & Sambralio, 1984). In cognitive-behavior groups, goal setting is almost always used to establish individual treatment goals.

Two authors have reported on psychoeducational groups (Connors, Johnson, & Stuckey, 1984; Wolchik, Weiss, & Katzman, 1986). These groups usually have an educational or teaching component as part of the group therapy and are highly structured and time limited.

The eating disorders program at the University of Minnesota has used intensive outpatient group treatment as its main treatment technique for BN in the past (Mitchell, Hatsukami, et al., 1985). The behavioral and cognitive-behavioral format consisted of three phases: (1) psychoeducational, (2) interruption of bulimic behavior, and (3) behavior stabilization. The expectation was that all members of the group would focus on reducing bulimic behavior on the first night of the second phase of the group program.

Stuber and Strober (1987) have noted that evaluation of group psychotherapy for adolescents with BN is needed and that there has been insufficient attention paid to this important group of patients. The authors noted that adolescents do not accept behavioral and psychoeducational techniques used for adult bulimia. They believe that group psychotherapy may better fit an adjunctive role for adolescents (1) to reduce the secrecy and the isolation that surround the illness, (2) to reduce the ridgidly fixed and irrational ideas concerning body weight or fasting, (3) to help patients develop alternative strategies to cope with stress and intrapsychic conflict, (4) to clarify and resolve psychically painful emotional states, and (5) to serve as a catalyst for movement in individual or family therapies.

Group Therapy for AN

Group therapy for AN is frequently a part of the therapeutic milieu of major inpatient programs. In order to participate in group therapy, the patient must not be at a stage of extreme starvation (Hall, 1985). In addition, the patient must have moved beyond the stage of denial and must have a mutually positive relationship with the therapist. Contrary to group therapy for other conditions, group therapy for AN is seen in the context of a variety of other forms of treatment in a specialized program, in both inpatient and outpatient psychotherapy, and it is seen as a mechanism to improve interpersonal relationships (Hall, 1985; Polivy, 1981). Group therapy for anorexia has received little attention in the literature. This may be related to the difficulty of involving patients with AN in group therapy (Hall, 1985). Anorectic patients have been described as withdrawn, anxious, rigid, egocentric, preoccupied with body weight and food, and less able to identify and express feelings. All of the aforementioned characteristics lend themselves poorly to group psychotherapy. In addition, the capacity of patients with AN to intellectualize tends to make them less accessible to therapists (Hall, 1985).

Family Therapy

Family therapy is viewed as an important component in the treatment of AN, mainly because of the influential writings of two groups of therapists: Minuchin and his colleagues (1978) at the Philadelphia Child Guidance Clinic, and Selvini-Palazzoli (1978) and co-workers in Milan. Both have based their treatment of AN on theoretical models that they have devised to explain the genesis of that illness. The structural family therapists (Minuchin and associates) seek to alter dysfunctional transactional patterns within the family system, by using active and straightforward directives around the symptom, as opposed to insight. The strategic therapists, with Selvini-Palazzoli most often associated with family treatment of anorexia nervosa, are also symptom oriented, but they attempt to uncover the hidden family gain, which they see as necessary to disrupt the maladaptive cycle. Both may use seemingly illogical and paradoxical interventions. Both of these therapeutic schools view family therapy as the primary treatment for AN. The work of both schools was exciting to therapists, and Minuchin's posttreatment and follow-up results (with a reported 86% recovery) created great interest. Minuchin, however, treated young inpatients with a short duration of illness coming from intact families—all characteristics associated with positive treatment outcome. However, the enmeshed family described by Minuchin et al. (1978) comprises only part of the families of patients with AN, limiting the applicability of the approach to a wider range of patients. In addition, many families of anorectic patients are unable to tolerate the anxiety and confrontation of these family approaches, and they discontinue therapy.

By the mid 1980s, there was a clear tendency to develop an eclectic and integrated treatment for most eating disorders, which led to the current trend of eclecticism and integration of family therapy into a multidemensional treatment program (Garfinkel & Garner, 1982). This approach led to abandonment of orthodox adherence to one particular school of family therapy. Instead, more family therapists started to combine concepts and strategies derived from different models. The writings of Vandereycken (Vandereycken & Meerman, 1984) are typical of the current generation of family therapists engaged in the treatment of AN. He advocates family therapy as a component to be integrated within a multidemensional approach that is guided by a constructive and positive attitude toward the family and is based on a pragmatic but flexible scientist-practitioner spirit (Vandereycken, 1987).

Although AN as an illness lends itself to the objective evaluation of the efficacy of psychological treatment, only one controlled trial with systematic follow-up has been reported for the family therapy of AN and BN. Russell et al. (1987) have completed a controlled evaluation of family therapy for AN and BN in a trial with 80 patients (57 with AN and 23 with BN). Patients were randomly assigned to family therapy or individual supportive therapy, and after one year of treatment they were reassessed, using body weight, menstrual function, and ratings on the Morgan and Russell scales. The positive results of Minuchin et al. (1978) with young anorectics with short-term illness were confirmed by this study, which demonstrated that young (under age 19 years) anorectics with brief duration of illness (under four years) responded to the family therapy at a higher rate (60% good results) than they did to individual supportive therapy (10% good results). However, family therapy was not superior to individual therapy for BN.

Family therapy has been used less frequently for patients with BN because of the large number of these patients who are separated from their families.

OTHER THERAPIES

Marital therapy may also be important in the treatment of individuals with eating disorders, as the marriage relationship may change dramatically when eating behavior becomes normalized and codependency is exposed. Local support groups and self-help groups for individuals recovering from eating disorders contribute to a comprehensive support network, provided that a majority of their members are in remission. It is likely that women with eating disorders may also benefit from groups focusing on feminists issues and sociocultural pressures. Assertiveness training, relaxation training, and training in stress management and problem solving may also be valuable supports in relapse prevention. Combination treatment with antidepressants and psychosocial treatment may be required for many patients. More than one adequate trial of antidepressant therapy may be required before the right medication is found (i.e., desipramine, fluoxetine, or tranylcypromine).

A treatment for AN at the Montreaux Counseling Center in Victoria B. C. Canada, places patients in an environment of constant nurturing. This focus on reducing the interpersonal estrangement and touch deprivation claims excellent outcome. The program requires high staff levels and enthusiasm, empathy, and persistence. Cost effective replication of the program might require expatient volunteers because semiskilled staff who would accept lower pay might lack the enthusiasm required to maintain successful outcome. Because long-term outcome is related to individual strength and self concept, one would have to conduct follow-up studies to assess the ability of program participants to progress from a very supportive environment to one requiring more self-sufficiency.

Case Illustration

Mary L. is a 23-year-old, single family who came for eating disorder evaluation, was self-referred, and was requesting BN treatment. She related a history of BN for five years following a diagnosed episode of anorexia nervosa six years prior to evaluation. During her bout of AN, she lost weight until she weighed 85 pounds. At evaluation, she weighed 124 pounds and was 64 inches tall. She binge-ate three to four times weekly at evaluation, down from a high of three to four times daily. She reported on six-month period of remission. She controls her weight by inducing vomiting each time she binge-eats. She goes on 24-hour fasts once or twice monthly. Her binges at time of evaluation occurred after eating a complete meal. The binges included ingestion of two handfuls of candy or a large number of crackers. Although much smaller than her earlier binges, they were associated with a feeling of loss of control. Symptoms include puffy cheeks, but she denied ever having calluses on her knuckles from inducing vomiting. At evaluation, she was also exercising to control weight and to maintain physical fitness, although she rigidly controls the duration so that she won't overdo it.

She was first treated five years prior to evaluation with cognitive-behavior therapy for three months. She also received three months of behavioral therapy, including extensive assertiveness training four years prior to the evaluation. She was treated one year prior to evaluation in group therapy for BN by her health maintenance organization, and she was also seen by a counselor at the University she was attending one year prior to and on the year of the evaluations. Although she believed that all these treatments were helpful to her, she stated that she had been unable to eliminate the bulimic behaviors. She related her six-month abstinence from bulimic behavior to going away to school and becoming more independent. Not surprisingly, she felt that her relapse was due to conflict with her mother over money and the discontinuation of her eating disorder group at the university, along with other stresses.

Psychiatric history was unremarkable, but medical history revealed a diagnosis of hiatal hernia $1\frac{1}{2}$ years prior to evaluation. In recent months, she reported developing more cavities in her teeth and was told by her dentist that she had erosion of her teeth. Evaluation of chemical use indicated a social drinking pattern once or twice a month without intoxication, the consumption of four to five cans of diet cola daily, and eight cups of coffee daily, along with caffeine to study for finals. Family history revealed that there were no eating disorders in her family, although her mother tended to watch her own weight. Mary L. related that she had an uncle who was depressed and was on medication for depression and may or may not have been hospitalized. There was a strong family loathing for alcoholism. A brother had been arrested for driving while intoxicated, and chemical dependency treatment; a sister also had problems with alcohol. A maternal grandmother and grandfather were untreated alcoholics, and a paternal grandfather was treated for alcoholism and recovered. At the time of evaluation, she was a senior at a state university, studying psychology, and working part-time as a waitress, although she reported no disordered eating behavior either during of after work. She had four or five good friends, all of whom know about her eating disorder. She was not dating at the time of evaluation, because she did not like herself in her present state. She expressed motivation for treatment. On mental status examination, mood and affect were appropriate to interview content, and there was no evidence of anxiety, symptoms of major depression, or thought disorder.

Mary L. was referred to an intensive outpatient group therapy program for BN, where she reduced her binge-purging behavior almost 50 percent during the meal planning and psychoeducational phase of treatment. She stopped behavior altogether during the second (intensive) phase, and she remained free of bulimic behavior until the tenth and final week of treatment, when she had two episodes of binge-purging behavior on a weekend. Because of this, she entered a maintenance support group for a period of four months maintenance treatment, she reported symptoms of intermittent sadness, irritability, and dysphoria. Following initiation of antidepressant treatment with 20mg of fluoxetine, there was an improvement in mood. In addition, she found it much easier to refrain from binge-purging behaviors, and after three months of improved mood and remission of bulimia symptoms, the antidepressant was successfully discontinued. On one-year follow-up, it was noted that she had experience two episodes of binge-purging behavior following a disappointment over an unsuccessful job interview. In general, she was quite happy with her lifestyle and her eating habits, although she had reduced the number of meals she ate from three to two daily.

ALTERNATIVE TREATMENT OPTIONS

ASSESSING ALTERNATIVE TREATMENTS

Despite the fact that psychotherapy makes good pragmatic sense in treatment of AN, the long-term effectiveness of the alternative psychotherapy techniques remains to be evaluated, in part because of the small population in treatment. More research should be directed toward prevention of relapse, in addition to comparison of inpatient, outpatient, and partial hospitalization programs to restore and maintain weight. The role of specific elements of the multimodal treatments that are now favored should be evaluated.

Factors other than the treatment being evaluated must also be considered (i.e., subjects motivation, treatment system, skill of therapists) for those studies reporting excellent results from all treatments being compared. Treatments that have been replicated in controlled studies at different centers are the most likely to have value for the clinician. Dropouts should be considered in any evaluation of treatment results, because retention of potential subjects in treatment is a legitimate measure of the effectiveness of that treatment. Unfortunately, treatments that are continued during follow-up or that are coincident with or followed by other treatments are difficult to evaluate.

Although reduction of bulimic behavior for bulimia nervosa and weight normalization and maintenance for AN are important outcome measures, treatment success and avoidance of relapse may relate to a number of other measures, such as preoccupation with body image, weight, and other attitudes about nutrition that may be measured through such instruments as the EDI (Garner & Olmstead, 1984). Psychological factors, including (1) depression, anxiety, and global improvement; (2) overall social adjustment; and (3) self-esteem, assertiveness, and self-control, may be associated with the outcome of treatment. Recently, Miller (1996) has recommended a much broader definition of treatment success, including more varied treatment outcome targets that include body related measures, medical health variables, exercise and eating habits, psychological health factors, body image, and quality of life measures.

Assessment of new treatments must emphasize not only effective but rapid treatment. Two new approaches that merit further assessment are motivation interviewing and enhancement and the constructive therapies.

MOTIVATIONAL INTERVIEWING AND ENHANCEMENT

This approach to encourage clients to take responsibility for changes they would make in their behavior has been increasingly used in the treatment of chemical dependency. Termed motivational interviewing (Miller & Rollnick, 1991) and motivational enhancement (Miller, Zwenben, DiClemente, & Rychtarik, 1992), much treatment offers a high degree of patient choice. Major elements are (1) presentation of data, (2) recognizing the problem, (3) setting goals for change, (4) development of a treatment menu, (5) assessment of treatment progress, and (6) menu modification to ensure success. The three main characteristics required by motivational enhancement practitioners include (1) accurate empathy, (2) nonpossessive warmth, and (3) genuiness. Such a therapist will engage in giving advice, removing barriers, providing choices, decreasing desirability of the unwanted behavior, practicing empathy, providing feedback, clarifying goals and active helping, which includes being available for follow-up.

A most important element of this method is the increasing sense of self-efficacy that program participants develop after choosing their own goals, selecting their own treatment, and being responsible for modifying goals and/or treatment based on outcome assessment.

Multiple factors need to be considered to enhance motivation for change. Research to date suggests that improvement of self-efficacy is quite important in motivational enhancement. Strong social support from families is an important motivator. In addition, desire for change and outcomes that are easily measurable and acceptable to the individual are critical. As part of a multicenter research study at the University of Washington, Seattle, college-age problem drinkers were placed in motivational enhancement therapy or a 12-step control group that stressed abstinence. It was noted that the motivational enhancement group had better treatment retention, had increased belief that abstinence was the best treatment solution, and reported a significantly higher abstinence rate than control subjects who had abstinence as their initial goal. Most of the experimental group had as their goal an acceptable degree of social drinking, but they had failed to achieve that goal and selected abstinence as an alternative (Miller et al., 1992).

CONSTRUCTIVE THERAPY

Another relatively recent therapeutic approach that is gaining increased attention comes from the child guidance literature (Hoyt, 1994). Constructive therapy focuses on strengths and resources rather than weaknesses and limitations (where they want to go, not where they have been). People are viewed as unique and resourceful creators of their own reality (for better or worse). Signposts associated with constructive therapies include the terms *competency based, future oriented, solution oriented, solution focused,* and *constructivist* (Hoyt, 1994). This therapeutic approach has a number of important principles. They include keeping the therapy simple and taking the patients seriously. This involves very careful listening on the part of the therapist, respect for patient goals and self-determination, identifying what works, and engaging in interviewing that will help patients reach attainable goals.

Desired changes should be small rather than large, very salient to the clients, and described in specific and concrete behavioral terms. They should be achievable within a practical context of the clients' lives and perceived by the clients as involving their own hard work. The goal should be treated as involving new behavior(s) rather than the absence or cessation of existing behavior(s). This approach involves a construction of useful solutions. It directs clients toward their own individual strength, success, and solution.

Dialogue with the client must remain sufficiently simple so that the client's resources can be utilized and so we express respect for them by accessing the information that they are able to share. Listening to clients and taking them seriously is required. In a single-session therapy project using constructive techniques, not only did the main complaint get resolved, but 67 percent of the patients described what they called ripple effects, that is, the clearing of other problems. Less than 10 percent of the improvements reported since the first session had anything to do with the presenting complaint.

The therapist must maintain therapeutic contacts that are useful. One of the major problems for clients are therapists who think that they know much better than the client what the problem is. Although this may be true, prescribing a treatment program may not be successful. There is a body of knowledge and a point of view that goes along with being a professional. Both have been acquired at considerable cost in time and money and, therefore, a large investment exists. Often, therapists get hooked into paying a lot of attention to what does not work and not what does.

PRESCRIPTIVE TREATMENT AND MANAGED CARE

The goal of managed care is to provide cost-effective treatment for clients. Low cost has been achieved, but superior treatment results with low cost have not. Therapists have argued that more expensive treatment is ultimately more effective, however, this premise has not been demonstrated in a convincing manner to those people who provide funding for treatment. There are several situations that have been quite frustrating for individuals engaged in treatment of eating disorders, especially AN. Therapists have had increasing frustration with their inability to conduct treatment in the way that has been demonstrated as effective over time. Many have felt the frustration of having third-party payors stop inpatient treatment when weight gain has reached a critical state that will be associated with relapse and long-term treatment failure if the patient is discharged. Another frustrating treatment situation is the complex patient who has several comorbid conditions and has experienced multiple treatment failures.

A Treatment Algorithm for AN

In the past four years we have applied the treatment techniques just reviewed to our treatment of women with AN. Our preliminary observations have not been systematically tested, but our clinical impressions have been reported (Pyle & Schmid, 1996).

Treatment for AN that will satisfy the managed-care system must achieve a rapid and complete alliance for treatment and goal attainment. The alliance for treatment-goal attainment requires education and genuine empathy and accepts education as being a *two way* process. This alliance must rapidly reach the point of accomplishing goal reversal by the client, using the techniques of therapeutic challenge, positive reinforcement, and the transfer of responsibility to arrive at a treatment solution that will work for our clients. Our task is to have sufficient knowledge to offer a menu of treatment options for consideration. Hsu (1986) was previously cited about the importance of therapeutic alliance. Many of his recommendations are consistent with recent treatment developments. Goal reversal involves the change in client goals, from winning the power struggle over weight, losing weight and being the most thin, to remaining with their peers in reaching program goals and eventually working with their peers to achieve success. The only requirement is that clients must gain weight during their stay. Consequences for treatment noncompliance, after a specific number of weekly reassessments, would include discharge. Relating to patients from this position rather than simply keeping them in therapy, will challenge them to stay with the peer treatment group and continue to succeed. A constant what-works-for-you approach, which increases self-esteem and motivation to take responsibility for success, is important. The most critical comment made about treatment selection is, "How does this approach fit with your previous experience." Phrases associated with goal reversal may be:

> "It must have taken a tremendous strength, focus, and resolve to lose weight in the face of all the social pressures opposing you."
>
> "From what you tell me, the feelings of accomplishment are much less than they used to be because of the weakness and physical problems, being dropped from activities, and recognizing that the need to be this is actually in control of you."
>
> "Even though you hate being hospitalized and you are confident you can eat outside the hospital, you have told us that you have had two opportunities to avoid hospitalization by eating."
>
> "It sounds like eating is very difficult."
>
> "Many people can lose weight, but the real challenge is gaining it back."
>
> "People sometimes need help to change."

The initial gains are supported by using paradoxical challenge and positive reinforcement. It is difficult for the therapist to accept a patient goal that states "I'll gain the weight to get out of here, but then I will lose it after discharge." Fortunately this can be discussed with the patient by recognizing the magnitude of this accomplishment, which would allow them to leave treatment. Clients are much more likely to further revise their goals to a more practical outcome. Phrases that might be used in treatment when future plans are formulated include:

"Although many people in this program are successful, we know how hard it is."

"I would understand if you couldn't succeed."

"As frightening as eating is for you it must be like taking poison."

"If you think about it, you won't be able to eat."

"The first week you may need to make yourself like a robot and not think."

"Since you feel that you might be able to eat if you were discharged, certainly it will be possible for you to leave within seven to fourteen days since the only criteria for leaving is to gain weight for seven days without any contingencies."

"There are a lot of options for your support that may be helpful and we will be happy to review some of those with you."

Slow progress in treatment is usually dealt with by emphasizing client responsibility for goal attainment, desire to keep up with their peer group, and to remain in the program. The success of these motivators is associated with the clients knowledge that we do what we say we will do and our knowledge that they will do what they say they are going to do. This adds a strong value to the process of discharge for people who are not ready for change and will make it easier for them to come back into the program when they are ready to complete it. Similar approaches are used as clients move to a position of independence and deal with relapse issues, support systems, follow-up visits, and possible volunteer work in the program.

THE PROBLEM PATIENT AND TREATMENT FAILURE

The techniques discussed above may also be effective with those patients described earlier in this chapter who have a history of sexual abuse, symptoms of alcohol abuse, personality disorder, abuse of other chemicals, or PTSD, in addition to an eating disorder. Although using the same basic treatment of philosophy, different comorbid conditions often have different levels of emphasis. The strong focus on education and empathy, paradoxical challenge, and positive reinforcement to establish the alliance for goal attainment in individuals with AN has been discussed. Attainment of those treatment goals also includes a strong emphasis on individual therapy, with ancillary use of cognitive behavioral problem solving, body image normalization, and constructive family therapy.

For individuals with BN, paradoxical challenge and positive reinforcement are the major tools for establishing an alliance for attainment of treatment goals. Ancillary approaches for attainment of treatment goals include education and empathy and motivational enhancement. Another major emphasis is on group therapy with ancillary use of cognitive-behavioral problem solving and pharmacotherapy, starting with one of the antidepressant selective serotonin reuptake inhibitors (SSRIs). For those individuals who have BN and comorbid alcohol abuse, we place a stronger emphasis on pharmacotherapy, offering a treatment menu of antibuse for at least the first 30 days in combination with an SSRI and the option of a narcotic antagonist when active craving is present. Individuals with significant personality problems are approached with shared education, empathy, paradoxical intent, positive reinforcement, and motivational enhancement to establish a therapeutic alliance. We believe individual therapy and family therapy are more helpful than group treatment for individuals with severe personality disorders.

The most important aspect of meeting the challenge from funders of managed care is to continue to promote psychotherapeutic solutions that empower the patient to choose from a treatment menu to accomplish desired change, or construct their own option to promote change. Their chances for success will be enhanced is they are willing to accept responsibility for reaching the goals they have defined.

Many types of prescribed treatment and clinical pathways require a chronological progression for completion of each step in the treatment. Our own philosophy is that success in following a treatment algorithm is not possible without strong patient motivation. Consequently we emphasize rapid movement through the treatment system to day treatment when medically stable and decreased daily hours of attendance and amount of structure until weekly outpatient contact is achieved. An important difference in this approach is that desire for change or acceptance of the status quo with later reentry into the treatment program are both successful outcomes.

SUMMARY

In summary, cognitive behavioral therapy for eating disorders remains the treatment of choice. There is ample evidence however, that alternative treatments such as interpersonal therapy may be equally effective. There are also studies that indicate that increasing self-esteem and normalizing body image are important in the success of these diverse treatments. Hopefully those factors that are related to long-term positive outcome after treatment exposure can be isolated from the existing and newly emerging approaches.

REFERENCES

American Psychiatric Association. (1987). *Diagnostic and statistical manual of mental disorders* (3rd ed., Rev.). Washington, DC: Author.

American Psychiatric Association. (1994). *Diagnostic and statistical manual of mental disorders* (4th ed.). Washington, DC: Author.

Beck, A.T., Rush, A.J., Shaw, B.F., & Emery, G. (1979). *Cognitive therapy of depression: A treatment manual.* New York: Guilford Press.

Boskind-Lodahl, M., & White, W.C. (1978). The defination and treatment of bulimarexia in college women—a pilot study. *Journal of the American College Health Association, 2,* 84–87.

Brotman, A.W., Alonso, A., & Herzog, D.B. (1985). Group therapy for bulimics: Clinical experience and practical recommendations. *Group, 9,* 15–23.

Brotman, A.W., Stern, T.A., & Herzog, D.B. (1984). Emotional reactions of house officers to patients with anorexia nervosa, diabetes, and obesity. *International Journal of Eating Disorders, 3,* 71–77.

Bruch, H. (1973). *Eating disorders: Obesity, anorexia nervosa and the person within.* New York: Basic Books.

Bruch, H. (1974). Perils of behavior modification in treatment of anorexia nervosa. *Journal of the American Medical Association, 230,* 1419–1422.

Bruch, H. (1978). *The golden cage.* Cambridge, MA: Harvard University Press.

Bruch, H. (1982). Anorexia nervosa: Therapy and theory. *American Journal of Psychiatry, 139,* 1531–1538.

Bruch, H. (1985). Four decades of eating disorders. In D.M. Garner & P.E. Garfinkel (Eds.), *Handbook of psychotherapy for anorexia nervosa and bulimia.* New York: Guilford Press.

Cantwell, D.P., Sturzenberger, S., Borroughs, J., Salkin, B., & Green, J.K. (1977). Anorexia nervosa—An affective disorder? *Archives of General Psychiatry, 34,* 1084–1093.

Casper, R.C. (1982). Treatment principles in anorexia nervosa. *Psychiatry, 10,* 431–454.

Connors, M.E., Johnson, C.L., & Stuckey, M.K. (1984). Treatment of bulimia with brief psychoeducational group therapy. *American Journal of Psychiatry, 141,* 1512–1516.

Crisp, A.H. (1980). *Anorexia nervosa—Let me be.* London: Academic Press.

Dally, P.J. (1969). *Anorexia nervosa.* London: Heinemann.

Fairburn, C.G. (1981). A cognitive behavioral approach to the management of bulimia. *Psychological Medicine, 141,* 631–633.

Fairburn, C.G. (1983). Bulimia: Its epidemiology and management. In A.J. Stunkard & E. Steller (Eds.), *Eating and its disorders.* New York: Raven Press.

Fairburn, C.G. (1985). Cognitive-behavioral treatment for bulimia. In D.M. Garner & P.E. Garfinkel (Eds.), *Handbook of psychotherapy for anorexia nervosa and bulimia.* New York: Guilford Press.

Fairburn, C.G., Kirk, J., O'Connor, M., & Cooper, P.J. (1986). A comparison of two psychological treatments for bulimia nervosa. *Behavioral Research and Therapy, 24,* 629–643.

Fairburn, C.G., Norman, P.A., Welch, S.L., O'Connor, M.E., Doll, H.A., & Peveler, R.C. (1995). A prospective study of outcome in bulimia nervosa and the long-term effects of three psychological treatments. *Archives of General Psychology, 52,* 304–312.

Frankenburg, F.R. (1984). Female therapists in the management of anorexia nervosa. *International Journal of Eating Disorders, 3,* 25–33.

Freeman, C.P.L., Barry, F., Dunkeld-Turnbull, J., & Henderson, A. (1988). Controlled trial of pychotherapy for bulimia nervosa. *British Medical Journal, 296,* 521–525.

Garfinkel, P.E., & Garner, D.M. (1982). *Anorexia nervosa: A multi-demensional perspective.* New York: Brunner/Mazel.

Garner, D.M. (1985a). Iatrogenesis in anorexia nervosa and bulimia nervosa. *International Journal of Eating Disorders, 4,* 701–726.

Garner, D.M. (1985b). Individual psychotherapy for anorexia nervosa. *Journal of Psychiatric Research, 19*, 423–433.

Garner, D.M., & Bemis, K.M. (1982). A cognitive behavioral approach to anorexia nervosa. *Cognitive Therapy and Research, 6*, 1–27.

Garner, D.M., & Bemis, K.M. (1985). Cognitive therapy for anorexia nervosa. In D.M. Garner & P.E. Garfinkel (Eds.), *Handbook for psychotherapy of anorexia nervosa and bulimia.* New York: Guilford Press.

Garner, D.M., & Garfinkel, P.E. (1980). Socio-cultural factors in the development of anorexia nervosa. *Psychological Medicine, 10*, 647–656.

Garner, D.M., & Garfinkel, P.E. (1985). Introduction. In D.M. Garner & P.E. Garfinkel (Eds.), *Handbook for psychotherapy of anorexia nervosa and bulimia.* New York: Guilford Press.

Garner, D.M., Garfinkel, P.E., & Irving, M.T. (1986). Integration and sequences of treatment approaches for eating disorders. *Psychotherapy and Psychosomatics, 46*, 246–251.

Garner, D.M., Garfinkel, P.E., & O'Shaughnessy, M. (1985). The validity of the distinction between bulimia with and without anorexia nervosa. *American Journal of Psychiatry, 142*, 581–587.

Garner, D.M., Garfinkel, P.E., Schwartz, D., & Thompson, A. (1980). Cultural expectation of thinness in women. *Psychological Reports, 47*, 483–491.

Garner, D.M., & Olmstead, M.P. (1984). *Manual for the eating disorders inventory.* Odessa, FL: Psychological Assessment Resources.

Garner, D.M., Olmstead, M.P., Davis, R.B., Rockert, W., Goldbloom, D.S., & Eagle, M. (1988, May 9). *Bulimia symptoms: Affect, state and trait measures.* Paper presented at the 141st annual meeting of the American Psychiatric Association, Montreal, Canada.

Garner, D.M., Rockert, W., Olmstead, M.P., Johnson, C., & Coscina, D.V. (1985). Psychoeducational principles in the treatment of bulimia and bulimia nervosa. In D.M. Garner and P.E. Garfinkel (Eds.), *Handbook for psychotherapy of anorexia nervosa and bulimia.* New York: Guilford Press.

Goodsitt, A. (1985). Self-psychology and the treatment of anorexia nervosa. In D.M. Garner & P.E. Garfinkel (Eds.), *Handbook for psychotherapy of anorexia nervosa and bulimia.* New York: Guilford Press.

Hall, A. (1985). Group psychotherapy for anorexia. In D.M. Garner & P. E. Garfinkel (Eds.), *Handbook for psychotherapy of anorexia nervosa and bulimia.* New York: Guilford Press.

Hatsukami, D., Owen, P., Pyle, R., & Mitchell, J.E. (1982). Similarities and differences on the MMPI between women with bulimia and women with alcohol or drug abuse problems. *Addictive Behaviors, 7*, 435–439.

Herzog, D.B., & Copeland, P.M. (1985). Eating disorders. *New England Journal of Medicine, 313*, 295–303.

Hoyt, M.F. (1994). Competency-based future oriented therapy. In M.F. Hoyt (Ed.), *Constructive therapies.* New York: Guilford Press.

Hsu, L.K.G. (1980). Outcome of anorexia nervosa—A review of the literature (1954–1978). *Archives of General Psychiatry, 37*, 1041–1046.

Hsu, L.K.G. (1986). The treatment of anorexia nervosa. *American Journal of Psychiatry, 143*, 573–581.

Hsu, L.K.G., Crisp, A.H., & Harding, B. (1979). Outcome of anorexia. *Lancet, 1*, 61–65.

Hsu, L.K.G., & Lieberman, S. (1982). Paradoxical intention in the treatment of chronic anorexia nervosa. *American Journal of Psychiatry, 139*, 650–653.

Hudson, J.E., Pope, H.G., Jonas, J.M., & Yurgelun-Todd, D. (1983). Family history study of anorexia nervosa and bulimia. *British Journal of Psychiatry, 142,* 133–138.

Hudson, J.I., Laffer, P.S., & Pope, H.G., Jr. (1982). Bulimia related to affective disorder by family history and response to the dexamethasone suppression test. *American Journal of Psychiatry, 137,* 693–695.

Johnson, C., Connors, M.E., & Stuckey, M. (1983). Short-term group treatment of bulimia: A preliminary report. *International Journal of Eating Disorders, 2,* 199–208.

Kirkley, B.G., Schneider, J.A., Agras, W.S., & Beckman, J.A. (1985). Comparison of two group treatments for bulimia. *Journal of Consulting and Clinical Psychology, 53,* 43–48.

Kohut, H. (1971). *The analysis of the self.* New York: International Universities Press.

Lee, N.F., & Rush, A.J. (1986). Cognitive-behavioral group therapy for bulimia. *International Journal of Eating Disorders, 5,* 599–615.

Miller, P.M. (1996). Redefining success in eating disorders. *Addictive Behaviors, 21,* 745–754.

Miller, W.R., & Rollnick, S. (1991). *Motivatoinal interviewing.* New York: Guilford Press.

Miller, W.R., Zwenben, A., DiClemente, C.C., & Rychtarik, R.G. (1992). *Motivational enhancement therapy manual.* U.S. Department of Health and Social Sciences.

Minuchin, S., Rosman, B.L., & Baker, L. (1978). *Psychosomatic families: Anorexia nervosa in context.* Cambridge, MA: Harvard University Press.

Mitchell, J.E., Hatsukami, D., Eckert, E.D., & Pyle, R.L. (1985). Characteristics of 275 patients with bulimia. *American Journal of Psychiatry, 142,* 482–485.

Mitchell, J.E., Hatsukami, D., Goff, G., Pyle, R.L., Eckert, E.D., & Davis, L.E. (1985). Intensive outpatient group treatment for bulimia. In D.M. Garner & P.E. Garfinkel (Eds.), *Handbook for psychotherapy of anorexia nervosa and bulimia.* New York: Guilford Press.

Ordman, A.M., & Kirschenbaum, D.S. (1985). Cognitive-behavioral therapy for bulimia: An initial outcome study. *Journal of Consulting and Clinical Psychology, 53,* 305–313.

Polivy, J. (1981). Group therapy for anorexia nervosa. *Journal of Psychiatric Research, 3,* 279–283.

Pyle, R.L., & Mitchell, J.E. (1985). Psychotherapy of bulimia: The role of groups. In W.T. Kaye & H.E. Gwirtsman (Eds.), *The treatment of normal weight bulimia.* Washington, DC: American Psychiatric Press.

Pyle, R.L., Mitchell, J.E., & Eckert, E.D. (1981). Bulimia: A report of 34 cases. *Journal of Clinical Psychiatry, 42,* 60–64.

Pyle, R.L., & Schmid, M. (1996, April). *A treatment algorhythm for anorexia nervosa in an era of managed care.* Workshop at 7th International Conference on Eating Disorders, New York.

Reiss, D., & Johnson-Sabine, E. (1995). Bulimia nervosa: Five year social outcome and relationship to eating pathology. *International Journal of Eating Disorders, 18,* 127–133.

Rodin, J., Silberstein, L.R., & Striegel-Moore, R.H. (1983). Women and weight: A normative discontent. In T.B. Sonderegger (Ed.), *Nebraska Symposium on Motivation: Psychology and gender* (Vol. 32, pp. 267–307).

Rorty, M., Yager, J., & Rossotto, E. (1994). Childhood sexual, physical, and psychological abuse in bulimia nervosa. *American Journal of Psychiatry, 151,* 1122–1126.

Rosen, B. (1979). A method of structured brief psychotherapy. *British Journal of Medical Psychology, 52,* 157–162.

Rosen, J.C., & Leitenberg, H. (1982). Bulimia nervosa: Treatment with exposure and response preventions. *Behavior Therapy, 13,* 117–124.

Russell, G.F.M. (1970). Anorexia nervosa—Its identity as an illness and its treatment. In J.H. Price (Ed.), *Psychological medicine* (Vol.2). London: Butterworths.

Russell, G.F.M., Szmukler, G.I., Dare, C., & Eisler, I. (1987). An evaluation of family therapy in anorexia nervosa and bulimia nervosa. *Archives of General Psychiatry, 44,* 1047–1056.

Schneider, J.A., & Agras, W.S. (1985). A cognitive behavioral group treatment of bulimia. *British Journal of Psychiatry, 146,* 66–69.

Selvini-Palazzoli, M. (1978). *Self-starvation.* New York: Aronson.

Strober, M. (1984). Stressful life events associated with bulimia and anorexia nervosa: Empirical findings and theoretical speculations. *International Journal of Eating Disorders, 3,* 1–16.

Strober, M., Salkin, B., Burroughs, J., & Morrell, W. (1982). Validity of the bulimia-restrictor distinction in anorexia nervosa. *Journal of Nervous and Mental Disease, 170,* 345–351.

Stuber, M., & Strober, M. (1987). Group therapy in the treatment of adolescents with bulimia: Some preliminary observations. *International Journal of Eating Disorders, 6,* 125–131.

Stunkard, A.J. (1980). *Obesity.* Philadelphia: Saunders.

Vandereycken, W. (1987). The constructive family approach to eating disorders: Critical remarks on the use of family therapy in anorexia nervosa and bulimia. *International Journal of Eating Disorders, 6,* 455–467.

Vandereycken, W., & Meerman, M. (1984). *Anorexia nervosa: A clinicians guide to treatment.* Berlin: de Gruyter.

Wardle, J. (1980). Dietary restraint and binge-eating. *Behavioral Analysis and Modification, 4,* 201–209.

Weiss, S.R., & Ebert, M.H. (1983). Psychological and behavioral characteristics of normal-weight bulimics and normal weight controls. *Psychosomatic Medicine, 45,* 293–303.

Wilson, G.T., Rossiter, E., Kleifeld, E.I., & Lindholm, L. (1986). Cognitive-behavioral treatment of bulimia nervosa: A controlled evaluation. *Behavior Research and Therapy, 24,* 277–288.

Wolchik, S.A., Weiss, L., & Katzman, M.A. (1986). An empirically validated, short-term psychoeducational group treatment program for bulimia. *International Journal of Eating Disorders, 5,* 21–34.

Yates, A.J., & Sambrailo, F. (1984). Bulimia nervosa: A descriptive and therapeutic study. *Behavior Research and Therapy, 22,* 503–517.

CHAPTER 20

Cognitive Behavior Therapy

LINDA K. PORZELIUS, SUSAN BEREL,
and CHRISTINE HOWARD

CONCEPTUALIZATION
OF THE DISORDER

Eating disorders are extremely complex, with multifaceted etiologies, including biological, psychological, and social factors. The consequences of the disorders can be severe. Anorexia nervosa (AN) has a mortality rate of 5 percent to 15 percent, higher than any other psychological disorder, and both AN and bulimia nervosa (BN) have potentially serious health, interpersonal, work, and academic consequences (Sullivan, 1995). The complex, refractory nature of eating disorders and seriousness of their impact present a challenge for the clinician.

AN is defined as a refusal to maintain normal body weight for fear of weight gain and body image disturbance, and an absence of regular menses (American Psychiatric Association, 1994). AN is classified as either restricting, or binge/purge type. Criteria for BN include a regular pattern of binge-eating, undue importance placed upon body image and weight in self-evaluation, and regular use of behaviors to compensate for calorie intake (APA, 1994). Purging type involves use of self-induced vomiting, laxative abuse, or diuretic abuse as compensatory behaviors. Nonpurging type includes either extreme dieting or exercise to compensate for food eaten during binges.

Prevalence among young females is estimated at about .28 percent for AN, and 1 percent for BN (for review, see Hoek, 1993). Rates are highest among western, industrialized cultures, and appear to be increasing among young women. Most people diagnosed with eating disorders are female; about 93 percent for AN, and 96 percent for BN (Hoek, 1993). Average age of onset for AN is 17 years (APA, 1994), and for BN is 21 years (Kendler et al., 1991).

SOCIOCULTURAL INFLUENCES

Nearly all theories, including cognitive behavioral theory, identify sociocultural factors as a central component in the development of eating disorders (for reviews see Gilbert & Thompson, 1996; Stice, 1994). Our society stigmatizes the overweight as lazy, ugly, and undisciplined, which results in pervasive fears of fat (Rothblum, 1994). Whereas obesity is stigmatized, thinness is equated with attractiveness, happiness, and success. The fashion and cosmetic industries make millions by instilling appearance anxiety and body dissatisfaction to sell their products. As a result, body dissatisfaction and fear of fat are rampant, and dieting is pandemic, with about 50 percent of adolescent girls (Grigg, Bowman, & Redman, 1996) and 30 percent of adult women dieting at any given time (Neumark-Sztainer, Jeffery, & French, 1997). Although many women experience body dissatisfaction and engage in frequent dieting, only a small portion of dieters develops an eating disorder (Wilson, 1993). Therefore, a complete understanding of the etiology of eating disorders requires the identification of additional risk factors.

COGNITIVE BEHAVIORAL MODELS

Bulimia Nervosa

Cognitive behavioral models of BN describe a diet/binge/purge cycle, articulated well by Fairburn and colleagues (Fairburn, Marcus, & Wilson, 1993). The model is described here for BN, but many components also apply to AN, particularly the binge/purge subtype. According to the cognitive behavioral model, the core self-schema in eating disorders, which drives the diet/binge/purge cycle, is a generally negative schema, with a narrow focus on body appearance and weight. This core negative, weight-related self-schema guides the individual's cognitive processing of experiences by influencing attention, perception, and memory (Vitousek & Hollon, 1990; Vitousek & Orimoto, 1993). General feelings of inadequacy and an overfocus on food and weight lead to extreme concerns about shape and weight, and extreme and rigid dieting. Vitousek and Hollon suggest that the narrow focus on weight and food may serve the function of reducing complexity and ambiguity in the individual's world. The negative, weight-related self-schema in eating disorders also contributes to characteristic distorted patterns of thinking, similar to those found in depressed individuals (Cooper & Fairburn, 1992; Dritschel, Williams, & Cooper, 1991; Mizes & Christiano, 1995; Zotter & Crowther, 1991). For example, black and white or dichotomous thinking is common, where a woman sees herself as either fat or thin, and as on or off a diet. Foods are either good or bad, with nothing inbetween.

The core self-schema contributes to distorted cognitions about shape and weight, leading the individual to diet, often in an extremely rigid manner, with many forbidden foods. Chronic and rigid dieting cannot be sustained indefinitely. When the individual encounters physiological, cognitive, or emotional events that disrupt dietary restraint, she loses control, resulting in a binge (Grilo & Shiffman, 1994; Polivy & Herman, 1993; Schlundt & Johnson, 1990). Physiological disinhibitors of dieting include hunger or consumption of alcohol. Cognitive disinhibition of dieting occurs when the dieter violates rigid dietary rules and believes that she has blown the diet anyway, and might as well binge. Emotional disinhibition occurs when strong negative emotions or mood fluctuations trigger binge episodes.

Binge-eating raises mood in the short term, thereby reinforcing the binge (Lingswiler, Crowther, & Stephens, 1989). Shortly after the binge, mood drops, with feelings of extreme guilt, depression, and self-loathing. In addition, the binge causes intense anxiety about weight gain. Purging serves to reduce anxiety about weight gain following a binge, acting as a negative reinforcer for the purge. In fact, the anxiety model identifies purging as the critical maintaining factor for binge-eating (Rosen & Leitenberg, 1988). According to the anxiety model, purging should be the primary target of intervention (see "Treatment Strategies" section). After purging, initial feelings of relief due to a reduction in anxiety give way to feelings of shame and disgust, which contribute to poor self-esteem, thereby strengthening the negative self-schema (Fairburn, Marcus, et al., 1993). The individual renews a commitment to rigid dietary rules as a means of overcoming feelings of inadequacy, and the diet/binge/purge cycle continues.

The diet/binge/purge cycle, maintained by a variety of negative and positive reinforcers, forms the basis of the cognitive-behavioral (CB) conceptualization of eating disorders. Increasingly, CB models of the eating disorders go beyond the diet/binge/purge cycle to include psychosocial factors related to both etiology and maintenance, such as problems with emotion regulation and interpersonal relationships. The two-component or dual pathway models propose that an eating disorder develops when risk factors for body dissatisfaction combine with risk factors for self-regulatory difficulties (Connors, 1996; Stice, Nemeroff, & Shaw, 1996; Stice, Ziemba, Margolis, & Flick, 1996). In the body dissatisfaction pathway, environmental, physical, and developmental risk factors lead to poor body image, weight concerns, and dieting. Body dissatisfaction and dieting will not lead to an eating disorder unless combined with self-regulatory problems. Risk factors for self-regulatory difficulties, such as poor parenting or trauma, lead to poor emotion regulation and low self-esteem. Emotional disturbance in the absence of body dissatisfaction would result in non-eating-disordered psychopathology, such as an affective disorder or personality disorder, but not to an eating disorder. Thus, the dual pathway model posits that both body dissatisfaction risk factors and self-regulatory risk factors are necessary for a clinical eating disorder to develop (Connors, 1996; Stice, Nemeroff, et al., 1996; Stice, Ziemba, et al., 1996).

Emotion Regulation

Several models identify affective instability as a central component in the development and maintenance of eating disorders, particularly BN (Polivy & Herman, 1993). Stress and negative affect are common antecedents of binge-eating episodes in both naturalistic and laboratory studies (Davis, Freeman, &

Garner, 1988; Elmore & deCastro, 1990; Rebert, Stanton, & Schwarz, 1991). In addition, binge-eating is associated with reductions in negative mood states, including depression, anger, boredom, shame, and anxiety (Fremouw & Heyneman, 1983; Steinberg, Tobin, & Johnson, 1990; Teusch, 1988). Binge-eating may soothe negative emotions or may serve as a means to avoid painful emotions by narrowing the individual's focus of attention and distracting from painful self-awareness (Heatherton & Baumeister, 1991; Polivy & Herman, 1993). Reduction in negative affect during and immediately after the binge re-inforces eating as a way to cope with negative affect. Foods eaten during a binge may have particularly strong reward potential when food intake is being restricted (Wardle, 1988).

Deficits in coping skills among individuals with eating disorders may con-tribute to frequent mood fluctuations and to use eating as a way to cope with emotions (for review, see Christiano & Mizes, 1997). Numerous studies have identified deficits in both stress appraisal and coping skills among individuals with eating disorders (Cattanach & Rodin, 1988; Hansel & Wittrock, 1997; Soukup, Beiler, & Terrell, 1990). Individuals with eating disorders are more likely to rate events as highly stressful and threatening than noneating disor-dered individuals, reflecting appraisal deficits. Another appraisal deficit in-volves difficulty in differentiating among emotional states or between emotional and physical states, such as hunger or fatigue (Cochrane, Brewerton, Wilson, & Hodges, 1993; de Groot, Rodin, & Olmsted, 1995; G. Smith, Amner, Johnsson, & Franck, 1997). Research also finds deficits in coping skills, such as frequent use of avoidant coping and emotion-oriented strategies (Koff & San-gani, 1997; Paxton & Diggens, 1997; Troop, Holbrey, & Treasure, 1998), which tend to be ineffective in reducing negative affect in the long run (Wills, 1997).

Interpersonal Relationships

Numerous studies have identified interpersonal problems among individuals with eating disorders, including nonassertiveness, difficulties in expressing anger, elevated interpersonal conflict, and inadequate social support (Grissett & Norvell, 1992; Herzog, Keller, Lavori, & Ott, 1987; Tiller et al., 1997). In addi-tion to strong fears about negative evaluation of their bodies, individuals with eating disorders also have general social evaluation concerns that may act as a risk factor (Striegel-Moore, Silberstein, & Rodin, 1993). High levels of social anxiety are common among individuals with eating disorders, and one study found that the anxiety usually appears years before the eating disorder (Schwalberg, Barlow, Alger, & Howard, 1992). Studies find a high need for ac-ceptance and approval among individuals with eating disorders (Bulik, Beidel, Duchmann, & Weltzin,1991; Friedman & Whisman, 1998), possibly reflecting apprehension about expressing their emotions or asserting their needs for fear of rejection.

Anorexia Nervosa

In cognitive behavioral models of AN, similar to BN, the core self-schema in-volves feelings of inadequacy and an overemphasis on body appearance. For the individual with AN, weight loss provides a source of self-worth and helps to combat feelings of inadequacy (Garner, Vitousek, & Pike, 1997; Vitousek & Hollon, 1990). Friends and families may give social reinforcement for weight loss in the early stages. A sense of accomplishment from achieving weight loss goals and maintaining control over hunger serve as strong positive reinforcers that maintain food restriction (Vitousek & Hollon, 1990).

Negative reinforcement may also maintain dieting. Crisp and colleagues (Crisp, Joughin, Halek, Bowyer, & Browne, 1996) conceptualize AN as a "fat phobia" in which individuals with AN greatly fear weight gain, and, therefore, diet stringently. Dieting and weight loss are maintained by negative reinforcement, by avoiding the feared stimulus of weight gain. The prepubertal woman may be avoiding normal weight gain associated with puberty by losing weight and preventing menarche. Attention and energy spent on weight loss may help the individual to avoid dealing with many anxieties of adolescence, including sexuality and separation from parents (Slade, 1982; Strober, 1997; Vitousek & Hollon, 1990).

A complicating factor is that starvation can cause many of the symptoms observed in AN. In the early 1940s, Keys and colleagues conducted experimental studies of starvation. The men who participated in these studies engaged in behaviors very similar to those of women with AN (Keys, Brozek, Henschel, Mickelson, & Taylor, 1950). Mood swings, irritability, and anxiety were common and had not been present prior to the starvation. Cognitive functioning was impaired. Physical changes, similar to those seen in AN, included decreased tolerance for cold, sensitivity to noise and light, fatigue, hair loss, and decreased sleep. The complex physiological and psychological responses to starvation serve to highlight, (1) the difficulties inherent in trying to determine causes of AN by observing symptoms, and (2) the importance of weight restoration in treating AN.

DIAGNOSTIC ISSUES AND PROBLEMS

DIAGNOSTIC CRITERIA

Anorexia Nervosa

DSM-IV criteria for AN include a refusal to maintain normal body weight, an intense fear of fat, body image disturbance, and amenorrhea (APA, 1994). *DSM-IV* provides a figure of 85 percent in determining low body weight, which allows for flexibility and use of clinical judgment (Walsh & Garner, 1997). Body image disturbance may involve a disturbance in the way body weight or shape is experienced, an undue influence of weight on self-evaluation, or denial of the seriousness of low body weight (APA, 1994).

DSM-IV defines amenorrhea as the absence of three consecutive menstrual periods (APA, 1994). The latest edition improved diagnostic specificity by applying the criterion only to postmenarchal girls, and including women who menstruate only as a result of oral contraceptive use (Walsh & Garner, 1997). However, the amenorrhea criterion remains complicated, because some women continue menstruating even at extremely low body weights (Cachelin

& Maher, 1998b). In addition, research raises questions about the criterion's utility, finding no differences between amenorrheaic AN and nonamenorrheaic AN in severity of eating-disorder symptoms or rates of comorbid psychopathology (Cachelin & Maher, 1998b; Garfinkel et al., 1996).

DSM-IV added subtypes for AN (APA, 1994). Restricting type describes the classical presentation of AN, whereby the individual attempts to lose weight by dieting, fasting, or engaging in excessive exercise. The binge-eating/purging type includes individuals who regularly binge and/or purge during an episode of AN. Although it is generally thought that the binge-eating/purging type is associated with greater psychological disturbance (Walsh & Garner, 1997), one study found no differences between the subtypes (Nagata, McConaha, Rao, Sokol, & Kaye, 1997). Other studies found that purging, but not binge-eating, is related to more severe psychopathology, suggesting the need to distinguish binge-eating AN from purging AN (Cachelin & Maher, 1998a; Garner, Garner, & Rosen, 1993).

Bulimia Nervosa

DSM-IV criteria for BN include the following: regular binge-eating, undue importance placed upon body image and weight in self-evaluation, and regular use of inappropriate behaviors to compensate for calorie intake (APA, 1994). The central feature of BN, binge-eating, is further defined as eating a large quantity of food during a discrete period of time, while experiencing a lack of control. Binge-eating and purging must occur at least two times per week for three months, although empirical support for this frequency level is not strong (Walsh & Garner, 1997; Wilson & Eldredge, 1991).

A large quantity of food is defined as ". . . more than most people would eat under similar circumstances" (APA, 1994, p. 549). The definition excludes subjective binges in which food quantity is normal, but the individual feels out of control because she ate more than she intended or broke a dietary rule. Some argue that subjective binges should be included in the binge definition, as research has not found a relationship between quantity of food eaten during a binge and associated psychopathology or treatment outcome (Niego, Pratt, & Agras, 1997; D. Smith, Marcus, & Eldredge, 1994). Furthermore, the quantity of food involved in a binge episode can vary tremendously between individuals and within one individual over the course of treatment (Rossiter & Agras, 1990; D. Smith et al., 1994). Judgments about whether an eating episode is considered a binge may be influenced by gender, mood, and a sense of loss of control (Beglin & Fairburn, 1992; La Porte, 1996, 1997), which underscores the importance of providing a clear definition of *binge* in discussions with clients.

DSM-IV introduced subtypes of BN according to type of compensatory behaviors used: purging and nonpurging types. Individuals with purging type engage in self-induced vomiting, or abuse of laxatives or diuretics. Those with nonpurging type use compensatory behaviors of extreme dieting or excessive exercise. The utility of the subtypes is not yet clear. Some studies have found that purging BN is associated with lower body weight and higher levels of psychopathology (Walsh & Garner, 1997). Other research has failed to support the subtypes (Tobin, Griffing, & Griffing, 1997).

Eating Disorder Not Otherwise Specified

Eating disorder not otherwise specified (EDNOS) is a frequently diagnosed category, and includes individuals with widely differing symptoms (APA, 1994; Walsh & Garner, 1997). EDNOS is diagnosed when most AN criteria are met, but weight loss is insufficient or menstruation continues. EDNOS is also diagnosed when most BN criteria are met, but binge-eating or purging occur once per week or less, or when binge episodes involve small quantities of food. A specific subtype of EDNOS, binge-eating disorder (BED), is defined in the *DSM-IV* appendix in order to determine the inclusion of BED in future *DSM* editions (APA, 1994). Individuals with BED binge regularly, but do not engage in regular compensatory behaviors.

COMORBID PSYCHOPATHOLOGY

Eating disorders are associated with considerable comorbid psychopathology, leading to extensive research. Two recent reviews summarize this literature (Herzog, Nussbaum, & Marmor, 1996; Wonderlich & Mitchell, 1997). Eating disorders are most commonly associated with affective and anxiety disorders, and are also associated with substance-use disorders and personality disorders. However, research support for a relationship between eating disorders and dissociative disorders is generally weak (Gleaves & Eberenz, 1997).

Lifetime prevalence rates of major depression in eating disorders range from 25 percent to 80 percent, with approximately equal rates across eating-disorder classifications (Herzog et al., 1996; Wonderlich & Mitchell, 1997). Depression symptoms in eating disorders may be less severe than that in major depression, with fewer melancholic features (Strober & Katz, 1988, as cited in Wonderlich & Mitchell). The most recent research suggests that eating disorders usually predate depression, supporting the view of depression as a reaction to the eating disorder rather than a vulnerability factor, although the relationship is likely complex (Herzog et al., 1996; Wonderlich & Mitchell, 1997). Some recent studies have investigated the relationship between seasonal affective disorder and eating disorders (e.g., Lam, Goldner, & Grewal, 1996), but more research is needed before drawing conclusions.

Symptoms of anxiety are also common in individuals with eating disorders, including obsessions about food and weight, morbid fear of fat, and social phobia. Lifetime prevalence rates of anxiety disorders are elevated in both AN and BN, but are somewhat higher in AN, ranging from 20 percent to 65 percent (Wonderlich & Mitchell, 1997). AN is most strongly related to obsessive compulsive disorder, BN to social phobia. Some studies have found that anxiety disorders most often predate the eating disorder, leading to questions about whether eating disorders are a variant of obsessive-compulsive disorder or social phobia (Bulik, Sullivan, Fear, & Joyce, 1997; Hsu, Kaye, & Weltzin, 1993; Schwalberg et al., 1992).

Substance abuse is more common in BN and the binge-purge type of AN than in restricting AN (for review, see Holderness, Brooks-Gunn, & Warren, 1994). The rate of comorbid substance abuse among those with BN is approximately

22.9 percent (Holderness et al., 1994), significantly higher than rates found among controls (Garfinkel et al., 1996). Some hypothesize that eating disorders and substance abuse may derive from similar underlying personality disturbances, representing features of an addictive personality or an impulse-control problem. Others argue that resemblances between eating disorders and addictive disorders are only superficial, and are not well supported by research (Holderness et al., 1994; Wilson, 1995). Some propose that substance abuse is found in only a small subgroup of individuals with BN, termed multi-impulsive BN, involving excessive alcohol use, drug abuse, self-mutilating, and stealing (Tuschen & Bents, 1995).

Rates of personality disorders are also elevated in eating disorders, ranging from 20 percent to 80 percent in AN, and from 22 percent to 77 percent in BN (Herzog et al., 1996; Wonderlich & Mitchell, 1997). Restricting AN is associated with avoidant, obsessive-compulsive, and dependent personality disorders. Purging, in both AN and BN, is associated with borderline and histrionic features. (for review, see Dennis & Sansone, 1997). However, Vitousek and Manke (1994) caution that personality disorder symptoms often remit along with remission of eating disorder symptoms, and recommend that the clinician defer diagnosing a personality disorder until after eating-disorder treatment.

TREATMENT STRATEGIES

EMPIRICAL SUPPORT FOR CBT

A large volume of research supports the efficacy of CBT (for reviews, see Wilson & Fairburn, 1998; Wilson, Fairburn, & Agras, 1997). Studies support CBT compared to wait-list or delayed-treatment control groups. In addition, studies have shown CBT to be more effective than supportive psychotherapy, behavior therapy, brief psychodynamic therapy, and pharmacotherapy. A recent meta-analysis found that CBT for bulimia resulted in substantial reduction in behavioral measures, such as binge eating and purging, and attitudinal measures, such as attitudes toward shape and weight, dietary restraint, and other psychopathology (Lewandowski, Gebing, Anthony, & O'Brien, 1997). The benefits of CBT appear to be well maintained at six-month and at one-year follow-ups (Lewandowski et al., 1997; Wilson et. al., 1997). Almost six years posttreatment, abstinence rates were 48 percent (Fairburn et al., 1995; Wilson & Fairburn, 1998).

In general, available evidence suggests that CBT should be considered the treatment of choice for BN. However, client problems that preclude participation in treatment, such as severe substance abuse, severe depression, or psychosis, may require alternative approaches (Wilson et al., 1997). Although some client characteristics predict poor treatment outcome (e.g., low self-esteem and borderline personality disorder), there is no evidence that other treatments are more effective than CBT with these individuals (Wilson et al., 1997).

Empirical support for CBT of AN is strikingly sparse, consisting primarily of case reports and uncontrolled treatment studies, rather than controlled empirical investigation. Garner et al. speculate that the lower incidence, lengthier treatment, lower motivation, and greater potential for hospitalization make research more challenging for AN than for BN (Garner et al., 1997). In the one controlled treatment trial of CBT for AN, CBT was equal in effectiveness to behavioral therapy, and both were superior to a control treatment (Channon, deSilva, Hemsley, & Perkins, 1989). However, attendance at sessions was greater in CBT than in standard behavioral treatment, indicating greater adherence. Thus, AN research provides preliminary support for the effectiveness of CBT.

DESCRIPTION OF TREATMENT

Excellent manuals (Agras & Apple, 1997; Fairburn, Marcus, et al., 1993) and client workbooks (Apple & Agras, 1997; Fairburn, 1995) are available for CBT treatment of BN. The Oxford CBT treatment manual, which has received the most research attention and empirical support, is briefly described below (Fairburn, Marcus, et al., 1993; Wilson, Fairburn, & Agras, 1997).

In the CBT approach, client and therapist work together in an explicit, open manner. Treatment is structured and directive, with specific goals across sessions and within each session (Wilson et al., 1997). The client learns new skills for changing behaviors and attitudes, which are practiced in weekly homework assignments. A solid therapeutic relationship is crucial, as clients are asked to work hard between sessions, completing many anxiety-provoking assignments.

Treatment consists of 19 sessions, comprised of three stages. The first stage of treatment, lasting eight weeks and aims to: (1) introduce the rationale behind the CBT approach and, (2) replace restrictive or chaotic eating with regular eating patterns. The therapist introduces the cognitive behavioral model, explaining how attitudes and behaviors work to maintain the diet/binge/purge cycle. The first stage includes education about weight regulation, the ineffectiveness of using laxatives and vomiting as a means of weight control, and the physical consequences of compensatory behaviors. Clients weigh themselves weekly.

Self-monitoring supplies essential information about antecedents and consequences of binge eating and purging, and provides a baseline of behavior for later comparison. Clients self-monitor all eating episodes, recording type and amount of foods eaten, time, binges and purge episodes, situations, and moods. To normalize eating, clients eat three meals plus two snacks each day. Self-control strategies (e.g., limiting eating to one location, substituting alternative behaviors for binge eating) help clients gain control over eating.

The goals in the second stage of CBT (sessions 9 to 16), are to (1) eliminate restrictive dieting, (2) prevent binge eating and purging through use of problem-solving skills, and (3) change dysfunctional beliefs about weight, shape, and eating, (Fairburn, Marcus, et al., 1993). To eliminate restrictive dieting, clients make a list of foods avoided, then practice eating each forbidden food in a safe, controlled manner, until food becomes less feared. Problem-solving skills provide a tool for coping with any situations that trigger binge episodes. Examples of triggers to binge-eating include interpersonal problems, hunger, fatigue, or negative thoughts or feelings.

Cognitive techniques address dysfunctional attitudes about body weight and shape, and eating. Cognitive restructuring, similar to Beck et al.'s treatment of depression (Beck, Rush, Shaw, & Emery, 1979), aims to "restructure" dysfunctional beliefs. Clients learn to identify automatic dysfunctional thoughts (e.g., "I am fat"), to question the validity of dysfunctional thoughts by finding evidence for and against them, and to generate more functional counterthoughts (e.g., "I may have gained weight, but I am certainly not fat"). Underlying dysfunctional beliefs (e.g., "I cannot be happy until I lose weight") are identified, examined, and challenged.

During the third stage (sessions 17 to 19), the focus turns to maintenance of change following treatment (Fairburn et al., 1997). The therapist assumes a less directive role in treatment, with more time between sessions. Relapse prevention involves teaching clients to anticipate and plan for slips or lapses that will occur in the future. Clients develop a detailed list of high-risk times, when they are likely to lapse. A step-by-step, written plan for dealing with lapses can keep the client from giving up when a small setback occurs.

CBT for AN involves many of the same components as CBT for BN, but requires much longer treatment (one to two years), for numerous reasons. Motivation for change is generally low in AN, psychological issues are complex, and weight gain goals must take precedence, possibly requiring hospitalization (Garner et al., 1997). Garner et al.'s treatment manual for AN emphasizes that the most important and first goal is to increase motivation by building a strong therapeutic alliance through a positive, nonjudgmental approach. The dangers of underweight demand setting explicit weight goals. Clients gain weight in a series of gradual experiments used to test dysfunctional attitudes and belief about weight. Once weight gain is achieved, cognitive techniques address dysfunctional attitudes about body weight and shape, as well as broader issues of self-concept, perfectionism, interpersonal functioning, and affective expression. In the final stage of treatment, clients prepare for termination, learning relapse prevention techniques.

Additional Treatment Components

Body Image

The CBT approach described above includes general interventions for body image problems, but does not require specific body-image techniques (Wilson et al., 1997). Body-image techniques include self-monitoring of body-image thoughts, cognitive restructuring of appearance beliefs, changing body-image behaviors (such as avoiding people, activities or tight clothing), and body image exposure and desensitization (Cash, 1996). Most treatment studies of CBT have not included these body image techniques, even though poor body image is associated with poor treatment outcome and greater relapse rates (Rosen, 1997).

Exposure and Response Prevention

Fairburn and colleagues recommend using exposure and response prevention methods for clients who are unable to eat forbidden foods on their own (Fairburn, Marcus, et al., 1993). Exposure and response prevention, based on the anxiety model, consists of exposure to feelings of anxiety after eating a forbidden food, and prevention of the purge response, with the goal of extinguishing anxiety about eating the food (Rosen & Leitenberg, 1988). Typically, the therapist sits with the individual while the individual eats the forbidden food, then the therapist stays until the urge to purge passes. Research support is currently mixed for the use of exposure and response prevention in the treatment of eating disorders (Bulik, Sullivan, Carter, McIntosh, & Joyce, 1998; Leitenberg, 1995).

Case Illustration

Jennifer, a 25-year-old student, came to a university-based clinic seeking treatment for an eating disorder. She was of normal weight, attractive, and well groomed. She completed the initial assessment during the first appointment, which included a semistructured interview of eating and weight history, and questionnaires concerning eating habits, weight history, body image, and general psychopathology. She was referred to her physician for a physical examination as a part of the initial evaluation.

Jennifer met criteria for BN, purging type. She reported binge eating, followed by self-induced vomiting, one to two times per day. She engaged almost every day in rigid dieting and excessive exercise (i.e., stairstepper and circuit training for 2 hours per day). Jennifer had begun binge eating and purging at age 19. Although bulimic episodes occurred more often when she was younger, Jennifer was motivated to seek treatment now because she would begin her student teaching in four months and was concerned that the bulimic symptoms could interfere with her work. She was extremely critical of herself for being so "undisciplined" and extremely fearful of getting fat. She had tried many times to get control of the problem by imposing strict rules about when, what, and where she ate, but always ended up losing control and feeling even worse about herself. Her self-esteem was quite low, and body image was poor.

Jennifer described a normal childhood and a good relationship with her family. Both parents were of normal weight. Her mother had always worked to control her own weight by serving healthful foods and limiting desserts in the house. Jennifer's sister had been hospitalized twice for AN and had once almost died. Jennifer had not revealed her own eating disorder to her family, believing that her family would be very disappointed in her.

At the time of the initial assessment, Jennifer was living by herself, attending school full time as a graduate student in education. She had always done very well in school, pushing herself to excel. She had been involved in a romantic relationship for two years with a man with whom she had discussed her eating disorder, and who supported her receiving treatment. Jennifer reported having no close friends other than her boyfriend. She attributed social isolation to her eating disorder, which involved a great deal of time and secrecy.

Jennifer was eager to begin treatment. The treatment program was explained and statistics about success rates were given. The role of the therapist was to teach

Jennifer the skills to regain control of her eating, coaching her so that she could ultimately act independently as her own coach. She was given food records and asked to monitor food eaten, time of day, binges, purges, and situations and emotions leading to binges. It was explained that self-monitoring would provide valuable information about her pattern of binges and purges. Records would also provide a baseline of information so that she could note improvements in the future. Jennifer initially expressed concern that she could not carry this record with her for fear that someone might discover it. She also expressed fears that writing down what she ate would make her feel more anxious about eating. She resolved the former concern by deciding to record on a pocket notebook, which she would then transfer to a food record in the evening, when she was alone. In response to Jennifer's reluctance to try recording every time she ate, the therapist acknowledged her feelings and agreed to continue exploring them with her, but emphasized that self-monitoring was a crucial part of treatment.

At the following session, Jennifer had successfully completed food records for each day, typing the forms to make them more legible. The therapist followed up on Jennifer's concern about the anxiety she might experience when recording what she ate. Jennifer reported that she felt somewhat uncomfortable with keeping the record, and that she did not write down the foods eaten during binges due to embarrassment. However, she understood that the record was an important part of treatment and agreed to continue recording.

The first part of each session was spent looking at Jennifer's food records to identify eating patterns, including antecedents and consequences of binge eating. Jennifer generally tried to put off eating for as long as possible each day and had many rules about avoiding fattening foods. On a typical weekday, Jennifer got up early, skipped breakfast, and went to school. She ate a light lunch, consisting of one cup of vegetable soup and one piece of fruit, and then avoided eating until returning home in the late afternoon. Feeling hungry, tired, and stressed about schoolwork, she started out eating a healthful snack, but was unable to stop eating until she was very full. Afterward, she felt extremely guilty and fearful about gaining weight and forced herself to vomit.

Jennifer was able to identify important triggers for the binge episodes, including hunger, stress, and being alone with unstructured time. To prevent hunger later in the day, the therapist recommended that she eat breakfast. She was somewhat reluctant to act on this suggestion because she was not hungry in the mornings. However, she eventually agreed to eat a piece of toast and drink a glass of milk before school. She also agreed to add a healthful food to her lunch. Later on in treatment, when binges were less frequent and Jennifer realized that she had not gained weight, she was able to add two healthful snacks. To avoid being alone at home at her high-risk time, she arranged to meet with her boyfriend to study and then ate supper with him. She also identified pleasurable activities that could replace afternoon binge eating.

Jennifer was given information on the health effects of purging. She was surprised to hear that vomiting does not get rid of most of the calories eaten. We worked together to find ways to postpone or eliminate purging by avoiding situations in which she could purge or by planning alternative activities after eating. In these ways she was quickly able to reduce her purging to less than once a week.

As Jennifer's purging decreased and her eating increased, her anxiety about weight gain became more intense. She had not gained weight since treatment began, but she was feeling fatter. The therapist explained that it was normal to experience changes in body fluids subsequent to quitting purging and returning to normal eating. Jennifer was encouraged to weigh herself once a week so that she would get used to seeing her weight. Regular weighing also allowed her to see that her less restrictive eating patterns were not causing weight gain.

Problem-solving techniques were introduced to help prevent the remaining episodes of binge-eating and purging. To continue decreasing dietary restraint, feared and forbidden foods were gradually incorporated into her diet. The rationale presented was that depriving oneself of foods leads to cravings, feelings of deprivation, and binge-eating. By learning to eat the food in moderate amounts, with some control, one is less vulnerable to binge eating with the food. Jennifer created a list of forbidden foods, rating each according to how much she feared and avoided the food. She was reluctant to eat many foods, including desserts, chips, red meat, nuts, cheese, margarine, and salad dressings. Starting with the least feared food, she introduced approximately one food every week, eating the food with her boyfriend, with whom she was unlikely to binge or purge. As she became more comfortable with a particular food, she took it off of her list of feared foods.

The week before her ninth session, Jennifer and her boyfriend had an argument and broke up for a brief time. The break-up provided an opportunity for Jennifer and the therapist to practice cognitive restructuring. She experienced many dysfunctional automatic thoughts, such as, "I have to lose weight to make him interested in me again." Jennifer learned to identify and challenge this type of negative automatic thought. She began to realize that there was a lack of evidence to support her belief that people liked or disliked her based upon her weight. She realized that placing such extreme importance on losing weight made her miserable, and may even lead to weight gain through binge-eating.

To further address the issue of body image, the therapist provided information about cultural pressures on women to be thin. Jennifer worked on developing a critical attitude toward the unrealistic female bodies portrayed in the media. She identified the qualities that she most respected in her friends and teachers, other than appearance and weight, in order to get a better perspective on the importance of weight. She was increasingly able to see her positive qualities and to view herself in more complex ways, rather than focusing narrowly on weight and appearance.

The final sessions of therapy focused on relapse prevention strategies. Sessions were decreased to one every two weeks. Jennifer was asked to anticipate future difficulties and prepare ways of handling them. For example, she had learned that a particularly high risk time for her was when she did not perform as well as she expected of herself in schoolwork. She would be overwhelmed with feelings of failure, and she would often binge and purge. Jennifer wrote out a plan to go to her boyfriend's apartment after getting the exam back so that she would not be tempted to binge.

Jennifer successfully completed treatment, attending a total of 22 sessions, over 25 weeks. At the end of treatment, she was not binge-eating or purging. Scores on questionnaire measures of body image, and eating- and weight-related attitudes were reduced to normal levels. She had expanded her social activities considerably and was feeling very positive about the changes she had made. At six-month follow-up, she had maintained her changes in binge-eating and purging.

ALTERNATIVE TREATMENT STRATEGIES

INTERPERSONAL THERAPY

Interpersonal therapy (IPT) is a short-term treatment, originally developed for depression (Klerman, Weissman, Rounsaville, & Chevron, 1984), which focuses on helping the client with current interpersonal problems. A description of IPT for BN can be found in Fairburn (1997). In controlled treatment studies, both IPT and CBT effectively reduced binge eating and vomiting at posttreatment, 12-month follow-up, and long-term follow-up (Fairburn, Jones, Peveler, Carr, et al., 1991; Fairburn, Kirk, O'Connor, & Cooper, 1986; Fairburn et al., 1995). Fairburn (1997) recommends using IPT as an alternative when CBT fails, rather than as the first intervention, because the volume of research on IPT is quite small compared to research supporting CBT for BN. Interestingly, although IPT is as effective as CBT, dysfunctional eating behaviors and attitudes are not directly addressed during IPT as they are in CBT (Fairburn, 1997). The question arises as to whether CBT and IPT may achieve a reduction in bulimic symptoms through different mechanisms.

FAMILY THERAPY

Clinical and empirical observation document the family's contribution to the development of eating disorders, including specific eating-disorder risk factors, such as weight-related teasing, preoccupation with appearances, or early mealtime practices, and nonspecific risk factors, such as family communication, achievement expectations, or childhood sexual abuse (Connors, 1996). Family therapy is widely used in treating eating disorders, including a disparate group of approaches, such as Structural Family Therapy (Fishman, 1996), Feminist Family Therapy (Kuba & Hanchey, 1991), Behavioral Family Therapy (Robin, Bedway, Siegel, & Gilroy, 1996), and Maudsley Systemic Family therapy (Dare & Eisler, 1997). Although widely used, most family therapy approaches have little or no empirical support. The strongest research support for family therapy comes from controlled treatment studies comparing Maudsley systemic family therapy to supportive individual therapy (Dare et al., 1995). The data indicate promising results in treating early onset AN with family therapy, although late onset AN and BN may respond better to individual therapy (Dare & Eisler, 1997). A few studies investigating behavioral family systems therapy also found good results in treating early onset AN (Robin et al., 1996).

PRESCRIPTIVE TREATMENT AND MANAGED CARE

The expense of treating the individual with an eating disorder is at odds with managed care's demand for low cost, short-term treatments. CBT for BN, with its strong empirical support, has tended to fare better with managed care companies than longer-term treatments. However, even short-term treatment lasts 19 sessions, which is long by managed-care standards, and treatment may need to be extended if complicating physical or psychological factors interfere. A multidisciplinary team including a therapist, a physician, and a dietitian is often needed to address the complex physical and psychological aspects of eating disorders. Obtaining adequate coverage for AN can be particularly problematic. Coverage may be denied because of a lack of research documenting treatment effectiveness (Kaye, Kaplan, & Zucker, 1996). In addition, CBT for AN is longer than treatment for BN and may require hospitalization to restore weight. Insurance companies often put a lifetime spending cap on payment for hospitalization, which may not even pay for one short-term stay (Fox, 1997).

The Academy of Eating Disorders, a multidisciplinary association of eating disorder professionals, recently published a position statement (1998) charging that, at present, insurance coverage for eating disorders is often minimal, leading to inadequate treatment. The statement contends that eating disorders should be covered on a par with other medical conditions, citing research on medical complications, treatment outcome, and the risks of inadequate treatment. In a recent Plenary Address at the International Conference on Eating Disorders, Dr. James Mitchell underscored the dangerous implications of reduced funding for treatment of AN, stating that this may actually increase mortality rates for this already dangerous mental and physical disorder (Mitchell, 1998).

Patients and their families are also becoming more vocal about their concerns. Articles on insurance problems in treating eating disorders have recently appeared in *USA Today, Chicago Tribune,* the *Wall Street Journal,* the *New York Times, Good Housekeeping,* and *Life.* In two recent cases, New York judges ordered insurance companies to pay for hospitalization of women with AN. *Life* magazine published a feature article on these cases and on more general issues in eating disorders and managed care (Fox, 1997).

These events offer some hope for improvements in the future, but practitioners need more immediate solutions as they negotiate with managed-care providers to obtain coverage. Two recent articles (Kaye et al., 1996; Zerbe, 1996) offer practical suggestions for the clinician, emphasizing the importance of: (1) designing a clear treatment plan with well-specified treatment targets, (2) documenting treatment outcomes, (3) choosing cost-effective treatments, and (4) developing good working relationships with managed-care reviewers. In addition, practitioners may find the academy's position statement of use in justifying treatment coverage when negotiating with managed-care reviewers.

SUMMARY

Eating disorders are extremely complex. The clinician working with a client who has an eating disorder needs to be attentive to the serious consequences of starvation and purging, the high potential for suicide, and the high rates of comorbidity. The clinician needs to appreciate society's role in promoting body dissatisfaction and dieting. In addition, the clinician faces challenges in obtaining adequate insurance coverage.

Despite the challenges inherent in treating these complex disorders, research provides encouragement that treatment works. Controlled treatment outcome studies provide strong support for the long-term effectiveness of cognitive-behavioral treatment of BN. Although little research is available on CBT for AN, initial results are promising. Cognitive-behavioral treatment manuals, available for BN and AN, provide specific, point-by-point instructions, which should promote use by clinicians and further research.

REFERENCES

Academy for eating disorders position statement: On equity in insurance coverage for eating disorders. (1998, Winter). *Academy for Eating Disorders Newsletter,* (12).

Agras, W.S., & Apple, R.F. (1997). *Therapist guide. Overcoming eating disorders: A cognitive-behavioral treatment for bulimia nervosa and binge-eating disorder.* San Antonio: Harcourt Brace.

American Psychiatric Association. (1994). *Diagnostic and statistical manual of mental disorders* (4th ed.). Washington, DC: Author.

Apple, R.F., & Agras, W.S. (1997). *Client workbook. Overcoming eating disorders: A cognitive-behavioral treatment for bulimia nervosa and binge-eating disorder.* San Antonia: Harcourt Brace.

Beck, A.T., Rush, A.J., Shaw, B.F., & Emery, G. (1979). *Cognitive therapy of depression.* New York: Guilford Press.

Beglin, S.J., & Fairburn, C.G. (1992). What is meant by the term "binge"? *American Journal of Psychiatry, 149,* 123–124.

Bulik, C.M., Beidel, D.C., Duchmann, E., & Weltzin, T.E. (1991). An analysis of social anxiety in anorexic, bulimic, social phobic, and control women. *Journal of Psychopathology & Behavioral Assessment, 13*(3), 199–211.

Bulik, C.M., Sullivan, P.F., Carter, F.A., McIntosh, V.V., & Joyce, P.R. (1998). The role of exposure with response prevention in the cognitive-behavioural therapy for bulimia nervosa. *Psychological Medicine, 28*(3), 611–623.

Bulik, C.M., Sullivan, P.F., Fear, J.L., & Joyce, P.R. (1997). Eating disorders and antecedent anxiety disorders: A controlled study. *Acta Psychiatrica Scandinavica, 96*(2), 101–107.

Cachelin, F.M., & Maher, B.A. (1998a). Is amenorrhea a critical criterion for anorexia nervosa? *Journal of Psychosomatic Research, 44,* 435–440.

Cachelin, F.M., & Maher, B.A. (1998b). Restricters who purge: Implications of purging behavior for psychopathology and classification of anorexia nervosa. *Eating Disorders: The Journal of Treatment and Prevention, 6,* 51–63.

Cash, T.F. (1996). The treatment of body image disturbances. In J.K. Thompson (Ed.), *Body image, eating disorders, and obesity* (pp. 83–107). Washington, DC: American Psychological Association.

Cattanach, L., & Rodin, J. (1988). Psychosocial components of the stress process in bulimia. *International Journal of Eating Disorders, 7*(1), 75–88.

Channon, S., deSilva, P., Hemsley, D., & Perkins, R.E. (1989). A controlled trial of cognitive-behavioural and behavioural treatment of anorexia nervosa. *Behavior Research & Therapy, 27,* 529–535.

Christiano, A., & Mizes, D. (1997). Appraisal and coping deficits associated with eating disorders: Implications for treatment. *Cognitive and Behavioral Practice, 4,* 263–290.

Cochrane, C.E., Brewerton, T.D., Wilson, D.B., & Hodges, E.L. (1993). Alexithymia in the eating disorders. *International Journal of Eating Disorders, 14,* 219–222.

Connors, M.E. (1996). Developmental vulnerabilities for eating disorders. In L. Smolak, M. Levine, & R. Striegel-Moore (Eds.), *The developmental psychopathology of eating disorders: Implications for research, prevention, and treatment* (pp. 285–310). Mahwah, NJ: Erlbaum.

Cooper, M.J., & Fairburn, C.G. (1992). Selective processing of eating, weight and shape related words in patients with eating disorders and dieters. *British Journal of Clinical Psychology, 31*(3), 363–365.

Crisp, A.H., Joughin, N., Halek, C., Bowyer, C., & Browne, N. (1996). *Anorexia nervosa: The wish to change: Self-help and discovery, the thirty steps* (2nd ed.). Hove, England: Erlbaum (UK) Taylor & Francis.

Dare, C., & Eisler, I. (1995). Family therapy. In G.I. Szmukler & C. Dare (Eds.), *Handbook of eating disorders: Theory, treatment and research* (pp. 333–349). Chichester, England: Wiley.

Dare, C., & Eisler, I. (1997). Family therapy for anorexia nervosa. In D.M. Garner & P.E. Garfinkel (Eds.), *Handbook of treatment for eating disorders* (2nd ed., pp. 307–326). New York: Guilford Press.

Dare, C., Eisler, I., Colahan, M., Crowther, C., Senior, R., & Agen, E. (1995). The listening heart and the chi square: Clinical and empirical perceptions in the family therapy of anorexia nervosa. *Journal of Family Therapy, 17,* 31–58.

Davis, R., Freeman, R.J., & Garner, D.M. (1988). A naturalistic investigation of eating behavior in bulimia nervosa. *Journal of Consulting and Clinical Psychology, 56,* 273–279.

de Groot, J.M., Rodin, G., & Olmsted, M.P. (1995). Alexithymia, depression, and treatment outcome in bulimia nervosa. *Comprehensive Psychiatry, 36*(1), 53–60.

Dennis, A.B., & Sansone, R.A. (1997). Treatment of patients with personality disorders. In D.M. Garner & P.E. Garfinkel (Eds.), *Handbook of treatment for eating disorders* (pp. 437–449). New York: Guilford Press.

Dritschel, B.H., Williams, K., & Cooper, P.J. (1991). Cognitive distortions amongst women experiencing bulimic episodes. *International Journal of Eating Disorders, 10,* 547–555.

Elmore, D.K., & deCastro, J.M. (1990). Self-related moods and hunger in relation to spontaneous eating behavior in bulimics, recovered bulimics, and normals. *International Journal of Eating Disorders, 9,* 179–190.

Fairburn, C.G. (1995). *Overcoming binge eating.* New York: Guilford Press.

Fairburn, C.G. (1997). Interpersonal psychotherapy for bulimia nervosa. In D.M. Garner & P.E. Garfinkel (Eds.), *Handbook of treatment for eating disorders* (2nd ed., pp. 278–294). New York: Guilford Press.

Fairburn, C.G., Agras, W.S., & Wilson, G.T. (1992). The research on the treatment of bulimia nervosa: Practical and theoretical implications. In G.H. Anderson & S.H. Kennedy (Eds.), *The biology of feast and famine: Relevance to eating disorders* (pp. 317–340). New York: Academic Press.

Fairburn, C.G., Jones, R., Peveler, R.C., Carr, S.J., Solomon, R.A., O'Connor, M.E., Burton, J., & Hope, R.A. (1991). Three psychological treatments for bulimia nervosa: A comparative trial. *Archives of General Psychiatry, 48,* 463–469.

Fairburn, C.G., Jones, R., Peveler, R.C., Hope, R.A., & O'Connor, M. (1993). Psychotherapy and bulimia nervosa: Longer-term effects of interpersonal psychotherapy, behavior therapy, and cognitive behavior therapy. *Archives of General Psychiatry, 50,* 419–428.

Fairburn, C.G., Kirk, J., O'Connor, M., & Cooper P.J. (1986). A comparison of two psychological treatments for bulimia nervosa. *Behaviour Research and Therapy, 24,* 629–643.

Fairburn, C.G., Marcus, M.D., & Wilson, G.T. (1993). Cognitive-behavioral therapy for binge eating and bulimia nervosa: A comprehensive treatment manual. In C.G.Fairburn & G.T.Wilson (Eds.), *Binge eating: Nature, assessment, and treatment* (pp. 361–404). New York: Guilford Press.

Fairburn, C.G., Norman, P.A., Welch, S.L., O'Connor, M.E., Doll, H.A., & Peveler, R.C. (1995). A prospective study of outcome in bulimia nervosa and the long-term effects of three psychological treatments. *Archives of General Psychiatry, 52,* 304–312.

Fishman, H.C. (1996). Structural family therapy. In J. Werne & I.D. Yalom (Eds.), *Treating eating disorders* (pp. 187–216). San Francisco: Jossey-Bass.

Fox, C. (1997, December). Discovery: Starved out. *Life, 20*(12), 78.

Fremouw, W.J., & Heyneman, N.E. (1983). Cognitive styles and bulimia. *Behavior Therapist, 6,* 143–144.

Friedman, M.A., & Whisman, M.A. (1998). Sociotropy, autonomy, and bulimic symptomatology. *International Journal of Eating Disorders, 23,* 439–442.

Garfinkel, P.E., Lin, E., Goering, P., Spegg, C., Goldbloom, D.S., Kennedy, S., Kaplan, A.S., & Woodside, D.B. (1996). Purging and nonpurging forms of bulimia nervosa in a community sample. *International Journal of Eating Disorders, 20,* 231–238.

Garner, D.M. (1986). Cognitive therapy for anorexia nervosa. In K.D. Brownell & J.P. Foreyt (Eds.), *Handbook of eating disorders* (pp. 301–327). New York: Basic Books.

Garner, D.M., Garfinkel, P.E., Schwarz, D.M., & Thompson, M.M. (1980). Cultural expectations of thinness in women. *Psychological Reports, 47,* 483–491.

Garner, D.M., Garner, M.V., & Rosen, L.W. (1993). Anorexia nervosa "restricters" who purge: Implications for subtyping anorexia nervosa. *International Journal of Eating Disorders, 13,* 171–185.

Garner, D.M., Olmstead, M.P., & Polivy, J. (1983). Development and validation of a multidimensional eating disorder inventory for anorexia nervosa and bulimia. *International Journal of Eating Disorders, 2,* 15–34.

Garner, D.M., Rockert, W., Davis, R., Garner, M.V., Olmsted, M.P., & Eagle, M. (1993). A comparison of cognitive-behavioral and supportive-expressive therapy for bulimia nervosa. *American Journal of Psychiatry, 150,* 37–46.

Garner, D.M., Vitousek, K.M., & Pike, K.M. (1997). Cognitive-behavioral therapy for anorexia nervosa. In D.M. Garner & P.E. Garfinkel (Eds.), *Handbook of treatment for eating disorders* (pp. 94–144). New York: Guilford Press.

Gilbert, S., & Thompson, J.K. (1996). Feminist explanations of the development of eating disorders: Common themes, research findings, and methodological issues. *Clinical Psychology-Science & Practice, 3,* 183–202.

Gleaves, D.H., & Eberenz, K.P. (1997). Correlates of dissociative symptoms among women with eating disorders. *Journal of Psychiatric Research, 29,* 417–426.

Grigg, M., Bowman, J., & Redman, S. (1996). Disordered eating and unhealthy weight reduction practices among adolescent females. *Preventive Medicine, 25,* 748–756.

Grilo, C.M., & Shiffman, S. (1994). Longitudinal investigation of the abstinence violation effect in binge eaters. *Journal of Consulting & Clinical Psychology, 62,* 611–619.

Grissett, N.I., & Norvell, N.K. (1992). Perceived social support, social skills, and quality of relationships in bulimic women. *Journal of Consulting and Clinical Psychology, 60,* 293–299.

Hansel, S.L., & Wittrock, D.A. (1997). Appraisal and coping strategies in stressful situations: A comparison of individuals who binge eat and controls. *International Journal of Eating Disorders, 21,* 89–93.

Heatherton, T.F., & Baumeister, R.F. (1991). Binge eating as escape from self-awareness. *Psychological Bulletin, 110,* 86–108.

Herzog, D.B., Keller, M.B., Lavori, P.W., & Ott, I.L. (1987). Social impairment in bulimia. *International Journal of Eating Disorders, 6,* 741–747.

Herzog, D.B., Nussbaum, K.M., & Marmor, A.K. (1996). Comorbidity and outcome in eating disorders. *Psychiatric Clinics of North America, 19,* 843–859.

Hoek, H.W. (1993). Review of the epidemiological studies of eating disorders. *International Review of Psychiatry, 5,* 61–74.

Holderness, C.C., Brooks-Gunn, J., & Warren, M.P. (1994). Co-morbidity of eating disorders and substance abuse review of the literature. *International Journal of the Eating Disorders, 16,* 1–34.

Hsu, L.K.G., Kaye, W., & Weltzin, T. (1993). Are the eating disorders related to obsessive-compulsive disorder? *International Journal of Eating Disorders, 14,* 305–318.

Kaye, W.H., Kaplan, A.S., & Zucker, M.L. (1996). Treating eating-disorder patients in a managed care environment: Contemporary American issues and a Canadian response. *Psychiatric Clinics of North America, 19,* 793–810.

Kendler, K.S., MacLean, C., Neale, M., Kessler, R.C., Heath, A., & Eaves, L. (1991). The genetic epidemiology of bulimia nervosa. *American Journal of Psychiatry, 148,* 1627–1637.

Keys, A., Brozek, J., Henschel, A., Mickelson, O., & Taylor, H.I. (1950). *The biology of human starvation.* Minneapolis: University of Minnesota Press.

Klerman, G.L., Weissman, M.M., Rounsaville, B.J., & Chevron, E.S. (1984). *Interpersonal psychotherapy of depression.* New York: Basic Books.

Koff, E., & Sangani, P. (1997). Effects of coping style and negative body image on eating disturbance. *International Journal of Eating Disorders, 22,* 51–56.

Kuba, S.A., & Hanchey, S.G. (1991). Reclaiming women's bodies: A feminist perspective on eating disorders. In N. Van Den Bergh (Ed.), *Feminist perspectives on addictions* (pp. 125–137). New York: Springer.

Lam, R.W., Goldner, E.M., & Grewal, A. (1996). Seasonality of symptoms in anorexia and bulimia nervosa. *International Journal of Eating Disorders, 19,* 35–44.

LaPorte, D.J. (1996). Influences of gender, amount of food, and speed of eating on external raters' perceptions of binge eating. *Appetite, 26,* 119–127.

LaPorte, D.J. (1997). Gender differences in perceptions and consequences of an eating binge. *Sex Roles, 36,* 479–489.

Leitenberg, H. (1995). Cognitive-behavioural treatment of bulimia nervosa. *Behaviour Change, 12,* 81–97.

Lewandowski, L.M., Gebing, T.A., Anthony, J.L., & O'Brien, W.H. (1997). Meta-analysis of cognitive-behavioral treatment studies for bulimia. *Clinical Psychology Review, 17,* 703–718.

Lingswiler, V.M., Crowther, J.H., & Stephens, M.A.P. (1989). Emotional and somatic consequences of binge episodes. *Addictive Behaviors, 14,* 503–511.

Mitchell, J. (1998). *Update on treatment research.* Plenary address given at the eighth New York International Conference on Eating Disorders, New York.

Mizes, J.S., & Christiano, B.A. (1995). Assessment of cognitive variables relevant to cognitive behavioral perspectives on anorexia nervosa and bulimia nervosa. *Behavior Research and Therapy, 33,* 95–105.

Nagata, T., McConaha, C., Rao, R., Sokol, M., & Kaye, W. (1997). A comparison of subgroups of inpatients with anorexia nervosa. *International Journal of Eating Disorders, 22,* 309–314.

Neumark-Sztainer, D., Jeffery, R.W., & French, S.A. (1997). Self-reported dieting: How should we ask? What does it mean? Association between dieting and reported energy intake. *International Journal of Eating Disorders, 22,* 437–449.

Niego, S.H., Pratt, E.M., & Agras, W.S. (1997). Subjective or objective binge: Is the distinction valid? *International Journal of Eating Disorders, 22,* 291–298.

Paxton, S.J., & Diggens, J. (1997). Avoidance coping, binge eating, and depression: An examination of the escape theory of binge eating. *International Journal of Eating Disorders, 22,* 83–87.

Polivy, J., & Herman, C.P. (1993). Etiology of binge eating: Psychological mechanisms. In C.G. Fairburn & G.T. Wilson (Eds.), *Binge eating: Nature, assessment, and treatment* (pp. 173–205). New York: Guilford Press.

Rebert, W.M., Stanton, A.L., & Schwarz, R.M. (1991). Influence of personality attributes and daily moods on bulimic eating patterns. *Addictive Behaviors, 16,* 497–505.

Robin, A.L., Bedway, M., Siegel, P.T., & Gilroy, M. (1996). Therapy for adolescent anorexia nervosa: Addressing cognitions, feelings, and the family's role. In E.D. Hibbs & P.S. Jensen (Ed.), *Psychosocial treatments for child and adolescent disorders: Empirically based strategies for clinical practice* (pp. 239–259). Washington, DC: American Psychological Association.

Rosen, J.C. (1997). Cognitive-behavioral body image therapy. In D.M. Garner & P.E. Garfinkel (Eds.), *Handbook of treatment for eating disorders* (2nd ed., pp. 188–201). New York: Guilford Press.

Rosen, J.C., & Leitenberg, H. (1988). The anxiety model of bulimia nervosa and treatment with exposure plus response prevention. In K.M. Pike, W. Vandereycken, & D. Ploog (Eds.), *The psychobiology of bulimia nervosa* (pp. 146–150). Heidelberg: Springer-Verlag.

Rossiter, E.M., & Agras, W.S. (1990). An empirical test of the *DSM-III-R* definition of a binge. *International Journal of Eating Disorders, 9,* 513–518.

Rothblum, E.D. (1994). "I'll die for the revolution but don't ask me not to diet": Feminism and the continuing stigmatization of obesity. In P. Fallon & M.A. Katzman (Eds.), *Feminist perspectives on eating disorders* (pp. 53–76). New York: Guilford Press.

Schlundt, D.G., & Johnson, W.G. (1990). *Eating disorders: Assessment and treatment.* Boston: Allyn & Bacon.

Schwalberg, M.D., Barlow, D.H., Alger, S.A., & Howard, L.J. (1992). Comparison of bulimics, obese binge eaters, social phobics, and individuals with panic disorder on comorbidity across *DSM-III-R* anxiety disorders. *Journal of Abnormal Psychology, 101,* 675–681.

Slade, P. (1982). Towards a functional analysis of anorexia nervosa and bulimia nervosa. *British Journal of Clinical Psychology, 21,* 167–179.

Smith, D.E., Marcus, M.D., & Eldredge, K.L. (1994). Binge eating syndromes: A review of assessment and treatment with an emphasis on clinical application. *Behavior Therapy, 25,* 635–658.

Smith, G.J.W., Amner, G., Johnsson, P., & Franck, A. (1997). Alexithymia in patients with eating disorders: An investigation using a new projective technique. *Perceptual & Motor Skills, 85,* 247–257.

Soukup, V.M., Beiler, M.E., & Terrell, F. (1990). Stress, coping style, and problem solving ability among eating-disordered inpatients. *Journal of Clinical Psychology, 46,* 592–599.

Steinberg, S., Tobin, D.L., & Johnson, C. (1990). The role of bulimic behaviors in affect regulation: Different functions for different patient subgroups? *International Journal of Eating Disorders, 9,* 51–55.

Stice, E. (1994). Review of the evidence for a sociocultural model of bulimia nervosa and an exploration of the mechanisms of action. *Clinical Psychology Review, 14,* 633–661.

Stice, E., Nemeroff, C., & Shaw, H. (1996). Test of the dual pathway model of bulimia nervosa: Evidence for dietary restraint and affect regulation mechanisms. *Journal of Social & Clinical Psychology, 15,* 340–363.

Stice, E., Ziemba, C., Margolis, J., & Flick, P. (1996). The dual pathway model differentiates bulimics, subclinical bulimics, and controls: Testing the continuity hypothesis. *Behavior Therapy, 27,* 531–549.

Striegel-Moore, R.H., Silberstein, L.R., & Rodin, J. (1993). The social self in bulimia nervosa: Public self-consciousness, social anxiety, and perceived fraudulence. *Journal of Abnormal Psychology, 102,* 297–303.

Strober, M. (1997). Consultation and therapeutic engagement in severe anorexia nervosa. In D.M. Garner & P.E. Garfinkel (Eds.), *Handbook of treatment for eating disorders* (pp. 229–247). New York: Guilford Press.

Strober, M., & Katz, J.L. (1988). Depression in the eating disorders: A review and analysis of descriptive, family, and biological findings. In D.M. Garner & P.E. Garfinkel (Eds.), *Diagnostic issues in anorexia nervosa and bulimia nervosa.* New York: Brunner/Mazel.

Sullivan, P.F. (1995). Mortality in anorexia nervosa. *American Journal of Psychiatry, 152,* 1073–1074.

Teusch, R. (1988). Level of ego development and bulimics' conceptualizations of their disorder. *International Journal of Eating Disorders, 7,* 607–615.

Tiller, J.M., Sloane, G., Schmidt, U., Troop, N., Power, M., & Treasure, J.L. (1997). Social support in patients with anorexia nervosa and bulimia nervosa. *International Journal of Eating Disorders, 21,* 31–38.

Tobin, D.L., Griffing, A., & Griffing, S. (1997). An examination of subtype criteria for bulimia nervosa. *International Journal of Eating Disorders, 22,* 179–186.

Troop, N.A., Holbrey, A., & Treasure, J.L. (1998). Stress, coping, and crisis support in eating disorders. *International Journal of Eating Disorders, 24,* 157–166.

Tuschen, B., & Bents, H. (1995). Inpatient treatment of multi-impulsive bulimia nervosa. In K.D. Brownell & C.G. Fairburn (Eds.), *Eating disorders and obesity: A comprehensive handbook.* New York: Guilford Press.

Vitousek, K.B., & Hollon, S.D. (1990). The investigation of schematic content and processing in eating disorders. *Cognitive Therapy and Research, 14,* 191–214.

Vitousek, K.B., & Manke, F. (1994). Personality variables and disorders in anorexia nervosa and bulimia nervosa. *Journal of Abnormal Psychology, 103,* 137–147.

Vitousek, K.B., & Orimoto, L. (1993). Cognitive-behavioral models of anorexia nervosa, bulimia nervosa, and obesity. In K.S. Dobson & P.C. Kendall (Eds.), *Psychopathology and cognition* (pp. 191–243). New York: Wiley.

Walsh, B.T., & Garner, D.M. (1997). Diagnostic issues. In D.M. Garner & P.E. Garfinkel (Eds.), *Handbook of treatment for eating disorders* (2nd ed., pp. 25–33). New York: Guilford Press.

Wardle, J. (1988). Cognitive control of eating. *Journal of Psychosomatic Research, 32,* 607–612.

Wills, T.A. (1997). Modes and families of coping: An analysis of downward comparison in the structure of other cognitive and behavioral mechanisms. In B.P. Buunk & F.X. Gibbons (Eds.), *Health, coping, and well-being: Perspectives from social comparison theory.* New Jersey: Erlbaum.

Wilson, G.T. (1993). Relationship of dieting and voluntary weight loss to psychological functioning and binge eating. *Annals of Internal Medicine, 119,* 727–730.

Wilson, G.T. (1995). Eating disorders and the addictive disorders. In K.D. Brownell & C.G. Fairburn (Eds.), *Eating disorders and obesity: A comprehensive handbook* (pp. 165–170). New York: Guilford Press.

Wilson, G.T., & Eldredge, K.L. (1991). Frequency of binge eating in bulimic patients: Diagnostic validity. *International Journal of Eating Disorders, 10,* 557–561.

Wilson, G.T., & Fairburn, C.G. (1998). Treatments for eating disorders. In P.E. Nathan & J.M. Gorman (Eds.), *A guide to the treatments that work* (pp. 501–530). New York: Oxford University Press.

Wilson, G.T., Fairburn, C.G., & Agras, W.S. (1997). Cognitive-behavioral therapy for bulimia nervosa. In D.M. Garner & P.E. Garfinkel (Eds.), *Handbook of treatment for eating disorders* (pp. 67–93). New York: Guilford Press.

Wonderlich, S.A., & Mitchell, M.D. (1997). Eating disorders and comorbidity: Empirical, conceptual, and clinical implications. *Psychopharmacology Bulletin, 33*(3), 381–390.

Zerbe, K. (1996). Extending the frame: Working with managed care to support treatment for a refractory patient. In J. Werne (Ed.), *Treating eating disorders.* San Francisco: Jossey-Bass.

Zotter, D.L., & Crowther, J.H. (1991). The role of cognitions in bulimia nervosa. *Cognitive Therapy and Research, 15,* 413–426.

Part Eight

BORDERLINE PERSONALITY DISORDER

ALTHOUGH THE behavioral patterns that characterize borderline personality disorder (BPD) have been known for many years and have received a fair number of labels (e.g., pseudoneurotic schizophrenia), it is only in the last decade or so that there has been any semblance of scientific study of this diagnostic entity. Contributing to more reliable diagnostic appraisals have been the criteria posted in *DSM-III-R* and *DSM-IV* and the several semistructured interview schedules that have emerged to study this most complicated phenomenon. However, even with improvement in the operational criteria to make the diagnosis, research indicates that there is much overlap between borderline personality disorder and other personality disorders and atypical affective disorders. Also, within the diagnosis of borderline personality disorder itself, various patients will not always evince the identical cluster of symptoms. Therefore, given the heterogeneity of the disorder, its complexity, its numerous behavioral manifestations, its biological components, its pervasiveness and chronicity, and its resistiveness to treatment, it should not be surprising that there are few standard treatments that can be implemented, as there are for the better defined affective disturbances.

In the chapters comprising this section, distinctive perspectives on etiology and treatment are apparent. However, despite differences, there is clear recognition of the disorder's extraordinary complexity. In light of the few controlled outcome studies that examine the differential efficacy of the psychoanalytic, behavioral, and pharmacological approaches at this point in time, an integrated multimodal approach seems to be indicated.

In the chapter on dynamic psychotherapy, Pollack describes various theoretical approaches to conceptualizing the disorder, including theories derived from the ego psychology homework (e.g., Knight) and object relations (Kernberg). When viewed as an object-relations disorder, BPD is conceived as the pathology of internalized object relations. This is brought about primarily as a result of excessive aggressive drive in infancy and early childhood—and the need to keep it from contaminating a sense of love toward one's caregiver. With respect to therapy, Pollack talks about an "integrated treatment paradigm" that focuses on "personal repair to the self."

In the chapter on behavior therapy, Comtois, Levensky, and Linehan examine borderline personality disorder (BPD) from a number of different perspectives: (1) conceptual underpinnings of the disorder, (2) diagnostic issues, (3) conceptual underpinnings of treatment, (4) specific treatment strategies, (5) other treatments for BPD, and finally, (6) treatment organization and funding under managed care.

The authors note that there are two behavioral treatments currently available that are designed specifically for borderline personality disorder: dialectical behavior therapy (DBT) and bio-cognitive-behavioral treatment, of which only the former has been validated in a randomized controlled trial. Both focus on treating emotional dysregulation and its cognitive and interpersonal consequences. DBT is a comprehensive principle-based treatment that is conceptualized in terms of levels of disorder and corresponding stages, targets, and functions of treatment. Although comprehensive treatments are both expensive to provide and difficult to learn, such would be the expectation for a disorder that is severe, persistent, and historically difficult to treat. Additional research is still needed to determine the necessary and sufficient components of a behavioral treatment for BPD.

Karvoussi and Coccaro review the diagnostic features of BPD and indicate which ones are responsive to particular psychotropic interventions. The authors note that psychotic-like traits (illusions, paranoia, ideas of reference) appear to respond preferentially to low dose antipsychotic medication (these are best used for acute periods of stress-related symptoms). Medicines with putative serotonergic properties (e.g., the serotonin reuptake inhibitors (SSRIs)—fluoxetine, sertraline, paroxetine, fluvoxamine) may be best suited for treating impulsive anger and aggression. Affective instability in borderlines appears to be related to Axis I affective disorders, and medications such as lithium and divalproex sodium may be most effective in reducing mood lability in these patients. Self-destructive behavior may benefit from antipsychotics, SSRIs, or opiate blockers (naltrexone). Rejection sensitivity appears to benefit from monoamine oxidase inhibitors (MAOIs) more than tricyclic antidepressants; whether other agents would also be helpful awaits further controlled trials.

However, as in the case of the dynamic and behavioral approaches, the enormous diagnostic complications and permutations obfuscate the clear choice of given approaches. Indeed, very much like the two previous chapters, the authors call for the study of an integrated approach that combines psychotherapy with pharmacotherapy. Much more work remains to be done with this seemingly intractible disorder. Controlled studies with larger Ns are first needed to determine the most effective psychotherapies, behavior therapies, and pharmacotherapies. This, then should be followed by more comprehensive evaluations in which modalities are both contrasted and examined in additive fashion. In short, research at this time is still in its early stages, but a promising foundation appears to be in place.

CHAPTER 21

Dynamic Psychotherapy

WILLIAM S. POLLACK

CONCEPTUALIZATION
OF THE DISORDER

For over half a century, clinicians have been bedeviled by the seemingly chaotic myriad of behaviors and symptoms manifested by patients who more recently have come to be diagnosed as suffering from borderline personality disorder. The current conceptualization of borderline personality disorder (BPD) and its psychotherapeutic treatment have arisen from a long and arduous history of clinical trial and error, empirical investigation, and the increasingly in-depth psychological immersion by psychotherapists into the feeling states of patients in severe distress. Based upon extensive clinical experience and empirically validated research outcome studies, clinicians today, however, should feel increasingly confident that, with adequate time frame, modern training, supervision, peer support, consultation, and multimodal treatment plans, the psychotherapeutic treatment of BPD has every reason to meet with excellent success.

As early as 1930, psychoanalytically oriented clinicians were beginning to draw attention to a group of patients who appeared to be neither neurotic nor psychotic, but who, rather, seemed to fall on a continuum between these two disorders (Glover, 1932; Oberndorf, 1930). Hoch and Polatin (1949) viewed such patients as suffering from "pseudoneurotic schizophrenia." Stern (1938), however, was the first to use the term *borderline* to describe those patients whose clinical presentations included disorders of narcissism, rigid personality, a sense of personal inferiority, hypersensitivity to insult, and a deeply rooted, almost unshakable sense of anxiety. He argued that this *borderline* syndrome constituted a distinct, clinical diagnostic entity. By the late 1940s and early 1950s, others had come to agree that borderline patients were indeed a distinct and distinguishable diagnostic group with definitive, even pathognomic clinical symptomatology (Deutsch, 1942; Wolberg, 1952).

Utilizing the newer psychodynamic theories of *ego psychology*, Knight (1953) argued that borderline patients suffered from severely weakened ego functions manifested in the areas of secondary-process thinking, realistic planning, adaptation to the environment, maintenance of object relations, and internal defenses against primitive aggressive and sexual impulses. More importantly, Knight put forth the seminal idea that the primary source of the observed ego dysfunctions were underlying developmental failures. These included problems with what Knight called constitutional development, disturbed early object relations, early traumatic events, and severe precipitating stress. It is this central concept of a developmental delay, dysfunction, or deficit—expressed in the borderline's often severe problems with internal affective tolerance, problematic interpersonal behaviors, and so on—that unifies most modern concepts of borderline disorder and provides a cohesive theme for many of the successful psychotherapeutic treatment strategies.

As a harbinger of modern clinical concerns, Knight stressed the difficulty in treating borderline patients in psychotherapy. He called attention to these patients' tendency to regress within the treatment setting itself, apparently becoming worse. Often, within an unmodified transference-oriented psychotherapy, such patients would express overt dependency and emit extreme rageful reactions directed at their therapists, sometimes in conjunction with suicidal threats and self-destructive actions. These behaviors would often frighten clinicians, who were made severely anxious by these indirect and confusing expressions of developmentally early needs for caring, holding, or soothing. In some cases, the greater the therapeutic zeal of the treaters, and the more inclusive the treatment setting, the more severe the regression! Indeed, hospitalization often led to even more regressed and primitive behaviors, which left the treatment staff feeling intensely helpless and angry (Adler, 1985). Evocation of such countertransference reactions has become a definable characteristic of patients with borderline psychopathology. Consequently, Knight argued for practical modifications of classic psychotherapeutic technique. He proposed that a central goal in the treatment of borderline patients should be the strengthening of the ego's control over the overwhelming internal impulses. This approach was popularized by Zetzel (1971).

It was not until the next decade that systematic empirical studies of borderline psychopathology were undertaken. Grinker, Werble, and Drye (1968), in one such study, postulated that what had been defined as the "borderline syndrome" was most reasonably a consequence of a developmental arrest in childhood, leading to later adult deficits of ego functioning. Their findings supported the hypothesis that this so-called borderline syndrome was not merely an affective state, but rather, an enduring personality trait or disorder. They also identified statistically distinct subgroups of borderline patients, but they highlighted four characteristics that were shared by all patients: (1) anger as the main or only affect; (2) defects in affectional relationships; (3) deficient sense of self-identity; and (4) depressive loneliness.

Gunderson and colleagues (Carpenter, Gunderson, & Strauss, 1977; Gunderson, 1977, 1982, 1984; Gunderson & Kolb, 1978; Gunderson & Singer, 1975) showed empirical distinctions between borderline patients and patients suffering from psychotic disorders, and they provided a basis for more reliable and valid diagnosis of borderline patients. Based on this research and clinical experience, Gunderson (1984) argued for a more narrow, empirically based definition of borderline personality disorder.

In contrast to Gunderson, Kernberg (1967, 1975) has argued for a broader definition of the disorder, which he terms *borderline personality organization* (BPO). Although agreeing that borderline patients are neither fully neurotic nor fully psychotic, he maintains that there is a core set of unique characteristics that argue for a conceptually separate and diagnostically distinct disorder: (1) a diffuse and unstable sense of identity, and (2) a use of more developmentally primitive internal defensive operations, especially those of splitting and projective identification. He sees these two characteristics as occurring within a generally intact capacity for reality testing. Regression to primary-process thinking is only transient and present under severe psychological pressure; secondary-process thinking returns with appropriate support.

In brief, Kernberg conceptualizes the borderline disorder as a disturbance within the self, particularly in self and object representations (introjects). He views these inner mental representations as being pathologically intertwined in borderline patients. This is said to occur as a result of a developmental fixation at, or a regression to an early stage of internalized object relations in which conflicting images of self and other are not adequately differentiated or integrated, and the balance among positively and negatively tinged (libidinal and aggressive) affects is not achieved.

Kernberg traces the defects in the borderline patient's ego to a predominance of pathological aggression and aggressive drive derivatives, tied either to primary biological predisposition, or developmental reactions to a frustrating environment. Regardless of the ultimate cause, the effect is both an inability to integrate such aggressive wishes, and a need to control them—in order to maintain a reservoir of positive connection with significant others—both in the present real world and in the internal representational world. Such a search for balance leads, in turn, to the regressive and defensive utilization of splitting.

According to Kernberg, splitting is used to keep apart good and bad introjects so that the person can preserve the limited, available good memories of the self and important others. Kernberg thus feels that borderline patients are using an unconscious primitive psychological defense to avoid noticing their own extremely angry feelings toward their early objects, and thereby desperately clinging to a modicum of positive connection with those on whom they are emotionally and physically dependent.

As one might imagine, however, splitting leads to major deficits in self-definition, self-versus-other differentiation, self-cohesion, and self-esteem. Peace is bought at a heavy price! Kernberg argues that the mechanism of splitting sets in motion other primitive defense mechanisms of the ego (e.g., projective identification, denial, idealization), which, in turn, prevent further integration from occurring and give rise to the symptoms so characteristic of borderline patients (Kernberg, 1967, 1975). The amalgam of cognitive, emotional, and clinical dysfunctions that emerges is termed *nonspecific manifestations of ego weakness.* They include primitive free-floating anxiety (with lack of anxiety tolerance), lack of impulse control, lack of sublimatory channels, and occasional breakthroughs of primary-process thinking, that is, transient psychosis.

In summary, then, Kernberg conceptualizes BPD as an object relations disorder, with pathology of internalized object relations. Such pathology is brought about primarily as a result of excessive aggressive drives in infancy and early childhood—and the need to keep them from contaminating a sense of love toward one's caregiver. Although Kernberg pays lip service to the developmental concepts of Mahler (1971) and the significance of the separation-individuation phase of development, he virtually ignores the real interpersonal and environmental contributions to the etiology of the disorder. His model is primarily a classic conflict-drive theory, in which conflict over the binding of an excessive amount of aggression and rage leads to ego or self deficits.

On the other end of the conceptual spectrum are Buie and Adler. They offer a view of BPD that relies heavily on the research of developmental psychology, cognitive structuralism, and psychoanalytic developmental psychology. They integrate the object relations work of Winnicott—his concepts of good-enough mothering and of the holding environment (Winnicott, 1965; see also Modell, 1976)—and Kohut's concept of the self-object (Kohut, 1977). Adler and Buie have identified a core existential state of frightening and painful aloneness, which they argue is the sine qua non of borderline psychopathology (Adler, 1985; Adler & Buie, 1979; Buie & Adler, 1982). They propose that such aloneness is the result of a developmental deficit in the capacity, during times of distress, to recall in memory a sustaining, holding, or soothing object—the "holding self-object." Because the resulting aloneness panic cannot be assuaged by the self, the affected individual engages in the intrapsychic defenses, interpersonal distancing operations, and the self-destructive activities for which borderline patients are only too well known.

Buie and Adler, unlike Kernberg, attribute this aloneness deficit to real deficiencies in the parents' capacity to hold and soothe their child early in life. They maintain that by age two years, individuals who will later suffer from BPD have already undergone disruptions in their caregiving environment—a holding environment. This disruption both impedes their capacity to learn how to use a transitional object to soothe themselves at times of distress and interferes with the normal development of evocative memory, a capacity to remember the caregiving functions of parental figures in their absence and during times of distress. The inability to achieve a solid form of evocative memory, or to utilize it at times of severe distress, leaves these individuals at an immense disadvantage in soothing or calming themselves when, in adulthood, they are most upset or hurt.

In addition, Adler and Buie emphasize the fact that the rage and *hurt* that these patients often display when faced with separations further damage whatever already fragile capacity they have to evoke a positively tinged memory of a supporting object. Consequently, at times of separation, they are left even further bereft and enraged. Intolerable panic and aloneness takes hold as their positive connection with a significant other is lost. The reactions to such overwhelming distress include the familiar attempts at either dependent clinging or rageful self-harm. Empirical research has now confirmed what many clinicians have long suspected (Pollack, 1990): A significant majority of patients suffering from BPD have experienced actual childhood trauma; a history of sexual and/or physical abuse (Bryer, Nelson, Miller, & Krol, 1987; Herman, Perry, & van der Kold, 1989; Zanarini, 1996; Zanarini, Gunderson, & Marino, 1989). Our knowledge of a potential past reality of traumatic harm demands modification in our conceptual and treatment models of the disorder, and raises significant questions of efficacy and ethics in carrying out psychotherapeutic approaches not informed by these more current findings. All successful modern psychotherapy models, therefore, must now take into account the patient's legitimate rage at caretakers who failed to protect, or actually abused; the need to empathically understand the experience of victimization, and the legitimacy of a number of characterological defenses that, although maladaptive in adult life, were life sustaining in an earlier environment of actual abandonment, impingement, or abuse (Gunderson & Chu, 1993; Herman, 1992; Pollack, 1990). (See "Psychodynamic Treatment Approaches," later in this chapter.)

Variations in the conceptualization of BPD have naturally led to a series of diagnostic approaches, issues, and problems, whose resolution and integration are made all the more salient by the life threatening pain of patients suffering from the disorder.

DIAGNOSTIC ISSUES AND PROBLEMS

PREVALENCE

Accurate estimates of the prevalence of BPD are somewhat elusive, but there is growing evidence that it may be the most commonly occurring *DSM-IV* personality disorder (American Psychiatric Association [APA], 1994; Frances, Clarkin, Gilmore, Hurt, & Brown, 1984; Kass, Spitzer, & Williams, 1983; Koenigsberg, Kaplan, Gilmore, & Cooper, 1985). A 1985 report suggests that up to 4 percent of the general population may suffer from this disorder (Institute of Medicine, 1985). Kroll, using Gunderson's Diagnostic Interview for Borderlines (DIB) in a cross-cultural study (Kroll, Carey, Sines, & Roth, 1982), found a diagnostic prevalence of 15 percent to 20 percent of an inpatient psychiatric population. Present prevalence is estimated to be about 2 percent of the general population, 10 percent of outpatient mental-health populations, 20 percent of psychiatric inpatients, and, "ranges from 30 percent to 60 percent among clinical populations with Personality Disorders" (APA, 1994, p. 652). Although more empirical studies are needed, BPD certainly represents a significant proportion of individuals who seek or are in need of psychological treatment.

It is noteworthy that the disorder appears to be more prevalent among women than among men. The female-to-male ratio ranges from 2:1 to 4:1, depending on the samples used (Gunderson, 1984; Stiver, 1988). Kass and colleagues (1983) have raised the possibility of gender bias in the application of BPD diagnostic criteria, but they do believe that there are genuine gender differences in prevalence of BPD. A study by Bardenstein and McGlashan (1988) highlights some of those differences. Pope and colleagues (Pope, Jonas, Hudson, Cohen, & Gunderson, 1983), however, raise the possibility that the differences are more apparent than real and that similarly disturbed male and female patients are simply labeled differently, specifically as "antisocial" and "borderline," respectively. The same often occurs in outpatient practices, where male and female patients with moderate to severe personality disorders tend to be diagnosed as "narcissistic" and "borderline," respectively. The *DSM-IV* estimates a 75 percent to 25 percent, female to male ratio for the BPD diagnosis (APA, 1994).

MORBIDITY

Although Axis I psychiatric disorders, especially schizophrenia and affective illness, are usually seen by clinicians as more serious than the personality disorders on Axis II, such an impression may be both erroneous and dangerous (Gunderson & Pollack, 1985). In fact, presence of personality disorders, especially BPD, may represent a serious risk of morbidity.

Even in samples of well-treated patients, the long-term risk of suicide and chronic dysfunction is relatively high. Several longitudinal empirical reports (Carpenter et al., 1977; Gunderson, Carpenter, & Strauss, 1975) have found surprising similarities in the course of borderline and schizophrenic patients. Both groups showed unremitting symptomatology, evidence of sustained recidivism, poor employment functioning, and difficulty in social relations. Pope et al. (1983) also provided evidence of severe impairments in long-term psychosocial functioning in patients with BPD.

Recent studies have been more optimistic, but they continue to caution clear risk of morbidity. For example, McGlashan (1986) found evidence for positive treatment outcome when borderline patients were followed for several decades, into middle age. However, even those patients showed severe, albeit, intermittent symptomatic psychopathology and ongoing urges toward impulsive solutions to pain; and the sample had a completed suicide rate of 3 percent. Stone, Hurt, and Stone (1987), in another long-term outcome study, also found a basis for some cautious optimism concerning morbidity, given appropriate treatment. Again, however, this is within a context of ongoing severe dysfunction, as well as an overall suicide rate of approximately 9 percent, with close to 8 percent of completed suicides occurring before the age of 30. In a review of current literature, Maltsberger and Lovett (1992) estimate that approximately 10 percent of BPD patients may complete a suicide, with close to 40 percent making one or more lethal attempts. With subgroups of patients who also meet the diagnosis for a major affective disorder and untreated alcoholism, the survival rate may reach a low of 58 percent (Stone, 1990).

In sum, available data suggest that if borderline patients can be provided optimal treatment early on, they can make reasonable adjustment and suicidal enactment can be controlled. However, the opposite also appears true: the younger the patient, the less well contained, the less appropriately geared the treatment to the illness, the greater the likelihood for severe dysfunction over time, as well as completed suicide. Such findings argue for careful diagnostic evaluation, and for early intervention with appropriate, well-tested treatment paradigms.

CLINICAL PRESENTATION

Despite some remaining diagnostic ambiguities, a reasonable consensus has been achieved concerning the diagnostic entity of BPD, first in the *DSM-III* and *DSM-III-R* (American Psychiatric Association [APA], 1980, 1987), and now in the *DSM-IV* (APA, 1994), where BPD is characterized as "a pervasive pattern of instability of interpersonal relationships, self-image, and affects, and marked impulsivity, beginning by early adulthood and present in a variety of contexts" (APA, 1994). To meet a distinct *DSM-IV* diagnosis of BPD, five out of eight of the following criteria must be manifest: efforts to avoid a feeling of abandonment, unstable and intense pattern of interpersonal relationships, identity disturbance, impulsivity in a self-damaging manner, recurrent suicidal behavior, threats of or actual self-mutilation, affective instability, chronic sense of emptiness, inappropriate intense anger, transient paranoid thinking, or dissociative symptoms. In addition, these problems must be characterological in nature (enduring and repetitive) and must lead to functional impairment (vocational/social) as well as to significant and ongoing internal distress (APA, 1994, pp. 633, 650–654).

Although *DSM-IV* guidelines are useful, I believe that a more complete and accurate picture of the borderline patient is achieved by focusing the diagnostic evaluation on the major psychodynamic aspects of the disorder. These can be dichotomized along two axes: (1) problems in and within the self, and (2) problems manifested along the lines of the self in interaction with others.

PROBLEMS WITHIN THE SELF

Noncohesive Sense of Self and an Unstable Identity

A core characteristic of borderline patients, and one of the most striking aspects of their presentation, is their developmental difficulty in establishing a cohesive self (Kohut, 1971, 1977) and a stable sense of personal identity. Although such disturbances run deep, they remain difficult to define objectively, especially because patients with other personality disorders (e.g., narcissistic personality), younger patients in late adolescence or early adulthood, and normal adults in life transitions or crises may sometimes manifest similar disturbances.

Related to this, theorists and clinicians have identified specific disturbances within borderline patients that are related to a fear of separation from significant objects. The inability to tolerate feeling or being alone is seen by Adler and Buie (1979) and Adler (1985) as the pathognomonic central core of borderline psychopathology. Masterson (1971) noted a similar vulnerability of borderline patients to "abandonment depression," and Mahler (1971) noted severe separation anxiety. Consequently, such patients may often be socially overactive or compulsively involved with others in order to avoid being alone. These attempts at interpersonal involvement are often frantic and short-lived.

Cognitive Disturbances—Transient Psychotic Experiences

Under severe stress, borderline patients often experience episodes of severe dissociation, including, at times, derealization or depersonalization, manifestations of paranoid thinking, and a host of primitive and regressive defenses. Such episodes cannot, however, be considered definitive for the diagnosis of BPD, because many other patients may have such experiences at times. In borderline patients, these experiences are almost always ego dystonic. They are not accepted by the patient as a consensual way of seeing the world. They often are accompanied by massive anxiety; and they may be the impetus for such patients seeking treatment.

Impulsive Behaviors

Impulsivity may manifest itself diversely, but it is usually linked to the borderline's unstable and noncohesive sense of self. Although compulsive gambling, shoplifting, or eating disturbances may occur, the most prevalent form of impulsive activity in borderline patients, especially in young adults, is the abuse of alcohol or other drugs. Sexual promiscuity or deviance, used in an equally addictive manner, is also quite common. Indeed, severity and prevalence of these impulsive behaviors has fueled the ongoing debate over their etiology. Psychoanalytic clinicians tie them to the underlying unstable, noncohesive self and the need for self-soothing (see Adler & Buie, 1979), whereas biologically oriented researchers take them as evidence that BPD may be part of a biological affective spectrum of disease (Akiskal, 1981).

Labile and Uncomfortable Affect

A striking characteristic of borderline patients, evident in the transferences they form and the countertransferences they evoke in therapy, is the experience of ongoing uncomfortable affects, including anger and a painful sense of emptiness or abandonment. At times, they express their anger in outbursts of extreme rage; at other times, they do so with an ongoing sense of bitterness or with apparently excessive demands on their primary objects. In my opinion, the anger is often a response to either past or present experiences of real hurt, trauma, and disappointment. With empathic probing, therapists often discover a terrifying sense of depression, loneliness, and loss lying behind the rage. They also are apt to uncover a sense of "badness" that these patients may feel about themselves (Gunderson, 1984; Kernberg, 1967, 1975, 1984).

Buie's Summary of Self-Functions

Buie (1997) has recently conceptualized a series of five "self-maintenance functions," which he feels "are essential for maintaining psychological self-stability." These include: a felt sense of self-realness, an inner capacity for secure holding-soothing, positive self-esteem, the capacity for self-love, and a felt sense of personal identity. The absence, dysregulation, or enfeeblement of all five of these bedrocks of self are often obvious in BPD, if we take a depth-psychological, empathic view of our patient's expressions of distress.

PROBLEMS OF THE SELF IN INTERACTION WITH OTHERS

Unstable and Intense Interpersonal Relationships

No therapist experienced in working with borderline patients can mistake their characteristic pattern of rapidly idealizing and then devaluing those on whom they depend, and their subtle, often nonverbal means of gaining support from significant others, usually through impulsive actions rather than words.

Some (e.g., Pollack, 1986; Stiver, 1985) have questioned the language used to describe the borderline patient's problematic relationships. Words such as *manipulative* often are used in a critical and pejorative manner and reflect a misunderstanding of the patient's needs. Therapist should seek, instead, to understand how such patients' developmental difficulties and present anxieties cause them to crave and seek, over and over again, close, dependent relationships, only to defend against acknowledging any need for them by pushing significant others away at times of stress. Such actions may also be linked to actual past traumatic experiences, including abuse, incest, and other forms of exploitation suffered at the hands of those on whom patients depended in childhood. (See "Case Illustration," later in this chapter.)

Self-Destructive Activity

Borderline patients are likely to engage in self-destructive behavior (including suicidal enactment) in a frantic effort to get others to intervene with or respond to them. Grunebaum and Klerman (1967) have delineated a subgroup of patients for whom acts of self-harm are a dynamic expression of inner feelings. Again, some have termed these acts manipulative, with no appreciation of their function, that is, to engage the response of those around them. However, such self-destructive activity should be neither countertransferentially denied nor minimized because, as noted previously, there is also a serious risk of completed suicide! Suicide attempts are often a cause of therapeutic failure, therapist anxiety, and hospitalization of patients with BPD.

In addition to suicidal and parasuicidal enactment, borderline patients often engage in a wide range of apparently self-mutilating behaviors (e.g., cutting of the body without attempt to suicide, painful mutilation of genitals). These behaviors may be understood as an expression of an attempt at self-soothing, as well as a possible repetition of an earlier trauma (Buie & Adler, 1982).

Functional Failures

Although not emphasized in the *DSM-III-R*, the inability of borderline patients to effectively apply their talents in order to achieve success in the world is an important diagnostic feature. Many such patients show a potential for high achievement that falls by the wayside, often due to the affective overloading of their cognitive skills.

Functional incapacity, especially in vocational and occupational domains, helps in the differential diagnosis of BPD: Patients who experience problems related to cohesion of the self and to affective stability, but who can indeed function well with minimal support and intervention, may well be suffering from depressive disorders with characterological aspects or from less severe characterological disturbances. They do not, however, usually meet the criteria for BPD.

THE BORDERS OF BORDERLINE

OTHER PERSONALITY DISORDERS

The capacity to make clear, empirically based distinctions among all the personality disorders is still difficult. Pope et al. (1983) found that although BPD could be distinguished from both affective illness and schizophrenia, it was not easily distinguishable from either histrionic or antisocial personality disorders. They, therefore, questioned whether these personality disorders are appropriately separate categories. The *DSM-IV* has attempted to make some dimensional distinctions amongst the personality disorders in general by dividing them into the three categories or clusters of A: odd-eccentric; B: dramatic-emotional (in which BPD falls); and C: anxious-fearful. I believe that clinicians can make differential diagnoses with practical, therapeutic meaning if certain distinctions are kept in mind.

Although borderline patients engage in acts that may be considered antisocial, they are likely to experience shame or remorse, and, although they may need to justify such acts for the survival of the self, the behaviors are usually ego-dystonic. In addition, borderline patients are less likely than antisocial or schizoid patients to be aloof and detached from their needs for people close to them. Rather, they engage in intense, unstable relationships with uncomfortable affects.

The border between borderline and histrionic personality disorder is less clear and requires greater differentiation. I would argue that the key distinction is functional incapacity. Histrionic patients are likely to perform at a much higher functional level and also to present a more stable inner sense of self than those with BPD; and the former are less apt to show evidence of repeated self-destructive activity.

Although borderline and narcissistic patients have some common features and disabilities, their expression of the need for a primary object on whom to depend differs radically. Borderline patients are likely to be open in their needs for support, whereas narcissistic patients tend to deny their dependency needs. On the other hand, when attached in a sustaining relationship, narcissistic patients are usually able to perform their roles effectively and to maintain a stable sense of themselves. By contrast, patients with BPD are more likely to have storms of affect that last longer and are much more disorganizing. Even in a supportive therapeutic environment, BPD patients may show persistent and major deficiencies in the role performance and social relationships.

AFFECTIVE ILLNESS AND OTHER AXIS I DISORDERS

It is now clear that patients with BPD do not share the diagnosis of schizophrenia, and that the latter must take precedence in any diagnostic characterization. Since the late 1970s, however, the debate has reemerged about whether patients with BPD actually suffer from some form of affective illness. Akiskal (1981, 1983) argues most strongly for viewing BPD as merely part of an affective spectrum of disease. Other researchers have highlighted the overlap between BPD and affective illness, but they have argued for two distinct, diagnosable disorders: BPD *and* major affective illness (Kroll et al., 1981; McGlashan, 1983, 1986; Pope et al., 1983; Stone et al., 1987). In the interest of brevity, this chapter does not fully air the debate concerning the overlap between affective illness and BPD. Gunderson and Elliott (1985) and Gunderson and Phillips (1991) have reviewed the relevant issues and raised several putative explanatory hypotheses.

For clinicians, however, it is important to recognize that patients with BPD may present prominent affective symptoms and may meet criteria for dysthymic disorder, for cyclothymia, or for a major depression. When patients with an uncomplicated acute or episodic unipolar depression recover from their particular episode of the disorder, their functioning intermorbidly will likely be more adaptive than that of depressed patients who continue to suffer from concurrent and severely disabling BPD. Psychopharmacologic consultation for underlying affective illness should be addressed.

DIFFERENTIAL DIAGNOSIS

INTERFACE WITH NEUROLOGICAL DISTURBANCE

Recently, there has been interest in the interface of BPD with seizure disorders, most noticeably atypical partial complex seizures (TLE). The advent of more sensitive brain scanning devices and more sophisticated analysis of electroencephalograph (EEG) activity [e.g., nuclear magnetic resonance imaging (MRI), positron emission tomography (PET) scans, and brain electrical activity mapping (BEAM) EEG] has allowed for evaluation of electromagnetic activity and structural abnormalities in the brains of patients with personality disorders (Cowdry & Gardner, 1988; Schatzberg, 1983). There is some evidence of seizure activity, subclinical seizures, or atypical neurological disturbance in patients with BPD (see Silk, 1994).

In addition, clinical trials of antiseizure medication (e.g., valproic acid and carbamazepine) in BPD raise questions about the overlap of these disorders. Although some argue that BPD is a subvariant of neurological dysfunction, the possibility remains of two distinct interactive disorders manifest simultaneously in certain patients. For the practicing clinician, it is important to note that neurological evaluation and, at times, trials of neurological medication may be useful in establishing a diagnosis and in alleviating some of the severe symptomatology of patients with BPD. It is unlikely, however, that this treatment alone will be sufficient.

OUTCOME MEASURES

Waldinger and Gunderson (1987), in a qualitative study, showed the significant effects on personality functioning for BPD patients in intensive long-term psychotherapy with a five-year course. Stevenson and Meares (1992) showed results with twice-weekly therapy of only one-year duration, including diminishing self-harmful behavior and substance abuse. Hoke (1989) and Howard (1986) have both demonstrated the salutary effects of intensive long-term psychodynamic psychotherapy for BPD, with treatments exceeding two years of constant work predicting the best results.

SUMMARY OF ISSUES

Although debate continues over conceptualization, categorization, and assessment of BPD, there has been growing clarity in the delineation of a distinct, circumscribed personality disorder that can be reliably and validly diagnosed. For patient and clinician alike, however, diagnosis has its greatest meaning in informing specific therapeutic strategies that may be successful in remediating the degree of severe human suffering that a diagnosis of BPD connotes.

PSYCHODYNAMIC TREATMENT STRATEGIES

Historically, it has been argued that the treatment of choice for BPD is a modified or specialized form of psychoanalytic psychotherapy. Other approaches have also been suggested, and within psychodynamic psychotherapy, a wide range of techniques has been advocated: Adler (1985), Buie (1997), Gunderson (1984), Kernberg (1984), Pollack (1986), and Waldinger and Gunderson (1987). Current controversies center around (1) how supportive or exploratory the process should be, (2) how empathic or confrontive the therapist should be, (3) how often the therapy should take place, and (4) what other adjunctive treatments should be used and under what conditions.

Addressing all these controversies is beyond the scope of this chapter. Rather, I highlight the major issues in the psychodynamic therapeutic treatment of BPD, and briefly describe other pragmatic treatment approaches. Some consensual components of all successful psychodynamic psychotherapies for BPD include creating a stable treatment frame; active, positive, and involved therapists; creating connections between patient's actions and feelings; dealing with the complexities of self-destructive behavior; and paying careful attention to the therapists' countertransference feelings (Waldinger & Gunderson, 1987).

Although there is debate about the conditions necessary for successful use of individual psychotherapy with BPD, the most consistent contraindication for any form of this treatment is an untrained or an emotionally unavailable psychotherapist. I strongly concur with Gunderson (1984) that a novice should not treat a BPD patient without intensive supervision and support. I also believe that psychotherapists who have not yet achieved substantial understanding of their own psychological functioning are apt to become confused by countertransference feelings. At the least, they will not be therapeutically available and useful to such patients. At most, they could easily do extreme harm.

SUPPORTIVE VERSUS EXPLORATORY-INTENSIVE PSYCHOTHERAPY

I have argued elsewhere that one of the *least* productive debates in the BPD treatment literature has been the argument over the merits of intensive, exploratory, insight-oriented psychotherapy versus supportive, nonintensive psychotherapy. It has been suggested that the BPD's fragile ego and self-structure require a more supportive approach, involving infrequent (usually once per week) meetings and an effort to support rather than to uncover defenses (Friedman, 1975; Grinker et al., 1968; Knight, 1953; Zetzel, 1971). The assumption is that the creation of a sustaining psychotherapeutic relationship will allow borderline patients to order their chaotic inner experiences and, consequently, to gain stability in their daily life functions. Given the concerns about regressive reactions to a more intensive psychotherapy, such an approach is believed to bolster the alliance and decrease the possibility of unmanageable transference enactments and self-destructive activity.

Kernberg et al. (1972) have argued against the supportive approach, feeling that it leads to iatrogenic toxic side effects. They maintain that borderline patients do equally well in an expressive approach and that the negative side effects encountered in this treatment are better handled by using short-term inpatient hospital stays, PRN, rather than by watering down the psychotherapy itself.

However, the distinctions between so-called supportive and intensive psychotherapies are rarely so clear cut. Kernberg himself argues for the supportive aspects of the intensity of the treatment, and this point has been echoed by Wallerstein (1983). In fact, the so-called supportive treatments may do more than bolster defenses or decrease suicide risks. They may also bring about internal structural changes usually ascribed only to insight-oriented psychotherapy. Most would agree with Greenberg (1977) and Levine (1979) that the establishment of a "sustaining object relationship" within psychotherapy is necessary. Indeed, most recent approaches to intensive psychotherapy for the character neuroses highlight the importance of the "holding environment" (Adler, 1985; Modell, 1976).

Clinical and common sense both dictate that any set of psychotherapeutic interventions that do not help the patient either to stem the tide of chaotic, overwhelming internal feelings or to limit suicidal enactment will not be very therapeutic in the long run. I believe that effective psychotherapists will, of necessity, blend supportive and interpretive techniques to react flexibly to varying needs and levels of functioning of their particular borderline patients.

TWO APPROACHES TO BPD

Having said that, it is worth examining two major psychoanalytically oriented paradigms for the individual psychotherapy of BPD: (1) Kernberg's "object relations" approach, and (2) Buie and Adlers' therapeutic "holding environment" approach. It is also valuable to consider what I believe is a more developmentally oriented multimodal, yet still a psychodynamic approach to BPD.

KERNBERG

There are major clinical implications of Kernberg's conceptualization of BPD as a pathology of internalized object relations brought about by the incapacity to tolerate primitive aggression: (1) It leads to the belief that in therapy, the borderline patient will experience "a premature activation in the transference of very early conflict-laden object relations" (Kernberg, 1982, p. 472). (2) These conflicts in turn will get played out in the transference as a pathological condensation of pregenital and genital aims *under the overriding influence of pregenital aggression* (Kernberg, 1982, p. 472, italics mine). (3) The end result will be a deep sense of distrust and fear of the therapist, who is often viewed as a potent "attacker."

Consequently, Kernberg's approach emphasized the need to control transference enactment. To this end, he recommends limiting the patient's enactment while interpreting the need for such limits from the perspective of the transference relationship itself. Kernberg recommends that this be done in an intensive psychoanalytic therapy organized around: (1) interpretation, (2) maintenance of neutrality, and (3) analysis of transference.

For Kernberg (1975, 1984), interpretation is fundamental, whereas suggestion, manipulation, and most other forms of active intervention should be eschewed. The only exception to this rule would be setting limits on the patient's acting out negative (especially self-destructive) impulses. To accomplish this, the therapist may add external structuring of the patient's life and/or may intervene in the patient's social network, but even such interventions should eventually be interpreted and should wither away.

Although Kernberg advocates empathic responsiveness to patients' needs, he maintains that patients must face and bear those aspects of their inner lives, which may at first be walled off or unbearable. He believes this goal can only be achieved through maintenance of clinical neutrality.

The active analysis of transference is the third aspect of Kernberg's approach and the major vehicle of therapeutic change. It is through transference interpretation that developmentally arrested object relations are finally integrated, making it possible for the BPD patient to tolerate ambivalent feelings. To accomplish this, Kernberg suggests that (1) the predominantly negative transference of borderline patients should be systematically elaborated and interpreted, highlighting the here-and-now aspect of the aggressive constellations; (2) typical defenses such as splitting and projective identification should be interpreted as soon as they enter the transference; and (3) limits must be set in order both to stop any acting out of the transference and to maintain the neutrality of the therapist (Kernberg, 1984).

Kernberg sees positive aspects of the transference as needing less interpretation and as forming the basis of a therapeutic alliance. Still, grossly exaggerated idealization should not be left unchallenged. It is just that the negative transference must be interpreted first if the patient is to develop the capacity to deal with primitive conflicts around aggression and the intolerance of ambivalence (Kernberg, 1984, p. 106). It is for this reason that Kernberg advocates interpreting any current defenses that distort reality, even is these are attempts at self soothing. Although Kernberg is aware of the need for holding or containing borderline patients (Bion, 1967; Winnicott, 1960), he cautions therapists not to lose their neutrality and gratify rather than interpret the patient's needs.

Clinicians will recognize in Kernberg's approach an opportunity to squarely face a patient's aggression without being overtly critical. By maintaining neutrality, the clinician calms and supports the patient and orders the intense chaotic feelings expressed in the treatment. Herein lies Kernberg's therapeutic optimism and the hope needed to sustain a very difficult treatment. Others, however, have criticized this approach.

Searles (1979a, 1979b) has raised questions about the Olympian nature of Kernberg's treatment. The requirement of strict neutrality may demand more than a psychotherapist can practically provide or than borderline patients can tolerate (Tolpin & Kohut, 1980). I also have argued that Kernberg's emphasis on aggression may leave patients feeling as though they are actually bad because they always seem so angry.

In addition, many clinicians view their patients' aggression not as primary but either as a secondary and legitimate response to early environmental trauma or hurt, or as a defense against a deeper sense of loneliness or abandonment. Kernberg's approach might then be experienced as a collusion with the patient's harsh superego, so that the patient begins to feel responsible for harm that was actually perpetrated by others. Indeed Gabbard et al. (1994) found that interpretation of a patient's aggression had a negative effect on the alliance, if the patient had sustained trauma in earlier life. Rather, empathic validation of the patient's rageful response to realistic pain led to a greater sense of "in sync" connection between therapist and patient, and eventually yielded greater mutative effect for the interpretive model.

Kernberg's approach may also be somewhat impractical. Economic and geographic considerations often require that the therapist play several roles, including a supportive one, in the midst of ongoing psychotherapy. This is not to diminish the importance of Kernberg's admonition against becoming too involved in the patients' real lives and thereby enacting transference fantasies. Rather, it highlights the fact that one must often do more than interpret in order to help borderline patients. This view is echoed by Adler and Buie.

ADLER AND BUIE

Based on the salient concepts of intolerable aloneness and developmental dysfunctions in the areas of holding introjects and self-soothing capacities Adler and Buie (Adler, 1985; Adler & Buie, 1979; Buie, 1997; Buie & Adler, 1982) have advocated a somewhat different psychotherapeutic approach. They maintain that in order to cure what they conceptualize as the primary sector of border-line psychopathology—an inability to sustain a holding or soothing memory of significant others at times of separation or distress—the therapist must pro-vide, actual, active, interpersonal (self-object) functions.

They suggest that the therapist begin the treatment by not disturbing the development of the supporting idealizing transference so as to gradually allow the issue of aloneness to unfold. As patients come to see the therapist as rela-tively reliable and sustaining, they may simultaneously begin to shed some of their characteristic distancing techniques. Then, the patient will come to con-sciously experience, or to reexperience, a vulnerable sense of dependence, es-pecially when the panic of separation becomes manifest. This is most likely to occur when there is an interruption in the therapy, for example, a vacation or a weekend. At those times, the patient's early-felt needs for self-object support will reemerge, sometimes abruptly in the form of rage toward the entire envi-ronment (and particularly the therapist) for not providing the desired amount of continuous soothing or holding. This may be accompanied by a loss of evoca-tive memory and a completely negative image of the therapist. A central thera-peutic task, therefore, becomes creation of an environment in which the patient can take in and hold onto real memories of sustaining the soothing at times of aloneness. From this develops an internal structure, which patients will even-tually use to soothe themselves.

To achieve this goal, Adler and Buie recommend that therapists use clarifi-cation, interpretation, and setting of limits to protect patients from destructive enactment of their abandonment fears and rage. Therapists also may have to extend themselves directly to forestall more pathological regression (e.g., by offering intermittent telephone calls between sessions, by negotiating extra ap-pointments, or by using brief periods of hospitalization). Adler and Buie argue that these holding actions sustain the patient and allow for the recognition that the therapist can tolerate the patient's rage, hurt, and loneliness and yet con-tinue to be helpful (Winnicott, 1965). Especially useful is their reliance on tran-sitional objects, such as postcards, stationery, or something that is specially valued in the context of the therapeutic work, to help sustain patients during times of need and separation.

If patient and therapist are able to see their way through this initial pres-sure, then the second phase of treatment ensues—that of optimal disillusion-ment. Borrowing from the work of Kohut (1977), Adler and Buie argue that patients can be helped to notice the reality of the transference and their need to idealize the therapist, and then to gradually relinquish that idealized view. Each moment of seeing the therapist as a real person with strengths and weak-nesses, helps the patient to integrate the soothing qualities once imagined to exist *only* in an idealized other person.

In the third and final phase of the treatment, the therapist admires and sup-ports the emerging autonomous capacities of the patient. Separation is valued as an important part of life, and, if all goes well, patients eventually come to treat themselves and the significant others in life with the same respect, admi-ration, understanding, and feeling once expected from the psychotherapist.

A major advantage of Adler and Buie's approach is the emphasis on empathic understanding of the existential pain of aloneness, which so many borderline patients manifest. Also important is their flexible support for an active interactional, approach to treatment, and their recognition of the legitimacy of the need for phase-appropriate dependency, upon others. By allowing for a much more mutually oriented therapeutic process, such an approach certainly helps avoid iatrogenic struggles over limits.

Critics say that therapists using this approach may confuse the real needs for support with inappropriate gratification of more libidinally or aggressively derived demands, so that instead of providing necessary holding, an addictive, collusive, and countertherapeutic enactment between therapist and patient may be created. I believe that this is unlikely when the therapist is experienced, empathic, and willing to seek appropriate supervision, or consultation. Another critique of this approach is that it allows the patient and the therapist to avoid facing and bearing the patient's aggression and rage. Adler and Buie, like Kernberg, see rage as being central, but unlike Kernberg, they see it as best understood as a response to loss of the supportive object. Their goal, then, is not to confront but to help patients understand and sympathize with their own anger, as part of an ongoing process of internalizing the soothing qualities of the empathic psychotherapist.

Although both Kernberg and Adler and Buie have set the standard for the psychodynamic treatment of BPD, the contributions of others should not be discounted. These include the contributions of Winnicott (1953, 1965, 1975) and Modell (1963, 1976, 1984), as well as Kohut and colleagues (Kohut, 1971, 1977; Kohut & Wolf, 1978; Tolpin, 1971). Their views, when understood within a developmental context, may be integrated into a new, theoretically sound, and practically useful series of treatment strategies for the borderline patient. As I show in this chapter, such an integrated empathic approach, which I have developed and practiced, can help to bridge the gap between the so-called confrontational camp of Kernberg and the holding camp of Adler and Buie.

AN INTEGRATED DEVELOPMENTAL-PSYCHODYNAMIC PSYCHOTHERAPEUTIC APPROACH

In my view, the frequency of psychotherapy must be intensive enough, and its duration extensive enough, to allow the distrusting borderline patient to develop a sense of trust. Only then will BPD patients openly share their distress, tolerate an investigation of the origins of their pain, and be willing to explore in the here-and-now more creative and less distracting solutions to past dilemmas to hurt and pain. I believe this requires fact-to-face psychotherapy sessions to occur from two to four times a week, at least through the early period of therapy.

Phases of Treatment

If all goes well, the treatment will likely unfold in three stages: (1) holding, (2) understanding, and (3) moving on.

(Flexible) Holding

The first phase centers around the provision of good enough holding (see Modell, 1984; Winnicott, 1965). The patient must be able to see that the therapist is a *reliable, reasonably present* object, who can be depended on to accept patients' manifest and latent feelings, to remember them, and to reflect them in the absence of the patient's own capacity to do so. This requires that the therapist be able to tolerate and bear a substantial level of the patient's painful affects, including both sadness and rage. The therapist also must recognize that most borderline patients have not experienced a significant positive holding in the past, and that this is a new interpersonal matrix—one that is both deeply wished for and suspiciously viewed. How can one expect that patients who have been hurt again and again by others, or who have been defeated by their own repetitive pushing away of others at times of need, will believe that this particular relationship will be different? The answer, of course, is that no reasonable person could have such trust. Empathically accepting the patient's inability to trust provides one of the greatest tools for later modification of the patient's own suspiciousness—tolerance of ambivalence.

The earliest phase of the therapy is usually marked by confused behavioral expressions of such ambivalence. There is a general disparaging of the psychotherapy and the therapist. Although there may be periods of idealization, the more severely disturbed the patient, the less likely it is that such a honeymoon phase will last. Usually, it gives way to a terrifying sense, on the patient's part, of the therapist's inadequacies—well before any form of optimal disillusionment can occur—and to rage at the therapist. The therapist must be able to survive these rageful attacks while understanding them as emanating from a deep sense of fear. The therapist also must be able to feel and to communicate the patient's sense of loss and loneliness even during moments of extreme rage and disconnection.

During this period, one cannot overestimate the patient's sensitivity to therapist rebuffs, misunderstanding, and hurt. The therapist must remain acutely aware of this, must be flexible to detect any derailment of trust or empathy, must analyze it openly and nondefensively, and must maintain an active empathic stance vis-à-vis the patient during times of defensive emotional withdrawal.

I have used the term flexible holding because, at times, the holding requires a certain letting go. Patients may need to enact a certain amount of disconnection from the treatment, and the therapist must tolerate this. To what extent and in what ways depends on both the particular needs of the patient and the capacities of the therapist. In all cases, however, titration of the holding and letting go must be a mutually discussed, interactive process between patient and therapist. By negotiating, the therapist forestalls more severe and bizarre forms of idealization/devaluation and communicates that relationships can be discussed, understood in depth, and changed over time. Through flexible holding, the therapist also provides an opportunity for the patient to soothe the self through the psychotherapy, and to internalize a sense of the caring therapist.

It is in this phase that the challenge first emerges of integrating both confrontation of the patient's aggression and soothing of the patient's self. Again, the therapist must be flexible and empathically attuned to the patient. Some patients may need to be given considerable latitude to experience and express their rage with quiet support from the therapist. Others may require an immediate active response and clarification, including, at times, the setting of limits. I believe it matters less whether one confronts the aggression than whether the aggression is understood like any other aspect of the patient, as something to be valued, explored, and mastered.

Often, borderline patients are much more frightened of their own rage than they let on. Indeed, they may be using the rage defensively to hide other feelings, especially sadness and aloneness. One must be open to exploring the rage in all its facets with the patient, recognizing that BPD patients are (1) almost always able to sense whether the therapist is comfortable with their aggression, and (2) exquisitely sensitive to the therapist's capacity to know when the anger might be getting out of control. In general, when one is able to achieve a balance between tolerating the patient's aggressive feelings and setting limits on aggressively motivated destructive actions, patients will feel increasingly secure and be able to share a whole range of difficult and painful feelings. This should ultimately lead to the patient's increased tolerance of those feelings— the internalization of the holding phase.

Some borderline patients go through this phase without much limit setting or reflection on their aggression. Others have a stormy early phase, requiring an approach that, to some extent, mirrors Kernberg's. What remains essential, however, is the use of limits within the context of the therapist's own sense of human limitations, which is shared genuinely with the patient, while eschewing educational moralism.

(Interpretive) Understanding

Given sufficient flexible holding and soothing of the self, patient and therapist can then turn to an exploration of the patient's particular developmental history and hurt. I emphasize the term hurt because I believe that borderline patients have usually experienced some trauma in their childhood, whether it be actual abuse, emotional coldness, tragic loss, or an overwhelming sense of affect again and again that is not tolerated or tolerable.

There is now growing evidence that the majority of patients with moderate to severe BPD have been the victims of actual childhood trauma and/or abuse. Such data must alert the clinician to the very real childhood hurts or traumas experienced by BPD patients and their effect on later adult functioning. It would not be extreme to suggest that at least some significant subgroup of BPD patients is suffering from a variant of posttraumatic stress in a characterological crystallization. The clinician must remain empathically aware of this reality and not retraumatize the patient through benign neglect or misunderstanding.

Therefore, I also emphasize the *particular* developmental history of the patient because there is no prototype of a borderline history. If a therapist begins to feel that the specific transference, or the unfolding of past history in the present, is stereotyped, the therapist is losing the empathic edge in understanding the patient. As the patient feels held and soothed, and as the patient in small doses attempts such self-functions in the absence of the therapist (or while the therapist looks on admiringly), the capacity for genetic reconstruction of the particular history is enhanced. Often, such a phase will be ushered in either by patients reporting their dreams or by patients' experiences in the therapy that remind them of past disappointments—most notable, disappointments about separation.

Without minimizing the importance of understanding here-and-now difficulties, I believe it is the linking of the patient's present sense of suspicion and hurt to the patient's past history that gives meaning to an otherwise obscurely disconnected sense of feelings and behaviors. It is, indeed, the remembering and understanding of the past, and the bringing of it into the present transference, that enables the patient both to make sense of an inner feeling of chaos and to integrate an intermittently dissociated sense of self into a real and cohesive whole.

At least initially, the patient must be helped to see that even the most defensive, maladaptive, and confusing maneuvers (including dissociative states, and rageful enactments) were meant, at one time, to protect and sustain the self. As patients can come to empathize with their own self-needs, they are less likely to need to stand at so far a distance from the self. Here, Kohut's suggestion of eschewing a maturity morality comes into play. Borderline patients are not necessarily primitive or immature; they are opening up and growing. The concept of the patient's thwarted need to grow makes a great deal of sense. It also requires an understanding that the therapist too, will be growing in the treatment. One might say that the therapeutic task is (1) to develop a mutually shared developmental story of the patient's experience, and (2) to connect and integrate this story into the experiences of the present in a way that sustains inner emotional growth and leads to outer behavioral change.

(Relative) Moving On

In my view, the final phase of the treatment consists of consolidating the gains of the self around cohesion and soothing and the esteem-regulating mechanisms that facilitate self-value, that is, to permit and foster the growth of an array of thriving, autonomous functions. It must be remembered, however, that all such growth, autonomy, and moving on is relative and occurs within a larger framework of interdependent relationships.

At one time, the hallmark of mental health was considered to be totally individuated functioning. The need for dependence on another object was considered not essential, or at best secondary. It is now recognized that individuals can gain greater flexibility for internalization and autonomous self-functioning without abandoning the need for mature dependency on others (Kohut, 1980). From this perspective, the pathway to mental health is achieved through what I have termed a balance between autonomy and affiliation. This includes the sobering recognition that we live in an interdependent world where relationships are required to sustain us emotionally, just (as Kohut has pointed out) as oxygen is required to sustain us biologically. Such an approach to human development has practical meaning for the borderline patient (see Pollack & Grossman, 1985).

Moving on in psychotherapy, then, must include the willing recognition, by both therapists and patients, that patients are able to understand themselves, soothe themselves, and help themselves, but also that some form of ongoing interdependence on significant others, including the psychotherapist, may be necessary for the patients to maintain psychological equilibrium and growth. Even more significantly, moving on requires that the patient and therapist view such continuing interpersonal needs not as evidence of residual pathology, but rather as evidence of health and cure!

Some patients will achieve almost complete internalization of the functions of the psychotherapy and not require an ongoing relationship with the therapist at all. Other patients may require some ongoing contact with the therapist, even if only intermittently. One must be careful and clear that such ongoing contact in no way represents therapeutic failure. This becomes more possible if one moves away from a purely autonomy-oriented focus toward a balanced approach in which the ongoing affiliative needs of the patient, especially as expressed toward the therapist, are tolerated and understood.

AUTONOMY AND AFFILIATION: ACHIEVING BALANCE

Most paradigms for the treatment of character disorders stress either the importance of separation-individuation (Kernberg, 1984; Mahler, 1971) or of human interconnection (Adler 1985; Adler & Buie, 1979; Kohut, 1977). However, growing evidence suggests that it is the balance of autonomy and affiliation that is critical. I have argued elsewhere (Pollack, 1982, 1983a, 1983b; Pollack & Grossman, 1985) that healthy development requires the capacities to experience and sustain both an independent sense of oneself (autonomy) and an interconnected relation with others (affiliation). Not only young children but also couples in the transition to parenthood and fathers engaged in ongoing parenting have been shown to benefit from the provision of a healthy balance of support for both autonomous and affiliative tendencies (Grossman, Pollack, & Golding, 1988; Grossman, Pollack, Golding, & Fedele, 1987).

I believe that the historical emphasis solely on autonomy as a measure of mental health may well reflect a masculine bias in psychology-psychiatry, and one with important clinical implication. We may, for example, become so preoccupied with the negative aspects of so-called dependency that we discount the normal, healthy needs to remain dependent on significant others or on our social network throughout the life cycle. Women's normal, healthy need for ongoing relational activity has long been recognized (see Stiver, 1985). Recent research on families in development indicates that such affiliative urges and actions are equally salient for men (Pollack, 1989, 1995). In the treatment of BPD, such dependency needs are paramount.

It is a central premise of the integrated treatment regime described herein that borderline patients are not suffering from overdependency as much as from the inability to recognize the legitimacy of their need to depend on others and to build an interdependent network of support. The therapeutic goal, then, is to help the patient to tolerate aloneness on the one hand, and to tolerate togetherness on the other.

COUNTERTRANSFERENCE: THE THERAPIST'S OWN AGGRESSION AND LOVE

A major component of intensive psychotherapy with BPD patients is the mobilization of the therapist's own hateful an loving countertransference. Whether this is an aspect of projective identification (see Kernberg, 1984) or simply a hurt and angry response to accusations either of being an inadequate self-object or of providing a deficient holding environment, the therapist must remain aware of his or her own hate or love (Madow & Pollack, 1986; Maltsberger & Buie, 1974).

Adler and Buie (1972) have highlighted the dangerous misuse of confrontation with borderline patients generated by countertransference. Most often, this involves clarifications or interpretations ostensibly aimed at making psychological change. In reality, these interventions may reflect the therapist's unconscious aggression and may be intended to convince patients that they have been bad and should desist from such behavior. The result may be an increase in patients' self-hate and an engendering of self-destructive behavior. One cannot underestimate the borderline patient's capacity to unconsciously experience the therapist's anger and act it out. In order to forestall such events, therapists must accept and bear their own experiences of hate toward the patient without enacting them and must, when needed, seek consultation. Therapists who are angry and unaware may confront a borderline patient who is in the midst of a struggle to survive, with disastrous results. Therapists may likewise confuse the need to rescue or love the patient with therapeutic holding. This, too, may lead to desperate attempts to separate through enactment or boundary violation (see Gabbard & Wilkinson, 1994). Thus, therapist self-awareness and collegial consultation are essential.

SELF-DESTRUCTIVE BEHAVIORS

As noted earlier, borderline patients often are at risk for suicide and parasuicidal acts. Therapists must be able not only to tolerate suicidal wishes and fantasies, but also to intervene when actual suicide threatens. Some patients with BPD may deal with the intolerance of their strong affects through minor forms of self-harm (cutting, minor accidents, head banging, sexual self-harm, etc.). Others may have the need to soothe themselves for long periods of time, with fantasies about death. One should not, however, intervene prematurely, because some self-destructive activity may represent the patient's best and only means of maintaining a psychological equilibrium. However, one must also recognize that rage and hurt may reach a point where self-destruction appears to patients as their only way out and may lead to dangerous life-threatening enactment.

Whatever the circumstances, the therapist must always take the patient's feelings, thoughts, and plans seriously. Gunderson (1984) has created a simple and practical taxonomy of two classes of self-destructive activity in borderline patients. The first occurs in the presence of an ongoing connection to the therapist. Here, patients may be asking the therapist through the action to, "Please change things for me, or help me differently." Such gestures can usually be clarified during the therapeutic hours or defused by rapid crisis intervention aimed at providing a safe environment in which the problem can be discussed.

The other type of self-destructive activity, however, occurs following an experience of abandonment, loss, or severe derailment in the psychotherapy, resulting in growing aloneness panic. Patients may need to harm themselves in small ways either to gain a sense of numbness or to expel the bad feelings. However, the guilt and emptiness may escalate quickly, leading to frantic requests for help and rapid reversion to serious self-destructive behavior. Often, psychotherapists mistake such desperate discussions and behaviors as attempts to manipulate the therapist to gain more time and caring. Failure to respond quickly and directly may well lead to a completed suicide.

Under these conditions, the therapist must be available and active and be willing to provide the patient with added structure, including more sessions, telephone calls, or, if necessary, hospitalization. The dangers of therapeutic passivity are especially great in early phases of treatment, before an alliance is established. At this time, therapists must be careful to inquire after missed appointments and must be willing to telephone the patient should there be any suspicion or concern. When patients discuss their suicidal wishes or plans, therapists should inquire actively about what they mean. This should help to differentiate a cry for help from a sense of despair that requires more active intervention.

RECOGNIZING ONE'S OWN LIMITS: HOSPITALIZATION AND CONSULTATION

When patients appear unable to use additional therapeutic support (e.g., telephone calls, more frequent sessions), short-term hospitalization should be considered. Hospitalization does not necessarily mean a failure of psychotherapy. Therapists' inner experiences of anxiety may serve as clues to the level of distress that patients cannot put into words. Should therapists' anxiety become so extreme that they are always worried about their patients' safety, then therapy and patient alike are both in jeopardy. This and the proposed interventions must be discussed openly with patients. When therapists are seriously concerned about patients' safety, it is better to act first to create a secure environment and then to discuss with patients what has occurred. An attempt to maintain outpatient psychotherapy at all costs is likely to cost too much. There will be little use for setting limits or for a therapeutically neutral working approach if the patient is no longer alive!

If patients are aware that their therapists do not believe in hospitalization or will not use it, they may have an unconscious need to push limits to the brink in a dangerous way. Indications for short-term inpatient hospitalization are (1) the failure of active structural additions to outpatient psychotherapy to stem the tide of self-destructive enactment; (2) the therapist's level of anxiety concerning the patient's safety reaching a point where reasonable comfort is no longer possible; (3) the abuse of substances, including food, requiring control or detoxification; and/or (4) countertransference experiences becoming so intense that patient and therapist need a breather in a setting where other skilled clinicians can help (see Gunderson, 1984; Madow & Pollack, 1986).

A day-treatment program is sometimes an excellent alternative to inpatient hospitalization. Not only are such programs cost-efficient and flexible, but they also may provide the proper balance between the holding and the separation and autonomy, with less chance of inducing regression (Pollack, 1983a). In either day treatment of full hospitalization, the psychotherapist should feel comfortable with the philosophy of the treating unit, and there should be mutual trust between therapist and milieu staff. There are, of course, times when psychotherapists feel that they have had enough and cannot continue. Candidly expressing this while the patient is in the hospital can be especially useful. Under these conditions, the hospital staff may be helpful in finding an alternative psychotherapeutic arrangement.

The place of long-term, intensive inpatient hospitalization in the treatment of BPD has been reviewed elsewhere (Frosch, 1983; Gunderson, 1984). Generally, it seems advisable to reserve such treatment for those patients who have shown an inability to sustain reasonable functioning in intensive outpatient psychotherapy even with occasional brief hospitalizations.

Whenever hospitalization is being considered, seeking consultation on an outpatient basis should be considered. Often, psychotherapists are wary of opening their treatments to colleagues, especially when this occurs under the somewhat angry or negative demands of dissatisfied patients. Therapists should remember that consultation, like hospitalization, is not an indication of therapeutic failure; if the consultation is discussed openly with the patient, as it should be, it may provide patients with a useful model for problem solving. I recommend that both the therapist and the patient talk to the consultant. As long as such a process is not misused, it has many potential benefits for the therapist and patient alike.

Case Illustration

Ms. B. began her psychotherapy during a severe personal crisis, and in a state of total disarray. Her marriage of many years was disintegrating (though she and her husband were not separated and had no immediate plans for doing so). Caring for her 3-year-old son seemed like an intolerable burden, and a series of relationships with previous psychotherapists and psychopharmacologists had left her feeling despondent, enraged, and suicidal. During the vacation of her treating psychotherapist, she took an overdose of her antidepressant medication, which had proven only moderately effective, and was hospitalized. After defeating the efforts of several senior psychopharmacologists to completely control her depression with medication—antidepressants, antipsychotics, anticonvulsants, and so on—she was referred for intensive psychotherapy. She began treatment with a senior psychoanalytic clinician, which ended quickly in a transference-countertransference impasse. The patient experienced quasipsychotic episodes—visual images of bloody faces—while the therapist felt helpless and intermittently enraged with the patient.

Ms. B.'s new psychotherapy began during her hospitalization, starting out with meeting four times weekly. Eventually, the patient made a transition to an aftercare environment, and finally to her home, resuming her parenting activities.

From the start, Ms. B. presented herself as an attractive, intelligent, and perceptive woman, who was alternatively either intensely demanding, hopeless, emotionally hyperactive, or enraged. She would often cry easily, and then quickly become infuriated at what might appear to an outside observer as a very minor slight, but to the patient, the slights felt like a major provocation.

Therapy began with a very brief phase of idealization—a honeymoon, in which the clinician was seen as extremely intelligent and caring. This quickly gave way to expressions of severe hopelessness, intense demand for help, and intermittent rage. One day, the patient was describing a tragic experience from her childhood, in what appeared to be so disassociated and distorted a manner that the therapist was unable to feel the emotional connection necessary to experience the pain with her. He began to realize a rising sense of disconnection in himself, and consequent boredom and removal. The therapist interrupted the patient's then emotionally flat monologue and inquired as to whether she might have been feeling somewhat overwhelmed by and, therefore, removed from, the sense of distress that she was discussing.

The patient responded by immediately falling silent, grimacing, and remaining in what appeared to be an angry removed stance for several moments:

T: You've become quiet.
P: (silence) . . .
T: Can you try to share what you're thinking or feeling?
P: (silence continues, with an angry look)
T: (after a long silence) I can only guess, but it feels like something I said may have hurt your feelings.
P: You're damn right! You seem to question my honesty, like everybody does, you bastard! . . . You're no different, you're just like the rest. Do you believe me or don't you?
T: When I interrupted and made some clarification, it seemed like I stopped believing you, started doubting you . . . that hurt your feelings and you became very hurt and then very angry with me. It's your experience that counts, it's not a question of whether you're right or wrong; this is what happened to you; this is how you feel, and you worry that I can't reflect that. But if you're hurt, and then you're angry, it's extremely important to talk about it here, to discuss it with me.
P: Like who the hell wants to talk to someone when you're hurt and you're angry with them!!
T: That's right, trust takes time. We can't expect this right away, of course. But I think it has to be our goal, together at least, to talk about the hurt, especially when it happen here in the therapy, and to look at the sadness before it becomes very confusing anger.

The next day, the patient reported a bizarre experience that unfortunately had become somewhat commonplace in her past—a seizure. Having been thoroughly worked up neurologically, it had become clear that these seizures were actually disturbing experiences of anxiety and syncope. The patient felt vulnerable, unable to protect and soothe herself, and she sensed an attack from a potential protector. In addition, however, she expressed her conflicts about wanting to be looked at and seen, as well as needing to hide such a wish—one that she felt was humiliating, shameful, and selfish.

Slowly, over a period of approximately two years, she and her therapist were able to discuss these experiences, first from the sense of self-acceptance rather than of blaming herself, and next attempting to understand them within the context of her personal history. Withing this context, as the therapist encouraged remembering, during the hours, the patient's history of having been severely abused and abandoned repeatedly as a child emerged. Only after reviewing these feelings time and time again, day after day, month in and month out, was the patient able to begin to discuss the nature of the wishes that were reemerging in the context of the transference itself: to be held like a baby by the therapist, to be looked upon, to have her needs reflected, and to be special in a way that also frightened her, as it had sexual connotations.

To a large extent, the issues were taken up from the perspective of the inconsistencies of the past caretaking, and the need for holding and understanding in the present. The patient's conflicts about being seen, reflected, and hidden/protected were also addressed within the context of her difficulties of vocational dysfunction and her parental anxieties in her present capacity to cherish and care for her young son—whom she loved very much. As the therapist actively encouraged the patient to explore these issues in depth, three events emerged almost simultaneously in the treatment, and they continued over time.

First, the patient became intermittently anxious, as she attempted to take up lifelong wishes for educational accomplishment, which she had put aside. She would make small steps in the direction of graduate school and then become extremely anxious. Coupled with this anxiety were suicidal thoughts, wishes, and at times, plans. Often the sense of guilt of making change and the fear of shame from abandonment that occurred each time the patient moved forward had to be met by active therapeutic interpretation and clarification, as well as by additional structure and support. There were frequent late-night telephone calls, which were reviewed in the subsequent psychotherapy hours. Discussion of the use of rehospitalization on an acute basis ensued, but the patient was able to use planned intercession telephone contact as an alternative. She also began to seek out a network of friends (many of whom had experienced similar abuse in their families of origin) as a means for additional structure between the therapeutic sessions.

Second, the patient also began to realize that the nature of her marital attachment was dysfunctional. For the first time, she engaged in a lengthy, thoughtful, and deep review about why she had chosen her present mate and the nature of their ongoing difficulties. She accepted the therapist's direct suggestion to attempt couples therapy to address these difficulties, but it met with little success. Her conceptualization of her husband as a caring but out-of-touch man who was quite enraged with her appeared to be verified by the context of the interpersonal work. The patient, her husband, and the couples therapist all came to the same conclusion—that an amicable parting or divorce was probably the most appropriate course.

Now, in the third year of intensive therapy, as the patient began to achieve real life change, to tolerate greater internal anxiety, and to differentiate the here-and-now difficulties from the traumas of the past, a broader and more mature interest in the nature of the psychotherapy emerged. This, in turn, was reflected in a series of more coherent transference paradigms, which were open to interpretation and genetic reconstruction. The patient was able to see the therapist, alternatively, as both mother and father. This father was brutal and uncaring, but promised some hope for the future. This mother was only intermittently available, but at times promised love. The cycling between maternal and paternal transference, love and hate, abandonment and understanding, now was interpretable within the treatment.

For the majority of this phase in treatment, the patient felt held and understood. Yet, there would be intermittent moments of therapeutic derailment in which the patient would become terribly enraged and, at times, suicidal. However, over time, the patient felt that the therapist was able to work through these issues with her. Occasionally, she would make a late-night phone call to discuss her distress. But increasingly, she was able to hold onto her feelings until the next session. She came to feel that the therapist was human, and this had both negative and positive effects. The patient and therapist were able to discuss her sense of hurt and ensuing rage, and the patient was able to feel generally that the therapist was attempting to understand her and was helping her to understand. As the patient remembered more of the hurt and pain of the past—particularly the pain of abandonment and attack— she sought to organize her present life in new ways.

She also sought additional psychopharmacology consultation to reduce her use of medication. She gravitated toward self-help groups and greater personal interaction with other people who, like herself, were struggling with pain from the past in an attempt to have a more proactive and positive view in the future. Significantly, she and her husband separated, and she began dating other men. She appeared ready to move on.

In the fourth year of therapy, the patient now became aware of her wish to reduce the frequency of her sessions but to continue in an intensive treatment; after discussion, her therapist agreed. Ms. B. now became more alive and interested in the nature of relationships. The treatment no longer focused on the patient alone or on her own history, but also on the nature of her interpersonal activity in the present. The patient craved information, and demanded that the therapist give her advice. At times, these demands were reasonable, but at other times, they seemed to be an attempt to deal with the conflictual wish about closeness to the therapist, which was interpreted rather than enacted. The patient would sometimes become angry, but she usually felt that the therapist was attempting to understand.

Ms. B. came to see herself as having a delayed adolescence. She felt very hurt and angry that she needed to go through the pain of relationships and the possibility of separation at such a late date. However, with the capacity to review these feelings of disappointment and disillusionment in the therapy, the growth continued outside the therapy sessions. The patient continued to build a series of relationships with increasingly appropriate males.

Equally important, the patient began to negotiate close personal friendships with a number of women. At times, the patient became upset and felt she was too selfish. Now the therapist clarified that the need to protect herself, rather than engaging in relationships, came from the early experience that she and the therapist had reviewed over and over again—that a balance between having her own needs and caring about herself, as well as being interested in others was both reasonable and healthy. This was mirrored, in turn, by her wish expressed in the therapy to be more assertive, to be more reasonably critical of the therapist and his own personal habits. The therapist responded to this with excitement, as it reflected an individuated sense within the work.

Again, as the patient felt more individuated and strong in these areas, her suicidality, guilt, shame, and anxiety reemerged. These were again interpreted in the context of the fear that if she became her own person, she would lose the people around her and behind her. The therapist was direct in reassuring the patient that her wishes to be her own person would not destroy the nature of the support, and that as she moved on, her need to come to the therapy would be decided by her rather than by the therapist. This relaxed the patient, and she continued during the fifth treatment year to pursue her independent needs in the context of an interpersonal connection.

This case vignette is left unfinished for two reasons: First, the treatment itself is not perfect and not complete. Therefore, it comes closest to the actual work between the clinicians and borderline patients engaged in intensive psychoanalytic psychotherapy. Second, it highlights the argument that I have made throughout the chapter: that the treatment need not lead to complete separation or achievement of absolute autonomy.

The patient presently is continuing in an intensive treatment, as she becomes increasingly involved in the world of relationships. It is expected that there will be stops and starts along that road, but that over the next year the patient will reduce the frequency of her therapy, to the extent that it will probably no longer be considered ongoing and intensive, but rather intermittent and supportive. As she explores the world of relationships and frees herself from the inhibiting pain of separation, she may use the therapy and the therapist from time to time, when anxieties reemerge. When and how to decide that the treatment is complete or that termination should or has taken place will be a mutual task between patient and therapist.

Above all, this case illustrates how genuine therapeutic change can ensue within the context of mutual understanding, transference interpretation, and a sense of flexible holding. The patient's past was understood from within her own perspective, and the therapist facilitated a balance between connectedness and independence within the treatment, a balance that Ms. B. struggled to internalize and succeeded in making her own.

ALTERNATIVE TREATMENT OPTIONS: PRESCRIPTIVE TREATMENT AND MANAGED CARE

Recently, alternative approaches for the treatment of BPD have been suggested. These include family treatment, vocational rehabilitation, structured group therapy, scientifically prescribed psychopharmacological interventions, and short-term psychotherapeutic approaches reframed from a cognitive and behavioral standpoint. Whether these treatments for BPD should be considered alternative to psychoanalytic psychotherapy or adjunctive interventions depends on one's philosophical approach. It is my contention that an integrated, multimodal approach is most reasonable and most consistent with clinical and research data. For example, there is now evidence that vocational and psychopharmacological interventions enhance the psychotherapeutic course of BPD and that cognitive approaches diminish self-destructive activity (Linehan, 1987a, 1987b; McGlashan, 1986; Stone et al., 1987). However, a definitive, longitudinal, empirical study of differential therapeutics in BPD has yet to be done.

Until all the votes are counted and integrated, multimodal approach, based on the patient's individual needs and capacities, seems warranted.

FAMILIES

In discussing psychotherapeutic approaches to BPD, Gunderson (1984) notes that some families of borderline patients are overinvolved with the patient. They can be contained within the context of family therapy. There also are neglectful families who are unlikely to stick with treatment and may enact their rage in a harmful way in a family therapy. Decisions regarding treatment of family members must, of course, take into account the characteristics and capacities of the patient. This view is echoed by E. Shapiro, and his colleagues (Shapiro, Shapiro, & Zinner, 1977; Shapiro, Zinner, Shapiro, & Berkowitz, 1975), who advocate a family therapeutic approach for borderline adolescents or young adults. They use conjoint weekly family therapy in conjunction with individual psychodynamic psychotherapy for the identified patient and ongoing couples treatment for the parents. The conjoint family treatment is carried out in tandem by the individual therapist and by the couples' therapist. When the borderline patient is older and married or is engaged in a significant relationship, ongoing couples treatment may also be a useful adjunct to individual psychotherapy.

COGNITIVE-BEHAVIORAL TECHNIQUES

Levendusky and colleagues (Berglas & Levendusky, 1985; Levendusky, Berglas, Dooley, & Landau, 1983; Levendusky & Dooley, 1985) have developed promising treatment regimen for borderline patients, which centers around a modification of cognitive-behavioral techniques and may be used in conjunction with psychodynamic psychotherapy. They use the concepts of the therapeutic contract, group feedback, and structured cognitive-behavioral planning in helping borderline patients to take increased responsibility for their lives and to begin to cope with the anxiety that ensues when such patients attempt greater social interaction or higher level of vocational functioning. Of particular interest is their adjunctive use of (1) assertiveness training to help patients who feel downtrodden but who behave overly aggressively to meet their needs; (2) mood monitoring to help patients understand their affective lability while connecting their mood states to external events; and (3) a form of group social-skill training to support the patients' acquisition of new behaviors.

Linehan and her research-clinical team (Linehan, 1981, 1987a, 1987b, 1993a, 1993b) also have created a comprehensive cognitive-behavioral treatment for BPD, specifically for patient who engage in parasuicide. Their approach of dialectical behavior therapy (DBT) has begun to show excellent results, and a full description of this approach is included elsewhere in this volume.

GROUP PSYCHOTHERAPY

Horwitz (1977, 1980) has summarized many of the advantages of group psychotherapy with borderline patients, including the following: (1) The intensity of transference and countertransference reactions can be positively diluted through use of multiple therapeutic objects in the group; (2) Peer members in the group can aid in reality testing, can support appropriate social interaction, and can help titrate the need for social and emotional distance; (3) Peer pressure may help patients who have difficulties with their anger to find more reasonable outlets than they might find in individual psychotherapy alone; and (4) the group can provide opportunities for multiple identifications and can enable members to focus on issues such as jealousy, competition, and narcissistic defenses in a way that can be quite powerful and therapeutic.

Clinical experience also indicates that borderline patients are more likely to accept confrontations and interpretations from other patients earlier in treatment than they would from an individual therapist. Negativism toward authority and feelings of being controlled are less likely to emerge among peers in the group.

Macaskill (1982) notes that the group therapist or the group itself achieves results by functioning along the lines of Winnicott's holding environment and becoming the good-enough mother. Macaskill also stresses the capacity to provide soothing interpretations while instilling hope as important ingredients in effective group psychotherapy for BPD. Whether groups should be diagnostically heterogeneous, as suggested by Wong (1980), or homogeneous, as argued by Stone and Weissman (1984), remains an open question.

VOCATIONAL REHABILITATION: IMPROVING WORK SKILLS

Rehabilitation aimed at enhancing work skills represents one of the greatest untapped resources in the treatment of BPD. Borderline patients are often severely deficient in vocational functioning. We have had good results in combining individual psychodynamic psychotherapy with a psychologically oriented approach to vocational rehabilitation outlined by Anthony (1977). Success in the workplace often enhances self-esteem and self-cohesion, and, in turn, positively affects progress in therapy. Nonetheless, analytically oriented clinicians have been reluctant to make full use of such approaches—although there is some evidence that such attitudes are changing (Pollack & Dion, 1985, 1987).

PSYCHOPHARMACOLOGY

Many researchers and clinicians advocate various psychopharmacological interventions for BPD. Medications suggested include (1) low-dose antipsychotics, (2) heterocyclic and serotonergic antidepressants, (3) monoamine oxidase inhibitors, (4) lithium, (5) pemoline or methylphenidate, (6) carbamazepine or valproic acid, and (7) benzodiazepines. The choice drug, of course, relates to the theoretical connection postulated between BPD and other more biologically linked illnesses, including: affective spectrum disorders, transient cognitive dysfunction, anxiety disorders, impulse disorders, posttraumatic stress disorder, ADHD, TLE, and so forth. Cole and Sunderland (1982), Cowdry and Gardner

(1988), Gunderson and Links (1996), Gunderson and Phillips (1994), Salzman et al. (1992), and Soloff et al. (1986, 1993) have described the current psychopharmacological treatment regimens for borderline patients.

Whatever the approach chosen, one should consider the possibility that patients with BPD may also suffer from other biologically based illnesses, and vice versa. For example, clinicians who are used to treating depression psychopharmacologically may overlook a comorbid personality disorder that could interfere with progress. On the other hand, therapists who tended to eschew medication may miss an opportunity to aid borderline patients by relieving biologically based depressive symptomatology. Once again, the issue of balance remains supreme.

It is also important to consider the psychodynamics of prescribing. The nature of the transitional object transference both to medication and to the prescribing treater (see Adelman, 1985; Waldinger & Frank, 1989) must be understood and addressed. Use of medication in psychotherapy is bound to have repercussions both within and outside of the treatment environment. Clinicians must consider the meaning of giving pills to patients with a yearning for closeness, and a need for early parenting; they should, therefore, proceed with caution and flexibility.

The need for a strong alliance between patient and therapist, or between patient and prescribing physician, is extremely important in BPD. Without it, patients may either not use their medication or use it in an inappropriate or self-destructive manner. If the prescribing physician and the psychotherapist are two different people, it is important to maintain frequent contact to void any splitting of these two helpers. It may be necessary to prescribe medication that is least likely to be lethal and, at times, to limit the number of pills per prescription, especially for patients who have suicidal impulses and are involved in an intensive psychotherapy.

Managed Care and Short-Term Treatment

The cognitive-behavioral approaches described earlier (especially Linehan's DBT), although not short-term in the strictest sense, do appear to shorten the length of time in treatment as well as to provide increased cost savings with reduced utilization of inpatient and emergency care. Silver (1983, 1985) has described the use of short-term intermittent therapy on a long-term basis with some success, and there is reason to believe that the utilization of the multimodal model suggested here (e.g., appropriate medication, attention to substance abuse, focused behavioral, plus more active, efficient psychodynamic psychotherapy), may, in the long run, provide excellent prescriptive care with important costs savings compared to either inpatient hospitalization, ongoing emergency intervention, or the treatment for life-threatening, suicidally induced medical crises. We must remain cognizant, however, that BPD is a serious, morbid disease untreated, and that all research to date suggests that those patients maintained in a sustained treatment alliance are likely to improve most (Hoke, 1989).

SUMMARY

The psychotherapy of BPD poses many challenges, but it offers significant rewards for clinician and patient. Modern empirical research has supported the hypothesis that dynamic treatment has positive results, but it also has raised important questions about etiology, adjunctive therapeutics, efficacy, and biological interface.

The conceptualization of BPD and the integrated treatment paradigm described and illustrated herein may offer more than a developmentally informed, biologically-aware, empathic psychotherapy matrix with clinical utility. At its deepest and broadest moments, it suggests the possibilities for personal repair to the self, a repair that, in borderline patients, strikes at the heart of questions of life and death, pain and joy. In this sense, the psychotherapy of BPD remains only too humanly cathected and too humanly imperfect.

REFERENCES

Adelman, S. (1985). Pills as transitional objects: A dynamic understanding of the use of medication in psychotherapy. *Psychiatry, 48,* 246–263.

Adler, G. (1985). *Borderline psychopathology and its treatment.* New York: Aronson.

Adler, G., & Buie, D. (1972). The misuses of confrontation with borderline patients. *International Journal of Psychoanalytic Psychotherapy, 1,* 109–120.

Adler, G., & Buie, D. (1979). Aloneness and borderline psychopathology: The possible relevance of child development issues. *International Journal of Psychoanalysis, 60,* 83–96.

Akiskal, H. (1983). Sub-affective disorders, dysthymic, cyclothymic and bipolar II disorders in the borderline realm. *Psychiatric Clinics of North America, 4,* 25–46.

Akiskal, H. (1983). The relationship of personality to affective disorders. *Archives of General Psychiatry, 40,* 804–810.

American Psychiatric Association. (1980). *Diagnostic and statistical manual of mental disorders* (3rd ed.). Washington, DC: Author.

American Psychiatric Association. (1987). *Diagnostic and statistical manual of mental disorders* (3rd ed., rev.). Washington, DC: Author.

American Psychiatric Association. (1994). *Diagnostic and statistical manual of mental disorders* (4th ed.). Washington, DC: Author.

Andrulonis, P., Glueck, B., Stroebel, C., Vogel, N., Shapiro, A., & Aldridge, D. (1981). Organic brain dysfunction and the borderline syndrome. *Psychiatric Clinics of North America, 4,* 47–66.

Anthony, W.A. (1977). Psychological rehabilitation: A concept in need of a method. *American Psychologist, 32,* 658–662.

Bardenstein, K.K., & McGlashan, T.H. (1988). The natural history of a residentially treated borderline sample: Gender differences. *Journal of Psychiatric Research, 4,* 213–228.

Barrash, I., Kroll, J., Carey, K., & Sines, L. (1983). Discriminating borderline disorder from other personality disorders: Cluster analysis of the diagnostic interview for borderlines. *Archives of General Psychiatry, 40,* 1297–1302.

Bauer, S., Hunt, H., Gould, M., & Goldstein, E. (1980). Personality organization, structural diagnosis and the structural interview. *Psychiatry, 22,* 36–45.

Bion, W.R. (1967). *Second thoughts: Selected papers on psychoanalysis.* New York: Basis Books.

Brandschaft, B., & Stolorow, R. (1984). The borderline concept: Pathological character or iatrogenic myth? In J. Lichtenberg, M. Bornstein, & D. Silver (Eds.), *Empathy* (Vol. 2, pp. 333–357). Hillside, NJ: Analytic Press.

Bryer, J.B., Nelson, B.A., Miller, J.B., & Krol, P.A. (1987). Childhood sexual and physical abuse as factors in adult psychiatric illness. *American Journal of Psychiatry, 144,* 1426–1430.

Buie, D. (1997). *Self maintenance functions.* Hazenbush Lecture, Harvard University.

Buie, D., & Adler, G. (1982). The definitive treatment of the borderline personality. *International Journal of Psychoanalytic Psychotherapy, 9,* 51–87.

Carpenter, W., Gunderson, J., & Strauss, J. (1997). Considerations of the borderline syndrome: A longitudinal comparative study of borderline and schizophrenic patients. In P. Hartocollis (Ed.), *Borderline personality disorders: The concept, the syndrome, the patient* (pp. 231–253). New York: International Universities Press.

Cole, J., & Sunderland, P. (1982). The drug treatment of borderline patients. In L. Grinspoon (Ed.), *Psychiatry* (Vol. 1, pp. 456–470). Washington, DC: American Psychiatric Press.

Cornell, D., Silk, K., Ludolph, P., & Lohr, N. (1983). Test-resist reliability of the diagnostic interview for borderlines. *Archives of General Psychiatry, 40,* 1307–1310.

Cowdry, R., & Gardner, D. (1988). Pharmacotherapy of borderline personality disorder: Alprazolam, carbamazepine, trifluoperazine and tranylcypromine. *Archives of General Psychiatry, 45,* 111–119.

Deutsch, H. (1942). Some forms of emotional disturbances and their relationship to schizophrenia. *Psychoanalytic Quarterly, 11,* 301–321.

Frances, A., Clarkin, J., Gilmore, M., Hurt, S.W., & Brown, R. (1984). Reliability of criteria for borderline personality disorder: A comparison of *DSM-III* and DIB. *American Journal of Psychiatry, 141,* 1080–1083.

Friedman, H. (1969). Some problems of inpatient management with borderline patients. *American Journal of Psychiatry, 126,* 299–304.

Friedman, H. (1975). Psychotherapy of borderline patients: The influence of theory on technique. *American Journal of Psychiatry, 132,* 1048–1052.

Frosch, J. (1970). Psychoanalytic considerations of the psychotic character. *Journal of the American Psychoanalytic Association, 18,* 24–50.

Frosch, J.P. (1983). *Current perspectives in personality disorders.* Washington, DC: American Psychiatric Press.

Gabbard, G.O., Horwitz, L., Allen, J.G., et al. (1994). Transference interpretation in the psychotherapy of borderline patients: A high-risk, high-gain phenomenon. *Harvard Review of Psychiatry, 2,* 59–69.

Gabbard, G.O., & Wilkinson, S.W. (1994). *Management of countertransference with borderline patients.* Washington, DC: American Psychiatric Press.

Gilligan, C. (1982). *In a different voice.* Cambridge, MA: Harvard University Press.

Giovacchini, P. (1979). *Treatment of primitive mental states.* New York: Aronson.

Glover, E. (1932). A psycho-analytic approach to classification of mental disorders. *Journal of Mental Science, 78,* 819–842.

Greenberg, S. (1977). *The supportive approach to therapy.* Unpublished manuscript, McLean Hospital, Belmont, MA.

Grinker, R., Werble, B., & Drye, R. (1968). *The borderline syndrome: A behavioral study of ego functions.* New York: Basic Books.

Grossman, F.K. (1985). *Autonomy and affiliation: Parents and children* (Conference paper series). Washington, DC: National Institute of Child Health and Development.

Grossman, F.K., Pollack, W.S., & Golding, E. (1988). Fathers and children: Predicting the quality and quantity of fathering. *Developmental Psychology, 24*(1), 82–91.

Grossman, F.K., Pollack, W.S., Golding, E.R., & Fedele, N.M. (1987). Affiliation and autonomy in the transition to parenthood. *Family Relations, 36,* 263–269.

Grunebaum, H., & Klerman, G. (1967). Wrist slashing. *American Journal of Psychiatry, 124,* 524–534.

Gunderson, J. (1977). Characteristics of borderlines. In P. Hartocollis (Ed.), *Borderline personality disorders: The concept, the syndrome, the patient* (pp. 173–192). New York: International Universities Press.

Gunderson, J. (1982). Empirical studies of the borderline diagnosis. In L. Grinspoon (Ed.), *Psychiatry* (Vol. 1, pp. 414–437). Washington, DC: American Psychiatric Press.

Gunderson, J. (1983a). Discussion of R. Chessick: Problems in the intensive psychotherapy of the borderline patient. *Dynamic Psychotherapy, 1,* 33–34.

Gunderson, J. (1983b, December). *Interfaces between psychoanalytic and empirical studies of borderline personality disorder.* Unpublished paper presented at the annual meeting of the American Psychoanalytic Association, New York.

Gunderson, J. (1984). *Borderline personality disorder.* Washington, DC: American Psychiatric Press.

Gunderson, J., Carpenter, W., & Strauss, J. (1975). Borderline and schizophrenic patients: A comparative study. *American Journal of Psychiatry, 132,* 1257–1264.

Gunderson, J., & Chu, J.A. (1993). Treatment implications of past trauma in borderline personality disorder. *Harvard Review of Psychiatry, 1,* 75–81.

Gunderson, J., & Elliott, G. (1985). The interface between borderline personality disorder and affective disorder. *American Journal of Psychiatry, 142,* 277–288.

Gunderson, J., & Englund, D. (1981). Characterizing the families of borderlines. *Psychiatric Clinics of North America, 4,* 159–168.

Gunderson, J., & Kolb, J. (1978). Discriminating features of borderline patients. *American Journal of Psychiatry, 135,* 792–796.

Gunderson, J., Kolb, J., & Austin, V. (1981). The diagnostic interview for borderline patients. *American Journal of Psychiatry, 138,* 896–903.

Gunderson, J., & Links, R. (1996). Borderline personality disorder. In G.O. Gabbard & S.D. Atkinson (Eds.), *Synopsis of treatments of psychiatric disorders* (pp. 969–977). Washington, DC: American Psychiatric Press.

Gunderson, J., Phillips, K.A. (1991). A current view of the interface between borderline personality disorder and depression (see comments). *American Journal of Psychiatry, 148*(8), 967–975.

Gunderson, J., & Pollack, W. (1985). Conceptual risks of the Axis I–II division, In H. Klar & L.J. Siever (Eds.), *Biological response styles: Clinical implications.* Washington, DC: American Psychiatric Press.

Gunderson, J., & Singer, M. (1975). Defining borderline patients: An overview. *American Journal of Psychiatry, 134,* 9–14.

Herman, J.L. (1992). *Trauma and recovery.* New York: Basic Books.

Herman, J.L., Perry, J.C., & van der Kold, B.A. (1989). Childhood trauma in borderline personality disorder. *American Journal of Psychiatry, 146,* 490–495.

Hoch, P., & Polatin, P. (1949). Pseudoneurotic forms of schizophrenia. *Psychiatric Quarterly, 23,* 248–276.

Hoke, L. (1989). *Longitudinal patterns of behaviors in borderline personality disorder*. Unpublished dissertation, Boston University Graduate School, Boston.

Horwitz, L. (1977). Group psychotherapy of the borderline patient. In P. Hartocollis (Ed.), *Borderline personality disorders: The concept, the syndrome, the patient* (pp. 399–422). New York: International Universities Press.

Horwitz, L. (1980). Group psychotherapy for borderline and narcissistic patients. *Bulletin of the Menninger Clinic, 44*, 181–200.

Hurt, S.W., Hyler, S.E., Frances, A., Clarkin, J.F., & Brent, R. (1984). Assessing borderline personality disorder with self-report, clinical interview, or semistructured interview. *American Journal of Psychiatry, 141*, 1228–1231.

Hyler, S.E., Rieder, R., Spitzer, R.L., & Williams, J.B.W. (1978). *Personality diagnostic questionnaire (PDQ)*. New York: State Psychiatric Institute.

Institute of Medicine. (1985, July). A report of the board on mental health and behavioral medicine: Research on mental illness and addictive disorders: Progress and prospects. *American Journal of Psychiatry, 142*(Suppl.).

Kass, F., Skodol, A.E., Charles, E., Spitzer, R.L., & Williams, J.B.W. (1985). Scaled ratings of *DSM-III* personality disorders. *American Journal of Psychiatry, 142*, 627–630.

Kass, F., Spitzer, R.L., & Williams, J.B.W. (1983). An empirical study of the issue of sex bias in the diagnostic criteria of *DSM-III* Axis II personality disorder. *American Psychologist, 38*, 799–801.

Kernberg, O. (1965). Countertransference. *Journal of the American Psychoanalytic Association, 13*, 38–56.

Kernberg, O. (1967). Borderline personality organization. *Journal of the American Psychoanalytic Association, 15*, 641–685.

Kernberg, O. (1971). Prognostic considerations regarding borderline personality organization. *Journal of the American Psychoanalytic Association, 19*, 595–615.

Kernberg, O. (1975). *Borderline conditions and pathological narcissism*. New York: Aronson.

Kernberg, O. (1976). *Object-relations theory and clinical psychoanalysis*. New York: Aronson.

Kernberg, O. (1977). The structural diagnosis of borderline personality organization. In P. Hartocollis (Ed.), *Borderline personality disorders: The concept, the syndrome, the patient* (pp. 87–121). New York: International Universities Press.

Kernberg, O. (1981). Structural interviewing. *Psychiatric Clinics of North America, 4*, 169–195.

Kernberg, O. (1982). Supportive psychotherapy with borderline conditions. In J. Cavenar & H. Brodie (Eds.), *Clinical problems in psychiatry* (pp. 180–202). Philadelphia: Lippincott.

Kernberg, O. (1984). *Severe personality disorders psychotherapeutic strategies*. New Haven, CT: Yale University Press.

Kernberg, O., Burnstein, E., Coyne, L., Appelbaum, A., Horwitz, L., & Voth, H. (1972). Final report of the Menninger Foundation's psychotherapy research project: Psychotherapy and psychoanalysis. *Bulletin of the Menninger Clinic, 34*, 1–2.

Kibel, H. (1980). The importance of a comprehensive clinical diagnosis for group psychotherapy of borderline and narcissistic patients. *International Journal of Group Psychotherapy, 30*, 427–440.

Klein, D. (1977). Psychopharmacological treatment and delineation of borderline disorders. In P. Hartocollis (Ed.), *Borderline personality disorders: The concept, the syndrome, the patient* (pp. 365–384). New York: International Universities Press.

Klein, M. (1946). Notes on some schizoid mechanisms. *International Journal of Psychoanalysis, 27*, 99–110.

Knight, R. (1953). Borderline states. *Bulletin of the Menninger Clinic, 17,* 1–12.

Koenigsberg, H., Kaplan, R.D., Gilmore, M.M., & Cooper, A.M. (1985). The relationship between syndrome and personality disorder in *DSM-III:* Experience with 2,462 patients. *American Journal of Psychiatry, 142,* 207–212.

Koenigsberg, H., Kernberg, O, & Schomer, J. (1983). Diagnosing borderline conditions in an outpatient setting. *Archives of General Psychiatry, 40,* 49–53.

Kohut, H. (1971). *The analysis of the self.* New York: International Universities Press.

Kohut, H. (1977). *The restoration of the self.* New York: International Universities Press.

Kohut, H. (1980). From a letter. In A. Goldberg (Ed.), *Advances in self-psychology.* New York: International Universities Press.

Kohut, H., & Wolf, E. (1978). The disorders of the self and their treatment: An outline. *International Journal of Psychoanalysis, 59,* 413–425.

Kolb, J., & Gunderson, J. (1980). Diagnosing borderline patients within semi-structured interviews. *Archives of General Psychiatry, 37,* 37–41.

Kroll, J., Carey, K., Sines, L., & Roth, M. (1982). Are there borderlines in Britain: A cross-validation of U.S. findings. *Archives of General Psychiatry, 39,* 60–63.

Kroll, J., Sines, L., Martin, K., Lari, S., Pyle, R., & Zander, J. (1981). Borderline personality disorder: Construct validity of the concept. *Archives of General Psychiatry, 38,* 1021–1026.

Levendusky, P.G., Berglas, S., Dooley, C.P., & Landau, R.J. (1983). Therapeutic contract program: A preliminary report on a behavioral alternative to the token economy. *Behavioral Research and Therapy, 21,* 137–142.

Levendusky, P.G., & Dooley, C.P. (1985). An inpatient model for the treatment of anorexia nervosa. In S. Emmett (Ed.), *Theory and treatment of anorexia nervosa and bulimia—Biomedical, sociocultural, and psychological perspectives* (pp. 211–213). New York: Brunner/Mazel.

Levine, H.B. (1979). The sustaining object relationship. *Annual of Psychoanalysis, 7,* 203–232.

Liebowitz, M. (1983). Psychopharmacological intervention in personality disorders. In J. Frosch (Ed.), *Current perspectives on personality disorders* (pp. 68–93). Washington, DC: American Psychiatric Press.

Linehan, M.M. (1981). A social behavioral analysis of suicide and parasuicides: Implications for clinical assessment and treatment. In H. Glazer & J. Clarkin (Eds.), *Depression: Behavioral and directive intervention strategies.* New York: Brunner/Mazel.

Linehan, M.M. (1987a). Dialectical behavioral therapy: A cognitive behavioral approach to parasuicide. *Journal of Personality Disorder, 1*(4), 328–333.

Linehan, M.M. (1987b). Dialectical behavior therapy in groups: Treating borderline personality disorder and suicidal behavior. In C.M. Broody (Ed.), *Women in groups.* New York: Springer.

Linehan, M.M. (1993a). *Cognitive-behavioral treatment of borderline personality disorder.* New York: Guilford Press.

Linehan, M.M. (1993b). *Skills training manual for treating borderline personality disorder.* New York: Guilford Press.

Loranger, A.W., Oldham, J.M., Russakoff, L.M., & Susman, V.L. (1984). *Personality disorder examination: A structured interview for making DSM-III Axis II diagnoses (PDE).* White Plains: The New York Hospital—Cornell Medical Center, Westchester Division.

Macaskill, N. (1982). Therapeutic factors in group therapy with borderline patients. *International Journal of Group Psychotherapy, 32,* 61–74.

Madow, M., & Pollack, W.S. (1986). *Countertransference and inpatient psychiatry.* Manuscript submitted for publication.

Mahler, M. (1971). A study of the separation-individuation process and its possible application to borderline phenomena in the psychoanalytic situation. *Psychoanalytic Study of the Child, 26,* 403–424.

Mahler, M. (1972). Rapprochement subphase of the separation-individuation process. *Psychoanalytic Quarterly, 41,* 487–506.

Mahler, M., & Kaplan, L. (1977). Developmental aspects in the assessment of narcissistic and so-called borderline personalities. In P. Hartocollis (Ed.), *Borderline personality disorders: The concept, the syndrome, the patient* (pp. 71–86). New York: International Universities Press.

Mahler, M., Pine, F., & Bergman, A. (1975). *The psychological birth of the human infant.* New York: Basis Books.

Maltsberger, J.T., & Buie, D.J. (1974). Countertransference hate in the treatment of suicidal patients. *Archives of General Psychiatry, 30,* 625–633.

Maltsberger, J.T., & Lovett, C.G. (1992). Suicide in borderline personality disorder. In D. Silver & M. Rosenblutn (Eds.), *Handbook of borderline personality disorder* (pp. 307–334). Madison, CT: International University Press.

Masterson, J. (1971). Treatment of the adolescent with borderline syndrome (a problem in separation-individuation). *Bulletin of the Menninger Clinic, 35,* 5–18.

Masterson, J. (1976). *Psychotherapy of the borderline adult.* New York: Brunner/Mazel.

McGlashan, T. (1983a). The borderline syndrome: II. Is borderline a variant of schizophrenia or affective disorder? *Archives of General Psychiatry, 40,* 1319–1323.

McGlashan, T. (1983b). The Chestnut Lodge follow-up study: II. Long-term outcome of schizophrenia and the affective disorders. *Archives of General Psychiatry, 41,* 586–601.

McGlashan, T. (1986). The Chestnut Lodge follow-up study: III. Long-term outcome of borderline personalities. *Archives of General Psychiatry, 43,* 20–30.

Meissner, W. (1978). Theoretical assumptions of concepts of the borderline personality. *Journal of American Psychoanalytic Association, 26,* 559–578.

Millon, T. (1981). *Disorders of personality, DSM-III.* New York: Wiley.

Modell, A. (1963). Primitive object relationships and the predisposition to schizophrenia. *International Journal of Psychoanalysis, 44,* 282–291.

Modell, A. (1976). The holding environment and the therapeutic action of psychoanalysis. *Journal of the American Psychoanalytic Association, 24,* 285–308.

Modell, A. (1984). *Psychoanalysis in a new context.* New York: International Universities Press.

Oberndorf, C. (1930). The psycho-analysis of borderline cases. *New York State Journal of Medicine, 30,* 648–651.

Oldham, J., Clarkin, J.F., Appelbaum, A., Carr, A., Kernberg, O., Lotterman, A., & Haas, G. (1984). *A self-report instrument for borderline personality organization.* White Plains: The New York Hospital—Cornell Medical Center, Westchester Division.

Perry, J. (1984). *The borderline personality disorder scale: Reliability and validity.* Unpublished manuscript.

Perry, J., & Klerman, G. (1980). Clinical features of the borderline personality disorder. *American Journal of Psychiatry, 137,* 165–173.

Pfohl, B., Stangl, D., & Zimmerman, M. (1983). *Structured interview for DSM-III personality disorder (SIDP).* Iowa City: University of Iowa Medical School, Department of Psychiatry.

Pollack, W.S. (1982). *"I-ness" and "we-ness": Parallel lines of development.* Unpublished manuscript, Boston University, Boston.

Pollack, W.S. (1983a). *The day hospital as a therapeutic holding environment.* The 1982 proceedings of the annual conference on Partial Hospitalization, Boston.

Pollack, W.S. (1983b). Object-relations and self-psychology: Researching children and their family systems. *The Psychologist-Psychoanalyst, 4,* 14.

Pollack, W.S. (1986). Borderline personality disorder. Definition, diagnosis, assessment and treatment considerations. In P.A. Keller & L.G. Ritt (Eds.), *Innovations in clinical practice* (Vol. 5, pp. 103–135). Sarasota, FL: Professional Resource Exchange.

Pollack, W.S. (1989). *Boys and men: Developmental ramifications of autonomy and affiliation.* Paper presented at the mid-winter meetings, American Psychological Association, Division of Psychotherapy, Orlando, FL.

Pollack, W.S. (1990). Borderline personality disorder: Psychotherapeutic approaches to treatment. In A.S. Bellack & M. Hersen (Eds.), *Comparative handbook of treatments for adult disorders* (pp. 393–419). New York: Wiley.

Pollack, W.S. (1995). Deconstructing dis-identification: Rethinking psychoanalytic concepts of male development. *Psychoanalysis and Psychotherapy, 12*(1), 30–45.

Pollack, W.S., & Dion, G. (1985). *Functional disability, severity of illness and DSM-III diagnosis: The creation of a scale.* Unpublished manuscript, Harvard Medical School, Belmont, MA.

Pollack, W.S., & Dion, G. (1987). Beyond *DSM-III* Axis V: Creating an alternative multiaxial measure of psychosocial functioning—Measuring severity of illness in hospitalized psychiatric patients. In S.M. Mirin (Ed.), *Current research in private psychiatric hospitals.* Washington, DC: National Association of Private Psychiatric Hospitals.

Pollack, W.S., & Grossman, F.K. (1985). Parent-child interaction. In L. L'Abate (Ed.), *The handbook of family psychology and therapy* (pp. 586–622). Homewood, IL: Dorsey Press.

Pope, H., Jonas, J., Hudson, J., Cohen, B.M., & Gunderson, J.G. (1983). The validity of *DSM-III* borderline personality disorder. *Archives of General Psychiatry, 40,* 23–30.

Rinsley, D. (1982). *Borderline and other self disorders.* New York: Aronson.

Roth, B. (1980). Understanding the development of a homogeneous identity-impaired group through countertransference phenomena. *International Journal of Group Psychotherapy, 30,* 405–426.

Roth, B. (1982). Six types of borderline and narcissistic patients: An initial typology. *International Journal of Group Psychotherapy, 32,* 9–27.

Salzman, C., Wolfson, A.B., Schatzberg, A., et al. (1992). *Effect of fluoxetine on anger in symptomatic volunteers with borderline personality disorder.* Paper presented at the annual meeting of the American College of Neuropsychopharmacology, San Juan, Puerto Rico.

Schatzberg, A. (1983). *Brain imaging in atypical depressions.* Paper presented at the McLean Hospital Symposium on Atypical Depressions, New York.

Searles, H. (1979a). *Countertransference and related subjects: Selected papers.* New York: International Universities Press.

Searles, H. (1979b). The countertransference with the borderline patient. In J. Leboit & A. Capponi (Eds.), *Advances in psychotherapy of the borderline patient* (pp. 347–403). New York: Aronson.

Shapiro, E., Shapiro, R., & Zinner, J. (1977). The borderline ego and the working alliance: Indications for family and individual treatment in adolescence. *International Journal of Psychoanalysis, 58,* 77–87.

Shapiro, E., Zinner, J., Shapiro, R., & Berkowitz, D. (1975). The influence of family experience on borderline personality development. *International Review of Psychoanalysis, 2,* 399–411.

Siever, L., & Gunderson, J. (1983). The search for a schizotypal personality: A review. *Comprehensive Psychiatry, 24,* 199–212.

Silk, K.R. (1994). *Biological and neurobehavioral studies of borderline personality disorder.* Washington: American Psychiatric Press.

Silver, D. (1983). Psychotherapy of the characterologically difficult patient. *Canadian Journal of Psychiatry, 28,* 513–521.

Silver, D. (1985). Psychodynamics and psychotherapeutic management of the self-destructive character-disordered patient. *Psychiatric Clinics of North America, 8,* 357–375.

Soloff, P.H., Cornelius, J., George, A., et al. (1993). Efficacy of phenelzine and haloperidol in borderline personality disorder. *Archives of General Psychiatry, 50,* 377–385.

Soloff, P.H., George, A., Natman, R.S., Schultz, P.M., Ulrich, R.F., & Perel, J.M. (1986). Progress in pharmacotherapy of borderline disorders: A double-blind study of amitriptyline, haloperidol, and placebo. *Archives of General Psychiatry, 43,* 691–697.

Spitzer, R., Endicott, J. (1979). Justification for separating schizotypal and borderline personality disorders. *Schizophrenia Bulletin, 5,* 95–104.

Spitzer, R., Endicott, J., & Gibbon, M. (1979). Crossing the border into borderline personality and borderline schizophrenia: The development of criteria. *Archives of General Psychiatry, 36,* 17–24.

Spitzer, R., Williams, J., & Skodol, A. (1980). *DSM-III:* The major achievements and an overview. *American Journal of Psychiatry, 137,* 151–164.

Stangl, D., Pfohl, B., Zimmerman, M., Bowers, W., & Corenthal, C. (1985). A structured interview for the *DSM-III* personality disorder. *Archives of General Psychiatry, 42,* 591–596.

Stern, A. (1938). Psychoanalytic investigation of and therapy in the borderline group of neuroses. *Psychoanalytic Quarterly, 7,* 467–489.

Stevenson, J., & Meares, R. (1992). An outcome study of psychotherapy for patients with borderline personality disorder (see comments). *American Journal of Psychiatry, 149*(3), 358–362.

Stiver, I. (1985). *The meanings of "dependency" in female male relationships* (Work in progress series, Stone Center). Wellesley, MA: The Stone Center for Developmental Services and Studies at Wellesley College.

Stiver, I. (1988). Developmental psychopathology: Introducing a consultant in the treatment of borderline patients. *McLean Hospital Journal, 13,* 89–113.

Stone, M.H. (1980). *Borderline syndromes.* New York: McGraw-Hill.

Stone, M.H. (1990). *The fate of borderline patients: Successful outcome and psychiatric practice.* New York: Guilford Press.

Stone, M.H., Hurt, S.W., & Stone, D.K. (1987). The PI 500: Long-term follow-up of borderline inpatients meeting *DSM-III* criteria: I. Global outcome. *Journal of Personality Disorders, 1*(4), 291–298.

Stone, M.H., & Weissman, R. (1984). Group therapy with borderline patients. In N. Slavinka-Holy (Ed.), *Contemporary perspectives in group psychotherapy.* London: Routledge & Kegan Paul.

Stororow, R.D., & Lachman, F.M. (1980). *Psychoanalysis of developmental arrests: Theory and treatment.* New York: International Universities Press.

Tolpin, M. (1971). On the beginnings of a cohesive self: An application of the concept of transmuting internalization to the study of the transitional object and signal anxiety. *The Psychoanalytic Study of the Child, 26,* 316–354.

Tolpin, M., & Kohut, H. (1980). The disorders of the self: The psychopathology of the first years of life. In S.I. Greenspan & G. Pollack (Eds.), *The course of life* (Vol. 1, pp. 425–442). Adelphi, MD: National Institute of Mental Health.

Waldinger, R.J., & Frank, A.F. (1989). Clinicians' experiences in combining medication and psychotherapy in the treatment of borderline patients. *Hospital Community Psychiatry, 40*(7), 712–718.

Waldinger, R.J., & Gunderson, J.G. (1987). *Effective psychotherapy with borderline patients.* New York: Macmillan.

Wallerstein, R. (1983, October 29). *Psychoanalysis and psychotherapy: Relative roles reconsidered.* Paper presented at the Boston Psychoanalytic Society and Institute Symposium, Boston.

Winnicott, D. (1953). Transitional objects and transitional phenomena. *International Journal of Psychoanalysis, 34,* 89–97.

Winnicott, D. (1960). The theory of the parent-infant relationships. *International Journal of Psychoanalysis, 41,* 585–595.

Winnicott, D. (1965). *The maturational process and the facilitating environment.* New York: International Universities Press.

Winnicott, D. (1975). Hate in the countertransference (1947, pp. 194–203) and the depressive position in normal emotional development (1954, pp. 262–277). In *Through pediatrics to psychoanalysis.* New York: Basic Books.

Wolberg, A.R. (1952). The "borderline" patient. *American Journal of Psychotherapy, 6,* 694–710.

Wong, J. (1980). Combined group and individual treatment of borderline and narcissistic patients: Heterogeneous vs. homogeneous groups. *International Journal of Group Psychotherapy, 30,* 389–404.

Zanarini, M. (1996). *The role of sexual abuse in the etiology of borderline personality disorder.* Washington: American Psychiatric Press.

Zanarini, M.C., Gunderson, J.G., Marino, M.F., et al. (1989). Childhood experiences of borderline patients. *Comprehensive Psychiatry, 30,* 18–25.

Zetzel, E. (1971). A developmental approach to the borderline patients. *American Journal of Psychiatry, 128,* 867–871.

CHAPTER 22

Behavior Therapy

KATHERINE A. COMTOIS, ERIC R. LEVENSKY, and MARSHA M. LINEHAN

THIS CHAPTER will review behavior therapy for borderline personality disorder (BPD) from a number of different perspectives: (1) conceptual underpinnings of the disorder, (2) diagnostic issues, (3) conceptual underpinnings of treatment, (4) specific treatment strategies, (5) other treatments for BPD, and, finally, (6) treatment organization and funding under managed care. To illustrate the treatment strategies, a case example is also presented.

There have been two experimental studies evaluating the effectiveness of behavior therapy with BPD. Both Linehan and colleagues (Linehan, Armstrong, Suarez, Allmon, & Heard, 1991; Linehan, Heard, & Armstrong, 1993; Linehan, Tutek, Heard, & Armstrong, 1994) and Turner (1989) have shown behavior therapy to be effective in treating BPD. Because only the structural strategies of Turner's Bio-Cognitive-Behavioral treatment for BPD have been described in detail (Turner, 1987, 1989), this chapter focuses on Dialectical Behavior Therapy and the concepts on which it is based. However, when the structural strategies of behavior therapy are discussed, Turner's structure will also be included.

CONCEPTUALIZATION OF THE DISORDER

Dialectical Behavior Therapy has been described in detail in Linehan's two treatment manuals (Linehan, 1993a, 1993b) as well as in subsequent topic-specific articles, chapters and manuals adapted for specific patient populations (Koerner et al., 1997; Linehan, 1997; Linehan, in press; Linehan & Dimeff, 1998; Linehan & Schmidt, 1995, 1998). The following is a summary of Linehan's theoretical position. The roots of Linehan's theory lie in two schools: dialectical

Writing of this manuscript was partially supported by grant RO1 MH34486 from the National Institute on Mental Health, Bethesda, MD.

philosophy and basic psychological research on social-learning and genetic-biological bases of behavior. These schools of thought are synthesized by Linehan into the Biosocial Theory of BPD.

DIALECTICAL PHILOSOPHY

A dialectical world view has been applied to socioeconomic history (Marx & Engels, 1970), the development of science, (Kuhn, 1970), biological evolution (Levins & Lewontin, 1985), analyses of sexual relations (Firestone, 1970), and the development of thinking in adults (Basseches, 1984). Wells (1972, cited in Kegan, 1982) has documented a shift toward dialectical approaches in almost every social and natural science during the past 150 years. Dialectical analysis is crucial to understanding the developmental analysis of both borderline personality disorder and the treatment process espoused by Linehan (1993a).

A dialectical framework stresses the fundamental interrelatedness and wholeness of reality, and it is in direct contradiction to traditional Cartesian reductionism. As Levins and Lewontin (1985) describe, in the Cartesian world view, parts are seen as homogeneous entities, existing separately from the whole they comprise. In contrast, a dialectical view sees the internal heterogeneity of elements at every level such that knowing the parts of the whole depends on what facets of the whole are being considered. Elements are nonreducible, and there is no *a priori* independent existence of parts, only parts as they relate to a particular whole. Wholes themselves are, in turn, not static but comprise internal opposing forces (*thesis* and *antithesis*) out of whose *synthesis* evolves a new set of opposing forces. Thus, parts and whole are in constant interaction and re-creation of each other. At the same time, the ever-changing nature of the whole influences and is influenced by the external world of which it is a part. Thus, the fundamental principles of a dialectical world view are the nonreducible nature of reality and the interconnectedness of all things, both of which lead to a wholeness continually in the process of change.

The behavioral, tripartite system's view of human functioning is compatible, with slight modification, with a dialectical approach. In the tripartite view, behavioral responses are partitioned into three general subsystems: (1) the overt-motor system, (2) the physiological-emotional system, and (3) the cognitive-verbal system (Staats, 1975). A systems orientation suggests that relationships among the three systems are dynamic, such that change in any one will produce system-wide changes (Schwartz, 1982). No one system is viewed as primary. In turn, equal significance is accorded to the reciprocal influence of the person system and the social-environmental system. From a dialectical point of view, addressing any one system in isolation from the others is not meaningful. Similarly, individuals cannot be isolated from their environment. Less obvious, but equally true, the environment cannot be isolated from the individual.

A dialectical-systems approach influences conceptualization on all levels. For example, a dialectical view favors a dimensional rather than a categorical classification system for mental disorders, inasmuch as categories create a myriad of self-contained, independent parts. Dimensions, on the other hand, are defined by their opposing poles. A dialectical approach, rather than identifying phenomena as static points on a dimensional continuum, emphasizes the continuous creation of the phenomena out of the tension exerted by the coexistence of the opposing poles.

For example, on the level of particular borderline behaviors, such as interpersonal dependence, a dialectical perspective would suggest that independence without dependence is a myth. A dialectical synthesis might suggest the problem for borderline patients is not too much dependence, as is commonly supposed by Western cultural norms, but too much *fear* of dependence, with good reason of course. (From our perspective, the question certainly can be raised of whether the world would not perhaps be better off if we emphasized dependence more and independence less!)

Most important, a dialectical account of psychopathology may allow greater compassion. Dialectics, with its systemic overtones in synthesizing truth from multiple perspectives, is incompatible with the assignment of blame, certainly a relevant issue with a label as stigmatized among mental-health professionals as *borderline* (for examples of the misuse of the diagnosis, see Reiser & Levenson, 1984).

Learning Theory and Social Psychology

Dialectical behavior therapy (DBT) is based on the application of principles of learning and contextual theory and on experimental psychology, including discrete emotions theory (Izard & Kobak, 1991; Malatesta, 1990) and self-verification theory (Swann, 1997). A detailed description of these theories and how they might account for much of BPD is complex and beyond the scope of this chapter. What follows, however, is a review of the biosocial theory of BPD, which integrates these theories and forms a conceptual core from which DBT was developed.

Biosocial Theory

Linehan's (1993a) theory of the etiology and maintenance of BPD is based on a biosocial theory of human functioning. The core concept of a biosocial theory of BPD is that pervasive dysregulation of emotion is the primary dysfunction in BPD and that all other behavioral problems associated with BPD are the result of, or are an attempt to manage, such dysregulation. The theory holds that this dysregulation of emotion is the result of a transactional process between individuals who are vulnerable to dysregulation of emotion as a function of their biological makeup (e.g., neurotransmitter systems) and a particular type of social environment in which such individuals develop, termed the "invalidating environment" by Linehan. Each of these concepts will be described in turn.

Emotionally vulnerable individuals, as compared to others: (1) are more sensitive to emotional stimuli (i.e., have a low threshold for emotional response), (2) experience and express quicker and more intense responses to emotional stimuli; and (3) take longer to return to baseline after becoming emotionally aroused. Regulating emotions requires the ability to: (1) increase or decrease the physiological arousal associated with emotion, (2) orient or reorient attention in the presence of strong emotion, (3) inhibit mood dependent actions, (4) experience emotions without attempting to escape or blunt them, and (5) organize behavior in service of non-mood-dependent goals (cf. Gottman & Katz, 1990). According to Linehan (1993a), borderline individuals are emotionally vulnerable and also lack the ability to regulate their strong emotions. It is this combination of an overly sensitive and reactive emotional response system with an inability to modulate the resulting strong emotions that constitutes the emotional dysregulation in borderline individuals.

According to the biosocial theory, the crucial link between biological emotional vulnerability and subsequent pervasive emotional dysregulation characteristic of BPD is the transactional process between the emotionally vulnerable individual and the "invalidating environment." The invalidating environment is a family or social environment that tends to respond in an erratic, inappropriate, or extreme way to an individual's communication of, or behavior that reflects, the individual's private experiences (e.g., thoughts, feelings, physiological responses). This style of responding can include disputing, trivializing, criticizing, pathologizing, or generally over- or under-responding to the individual's private experiences (e.g., responding to an individual's statement "I'm trying my best" with "No, you aren't, try harder"). An invalidating environment communicates to an individual that that individual's experiences (or interpretations of the individual's experiences) are incorrect, inaccurate, faulty, inappropriate, or otherwise not valid.

This process of invalidating the emotionally vulnerable individual's private experiences has two main consequences. First, the individual does not learn to label private experiences in a way that is consistent with the larger social community. For example, an individual may label an experience of crying as reflecting stupidity or inappropriateness as opposed to a normative label of sadness, fear, or anger. Second, the invalidating environment teaches individuals to not trust their private experiences as valid responses to environmental events and instead teaches them to search the social environment for cues about how to respond, such as trying not to cry when inclined to do so unless others around give cues that crying is an appropriate response.

Invalidating environments also tend to punish behavior that is not congruent with that of the family or social environment or behavior that puts a demand on the environment that is above the preferred level. For example, an individual may be yelled at for crying at a family party or, conversely, chastised for not crying at a funeral. The consequence of this environmental suppression of the individual's natural emotional responses is that the individual does not learn to accurately express emotions or communicate pain so they can be interpreted correctly by the larger social environment. In addition, the invalidating environment does not respond to moderate expressions of emotion, which results in the individual learning that only extreme expressions of emotion will be attended to. Thus, the environment teaches the individual to oscillate between emotional inhibition or suppression and extreme emotional expression.

Finally, an invalidating environment tends to respond to problems as though they are easily solved and to goals as though they are easily reached. Both the practical problems and goals experienced in day-to-day living, as well as the problem of overwhelming emotional responses (i.e., what to do when one is upset) are minimized in this way. Therefore, the individual does not learn to go through the process of identifying a problem, developing options, and solving it nor does the individual learn the process of choosing a goal, working toward it, and attaining it. This environment teaches the individual to form unrealistic goals and expectations for what solutions are possible. In addition, the individual does not learn how to tolerate distress when a problem cannot be solved or a goal cannot be met. This results in the individual having perfectionistic standards and being unprepared for failures, which are in turn responded to with excessive distress.

In describing the deleterious effects of the invalidating environment on the emotionally vulnerable individual, it is important to point out that the interplay between the individual and the environment is a transactional process. The term *transaction* is used to describe this process because the individual is both affected by and has an effect on the environment. Just as the invalidating social environment can cause the emotionally vulnerable individual to become more emotionally dysregulated by invalidating that individual's experiences, the individual can elicit and maintain new invalidating responses from the environment. For example, constant emotional sensitivity (e.g., irritability, whininess) requires constant responsiveness that can be very frustrating to a parent who eventually tries to suppress the child's emotional responses (e.g., "You are fine" or "Don't make such a big deal of nothing"). Through this transaction, the emotionally vulnerable individual and the invalidating environment operate together and mutually influence one another resulting in the individual becoming increasingly dysregulated.

From the biosocial perspective, BPD behavioral patterns outlined in the *Diagnostic and Statistical Manual, Fourth Edition* (American Psychiatric Association [APA], 1996) can be seen as three expressions of emotion dysregulation. First, the diagnostic criteria of affective instability, inappropriate intense anger, and transient stress-related paranoid ideation or severe dissociative symptoms are examples of the dysregulation itself. Although the latter two criteria are cognitive in nature, they are paired with emotion dysregulation because they are immediate, short-term responses that directly reflect the dysregulated emotion.

Second, criteria of frantic efforts to avoid abandonment, recurrent suicidal behavior, and impulsivity can be seen as maladaptive attempts to regulate emotion. These behaviors are attempts to regulate emotion both directly (i.e., emotional relief or reorientation of attention frequently follows parasuicidal behavior and other impulsive behaviors such as substance abuse, eating binges, or risky sexual behavior) and indirectly by communicating distress to others who then provide help to the individual who regulates distress.

Third, chronic emotion dysregulation results in identity disturbance and a pattern of unstable and intense interpersonal relationships. A pervasive inability to regulate emotions interferes with development and maintenance of a sense of self and stable relationships with others. Emotional consistency and predictability across time and similar situations are prerequisites of both identity development and stable relationships. In addition, successful relationships require a capacity to adaptively self-regulate emotions and to tolerate some emotionally painful stimuli. Lack of a sense of self and stable relationships with others in turn lead to the final criteria: a chronic sense of emptiness.

DIAGNOSTIC ISSUES AND PROBLEMS

BPD as a diagnostic category has become increasingly established over the past ten years. The diagnosis has been codified in both the *Diagnostic and Statistical Manual, Fourth Edition* (American Psychiatric Association, 1994) and the *International Classification of Disorders, Tenth Edition* (World Health Organization, 1993). Considerable research based on these criteria has been conducted regarding etiology and course, family history and other biological correlates, and development and outcome of treatments. Despite establishment of behavioral treatments for BPD, the diagnosis itself remains controversial to behaviorists with regard to the construct of personality on which it is based.

DSM-IV DIAGNOSIS AND ITS ASSESSMENT

A number of semistructured interviews have been developed to assess personality disorders in general and BPD specifically. Three instruments have come to the fore in research studies regarding BPD. The Diagnostic Interview for Borderlines-Revised (DIB-R) was developed by Kolb and Gunderson (1980) and revised by Zanarini, Gunderson, Frankenburg, & Chauncey (1989). The instrument includes subscales assessing the personality dimensions of Gunderson's conceptualization of BPD as well as a dimensional scale assessing "borderline-ness." The DIB-R has been used widely in research studies of borderline patients, but it is limited because it is too overinclusive to result in a *DSM* or *ICD* diagnosis, although specificity has improved in the *DIB-R* (Zanarini et al., 1989). Other instruments include the Structured Clinical Interview for *DSM-IV* for Axis II (SCID-II) (First, Spitzer, Gibbons, Williams, & Benjamin, 1996) which was developed in combination with the SCID for Axis I disorders (First, Spitzer, Gibbons, & Williams, 1995) and the International Personality Disorders Examination (IPDE) (Loranger et al., 1994) which was developed in conjunction with the World Health Organization to facilitate cross-national studies of personality disorders.

Paper and pencil questionnaires, such as that accompanying the SCID-II as well as the Personality Diagnostic Questionnaire-Revised (Hyler, Skodol, Oldham, Kellman, & Doidge, 1992), have been developed to assess BPD, but they result in so many false positives (as compared to clinical interview) that they are unsuitable for differential diagnosis (Loranger, 1992; Perry, 1992). However, paper and pencil questionnaires can serve as useful screening tools (Ekselius, Lindstrom, von Knorring, Bodlund, & Kullgren, 1994; Jacobsberg & Perry, 1995; Patrick, Links, van Reekum, & Mitton, 1995). No interviews for lay interviewers have been developed that assess personality disorders (Loranger, 1992).

THEORETICAL AND DIAGNOSTIC DILEMMAS

Construct of Personality

A major problem with BPD from a behavioral point of view is its reliance on the construct of personality. How does one operationalize personality? At a minimum, the notion of a personality disorder requires one to assume that individual behavior patterns (including patterns of action, cognitive processes, and physiological-emotional responses) are reasonably consistent across both time and situations. This assumption, however, has long been questioned by behaviorists. Mischel's (1968) now-classic summary of the empirical data underlying the premise that behavior is a function of person characteristics (i.e., personality) concluded that much behavioral variation formerly attributed to personality is instead due to situational characteristics. With some additional limits, Mischel's conclusion has withstood the test of intensive critical scrutiny over the years (Mischel, 1990).

Categorical versus Behavioral Focus

From a behavioral perspective, a categorical classification system is a problematic match for BPD, because, by definition, a categorical approach espouses a different scientific paradigm from behaviorism, and because, even within the context of a categorical classification system, BPD is unable to satisfy that system's requirements for validity (Follette, 1997). A fundamental problem is that a categorical approach assumes existence and significance of some underlying essence of "borderline-ness" that is not immediately accessible to investigation. Independent verification of the existence of this phenomenon, such as locating a borderline gene or a particular ratio of various neurotransmitters that adds up to "borderline-ness," has not been achieved. In fact, recent reviews of the family and genetic research on BPD has shown only moderate family-history effects, much of which can be explained by nonspecific factors equally true of non-BPD subjects (Nigg & Goldsmith, 1994; Paris, 1994; Torgersen, 1994). Further problems with the validity of a categorical classification are reflected in the debate about whether BPD reflects an affective disorder (Akiskal, 1994; Nigg & Goldsmith, 1994) or a pattern of symptoms resulting from childhood abuse (Briere, 1984; Zweig-Frank & Paris, 1995).

In the absence of knowing what core problem constitutes "borderline-ness," it is unclear what characteristics are its direct expression. As Widiger and Frances (1987) point out, the criteria sets of the *DSM-IV* are at times used as indicators of some underlying pathology (diagnostically), and at other times, they are used as operational criteria of a disorder (definitionally). Research, in many cases, does not sufficiently distinguish which criteria are definitional and which (if any) are diagnostic. Problems with validity and diagnosis are, thus, for the *DSM-IV* categorical classification system, inextricably intertwined.

From a behavioral point of view, a final problem involves the treatment utility of a categorical system of classification. Taken at face value, the generally good interrater reliability of some measures of BPD might seem to support the notion that a pattern of behaviors exists that, for simplicity's sake, may be labeled "borderline." However, as Clarkin and colleagues (Clarkin, Widiger, Frances, Hurt, & Gilmore, 1983) point out, reliability of *DSM* criteria does not guarantee homogeneous groupings of behaviors across subjects. That is, the *DSM-IV* calls for meeting five out of nine criteria to receive the diagnosis, resulting in more than 100 different ways to qualify for BPD, thus limiting the construct validity of the diagnosis (Clark, Livesley, & Morey, 1997). High interrater reliability can be achieved for the diagnosis even when behavioral clusters are nonoverlapping across subjects. Heterogeneity of criteria clusters across subjects is also suggested by mixed findings on intermeasure agreement. Clearly, this presents a formidable problem for treatment when treatment is aimed at reducing behaviors associated with the diagnosis. Ideally, treatment would consist of a flexible series of strategies that could be used singly or in different combinations to accommodate the specific constellation of behaviors engaged in by any one borderline patient (Follette, 1997).

BEHAVIORAL PERSPECTIVES

Construct of Personality

Personality, from the behaviorist's perspective, may best be regarded as a set of behavioral capabilities (Wallace, 1966). Defining personality or personality disorder from this framework, therefore, consists of defining the relevant behavioral and associated environmental domains and choosing behaviors thought to be representative samples of the domains of interest. Content validity then becomes the issue. Are the behaviors identified by current measures of BPD representative samples of the behavioral domains constituting borderline behaviors? The first step in answering such a question involves the development of instruments that assess measurable behavioral criteria. Both the SCID II and IPDE operationalizations of *DSM-IV* criteria and the DIB-R fulfill this requirement and are sufficiently reliable for research purposes. Then, the crucial question from a behavioral point of view is whether these behaviors truly co-occur with each other more than other behaviors. Recent studies have indicated moderate empirical support for three factors of the BPD criteria (i.e., interpersonal and identity instability, impulsivity, and affective instability) (Blais, Hilsenroth, & Castlebury, 1997; Clarkin, Hull, & Hurt, 1993) suggesting the behaviors co-occur. However, frequency of overlap with numerous other diagnoses and absence of data supporting a fundamental, underlying organizational principle of BPD does not support this co-occurrence as more distinctive than the relationship of the BPD criteria to other (non-BPD) behaviors.

Dimensionality as an Alternative Construct

In addition, Frances, Clarkin, Gilmore, Hurt, and Brown (1984) highlight the poorness of fit between a categorical classification system and BPD. They argue that in cases where the distribution of scores for a diagnosis is uniform, as was the case with their sample's scores on the DIB, cutoffs are arbitrary. The boundaries of classically defined categories depend upon points of rarity.

Absence of points of rarity to define categories suggests that alternative systems of classification should be considered. Rather than discrete or prototypical categories, continuums may provide the best fit to the data. Continuums are, in turn, best represented by dimensional rather than categorical approaches to classification.

From a behavioral point of view, there are several advantages to a dimensional system of classification and diagnosis. First, dimensions may provide a more accurate and flexible fit to the data, because (1) dimensions can take account of phenomena excluded from consideration by diagnostic categories, (2) dimensions depend on finer measurements than do categorical data, which suggests that phenomena must be more carefully operationalized and more tied to observables, and (3) the fit between dimensions and the natural characteristics of the phenomenon in question may be closer. Second, as Cloninger (1987) points out, there is little evidence of bimodal or multimodal distributions in the observed variation of so-called normal personality traits, suggesting that cognitive and social styles vary along continuums. Third, dimensions are defined by specific classes of behaviors and, therefore, clearly specify the targets of treatment. Last, a dimensional approach has advantages over a categorical approach for research and theory building analogous to the advantages of a phenomena-over-diagnosis approach endorsed by Persons (1986). By including more of the overt phenomena organized into smaller chunks, a dimensional approach enables the study of a single phenomenon in isolation and permits the theory-rich recognition of the continuity of clinical phenomena with normal phenomena. By allowing attention to detail, it will most likely improve the validity diagnosis.

The behavioral treatments for BPD offered to date represent an interesting blend of categorical and dimensional approaches. The treatments are modular, focused on specific behavioral targets, and, thus, fit a dimensional perspective. However, inclusion criteria for patients in the research studies, theoretical underpinnings of the treatments, and strategies for applying the treatment modules are based largely on categorical assumptions. Some inherent "borderline-ness" (i.e., some characteristic setting these patients apart from other patients) is presumed to moderate the influence of specific treatments targeted to specific behavioral phenomena.

OVERVIEW OF TREATMENT STRATEGIES

In considering comprehensive treatments for mental disorders, in general, Linehan (1997) has conceptualized five functions to which treatment must attend if the patient's goals are to be realized. The first function, capability enhancement, includes the ability to function skillfully in general and to match skill to situation. Typical modes of treatment for capability enhancement are skills training (either individually or in a group format), psychoeducational programs, or providing written materials.

Behavioral capabilities without motivation, however, will not lead to changed behavior. Thus, the second function of treatment is motivational enhancement.

Motivation from a behavioral framework does not imply a personality trait or other internal characteristic. Rather, motivation is conceptualized in terms of the environmental contingencies. In this view, a patient is always motivated for something—the question is for what? The goal of psychotherapy is that functional behaviors or their approximations are reinforced by the environment and dysfunctional behaviors are not. This requires that the therapist have an acute understanding of the contingencies operating in the patient's environment. Enhancing motivation requires the therapist (1) to clarify and make salient to the patient the contingencies that exist between the patient's behavior and environmental events, (2) to assist the patient to find reinforcers for functional behavior and avoid those for problem behavior, and (3) to reduce behaviors that interfere with or inhibit functional behaviors (including overwhelming emotions and dysfunctional cognitions). When treating patients with BPD, it is often necessary to use arbitrary reinforcers (such as treatment rules) to reinforce functional behaviors that can be removed or become irrelevant as natural reinforcers in the environment become salient. For instance, patients who are cutting or burning themselves may be unable to sustain intimate relationships. In the absence of such relationships, there is little to reinforce more functional alternatives to self-injury. Thus, the DBT therapist uses arbitrary contingencies such as refusing to take calls within 24 hours of self-injury or requiring an in-depth analysis of self-injury in session after each time it occurs. These contingencies lead the patient to use coping strategies other than self-injury. Over time, as self-injury stops, the patient is more likely to develop intimate relationships, and the potential loss of those relationships serves as a natural contingency for using the alternative coping strategies long term. Motivational enhancement in standard DBT is the focus of individual psychotherapy but can also be provided in other treatment modalities including group therapy, the milieu of a residential setting, or contingency management programs, such as the voucher system of Higgins and colleagues (Higgins et al., 1993) and the community reinforcement approach (Barley, 1996; Higgins, 1997).

Assuming that the patient is now capable and motivated, the patient might be extremely effective in the therapy session. The third function of treatment is generalization. The patient must be able to be effective in all relevant contexts: in different environments, with different people, and, for emotionally dysregulated patients, in different moods. This function can be served by homework, telephone or email coaching, or in vivo interventions.

In addition to the patients' ability to generalize their skills to the natural environment, it is often a function of therapy to ensure that the patients' natural environment be as reinforcing of progress as possible. This fourth function is termed structuring the environment. This may involve case-management interventions to change housing situations, to facilitate employment, or to otherwise assist patients to make concrete changes in their environment. However, it may also be the case that there are contingencies acting on the therapist that reinforce dysfunctional patient behaviors. For example, risk-management policies may dictate hospitalization as the strategy for patients reporting significant suicidal ideation, despite the therapist's belief that hospitalization reinforces (i.e., increases the frequency of) suicidal behavior in the face of environmental stress.

Finally, the therapist must conduct effective therapy. Treating patients with BPD is often demoralizing and demands a sophistication requiring special training. Thus, the final function, enhancing therapist capabilities and motivation, is needed to ensure that therapists are capable of providing the treatment. This includes providing training and analyzing problems in therapy to assure that lack of skill is not leading to ineffective treatment. In addition, patients, especially patients with BPD, often provide little of no reinforcement to the therapist. Thus, therapists need to ensure that they find reinforcement in other settings. The most typical mode for enhancing therapist capability and motivation is the consultation group where cases are reviewed, therapist motivation is monitored and addressed, and training can occur. Other modes of therapist enhancement include continuing education, supervision, and informal discussions (i.e., catching up with other therapists in the course of the day to discuss patients, aspects of the therapy, feelings of burnout, etc.).

SPECIFIC TREATMENT STRATEGIES

There are five basic types of treatment strategies in any behavior therapy treatment program. Although various strategies are more or less specified depending on the particular therapy manual, most treatments combine some version of the following strategies in a comprehensive treatment: (1) structural strategies (how to organize sessions and how to choose appropriate treatment targets at specific points), (2) problem-solving strategies (how to organize specific behavior-therapy interventions and procedures, including (when applicable) skills acquisition, exposure, contingency management, and cognitive modification procedures), (3) empathic and/or validation strategies, (4) communication strategies (or how to deliver the what of the other strategies), and (5) special protocols that describe how to integrate strategies for certain common situations, such as crises, relationship difficulties, etc. In addition, Linehan in DBT adds (6) dialectical strategies (concerned with the balance, movement, and flow of treatment), and (7) case-management strategies (concerned with interactions of the therapist with the patient and the environment in meeting demands of the patient's personal and professional network).

Structural Strategies

A core component of both Linehan's and Turner's treatments for BPD is the notion that borderline individuals have several important behavioral deficits. Turner (1989) focuses on interpersonal skills, information processing, and anxiety management. Linehan also targets interpersonal skills and cognitive restructuring, but expands anxiety management to encompass emotional regulation in general, and she adds a focus on distress tolerance, acceptance, and dialectics. We will briefly review Turner's treatment structure and then discuss DBT in more detail.

Turner's Bio-Cognitive-Behavioral Treatment. Turner proposes that maladaptive schema learned early in life are responsible for rapid disjunctive shifts in mental and emotional sets characteristic of borderline individuals. These shifts lead to a disturbance in the sense of temporal continuity and to cognitive confusion, disorientation, and derealization whenever a feared stressor occurs. Among the behavioral sequelae to these difficulties are interpersonal problems, micro-psychotic episodes, social anxiety, cognitive dysfunction, depression, and impulsive behavior.

Turner's (1987) treatment consists of four sequential phases: (1) pharmacotherapy stabilization, (2) flooding procedures to inoculate patients against cognitive and mood experiences associated with their worst symptoms, (3) covert rehearsal and in vivo practice of coping strategies, and (4) interpersonal problem solving. These phases are completed in the first three months and followed by nine months of supportive psychotherapy with return to earlier treatments as needed.

Levels of Disorder and Stages of Treatment in DBT.   DBT is conceptualized in terms of levels of disorder and corresponding targets of treatment (Linehan, in press). Specific treatment modalities are expected to vary according to the treatment setting and funding structure. There are four levels of disorder conceptualized by Linehan (in press); each level having a corresponding stage of treatment.

Level 1 disorders are characterized by behavioral dyscontrol and typically include disorders that are both severe and pervasive. Stage 1 treatments for level 1 disorders have, as an overall treatment goal, to help these patients be in control of their behavior and their lives. Behaviors that are targeted for treatment in stage 1 are arranged hierarchically as follows: (1) suicidal behaviors (parasuicide, high-risk suicidal ideation), (2) behaviors interfering with the conduct of therapy, (3) behaviors interfering with a reasonably high quality of life (e.g., substance abuse, poor work behaviors, criminal behaviors, poor judgment), (4) behavioral-skill acquisition (emotion regulation, interpersonal effectiveness, distress tolerance, mindfulness, and self-management), and (5) other goals on which the individual wishes to focus. Attention is shifted from a later target to a target earlier on the list when problems in that area resurface. Thus, therapy is somewhat circular, because target focal points revolve over time.

The second level of disorder is best described as quiet desperation (in contrast to the loud desperation of level 1). At this level, the experience of emotions is traumatic, and the key problem is avoidance of emotions and the environmental cues associated with them. Simple posttraumatic stress disorder is an example of a level 2 disorder in which the patient is in enough control to show up for treatment and avoid substance abuse, but is unable to function normally because of emotional avoidance. The goal for stage 2 treatment is the ability to experience emotions in a way that is both modulated and provides corrective information. The third level of disorders is best thought of as problems in living (in which problems the patient experiences may be very serious, as in a troubled marriage or job stress), but are not themselves disabling. The goal of treatment at Stage 3 is ordinary happiness and unhappiness as well as a stable sense of self respect. Finally, the fourth level of disorder reflects a sense of incompleteness experienced by many individuals who are for the most part content with their lives. The goal of treatment for Stage 4 is a sustained capacity for joy via psychological insight, spiritual direction or practices, or other experiential treatments or activities.

Standard DBT is a Stage 1 treatment specifically designed to address all five functions of treatment for level 1 disorders. The standard modes of treatment are individual psychotherapy, group skills training, phone consultation, and a therapist consultation group. Case management, pharmacotherapy, and other capability enhancement and generalization modes are provided on an *as needed* basis. Because DBT is based on principles of function, level, stage, and target, rather than on form (i.e., modality), the treatment might appear quite different in a setting such as an inpatient unit or day treatment program, which is characterized by quite different treatment modalities. The key, however, is that functions are attended to for targets of that stage of treatment, regardless of the treatment modalities used.

Problem-Solving Strategies

Linehan includes at the center of her treatment a broad array of standard behavioral assessment strategies and behavior therapy techniques. A wide array of empirical studies supports efficacy of these techniques in achieving specified treatment goals for other populations. The specific behavioral strategies are organized by Linehan under the general rubric of problem solving, because behavior therapy, in general, can be considered a set of procedures to solve behavioral problems brought to them by patients.

Although it may seem obvious, problem solving first requires an acceptance of the existence of a problem. Therapeutic change commonly occurs within the context of acceptance of the existing situation. In the case of borderline patients, problem solving is enormously complicated by their frequent tendency to view themselves in a negative manner and their inability to regulate consequent emotional distress. On the one pole, they often have difficulty correctly identifying problems in their environment, tending instead to view all problems as somehow self-generated. On the other pole, the view that all problems are self-generated is so painful that the patient often responds by inhibiting the process of self-reflection. By acknowledging the problem, therapist and patient have already begun the process of change by helping the patient frame the problem in a more realistic way.

Identification of the problem(s) causing distress is often not easy. The usual tactic is to teach the patient to view dysfunctional responses, such as parasuicide, as signals of a problem that needs to be solved. The therapist and the patient then conduct a thorough behavioral analysis of these signal responses. The chain of events leading up to the dysfunctional responses is examined in minute detail, including the reciprocal interaction between the environment and the patient's responses (cognitive, emotional, and overt-behavioral). Hypotheses about variables influencing or controlling the dysfunctional behaviors are generated and evaluated.

Next, alternative response chains (i.e., adaptive solutions), which could have been made, and which could be made in the future, are generated and analyzed, as well as the patient's response capabilities (skills). It often becomes clear that the individual does not have the requisite response capabilities to implement the alternative responses or is too emotionally aroused to use them. The therapist then moves to capability-enhancement or exposure strategies. At times, it may be that the patient has the requisite capabilities but is inaccurate in predicting current environmental contingencies. At other times, current contingencies that do operate favor dysfunctional over functional behaviors. For example, a busy friend or family member may become more attentive to the patient when the patient threatens suicide. The therapist then moves to contingency strategies. Finally, cognitive distortions or rigidity in cognitive processing might inhibit functional behavior. In that case cognitive restructuring would be used.

Capability-Enhancement Procedures.   Using these strategies, the therapist acts as a teacher, insisting at every point that the patient actively engage in acquiring and practicing the capabilities needed to cope with everyday life. The borderline individual's passive problem-solving style is challenged directly, forcefully, and repeatedly. Behavioral-skill acquisition techniques are used, as well as techniques for skills strengthening and generalization. These techniques are discussed at length in the skills-training manual (Linehan, 1993b).

Exposure Procedures.   In DBT, the therapist is alert for emotional avoidance and its cues. Frequently, overwhelming emotion precludes many functional behaviors that might substantially improve an individual's life. The first step of exposure procedures is to recognize emotional avoidance and identify the specific cues triggering the avoidance. Once cues are identified, therapists assist patients to expose themselves to the cues that elicit problematic emotions without engaging in the avoidance or escape behaviors. At the same time, therapists encourage patients to engage in actions that reflect the opposite of the avoided emotion. All three steps—exposure to the cue, prevention of the avoidance response, and engagement in the opposite action—must occur together. Therapists spend significant amounts of time orienting patients to the procedure and its efficacy and fostering a commitment by patients to engage in exposure before beginning the procedure.

Contingency-Management Procedures.   Contingency includes two primary procedures: contingency clarification and use of the relationship as a contingency. First, contingency clarification and "professor" strategies involve giving patients information about what can be reasonably expected from the therapist and about the process and requirements of therapy. In addition, the therapists teaches patients about factors that are known to influence behavior in general, and explain to patients any theories and data that might cast light on a particular patient's behavior patterns. Second, the therapy relationship is used as a major contingency. This requires, as far as possible, arrangement of therapist responses to reinforce adaptive, nonsuicidal behaviors and to extinguish maladaptive and suicidal behaviors. Because of the life-threatening nature of suicidal behavior, the therapist necessarily walks a dialectical tightrope, so to speak, neither reinforcing suicidal responses excessively nor ignoring them in such a manner that the patient escalates them to a life-threatening level. The DBT therapist takes some short-term risks to enhance long-term advantage.

Cognitive Modification Procedures. Cognitive modification in DBT addresses several areas of cognition: dysfunctional descriptions of situations and of others, faulty rules that govern the patient's behavior, rigid (nondialectical) thinking, and dysfunctional allocation of attention. A central technique is to teach patients how to observe and describe their own way of thinking, to challenge their dysfunctional cognitions, and to generate alternative ways of thinking that would prove to be more functional. Other cognitive modification techniques include teaching patients to redirect their attention away from stimuli that cue emotional arousal, self-monitoring to increase awareness of their behaviors, and thinking in specific rather than global terms.

Validation Strategies

The essence of the validation strategies is the active acceptance of the patient by the therapist and the communication of such acceptance to the patient. Validation strategies lead the therapist to search for the inherent validity and functionality of the patient's responses. This is in contrast to the usual cognitive and behavior therapies, in which a primary focus of treatment is to search for and replace dysfunctional behavioral processes. The therapist serves as a contrast to the invalidating environments often experienced by the patient.

For heuristic purposes, validation can be conceptualized in six levels (Linehan, 1997). The first three levels are essentially basic therapeutic strategies for building and maintaining rapport. The second three focus on communicating accurately the valid and invalid nature of the patient's behavior and emotional responses. Level 1 validation is concerned with staying awake. That is, the therapist communicates to the patient that he or she is actively listening and attuned to that patient's subtle behaviors. Level 2 involves accurately reflecting the content of the patient's verbalizations to assure that the patient is being heard accurately. Level 3, termed *mind-reading,* consists of stating the content of the patient's communications and experiences that is not explicitly verbalized. Mind reading is unlike interpretation or inference, because it requires explicit (although potentially nonverbal) verification of its accuracy from the patient. Level 4 consists of communicating to the patient that the patient's behavior is completely understandable (i.e., valid) given the patient's learning history and/or biological makeup. Level 5, by contrast, conveys to patients that their behaviors are valid in terms of current circumstances and/or are normative. Finally, Level 6 is a higher level of validity termed *radical genuineness.* The radically genuine therapist recognizes the patient as the patient is in terms of both strengths and capacities as well as difficulties and incapacity. The patient is responded to as a person of equal status who is due equal respect, that is, as more than a disorder. Radical genuineness involves treating the patient as capable of effective and reasonable behavior rather than treating the patient in a condescending manner or as an invalid. One example of radical genuineness is to use the question, "What would I do if this patient were my brother, colleague, or friend?" as a method of choosing an appropriate response. There are no explicit guidelines in DBT for levels of validation as to when and how much each should be used. However, when multiple levels are possible, higher levels are emphasized over lower ones.

Communication Strategies

There are two communication styles in DBT, reciprocal communication and ir-reverence. In reciprocal communication, the therapist strives to reciprocate the engagement, genuineness, and vulnerability of the patient rather than to focus on how the therapy relationship represents other relationships (i.e., interpret transference). Much of reciprocal communication is validation as already de-scribed (especially, levels 1, 5, and 6) and emphasizes acceptance of the patient as an equal member of a real, intimate relationship with the therapist.

In contrast, irreverence is not designed to promote acceptance but to provoke change. Irreverence is designed to get the patient's attention (i.e., to shift the patient's affective response by a comment or response outside the patient's frame of reference). For instance, a therapist might respond to a patient ra-tionalizing why she should quit her job by saying, "You weren't for a second actually believing I would think that this is a good idea, were you?" Irrever-ence serves to save time in therapy by tackling a problem as directly as possible rather than trying to gently work toward it. It is important that irreverence and reciprocal communication balance each other. Too much reciprocity leads to a safe relationship in which nothing changes, whereas shake-up of irreverence can lead to greater changes in the patient's thinking and behavior but risks hurting the patient's feelings.

Dialectical Strategies

The primary dialectic in DBT is that patients need to change their behavior while accepting themselves as they are now. The therapist facilitates change by highlighting dialectical oppositions arising in sessions and in everyday life, and by fostering their successive reconciliation and resolution at increasingly functional levels. Rigid adherence to either pole of the dialectic increases ten-sion between patient and therapist, and it inhibits reconciliation and synthesis.

The dialectical focus involves two levels of therapeutic behavior. First, the therapist is alert to the dialectical balance occurring within the treatment rela-tionship itself. Second, the therapist teaches and models dialectical thinking. (See Basseches, 1984, for a very useful discussion of the characteristics of di-alectical thinking.) Strategies include extensive use of metaphor and paradox, nonresolution of ambiguity, focus on reality as constant change, cognitive chal-lenging and restructuring, and reinforcement for use of intuitive, nonrational knowledge bases.

Case-Management Strategies

In DBT, the therapist's role is that of consultant to the patient, but not to other treatment professionals interacting with the patient. Thus, the therapist helps patients modify their own behavior in order for them to interact effectively with other community professionals. As a rule, the DBT therapist does not as-sist other professionals in planning or modifying their behavior to be effective with the patient. When asked directly, other professionals are advised to fol-low normal procedures. Patients are taught interpersonal skills; other profes-sionals are not.

There are two exceptions to this rule. First, direct intervention is used when substantial harm may come to the patient from professionals who are unwilling to modify their treatment unless a high-power person intervenes. The mental health and judicial systems and public assistance programs are examples where intervention may be necessary. Second, DBT group and individual therapists are in constant contact. From the point of view of DBT, the well-known phenomenon of staff splitting is seen as a problem of the treatment professionals rather than a patient problem. Treatment staff are encouraged to use their interpersonal skills to work out these problems as they arise.

Case Illustration

Background

Jane S. is a white, divorced, single woman, with a seizure condition that is only partially controlled. She has a high school education and is gifted with her hands. An accomplished mechanic who "can fix anything," she also draws well and plays banjo and guitar. Jane was referred at age 28 years to one of the authors (MML) by a psychiatric inpatient unit that had planned to commit her to the state hospital if the referral was not accepted. Although she voluntarily entered the inpatient unit because of suicidal ideation, once there, she had recommenced a characteristic form of parasuicide-strangulation. A different therapist whom Jane had seen for two years had just terminated treatment with her because Jane had taken a nearly lethal drug overdose. In addition, Jane had been fired from her job and evicted from her apartment.

Jane had been hospitalized at least 30 times since the age of twelve years. Among the diagnoses she had accrued were schizophrenia, latent type, with minimal cerebral dysfunction; major depressive episode; organic brain syndrome with seizure disorder; passive-aggressive personality with suicidal acting-out; and BPD with depressive symptoms. At the time of referral, she met criteria for BPD on *DSM-III* and on Gunderson's DIB. Over the years, therapists had placed Jane on a variety of antidepressant and antipsychotic drugs, none of them having lasting effect. She was continuously on either phenytoin (Dilantin) or carbamazepine (Tegretol) for her seizure disorder, although dosages were frequently changed due to side effects and problems in controlling seizures. She had been in individual psychotherapy for nine years, but the longest stretch with any one therapist was the previous two years.

Hospital and school records, and Jane's self-reports, strongly suggest invalidating environments at home and at school, environments in which real problems, such a sibling rivalry and learning disabilities, were left untreated and unsolved. Hospital records reported that her mother had not wanted her pregnancy with Jane and had attempted to miscarry several times. After birth, Jane was sent to live with her grandparents for her first few months. She was then returned to her biological parents, who raised her and two sisters: one older, and one younger, both only a year apart from Jane in age. Jane reports memories of always "losing" in verbal confrontations with her sisters and at school. She apparently has never been able to articulate her emotions well, and she coped either by withdrawing to her room for days at a time or by resorting to physical aggression.

Jane's parasuicidal behavior began at age nine years when, during an argument with her sisters, she tried to jump out of a camper moving at highway speeds. At twelve, the age Jane dates as the beginning of her troubles, she took an overdose and slit her wrists. This was about a year after her father was convicted of embezzlement at his job as a mailman and the family "went into seclusion," withdrawing from social activities. Jane began running away and would stay away two to three days at a time. Over the years, she had continued to cut, head-bang, and overdose. Jane remembers having always been referred to as the "different" one in the family.

Unfortunately, invalidation extended to Jane's school environment as well. Although Jane's hospital records report her as average to superior in intelligence, she was labeled as mentally retarded for most of her school years and was placed in special education classes from second grade on, until it was discovered she had dyslexia at age eighteen years. When Jane asked for remedial training at age eighteen to help her get a job, she was again put in a class with mentally retarded students. She quit and a year later was refused further help because she could *not* demonstrate an ability to keep a job if trained to get one. After keeping a job for two years but being fired because of her epilepsy, she was refused training because she had demonstrated that she *could* find and keep a job.

When treatment began, Jane was going to sleep with a belt wrapped around her neck, tightly enough to seriously constrict circulation. She reported that this was the only way she could stop her painful emotions. During the previous year, she had on six occasions stopped taking her antiseizure medications. Typically, her failure to comply precipitated a series of seizures that would leave her in a deep sleep for two to three days at a time. In addition, there were numerous minor drug overdoses and one nearly lethal one.

Treatment

The first targets of treatment were to reduce parasuicidal activity and form a treatment alliance with the therapist. An important step in forming the alliance had already been taken by virtue of the therapist being the only person willing to accept her in therapy and thereby keep the state from involuntarily committing her once again. Acceptance into therapy was presented as a positive contingency for a strong verbal commitment on Jane's part to actively work at eliminating parasuicide from her coping repertoire. A dialectical frame had been created. By accepting her into treatment, the therapist communicated acceptance of Jane as she was, with compassion for her misery. At the same time, the conditions for acceptance redefined their supportive alliance as one committed to inducing change.

Behavioral analysis and insight strategies were used in sessions to begin tracing the sequence of events that elicited Jane's suicidal urges and behaviors. On diary cards, which she was asked to fill out daily, Jane reported a high frequency of suicidal images that would suddenly appear, as if out of the blue. For example, upon going to clean a plate glass window, Jane would suddenly see the window smashing inward, the thousand shards of glass lacerating and gouging her body. It became clear from the diaries that long hours alone in her apartment correlated highly with suicidal images, which in turn were frequently followed by parasuicide. In contrast, hours spent on manual work activities, such as gardening, construction work, and fixing cars were correlated with low daily misery, low suicidal ideation, and low urges toward parasuicide.

Concurrently, it became apparent that Jane's major therapy-interfering behavior was withdrawal. She would wear mirrored sunglasses, sink down into her chair, lower her head slightly, and remain silent. Therapist questions or comments were followed by long latencies, and many were not responded to at all. (Jane reported that in previous therapies, she would often go entire sessions without speaking.)

Behavioral analysis revealed that withdrawal increased in sessions following family interactions that Jane interpreted as rejecting, following interactions with the therapist in which Jane believed that her therapist took other people's side rather than hers (a common occurrence in the group-skills training), or following unsuccessful assertive attempts directed at institutional systems (e.g., welfare, her bank). Generally, three weeks or so of rather extreme in-session withdrawal was the norm. Withdrawal also followed attempts by the therapist to direct therapy discussions toward previous interpersonal losses and rejections, toward unsuccessful assertion directed toward the "system," or toward current feelings in the session. Such withdrawal could usually be reversed if the therapist redirected the discussion to more neutral topics. The therapist hypothesized that behavioral and verbal withdrawal was a way of avoiding and/or inhibiting intense emotional responses, especially anger. Jane reported that her silences during sessions were attempts to ward off what she felt to be imminent uncontrollable emotions. She felt that if she talked, she would lose control. Her fears of "loss of control" included those of attacking others physically. Also, if she talked, she would experience an emotional intensity that she would then have to tolerate alone after she left the session. These expectations appeared grounded in many previous experiences in which those outcomes were the norm, not the exception. Subsequent close observation of Jane during silences in sessions revealed that during these periods, she tensed most of her cheek, jaw, and throat muscles, and she appeared to have difficulty breathing. At times, she got up, saying she had to leave; at other times, she requested that a window be opened so she could breathe.

These in-session behaviors corresponded to a between-session style of withdrawal from and avoidance of any situation that either did or might elicit negative affect. Between-session withdrawal included staying in her apartment, lying in bed or on the floor; not opening mail, picking up clothes, washing dishes, or bathing; and avoiding contact with her family. As with in-session withdrawal, these behaviors could last for up to three weeks and characteristically followed perceived family, "system," or therapist rejections.

Over the first four months, a characteristic chain of events leading to parasuicide was established: (1) rejection or problem→ (2) painful emotion→ (3) suicide fantasies→ (4) if still in emotional pain, psychological withdrawal→ (5) if still in pain, overdose or strangulation. Suicidal images appeared to be linked with current anger-eliciting incidents or reminders of previous losses and were reframed as signals of anger and/or grief that had not yet been resolved.

A number of strategies were used to treat the parasuicide and the therapy-interfering behaviors. Problem-solving strategies consisted of ongoing behavioral analyses, insight into repetitive patterns, and generation of alternative behaviors to preclude suicidal ideation or to cope with intense emotions and parasuicide urges when they arose. Jane agreed on a goal of spending at least six hours outside her apartment each day, and she kept track of the number of hours out and the nature of the activities undertaken on her diary cards. In addition, behaviors incompatible with parasuicide were generated, such as inducing other intense internal stimuli (e.g., by squeezing ice cubes, standing under a hot shower), listening to relaxation tapes, working on projects, calling friends (or the therapist), mentally reviewing reasons against parasuicide, or leaving her apartment. Further, the alternative of simply experiencing and observing painful emotions (i.e., inhibiting maladaptive and impulsive escape behaviors) had been a goal of therapy from the beginning. This alternative behavior was shaped primarily during group and individual sessions and during phone calls to the therapist.

Contingency strategies, primarily using the relationship with the therapist as the contingent outcome, proved to be a powerful approach to reducing parasuicidal behaviors, increasing the amount of verbal discourse in sessions, and decreasing some between-session withdrawal-avoidance behaviors. At first, this consisted of reminding Jane of her initial commitment to work on stopping parasuicide and eliciting a new commitment, which now also included a good faith effort to approach experiencing at least some of the unbearably painful feelings of anger and grief she worked so hard to escape. Over time, Jane disclosed some of the searing losses she had endured. The only two people Jane ever felt loved her, her grandfather and an aide at the state mental hospital, had died. When she was married, a baby she desperately wanted had to be aborted due to medical complications. Not long after, she returned home from work to find a note from her husband of several months saying goodbye and his clothes and all the furniture gone. She called her parents and asked them to come get her. They refused, saying that because her father had to go to work the next day, there was not time.

Eight months into therapy, Jane's strangling behavior had receded. The focus of therapy became experiencing and expressing her feelings of grief over the sense of never belonging to a family. During this period, Jane disclosed to the therapist an activity that she had engaged in for years but had never revealed to anyone. It involved fantasy activity where she played the role of a reclusive, helpless, frightened damsel in distress, always rescued by a family member. Diary accounts indicated an average of six to eight hours daily devoted to such fantasy activity. The reinforcing effects of this fantasy on helpless and passive behavior patterns were explained to Jane repeatedly, and reducing the hours devoted to this fantasy became a new target of treatment. Jane contended that after parasuicide, this activity was her most effective mode of affect control. Thus, until other more effective methods could be taught, the only treatment was daily self-monitoring.

During the next few months, Jane began to express fears of getting too close to the therapist and thereby setting herself up for another interpersonal rejection and subsequent unendurable emotional experience. Phone calls and therapy sessions were marked by long silences. At the same time, her noncompliance with antiseizure medications became more frequent. Dialectical strategies employed here involved simultaneous validation of Jane's emotional pain with exhortations to expose herself to the painful stimuli and affect she was inhibiting. (Attempts to arrange inpatient flooding sessions to control Jane's behaviors were rejected by inpatient staff afraid of not being able to control her behaviors subsequent to flooding sessions.) Medication noncompliance was framed as another way of avoiding difficult topics and painful emotions, because generally noncompliance resulted in several days of seizures, hospitalization, cessation of discussions of other problems, and so on. It was pointed out that with this continuous quitting and avoidance, Jane's problems never were confronted. This point was made over and over again throughout therapy, using stories, metaphor, and what Jane accurately referred to as "lectures" from the therapist. In addition, therapist contingencies were used; the therapist often remarked that she was getting tired of "pulling Jane back up when she kept jumping off the mountain" (the therapy metaphor here was mountain climbing).

Over time, the therapist shaped therapy work and nonavoidance by both threatening withdrawal of therapy if Jane did not work in therapy and providing praise, encouragement and warmth when Jane reported problem confrontation between sessions or reduced within session avoidance behaviors within sessions. A gradual reduction in emotional inhibition was shaped by combining validation of emotional pain—a reinforcing consequence for both the experience and expression of emotion—with continued emphasis on appropriate emotion-control strategies.

Although at fourteen months into therapy, strangling briefly reappeared in response to a series of major life crises (including bankruptcy, probably incurable neurological problems with one hand, etc.), it again receded. Jane threw out her belt and agreed to discontinue strangling behaviors. Her ability to confront problem situations increased, including the ability to confront her therapist when she felt criticized and her mother in minor incidents when she felt rejected. She also agreed to continue group treatment. These gains were made despite new stresses: her father was accused of child molestation, and, because of her chronic neurological pain in her hand, she became unable to continue many activities, such as mechanics, that had been not only sources of satisfaction, but also potential sources of future income.

At three years in therapy, she had had no hospitalizations for over two years and no parasuicide for 18 months, and was considered to have moved to stage 2 of treatment. It was then that she revealed, for the first time, a history of six years of childhood incest by her father. She and her therapist then conducted ten sessions of formal exposure regarding that trauma. It took some time to identify that the relevant cue for her distress was the size differential between herself and her father. This discovery was made when, in the process of a behavioral analysis, the therapist tested a cue of standing on a chair. With exposure, Jane's ability to experience her emotions became substantively more manageable. This also generalized to her accepting increasing physical pain due to her neurological problems. During this time she also learned that her father had propositioned both of her sisters who had said no.

At this time, Jane was considered to be in stage 3 treatment. Therapy was reduced in frequency to one session per month due to her therapist's need to reduce her clinical work. Jane moved into a better apartment and began a volunteer job. However, her neurological problems continued to progress and she was eventually directed by her doctor to discontinue volunteer work. Acceptance of the severity and progressive nature of her medical problems precipitated a brief episode of suicidal ideation, which was addressed in therapy and resolved quickly. Suicidal ideation was treated as a signal of the need for greater problem solving with regard to her neurological problems, and she was referred to a pain clinic for evaluation. Their assessment was that she was doing well given the level of damage, and they worked with her to minimize her disability. Jane has had continued interaction with her family, although, interestingly, during this time both of her sisters have been doing much worse emotionally due to marital and substance-abuse problems.

Jane now walks with a cane but is able to continue some gardening and is able to drive. She works with computers and the Internet and has become the "together" person in her family. She decided to terminate her monthly therapy with her therapist so she could begin weekly counseling elsewhere.

ALTERNATIVE TREATMENT OPTIONS

There are four treatments that are common alternatives to behavior therapy in the treatment of BPD: pharmacotherapy, psychiatric inpatient treatment, cognitive therapy, and long-term psychodynamic therapy. We will review each of these in turn from a behavioral perspective.

PHARMACOTHERAPY

The utility of pharmacotherapy for the treatment of borderline patients is discussed extensively elsewhere (for review, see Dimeff, McDavid, & Linehan, in press). There are no available data to support a psychotropic medication as a sufficient stand-alone treatment for BPD. Many of the studies of pharmacotherapy have been conducted among inpatients and all included at least some minimal form of psychotherapy. Additionally, no single psychotropic medication has emerged as the preferred adjunctive medication in treating individuals with BPD.

There are also very few studies of pharmacotherapy with highly suicidal outpatient borderline patients. To our knowledge, there is no direct evidence that pharmacotherapy of any type substantially reduces suicide risk in an outpatient population. Furthermore, risk of overdose poses a lethal side effect, so to speak, that cannot be ignored. Thus, the general protocol in DBT is to eliminate lethal drugs, including antidepressants and oral neuroleptics, from the treatment regime, at least until suicidal behaviors are well under control. When potentially lethal medication is required (e.g., lithium in a patient also meeting criteria for bipolar disorder), attempts are made to induce the patient to arrange for control of the lethal medication by a third party (consultant strategy). At times, a therapist might require such control or monitoring of blood levels to prevent medication hoarding.

In the first study of the efficacy of DBT, neither the DBT group nor the treatment-as-usual group reported decreases in negative affect following one year of treatment (Linehan, Armstrong, Suarez, Allmon, & Heard, 1991). This is in contrast to clear reductions in parasuicidal behavior among the DBT patients. In other words, DBT patients learned more adaptive ways to cope, although they did not feel they were experiencing less intense emotional pain. These findings suggest that the addition of pharmacotherapy to address depressed moods, at least during the second year if not earlier, might be very helpful to these patients.

PSYCHIATRIC INPATIENT TREATMENT

There are no empirical data showing that hospitalizing suicidal borderline patients actually reduces suicide risk. Indeed, among 10 studies that randomly assigned serious psychiatric patients, including presumably suicidal borderline patients, to either inpatient or outpatient treatment, none showed a superiority for inpatient treatment (Kiesler, 1982). In light of these points, DBT rarely recommends psychiatric hospitalization as a response either to suicide risk or to actual parasuicidal behavior. Generally, hospitalization is only recommended when a therapist feels unable to provide or arrange for the minimum level of support believed absolutely essential to keep the patient alive at the moment. Hospitalization is often viewed as a treatment strategy to benefit the therapist rather than the patient—a worthy goal.

In contrast to reservations about the efficacy of hospitalization held by a DBT therapist, our experience is that suicidal borderline patients often insist that they need to be hospitalized. Our strategy here is to validate the inherent wisdom of patients in determining what is best for them while also maintaining our own point of view. When we disagree about the wisdom of hospitalization, we instruct the patient in how to go about getting into a hospital, but we refuse to get actively engaged in the process. Every attempt is made to reinforce patients for both accurately estimating their capacities to endure and cope out of a hospital, as well as for trusting their own wise judgment in making decisions about care. Interestingly, with this approach, DBT subjects in the aforementioned treatment outcome study did not differ from community treatment-as-usual subjects in the number of admissions to a psychiatric inpatient unit. In addition, the average days per visit appeared lower among the DBT subjects.

COGNITIVE THERAPY

Application of cognitive therapies to BPD is receiving increasing attention (Pretzer & Beck, 1996; Young, 1994; Young & Swift, 1988). In general, these treatments are modified versions of Beck's (1976) cognitive therapy. Young's (1994) treatment, for example, identifies and focuses on changing long-standing maladaptive schemas hypothesized to be significant in terms of etiology and maintenance of BPD. Unfortunately, there are no empirical data on the efficacy of these strategies with borderline patients.

Both Turner's treatment and DBT incorporate many cognitive therapy strategies. In many ways, DBT grew out of initial unsuccessful attempts by Linehan to apply cognitive-restructuring procedures to borderline patients. Borderline patients are particularly sensitive to the emotionally invalidating message that can sometimes be incorporated unwittingly within a cognitive approach (e.g., "if you just think straight, you will not have these problems;" that logical, rational thought is superior to intuitive thought). In addition, behavioral change is not always preceded by cognitive restructuring. In fact, it is frequently seen in DBT that cognitive restructuring occurs naturally when behavior is changed directly (i.e., through contingency management, exposure, skills training, etc.).

LONG-TERM PSYCHODYNAMIC THERAPY

Several psychodynamic therapies have been developed over the past 30 years by Kernberg, Masterson-Rinsley, and Kohut (for review, see Chatham, 1985). All three of these treatments are based on a developmental perspective rooted in parent-child interactions. There are many commonalties between the developmental issues identified by these theorists and the invalidating environment described by Linehan (1993a). Also, as in behavioral treatments, motivation is considered a central concept. However, the conceptual basis of motivation is quite different between psychodynamic and behavioral treatments. In the former, motivation is a function of unconscious processes resulting from early-developed personality traits. In behavioral treatments, by contrast, motivation is conceptualized as a function of both the present environment and the individuals learning history. Environmental contingencies and contexts, skill deficits, and overly rigid thinking are identified as the basis of a patient's motivation. Both DBT and psychodynamic treatments emphasize the need for in-depth analysis of factors maintaining disordered behavior. Unlike psychodynamic treatments, however, behavioral treatments maintain the need for behavior change strategies in addition to the insight gained from analysis of the behaviors. Finally, both treatments focus on the relationship as a vehicle for change. However, whereas psychodynamic treatments emphasize the therapy relationship as a representation of other outside relationships, behavioral treatments emphasize the reality of the relationship and use the relationship as a practice ground for teaching interpersonal skills that will then generalize to other intimate relationships.

PRESCRIPTIVE TREATMENT AND MANAGED CARE

Based on its demonstrated efficacy, DBT is considered a prescriptive treatment for both borderline personality disorder and suicidal behavior. Replication of the efficacy of DBT has been shown in a sample of female veterans with BPD (Koons & Robins, 1998), suicidal adolescents (Miller, Rathus, Linehan, Wetzler, & Leigh, 1997), and is underway at our clinic for parasuicidal women with BPD. In addition, DBT has been modified and evaluations are underway for the DBT treatment of substance abuse (Linehan et al., 1998), of binge-eating disorder (personal communication with Christy Telch), and of chronic depression in the elderly (personal communication with Thomas Lynch).

Historically, many public and private funders of behavioral health services have been unwilling to fund services for patients with BPD because of the long-standing belief that BPD, and personality disorders in general, are untreatable disorders. Others, often public mental-health systems, provide outpatient treatment as a more affordable alternative to inpatient treatment with the target of decreasing hospitalization rather than improving quality of life or completing a course of treatment. Short-term follow-up studies of BPD patients have found little change in the level of functioning and consistently high rates of psychiatric hospitalization over two to five years (Barasch, Frances, & Hurt, 1985; Dahl, 1986; Richman & Charles, 1976). Other studies have found that four to seven years after index assessment, 57 percent to 67 percent of patients continued to meet criteria (Kullgren, 1992; Pope, Jonas, Hudson, Cohen, & Gunderson, 1983).

However, since publication of DBT's efficacy in randomized controlled trials, DBT has been approved for treatment for borderline personality disorder by many behavioral health-maintenance organizations. This is also true of several state departments of mental health who fund DBT as the Medicaid treatment for BPD and suicidal behavior. DBT is a comprehensive treatment that generally involves multiple weekly sessions, phone contact, and consultation meetings for therapists. As such, it is a more expensive treatment than many outpatient mental health services covered by health maintenance organizations. Interestingly in today's environment of limited services, DBT is generally only funded when all functions and modes of standard DBT are included (i.e., including skills training and therapist consultation).

This emphasis on empirical validation of psychosocial treatments appears to be taking firm root in the behavioral health services field. Treatments long considered to be the standard of care are increasingly less likely to be funded. This is in stark contrast to the medical services field in which most treatments reflect standard of care and relatively few have been empirically validated and where standard of care is often funded despite empirically validated alternatives. This may largely reflect the relative youth of behavioral interventions as well as the difficulties in measuring mental health treatment outcomes as compared to medicine where death or medical disability is more easily measured. For whatever reason, it is clear that studies of the efficacy and effectiveness of treatments for BPD, as well as component analysis within treatments, for this population are critical.

SUMMARY

There are two behavioral treatments currently available that are designed specifically for BPD: dialectical behavior therapy (Linehan, 1993a, 1993b) and bio-cognitive-behavioral treatment (Turner, 1987, 1989), of which only the former has been validated in a randomized controlled trial. Both treatments focus on treating emotional dysregulation and its cognitive and interpersonal consequences. DBT is a comprehensive principle-based treatment that is conceptualized in terms of levels of disorder and corresponding stages, targets, and functions of treatment. Although comprehensive treatments are both expensive (relatively) to provide as well as to learn, such comprehensive treatments could be expected for a disorder that is severe and persistent and historically difficult to treat. Future research is needed to determine the necessary and sufficient components of a behavioral treatment for BPD.

REFERENCES

Akiskal, H.S. (1994). The temperamental borders of affective disorders. *Acta Psychiatrica Scandinavica, 89*(Suppl. 379), 32–37.

American Psychiatric Association. (1994). *Diagnostic and statistical manual of mental disorder* (4th ed.). Washington, DC: Author.

Barasch, A., Frances, A.J., & Hurt, S.W. (1985). Stability and distinctness of borderline personality disorder. *American Journal of Psychiatry, 142*, 1484–1486.

Barley, W.D. (1996). Health care policy, psychotherapy research, and the future of psychotherapy. *American Psychologist, 51*, 1050–1058.

Basseches, M. (1984). *Dialectical thinking and adult development.* Norwood, NJ: Ablex.

Beck, A.T. (1976). *Cognitive therapy and the emotional disorders.* New York: International University Press.

Blais, M.A., Hilsenroth, M.J., & Castlebury, F.D. (1997). Content validity of the *DSM-IV* borderline and narcissisti personality disorder criteria sets. *Comprehensive Psychiatry, 38*, 31–37.

Briere, J. (1984). *The effects of childhood sexual abuse on later psychological functioning: Defining a post-sexual-abuse syndrome.* Unpublished manuscript.

Chatham, P.M. (1985). *Treatment of the borderline personality.* New York: Aronson.

Clark, L.A., Livesley, W.J., & Morey, L.C. (1997). Personality disorder assessment: The challenge of construct validity. *Journal of Personality Disorders, 11,* 205–231.

Clarkin, J., Hull, J., & Hurt, S.W. (1993). Factor structure of borderline personality disorder criteria. *Journal of Personality Disorders, 7,* 137–143.

Clarkin, J., Widiger, T.A., Frances, A.J., Hurt, F.W., & Gilmore, M. (1983). Prototypic typology and the borderline personality disorder. *Journal of Abnormal Psychology, 92*(3), 263–275.

Cloninger, C. (1987). A systematic method for clinical description and classification of personality variants. *Archives of General Psychiatry, 44,* 573–588.

Dahl, A.A. (1986). Prognosis of the borderline disorders. *Psychopathology, 19,* 68–79.

Dimeff, L.A., McDavid, J., & Linehan, M.M. (in press). Pharmacotherapy for borderline personality disorder: A review of the literature and recommendations for treatment. *Clinical Psychology in Medical Settings.*

Ekselius, L., Lindstrom, E., von Knorring, L., Bodlund, O., & Kullgren, G. (1994). SCID II interviews and the SCID screen questionnaire as diagnostic tools for personality disorders in *DSM-III-R. Acta Psychiatrica Scandinavica, 90,* 120–123.

Firestone, S. (1970). *The dialectic of sex: The case for feminist revolution.* New York: Bantam Books.

First, M.B., Spitzer, R.L., Gibbons, M., & Williams, J.B.W. (1995). *Structured clinical interview for axis I* DSM-IV *disorders—patient edition (SCID-I/P).* New York: Biometrics Research Department, NY State Psychiatric Institute.

First, M.B., Spitzer, R.L., Gibbons, M., Williams, J.B.W., & Benjamin, L. (1996). *User's guide for the structured clinical interview for* DSM-IV *axis II personality disorders (SCID-II).* New York: Biometrics Research Department, New York State Psychiatric Institute.

Follette, W.C. (1997). A behavior analytic conceptualization of personality disorders: A response to Clark, Livesley, and Morey. *Journal of Personality Disorders, 11,* 232–241.

Frances, A., Clarkin, J., Gilmore, M., Hurt, S.W., & Brown, R. (1984). Reliability of criteria for borderline personality disorder: A comparison of *DSM-III* and the diagnostic interview for borderline patients. *American Journal of Psychiatry, 141,* 1080–1084.

Gottman, J., & Katz, L.F. (1990). Effects of marital discord on young children's peer interaction and health. *Developmental Psychology, 25,* 373–381.

Higgins, S.T. (1997). Potential contributions of the community reinforcement approach and contingency management to broadening the base of substance abuse treatment. In J.A. Tucker, D.A. Donovan, & G.A. Marlatt (Eds.), *Changing addictive behavior: Moving beyond therapy assisted change.* New York: Guilford Press.

Higgins, S.T., Budney, A.J., Bickel, W.K., Hughes, J.R., Foeg, F., & Badger, G. (1993). Achieving cocaine abstinence with a behavioral approach. *American Journal of Psychiatry, 150,* 763–869.

Hyler, S.E., Skodol, A.E., Oldham, J.M., Kellman, H.D., & Doidge, N. (1992). Validity of the personality diagnostic questionnaire—revised: A replication in an outpatient sample. *Comprehensive Psychiatry, 33,* 73–77.

Izard, C.E., & Kobak, R.R. (1991). Emotions systems functioning and emotion regulation. In J. Garber & K.A. Dodge (Eds.), *The development of emotion regulation and dysregulation* (pp. 303–322). England: Cambridge University Press.

Jacobsberg, L., & Perry, S. (1995). Diagnostic agreement between the SCID-II screening questionnaire and the personality disorder examination. *Journal of Personality Assessment, 65,* 428–433.

Kegan, R. (1982). *The evolving self: Problem and process in human development.* Cambridge, MA: Harvard University Press.

Kiesler, C.A. (1982). Mental hospitals and alternative care: Noninstitutionalization as potential public policy for mental patients. *American Psychologist, 37*, 349–360.

Koerner, K., & Linehan, M.M. (1997). Case formulation in dialectical behavior therapy for borderline personality disorder. In T. Eells (Ed.), *Handbook of psychotherapy case formulation* (pp. 340–367). New York: Guilford Press.

Kolb, J.E., & Gunderson, J.G. (1980). Diagnosing borderline patients with a semi-structured interview. *Archives of General Psychiatry, 37*, 37–41.

Koons, C.R., & Robins, C.J. (1998). *Efficacy of dialectical behavior therapy with borderline women veterans: A randomized controlled trial.* Unpublished manuscript. Durham, NC: Duke VA Medical Center.

Kuhn, T.S. (1970). *The structure of scientific revolutions.* Chicago: University of Chicago Press.

Kullgren, G. (1992). Personality disorders among psychiatric inpatients. *Nordisk Psykiastrisktidsskrift, 46*, 27–32.

Levins, R., & Lewontin, R. (1985). *The dialectical biologist.* Cambridge, MA: Harvard University Press.

Linehan, M.M. (1993a). *Cognitive behavioral therapy of borderline personality disorder.* New York: Guilford Press.

Linehan, M.M. (1993b). *Skills training manual for treating borderline personality disorder.* New York: Guilford Press.

Linehan, M.M. (1997). Validation and psychotherapy. In A. Bohart & L. Greenberg (Eds.), *Empathy reconsidered: New directions in psychotherapy.* Washington, DC: American Psychological Association.

Linehan, M.M. (in press). Development, evaluation, and dissemination of effective psychosocial treatments: Stages of disorder, levels of care, and stages of treatment research. In M.D. Glantz & C.R. Hartel (Eds.), *Drug abuse: Origins and interventions.* Washington, DC: American Psychological Association.

Linehan, M.M., Armstrong, H.E., Suarez, A., Allmon, D., & Heard, H.L. (1991). Cognitive-behavioral treatment of chronically parasuicidal borderline patients. *Archives of General Psychiatry, 48*, 1060–1064.

Linehan, M.M., & Dimeff, L.A. (1998). *Dialectical behavior therapy manual of treatment interventions for substance abusers with borderline personality disorder.* Unpublished manual. Department of Psychology, University of Washington.

Linehan, M.M., Heard, H.L., & Armstrong, H.E. (1993). Naturalistic follow-up of a behavioral treatment for chronically parasuicidal borderline patients. *Archives of General Psychiatry, 50*, 971–974.

Linehan, M.M., & Schmidt, H.I. (1995). The dialectics of effective treatment of borderline personality disorder. In W.O. O'Donohue & L. Krasner (Eds.), *Theories in behavior therapy: Exploring behavior change* (pp. 553–584). Washington, DC: American Psychological Association.

Linehan, M.M., Schmidt, H.I., Kanter, J.S., Craft, J.C., Dimeff, L.A., Comtois, K., & McDavid, J. (1998). Randomized control trial of DBT-S vs. treatment-as-usual with BPD substance abusers. In S.T. Higgins (Chair.), *Therapy for borderline personality and substance abuse.* Symposium conducted at the American Psychiatric Association Convention, Toronto, Canada.

Linehan, M.M., Tutek, D.A., Heard, H.L., & Armstrong, H.E. (1994). Interpersonal outcome of cognitive behavioral treatment for chronically suicidal borderline patients. *American Journal of Psychiatry, 151*, 1771–1776.

Loranger, A.W. (1992). Are current self-report and interview measures adequate for epidemiological studies of personality disorders? *Journal of Personality Disorders, 6,* 313–325.

Loranger, A.W., Sartorius, N., Andreoli, A., Berger, P., Buchheim, P., Channabasavanna, S.M., Coid, B., Dahl, A., Diekstra, R.F., Ferguson, B., & et al. (1994). The international personality disorder examination. The World Health Organization/alcohol, drug abuse, and mental health administration international pilot study of personality disorders. *Archives of General Psychiatry, 51,* 215–224.

Malatesta, C.Z. (1990). The role of emotions in the development and organization of personality. In R.A. Thompson (Ed.), *Socioemotional development: Nebraska Symposium on Motivation, 1988* (pp. 1–56). Lincoln and London: University of Nebraska.

Marx, K., & Engels, F. (1970). *Selected works.* New York: International Press.

Miller, A., Rathus, J.H., Linehan, M.M., Wetzler, S., & Leigh, E. (1997). Dialectical behavior therapy adapted for suicidal adolescents. *Journal of Practical Psychiatry and Behavioral Health, 3,* 78–86.

Mischel, W. (1968). *Personality and assessment.* New York: Wiley.

Mischel, W. (1990). Personality dispositions revisited and revised: A view after three decades. In L.A. Pervin (Ed.), *Handbook of personality theory and research* (pp. 111–134). New York: Guilford Press.

Nigg, J.T., & Goldsmith, H.H. (1994). Genetics of personality disorders: Perspectives from personality and psychopathology research. *Psychological Bulletin, 115,* 346–380.

Paris, J. (1994). The etiology of borderline personality disorder: A biopsychosocial approach. *Psychiatry, 57,* 316–323.

Patrick, J., Links, P., van Reekum, R., & Mitton, J.E. (1995). Using the PDQ-R scale as a brief screening measure in the differential diagnosis of personality disorder. *Journal of Personality Disorders, 9,* 266–274.

Perry, J.C. (1992). Problems and considerations in the valid assessment of personality disorders. *American Journal of Psychiatry, 149,* 1645–1653.

Persons, J.B. (1986). The advantages of studying psychological phenomena rather than psychiatric diagnoses. *American Psychologist, 41,* 1252–1260.

Pope, H.G., Jonas, J.M., Hudson, J.I., Cohen, B.M., & Gunderson, J.G. (1983). The validity of *DSM-III* borderline personality disorder: A phenomenologic, family history, treatment response, and long term follow-up study. *Archives of General Psychiatry, 40,* 23–30.

Pretzer, J., & Beck, A.T. (1996). A cognitive theory of personality disorders. In J.F. Clarkin, M.F. Lenzenweger, & et al. (Eds.), *Major theories of personality disorder* (pp. 36–105). New York: Guilford Press.

Reiser, D.E., & Levenson, H. (1984). Abuses of the borderline diagnosis: A clinical problem with teaching opportunities. *American Journal of Psychiatry, 141*(12), 1528–1532.

Richman, J., & Charles, E. (1976). Patient dissatisfaction and attempted suicide. *Community Mental Health Journal, 12*(3), 301–305.

Schwartz, G.E. (1982). Psychophysiological patterning of emotion revisited: A systems perspective. In C.E. Izard (Ed.), *Measuring emotions in infants and children* (pp. 67–93). Cambridge, England: Cambridge University.

Staats, A.W. (1975). *Social behaviorism.* Homewood, IL: Dorsey Press.

Swann, W.B. (1997). The trouble with change: Self-verification and allegiance to the self. *Psychological Science, 8,* 177–179.

Torgersen, S. (1994). Genetics in borderline conditions. *Acta Psychiatrica Scandinavica, 89*(Suppl. 379), 19–25.

Turner, R.M. (1987). Treating borderline personality disorder in the partial hospital setting. *International Journal of Partial Hospitalization, 4*(4), 257–269.

Turner, R.M. (1989). Case study evaluations of a bio-cognitive-behavioral approach for the treatment of borderline personality disorder. *Behavior Therapy, 20,* 477–489.

Turner, R.M. (1995). *A bio-social learning approach to borderline personality disorder.* Unpublished document.

Wallace, J. (1966). An abilities conception of personality: Some implications for personality measurement. *American Psychologist, 21,* 132–138.

Widiger, T.A., & Frances, A. (1987). Definitions and diagnoses: A brief response to Morey and McNamara. *Journal of Abnormal Psychology, 96,* 286–287.

World Health Organization. (1993). *The ICD-10 classification of mental and behavioural disorders: Diagnostic criteria for research.* Geneva: Author.

Young, J.E. (1994). *Cognitive therapy for personality disorders: A schema-focused approach* (2nd ed.). Sarasota, FL: Professional Resource Press.

Young, J.E., & Swift, W. (1988). Schema-focused cognitive therapy for personality disorders. *International Cognitive Therapy Newsletter, 4*(1), 5–14.

Zanarini, M.C., Gunderson, J.G., Frankenburg, F.R., & Chauncey, D.L. (1989). The revised diagnostic interview for borderlines: Discriminating borderline personality disorder from other axis II disorders. *Journal of Personality Disorders, 3*(1), 10–18.

Zweig-Frank, H., & Paris, J. (1995). The five-factor model of personality in borderline and nonborderline personality disorders. *Canadian Journal of Psychiatry, 40,* 523–526.

CHAPTER 23

Pharmacotherapy

RICHARD KAVOUSSI and EMIL F. COCCARO

CONCEPTUALIZATION

Although borderline personality disorder (BPD) is widely diagnosed in clinical settings, treatment of these patients poses a significant problem for clinicians. Borderline patients are difficult to treat, and their long-term outcomes are often poor (Trull, Useda, Conforti, & Doan, 1997). Just as psychotherapy with these patients can be fraught with problems, the appropriate treatment of the borderline patient with medicines can be difficult. One of the reasons for this is that BPD describes a heterogeneous group of patients, some with more affective symptoms, some with more anger and behavioral problems, and some with more psychotic-like or dissociative symptoms. As we will discuss later, there is also a great deal of overlap between borderline personality and other disorders. Such diagnostic problems make it difficult to conduct and interpret studies of pharmacologic treatment of these patients.

In fact, there is no single agent that has been shown to be of benefit in treating BPD as a discrete entity. This differs from the pharmacological treatment of other psychiatric disorders, which may have specific medications indicated for their treatment (i.e., antidepressants for major depression, antimanic agents for bipolar disorder, antipsychotic medicines for schizophrenia). There is emerging evidence, however, that medicines can be used successfully to treat specific target symptoms in borderline patients. This suggests that the best approach to treating a patient with BPD with medication is to identify particular pathological behaviors or traits and then target those behaviors with specific medications.

Our chapter reviews some of the diagnostic problems inherent in the borderline construct. Then we review the literature on medication treatment of borderline personality, and we attempt to define possible pathological traits and behaviors that may benefit from medication treatment. These traits include impulsive aggression, affective lability, transient psychotic phenomenon, self-destructive behavior, and extreme responses to rejection. We conclude with a discussion of the overall clinical implications of these findings and make recommendations for future research.

DIAGNOSTIC ISSUES AND PROBLEMS

Unfortunately, diagnosis of BPD has not been adequately validated because of inconclusive and discordant findings across studies of phenomenology, familial transmission, biology, and treatment response. Since the diagnosis was first used by psychoanalysts to describe patients with pathology "on the border" between their "neurotic" and psychotic patients, there have been multiple criteria sets developed (e.g., Gunderson & Singer, 1975; Kernberg, 1967; Knight, 1953; Spitzer, Endicott, & Gibbon, 1979). Even with use of a single criteria set, such as that found in *DSM-IV*, there is still debate concerning such categorical models of personality disorders. Many investigators propose that personality psychopathology occurs on a continuum with "normal" personality traits, rather than as discrete diagnoses (Frances, 1982). Such dimensional models have been proposed in the past to explore personality pathology in general (e.g., the Minnesota Multiphasic Personality Inventory [MMPI] scales, the personality disorder clusters of *DSM-IV*). The advantage of such a dimensional classification is that personality-disorder symptom clusters, rather than discrete diagnoses, appear to correlate with biologic markers and treatment response.

Another problem is that there is a great deal of overlap between borderline personality disorder (BPD) and other *DSM-IV* disorders (both Axis I and Axis II). In particular, there is much overlap between BPD and somatization disorders, substance abuse disorders, affective disorders, and anxiety disorders (Hudziak et al., 1996). Most borderline patients meet more than one personality disorder diagnosis, and there is a great deal of comorbidity with schizotypal personality disorder (Kavoussi & Siever, 1992) and antisocial personality disorder (Paris, 1997). This overlap makes it difficult to investigate treatments for pure BPD, and it complicates much of the literature on the treatment of this disorder.

Based on the foregoing discussion, it appears prudent to attempt to postulate several symptom clusters for BPD and then to target medication treatment to those dimensions. Recent biological and treatment studies suggest the following as candidates for treatment: (1) impulsivity and intense anger, (2) affective lability, (3) transient psychotic symptoms, (4) self-destructive behavior, and (5) extreme rejection sensitivity. In the next section, we will explore each of these dimensions and the evidence for selective treatment response in each cluster.

TREATMENT STRATEGIES

IMPULSIVITY AND INTENSE ANGER

Abnormalities in central serotonin (5HT) function correlate with impulsive aggression. This finding has been replicated in many studies and in many different populations. For example, numerous studies show that the major metabolite of serotonin, 5-hydroxyindolacetic acid (5-HIAA), is reduced in the cerebrospinal fluid (CSF) of subjects with a history of aggression (violence toward others and violent suicide attempts) compared with those with no such history (Brown, Goodwin, Ballenger, Goyer, & Major, 1979; Linnoila et al., 1983).

Other biological studies also show evidence of a relationship between decreased central 5-HT function and impulsive aggression in borderline personality. Borderline patients with high degrees of lifelong irritability and impulsive aggression have a lower prolactin response to fenfluramine compared with normal controls. In fact, there is a strong inverse relationship between the prolactin response to fenfluramine challenge and measures of irritable, impulsive aggression in personality-disorder patients, whatever the particular personality disorder (Coccaro et al., 1989). Abnormal serotonin functioning in borderline patients has also been found using m-chlorophenylpiperazine (m-CPP) (Hollander et al., 1994) and the 5HT1A receptor agonists buspirone (Coccaro, Gabriel, & Siever, 1990) and ipsapirone (Coccaro, Kavoussi, & Hauger, 1995). Reduced numbers of platelet 5HT transporter sites are associated with a life history of aggressive behavior in patients with borderline personality disorder (Coccaro, Kavoussi, Sheline, Lish, & Cszernansky, 1996).

Given that abnormalities in serotonin function produce a vulnerability to impulsive anger and aggression, medications that selectively enhance serotonin function should be particularly effective in reducing these maladaptive traits. In fact, several studies have now shown just that. In a 13-week, double-blind study of 21 patients with BPD, there was a clinically and statistically significant decrease in anger among patients receiving fluoxetine, independent of changes in depression (Salzman et al., 1995). In an open trial of 11 patients, sertraline was effective in reducing impulsive aggression and irritability in nondepressed patients with a variety of personality disorders (Kavoussi, Liu, & Coccaro, 1994). Fluoxetine was generally effective during an open treatment trial of inpatients with BPD, reducing both suicidal ideation and impulse control problems (Cornelius, Soloff, Perel, & Ulrich, 1991). In a 14-week, double-blind, placebo-controlled trial, fluoxetine treatment was associated with substantial reductions in overt aggressive behavior and irritability in 39 nondepressed personality-disordered outpatients with histories of prominent impulsive aggressive behavior (Coccaro & Kavoussi, 1997). This improvement was independent of any changes in Hamilton anxiety or depression scores. Effective doses of fluoxetine ranged from 20 mg/day to 60 mg/day.

As if to confirm the hypothesis that selective serotonin medicines are of value in treating impulsive anger and aggression in borderline personality, studies of nonselective medicines have demonstrated significantly less efficacy. For example, tricyclic antidepressants (which do not selectively enhance serotonin functioning) have been associated with increased impulse control problems in some borderline patients—almost half of the amitriptyline treated patients had more acting-out behavior than at baseline (Soloff, George, Nathan, Schulz, & Perel, 1986). In another double-blind study, desipramine was no better than a placebo in reducing aggression in patients with BPD (Links et al., 1990).

Although serotonin-enhancing medicines hold the most promise for reducing impulsivity and anger in borderline patients, other medicines may also be of benefit in reducing anger and impulsivity in borderline patients. Lithium has been found to decrease impulsive and aggressive behaviors in various populations of patients. A study comparing lithium, desipramine, and placebo in patients with BPD found lithium to be superior to desipramine and placebo on behavioral measures of aggression (Links, Steiner, Boiago, & Irwin, 1990). Other studies (Sheard, Marini, Bridges, & Wagner, 1976; Tupin et al., 1973) have shown lithium to be effective in suppressing impulsive aggressive behaviors in aggressive prison inmates. A blinded, placebo-controlled trial found the antiseizure and antimanic agent carbamazepine to be the only medicine that selectively decreased behavioral outbursts in patients with BPD (Cowdry & Gardner, 1988).

The antipsychotic medication thioridazine has been reported to reduce impulsive behavior in patients with BPD (Teicher et al., 1989). Similarly, treatment with low-dose haloperidol was associated with significant improvement in ratings of hostility and impulsivity compared to amitriptyline and placebo in a large sample of patients with borderline and/or schizotypal personality disorder (Soloff et al., 1989). However, these findings were not reproduced in two other double-blind, placebo-controlled studies of borderline and schizotypal personality-disordered patients treated with thiothixine (Goldberg et al., 1986) or trifluoperazine (Cowdry & Gardner, 1988). On the other hand, the newer, atypical antipsychotic agents (i.e., clozapine, risperidone, olanzapine, sertindole, quetiapine) may be more effective and have fewer side effects than traditional antipsychotic drugs in treating anger and aggression in BPD.

AFFECTIVE LABILITY

Affective instability is a prominent symptom of BPD. Some authors suggest that affective lability occurs on a spectrum with other disorders of mood—dysthymia, cyclothymia, hypomania, bipolar illness (Akiskal, 1981). This would imply that affective lability should respond to medicines that treat mood swings in other affective disorders (e.g., antimanic medications). In fact, studies do suggest that these medicines (i.e., lithium, divalproex, carbamazepine) can be effective in reducing affective lability in borderline patients. Prior to the development of *DSM-III* criteria, psychopharmacologists diagnosed some patients with "emotionally unstable character disorder," that is, rapidly shifting and intensely felt affective states (Rifkin et al., 1972). Patients with this diagnosis responded better to lithium than to placebo or imipramine. In several open trials, borderline patients have also shown decreased mood lability and irritability following open treatment with divalproex sodium, another treatment for mania (Stein, Simeon, Frenkel, Islam, & Hollander, 1995; Wilcox, 1995). These responses support the possibility, noted above, that borderline patients suffer from a subclinical affective disorder similar to bipolar disorder or cyclothymia.

PSYCHOTIC SYMPTOMS

Psychotic episodes are common in patients with BPD, regardless of whether a concurrent Axis I disorder is present. Such episodes increase the risk of hospitalization in these patients (Miller, Abrams, Dulit, & Fyer, 1993). In fact, an additional criterion—"transient, stress-related paranoid ideation or severe dissociative symptoms" was added to the *DSM-IV* criteria for BPD. It is not surprising that several studies report that low doses of antipsychotic medications are effective in treating borderline patients. Early reports suggested that antipsychotic medicines were mildly to moderately effective in improving the global status of these patients (Brinkley, Beitman, & Friedel, 1979; Leone, 1982; Serban & Siegel, 1984).

Some studies suggest further that these medicines are specifically effective in treating psychotic symptoms in borderline patients, including suspiciousness, ideas of reference, odd communication, social isolation, impulse-action, and hostility. In a controlled study (Goldberg et al., 1986), investigators examined efficacy of the antipsychotic thiothixene compared with placebo in 50 patients who were either borderline or schizotypal and who also had a history of a brief psychotic episode. Overall, thiothixene demonstrated significant drug-placebo differences for the SCL-90 subscales related to psychoticism, illusions, ideas of reference, and phobic anxiety. The medication's effects were limited to these psychotic-like personality symptoms. Another controlled study (Soloff et al., 1989) compared the antipsychotic medicine haloperidol, the antidepressant amitriptyline, and placebo in 90 borderline patients. The antipsychotic was superior to placebo and amitriptyline in a variety of symptom areas related to psychosis: schizotypal symptoms, hostility, and suspiciousness. These results support the idea that low doses of antipsychotics are most useful in treating psychotic-like traits in borderline patients.

Unfortunately, risks of side effects (such as tardive dyskinesia) make most clinicians wary of using these medicines indiscriminately. The newer antipsychotics, such as clozapine, risperidone, olanzapine, sertindole, and quetiapine, have lower rates of side effects than the older antipsychotics and may replace them as treatments for psychotic symptoms in borderline patients. In a study of fifteen patients with BPD and psychotic symptoms, clozapine was effective in reducing psychotic symptoms (Frankenburg & Zanarini, 1993). Further controlled trials of the newer antipsychotics in BPD are warranted.

SELF-DESTRUCTIVE BEHAVIOR

One of the most troubling aspects of working with borderline patients is the risk of impulsive suicide attempts and repeated self-injury. Although there are no magic pills to prevent this behavior and there are few controlled studies, there are reports that appropriate use of certain medicines may be helpful in reducing self-destructive behavior. For instance, there is evidence that some antipsychotic medicines may reduce suicide proneness in recurrent suicide attempters with severe personality disorders (Montgomery & Montgomery, 1982). There are also case reports of newer antipsychotic agents such as risperidone reducing self-injurious behavior (Khouzam & Donnelly, 1997).

Recently, there has been a great deal of interest in the brain's opiate system and its relationship to self-injurious behavior. A subset of borderline patients reports relief from dysphoria and absence of pain when engaging in self-injurious behavior (e.g., burning, cutting of extremities). Several open trials suggest that the opiate antagonist naltrexone may be helpful in reducing this behavior (McGee, 1997; Roth, Ostroff, & Hoffman, 1996; Sonne, Rubey, Brady, Malcolm, & Morris, 1996).

REJECTION SENSITIVITY

Anyone who works with borderline patients has seen intense reactions (depression, anger, impulsivity, self-destructive behavior) following real or imagined rejection. Such rejection may be from anyone important to the patient: spouse, sexual partner, family, hospital staff, or therapist. Before BPD was included in *DSM-III*, psychopharmacologists had described a group of patients with very similar symptoms—intense dysphoria, self-destructive behavior, impulsivity—all usually triggered in response to rejection. These patients were diagnosed with hysteroid dysphoria and appeared to benefit from monoamine oxidase inhibiting (MAOI) antidepressants (Liebowitz & Klein, 1981). Such medications (phenelzine, tranylcypromine) appeared to improve mood in general and offered some protection from this severe sensitivity to rejection. One study compared the MAOI phenelzine with the tricyclic antidepressant imipramine in depressed patients and found phenelzine to be more effective in patients who also met criteria for BPD (Parsons et al., 1989). Thus it appears that MAOIs may be more effective than other antidepressants in treating rejection sensitivity. In a comprehensive trial of medications in BPD, four different agents were compared to placebo in 16 female patients (Cowdry & Gardner, 1988). The four comparison agents were trifluoperazine, tranylcypromine, carbamazepine, and alprazolam. Each agent was given for a total of six weeks followed by a two-week placebo washout, after which the patient was crossed over to another agent. This study found that tranylcypromine was most effective in reducing depressive symptoms, again suggesting that MAOI antidepressants may have specific efficacy in treating dysphoria secondary to rejection. Another study compared long-term (16-week) treatment with haloperidol and phenelzine (Cornelius, Soloff, Perel, & Ulrich, 1993). Although the haloperidol-treated group had little benefit and high drop-out rates, the phenelzine treated patients reported improvement in mood and irritability. Unfortunately, the MAOI antidepressants have many side effects and interact negatively with many foods and medicines, making them difficult to use in clinical practice. Hopefully, safer medicines with similar mechanisms of action will become available for treatment and future studies of their efficacy in borderline patients completed.

ALTERNATIVE TREATMENT OPTIONS

Other medicines may prove to be of benefit in certain borderline patients. Some patients with BPD (especially those with symptoms resembling those of attention deficit disorder) may respond to noradrenergic enhancing medicines, such as stimulants or the antidepressant bupropion. In several early studies, subgroups of patients diagnosed as having pseudoneurotic schizophrenia (a precursor to the diagnosis of borderline personality) appeared to respond better to agents that enhanced noradrenergic function (e.g., stimulants, tranylcypromine) than either placebo or agents that decreased noradrenergic function (e.g., chlorpromazine, trifluoperazine) (Hedberg, Hauch, & Glueck, 1971; Vilkin, 1964). Venlafaxine, a norepinephrine and serotonin reuptake inhibitor, was found to have efficacy in reducing aggression and dysphoria in an open trial on borderline patients (Markovitz & Wagner, 1995).

As with medicine treatment, there has been little empirical research on the treatment of borderline patients with psychotherapy. Linehan (1987), however, has devised an innovative cognitive-behavioral treatment program for self-destructive patients with BPD. This treatment is directed toward teaching the patient various skills to deal with and to tolerate rapidly shifting, intense affective states. This approach uses instruction, modeling, behavioral and cognitive rehearsal, cognitive restructuring, and operant conditioning (reinforcement). Several empirical trials suggest that this treatment reduces anger, reduces self-destructive behavior, and improves interpersonal functioning (Linehan, Heard, & Armstrong, 1993).

Unfortunately, there have been no well-designed studies of the relative efficacies of medication and psychotherapy separately and in combination for this disorder. It would be foolish to suggest that medications alone will treat BPD. With occasional exceptions, the medication is not a cure for the personality disorder and at best will only be effective in reducing intensity of symptom clusters. This reduction in symptom intensity, however, often assists in allowing the patient to participate in psychotherapy. Current medications should almost always be used in addition to psychotherapy, and most patients will require a combination of behavioral, dynamic, and family interventions at various points in treatment. The following case reports illustrate the different responses that borderline patients may have to medication treatment and the integration of medication and therapy in their treatment.

Case Illustration: Ms. X.

The patient, Ms. X., was a 27-year-old single woman who presented for treatment at the insistence of her family. The patient admitted to frequent violent arguments with her family, friends, and often strangers. She had lost many jobs due to her mood lability and intense, inappropriate anger. For example, she had lost her most recent job in a restaurant when she had an argument with a fellow worker and the patient had tried to strangle her coworker in the restaurant. She had gotten into similar violent arguments with her sister and mother and had been unable to maintain any consistent relationships. Ms. X. would usually feel guilt after these events and had attempted suicide three times. She had been hospitalized at least 10 times over the course of her life. Previous treatment with haloperidol, amitriptyline, and supportive psychotherapy had been unsuccessful. The patient began taking sertraline 50 mg/day, and the dose was gradually increased by 50 mg every two weeks to 150 mg/day. After five weeks of treatment, Ms. X. noted a marked decrease in her irritability. She had a dramatic decrease in temper outbursts and was able to return to school. Ms. X. stopped the medication on her own after six months but noted a return of irritability and anger, leading her to restart treatment with sertraline. The patient stopped and restarted medication several times over the next few years before deciding to remain on medication indefinitely. She also restarted individual psychodynamic therapy. Both she and her therapist reported significant progress compared to her previous trials of therapy.

Mr. Y.

The patient, Mr. Y., was a 42-year-old single man who had seen many therapists and psychiatrists (more than twenty) since his adolescence. He had a history of multiple hospitalizations and at least 10 suicide attempts, often serious. He also had a history of alcohol dependence until age 34. He had been on many medicines, including many tricyclic antidepressants, selective serotonin reuptake inhibitors (SSRIs), and lithium. On presentation to our clinic, he complained of generalized dysphoria, but he could not verbalize more than that when asked about his affective states. On evaluation, Mr. Y. was noted to have significant mood lability, extreme rejection sensitivity, and chronic self-destructive thoughts. He was placed on divalproex sodium 2000 mg/day with a reduction in the intensity of his mood swings. He was then placed on olanzapine 5 mg/day with a reduction in suicidal ruminations. Although he had been in supportive psychotherapy in the past, he had never been in structured treatment. He started cognitive-behavioral therapy and was able to benefit from treatment. His attempts to stop treatment on several occasions led to a worsening of his symptoms, requiring him to restart the medicines.

There is a lack of basic research on the relationship between life experiences and biological vulnerabilities in the development of BPD. There is evidence that certain traits of borderline personality have a biological component whereas others are more clearly learned. For example, a history of abuse in borderline patients correlates with the criteria of unstable relationships, feelings of emptiness, abandonment fears, and histories of neglect correlate with suicidal behavior (Oldham, Skodol, Gallaher, & Kroll, 1996). On the other hand, affective instability, intense anger, and identity disturbance do not seem to correlate with a history of abuse or neglect, consistent with the idea that these dimensions might particularly benefit from medication treatment.

PRESCRIPTIVE TREATMENT AND MANAGED CARE

Difficulties in diagnosis and treatment selection make it difficult to come up with uniform treatment plans for patients with BPD. At this point, most patients with BPD will require long-term treatment (i.e., years) with a combination of modalities. At various times, patients may need brief (i.e., 3- to 5-day) inpatient hospitalizations during times of stress, outpatient crisis management, family therapy, cognitive-behavior therapy, and medication therapy. Medication management can be complicated and requires frequent visits with an experienced psychopharmacologist during times of medication adjustment. (See Table 23.1.)

Table 23.1
Medication Interventions of Abnormal Personality Traits

Symptom Cluster	Medications
Impulsive aggression	Serotonin medications (fluoxetine, sertraline)
Affective lability	Mood-stabilizing agents (lithium, divalproex)
Psychotic-like phenomenon	Antipsychotics
Self-destructive behavior	Antipsychotics, naltrexone
Rejection sensitivity	MAOIs

SUMMARY

It appears that the dimensions or clusters of abnormal personality traits in borderline patients respond to specific medication interventions (Table 23.1). Psychotic-like traits (illusions, paranoia, ideas of reference) appear to respond preferentially to low-dose antipsychotic medication (these are best used for acute periods of stress-related symptoms). Medicines with putative serotonergic properties (e.g., the serotonin reuptake inhibitors—fluoxetine, sertraline, paroxetine, fluvoxamine) may be best suited for treating impulsive anger and aggression. Affective instability in borderlines appears to be related to Axis I affective disorders; and medications, such as lithium and divalproex sodium, may be most effective in reducing mood lability in these patients. Self-destructive behavior may benefit from antipsychotics, SSRIs, or opiate blockers (naltrexone). Rejection sensitivity appears to benefit from MAOIs more than tricyclic antidepressants. Whether other agents would also be helpful awaits further controlled trials.

The biggest hurdles in the treatment of BPD are related to diagnostic issues. Although we have tried to paint a neat picture of separate dimensions of psychopathology in BPD, it is often difficult to determine whether a particular behavior is due to one dimension or another. For example, an individual born with a vulnerability to intense affective shifts may be predisposed to impulsive, angry outbursts if the individual never learns to label emotions or is told by family or caregivers that there is nothing wrong with them. Many borderline patients with self-injurious behavior report that they engage in such behavior to reduce intense dysphoria or anger. Patients who are very sensitive to rejection may manifest intense anger rather than depression in response to perceived rejection. Psychotic-like symptoms and paranoia in the borderline patient may be closely associated with intolerable, intense, and rapidly changing affective states (guilt, anger, sadness, etc.). At this time, therefore, the management of BPD remains a clinical challenge. It is our hope that development of new medications and new psychotherapeutic interventions in combination will improve our ability to care for borderline patients.

REFERENCES

Akiskal, H.S. (1981). Subaffective disorders: Dysthymic, cyclothymic and bipolar II disorders in the "borderline" realm. *Psychiatric Clinic of North America, 4,* 25–46.

Brinkley, J.R., Beitman, B.D., & Friedel, R.O. (1979). Low-dose neuroleptic regimens in the treatment of borderline patients. *Archives of General Psychiatry, 36,* 319–326.

Brown, G.L., Goodwin, F.K., Ballenger, J.C., Goyer, P.F., & Major, L.F. (1979). Aggression in humans correlates with cerebrospinal fluid metabolite. *Psychiatry Research, 1,* 131–139.

Coccaro, E., Siever, L., Klar, H., Maurer, G., Cochrane, K., Cooper, T.B., Mohs, R.C., & Davis, K.L. (1989). Serotonergic studies in affective and personality disorder patients: Correlations with behavioral aggression and impulsivity. *Archives of General Psychiatry, 46,* 587–599.

Coccaro, E.F., Gabriel, S., & Siever, L.J. (1990). Buspirone challenge: Preliminary evidence for a role for central 5HT-1A receptor function in impulsive aggressive behavior in humans. *Psychopharmacological Bulletin, 26,* 393–405.

Coccaro, E.F., & Kavoussi, R.J. (1997). Fluoxetine reduces impulsive aggressive behavior in personality disordered subjects: Results from a double blind placebo controlled trial. *Archives of General Psychiatry, 54,* 1081–1088.

Coccaro, E.F., Kavoussi, R.J., & Hauger, R.L. (1995). Physiological responses to d-fenfluramine and ipsapirone challenge correlate with indices of aggression in males with personality disorder. *International Clinical Psychopharmacology, 10,* 177–179.

Coccaro, E.F., Kavoussi, R.J., Sheline, Y.I., Lish, J.D., & Csernansky, J.G. (1996). Impulsive aggression in personality disorder correlates with tritiated paroxetine binding in the platelet. *Archives of General Psychiatry, 53,* 531–536.

Cornelius, J.R., Soloff, P.H., Perel, J.M., & Ulrich, R.F. (1991). A preliminary trial of fluoxetine in refractory borderline patients. *Journal of Clinical Psychopharmacology, 11,* 116–120.

Cornelius, J.R., Soloff, P.H., Perel, J.M., & Ulrich, R.F. (1993). Continuation pharmacotherapy of borderline personality disorder with haloperidol and phenelzine. *American Journal of Psychiatry, 150,* 1843–1848.

Cowdry, R.W., & Gardner, D.L. (1988). Pharmacotherapy of borderline personality disorder: Alprazolam, carbamazepine, trifluoperazine, and tranylcypromine. *Archives of General Psychiatry, 45,* 111–119.

Frances, A. (1982). Categorical and dimensional systems of personality diagnosis: A comparison. *Comprehensive Psychiatry, 23,* 516–527.

Frankenburg, F.R., & Zanarini, M.C. (1993). Clozapine treatment of borderline patients: A preliminary study. *Comprehensive Psychiatry, 34,* 402–405.

Goldberg, S.C., Schulz, S.C., Schulz, P.M., Resnick, R.J., Hamer, R.M., & Friedel, R.D. (1986). Borderline and schizotypal personality disorders treated with low-dose thiothixene versus placebo. *Archives of General Psychiatry, 43,* 680–686.

Gunderson, J.G., & Singer, M.T. (1975). Defining borderline patients: An overview. *American Journal of Psychiatry, 132,* 1–10.

Hedberg, D.C., Hauch, J.H., & Glueck, B.C. (1971). Tranylcypromine-trifluoperazine combination in the treatment of schizophrenia. *American Journal of Psychiatry, 127,* 1141–1146.

Hollander, E., Stein, D.J., Decaria, C.M., Cohen, L., Saund, J.B., Shodol, A.E., Kellman, D., Resnick, L., & Oldham, J.M. (1994). Serotonergic sensitivity in borderline personality disorder: Preliminary findings. *American Journal of Psychiatry, 151,* 277–280.

Hudziak, J.J., Boffeli, T.J., Kreisman, J.J., Battaglia, M.M., Stanger, C., & Guze, S.B. (1996). Clinical study of the relation of borderline personality disorder to Briquet's syndrome (hysteria), somatization disorder, antisocial personality disorder, and substance abuse disorders. *American Journal of Psychiatry, 153,* 1598–1606.

Kavoussi, R.J., Liu, J., & Coccaro, E.F. (1994). Sertraline in the treatment of impulsive aggression in personality disordered patients. *Journal of Clinical Psychiatry, 55,* 137–141.

Kavoussi, R.J., & Siever, L.J. (1992). Overlap between borderline and schizotypal personality disorders. *Comprehensive Psychiatry, 33,* 7–12.

Kernberg, O. (1967). Borderline personality organization. *Journal of the American Psychoanalytic Association, 15,* 641–685.

Khouzam, H.R., & Donnelly, N.J. (1997). Remission of self-mutilation in a patient with borderline personality during risperidone therapy. *Journal of Nervous & Mental Disease, 185,* 348–349.

Knight, R. (1953). Borderline states. *Bulletin of the Menninger Clinic, 17,* 1–12.

Leone, N.F. (1982). Response of borderline patients to loxapine and chlorpromazine. *Journal of Clinical Psychiatry, 43,* 148–150.

Liebowitz, M.R., & Klein, D.F. (1981). Interrelationship of hysteroid dysphoria and borderline personality disorder. *Psychiatric Clinics of North America, 4,* 67–87.

Linehan, M.M. (1987). Dialectical behavior therapy for borderline personality disorder: Theory and method. *Bulletin of the Menninger Clinic, 51,* 261–276.

Linehan, M.M., Heard, H.L., & Armstrong, H.E. (1993). Naturalistic follow-up of a behavioral treatment for chronically parasuicidal borderline patients. *Archives of General Psychiatry, 50,* 971–974.

Links, P.S., Steiner, M., Boiago, I., & Irwin, D. (1990). Lithium therapy for borderline patients: Preliminary findings. *Journal of Personality Disorders, 4,* 173–181.

Linnoila, M., Virkkunen, M., Scheinin, M., Nuntila, A., Rimon, R., & Goodwin, F.K. (1983). Low cerebrospinal fluid 5 hydroxyindoleacetic acid concentration differentiates impulsive from nonimpulsive violent behavior. *Life Sciences, 33,* 2609–2614.

Markovitz, P.J., & Wagner, S.C. (1995). Venlafaxine in the treatment of borderline personality disorder. *Psychopharmacology Bulletin, 31,* 773–777.

McGee, M.D. (1997). Cessation of self-mutilation in a patient with borderline personality disorder treated with naltrexone. *Journal of Clinical Psychiatry, 58,* 32–33.

Miller, F.T., Abrams, T., Dulit, R., & Fyer, M. (1993). Psychotic symptoms in patients with borderline personality disorder and concurrent Axis I disorder. *Hospital & Community Psychiatry, 44,* 59–61.

Montgomery, S.A., & Montgomery, D. (1982). Pharmacological prevention of suicidal behavior. *Journal of Affective Disorders, 4,* 219–298.

Oldham, J.M., Skodol, A.E. Gallaher, P.E., & Kroll, M.E. (1996). Relationship of borderline symptoms to histories of abuse and neglect: A pilot study. *Psychiatric Quarterly, 67,* 287–295.

Paris, J. (1997). Antisocial and borderline personality disorders: Two separate diagnoses or two aspects of the same psychopathology? *Comprehensive Psychiatry, 38,* 237–242.

Parsons, B., Quitkin, F.M., McGrath, P.J., Steward, J.W., Tricame, E., Ocepek-Welikson, K., Harrison, W., Rabkin, J.G., Wager, S.G., & Nunes, E. (1989). Phenelzine, imipramine, and placebo in borderline patients meeting criteria for atypical depression. *Psychopharmacology Bulletin, 25,* 524–534.

Rifkin, A., Quitkin, F., Carrillo, C., Blumberg, A.G., & Klein, D.F. (1972). Lithium carbonate in emotionally unstable character disorders. *Archives of General Psychiatry, 27,* 519–523.

Roth, A.S., Ostroff, R.B., & Hoffman, R.E. (1996). Naltrexone as a treatment for repetitive self-injurious behavior: An open-label trial. *Journal of Clinical Psychiatry, 57,* 233–237.

Salzman, C., Wolfson, A.N., Schatzberg, A., Cooper, J., Henke, R., Albanese, M., Schwartz, J., & Miyawaki, E. (1995). Effect of fluoxetine on anger in symptomatic volunteers with borderline personality disorder. *Journal of Clinical Psychopharmacology, 15,* 23–29.

Serban, G., & Siegel, S. (1984). Responses of borderline and schizotypal patients to small doses of thiothixene and haloperidol. *American Journal of Psychiatry, 141,* 1455–1458.

Sheard, M., Marini, J., Bridges, C., & Wagner, E. (1976). The effect of lithium on impulsive aggressive behavior in man. *American Journal of Psychiatry, 133,* 1409–1413.

Soloff, P.H., George, A., Nathan, S., Schulz, P.M., Cornelius, J.R., Herring, J., & Perel, J.M. (1989). Amitriptyline versus haloperidol in borderlines: Final outcomes and predictors of response. *Journal of Clinical Psychopharmacology, 9,* 238–246.

Soloff, P.H., George, A., Nathan, S., Schulz, P.M., & Perel, J.M. (1986). Paradoxical effects of amitriptyline in borderline patients. *American Journal of Psychiatry, 143,* 1603–1605.

Sonne, S., Rubey, R., Brady, K., Malcolm, R., & Morris, T. (1996). Naltrexone treatment of self-injurious thoughts and behaviors. *Journal of Nervous & Mental Disease, 184,* 192–195.

Spitzer, R.L., Endicott, J., & Gibbon, M. (1979). Crossing the border into borderline personality and borderline schizophrenia. *Archives of General Psychiatry, 36,* 17–24.

Stein, D.J., Simeon, D., Frenkel, M., Islam, M.N., & Hollander, E. (1995). An open trial of valproate in borderline personality disorder. *Journal of Clinical Psychiatry, 56,* 506–510.

Teicher, M.H., Glod, C.A., Aaronson, S.T., Gunter, P.A., Schatzberg, A.F., & Cole, J.D. (1989). Open assessment of the safety and efficacy of thioridazine in the treatment of patients with borderline personality disorder. *Psychopharmacology Bulletin, 25,* 535–549.

Trull, T.J., Useda, J.D., Conforti, K., & Doan, B.T. (1997). Borderline personality disorder features in nonclinical young adults: Two-year outcome. *Journal of Abnormal Psychology, 106,* 307–314.

Tupin, J., Smith, D., Clanon, T., Kim, L., Nugent, A., & Groupe, A. (1973). The long term use of lithium in aggressive prisoners. *Comprehensive Psychiatry, 14,* 311–317.

Vilkin, M.I. (1964). Comparative chemotherapeutic trial in treatment of chronic borderline patients. *American Journal of Psychiatry, 120,* 1004.

Wilcox, J.A. (1995). Divalproex sodium as a treatment for borderline personality disorder. *Annals of Clinical Psychiatry, 7,* 33–37.

PART NINE

ALCOHOLISM AND SUBSTANCE ABUSE

OF THE disorders listed in *DSM-III-R*, few are as recalcitrant to treatment as alcoholism and other substance abuse. Although alcoholism and other substance abuse have been well-studied from numerous vantage points, and many psychotherapeutic and pharmacological interventions have been developed and tried, the long-term results are still quite disappointing. In general, the vast majority of patients treated for any sort of substance abuse eventually return to their favored substance, be it alcohol, nicotine, or illicit drugs.

The contributors to this section (Glanter & Castañeda; Kassel, Wagner, & Unrod; and Moss) are painfully aware of the resistant nature of the disorders they are treating, and they are most humble in the presentation of strategies that they pursue consistent with their theoretical bents. In each of the chapters, the importance of following a multimodal approach to treatment is fully acknowledged. Thus, the unitary development of psychotherapy, of behavior therapy, or of pharmacotherapy is discouraged. To the contrary, it is clear that many concurrent modalities must be carried out, including the use of an adjunctive network of individuals such as Alcoholics Anonymous (AA) with a family-oriented psychotherapy (Galanter & Castaneda), use of drugs in addition to behavioral self-management (BSM) techniques (Sobell et al.), or use of self-help groups in addition to other psychotherapies and a comprehensive pharmacological approach (Moss).

Difficulties encountered in treatment are identified in each of the chapters: First, alcoholism and other substance abuse represent approach behaviors that eventuate in short-term pleasurable responses that are mediated by the central nervous system (CNS). Indeed, the long-term negative medical and psychological sequelae of prolonged use are obfuscated by the immediate pleasure that alcoholics or other drug abusers receive from their favorite substance. Thus, motivating patients to consider the long-term effects of their abuse is a highly difficult therapeutic task. Second, for those who have become physiologically and/or psychologically dependent on the substance, the process of withdrawal can be painful and/or distressing. Third, in many instances, polydrug abuse is the norm, and the eradication of one addiction simply leads to the intensification of a concomitant addiction (e.g., switching from opiates to alcoholism). Moreover, alcoholics and other drug addicts tend to be heavy smokers as well. Fourth, in addition to the possible effects of genetic and familial influences for a given form of substance abuse (e.g., alcoholism), many individuals find it difficult to quit because of the negative impact of their particular peer group. Fifth, a most recent impediment to treatment is the use of newly developed ("designer") illicit drugs because very little is known about their chemical actions or possible antagonists. Sixth, in some instances, the substance abuse masks an underlying psychiatric condition (e.g., anxiety, affective disorder) that requires separate treatment. Seventh, conversely, prolonged used of psychoactive substances that affect the CNS may result in psychiatric and neurological symptoms that require medical management.

As pointed out by Moss in his chapter, the costs of alcohol abuse and other drug abuse are staggering from both an economic and a societal perspective. In addition to costing our society over 150 billion dollars per year, alcohol and drug abuse are implicated in family dissolution, rape, child abuse, automobile accidents, burglary, theft, and other kinds of legal transgressions. But despite the tremendous problems of abuse (e.g., costliness to society, the difficulties in motivating the abuser to consider treatment, the medical sequelae of abuse, and the repeated recidivism of treated abusers), the authors of the three chapters do point out some encouraging trends in remediation. For example, Galanter and Castañeda provide a very optimistic view of network and family approaches, in which multiple agents and modalities are brought together to influence the patient. There is clear recognition that alcoholism, and other forms of substance abuse, are as much lifestyle issues as psychiatric disorders, and treatment cannot be compartmentalized.

Kassel et al. describe a host of new behavioral and cognitive behavioral interventions. Initial approaches, such as aversion therapy, based on narrow conditioning models have given way to cognitive behavioral and skills based approaches. There is also much greater recognition of the motivational component of change, as exemplified by the Prochaska and DiClemente transtheoretical model. People with substance problems do not simply decide to change once and achieve life-long abstinence or controlled consumption regardless of treatment. Motivation to change waxes and wanes, and relapses are to be expected. Thus, treatment must be geared to motivation at the time and must anticipate long-term involvement with the patient. Not only may different patients require different types of treatment, but each patient may require different types of treatment at different times. Unfortunately, as evidenced by Project Match, this awareness of significant individual differences in treatment needs has not yet translated into effective patient-treatment matching.

Moss, in his chapter on pharmacotherapy, details progress in the biological approach to alcoholism and other substance abuse. He argues that there are three specific targets in the pharmacological approach to chemical dependency: (1) alleviation of withdrawal symptoms, (2) either reduction of reinforcement or development of aversion to alcohol or other drugs, and (3) reduction of craving for the abused substance. Examples of the first category are the substitution of the long-acting opiate methadone for heroin, the use of chlordiazepoxide for alcohol withdrawal symptoms, and introduction of bromocriptine, a dopamine agonist for cocaine withdrawal. As for the second category, lithium carbonate has been administered to diminish the euphoria associated with stimulant compounds (e.g., amphetamines), whereas disulfiram (Antabuse) has been used to discourage chronic alcoholics from drinking. Finally, with respect to the third category, the administration of chronic benzodiazepine therapy has been recommended as a deterrent to craving for alcohol.

However, application of pharmacological strategies in the chemical dependency area is controversial, given that (1) the patient may not comply with the medical regimen, and (2) unpleasant side effects may develop in some instances. Furthermore, self-help groups, such as AA, are not reinforcing of the medical-model approach to treatment.

The future looks promising for treatment of substance abuse. New pharmacological agents (e.g., naloxone, naltrexone) have recently come on the market, and a number of creative new behavior-therapy strategies have shown promising results. Assessment and diagnosis have improved, which should facilitate comparison of findings across trials. There also continues to be great interest in reducing alcohol and drug use by the public and government leaders. Major public-health campaigns, especially preventive efforts directed to children and adolescents, can be helpful, even if they do not eradicate the problem. Broader recognition of these conditions as diseases, rather than as absence of willpower, will also foster broader recognition of the value of treatment, rather than admonition and incarceration, and increased research funding at NIH.

CHAPTER 24

Psychotherapy and Family Network Therapy

MARC GALANTER and RICARDO CASTAÑEDA

CONCEPTUALIZATION

GENERAL CONSIDERATION

Development of effective preventive and thereapeutic strategies for substance abuse disorders constitutes an important challenge for present-day society. The level of alcohol consumption in 1996 in the United States is lower than that observed in the 1980s. In fact, the alcohol amount consumed in this country has consistently declined since 1981. Yet, according to the last large epidemiological assessment, 19 million people are problem drinkers, including 8 million, or 7.5 percent of adults, who can be classified as alcoholic. The lifetime rate of alcohol abuse/dependence was estimated to be 13.3 percent (Regier et al., 1988). Consumption of other drugs has also declined since 1980. Lifetime prevalence of substance abuse other than alcohol reported in the last Epidemiologic Catchment Area Study was 6.1 percent, 4 percent for cannabis, 2 percent for amphetamines, and 0.7 for opiates (Regier, Myers, & Kramer, 1984). In 1996 probably less than six million people in this country use some form of cocaine regularly (Resnick & Resnick, 1984).

Males have higher lifetime prevalences for alcohol and other substance abuse (Ray & Braude, 1986; Regier et al., 1984), and gender differences regarding patterns of use, such as age of onset and severity of clinical course, also have been confirmed (Brady, Grice, & Dustan, 1993; Kosten, Gawin, & Kosten, 1993; White, Brady, & Sonne, 1996). Gender, however, is not the only factor that affects incidence of these disorders; cultural and ethnic contexts also determine wide differences in drinking practices (Castañeda & Galanter, 1988; Heath, Waddell, & Topper, 1981; Kane, 1981). Contrasting drinking patterns among ethnic groups are associated with variations in the expression of alcoholism and abuse of illegal drugs (National Institute on Drug Abuse, 1990).

Both inner-city American black (Fernandez-Pol, Bluestone, Missouri, Morales, & Mizruchi, 1986) and urban Puerto Rican groups, for example, have been observed to display not only more severe drinking patterns, but also higher rates of cognitive impairment and more intense symptomatology during alcohol withdrawal than their urban white counterparts.

RISK FACTORS

There is no evidence to suggest existence of a common personality organization among alcoholics or other drug abusers (Vaillant, 1983). Nonetheless, psychoanalysts have proposed a series of personality structures that predispose an individual to addictive behavior. In common, such personalities are said to have basic deficits in object relations (Balint, 1969) and self-concept (Kernberg, 1975) that determine reliance by the ego on compensatory mechanisms, such as denial and grandiosity. The alcoholic's frequent inability to satisfactorily manage impulses and regulate emotions are seen, in this context, as consequences of a weak self or a deficient ego (Khantzian, 1982).

From a slightly different perspective, a large number of personality characteristics have, at some point or another, been identified as markers for alcoholism and other drug abuse. It seems, however, that because these clinical characteristics are as likely determinants of alcoholism and other drug abuse as they are the consequence of them, their value as diagnostic markers is questionable.

On the other hand, it has been definitely established that alcoholism and other drug abuse are familially transmitted (Cotton, 1979). Several studies of alcoholic groups have reported alcoholism rates of 50 percent among their fathers, 30 percent among their brothers, and 6 percent among their mothers (Goodwin, 1981). Among first- and second-degree male relatives of alcoholic males, the risk is 25 percent (Cotton, 1979).

Environmental factors, such as home disruption, a disadvantaged urban upbringing, or a history of parental substance abuse and/or mental illness are not the only factors that have been found to explain such a familial transmission (Frances, Timm, & Bucky, 1980; Haarstrup & Thomsen, 1972; Helzer, Robins, & Davis, 1976; Rosenberg, 1969). Twin, adoption, and family illness studies, and neuropsychiatric investigations as well, have demonstrated that genetic factors may also contribute to the familial transmission of alcoholism and other drug abuse. Frances et al. (1980), for example, reported a higher frequency of severe alcoholism, conduct disorders, sociopathy, and mental illness in general among relatives of individuals with a strong family history of alcoholism than among those relatives of problem drinkers who had no such family history. Winokour (1979) also has studied first-degree relatives of alcoholics. They have reported high prevalence of sociopathy and alcoholism among males, and high rates of early onset depression among females.

Twin studies have added support to the notion of a genetic predisposition toward alcoholism, mainly by demonstrating that monozygotic twins generally have higher concordance rates for alcoholism than dizygotic twins (Kaij, 1960). Adoption studies by Goodwin, Schlusinger, Hemansen, Guze, and Winokour

(1973) revealed that incidence of alcoholism among sons of alcoholic fathers was four times higher than that observed among a control group without such family history, irrespective of whether subjects were raised by their own parents or by foster parents.

Multiple studies of several populations of subjects at high-risk of developing alcoholism, such as children, twins, and relatives of alcoholics suggest that there may be several genetic markers for alcoholism (Anthenelli & Schuckit, 1990). Those studies that assessed various responses among high-risk populations to challenges with alcohol in experimental settings suggest that relatives of alcoholics display a decreased intensity of motor, subjective, hormonal and electrophysiologic reactions to alcohol when compared with subjects who are not at apparent risk of becoming alcoholics (1990). Evidence has, as well, accumulated to suggest the need to consider alcoholism as an expression of predisposing neurological deficits. Begleiter, Porjesz, Bihari, and Kissin (1984), for example, found a defect in the P3 component of the evoked brain potentials of a group of boys of alcoholic fathers that was similar to the defect observed in adult alcoholic males. Such a deficit, they propose, would determine specific decrements in memory processing. Multiple investigations on the biological sons of alcoholics have also reported an abnormally high incidence of attention-deficit hyperactivity disorder (Goodwin, Schlusinger, & Hemansen, 1975) and impairments of other neuropsychological functions, including memory, processing of language, regulation of emotions, and perceptual-motor functioning (Tarter, Hegedus, & Goldstein, 1984).

ABUSE AND DEPENDENCE

The multiplicity of substance-abuse disorders, along with the frequent revisions of concepts and terminology used to describe them in the past 100 years, have hindered development of an acceptable classification. At present, two concepts prevail in the substance-abuse literature—substance dependence and substance abuse—both of which are described in the *DSM-IV* published in 1994 (American Psychiatric Association, 1994).

Psychoactive Substance Dependence

This concept refers to a group of behavioral and physiologic symptoms that confirm that an individual continues to use alcohol and other drugs despite the serious problems that derive from such use. At least some of the clinical features required to make this diagnosis must have persisted for at least one month or must have occurred repeatedly for a longer period of time. They include at least three of the following:

1. Alcohol or other drug often taken in larger amounts or over a longer period of time than the individual originally intended.
2. Repeated and unsuccessful attempts to cut down or control substance use.
3. Large investment of time spent (a) in activities necessary to get the substance, (b) in taking the substance, or (c) in recovering from its effects.

4. Interference with work, school, or home obligations caused by frequent intoxication or withdrawal symptoms.
5. Elimination or reduction of important social, occupational, or recreational activities because of substance use.
6. Continued substance use despite the individual's knowledge of having a persistent or recurrent social, psychological, or physical problem that is either caused by or made worse by the use of the substance.
7. Existence of *tolerance*: The need to increase the amount of the substance in order to achieve intoxication or a desired effect, or markedly diminished effect with continued use of the same amount.

Additionally, substance dependence may be associated with withdrawal, which is a substance-specific array of cognitive, psychiatric, and physiologic symptoms that develops upon the marked reduction in the habitual level of substance consumption. Characteristic withdrawal symptoms have been recognized for alcohol, opioids, sedatives, caffeine, nicotine, and stimulants, such as cocaine and amphetamines. This diagnostic criterion may not apply to cannabis, hallucinogens, or phencyclidine (PCP) (the latter, however, has been observed in animals).

Psychoactive Substance Abuse

This diagnosis is made when an individual engages in a maladaptive pattern of substance use, which leads to clinically significant impairment or distress, as manifested in at least one of the following behavioral symptoms: (1) failure to fulfill major role obligations at work, school, or home; (2) recurrent substance use in situations in which it is physically hazardous; (3) recurrent substance-use legal problems; and (4) substance use despite persistent or recurrent social or interpersonal problems secondary to the effects of the substance.

DIAGNOSTIC ISSUES AND PROBLEMS (DSM-IV)

DIAGNOSTIC PROBLEMS

Self-Report

Several circumstances contribute to the clinician's difficulties in making a correct substance-abuse diagnosis. First, information available to the diagnostician frequently derives from the patient's self-report. Although self-report of alcoholic behavior has been found to be a reliable tool in research settings (Sobell, 1979), the clinician should interpret it with caution. The individual engaged in some form of substance abuse will frequently misrepresent amount, frequency, and consequences of drug use, not only because of defensive denial, but also because of frequently impaired memory and perception of reality. A chronic drug-dependent individual may, in fact, be utterly unable to provide a good history. It is always advisable to interview other people, such as family members, friends, or work associates, in order to clarify the history. A spouse, for example, might voice complaints of abusive or intoxicated behavior. Work and social associates might reveal the true magnitude of the time spent in obtaining the substance and recovering from its effects.

Psychiatric Symptoms

An important diagnostic consideration for the clinician is the need to differentiate between primary and secondary psychiatric symptoms. On the one hand, several psychiatric conditions, such as mood, conduct, and personality disorders, may predispose affected individuals to developing substance abuse. At a minimum, their primary symptomatology is frequently exacerbated by drug use (Galanter, Castañeda, & Ferman, 1988). On the other hand, chronic substance abuse or dependence is generally associated with a large variety of symptoms. These include, for example, behavioral disturbances frequently related to the need to obtain money or illegal drugs, which may wrongly suggest antisocial or other personality disorders. Complicating matters, the association between sociopathy and drug abuse often has been documented to be the source of diagnostic confusion (Schuckitt, 1985).

Mood disorders, mostly depression, are also frequent complications of drug abuse. This was illustrated by Minnesota Multiphasic Personality Inventory (MMPI) studies, which found that while 60 percent of recently detoxified alcoholics were depressed (Keeler, Taylor, & Miller, 1979), no evidence of depression could be obtained in a group of abstinent alcoholics (Pettinati, Sugarman, & Maurer, 1982). A general consensus exists that in 90 percent of heavy drinkers with symptoms of both alcoholism and depression, the correct diagnosis is alcoholism and not primary affect illness (Galanter et al., 1988). Presence of such symptoms, however, warrants prompt consideration by the clinician, as suicidal behavior in this population is by no means uncommon. Among heroin-dependent individuals, for example, the suicide rate is 25 percent, and among alcoholics, suicide has been observed to occur in at least 15 of every 100 patients (Galanter & Castañeda, 1985). Psychotic symptoms, such as hallucinations, delusions, and other disorders of thought, affect the behavior. Such psychotic symptoms can also cloud the diagnostic picture of the abuse of or dependence on hallucinogens, cocaine, amphetamines, marijuana, PCP, and inhaled substances, as well as withdrawal episodes from alcohol and other depressants. Simultaneous use of alcohol and other drugs by schizophrenic individuals can, in addition, obscure the expression of primary psychotic symptoms.

In addition to occurrence of psychotic symptoms, associated features of drug abuse are anxiety, irritability, mood lability, and impairment of social and occupational functioning, all of which should be considered in the appropriate context of the existing addictive disorder, in order to prevent premature diagnoses and treatments. Final diagnosis should be postponed in the presence of any of these disturbances for at least two weeks because secondary symptoms are likely to recede after a period of recovery (Galanter et al., 1988).

A multitude of medical problems also contributes to diagnostic confusion. Alcoholism, for example, can result in permanent dementia; hallucinogen use can lead to protracted delusional states; and drugs such as marijuana, phencyclidine

(PCP), and hallucinogens can induce motivational and cognitive deficits. Neuropsychological assessments in these circumstances are clearly indicated.

POLYSUBSTANCE DEPENDENCE

Is simultaneous or sequential abuse of multiple substances another frequent source of diagnostic-confusion among a group of abstinent alcoholics? In much the same way as depressed or anxious patients may develop a secondary addiction in their efforts to self-medicate their symptoms, primary-drug abusers may also become dependent on another substance that counteracts distressing feelings and drug reactions. Characteristic among stimulant-dependent individuals, for example, is the consumption of sedatives and/or alcohol, to ameliorate the anxiety associated with withdrawal states and chronic dependence.

Polydrug abuse is not uncommon, and in certain age and cultural subgroups may, indeed, be the rule more often than the exception. The frequently incongruous and even bizarre constellations of symptoms characteristic of this condition should not deter the clinician from trying to diagnose all the existing drug-abuse disorders.

TREATMENT STRATEGIES

A pragmatic psychotherapeutic approach to the alcohol-dependent patient is worth consideration. The origins of this approach lie in network therapy, as developed by Speck (1967) and others, and in more widely used family-therapy techniques.

This approach can be useful in addressing a broad range of addicted patients. These patients are characterized by the following clinical hallmarks of addictive illness relevant to this treatment model. First, when they initiate consumption of their addictive agent, be it alcohol, cocaine, opiates, or depressant drugs, they frequently cannot limit that consumption to a reasonable and predictable level; this phenomenon has been termed *loss of control* by clinicians who treat alcohol- or other drug-dependent persons. Second, they have consistently demonstrated relapse to the agent of abuse, that is, they have attempted to stop using the drug for varying periods of time but have returned to it despite a specific intent to avoid it (Vaillant, 1981).

This treatment approach is not necessary for those abusers who can, in fact, learn to set limits on their alcohol or drug use; their abuse may be treated as a behavioral symptom in a traditional psychotherapeutic fashion. It is also not directed to those patients for whom the addictive pattern is most unmanageable, such as long-term intravenous opiate addicts and others with unusual destabilizing circumstances, such as homelessness, severe character pathology, or psychosis. These patients may need special supportive care, such as drug substitution (e.g., methadone maintenance), inpatient detoxification, or long-term residential treatment.

Therapists should focus on those aspects of the treatment outlined here that are at variance with their usual therapeutic approach. Although it is essential to rely on acquired clinical judgment and experience, it is equally important for therapists to be prepared to depart from the usual mode of psychotherapeutic treatment. For example, an active rather than a passive role is essential when drug exposure is suggested. The concept of therapist and patient enclosed in an inviolable envelope must be modified, because immediate circumstances that may expose the patient to drug use must take precedence over long-term understanding and insight. These principles are applicable within the technique outlined here. Other approaches, too, such as the use of couples' group therapy and other techniques discussed by Gallant, Rich, Bey, and Terranova (1970) may incorporate most of these principles.

THE INITIAL ENCOUNTERS

The patient should be asked to bring a spouse or a close friend to the first session. Drug-dependent patients often do not like certain things they hear when they first come for treatment, and they may deny or rationalize even if they have voluntarily sought help. Because of their denial of the problem, a significant other is essential both to history taking and to implementing a viable treatment plan. A close relation can often cut through denial in the way that an unfamiliar therapist cannot and can, therefore, be invaluable in setting a standard of realism about the addiction.

Some patients make it clear that they wish to come to the initial session on their own. This is often associated with the desire to preserve the option of continued substance abuse and is borne out of the fear that an alliance will be established independent of them to prevent this. Although a delay may be tolerated for a session or two, there should be no ambiguity at the outset that effective treatment can only be undertaken on the basis of a therapeutic alliance around the drug issue. This includes the support of significant others, and it is expected that a network of close friends and/or relations will be brought in within a session or two at the most.

Not only are the patients sometimes reluctant to establish a network, but their relatives may also be resistant. For example, it may be necessary to develop a strategy for engaging a resistant spouse to enter a cooperative role:

Case Illustration: Case 1

A 40-year-old lawyer came for treatment of his drinking problem primarily because his marriage was doing poorly. He secured his wife's agreement to come to the initial session and hoped that the therapy would serve as a bridge for improving their failing relationship. She was actually reluctant to establish closer ties to him and told me that she preferred not to be involved in the treatment. She came a half hour late for the second conjoint session, citing heavy rains along the route from their home in an outlying suburb. She was in an angry mood, announcing that she could not come again, because she had to tend to their four children and organize their after-school activities. Rather than retreating from his position, the therapist expressed considerable regret that she was compromised by the plan and stated his own appreciation that she had gone so far out of her way to help out. He pointed out to her how valuable she was to the plan (never noting that, in fact, she was being much less than positive to date) and that he needed her to support his own imperfect ability to help her husband achieve sobriety, underlying the serious limitations of the individual therapist who alone treats the alcoholic. He agreed to her skipping a session the next week, giving acknowledgment to a relatively unimportant conflicting appointment, in exchange for her agreement to come the week thereafter. After a month, it became clearer to her that it was in her interest—on a pragmatic level—to participate.

Therapists are used to thinking that they are right and expecting (or at least hoping for) a good measure of respect for their views. This example is given to underline the strategic importance of generating whatever understanding may be necessary to achieve a viable relationship with a network member, even at the risk of feeling rejected. This may also take a good measure of cajoling and even manipulation at the outset of treatment.

The weight of clinical experience supports the view that abstinence is the most practical goal to propose to the addicted person for rehabilitation (Gitlow & Peyser, 1980; Zimberg, 1982). For abstinence to be expected, however, the therapist should assure the provision of necessary social supports for the patient. Consider how a long-term support network is initiated for this purpose, beginning with availability of the therapist, significant others, and a self-help group.

First, the therapist should be available for consultation on the telephone and should indicate to patients that the therapist wants to be called if problems arise. This makes the therapist's commitment clear and sets the tone for a team effort. It begins to undercut one reason for relapse: Patients' sense that they will be on their own if they are unable to manage the situation. The astute therapist, though, will assure the patient that the therapist does not spend excessive time at the telephone or in emergency sessions, and, therefore, the patient will develop a support network that can handle the majority of day-to-day problems. This will generally leave the therapist only to respond to occasional questions of interpreting the terms of the understanding between therapist, patient, and support network members. If there is a question about availability of a given patient and network to manage the period between initial sessions, the first few scheduled sessions may be arranged at intervals of only one to three days. In any case, frequent appointments should be scheduled at the outset of a pharmacological detoxification (as with benzodiazepines for alcoholism), so that the patient need never manage more than a few days' medication at a time.

The next section will discuss membership that ranges from one to several persons who are close to the patient. Larger networks have been used effectively by Speck (1967) in treating schizophrenic patients. Contacts among network members at this stage typically include telephone calls (usually at the patient's initiative), dinner arrangements, and social encounters, and they should be pre-planned to a fair extent during the joint session. These encounters are most often undertaken at the time when alcohol or other drug use is likely to occur. In planning, however, it should be made clear to network members that relatively little unusual effort will be required for the long term, that after the patient is stabilized, participation will come to little more than attendance at infrequent meetings with the patient and therapist. This requires a major time commitment from the network members initially, but eventually, reduction in commitment relieves both the network members and those patients who do not want to be placed in a dependent position.

TECHNIQUES IN SOCIAL AND FAMILY NETWORK THERAPY

Introducing Alcoholics Anonymous and Disulfiram

Use of self-help modalities is desirable whenever possible. For the alcoholic, certainly, participation in Alcoholics Anonymous (AA) as described by Zimberg (1977), is strongly encouraged. Groups, such as Narcotics Anonymous (NA), Pills Anonymous (PA), and Cocaine Anonymous (CA in some communities), are modeled after AA, and they play a similarly useful role. One approach is to tell the patient that attendance is expected at two AA meetings in a week at least, in order to become familiar with the program. If, after a month, the patient is quite reluctant to continue and other aspects of the treatment are going well, nonparticipation may have to be accepted. Such acceptance, as illustrated later herein, may sometimes be used as one bargaining chip in the game of securing compliance with other aspects of the treatment.

For the alcoholic, disulfiram (Antabuse) may be a useful tool in assuring abstinence, but it becomes much more valuable when carefully integrated into work with the patient and network. For example, it is a good idea to use the initial telephone contact to engage the patient's agreement to be abstinent from alcohol for the day immediately prior to the first session. The therapist then has the option of prescribing or administering disulfiram at that time. For a patient who is earnest about seeking assistance for alcoholism, this is often not difficult, if some time is spent on the phone making plans to avoid a drinking context during that period. If it is not feasible to undertake this on the phone, it may be addressed in the first session. Such planning with the patient will almost always involve organizing time with significant others and, therefore, serves as a basis for developing the patient's support network. Disulfiram is typically initiated with a dose of 500 mg, and then 250 mg. It is taken every morning, when the urge to drink is generally lowest.

Anticipating the Recurrence of Drug Use

Most individual therapists, as described by Hayman (1956), see the alcoholic or other drug abuser as a patient with poor prognosis. This is largely because, in the context of traditional psychotherapy, there are no behavioral controls to prevent recurrence of drug use, and resources are not available for behavioral intervention if a recurrence takes place, which it usually does. A system of impediments to the emergence of relapse, which rests heavily on the actual or symbolic role of the network, must, therefore, be established. The therapist must have assistance in addressing any minor episode of drug use so that this ever-present problem does not lead to an unmanageable relapse or an unsuccessful termination of therapy.

Preventing Relapse

How can the support network be used to deal with recurrences of drug use when, in fact, the patient's prior association with these same persons did not prevent use of alcohol or other drugs? In answering this question, it is necessary to clarify what the therapist must do to construct an effective support network. The following examples illustrate how this may be done. In Case 2, a specific format was defined with the network to monitor a patient's compliance with a disulfiram regimen:

Case Illustration: Case 2

A 33-year-old female public relations executive had moved to New York from a remote city three years before coming to treatment. She had no long-standing close relationships in the city, a circumstance not uncommon for a single alcoholic in a setting removed from her origins. She presented a 10-year history of heavy drinking that had increased in severity since her arrival, no doubt associated with her social isolation. Although she consumed a bottle of wine each night and additional hard liquor, she was able to get to work regularly. Six months before beginning treatment, she had attended AA meetings for two weeks and had been abstinent during that time. She had then relapsed, though, and she became disillusioned with the possibility of maintaining abstinence. At the outset of treatment, it was necessary to reassure her that her prior relapse was in large part a function (1) of not having established sufficient outside supports (including a more sound relationship with AA), and (2) of having seen herself as having failed after only one slip. The therapist realized, though, that there was a basis for concern about whether she should do any better now, if the same formula were reinstituted in the absence of sufficient reliable supports, which she did not seem to have. Together, therapist and patient came on the idea of bringing in an old friend whom she saw occasionally, and whom she felt she could trust. They made the following arrangement with her friend. The patient came to sessions twice a week. She would see her friend once each weekend. On each of these thrice-weekly occasions, the patient would be observed taking disulfiram, so that even if she missed a daily dose in between, it would not be possible for her to resume drinking on a regular basis undetected. The interpersonal support inherent in this arrangement, bolstered by conjoint meetings with her and her friend, also allowed her to return to AA with a sense of confidence in her ability to maintain abstinence.

The ensuing example illustrates how an ongoing network may be used to abort an emerging relapse. A high index of suspicion for signs of trouble was important, as was a clear understanding with the network members that they would be mobilized when necessary. Also illustrated, however, is the serious vulnerability of the network whose members may deny or rationalize because of their own drug use.

Case Illustration: Case 3

A 34-year-old cameraman became addicted to cocaine and used it heavily on a daily basis. He acquired a considerable amount of capital by extensively dealing (i.e., selling) the drug, primarily among friends and acquaintances, to support his habit.

After a point, though, his wife moved out of the house and took their baby, saying she could no longer tolerate his heavy drug use. Ironically, she had been using cocaine herself, but to a lesser extent. The couple reunited in the context of a therapy predicated on the patient's abstinence (and secondarily, on hers, too). It was supported by a network consisting of his wife, the patient's brother, and a good friend.

The issue of relapse arose in an interesting context, one that illustrates how the subtleties of attitude among network members influence the patient's attitudes. Each network member had a contributing role. The wife, seeing her husband's boredom and disillusionment at the contraction of his successful but illicit drug-sales career, suggested that he might be able to sell cocaine, although not use it himself. His friend had previously experienced difficulties with cocaine and had stopped on his own, but he still used it occasionally. The brother, a staunch advocate of abstinence from all drugs (and all other human frailties, for that matter), was feared by the patient as unable to empathize with his problems, although the patient did feel considerable affection toward him. No network members provided a suitable model for comfortable abstinence, given these circumstances.

Difficulties gradually emerged when the patient had been in treatment for six months, with only one occasion of use of a small amount. The therapist was away on vacation for a month and returned to find that the patient had again taken cocaine on two occasions. On a third occasion, he had brought some over to the home of his friend from the network and was fortunately persuaded to return it to the supplier. Although he had not taken the drug on this third occasion, it seemed essential to seize on the circumstances to reverse his orientation toward intermittent use. The therapist, therefore, summoned the network for weekly meetings, three in all, during which the risks inherent in the patient's occasional use of drugs were examined in a nonjudgmental way. The group affirmed what had seemingly been clear, but had not been fully adopted: the need for total abstinence in order to avoid the vulnerability to serious relapse. In this situation, it became necessary to explore the ambivalence of the wife and the friend. The brother's rigidity was also addressed, to underline that a judgmental attitude was not constructive in this situation.

The Network for Treatment Monitoring

Administration of disulfiram under observation is a treatment option that is easily adapted to work with social networks. A patient who has taken disulfiram cannot drink; a patient who agrees to be observed by a responsible party while taking disulfiram will not miss a dose without the observer's knowing. This may take a measure of persuasion and, above all, the therapist's commitment that such an approach can be reasonable and helpful, Case 4 shows one example of how this can take place.

Case Illustration: Case 4

Ted is a 55-year-old musician who, like may colleagues in his field, has had a successful career in the context of alcohol addiction. He is a man whose discomfort with dependency and compliance leads him to disregard some of the most routine of social norms; he drives without a license, for example. Although he acknowledges no responsibility or concern for those who hold authority over him, he is solicitous and responsible toward those who rely on him. It is because of this that he decided to take action about his drinking when his wife was soon to deliver their first child, even though he had paid little attention to her concern previously. The two had a tacit understanding that they would not place demands on each other.

The patient presented himself saying that he wanted to have disulfiram prescribed and made it implicitly clear that he was not too interested in a great deal of professional advice. The therapist was concerned, though, because the therapist had little faith that the patient would continue taking disulfiram for a day longer than he wanted to, and that he might not want to for very long. Because compliance based on trust was hardly this patient's style, it seemed necessary to corral him into an arrangement whereby he would agree to be monitored for at least the initial months of abstinence.

The network began with his wife alone. The therapist had pressed him to attend AA meetings and to bring his college-aged daughter from a previous marriage into the network. It seemed feasible to stage a negotiation in which the therapist would concede some points to him so that he could save face; he might then agree to having his wife observe him taking disulfiram. The therapist also conceded that the daughter's involvement should be a matter for his own decision, thereby making it clear that there was room for his own decision making in defining the therapeutic contract.

The therapist then said that the odds for his maintaining stable abstinence were significantly decreased if he did not go to AA meetings (it was clear to the therapist that he never would, anyway). The therapist told him, though, that the therapist could not, in good conscience, treat him if he neither went to AA nor participated in the observed disulfiram regimen. The odds of the treatment having a meaningful impact under such circumstances were not very good. The therapist was earnest, and this seemed to be a fair test of his commitment to treatment, anyway.

The patient agreed to comply to observation by his wife for a year, but he did not agree to long-term AA attendance. He continued with this disulfiram regimen with good reliability, as agreed, thus allowing him to get through his most vulnerable period. He then, subsequently, took the disulfiram on an ad hoc basis, while remaining abstinent and continuing in therapy.

Some patients are more easily convinced to attend AA meetings than the musician in this case. Others, although no more interested than the patient just described, may be more compliant. Therefore, the therapist must use compliance, mobilizing the support network as appropriate, in order to continue pressure for the patient's involvement with AA for a reasonable trial. It may take a considerable period of time, but ultimately, a patient may experience something of a conversion, wherein he adopts the group ethos and expresses a deep commitment to abstinence, a measure of commitment rarely observed in patients who experience psychotherapy without AA. When this occurs, the therapist may assume a more passive role in monitoring the patient's abstinence and in keeping an eye on the patient's ongoing involvement in AA.

TECHNICAL CONSIDERATIONS

Defining the Network's Membership

Establishing a network is a task that requires the active collaboration of patient and therapist. The two, aided by those parties who initially join the network, must search for the right balance of members. This process is not without problems, and the therapist must think in a strategic fashion. The following case illustrates this point.

Case Illustration: Case 5

A 25-year-old male graduate student had been abusing cocaine since high school, in part drawing on funds from his affluent family, who lived in a remote city. At two points in the process of establishing his support network the reactions of his live-in girlfriend (who worked with the therapist from the outset) were particularly important. Both he and she agreed to being in his 19-year-old sister, a freshman at a nearby college. He then mentioned a friend of his, apparently a woman whom he found attractive, even though there was no history of an overt romantic involvement. The therapist sensed that his girlfriend did not like the idea, although she offered no rationale for excluding this potential rival. The idea of having to rely for assistance solely on a younger sister and two women who might see each other as competitors was unappealing. The therapist, therefore, suggested dropping the idea of including the friend. The network then fell to evaluating the patient's uncle, whom he preferred to exclude, but whom his girlfriend thought appropriate. It later turned out (as the therapist had expected) that the uncle was in many ways a potentially disapproving representative of the parental generation. In this case, the therapist encouraged the patient to accept the uncle as a network member in order to round out the range of relationships within the group, and the therapist spelled out the rationale for this. In matter of fact, the uncle turned out to be caring and supportive, particularly after he was helped to understand the nature of the addictive process.

The therapist must carefully promote the choice of appropriate network members, just as the platoon leader selects those who will accompany her or him in combat. The network is crucial in determining the balance of therapy.

Defining the Network's Task

As conceived here, the therapist's relationship to the network is like that of a team leader rather than that of a family therapist. The network is established to implement a straightforward task: that of aiding the therapist to sustain the patient's abstinence. It must be directed with the same clarity of purpose that an organizational task force is directed to build more cars, to open a branch office, or to revise its management procedures. Competing and alternative goals must be suppressed or at least prevented from interfering with the primary task.

Unlike those involved in traditional family therapy, network members are not led to expect symptom relief or self-realization. This prevents development of competing goals for the network's meetings. It also assures the members protection from having their own motives scrutinized and thereby supports their continuing involvement without the threat of an assault on their psychological defenses. Because network members have kindly volunteered to participate, their motives must not be impugned. Their constructive behavior should be commended. It is useful to acknowledge appreciation for the contribution they are making to the therapy. There is always a counterproductive tendency on their part to minimize the value of their contribution.

The network must, therefore, be structured as an effective working group with good morale. This is not always easy, as the following case shows.

Case Illustration: Case 6

A 45-year-old single woman served as an executive in a large family-held business except when her alcohol problem led her into protracted binges. Her father, brother, and sister were prepared to banish her from the business, but they decided first to seek consultation. Because they had initiated the contract, they were included in the initial network and indeed were very helpful in stabilizing the patient. Unfortunately, however, the father was a domineering figure who intruded into all aspects of the business and often evoked angry outbursts from his children. The children typically reacted with petulance, which provoked him in return. The situation came to a head when both of the patient's siblings angrily petitioned the therapist to exclude the father from the network two months into the treatment. This presented a problem, because the father's control over the business made his involvement important in securing the patient's compliance. The patient's relapse was still a real possibility. This potentially coercive role, however, was an issue that the group could not easily handle. The therapist decided to support the father's membership in the group, indicating the constructive role he had played in getting the therapy started. It seemed necessary to support the earnestness of his concern for his daughter, rather than the children's dismay at their father's character pathology directly. The hubbub did, in fact, quiet down with time. The children became less provocative themselves, as the group responded to the therapist's pleas for civil behavior.

Frequency of Network Sessions

At the outset of therapy, it is important to see the patient with the group on a weekly basis for at least the first month. Unstable circumstances demand more frequent contacts with the network. Sessions can be tapered off to biweekly and then monthly intervals after a time. In order to sustain the continuing commitment of the group (particularly that between the therapist and the network members), network sessions should be held every three months or so for the duration of the individual therapy. Once the patient has stabilized, meetings tend less to address day-to-day issues. They may begin with a recounting by the patient of the drug situation. Reflections on the patient's progress and goals, or sometimes on the relations among the network members, may then be discussed. In any case, it is essential that an agreement be made that network members contact the therapist if they are concerned about the patient's possible use of alcohol or other drugs, and that the therapist contact the network members if concern increases about a potential relapse.

Confidentiality

Use of the network raises the issues of confidentiality and the nature of the therapist's commitment to the patient. The overriding commitment of the therapist to the patient is that the therapist support the patient in maintaining the drug-free state. Open communication on matters regarding alcohol and other drugs should be maintained among the network, the patient, and the therapist. The therapist must set the proper tone of mutual trust and understanding so that the patient's right to privacy is not otherwise compromised. It is also made explicit that absolute confidentiality applies to all other (non-drug-related) communications between therapist and patient and that network members should not expect to communicate with the therapist about any matter that does not directly relate to alcohol or other drug problems.

Intrusive Measures

Certain circumstances may necessitate further incursions on the patient's autonomy in order to assure compliance with treatment. This is particularly true when the patient has begun treatment reluctantly, as with overt pressure from family or employer, or when the possibility of relapse will have grave consequences. Optional measures may include financial constraints, spousal separation, and urine monitoring. These, of course, can only be undertaken with the patient's agreement, based on the fact that greater or more immediate loss is being averted. Such steps may also provide greater certitude against relapse to all concerned, including an uneasy therapist and family.

Cse Illustration: Case 7

A 35-year-old man had used heroin intranasally for two years and then intravenously for eight months; he had previously used other drugs. He was stealing money from the family business in which he worked. The patient underwent ambulatory detoxification, but he relapsed to heroin use and finally underwent a hospitalization that lasted five weeks. On discharge from the hospital, he was referred to the therapist and was to continue with meetings of Narcotics Anonymous. His network consisted of his mother and his wife and the following family members involved in the family business: his father, his younger sister and brother, and his uncle. His family was very concerned about allowing him to get involved again in the business. He, therefore, agreed to do two things so that he might be included with less concern on everyone's part: (1) The patient agreed to have his urine spot-checked on a regular basis, and (2) he and the therapist, along with the network, discussed his financial circumstances in the firm, clarifying what consequences might result should he return to active addiction. An informal but explicit agreement was reached in this matter, thereby helping the patient understand the constraints under which he was operating and leaving the family more comfortable about his return to work. Because this agreement was undertaken with the network, it became a part of the treatment plan.

Adapting Individual Therapy to the Network Treatment

As noted, network sessions are scheduled on at least a weekly basis at the outset of treatment. This is likely to compromise the number of individual contacts. Indeed, if sessions are held once a week, the patient may not be seen individually for a period of time. This may be perceived as a deprivation by the patient unless the individual therapy is presented as an opportunity for further growth predicated on achieving stable abstinence assured through work with the network.

When individual therapy does begin, the traditional objectives of therapy must be ordered to accommodate the goals of the substance abuse treatment. For insight-oriented therapy, clarification of unconscious motivations is a primary objective; for supportive therapy, the bolstering of established constructive defenses is primary. In the therapeutic context that we are describing, however, the following objectives are given precedence:

1. *Exposure to the substance and to relevant cues.* The therapy first must address the patient's exposure to substances of abuse, or exposure to cues that might precipitate alcohol or other drug use, as describe by Galanter (1983). Both patient and therapist should be sensitive to this matter and should explore these situations as they arise.

2. *Stable and appropriate social context.* The therapy should support a stable social context in an appropriate social environment—one conducive to abstinence with minimal disruption of life circumstances. Considerations of minor disruptions in place of residence, friends, or job need not be a primary issue for the patient with character disorder or neurosis, but they cannot go untended here. For a considerable period of time, the substance abuser is highly vulnerable to exacerbations of the addictive illness and must be viewed with considerable caution (i.e., in some respects as one treats the recently compensated psychotic).

3. *Individual priorities related to psychological conflict.* After attending to the first two priorities, psychological conflicts that the patient must resolve, relative to the patient's own growth, are considered. As the therapy continues, these come to assume a more prominent role. In the earlier phases, they are likely to directly reflect issues associated with previous drug use. Later, however, the tenor of treatment will come to resemble increasingly the traditional psychotherapeutic context. At this point, the therapist is in the admirable position of working with a patient who, while exercising insight into his or her problems, is also motivated by the realization of a new and previously untapped potential.

Empirical Research

Two studies have recently been added to empirical research on network therapy. In one, the technique was standardized relative to a structured treatment manual, and in the second, an assessment was made of the feasibility of training clinicians in the technique.

Standardization

Contemporary research on psychosocial treatment modalities requires the development of a structured manual that explicates the way in which the treatment is carried out in the clinical setting. It is only in this manner that reliability can be achieved across clinicians in the application of therapy techniques.

Such a manual, 122 pages in length, was developed for Network Therapy (Galanter & Keller, 1994). Seventeen clinicians were then trained in the network technique and tested for their ability to distinguish network procedures in a reliable manner from conventional family systems therapy framed for the treatment of substance abusers. For both modalities, videotape segments of respective sessions were shown and scored by mental health professionals. The treatments were found differentiable with a high degree of reliability.

Clinical Training Study

The Network Therapy Rating Scale, which was employed with this latter group fo subjects was then applied in a second study, in which the efficacy of clinical training was assessed in terms of the results of treatment of substance abusers in the clinical context. In this second study (Galanter, Keller, & Dermatis, 1997), 19 third-year psychiatric residents without experience in substance abuse treatment or in outpatient therapy were given a 13-hour course in network therapy. They then undertook the treatment of cocaine addicts, and were supervised by clinicians experienced in the network therapy technique. Altogether, 24 patients were each treated over the course of a 24-week treatment episode. Seventy-nine percent of the urine samples obtained each week from these patients while in treatment were negative for cocaine, and 42 percent of the patients produced clean urines during the three weeks immediately prior to their termination. Overall, this outcome, along with treatment retention rates, compared favorable with that reported in several studies on cocaine treatment in the medical literature in which experienced therapists were employed. These results suggest that naive mental health trainees can be taught to apply network therapy for effective substance-abuse management.

ALTERNATIVE TREATMENT OPTIONS

TREATMENT SETTINGS OTHER THAN THE CLINICIAN'S OFFICE

Inpatient Detoxification

Inpatient detoxification units allow for the removal of patients from their habitual environments into a drug-free setting. This intervention not only interrupts drug use but also helps prevent the progression of the withdrawal process.

Once admitted, the patient can be thoroughly evaluated for psychiatric status and medical and cognitive conditions. Proper diagnosis and treatment of psychiatric and medical complications can be extremely difficult to complete on an unstable ambulatory patient.

Inpatient settings constitute the ideal forum for the initial assessment of the patient's social and family support networks. Frequently, initial family interventions are only accomplished in the safe room of an inpatient detoxification unit.

Inpatient Rehabilitation

Very often when immediate reinstatement to the community of the recently detoxified individual is not clinically advisable, the clinician may suggest referral to a drug rehabilitation facility. These settings provide such patients with a temporary residence until an appropriate living arrangement can be finally worked out, and they constitute an adequate environment for long-term treatment planning.

The typical rehabilitation unit is a residential community of recovering drug users whose experiences and feelings are shared in a new substance-free context. Average patient stays are about 28 days, and the programs generally adhere to a treatment model that incorporates addiction counselors as their primary therapists and, in the case of alcoholism rehabilitation centers, a strong AA orientation. Characteristically, attempts are made to recruit family members and employers into the process of restructuring the patient's social network. The treatment per se is delivered in the context of small groups, but often, appreciable changes are attributed to the application of systems therapy and crisis interventions (Stuckey & Harrison, 1982).

Therapeutic Communities

Protracted maladaptive behaviors and severe disaffiliation from the community are both adequate indications for patient referral to therapeutic communities for the treatment of drug abuse. These treatment settings provide inmates with a fairly structured environment and a lifestyle that generally is organized around a specific treatment philosophy and schedule of recovery. Most therapeutic communities follow a three-phase treatment program that aims at reshaping the individual patient under the influence of daily enforcement of specific behaviors and values strongly espoused by the commune. Initially, most of these programs have residents both participate in various forms of structured therapies and advance in some kind of job-privilege hierarchy. Eventually, each resident undergoes a period of transisiton back into the home community, following psychological and frequently vocational rehabilitation. It has been suggested that there is a positive association between time spent in a therapeutic community and posttreatment outcome (De Leon, 1984; Holland, 1983; Stuckey & Harrison, 1982). Attrition rates, however, have traditionally been very high, up to 50 percent in fact, during the initial months of treatment.

Multimodality Outpatient Clinics

Most alcoholics in professional treatment in the United States attend multimodality outpatient clinics. For those alcoholics with associated nonacute medical or psychiatric disorders in particular, such a treatment setting represents an appropriate choice. Usually, this kind of clinic offers a variety of treatment modalities that include individual and group therapies, and recreational and vocational rehabilitation. Given their frequent association with medical institutions, these clinics can often assess and treat mild medical complications, and they serve as a referring source for the patient to those services and resources available in the community, such as vocational rehabilitation programs, medical facilities, and AA, NA, or CA.

Those patients capable of benefiting from these programs need to meet some minimal degree of stability regarding their social and medical statuses. The more socially intact and the more motivated and healthy the patient is, the more likely he or she will be to achieve and maintain abstinence from alcohol or other drugs.

OTHER TREATMENT MODALITIES

FAMILY THERAPIES

Contrary to a widely held belief, alcoholics and other drug abusers are far more often found in the context of intact family situations than on Skid Row. Only a minority of alcoholics and other drug abusers live in social isolation and homelessness (World Health Organization, 1977). We already reviewed the evidence supporting the association between hereditary-environmental factors and alcoholism and other drug dependence. Substance abuse runs in families. Additionally, family interactions are intimately intertwined with substance-abuse behavior, and they represent an important area of clinical study, because they are valuable from both diagnostic and treatment perspectives.

SYSTEMS FAMILY THERAPY

Reflecting this view, systems family therapists have proposed a model for both classifying and treating families with substance-abusing members. (Steinglass, Weiner, & Mendelson, 1971). A key concept in the formulation of their topological scheme and methodology of treatment is that of the alcoholic system. According to this model, families are classified according to the degree to which family patterns of interaction are structured around the behavior of the alcoholic member, from "a family with an alcoholic member" (when the behavioral patterns are only minimally organized around alcoholic behavior) to "an alcoholic family" (whose interactions are maximally dependent on the alcoholic member). Treatment success is measured according to not only the quality of abstinence achieved by the identified patient, but also the magnitude of improvement in the level of functioning of the family system or unit.

STRATEGIC AND STRUCTURAL FAMILY THERAPIES

Stanton and Todd (1982) have proposed a family model of addiction and treatment based on their extensive experience in applying a strategic-structural therapy approach to families with a heroin-dependent member. They see drug addiction as part of a cyclical process involving parents (or parent surrogates) and addict in an interdependent system. Addicted behavior serves an important protective function and helps to maintain the homeostatic balance of the family system. Central to this model is their contention that drug addiction also serves in a number of ways to resolve the dilemma of whether the addict can become an independent adult. Addicts, in fact, maintain close contact with their families of origin, and the addicted behavior attempts to ameliorate serious parental problems and generally reflects family conflicts.

This therapy approach requires a different perspective of the addiction process and of the people and systems involved in it. Treatment strategies focus on the consequences of interactional behavior and specific acts, rather than on the content of family verbalizations. The goals of treatment are (1) total abstinence by the addicted member of both illegal and legal drugs (such as methadone); (2) a productive use of time by the addict, through gainful employment or through stable school or vocational training; (3) stable and autonomous living conditions by the addicted member.

Therapy is concerned mostly in correcting the repetitive interactional patterns that maintain drug use. The thrust of treatment is to alter their behavioral sequences, usually by taking advantage of spontaneous or induced crises in the family.

LARGE SELF-HELP GROUPS FOR SUBSTANCE ABUSERS

By far, the most notable example of self-help groups for substance abusers is AA. Derivative groups such as CA and NA are organized along the basic AA model that includes a fellowship of men and women who share their individual experiences with alcohol or other drugs and who derive support from one another in the context of large group gatherings.

The organization is premised on a list of beliefs known as the twelve steps as their basic philosophy of recovery, to be accepted and strictly followed by all members. The cohesiveness generated by self-disclosure, the adherence to a shared belief system, and a strong sense of mutual affiliation achieved in these twelve-step programs have proved indisputably efficacious in inducing and maintaining long-term abstinence. In this respect, Emerick, Lasse, and Edwards (1977) have noted that AA has been more effective as an enforcer of abstinence among its members than traditional psychotherapies, which, on the other hand, have proved more successful at effecting reduction and control of drinking behavior. Multiple internal surveys of AA members, for instance, have yielded the following statistics: More than half of new members who remain in the fellowship for at least three months maintain abstinence for a consequent year. Then, members' chances of remaining sober for another year are an average of 86 percent.

This self-help movement originated in the 1930s as a social response to the lack of available professional treatment for alcoholics. It is now a worldwide organization with close to one million members in the United States and Canada alone (Castañeda & Galanter, 1987). AA, CA, and NA are by now widely regarded by professional treatment centers as a vital adjunct to the treatment of alcohol and other drug abuse. As AA itself has observed, more than 30 percent of its members credit a rehabilitation center or some form of professional counseling for their initial referral to AA.

The demonstrated success of the model of recovery promulgated by these self-help groups, and the identification through a series of controlled studies of mechanisms of psychological influence in contemporary charismatic religious sects (Galanter, 1984), have inspired the institution (in otherwise traditional treatment settings) of groups that attempt to capture in their de-sign and overall organization the basic traits that characterize such large self-help groups and religious sects. Controlled studies have demonstrated that these peer-led therapy groups can yield improved cost-effectiveness and clin-ical outcome when compared to traditional small treatment groups currently employed by most alcoholism treatment facilities (Galanter, Castañeda, & Salamon, 1987).

MANAGED CARE

Managed care has had a profound impact on the availability of treatment for substance abuse. Whereas long-term inpatient treatment (such as the Hazelden model) was widely available in the 1970s, there is now considerable pressure to truncate any period of inpatient treatment. Such treatment is usually restricted to no more than several days, and movement is afoot to apply such treatment only to substance abusers suffering major and severe sequelae of withdrawal or comorbid illness.

Ironically, comprehensive ambulatory care is not necessarily provided as an alternative to diminished inpatient treatment. The number of visits available to the substance abuser in psychosocially based ambulatory care is often quite limited, and parties monitoring the treatment typically require a justification of continued care after each sequence of several visits. Furthermore, reim-bursement for each session is often quite limited, so that rates for ambulatory sessions may be appropriate only to therapists with limited training.

Despite these trends, there is a growing awareness of the limitations of such abbreviated treatment in terms of both the vulnerability to relapse and the cost offset of treatment that is associated with more effective care. These factors are coming to provide a greater appreciation among corporate employers, and cer-tainly health professionals, of the importance of providing a broad spectrum of treatment options tailored to the level of care suitable to each given patient. Hopefully, this latter trend will emerge further and assure the appropriate care needed for addictive illness, since appropriate care is generally provided for other medical diseases.

PRESCRIPTIVE TREATMENT

The modalities usually employed in addiction treatment are not specific to any subgroups of patients. That is to say, there is no unanimity in the empirical lit-erature on which patients are more appropriate for group therapy or for individ-ual therapy; or for twelve-step treatment of less spiritually oriented approaches. Each modality could be appropriate either to beginning therapy or to later stages of treatment.

Patients, however, may be at different stages of readiness for treatment and require attention appropriate to that stage. Thus, the enhancement of a pa-tient's motivation for abstinence is most relevant for patients who are not yet aware of the nature and severity of their illness. Similarly, patients in severe relapse may be suitable for more assertive interventions that employ family confrontation with support from a professional.

The choice of a proper level of care, reflected in the intensity of the therapeutic support system in which the patient is placed, is an issue that confronts the clinician. Medically managed intensive inpatient treatment is more suitable for patients who are unable to deal with their detoxification from alcohol or other drugs while at home, or who have acute medical or psychiatric problems associated with their substance abuse. Medical monitoring in a nonhospital residential setting (like a sobering-up station) may be appropriate for patients with less server problems associated with their detoxification. Intensive outpatient treatment or partial hospitalization is suited to stabilized patients who require some additional support, whereas more attenuated outpatient treatments, as with weekly ambulatory sessions, is suitable for stabilized patients in a well-established pattern of recovery.

SUMMARY

In this chapter we have looked at the risk factors that contribute to the onset of substance abuse, including social, genetic, and physiologic issues. Following this, the diagnostic criteria for substance abuse and dependence were reviewed, along with the problems associated with making a diagnosis, particularly issues of comorbidity and polysubstance dependence.

The overall strategies for addiction treatment have been reviewed, ranging from the initial patient encounter to techniques for family therapy and network therapy. In this regard, case descriptions were used to illustrate the particulars of the respective approaches, including the introduction of family supports, and monitoring the course of the patient's treatment. Specifics of Network Therapy, which include family and peer supports along with relapse prevention, were reviewed, along with the results of training in this technique.

In addition to this, particulars of inpatient treatment, therapeutic communities, multimodality outpatient treatment, and twelve-step groups are discussed relative to their integration into a comprehensive approach to the treatment. Finally, the impact of managed care and the proper placement of patients in treatment have been considered.

REFERENCES

American Psychiatric Association. (1994). *Diagnostic and statistical manual of mental disorders* (4th ed.), Washington, DC: Author.

Anthenelli, R.M., & Schuckit M.A. (1990). Genetic studies of alcoholism. *International Journal of Addiction, 3,* 31–94.

Balint, M. (1969). *The basic fault.* London: Tavistock.

Begleiter, H., Porjesz, B., Bihari, B., & Kissin, B. (1984). Event-related brain potentials in boys at risk for alcoholism. *Science, 225,* 1493–1496.

Brady, K.T., Grice, D.E., & Dustan, L. (1993). Gender differences in substance use disorders. *American Journal of Psychiatry, 150,* 1708–1711.

Castañeda, R., & Galanter, M. (1987). A review of treatment modalities for alcoholism and their outcome. *American Journal of Social Psychiatry, 7*(4), 237–244.

Castañeda, R., & Galanter, M. (1988). Ethnic differences in drinking practices and cognitive impairment among detoxifying alcoholics. *Journal of Studies on Alcohol, 49,*(4), 335–339.

Cotton, N.S. (1979). The familial incidence of alcoholism. *Journal of Studies on Alcohol, 40,* 89–115.

De Leon, G. (1984). *The therapeutic community: Study of effectiveness* (National Institute of Drug Abuse Treatment Monograph Series). Rockville, MD: National Institute of Drug Abuse Treatment.

Emerick, C., Lasse, D.L., & Edwards, M.T. (1977). Nonprofessional peers as therapeutic agents. In A.M. Razin & A.S. Gurman (Eds.), *Effective psychotherapy: A handbook of research.* New York: Pergamon Press.

Fernandez-Pol, B., Bluestone, H., Missouri, C., Morales, G., & Mizruchi, M.S. (1986). Drinking patterns of inner-city black Americans and Puerto Ricans. *Journal of Studies on Alcohol, 47*(2), 156–160.

Frances, R.J., Timm, S., & Bucky, S. (1980). Studies of familial and nonfamilial alcoholism. *Archives of General Psychiatry, 37,* 564–566.

Galanter, M. (1983). Cognitive labelling: Adapting antecedents of narcotic use and addiction: A study psychotherapy to the treatment of alcohol abuse. *Journal of Psychiatric Treatment and Evaluation, 5,* 551–556.

Galanter, M. (1984). Self-help large group therapy for alcoholism: A controlled study. *Alcoholism: Clinical and Experimental Research, 8*(1), 16–23.

Galanter, M., & Castañeda, R. (1985). Self-destructive behavior in the substance abuser. *Psychiatric Clinics of North America, 8*(2), 251–261.

Galanter, M., Castañeda, R., & Ferman, J. (1988). Substance abuse among general psychiatric patients: A review of the "dual diagnosis" problem. *American Journal of Drug and Alcohol Abuse, 14*(2), 211–235.

Galanter, M., Castañeda, R., & Salamon, I. (1987). Institutional self-help therapy for alcoholism: Clinical outcome. *Alcoholism: Clinical and Experimental Research, 11*(5), 1–6.

Galanter, M., Keller, D., & Dermatis, H. (1997). Network therapy for addiction: Assessment of the clinical outcome of training. *American Journal of Drug and Alcohol Abuse, 23,* 355–367.

Gallant, D.M., Rich, A., Bey, E., & Terranova, L. (1970). Group psychotherapy with married couples: A successful technique in New Orleans Alcoholism Clinic patients. *Journal of Louisiana State Medical Society, 122,* 41–44.

Gitlow, S.E., & Peyser, H.S. (Eds.). (1980). *Alcoholism: A practical treatment guide.* New York: Grune & Stratton.

Goodwin, D.W. (1979). Alcoholism and heredity. *Archives of General Psychiatry, 36,* 57–61.

Goodwin, D.W. (1981). *Alcoholism: The facts.* New York: Oxford University Press.

Goodwin, D.W., Schlusinger, F., & Hemansen, L. (1975). Alcoholism and the hyperactive child syndrome. *Journal of Mental and Nervous Disease, 150,* 349–353.

Goodwin, D.W., Schlusinger, F., Hemansen, L., Guze, S.B., & Winokour, G. (1973). Alcohol problems in adoptees raised apart form alcoholic biological parents. *Archives of General Psychiatry, 28,* 238–243.

Haarstrup, S., & Thomsen, K. (1972). The social backgrounds of young addicts as elicited in interviews with their parents. *Acta Psychiatrica Scandinavica, 48,* 146–173.

Hayman, M. (1956). Current attitudes to alcoholism of psychiatrists in Southern California. *American Journal of Psychiatry, 112,* 484–493.

Heath, D.B., Waddell, J.D., & Topper, M.T. (Eds.). (1981). Cultural factors in alcohol research and treatment of drinking problems. *Journal of Studies on Alcohol Supplement, 9,* 217–240.

Helzer, J.E., Robins, I.N., & Davis, D.H. (1976). Antecedents of narcotic use and addiction: A study of 898 Vietnam veterans. *Drug and Alcohol Dependence, 3,* 183–190.

Holland, S. (1983). Evaluating community-based treatment programs: A model for strengthening inferences about effectiveness. *International Journal of Therapeutic Communities, 4,* 285–306.

Kaij, L. (1960). *Alcoholism in twins.* Stockholm: Almqvist & Wiksell.

Kane, P. (1981). *Inner-city alcoholism and ecological analysis, a cross-cultural study.* New York: Human Resources Press.

Keeler, M.H., Taylor, C.I., & Miller, W.C. (1979). Are all recently detoxified alcoholics depressed? *American Journal of Psychiatry, 136,* 586–588.

Keller, D., Galanter, M., & Weinberg, S. (1997). Validation of a scale for Network Therapy: A technique for systematic use of peer and family support in addiction treatment. *American Journal of Drug and Alcohol Abuse, 23,* 115–127.

Kernberg, O. (1975). *Borderline conditions and pathological narcissism.* New York: Aronson.

Khantzian, E.S. (1982). Psychopathology, psychodynamics, and alcoholism. In E. Kaufman & E.M. Pattison (Eds.), *Encyclopedia handbook of alcoholism.* New York: Gardner Press.

Kohut, H. (1971). *The analysis of the self.* New York: International Universities Press.

Kosten, T.K., Gawin, F.H., & Kosten, T.R. (1993). Gender differences in cocaine use and treatment response. *Journal of Substance Abuse Treatment, 10,* 63–66.

National Institute on Drug Abuse. (1990). *National household survey on drug abuse: Main findings 1988.* Rockville, MD: National Institute on Drug Abuse.

Pattison, E.M., Sobell, M.B., & Sobell, I.C. (1977). *Emerging concepts of alcohol dependence.* New York: Springer.

Pettinati, H.M., Sugarman, A.A., & Maurer, H.S. (1982). Four year MMPI changes in abstinent and drinking alcoholics. *Alcoholism: Clinical and Experimental Research, 6,* 487–494.

Ray, B.A., & Braude, M.C. (Eds.). (1986). *Women and drugs: A new era for research.* Rockville, MD: National Institute on Drug Abuse.

Regier, D., Myers, J.K., & Kramer, M. (1984). The NIMH epidemiological catchment area program. *Archives of General Psychiatry, 41,* 934–958.

Regier, D.A., Boyd, J.D., Burke, J.D., Jr., Rae, D.S., Myers, J.K., Kramer, M., Robins, L.N., George, L.K., Karns, M., & Locke, B.Z. (1988). One month prevalence of psychiatric disorders in the United States. *Archives of General Psychiatry, 45,* 977–985.

Resnick, R.B., & Resnick, E. (1984). Cocaine abuse and its treatment. *Psychiatric Clinics of North America, 7,* 713–728.

Rosenberg, C.M. (1969). Young drug addicts: Background and personality. *Journal of Nervous and Mental Disease, 148,* 65–73.

Schuckitt, M.A. (1985). The clinical implications of primary diagnostic groups among alcoholics. *Archives of General Psychiatry, 42,* 1043–1049.

Sobell, I.C. (1979). Reliability of alcohol abusers' self-reports of drinking behavior. *Behaviour Research and Therapy, 17,* 157–160.

Speck, R. (1967). Psychotherapy of the social network of a schizophrenic family. *Family Process, 6,* 208.

Stanton, D., & Todd, T. (1982). *The family therapy of drug and addiction.* New York: Guilford Press.

Steinglass, P., Weiner, S., & Mendelson, J.H. (1971). A systems approach to alcoholism: A model and its clinical applications. *Archives of General Psychiatry, 24,* 401–408.

Stuckey, R.F., & Harrison, J.S. (1982). The alcoholism rehabilitation center. In E. Kaufman & E.M. Pattison (Eds.), *Encyclopedic handbook of alcoholism* (pp. 865–873). New York: Gardner Press.

Tarter, R.E., Hegedus, A.M., & Goldstein, G. (1984). Adolescent sons of alcoholics: Neuropsychological and personality characteristics. *Alcoholism, Clinical and Experimental Research, 8,* 216–222.

Vaillant, G.E. (1981). Dangers of psychotherapy in the treatment of alcoholism. In M.H. Bean & N.E. Zimberg (Eds.), *Dynamic approaches to the understanding and treatment of alcoholism.* New York: Free Press.

Vaillant, G.E. (1983). *The natural history of alcoholism.* Cambridge, MA: Harvard University Press.

Vishi, T.R., Jones, K.R., Shank, E.L., & Lima, I.H. (1980). *The alcohol, drug abuse and mental health national data book.* Washington, DC: Department of Health and Human Services.

White, K.A., Brady, K.B., & Sonne, S. (1996). Gender differences in patterns of cocaine use. *American Journal of Addictions, 5,* 259–261.

Winokour, G. (1979). Alcoholism and depression in the same family. In D.W. Goodwin & C.K. Erickson (Eds.), *Alcoholism and affective disorders.* New York: Medical & Scientific Books.

World Health Organization. (1977). *Manual of international statistical classification of diseases, injuries and causes of death* (ICD-9). Geneva: Author.

Zimberg, S. (1977). Alcoholics Anonymous and the treatment and prevention of alcoholism. *Alcoholism: Clinical and Experimental Research, 1,* 91–102.

Zimberg, S. (1982). *The clinical management of alcoholism.* New York: Brunner/Mazel.

CHAPTER 25

Alcoholism-Behavior Therapy

JON D. KASSEL, ERIC F. WAGNER, and MARINA UNROD

CONCEPTUALIZATION

Perhaps more than any other behavioral disorder, the study of alcoholism* has been plagued by ideological controversy. Dogmatic approaches to the conceptualization, prevention, and treatment of this disorder have persisted in the field for years, often resulting in a chasm between science and practice. Questions such as whether alcoholism is a disease, inheritable, controllable, a reflection of moral weakness, a habit, has an inevitable and predictable course, and is socioculturally determined, still evoke discussion and debate. At the same time, our conceptualizations and understanding of the etiology of alcoholism inevitably and necessarily affect the formulation of treatment strategies. Thus, pertinent questions, such as whether total abstinence or controlled drinking are acceptable treatment goals, have also generated passionate discussion over the years (Maltzman, 1994; Miller, 1983a; M. Sobell & Sobell, 1995).

Acknowledging that our understanding of the processes governing development of alcohol-related problems is quite limited, we must still face the fact that costs of alcoholism to our society are large in every respect. Alcohol dependent individuals suffer from a variety of medical disorders directly attributable to their drinking (e.g., Merrill, Fox, & Chang, 1993) and are among the highest cost users of medical care in the country (Zook & Moore, 1980). Estimates suggest that over 7 percent of individuals 18 and older currently meet diagnostic criteria for alcohol abuse or dependence, with an additional segment of the population manifesting less severe, though still problematic, forms of

---

*The terms *alcoholism* and *alcohol dependence* will be used interchangeably throughout this chapter. Though some might argue that they denote different constructs, we believe that their differential use stems from an ideological, rather than an empirical basis. *Alcohol abuse*, on the other hand, is viewed as a different entity, as discussed in the section on Diagnosis. The terms *alcohol-related problems* and *disorders* encompass the entire spectrum of both abuse and dependence.

alcohol use disorders (Regier et al., 1993). Moreover, the number of people using alcoholism treatment services has risen dramatically, culminating in over 500,000 patients on any given day during the late 1980s (Weisner, Greenfield, & Room, 1995).

As such, the quest for effective treatments for this disorder is a critical one. Research has revealed that clinical outcomes are determined by multiple factors, including patient characteristics, psychosocial functioning, life context factors, as well as the treatment itself (Institute of Medicine, 1989; Moos, Finney, & Cronkite, 1990). Recognizing that the disorder is an inherently complex one, it is unlikely that any single treatment approach will work for all patients. Furthermore, much of the available treatment for alcoholism is steeped in approaches (e.g., confrontational interventions, general counseling, educational lectures) that, when subjected to empirical scrutiny, do not fare well (Finney & Monahan, 1996; Holder, Longabaugh, Miller, & Rubonis, 1991; Miller et al., 1995). The good news, however, is that there is accumulating evidence supporting effectiveness of certain interventions. Finney and Moos (1998) assert that "... the most effective treatments are those that help patients shape and adapt to their life circumstances" (p. 157). Indeed, as will be discussed in some detail in this chapter, behavioral and cognitive-behavioral models of alcoholism have emerged as particularly helpful in conceptualizing the disorder and in treating it.

It is important to note that multiple factors influence treatment outcome. Although space limitations prevent a thorough discussion of these factors, the following conclusions drawn by Finney and Moos (1998) are offered. Regarding characteristics of the therapist and their affect on treatment, the literature suggests that patients whose therapists are interpersonally skilled, less confrontational, and/or more empathic fare better. Another hotly debated issue has been whether longer treatment is better than brief treatment. Available data suggest that treatment is more effective when spread out over a long period of time and of low intensity. Finally, the question about whether inpatient or outpatient treatment is ultimately more effective yields an equivocal answer: Overall, it appears that there is little to no difference in outcomes of inpatient versus outpatient treatment. However, inpatient treatment appears to be more effective for those patients who are more seriously impaired and who are less socially stable.

DIAGNOSTIC ISSUES AND PROBLEMS

Diagnostic clarity provides a common language for treatment providers and the basis for effective treatment planning. Diagnostic criteria for alcohol problems reflect the consensus of clinical researchers as to the patterning of behavioral, cognitive, and physiological characteristics that constitute symptoms of these conditions. Diagnostic formulations of alcoholism have changed dramatically in recent years (Nathan, 1991). Earlier versions of the American Psychiatric Association's *Diagnostic and Statistical Manual of Mental Disorders* (DSM) grouped alcoholism along with a general set of problems including personality disorders, homosexuality, and neuroses. Edwards and Gross' (1976; Edwards, 1986) influential work later resulted in the formulation of an alcohol dependence syndrome, defined as a narrowing of the drinking repertoire, drink-seeking behavior, tolerance, withdrawal, drinking to relieve or avoid withdrawal symptoms, subjective awareness of the compulsion to drink, and a return to drinking after a period of abstinence.

In *DSM-III* (American Psychiatric Association, 1980), the term alcoholism was dropped in favor of two separate categories, labeled "alcohol abuse" and "alcohol dependence." Subsequent revisions in *DSM-III-R* (APA, 1987) regarded alcohol abuse as a residual category for diagnosing those individuals who, although they did not meet criteria for dependence, nonetheless exhibited problematic drinking behavior. The *DSM-IV* (APA, 1994) represents further refinement of alcohol-related diagnoses. Alcohol abuse is diagnosed by presence of any of four symptoms: hazardous use, interference with role obligations, legal problems caused by drinking, or continued drinking despite social or interpersonal problems. Alcohol dependence is diagnosed when three of the following criteria are present: tolerance, withdrawal, drinking in larger amounts or over a longer period of time than intended, unsuccessful attempts or a desire to cut down or quit, a great deal of time spent drinking, activities given up or reduced to drink, and continued drinking despite knowledge of negative consequences. It should be noted that these criteria reflect, to a great extent, the previously described alcohol dependence syndrome. *DSM-IV* also permits the subtyping of dependence based on presence or absence of tolerance and withdrawal. Finally, *DSM-IV* highlights the fact that symptoms of other psychological disorders, such as depression or anxiety, may be related to the individual's use of alcohol or other drugs.

Use of valid assessment measures is crucial in formulating diagnoses and treatment plans. Such measures need to tap the heterogeneity of the disorder, the high rates of psychiatric comorbidity, and alcohol-related problems that fall below the diagnostic threshold. Proper assessment is also critical given that alcohol-related problems are often underdetected by health professionals (Moore et al., 1980). Fortunately, there are numerous instruments now available that possess excellent psychometric properties. Paper-and-pencil questionnaires, such as the Michigan Alcohol Screening Test (MAST), Alcohol Use Disorders Identification Test (AUDIT), and CAGE have yielded adequate sensitivities and specificities and are easily administered (see Allen & Columbus, 1995, for an excellent compendium of instruments to assess alcohol problems). Interview methods, such as the Structured Clinical Interview for *DSM-IV* (First, Gibbon, Spitzer, & Williams, 1995), are also available and can further facilitate detection and diagnosis of alcohol problems. In sum, proper assessment and diagnosis is clearly a critical component of treatment planning. McCrady and Langenbucher (1996) provide a succinct summary when they assert, "The use of appropriate tools to determine the severity of dependence and to establish formal diagnosis should enhance selection of appropriate treatments and treatment settings" (p. 739).

TREATMENT STRATEGIES

During the past decade, considerable research has been devoted to determining effectiveness of interventions for alcohol abuse and dependence. Of extant treatments, behavioral and cognitive-behavioral interventions have shown great promise and, indeed, have received substantial empirical support (Finney & Moos, 1998; Holder et al., 1991; Miller & Hester, 1986; Morgan, 1996). According to the cognitive-behavioral conceptualization, drinking is best regarded as a learned behavior than can be modified by identifying its antecedents and consequences, and modifying the drinker's cognitive, behavioral, and affective responses to them. The treatment approaches reviewed in this chapter all reflect this basic premise. Evidence continues to grow in support of longstanding behavioral interventions, such as self-management/self-control training and relapse prevention. More recent behavioral treatments for alcohol problems also have shown promise. These include cue exposure treatment, skills training, and behavioral marital therapy (see Hester & Miller, 1995; Holder et al., 1991; Morgan, 1996).

The following section provides a brief review of the literature on behavioral treatments of alcohol abuse and alcohol dependence, with a focus on empirical studies conducted over the past 10 years (see L. Sobell, Toneatto, & Sobell, 1990, for a review of earlier studies assessing behavioral treatment of alcoholism and drug abuse). Our review is not intended to be an exhaustive one. Rather, our goal is to present an overview of several behavioral interventions currently available and to assess their effectiveness by highlighting a number of well-controlled, representative studies. For a more comprehensive review and detailed discussion of current alcoholism interventions and treatment outcome, the interested reader is referred to Finney and Moos (1998), Hester and Miller (1995), Kadden (1994), McCrady and Langenbucher (1996), and Morgan (1996).

It is important to note that, although various interventions will be presented and discussed separately, there is considerable overlap among them. We should also point out that our review includes both behavioral and cognitive-behavioral treatments. We chose to do this given that many variants of modern behaviorism acknowledge the role of cognition (e.g., Locke, 1995; Mischel, 1997), and the alcoholism-treatment field has come to recognize that behavioral and cognitive factors are often inextricably linked, with both playing a crucial role in the development and maintenance of the disorder.

BEHAVIORAL SELF-CONTROL TRAINING

Behavioral Self-Control Training (BSCT) is a brief-treatment approach in which clients learn specific self-regulation techniques (Hester, 1995). Although it can be used with clients pursuing the goal of abstinence, BSCT is probably most often thought of as a moderation-oriented treatment. Eight self-control strategies, as described by Hester (Hester, 1995; Hester & Miller, 1989), may be implemented in the following order: (1) setting limits on the number of drinks consumed and on peak blood alcohol concentrations (BACs) per day, (2) self-monitoring of drinking that involves filling out information (e.g., location, mood state) about each drink on special cards, (3) changing the rate of drinking by switching to weaker and less tasty drinks, learning to sip drinks, spacing of sips, and spacing drinks over time, (4) assertiveness-skills training in drink refusal through role play, (5) development of tailor-made reward systems for success with emphasis on easily accessible, immediate, and tangible rewards, (6) gaining an understanding of the antecedents of overdrinking, and learning to modify those factors, (7) learning alternative coping skills (in lieu of drinking), including relaxation training, problem solving, assertiveness training, and social-skills training, and (8) relapse prevention strategies (which will be described in more detail later in this chapter). BSCT may be conducted either in a group format or through individually tailored treatment plans. Individual treatment can be either self- (with a self-help manual) or therapist-directed.

BSCT is one of the most extensively studied interventions for alcohol abuse and alcoholism (Hester, 1995; Hester & Miller, 1989). In the late 1970s and early 1980s, efficacy of BSCT was frequently compared to that of abstinence-oriented treatments. Results support the effectiveness of BSCT (see Hester & Miller, 1989; Holder, Longabaugh, Miller, & Rubonis, 1991; Morgan, 1996), indicating that BSCT is more effective than no treatment and at least as effective as more traditional, abstinence-oriented approaches.

Several recent studies offer further support for the effectiveness of BSCT. Miller, Leckman, Delaney, and Tinkcom (1992) evaluated the long-term outcome of outpatient BSCT. Four cohorts of problem drinkers treated with BSCT were assessed at three-and-one-half, five, seven, and eight years. Of the 71 percent of cases accounted for at follow-up, 23 percent were abstinent, 14 percent were controlled/asymptomatic drinkers, 22 percent were improved but still impaired, 35 percent were unremitted, and 5 percent were deceased. Additionally, 39 percent of the improved patients were abstainers at long-term follow-up despite the fact that most clients initially set a goal of moderation. It is important to note the Miller, Leckman, et al. (1992) study excluded severely dependent and impaired drinkers. Thus, consistent with previous research, the authors concluded that clinically significant changes in drinking can be obtained and sustained over the long-term for a subset of individuals with less severe alcohol problems.

As noted earlier, there is much controversy in the alcohol literature regarding treatment goal selection (i.e., abstinence vs. moderation). This stems from the popularly held belief that the best way to address drinking problems is to not drink at all. This controversy is particularly pertinent with respect to the application of BSCT. Hodgins, Leigh, Milne, and Gerrish (1997) examined the effects of drinking goal selection on treatment outcome of BSCT with chronic alcoholics. Patients' treatment goals were assessed before and after treatment. Pretreatment data revealed that 46 percent of clients chose abstinence, 44 percent chose moderation, and 9 percent were uncertain as to treatment goal. By the end of the BSCT, clients shifted from a goal of moderation to one of abstinence, with 65 percent choosing abstinence and 32 percent choosing moderation. This study's findings also suggest that end-of-treatment (but not pre-treatment) goal choice was related to outcome: Patients with a final goal of abstinence (53%) were more likely than those with a final goal of moderation (9%) to be classified as abstinent (no alcohol during entire follow-up period) and successful (12 or fewer drinks per week) at the 12-month follow-up. Results from this study suggest that chronic alcoholics' treatment goals vary over the course of treatment and tend to move toward the goal of abstinence. These data also support utility of BSCT for chronic alcoholics with a goal of abstinence. The authors concluded that rather than initially imposing treatment goals upon patients, it may be more beneficial to gently move individuals toward an appropriate goal over the course of treatment, based on their severity of dependence.

A computer-based version of BSCT recently was evaluated for the treatment of nonalcoholic heavy drinkers (Hester & Delaney, 1997). The program consisted of eight weekly computer-interactive sessions, incorporating BSCT techniques. Participants in the treatment group reduced their drinking from an average of 5.1 drinking days per week to 3.2 days per week and from a mean of 38.7 standard ethanol content (SECs) per week to 14.5 SECs per week at the 12-month follow-up. This represented a significant improvement relative to a wait-list control group.

In summary, behavioral self-control training is a multicomponent treatment approach that has received extensive empirical support and scrutiny over the last two decades. Although most frequently associated with achieving a goal of drinking moderation, BSCT also has been successfully used with clients seeking a goal of abstinence. Research suggests that BSCT is effective in helping mildly to moderately dependent problem drinkers achieve clinically significant changes in their drinking. When implemented with moderately to severely dependent problem drinkers, BSCT shows promise as an effective means of ultimately achieving abstinence.

AVERSION THERAPY

Based on learning theory and classical conditioning, aversion therapy employs a number of techniques whereby aversive stimuli are paired with alcohol consumption. Thus, the ultimate goal of this behavioral treatment is to eliminate the client's desire to drink alcohol through aversive conditioning. The primary variants of aversion therapy include electric shock aversion, chemical aversion, and covert sensitization or imagery. Chemical aversion therapy has been implemented with some success as part of a multi-component inpatient treatment program (Nathan, 1985; J.W. Smith & Frawley, 1990). However, due to the stressful and sometimes painful nature of both electric shock and chemical aversion, high dropout rates, and insufficient evidence of effectiveness (Howard, Elkins, Rimmele, & Smith, 1991), it is generally accepted that these approaches are unwarranted for the treatment of alcohol abuse (Holder et al., 1991; Morgan, 1996). As such, covert sensitization has emerged as the most pragmatic choice among aversion therapy techniques.

As described by Rimmele and colleagues (Rimmele, Howard, & Hilfrink, 1995; Rimmele, Miller, & Dougher, 1989), covert sensitization involves pairing vividly imagined unpleasant scenes with imagery of drinking. The scenarios include graphic descriptions of nausea, vomiting, and other unpleasant consequences of alcohol consumption. The scenes are presented repeatedly until the images become associated with alcohol consumption, thereby reducing the client's desire to drink. Covert sensitization is not invasive or painful, has minimal risk to clients, requires no special equipment or medical supervision, and, therefore, can be easily implemented in an outpatient setting.

Early research on effectiveness of covert sensitization has yielded inconsistent findings, and we were unable to find any published studies in the 1990s on covert sensitization and alcoholism. In their review of the literature, Holder et al. (1991) cited seven controlled studies examining the efficacy of covert sensitization and, of these, four produced positive results. In summary, some research suggests that covert sensitization procedures can result in a reduction in drinking behavior (Rimmele et al., 1989). However, such benefits are likely to be produced in the context of a multicomponent treatment program. In addition, the duration of treatment gains resulting from covert sensitization is not yet known.

CUE-EXPOSURE TREATMENT

Cue-exposure treatment also draws upon the principles of classical conditioning. This approach aims to diminish the client's responsiveness to stimuli that, through repeated pairing with drinking, have come to be associated with, and elicit, drinking behavior. Thus, in cue-exposure treatment, clients are repeatedly presented with numerous alcohol-related cues while being prevented from exhibiting the conditioned response of drinking. Through such repeated exposure, other conditioned responses (e.g., physiological reactivity, subjective craving) are diminished as well. Overall, the goal of cue-exposure treatment is to reduce or eliminate alcohol consumption by inoculating clients against high-risk triggers of alcohol use and diminishing alcohol craving. Treatment typically is provided in an inpatient setting and may consist of six to eight sessions. Importantly, this approach may also provide opportunities for patients to practice coping skills in the presence of alcohol and alcohol-related cues (Monti, Abrams, Kadden, & Cooney, 1989). It must be noted, however, that extinction can only take place if cue exposure occurs in the absence of the conditioned response (drinking). Thus, implementation of cue-exposure therapy on an outpatient basis may be risky because it cannot be assured that clients abstain from alcohol use between sessions, which would prevent extinction (Rohsenow, Niaura, Childress, Abrams, & Monti, 1991).

In a recent controlled trial of cue-exposure treatment, Drummond and Glautier (1994) randomly assigned severely alcohol dependent patients to either cue-exposure (CE) or relaxation-control (RC) treatment groups, following detoxification. Patients in the CE group underwent 10 sessions with a total alcohol stimulus exposure of 400 minutes, whereas patients in the RC group received a total of 20 minutes of alcohol stimulus exposure, the balance of the time spent on progressive relaxation training. At the 6-month follow-up, the CE group faired better than the RC group as measured by total alcohol consumption and length of time to full relapse. Moreover, 20 percent of the CE group remained completely abstinent compared to 13 percent of the RC group, at 6 months posttreatment.

Other researchers have proposed that although cue exposure alone may not be adequate as a treatment for alcohol abuse, combining this technique with coping-skills training may enhance treatment outcome (Monti et al., 1989, 1993). Heather, Tebbutt, and Greeley (1993) reported a case study in which cue exposure was followed by supervised practice in resistance to drinking in tempting situations. Improvements on drinking status and decreased desire to drink were maintained at 12-month follow-up. Monti et al. (1993) randomly assigned patients to either cue-exposure treatment with urge reduction coping-skills training (CET) or to a contrast condition (CC), to control for daily contact. All patients received a standard inpatient alcohol abuse treatment. Results indicated the groups did not differ on any outcome measures at the three-month follow-up. At six months, the CET group had more abstinent patients, reported fewer drinks per day, and reported more abstinent days than the CC group. With regard to drinking status, 31 percent of the CET patients drank heavily (defined as more than six standard alcoholic drinks on any one day) at the six-month follow-up compared to 50 percent of the CC group patients. Given the pattern of these results, Monti et al. (1993) proposed that learning coping skills while being exposed to alcohol triggers allows patients to apply these skills over time, even as the benefits of the standard treatment diminish.

In summary, cue exposure treatment appears to be a promising technique when used as part of a multicomponent alcohol dependence program. Although empirical evidence is still scarce, CET appears to be particularly effective in combination with coping-skills training, following an inpatient alcohol-abuse treatment program. Further research is needed to determine CET's efficacy in conjunction with other interventions, as well as its long-term impact.

SKILLS TRAINING

The skills-training approach to the treatment of alcohol-related problems stems from the social learning theory perspective on alcoholism (Abrams & Niaura, 1987). This perspective posits that alcohol use can serve as a coping method for individuals who may be deficient in their mastery of alternate, more effective strategies (Wills & Shiffman, 1985). Hence, the skills-training model stresses the development of more adaptive and active coping skills in lieu of drinking. Skills training is usually implemented in conjunction with other treatment approaches, such as behavioral self-control training, and focuses on the development of a variety of skills, including social, problem solving, relaxation, and assertiveness. These skills are acquired through use of modeling, role playing, and other cognitive-behavioral techniques.

Although skills training is still a relatively new approach to the treatment of alcohol problems, its efficacy when implemented as part of a multicomponent alcoholism treatment program has been empirically supported and validated

(Chaney, 1989). Several studies that specifically evaluated social skills and stress management/coping training have also reported promising findings; of 10 controlled studies recently reviewed all produced positive results (Holder et al., 1991).

The effect of adding coping skills training to a standard inpatient alcoholism intervention on long-term treatment outcome was recently examined (Vogel, Eriksen, & Bjornelv, 1997). Chronic alcohol-dependent patients in the coping skills group showed significant improvement on a measure of self-efficacy to withstand relapse. Moreover, patients' self-efficacy scores predicted their 16-month follow-up drinking status. Monti, Abrams, Binkoff, and Zwick (1990) evaluated the relative effectiveness of individual communication-skills training (CST), communication-skills training with family participation (CSTF), and cognitive-behavioral mood management training (CBM). At a six-month follow-up, patients in the CST and CSTF groups drank less per drinking day than those in the CBM group. Finally, as noted in the section on cue-exposure therapy, coping-skills training in conjunction with cue-exposure training produced superior results to cue exposure alone (Monti et al., 1993).

In summary, skills training appears to be an important component of a comprehensive alcohol-dependence treatment program. It encompasses a variety of skills, the most empirically supported of which are social-skills and coping-skills training. It should be noted that there is much overlap between a number of behaviorally oriented treatments, many of which incorporate skills training into their treatment program. As such, skills training has been most frequently evaluated in the context of other intervention approaches, such as behavioral self-management and relapse prevention.

BEHAVIORAL MARITAL THERAPY

Behavioral Marital Therapy (BMT; O'Farrell, 1994) represents one of the newest approaches to the treatment of alcohol problems and incorporates active involvement of the client's spouse. The rationale behind BMT stems from the observation that there is a relationship between quality of marital interactions and problem drinking (O'Farrell & Cowles, 1989). BMT is a relatively brief intervention (10 to 12 sessions) and is usually used in combination with an individually based treatment approach. Through use of behavioral rehearsal, homework assignments, and an Antabuse (disulfiram) contract, BMT promotes sobriety while focusing on increasing positive couple activities and teaching communication and negotiation skills (O'Farrell, 1994). In order to increase positive activities, couples are taught to list and plan mutually rewarding activities and to regularly notice, acknowledge, and initiate pleasing behaviors. Couples learn communication skills such as listening and expressing feelings directly, which enhance and promote conflict resolution. They are also taught to negotiate and compromise, skills that promote agreed-upon behavior change. Finally, BMT also places emphasis on changing alcohol-related interactional patterns.

Although relatively new in the treatment of alcohol abuse, BMT is gaining empirical support with respect to its ability to enhance treatment outcome, particularly when used as a supplement to individual alcoholism intervention (O'Farrell & Cowles, 1989). A comprehensive research review indicated that of seven controlled studies on BMT considered, all yielded positive outcomes (Holder et al., 1991). McCrady, Stout, Noel, Abrams, and Nelson (1991) compared effectiveness of various levels of spousal involvement in the treatment of alcoholism. Clients were randomly assigned to one of three groups: (1) minimal spouse involvement (MSI), in which behavioral self-control and coping-skills training were directed toward the problem drinker in the presence of the spouse, (2) alcohol-focused spouse involvement (AFSI), in which the skills from group 1 were taught to both the problem drinker and the spouse, and (3) alcohol behavioral marital therapy (ABMT), in which marital intervention was added to the techniques of groups 1 and 2. Compared to the clients in the MSI and AFSI groups, who deteriorated over the nine months following treatment, clients in the ABMT group exhibited gradual improvement in the number of abstinent days and number of light drinking days experienced. In addition, clients in the ABMT group experienced greater marital satisfaction and were less likely to undergo marital separation than clients in the other two groups.

In a two-year longitudinal study, O'Farrell, Cutter, Choquette, Floyd, and Bayog (1992) examined the impact of BMT versus interactional couples therapy (ICT) versus no marital treatment, in addition to individual alcoholism counseling, on treatment outcome. Although results indicated that the BMT group was superior to both the ICT and the no-marital-treatment groups at the end of treatment, these findings did not extend to the two-year follow-up. At two years posttreatment, all three groups exhibited comparable treatment gains with regard to drinking behavior. Both BMT and ICT produced better marital adjustment than did no-marital-treatment condition.

In a cost-effectiveness analysis, O'Farrell, Choquette, Cutter, and Floyd (1996) compared outpatient individual alcoholism treatment supplemented by behavioral marital therapy (BMT), interactional couples therapy (ICT), or no marital therapy. Results revealed that addition of BMT to the individual treatment decreased health care and legal costs to a greater degree than did the addition of ICT, in the two years following treatment.

In summary, research suggests that addition of BMT to individual treatment for alcohol-related problems results in better marital-satisfaction and alcohol-consumption outcomes than individual treatment alone or the addition of nonbehavioral marital intervention (O'Farrell, 1993). However, more research is needed to evaluate long-term effects of BMT in the treatment of alcoholism.

RELAPSE PREVENTION

Based on self-efficacy theory, the influential relapse prevention (RP) model posits that clients' self-efficacy expectations regarding their ability to handle high-risk situations, determine, in great part, whether relapse occurs. The goals of relapse prevention training are to increase client's self-efficacy with respect to their ability to successfully cope with high-risk situations and to prevent a lapse (single instance of substance use) from turning into full-blown relapse. RP can be implemented on an outpatient basis and typically lasts eight sessions. It can be used as a supplement to other interventions or it can be fully integrated with other approaches. Several RP strategies have been outlined by Marlatt (1985). In the first step of RP, clients are instructed to identify high-risk situations that can potentially trigger a lapse. Clients are then taught to effectively use a number of coping strategies (both cognitive and behavioral) to apply in high-risk situations. Through role play and rehearsal, clients explore utilizing adaptive responses, and they practice those responses in increasingly difficult high-risk situations. Finally, clients are prepared for the occurrence of a lapse through the use of cognitive restructuring. By learning to reconceptualize a lapse as a single mistake rather than as indicative of personal failure, it is believed that clients are less likely to fully relapse as a result of one episode of alcohol consumption.

In an attempt to test the self-efficacy model of RP, McKay, Maisto, and O'Farrell (1993) examined the contribution of self-efficacy to treatment outcome. Alcoholic men who completed outpatient behavioral marital therapy (BMT) were assigned either to an aftercare condition that focused on RP or to a no-aftercare control group. Results revealed that low end-of-BMT-treatment self-efficacy was associated with poorer outcomes, but only in those patients who received no RP training. Hence, one explanation proposed by McKay et al. (1993) for these findings is that the addition of RP was most effective in increasing self-efficacy in those patients who were low on this measure at the end of BMT treatment. O'Farrell, Choquette, Cutter, and Brown (1993) evaluated the effect of providing couples with RP training (15 sessions over 12 months) subsequent to BMT. Patients who received RP reported fewer drinking days, more abstinent days, and improved marital relations relative to those patients who received BMT alone.

In sum, the relapse prevention model of alcoholism treatment has been evaluated in a relatively small number of studies and has been most frequently subsumed within a skills-training approach (for a more comprehensive review, the reader is referred to M. Sobell & Sobell, 1993). To date, findings have generally indicated that patients who receive RP training tend to experience better treatment outcome than those who do not, as evidenced by decreased alcohol consumption per week, longer time to first drink, decreased duration and severity of relapse episodes, longer periods of abstinence, and fewer symptoms of dependence. Some studies have also shown that such differences do not become manifest until 1 year posttreatment, suggesting delayed learning effects (M. Sobell & Sobell, 1993).

COMMUNITY REINFORCEMENT

The community reinforcement approach (CRA) is a broad-spectrum behavioral approach to the treatment of alcohol and drug abuse developed in the early 1970s by Azrin and colleagues (Azrin, 1976; Azrin, Sisson, Meyers, & Godley, 1982; see Sisson & Azrin, 1993; J.E. Smith & Meyers, 1995, for reviews of CRA).

CRA can be used with clients who strive to achieve abstinence from alcohol, as well as with those for whom moderation is a desired goal. At the root of CRA is the belief that in order for individuals to alter their drinking behavior, environmental contingencies must be modified. Thus, clients are taught ways by which they can develop a reinforcing lifestyle in the absence of drinking. Toward this end, CRA employs multiple interventions, many of which emphasize making use of community-based supports. Some critical aspects of CRA include (1) social skills training in order to bolster social contingencies in the recovery process, (2) use of a social club where clients can enjoy social activities without alcohol, (3) communication skills and problem-solving training, (4) drink refusal training, (5) use of a job club through which unemployed clients learn how to find and keep a job, (6) behavioral marital therapy, (7) functional analysis of drinking behavior (i.e., delineation of the antecedents and consequences of drinking), and (8) use of disulfiram, a medication that induces nausea if an individual drinks alcohol while taking it.

CRA has been empirically tested in only four published studies, all of which were conducted prior to 1990. However, in each instance it has fared extremely well. In their comprehensive review of the alcoholism treatment outcome literature, Finney and Monahan (1996) report that CRA is the most cost effective of the over 30 interventions that were examined. In one of the earliest studies, six-month follow-up results revealed that CRA clients drank on 14 percent of the follow-up days compared to 79 percent for those in the standard treatment group (Hunt & Azrin, 1976). Even better findings emerged in a subsequent study that also incorporated the use of disulfiram: Relative to a standard disease model intervention, clients who received CRA drank on only 2 percent of the follow-up days compared to 56 percent for those receiving standard treatment (Azrin, 1976).

In sum, although CRA is clearly a most promising approach, further evaluation of its effectiveness is needed. Furthermore, most of the published studies have been conducted by the same research group. Thus, studies of CRA by other investigators can help determine the generalizability of these findings.

Case Illustration

Joe T. is a 34 year-old married, white male who described being ordered by his wife and employer, to seek therapy for his drinking. Although Mr. T. did not initially view his drinking as problematic, he acknowledged, "Once in a while, I probably have a bit too much." During the first session, a thorough psychosocial history was taken and several questionnaires were administered. The findings indicated that although Mr. T. was presently suffering from some mild depressive and anxiety-related symptomatology, these symptoms were secondary to his marital problems and drinking. The *Timeline Followback Method* (L. Sobell & Sobell, 1992) was used to assess his drinking patterns over the previous 90 days, and revealed that the client drank almost daily, with a range of two to over 10 drinks per occasion. The Inventory of Drinking Situations (Annis, 1982) revealed that the client's drinking was predominantly associated with negative affective states, indicating that his heaviest drinking occurred most often when he felt bad or had been involved in interpersonal conflicts. Mr. T.'s score on the Alcohol Dependence

Scale (Skinner & Horn, 1984) was 15, placing him well within the problem-drinking range, although when all the data were considered together, he did not meet criteria for alcohol dependence. Further discussion revealed that Mr. T. did believe that his alcohol was impacting negatively on his job performance (as a sales manager) and that it likely contributed to arguments with his wife.

Based on findings from the first session, the therapist recommended that Mr. T. participate in both short-term (~10 sessions) individual and BMT. The rationale for both of these recommendations was explained to the client, and he begrudgingly agreed to commit to 10 sessions. When asked what his goals were for treatment, Mr. T. replied that he would like to reduce his drinking to no more than two days a week, limit his drinking to weekends, drink no more than two drinks per occasion, and get along better with his wife. Individual therapy proceeded and primarily involved behavioral self-control training. Hence, limit setting, self-monitoring of subsequent drinking situations, coping-skills training, mood management, and relapse prevention training were all essential components of the individual therapy.

Weekly sessions of BMT were also initiated. Although Mr. T.'s wife was initially disappointed with her husband's goal of moderating his drinking rather than totally abstaining, she conceded that were he able to realize his goal, their marriage would likely improve. The course of BMT focused on communication training, increasing positive couple activities, behavioral rehearsal, and negotiation skills.

By the end of the third session, Mr. T. had significantly modified his drinking behavior: He had not had a drink on a weeknight, and in fact, had only consumed alcohol on two occasions, adhering to his goal of having no more than two drinks per occasion. Both the client and his wife expressed initial satisfaction over his behavior change. Moreover, Mr. T. expressed that he felt sharper and more productive at work. At the same time, the client described that he missed drinking, and was unsure about whether he could maintain this restraint. Such feelings were normalized, and emphasis was placed on the development of alternate coping skills and mood management.

Throughout the course of BMT, Mrs. T. revealed that she had built up years of resentment toward her husband's drinking behavior, describing that he was mean and distant when intoxicated. The expression of these previously repressed feelings was integral to the success of the therapy, as Mr. T. began to understand how his drinking had profoundly impacted his marriage. Scheduling of pleasant activities became an important venue for the couple, as they began to experience reinforcing, shared experiences for the first time. Mrs. T. occasionally reiterated her fear that her husband could not maintain this limited drinking, yet was clearly proud of his accomplishments thus far.

By the tenth session of both individual treatment and BMT, Mr. T. had successfully achieved his goal, with only one instance of consuming more than two drinks. Their marriage was clearly improving, as they were learning how to openly communicate with one another as well as more thoroughly enjoy each other's company. A follow-up appointment was made for three months posttreatment. At this session, Mr. T. completed a Timeline Followback Form revealing that he was actually drinking only one evening per week, usually consuming no more than one drink. The client expressed that his marriage was continuing to improve, as was his job satisfaction.

ALTERNATIVE TREATMENT OPTIONS

Treatments selected for inclusion in this section (motivational enhancement, guided self-change, and Alcoholics Anonymous) could have just as easily been listed in the previous section on "Treatment Strategies." We include the first two here because both motivational interviewing and guided self-change represent relatively novel, yet highly promising cognitive-behavioral approaches to the treatment of alcohol-related problems. Although Alcoholics Anonymous (AA) is hardly a novel approach, we believe that its hegemony, as well as its implementation of basic behavioral principles, justify its inclusion in this chapter.

MOTIVATIONAL ENHANCEMENT

Motivational enhancement (ME) (Miller, 1983b, 1985; Miller & Rollnick, 1991; Miller, Zweben, DiClemente, & Rychtarik, 1992) is an approach to treating alcohol abuse and dependence designed to produce rapid, internally motivated changes in drinking problems. To prompt clients to initiate making changes in their drinking, ME relies on a variety of empirically supported motivational strategies (Miller, 1985), including: (1) providing feedback of personal risk or impairment, (2) emphasizing personal responsibility for change, (3) providing clear advice on how to change, (4) offering a menu of alternative change options, (5) empathic therapist behavior, and (6) facilitating client self-efficacy or optimism. The approach also draws from research on the processes of natural (e.g., untreated) recovery from addictive behaviors (e.g., DiClemente & Prochaska, 1982; Prochaska, 1983) and utilizes the stages-of-change model (Prochaska & DiClemente, 1986) to adjust intervention to match the client's readiness to change. In natural recovery, the typical process of change progresses from (1) precontemplation to (2) contemplation to (3) determination to (4) action to (5) maintenance of change. ME begins wherever the client is in the change process and facilitates the client's movement through the cycle of change toward lasting change. Ultimately, responsibility and capability for change is placed with the client.

ME was one of the three treatment strategies utilized in Project MATCH, the multisite treatment outcome study initiated by the Treatment Research Branch of the National Institute on Alcohol Abuse and Alcoholism. The ME treatment manual developed for Project MATCH (Miller, Zweben, et al., 1992) sets the prototypical course of ME treatment as the following: a comprehensive assessment session using a battery of standardized self-report and interview measures, an intensive initial treatment session soon after the assessment, and three "follow-through" sessions spaced in varying intervals across 12 weeks. Session 1 involves presentation of the rationale and limitations of treatment and provision of personalized feedback on the findings from the assessment. An important component of the session is provision of feedback such that it serves as persuasive input for convincing clients that they are not where they ought (or want) to be. Session 2 involves reviewing what transpired during the first session and continuing to provide personalized feedback such that the client is moved along in the change process. Sessions 3 and 4 are conceptualized as booster sessions that reinforce and further motivate clients' efforts to make changes in their drinking behavior. Across the assessment and treatment sessions, ME treatment is viewed as proceeding through three distinct phases: (1) building motivation for change, (2) strengthening commitment to change, and (3) helping the client develop follow-through strategies for making and maintaining changes. Variations on prototypical ME treatment also have been developed including a one-session format and a format that includes client's significant others (see Miller, 1995).

Empirical research concerning the effectiveness of ME treatment is just beginning to be conducted. Although several reports have confirmed the importance of motivational strategies in successfully treating alcohol abuse and dependence (Bien, Miller, & Tonigan, 1993; Miller, Benefield, & Tonigan, 1993), controlled clinical trials of ME treatment are scant (B. Saunders, Wilkinson, & Phillips, 1995). Overall, findings thus far suggest that ME treatment can be as effective as more extensive treatments for addressing mild to moderate alcohol problems and may be particularly effective for clients at earlier stages of change or who demonstrate antisocial behavior (Heather, Rollnick, Bell, & Richmond, 1996; Waldron & Miller, in press). ME also appears to hold promise for use as a brief adjunctive intervention that can improve the effectiveness of more extensive alcohol treatments (Brown & Miller, 1993) or in "window of opportunity" situations (e.g., emergency room visits, patients in general hospital wards) during which motivation to change may be especially malleable (Heather et al., 1996; Monti, 1997).

GUIDED SELF-CHANGE

Guided Self-Change (GSC) treatment (M. Sobell & Sobell, 1998) is a brief motivational intervention designed for use with individuals who have alcohol and drug problems. Originally, this treatment approach was developed for problem drinkers, a group not severely dependent on alcohol but still demonstrating alcohol problems. The focus on problem drinking derived from research showing that this type of alcohol problem is more prevalent than more severe drinking problems (Calahan & Room, 1974; Institute of Medicine, 1990) and does not necessarily progress to become more severe (Pattison, Sobell, & Sobell, 1977; M. Sobell & Sobell, 1987, 1993). Another important influence on the development of the GSC treatment was Edwards and colleagues' finding (Edwards et al., 1977; Orford, Oppenheimer, & Edwards, 1976) that one session of advice and counseling was more effective in addressing alcohol problems of mild to moderate severity than more traditional and intensive treatment. Additional influences included research documenting recovery from alcohol and other drug problems without treatment or help (W. Saunders & Kershaw, 1979; Tuchfeld, 1976; Waldorf & Biernacki, 1982), the importance of client's motivation to change in determining treatment outcome (DiClemente & Prochaska, 1982; Miller, 1983b, 1985; Prochaska, 1983), and the social-learning premise that allowing goal choice (e.g., abstinence from alcohol vs. moderation) increases an individual's commitment to a goal (M. Sobell & Sobell, 1995).

GSC treatment can be used individually, with couples, or with groups, with minor variations in format and materials. Individual GSC treatment represents the prototype and has been standardized and manualized for clinical and research applications (M. Sobell & Sobell, 1993). A typical course of GSC treatment includes a two-hour assessment using several standardized measures, followed by four 60-minute intervention sessions utilizing motivational and cognitive-behavioral techniques. Session 1 involves explaining the rationale behind GSC treatment, providing feedback on drinking patterns based on the assessment findings, reviewing a decisional balance exercise assigned as homework during the assessment, setting goals for treatment, and assigning self-monitoring and drinking-triggers homework exercises. Session 2 involves reviewing homework assignments, discussing two high-risk drinking situations, providing feedback on drinking situation profiles based on the assessment session, and assigning an options/action plan for managing triggers homework exercise. Session 3 involves reassessment of drinking situations, reviewing ongoing self-monitoring, reviewing the homework assignment, discussing any anticipated situations in which the option/action plan can be put into practice, and assigning homework exercises that include a reassessment of treatment goals and the client's assessment of the treatment and the need for additional sessions. Session 4 involves reviewing ongoing self-monitoring, reviewing the second goal statement, revisiting the first decisional balance exercise, discussing any behavioral or attitudinal changes that may have occurred during treatment, and assessing the client's current status and the need for aftercare support.

Several studies have been conducted evaluating the effectiveness of GSC for treating problem drinking. An initial study compared the effectiveness of GSC treatment with and without a relapse prevention component (M. Sobell & Sobell, 1993). The two approaches proved equally effective, with a total reduction in reported alcohol consumption of 53.8 percent compared to the year preceding treatment, a near doubling of abstinence rates from the year prior to treatment to the one-year posttreatment follow-up, and very high consumer satisfaction ratings. A second study examined effectiveness of GSC treatment involving both clients and their spouse. In one treatment condition, the spouse intervention focused only on providing an understanding of the clients' treatment program and a realistic perspective for viewing recovery from alcohol problems; in a second treatment condition, the spouse intervention also included explicit instructions about how to be supportive of their partners' attempts to change their drinking; and in both treatment conditions the clients received standard GSC treatment. Clients in both groups showed significant decreases in drinking from one year pretreatment to one year posttreatment, with a doubling of abstinent days and overall decreases in drinking (L. Sobell, Sobell, & Leo, 1993). Although there were no significant differences in drinking outcomes between treatment groups, clients lacking confidence in their own ability to recover did better when treatment included explicit spousal instruction in how to be supportive. A third study compared effectiveness of GSC administered to individuals versus groups and to alcohol versus drug abusers (L. Sobell, Sobell, Brown, & Cleland, 1995; M. Sobell, Buchan, & Sobell, 1996; M. Sobell & Sobell, 1998). Results indicated that individual and group GSC treatment were equally effective, alcohol and drug clients were similarly responsive to treatment (although more drug clients dropped out of treatment), and changes in substance use paralleled those seen in earlier studies. Additional studies have found GSC treatment to be highly effective in managed care settings (Breslin, Sobell, Sobell, Cunningham, & Kwan, 1995) and with Spanish-speaking populations (Ayala-Velazquez, Echeverria, Sobell, & Sobell, 1997).

ALCOHOLICS ANONYMOUS

Steeped within a disease-model perspective of alcoholism, Alcoholics Anonymous (AA) is a highly influential organization whose philosophy has been incorporated into the vast majority of treatment programs in the United States. The only acceptable treatment goal, according to AA, is total abstinence from alcohol. AA views alcoholism as a threefold disease, comprised of physical, emotional, and spiritual factors (Alcoholics Anonymous, 1976). According to AA, critical aspects of recovery include (1) admitting one is powerless over alcohol, (2) accepting the concept of a higher power, (3) writing and expressing to another person a "fearless moral inventory" of oneself, (4) making amends to all those whom the alcoholic harmed, and (5) "passing on" the AA message to others who suffer from the disease of alcoholism (see Alcoholics Anonymous, 1984, for an in-depth discussion of the 12 steps and 12 traditions of AA).

As pervasive as AA is, it remains somewhat controversial, because there are few data to support its claims of success (McCrady & Irvine, 1989), although several recent and well-designed studies supported the efficacy and effectiveness of AA (Ouimette, Finney, & Moos, 1997; Project MATCH Research Group, 1993). Although there has been a great deal of armchair speculation about what makes AA work, few empirical studies have examined processes of change associated with success in AA (Emrick, Tonigan, Montgomery, & Little, 1993; Kassel & Wagner, 1993). AA is unquestionably ideologically bound, and, though many have suggested that its powerful ideology is central to its alleged success, it may also act as a deterrent to potential initiates (Kassel & Wagner, 1993). Correspondingly, as AA was initially developed to serve the needs of older, chronic alcoholics, the appropriateness of this approach to other types of problem drinkers must still be questioned.

Although the theoretical underpinnings of AA and behavior therapy are markedly different (McCrady, 1994), integration of AA and behavior therapy is certainly possible. In support of this notion, Kassel (1998) identified the following behavioral strategies as intrinsic to AA: (1) stimulus control: avoid drinking environments, develop interests and habits incompatible with drinking, (2) behavioral coping: "bring your body and your mind will follow," "don't drink; go to meetings," call your sponsor, (3) cognitive coping:

recite the "serenity prayer," tell yourself to take it "one day at a time," (4) covert sensitization: remember the consequences of your drinking, tell your "story" at meetings, (5) self-management: stress delayed reinforcers versus immediate reinforcers despite initial punishments (e.g., craving, social anxiety), (6) expanding behavioral repertoire: learn social skills, implement new reinforcers, and (7) modeling: watch and learn from successful AA members. It appears that behavioral strategies clearly complement, and may be integral to, the AA approach.

PRESCRIPTIVE TREATMENT AND MANAGED CARE

Prescriptive treatment involves matching specific types of clients to specific types of interventions according to a set of well-defined and strict rules. The rules should derive from empirical research documenting the precise conditions under which specific interventions are and are not effective. The goal of prescriptive treatment is to provide clients with the most effective intervention given their presenting complaints, personal circumstances, personal characteristics, and social resources. In both the behavior therapy and alcohol treatment fields, there is considerable interest in developing prescriptive or matching rules to guide the process of prescribing treatments to individuals (Acierno, Hersen, Van Hasselt, & Ammerman, 1994; Miller & Hester, 1995). However, few empirical data currently exist from which to develop prescriptive rules, especially in regard to alcohol problems.

Project MATCH, the multisite treatment outcome study initiated by the Treatment Research Branch of the National Institute on Alcohol Abuse and Alcoholism, was designed to compare the effectiveness of three different approaches to the treatment of alcohol problems across different subgroups of alcoholics. The three approaches included 12-step facilitation therapy, cognitive-behavioral coping-skills therapy, and motivational enhancement therapy. One of the study's primary goals was to assess whether subgroups of alcoholics responded differentially to the respective treatments offered. Based on the extant literature, several primary and secondary matching hypotheses were proposed. Findings released thus far have been disappointing, to the extent that the majority of hypothesized matching effects were not supported (see Longabaugh, in press). However, all three treatments proved generally (and equally) effective, with well-specified and tested manuals for conducting each of the three treatments now available from the National Institute on Alcohol Abuse and Alcoholism.

Researchers in the area of treatment matching remain hopeful that subsequent research will result in the development of valid prescriptive rules in the near future. For alcohol problems, promising matching variables include: (1) Treatment goals (e.g., abstinence vs. moderation), (2) treatment intensity, ranging from brief to long-term residential, (3) treatment context (e.g., disease-oriented vs. skill-based), (4) aftercare options (e.g., self-help groups, individual psychotherapy, etc.), (5) demographic characteristics of the client, (6) alcohol-related individual differences across clients (e.g., degree of alcohol dependence, drinking patterns and motives), (7) personality/ psychological variables, such as self-efficacy and anger, and (8) social support (Allen & Kadden, 1995; Longabaugh, in press; Miller, 1989). Although some intriguing matching effects have been suggested in isolated studies (e.g., Cooney, Kadden, Litt, & Getter, 1991; Rohsenow, Monti, et al., 1991; Waldron & Miller, in press; see Mattson et al., 1994 for an extensive review), these findings are in need of replication and extension. At present, two tentative conclusions can be drawn about the prescriptive treatment of clients with alcohol problems: First, clients with more severe problems (e.g., greater alcohol dependence, more psychopathology, and/or less social support) appear to do better with more intensive treatment. Second, clients high in sociopathy appear to do better with coping-skills-based interventions (Allen & Kadden, 1995).

SUMMARY

Alcoholism is a complex problem, likely governed by diverse etiologic pathways. As noted earlier, passionate debate has ensued over the years as differing conceptualizations of the disorder have been considered and put forth. Not surprisingly, equally lively discussion has centered around how alcohol problems should be best treated. We have provided a brief overview of several treatments originating from a behavioral or cognitive-behavioral model of alcoholism. Although our review was not intended to be an exhaustive one, we believe that there is an ever emerging empirical basis supportive of these approaches. Moreover, there is reason to believe that behavioral and cognitive-behavioral approaches are more cost effective than other popular treatments (McCrady & Langenbucher, 1996; Miller et al., 1995).

In conclusion, most of the treatments reviewed here fall under the rubric of what has been referred to as "broad spectrum behavior therapy." As such, it is important to reiterate these approaches are best viewed as complimentary, rather than as competitive. Put simply, few of these behaviorally based treatments are ever implemented in isolation from one another in the real world. Complex patient presentations, dual diagnoses, and severity of the disorder all affect the choice of appropriate interventions. Indeed, combining theoretically diverse orientations, such as Alcoholics Anonymous and behavioral self-control training, is not only feasible, but highly effective for some patients (Franco, Galanter, Castaneda, & Patterson, 1995). As a field, we can no longer afford to be wed to ideology and dogma. The good news is that the chasm between science and practice appears to be growing smaller, and as a result, behavioral treatments are becoming more widely utilized.

REFERENCES

Abrams, D.B., & Niaura, R.S. (1987). Social learning theory. In H.T. Blane & K.E. Leonard (Eds.), *Psychological theories of drinking and alcoholism* (pp. 131–178). New York: Guilford Press.

Acierno, R., Hersen, M., Van Hasselt, V.B., & Ammerman, R.T. (1994). Remedying the Achilles heel of behavior research and therapy: Prescriptive matching of intervention and psychopathology. *Journal of Behavior Therapy and Experimental Psychiatry*, 25, 179–188.

Alcoholics Anonymous. (1976). *Alcoholics Anonymous: The story of how many thousands of men and women have recovered from alcoholism.* New York: AA World Services.

Alcoholics Anonymous. (1984). *Twelve steps and twelve traditions.* New York: AA World Services.

Allen, J.P., & Columbus, M. (1995). *Assessing alcohol problems: A guide for clinicians and researchers* (National Institute on Alcohol Abuse and Alcoholism, Treatment Handbook Series 4). Bethesda, MD: U.S. Department of Health and Human Services.

Allen, J.P., & Kadden, R.M. (1995). Matching clients to alcohol treatments. In R.K. Hester & W.R. Miller (Eds.), *Handbook of alcoholism treatment approaches: Effective alternatives* (2nd ed., pp. 278–291). Boston: Allyn & Bacon.

American Psychiatric Association. (1980). *Diagnostic and statistical manual of mental disorders* (3rd ed.). Washington, DC: Author.

American Psychiatric Association. (1987). *Diagnostic and statistical manual of mental disorders* (3rd ed., rev.). Washington, DC: Author.

American Psychiatric Association. (1994). *Diagnostic and statistical manual of mental disorders* (4th ed.). Washington, DC: Author.

Annis, H.M. (1982). *Inventory of drinking situations.* Toronto: Addictions Research Foundation of Ontario.

Ayala-Velazquez, H.E., Echeverria, L.S., Sobell, M., & Sobell, L. (1997). Auto control dirigido: Intervencioines breves para bebedores problema en Mexico. *Revista Mexicana de Psicologia [Mexican Journal of Psychology]*, 14, 113–127.

Azrin, N.H. (1976). Improvements in the community reinforcement approach to alcoholism. *Behaviour Research and Therapy*, 14, 339–348.

Azrin, N.H., Sisson, R.W., Meyers, R., & Godley, M. (1982). Alcoholism treatment by disulfiram and community reinforcement therapy. *Journal of Behavior Therapy and Experimental Psychiatry*, 13, 105–112.

Bien, T.H., Miller, W.R., & Tonigan, J.S. (1993). Brief interventions for alcohol problems: A review. *Addiction*, 88, 315–336.

Breslin, F.C., Sobell, L.C., Sobell, M.B., Cunningham, J.C., & Kwan, E. (1995, November). *Prognostic markers for a stepped care approach: The utility of within treatment drinking variables.* Paper presented at the 29th annual meeting of the Association for Advancement of Behavior Therapy, Washington, DC.

Brown, J.M., & Miller, W.R. (1993). Impact of motivational interviewing on participation and outcome in residential alcoholism treatment. *Psychology of Addictive Behaviors*, 7, 211–218.

Calahan, D., & Room, R. (1974). *Problem drinking among American men.* New Brunswick, NJ: Rutgers Center of Alcohol Studies.

Chaney, E.F. (1989). Social skills training. In R.K. Hester & W.R. Miller (Eds.), *Handbook of alcoholism treatment approaches: Effective alternatives* (pp. 206–221). New York: Pergamon Press.

Cooney, N.L., Kadden, R.M., Litt, M.D., & Getter, H. (1991). Matching alcoholics to coping skills or interactional therapies: Two year follow-up results. *Journal of Consulting and Clinical Psychology*, 59, 598–601.

DiClemente, C.C., & Prochaska, J.O. (1982). Self-change and therapy change of smoking behavior: A comparison processes of change in cessation and maintenance. *Addictive Behaviors*, 7, 133–142.

Drummond, D.C., & Glautier, S. (1994). A controlled trial of cue exposure treatment in alcohol dependence. *Journal of Consulting and Clinical Psychology, 62,* 809–817.

Edwards, G. (1986). The alcohol dependence syndrome: A concept as stimulus to enquiry. *British Journal of Addiction, 81,* 171–183.

Edwards, G., & Gross, M.M. (1976). Alcohol dependence: Provisional description of a clinical syndrome. *British Medical Journal, 1,* 1058–1061.

Edwards, G., Orford, J., Egert, S., Guthrie, S., Hawker, A., Hensman, C., Mitcheson, M., Oppenheimer, E., & Taylor, C. (1977). A controlled trial of "treatment" and "advice." *Journal of Studies on Alcohol, 38,* 1004–1031.

Emrick, C., Tonigan, J.S., Montgomery, H., & Little, L. (1993). Alcoholics Anonymous: What is currently known? In B.S. McCrady & W.R. Miller (Eds.), *Research on Alcoholics Anonymous: Opportunities and alternatives* (pp. 41–76). New Brunswick, NJ: Alcohol Research Documentation, Rutgers—The State University of New Jersey.

Finney, J.W., & Monahan, S.C. (1996). The cost effectiveness of treatment for alcoholism: A second approximation. *Journal of Studies on Alcohol, 47,* 122–134.

Finney, J.W., & Moos, R.H. (1998). Psychosocial treatments for alcohol use disorders. In P.E. Nathan & J.M. Gorman (Eds.), *A guide to treatments that work* (pp. 156–166). New York: Oxford University Press.

First, M.B., Gibbon, M., Spitzer, R.L., & Williams, J.B.W. (1995). *User's guide for the structured clinical interview for DSM-IV axis 1 disorders.* New York: Biometrics Research Department, New York State Psychiatric Institute.

Franco, H., Galanter, M., Castaneda, R., & Patterson, J. (1995). Combining behavioral and self-help approaches in the inpatient management of dually diagnosed patients. *Journal of Substance Abuse Treatment, 12,* 227–232.

Heather, N., Rollnick, S., Bell, A., & Richmond, R. (1996). Effects of brief counseling among male heavy drinkers identified in general hospital wards. *Drug and Alcohol Review, 15,* 29–38.

Heather, N., Tebbutt, J.S., & Greeley, J.D. (1993). Alcohol cue exposure directed at a goal of moderate drinking. *Journal of Behavior Therapy & Experimental Psychiatry, 24,* 187–195.

Hester, R.K. (1995). Behavioral self-control training. In R.K. Hester & W.R. Miller (Eds.), *Handbook of alcoholism treatment approaches: Effective alternatives* (2nd ed., pp. 148–159). Boston: Allyn & Bacon.

Hester, R.K., & Delaney, H.D. (1997). Behavioral self-control program for windows: Results of a controlled clinical trial. *Journal of Consulting and Clinical Psychology, 65,* 686–693.

Hester, R.K., & Miller, W.R. (1989). Self-control training. In R.K. Hester & W.R. Miller (Eds.), *Handbook of alcoholism treatment approaches: Effective alternatives* (pp. 141–150). New York: Pergamon Press.

Hester, R.K., & Miller, W.R. (1995). *Handbook of alcoholism treatment approaches: Effective alternatives* (2nd ed.). New York: Pergamon Press.

Hodgins, D.C., Leigh, G., Milne, R., & Gerrish, R. (1997). Drinking goal selection in behavioral self-management treatment of chronic alcoholics. *Addictive Behaviors, 22,* 247–255.

Holder, H., Longabaugh, R., Miller, W.R., & Rubonis, A.V. (1991). The cost effectiveness of treatment for alcoholism: A first approximation. *Journal of Studies on Alcohol, 52,* 517–540.

Howard, M.O., Elkins, R.L., Rimmele, C., & Smith, J.W. (1991). Chemical aversion treatment of alcohol dependence. *Drug and Alcohol Dependence, 29,* 107–143.

Hunt, G.M., & Azrin, N.H. (1976). A community-reinforcement approach to alcoholism. *Behaviour Research and Therapy, 11*, 91–104.

Institute of Medicine. (1989). *Prevention and treatment of alcohol problems: Opportunities for research: Report of a study.* Washington, DC: National Academy Press.

Institute of Medicine. (1990). *Broadening the base of treatment for alcohol problems.* Washington, DC: National Academy Press.

Kadden, R.M. (1994). Cognitive-behavioral approaches to alcoholism treatment. *Alcohol Health and Research World, 18*, 279–286.

Kassel, J.D. (1998). *A cognitive-behavioral analysis of Alcoholics Anonymous.* Manuscript under review, University of Florida.

Kassel, J.D., & Wagner, E.F. (1993). Processes of change in Alcoholics Anonymous: A review of possible mechanisms. *Psychotherapy, 30*, 222–234.

Locke, E.A. (1995). Beyond determinism and materialism, or isn't it time we took consciousness seriously? *Journal of Behavior Therapy and Experimental Psychiatry, 26*, 265–273.

Longabaugh, R. (in press). *Client-treatment matching.* Rockville, MD: NIAAA Monograph.

Maltzman, I. (1994). Why alcoholism is a disease. *Journal of Psychoactive Drugs, 26*, 13–31.

Marlatt, G.A. (1985). Relapse prevention: Theoretical rationale and overview of the model. In G.A. Marlatt & J.R. Gordon (Eds.), *Relapse prevention: Maintenance strategies in the treatment of addictive behaviors* (pp. 3–67). New York: Guilford Press.

Mattson, M.E., Allen, J.P., Longabaugh, R., Nickless, C.J., Connors, G.J., & Kadden, R.M. (1994). A chronological review of empirical studies matching alcoholic clients to treatment. *Journal of Studies on Alcohol*, (Suppl. 12), 16–29.

McCrady, B.S. (1994). Alcoholics Anonymous and behavior therapy: Can habits be treated as diseases? Can diseases be treated as habits? *Journal of Consulting and Clinical Psychology, 62*, 1159–1166.

McCrady, B.S., & Irvine, S. (1989). Self-help groups. In R.K. Hester & W.R. Miller (Eds.), *Handbook of alcoholism treatment approaches: Effective alternatives* (pp. 153–169). Elmsford, NY: Pergamon Press.

McCrady, B.S., & Langenbucher, J.W. (1996). Alcohol treatment and health care system reform. *Archives of General Psychiatry, 53*, 737–746.

McCrady, B.S., Stout, R., Noel, N., Abrams, D., & Nelson, H.F. (1991). Effectiveness of three types of spouse-involved behavioral alcoholism treatment. *British Journal of Addiction, 86*, 1415–1424.

McKay, J.R., Maisto, S.A., & O'Farrell, T.J. (1993). End-of-treatment self-efficacy, aftercare, and drinking outcomes of alcoholic men. *Alcoholism: Clinical and Experimental Research, 17*, 1078–1083.

Merrill, J., Fox, K., & Chang, H.-H. (1993). *The cost of substance abuse to America's health care system, Report 1: Medicaid hospital costs.* New York: Center on Addiction and Substance Abuse at Columbia University.

Miller, W.R. (1983a). Controlled drinking: A history and critical review. *Journal of Studies on Alcohol, 44*, 68–83.

Miller, W.R. (1983b). Motivational interviewing with problem drinkers. *Behavioural Psychotherapy, 11*, 147–172.

Miller, W.R. (1985). Motivation for treatment: A review with special emphasis on alcoholism. *Psychological Bulletin, 98*, 84–107.

Miller, W.R. (1989). Matching individuals with interventions. In R.K. Hester & W.R. Miller (Eds.), *Handbook of alcoholism treatment approaches: Effective alternatives* (pp. 261–271). New York: Pergamon Press.

Miller, W.R. (1995). Increasing motivation for change. In R.K. Hester & W.R. Miller (Eds.), *Handbook of alcoholism treatment approaches: Effective alternatives* (2nd ed., pp. 89–104). New York: Allyn & Bacon.

Miller, W.R., Benefield, R.G., & Tonigan, J.S. (1993). Enhancing motivation for change in problem drinking: A controlled comparison of two therapist styles. *Journal of Consulting and Clinical Psychology, 61,* 455–461.

Miller, W.R., Brown, J.M., Simpson, T.L., Handmaker, N.S., Bien, T.H., Luckie, L.F., Montgomery, H.A., Hester, R.K., & Tonigan, J.S. (1995). What works? A methodological analysis of the alcohol treatment outcome literature. In R.K. Hester & W.R. Miller (Eds.), *Handbook of alcoholism treatment approaches: Effective alternatives* (pp. 12–44). Boston: Allyn & Bacon.

Miller, W.R., & Hester, R.K. (1986). The effectiveness of alcoholism treatment: What research reveals. In W.R. Miller & N. Heather (Eds.), *Treating addictive behaviors: Processes of change* (pp. 121–174). New York: Plenum Press.

Miller, W.R., & Hester, R.K. (1995). Treatment for alcohol problems: Toward an informed eclecticism. In R.K. Hester & W.R. Miller (Eds.), *Handbook of alcoholism treatment approaches: Effective alternatives* (2nd ed., pp. 1–11). Boston: Allyn & Bacon.

Miller, W.R., Leckman, A.L., Delaney, H.D., & Tinkcom, M. (1992). Long-term follow-up of behavioral self-control training. *Journal of Studies on Alcohol, 53,* 249–261.

Miller, W.R., & Rollnick, S. (Eds.). (1991). *Motivational interviewing: Preparing people to change addictive behavior.* New York: Guilford Press.

Miller, W.R., Zweben, A., DiClemente, C.C., & Rychtarik, R.G. (1992). *Motivational enhancement therapy manual: A clinical research guide for therapists treating individuals with alcohol abuse and dependence* (Publication No. (ADM) 92-1894). Washington, DC: U.S. Department of Health and Human Services.

Mischel, W. (1997). Was the cognitive revolution just a detour on the road to behaviorism? On the need to reconcile situation control and personal control. In R.S. Wyer, Jr. (Ed.), *The automaticity of everyday life: Advances in social cognition* (Vol. 10, pp. 181–186). Mahway, NJ: Erlbaum.

Monti, P.M. (1997, July). Motivational interviewing with alcohol-positive teens in an emergency department. In E. Wagner (Chair.), *Innovations in adolescent substance abuse intervention.* Symposium conducted at the annual meeting of the Research Society on Alcoholism, San Francisco.

Monti, P.M., Abrams, D.B., Binkoff, J.A., & Zwick, W.R. (1990). Communication skills training, communication skills training with family and cognitive behavioral mood management training for alcoholics. *Journal of Studies on Alcohol, 51,* 263–270.

Monti, P.M., Abrams, D.B., Kadden, R.M., & Cooney, N.L. (1989). *Treating alcohol dependence: A coping skills training guide.* New York: Guilford Press.

Monti, P.M., Rohsenow, D.J., Rubonis, A.V., Niaura, R.S., Sirota, A.D., Colby, S.M., Goddard, P., & Abrams, D.B. (1993). Cue exposure with coping skills treatment for male alcoholics: A preliminary investigation. *Journal of Consulting and Clinical Psychology, 61,* 1011–1019.

Moore, R.D., Bone, L.R., Geller, G., Mamom, J.A., Stokes, E.J., & Levine, D. (1980). Prevalence, detection, and treatment of alcoholism in hospitalized patients. *Journal of the American Medical Association, 261,* 403–407.

Moos, R.H., Finney, J.W., & Cronkite, R.C. (1990). *Alcoholism treatment: Context, process, and outcome.* New York: Oxford University Press.

Morgan, T.J. (1996). Behavioral treatment techniques for psychoactive substance use disorders. In J. Rotgers, R. Keller, & S. Morgenstein (Eds.), *Treating substance abuse: Theory and technique* (pp. 202–240). New York: Guilford Press.

Nathan, P.E. (1985). Aversion therapy in the treatment of alcoholism: Success and failure. *Annals of the New York Academy of Sciences, 443,* 357–364.

Nathan, P.E. (1991). Substance use disorders in the DSM-IV. *Journal of Abnormal Psychology, 100,* 356–361.

O'Farrell, T.J. (1993). A behavioral marital therapy couples group program for alcoholics and their spouses. In T.J. O'Farrell (Ed.), *Treating alcohol problems: Marital and family interventions* (pp. 170–209). New York: Guilford Press.

O'Farrell, T.J. (1994). Alcohol dependence and abuse. In C.G. Last & M. Hersen (Eds.), *Adult behavior therapy casebook* (pp. 61–78). New York: Plenum Press.

O'Farrell, T.J., Choquette, K.A., Cutter, H.S.G., & Brown, E.D. (1993). Behavioral marital therapy with and without additional couples relapse prevention sessions for alcoholics and their wives. *Journal of Studies on Alcohol, 54,* 652–666.

O'Farrell, T.J., Choquette, K.A., Cutter, H.S.G., & Floyd, F.J. (1996). Cost-benefit and cost-effectiveness analyses of behavioral marital therapy as an addition to outpatient alcoholism treatment. *Journal of Substance Abuse, 8,* 145–166.

O'Farrell, T.J., & Cowles, K.S. (1989). Marital and family therapy. In R.K. Hester & W.R. Miller (Eds.), *Handbook of alcoholism treatment approaches: Effective alternatives* (pp. 183–205). Elmsford, NY: Pergamon Press.

O'Farrell, T.J., Cutter, H.S.G., Choquette, K.A., Floyd, F.J., & Bayog, R.D. (1992). Behavioral marital therapy for male alcoholics: Marital and drinking adjustment during the two years after treatment. *Behavior Therapy, 23,* 529–549.

Orford, J., Oppenheimer, E., & Edwards, G. (1976). Abstinence or control: The outcome for excessive drinkers two years after consultation. *Behaviour Research and Therapy, 14,* 409–418.

Ouimette, P.C., Finney, J.W., & Moos, R.H. (1997). Twelve-step and cognitive-behavioral treatment for substance abuse: A comparison of treatment effectiveness. *Journal of Consulting and Clinical Psychology, 65,* 230–240.

Pattison, E.M., Sobell, M.B., & Sobell, L.C. (1977). *Emerging concepts of alcohol dependence.* New York: Springer.

Prochaska, J.O. (1983). Self-changers versus therapy versus Schachter [Letter for the editor]. *American Psychologist, 38,* 853–854.

Prochaska, J.O., & DiClemente, C.C. (1986). Toward a comprehensive model of change. In W.R. Miller & N. Heather (Eds.), *Treating addictive behaviors: Processes of change* (pp. 3–27). New York: Plenum Press.

Project MATCH Research Group. (1993). Project MATCH: Rationale and methods for a multisite clinical trial matching alcoholic patients to treatment. *Alcoholism: Clinical and Experimental Research, 17,* 1130–1145.

Regier, D.A., Narrow, W.E., Rae, D.S., Manderscheid, R.W., Locke, B.Z., & Goodwin, F.K. (1993). The de facto U.S. mental and addictive disorders service system. *Archives of General Psychiatry, 50,* 85–93.

Rimmele, C.T., Howard, M.O., & Hilfrink, M.L. (1995). Aversion therapies. In R.K. Hester & W.R. Miller (Eds.), *Handbook of alcoholism treatment approaches: Effective alternatives* (2nd ed., pp. 134–147). Boston: Allyn & Bacon.

Rimmele, C.T., Miller, W.R., & Dougher, M.J. (1989). Aversion therapies. In R.K. Hester & W.R. Miller (Eds.), *Handbook of alcoholism treatment approaches: Effective alternatives* (pp. 128–140). New York: Pergamon Press.

Rohsenow, D.J., Monti, P.M., Binkoff, J.A., Liepman, M.R., Nirenberg, T.D., & Abrams, D.B. (1991). Patient-treatment matching for alcoholic men in communication skills versus cognitive-behavioral mood management training. *Addictive Behaviors, 16,* 63–69.

Rohsenow, D.J., Niaura, R.S., Childress, A.R., Abrams, D., & Monti, P.M. (1991). Cue reactivity in addictive behaviors: Theoretical and treatment implications. *International Journal of the Addictive Behaviors, 25,* 957–993.

Saunders, B., Wilkinson, C., & Phillips, M. (1995). The impact of a brief motivational intervention with opiate users attending a methadone programme. *Addiction, 90,* 415–424.

Saunders, W.M., & Kershaw, P.W. (1979). Spontaneous remission from alcoholism: A community study. *British Journal of Addiction, 74,* 251–265.

Sisson, R.W., & Azrin, N.H. (1993). Community reinforcement training for families: A method to get alcoholics into treatment. In T.J. O'Farrell (Ed.), *Treating alcohol problems: Marital and family interventions* (pp. 34–53). New York: Guilford Press.

Skinner, H.A., & Horn, J.L. (1984). *Alcohol dependence scale: Users guide.* Toronto: Addiction Research Foundation.

Smith, J.E., & Meyers, R.J. (1995). The community reinforcement approach. In R.K. Hester & W.R. Miller (Eds.), *Handbook of alcoholism treatment approaches: Effective alternatives* (2nd ed., pp. 251–266). Boston: Allyn & Bacon.

Smith, J.W., & Frawley, P.J. (1990). Long-term abstinence from alcohol in patients receiving aversion therapy as part of a multimodal inpatient program. *Journal of Substance Abuse Treatment, 7,* 77–82.

Sobell, L.C., & Sobell, M.B. (1992). Timeline follow-back: A technique for assessing self-reported ethanol consumption. In J. Allen & R.Z. Litten (Eds.), *Measuring alcohol consumption: Psychosocial and biological methods* (pp. 41–72). Totowa, NJ: Humana Press.

Sobell, L.C., Sobell, M.B., Brown, J., & Cleland, P.A. (1995, November). *A randomized trial comparing group versus individual Guided self-change treatment for alcohol and drug abusers.* Paper presented at the 29th annual meeting of the Association for Advancement of Behavior Therapy, Washington, DC.

Sobell, L.C., Sobell, M.B., & Leo, G.I. (1993, November). *Spousal social support: A motivational intervention for alcohol abusers.* Paper presented at the annual meeting of the Association for Advancement of Behavior Therapy, Atlanta, GA.

Sobell, L.C., Toneatto, A., & Sobell, M.B. (1990). Behavior therapy. In A.S. Bellack & M. Hersen (Eds.), *Handbook of comparative treatments for adult disorders* (pp. 479–505). New York: Wiley.

Sobell, M.B., Buchan, G., & Sobell, L.C. (1996, November). *Relationship of goal choices by substance abusers in guided self-change treatment to subject characteristics and treatment outcome.* Poster presented at the 30th annual meeting of the Association for Advancement of Behavior Therapy, New York.

Sobell, M.B., & Sobell, L.C. (1987). *Conceptual issues regarding goals in the treatment of alcohol problems.* New York: Haworth Press.

Sobell, M.B., & Sobell, L.C. (1993). *Problem drinkers: Guided self-change treatment.* New York: Guilford Press.

Sobell, M.B., & Sobell, L.C. (1995). Controlled drinking after 25 years: How important was the great debate? *Addiction, 90,* 1149–1153.

Sobell, M.B., & Sobell, L.C. (1998). Guided self-change treatment. In W.R. Miller & N. Heather (Eds.), *Treating addictive behaviors: Processes of change* (2nd ed., pp. 189–202). New York: Plenum Press.

Tuchfeld, B.S. (1976). *Changes in patterns of alcohol use without the aid of formal treatment: An exploratory study of former problem drinkers.* Research Triangle Park, NC: Research Triangle Institute.

Vogel, P., Eriksen, L., & Bjornelv, S. (1997). Skills training and prediction of follow-up status for chronic alcohol dependent inpatients. *European Journal of Psychiatry, 11*(1), 51–63.

Waldorf, D., & Biernacki, P. (Eds.). (1982). *Natural recovery from heroin addiction: A review of the incidence literature.* New York: Human Science.

Waldron, H.B., & Miller, W.R. (in press). Client anger as a predictor of differential response to treatment. In R. Longabaugh (Ed.), *Client-treatment matching.* Rockville, MD: NIAAA Monograph.

Weisner, C., Greenfield, T., & Room, R. (1995). Trends in the treatment of alcohol problems in the U.S. general population, 1979 through 1990. *American Journal of Public Health, 95,* 55–60.

Wills, T.A., & Shiffman, S. (1985). Coping and substance use: A conceptual framework. In S. Shiffman & T.A. Wills (Eds.), *Coping and substance use* (pp. 1–24). New York: Academic Press.

Zook, C.J., & Moore, F.D. (1980). High-cost users of medical care. *New England Journal of Medicine, 302,* 996–1002.

CHAPTER 26

Pharmacotherapy

HOWARD B. MOSS

CONCEPTUALIZATION OF THE DISORDER

Abuse and dependence on habituating drugs represents a significant public-health problem. Among the major causes of mortality in the United States in 1990, tobacco use was estimated to account for about 400,000 deaths, alcohol use accounted for 100,000 deaths, and illicit drugs for 20,000 deaths (McGinnis & Foege, 1993). Despite its societal importance, with a few notable exceptions, the clinical psychopharmacological treatment of substance abuse disorders remains an underdeveloped area. Basic scientists, psychopharmacologists, and clinicians are now constantly challenged by the rapidly changing trends in drugs of abuse. In recent years, the illicit market has introduced more potent and dangerous forms of drugs of abuse, and new designer drugs (i.e., chemically redesigned psychoactive substances) have been developed. At the same time, historically well-established drugs of abuse such as alcohol, opiates, cannabis, nicotine, and cocaine continues to plague society. However, substantial progress has been made in terms of biological mechanisms of drug action, the phenomenon of drug reinforcement, the psychobiology of addiction, and the clinical syndromes associated with their abuse. Hopefully, these advances in research will potentially yield a new pharmacological armamentarium with which to treat abusers of habituating drugs.

Despite these technological advances in pharmacology, it is apparent from clinical experience that these new pharmacotherapies are useful primarily as adjuncts to psychosocial interventions. Thus, it is doubtful that successful treatment can neglect the social, cultural, and psychological factors leading to substance abuse while attending only to the biological and pharmacological domains.

BASIC PHARMACOLOGICAL CONCEPTS
RELEVANT TO THE SUBSTANCE USE DISORDERS

Central to the pharmacological approach to substance abuse treatments are the concepts of intoxication, tolerance, dependence, and the intrinsic reinforcing properties of drugs.

INTOXICATION

Intoxication refers primarily to the complex alterations of the normal functioning of the central nervous system (CNS) produced by the pharmacological characteristics of a drug. This process includes disturbances in arousal, sensation, cognition, mood, and motor function. Each psychoactive drug produces its own pattern of perturbation of these brain processes, which depend on the specific nature of the drug's actions. For example, alcohol produces incoordination, memory deficits, attentional deficits, sedation, impairment in judgment, euphoria or dysphoria, and decrements in performance on a variety of tasks. The extent to which an individual displays the CNS effects of a drug depends on a variety of factors, including dose, route of administration, time of day, and individual constitutional factors such as gender and body habitus, liver functioning, phenotype of drug metabolizing enzymes, rate of gastric emptying, renal functioning, and prior exposure to the drug. The effects of prior exposure to the drug or to a similarly acting compound are aspects of the concept of tolerance.

TOLERANCE

Tolerance refers to the changes that occur in an individual as a result of repeated exposure to alcohol or other drug (or another closely related compound) such that an increased amount of the drug is required to produce the same effect or less effect is produced by the same dose of drug (Kalant, LeBlanc, & Gibbins, 1971). The mechanisms of tolerance are generally described as either dispositional or functional. *Metabolic* or *dispositional tolerance* refers to changes in drug absorption, distribution, biotransformation, and excretion that lead to a reduction in the intensity and duration of exposure of an organ (e.g., the brain) to the drug. *Functional tolerance* refers to the changes in the target organ that render it less sensitive to the drug. The role of conditioned learning in the development of functional tolerance has stimulated much controversy. Tabakoff and colleagues (Tabakoff, Melchior, & Hoffman, 1984) have suggested further dividing the concept of functional tolerance into environment-dependent and environment-independent tolerance with respect to forms of tolerance in which learning plays a major or a minor role.

DEPENDENCE

Current conceptualizations of drug dependence are, to a great extent, indebted to the alcohol dependence syndrome described by Edwards and Gross (Edwards & Gross, 1976). Beginning with the *Diagnostic and Statistical Manual of*

Mental Disorders, (3rd ed., rev., DSM-III-R: American Psychiatric Association, 1987), there has been a significant broadening of the definition of *dependence* to "a syndrome of clinically significant behaviors, cognitions, and other symptoms that indicate loss of control of substance use and continued use of the substance despite adverse consequences." Thus, the concept now includes aspects of both physical and psychological dependence. Psychological dependence refers to the subjective compulsion to use the drugs, and the salience of drug use in the lifestyle of the patient. The physical-dependence aspect of the syndrome refers to the presence of tolerance and a withdrawal syndrome when use ceases or there is a reduction in drug use. The current psychiatric nosologies of *DSM-IV* and the 10th edition of the International Classification of Diseases (ICD-10) includes both of these specific physiological and psychological aspects of a substance dependence syndrome and permits an additional coding for physiological dependence based upon the presence of a withdrawal syndrome upon reduction or cessation of use.

DRUGS AS REINFORCERS

Animal studies carried out in the mid-1950s first suggested that drugs might be self-administered for their intrinsic reinforcing effects (Nichols, Headlee, & Coppock, 1956). Since that time, the application of behavioral pharmacological techniques has revealed that the inherent reinforcing properties of some drugs do contribute to drug-seeking behavior in humans. Highly reinforcing drugs of abuse such as cocaine (Fischman & Schuster, 1982), nicotine (Henningfield & Griffiths, 1980), morphine (Wikler, 1952), alcohol (Mendelson & Mello, 1966), heroin (Mello & Mendelson, 1980), and marijuana (Mello & Mendelson, 1978) produce high rates of self-administration in laboratory settings. These effects may occur independent of the pharmacological phenomena of dependence and withdrawal. It is unclear, however, how much one can generalize from the human operant laboratory to a naturalistic setting. Further, most of these studies have been conducted with drug abusers as subjects. There may be specific characteristics about such preselected individuals that make them especially sensitive to the reinforcing properties of these drugs.

Considerable progress has been made in identifying the neurobiological substrate for the reinforcing properties of drugs of abuse. Most habituating drugs activate a circuit in the brain running from the ventral tegmental area of brainstem, through the nucleus accumbens to the prefrontal cortex (Koob, 1992). This pathway consists of primarily dopaminergic neurons. For this reason, it is referred to as the mesolimbic dopaminergic pathway. Dopamine release in either nucleus accumbens or prefrontal cortex is associated with administration of reinforcing drugs.

DIAGNOSTIC ISSUES AND PROBLEMS

The conceptualization of diagnostic constructs for psychoactive substance abuse disorders has evolved since Jellinek's time into various operationalized schemes. The most recent nosological constructs are the revised criteria now accepted by the American Psychiatric Association (APA, 1994) in its *DSM-IV*. Under this taxonomy, substance use disorders are dichotomized into two categories: (1) substance abuse, and (2) substance dependence. Although the drug dependence construct is well-characterized and explicit in its requirement for any three criteria referring to either physical or psychological aspects of dependence, the abuse construct appears to be more of a diagnosis of exclusion. Therein, any maladaptive pattern of substance use that occurs over a 12-month period may be sufficient for diagnostic labeling. Recent evidence suggests that abuse may simply be the prodromal stage in the development of a drug dependence disorder (Langenbucher & Chung, 1995).

Previous diagnostic systems have been plagued with problems. For example, the construct validity of these taxonomic systems have frequently been without empirical verification. For example, it was reported that three prior diagnostic criteria for alcoholism, specifically the Research Diagnostic Criteria (RDC), the Feigner Criteria, and the *DSM-III* (APA, 1980) criteria appeared not to be concordant for classifying alcoholic individuals (Leonard, Bromet, Parkinson, & Day, 1984). Similarly, the *DSM-III* criteria for alcohol abuse correlated poorly with self-reported drinking pattern, quantity, and consequences of alcohol consumption (Tarter, Arria, Moss, Edwards, & Van Thiel, 1987).

TREATMENT STRATEGIES

In general, three specific strategies have been applied to the pharmacological approach to chemical dependency: (1) attenuation of withdrawal symptoms, (2) alteration of the drug's stimulus properties in order to reduce drug-seeking behaviors, and (3) reduction of the craving for the abused substance in an effort to forestall relapse. The first is the attenuation of withdrawal symptoms. In the past, compulsive alcohol-seeking and other drug-seeking behavior was thought to be motivated by the desire to avoid the unpleasant symptoms of the specific withdrawal syndromes. However, it is now known that not all abusable drugs produce a withdrawal syndrome upon cessation of use and that some abusable drugs cause a withdrawal state that is clinically insignificant. Thus, the focus of pharmacological control of withdrawal states is directed toward reduction of the morbidity and mortality associated with acute abstinence, as well as toward making patients more comfortable so that they may competently participate in psychosocial therapies. In particular, the most severe form of alcohol withdrawal, delirium tremens, was associated with a 15 percent mortality rate earlier in this century (Thompson, Johnson, & Maddrey, 1975). Advances in pharmacotherapy in the form of rational use of benzodiazepines have significantly reduced this death rate.

The second strategy for the pharmacotherapy of substance abuse problems involves alteration of the stimulus properties of the drug such that it no longer promotes drug-seeking behavior. This may take the form of either the reduction of reinforcement from alcohol or other drugs (i.e., "antagonist drugs") or the development of aversion to them (i.e., "deterrent drugs").

Examples of reinforcement-reduction techniques include naltrexone (Revia) therapy and high-dose methadone maintenance for opiate abuse. An example of an aversive approach that is widely used clinically is disulfiram (Antabuse) treatment for alcoholism.

The third strategy involves using medications to reduce craving for the abused substance. Craving is a theoretical construct that represents the internal drive state propelling drug-seeking or other alcohol-seeking behavior (Rankin, Hodgson, & Stockwell, 1979). Although heightened during the withdrawal syndrome, craving appears to persist beyond the expression of physical withdrawal symptoms into the postwithdrawal interval. The existence of a subacute, protracted abstinence syndrome, extending weeks after the signs of the physical withdrawal syndrome have abated, has been noted by clinicians in opiate and alcohol addicts, but it is yet without careful empirical investigation (Meyer, 1986). Neuroadaptive changes may still be taking place beyond the classical withdrawal period. For example, the sleep disturbances of newly abstinent alcoholics may not normalize for 9 to 21 months (Williams & Rundell, 1981). Nonsuppression on the dexamethasone suppression test may persist for more than three weeks after classical physical alcohol withdrawal (Khan et al., 1984). During this postwithdrawal interval, craving appears to be at its peak.

Two approaches have been taken to the reduction of craving. Drug substitution has been a frequently used means of modifying or eliminating craving and drug-seeking behavior. Methadone maintenance for heroin addiction is a classic example. Substitution of nicotine-containing gum for cigarettes (Hughes et al., 1984) is another example. Chronic benzodiazepine treatment of alcoholics was suggested by Kissin (1975). Unfortunately, this approach involves first the re-addiction of the patient to another drug (though it is considered a socially acceptable choice) and then the gradual reduction of that drug's dosage. This may have short-term benefits, such as retention of the patient in treatment or reduced involvement in criminal activities, but ultimately the patient still needs to undergo withdrawal of the drug and some degree of drug craving.

Correction of underlying physiological disturbances produced by the chronic presence of a drug in the body is another approach. The attenuation of cocaine craving was initially reported with bromocriptine (Parlodel), a dopamine agonist (Dackis & Gold, 1985), and with desipramine, a tricyclic antidepressant (Kleber & Gawin, 1986). The rationale for each approach is the reversal of cocaine-induced pathophysiology in the central dopaminergic and noradrenergic systems, respectively. Subsequent studies however, have failed to demonstrate clinical benefit. Bromocriptine has also been reported by one researcher to be efficacious in the treatment of alcohol craving (Borg, 1983); however, further experience with bromocriptine in alcoholics is obviously needed.

PHARMACOLOGICAL TREATMENT OF THE WITHDRAWAL SYNDROME

Withdrawal syndromes are generally treated either with drug substitutions that: (1) possess cross-tolerance with the abused substance and possess a favorable pharmacokinetic profile, or (2) with drugs that indirectly suppress physiological symptoms of the withdrawal syndrome through their separate actions on the autonomic nervous system (ANS) or on central neurotransmission.

Opiate Withdrawal

Opiate withdrawal is commonly managed in inpatients through the substitution method. The long-acting opiate methadone (half-life 15 to 22 hours) is substituted for heroin, morphine, or other opioids. Methadone is used because of its cross-tolerance with other opiates and its prolonged apparent half-life, and because it is well absorbed from the gastrointestinal tract (Jaffe & Martin, 1980). Typically, when withdrawal symptoms become apparent, a patient is given an initial oral dose of 15 to 20 mg of methadone. Doses are titrated against withdrawal symptoms during the first 24 hours up to a maximum of 80 mg. Once the patient is stabilized on an adequate amount of methadone to keep the patient symptom free for a 24-hour interval, gradual daily reduction may take place. Usually, a dose reduction of about 20 percent per day is well tolerated (Jaffe, 1980). Thus, the methadone substitution protocol may take anywhere from 10 days to one month for successful detoxification.

An important discovery in the treatment of the opiate withdrawal syndrome was the finding that clonidine, an alpha-2 adrenergic receptor agonist when used clinically as an antihypertensive agent, effectively reduces signs and symptoms of opiate withdrawal (Gold, Redmond, & Kleber, 1978). Typically, oral doses of 1 to 2 mg/day of clonidine are used to suppress the withdrawal symptoms of opiate addicts. Up to 10 days of clonidine treatment may be required, particularly if a longer-acting opiate is the drug of abuse or if clonidine is used for the purpose of methadone withdrawal (Charney, Sternberg, Kleber, Heninger, & Redmond, 1981). Clonidine, in combination with the long-term opiate antagonist naltrexone, has been found to be effective for an even more rapid opiate detoxification regimen (Charney, Heninger, & Kleber, 1986). Detoxification from methadone can be successfully accomplished in 4 to 5 days using these two agents to simultaneously precipitate and suppress the opiate withdrawal syndrome.

Recently, considerable interest has been aroused by the prospect of ultra-rapid (<24-hour) opiate withdrawal employing midazolam-induced general anesthesia, substantial doses of naltrexone and clonidine or guanfacine (another alpha-2 agonist), and adjunctive medication to reduce diarrhea (Legarda & Gossop, 1994). This procedure is conducted in an intensive care setting with ongoing cardiorespiratory monitoring. Although this technique has the significant benefit of rapidly reversing the process of neuroadaptation to opiates, to date clinical trials formally investigating the clinical efficacy, safety and toleration of this protocol have yet to be accomplished, thus it is unclear as to the strengths and limitations of this method.

Alcohol Withdrawal

In the classic study by Isbell and associates (Isbell, Fraser, & Wikler, 1955), six volunteers maintained an excellent diet and consumed large amounts of alcohol for 48 days. Upon abrupt discontinuation of alcohol, these volunteers developed a broad spectrum of withdrawal symptoms, including seizures, hallucinations with a clear sensorium, and delirium tremens. Because a nutritional deficiency could be ruled out by the adequate dietary intake, the authors concluded that the withdrawal of alcohol alone was responsible for this syndrome. Since this report, a variety of pharmacological approaches have been applied to the treatment of the withdrawal syndrome. The two most successful treatments have involved: (1) substitution with drugs that have some degree of cross-tolerance with alcohol, yet have a different pharmacokinetic profile, and more recently, (2) treatment with those agents that decrease activity of the sympathetic nervous system (SNS). The safety and efficacy of benzodiazepine therapy in the treatment of the alcohol withdrawal syndrome is now well established. Clinical trials have demonstrated the superiority of benzodiazepine therapy over a variety of other pharmacological approaches, including antipsychotics (Kaim, Klett, & Rothchild, 1969), anticonvulsants (Sampliner & Iber, 1974), paraldehyde (Thompson et al., 1975), hydroxyzine (Runion & Fowler, 1978), and meprobamate (Wegner & Fink, 1965).

The first introduced benzodiazepine, chlordiazepoxide (Librium), has in recent years been the standard for treating the alcohol withdrawal syndrome. However, the appropriate dosing regimen for this drug is often problematic. The relatively slow rate of absorption following oral administration produces a delay of several hours for peak plasma concentrations. As a consequence of this delay, overtreatment with this pharmacological agent is not uncommon. Patients may, therefore, remain lethargic, ataxic, or confused for several days after the withdrawal state has resolved (Baskin & Easdale, 1982). A more rational approach involves the titration of a dose of a rapidly absorbed benzodiazepine against the presentation of clinical symptoms (e.g., the diazepam loading method of Sellers and associates, 1983). Diazepam is highly lipid-soluble, and oral administration results in peak plasma concentrations occurring in approximately one hour. Thus, the physician can administer a dose and readily observe for its effect on the alcohol withdrawal syndrome. As an additional benefit, the favorable pharmacokinetic profile of diazepam allows for the oral loading of the drug on the first day of treatment only. Because the half-life of diazepam is about 33 hours, and that of its active metabolite desmethyldiazepam is about 50 hours, therapeutic plasma concentrations will be present after only one day's loading for more than the 72 hours duration of a typical alcohol withdrawal syndrome. Briefly, the method protocol involves oral administration of 20 mg of diazepam every two hours until the patient is asymptomatic. After the first day, patients are then permitted to continue on diazepam and its active metabolite with additional medication given only on an as-needed (PRN) basis.

There is one limitation to this method. Patients with severely compromised liver function will not metabolize the drug, thereby causing an accumulation of the compound in the body. For patients with severe hepatic dysfunction, lorazepam may be a safer benzodiazepine. This drug does not depend on hepatic biotransformation for its excretion. Although the oral form of lorazepam has a similar delay in absorption as chlordiazepoxide, a rapidly absorbed sublingual preparation (Caille et al., 1980) and a parenteral form (Spencer, 1980) may be very useful in the rational treatment of the alcohol withdrawal syndrome.

Clonidine has also been demonstrated to have efficacy in treatment of the alcohol withdrawal state (Wilkins, Jenkins, & Steiner, 1983). Clonidine stimulates the presynaptic alpha adrenoceptors, which reduces noradrenergic transmission and thereby attenuates the activation of the SNS. In a comparative study of the relative efficacy of clonidine versus chlordiazepoxide, clonidine was found to be both more effective in reducing cardiovascular symptoms of withdrawal and as effective at improving cognitive capacity, reducing anxiety, and reducing subjective complaints of withdrawal (Baumgartner & Rowen, 1987). Although it lacks anticonvulsant properties, it also is without any intrinsic abuse potential. Thus, clonidine should be seriously considered as an alternative to benzodiazepines.

Nicotine Withdrawal

Nicotine withdrawal begins a few hours after acute abstinence, peaks within a few days, and frequently lasts for about four weeks. (Henningfield, 1995). Symptoms include a dysphoric or depressed mood, insomnia, irritability, anxiety, difficulty concentrating, restlessness, decrease heart rate and increased appetite. Nicotine replacement paradigms have been successfully utilized to reduce the severity of nicotine withdrawal while patients are learning to change their lifestyle and live without tobacco (Gross & Stitzler, 1989). In general, nicotine replacement seeks to administer less nicotine than the habitually smoked cigarettes, but sufficient to suppress the withdrawal syndrome. Two nicotine delivery systems are currently available as over-the-counter medications. Nicotine polacrilex (nicotine gum) releases about 50 percent of its nicotine into the mouth with chewing. The dose is usually titrated against the patient's withdrawal symptomatology, and may require 10 to 15 doses per day depending upon the severity of physical dependence. Transdermal nicotine delivery (nicotine patch) is the other major method for administering nicotine in smoking cessation efforts. The patch requires the passage of two to three days before maximal plasma concentrations are achieved (H. Ross, Chan, Piraino, & John, 1991). Thus, severely dependent patients may find themselves experiencing a significant withdrawal syndrome upon immediate smoking cessation once the patch is administered, and they may be at greater risk for relapse. Henningfield has recently recommended that those patients receiving the patch, who smoke more than 10 cigarettes per day, should start on the highest nicotine patch dose as possible. Similarly, those patients who smoke more than 20 cigarettes per day should start with one 4-mg dose of nicotine polacrilex for every three to four cigarettes typically smoked. In either case, underdosing with nicotine significantly increases the risk of uncomfortable withdrawal symptoms and an augmented risk for relapse.

At the time of this writing, an aerosolized nicotine spray is under consideration by the Food and Drug Administration for approval as another nicotine delivery system. It also appears to have potential as nicotine replacement to assist smokers in achieving abstinence.

Cocaine Withdrawal

The nature and manifestations of a physical cocaine withdrawal syndrome or "crash" have been a relatively controversial phenomenon. Initially, the syndrome of cocaine cessation was described in terms of three phases: the crash, the withdrawal phase, and the extinction phase (Gawin & Kleber, 1986). The crash phase was described as a syndrome comprising those symptoms that are generally the opposite of those found with cocaine intoxication. Specifically, these included anergy, intense craving, hypersomnia, hyperphagia, decreased libido, irritability, psychomotor retardation, amotivation, and decreased attentional concentration. It was thought to last anywhere from nine hours to four days. The withdrawal phase was thought to last for from 1 to 10 weeks and was characterized at its terminus by anhedonia, anergia, anxiety, and high levels of drug craving. The extinction phase was described as an indefinite time period of euthymic mood, and episodic cocaine craving. However, a subsequent study in a controlled environment revealed that the greatest craving for cocaine occurs within 24 hours of the last administration and the greatest effects of cocaine abstinence on mood appeared to be on the first day after last administration (Weddington et al., 1990). All symptoms improved with abstinence over time, and there was no evidence of phases or cycles in the withdrawal picture. In general, a dramatic physiological abstinence syndrome has not been demonstrated.

The catecholaminergic system is thought to be implicated both in the actions of cocaine and the manifestations of withdrawal. Cocaine is a releaser of dopamine (Van Rossum & Hurkmans, 1964) and a potent inhibitor of the neuronal reuptake of dopamine and other catecholamines (S. Ross & Renyi, 1966). Chronic cocaine administration is associated with a depletion of catecholamines. Brain dopamine levels have been reported to fall after repeated administration of cocaine (Taylor & Ho, 1977). Chronic cocaine administration also results in a compensatory increase in the number of dopamine receptors in the brain (Taylor, Ho, & Fagan, 1979) consistent with reduced dopaminergic transmission. A reduction in the urinary metabolite of central and peripheral norepinephrine has been reported in chronic cocaine abusers (Tennant, 1985). Increases in the number of beta adrenoceptors have also been reported with chronic cocaine administration (Banerjee, Sharma, Kung-Cheung, Chanda, & Riggi, 1979). Therefore, the pathophysiology of this withdrawal condition has been hypothesized to result from a diminution of dopaminergic and/or noradrenergic neurotransmission produced by the chronic effects of cocaine.

Guided by these findings, two initially successful, but subsequently disconfirmed approaches to cocaine withdrawal were reported. First, bromocriptine (a dopamine agonist) was suggested in low doses for the treatment of cocaine withdrawal (Dackis & Gold, 1985). Its use followed a physiological replacement strategy in which a dopamine agonist compensates for presynaptic depletion and regulates down postsynaptic receptors until natural physiological dopamine synthesis catches up with its losses.

Second, a similar observation was that tricyclic antidepressants such as desipramine and imipramine downregulate supersensitive beta adrenoceptors

(Charney, Menkes, & Heninger, 1981) and dopamine receptors (Koide & Matshushita, 1981). This observation has led to an initially successful clinical trial using these agents in the treatment of cocaine withdrawal (Kleber & Gawin, 1986). To date, no effective therapeutic has proven itself efficacious in the treatment of the cocaine abstinence syndrome. Given the self-limiting nature of this condition, pharmacotherapy is in all probability unnecessary.

REINFORCEMENT REDUCTION OR AVERSION DEVELOPMENT

Disulfiram for Alcoholism

Disulfiram (Antabuse) use was first initiated in Europe as a treatment for alcoholism in 1948 (Hald & Jacobsen, 1948). It was later introduced in the United States and has since remained one of the two pharmaceuticals available here that are specifically indicated for alcoholism therapy.

Disulfiram alters the intermediary metabolism of alcohol. Specifically, it inhibits the activity of the enzyme acetaldehyde dehydrogenase. Thus, when ethyl alcohol is ingested, blood acetaldehyde concentrations rise, resulting in acetaldehyde reaction. This disulfiram-ethanol reaction (DER) consists of the rather unpleasant combination of vasodilatation, sweating, intense throbbing in the head and neck, respiratory difficulties, nausea, vomiting, vertigo, chest pain, and hypotension. The hypotension may be severe and cause postural syncope. This reaction may last anywhere from 30 minutes to several hours.

The DER obviously reduces the reinforcing aspects of alcohol consumption. However, the clinical reality is that most alcoholics never drink while taking disulfiram. The knowledge of the possibility of having a DER is a sufficient deterrent to the consumption of alcohol. Thus, disulfiram may be viewed as an active placebo.

The efficacy of disulfiram in the treatment of alcoholism is quite controversial. Fuller and Williford (1980) used life-table or actuarial methods to describe the outcome of three randomly assigned groups of alcoholic patients who were receiving counseling and medical care. The first group was given a daily therapeutic dose (250 mg) of disulfiram. The second group was told that they, too, would be receiving disulfiram, but they were given the markedly subtherapeutic dose of 1 mg. The third group was told they would not be treated with the drug. The abstinence rates measured one year after discharge from the program indicated no difference between disulfiram therapeutic dose, and the 1 mg subtherapeutic dose. Both of these groups, however, had superior outcome in comparison to the no-drug group. Thus, therapeutic doses of disulfiram may be no better than placebo. A similarly designed, large-scale, multicenter study was conducted by the Veterans Administration, which also looked at the effects of counseling in addition to disulfiram (Fuller et al., 1986). This time, there were no differences among the three groups in terms of abstinence. Thus, counseling alone appeared as effective as disulfiram or the low-dose active placebo. However, among the patients who relapsed, those receiving therapeutic doses of disulfiram had fewer drinking days than their counterparts in the subtherapeutic or counseling-only groups.

If disulfiram was a totally innocuous compound, there would be little controversy surrounding its use despite its placebo-like status. However, the literature is riddled with suggestions that disulfiram may be responsible for a variety for adverse side effects. These include hepatotoxicity (Goyer & Major, 1979), carbon disulfiram poisoning with polyneuropathy (Rainey, 1977), psychotic reactions (Bennett, McKeever, & Turk, 1951; Major et al., 1979), acute organic brain syndrome (Knee & Razani, 1974), and a worsening of preexisting schizophrenia (Heath, Nesselhof, Bishop, & Byers, 1965).

The majority of these adverse sequelae now appear to be dose related, because early dosing schedules exceeded the now-recommended 250 mg to 500 mg dose range. Two recent reports of disulfiram side effects at this lower dose did not implicate disulfiram in the production of either physical (Christensen, Ronsted, & Vaag, 1984) or psychiatric complications (Branchey, Davis, Lee, & Fuller, 1987). However, the former study was flawed by being only six weeks in duration, and the latter study carefully screened out subjects who had a history of organic mental disorder, schizophrenia, affective disorder, or a history of psychotropic drug abuse. Therefore, a longer duration of treatment, higher doses, and the use with patients who have preexisting psychiatric disorders could account for many of the earlier reports of problematic side effects. Until these issues are clarified, clinicians who believe in the clinical value of this compound should restrict their prescriptions to lower doses for a limited duration of treatment, and they should exercise restraint in the administration of disulfiram to those patients with preexisting hepatic, myocardial, neurological, or psychiatric illnesses.

Lithium Carbonate for Alcoholism

Chronic lithium pretreatment has been reported to attenuate the euphoria and activation associated with a variety of stimulant compounds, including amphetamine (Flemenbaum, 1974; Van Kammen & Murphy, 1975), cocaine (Cronson & Flemenbaum, 1978), and intravenous (IV) methylphenidate (Huey et al., 1981). Although these initial reports were promising, later trials revealed less consistency in this effect (Angrist & Gershon, 1979). In an open trial of the comparative efficacy of lithium versus desipramine in the treatment of cocaine abuse, lithium was apparently not clinically effective (Gawin & Kleber, 1984). Therefore, routine use of lithium for stimulant abuse cannot be recommended.

Since the mid-1970s, there have been a number of reports in the literature both suggesting that lithium antagonizes some of the effects of alcohol intoxication and advocating its use in treatment of clinical alcoholism. Early reports from Kline and associates (Kline, Wren, Cooper, Varg, & Canal, 1974) and from Merry and associates (Merry, Reynolds, Baily, & Coppen, 1976) suggested that lithium might be of benefit only in depressed alcoholics. However, studies on normal volunteers revealed that lithium reduced the subjective intoxication "high" from alcohol, and that lithium reduced alcohol-induced psychomotor performance deficits (Judd, Hubbard, & Huey, 1977; Linnoila, Saario, & Maki, 1974). Subsequently, a double-blind, placebo-controlled study of detoxified alcoholics receiving chronic lithium treatment demonstrated less intoxication, less of a desire to continue drinking, and less cognitive and psychomotor performance deficits when challenged with doses of alcohol (Judd & Huey, 1984). Then, in a double-blind, placebo-controlled clinical trial of lithium carbonate therapy for alcoholism initiated during inpatient treatment, Fawcett and associates (1987) found that subjects with a therapeutic lithium level demonstrated a better treatment outcome than the placebo group, and that these results were independent of the presence of affective symptoms. However, a subsequent multisite Veterans Affairs Cooperative Study, which included alcoholics with and without major depression revealed no differences between alcoholics who took lithium versus placebo in terms of abstinence rates, drinking days, alcohol-related hospitalizations, and changes in severity of either alcoholism or depression (Dorus et al., 1989). Thus, lithium may not have the clinical utility that was initially indicated by smaller studies.

Naltrexone for Alcoholism and Opiate Dependence

Naltrexone is an essentially pure opiate antagonist, which is orally effective, and structurally it is similar to oxymorphone. It appears to have little or no agonist activity and binds selectively to *mu* opiate receptors. When patients are pretreated with naltrexone and then given doses of morphine, heroin, or other opiates, naltrexone significantly reduces or blocks the pharmacological effects of the opiates. Such blockade of opiate effects includes the subjective high from the opiate, as well as drug craving and the production of physical dependence. Thus, naltrexone pretreatment eliminates much of the intrinsically reinforcing properties of opiates.

Unfortunately, the clinical utility of this opiate-blocking drug for opiate-dependent individuals appears to be limited. Poor patient compliance has plagued naltrexone programs. In one multicenter trial of naltrexone therapy, client retention in the program was reported to be as low as six weeks (Ginzburg, 1986). However, programs that combine pharmacotherpy with psychosocial support services do appear to have better superior treatment outcome (Resnick, Schuyten-Resnick, & Washton, 1980).

The endogenous opioid system has also been implicated in alcohol drinking behavior. Rats will increase alcohol consumption following administration of low doses of morphine (Hubbell, Abelson, Burkhardt, Herlands, & Reid, 1988). Opioid receptor antagonists, such as naltrexone and naloxone decrease alcohol consumption in animal models (Altshuler, Philips, & Feinhandler, 1980; Myers, Borg, & Mossberg, 1986; Samson & Doyle, 1985; Volpicelli, Davis, & Olgin, 1986). In clinical trials with alcoholics, the drug naltrexone has also been shown to decrease alcohol consumption (O'Malley et al, 1992; Volpicelli, Alterman, Hayashida, & O'Brien, 1992). Consequently, naltrexone (Revia) has been remarketed as an adjunctive treatment for alcoholism, though its efficacy in larger clinical samples remains to be investigated.

Methadone and Buprenorphine for Opiate Dependence

Methadone maintenance as a method for treating opiate dependence was initially proposed by Dole and Nyswander (1965). Part of the original rationale for this approach was that methadone would induce the development of cross-tolerance to heroin, such that heroin addicts would not experience a subjective high from illicit opiates. Subsequently, this effect has been attributed to a saturation of the *mu* opiate receptors, and to a lessor extent to the consequences of drug tolerance. Methadone maintenance has been found to decrease the addict's criminal activity and to reduce both opiate and nonopiate drug use (Gearing & Schweitzer, 1974; McLellan, Luborsky, & O'Brien, 1982). The weight of evidence also suggests that opiate addicts remain in methadone maintenance for a year or more, despite longer and more serious histories of addiction, than those in drug-free programs (Hubbard & Marsden, 1986). Importantly, addicts in methadone maintenance have lower rates of HIV seropositivity than do addicts not in treatment (Ball, Lange, Myers, & Friedman, 1988). This is due to reduced IV drug use, and reduced needle sharing among addicts in methadone maintenance. The success of methadone maintenance in attenuating the reinforcing effects of heroin appears largely to be a dose-dependent phenomenon. Inadequate plasma levels of methadone (Tennant, 1987) or lower oral doses of methadone (Jaffe, 1987) may have limited impact on drug-seeking behavior. These authors suggest that both higher oral doses (> 80 mg/day) and concurrent measurement of plasma methadone levels with dose adjustment may benefit those in methadone who continue to engage in drug use and attendant criminality. Typically, dosage of methadone is established through clinical titration. Patients in most methadone maintenance programs also receive some form of counseling and/or psychotherapy. McLellan and colleagues (McLellan, Arndt, Metzger, Woody, & O'Brien, 1993) have clearly demonstrated that the efficacy of methadone maintenance can be enhanced by such psychotherapeutic interventions.

Buprenorphine is a partial *mu* opioid agonist with minimal ability to produce physical dependence. It combines the characteristics of both opioid agonists (e.g., morphine, heroin, methadone) and antagonists (e.g., naltrexone) drug therapies for opiate addiction. A single dose of buprenorphine antagonizes the effects of opiates for up to 30 hours. It offers two advantages over methadone treatment for opiate addiction: (1) abrupt cessation of buprenorphine maintenance does not result in severe withdrawal signs and symptoms, and (2) the potential for lethal overdose is reduced because of the opiate antagonist properties of the drug (Mello et al., 1993). Importantly, reports have demonstrated that buprenorphine maintenance reduces opiate abuse by opiate dependent patients (Johnson, Jaffe, & Fudala, 1992; Kosten, Morgan, & Kleber, 1991). It is currently a Schedule V drug according to the U.S. Food and Drug Administration, although the drug is not in distribution.

Serotonergic Agents for Alcoholism

Several specific serotonin reuptake-inhibiting (SSRIs) antidepressant drugs appeared to have some limited efficacy in the attenuation of alcohol consumption independent of their effects on depression. Zimelidine has been reported to reduce alcohol intake among nondepressed heavy drinkers (Naranjo et al., 1984). Unfortunately, the manufacturer had withdrawn this drug from clinical trials due to untoward side effects. However, other similarly acting agents, such as citalopram, fluoxetine, and fluvoxamine also appeared to have potential in reduction of alcohol consumption (Naranjo, Sellers, & Lawrin, 1985). The mechanism of action for these drugs is unclear; however, it has been suggested that they inhibit the neurobiological substrate for positive reinforcement that maintains alcohol drinking behavior (Naranjo, Cappel, & Sellers, 1981). Nonetheless, in a more recent double-blind, placebo-controlled clinical trial of the SSRI fluoxetine in outpatient alcoholics over a 12-week period, no differences in relapse rate or drinking were found between patients receiving active drug or placebo (Kranzler et al., 1995). Similarly, in a placebo controlled trial of the serotonergic agent buspirone in VA inpatient alcoholics, the drug did not appear to be superior to placebo (Malcolm et al., 1992). Although serotonergic agents may have utility in treating psychiatric conditions that are comorbid with alcoholism, to date they have not proven to be effective therapeutics for the treatment of primary alcoholism.

PHARMACOLOGICAL ATTENUATION OF CRAVING

Opiate Craving

Opiate craving is successfully attenuated primarily by drug substitution employing long-acting opioid drugs such as methadone, buprenorphine or l-alpha-acetylmethadol (LAAM). This successful method for attenuation of craving and opiate-seeking behavior does not readily reduce craving for other drugs of abuse. For example, methadone maintenance does not reduce the desire to use cocaine (Kosten, Rounsaville, & Kleber, 1987). It is noteworthy that methadone maintenance also has some psychological drawbacks. Reports suggest that anywhere from 20 to 30 percent of individuals on chronic methadone maintenance acquire a morbid fear or phobia of detoxification, which complicates subsequent successful methadone detoxification (Milby et al., 1986).

Cocaine Craving

Despite a host of initially promising candidates, to date no pharmacotherapy for cocaine craving exists that favorably compares with methadone's impact on heroin craving. The National Institute on Drug Abuse's Medication Development Division has labeled buprenorphine, carbamazepine, desipramine, imipramine, and nifedipine as "disappointing" (GAO Report, 1996). For a host of other compounds, results have been mixed such that one study shows therapeutic benefit whereas subsequent research shows no effect.

Alcohol Craving

Kissin (1975) first argued for the use in alcoholics of chronic benzodiazepine therapy. He noted that because many patients are unable to deal with the symptoms of a protracted withdrawal syndrome, benzodiazepine therapy would reduce craving for alcohol and would retain patients in treatment. However, clinical experience diminished the enthusiasm for this approach.

Benzodiazepines appear to have abuse potential in alcoholics. They clearly potentiate the effects of alcohol, and cross-addiction to benzodiazepines is not an uncommon occurrence.

Buspirone, a nonbenzodiazapine anxiolytic, has been suggested as an alternative therapy for alcoholics, based on its apparent lack of abuse potential and its lack of potentiation of the effects of alcohol (Meyer, 1986). However, few data exist concerning the effect of buspirone on alcohol craving, although it appears to have some utility for patients with concurrent generalized anxiety symptoms and alcoholism (Kranzler et al., 1994).

Dopaminergic drugs may have some utility in the treatment of alcoholic craving. Two dopamine agonists, bromocriptine (Borg, 1983) and apomorphine (Jensen, Christoffersen, & Noerregaard, 1977), have been reported to control withdrawal symptoms and reduce craving for alcohol for two to six weeks after detoxification. However, another report failed to find any benefit of apomorphine therapy on post-intoxication symptoms (Wadstein, Ohlin, & Stenberg, 1978). Further controlled studies of these agents clearly should be done before routine clinical prescription can be recommended.

Clinical trials of naltrexone have found that subjects receiving the drug were less likely to relapse than those receiving placebo (O'Malley et al., 1992; Volpicelli et al., 1992). One potential mechanism for this reduction in relapse is the attenuation of alcohol craving associated with alcohol-related stimuli or alcohol consumption. Both Volpicelli and colleagues (1992), and O'Malley, Jaffe, Rode, and Rounsaville (1996) have independently demonstrated that naltrexone modifies alcohol-induced craving. Thus, naltrexone appears to be an efficacious therapeutic for attenuation of alcohol craving.

Case Illustration

Mr. E. is a 55-year-old divorced Caucasian man, who was admitted into an inpatient alcohol and other drug treatment program, upon the referral of his family physician. He had a 10-year history of heavy daily alcohol consumption. In the year prior to admission, he had been reprimanded and placed on probation at his work for having reduced productivity and for having alcohol on his breath. He also had gotten two motor vehicle citations in the preceding year for driving under the influence of alcohol. His divorce was prompted by incidents of verbal and physical abuse of his wife and children while he was intoxicated. Prior to admission, the patient still did not believe that he was an alcoholic.

Mr. E. was admitted to the inpatient unit mildly intoxicated, with a blood alcohol level of 90 mg/dl (per deciliter). His vital signs were initially within normal limits. His initial clinical withdrawal syndrome rating scale scores were low. He was given oral fluid and electrolyte replacements and made comfortable by the nursing staff. Approximately five hours later, Mr. E. was found to have a rapid pulse, a slightly elevated temperature, and an elevated systolic blood pressure. He became tremulous, diaphoretic, and agitated. His clinical withdrawal score was moderately elevated. The decision was made to institute pharmacotherapy.

The patient was given an initial oral dose of 20 mg of diazepam. When clinical withdrawal ratings were performed one hour later, his severity of withdrawal score was slightly higher than the previous rating. He was then given another oral dose of 20 mg of diazepam and allowed to rest. One hour later, his clinical withdrawal score was unchanged from the previously elevated clinical rating. One hour later, his withdrawal score, although still elevated, was lower than at the two previous ratings. The decision was made to withhold medication and to observe the patient for another hour. His next hourly withdrawal rating was even lower than the two previous ratings, but his vital signs were still abnormal. The clinical decision was made to give one last oral dose of diazepam. Two hours later, the patient had normal vital signs, and his clinical withdrawal rating scores were only slightly elevated. The patient appeared comfortable and in no acute distress. That night he got five hours of sleep. No additional medications were given to treat the alcohol withdrawal syndrome, and the patient remained stable.

Five days later, Mr. E. was actively participating in the psychotherapy program on the ward. He attended the psychoeducational programs, participated in the individual and group therapies, and was introduced to the fellowship of Alcoholics Anonymous (AA). Despite all these interventions, Mr. E. was concerned that he "wouldn't be able to stay away from the booze" after he was discharged. Therefore, the treatment team elected to suggest disulfiram therapy upon discharge, to give the patient the psychological crutch he needed to remain abstinent outside the hospital.

The patient met with the program physician, who explained to him what disulfiram was, what it did, and the details of the reaction he would have if he drank, and the physician warned him of the potential risks versus its benefits. After thinking this option over, the patient agreed to a six-week trial of the drug as part of his aftercare plan. Mr. E. felt that taking disulfiram was "just the insurance I need to stay sober," and he consented to treatment. It was agreed that the treatment team would reevaluate his need for the drug at six-week intervals.

Mr. E. was started on disulfiram 250 mg/day during his last week in the hospital, and this dose was continued after discharge. In addition to pharmacotherapy, the patient also attended twice weekly AA meetings, and returned for weekly aftercare therapy groups. Although the patient remained totally abstinent during his first six weeks outside of the hospital, and he never experienced a DER, he felt strongly that the drug helped his recovery. He requested another six-week treatment interval with disulfiram as a crutch. The treatment team agreed. Mr. E. continued abstinence and actively participated in AA, as well as in aftercare therapy. At the next six-week evaluation however, the team felt that it was time to phase out the drug because his new behaviors seemed firmly established. Mr. E. was gradually tapered off disulfiram over about a week. Although he was somewhat anxious about how he would maintain sobriety without the drug, at the time of this writing, he has now totally abstained from alcohol for 14 months without the reinitiation of pharmacotherapy.

ALTERNATIVE TREATMENT OPTIONS

The central controversy in the pharmacological management of substance abuse disorders may be whether to use pharmacotherapy at all. For example, several uncontrolled studies suggest that otherwise healthy patients in alcohol withdrawal can be safely treated without the use of psychoactive drugs (Shaw, Kolesar, Sellers, Kaplan, & Sandor, 1981; Whitfield et al., 1978). Thus, pharmacotherapy is apparently not always mandatory.

In addition, front-line, nonphysician clinicians are frequently opposed to the use of psychoactive drugs for individuals with a preexisting psychoactive substance abuse disorder. In part, this perspective is due to the prominent influence of AA and Narcotics Anonymous (NA) as part of the treatment regimen of substance abusers. These self-help groups warn their members about the potential dangers of dependence on physician-prescribed or illicit psychoactive drugs as a substitute for the original addiction. In particular, AA warns alcoholics about the danger of becoming addicted to sedatives and hypnotics (Alcoholics Anonymous, 1984). In general, these highly influential self-help groups advocate that their members seek "nonchemical solutions for the aches and discomforts of everyday living."

Given the efficacy, proliferation, and well-deserved prestige of these self-help groups, the search for effective pharmacotherapeutic agents for alcohol and drug abuse disorders has generated limited interest among pharmaceutical concerns. For example, disulfiram, which was the only drug available in the United States that was indicated for the treatment of alcoholism, was first introduced in Europe in 1948, and later in the United States. No American pharmaceutical company has, until the recent remarketing of naltrexone, undertaken a research and development program to find other novel drug treatments for alcoholism, despite the lack of convincing empirical support for the notion that all psychoactive drugs are a danger to the alcoholic, the drug-free approach espoused by the substance abuse treatment community has reigned for nearly 40 years.

PRESCRIPTIVE TREATMENT

Evidence-based approaches to the clinical care of substance dependent patients support the use of psychopharmacological interventions for alcohol, nicotine, and opiate withdrawal syndromes, though as noted in the above section, pharmacological intervention is not always necessary or indicated.

However, the evidence is mixed in terms of the use of pharmacological treatments in the postdetoxification period. At the time of this writing, no psychopharmacological intervention for cocaine abuse has met empirical standards of efficacy. However, for severe opiate addiction, the empirical evidence strongly supports the use of substitution therapies (e.g., methadone, buprenorphine), particularly for intravenous drug abusers or those with criminal careers. For alcohol use disorders, preliminary evidence supports the utility of naltrexone therapy as an adjunctive treatment. However, the evidence is less compelling for other pharmacological approaches, including disulfiram, which may have utility only among a more narrow range of patients.

A more complex picture is presented by the patient suffering a concurrent substance use disorder and another psychiatric condition. Here, clinical evidence supports the usefulness of specific pharmacological treatments for the comorbid mental disorder (i.e., anxiety, depression or schizophrenia) having a beneficial effect on the psychosocial treatment for the substance use disorder. Thus, pharmacotherapies may have indirect efficacy in the treatment of some substance abusing patients.

MANAGED CARE

Over the past five years, managed healthcare has emerged as the dominant force in the structuring of addictive disorder treatment. The emphasis on cost cutting, and the provision of the least restrictive and most cost-effective approaches has all but eliminated the 28-day inpatient program formats that typified chemical dependency treatment since the late 1950s. In its stead, is a continuum of care that ranges from short-stay inpatient programs to a bolstered menu of outpatient services ranging from standard outpatient treatment to intensive outpatient and partial hospital programs. Of course, methadone maintenance programs have operated almost exclusively in outpatient settings since their initiation. Detoxification services, which in the past were regularly provided in inpatient or residential settings, have also now moved to the outpatient clinic where they are provided with a lower level of medical supervision, and rely heavily on the patients own resources. Alternatively, there has been increasing interest in ultra-fast methods for detoxification that can be accomplished in a matter of hours using general anesthesia (e.g., Legarda & Gossop, 1994), though controlled clinical trials are currently lacking. Given the emphasis on outpatient treatments, one can anticipate that pharmacotherapeutic approaches may be relied upon increasingly in this new treatment climate due their perceived efficiency. Hopefully, this trend will not exclude the provision of concurrent psychosocial treatments. As demonstrated in the case of methadone maintenance by McLellan and colleagues (1993), the efficacy of outpatient medication therapies can be significantly enhanced by psychosocial interventions.

SUMMARY

Major federal initiatives in medications development have resulted in significant progress in both our understanding of the appropriate role of pharmacotherapies for the addictive disorders and in the expansion of our clinical armamentarium. Pharmacological treatments have been most successful in attenuating the adverse effects of physiological drug withdrawal. Replacement therapies for intravenous opiate addiction continue to be efficacious in reducing intravenous drug use behavior and its associated criminality. Replacement therapies for nicotine dependence is also useful in attenuating nicotine withdrawal and craving. Pharmacological approaches to the reduction of other forms of drug craving have not been wholly successful, although naltrexone therapy for alcoholism appears to be promising. However, research advances in the pharmacology of alcohol, cocaine, and other drugs of abuse, and recent investigations into the biological basis of heritable forms of substance abuse disorders, have renewed interest in potential psychopharmacological approaches to these conditions. Should new therapeutics be developed, the proof of the clinical safety and the efficacy of these compounds in substance abuse treatment is a burden that falls squarely on the shoulders of researchers, pharmacologists, and clinicians.

REFERENCES

Alcoholics Anonymous. (1984). *The A.A. member—Medications and other drugs: A report from a group of physicians in A.A.* New York: Alcoholics Anonymous World Services.

Altshuler, H.L., Philips, P.E., & Feinhandler, D.E. (1980). Alteration of ethanol self-administration by naltrexone. *Life Science, 26,* 679–688.

American Psychiatric Association. (1980). *Diagnostic and statistical manual of mental disorders* (3rd ed.). Washington, DC: Author.

American Psychiatric Association. (1987). *Diagnostic and statistical manual of mental disorders* (3rd ed., rev.). Washington, DC: Author.

American Psychiatric Association. (1994). *Diagnostic and statistical manual of mental disorders* (4th ed.). Washington, DC: Author.

Angrist, B., & Gershon, S. (1979). Variable attenuation of amphetamine effects by lithium. *American Journal of Psychiatry, 136,* 806–810.

Ball, J.C., Lange, W.R., Myers, C.P., & Friedman, S.R. (1988). Reducing the risk of AIDS through methadone maintenance treatment. *Journal of Health and Social Behavior, 29,* 214–226.

Banerjee, S.P., Sharma, V.K., Kung-Cheung, L.S., Chanda, S.K., & Riggi, S.J. (1979). Cocaine and amphetamine induce changes in ceneral beta-andrenoceptor sensitivity: Effects of acute and chronic drug treatment. *Brain Research, 175,* 119–130.

Baskin, S.I., & Easdale, A. (1982). Is chlordiazepoxide the rational choice among benzodiazepines? *Pharmacotherapy, 2,* 110–119.

Baumgartner, G.R., & Rowen R.C. (1987). Clonidine vs. chlordiazepoxide in the management of alcohol withdrawal. *Archives of Internal Medicine, 147,* 1223–1226.

Bennett, A., McKeever, L., & Turk, H. (1951). Psychotic reactions during tetraethylthiuram disulfide (Antabuse) therapy. *Journal of the American Medical Association, 145,* 483.

Borg, V. (1983). Bromocriptine in the prevention of alcohol abuse. *Acta Psychiatrica Scandinavia, 68,* 100–110.

Branchey, L., Davis, W., Lee, K.K., & Fuller, R.K. (1987). Psychiatric complications in disulfiram treatment. *American Journal of Psychiatry, 144,* 1310–1312.

Caille, G., Lacasse, Y., Vezina, M., Porter, R., Shaar, S., & Darke, A. (1980). A novel route for benzodiazepine administration: A sublingual formulation of lorazopam. In L. Manzo (Ed.), *Advances in neurotoxicity* (pp. 375–389). New York: Pergamon Press.

Charney, D.S., Heninger, G.R., & Kleber, H.D. (1986). The combined use of clonidine and naltrexone as a rapid, safe, and effective treatment of abrupt withdrawal from methadone. *American Journal of Psychiatry, 143,* 831–837.

Charney, D.S., Menkes, D.B., & Heninger, G.R. (1981). Receptor sensitivity and the mechanisms of action of antidepressant treatment. *Archives of General Psychiatry, 38,* 1160–1180.

Charney, D.S., Sternberg, D.E., Kleber, H.D., Heninger, G.R., & Redmond, D.E. (1981). The clinical use of clonidine in abrupt withdrawal from methadone. *Archives of General Psychiatry, 38,* 1223–1227.

Christensen, J.K., Ronsted, P., & Vaag, U.H. (1984). Side effects after disulfiram. *Acta Psychiatrica Scandinavia, 69,* 265–273.

Cronson, A.J., & Flemenbaum, A. (1978). Antagonism of cocaine highs by lithium. *American Journal of Psychiatry, 135,* 856–857.

Dackis, C.A., & Gold, M.S. (1985). Pharmacological approaches to cocaine addiction. *Journal of Substance Abuse Treatment, 2,* 139–145.

Dole, U.P., & Nyswander, M. (1965). A medical treatment for diacetylmorphine (heroin) addiction: A clinical trial with methadone hydrochloride. *Journal of the American Medical Association, 193*, 646–650.

Dorus, W., Ostrow, D.G., Anton, R., Cushman, P., Collins, J.F., Schaefer, M., Charles, H.L., Desai, P., Hayashida, M., Malkerneker, U., Willenbring, M., Fiscella, R., & Sather, M.R. (1989). Lithium treatment of depressed and nondepressed alcoholics. *Journal of the American Medical Association, 262*, 1646–1652.

Edwards, G., & Gross, M.M. (1976). Alcohol dependence: Provisional description of a clinical syndrome. *British Medical Journal, 1*, 1058–1061.

Fawcett, J., Clark, D.C., Aagesen, C.A., Pisani, V.D., Tilkin, J.M., Sellers, D., McGuire, M., & Gibbons, R.D. (1987). A double-blind placebo-controlled trial of lithium carbonate therapy for alcoholism. *Archives of General Psychiatry, 44*, 248–256.

Fischman, W.M., & Schuster, G.R. (1982). Cocaine self-administration in humans. *Federation Proceedings, 41*, 241–246.

Flemenbaum, A. (1974). Does lithium block the effects of amphetamine? *American Journal of Psychiatry, 131*, 7.

Fuller, R.K., Branchey, L., Brightwell, D.R., Derman, R.M., Emrick, C.D., Iber, F.L., James, K.E., & Lacoursiere, R.B. (1986). Disulfiram treatment of alcoholism: A veteran administration cooperative study. *Journal of the American Medical Association, 256*, 1449–1455.

Fuller, R.K., & Williford, W.O. (1980). Life-table analysis of abstinence in a study evaluating the efficacy of disulfiram. *Alcoholism: Clinical and Experimental Research, 4*, 298–301.

Gawin, F.H., & Kleber, H.D. (1984). Cocaine abuse treatment: An open pilot trial with lithium and desipramine. *Archives of General Psychiatry, 41*, 903–910.

Gawin, F.H., & Kleber, H.D. (1986). Abstinence symptomatogy and psychiatric diagnoses in cocaine abusers: clinical observation. *Archives of General Psychiatry, 43*, 107–113.

Gearing, F.R., & Schweitzer, M.D. (1974). An epidemiological evaluation of long-term methadone maintenance. *American Journal of Epidemiology, 100*, 101–105.

General Accounting Office: Report to Congressional Requesters. (1996). *Cocaine treatment: Early results from various approaches.* Washington, DC: USHEHS.

Ginzburg, H.M. (1986). Naltrexone: Its clinical utility. In B. Stimmd (Ed.), *Advances in alcohol and substance abuse* (pp. 83–101). New York: Haworth Press.

Gold, M.E., Redmond, D.C., & Kleber, H.D. (1978). Clonidine blocks acute opiate-withdrawal symptoms. *Lancet, 2*, 599–602.

Goyer, P.F., & Major, L.F. (1979). Hepatotoxicity in disulfiram-treated patients. *Journal of Studies on Alcohol, 40*, 133–137.

Gross, J., & Stitzler, M.L. (1989). Nicotine replacement: Ten-week effects on tobacco withdrawal symptoms. *Psychopharmacology, 98*, 334–341.

Hald, J., & Jacobsen, E. (1948). A drug sensitizing the organism to ethyl alcohol. *Lancet, 255*, 1001–1004.

Heath, R.G., Nesselhof, W., Bishop, M.P., & Byers, L.W. (1965). Behavioral and metabolic changes associated with administration of tetraethylthiuram disulfide (Antabuse). *Diseases of the Nervous System, 26*, 99–105.

Henningfield, J.E. (1995). Nicotine medications for smoking cessation. *New England Journal of Medicine, 333*, 1196–1203.

Henningfield, J.E., & Griffiths, R.R. (1980). Effects of ventilated cigarette holders on cigarette smoking by humans. *Psychopharmacology, 63*, 115–119.

Hubbard, R.L., & Marsden, M.E. (1986). Relapse to use of heroin, cocaine and other drugs in the first year after treatment. In F.M. Tims & C.G. Leukefeld (Eds.), *Relapse and recovery in drug abuse* (NIDA Research Monograph 72). Washington, DC: U.S. Department of Health and Human Services.

Hubbell, C.L., Abelson, M.L., Burkhardt, C.A., Herlands, S.W., & Reid, L.D. (1988). Constant infusions of morphine and intakes of sweetened ethanol solution among rats. *Alcohol, 5*, 409–415.

Huey, L., Janowsky, D., Lewis, J., Abrams, A., Parker, D., & Clopton, P. (1981). Effects of lithium carbonate on methylphenidate induced mood, behavior and cognitive processes. *Psychopharmacology, 73*, 161–164.

Hughes, J.R., Hatsukami, D.K., Pickens, R.W., Krahn, D., Malin, S., & Luknic, A. (1984). Effect of nicotine on the tobacco withdrawal syndrome. *Psychopharmacology (Berlin), 83*, 82–87.

Isbell, H., Fraser, H.F., & Wikler, A. (1955). An experimental study of the etiology of "rum fits" and delirium treatments. *Quarterly Journal of Studies on Alcohol, 16*, 1–13.

Jaffe, J.H. (1980). Drug addiction and drug abuse. In A.G. Gilman, L.S. Goodman, & A. Gilman (Eds.), *The pharmacological basis of therapeutics* (pp. 535–584). New York: Macmillan.

Jaffe, J.H. (1987). Pharmacological agents in treatment of drug dependence. In H.Y. Meltzer (Ed.), *Psychopharmacology: The third generation of progress* (pp. 1605–1616). New York: Raven Press.

Jaffe, J.H., & Martin, W.R. (1980). Opioid analgesics and antagonists. In A.G. Gilman, L.S. Goodman, & A. Gilman (Eds.), *The pharmacological basis of therapeutics* (pp. 494–534). New York: Macmillan.

Jensen, S.B., Christoffersen, C.B., & Noerregaard, A. (1977). Apomorphine in outpatient treatment of alcohol intoxication and abstinence: A double-blind study. *British Journal of Addiction, 72*, 325–330.

Johnson, R.E., Jaffe, J.H., & Fudala, P.J. (1992). A controlled trial of buprenorphine treatment for opioid dependence. *Journal of the American Medical Association, 267*, 2750–2755.

Judd, L.L., Hubbard, R.B., & Huey, L.Y. (1977). Lithium carbonate and ethanol induced "highs" in normal subjects. *Archives of General Psychiatry, 34*, 463–467.

Judd, L.L., & Huey, L.Y. (1984). Lithium antagonizes ethanol intoxication in alcoholics. *American Journal of Psychiatry, 141*, 1517–1521.

Kaim, S.C., Klett, C.J., & Rothchild, B. (1969). Treatment of the acute alcohol withdrawal state: A comparison of four drugs. *American Journal of Psychiatry, 125*, 1640–1646.

Kalant, H., LeBlanc, A.E., & Gibbins, R.J. (1971). Tolerance to, and dependence on, some non-opiate psychotropic drugs. *Pharmacological Reviews, 23*, 135–191.

Khan, A., Ciraulo, D.A., Nelson, W.H., Becker, J.T., Nies, A., & Jaffe, J.H. (1984). Dexamethasone suppression test in recently detoxified alcoholics: Clinical implications. *Journal of Clinical Psychopharmacology, 4*, 94–97.

Kissin, B. (1975). The use of psychoactive drugs in the long-term treatment of chronic alcoholics. *Annals of the New York Academy of Sciences, 252*, 385–395.

Kleber, H., & Gawin, F. (1986). Psychopharmacological trials in cocaine abuse treatment. *American Journal of Drug and Alcohol Abuse, 12*, 235–246.

Kline, N.S., Wren, J.C., Cooper, T.B., Varg, E., & Canal, O. (1974). Evaluation of lithium therapy in chronic and periodic alcoholism. *American Journal of Medical Science, 268*, 15–22.

Knee, S.T., & Razani, J. (1974). Acute organic brain syndrome: A complication of disulfiram therapy. *American Journal of Psychiatry, 131*, 1281–1282.

Koide, T., & Matshushita, H. (1981). An enhanced sensitivity of muscarinic cholinergic receptors associated with dopaminergic receptor sub-sensitivity after chronic antidepressant treatment. *Life Sciences, 28,* 1139.

Koob, G.E. (1992). Drugs of abuse: Anatomy, pharmacology, and function of reward pathways. *Trends in Pharmacological Science, 13,* 177–184.

Kosten, T.R., Morgan, C., & Kleber, H.D. (1991). Treatment of heroin addicts using buprenorphine. *American Journal of Drug and Alcohol Abuse, 17,* 119–128.

Kosten, T.R., Rounsaville, B.J., & Kleber, H.D. (1987). A 25 year follow-up of cocaine use among treated opioid addicts: Have our treatments helped? *Archives of General Psychiatry, 44,* 281–284.

Kranzler, H.R., Burleson, J.A., Del Boca, F.K., Babor, T.F., Korner, P., Brown, J., & Bohn, M.J. (1994). Buspirone treatment of anxious-alcoholics: A placebo-controlled trial. *Archives of General Psychiatry, 51,* 720–731.

Kranzler, H.R., Burleson, J.A., Korner, P., Del Boca, F.K., Bohn, M.J., Brown, J., & Liebowitz, N. (1995). Placebo-controlled trial of fluoxetine as an adjunct to relapse prevention in alcoholics. *American Journal of Psychiatry, 152,* 391–397.

Langenbucher, J.W., & Chung, T. (1995). Studies in illness onset and staging: *DSM-IV* alcohol dependence using mean-age and survival/hazards methods. *Journal of Abnormal Psychology, 104,* 346–354.

Legarda, J.J., & Gossop, M. (1994). A 24-hour inpatient detoxification treatment for heroin addicts: A preliminary investigation. *Drug and Alcohol Dependence, 35,* 91–93.

Leonard, K.E., Bromet, E.J., Parkinson, D.K., & Day, N. (1984). Agreement among Feigner, RDC, and *DSM-III* criteria for alcoholism. *Addictive Behaviors, 9,* 319–322.

Linnoila, M., Saario, I., & Maki, M. (1974). Effect of treatment with diazepam or lithium and alcohol on psychomotor skills related to driving. *European Journal of Clinical Pharmacology, 7,* 337–342.

Major, L.F., Lemer, P., Ballenger, J.C., Brown, G.L., Goodwin, F.K., & Lovenbag, W. (1979). Dopamine-beta-hydroxylase in the cerebrospinal fluid: Relationship to disulfiram-induced psychosis. *Biological Psychiatry, 14,* 337–344.

Malcolm, R., Anton, R.F., Randall, C.L., Johnston, A., Brady, K., & Thevos, A. (1992). A placebo-controlled trial of buspirone in anxious inpatient alcoholics. *Alcoholism: Clinical and Experimental Research, 16,* 1007–1013.

McGinnis, J.M., & Foege, W.H. (1993). Actual causes of death in the United States. *Journal of the American Medical Association, 270,* 2207–2212.

McLellan, A.T., Arndt, I.O., Metzger, D.S., Woody, G.E., & O'Brien, C.P. (1993). The effects of psychosocial services in substance abuse treatment. *Journal of the American Medical Association,* 1953–1959.

McLellan, A.T., Luborsky, L., & O'Brien, C.P. (1982). Is substance abuse treatment effective? Five different perspectives. *Journal of the American Medical Association, 247,* 1423–1427.

Mello, N.K., & Mendelson, J.H. (1978). Behavioral pharmacology of human alcohol, heroin, and marijuana use. In J. Fishman (Ed.), *The bases of addiction* (pp. 101–116). Berlin: Dahlem Konferenzen.

Mello, N.K., & Mendelson, J.H. (1980). Buprenorphine suppress heroin use by heroin addicts. *Science, 207,* 657–659.

Mello, N.K., Mendelson, J.H., Lukas, S.E., Gastfriend, D.R., Teoh, S.K., & Holman, B.L. (1993). Buprenorphine treatment of opiate and cocaine abuse: Clinical and preclinical studies. *Harvard Review of Psychiatry, 1,* 168–183.

Mendelson, J.H., & Mello, N.K. (1966). Experimental analysis of drinking behavior of chronic alcoholics. *Annals of the New York Academy of Science, 133,* 828.

Merry, J., Reynolds, C.M., Baily, J., & Coppen, A. (1976). Prophylactic treatment of alcoholism by lithium carbonate: A controlled study. *Lancet, 2,* 481–482.

Meyer, R.E. (1986). Anxiolytics and the alcoholic parent. *Journal of Studies on Alcohol, 47,* 269–273.

Milby, J.B., Gurwitch, R.H., Wiebe, D.J., Ling, W., McLellan, A.T., & Woody, G.E. (1986). Prevalence and diagnostic reliability of methadone maintenance detoxification fear. *American Journal of Psychiatry, 143,* 739–743.

Myers, R.D., Borg, S., & Mossberg, R. (1986). Antagonism by naltrexone of voluntary alcohol selection in the chronically drinking macaque monkey. *Alcohol, 3,* 383–388.

Naranjo, C.A., Cappel, H., & Sellers, E.M. (1981). Pharmacological control of alcohol consumption: Tactics for identification and testing of new drugs. *Addictive Behaviors, 6,* 261–269.

Naranjo, C.A., Sellers, E.M., & Lawrin, M.O. (1985). Moderation of ethanol intake by serotonin uptake inhibitors. In C. Shagass (Ed.), *Biological psychiatry 1985* (pp. 708–710). Amsterdam, The Netherlands: Elsevier Science.

Naranjo, C.A., Sellers, E.M., Roach, C.A., Woodley, D.V., Sanchez-Craig, M., & Sykora, K. (1984). Zimelidine-induced variations in alcohol intake by nondepressed heavy drinkers. *Clinical Psychopharmacology and Therapeutics, 35,* 374–381.

Nichols, J.R., Headlee, C.P., & Coppock, H.W. (1956). Drug addiction: I. Addiction by escape training. *Journal of the American Pharmaceutical Association, 45,* 788–791.

O'Malley, S.S., Jaffe, A.J., Chang, G., Schottenfeld, R.S., Meyer, R.E., & Rounsaville, B. (1992). Naltrexone and coping skills therapy for alcohol dependence: A controlled study. *Archives of General Psychiatry, 49,* 881–887.

O'Malley, S.S., Jaffe, A.J., Rode, S., & Rounsaville, B. (1996). Experience of a "slip" among alcoholics treated with naltrexone or placebo. *American Journal of Psychiatry, 153,* 281–283.

Rainey, J.M. (1977). Disulfiram toxicity and carbon disulfide poisoning. *American Journal of Psychiatry, 134,* 371–378.

Rankin, H., Hodgson, R., & Stockwell, T. (1979). The concept of craving and its measurement. *Behaviour Research and Therapy, 17,* 389–396.

Resnick, R.B., Schuyten-Resnick, E., & Washton, A.M. (1980). Assessment of narcotic antagonists in the treatment of opioid dependence. *Annual Review of Pharmacology and Toxicology, 20,* 463–474.

Ross, H.D., Chan, K.K., Piraino, A.J., & John, V.A. (1991). Pharmacokinetics of multiple daily transdermal doses of nicotine in healthy smokers. *Pharmacology Research, 8,* 385–388.

Ross, S.B., & Renyi, A.L. (1966). Uptake of some tritiated sympathomimetic amines by mouse brain cortex in vitro. *Acta Pharmacologica Toxicologica, 24,* 297–309.

Rounsaville, B.J., Spitzer, R.L., & Williams, J.B.W. (1986). Proposed changes in *DSM-III* substance abuse disorders: Descriptions and rationale. *American Journal of Psychiatry, 143,* 463–468.

Runion, H.L., & Fowler, A. (1978). A double-blind study of chlordiazepoxide and hydroxyzine HCI therapy in acute alcohol withdrawal. *Proceedings of the Western Pharmacologic Society, 21,* 303–309.

Sampliner, R., & Iber, P.L. (1974). Diphenylhydantoin control of alcohol withdrawal seizures. *Journal of the American Medical Association, 230,* 1430–1437.

Samson, H.H., & Doyle, T.F. (1985). Oral ethanol self-administration in the rat: Effects of naloxone. *Pharmacology, Biochemistry and Behavior, 22,* 91–99.

Sellers, E.M., Naranjo, C.A., Harrison, B., Devenyi, P., Roach, C., & Sykora, K. (1983). Diazepam loading: Simplified treatment of alcohol withdrawal. *Clinical Pharmacology and Therapeutics, 34,* 822–826.

Shaw, J.M., Kolesar, G.S., Sellers, E.M., Kaplan, H.L., & Sandor, P. (1981). Development of optimal treatment tactics for alcohol withdrawal: I. Assessment and effectiveness of supportive care. *Journal of Clinical Psychopharmacology, 1,* 382–389.

Spencer, J. (1980). Use of injectable lorazepam in alcohol withdrawal. *Medical Journal of Australia, 2,* 211–212.

Tabakoff, B., Melchior, C.L., & Hoffman, P. (1984). Factors in ethanol tolerance. *Science, 224,* 523–524.

Tarter, R.E., Arria, A.M., Moss, H., Edwards, N.J., & Van Thiel, D. (1987). *DSM-III* criteria for alcohol abuse: Associations with alcohol consumption. *Alcoholism: Clinical and Experimental Research, 11,* 541–543.

Taylor, D.L., & Ho, B.T. (1977). Neurochemical effects of cocaine following acute and repeated injection. *Journal of Neuroscience Research, 3,* 95–101.

Taylor, D.L., Ho, B.T., & Fagan, J.D. (1979). Increased doparnine receptor binding in rat brain by repeated cocaine injections. *Communications in Psychopharmacology, 3,* 137–142.

Tennant, F.S. (1985). Effect of cocaine dependence on plasma phenylalanine and tyrosine levels and on urinary MHPG excretion. *American Journal of Psychiatry, 142,* 1200–1201.

Tennant, F.S. (1987). Inadequate plasma concentrations in some high-dose methadone maintenance patients. *American Journal of Psychiatry, 144,* 1349–1350.

Thompson, W.L., Johnson, A.D., & Maddrey, W.L. (1975). Diazepam and paraldehyde for treatment of severe delirium tremens. *Annals of Internal Medicine, 82,* 175–180.

U.S. Department of Health and Human Services. (1987). *Sixth special report to congress on alcohol and health from the secretary of health and human services.* Rockville, MD: Author.

Van Kammen, D.P., & Murphy, D.L. (1975). Attenuation of the euphoriant and activating effects of d- and l-amphetamine by lithium carbonate treatment. *Psychopharmacologia (Berlin), 44,* 215–224.

Van Rossum, J.M., & Hurkmans, J.A. (1964). Mechanism of action of psychomotor stimulant drugs: Significance of dopamine in locomotor stimulant action. *International Journal of Neuropharmacology, 3,* 227–236.

Volpicelli, J.R., Alterman, A.I., Hayashida, M., & O'Brien, C.P. (1992). Naltrexone in the treatment of alcohol dependence. *Archives of General Psychiatry, 49,* 876–880.

Volpicelli, J.R., Davis, M.A., & Olgin, J.E. (1986). Naltrexone blocks the post-shock increase of ethanol consumption. *Life Science, 38,* 841–847.

Wadstein, J., Ohlin, H., & Stenberg, P. (1978). Effects of apomorphine and apomorphine-L-Dopa carbidopa on alcohol postintoxication symptoms. *Drug and Alcohol Dependence, 3,* 281–287.

Weddington, W.M., Brown, B.S., Haertzen, C.A., Cone, E.J., Dax, E.M., Herning, R.I., & Michaelson, B.S. (1990). Changes in mood, craving, and sleep during short-term abstinence reported by male cocaine addicts: A controlled, residential study. *Archives of General Psychiatry, 47,* 861–868.

Wegner, M.E., & Fink, D.W. (1965). Chlordiazepoxide compared to meprobamate and pormazine for the withdrawal symptoms of acute alcoholism. *Wisconsin Medical Journal, 64,* 436–440.

Whitfield, E.L., Thompson, G., Lamb, A., Spencer, U., Pfeifer, M., & Browning-Ferrando, M. (1978). Detoxification of 1,024 alcoholic patients without psychoactive drugs. *Journal of American Medical Association, 293,* 1409–1410.

Wikler, A. (1952). A psychodynamic study of a patient during self-regulated readdiction to morphine. *Psychiatric Quarterly, 26,* 270–293.

Wilkins, A.J., Jenkins, W.J., & Steiner, J.A. (1983). Efficacy of clonidine in treatment of alcohol withdrawal state. *Psychopharmacology, 81,* 78–80.

Williams, H.L., & Rundell, O.H. (1981). Altered sleep physiology in chronic alcoholics: Reversal with abstinence. *Alcoholism: Clinical and Experimental Research, 5,* 318–325.

Author Index

Subject Index